Contents

Acknowledgments

It had been understood for the last twenty years by the Antiquarian, Archæological, and other societies that he was the projector of a new theory about Stonehenge, and that his book on the subject was almost ready.

Anthony Trollope, *The Vicar of Bulhampton* (1870)

This book has been many years in gestation, and I have above all to thank my beloved and long-suffering wife Georgina for her patience and care throughout this time. How many times at social gatherings has she been obliged to overhear someone kindly enquire what I am writing, only to receive the wearisome response: 'It's about Stonehenge – but *not* the archæology!' The book alone can explain what I have been up to all these years, for there seemed no succinct way of summarizing what has been a long and winding trail.

Stonehenge in fact provides the appropriate focus of this enquiry, rather than its totality. In order to penetrate the persisting *mysterium*, I have found it necessary to engage with many related aspects of our forebears' most profound cosmological beliefs. Although it was as I recall not altogether my original intention, I believe the picture which emerges illuminates many significant aspects of early myth and legend, principally in Celtic Britain and Ireland.

Professor Mike Parker Pearson, lately of the University of Sheffield, and now of University College London, kindly read the second chapter (the only one that *is* exclusively about archæology), making helpful comments from which I have profited. As his team's remarkable discoveries on the site of Stonehenge and its environs gradually became public, it is gratifying to discover the extent to which they are corroborated by my own findings, in entirely distinct fields of study. I am grateful, too, to Professor John Waddell, of the National University of Ireland at Galway, for writing the preface to the book, as well as drawing my attention to some significant sources which had escaped my attention.

Above all, I wish to thank two scholars in related fields, who have been exceptionally generous with critical appraisal. Despite being committed to a busy programme of his own, at the suggestion of my old friend Dr Roger Pearson, Dean A. Miller, Professor Emeritus of History and Comparative Religion at the University of Rochester, NY, painstakingly read an earlier draft of the book. Eventually he sent me a lengthy catalogue of detailed comments, many noting embarrassing solecisms (in consequence thankfully corrected), while others suggested fruitful sources of information I had overlooked. Any remaining errors are entirely my own, and should the book be thought to possess any virtue much credit must be laid at Professor Miller's door.

Sometime after this thorough overhaul of my text, my friend Dr Andrew Breeze of the University of Pamplona similarly set aside labours of his own to subject my work to renewed searching appraisal, with particular attention to his own field of Celtic studies. He too proved meticulous in suggesting neglected critical sources, correcting remaining small but irritating errors, and suggesting fruitful improvements to technical arguments.

Finally, although she could play no part in my recent labours, I must as in previous books on related subjects thank my late dear friend Rachel Bromwich, who, from that long-distant day when we first met at Griff's bookshop in Cecil Court, never failed to encourage, guide, and inspire me in the enthralling study of Celtic history and mythology.

Nikolai Tolstoy, 2016

Preface by Professor John Waddell

For many, the phrase 'the legacy of the Middle Ages' conjures up a picture of great architecture and rich metalwork, but there is an extraordinary literary heritage as well. The literatures of mediæval Ireland and Wales are by far the most substantial body of written material in a vernacular tongue in western Europe and, as is well known, are supplemented by a large corpus of writing in Latin. Nikolai Tolstoy's impressive work confronts not just some of the mysteries of Stonehenge, but the crucial question of the preservation of ancient motifs in mediæval literature, a topic which has been the focus of much debate. Once upon a time it was widely accepted that much of this written material, most notably the narrative literature, had derived from a pre-mediæval oral tradition with deep roots in an even more ancient pre-literate past. Some tales, like the great Irish epic, the *Táin Bó Cúailnge* (The Cattle Raid of Cooley), were thought to be a 'window on the Iron Age', offering a partial but nonetheless reasonably accurate picture of a prehistoric world populated by heroic warriors and great kings and queens. It was even believed that differences in the Iron Age archæological record of Connacht and Ulster were a reflection of the rivalry between those ancient provinces recounted in the *Táin*.

Even older ancestries were explored, and some scholars highlighted intriguing similarities between elements in these Celtic texts and details in the early literature of faraway India. Since horizontal transmission over such a great geographical distance seemed unlikely at any time, they argued that these parallels indicated a common Indo-European source, and meant that some features in these insular writings offered a glimpse of customs and beliefs thousands of years old. It did seem possible that the great chronological gap between prehistoric archæology and mediæval text might be bridged and the preliterate past illuminated by the written word.

The terms nativist and anti-nativist gradually entered the lexicon of Celtic studies over half a century ago, marking the slow beginning of a paradigm shift. Those of an anti-nativist or revisionist persuasion questioned any significant contribution by an older oral tradition to mediæval texts, viewing them as original compositions created *de novo* in a Christian environment. A series of archæological and literary studies in the 1980s were especially important, and gave impetus to this process. An analysis of the sword types described in the *Táin Bó Cúailnge*, for instance, was just one of several studies which demonstrated that various objects featured in epic literature bore little resemblance to Iron Age material, but found their closest parallels in objects of the mediæval period. Consequently, it was argued the writer was actually describing contemporary and familiar items. Furthermore, excavations at Navan Fort or Emain Macha, the legendary capital of ancient Ulster and kingly settlement in Co. Armagh, had revealed that this was a great ritual centre rather than a fortified royal court, and this fact was considered further evidence of a total disassociation between prehistoric archæology and mediæval text. The seemingly logical conclusion was that early Irish epic literature did not constitute a legitimate source for the study of pagan Celtic society.

The rich heritage of saga, legal and genealogical literature was also subjected to critical scrutiny, demonstrating that the Christian Church and classical learning had had a much greater impact on this material than had been supposed. Indeed, it was argued that all of this great body of mediæval literature was the product of a monastic milieu that presented a version of a past which was profoundly transformed if not actually created by Christian writers. With great erudition, a number of fierce philologists and dogmatic historians effectively created a new and influential orthodoxy, in which pre-Christian traditions had a minimal role to play. In Irish tradition, figures like Medb, associated with Rathcroghan, and Macha, associated with Emain Macha, who had long been held to be pagan sovereignty goddesses in origin, were re-evaluated. In the case of Medb, the limited nature of her mythical qualities, found mainly in later mediæval texts, has been emphasized and her rôle as an ancient goddess questioned. As for Macha, her several manifestations have been deemed to be either late scholastic inventions or simply representations of an ancient war-goddess.

Notwithstanding these objections, for an archæologist, faced with the exceptional evidence for protracted pagan ritual activity at Emain Macha and Rathcroghan over many centuries, an obvious question to ask is what was the purpose of all of this, and to what supernatural entity was this activity addressed? The fact that these female figures with their specific supernatural qualities were intimately linked to great ceremonial centres is a telling one, and cannot be ignored. Their diminished status in mediæval texts has certainly something to tell us about the objectives of Christian scribes who, however, had no qualms about including tantalizing scraps of pagan material when it suited their purpose. Of course, these myths might, perhaps, have been invented, but more often than not pre-existing material was reutilized or distorted. There is an interesting parallel here with the actions of the forerunners of these Irish scribes who wrote the Christian gospels, and who also were content to include fragments of older eastern mythic themes such as virgin birth, the divine child and slain god in the creation of a new and powerful story.

The transmission of tradition is not a straightforward transference. It is a process of change at every stage, and so the reduced stature of pagan figures in mediæval contexts is not surprising. What is surprising today is a passion for further demotion displayed by a few modern commentators, who still prefer to see little significance in the supernatural dimensions of these personages. The author of a recent learned study of druids, ancient and modern, takes a very negative view of the Irish and Welsh material. This sceptical approach effectively involves the complete dismissal of all mediæval evidence. What are described as the morsels picked from early Irish texts that provide apparent evidence for the nature of ancient druids are held to be without value. Fortunately, not all Celtic scholars share this pessimistic view.

The famous Welsh figure Rhiannon has not escaped this sort of anti-nativist attention. The process of converting her 'into a pagan deity' has lately been presented as a nineteenth-century development, and other more mundane explanations offered for her equine associations. Like other aristocratic personages in what have been dismissively called mediæval wonder tales – where the line between the natural and the supernatural is blurred – she has been seen as just one of a series of apparently human figures who frequently possess magical abilities. Yet her supernatural qualities are noteworthy and well documented by Nikolai Tolstoy in this volume. The importance of the Preseli Hills in her story is intriguing, for this part of south-west Wales is now recognized as a sacral landscape of exceptional archæological significance. It was from here that the so-called bluestones, conceivably endowed with magical healing properties, were transported to Stonehenge.

It has been claimed that the equine associations that linked Rhiannon to Macha and Epona have nothing to do with the notion of a sovereignty goddess. The accumulated evidence remains compelling, however, and the steadily growing archæological data on horse-related ritual activities in the Celtic world lend support to the concept of equine cults anterior to that of the Gallo-Roman Epona, and to the belief that the mythic themes associated with Macha and Rhiannon could have ancient prehistoric origins. Even the horse sacrifice associated with the Cenél Conaill in Donegal recorded by Giraldus Cambrensis in the twelfth century has recently been rejected as gossip picked up by a foreigner, despite the fact that Giraldus himself deliberately declared he was recording events and scenes of time past, as he put it. The rite has generally been accepted as a valuable piece of antiquarian lore with parallels in ancient India.

The well-established belief that sovereignty and sacral kingship, a feature of both Irish and Indian tradition, have Indo-European roots is sometimes questioned – even though, ironically, no scholar of Irish, Welsh or Continental Celtic will deny the Indo-European origins of these languages. Language was not just a vehicle for the transmission of phonemes and semantemes, and many will agree that mythic themes (akin to the mythemes of Claude Lévi-Strauss) travelled too. Embedded in mediæval texts, their careful excavation does have something to tell us about both the mediæval mind and the distant past.

It is possible to offer a satisfactory explanation for the apparent mismatch between the archæological reality at Emain Macha and the textual material relating to that famous site. We know Christian writers had their own agendas. They were creating a heroic past for their mediæval audience, a past peopled by intrepid warriors and illustrious kings who lived in splendidly decorated dwellings. At the same time, they were anxious to obscure the potent pagan symbolism linked to rites of kingship. Paradoxically, it was this primordial past that might also lend support to claims of political legitimacy and antiquity, and this was a very good reason to include some mythic credentials. One interesting illustration of this tendency involves the Celtic deity Lug (Lugh in modern Irish), who makes an appearance in the Irish tale *Baile in Scáil* (The Vision of the Spectre). Seated on a throne and accompanied by a woman who is described as the 'eternal Sovereignty of Ireland', his rôle is to foretell the future of the legendary king of Tara, Conn of the Hundred Battles, who has been transported to the Otherworld. He introduces himself as no spectral apparition, declaring that he is Lug, son of Ethliu (his supernatural mother's name), who is to prophesy Conn's future and that of every future ruler in Tara. The mediæval author of the tale ensures that Lug also declares that he has come back from the dead, and is of 'the race of Adam'. The fact that Lug is now given a respectable human pedigree (as the ultimate ancestor of Conn) in a clear case of clerical manipulation in no way diminishes his supernatural pagan aspects. The point of the episode is to portray the immortal legitimacy of the kingship of Tara.

Both Lug and his Welsh counterpart Lleu have long been considered the insular counterparts of a pan-Celtic deity (the Lugus found in Gaul and Iberia). Not surprisingly, this concept too has been questioned. True, muddled nineteenth-century scholarship and fragmentary evidence are easy targets, but for at least one historian the long-running argument, promoted for the most part by a few British writers, that the ancient European Celts were never a distinct people but were a nineteenth-century construct also has a part to play in this assessment. Quite simply, a Celt of old was someone who spoke a Celtic language. Fixated on the archæological diversity that does exist across a large part of Europe, and on the fact that some Celtic-speaking peoples had a distinctive art style, and some did not, and perplexed by the largely irrelevant (and incorrect) detail that those Celts never used this label of themselves, statements such as 'there was no single language' fail to grasp the facts of linguistic geography. In this case, abundant evidence demonstrates the existence of a language family that facilitated communication and shared belief systems.

In the context of Emain Macha, the Christian scribe's integration of some of Macha's supernatural traits and equine links in the story of that complex figure is unlikely to have been conjured out of nowhere. It is far more probable that they draw on pre-existing beliefs and mythic narratives. These suggest that ceremonies such as horse sacrifice may have been a part of the prehistoric rituals once practised there. Of course, archæological proof is hard to come by – even though a few horse bones were found in the Navan excavations, some displaying signs of butchery, and implying the occasional consumption of horse flesh or horse sacrifice. Here, in peering into the past – from a great distance – we may perceive traces of rites obliquely reflected by myth.

The anti-nativist approach has not always been marked by unanimity or consistency, and not all Celtic scholars have subscribed to it, but it has been very valuable in promoting a more critical appraisal of Irish and Welsh tradition. Unfortunately, it has sometimes had its own narrowness of vision and it has, to a degree, succeeded in discouraging the study of mythic discourse in early literature.

Many would agree it is now time for a more nuanced approach, open to comparative studies and embracing archæology, anthropology, folklore and discourse analysis – to name but a few relevant disciplines. While a small minority persist in arguing that none of these mediæval writings bears any of the hallmarks of orally transmitted material, and show all the signs of original literary creation, there are eminent Celtic scholars and historians who are not so dismissive, and who do recognize that there are numerous pagan motifs in mediæval texts that represent an avenue of enquiry worthy of study. After all, these written works, like archæological artefacts, are statements of their respective pasts. The question posed by Nikolai Tolstoy as to what extent ancient lore was preserved in mediæval writing must be addressed with an open and enquiring mind, and not summarily dismissed. In demonstrating just how such a substantial amount of pagan mythology is preserved in ancient Welsh literature, he rightly argues that if this is accepted as a feasible proposition, then the onus is on any entrenched sceptic to disprove it.

John Waddell,
Emeritus Professor of Archæology at the National University of Ireland at Galway

Introduction

This book is only tangentially concerned with the archæology of Stonehenge, a perennially fascinating topic of universal interest, which has of late undergone extensive reinterpretation in light of continuing fresh discoveries. These have largely resulted from excavations at the site and its vicinity, conducted over the years 2003 to 2009 by the Stonehenge Riverside Project, under the supervision of Professor Mike Parker Pearson of the University of Sheffield, now at the University College of London Institute of Archaeology.[1] In Chapter Two, I summarize the state of archæological knowledge as it stands at the time of writing.

My exploration of the essential meaning of Stonehenge follows a distinct path from that of the archæologists, and if nothing else possesses the quality of being almost entirely novel. Over long years of study, I have become increasingly persuaded that an extensive body of knowledge relevant to understanding of the numinous *purpose* and *functions* of the monument, traces of which I shall argue being chiefly preserved in mediæval Welsh and Irish texts, has been largely overlooked in the context. These records in turn are illuminated by explorations in comparative mythology, folklore studies, and the lore of early cultures analogous in varying degree to those of early Britain and Ireland.

My intention is to demonstrate that discoveries may be effected through the medium of early literatures and comparative religion, which may prove as revealing in their way as those grounded in analysis of artefacts. At the same time, the present work is emphatically not intended to compete with archæological researches, which constitute the fundamental basis for understanding the great monument on Salisbury Plain. Rather, I hope to complement and extend them in hitherto unexplored directions. It was the eminent archæologist Stuart Piggott, an experienced excavator at Stonehenge, who in the dark days of 1941 published a brilliant pioneering paper, which first suggested avenues whereby significant advances might be effected through investigation of literary sources combined with archæological revelations.[2]

I am aware that there are even today historians who find it hard to contemplate the possibility of gaining any useful understanding of the functions of Stonehenge through such an approach.[3] After all, the great sarsen stones we see today were erected about the

---

1   Cf. Caroline Alexander, 'If the Stones Could Speak: Searching for the Meaning of Stonehenge', *National Geographic* (Washington, June 2008), ccxiii, pp. 34–59.

2   Piggott may have enhanced and refined a suggestion by H. J. Fleure, 'Archaeology and Folk Tradition', *The Proceedings of the British Academy* (London, 1932), xvii, p. 379.

3   Heated emotions liable to arise on occasion between specialists in the 'rival' fields of history, archæology, and philology were amusingly dissected by F. T. Wainwright in his *Archaeology and Place-Names and History: An Essay on Problems of Co-ordination* (London, 1962), pp. 97–100. He illustrated the point by

middle of the third millennium BC, while the earliest certain historical allusion to the site was recorded in the fourth decade of the twelfth century AD! As Piggott himself warned long ago:

> It is hard doctrine for the non-specialist to accept that we do not know what sort of religion lay behind the building of Stonehenge, nor what ceremonies were performed there: it is harder, too, when you add that such things just cannot be discovered by archæological means, however much techniques may be refined and elaborated, but only by the medium of the historical documents which in the nature of things are non-existent for the period and monuments in question.[4]

In view of his seminal paper published fourteen years earlier, Piggott's concluding reservation may perhaps be taken in an ambivalent light. While there clearly can have existed no written records remotely contemporary with any stage of the building of Stonehenge, there are nevertheless historical sources of a much later era which repay examination. Most of what follows in this book is concerned with such literary evidence. For this reason I set out *in extenso* the original sources on which my arguments depend, together with critical appraisals by leading scholars in relevant fields of study. In consequence, I believe any reader instinctively desirous of rejecting my conclusions will find the necessary ammunition conveniently to hand!

The nature of the records on which this enquiry largely depends requires that some arguments, or elements of them, must inevitably draw on circumstantial evidence. I shall not attempt to apologize for this. The anthropologist A. M. Hocart sharply rejected the 'popular, but natural, delusion that direct evidence is necessarily better than circumstantial, in fact that it is the only satisfactory kind of evidence'. He continued:

> The historian as a rule shares the popular prejudice: he pins his faith to direct evidence, to the writings of contemporaries, to coins, to ruins. Circumstantial evidence he distrusts and even fears. He clings to his direct evidence like a timid sailor to the coast. If anyone proposes to strike across the sea with the guidance of a compass alone he makes a virtue of his timidity, and converts it into a lofty superiority …
>
> Man was given a cerebral cortex to make good the deficiencies of his senses by combining their fragmentary messages into a body of knowledge on which he can act. Whether the historical sciences survive as such a body of knowledge, or perish as a mere mass of erudition, will depend on whether they have the courage to use the gift of nature or continue to believe only what they can see.[5]

---

citing broadly irreconcilable interpretations arising from a single entry in the *Anglo-Saxon Chronicle* (pp. 93–94), and suggested collaboration by scholars from differing appropriate disciplines as the solution (pp. 89–91).

4   Stuart Piggott, 'The Druids and Stonehenge', in Glyn E. Daniel (ed.), *Myth or Legend?* (London, 1955), p. 103. 'The world view and belief system of the builders of Stonehenge are not our world and belief system, and it is difficult for us to appreciate what their motivations may have been', Mark Bowden, Sharon Soutar, David Field, and Martyn Barber, *The Stonehenge Landscape* (Swindon, 2015), p. 45.

5   Rodney Needham (ed.), *Imagination and Proof: Selected Essays of A. M. Hocart* (Tucson, 1987), pp. 15–28. This recalls Sherlock Holmes's observation that 'There is nothing more deceptive than an obvious fact … Besides, we may chance to hit upon some other obvious facts which may have been by no means obvious to Mr Lestrade' ('The Boscome Valley Mystery').

Alec Fisher's practical aphorism is also worth consideration:

> You have to make a judgement about 'appropriate standards'. That judgement will be *yours*; it is a judgement which requires justification and which is open to criticism. Set too severe a standard and it will seem that nothing can be known with certainty; set too unimaginative a standard and you will be easily led into error.[6]

The enquiry which follows is directed in the main towards reconstruction of salient aspects of British pagan ideology of the pre-Roman Iron Age. Without further anticipating the matter of this book, I conclude from converging evidence that Stonehenge was regarded from earliest times as the 'Sacred Centre' of Britain, its *omphalos* (or navel), from which the island was believed to have emerged at its beginning, and to which it was anticipated to contract at its cataclysmic end. Fortunately, the process was envisaged as cyclical, and after each eschatological catastrophe a new Britain is destined to emerge, the procedure repeating itself throughout succeeding eras of elemental destruction and rebirth.[7] Fundamental elements of the mythologies of Celtic peoples, many of which focus on the umbilical centre, are examined in successive chapters of this book. Finally, evidence suggesting possible reconstruction of pre-Christian rituals conducted at Stonehenge is set out in the concluding chapter.

To the extent that the reconstruction may be achieved at all is largely owing to the survival of strata of archaic lore embedded in the mediæval literatures of Celtic Britain and Ireland. Interpretation of this category of evidence may at times require detailed evaluation of relevant texts, to most of which intensive scholarly labours have fortunately been devoted for well over a century.

The concept of the *omphalos* provided a national focus of belief and ritual in many (probably most) early societies. In the fourth decade of the twelfth century AD, Geoffrey of Monmouth compiled his *History of the Kings of Britain*. Most of that enduringly popular work sprang from his own lively imagination, but it nevertheless contains (as might be expected from an inquisitive author, whose impressionable early years were spent on the Welsh side of the border) valuable glimpses of authentic Celtic tradition tucked here and there among the quaint meanderings of his fiction. At the same time, the authenticity of such instances can never be assumed, but in each case requires demonstration on the basis of relevant evidence.

Geoffrey described how, through the ingenuity of Merlin, the great megaliths of Stonehenge were brought from the Hill of Killare in Ireland to Salisbury Plain. In reality, I believe it can be shown that the connexion was (obviously) not physical, but ideological. The obscure township of Killare is situated beside Uisneach, a spot celebrated in ancient lore as the Omphalos of Ireland. The site's legendary history and ideological functions are extensively described in early Irish literature, and it is clear that the tradition which Geoffrey adapted related to corresponding *functions* of the respective insular *omphaloi*. This misunderstanding could in turn only have occurred had the unknown originators of the legend *already* been aware of Stonehenge's identity as the Omphalos of Britain. The notion that the stones of Stonehenge were transported from Uisneach to Salisbury Plain could have appeared confirmed by the fact that a comparable megalithic structure was no longer to be found at the former site. If this ideological identity be accepted, then it seems that, like Uisneach,

---

6   Alec Fisher, *The Logic of Real Arguments* (Cambridge, 2004) , p. 27.

7   Mircea Eliade, *Birth and Rebirth: The Religious Meanings of Initiation in Human Culture* (London, 1961), pp. xii–xiii.

Stonehenge was the focus of myths and rituals linked to the concept of the umbilical centre, together with associated lore of the Celtic doctrine of the soul, national kingship, and related cosmological beliefs of our pre-Christian forebears. Naturally, all this must be scrupulously demonstrated on the basis of evidence.

Preseli Mountain in Pembrokeshire, whence the smaller (but nonetheless substantial) bluestones were transported to the *omphalos* site on Salisbury Plain, features in the early eleventh-century Welsh story 'Pwyll, Prince of Dyfed' (*Pwyll Pendeuic Dyuet*) as setting for rites ensuring perpetuation of the royal dynasty of Dyfed. This in turn suggests the motive for the stupendous operation required for transportation of sacred monoliths from the great mountain by the Western Sea to the national *omphalos* at Stonehenge.

Stuart Piggott conjectured that Geoffrey of Monmouth's colourful story of the bodily transfer of Stonehenge from Ireland represents a relic of what must once have been an extensive Bronze Age literature. I hope to demonstrate, not only that the essence of his hypothesis is validated by evidence unavailable at a time when military service denied him access to specialist libraries, but that other mediæval texts, ranging from the Welsh tales of 'The Dream of Maxen the Emperor' (*Breudwyt Maxen Wledic*) and 'The Conversation of Lludd and Lleuelys' (*Cyfranc Lludd a Lleuelys*), to Latin Lives of the Welsh saints Samson, Cadog, and Illtud, preserve hitherto unrecognized precious aspects of pagan beliefs and rites associated with the Omphalos of Britain.[8]

Furthermore, myths attached to national *omphaloi* in other cultures, such as the celebrated navel-stone at the temple of Apollo at Delphi in Greece, may throw refracted light on those of Britain and Ireland. That the course of the ensuing investigation involves consideration of wide-ranging aspects of Celtic paganism does not arise from chance, but because Celtic religion was (like that of most pre-modern societies) enduringly focussed on the concept of the centre.

Finally, at the latter end of the chronological spectrum, I shall argue that paganism in Britain flourished as a living creed to a considerably later period than is generally allowed. This makes the survival of archaic lore in extant sources a more likely proposition than might otherwise be the case. Effectively, however, this represents a subsidiary consideration, and the cautious reader may if he or she chooses remain content to direct attention to the greater part of the book, which is primarily concerned with the pagan lore and ritual of the Celtic Britons and Irish, and the extent to which they can throw light on the all-important concept of the national centre, or *omphalos*. How far they in turn may have absorbed and perpetuated elements of their religious beliefs from those who originally constructed and frequented Stonehenge is examined in the light of similar transmissions found in more fully-documented early societies.[9]

---

8   Throughout this book early literary sources are for the most part cited from editions whose texts are published in their original languages. This is not motivated by pedantry, but because their precise interpretation is frequently fundamental to the argument. However, to ensure comprehensibility such passages are throughout fully paraphrazed or translated. The best translation of the mediæval Welsh tales, which play a particularly significant part in what follows, is by Sioned Davies (tr.), *The Mabinogion* (Oxford, 2007).

9   While even the possibility of this having occurred may alarm one or two mediævalists, I suspect it is less likely to raise eyebrows among archæologists, accustomed as they are to assessing issues over the *longue durée*. To provide but one example highly relevant to the present study (others will be cited in due course), 'Although there are outstanding questions regarding the dating of many monuments at Uisneach, it is quite evident that the sacral significance of the hill was established early in prehistory, and subsequently sustained over many millennia', Roseanne Schot, 'From cult centre to royal centre:

Overall, the approach I adopt has been encapsulated with admirable clarity by Professor Thomas Charles-Edwards, in his introduction to the study of the Old English land measurement, the hide:

> This is the theory I shall put forward. It is, however, an avowedly hypothetical theory: I can provide no conclusive proof of several of its main propositions. It is a theory about a pre-historic period based upon historical evidence. The arguments which support it can only lead to probable conclusions. On the other hand, the interest of the problem justifies recourse to such fragile methods of investigation.[10]

Nikolai Tolstoy, St David's Day 2016

---

monuments, myths and other revelations at Uisneach', in Roseanne Schot, Conor Newman, and Edel Bhreatnach (ed.), *Landscapes of Cult and Kingship* (Dublin, 2011), p. 99.

10 T. M. Charles-Edwards, 'Kinship, Status, and the Origins of the Hide', *Past & Present* (Oxford, 1972), lvi, p. 3. Cf. Alwyn D. Rees's perceptive comments on reconstruction of Celtic mythology and religion by the comparative method ('Modern Evaluations of Celtic Narrative Tradition', in *Proceedings of the Second International Congress of Celtic Studies* (Cardiff, 1966), pp. 31–61). Few if any scholars today espouse the entrenched scepticism against which the brothers Rees were compelled to battle.

1

The Riddle of Stonehenge

A millennium of mystery

Every year a million or more visitors arrive to gaze upon Stonehenge. Among great monuments of antiquity it is likely that the Pyramids of Egypt alone attract comparable interest. However, Stonehenge possesses a uniquely mysterious quality which sets it apart from the Pyramids. The latter were largely constructed by a literate civilization, and their function as tombs of in many cases identifiable pharaohs has long been established by archæologists. Thus, there exists no fundamental mystery, such as is posed by the mighty monument on Salisbury Plain.

In striking contrast, almost everything about Stonehenge appears bafflingly enigmatic. Although the western seaboard of Europe abounds in megalithic monuments, some like Carnac and Avebury constructed on an even more grandiose scale, none has excited the curiosity of succeeding generations to a comparable extent. In the 1130s the historian Henry of Huntingdon provided the earliest extant description of

> *Stanenges*, where stones of wonderful size have been erected after the manner of doorways [*in modo portarum*], so that doorway appears to have been raised upon doorway; and

Stonehenge. (Courtesy Flickr Waaghals)

no one can conceive how such great stones have been so raised aloft, nor why they were built there.

He accordingly included the monument among the four wonders of England.[1]

The name of Stonehenge derives from Old English *stān*, 'stone', and *hencg*, 'hinge', or *hencgen*, 'hanging; gallows': in either case the allusion is clearly to the majestic sarsen trilithons.[2]

Henry's description suggests that he may not himself have visited the site, but relied on accounts by others. The earliest likely eyewitness accounts would in that case be those of the imaginative 'historian' Geoffrey of Monmouth, who completed his work about 1136, and Gerald of Wales, writing towards the end of the same century.[3] Geoffrey's colourful account of Merlin's use of engineering skills to transport the stones from Ireland, in order to re-erect them on Salisbury Plain as a memorial to valiant British nobles treacherously slaughtered by the Saxons, will be examined later in this book. It will be argued that it contains a core of authentic tradition, whose ultimate origins (as Stuart Piggott was first to suggest) ascend to the Bronze Age.

Apart from Geoffrey's 'history' of Stonehenge, tradition has frustratingly little to recount of its legendary origin and function. It is possible for folklore to preserve collective memory over astonishingly long periods of time, appearing on occasion to be as reliable as written historical records.[4] The most consistently recorded piece of traditional lore concerning Stonehenge is the supposed impossibility of counting its monoliths more than once, and arriving at the same number. This belief was cited and disproved by King Charles II, who coolly rode out to inspect the site during his escape from Cromwell's vengeful troops after the battle of Worcester in 1651. (Later, Dryden envisaged the fugitive monarch as 'Watch'd by the Genius of this Kingly Place' – as will be seen, a remarkably apt conjecture). In the following century, the same superstition was noted by the antiquary William Stukeley, who, remarking on its general acceptance, added the detail that 'in the mouth of the vulgar ... tis an ominous thing & great danger that people will dye after it'.[5] However a similar tradition

1   Diana Greenway (ed.), *Henry, Archdeacon of Huntingdon, Historia Anglorum: The History of the English People* (Oxford, 1996), p. 22.

2   J. E. B. Gover, Allen Mawer, and F. M. Stenton, *The Place-Names of Wiltshire* (Cambridge, 1939), pp. 360–61; Max Förster, *Der Flußname Themse und seine Sippe: Studien zur Anglisierung keltischer Eigennamen und zur Lautchronologie des Altbritischen* (Munich, 1941), p. 326.

3   'Here Gerald was following Geoffrey of Monmouth, who had also apparently seen Stonehenge' (Antonia Gransden, *Legends, Traditions and History in Medieval England* (London, 1992), p. 195).

4   Eoin MacNeill and Gerard Murphy (ed.), *Duanaire Finn: The Book of the Lays of Finn* (London and Dublin, 1908-53), iii, pp. xliii-xlv, 192–94. Oliver Padel has presented a closely argued case for the priority of Arthurian folklore and legend over the 'historical' king featured in mediæval records ('The Nature of Arthur', *Cambrian Medieval Celtic Studies* (Aberystwyth, 1994), xxvii, pp. 1–31).

5   Allan Fea, *After Worcester Fight* (London, 1904), p. 36; Aubrey Burl and Neil Mortimer (ed.), *Stukeley's 'Stonehenge': An Unpublished Manuscript 1721-1724* (Cambridge, 2005), p. 80. Cf. Christopher Chippindale, *Stonehenge Complete* (London, 1983), pp. 44–47. A more interesting point about Inigo Jones lies in the ideological perception projected in his 1655 work on Stonehenge. 'Jones thought that the Romans erected Stonehenge so its ordered proportions would civilize the barbarous ancient Britons. The building of Covent Garden, the renovation of St. Paul's, and the planned construction of a new royal palace for Charles I reflected the same view: these projects were intended to function, simultaneously, as civilizing influences on Jones's contemporaries and as monuments of the "admired achievements" of Charles I', (Malcolm Smuts, *Court Culture and the Origins of a Royalist Tradition in Early Stuart England* (Philadelphia, 1987), p. 166). This, together with Charles II's concern with Stonehenge and Avebury, echoes the concept of Stonehenge as primæval royal Centre, as well as the Jacobite ideology of the lawful king acting as legitimating focus of society (Paul Kléber Monod, *Jacobitism and the English people 1688-1788* (Cambridge, 1989), pp. 343–50).

is associated with other megalithic complexes,[6] and the concept is besides explicable on rational grounds. Seven years before King Charles's dangerous visit, the diarist John Evelyn observed that 'to number them exactly, is very difficult, in such variety of postures they lie & confusion.'[7]

Beyond this, little attests to the survival of any tradition of significance among the local inhabitants, who largely comprised shepherds and shepherdesses tending their flocks across the great plain. From at least the early seventeenth century onward a regular trickle of inquisitive visitors came to marvel at the monument, and it is hard to believe that none conducted enquiries among the local inhabitants.

The florid terminology of a curious Lieutenant Hammond, who visited the site in 1635, is apt to the mystifying spectacle.

> I tooke my Nag and made a 6 Mile step ouer the pleasant Plaines to goe see one of our Islands wonders, those admir'd, strange, confus'd, huge, fixt astonishing Stones … I found them in compasse in a round ring, on an ascending hill, in 3 Circular Rankes on a faire Plaine, euery way 30 of my Paces … and I found them (if you dare credit my telling) iust 90. These stones are of an exceeding length, neere 30 Foote, and and of a great bignes, being 10 foot broad, and stand most confusedly, some in a hanging and tumbling Posture, and some twyn'd togeather on the top like a hideous payre of Gallowes, so strangely, as makes any Spectator to gaze and greatly to wonder at them.

He also remarked upon the great array of neighbouring barrows, 'about the number of 50 high, round little Hills, artificially cast vp …'[8]

During the Great Rebellion the antiquary and inimitable gossip John Aubrey, who lived a few miles away at Broadchalke on the edge of the plain, evinced keen interest in the monument. Not long after the Restoration King Charles II urged him to write a work on the neighbouring megalithic complex at Avebury.[9] Aubrey complied, and although his 'discourse' was never published, he conducted extensive researches into both monuments. As he hunted regularly in the neighbourhood, observing the attractions of 'the nut-brown Shepherdesses' encountered

---

6   D. H. Moutray Read, 'Hampshire Folklore', *Folk-Lore* (London, 1911), xxii, p. 308; Grinsell, *The Folklore of Stanton Drew* (St Peter Port, Guernsey, 1973), pp. 10–11. Similar beliefs recur in Celtic tradition. The measurements of the tomb of a son of King Arthur in South Wales were thought to be impossible to reckon twice – a belief which its early ninth-century recorder declared he had confirmed on the spot (Theodor Mommsen (ed.), *Monvmenta Germaniae Historica* (xiii): *Chronica Minora saec. IV. V. VI. VII* (Berlin, 1894), iii, pp. 217–18). In Ireland a herd of diabolical swine could not be accurately counted twice (Máirín O Daly (ed.), *Cath Maige Mucrama: The Battle of Mag Mucrama* (Dublin, 1975), p. 48). It seems that the act of counting provided means of exerting potentially damaging control over its objects, with its prevention correspondingly representing a form of protective magic. With this may be compared the rooted antipathy of the Israelites (in common with other societies around the world) to acceptance of a census (Sir James George Frazer, *Folk-Lore in the Old Testament: Studies in Comparative Religion Legend and Law* (London, 1918), ii, pp. 555–63).

7   E. S. de Beer (ed.), *The Diary of John Evelyn* (Oxford, 1955), iii, p. 116. A Dutch visitor in 1662 noted the same problem: 'The stones are difficult to count, as some have fallen and lie on top of each other' (Maurice Exwood and H. L. Lehmann (ed.), *The Journal of William Schellinks' Travels in England 1661–1663* (London, 1993), p. 134).

8   L. G. Wickham Legg (ed.), *A Relation of a Short Survey of the Western Counties: Made by a Lieutenant in the Military Company in Norwich in 1635 (Camden Miscellany)* (London, 1936), xvi, p. 65.

9   The King may have been influenced by more than antiquarian curiosity. As Lorraine Madway has shown, he was concerned to exalt the ancient provenance of his illustrious dynasty ('Charles II and Royal Reshaping of Ancient British History', *Royal Stuart Journal* (Glanton, 2011), iii, pp. 1–27).

on his way, he enjoyed ample opportunity for garnering popular traditions.[10] All he appears to have learned, however, was that an 'errour runnes from generation to generation concerning Stoneheng, that the stones there are artificial'.[11] This, together with the belief that the stones could not be counted more than once with the same result, perhaps reflects no more than popular speculation on the uniquely ordered form of the megalithic complex, together with confusion as to the number of stones arising from its current delapidated condition.

In 1668 the indefatigably curious Samuel Pepys, having purchased a recent book on the subject before his arrival, declared the megaliths to be 'as prodigious as any tales I ever heard of them and worth going this journey to see'. At the same time, he acknowledged 'God knows what their use was'. He bestowed fourpence on the shepherdess who led his party's horses, but it appears that she imparted no information worth his recording.[12] About the same time a Puritan clergyman coldly conjectured that God had preserved the desolate ruin,

> so we should remember, that these forlorne Pillars of Stone are left to be our remembrancers, dissuading us from looking back in our hearts upon any thing of Idolatry, and persuading us, in imitation of Moses and the Prophets, so to describe, and deride, in it's uglie Coullers, that none of us, or our posteritie, may returne, with Doggs to such Vomit, or Sows to wallowing in such mire.[13]

However, it was largely the gigantic yet ordered appearance of 'these forlorne Pillars of Stone' that provoked their visitors' baffled curiosity. When was it erected? By whom? For what purpose? Until early nineteenth-century geologists began to demonstrate that the earth had passed through successive eras of unimaginable antiquity,[14] for most people there appeared little choice but to rely on Archbishop Ussher's tentative calculation, arrived at by the then plausible approach of reckoning biblical genealogies back to Adam, that the earth was created by God in 4004 BC.[15] Archæology being likewise in its infancy, that there existed complex societies in Western Europe prior to those described by classical historians occurred to few. The earliest recorded inhabitants of Britain were those encountered by Julius Caesar during his two visits to the island in the middle of the first century BC. Accordingly, apart from enthusiasts like Inigo Jones, who assigned the design

---

10 Christopher Chippindale, *Stonehenge Complete* (London, 1983), pp. 66–71; Alexandra Walsham, *The Reformation of the Landscape: Religion, Identity, and Memory in Early Modern Britain and Ireland* (Oxford, 2011), pp. 297–302; David Tylden-Wright, *John Aubrey: A Life* (London, 1991), pp. 69–77.

11 James Britten (ed.), *Remaines of Gentilisme and Judaisme. by John Aubrey, R.S.S. 1686–87* (London, 1881), p. 252. 'ARTIFICIAL ... artful, done according to the Rules of Art' (N. Bailey, *An Universal Etymological Dictionary* (London, 1723), *s.v.*, i.e. carved and rendered, rather than created from some early form of concrete.

12 Robert Latham and William Matthews (ed.), *The Diary of Samuel Pepys* (London, 1970–83), ix, pp. 226, 229–30. Pepys also visited Avebury and Silbury Hill (p. 240).

13 Walsham, *The Reformation of the Landscape*, p. 149.

14 William B. N. Berry, *Growth of a Prehistoric Time Scale: Based on Organic Evolution* (San Francisco, 1968), pp. 64–114.

15 R. Buick Know, *James Ussher Archbishop of Armagh* (Cardiff, 1967), pp. 105–6. By the eighteenth century, enlightened people had already begun to appreciate that the earth must be far older than was allowed by the Adamite reckoning. In 1786 Mrs Piozzi noted that 'the modern Philosophy holds the Eternity of the Earth, or at least an Antiquity of 50,000 Years' (Katharine C. Balderston (ed.), *Thraliana: The Diary of Mrs. Hester Lynch Thrale (Later Mrs. Piozzi) 1776–1809* (Oxford, 1951), p. 647). However, she was dismayed by a backsliding clergyman's declaration, 'in my hearing three Days ago, that Adam & Eve and the Apple was an old Woman's Story – that he believed the world was five Hundred thousand years old at least' (ibid., p. 776). Nevertheless, in 1816 Beethoven could still declare that 'Our world history has now lasted for 5,816 years' (Maynard Solomon, *Beethoven Essays* (Cambridge, Mass., 1988), p. 270).

of the great monument to Roman architects,[16] and others favouring the Danes, in the eyes of most enquirers the druids appeared the likely authors of its construction.

It would be unjust to be dismissive of the hypotheses of pioneer investigators like Aubrey and Stukeley, who carefully surveyed Stonehenge in the seventeenth and eighteenth centuries.[17] Their ascription of its construction to the druids was not implausible in light of knowledge then available. Whatever the rites and beliefs associated with the structure and its creation, it remains reasonable to assume that they were supervised and expounded by a class of religious specialists not dissimilar in function to the druids. Julius Caesar possessed the advantage, denied modern investigators, of conversing with learned druids in Gaul over a period of years, and his report of their assertion that the druidic *disciplina* originated in Britain and was brought thence to Gaul is certainly not to be dismissed out of hand.[18]

The word *druid* being of Celtic origin, it is consequently unlikely to be associated with the early period of a monument likely to have been constructed long before the arrival of Celtic-speaking peoples in Britain. On the other hand, scholars have suggested the probability that druidism in Britain was influenced by pre-Celtic cultic beliefs and practices, the legacy of priestly hierarchies originating in the Bronze Age, or the still earlier Neolithic.[19]

Desultory attempts by early enthusiasts, like Charles I's able favourite the Duke of Buckingham, to discover evidence in the ground from excavation achieved little to advance understanding. Indeed, critics complained that these pioneer efforts had caused considerable damage to the unique architectural monument.[20] Even the intelligent John Evelyn blithely recorded that the stones were 'so exceeding hard, that all my strength with an hammer, could not break a fragment'.[21] Archbishop Ussher's colleague William Camden, the greatest topographic scholar of his age, was obliged to be content with citing legendary accounts derived from his mediæval predecessors.[22]

To some, Stonehenge appeared little more than a remarkable curiosity. In 1735 the playwright John Gay cheerfully advised Dean Swift: 'You might ride upon the Downs & write conjectures upon Stonhenge.' In 1769 Parson Woodforde rode out of his way to allow his servant to gaze upon its majestic appearance.[23] More serious was the intent of two intellectual giants of the eighteenth

16 Following a visit to the site, the erudite King James I commissioned Inigo Jones to write a survey of Stonehenge, which was published posthumously (Chippindale, *Stonehenge Complete*, pp. 48–61).

17 Good accounts of Stukeley's valuable work on Stonehenge are to be found in ibid., pp. 71–81; David Boyd Haycock, *William Stukeley: Science, Religion and Archaeology in Eighteenth-Century England* (Woodbridge, 2002), pp. 121–32; Rosemary Sweet, *Antiquaries: The Discovery of the Past in Eighteenth-Century Britain* (London, 2004), pp. 128–33.

18 Otto Seel (ed.), *C. Ivlii Caesaris Commentarii Rervm Gestarvm: Bellvm Gallicvm* (Leipzig, 1961), p. 185.

19 John Rhŷs, 'Studies in Early Irish History', *The Proceedings of the British Academy* (London, 1903), i, pp. 8, 35–36; Julius Pokorny, 'The Origin of Druidism', *The Smithsonian Report for 1910* (Washington, 1911), pp. 583–97; T. Rice Holmes (ed.), *C. Iuli Caesaris Commentarii: Rerum in Gallia Gestarum VII; A. Hirti Commentarius VIII.* (Oxford, 1914), p. 245; T. D. Kendrick, *The Druids: A Study in Keltic Prehistory* (London, 1927), pp. 72, 194–211; Eoin MacNeill, *Early Irish Laws and Institutions* (Dublin, 1935), pp. 66–67; Adolf Mahr, 'New Aspects and Problems in Irish Prehistory: Presidential Address for 1937', *Proceedings of the Prehistoric Society* (Cambridge, 1937), iii, pp. 417–18; Nora K. Chadwick, *The Druids* (Cardiff, 1966), pp. 15–16; Stuart Piggott, *The Druids* (London, 1968), pp. 184–89; Anne Ross, 'Chartres: the *Locus* of the Carnutes', *Studia Celtica* (Cardiff, 1979/1980), xiv/xv, p. 266.

20 Burl and Mortimer (ed.), *Stukeley's 'Stonehenge'*, p. 66.

21 de Beer (ed.), *The Diary of John Evelyn*, iii, pp. 115–16. Further instances of destructive delapidation are recounted by Chippindale, *Stonehenge Complete*, pp. 72, 73, 91, 92.

22 William Camden, *Britannia* (London, 1600), pp. 218–21.

23 C. F. Burgess (ed.), *The Letters of John Gay* (Oxford, 1966), p. 93; John Beresford (ed.), *The Diary of a Country Parson: The Reverend James Woodforde* (London, 1924–31), i, p. 87.

century, Samuel Johnson and Edmund Burke, who on 7 October 1783 spent an evening discussing their impressions of Stonehenge, which each had independently visited that summer. Johnson believed that his examination enabled him to refute two theories advanced by the curious: first, that the stones were artificially created from some form of concrete; and, second, that the Danes were responsible for its erection. He rejected both hypotheses on the same grounds, viz. that the knobs on top of the perpendicular stones, designed as tenons for the transverse stones, proved the architects to have been unaware of the existence of mortar. This consideration further excluded the Danes, 'who came hither in Ships, and were not ignorant certainly of the arts of life'. Johnson sagely concluded that the work should

be refered to the earliest habitation of the Island, as a Druidical monument of at least two thousand years, probably the most ancient work of Man upon the Island. Salisbury Cathedral and its Neighbour Stonehenge, are two eminent monuments of art and rudeness, and may show the first essays and the last perfection of architecture.[24]

Judging by his detailed description, Johnson's friend Oliver Goldsmith also visited the 'eminent monument'. He concluded:

In viewing the whole of this stupendous work, an awful kind of pleasure, not to be expressed, arises in the mind, owing to that geometrical proportion which was observed by the founders of *Stone-Henge* ... the most probable conjecture is that of Mr. *Aubrey* and Dr. *Stukeley* who strenuously contend that it was a British temple, and erected in the time of the druids. There was a tablet of tin with an inscription found here in the reign of King Henry VIII. which might probably have set this mystery in a clear light. But as the characters were not then understood by those who were consulted on the occasion, the plate was destroyed, or at least thrown by and lost.[25]

The tantalizing possibility that there had once existed a written record of the monument's construction was not unreasonable, in view of the assumption that it was erected in the Roman or immediate pre-Roman period.

The numinous effect of the colossal pillars, standing eerily silent in the midst of the windy plain, affected many pilgrims. William Stukeley, who earlier in the century spent long hours on the spot pondering its druidical origins, was moved to record:

Often when I have been in Stonehenge have I been rapt up in Jacobs soliloquy, how dradful is this place this is none other but the house of God & this is the gate of heaven.[26]

---

24   Bruce Redford (ed.), *The Letters of Samuel Johnson* (Oxford, 1992–94), iv, pp. 221–22. Johnson had presumably learned of the popular belief reported by John Aubrey. Boswell further recorded that, 'Whilst Dr. Johnson was in Wiltshire he viewed Stonehenge which he declared surpassed his ideas and was more curious than he expected to have found it' (Marshall Waingrow (ed.), *The Correspondence and Other Papers of James Boswell Relating to the Making of The Life of Johnson* (Edinburgh, 2001), p. 196). The Cornish antiquary William Borlase likewise ascribed the monument to the druids, in preference to the Romans (*Antiquities, Historical and Monumental, of the County of Cornwall* (London, 1769), p. 197). Thomas Rowlandson sketched the monument in the year after Johnson's visit (Robert R. Wark (ed.), *Rowlandson's Drawings for a Tour in a Post Chaise* (San Marino, CA, 1964), plate 19; cf. p. 128).

25   *The Geography and History of England: Done in the Manner of Gordon's and Salmon's Geographical and Historical Grammars* (London, 1765), pp. 184–85.

26   Burl and Mortimer (ed.), *Stukeley's 'Stonehenge'*, p. 112.

In 1791 Fanny Burney's taste was initially dismayed

> by the little shape, or intelligence, of the huge masses of stone so unaccountably piled
> at the summit of Salisbury Plain. However, we alighted, and the longer I surveyed &
> considered them, the more augmented my Wonder, & diminished my disappointment.
> There is enough remnant to prove the form had been circular, & the pile a Temple;- but
> I shall enter into no disquisitions of what is nearly proved undisquisitionable – even
> though I spent *half an Hour* in examining the premises![27]

Not long afterwards a knowledgable French traveller adopted a more rational approach, while
remaining no less baffled by the astonishing feat of engineering involved:

> The great pillars may contain 600 cubic feet of stone, and weigh 45 tons each. There is no
> quarry on the spot. Fifteen or sixteen miles from thence, on Marlborough Downs, there is,
> I am told, a quarry of sandstone like these; but by what means could a barbarous people
> transport these enormous blocks, and, what is full as incomprehensible, plant them
> upright in the ground, and place the cross blocks on the top?[28]

At the same time the Romantics, like Wordsworth and Blake, were profoundly impressed by the
grandeur of Stonehenge's spectacular size and setting. Unfortunately, the current prevailing belief
in druidic construction led them to associate it with lurid accounts by classical authors of human
sacrifices, conveying feelings of sublime terror as much as religious awe. Blake adjudged it

> Labour unparallelld! A wondrous rocky World of cruel destiny,
> Rocks piled on rocks reaching the stars; stretching from pole to pole.
> The Building is Natural Religion & its Altars Natural Morality,
> A building of eternal death: whose proportions are eternal despair.[29]

It must have been a comparable assumption that led Thomas Hardy in *Tess of the d'Urbervilles*
to locate the capture of his tragic heroine at Stonehenge, where she inadvertently sleeps on
the supposed sacrificial 'altar stone' as a prelude to her own unjust sacrifice. Hardy visited the
site more than once, and remarked on 'the misfortune of ruins – to be beheld nearly always at
noonday by visitors, and not at twilight'.[30]

Perhaps the most evocative of travellers' accounts is that of Francis Kilvert, who paid his
respects to the colossal shrine in August 1875. After a 'merry luncheon' with friends at the
Druid's Head Inn, the party set off across the Plain among 'great and solemn barrows', the 'grassy

27   Joyce Hemlow (ed.), *The Journals and Letters of Fanny Burney (Madame d'Arblay)* (Oxford, 1972-84), i,
       pp. 21–22.

28   [Louis Simond], *Journal of a Tour and Residence in Great Britain, during the Years 1810 and 1811, by
       a French Traveller* (Edinburgh, 1815), i, pp. 195–96. After citing the views of Stukeley and others, the
       contemporary *Encyclopaedia Britannica* advanced a classical etymology for Geoffrey's *mons Ambrii*:
       'The ancients distinguished stones erected with a religious view, by the name of *amber*; by which
       was signified anything solar and divine. The Grecians called them πετραι αμδροσιαι, *petrœ ambrosiœ*'
       (*Encyclopaedia Britannica; or, a Dictionary of Arts, Sciences, and Miscellaneous Literature* (Edinburgh,
       1810), xix, pp. 729–30).

29   Stephen Gill (ed.), *The Salisbury Plain Poems of William Wordsworth* (Ithaca, New York, 1975),
       pp. 22–27, 127–28, 232–35; G. E. Bentley, Jr. (ed.), *William Blake's Writings* (Oxford, 1978), pp. 560–62.

30   Florence Emily Hardy, *The Later Years of Thomas Hardy 1892–1928* (London, 1930), p. 72.

barrows of the happier dead'. It seemed to be 'holy ground and the Acre of God'. Before long they arrived at

the grey cluster of gigantic Stones. They stood in the midst of a green plain, and the first impression they left on my mind was that of a group of people standing about and talking together. It seemed to me as if they were ancient giants who suddenly became silent and stiffened into stone directly anyone approached, but who might at any moment come alive again, and at certain seasons, as at midnight and on Old Christmas and Midsummers Eve, might form a true 'Chorea Gigantum' and circle on the Plain in a solemn and stately dance.

It is a solemn awful place. As I entered the charmed circle of the sombre Stones I instinctively uncovered my head. It was like entering a great Cathedral Church. The great silent service was going on and the Stones inaudibly whispered to each other the grand secret. The Sun was present at the service in his Temple and the place was filled with his glory ...

It must be a solemn thing to pass the night among the silent shadows of the awful Stones, to see the Sun leave his Temple in the evening with a farewell smile, and to watch for him again until morning he enters once more by the great Eastern gate and takes his seat upon the altar stone.

As we went down the southern slope of the green plain we left the Stones standing on a hill against the sky, seeming by turns to be the Enchanted Giants, the Silent Creatures, the Sleepless Watchers, the great Cathedral on the Plain.[31]

Throughout the nineteenth century Stonehenge continued to provide increasing attraction for painters and writers, tourists and excursions, as well as enthusiasts eccentric and serious. Among scholars who paid their respects was Charles Darwin, who, together with his wife Emma, spent a day on the spot in June 1877 investigating the effect earthworms exercized on the subsidence of stones. Mrs Darwin reported with wifely resignation that 'they did not find much good about the worms, who seem to be very idle out there'.[32]

In 1895 Beatrix Potter was, by contrast, 'more impressed by the Plain than by Stonehenge', finding her first view 'disappointing, not because it is small, but because the place whereon it stands is so immense'. Regrettably, the wild setting was already becoming blighted by intrusions of modernity: 'Behold the ubiquitous game of golf, two other carriages and a camping-photographer; his pony was wandering about in a sack'.[33]

One wonders whether it may not in fact have been, at least in part, the eerie encircling void that induced the original builders to sanctify the spot. When Blake wrote of 'Rocks piled on rocks reaching the stars; stretching from pole to pole', his poetic intuition touched on a fundamental aspect of the essence of the shrine.

Investigation of the origins of the monument proceeded initially at a fairly leisurely but ultimately constructive pace during the reign of Queen Victoria. In the middle of the century

---

31 William Plomer (ed.), *Kilvert's Diary: Selections from the Diary of the Rev. Francis Kilvert* (London, 1977), iii, pp. 223–24. Kilvert's mystical experience provides a fine instance of Otto's *mysterium tremendum* (Rudolf Otto, *The Idea of the Holy: An Inquiry into the Non-rational Factor in the Idea of the Divine and its Relation to the Rational* (Oxford, 1926), pp. 12–24).

32 Chippindale, *Stonehenge Complete*, pp. 136, 141–56.

33 Leslie Linder (ed.), *The Journal of Beatrix Potter 1881–1897* (London, 1989), pp. 381, 382.

'Stonehenge, near Salisbury, England', photochrome taken between 1890 and 1900. (Courtesy Library of Congress)

scholars could still argue for a date of construction *after* the Roman occupation, or at earliest a couple of centuries before that period.[34] However, by the conclusion of her reign excavations showed incontrovertibly that Stonehenge could not have been built later than the Bronze Age.[35] The time had arrived when investigation was to become increasingly conducted according to scientific principles, with rewarding results.

Early scholarly explanations

The date of the construction of Stonehenge, together with the related issue of the identity of the people who raised it, has endured as a topic of perennial fascination from the twelfth century onwards. As I write, remarkable fresh discoveries by archæologists under the direction of Professors Mike Parker Pearson and Vincent Gaffney are revolutionizing our understanding, not only of the erection of the edifice itself, but of a vast complex of previously ignored related structures on the surrounding plain.

Above all, there remains the intriguing and elusive enigma of the purposes it served. The influence of Geoffrey of Monmouth's pioneering account is accounted for, not only by the fact that it provided the first explanation, but that it remained for centuries the fullest and most specific. According to his 'history', the stones were transported from Ireland in the fifth century AD at the instance of King Aurelius, under the direction of Merlin, in order to provide a fitting memorial to British nobles massacred by Saxon ruffians under the command of their

---

34   Edwin Guest, *Origines Celticae (A Fragment) and other Contributions to the History of Britain* (London, 1883), ii, pp. 200–17; Thomas Wright, *The Celt, the Roman, and the Saxon: A History of the Early Inhabitants of Britain, Down to the Conversion of the Anglo-Saxons to Christianity* (London, 1852), pp. 82–83.

35   T. Rice Holmes, *Ancient Britain and the Invasions of Julius Caesar* (Oxford, 1907), pp. 215–16.

treacherous chieftain Hengist. Geoffrey was careful to explain that this extraordinary feat was accomplished, not by magic, but by means of the prophet's superior engineering skills (*machinationes*).[36] Interment of the heroic victims established the sanctuary as burial place of British kings, notably Aurelius himself, and his successors Uther Pendragon and Constantine.

Had Geoffrey not introduced the seemingly fantastic account of the transportation of the stones across the Irish Sea and much of southern Britain, the credibility of his story might have endured longer than it did. Yet, although his account clearly cannot be literally true, it is paradoxically likely to be this aspect that substantially reflects authentic prehistoric lore.

However, it was not long before Geoffrey's colourful *History* came under attack. Towards the close of the twelfth century, the Yorkshire chronicler William of Newburgh launched a devastating criticism of its Arthurian section in particular. It was not difficult to show that it conflicted with what was recorded of the period in accounts by reputable early historians such as Bede, while the silence of contemporary Continental historians made Geoffrey's heady account of Arthur's extensive conquests in Europe impossible to countenance. Although he made no allusion to the Stonehenge episode, William's scepticism must have been evident from his denunciation of Merlin as a pseudo-historical pagan magician.[37] However, it appears that William's ire was directed less against the *Historia Regum Britanniæ* itself, than to its increasing acceptance by subsequent historians such as Gervase of Canterbury.[38]

Despite this early assault, the veracity of Geoffrey's *Historia* generally, and his account of Stonehenge in particular, remained widely accepted throughout the Middle Ages. Within decades of its completion there appeared two popular verse adaptations, known as *Bruts*. The Anglo-Norman Wace composed a French version in 1155, which was followed at the beginning of the thirteenth century by Layamon's English verse epic. Both included the story of Merlin's transfer of the stones of Stonehenge, together with the royal burials, as veracious history.[39]

Despite William of Newburgh's trenchant criticism, it was only occasionally that subsequent mediæval chroniclers ventured tentative doubts. In the middle of the fourteenth century Ranulph Higden, in his *Polychronicon*, while prepared to accept the royal burials at the site, expressed misgiving over the transmarine removal of the stones. Fifty years later Richard of Cirencester appeared to share this scepticism, since he omitted the foundation legend of Stonehenge and other marvellous episodes from his history altogether. However, so dramatic a tale was not to be dismissed by a public eager for wonders, and in 1420 Thomas Otterbourne

36   According to Olympiodorus, the Argonauts employed 'machines' (μηχανῆς) to transport their ship Argo 400 stades overland in Italy (R. C. Blockley (ed.), *The Fragmentary Classicising Historians of the Later Roman Empire: Eunapius, Olympiodorus, Priscus and Malchus* (Liverpool, 1983), p. 154).

37   Richard Howlett (ed.), *Chronicles of the Reigns of Stephen, Henry II, and Richard I* (London, 1884), i, pp. 17–18. Cf. Catherine Daniel, *Les prophéties de Merlin et la culture politique (XIIe-XVIe siècle)* (Turnhout, 2006), pp. 100–101.

38   R. William Leckie, Jr, *The Passage of Dominion: Geoffrey of Monmouth and the Periodization of Insular History in the Twelfth Century* (Toronto, 1981), pp. 93–97.

39   Ivor Arnold (ed.), *Le Roman de Brut de Wace* (1938–40), pp. 424–31, 436–37, 475; G. L. Brook and R. F. Leslie (ed.), *Laȝamon: Brut* (Oxford, 1963–78), pp. 440–454.

included in his *Chronica Regum Angliæ* Merlin's feat among other wild and wonderful matter adopted from Geoffrey's *Historia*.[40]

It was the new humanism of the Renaissance which began irreversible inroads into Geoffrey's narrative. At the beginning of Henry VIII's reign, the Italian Polydore Vergil ignored his account of the origin and erection of the stones. However, he accepted Stonehenge as burial-place of Ambrosius (Geoffrey's Aurelius),

> for whome, in the meane time, in that hee hadde well deserved of the common wealthe, thei [the Britons] erected a rioll sepulcher in the fashion of a crowne of great square stones, even in that place wheare in skirmished hee receaved his fatall stroke. The tumbe is as yet extante in the diocesse of Sarisburie, neare to the village, called Aumsburie.[41]

Such inconsistencies, or compromises, illustrate the reluctance with which even Geoffrey's most trenchant critics contemplated discarding his *Historia* in its entirety. For without it, what was there to occupy the vast historiographical void prior to the Roman conquest, or that which ensued for a century and more after the end of Roman Britain? At the close of Elizabeth's reign, two of her greatest topographical historians were found ranged on either side of the divide. While John Stow credited Geoffrey's account of Stonehenge, William Camden rejected Merlin's transportation of the stones as altogether unworthy of consideration.[42]

From the seventeenth century onwards Geoffrey's account of Stonehenge became increasingly discarded, not infrequently to be replaced by explanations fully as extravagant. While the architect Inigo Jones pronounced it a temple to the god Coelus, probably erected in the time of Agricola, Edmund Bolton with equal confidence pronounced it the tomb of Boadicea. Meanwhile Walter Charleton, in his *Chorea Gigantum*, identified the complex as the ancient coronation site of the Danish kings of England, which explained its being shaped (so he claimed) like a crown. However such extravagant theories were sidelined by increasing endorsement of John Aubrey's pioneering assertion that Stonehenge was a druidic temple.[43]

Given the state of knowledge available at the time, the druidic hypothesis appeared the most plausible. But since all that was then known of the druids comprised a scattering of allusions in the works of Roman historians, this frustrating void came to be filled by vagaries of speculative imagination. Stukeley's admirable pioneering surveys of the site of Stonehenge became absorbed into his subsequent weird and wonderful reconstructions of druidic rites and beliefs, serpent-cults and the like, originating almost entirely in his enthusiastic imagination. Stukeley's contemporary John Wood aroused the great antiquary's wrath by asserting in his book *Choir Gaure* (1747) that Stonehenge was created by the prehistoric King Bladud of Bath, as

---

40 Laura Keeler, *Geoffrey of Monmouth and the Late Latin Chroniclers 1300–1500* (Berkeley, 1946), pp. 19, 32, 38.

41 Sir Henry Ellis (ed.), *Polydore Vergil's English History, from an Early Translation Preserved among the MSS. of the Old Royal Library in the British Museum* (London, 1846), i, p. 117. A good account of Vergil's antiquarian writing is to be found in T. D. Kendrick, *British Antiquity* (London, 1950), pp. 80–84. Thundering Welsh patriotic ripostes to the 'wilful ignorance and dogged envie' of such detractors of the British History are cited on pp. 87 and 100.

42 John Stow, *The Annales of England* (London, 1601), pp. 57–58. *Gigantum verò chorea quam hoc in agro statuit Giraldus, fabulosæ antiquitatis admiratoribus libenter relinquo. Non enim ego fabellis indulgere decreui* (Camden, *Britannia*, p. 774).

43 Chippindale, *Stonehenge Complete*, pp. 57, 61, 70–71.

focus of a moon-cult. Bath was where Wood plied his trade as a gifted architect, its magnificent Circus being inspired by his vision of Stonehenge.

A total absence of genuinely fresh information was far from inhibiting continuing controversy. With a blast of robust eighteenth-century invective, the deviser of one fanciful hypothesis denounced another's no less eccentric brainchild as 'the fermented dregs and settlement of the dullest, and most inveterate mixture of ignorance, malice and malevolence'.[44]

Critics failed to note the illogicality of replacing Geoffrey of Monmouth's own account with the ascription to King Bladud of Bath, who was no authentic figure of legend like Merlin but a dynast whose fanciful career was cobbled together by Geoffrey himself.[45]

Meanwhile, Welshmen, proudly conscious of their status as heirs of the ancient Britons, extolled Stonehenge as a work constructed by their forebears. Edward Williams (1746–1826), better known by his bardic name Iolo Morganwg, was a noted eccentric and colourful radical, who denounced Pitt and Burke for their opposition to the French Revolution, and declared himself a

'Democrate, Leveler, Jacobin, Sansculotte, or anything that may be manufactured from the cream that swims on the surface of their malevolence'.[46]

In 1801 Iolo published a collection of Welsh triads. These included allusions to Stonehenge, whose flavour is best conveyed by two associated entries:

> The Three powerfully strong men of the Island of Britain GWRNERTH OF PIERCING STROKE, who killed the largest Bear that was ever seen with an Arrow of Straw; GWGAN OF POWERFUL HAND who rolled the STONE OF MAENARCH from the Glen up to the top of the Mountain, tho' to drag it required no less than sixty oxen, and EIDIOL THE MIGHTY, who in the Massacre of Salisbury Plain, with a mountain-ash bludgeon, killed six hundred and sixty Saxons between the setting of the sun and dark night.

Another triad catalogued

> The Three Mighty works of the Island of Britain: the erection of the STONE of CETTI; the WORK OF EMRYS [i.e. Stonehenge] and the raising of the HEAP OF BATTLES.[47]

Unfortunately Iolo's Triads have since been exposed as an entertaining forgery.[48] Throughout the nineteenth and early twentieth centuries, however, they exerted considerable influence upon contemporary Romantics and even historians. Another imaginative enthusiast for ancient Welsh bardic lore, Edward Davies (1756–1831), published in 1804 an exposition of the wisdom of the druids. Davies's reconstructed druidical doctrines appear mystical to the point of obfuscation, of which his explanation of the significance of Stonehenge provides a fair sample.

---

44   Ibid., pp. 82–86, 94–95; Sweet, *Antiquaries*, p. 131.

45   Edmond Faral, *La légende arthurienne - Études et documents* (Paris, 1929), ii, pp. 102–9; Bernard Merdrignac, 'Une course en char dans l'hagiographie bretonne? Saint Samson contre la *Theomacha*', in John Carey, Máire Herbert, and Pádraig Ó Riain (ed.), *Studies in Irish Hagiography: Saints and Scholars* (Dublin, 2001), p. 145.

46   Geraint H. Jenkins, 'The Bard of Liberty during William Pitt's Reign of Terror', in Joseph Falaky Nagy and Leslie Ellen Jones (ed.), *Heroic Poets and Poetic Heroes in Celtic Tradition: A Festschrift for Patrick K. Ford* (Dublin, 2005), pp. 183–206.

47   Rachel Bromwich, 'Trioedd Ynys Prydain: The *Myvyrian* "Third Series"', *The Transactions of the Honourable Society of Cymmrodorion: Session 1969* (London, 1969), pp. 131–32, 138.

48   G. J. Williams, *Iolo Morganwg* (Cardiff, 1956), pp. 396–97.

The sacred *precinct,* and the *temple,* are to be seen, at this day, upon *Salisbury plain.* It was called … *Gwaith Emrys,* or *Emreis,* the structure of the *revolution,* evidently that of the sun, for the name has been so contrived, that the letters which form it, when valued as the *Celtic* or *Greek* numerals, mark the day on which that revolution is completed, *viz.*

η' 8, μ' 40, ς 100, η' 8, ι' 10, ς 200 = 366.[49]

Despite, or perhaps because of, its baffling obscurity, the legacy of Iolo and Davies tenaciously endures to the present day as inspiration for many of those white-clad druids who may annually be glimpsed celebrating the summer solstice at Primrose Hill or Stonehenge. In my youth I participated in assemblies of The Druid Order ('The British Circle of The Universal Bond'), and see from my invitation to attend at Stonehenge in 1961 that 'Cheques etc. should be made payable to the DRUID ORDER and will be acknowledged immediately upon receipt'. Evidently the modern pacific Order had replaced the dark inheritance of human sacrifice, described by Caesar and Lucan, with a more commercial ethos.

It is however fruitless to mock the wilder extravagances of enthusiasts, nor need the harmless pleasure they continue to afford their flocks be severely dismissed.[50] Romantic druids inspire gratifying appeal for their devotees, and so long as real evidence remains lacking, curiosity will inevitably continue to lure enquirers into enticing byways of imaginative speculation. Nor, indeed, is modern 'scientific' thinking entirely averse to voyaging along the wilder shores of conjecture. One example among many illustrates the extent to which today's scholarly theory may appear little less speculative than imaginative interpretations hazarded by our mediæval forebears.

In short, Stonehenge can be seen as the product of matrilineal social organizations descended from the Neolithic and practising goddess religion.[51]

In fact, there exists no more evidence to support this confident hypothesis than that buttressing the mystic calculations of Edward Davies.

Not long ago, a Canadian scholar sought to 'prove' that religion played no significant part in the ideology of the builders of Stonehenge, by offering his students $1,000 if they could persuade sufficient people to quarry and convey a ten-ton megalith to Simon Fraser University,

49 Edward Davies, *Celtic Researches, on the Origin, Traditions & Language, of the Ancient Britons* (London, 1804), p. 191. The third letter appears to be *sigma,* but should surely be *rho*: ημρηις. My copy bears the autograph of its previous owner, Sir John Edward Lloyd: one wonders what that eminent historian of Wales made of Davies's baffling work.

50 Cf. Stewart F. Sanderson, 'Druids-As-Wished-For', in J. V. S. Megaw (ed.), *To illustrate the monuments: Essays on archaeology presented to Stuart Piggott* (London, 1976), pp. 23–26. Piggott himself compiled an entertaining account of romantic evocations of Stonehenge and its votaries (*The Druids*, pp. 131–81).

51 Frank Battaglia, 'Goddess Religion in the Early British Isles', in Miriam Robbins Dexter and Edgar C. Polomé (ed.), *Varia on the Indo-European Past: Papers in Memory of Marija Gimbutas* (Washington, 1997), p. 56. Gimbutas's more sober account remains nevertheless *au fond* speculative (Marija Gimbutas, *The Language of the Goddess* (London, 1989), p. 313). Penetrating dismissals of the 'goddess religion' hypothesis are assembled in essays collected by Lucy Goodison and Christine Morris (ed.), *Ancient Goddesses: The Myths and the Evidence* (Madison, Wis., 1998). Cf. also Ronald Hutton, 'Medieval Welsh Literature and Pre-Christian Deities', *Cambrian Medieval Celtic Studies* (Aberystwyth, 2011), lxi, p. 63.

and erect it using *only* their powers of persuasion concerning supernatural concepts (i.e., no rewards or monetary benefits can be offered to people to induce them to undertake this task). I have never had anyone take me up on such an offer and I do not expect to be paying anyone in the future.[52]

Possibly volunteers for this exotic proposal might after all have been found, had the cheque been made out in druidic currency, reflecting the considerably more modest sum I was happy to proffer at Stonehenge in 1961.

There is a tendency for successive generations of scholars to interpret the monument in light of prevailing contemporary ideological conceptions. Whether it be Stonehenge as astronomical observatory, or more recent hypotheses of 'the archæology of power' or an imagined primæval matriarchate, all too often such visionary reconstructions do indeed appear to owe more to current fashionable predilections than prehistoric reality.[53]

The time has surely arrived when serious discussion of the purpose and associated ideology of Stonehenge should be rigorously confined to reconstructions based on sound evidence, else the investigation may be abandoned as fruitless. However, before entering on the challenging task of assembling and examining the sources, it is necessary to summarize the spectacular advances achieved by archæologists over the past century and more. If archæology cannot of itself be expected to explain *why* the monument was erected, nor what were its continuing functions, it can convincingly establish with increasing certitude *when* and *how* there occurred Stonehenge's protracted coming into being. Many years ago, a perceptive archæologist observed that:

> We can say that Stonehenge is a large impressive structure, not obviously a house or a tomb; it is by inference a great ritual centre, perhaps one might say a great magico-religious centre – but if we say more, we are guessing. It is easier to date Stonehenge than to say what went on inside it.[54]

---

52 Brian Hayden, *Shamans Sorcerers and Saints* (Washington, 2003), pp. 18–19.

53 C. C. Wrigley, 'Stonehenge from without', *Antiquity* (Cambridge, 1989), lxiii, pp. 746–52. For a useful survey of some modern theories, cf. John North, *Stonehenge: Neolithic Man and the Cosmos* (London, 1996), pp. 393–408. That Stonehenge was at least in part aligned to accord with astronomical considerations seems clear: what is not is that this made it *primarily* an observatory.

54 G. E. Daniel, 'The Peoples of Prehistoric Britain', in M. P. Charlesworth and M. D. Knowles (ed.), *The Heritage of Early Britain* (London, 1952), p. 16.

2

Archæology and Stonehenge

What follows makes no claim towards providing a comprehensive account of the building of Stonehenge, and comprises a summary outline of the chronology of successive stages of its evolution relevant to the present investigation. Especially significant, for reasons which will become apparent as the story unfolds, is the manner in which the celebrated bluestones came to be incorporated within the structure.

It is now known that the area where Stonehenge subsequently came to be built was regarded as possessed of peculiar sanctity from a very early period. In the eighth millennium BC hunter-gatherers on Salisbury Plain erected huge posts close to the site, made from the trunks of pine trees.[1] It may be that these early inhabitants experienced some form of theophany, revealing the spot as especially holy.[2]

It was surely the continuing sanctity of the spot that induced early farmers to begin building large tombs ('long barrows') in the locality from about 3800 BC.[3] Throughout this period scrub and woodland were cleared, gradually making way for 'a stable and quite open grassland by late Neolithic times or the third millennium BC'.[4] Thus, it was no later than 3500 BC that the region

---

1   Michael J. Allen, 'Before Stonehenge: Mesolithic human activity in a wildwood landscape', in Rosamund M. J. Cleal, K. E. Walker, and R. Montague (ed.), *Stonehenge in its landscape: Twentieth-century excavations* (London, 1995), pp. 470–72; Sally Exon, Vince Gaffney, Ann Woodward, and Ron Yorston, *Stonehenge Landscapes: Journeys through real-and-imagined worlds* (Oxford, 2000), pp. 30–31; Mike Parker Pearson, *Stonehenge: Exploring the Greatest Stone Age Mystery* (London, 2012), pp. 134–37; Mark Bowden, Sharon Soutar, David Field, and Martyn Barber, *The Stonehenge Landscape* (Swindon, 2015), pp. 13–15.

2   'In actual fact, the place is never "chosen" by man; it is merely discovered by him; in other words, the sacred place in some way or another reveals itself to him' (Mircea Eliade, *Patterns in Comparative Religion* (London, 1958), p. 369; cf. pp. 369–71). Cf. William James, *The Varieties of Religious Experience: A Study in Human Nature* (Cambridge, Mass., 1902), pp. 53–77; Rudolf Otto, *The Idea of the Holy: An Inquiry into the Non-rational Factor in the Idea of the Divine and its Relation to the Rational* (Oxford, 1926), pp. 12–24; Ivar Lissner, *Man, God and Magic* (London, 1961), pp. 37–38; Joan M. Vastokas and Romas K. Vastokas, *Sacred Art of the Algonkians: A Study of the Peterborough Petroglyphs* (Peterburgh, Ontario, 1973), pp. 49–50; Thomas A. Idinopulos, 'Understanding and Teaching Rudolph Otto's The Idea of the Holy', in Thomas A. Idinopulos and Edward A. Yonan (ed.), *The Sacred and its Scholars: Comparative Methodologies for the Study of Primary Religious Data* (Leiden, 1996), pp. 139–55. Striking evidence of paranormal and supernatural manifestations is recorded by C. R. Hallpike, *The Foundations of Primitive Thought* (Oxford, 1979), pp. 474-79.

3   Exon, Gaffney, Woodward, and Yorston, *Stonehenge Landscapes*, pp. 34–42; Pearson, *Stonehenge*, pp. 138–39.

4   Charles French, Rob Scaife, and Michael J. Allen, 'Durrington Walls to West Amesbury by Way of Stonehenge: A Major Transformation of the Holocene Landscape', *The Antiquaries Journal* (Cambridge, 2012), xcii, pp. 1–36. 'The landscape is open and would have been so in prehistory: the latest research indicates that this downland never was heavily wooded but has remained since the last Ice Age broadly as we see it today' (Bowden, Soutar, Field, and Barber, *The Stonehenge Landscape*, p. 1).

became focus to major ceremonial activities, to an extent suggesting that they radiated across a region considerably more widespread even than Salisbury Plain.

Creation of the sanctuary commenced at the beginning of the fourth millennium BC, with the establishment of an enclosure by digging its encircling ditch and bank.

> It is accepted here that the construction of the Ditch marks the beginning of use of the monument site in a way which differed markedly from what had gone before. There is no indication that the site was marked out as special, or selected for particular use in any way prior to the excavation of the Ditch.[5]

Its purpose was to establish a sacred space, distinguished from the profane world without.

> In the British Isles, circular embanked enclosures, sometimes containing rings of upright stones or wooden posts, are interpreted as open-air temples or sanctuaries, comparable to the embanked circles and rings of carved wooden posts created by North American Indians.[6]

The huge sarsen stones weighing around thirty-five tons apiece which now dominate the site were in BC 2620–2480 dragged overland from locations to the north, in the region of Avebury and Clatford, where they had been deposited by melting glaciers at the close of the Ice Age, and erected to form the great lintelled circle of trilithons which remains partially intact to this day.[7]

About the same time the Aubrey Holes (named after their seventeenth-century discoverer, John Aubrey) were dug. Recent work at the site has established that they were excavated to receive fifty-six bluestones.[8] Although less striking in appearance than the massive sarsens which now dominate the monument, their erection represents a feat of engineering yet more extraordinary. Later, the bluestones were taken from their original setting, and re-erected within the sarsen circle. Their singular importance (sacrality) is confirmed by the fact that they were twice further rearranged within the sanctuary in 2480–2280 and 2280–2020 BC.[9]

Since 1923, the prevailing conclusion among archæologists and geologists has been that the bluestones, weighing up to four tons apiece (the Altar Stone, however, weighs some eight to ten

---

5   Cleal, Walker, and Montague (ed.), *Stonehenge in its landscape*, p. 65. 'The earliest phase (Phase 1) is closely dated to *3015–2935 cal BC*' (Mike Parker Pearson *et al.*, 'The age of Stonehenge', *Antiquity: A Quarterly Review of World Archaeology* (Cambridge, 2007) , lxxxi, p. 618).

6   Stuart Piggott, *Ancient Europe from the beginnings of Agriculture to Classical Antiquity* (Edinburgh, 1965), p. 115. Cf. D. M. Waterman, *Excavations at Navan Fort 1961–71* (Belfast, 1997), pp. 218–24. Circular enclosures and rites traditionally demarcated sacred from profane space (Mircea Eliade, *Patterns in Comparative Religion* (London, 1958), p. 371.)

7   Michael J. Allen and Alex Bayliss, 'The radiocarbon dating programme', in Cleal, Walker, and Montague (ed.), *Stonehenge in its landscape*, p. 532; Cunliffe and Renfrew (ed.), *Science and Stonehenge*, pp. 31, 45, 56, 146; Pearson, *Stonehenge*, pp. 128–32, 292–302.

8   'It seems very likely that Stonehenge was a stone circle from its very beginning. From the sizes of the Aubrey Holes it is evident that the stones they once held were small and narrow. This rules out the sarsens, so we're confident that Stonehenge most likely started as a circle of 56 bluestones' (Pearson, *Stonehenge*, p. 193).

9   The revised Stonehenge chronology is conveniently tabulated in Mike Parker Pearson *et al.*, 'The age of Stonehenge', *Antiquity: A Quarterly Review of World Archaeology* (Cambridge, 2007), lxxxi, pp. 623, 627; idem, *Stonehenge*, pp. 309–313.

Summit of Carn Goedog.

tons),[10] were transported to the site of Stonehenge from the Preseli Mountains of Pembrokeshire in south-west Wales: a distance as the crow flies of some 135 miles, though much greater in practical terms.[11] The precise location of their origin has recently been established by geologists as a hill called Carn Goedog and its vicinity.[12] Their name derives from their greyish-blue colour.

Experiments funded by the BBC in 1954, and manned by scores of volunteers under the direction of archæologists, sought to re-enact this extraordinary feat. It was then conjectured that the stones were dragged on sleds over log rollers from their original site to the sea near Milford Haven (thus avoiding the navigationally perilous voyage around St David's Head), rowed on rafts the length of the Bristol Channel, and so upstream along the Somerset Avon. Thence it was conjectured that they were hauled overland to the headwater of the River Wylye in Hampshire, floated downstream to its confluence with the Avon, and finally rowed upstream, until near Amesbury they were pulled on rollers for a third stretch up to the site where they have remained for the ensuing five millennia.[13] Unlike the crow's flight, this represents a journey of well over 200 miles, including at least 24 of arduous land transport.[14]

---

10 Ibid., p. 266.

11 J. D. Scourse, 'Transport of the Stonehenge Bluestones: Testing the Glacial Hypothesis', in Barry Cunliffe and Colin Renfrew (ed.), *Science and Stonehenge* (Oxford, 1997), pp. 271–314 (cf. the discussion on pp. 315–18); Olwen Williams-Thorpe, M. C. Jones, P. J. Potts, and P. C. Webb, 'Preseli Dolerite Bluestones: Axe-heads, Stonehenge Monoliths, and Outcrop Sources', *Oxford Journal of Archaeology* (Oxford, 2006), xxv, pp. 29–46; Pearson, *Stonehenge*, pp. 268–72.

12 Richard Bevins, Rob Ixer, and Nick Pearce, 'Carn Goedog is the likely source of Stonehenge doleritic bluestones: evidence based on compatible element geochemistry and Principal Component Analysis', *Journal of Archaeological Science* (London, 2014), xlii, pp. 179–93.

13 The BBC reconstruction did not attempt the full land and sea voyage, its purpose being confined to demonstrating a feasible method of transportation.

14 Cf. R. J. C. Atkinson, *Stonehenge* (London, 1956), pp. 99–110. 'The distribution of finds in Pembrokeshire on Map C of this publication [p. xxv] shows a belt between the estuary of the Taf, and Fishguard harbour,

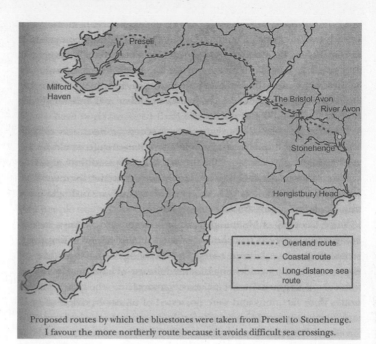

Possible routes for transportation of the Stonehenge bluestones.[16]

Proposed routes by which the bluestones were taken from Preseli to Stonehenge. I favour the more northerly route because it avoids difficult sea crossings.

It was further suggested that riverine transport of the huge blocks could have been conducted on the model of possible flotation of giant oak logs required for the construction of the neighbouring shrine at Woodhenge. Since oak was not indigenous to the region around Stonehenge, a likely source for the latter is the Vale of Pewsey, whence logs could be floated downstream along the Avon.[15]

On the other hand, recent work by the Stonehenge Riverside Project, under the direction of Professor Parker Pearson, suggests that transport by sea could have been impractical. For a start, some stones must surely have sunk on leaving Milford Haven.[17] Yet none has been found on the seabed. For this and other reasons, it is at present considered more likely that the stones were transported overland.[18]

The motive for accomplishing this extraordinary feat, based on detailed examination of archæological considerations, is summarised in a recent study:

---

surely representing a cross-peninsula route for sea-traders unwilling to face the dangers of the all-sea route to Ireland around St. Anne's Head and St. David's Head with their scattered rocky islets' (Sir Cyril Fox, *Life and Death in the Bronze Age: An Archaeologist's Field-Work* (London, 1959), p. xix. Cf. p. 184).

15 G. J. Wainwright and I. H. Longworth, *Durrington Walls: Excavations 1966–1968* (London, 1971), p. 223.

16 Pearson, *Stonehenge*, p. 279.

17 There was also a lack of suitable havens along much of the proposed coastal route: '*All* along the Coaste upon any storme or tempest but inevitable danger in every place even from Wormes head in *Glamorganshire* till they passe S^ce Davids head and soe all alonge the Coaste of *Wales* northwarde fewe good Rodes are to be founde even up to Holy head' (Henry Owen (ed.), *The Description of Pembrokeshire, by George Owen of Henllys, Lord of Kemes* (London, 1892–1936), ii, p. 555).

18 Pearson, *Stonehenge*, pp. 266–68. One may however note the Assyrian method of transporting huge stones on rafts known as *kelek*, which were sustained by inflated animal skins (Michel Tardieu, *Les paysages reliques: Routes et haltes syriennes d'Isidore à Simplicius* (Louvain and Paris, 1990), pp. 171, 174–5).

We propose that, after the earthwork enclosure at Stonehenge ceased to be a major cremation cemetery sometime about 2500 BC, bluestones from Carn Menyn and other nearby outcrops in west Wales were brought to Stonehenge and set up within a temple whose structure had already been built from sarsen stones. From that time onwards, pilgrims and travellers were drawn to Stonehenge because of the special properties that had empowered Stonehenge to provide pastoral and medical care of both body and soul: tending the wounded, treating the sick, calming troubled minds, promoting fecundity, assisting and celebrating births and protecting people against malevolent forces in a dangerous and uncertain world. *The bluestones hold the key to the meaning of Stonehenge* [italics inserted], and Preseli was the special place from whence they came at a high cost to society in labour and time, as befitted such important talismans.[19]

In Chapter Eight of the present work I adduce discrete historical reasons for arriving at a comparable conclusion.

The religious function of Stonehenge is further indicated by construction *c.* 2580–2280 BC of a great ditch-lined avenue, aligned on the midsummer sunrise, stretching from the river Avon to Stonehenge. This was plainly devised for a ritual purpose.[20]

The elaborate redeployment of the bluestones in the period 2280–2020 BC confirms their primary significance in the evolution of the monument. Their number was increased to a total of eighty by the addition of a further twenty-four or so bluestones.[21]

It is most likely that the dressing of bluestones took place inside Stonehenge. That certainly makes sense if the bluestones were already there, in the Aubrey Holes, ready to be rearranged in the Q and R Holes. Not all the bluestones have been dressed: of the 43 survivors, only 17 have been worked to create smooth surfaces. Although moved around several times, presumably the bluestones have never left the premises since their arrival about 2950 BC.[22]

It is thought that these additional stones were brought from a recently identified structure known as Bluestonehenge, beside the Avon.[23] This was probably erected at the time the bluestones were originally brought from Preseli Mountain.

It is hard to overestimate such extraordinary feats of engineering, above all the stupendous feat of bringing the bluestones from the far west of Britain. Describing an inspiring night-time visit to the site, the archæologist Geoffrey Wainwright reflected:

In the end, it was clear to me that the secret as to why Stonehenge was built lay in the bluestones, the first stones to be erected at the site. They had been brought from north

---

19   Timothy Darvill and Geoff Wainwright, 'Beyond Stonehenge: Carn Menyn Quarry and the origin and date of bluestone extraction in the Preseli Hills of south-west Wales', *Antiquity: A Quarterly Review of World Archaeology* (Cambridge, 2014), lxxxviii, pp. 1112–13. I am grateful to Professor John Waddell for drawing my attention to this valuable paper.

20   R. Montague, 'Construction and use of the Avenue', in Cleal, Walker, and Montague (ed.), *Stonehenge in its landscape*, pp. 291–317; *Antiquity*, lxxxi, p. 628.

21   Rosamund M. J. Cleal, 'The stone monument, phase 3', in Cleal, Walker, and Montague (ed.), *Stonehenge in its landscape*, pp. 167–331; Pearson, *Stonehenge*, pp. 32, 33, 193.

22   Ibid., p. 253.

23   Ibid., pp. 221–29.

Pembrokeshire to Stonehenge, and if one could find out why that was so, one would have a lead into one of the reasons why Stonehenge was built – I say one of the reasons because, quite clearly, it must have had a variety of functions.[24]

Recently, Mike Parker Pearson has advanced this hypothetical explanation of the conundrum:

The first stage of Stonehenge was built in that pivotal period around 3000 BC when this pan-island solidarity was gathering momentum. Within this wider context it's possible to understand how Stonehenge might have been designed as a monument for unity, embodying the spirit of the age. The designers of that first Stonehenge had big plans: it wasn't just a unification of people and places, drawing bluestones from an ancestral place of power in Wales, but also a unification of the entire cosmos – the earth, the sun and the moon.

Those who brought the stones from Wales were not simply laying claim to some good grazing land here on Salisbury Plain; they were also taking control of something akin to the *omphalos*, the navel of the world, or the birthplace of gods – the place where the movement of the sun was marked in the land. The work of moving the bluestones was not that of a small devoted sect but entailed the mobilization of an entire society, possibly a growing political domain or kingdom.[25]

This reconstruction appears wholly persuasive. What follows will I believe confirm the essential soundness of these archæologists' conclusions by a fresh approach to the question – one, moreover, grounded on wholly distinct categories of evidence.

---

24 Timothy Darvill and Geoffrey Wainwright, 'Stonehenge Excavations 2008', *The Antiquaries Journal* (Cambridge, 2009), lxxxix, p. 1; cf. pp. 17–18.

25 Pearson, *Stonehenge*, pp. 330–31.

3

The Sacred Centre and the Ancient Roads of Britain

Stonehenge as Omphalos

Distinct considerations indicate that Stonehenge was the *omphalos* of early Britain.[1] It has been suggested that the focus of the monument was a column identified with the Tree of Life, which in early cosmologies was believed to stand at the centre of the earth supporting the heavens.[2] Such a concept might explain cryptic allusion to 'the sun chamber of the single pillar' (*grianán in énúaitne*) at Tara, the twin Omphalos of Ireland.[3] Certainly, the concentric design of Stonehenge suggests an emphasis on *focus*.

> There could be no better symbolic assurance of continuity than a circle of imperishable rocks, linked in various ways with the intermittent but ever-returning lights of heaven.[4]

The *permanence* of the Navel, from which the earth emerged and to which it will in time contract, is one of its most marked ideological characteristics found in cosmologies around the world, while its *centrality* links it simultaneously to heaven and the underworld.[5]

Material confirmation of these conjectures has lately come to light in the course of excavations conducted under the auspices of the Stonehenge Riverside Project. It was on the Stonehenge Avenue, some thirty yards from the Heel Stone, that Professor Parker Pearson made one of his more remarkable discoveries.

> Here were ... periglacial features, this time long, thin erosion gullies created by freeze-thaw conditions and filled with sediment formed from the grinding of chalk by ice into a clay 'flour'. The Wessex chalklands are covered in these periglacial stripes ...

---

1 'A travers toute l'Europe antique a existé ce que nous pourrions appeler un réseau d'omphaloï, réseau certainement tres dense, dont nous ne possédons plus que des débris et dont les points culminants, Delphes, les Exernsteine, le Magdalensberg, Stonehenge, Uisnech, ont tous joué un rôle fondamentale dans l'histoire religieuse de l'Europe' (Françoise Le Roux, 'Le Celticvm d'Ambigatvs et l'omphalos gaulois: La royauté suprême des Bituriges', *Celticvm I: Actes du Premier Colloque International d'Etudes Gauloises, Celtiques et Protoceltiques; Medolanvm Bitvrigvm MCMLX* (Rennes, 1961), p. 184). Cf. Christian-J. Guyonvarc'h and Françoise Le Roux, *Les Druides*, pp. 228, 308.

2 E. O. James, *The Tree of Life: An Archaeological Study* (Leiden, 1966), p. 62; North, *Stonehenge: Neolithic Man and the Cosmos*, p. 546; Brian Hayden, *Shamans Sorcerers and Saints* (Washington, 2003), p. 164.

3 Ruth Lehmann (ed.), *Fled Dúin na nGéd* (Dublin, 1964), p. 2.

4 C. C. Wrigley, 'Stonehenge from without', *Antiquity: A Quarterly Review of Archæology* (Cambridge, 1989), lxiii, p. 751.

5 Mircea Eliade, *Le mythe de l'éternel retour: Archétypes et répétition* (Paris, 1949), pp. 30–37.

However, this particular stretch was possessed of a remarkable property. It is 'aligned on the midsummer sunrise/midwinter sunset solstice axis', for which reason 'we'd wrongly assumed that they would *not* be geological'. Further examination showed that

> in the early part of the post-glacial period, these gullies would have been very plain to see; they would have been clearly visible as stripes in the thin grass cover on the slowly developing soil.

By the Neolithic period they would have become less obvious, in consequence of accretion of earth and grass cover, but nonetheless plain to see in times of drought.

That they did indeed remain visible was confirmed by a discovery that ridges on either side of the gullies had been manually enhanced 'by digging the avenue's ditches along their outside edges and heaping soil on top of each ridge to form parallel banks':

> Looking more carefully at the landscape, we could also see that the natural pair of ridges ran only for about 200 meters whereas the avenue banks continued on well beyond them.

The explanation now became apparent:

> The natural ridges would have formed what anthropologists call an *axis mundi*, an axis or centre of the world. For Neolithic people this was where the passage of the sun was marked on the land, where heaven and earth came together. Such a place might have been regarded as the centre or origin of the universe. It would certainly have been worthy of celebrations involving the transport of Welsh bluestones and, later on, the huge sarsens.[6]

Professor Pearson's conclusion accords with attributes ascribed to *omphaloi* the world over:

> Stonehenge was a monument of unification, bringing together groups with different ancestries in a coalition that encompassed the entirety of southern Britain, if not the entire island. Its design embodied cosmic unity, geometrical harmony and inter-connectedness.[7]

Stonehenge and the prehistoric roads of Britain

Another significant material factor suggests Stonehenge to have been the Sacred Centre of Britain in early times. In Ireland, the Centre was believed to constitute the hub of five great roads, extending the length and breadth of the country. Although they had existed since the beginning of creation, their presence remained unknown until they were revealed by a fairy woman on the eve of the feast of Samain (1 November). Their focal point of intersection was variously

---

6   Mike Parker Pearson, *Stonehenge: Exploring the Greatest Stone Age Mystery* (London, 2012), pp. 243–48, 341–42. Cf. Mark Bowden, Sharon Soutar, David Field, and Martyn Barber, *The Stonehenge Landscape* (Swindon, 2015), p. 28.

7   Pearson, *Stonehenge*, p. 328. 'One of the principal implications of the cosmological model is that the center ideologically represents the totality and embodies the unity of the whole' (Stanley J. Tambiah, *Culture, thought, and social action* (Cambridge, MA, 1985), p. 266). In Islamic cosmology, 'The Holy One created the world like an embryo. As the embryo proceeds from the navel onwards, so God began to create the world from its navel onward, and from there it spread out in different directions' (A. J. Wensinck, *The Ideas of the Western Semites Concerning the Navel of the Earth* (Amsterdam, 1916), p. 19).

identified as Tara and Uisneach, each being regarded as Centre of Ireland in early times.[8] Although much of this radiating road-system existed in material fact, in Irish mythological tradition: 'The roads, as a vital organ of the land, are divine, eternal, and uncreated.'[9] They also served a numinous function, providing routes for pilgrimages to holy places.[10]

Julius Caesar reported that the inhabitants of Gaul converged annually on a nodal site,

within the bounds of the Carnutes, which is regarded as the centre of the whole of Gaul, they [the druids] sit in judgment in a holy place (*in loco consecrato*).[11] Hither all from every side, who have disputes, come and accept their decisions and judgments.

It is likely that this sanctuary was in or near the town of *Cenabum* (Orléans), which was also the major mart of Gaul.[12] This suggests, both in a sacral context and most likely in reality also, that the communications of Gaul were conceived as focussed on the national *omphalos*.

A parallel concept existed in early Britain. The mediæval Welsh tale *Breuddwyd Maxen* opens with the marriage of the Roman Emperor Maxen (Maximus) at Caernarvon to the beautiful British princess Elen. Next morning, in accordance with Welsh legal practice, she claimed her marriage portion (*agweddi*). This included:

Three major castles to be built for her in three places of her choosing in the Island of Britain. Then she asked that the highest castle be built for her in Arfon … After that the other two castles were built for her, namely Caerllion and Caerfyrddin.

Next,

Elen decided to build great roads from one castle to the other across the Island of Britain. Because of that they are called the Roads of Elen Lluyddawg ['Elen of the Hosts'], since she came from the Island of Britain.[13]

Although there are ambiguities in this account, its broad intent is clear. The expression for 'the highest castle' built for Elen in Arfon is *e gaer uchaf*, where the superlative *uchaf* means 'highest', whether in

---

8   R. I. Best, Osborn Bergin, M. A. O'Brien, and Anne O'Sullivan (ed.), *The Book of Leinster Formerly Lebar na Núachongbála* (Dublin, 1954–83), pp. 672–75; Joseph Vendryes (ed.), *Airne Fíngein* (Dublin, 1953), pp. 9–11; L. MacKenna, 'A Poem by Gofraidh Fionn Ó Dálaigh', *Ériu: The Journal of the School of Irish Learning, Dublin* (Dublin, 1952), xvi, p. 133. It seems likely that identification of Tara, rather than Uisneach, as focus of the mythological road system arose in consequence of the former's political importance in the early historical period (cf. Colm O Lochlainn, 'Roadways in Ancient Ireland', in Rev. John Ryan (ed.), *Féilsgríbinn Eóin Mhic Néill* (Dublin, 1940), p. 470). Tara was regarded as a Sacred Centre of Ireland: *Ic imlican urgna na hErenn, ic raith na rigraide i Temraig*, 'at the navel of Ireland, in the rath of the kings in Tara' (J. Fraser, 'The First Battle of Moytura', *Ériu* (1915), viii, p. 24: cf. p. 61).

9   A. G. van Hamel, 'Aspects of Celtic Mythology', *The Proceedings of the British Academy* (London, 1935), xx, p. 248.

10 Proinsias Mac Cana, 'Placenames and Mythology in Irish Tradition: Places, Pilgrimages and Things', in Gordon W. MacLennan (ed.), *Proceedings of the First North American Congress of Celtic Studies held at Ottawa from 26th-30th March 1986* (Ottawa, 1988), pp. 328–31.

11 Caesar's *locus consecratus* is presumably a translation of Gaulish *nemeton*, 'sacred place' (Xavier Delamarre, *Dictionnaire de la langue gauloise: Une approche linguistique du vieux-celtique continental* (Paris, 2001), pp. 197–78).

12 Christopher Hawkes, 'Britain and Julius Caesar', *The Proceedings of the British Academy* (London, 1977), lxiii, p. 178.

13 Brynley F. Roberts (ed.), *Breudwyt Maxen Wledic* (Dublin, 2005), p. 8.

altitude or importance. The latter interpretation is adopted by the latest editor of the text, who took the allusion to be to Caernarvon.[14] However, since the 'faery palace' at Aber Seint visited by Maxen must be the ruined Roman fortress at Caernarvon, whose delapidated but still impressive state at the time of composition enabled it to be envisaged as a vanished gorgeous palace of silver and gold, the new citadel built by Maxen for Elen implicitly lay elsewhere. In the early tenth century, to which I tentatively assign the story's composition (see Chapter Nine *infra*), there was no other stronghold in the vicinity. In any case, it would be incongruous to suppose that the new palace was erected alongside that gorgeous dwelling in which Maxen first discovered his bride.

Earlier scholars identified the *caer uchaf* with the hillfort of Dinas Emrys in Snowdonia, with which Elen was associated in local tradition.[15] This indeed appears an appropriate choice, given that mediæval Welsh sources describe Dinas Emrys as 'the strongest place' (*tutissima ... in aeternum*; *y lle kadarnhaf*) and 'the safest place' (*y lle diogelaf*) in the whole of Britain.[16] It is implicit in the narrative of *Cyfranc Lludd a Lleuelys* that Dinas Emrys was regarded as the inviolate Centre (*omphalos*) of Gwynedd, following its emblematic transfer from southern Britain. If Elen selected it as seat of her power, it would reflect this concept. Again, emphasis on its being linked by roads to cities situated at the furthest extremities of her realm suggests a mandala-like pattern, comparable to that of Ireland's five great roads centred on Uisneach or Tara. In *Breuddwyd Maxen*, Elen is unmistakably a personification of the Maiden Sovereignty of Britain, and her rôle as creator of roads traversing the entire island at the genesis of British history suggests a mythological paradigm, comparable to the miraculous revelation by a fairy maiden of the great roads of Ireland.[17]

Mediæval England preserved a tradition of the Four Great Roads of Britain. The Laws of William the Conqueror (*Leis Willelme*), and a later code erroneously ascribed to Edward the Confessor, list four mighty highways traversing the kingdom: *Watlingestrete, Ermingestrete, Fosse, Hykenild*.[18] In the early twelfth century, Henry of Huntingdon described them as extending from end to end of the island. Icknield Way, he asserted, reached from east to west, Ermine Street from south to north, Watling Street from Dover to Chester, and the Fosse Way from Land's End to Caithness in the north of Scotland.[19]

Geoffrey of Monmouth, writing about the same time, provided a variant account. According to him, King Belinus constructed a road spanning the length of Britain from Cornwall to Caithness, another traversed its breadth from St Davids in south-west Wales to Southampton (*Portus*

---

14   Ibid., pp. 40–42.

15   John Rhys, *Lectures on the Origin and Growth of Religion as Illustrated by Celtic Heathendom* (London, 1888), p. 161; Ifor Williams (ed.), *Breuddwyd Maxen* (Bangor, 1908), pp. 25, 27.

16   Theodor Mommsen (ed.), *Monvmenta Germaniae Historica* (xiii): *Chronica Minora saec. IV. V. VI. VII* (Berlin, 1894), iii, p. 181; Brynley F. Roberts (ed.), *Cyfranc Lludd a Llefelys* (Dublin, 1975), pp. 4–5.

17   In Breton tradition a legendary female figure named Ahès fulfilled a road-building function comparable to that ascribed Elen in Britain (Rachel Bromwich, 'Cantre'r Gwaelod and Ker-Is', in Sir Cyril Fox and Bruce Dickins (ed.), *The Early Cultures of North-West Europe (H. M. Chadwick Memorial Studies)* (Cambridge, 1950), pp. 236–37; Mary-Anne Constantine, 'Prophecy and Pastiche in the Breton Ballads: Groac'h Ahès and Gwenc'hlan', *Cambrian Medieval Celtic Studies* (Aberystwyth, 1995), xxx, pp. 89–99). Ascription of the discovery or creation of national roads to a goddess in all three Celtic realms presumably reflects the archaic concept of the land as a woman.

18   Felix Liebermann (ed.), *Die Gesetze der Angelsachsen* (Halle, 1903–16), i, pp. 510–11. For the reference in the twelfth-century 'Laws of Edward the Confessor', cf. ibid., pp. 637–38; Bruce R. O'Brien, *God's Peace and King's Peace: The Laws of Edward the Confessor* (Philadelphia, 1999), pp. 270–71.

19   Diana Greenway (ed.), *Henry, Archdeacon of Huntingdon, Historia Anglorum: The History of the English People* (Oxford, 1996), p. 22. Etymologies of the traditional names of the roads are examined by A. Mawer and F. M. Stenton, *The Place-Names of Bedfordshire & Huntingdonshire* (Cambridge, 1926), pp. 1–7.

Hamonis), and two further unnamed highways passed at oblique angles in order to link the remaining cities.[20] Ascription of their construction to Belinus probably reflects archaic tradition. Beli Mawr was the Welsh primal divinity, after whom Britain was believed to have been initially named *Ynys Veli*, 'the Island of Beli'.[21] The great roads of Ireland were believed to have sprung into existence in the reign of the primal King Conn, and it is likely enough that a comparable tradition existed in early Britain. In *Breuddwyd Maxen*, creation of the primæval road system is ascribed to the princess Elen, personification of the Sovereignty of Britain. After the Roman Maxen (Maximus) arrived in Britain and wedded her, he expelled Beli and his sons into the sea.[22] As personification of the Maiden Sovereignty, Elen would naturally have been wed to Maxen's predecessor as ruler of Britain. Implicitly, therefore, construction of the ancient road system was associated with Beli, in a tradition independent of Geoffrey of Monmouth's literary creation.

In *Cyfranc Lludd a Lleuelys*, Lleuelys discovers the exact centre of Britain by measuring it from end to end and side to side. There is a correlation between this procedure, and the magical revelation of a great national road system converging on a central focus. In this context it is pertinent to note the salient functions of the Gaulish god identified by Julius Caesar with the Roman Mercurius:

> The god they reverence most is Mercury. They have very many images of him, and regard him as the inventor of all arts, and their most powerful helper in trading and getting money.[23]

That he was 'inventor of all arts' recalls the Irish god Lug, who in *Cath Maige Tuired* is ascribed the sobriquet *samildánach*, meaning 'possessing many skills or accomplishments'. When challenged by the porter at Tara as to his qualification for entering the royal court, he responds by recapitulating his mastery of effectively every art. His Welsh counterpart Lleu acquires the epithet *llawgyffes*, 'skilful hand', which broadly corresponds to the sobriquet borne by Lug.[24] Caesar's *Mercurius* is probably to be identified with Gaulish *Lugus*, whose cult is attested in Gaul.[25] The other function Caesar ascribes to Mercury is that of guiding travellers and protecting merchants. He may in that case be the unnamed

---

20 Michael D. Reeve and Neil Wright (ed.), *Geoffrey of Monmouth: The History of the Kings of Britain* (Woodbridge, 2007), p. 53.

21 Rachel Bromwich (ed.), *Trioedd Ynys Prydein: The Welsh Triads* (Cardiff, 1978), p. 228.

22 Roberts (ed.), *Breudwyt Maxen Wledic*, p. 7.

23 §VI.xvii. *Deorum maxime Mercurium colunt. huius sunt plurima simulacra, hunc omnium inventorem artium ferunt, hunc viarum atque itinerum ducem, hunc ad quaestus pecuniae mercaturasque habere vim maximam arbitrantur* (Otto Seel (ed.), *C. Ivlii Caesaris Commentarii Rervm Gestarvm: Bellvm Gallicvm* (Leipzig, 1961), p. 187). Bernhard Maier in a critical study casts doubt on the identification of Mercurius with Lug ('Is Lug to be Identified with Mercury' (*Bell. Gall.* VI 17, 1)? 'New Suggestions on an Old Problem', *Ériu* (1996), xlvii, pp. 127–35; idem, *Die Religion der Kelten: Götter – Mythen – Weltbild* (Munich, 2001), pp. 87–90). This sceptical view was first advanced by Ernst Windisch, *Das Keltische Brittannien bis zu Kaiser Arthur* (Leipzig, 1912), pp. 99–100. However, the issue remains unsettled: cf. John T. Koch, 'A Swallowed Onomastic Tale in Cath Maige Mucrama?', in John Carey, John T. Koch, and Pierre-Yves Lambert (ed.), *Ildánach Ildírech: A Festschrift for Proinsias MacCana* (Andover and Aberystwyth, 1999), pp. 75–76. Koch's *caveat* is strengthened if my suggestions posed above be accepted, viz. that Lug, both as Lleuelys and as the Brittonic divinity replaced by Maxen Gwledig, was associated with the legendary foundation of British roads. Caesar's assertion that *plurima simulacra* were erected in Gaul to their supreme god corresponding to Mercurius, of which none now survives, is dismissed by Maier as an erroneous identification. However, Caesar for years travelled the length and breadth of Gaul, and his categorical assertion is entitled to respect. Since few if any *simulacra* of identifiable Gaulish deities contemporary with his time have survived, may it not be they were made of wood?

24 Ifor Williams (ed.), *Pedeir Keinc y Mabinogi* (Cardiff, 1930), p. 275.

25 Jan de Vries, *Keltische Religion* (Stuttgart, 1961), p. 54; Heinrich Wagner, 'Studies in the Origins of Early Celtic Civilisation', *Zeitschrift für celtische Philologie* (Tübingen, 1971), xxxi, p. 21. The form *Lug-* was

divinity commemorated in an inscription found at Catterick in Yorkshire, dedicated 'To the god who devized roads and paths'.[26] This suggests a continuing belief in Roman Britain that the primæval roads of the island were the work of a divinity. Clearly, a distinction was drawn between the Roman roads of Britain, whose origin would have been known to every Roman officer, and the ancient meandering British highways which preceded them.

Caesar's account of the annual gathering of druids, who converged from all Gaul on the centre of the land in the territory of the Carnutes, carries a suggestion of 'all roads lead to Rome'. It is thought that Orleans (*Cenabum*), which was probably the town of the Carnutes in question, was selected by the Frankish king Clovis as location for his great Church council of 511, on account of its centrality to all France.[27] Once again, this suggests convergence of the road system on the centre.

That Lleuelys is represented as delineating lines across Britain from coast to coast, crossing at the centre, correspondingly suggests that it was he who was regarded as having established the four great roads of Britain in the primal time. A connexion between the gods Lleu and Belinus, legendary creator of roads, is indicated by the Welsh name *Llewelyn*, earlier British *Lugubelinos* – a combination of the two divine names.[28]

Geoffrey's account of the British roads may be more archaic in origin than those of his contemporaries. Henry of Huntingdon's system is suspiciously neat, with four roads spanning the island in almost perfect radial pattern. Geoffrey's roads follow a more irregular arrangement. Contrary to his usual practice, he ascribes them no names. The location of his second pair remains obscure. His uncharacteristic failure to identify the British roads by name implies that he did not know them, which may again suggest independent tradition.[29] Be this as it may, Britain in prehistoric times was indeed traversed by four major highways, which met at or near a single focal point.[30]

---

popular in Gaulish onomastics and features in Gaulish epigraphy (Antonio Tovar, 'The God Lugus in Spain', *The Bulletin of the Board of Celtic Studies* (Cardiff, 1982), xxix, pp. 594–95).

26   *Deo qui uias / et semitas commentus est* (R. G. Collingwood and R. P. Wright (ed.), *The Roman Inscriptions of Britain: I Inscriptions on Stone* (Oxford, 1965), p. 244).

27   Jean Heuclin, 'Le concile d'Orléans de 511, un premier concordat?', in Michel Rouche (ed.), *Clovis: histoire & mémoire* (Paris, 1997), i, p. 438. A differing purpose is suggested by Alain Dierkens and Patrick Périn, 'Les sedes regiae mérovingiennes entre Seine et Rhin', in Gisela Ripoll and Josep M. Gurt (ed.), *Sedes regiae (ann. 400–800)* (Barcelona, 2000), p. 297.

28   Kenneth Jackson, *Language and History in Early Britain: A Chronological Survey of the Brittonic Languages First to Twelfth Century A.D.* (Edinburgh, 1953), p. 442.

29   For this reason it seems unlikely that 'Geoffrey borrowed his account of the four great roads from Henry of Huntingdon' (Antonia Gransden, *Historical Writing in England c. 550 to c. 1307* (London, 1974), p. 207); cf. J. S. P. Tatlock, *The Legendary History of Britain: Geoffrey of Monmouth's Historia Regum Britanniae and its Early Vernacular Versions* (Berkeley and Los Angeles, 1950), p. 281. This is not to say that Geoffrey was unaware of contemporary allusions to the major roads of Britain, which may in some degree have coloured his description.

30   Cf. O. G. S. Crawford, *Archaeology in the Field* (Plymouth, 1953), p. 78; Colin Burgess, *The Age of Stonehenge* (London, 1980), pp. 283–87. More recent research has shown that the great ridgeways did not, as was earlier believed, constitute single undeviating tracks, but pursued divergent routes evolved over time (Christopher Taylor, *Roads and Tracks of Britain* (London, 1979), pp. 38–39; David Miles, Simon Palmer, Gary Lock, Chris Gosden, and Anne Marie Cromarty, *Uffington White Horse and its Landscape: Investigations at White Horse Hill, Uffington, 1989–95, and Tower Hill, Ashbury, 1993–4* (Oxford, 2003), pp. 131–33). This consideration does not materially affect the present discussion. In sixteenth- and seventeenth-century Britain, major highroads could be as much as two miles wide, owing to the absence of metalled surfaces, and obstructions caused by flooding, fallen trees, and the like (J. Crofts, *Packhorse, Waggon and Post: Land Carriage and Communications under the Tudors and Stuarts* (London, 1967), pp. 14–21).

1. The Icknield Way extended from a location in Norfolk near the Wash, passing across central southern England in a south-westerly direction until it bifurcated, with one section traversing the Vale of the White Horse, and a lateral trackway passing along the Ridgeway high above on the Berkshire Downs. These were reunited at the western end of the Downs, where the road turned south to Salisbury Plain.[31]

2. In the south, the North Downs Ridgeway (Pilgrims' Way) extended from the eastern coast of Kent to Guildford, whence (as the Harroway) it crossed the Hampshire Avon and spanned Salisbury Plain on its course to the West Country.[32] It has even been suggested that the name of the Harroway reflects its relationship to Stonehenge:

    > There are no early forms of the word on record; a possible derivation is from an Old English *hearg-weg, the shrine-way, i.e. the way to Stonehenge. This would be closely parallel in form to the name 'Pilgrims' Way', which is in fact a branch of it.[33]

3. The South Downs Ridgeway passed from the vicinity of Beachy Head in a westerly direction, until it joined the North Downs Trackway at a juncture near the crossing of the Hampshire Avon.[34]

4. To complete this picture of Stonehenge as hub of ancient roads radiating to different points of the compass, the Great Western Ridgeway, 'forming a continuous line of communication from SW England to the Straits of Dover', stretched from the Salisbury Plain area into the south-west, providing access to the lead mines of Mendip and tin mines of Cornwall.[35]

It was thought that a fifth great prehistoric road, termed the Jurassic Way, extended from the Humber to the Mendips, and onward into the South-West. It was further conjectured that it was linked by a lateral route to the radial junction of the Wessex trackways at a point on Salisbury Plain. Latterly, however, the existence of this road has been called in doubt.[36]

---

31 Donald Atkinson, *The Roman-British Site on Lowbury Hill in Berkshire* (Reading, 1916), pp. 29–30; Cyril Fox, *The Archaeology of the Cambridge Region: A Topographical Study of the Bronze, Early Iron, Roman and Anglo-Saxon Ages, with an Introductory Note on the Neolithic Age* (Cambridge, 1923), pp. 143–47; E. T. Leeds, 'The West Saxon Invasion and the Icknield Way', *History: The Quarterly Journal of the Historical Association* (London, 1925), x, pp. 99–100; Crawford, *Archaeology in the Field*, pp. 79–80; Gordon J. Copley, *An Archaeology of South-East England: A Study in Continuity* (London, 1958), pp. 20, 54, 132; Taylor, *Roads and Tracks of Britain*, pp. 16–17, 36–38, 183–84; Richard Muir, *History from the Air* (London, 1983), pp. 232–33; Miles, Palmer, Lock, Gosden, and Cromarty, *Uffington White Horse and its Landscape*, p. 248.

32 D. H. Moutray Read, 'Hampshire Folklore', *Folk-Lore. Transactions of the Folk-Lore Society* (London, 1911), xxii, pp. 310–11; Ivan D. Margary, 'The North Downs' Main Trackways', *Surrey Archaeological Collections* (Guildford, 1952), lii, pp. 29–31; Crawford, *Archaeology in the Field*, pp. 77–79; Copley, *An Archaeology of South-East England*, pp. 50, 132, 138; Taylor, *Roads and Tracks of Britain*, pp. 7, 17, 185.

33 Crawford, *Archaeology in the Field*, p. 78. An alternative derivation is from 'here-weg OE, 'a highway'' (A. H. Smith, *English Place-Name Elements* (Cambridge, 1956), i, p. 245).

34 Crawford, *Archaeology in the Field*, p. 77; Copley, *An Archaeology of South-East England*, p. 84; Taylor, *Roads and Tracks of Britain*, p. 184.

35 G. B. Grundy, 'The Ancient Highways of Dorset, Somerset, and South-West England', *The Archaeological Journal* (London, 1938), xciv, pp. 262–70; Crawford, *Archaeology in the Field*, p. 78.

36 W. F. Grimes, 'The Jurassic Way', in idem (ed.), *Aspects of Archaeology in Britain and Beyond: Essays presented to O. G. S. Crawford* (London, 1951), pp. 144–71; Crawford, *Archaeology in the Field*, pp. 81–86. For doubts regarding the 'Jurassic Way', cf. Taylor, *Roads and Tracks of Britain*, pp. 32–36, 184; John Steane, 'How old is the Berkshire Ridgeway?', *Antiquity* (Cambridge, 1983), lvii, p. 104.

The hub of this national communications network is located in the vicinity of Stonehenge:

The three roads we have been discussing [the Berkshire Ridgeway and the North and South Downs Trackways] all converge on Salisbury Plain; and if the course suggested for each is even approximately correct they must have crossed within a couple of miles of Stonehenge.

In other words, 'the earliest Stonehenge ... is nodal to prehistoric communications'.[37]

When the Romans 'straightened' the ancient British trackways, they established the focus of their southern road system at Old Sarum (*Sorviodunum*) near Stonehenge, possibly because its massive Iron Age ramparts made it a strategically defensible point, in contrast to the exposed monument on Salisbury Plain.[38] Could it also be that the Roman authorities were also concerned to deflect native concern with Stonehenge?

In addition, it is likely that a major road linked the Stonehenge region to the Channel.[39] The most important emporium for prehistoric trade on the south coast of Britain was situated at Hengistbury Head, overlooking the mouth of the Hampshire Avon. The greater part of cross-Channel trade between the wealthy region of 'Wessex' and Northern France was handled by this uniquely important port.[40] It is hard to believe that there was not a ready system of communication between the Channel emporium and the national road-system.

Could this account for the anomalous route pursued by the eastern section of Geoffrey of Monmouth's second road? Instead of following the logical course of spanning Britain laterally from St Davids in South Wales to a corresponding extremity on the coast of south-east England (a pattern which underlay Welsh geographical tradition from as early as the tenth century),[41] his route unaccountably abandons the bisection of the island, instead dropping down to Southampton.

---

37 O. G. S. Crawford, *Man and his Past* (Oxford, 1921), pp. 158–60; idem, *Archaeology in the Field*, p. 80; Copley, *An Archaeology of South-East England*, p. 54. '... these ridgeways are certainly of high antiquity (Dark Ages), and almost certainly prehistoric ... every one of the belts of downland has one. (It is to its accessibility, as well as its use of pastoral land, that the undoubted primacy of Salisbury Plain in early times as a religious centre, in wealth, and in culture must be referred.)' (Sir Cyril Fox, *The Personality of Britain: Its Influence on Inhabitant and Invader in Prehistoric and Early Historic Times* (Cardiff, 1959), p. 66). Cf. V. Gordon Childe, *Prehistoric Communities of the British Isles* (London, 1940), p. 5. It is likely that access to Stonehenge and Avebury was gained by local tracks branching off the principal ridgeways (Aubrey Burl, *Prehistoric Avebury* (London, 1979), pp. 12–14, 140; Taylor, *Roads and Tracks of Britain*, pp. 19–20, 21).

38 Cf. W. Boyd Dawkins, 'The Retreat of the Welsh from Wiltshire', *Archæologia Cambrensis* (London, 1914), xiv, pp. 7–8; Ivan D. Margary, *Roman Roads in Britain* (London, 1955–57), i, pp. 91–97. The ramparts surrounding Old Sarum are impressively formidable (J. Forde-Johnston, *Hillforts of the Iron Age in England and Wales: A Survey of the Surface Evidence* (Liverpool, 1976), pp. 135–37).

39 A unique allusion from the reign of Edward III indicates that *Ykenelde Strete* continued south as 'the Roman road from Old Sarum to Winchester' (G. B. Grundy, 'The Ancient Woodland of Wiltshire', *The Wiltshire Archaeological & Natural History Magazine* (Devizes, 1939), xlviii, p. 569).

40 Barry Cunliffe (ed.), *Hengistbury Head Dorset; Volume 1: The Prehistoric and Roman Settlement, 3500 BC–AD 500* (Oxford, 1987), pp. 332–33). 'Cross-channel links with Brittany, forged during the later Neolithic, continued during this period and it is probable that Hengistbury was a main point of entry for the imported metalwork found in Wessex graves located in those areas of chalk to which it is linked by major rivers' (ibid., p. 335).

41 The Britons were assured they would recover their Island 'from Dyfed to Thanet' (Sir Ifor Williams and Rachel Bromwich (ed.), *Armes Prydein: The Prophecy of Britain From the Book of Taliesin* (Dublin, 1972), p. 12). For similar measurements independent of Geoffrey's version, cf. Egerton G. B. Phillimore, 'A Fragment from Hengwrt MS. No. 202', *Y Cymmrodor* (London, 1887), vii, p. 124; Aled Rhys Wiliam (ed.), *Llyfr Iorwerth: A Critical Text of the Venedotian Code of Medieval Welsh Law Mainly from BM. Cotton MS. Titus Dii* (Cardiff, 1960), p. 59; Melville Richards (ed.), *Cyfreithiau Hywel Dda o Lawysgrif Coleg yr Iesu Rhydychen LVII* (Cardiff, 1957), p. 119; Dafydd Jenkins (ed.), *Llyfr Colan: Y Gyfraith Gymreig un ôl Hanner Cyntaf Llawysgrif Peniarth 30* (Cardiff, 1963), p. 39; Timothy Lewis (ed.), *The Laws of Hywel Dda: A Facsimile Reprint of Llanstephan MS. 116 in the National Library of Wales, Aberystwyth* (London, 1912), p. 72. Cf. further Iwan Wmffre,

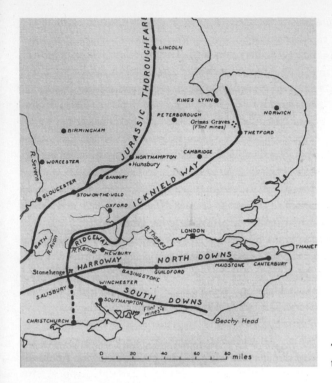

The four main prehistoric
thoroughfares. (Author's collection)

Southampton first appears as a town of significance in Saxon times, and by Geoffrey's day had become the principal port for communication with Normandy and Brittany. Accordingly it plays a prominent rôle in his imaginative *Historia*.[42] Could one of the four great roads in Geoffrey's source have terminated at an unnamed port on the Channel coast (Hengistbury?), which he identified with Southampton to its east?

Ancient road-systems as cosmic paradigms

That the early road-system converging on the Navel of Britain was believed, like that of Ireland, to reflect an ideological palimpsest superimposed on the physical landscape is further suggested by the belief, noted by Chaucer and others, that Watling Street corresponded to the Milky Way in the night sky, across which the hosts of the dead were believed to pass.[43]

Like much else in pagan Celtic tradition, the concept of the Centre as hub of radiating threads probably derives from pre-Celtic shamanist cosmology. In Finnish mythology:

'Penrhyn *Blathaon* ac Amgyffred yr Hen Gymry o Eithafion Gogledd Prydain', *Studia Celtica* (2004), xxxviii, pp. 59–68.

42   Tatlock, *The Legendary History of Britain*, pp. 48–49.

43   'See, yonder, lo, the Galaxyë, / Which men clepeth the Milky Wey, / For hit is whyt: and somme, parfey, / Callen hit Watlinge Strete' (Walter W. Skeat (ed.), *The Complete Works of Geoffrey Chaucer* (Oxford, 1894), iii, p. 28). Cf. Michael John Petry, *Herne the Hunter: A Berkshire Legend* (Reading, 1972), pp. 70–71; John MacQueen, *Numerology: Theory and outline history of a literary mode* (Edinburgh, 1985), p. 105. The Bering Eskimos identified the Milky Way as the road to the land of the dead (Åke Hultkrantz, 'Die Religionen der amerikanischen Arktis', in Ivar Paulson, Åke Hultkrantz, and Karl Jettmar, *Die Religionen Nordeurasiens und der amerikanischen Arktis* (Stuttgart, 1962), p. 407). Similarly, the Finns regarded the galaxy as route to the celestial Otherword: i.e. *Kalevanporras*, 'Stairs of Kaleva' (V. V. Napolskikh, 'Proto-Uralic World Picture: A Reconstruction', in Mihály Hoppál and Juha Pentikäinen (ed.), *Northern Religions and Shamanism* (Budapest, 1992), p. 6).

This mythical centre was also where everything was seen as ultimately originating. It was here that man was born again to continue his life in the hereafter; it was here that fire, frost, iron, disease, and healing balms originated; it was here that the bear was reborn from his bones, in the same way as all other game animals. It was also the source of the 'boneless flesh' which seers used in their healing charms to tempt away 'hungry' afflictions from tormenting man. It was also the place, in the form of the mountain of steel, the rock of iron, to which seers exorcised diseases, 'to the heart of the sea's navel, into a blue rock, a liver-coloured crevice'. And here, at the centre of all power, new worlds were given birth to during the cycle of the season ...

Links to this mythical centre are described as taking the form of threads in hunting charms. Hunters called on Tapio's daughter to blow a red or blue silken thread as a bridge for the game to run 'across Pohjola's river'. The image of brightly-coloured strands points to the rays of light seen in auroral displays. Auroral arcs and rainbows themselves acted as bridges to this centre. Both auroral arcs and rainbows could act as a route for abducting a person to the other world. A blue bridge was described by singers as leading to the 'back of a blue stone', or a 'pitching stone' was depicted as lying beyond a red gate.

The Milky Way has also been seen in folk poetry as a road to the mythical centre of the world. One metaphor used for the Milky Way is a river. The great oak, another metaphor for the Milky Way, also serves as a bridge to Tuonela [the realm of death].[44]

Similar beliefs are found on the other side of the world, in the Late Classic Maya civilization of Mexico:

> The perimeter of the quadrilateral world was conceived to be a road. Four roads also radiated from the centre to each midpoint on the side ... These ran on an east/west and north/south axis. The roads did not end at the midpoint but continued into the cave. The midpoint, where the road crossed the perimeter, was called a crossroads, as was the center where all four roads joined.

These Mayan roads provided access to the supernatural world of the deities, some of whom bore particular responsibility for their maintenance, being in consequence invoked by ritual specialists.[45]

Although the present work is not directly concerned with the relationship of Stonehenge to the heavenly bodies, it is worth noting that the cosmic geography of the Maya illuminates the association of earthly roads and their centre with their mirror image in the sky.

> There has been considerable debate over what established the corners of the [world] square; modern sources indicate it was either the intercardinal points or the rise and set points of the sun on the solstices ... Both models ultimately derive from the rise and set points of the sun. In a model based on the intercardinal directions, the corners of the

---

44   Brita Polttila, 'The Cosmology of Finnish Shamanistic Folk Poetry', in Mihály Hoppál and Juha Pentikäinen (ed.), *Northern Religions and Shamanism* (Budapest, 1992), pp. 168–69. 'Now the oak-tree had been felled / across Pohjoinen's river / for a traveller to go / a man to dark Pohjola ...' (Matti Kuusi, Keith Bosley, and Michael Branch (ed.), *Finnish Folk Poetry Epic: An Anthology in Finnish and English* (Helsinki, 1977), p. 267). Cf. Y. H. Toivonen, 'Le gros chêne des chants populaires finnois', *Journal de la Société Finno-Ougrienne* (Helsinki, 1947), liii, pp. 41–43.

45   Karen Bassie-Sweet, *At the Edge of the World: Caves and Late Classic Maya World View* (Norman and London, 1996), pp. 22–23, 44–45.

square are calculated by observing the east and west rise and set points of the equinox sun and using these to extrapolate north, south, and the intercardinal points. In a solstice-based model, the corners of the quadrilateral space established by direct observation of the solstice sun (observing where the sun 'turns' and begins to rise and set at points closer to the equinox points). This is still an important event for the Maya, who beseech the sun to come back at this time.[46]

Like the early Britons, the Maya believed that the sky was traversed by roads paralleling those on earth, which were

formed by the daily paths of the sun, moon, and stars across the heavens, by the ecliptic (the apparent annual path of the sun), by the Milky Way, and by rainbows ... In the *Popol Vuh* the brothers Hun Hunahpu (Sun) and Vucub Hunahpu (Venus) are said to follow the rift road to the underworld. This event must take place when the rift road is in conjunction with the horizon, and this occurs during to important times in the early cycle: the summer and winter solstices. The rift road is at the east midpoint on winter solstice sunrise and summer solstice sunset. Conversely, it is over the west midpoint on winter solstice sunset and summer solstice sunrise.

Furthermore, as in prehistoric Britain and Ireland, the key junctures of the Mayan year were the solstices.

The Milky Way also intersects the terrestrial crossroads on the solstices. At sunrise on the summer solstice and sunset on the winter solstice, the Milky Way arches across the sky from the north-east corner to the southwest corner. At these two important times for Maya calculations, the white road marks the exodus of the sun from under the earth (summer solstice) and the setting sun appears to follow the black road into the underworld (winter solstice). It is likely that the Maya used the movements in the night sky to order their world in the same manner that they used the day sun.[47]

The archaic character of this geocosmic 'atlas' is further indicated by the belief of Australian tribes in the establishment of natural features of the landscape at the primæval era known as the Dreaming. It was then that mythic beings left eternal signs of their presence: outcrops, ridges, unusual trees, springs, and the like, whereby past and present are established as interchangeably one.

Almost everywhere, throughout the continent, "'tribal territory is or was criss-crossed with a network of mythical tracks or "pathways" along which such beings are believed to have travelled' ... Along such tracks contemporary Aborigines too move in their quest for food – following traditional patterns. Even in this mundane task, then, they virtually replicate the travels of the mythic beings. Further, the movements and the incidents in

---

46   Ibid., p. 28.

47   Ibid., pp. 47–48. Cf. Dennis Tedlock (tr.), *Popol Vuh: The Definitive Edition of the Mayan Book of the Dawn of Life and the Glories of Gods and Kings* (New York, 1985), pp. 105–13.

the life of these beings, *vis-à-vis* the land, are immortalized in song and myth as well as in ritual re-enactment.[48]

Finally, we should not ignore the intrinsic likelihood that Stonehenge represented the umbilical centre of Britain.[49] The monument's two most striking characteristics are its cyclopean size, and its near-perfect circularity. So familiar and unique is its iconic image, that it remains the sole prehistoric monument in the British Isles to be instantly recognizable to millions of people around the globe. Yet its very familiarity may in part blind us to its significance. Why was no comparable megalithic structure erected – even on a modest scale – in Late Neolithic or Bronze Age Britain? The answer, surely, is that its rôle was as unique as its architecture, its design being appropriate to its function. Circularity is an essential aspect of the *omphalos*: like the hub of a chariot wheel, it stands equidistant from the encircling bounds of earth and cosmos. In the words of Angela Della Volpe, 'through the rite of circumambulation and the worship of the sacred fire, the circle was the symbol of the sun, the dead ancestors, the hearth, and consecrated space.'[50]

The British Omphalos and the national roads

In the ensuing section of this chapter, and in Chapter Ten below, I seek to show that the authors of the mediæval Lives of Saints Cadog and Illtud incorporated into their biographies archaic elements of the pagan Celtic myth of the Sacred Centre of Britain. It was characteristic of the mediæval hagiographer's *modus operandi* to appropriate what appeared apt legendary motifs – above all, those imbued with colourful aspects of the wonderful – and meld them into his imaginative biography. Of the real facts of the saint's life he generally knew little, but in this way he could portray his hero's career as corresponding to – while, at the same time, superseding – familiar pagan mythological paradigms.

In Elissa Henken's words,

> The saint is in some ways like the culture heroes of mythology. He, too, helps to create and define the world. He is a geomorphic constructor – making wells, raising hills, changing the course of rivers, confining the sea, draining marshes, and creating causeways. He helps to define the world by giving it names – through his ancestors, his own name, or with names derived from his actions. He is a benefactor of mankind, providing man with both physical and cultural necessities – food (which he often creates), healing, law. He provides both an explanation for why things are as they are and a standard for how they should be.[51]

The eleventh-century Life of Saint Cadog contains a remarkably explicit description of what appears to be the national *omphalos* of Britain: one deviating remarkably little from its pagan

---

48 Ronald M. Berndt, *Australian Aboriginal Religion* (Leiden, 1974), i, pp. 7–9; iv, pp. 6-8, 13–14. Cf. Harry Allen, 'The distribution of large blades: evidence for recent changes in Aboriginal ceremonial exchange networks', in Patrick McConvell and Nicholas Evans (ed.), *Archaeology and Linguistics: Aboriginal Australia in Global Perspective* (Melbourne, 1997), pp. 373–74.

49 *Celticvm I*, p. 184; Christian-J. Guyonvarc'h and Françoise Le Roux, *Les Druides* (Rennes, 1986), pp. 228, 308.

50 'From the Hearth to the Creation of Boundaries', *The Journal of Indo-European Studies* (Washington, 1990), xviii, p. 169. Of the king in early India, the *Satapatha* declares, '"he wheels round in a sunwise direction". The Vedic king is Indra, and Indra is the sun' (A. M. Hocart, *Kingship* (Oxford, 1927), p. 26).

51 Elissa R. Henken, *The Welsh Saints: A Study in Patterned Lives* (Cambridge, 1991), p. 6.

original. It appears that the hagiographer has pressed a floating myth into his service. As the editor of the *Vita*, the Rev. A. W. Wade-Evans, observed:

> He uses older material, some of a poetical nature, which he does not always seem to understand, often curiously reminiscent of incidents in the Four Branches of the *Mabinogi* and kindred tales.[52]

The chapter in question (§9) appears randomly included in the *Vita Sancti Cadoci*, bearing as it does scant relationship to anything coming before or after. Although its heading reads 'How the man of God constructed his first monastery' (*Qualiter uir Dei primum monasterium construxit*), the text is little concerned with that event. Cadog's erection of his *monasteriolum* has already been described at the conclusion of the previous chapter, while §9 is primarily concerned with extraneous factors. First, there is the construction of a magnificent cemetery (*cimiterium*), comprising a huge heap of earth (*uastum aceruum de terra*), which was designed as a place of interment for the holiest persons of all Britain (*totius Britanniae*). The author Lifris explains that this unusual arrangement enabled the corporeal remains of the faithful to be interred around the monastery: *quo fidelium corpora circa templi ambitum sepelirentur*.

Next, Cadog constructed four large roads, which traversed four formerly steep, impassable hills surrounding the monastery (*cella*). These were implicitly designed to provide universal access to the monastery, and its surrounding cemetery.

These works completed, Cadog is oddly said to have raised a duplicate earthen tumulus 'like a round fortress' (*in modum urbis rotundum*), on whose summit he erected a structure which became known in Welsh as Cadog's Castle, *Kastil Cadoci*. This curious detail may have been designed to account for an existing place name, which Lifris connected with the protagonist of his story. However, it would be anomalous for a saint to build a fortress,[53] and it may be questioned whether the toponym (of which no other record exists) did not rather commemorate an unconnected lay chieftain of the same name.

Be that as it may, nothing in the text suggests that Cadog inhabited the fortress, nor indeed put it to any purpose whatever. It seems safe to infer that Lifris knew nothing of it beyond its suggestive name, and added the allusion for completeness. It fulfils no function in the narrative beyond complementing the first tumulus, and overall it looks as though the content of §9 originally existed independent of the Saint's Life.

§9 concludes with the explanation that, although he owned very many fields, Cadog sowed grain in a particular one, which became known in Old Welsh as *Eruguenn*, or 'holy meadow'. It was this fertile acre alone that he sowed. Although unspecified, it is implicit that all crops derived their fertility from this hallowed plot sanctified by the Saint.[54]

As noted, §9 appears wholly inconsequential in terms of Cadog's biography. On no subsequent occasion is the Saint described as making use of the cemetery, the roads, or the castle. In fact, every feature of this episode suggests a characteristic piece of *omphalos* mythology. That the *templum* was approached by four roads of semi-miraculous construction

---

52   A. W. Wade-Evans (ed.), *Vitae Sanctorum Britanniae et Genealogiae* (Cardiff, 1944), p. xi.

53   St Samson and his companions sojourned for a while in a delightful castle beside the Severn (*iuxta Habrinum flumen castellum admodum delicatum*), but there is no suggestion that it became permanently sanctified, nor was it assigned the name of the Saint (Pierre Flobert (ed.), *La vie ancienne de saint Samson de Dol* (Paris, 1997), pp. 204, 206).

54   Wade-Evans (ed.), *Vitae Sanctorum Britanniae et Genealogiae*, pp. 44–46.

converging on a *tumulus* suggests a focus established at the precise centre (*y pwynt perued*) of the four quarters of the landscape.[55] The shape of the tumulus evokes the concept of circularity, which is fundamental to *omphalos* ideology.[56] Interment of the bodies of distinguished notables from the length and breadth of Britain around the *templum* at the focal point of four converging roads suggests the practice of burying royal and noble dead in a *cimiterium* surrounding the *omphalos*, in the belief that it was destined to survive the eventual eschatological cataclysm.[57]

Finally, as was seen earlier, the name and property of the Holy Field indicate the fertile source of the country's prosperity. This motif features also in the story of *Manawydan uab Llŷr*. There, the eponymous hero, originally a powerful Celtic deity, brings wheat from *Lloegr* to Arberth, whose characteristics identify it as the Sacred Centre of Dyfed. There he spends time catching fish and wild animals, indicating that, prior to his arrival, the land constituted a primordial wilderness. Next, he tills the soil, planting three fields producing the best wheat in the world. From the odd assertion that the wheat came from alien *Lloegr* (England), it may be inferred that, in an earlier version, it originated in the Otherworld. The concluding words of the story make it clear that it is from these three exemplary crops that the fertility of the kingdom as a whole derives.[58]

The introductory wording of §9 in the *Vita Cadoci* contains a suggestive allusion. After a back-reference to 'all the Britons of the western parts' (*cunctis occidentalium Brittonibus*) mentioned in the preceding chapter, the tale moves on uninterruptedly to explain how swarms of clerics flocked to Saint Cadog 'from various regions of the whole of Britannia' (*ex uariis totius Britanniae oris*), an irruption which caused him to build his cemetery and temple. In

---

55   Cf. Proinsias Mac Cana, *The Cult of the Sacred Centre: Essays on Celtic Ideology* (Dublin, 2011), pp. 91–107.

56   A common symbol of the *omphalos* was a dot within a circle (E. A. S. Butterworth, *The Tree at the Navel of the Earth* (Berlin, 1970), pp. 37–40, 162–63). The Centre must by definition be equidistant from every point on the earth's periphery. The account in the *Vita Cadoci* bears close resemblance to cosmic proportions accorded, both in theory and practice, to construction of cities in the ancient world. Surrounded by a circular fosse, the city is spanned by 'Two axis streets, one running north-south and the other east-west [which] divide the city into four quadrants which reflect the four quarters of the world' (H. P. L'Orange, *Studies on the Iconography of Cosmic Kingship in the Ancient World* (Oslo, 1953), p. 13; cf. pp. 9–17).

57   'Structures such as St Patrick's Bed and the various barrows and ring-ditches, for example, suggest that an important part of Uisneach's role in prehistory was sepulchral: it was, or so it would appear, a necropolis' (Roseanne Schot, 'From cult centre to royal centre: monuments, myths and other revelations at Uisneach', in Roseanne Schot, Conor Newman, and Edel Bhreatnach (ed.), *Landscapes of Cult and Kingship* (Dublin, 2011), p. 105). Scottish kings were believed to have been interred at Iona in consequence of a prophecy that the sacred island would survive the final Flood (Thomas Pennant, *A Tour in Scotland and Voyage to the Hebrides. MDCCLXXII. Part I.* (London, 1776), pp. 284–85). Cf. Alexander Carmichael (ed.), *Carmina Gadelica: Hymns and Incantations with Illustrative Notes on Words, Rites, and Customs, Dying and Obsolete: Orally Collected in the Highlands and Islands of Scotland* (Edinburgh, 1900–71), ii, p. 348. It was characteristic of *omphalos* cosmology that the Centre could not be submerged by the Flood (Mircea Eliade, *Patterns in Comparative Religion* (London, 1958), pp. 233, 375, 376). This suggests a conception comparable to that held by the early Semites: 'In Semitic literature this pre-existent spot in the midst of the primaeval waters, the origin of the later sanctuary and the centre of the future earth, is called the navel of the earth' (A. J. Wensinck, *The Ocean in the Literature of the Western Semites* (Amsterdam, 1918), p. 8; cf. p. 14). Again, 'It is a common idea among the Muslims, taken over from the Jews that the gathering of mankind before the last Judgment will take place at Jerusalem … It is not only in this connection that we meet the navel as seat of the judge' (idem, *The Ideas of the Western Semites Concerning the Navel of the Earth* (Amsterdam, 1916), p. 23).

58   Ian Hughes (ed.), *Manawydan Uab Llyr: Trydedd Gainc y Mabinogi* (Cardiff, 2007), pp. 7–11. Since the crops of the first two fields were destroyed by an Otherworld power, there remained but one exemplary field. It is probable that the original field became at some stage triplicated, in order to conform to the familiar Welsh typology of a triad.

mediæval Wales, *Britannia* could signify alike 'Wales' or 'Britain', context alone indicating which was intended.[59] Here, however, there is an unmistakable semantic shift from 'the Britons of the western parts' (i.e. the Welsh) of the previous chapter, to those of 'the whole of *Britannia*' (i.e. Britain) in the current one. It seems that, in the source of §9 in the *Vita Cadoci*, the cemetery and temple were envisaged as lying at the heart of Britain, not just Wales.

It appears that Lifris is here following the time-honoured hagiographical approach of appropriating a pre-Christian mythic theme to his narrative. The Four Branches of the *Mabinogi*, which were compiled earlier in the same century, attest the extent to which such stories survived in the repertoire of the bards, as also their widespread appropriation for use as 'building blocks' in Christian narratives. While this practice doubtless in part reflected the literary value of 'a good story', there existed also a perceived requirement to appropriate to the saints magical faculties comparable to those possessed by their superseded rivals, the druids.[60]

Myths attached to Stonehenge as *omphalos* could have originated in a very early era, since it seems likely that the monument was built in consequence of a belief that the site already represented the umbilical centre prior to its construction.[61] Extraordinary as this indicates the antiquity of the tradition to be, there is nothing incredible in the idea of its preservation over a period of millennia. The myth of the Centre preserved in *Cyfranc Lludd a Lleuelys* undoubtedly belongs to a tradition of great antiquity, transmitted orally for untold centuries, until it came eventually to be set down in writing. That Lifris, author of the *Vita Cadoci*, was familiar with legends associated with the British *omphalos* will shortly be shown to be confirmed by his use of the story of Illtud's escape from cosmic annihilation, which had become attached to a spot in the vicinity of Llancarfan fortuitously bearing the name *Medgarth*, 'Middle Enclosure'.

At one time there there must have existed a substantial corpus of legendary material relating to the ideology of the Omphalos of Britain, which became in time attached to what appeared appropriate geographical or toponymic locations, whether Dinas Emrys in Gwynedd, *Medgarth* in Morgannwg, or the important Saxon city of Oxford standing at the heart of *Lloegr* (England).

To recapitulate: the myth of the Centre appropriated by Lifris as §9 of his *Vita Cadoci* comprised the following motifs:

1. Cadog constructs a 'temple'.
2. Sanctified men flock from all over Britain to participate in his holy work.
3. About it, he creates a splendid 'round' (*rotundus*) cemetery, in which the bodies of the faithful could be buried (*quo fidelium corpora circa templi ambitum sepelirentur*).
4. He builds four large roads, implicitly converging on the temple and its surrounding cemetery. Evidently, these roads were designed to facilitate passage of the elect from the four corners of the land.
5. Like the pagan deity Manawydan, he creates a fertile enclosure at the Sacred Centre of the land, wherein he plants grain of supernatural quality. From this proliferates the wealth of the land of Britain.

---

59 Wade-Evans (ed.), *Vitae Sanctorum Britanniae et Genealogiae*, p. vii.

60 Carolus Plummer (ed.), *Vitae Sanctorum Hiberniae: Partim Hactenvs Ineditae ad Fidem Codicvm Manvscriptorvm Recognovit Prolegominis Notis Indicibvs Instrvxit* (Oxford, 1910), i, pp. clxvii–clxxvi.

61 Similarly, when St Patrick is represented by Tirechán as ascending the mountain of Cruachán Aigle to conduct his vigil, 'the clear implication is that it was already a site of national importance under the old dispensation' (Mac Cana, *The Cult of the Sacred Centre*, p. 121). The vigil was intended 'in effect to appropriate for Christianity and for Armagh the traditional associations of the holy mountain' (p. 123).

Apart from the possibility that §9 of the *Vita Cadoci* has preserved a pagan myth of the national *omphalos*, we may consider further intimations that it originally described Stonehenge itself:

1. 'Pilgrims' converged on Stonehenge, not only from the length and breadth of Britain, but also (as archæological evidence indicates) far-flung regions of Europe.
2. Stonehenge is a circular temple, possibly to be identified with the 'round' northern temple of Apollo described by Hecataeus of Abdera in the fourth century BC.
3. Geoffrey of Monmouth implicitly describes Stonehenge as being surrounded by an unequalled cluster of princely barrows, which he collectively terms a *cimiterium*.[62] St Cadog is described as creating a *cimiterium* for a comparable purpose, which likewise surrounded his central temple.
4. As O. G. S. Crawford observed, 'Wessex in the Early Bronze Age must have been the centre of gravity of England, to which all roads led'.[63] Four radial national roads converged in the vicinity of Stonehenge. Similarly, in Buganda, an African state ruled by a sacral king (*Kabaka*),

   Most of the time, the king stayed in his palace, located within the capital at the juncture of the kingdom's system of roads. The royal palace was both the center of communication within the kingdom and the source of its wealth. Along the roads ran the king's messengers, who carried information by word of mouth directly to and from the monarch. The roads also conveyed the royal taxes in the form of livestock and produce, and, most important, they conveyed the king's armies, which were raised during wartime to plunder Buganda's neighbors of slaves and livestock.[64]

   Similarly, four royal roads were held to lead from the Inca capital Cuzco to the four quarters of the earth.[65]
5. Stonehenge lay at the heart of 'Wessex', the most prosperous region of Bronze Age Britain, which might with reason have been regarded as source of the Island's wealth, *Eruguenn*.

Saint Cadog 'made four large roads across four steep and previously impassable hills around his *cella*' (*quattuor inmensas calles in transuersum quattuor decliuia moncium suam cellam ambientum*). That each *callis* was ranged across a hill evokes the ancient ridgeways, by means of which men were enabled to traverse or avoid swampy regions and those liable to flooding.[66] Thus, the sixth-century St Gudwal is described as travelling along a highroad in Cornwall which remained dry, while the countryside around was drenched in rain.[67] Clearly this miraculous faculty was ascribed to the Saint, in order to account for an existing ridgeway. St Cadog's four roads spanning steep surrounding hills, by means of which pilgrims from all Britannia converged on the sanctuary at the centre, recall the four national ridgeways converging on Stonehenge.

---

62 Michael D. Reeve and Neil Wright (ed.), *Geoffrey of Monmouth: The History of the Kings of Britain* (Woodbridge, 2007), p. 135.

63 Crawford, *Man and his Past*, p. 158.

64 Benjamin C. Ray, *Myth, Ritual, and Kingship in Buganda* (Oxford, 1991), p. 106; cf. p. 133.

65 Sir James George Frazer, *The Scapegoat* (London, 1913), p. 130.

66 William Bottrell, *Stories and Folk-Lore of West Cornwall* (Penzance, 1870–80), i, p. 28; H. P. R. Finberg, *Roman and Saxon Withington: A Study in Continuity* (Leicester, 1955), pp. 10–11.

67 Gilbert H. Doble, *The Saints of Cornwall* (Chatham and Oxford, 1960–70), i, p. 67.

4

Geoffrey of Monmouth's *Historia Regum Britanniæ*

Geoffrey's life and work

Since Geoffrey of Monmouth's account of the erection of Stonehenge provides (as I shall suggest) a unique description of that 'event', in part derived from earlier independent tradition, it is well to begin by considering the nature of the man and his idiosyncratic literary creation. While no serious scholar today believes that his book represents authentic history, judgments range from its wholesale dismissal as egregious fiction from beginning to end (save where it draws on the works of earlier, known writers), to cautious acceptance of the independent origin of some at least of those scattered passages which are original to the *Historia Regum Britanniæ*.

First, there is what is known of his life. Could he understand Welsh, the language of the book he claims in his preface to have translated? What opportunities did he have for obtaining access to early source material? Is it conceivable that he was familiar with evidence unknown to contemporary historians like Henry of Huntingdon and William of Malmesbury? Was he simply an inveterate liar, or was he struggling in his own way to compile a veracious history?

Unfortunately, the sources for Geoffrey's life are tantalizingly sparse and enigmatic. Contemporary allusions span the years from 1120 to his death in 1155, making it likely that he was born towards the end of the eleventh century. In his literary works he styles himself 'Geoffrey of Monmouth' (*Gaufridus Monemutensis, Gaufridus de Monemuta*), which indicates that town as the place of his upbringing, and probably birth. It is likely, but again uncertain, that he was attached to the Benedictine priory at Monmouth. A charter of the priory dating from 1120 is witnessed by one *Galfridus scriba*, 'Geoffrey the scribe': an office which 'fits the probable age, implied upbringing and future career of Geoffrey'.[1]

Monmouth lay within the district of Archenfield, Welsh *Ergyng*. Although it fell under the influence of Mercia from an early date, Archenfield remained part of Wales well into the Norman period, and continued to be predominantly Welsh in language, institutions, and ecclesiastical benefices.[2] A tract entitled *De terra ercycg* ('Concerning the Region of Ergyng'), compiled towards the end of the reign of William the Conqueror, lists its churches, whose

---

1   Basil Clarke (ed.), *Life of Merlin; Geoffrey of Monmouth: Vita Merlini* (Cardiff, 1973), p. 27.

2   Cf. Phillimore's note in Henry Owen (ed.), *The Description of Pembrokeshire, by George Owen of Henllys, Lord of Kemes* (London, 1892–1936), iii, pp. 264–67; John Edward Lloyd, *A History of Wales from the Earliest Times to the Edwardian Conquest* (London, 1911), p. 275; B. G. Charles, 'The Welsh, their Language and Place-names in Archenfield and Oswestry', in Henry Lewis (ed.), *Angles and Britons* (Cardiff, 1963), pp. 85–96; Margaret Gelling, *The West Midlands in the Early Middle Ages* (Leicester, 1992), pp. 114–18; Andrew Breeze, 'The Provenance of the Rushworth Mercian Gloss', *Notes and Queries* (London, 1996), ccxli, pp. 394–95.

dedications and incumbents are almost entirely Welsh in nomenclature. The South Welsh kings Caradog ap Gruffydd and Rhydderch ap Caradog were called in evidence as approving preferments in the district, and formally upheld the ecclesiastical jurisdiction of the Bishop of Llandaff over Ergyng.[3] Although the authority of the Welsh see was forcibly replaced by that of the diocese of Hereford at the close of William I's reign, the Welsh character of the region continued little affected by the change.

Originally William bestowed the earldom of Hereford on his cousin William Fitz Osbern, who built the castle at Monmouth. However the power of Caradog ap Gruffydd continued little diminished in South Wales, and in 1072 Fitz Osbern is found fighting as his ally against a Welsh rival. Three years later Caradog attended the consecration of the church of St Mary in Monmouth Castle.[4] However, Fitz Osbern's son Roger rashly became involved in rebellion against the King, which brought about the family's downfall. As Sir John Lloyd commented:

> A catastrophe of these dimensions must have had a chilling effect upon the ardour of the [Norman] colonisers of the South Welsh border; the king marked his distrust of the situation by creating no new Earl of Hereford …

That the Conqueror appears to have reverted to a policy of coexistence with the native princes of South Wales, is confirmed by a peaceful progress he undertook to St Davids in 1081 – although characteristically at the head of a substantial body of armed men.[5]

Nor was this the only manner in which the alien presence came to rest more lightly on the native Welsh of Ergyng and Monmouth. William had been supported during his invasion and conquest of England by a large contingent of Breton nobles and their following, to whom he granted extensive estates in his new kingdom. It was to one of these that he now turned to hold Monmouth. Not long after his appointment as castellan of Monmouth castle, the Breton Wihenoc bestowed the priory church on the abbey of St Florent, at Saumur on the border of Normandy and Brittany, where he himself eventually withdrew to become a monk. His authority as castellan of Monmouth and local magnate in Archenfield was transmitted to his brother Baderon, who in due course passed it on to his son William.[6]

Although it uncertain to what extent eleventh-century Breton nobles spoke Breton, it seems on the whole likely that Wihenoc and his heirs at Monmouth were bilingual. Despite the baneful effects of Viking attacks and increasing Norman-French aggrandisement, Breton language and culture persisted at all levels of society in Brittany in the early Middle Ages.[7] In the case of Wihenoc and his heirs, this broad probability is enhanced by interest displayed by the Breton monks of Monmouth in prominent Welsh saints, above all St Cadog, sixth-century patron of

---

3   J. Gwenogvryn Evans and John Rhŷs (ed.), *The Text of the Book of Llan Dâv Reproduced from the Gwysaney Manuscript* (Oxford, 1893), pp. 275–80.

4   Ibid., p. 278; Thomas Jones (ed.), *Brut y Tywysogion: Peniarth MS. 20* (Cardiff, 1941), pp. 20–21.

5   Lloyd, *A History of Wales*, pp. 376, 378, 393–94; R. R. Davies, *Conquest, Coexistence, and Change: Wales 1063–1415* (Oxford, 1987), p. 29. For the two FitzOsbern earls of Hereford, cf. G. E. C[ockayne]. *et al.* (ed.), *The Complete Peerage: or a History of the House of Lords and all its Members from the Earliest Times* (London, 1910–59), vi, pp. 447–50.

6   Gwenogvryn Evans and Rhŷs (ed.), *The Text of the Book of Llan Dâv*, pp. 37, 93, 278.

7   Caroline Brett, 'Breton Latin Literature as Evidence for Literature in the Vernacular, A.D. 800–1300', *Cambridge Medieval Celtic Studies* (Cambridge, 1989), xviii, pp. 1–25; Noël-Yves Tonnerre, 'Celtic literary tradition and the development of a feudal principality in Brittany', in Huw Pryce (ed.), *Literacy in Medieval Celtic Societies* (Cambridge, 1998), pp. 166–82.

the ancient church used by Wihenoc's community.[8] Close connexions were maintained between the abbey of St Florent and the priory of St Mary at Monmouth. St Florent was an exclusively Breton foundation, and many of the monks at Monmouth were Bretons. Thus, 'distinctively Breton influences surrounded the birth of Monmouth Priory, and to that extent set it apart, as compared with similar Norman foundations.'[9]

Relations between Bretons and Welsh at Monmouth must have been close, given that many of the monks are likely to have been able to converse with local people in their own tongue. Brittany (hence its name) had been colonized by Britons from Devon and Cornwall in the post-Roman period, and in the twelfth century the Breton and Welsh languages continued mutually intelligible.[10] As has been seen, when Wihenoc dedicated the chapel of Monmouth castle, a prominent participant at the service was King Caradog of South Wales.

These circumstances provided an appropriate setting for the upbringing of the most celebrated historian of early Britain in the mediæval era.[11] During his youth, among the streets of Monmouth, its priory, and even the castle, it would have been impossible for him not to encounter native Welsh-speakers on a daily basis.[12]

Nothing is known of Geoffrey of Monmouth's parentage. A unique allusion to his ethnicity is provided by his description of himself as *pudibundus Brito*, 'an abashed Briton'.[13] At that time *Brito* could signify equally 'Welsh', 'Cornish', or 'Breton'. However, it seems unlikely that he was a Welshman: contemporary Welsh are depicted slightingly in his *Historia* as degenerate offspring of their warlike ancestors, and it is unlikely that a Welshman in the eleventh century would have borne a Norman name such as Geoffrey.[14]

---

8   Silas M. Harris, 'The Kalendar of the *Vitae Sanctorum Wallensium* (B. M. Cotton MS., Vespasian A.xiv)', *Journal of the Historical Society of the Church in Wales* (Cardiff, 1953), iii, pp. 16, 27–28.

9   Ibid., p. 15.

10 Gwenogvryn Evans and Rhŷs (ed.), *The Text of the Book of Llan Dâv*, p. 181; J. S. Brewer, James F. Dimock, and George F. Warner (ed.), *Giraldi Cambrensis Opera* (London, 1861–91), vi, p. 177. Cf. further B. Lynette Olson and O. J. Padel, 'A Tenth-Century List of Cornish Parochial Saints', *Cambridge Medieval Celtic Studies* (1986), xii, pp. 38–41. A legendary explanation of the origins of Breton implies that Bretons retained their mother tongue into the early Middle Ages (Brynley F. Roberts (ed.), *Breudwyt Maxen Wledic* (Dublin, 2005), p. 11).

11 Julia C. Crick, *The Historia Regum Britannie of Geoffrey of Monmouth IV: Dissemination and Reception in the Later Middle Ages* (Cambridge, 1991), pp. 8–9.

12 Tatlock made the point that Geoffrey is unlikely to have learned to speak English in Monmouth, which he would have acquired 'rather in Oxford, where it was the vernacular' (J. S. P. Tatlock, *The Legendary History of Britain: Geoffrey of Monmouth's Historia Regum Britanniae and its Early Vernacular Versions* (Berkeley and Los Angeles, 1950), p. 445).

13 Edmond Faral, *La légende arthurienne - Études et documents* (Paris, 1929), ii, p. 26; iii, p. 189. Cf. Crick, *The Historia Regum Britannie of Geoffrey of Monmouth IV*, pp. 98, 179–80. Affected modesty was a regular *topos* espoused by mediæval writers (Ernst Robert Curtius, *European Literature and the Latin Middle Ages* (London, 1953), pp. 83–85).

14 '... il été de race bretonne' (Faral, *La légende arthurienne*, ii, p. 1); 'Geoffrey's own Norman name suggests a Breton rather than a Welshman' (Tatlock, *The Legendary History of Britain*, p. 443). There appears to be no recorded instance of a Welshman called Geoffrey at this time. The Life of St Teilo in the Book of Llandaff was written '*a magistro Galfrido fratre Vrbani Landavensis episcopi*' (Gwenogvryn Evans and Rhŷs (ed.), *The Text of the Book of Llan Dâv*, p. 360). However, *Galfrido* is glossed *.i. Stephano*, which is probably correct (Christopher Brooke, 'The Archbishops of St David's, Llandaff and Caerleon-on-Usk', in Nora K. Chadwick (ed.), *Studies in the Early British Church* (Cambridge, 1958), p. 219). Either way, the names borne by the Bishop and his brother suggest Anglo-Norman origin.

Norman names were in contrast not infrequently bestowed on the indigenous inhabitants of contemporary Cornwall and Brittany, while Geoffrey was a popular name in the latter realm.[15] Moreover, in contrast to the Welsh, both peoples are accorded flattering rôles in the *Historia*. Cornwall is repeatedly singled out as home of national kings and heroes, while Geoffrey diplomatically assigned hopes of a recovery of the fortunes of the Britons to their favoured transmarine cousins from Brittany. However, neither consideration bears any necessary relation to Geoffrey's own origins. As will be seen shortly, he evinced particular interest in Cornwall and Cornish legendary lore, which could suffice to account for the exaggerated importance he assigned the duchy. His exaltation of the Bretons probably sprang from a combination of awareness of their rôle in Welsh prophetic verse as destined liberators of Britain, and the distinguished part they played as allies of Duke William during and after the conquest, which made them 'respectable' Britons whom it was safe to praise.

Taking these considerations together, and given the Breton associations of Monmouth castle and priory, the likelihood is that Geoffrey was 'a modest Breton'.[16] This need not necessarily imply that he spoke Breton, or was born in Brittany. Nevertheless, he could scarcely have escaped speaking some Welsh, which at the time effectively amounted to the same thing. Although nothing is known of the status of his family, it seems unlikely that they were too impoverished to employ a servant or servants, who would almost certainly have been Welsh.[17] As a scribe, comfortably paid and hard-working,[18] Geoffrey must in any case surely have had a servant of his own. As noted earlier, he would necessarily have heard Welsh (and possibly Breton) spoken around him on a daily basis.

It has been suggested that Geoffrey's 'knowledge of Welsh cannot be assumed to have been extensive'.[19] Nevertheless, at some point following his arrival in Oxford in the 1120s, he was invited by Archdeacon Walter to translate the 'very old book', written in Welsh or Breton, which Geoffrey claimed to have transformed into the attractive Latin of the *Historia Regum Britanniæ*. The Archdeacon possessed some knowledge of indigenous Welsh lore, particularly in relation to legends of King Arthur.[20] The two men were evidently closely acquainted,[21] and Walter surely possessed reason to believe that Geoffrey was versed to some degree in the language of

15 Variant forms of the name Geoffrey (*Gaufredus, Gaufridus, Ioffredus, Gefre*) recur in early Breton charters (Hubert Guillotel, André Chédeville, Bernard Tanguy, Jean-Pierre Brunterc'h, Alain Duval, Hélène Guicharnaud, and Sandrine Pagès-Camagna (ed.), *Cartulaire de l'abbaye Saint-Sauveur de Redon* (Rennes, 2004), ii, p. 82).

16 A. O. H. Jarman, *Sieffre o Fynwy: Geoffrey of Monmouth* (Cardiff, 1966), p. 10.

17 Welsh loanwords in the thirteenth-century English *Ancrene Wisse* reflect a master-servant relationship, with linguistic connotations of Welsh people nursing, waiting at table, etc. (Andrew Breeze, 'Welsh loanwords in the AB Language', in Yoko Wada (ed.), *Europe Without Boundaries* (Osaka, 2010), pp. 9–14).

18 Cf. M. T. Clanchy, *From Memory to Written Record: England 1066–1307* (London, 1979), pp. 89–91.

19 Brynley F. Roberts, 'Geoffrey of Monmouth, *Historia Regum Britanniae* and *Brut y Brenhinedd*', in Rachel Bromwich, A. O. H. Jarman, and Brynley F. Roberts (ed.), *The Arthur of the Welsh: The Arthurian Legend in Medieval Welsh Literature* (Cardiff, 1991), pp. 109, 116. Cf. Tatlock, *The Legendary History of Britain*, p. 445.

20 Michael D. Reeve and Neil Wright (ed.), *Geoffrey of Monmouth: The History of the Kings of Britain* (Woodbridge, 2007), p. 249.

21 M. Dominica Legge, 'Master Geoffrey Arthur', in Kenneth Varty (ed.), *An Arthurian Tapestry: essays in memory of Lewis Thorpe* (Cambridge, 1983), pp. 23–24.

the province of his upbringing.[22] Had he been ignorant of Welsh, it could scarcely have been concealed from his colleagues at Oxford.

Nevertheless, the question remains how Geoffrey could have expected to get away with his imposture. What if someone had demanded to see the original of the 'British book'? That danger might conceivably have been discounted, given that few if any of his readers are likely to have been able to read Welsh, the language in which the source was purportedly written. (An exception was the Welsh historian Caradog of Llancarfan, who may however have been party to the deception.) Also significant is the fact that the dedicatees of Geoffrey's book were among the most powerful and wealthy notables of the land: King Stephen, Earl Robert of Gloucester, Count Waleran de Meulan, and Bishop Alexander of Lincoln. Not only this, but all were in varying degree sophisticated men, patrons and devotees of the realm of letters.[23] Might not lesser figures be reasonably expected to abide by the judgment of such highly placed intellectual figures?

Traditional Welsh lore in the Historia Regum Britanniæ

It has long been accepted by historians that by far the greater part of Geoffrey's work constitutes imaginative fiction. Nevertheless, we are not entitled to reject its authority *in toto*. For a start, the account by his contemporary Henry of Huntingdon of *Belinus*, *Cassibellanus*, and *Luid* as successive kings of Britain proves that their absorption into the British pseudo-historical tradition had occurred prior to Geoffrey of Monmouth's work.[24]

Again, a significant point which, so far as I am aware, has been hitherto overlooked is to be found in his dramatic account of the construction of Stonehenge. Geoffrey begins by naming the monument *chorea gigantum*, 'the Giants' Dance'. This must reflect the widely recorded folktale explanation of standing stones as petrified dancers.[25] However, the monoliths are accorded a quite different interpretation in Geoffrey's ensuing narrative, where it is their healing power described by Merlin that leads to their removal from Ireland. It is consequently likely that the name Geoffrey accorded the monument existed in contemporary independent tradition, of which no trace has survived in other sources. This is scarcely surprising, since it would be strange were Geoffrey to have made *no* enquiry of his own into Stonehenge, which plays so prominent a part in his narrative. Here we have an unmistakable intimation that he did indeed do so. It will be seen shortly that he also appears to have travelled to investigate local traditions attached to remote Tintagel, which likewise plays a significant part in his history.

---

22   Tatlock suggested that fluency in Breton (or Welsh) could have been a factor in Geoffrey's subsequent appointment to the see of St Asaph (Tatlock, *The Legendary History of Britain*, p. 442). He and the Archdeacon were witnesses to the foundation charter of Oseney Abbey in 1129 (H. E. Salter (ed.), *Cartulary of Oseney Abbey* (Oxford, 1929–36), iv, p. 12). Cf. H. L. D. Ward and J. A. Herbert, *Catalogue of Romances in the Department of Manuscripts in the British Museum* (London, 1883–1910), i, pp. 206–7.

23   Bromwich, Jarman, and Roberts (ed.), *The Arthur of the Welsh*, p. 99. Stephen was a ruler of culture and taste (David Crouch, *The Reign of King Stephen, 1135–1154* (Harlow, 2000), p. 19).

24   Diana Greenway (ed.), *Henry, Archdeacon of Huntingdon, Historia Anglorum: The History of the English People* (Oxford, 1996), pp. 32. Cf. Rachel Bromwich, 'The Character of the Early Welsh Tradition', in Nora K. Chadwick (ed.), *Studies in Early British History* (Cambridge, 1954), pp. 109–10; Roberts (ed.), *Cyfranc Lludd a Lefelys*, pp. xiii–xv.

25   Tatlock, *The Legendary History of Britain*, p. 40; Helmut Birkhan, *Kelten: Versuch einer Gesamtdarstellung ihrer Kultur* (Vienna, 1997), p. 1099. For the folklore explanation of stones as dancers, cf. L. V. Grinsell, *The Folklore of Stanton Drew* (St Peter Port, Guernsey, 1973), pp. 6–10.

Again, it has long been noted that Geoffrey was familiar with local legends of his home district of Ergyng, as well as neighbouring Gwent, which he utilized for dramatic events in his *Historia*.[26] A telling instance is provided by his account of the death of the British tyrant Vortigern. While his literary source, the ninth-century *Historia Brittonum*, locates the king's demise on the banks of the Teifi in Dyfed, Geoffrey places his end at Little Doward Hill on the Wye, some three miles north-east of Monmouth. This suggests acqaintance with local lore.[27]

Oral tradition of this nature is likely to have been familiar to Geoffrey from his youthful days at Monmouth, and substantiates the intrinsic likelihood of his familiarity with popular lore. Other Welsh legendary material could have been acquired after his move to Oxford. While nothing is known of his activities during his time there, it is reasonable to suppose that he returned occasionally to his old home at Monmouth, where members of his family and friends could still have been living. There are indications that Monmouth was a centre of literary production at the time, with a focus on the ecclesiastical and secular history of South Wales.[28] Particularly apt to Geoffrey's area of interest is a suggestion that an early version of the Welsh Arthurian romance of *Peredur* was composed at Monmouth Priory about the time of his youth.[29]

It is possible that Geoffrey was familiar with a version of this romance. His account of Arthur's expedition to fight the Romans on the Continent is prefaced by a dramatic description of the king's slaying of a lecherous giant at Mont St Michel. On landing, he and his trusty companions *Kaius* and *Beduerus* (the Kay and Bedivere of Arthurian romance) were drawn by the sound of an anguished scream. Hastening forward, they discovered the tomb of Helena, who had been murdered by the giant. Beside it was her nurse (*altrix*), who screamed on being raped by the lustful ogre. Arthur slew the ravisher, whose head was exhibited at a prominent spot, and the trio took their departure from the maiden's tomb, which continued to be known up to the time of writing as *Tumba Helenae*.[30]

This episode represents a digression from the narrative proper, suggesting that it 'may be a traditional onomastic story given a new Arthurian context'. This seems likely enough, in view of the king's being accompanied by *Caius* and *Beduerus,* who feature in prior native Welsh literature as his regular companions.[31] Arthur's reflexion on a previous giant-killing exploit is generally held to allude to a Welsh folktale, and the decapitation of an oppressive giant and display of his head on a post conclude the earliest Welsh Arthurian tale, *Culhwch ac Olwen*.[32]

26 Tatlock, *The Legendary History of Britain*, pp. 72–77; Jarman, *Sieffre o Fynwy*, p. 13, 68–70; Clarke (ed.), *Life of Merlin*, pp. 27, 31.

27 *Erat oppidum illud in natione Hergign* [Ergyng] *super fluuium Guaiae in monte qui Doartius nuncupatur* (Reeve and Wright (ed.), *Geoffrey of Monmouth: The History of the Kings of Britain*, p. 161). Cf. Lloyd, *A History of Wales*, pp. 526–27; Tatlock, *The Legendary History of Britain*, pp. 72–73; Andrew Breeze, 'The Name of Ganarew', *Journal of the English Place-Name Society* (Nottingham, 1999), xxxi, pp. 113–14.

28 R. M. Jones, 'Narrative Structure in Medieval Welsh Prose Tales', in D. Ellis Evans, John G. Griffith, and E. M. Jope (ed.), *Proceedings of the Seventh International Congress of Celtic Studies* (Oxford, 1986), pp. 174–75.

29 Glenys Goetinck, '*Peredur* ... Upon Reflection', *Études Celtiques* (Paris, 1988), xxv, pp. 221–32.

30 Reeve and Wright (ed.), *Geoffrey of Monmouth: The History of the Kings of Britain*, pp. 225–29.

31 Linda M. Gowans, *Cei and the Arthurian Legend* (Cambridge, 1988), pp. 4–36.

32 Robert Huntington Fletcher, *The Arthurian Material in the Chronicles especially those of Great Britain and France* (Boston, 1906), pp. 90–91; Tatlock, *The Legendary History of Britain*, pp. 64, 65; Chris Grooms, *The Giants of Wales: Cewri Cymru* (Lampeter, 1993), pp. 214–18, 300; Bromwich, Jarman, and Roberts (ed.), *The Arthur of the Welsh*, p. 108; O. J. Padel, *Arthur in Medieval Welsh Tradition* (Cardiff, 2000), p. 74.

It may be that originally it was the fair Helena herself who was raped by the giant, the intrusive nurse being a 'ghost' character created by Geoffrey. Helena's name here originated through misinterpretion of an eminence called *Tumbelaine* at Mont St Michel as 'tomb of Helena'.[33] It is further possible that the author of the original legend transferred the story from a prior location at St Michael's Mount in Cornwall. There a local folktale related how a neighbouring giant Trecrobben flung his hammer at the Mount, where it accidentally killed its giant owner's wife. Versions of the tale laid emphasis on the burial-place of the giantess on St Michael's Mount.[34]

Oliver Padel has shown that Geoffrey was particularly drawn to Cornwall, which is ascribed disproportionate importance in his *Historia*, and of whose topography and relatively obscure local affairs of his own day he displays detailed knowledge. After setting out the evidence, Padel concluded:

> After all, Geoffrey in his Monmouth days, may have known either the story of *Culhwch* itself (whether or not in the exact form in which we have it), or other south Welsh traditions which associated Arthur particularly with Cornwall, and may have followed them. It would thus have been his interest in the figure of Arthur which prompted him to visit Cornwall and see for himself the land of his great hero, and to give it such an honourable place in his *History*.[35]

A suggestive parallel may be drawn between the Welsh romance of *Peredur* and Arthur's adventure at Mont St Michel in Geoffrey's *Historia*. *Peredur* begins with the untutored boy leaving his forest home to seek his fortune in the wide world. His mother's parting advice, which provides a preface to several of his adventures, includes the admonition, 'If you hear a scream, go towards it, and a woman's scream above any other scream in the world.' Later, while riding through a dense forest, Peredur hears a loud shriek. Hastening to the spot, he discovers a beautiful auburn-haired girl, who explains that her husband had been slain by a knight in the wood. Peredur inters the corpse, overcomes the knight, and despatches him a prisoner to Arthur's court.[36]

The theme of the woman's scream as prefatory to the adventure occurs (so far as I am aware) nowhere else in early Welsh literature. Equally, Geoffrey and the author of *Peredur* could have drawn on a common source, rather than one borrowing from the other.

Geoffrey also appears to have been acquainted with Welsh poetry. In the lengthy prophecy he places in the mouth of Merlin in his *Historia*, cryptic allusion is made to 'the river *Periron*'.[37] The Welsh prophetic poem *Armes Prydein*, which was probably composed in AD 940, declares that 'Myrddin [the Welsh name for Merlin] foretells that they [the Saxons] will meet at *Aber Perydon*'.[38] *Aber Peryddon* is either an old name for the estuary of the Dee, or a tributary of that river, which Geoffrey mistakenly identified with *Aber Periron*, the confluence of an obscure

---

33 Faral, *La légende arthurienne*, ii, pp. 287–89; Tatlock, *The Legendary History of Britain*, pp. 88–89.

34 Robert Hunt, *Popular Romances of the West of England; or, The Drolls, Traditions, and Superstitions of Old Cornwall* (London, 1865), i, pp. 30–31.

35 O. J. Padel, 'Geoffrey of Monmouth and Cornwall', *Cambridge Medieval Celtic Studies* (Cambridge, 1984), viii, pp. 1–28.

36 Glenys Witchard Goetinck (ed.), *Historia Peredur vab Efrawc* (Cardiff, 1976), pp. 9, 20–22.

37 Reeve and Wright (ed.), *Geoffrey of Monmouth: The History of the Kings of Britain*, p. 149.

38 Sir Ifor Williams and Rachel Bromwich (ed.), *Armes Prydein: The Prophecy of Britain From the Book of Taliesin* (Dublin, 1972), p. 2. Cf. Nikolai Tolstoy, 'When and where was *Armes Prydein* Composed?', *Studia Celtica* (Cardiff, 2008), xlii, pp. 145–49.

brook flowing into the Wye near his home at Monmouth.[39] The influence of *Armes Prydein* (or a similar prophetic poem) is further suggested by Geoffrey's unhistorical account of the last British King Cadwaladr's withdrawal to Brittany. In the poem Cadwaladr is invoked as heading a gallant army from *Llydaw* (Brittany) to liberate Britain from the recreant Saxons.[40]

Overall, the indications are that Geoffrey possessed some familiarity with the works of Welsh storytellers (*cyfarwyddiaid*).[41] His failure to make greater use of their work than he did may have arisen in part from its rejection as a category of learning he deemed inappropriate to the serious history he claimed to be writing. Thus, he advances a pretext for declining to relate 'the contention of Lud and Nennius', which was most likely a version of the extant Welsh story of enchantments inflicted on the island of Britain, entitled 'The Discussion of Lludd and Lleuelys' (*Cyfranc Lludd a Lleuelys*). Elsewhere Geoffrey alludes to a prophecy uttered by an eagle at the foundation of Shaftesbury, which he discreetly refrained from repeating on grounds of its being incredible. It is possible that he had in mind a version of the Welsh poem 'The Conversation of Arthur and the Eagle' (*Ymddiddan Arthur a'r Eryr*).[42]

Geoffrey's selective use of Welsh lore is further attested by the extent to which he made use of a tale or tales similar to 'The Dream of Maxen the Emperor' (*Breuddwyd Maxen Gwledig*), which purports to recount historical events on the eve of the collapse of Roman rule in Britain.[43] All in all, it would be prudent not to be overly dismissive of Geoffrey's familiarity with the legendary lore of Celtic Britain.

Mention has been made of his especial concern with the topography and traditions of Cornwall, as well as the likelihood that he visited the region and acquired helpful contacts there. His famous account of the conception of Arthur at Tintagel reflects the familiar Celtic theme of a divinity, who sleeps with the mother of a king or hero on the night of her conceiving an infant prodigy. Impregnation of a closely guarded maiden in a sea-girt fortress is found also in legends of the begetting of the Irish god Lug on Tory Island, a similarly craggy outcrop of the coast of Donegal. The father of Lug's virgin mother was a tyrannical giant named Balor, who kept her confined in his stronghold, and whom Lug killed when grown to manhood.[44] The thirteenth century Welsh poet Bleddyn Vardd alludes to a tradition that Arthur attacked a giant Benlli in his castle, while Benlli and his son Beli correspond in British tradition to Balor in the Irish.[45]

---

39 Bromwich and Williams (ed.), *Armes Prydein*, pp. xxxv–xl.

40 Ibid., p. 12.

41 That Geoffrey possessed some knowledge of Welsh prophetic verse is generally accepted. Cf. Margaret Enid Griffiths, *Early Vaticination in Welsh with English Parallels* (Cardiff, 1937), pp. 59–83, 146, 152, 154; Rachel Bromwich (ed.), *Trioedd Ynys Prydein: The Welsh Triads* (Cardiff, 1978), p. xcvii; Brynley F. Roberts, 'Geoffrey of Monmouth and Welsh Historical Tradition', *Nottingham Mediaeval Studies* (Cambridge, 1976), xx, pp. 38–40; Doris Edel, 'Geoffrey's So-called Animal Symbolism and Insular Celtic Tradition', *Studia Celtica* (1983/1984), xviii/xix, pp. 96–109.

42 Reeve and Wright (ed.), *Geoffrey of Monmouth: The History of the Kings of Britain*, pp. 37, 281; Ifor Williams, 'Ymddiddan Arthur a'r Eryr', *The Bulletin of the Board of Celtic Studies* (Oxford, 1925), ii, pp. 269–86.

43 'The ... extended narrative of Maximianus, his British wife and the settlement of Brittany offers a number of points of comparison with the Welsh Dream of Maxen and with Breton Latin texts' (Bromwich, Jarman, and Roberts (ed.), *The Arthur of the Welsh*, p. 109).

44 Michael Herity (ed.), *Ordnance Survey Letters Donegal: Letters Containing Information relative to the Antiquities of the County of Donegal Collected during the Progress of the Ordnance Survey in 1835* (Dublin, 2000), pp. 40–44; Jeremiah Curtin, *Hero-Tales of Ireland* (London, 1894), pp. 283–95.

45 John Morris-Jones and T. H. Parry-Williams (ed.), *Llawysgrif Hendregadredd* (Cardiff, 1933), p. 68. For Benlli and Balor, cf. W. J. Gruffydd, *Math vab Mathonwy: An Inquiry into the Origins and Development*

Details of Geoffrey's description of Tintagel suggest that he visited the dramatic site.[46] It is unlikely that he was unaccompanied during his expedition, nor that he failed to conduct enquiries among informed Cornishmen of the neighbourhood. His account includes the odd detail that Uther and Merlin were guided to Tintagel by one *Vlfin de Ridcaradoch*, a character otherwise unmentioned in the *Historia*. Ulfin's sole function in the story is to provide a lively description of the peninsular fortress. In fact, his epithet derives from the name of a manor called Rosecraddock, situated about eighteen miles south-east of Tintagel.[47] This Caradog may well have been the contemporary owner of the manor, who related the birth-tale of Arthur to Geoffrey while escorting him on a visit to Tintagel.

Other names in the story of Arthur's birth likely to have been obtained by Geoffrey in the course of local enquiries are those of Gorlois (found in the placename Treworlas), husband of Arthur's mother Igerna; and Dimilioc, the castle to which Gorlois repairs after securing Igerna in Tintagel.[48]

From 1129 to 1151 Geoffrey's name features as witness to a succession of Oxford charters, to which city he had moved in advancement of his career. In two of these he describes himself as *magister*, a post which it has been suggested implies teaching responsibilities, probably as a secular canon of the College of St George in the castle of the city.[49] In others, starting with that witnessed in 1129, he signs himself 'Geoffrey Arthur' (*Galfridus Artur*). It was formerly thought that Arthur was the name of Geoffrey's father, but it is now more plausibly considered that he had become so besotted with matters Arthurian as to add the great king's name to his own as a sobriquet.[50]

It is surely likely that Geoffrey returned to Monmouth from time to time after his move to Oxford.[51] He appears to have retained close interest in the affairs of his home town. At the conclusion of his *Historia*, he describes how *Cadualadrus*, the last great British king, retired to Rome, where he foretold that the Britons, by the merit of their faith, should again recover their island when the time was come. To this he added that his body would then be returned from Rome to Britain, when the relics of other British saints, concealed up to that time, would be restored to the Britons.[52] In Geoffrey's day the mother-abbey of Monmouth at Saumur boasted possession of relics of a number of important Breton saints, including the body of the British St Paul Aurelian. Cadwaladr, a monarch famed for his piety, is commemorated by three church

_____

   of the Fourth Branch of the Mabinogi with the Text and a Translation (Cardiff, 1928), pp. 179–86; Grooms, *The Giants of Wales*, pp. 131–39.

46 *Cambridge Medieval Celtic Studies*, viii, p. 11; Charles Thomas, *Tintagel: Arthur and Archaeology* (London, 1993), pp. 24–25.

47 J. Loth, *Contributions à l'Étude des Romans de la Table Ronde* (Paris, 1912), p. 63.

48 W. Howship Dickinson, *King Arthur in Cornwall* (London, 1900), pp. 66–70; C. L. Wrenn, 'Saxons and Celts in South-West Britain', *The Transactions of the Honourable Society of Cymmrodorion: Session 1959* (London, 1959), p. 61; *Cambridge Medieval Celtic Studies*, viii, p. 12.

49 H.E. Salter, 'Geoffrey of Monmouth and Oxford', *The English Historical Review* (London, 1919), xxxiv, pp. 382–85; Bromwich, Jarman, and Roberts (ed.), *The Arthur of the Welsh*, pp. 99–100.

50 *Cambridge Medieval Celtic Studies*, viii, pp. 1–4; Bromwich, Jarman, and Roberts (ed.), *The Arthur of the Welsh*, p. 106; Neil Wright (ed.), *The Historia Regum Britannie of Geoffrey of Monmouth I: Bern, Burgerbibliothek, MS. 568* (Cambridge, 1984), p. x.

51 Clarke (ed.), *Life of Merlin*, pp. 29–31.

52 Reeve and Wright (ed.), *Geoffrey of Monmouth: The History of the Kings of Britain*, p. 279.

dedications in Monmouthshire.[53] Was Geoffrey dropping a genial hint to his monastic *confrères* at Monmouth, that the time had come to repatriate the collection of Welsh relics?

His account of the process which led to his writing the *Historia* is related in its preface. There he explains how he had often asked himself why contemporary historians (presumably Henry of Huntingdon and William of Malmesbury, whom he mentions in his epilogue) confined their accounts of the early part of British history to matter drawn from the writings of Gildas and Bede. Admirable as such writers were, why did they not describe the reigns of kings who lived before the Incarnation of Christ? Above all, how had had they come to overlook Arthur and other British monarchs who reigned subsequent to the departure of the Romans?

Eventually (he went on), Walter, Archdeacon of Oxford, proffered him that very ancient book in the British language, which filled the gap which had so long puzzled him. It described in exquisite language everything which passed from the arrival of Brutus, first king of Britain, to the reign of the Welsh king Cadwaladr. At Walter's request, Geoffrey undertook the task of turning the book into Latin, being careful not to adorn the text with flowery expressions of his own devising, which might come between the reader and the plain historical narrative.[54] Here Geoffrey was undoubtedly writing tongue-in-cheek with assumed modesty, for there can be no doubt that the widely admired rhetorical style and embellished narrative are entirely his own.

Nevertheless, there is some reason to believe that the 'certain very ancient book' really existed, if in very different form from that claimed by Geoffrey. Throughout the Middle Ages general opinion ran strongly in favour of the book's authenticity, as did also the belief that Geoffrey's *Historia* represented an authentic translation of an original work in Welsh. As late as the early twentieth century lingering attempts were made to propound this view, which had by then become otherwise generally discredited. The great Egyptologist Sir Flinders Petrie pronounced the *Historia* to be 'of the highest value, for … the internal evidence shows that it is based on British documents extending back to the first century'. His argument was largely grounded on a belief that mediæval Welsh translations of the text are older than the Latin *Historia*, and could in consequence reflect its source. Although this view was endorsed by one of the work's first scholarly editors,[55] it has long been rejected by serious authorities. All Welsh versions have been shown to derive from the *Historia*, and can consequently throw no light on its origins.[56]

The rejection of Geoffrey's *Historia* as authentic history in its entirety is unlikely ever again to be subjected to serious challenge. Two centuries ago Lord Byron cheerfully categorized him as 'Geoffrey of Monmouth, a noted liar in his way',[57] and there can be no disputing the fact that

---

53   S. Baring-Gould and John Fisher, *The Lives of the British Saints: The Saints of Wales and Cornwall and such Irish Saints as have Dedications in Britain* (London, 1907–13), ii, p. 45.

54   Reeve and Wright (ed.), *Geoffrey of Monmouth: The History of the Kings of Britain*, p. 5.

55   W. M. Flinders Petrie, 'Neglected British History', *The Proceedings of the British Academy* (London, 1917–18), viii, pp. 251–78; Acton Griscom (ed.), *The Historia Regum Britanniæ of Geoffrey of Monmouth with Contributions to the Study of its Place in Early British History* (London, 1929), pp. 99–147.

56   Patrick Sims-Williams, *Rhai Addasiadau Cymraeg Canol o Sieffre o Fynwy* (Aberystwyth, 2011). For an excellent survey of Welsh attitudes towards the 'British history', cf. Brynley F. Roberts (ed.), *Brut y Brenhinedd: Llanstephan MS. 1 Version* (Dublin, 1971), pp. 55–74. The translators occasionally incorporated fragments of independent Welsh lore, which were intended 'to reconcile the scheme of Geoffrey's narrative with the pre-existing, but in comparison certainly much less organised, native traditions' (Rachel Bromwich (ed.), *Trioedd Ynys Prydein: The Welsh Triads* (Cardiff, 1978), p. lxxx).

57   Leslie A. Marchand (ed.), *Byron's Letters and Journals* (London, 1973–82), i, p. 178. For the less sceptical, a visit to Monmouth afforded opportunity to view 'a very old house, which … is said to have been the abode of Geoffrey of Monmouth, and they show his study' (Henry Reeve (ed.), *The Greville Memoirs (Second Part): A Journal of the Reign of Queen Victoria from 1837 to 1852* (London, 1885), i, p. 219).

the greater part of his narrative was the creation of his own ebullient imagination. The historical value ascribable to his work has been well expressed by Brynley Roberts:

> The *Historia* ... cannot be a mere translation, even in the extended medieval sense. Almost every study of the work reveals its imaginative and creative use of a range of literary sources, the majority of which are in Latin, and it becomes increasingly clear that one of Geoffrey's most fruitful talents was his ability to create episodes and characters from a variety of disparate and unconnected elements. The firm narrative structure of the *Historia* and a developed authorial view of British history further mark this as an individually composed narrative.[58]

Aspects of his work which strike today's readers as obvious embroidery would not have appeared so to most mediæval readers. Contemporary expectations permitted Geoffrey to indulge in literary devices, such as placing flowery speeches in the mouths of his leading characters, and elaborating descriptions of battles and other dramatic events. Such artistic encrustations were regarded by contemporary historians (as well as some of the greatest historians of classical antiquity) as a proper function of the historian.[59]

Geoffrey's prime sources included the *Aeneid* of Virgil, and it has been suggested that his aim in part was to provide a British counterpart to the Latin epic.[60] Although the greater part of the *Aeneid* represents a compound of myth and poetical imagining, Virgil grounded his narrative in legendary Roman history, which recounted Aeneas's escape from Troy, his adventures en route, and his eventual foundation of Rome.[61] While the Roman poet's purpose was not that of providing a definitive account of Rome's origins, Geoffrey expressly intended his work to be regarded as *the* authoritative history of Britain from its earliest era to the close of the seventh century AD.

He must surely have been proud also of his literary achievement, despite his assertion of his work as pure historiography. In reality, it is as a work of visionary 'history' that it must be considered, and in that respect deserves its extraordinary reputation throughout the Middle Ages, and beyond.

58　H. E. Salter, 'Geoffrey of Monmouth and Oxford', *The English Historical Review* (London, 1919), xxxiv, pp. 382–85; Bromwich, Jarman, and Roberts (ed.), *The Arthur of the Welsh*, p. 101.

59　As early as the fourth century BC, Callisthenes of Olynthus declared it the historian's duty 'not to fail to hit off the character, but to match his speeches to the person and the situation' (F. W. Walbank, *Speeches in Greek Historians* (Oxford, 1970), p. 5). Likewise, in Geoffrey's day formal rhetorical art required skilful composition of speeches to be placed in the mouths of historical characters (Greenway (ed.), *Henry, Archdeacon of Huntingdon, Historia Anglorum*, pp. xxxvii–xxxviii).

60　For Geoffrey's use of Virgil, cf. Griscom (ed.), *The Historia Regum Britanniæ of Geoffrey of Monmouth*, pp. 49–50. The suggestion that he may have sought to emulate the Roman epic was advanced *inter alia* by W. Lewis Jones, *King Arthur in History and Legend* (Cambridge, 1914) pp. 67–68, and David Greene, *Makers and Forgers* (Cardiff, 1975), pp. 7–8. Chaucer acknowledged Geoffrey as an authority on the Trojan history: 'And English Gaufride eek, y-wis; / And ech of these, as have I Ioye, / Was besy for to bere up Troye' (Walter W. Skeat (ed.), *The Complete Works of Geoffrey Chaucer* (Oxford, 1894), iii, p. 44). Another appropriate source was the Bible, given that the Old Testament effectively constitutes the early history of Israel (Jacob Hammer, 'Geoffrey of Monmouth's Use of the Bible in the "Historia Regum Britanniae"', *Bulletin of the John Rylands Library* (Manchester, 1947), xxx, pp. 293–311). Geoffrey's own versification in the *HRB* received high praise from no less a judge than John Milton (John J. Parry and Robert A. Caldwell, 'Geoffrey of Monmouth', in Loomis (ed.), *Arthurian Literature in the Middle Ages: A Collaborative History* (Oxford, 1959), pp. 85–6).

61　Cf. Arnaldo Momigliano, *On Pagans, Jews, and Christians* (Middletown, Conn., 1987), pp. 264–88.

This imaginative apprehension of the past was the great legacy of Geoffrey of Monmouth: to look into the successive layers of time and see the kingdoms and peoples that had once flourished in your own land.[62]

My present concern, however, is with the possible historical value of his work. It is likely that the 'British book', on which Geoffrey based his *Historia Regum Britanniæ*, was a version of Nennius's *Historia Brittonum*, the earliest extant version of which was completed in AD 829-30, and whose text effectively provides a skeleton version of the greater part of Geoffrey's historical chronology.

The author of the *Historia Brittonum*, who identifies himself in the prologue as Nennius,[63] explains that, having failed despite exhaustive researches to discover any existing history of Britain (incidentally, a telling point against Geoffrey's claim to have discovered such a work three centuries later!), he gathered together what he could of relevant material from classical authors, works of the fathers of the Church, and native traditions preserved by the Irish, Saxons, and Welsh. These he assembled in what he took to be their chronological order, conferring on his finished work the modest title of 'excerpts'. Thus, it represents an historical anthology rather than history proper.

A brief comparison demonstrates the extent to which the structure of Geoffrey's work derived from a version of the *Historia Brittonum*.

HISTORIA BRITTONUM	GEOFFREY OF MONMOUTH
§§7–9. Description of Britain.	§2. Description of Britain.
§§10–11. Adventures and eventual settlement of Britain by Britto, grandson of Aeneas.	§§6–22. Adventures and settlement of Britain by Brutus, grandson of Aeneas.
§11. Synchronism of the reign of Britto with biblical chronology.	§22. Synchronism of the reign of Brutus with biblical chronology.
§§12–18. Assorted traditions of early Britain.	§§23–53. Chronological history of descendants of Brutus.
§§19–29. History of Roman Britain.	§§54–88. History of Roman Britain.
§§30–49. Post-Roman history of the Saxon invaders, Vortigern, Emrys, and St Germanus.	§§89–108. Post-Roman history of the Saxon invaders, Vortigern, Merlin (Emrys), and St Germanus.
-	§§109–17. Prophecies of Merlin.
§§50–55. Life of St Patrick.	-
§56. List of Arthur's victories.	§§135–78. Triumphant reigns of Uther and Arthur.
§§57–61. Saxon genealogies.	§§179–83. Reigns of four successor kings to Arthur.
§§61–83. Northern wars of Britons and Angles to the death of Cadwalader.	§§189–206. History of British Kings to the death of Cadwalader in 689.

62   Margaret Gibson, 'History at Bec in the twelfth century', in R. H. C. Davis and J. M. Wallace-Hadrill (ed.), *The Writing of History in the Middle Ages: Essays Presented to Richard William Southern* (Oxford, 1981), p. 186.

63   The authorship of Nennius was rejected by Professor Dumville as a mediæval imposture (David N. Dumville, "'Nennius' and the *Historia Brittonum*', *Studia Celtica* (Cardiff, 1975-6), x-xi, pp. 78–95). However, Professor Field has argued convincingly for the authenticity of the prologue, and consequently Nennius's authorship (P. J. C. Field, 'Nennius and his History', ibid. (1996), xxx, pp. 159–65).

From this it can be seen how closely Geoffrey's history reflects the structure of the *Historia Brittonum*. The latter represented his basic source, above all in providing a chronological framework for the *Historia Regum Britanniæ*. The approach of Geoffrey's adaptation is also plain. Using the *Historia Brittonum* as basis of his book, he expanded each section with additional source material (much of it identifiable), seasoned with extensive input from his own literary talent and efflorescent imagination.

The account of the original settlement of Britain by Brutus derives, with minor variations, from St Jerome's Latin translation of the Chronicle of Eusebius. While Jerome drew for his account of the founding of Rome on Virgil's *Aeneid*, there is no indication that Nennius possessed direct knowledge of the poem.[64] Geoffrey, however, was familiar with it, and employed it in his earlier section to expand the brief summary he evidently found in a version of the *Historia Brittonum*.

The notion that Brutus was founder of Britain's first royal dynasty appears to have originated in simple misunderstanding, or misappropriation, of an entry in Jerome's chronicle, which states that 'at Rome, after the kings ended, consuls began to be from Brutus' (*Romae post exactos reges primum consules a Bruto esse coeperunt*). The *Historia Brittonum* begins with a declaration that 'the island of Britain [is] named after a certain Brutus, a Roman consul' (*Britannia insula a quodam Bruto consule Romano dicta*).[65]

The account of the Roman conquest and occupation of Britain compiled by Nennius relies principally on Jerome's Chronicle and the early fifth-century Roman history of Orosius, together with valuable snippets of native traditional lore. Geoffrey, who was familiar with a considerably wider range of Roman history than was Nennius, built on this to concoct his long and fanciful account of the resistance of British kings to their Roman conquerors.

Nennius's narrative of the post-Roman era drew in turn on native Welsh sagas, which provided welcome grist to Geoffrey's mill. He expanded his source material into an increasingly lengthy and dramatic romance. It was at this point, too, that he introduced the towering figure of Merlin, whose fame as a prophet had recently spread dramatically from Wales across England, at a time when people apprehensively anticipated dire consequences from the disputed succession anticipated to follow on the death of Henry I.[66] Geoffrey substituted Merlin for the prophetic child Ambrosius who features in the *Historia Brittonum*, and devoted an entire book of his *Historia* to an extended prophecy ascribed to Merlin. While this prophecy largely represents his own invention, it was modelled on genuine Welsh vaticinatory poems ascribed to the seer.

From Merlin, Geoffrey directed his story effortlessly into a detailed history of the most vivid and popular figure of his work, the illustrious King Arthur. All Nennius had supplied on the topic was a bare list of Arthur's twelve victories over the Saxons (§56). Geoffrey utilized this skeleton framework as basis for a greatly expanded narrative, including imaginative descriptions of Arthur's glittering court at Caerleon, his conquests of foreign lands extending from Ireland and Iceland (the latter yet to be discovered in the real King Arthur's day!), to Norway and Dacia

---

64 Nennius cites *Virgilius* at one point, but the quotation is from the *Georgics* (Mommsen (ed.), *Chronica Minora*, iii, p. 164).

65 John Knight Fotheringham (ed.), *Evsebii Pamphili Chronici Canones: Latine Vertit, Adavxit, ad sva Tempora Prodvxit S. Evsebivs Hieronimvs* (London, 1923), p. 188; Theodor Mommsen (ed.), *Monvmenta Germaniae Historica* (xiii): *Chronica Minora saec. IV. V. VI. VII* (Berlin, 1894), iii, p. 147. In the seventh century, Isidore of Seville unkindly derived *Britons* from 'brutes': *Brittones quidam Latine nominatos suscipantur, eo quod bruti sint* (W. M. Lindsay (ed.), *Isidori Hispalensis Episcopi Etymologiarvm sive Originvm: Libri XX* (Oxford, 1911), §IX.ii,101–102).

66 Nikolai Tolstoy, 'Geoffrey of Monmouth and the Merlin Legend', in Elizabeth Archibald and David F. Johnson (ed.), *Arthurian Literature XXV* (Cambridge, 2008), p. 12.

(modern Romania), and culminating in his tragic end and withdrawal to the enchanted island of Avallon.

Geoffrey's Arthurian romance was to grip the imagination of Europe for centuries to come. It would be wrong, however, to suppose that it emerged *ex nihilo*. In his preface he alludes to the fact that Arthur's deeds were widely celebrated in popular tales, presumably recited by minstrels and storytellers: *gesta eorum digna eternitate laudis constarent et a multis populis quasi inscripta iocunde et memoriter predicarent*.[67] Ample evidence attests to the contemporary popularity of such stories in England on the eve of Geoffrey's writing.[68] Although he made limited use of such material, it might well have appeared anomalous that so celebrated a ruler was all but ignored by historians.

In his epilogue Geoffrey warned off the three best-known contemporary historians, Caradog of Llancarfan, William of Malmesbury, and Henry of Huntingdon, from trespassing on subject-matter which he alone possessed adequate information to describe. Of these, Caradog as a Welsh scholar may be assumed to have been familiar with the *Historia Brittonum*, while the two English historians expressly cite it.[69]

Two extensive sections of Geoffrey's work owe nothing to the *Historia Brittonum*. There is no correspondence between Nennius's concluding section on the one hand, and the latter part of Geoffrey's Book XI and the entirety of his Book XII on the other. Where Nennius rounds off his history with a heterogeneous collection of Anglian royal genealogies and historical entries relating to Northern Britain up to the death of St Cuthbert in AD 687, Geoffrey continues his linear history of British kings up to the withdrawal of their last King Cadwalader to Rome, where he died in an odour of sanctity in 689.

Geoffrey's sources for this section are readily detectable. He followed the death of Arthur with the reigns of four British kings: Constantine, Aurelius Conanus, Wortiporius, and Malgo. Here he has shamelessly converted four of five *contemporary* provincial kings excoriated by the sixth-century writer Gildas into *successive* monarchs of all Britain. Next he briefly recast a version of the French romance *Gormond et Isembard* (composed a generation or so before Geoffrey's day) as a barbarian invasion of Britain,[70] and concluded his work with a chronicle of British (Welsh) kings to the death of King Cadwalader in Rome – all blithely transmuted from a century and a half of West Saxon history. The source for almost all this section is the *Historia Ecclesiastica* of the Venerable Bede. Although Geoffrey was aware of the historical Cadwalader, who ruled over Gwynedd (North Wales) in the latter part of the seventh century, everything recounted of him is taken from Bede's account of the entirely distinct West Saxon King Cædwalla.[71]

---

67   Reeve and Wright (ed.), *Geoffrey of Monmouth: The History of the Kings of Britain*, p. 5. Earlier, in his *Prophetia Merlini*, Geoffrey had placed a prophecy in the mouth of Merlin, prognosticating that the deeds of the Boar of Cornwall (*aper Cornubiae* – i.e. Arthur) would become celebrated among the nations, providing material reward for those who related them (ibid., p. 145).

68   Faral, *La légende arthurienne*, i, pp. 257–61; Roger Sherman Loomis, *Arthurian Tradition & Chrétien de Troyes* (New York, 1949), pp. 12–20.

69   R. A. B. Mynors, R. M. Thomson, and M. Winterbottom (ed.), *William of Malmesbury, Gesta Regvm Anglorvm; The History of the English Kings: Volume I* (Oxford, 1998), pp. 20, 26; Greenway (ed.), *Henry, Archdeacon of Huntingdon, Historia Anglorum*, pp. 82, 84, 98–100. Caradog's account of Gildas writing 'the history of the kings of Britain' (Mommsen (ed.), *Chronica Minora*, iii, p. 109) may reflect those versions of the *Historia Brittonum* which ascribe its authorship to Gildas rather than Nennius.

70   Faral, *La légende arthurienne*, ii, pp. 312–13; Tatlock, *The Legendary History of Britain*, pp. 45–46, 135–38.

71   Faral, *La légende arthurienne*, ii, p. 336. Bede concludes his references to the kingdom of Wessex with the reigns of Cædwalla and his successor Ine (Geoffrey's *Ini*) (Charles Plummer (ed.), *Venerabilis Baedae Historiam Ecclesiasticam Gentis Anglorum; Historiam Abbatum, Epistolam ad Ecgberctum una cum Historia Abbatum Auctore Anonymo* (Oxford, 1896), i, pp. 292–94). It is possible that Geoffrey

It may be that Geoffrey was genuinely confused, since not only were the two kings contemporaries, but the Saxon name *Cædwalla* is a borrowing of Welsh *Cadwallon*, name of the father of Cadwalader.[72] Elsewhere Geoffrey confused *Gewisse*, an archaic name for Wessex, with that of the district of Ewyas in South Wales, which was significantly situated not far from Geoffrey's home town of Monmouth.[73] This might have misled him into believing that Bede's Cædwalla ruled over a British kingdom.

In this way Geoffrey ransacked the pages of Bede for his account of the final century and a half of his British history, substituting them for the assorted matter contained in §§57-65 of the *Historia Brittonum*. At first glance the imposition appears unnecessary, since the latter source could have supplied him with more than enough authentic Welsh lore to complete his history.[74] However, it is precisely those chapters that are omitted in a number of manuscripts of the *Historia Brittonum*, which also happen to be those ascribing its authorship to Gildas:

> There survive today five medieval manuscripts of the *Historia Brittonum* which assign the text to 'Nennius'. Of the remaining manuscripts, approximately thirty in number, the overwhelming majority attribute it anachronistically to Gildas whose claim was to be the only early British 'historian' identified by name.[75]

Thus, it may be that the version of the *Historia Brittonum* consulted by Geoffrey was a copy of this truncated edition, which could also explain why he occasionally cites Gildas as his authority, where reference is in fact to the work of Nennius.

Since this family of manuscripts concludes with §56 (the catalogue of Arthur's battles), no evident anachronism arose from ascribing authorship of the *Historia Brittonum* to Gildas, who features in the *Annales Cambriæ* and Caradog of Llancarfan's Life of Gildas as Arthur's

    did not originate the confusion between Welsh Cadwallon/Cadwaladr and English Cædwalla (David N. Dumville, 'Brittany and «Armes Prydein Vawr»', *Études Celtiques* (Paris, 1983), xx, pp. 154–55). However, there can be no question but that overall his detailed account of the career of *Cadualadrus* represents his own inventive construct, albeit compounded by genuine misunderstandings (cf. Faral, *La légende arthurienne*, ii, p. 336–37; Tatlock, *The Legendary History of Britain*, pp. 251–56).

72   Kenneth Jackson, *Language and History in Early Britain: A Chronological Survey of the Brittonic Languages First to Twelfth Century A.D.* (Edinburgh, 1953), p. 244. That there existed contemporary British kings bearing names so similar to that of the English *Cædwalla* served to occlude Geoffrey's distortion of Bede. Geoffrey refers to *Cadualadrus ... quem Beda Cheduallam Iuuenum uocat* (Reeve and Wright (ed.), *Geoffrey of Monmouth: The History of the Kings of Britain*, p. 277). Furthermore, earlier writers had confused the Welsh and Saxon monarchs (Plummer (ed.), *Venerabilis Baedae Historiam Ecclesiasticam Gentis Anglorum*, ii, pp. cxvi–vii). As Tatlock commented, 'Who would have expected two nearly contemporary kings bearing the same name to be unrelated and of different races?' (*The Legendary History of Britain*, p. 252).

73   William Henry Stevenson (ed.), *Asser's Life of King Alfred: Together with the Annals of Saint Neots Erroneously Ascribed to Asser* (Oxford, 1904), pp. 161–62; Williams and Bromwich (ed.), *Armes Prydein*, pp. 49–50.

74   Presumably the coincidence of the *Historia Brittonum*'s concluding with the same period as Bede's history led Geoffrey to end his history at about the same time.

75   David N. Dumville, "Nennius' and the *Historia Brittonum*', *Studia Celtica* (Cardiff, 1975–6), x–xi, p. 78. Cf. Mommsen (ed.), *Chronica Minora*, iii, p. 121–22; Ferdinand Lot, *Nennius et l'Historia Brittonum* (Paris, 1934), pp. 2, 6.

contemporary. Caradog's work, which Geoffrey had read,[76] states that Gildas compiled 'the histories of the kings of Britain' at Glastonbury during the time of Arthur.[77]

The other major lacuna in the *Historia Brittonum* occurs near its beginning, where §11 concludes the story of Brutus's settlement in Britain by synchronizing his reign with the era of the high priest Heli in Israel, *c.* 1120 BC. This left Nennius with no option but to confess his ignorance of a vast span of British history. §12 continues:

> After an interval of many years, not less than eight hundred, the Picts came and occupied the islands which are called *Orcades'* (Orkneys), from which they occupied Northern Britain.[78]

Geoffrey, who like nature abhorred a vacuum, interposed at this juncture two entire books of his *Historia*, in which he described at length events purportedly covering the eight missing centuries. The manner in which he achieved his purpose has been satisfactorily explained by historians, and here a brief summary will suffice. The first few reigns following Brutus are concocted from toponyms (e.g. King *Locrinus* < *Lloegr*, the Welsh name for England), and colourful accounts of the reigns of Bladud (< Old Welsh *Bleiddit*),[79] whom Geoffrey associated with *Badon*, a Welsh name for Bath), and Leir (the legendary Welsh king *Llŷr*, originally a divinity), the King Lear of Shakespeare's tragedy.

This section concludes with a purely imaginary account of the usurpation of Cunedagius, a name taken by Geoffrey from *Cunedag* (Cunedda), who in §14 of the *Historia Brittonum* is described as having expelled Irish colonists from Wales. In fact this event implicitly belongs to the period following the Roman evacuation of Britain *c.* 410 AD. As Cunedda is the last figure to receive mention in Nennius's brief account of Britain between the reign of Brutus and the coming of the Romans, Geoffrey evidently assumed that his reign concluded the pre-Roman era of British history. Accordingly he provided linking biblical synchronisms for the successors of Brutus to the time of Cunedagius and his immediate heirs.[80]

This however covered only 320 of the 800 missing years noted by Nennius, and Geoffrey clearly appreciated that there remained a gulf to fill. This he achieved by adding what amounted in the main to little more than a bare catalogue of names of successive kings of Britain, expanded by an occasional curt biographical notice. Stuart Piggott demonstrated that Geoffrey's dynastic catalogue was appropriated (with tell-tale misunderstandings) from a collection of Welsh pedigrees, similar to that appended to the best exemplar of the *Historia Brittonum*, contained in BM Harleian MS 3859 (*c.* 1100).[81] The only major addition was his conversion of the historical

---

76   Mommsen (ed.), *Chronica Minora*, iii, p. 109. In Caradog's Life of Gildas the Saint is struck dumb in the presence of the pregnant mother of St David, an incident to which Geoffrey alludes in the prophecy he places in the mouth of Merlin (ibid., pp. 107–8; Reeve and Wright (ed.), *Geoffrey of Monmouth: The History of the Kings of Britain*, p. 145).

77   *Ibi scripsit historias de regibus Britanniae* (Mommsen (ed.), *Chronica Minora*, iii, p. 109).

78   Mommsen (ed.), *Chronica Minora*, iii, p. 154.

79   Cf. Phillimore's note in Henry Owen (ed.), *The Description of Pembrokeshire, by George Owen of Henllys, Lord of Kemes* (London, 1892–1936), iii, p. 214.

80   Faral, *La légende arthurienne*, ii, pp. 113–115.

81   E. Williams B. Nicholson, 'The Dynasty of Cunedag and the 'Harleian Genealogies', *Y Cymmrodor* (London, 1908), xxi, p. 86; Stuart Piggott, 'The Sources of Geoffrey of Monmouth: I. The 'Pre-Roman' King-List', *Antiquity* (Gloucester, 1941), xv, pp. 275–84; John J. Parry and Robert A. Caldwell, 'Geoffrey

Gaulish leader Brennus, who conquered Rome in 390 BC, into a British King Brennius, whose exploits, part-historical and part-invented, he recapitulated at some length.[82]

Thus, it is this part alone of Geoffrey's work that might be held to justify his claim to have translated a 'very old book' from Welsh, seeing that it is the sole extended section of his work to be wholly independent of Nennius, Gildas, and Bede. Although the Harleian royal pedigrees consist almost in their entirety of dry lists of names, they include additional aspects which might partially exonerate Geoffrey from the charge of wholesale fabrication. Firstly, they contain the occasional laconic historical notice. In the Harleian manuscript these appear for the most part in Latin, but it is not unlikely that a comparable collection now lost contained glosses written in Old Welsh. The Jesus MS 20 collection of royal pedigrees, which is written entirely in Welsh, in addition to lists of names and patronymics includes gnomic allusions to otherwise largely lost early Welsh history and legend. Even were Geoffrey's ability to read Welsh restricted, he was probably capable of making something of brief narrative passages, such as:

> *yr anna hon oed verch y amhera6dyr rufein. Yr anna hono a dywedei wyr yr eifft y bot yn gyfinnithder6 y veir vor6yn;*
> This Anna was daughter of the Emperor of Rome. This Anna was said by the men of Egypt to be the cousin of the Virgin Mary.[83]

While the Jesus MS was compiled later than Geoffrey's day, its genealogies derive from an earlier collection related to the Harleian pedigrees, antedating Geoffrey's work.[84] As Piggott explained in his classic essay, Geoffrey's evident confusion in interpreting the pedigrees is likely to have arisen from a text similar to the Jesus MS, rather than the Harleian.[85]

While this does not absolve Geoffrey from the charge of deception, much of his book being demonstrably adapted from the Latin works of Gildas, Nennius and Bede, it has been suggested that there existed prior to Geoffrey a Welsh 'Book of Conquests' of Britain.[86] That is the sort of work likely to have been conjoined with a genealogical tract, and it could be that Geoffrey's *liber vetustissimus* was a manuscript containing matter written in part at least in Welsh, including royal pedigrees, glossed with occasional explanatory notes, and combined with a version of the *Historia Brittonum* concluding with the Arthurian passage in §56, such as is known to have been circulating in Wales before his day.[87]

Regrettably, it is difficult to exonerate Archdeacon Walter from the charge of being 'evidently his [Geoffrey's] accomplice'.[88] His concern with Geoffrey's 'translation' extended beyond merely lending him 'ye olde booke'. At the beginning of his §178, Geoffrey explains that what follows

---

of Monmouth', in Roger Sherman Loomis (ed.), *Arthurian Literature in the Middle Ages: A Collaborative History* (Oxford, 1959), p. 81; Bromwich, Jarman, and Roberts (ed.), *The Arthur of the Welsh*, p. 101.

82   Faral, *La légende arthurienne*, ii,, pp. 134–36.

83   J. G. Evans, 'Pedigrees from Jesus College MS. 20', *Y Cymmrodor* (1887), viii, p. 84.

84   Nora K. Chadwick, 'Early Culture and Learning in North Wales', in Chadwick (ed.), *Studies in the Early British Church*, pp. 49, 75–76.

85   *Antiquity*, xv, p. 277. Piggott acknowledged assistance in his investigations from the eminent Welsh scholars Sir Ifor Williams and Professor Henry Lewis (ibid., pp. 269, 282).

86   Peter C. Bartrum, 'Was there a British 'Book of Conquests?', *The Bulletin of the Board of Celtic Studies* (Cardiff, 1968), xxiii, pp. 1–6.

87   Bromwich (ed.), *Trioedd Ynys Prydein*, pp. cxxvi–vii.

88   Christopher Brooke, 'The Archbishops of St David's, Llandaff and Caerleon-on-Usk', in Nora K. Chadwick (ed.), *Studies in the Early British Church* (Cambridge, 1958), p. 231. '… it is not impossible that even an archdeacon

derived only partly from his manuscript, being amplified with information provided by the learned Archdeacon. The episode in question comprises the dramatic story of Modred's bigamous marriage with Arthur's Queen *Ganhumara* (Guenevere), his usurpation of the kingdom while the king was abroad fighting the Romans, Arthur's return and initial defeat of Modred, their final combat on the River Camblan in Cornwall in which Modred was slain and Arthur mortally wounded, and Arthur's removal to be healed in the Isle of Avallon.[89]

As Brynley F. Roberts observed:

The account of Arthur's end appears to have a progression which may derive from an established coherent narrative. It is significant that Geoffrey's sole explicit reference to an oral source is made in connection with this part of his account of Arthur's reign. Even in the native tradition it would appear that the circumstances of Arthur's death, real or apparent, were the tragic consequences of plotting, dissension at court, and perhaps a nephew's betrayal. There may well have been a *chwedl* (saga) of Camlan … which was … an integral part of the Welsh legend of Arthur.[90]

That Archdeacon Walter's account of Arthur's end was recorded in writing (whether Welsh or Latin) is indicated by Geoffrey's misspelling of the name of Arthur's queen as Ganhumara, which reflects orthographical error.[91]

This is the only episode – a major one, nonetheless – that Geoffrey acknowledged as originating in a source other than his *vetustissimus liber*. However, there are other extended episodes which from internal evidence are also likely to be of distinct origin. Some, like the story of Brennus discussed earlier, and that of King Bladud's foundation of Bath, with its hot fires and his untimely death while attempting to fly, may represent little more than Geoffrey's invention. On the other hand, the story of Lear and his three daughters derives from a motif found in Roman literature.[92]

Elsewhere, however, Geoffrey introduces what are probably authentic elements of Celtic legend into his narrative. Thus, allusion to an enchanted sword known as the Yellow Death (*crocea mors*), the effect of whose deadly blade none could avoid, may derive from a marginal note alluding to the great plague of the mid-sixth century, familiar to Welsh tradition under the name of the Yellow Death (*y fad felen*).[93] Attention has likewise been drawn to saga-like episodes not found in other extant sources, such as those describing the erection of Stonehenge, the death of Vortigern on Little Doward Hill, and the conception of Arthur at Tintagel – all of which bear appearance of originating in native tradition.

---

at that time should have countenanced so innocent an imposture' (W. Lewis Jones, 'Geoffrey of Monmouth', *Transactions of the Honourable Society of Cymmrodorion: Session 1898-1900* (London, 1900), p. 78).

89   Reeve and Wright (ed.), *Geoffrey of Monmouth: The History of the Kings of Britain*, pp. 249–53.

90   Bromwich, Jarman, and Roberts (ed.), *The Arthur of the Welsh*, pp. 81, 84–85, 110. Cf. Bromwich (ed.), *Trioedd Ynys Prydein*, p. cxii.

91   'La curieuse forme Guanhumara, par laquelle Geoffrey de Monmouth rend en latin le nom de la femme d'Arthur résulte d'une mauvaise lecture de Gwenhwyfar, dont la graphie ancienne Guenhuiuar a été lue avec m au lieu de iu' (J. Vendryes, 'Les éléments celtiques de la légende du Graal', *Études celtiques* (Paris, 1949), v, p. 34). Cf. R. Thurneysen, 'Zu Nemnius (Nennius)', *Zeitschrift für Celtische Philologie* (Halle, 1936), xx, p. 133).

92   Faral, *La légende arthurienne*, ii, pp. 104–8, 111-12.

93   *Antiquity*, xv, p. 285.

Geoffrey's regard for and use of indigenous material is convincingly summarized by Brynley F. Roberts:

> The *Historia* was written by one who was an outsider to British tradition, one with sympathy and interest but one for whom the tradition was not an integral part of his cultural make-up, and who was living far removed from the living waters of that tradition. It is not surprizing that Geoffrey sometimes misunderstood native material and that the majority of the episodes which he recounts in the *Historia* is not based on traditional tales. The pieces of genuine tradition found here are insertions rather than the basic content of the work; but that there are genuine pieces cannot be doubted and in his attitude to British history it may well be that Geoffrey is not only true to the myth but that it has meaning for him.

Furthermore, although the succession of dynasts in the *Historia Regum Britanniæ* was for the most part arbitrarily cobbled together from names found in Welsh genealogies, the underlying theme of Britain as a united monarchy is undoubtedly archaic:

> The sovereignty of Britain is the thread which runs through the whole book. Geoffrey accepted both the unity of Britain and its traditional divisions ... Geoffrey stresses the unity and single kingship of Britain ... The concept of a succession of single kings which is at the root of Geoffrey's view of British history is wholly traditional.[94]

All in all, consideration of Geoffrey's life and literary work suggests that his *Historia* represents what would now be considered a tolerably researched popular historical novel, rather than sober historiography.[95] It includes a sufficient leavening of independent traditional lore to make it unwise to dismiss out of hand as creative fiction any theme not demonstrably based on identifiable literary sources, or (as is not infrequently the case) patently fictitious.

Only through detailed examination of internal evidence can it be determined to what extent any given episode reflects genuinely independent tradition, employed by Geoffrey of Monmouth as a 'building block' in the creation of his *Historia Regum Britanniæ*. That he employed this technique when opportunity offered, and that he felt a certain pride in appropriating archaic lore to his purpose, has I believe been sufficiently demonstrated.

---

94 Brynley F. Roberts, 'Geoffrey of Monmouth and Welsh Historical Tradition', *Nottingham Mediaeval Studies* (Cambridge, 1976), xx, pp. 36, 37, 38.

95 Kendrick, *British Antiquity*, pp. 5–6. Still worth perusal is the measured analysis of Geoffrey's approach by Fletcher, *The Arthurian Material in the Chronicles*, pp. 57–65.

5

'The Giants' Dance'

Geoffrey's account of Stonehenge
The first explicit allusion to Stonehenge does not appear until some four thousand years after work first began on the monumental structure. About 1133 the Anglo-Norman historian Henry of Huntingdon included it among the Wonders of Britain. Then, a mere four or five years later, to the delight and astonishment of all Christendom, there unexpectedly appeared a sensational explanation of the mystery that had excited Henry's bewildered awe.

Of all the remarkable stories related by Geoffrey of Monmouth in his *History of the Kings of Britain* (*Historia Regum Britanniæ*), that of the transportation of Stonehenge from Ireland to Britain appears the most fantastic. Where Henry of Huntingdon confessed to bafflement as to how or why the gigantic boulders came to be erected, Geoffrey gratified his readers with a detailed description of their origin and purpose.

In §§104-105 of the *Historia* he recounts the duplicitous crime of the crafty Saxon leader Hengist, who, with the compliance of the besotted British King Vortigern, invited the nobles of Britain to a peace conference. Once assembled, at a prearranged signal the Saxon delegates drew concealed knives, with which they slaughtered the whole of the British party, save the captured Vortigern and a valiant nobleman named Eldol of Gloucester, who succeeded in escaping. Eventually the victims were avenged by Vortigern's doughty successor Aurelius, who overthrew the inept Vortigern and executed his brutal ally Hengist. Having restored the realm to its former prosperity, Aurelius, accompanied by Eldol, repaired to the Hill of Ambrius (*in monte Ambrii*), where the victims of the slaughter of the long knives had been interred. Deeply moved by the tragic scene, Aurelius decided to erect a fitting memorial to the noble slain. His masons and carpenters set to work, but despite determined efforts proved unequal to the task.

In view of this obstruction, the Archbishop of Caerleon counselled Aurelius to send for Merlin, the celebrated prophet who had foretold the future of Britain to Vortigern. The seer was accordingly brought before the king, whom he advised to arrange the transfer to the site of the Giants' Dance, a mighty structure whose stones were possessed of magical healing properties. However, Aurelius could not contain his laughter when Merlin went on to explain that the sanctuary was located beyond the sea, at the hill of Killare in Ireland: *chorea gigantum quae est in Killarao monte Hiberniae*. The king derisively questioned the purpose of transporting such colossal stones from so distant a country, as though suitable stones were not more conveniently available in Britain.

Merlin patiently explained that the Irish monoliths were imbued with unique power. Long ago giants had brought them from distant Africa. Every sickness could be cured by means of water washed upon the stones, and wounds healed with additional application of herbs. On hearing this, the Britons resolved to despatch an army to Ireland in order to take the stones by force, should the Irish resist their removal. Uther Pendragon was placed in command of the expedition, which was accompanied by Merlin.

'Merlin re-erects the Giant's Dance'. (Courtesy British Library, Egerton MS 3028)

The British host crossed to Ireland, where it routed an army raised by the inhabitants to oppose their progress. Once arrived at the Giants' Dance, Merlin invited the soldiers to remove the stones as planned. However, despite every effort, they were unable to shift the colossal monoliths. At this Merlin laughed,[1] and gave his own instructions as to how the task should be accomplished. The engineering techniques he recommended immediately proved effective. In no time at all the stones were transported to the coast, whence they were borne home by the British fleet and transferred to *mons Ambrii*. Aurelius repaired to the site, where after majestic ceremonies Merlin arranged for the stones to be re-erected in precisely the same manner as that in which they had stood upon the hill of Killare.

When in due course Aurelius died, he was interred at the Giants' Dance, which thereafter became the early British equivalent of Westminster Abbey as resting place of her kings. Geoffrey's description of the burials of Aurelius's successors Uther Pendragon and Constantine at the site includes an explicit identification which must have already been apparent to many of his readers. The kings, he states, were buried within the stones 'which were erected with wonderful skill not far from Salisbury, being known in English as *Stanhenge*'.[2]

Such in outline is Geoffrey's account of the erection of Stonehenge, which provided a graphic response to Henry of Huntingdon's baffled enquiry. Given that much of the *History of the Kings of Britain* is either derived from identifiable classical and mediæval sources, or Geoffrey's resourceful invention, it might be assumed that his fantastic account of the transportation of the stones across the Irish Sea arose from nothing more than brimming imagination. Indeed, it is

---

1   Merlin's laughter is a recurring motif in the tradition (Paul Zumthor, *Merlin le Prophète: Un thème de la littérature polémique de l'historiographie et des romans* (Lausanne, 1943), pp. 45–47; Lewis Thorpe, 'Merlin's sardonic laughter', in W. Rothwell, W. R. J. Barron, David Blamires, and Lewis Thorpe (ed.), *Studies in medieval literature and languages in memory of Frederick Whitehead* (Manchester, 1973), pp. 323–39; Alexandre Micha, *Étude sur le «Merlin» de Robert de Boron: Roman du XIIIᵉ siècle* (Geneva, 1980), pp. 184–85).

2   Michael D. Reeve and Neil Wright (ed.), *Geoffrey of Monmouth: The History of the Kings of Britain* (Woodbridge, 2007), pp. 171–81, 193, 255.

possible that Henry of Huntingdon regarded the account with scepticism, since he omitted the episode from a detailed summary of Geoffrey's work he sent to a colleague.[3]

Nevertheless, the story became widely accepted throughout the Middle Ages as a piece of veracious history. Later in the same century, Giraldus Cambrensis endorsed the story of Merlin's transfer of the stones from Ireland.[4] However, by the middle of the fourteenth century the chronicler Ranulph Higden had come to question its authenticity.[5] Eventually, Renaissance scholarship came largely to reject the account of Merlin's achievement. Polydore Vergil at the beginning of the sixteenth century loftily ascribed belief in Vortigern's collaboration with 'a certaine soothesayer, called Merline' to 'the common sorte of menne'; while the great Elizabethan topographer William Camden dismissed Geoffrey's story as too implausible to be worth repeating.[6]

Origins of Geoffrey's account

Whatever Geoffrey's failings as an historian, there are indications that he was not the inventor of his account of the transportation of the megaliths. So fantastic did Merlin's feat appear, that two popular versifications of the *Historia* composed in the twelfth century suggest that he employed supernatural arts to remove and re-erect the monumental stones.[7] Even the variant version of Geoffrey's *Historia* ascribes Merlin's achievement to magical power: *paulisper insusurrans motu labiorum tamquam ad oracionem.* This too is what Giraldus appears to have assumed, when he wrote that the task was accomplished through 'the divine effort of Merlin' (*diuina Merlini diligentia*).[8] However, Geoffrey himself emphasized that the prophet achieved the task by means of ingenious mechanical devices (*in operationibus machinandis*).[9]

Geoffrey was generally at pains to rationalize the supernatural in his *Historia*. The impregnation of Merlin's mother by an incubus is alluded to only in direct speech, and justified by a learned reference to the classical author Apuleius. He ascribes the burning of Vortigern's tower to an attack by his enemy Aurelius, whereas his source (the ninth-century *Historia Brittonum*) had represented it as destroyed by fire from heaven. When Merlin transforms Uther into the form of Duke Gorlois of Tintagel in order that he may enjoy the favours of the Duke's wife Igerna, Geoffrey makes the wizard explain that the transformation was achieved solely through application of his 'potions' (*medicaminibus meis*).[10]

It looks as though Geoffrey possessed access to a legendary source (or sources), which he adapted for his account of the erection of Stonehenge, and that his description of Merlin's engineering skills deployed in the transportation and erection of the megaliths represents

3   Diana Greenway (ed.), *Henry, Archdeacon of Huntingdon, Historia Anglorum: The History of the English People* (Oxford, 1996), p. 576.

4   John J. O'Meara, 'Giraldus Cambrensis in Topographia Hibernie: *Text of the First Recension*', *Proceedings of the Royal Irish Academy* (Dublin, 1949), lii, p. 143.

5   Laura Keeler, *Geoffrey of Monmouth and the Late Latin Chroniclers 1300–1500* (Berkeley, 1946), pp. 32, 34.

6   Sir Henry Ellis (ed.), *Polydore Vergil's English History, from an Early Translation Preserved among the MSS. Of the Old Royal Library in the British Museum* (London, 1846), i, p. 115; William Camden, *Britannia* (London, 1600), p. 774.

7   Ivor Arnold (ed.), *Le Roman de Brut de Wace* (Paris, 1938–40), i, pp. 420–31; G. L. Brook and R. F. Leslie (ed.), *Laȝamon: Brut* (Oxford, 1963–78), ii, pp. 440–54.

8   Neil Wright (ed.), *The Historia Regum Britannie of Geoffrey of Monmouth II: The First Variant Version: a critical edition* (Cambridge, 1988), p. 125; *Proceedings of the Royal Irish Academy*, lii, p. 143. Wace similarly ascribes Merlin's feat to a 'prayer' (*preiere*) he uttered (Arnold (ed.), *Le Roman de Brut de Wace*, i, p. 430).

9   Reeve and Wright (ed.), *Geoffrey of Monmouth: The History of the Kings of Britain*, p. 175.

10   Ibid., pp. 37, 72, 139, 171, 175, 187. In addition Geoffrey appears to have been careful to omit the more fanciful Arthurian *Mirabilia* in the *Historia Brittonum*.

rationalization of a process which had earlier been ascribed to magical enchantment. This is further indicated by his account of Merlin's previous appearance before Vortigern. There Geoffrey followed the tale of the fatherless boy Ambrosius contained in the *Historia Brittonum*. Striking parallels between Nennius's account of the wonderful erection of Vortigern's Snowdonian fortress in the *Historia Brittonum* on the one hand, and that of Stonehenge in Geoffrey's work on the other, are evident

1. Nennius: Vortigern orders the construction of a tower. However, no matter how much is achieved by his craftsmen in a day, it vanishes by the following morning.
   Geoffrey: Aurelius summons his workmen to build a memorial. They are compelled to abandon the task, which they unaccountably find beyond their capacity.
2. Nennius: Vortigern is advised by his druids (*magi*) to find a fatherless boy, whose sacrifice will preserve the edifice intact. After extensive searching, the prophetic boy Ambrosius is found and brought before the king.
   Geoffrey: Aurelius is advised by his archbishop to seek out Merlin, the prophet of Vortigern (*Merlinus uates Uortigirni*). After a wide-ranging search, the infant seer is found and brought before the king.
3. Nennius: Ambrosius provides advice which ensures the completion of Vortigern's tower.
   Geoffrey: Merlin's skills make possible erection of the monument proposed by Aurelius.
4. In the *Historia Brittonum*, the prophetic boy is named Ambrosius.
   According to Geoffrey, the place where the Britons' memorial is erected was called the plain of Ambrius (*pagus Ambrii*), where stood the hill (*mons*) of Ambrius (*Ambrii*).

These detailed parallels suggest that Geoffrey's account of Stonehenge drew on an independent version (or versions) of the legend recorded by Nennius three centuries earlier. Minor distinctions of detail and setting in his successive treatments of the theme of the Collapsing Castle point to use of disparate sources, rather than Geoffrey's recycling the same legend to furnish distinct passages in his history (a device featured nowhere else in his *History*). However, it was almost certainly Geoffrey who introduced Merlin as protagonist of the second story, a figure with whom he was familiar from Welsh bardic tradition as the great prophet of the British race.[11]

Stonehenge and Uisneach
In his discussion of Geoffrey of Monmouth's sources, Stuart Piggott urged that cavalier dismissal of his account of the transportation of megaliths to Salisbury Plain had become hard to sustain, given recent discovery of the provenance of the Stonehenge bluestones in the Irish Sea zone. Although Geoffrey's story located their original home in Ireland, rather than Pembrokeshire (whence they actually derived), for Piggott this represented no more than modification of the original event.[12]

---

11   Cf. *Arthurian Literature XXV*, pp. 1–42.

12   Stuart Piggott, 'The Sources of Geoffrey of Monmouth. II. The Stonehenge Story', *Antiquity: A Quarterly Review of Archæology* (Gloucester, 1941), xv, pp. 306–308. 'The correspondence between the legend and the fact is so striking that it cannot be dismissed as mere coincidence; for to do so imposes at least as great a strain upon credulity as to suppose that behind this correspondence there lies a genuine memory of

Navel of Ireland at Uisneach.[14] (Courtesy Flickr Abi Skipp)

It was presumably wartime deprivation of access to libraries that led him to overlook the fact that the pioneering Welsh scholar Sir John Rhŷs had in the previous century advanced an explanation yet more consonant with the evidence.[13] The latter had noted, firstly, that 'this story proves, among other interesting things, that formerly a circle of stones like that of Stonehenge or like a portion of it, was well known to exist in Ireland'. Next he showed Geoffrey's location of the source of the Irish stones at *Killaraus mons* to be an allusion to Killare in County Westmeath, a location close to the site of Uisneach, a site of unique cosmological significance in the Irish mythological tradition.[15] It is curious that Rhŷs's perceptive observation has remained almost entirely ignored by scholars.

---

recorded events … For the story of the carriage of so many stones over so great a distance would be one worthy of note and remembrance even in the Middle Ages, and still more so among the illiterate societies of prehistoric times, in which the oral transmission of tales of legendary and heroic feats was a commonplace' (R. J. C. Atkinson, *Stonehenge* (London, 1956), pp. 184–85). Cf. M. E. Cunnington, *An Introduction to the Archæology of Wiltshire from the Earliest Times to the Pagan Saxons* (Devizes, 1934), pp. 53–54.

13   Writing on military service in 1941, Piggott explained that his researches were of necessity conducted 'in those enforced circumstances in which the only really accessible works of reference are the *King's Regulations* and the *Manual of Military Law*' (*Antiquity*, xv, p. 269). I discussed and augmented Rhŷs's argument in my book *The Quest for Merlin* (London, 1985), pp. 127–29.

14   Another picture appears in Helmut Birkhan, *Kelten/Celts: Bilder ihrer Kultur/Images of their Culture* (Vienna, 1999), plate 468. An aerial view of the double rath of Uisneach is found in E. R. Norman and J. K. St Joseph, *The Early Development of Irish Society: The Evidence of Aerial Photography* (Cambridge, 1969), p. 50.

15   John Rhys, *Lectures on the Origin and Growth of Religion as Illustrated by Celtic Heathendom* (London, 1888), pp. 192–93. The connexion of Geoffrey's Killare with Uisneach was independently remarked by Andrew Breeze, 'Merlin, Stonehenge, and the Hill of Uisneach, Ireland', in Rosamund Allen, Lucy Perry, and Jane Roberts (ed.), *Laȝamon: Contexts, Language, and Interpretation* (Exeter, 2002), pp. 97–101.

Half a century after Geoffrey wrote, Giraldus Cambrensis remarked in his *History and Topography of Ireland* that the bounds of the five provinces of Ireland met at a stone in Meath, near the castle of Killare (*iuxta castrum de Kilair*). This stone was called 'the Navel of Ireland' (*qui lapis et umbilicus Hibernie dicitur*), as it was held to lie at the very centre of the island.[16]

In early cosmologies, the Navel or Omphalos (Celtic **ambliyon-*, Greek ὀμφαλός, Latin *umbilīcus* < Indo-European *embh-, ombh-*)[17] represents the navel of the country: its birthplace and Sacred Centre.[18] As umbilical centre of Ireland, Uisneach was rich in legendary associations, which cast revealing light on the ideology of the country's principal sacred Centre. The stone which marked the meeting-point of the five provinces of Ireland was held to have been first erected by Fintán mac Bochra, a pagan Irish Noah who survived successive cataclysms, eventually re-establishing the human race in Ireland.[19] The Life of Saint Fintán describes how Saint Mochoma discovered the young Fintán at Uisneach in Meath and blessed him. Since nothing of historical value is known of this Saint, it is evident that here as elsewhere the early Church has co-opted a potent pagan figure into hagiographical tradition.[20]

---

16 A full discussion of the archæology and ideological significance of the site is given by Roseanne Schot, 'From cult centre to royal centre: monuments, myths and other revelations at Uisneach', in Roseanne Schot, Conor Newman, and Edel Bhreatnach (ed.), *Landscapes of Cult and Kingship* (Dublin, 2011), pp. 87–113. Artefacts from the site suggest continuous usage from the Bronze Age (Adolf Mahr, 'New Aspects and Problems in Irish Prehistory: Presidential Address for 1937', *Proceedings of the Prehistoric Society* (Cambridge, 1937), iii, pp. 407–408; Harold Mytum, *The Origins of Early Christian Ireland* (London, 1992), pp. 194, 199; N.B. Aitchison, *Armagh and the Royal Centres in Early Medieval Ireland: Monuments, Cosmology, and the Past* (Woodbridge, 1994), p. 118. For the five provinces and their ideological convergence on the Centre, cf. Alwyn Rees and Brinley Rees, *Celtic Heritage: Ancient Tradition in Ireland and Wales* (London, 1961), pp. 118–39; Georges Dumézil, *Mythe et Épopée* (Paris, 1968–73), ii, pp. 253–55; Proinsias Mac Cana, *The Cult of the Sacred Centre: Essays on Celtic Ideology* (Dublin, 2011), pp. 251–61.

17 Julius Pokorny, *Indogermanisches Etymologisches Wörterbuch* (Berne, 1959–69), i, pp. 314–15; Hjalmar Frisk, *Griechisches Etymologisches Wörterbuch* (Heidelberg, 1954–72), ii, pp. 391–92; Ranko Matasović, *Etymological Dictionary of Proto-Celtic* (Leiden, 2009), p. 33. The Hill of Uisneach is regrettably to be avoided today, being shamefully disfigured by vulgar pseudo-Celtic carved effigies – just as the former enchantment of the Hill of Tara I experienced in May 1960 has been wantonly destroyed by a motorway gratuitously routed beside its ramparts. Nor is official Britain behindhand in inflicting senseless destruction on the country's most evocative sites. As I write, English Heritage [*sic*!] has announced ambitious plans for the wholesale Disneyfication of Tintagel, including scarring the castle and surroundings with 'humorous' effigies and crude graffiti, representing such well-attested local worthies as King Arthur and Merlin.

18 'We cannot dismiss this "navel" as a mere picturesque metaphor for a central protuberance. Behind it there may lie an old myth that this was the place where heaven and earth were once joined, and where their separation was effected, or where there is still a line of communication between them' (M. L. West, *The East Face of Helicon: West Asiatic Elements in Greek Poetry and Myth* (Oxford, 1997), p. 50). The Komi of northern Siberia believe that 'the umbilical cord ... symbolized a particular connexion of the baby with the other world' (Vladimir Napolskikh, Anna-Leena Siikala, and Mihály Hoppál (ed.), Komi Mythology (Budapest, 2003), p. 148).

19 R. I. Best, 'The Settling of the Manor of Tara', *Ériu: The Journal of the School of Irish Learning* (Dublin, 1910), iv, pp. 152, 154; R. I. Best, Osborn Bergin, M. A. O'Brien, and Anne O'Sullivan (ed.), *The Book of Leinster Formerly Lebar na Núachongbála* (Dublin, 1954–83), p. 33. For the concept of a holy rock as summit of the earth at its centre, cf. Eric Burrows, 'Some Cosmological Patterns in Babylonian Religion', in S. H. Hooke (ed.), *The Labyrinth: Further Studies in the Relation between Myth and Ritual in the Ancient World* (London, 1935), p. 54; Mircea Eliade, *Patterns in Comparative Religion* (London, 1958), pp. 231–35.

20 *Venit Mochoma de regionibus Chonnact et invenit puerum Fintanum apud Huisnech Midi et benedixit puerum* (W. W. Heist (ed.), *Vitae Sanctorum Hiberniae ex Codice olim Salmanticensi nunc Bruxellensi* (Brussels, 1965), p. 199).

Giraldus's account of the peculiar property of Uisneach is extensively confirmed in early Irish literature, where it is widely designated the Centre of Ireland. Every road was said to lead to the site. It was there in the primal time that the goddess Ériu conferred with the ancestors of the Irish, the Sons of Míl, to whom she stipulated that the island should henceforth bear her name.[21] The four provincial kings of Ireland used to convene at Uisneach every seventh year, as well as at their succession, under the ægis of the king of the surrounding province of Meath.[22] One of the three treasures of Ireland, the *fidchell* (a boardgame bearing cosmic implications) of Crimthann Nia Nair, was brought from a fairy mound to be concealed in the stronghold (*rath*) of Uisneach. The wizard Mide (a name abstracted from that of the district Meath) kindled a mystic fire on the spot, which blazed over the four quarters of Ireland. When the druids of the land complained of the smoke, he cut off their tongues and buried them at Uisneach: a legend which may reflect the sacred hill's reputation as primary source of wisdom in Ireland.[23]

Uisneach provided a point of access to the Happy Otherworld,[24] reflecting the widespread belief that this world and the other are linked at the Navel, from which the world emerged at the beginning of time. Conle the Red was standing with his father Conn on the Hill of Uisneach, when he was approached by an Otherworld woman who invited him to a delightful land wherein dwelt none but women and maidens.[25] It is possible that this happy Otherworld was originally believed to lie within the hill. The god Lug mac Eithne was variously believed to have been mortally wounded or slain at Uisneach.[26] When King Diarmaid mac Cerbaill held court there, a long-concealed enchanted well was revealed, in which the bard Oisín (Ossian) caught eight magical salmon.[27] A great national fair or festival called *Mórdáil Uisnig* was said to have been held on the spot at the feast of Beltane (1 May), when legal judgments were delivered and royal tributes conferred.[28]

21 Best, Bergin, O'Brien, and O'Sullivan (ed.), *The Book of Leinster*, p. 50.

22 Myles Dillon, 'The Taboos of the Kings of Ireland', *Proceedings of the Royal Irish Academy* (Dublin, 1951), liv, pp. 23–24. That this occurred in the mythical era is indicated by the assertion that the ceremony was transferred to the subsequent political capital at Tara.

23 Osborn Bergin and R. I. Best, 'Tochmarc Étaíne', *Ériu* (1938), xii, p. 144; Joseph Vendryes (ed.), *Airne Fíngein* (Dublin, 1953), p. 23; Best, Bergin, O'Brien, and O'Sullivan (ed.), *The Book of Leinster*, pp. 646, 941–42; R. A. Stewart Macalister (ed.), *Lebor Gabála Érenn: The Book of the Taking of Ireland* (Dublin, 1938–56), iv, p. 74; Standish H. O'Grady (ed.), *Silva Gadelica: A Collection of Tales in Irish with Extracts Illustrating Persons and Places* (London, 1892), ii, p. 475; Edward Gwynn (ed.), *The Metrical Dindshenchas* (Dublin, 1903–35), ii, p. 44; L. MacKenna, 'A Poem by Gofraidh Fionn Ó Dálaigh', *Ériu* (1952), xvi, p. 133. For Uisneach as druidic fount of learning cf. O'Grady (ed.), *Silva Gadelica*, i, pp. 154, 170; Philippe Jouët, 'La parole dans la civilisation celtique: mythes et figures', in Venceslas Kruta (ed.), *Les Celtes et l'écriture* (Paris, 1997), pp. 77–78; Séamus Mac Mathúna, 'The Relationship of the Chthonic World in Early Ireland to Chaos and Cosmos', in Jacqueline Borsje, Ann Dooley, Séamus Mac Mathúna, and Gregory Toner (ed.), *Celtic Cosmology: Perspectives from Ireland and Scotland* (Toronto, 2014), pp. 57–59.

24 On emerging from his visit to the palace within the hill, Mongan's year of absence seemed like one night – apparent diminution of time being a characteristic attribute of the Otherworld (Nora White (ed.), *Compert Mongáin and Three Other Early Mongán Tales* (Maynooth, 2006), p. 77).

25 Kim McCone (ed.), *Echtrae Chonnlai and the Beginnings of Vernacular Narrative Writing in Ireland* (Maynooth, 2000), pp. 121–23. The woman appears to have been a manifestation of the Maiden Sovereignty of Ireland (idem, *Pagan Past and Christian Present in Early Irish Literature* (Naas, 1990), pp. 157–58).

26 Edward Gwynn (ed.), *The Metrical Dindshenchas* (Dublin, 1903-35), iv, p. 278; David Comyn and Rev. Patrick S. Dinneen (ed.), *The History of Ireland by Geoffrey Keating, D.D.* (London, 1902–14), i, p. 220.

27 R. I. Best and Osborn Bergin (ed.), *Lebor na Huidre: Book of the Dun Cow* (Dublin, 1929), p. 337; O'Grady (ed.), *Silva Gadelica*, i, pp. 145–46.

28 T. P. McCaughey, 'Tract on the Chief Places of Meath', *Celtica* (Dublin, 1960), v, p. 173; *Proceedings of the Royal Irish Academy*, liv, pp. 29, 35; Comyn and Dinneen (ed.), *The History of Ireland by Geoffrey*

It is small wonder that the Church was concerned to appropriate the site to its own tradition. Writing in the seventh century, Tirechán recorded of Saint Patrick that 'in Uisnech of Meath he stayed next to the Rock of Coithrige'. *Coithrige* is an Irish version of *Patrick*, and the story was plainly intended to christianize the pagan fulcrum.[29] Patrick is represented as seated beside King Diarmaid mac Cerbaill when Uisneach's secret spring was revealed. At one celebration of *Mórdáil Uisnig* Saint Ciaran averted a national drought by joining Diarmaid in prayer. The resultant downpour of rain caused the twelve principal rivers of Ireland to flow from the hill.[30] Adomnan of Iona, travelling on a circuit of Ireland, arrived at *Uisnech Mide*, where a cleric called Oengus mac Tipraite promptly composed a hymn.[31] Nothing more is known of this personage, and as his patronymic means 'well' he is probably a ghost figure, reflecting the tradition of Uisneach's enchanted well as source of poetic inspiration and wisdom.

The archaic character of Uisneach's function as Sacred Centre of Ireland is implicit in its etymology. According to O'Rahilly:

The name Uisnech, which is unique in Irish topography, was probably given to it on account of its quadrilateral aspect as being the centre of the country. I take it to stand for **Ostināko-*, 'the angular place', connected with Ir. *uisin*, 'the temples', Sc. *Oisinn*, 'angle'.

The American philologist Eric P. Hamp suggested an alternative derivation from **us-tin-āko-*, 'place of hearth, or of cinders', recalling the traditional connexion of the hill with a fire festival.[32]

Keating, ii, pp. 246–48. Binchy doubted the authenticity of the assembly, considering it invented to correspond to the Fair of Tailtiu and the Feast of Tara. However, he conceded that even invention may reflect 'an aura of ancient sanctity' attached to the site (D. A. Binchy, 'The Fair of Tailtiu and the Feast of Tara', *Ériu* (1958), xviii, pp. 113–15), and while some details of the assembly may be imaginative it is hard to believe that so important a sacred centre was not also focus of significant tribal gatherings. Cf. Rees and Rees, *Celtic Heritage*, pp. 159–62; Schot, Newman, and Bhreatnach (ed.), *Landscapes of Cult and Kingship*, pp. 111–13. The king of Ulster was assigned the right to feast every seventh year at Uisneach in Meath (John O'Donovan (ed.), *leabhar na g-ceart, or The Book of Rights* (Dublin, 1847), pp. 6, 22).

29   *Inhuisniuch midi mansit iuxta petram coithrigi* (John Gwynn (ed.), *Liber Ardmachanus: The Book of Armagh, Edited with Introduction and Appendices* (Dublin, 1913), p. 21. 'L'assimilation s'est faite principalement par la voie étymologique. Le nom irlandais de l'apôtre «serviteur des quatre» a été adapté en Coithraige, d'où Ail Coithrige «la pierre de Coithraige» au lieu de Ail Coic-rige «la pierre aux cinq royaumes»' (Françoise Le Roux, 'Le Celticvm d'Ambigatus et l'Omphalos Gaulois: La royauté suprême des Bituriges', *Celticvm I: Actes du Premier Colloque International d'Etudes Gauloises, Celtiques et Protoceltiques; Medolanvm Bitvrigvm MCMLX* (Rennes, 1961), p. 176).

30   O'Grady (ed.), *Silva Gadelica*, i, pp. 73–74. Cf. Borsje, Dooley, Mac Mathúna, and Toner (ed.), *Celtic Cosmology*, pp. 60–61. The same story is told of Mongán (White (ed.), *Compert Mongáin*, p. 77). That Uisneach was regarded as a supernatural source of waters is implicit in an account of its function as source of three lakes (Macalister (ed.), *Lebor Gabála Érenn*, iv, p. 136). The mountain Pumlumon ('Five Peaks') was regarded as the centre of Wales, from which miraculously sprang one sunny day the rivers Rheidol, Wye, and Severn (John Rhŷs, *Celtic Folklore: Welsh and Manx* (Oxford, 1901), pp. 391–92).

31   J. H. Bernard and R. Atkinson (ed.), *The Irish Liber Hymnorum* (London, 1898), i, p. 460. On another occasion four of the greatest saints of Ireland conferred *in vnum locum, nomine Huysneach* (Plummer (ed.), *Vitae Sanctorum Hiberniae*, i, p. 248; Heist (ed.), *Vitae Sanctorum Hiberniae ex Codice olim Salmanticensi nunc Bruxellensi*, p. 364).

32   Thomas F. O'Rahilly, *Early Irish History and Mythology* (Dublin, 1946), p. 171; J. Vendryes, E. Bachellery, and P-Y. Lambert, *Lexique étymologique de l'irlandais ancien* (Dublin and Paris, 1959-), U-22. A valuable discussion of the Indo-European concept of the hearth as cosmic centre is provided by Gregory Nagy, *Greek Mythology and Poetics* (Ithaca, NY, 1990), pp. 143–80. Cf. also J. P. Mallory and D. Q. Adams (ed.), *Encyclopedia of Indo-European Culture* (Chicago and London, 1997), p. 263.

That Geoffrey of Monmouth possessed access to information associating Stonehenge with the hill at Killare (i.e. Uisneach) is evident. His knowledge of Ireland was minimal: significantly, *Killaraus mons* is the sole Irish location named in his *Historia*.[33] The name *Killare* (as opposed to Uisneach) features sparsely in Irish literary sources, and must have been a relatively obscure location in Geoffrey's day, its Norman castle not having been built until half a century after he wrote.[34] Since there is no hill at Killare itself, the Irish source upon which his account ultimately drew most likely referred to Uisneach as 'the hill at (or beside) Killare'. Uisneach lies hard by Killare (*Cell áir*), but nowhere in extant Irish sources is it termed the 'hill of Killare'.[35]

Two related questions arise. What precisely was the connexion between Stonehenge and Uisneach, and how might information concerning the Irish site have reached Geoffrey? In the first place, the possibility may safely be dismissed that his account of Merlin's feat reflected the archæologically proven transportation of the bluestones from Preseli Mountain to Stonehenge (although this factor may well have influenced tradition). Since the latter's stones did *not* originate in Uisneach, the Irish site must have entered the tradition for a distinct reason. Equally, the lack of any physical connexion between the two sites on either side of the Irish Sea suggests that they possessed some other common factor: one sufficiently striking as to suggest a common identity.

This factor is indicated by Geoffrey's identification of Killare (i.e. Uisneach) as the original home of the Stonehenge megaliths. According to his account, a stone circle formerly at Killare now stood in Britain, where it had become known as Stonehenge. Thus, *Stonehenge and Uisneach were effectively regarded as one and the same*. This is confirmed by Geoffrey's curious emphasis on the fact that that Merlin arranged for the stones to be arranged *in precisely the same pattern* as they had stood at *mons Killaraus* in Ireland.[36] This detail is the more striking, in that Geoffrey confines the value ascribed the stones to their curative powers, so that their arrangement would appear to be irrelevant.[37] As mentioned earlier, it has been suggested that identification of an Irish site as source of the Stonehenge monoliths arose from the existence of a megalithic site in the sister-island, which had for some reason become identified with Stonehenge. In fact, the opposite must be the case, since according to Geoffrey the Irish stones were *removed* to be re-erected on Salisbury Plain. The appropriate site of origin in Ireland must consequently have been one where no complete monument remained *in situ*, but which nevertheless possessed sufficient reason to be regarded as *the spot where it once stood*. The belief that the Omphalos of Ireland had been transferred to the site of Stonehenge can only have arisen to account for the fact that the latter was the corresponding Omphalos of Britain.

---

33   Tatlock, *The Legendary History of Britain*, pp. 78–82.

34   A. B. Scott and F. X. Martin (ed.), *Expugnatio Hibernica: The Conquest of Ireland by Giraldus Cambrensis* (Dublin, 1978), p. 341.

35   Edmund Hogan, S. J., *Onomasticon Goedelicum: Locorum et Tribuum Hiberniae et Scotiae; An Index, with Identifications, to the Gaelic Names of Places and Tribes* (Dublin, 1910), pp. 174, 678.

36   *At ille, praeceptis eius oboediens, eodem modo quo in Killarao monte Hiberniae positi fuerant erexit illos circa sepulturam ingeniumque uirtuti* ... (Reeve and Wright (ed.), *Geoffrey of Monmouth: The History of the Kings of Britain*, p. 175).

37   Aubrey Burl rejects Geoffrey's account as 'nothing more than a monkish mixture of Merlin, magic and imagination' (*Stonehenge: a new history of the world's greatest stone circle* (London, 2006), p. 136). Unfortunately, his indignant dismissal of the tainted source in its entirety seems to have led him to pay it insufficient attention. His argument is vitiated throughout by the erroneous assumption that Geoffrey and Giraldus refer to *Kildare*. From this he assumed that monks at that monastery spun yarns about a stone circle in its vicinity. In fact, Geoffrey names the site *Killaraus mons*, as does Giraldus. It is only in a single inferior manuscript of the latter's work that the celebrated Kildare is substituted for obscure Killair: clearly, the *lectio difficilior* is to be preferred. Burl's misconception was anticipated by Robert Huntington Fletcher, *The Arthurian Material in the Chronicles especially those of Great Britain and France* (Boston, 1906), p. 93.

Although dating of the separation of the Irish (Goidelic) tongue from British remains controversial, it is accepted that the two languages continued to be mutually comprehensible for many centuries after the break-up of their Common Celtic predecessor *c.* 600 BC. David Dumville believes that this state of affairs outlasted even the Roman occupation of Britain:

> In the fifth century [AD], British and Irish must have been mutually intelligible; in the sixth century they may have been; and in the seventh century, it is absolutely inconceivable that they were. The changes were so great that the languages became mutually unintelligible.[38]

Nevertheless, following bifurcation of their related languages, Ireland and Wales maintained close relations at all levels.[39] Informed people in Britain must have known of the Irish *omphalos* from a very early period.[40] *Omphaloi* worldwide were characterized by similar ideological conceptions, and correspondences between those attached to the great umbilical centres at Uisneach and Stonehenge would surely have been matter of common knowledge and curiosity in both islands, from at latest the early Iron age. It is surely perverse to suggest otherwise. At the turn of the eighth and ninth centuries, the British cleric Nennius conferred in North Wales with 'the most erudite of the Irish' (*peritissimi Scottorum*). They regaled him with the legendary history of their country's original settlements, together with mythological tales of a glass-walled Otherworld tower in the midst of the ocean, and the miraculous properties of two Irish swamps.[41] The second settlement was led by *Nimeth filius quidam Agnominis*, in whose reign Irish tradition ascribed the discovery of Uisneach with its mystic fire.[42] Nennius's account reveals the profound interest held by an educated Briton in Irish 'history', as it was then understood, and clearly believed that his readers (including his dedicatee, King Merfyn of Gwynedd) shared that interest. Independent evidence attests to the fact that Irish scholars were welcome visitors to the cultured court of Nennius's royal patron.[43] Is it to be credited that these discursive Gaels *never* alluded to the celebrated Navel of their country at Uisneach? It seems unlikely: after all, Nennius himself provides what can be shown to have been a detailed description of the mythical properties of the British *omphalos*, in his dramatic account of the nightly ruination of Vortigern's tower.

---

38   G. Ausenda (ed.), *After Empire: Towards an Ethnology of Europe's Barbarians* (Woodbridge, 1995), p. 213. The linguistic situation on either side of the Irish Sea suggests much interplay between Ireland and Britain in prehistory, reinforced by the existence of tribal groupings common to both islands (Patrick Sims-Williams, 'Common Celtic, Gallo-Brittonic and Insular Celtic', in Pierre-Yves Lambert and Georges-Jean Pinault (ed.), *Gaulois et celtique continental* (Geneva, 2007), pp. 329–31). The chronology of dramatic linguistic change from the fifth century AD in Britain and Ireland is plausibly ascribed by Koch to the promulgation in both islands of Christian Latin culture (John T. Koch, 'Windows on the Iron Age: 1964–1994', in J. P. Mallory and Gerard Stockman (ed.), *Ulidia: Proceedings of the First International Conference on the Ulster Cycle of Tales* (Belfast, 1994), pp. 234–35).

39   Cecile O'Rahilly, *Ireland and Wales: Their Historical and Literary Relations* (London, 1924), pp. 67–80; Proinsias Mac Cana, 'Ireland and Wales in the Middle Ages: an overview', in Karen Jankulak and Jonathan M. Wooding (ed.), *Ireland and Wales in the Middle Ages* (Dublin, 2007), pp. 17–45.

40   Artefacts from Roman Britain have been found at Uisneach and other Irish pre-Christian ceremonial sites (Schot, Newman, and Bhreatnach (ed.), *Landscapes of Cult and Kingship*, p. 105).

41   Theodor Mommsen (ed.), *Monvmenta Germaniae Historica* (xiii): *Chronica Minora saec. IV. V. VI. VII* (Berlin, 1894), iii, pp. 154–57, 219. The Irish *Mirabilia* in the Historia Brittonum presumably originally derived from an early version of the *Dindshenchas Dindshenchas Éireann,* attesting to concern with Irish topography in early Wales.

42   Best, Bergin, M. A. O'Brien, and O'Sullivan (ed.), *The Book of Leinster,* pp. 941–42.

43   Nora K. Chadwick, 'Early Culture and Learning in North Wales', in eadem (ed.), *Studies in the Early British Church* (Cambridge, 1958), pp. 93–103.

Just as the druids of Gaul repaired to Britain to acquire arcane knowledge from their British counterparts, so Irish druids are described as visiting Britain for the same purpose. Through a characteristic piece of folk rationalization, the striking correspondence of the two *omphaloi* led to the assumption recorded by Geoffrey of Monmouth that the one physically derived from the site of the other.[44] However, this in turn could scarcely have occurred unless there existed a pre-existing tradition identifying Stonehenge as the Omphalos of Britain.

It seems that the stones of Uisneach were credited with some form of curative quality similar to that ascribed by Merlin to the stones of Stonehenge. The giants who brought them from Africa, so the prophet explained, set up baths among them, which they filled with water with which the stones had been washed. This odd arrangement (of which more *infra*) was employed as efficacious means of curing wounds and sickness.[45]

In the legendary Tripartite Life of Saint Patrick, a text dating from the early ninth century and drawing on earlier traditions,[46] Patrick is described as arriving from Tara to found a church at Uisneach. There the two sons of Níall opposed him, eliciting a curse from the testy Saint which he was barely induced to deflect onto the stones of Uisneach. Consequently, 'no good use has been made of them from that day onwards: they are not even made into washing-stones'.[47] The point of the story is twofold: the curse, originally directed against the impudent royal youths, was transferred to the stones of Uisneach, which in consequence lost the power they formerly possessed.[48] As it stands, the parenthesis might be taken to assert that their state became so abject that they were unfit even for menial usage as washing-stones. However, both their size and distance from a river makes this interpretation unlikely. Given Geoffrey of Monmouth's allusion to healing powers accorded water washed over stones at Uisneach, it is possible that the hagiographer reinterpreted an earlier account, in which Patrick's curse deprived the stones of the potency ascribed by Geoffrey's Merlin to the stones on the hill at Killare. In that case, the tradition to which confused reference is made in the Tripartite Life, might have recorded something to the effect that 'the stones lost their (magical) power from that day onwards, and consequently ceased to function as "washing-stones"'.

At Stonehenge a local belief was recorded in the early eighteenth century that 'if they [the stones] be rubbed, or scraped, and Water thrown upon the Scrapings, they will (some say) heal any green Wound, or old Sore'.[49] Unfortunately, there is no means of knowing whether this reflects authentic tradition, or originated in comment by visitors conversant with reports originating from Geoffrey of Monmouth's *Historia*.

Reverting to the Hill of Uisneach, its functions and qualities may be enumerated as follows.

---

44 A similar legend arose in connexion with the Israelite *omphalos* at Shechem, which was held to be the tomb of Joseph. Relics of the patriarch were thought to have been brought from the *omphalos* of Osiris at Ausīm-Letopolis: 'the patriarch Joseph is derived from the divinity of the Shechem sanctuary, whose cult was established (or renovated) there by relics brought from Egypt' (G. R. H. Wright, *As on the First Day: Essays in Religious Constants* (Leiden, 1987), pp. 60–85). As will be seen, Welsh tradition held that artefacts were removed from the national *omphalos* in central Britain to create the local *omphalos* of Gwynedd at Dinas Emrys.

45 Reeve and Wright (ed.), *Geoffrey of Monmouth: The History of the Kings of Britain*, p. 173.

46 T. M. Charles-Edwards, *Early Christian Ireland* (Cambridge, 2000), pp. 11–13.

47 *Ní fuil nách maith dogníther díb o sin amach: ní dénaiter cid clocha fotraicthi díb* (Kathleen Mulchrone (ed.), *Bethu Phátraic: The Tripartite Life of Patrick* (Dublin, 1939), pp. 50–51).

48 Charles-Edwards, *Early Christian Ireland*, pp. 28–29.

49 Christopher Chippindale, *Stonehenge Complete* (London, 1983), p. 44.

1. It was regarded as the Navel (Irish *imbliu*) of Ireland.[50]
2. The Primordial Man, Fintán mac Bochra, first appeared at this spot.
3. Both he and the Navel represent inspired sources of ancient wisdom.
4. A stone on its summit was believed to embody the exact centre of Ireland.
5. From this axis radiated the twelve great rivers and five principal roads of the island.
6. The province of Meath, in which the hill lay, adjoined the other four provincial kingdoms of Ireland, of which it represented the microcosm.[51]
7. According to legend, a mystic fire burned at Uisneach.
8. The site is enigmatically termed in one source *Orainech n-Uisnig*, 'Uisneach Golden Face'.[52] Was this a general attribute of splendour, or an allusion to the sun? An Irish tale describes the god Lug's appearance at Uisneach, where his radiant features are likened to the burning glow of the sun.[53]
9. It was associated with the druids.
10. Within the hill lay a subterranean hall of great magnificence housing splendid treasures, to which on occasion privileged mortals gained access. This suggests a description of the Otherworld.
11. It also contained an enchanted well wherein swam magical salmon, which remained hidden for centuries. Points 10 and 11 indicate that the site was regarded as a point of access to the Otherworld, whence the land and people originated at the beginning. In addition, 11 confirms Uisneach's function as source of wisdom, the Salmon of Knowledge being a concept familiar from Irish mythology.[54]
12. An assembly or festival was regularly held on the spot: according to some sources on the feast of Beltane (1 May).

Most of these related factors are redolent of the ideology of the *omphalos*, recounted worldwide, and hence unlikely to have been fabricated by mediæval *literati*.[55] Much less is recorded of

---

50 It is alluded to as such by Fintán (*Ériu*, iv, p. 150). For related meanings of *imbliu* and its Indo-European cognates, cf. E. G. Quin *et al.* (ed.), *Dictionary of the Irish Language: Based mainly on Old and Middle Irish Materials* (Dublin, 1913–76), 'I', col. 99; Karin Stüber, *The Historical Morphology of N-Stems in Celtic* (Maynooth, 1998), pp. 114–15; J. P. Mallory and D. Q. Adams, *The Oxford Introduction to Proto-Indo-European and the Proto-Indo-European World* (Oxford, 2006), p. 181.

51 The original Meath was much smaller than the later province, being confined to a district surrounding Uisneach (O'Rahilly, *Early Irish History and Mythology*, pp. 166, 171). According to legend, the prehistoric king Tuathal Techtmar 'severed the heads of the provinces of Ireland for the first time ever, i.e. [to create] Mide' (Sharon Arbuthnott (ed.), *Cóir Anmann: A Late Middle Irish Treatise on Personal Names* (Dublin, 2005–7), i, p. 117).

52 Vendryes (ed.), *Airne Fíngein*, p. 2.

53 Seán Ua Ceallaiġ (ed.), *Trí Truaġa na Scéaluiḋeaċta* (Dublin, 1927), pp. 13–14.

54 O'Rahilly, *Early Irish History and Mythology*, pp. 318–21, 326–36; Françoise Le Roux, 'Le dieu-roi NODONS/NUADA', *Celticvm VI: Actes du Troisième Colloque International d'Études Gauloises, Celtiques et Protoceltiques* (Rennes, 1963), pp. 442–43; Dáithi Ó hÓgáin, *Fionn mac Cumhaill: Images of the Gaelic Hero* (Dublin, 1988), pp. 55–60.

55 Significant studies of the symbolism of the *omphalos* include Jane Ellen Harrison, *Themis: A Study of the Social Origins of Greek Religion* (Cambridge, 1912), pp. 396–424; A. J. Wensinck, *The Ideas of the Western Semites Concerning the Navel of the Earth* (Amsterdam, 1916); Eric Burrows, 'Some Cosmological Patterns in Babylonian Religion', in S. H. Hooke (ed.), *The Labyrinth: Further Studies in the Relation between Myth and Ritual in the Ancient World* (London, 1935), pp. 45–70; Mircea Eliade, *Patterns in Comparative Religion* (London, 1958), pp. 231–35; Hans-Volkmar Herrmann, *Omphalos* (Münster, 1959); Rees and Rees, *Celtic Heritage*, pp. 146–72; Paul Wheatley, *The Pivot of the Four*

the functions of Stonehenge than those of Uisneach, and what there is requires judicious assessment. We may begin with Geoffrey of Monmouth's account.

1. In the time of Vortigern the principal British and Saxon chieftains met to confer at the Kalends of May 'on the Plain of Ambrius' (*in pago Ambrii*). The invaders had prepared a treacherous ambush, at which they slew all the Britons save a valiant nobleman named Eldol.
2. At Merlin's instruction a stone structure known as *chorea gigantum*, 'the Giants' Dance', was subsequently brought from *mons Killaraus* in Ireland *in pago Ambrii*, where it was re-erected as a memorial to the 460 slaughtered British nobles.
3. The site was used as the burial place of mighty kings of Britain.

The most plausible explanation of Geoffrey's account of the otherwise improbable transfer of Stonehenge megaliths from Uisneach to Salisbury Plain is that it reflects awareness that Stonehenge and Uisneach fulfilled parallel functions. His version of events could have been further influenced by a lingering tradition relating to the transfer of the bluestones to the site from Pembrokeshire. Clearly, there existed *some* pre-existing factor that led Geoffrey to associate Uisneach with Stonehenge. It is hard to envisage it as other than that Stonehenge was the Omphalos of Britain, as Uisneach was that of Ireland. From this, it might naturally be inferred that the one physically originated from the other, possibly confirmed by the fact that no megalithic structure of substance remained on the Hill of Uisneach. The unflattering assertion that Ireland had lost her pillar-stones to Britain suggests that the tradition was of British origin, as is the fact that the story was designed to explain the origin of Stonehenge.[56]

A strikingly similar ideological assimilation occurred in the case of the famous Stone of Destiny at Scone, on which the kings of the Picts, and subsequently the Scots, were inaugurated. The Stone was regarded as the umbilical Centre of the Pictish kingdom. At the same time, it was identified with the Irish Stone of Destiny (*Lia Fáil*) at Tara, a belief originating in the fact that they fulfilled similar functions associated with the kingship of their respective realms. Legends evolved, recounting how the Irish stone was brought first from Spain to Tara, whence it was later transferred by one or other early Scottish king to Scone.[57] In reality, of course, there was no physical connexion between the two stones, but rather an ideological one.

Thus, the likeliest explanation of Geoffrey's story of the transfer of stones from the *omphalos* at Uisneach to the site of Stonehenge, is that it originated in similar legendary traditions adhering to umbilical Centres on either side of the Irish Sea.

Quarters: A Preliminary Enquiry into the Origins and Character of the Ancient Chinese City (Edinburgh, 1971), pp. 428–36; Mac Cana, *The Cult of the Sacred Centre*, pp. 79–87.

56   The phraseology of Geoffrey's account of Merlin's creation of Stonehenge was conceivably influenced by Joshua's erection of the shrine at Gilgal (Jacob Hammer, 'Geoffrey Monmouth's Use of the Bible in the "Historia Regum Britanniae"', *Bulletin of the John Rylands Library* (Manchester, 1947), xxx, p. 306.)

57   William F. Skene (ed.), *Chronicles of the Picts, Chronicles of the Scots, and Other Early Memorials of Scottish History* (Edinburgh, 1867), pp. 196–97; idem (ed.), *Johannis de Fordun Chronica Gentis Scotorum* (Edinburgh, 1871–72), i, pp. 23–24; *The History and Chronicles of Scotland: Written in Latin by Hector Boece, Canon of Aberdeen; and Translated by John Bellenden, Archdeacon of Moray, and Canon of Ross* (Edinburgh, 1821), i, p. 5. Cf. William F. Skene, *The Coronation Stone* (Edinburgh, 1869), pp. 15–22; Nick Aitchison, *Scotland's Stone of Destiny: Myth, History and Nationhood* (London, 2000), pp. 20–28.

6

Avenues of Transmission
in Archaic Tradition

Preservation and transmission of archaic lore

Stonehenge is vastly older than the Iron Age: older by some two thousand years. If, as was until recently generally accepted, Celtic immigrants began arriving in Britain no earlier than the Iron Age, it is the cosmology and mythology of that era which may primarily be expected to have left traces in early Welsh and Irish literarature. Of necessity, this implies that such traditions of the pre-Roman era as may be reconstructed from literary sources are in the main likely to reflect those of a culture or cultures introduced from the Continent long after the construction of Stonehenge. Consequently, any conclusions drawn from that evidence must be considered as primarily applicable to myths and rituals inhering to Stonehenge in an era long subsequent to the monument's original construction.

How far the imported ideology of the Celts may have absorbed aspects of pre-existing belief systems in Britain is a secondary question difficult to assess, but nonetheless one which it would be unsatisfactory to dismiss without consideration. In fact, I have long come to share Stuart Piggott's view that traces are detectable of archaic lore relating to Stonehenge and other prehistoric sites, which indicate the possibility of transmission of elements of the tradition from the Bronze and even Neolithic Ages. Here again the archæological record is of inestimable value, demonstrating *inter alia* widespread continuity in use of religious sanctuaries from Neolithic times to the Roman occupation of Britain. Such shrines represent likely havens for preservation of archaic lore.

Many scholars accept the intrinsic likelihood that early Celtic settlers absorbed and preserved aspects of the cosmology of their pre-Indo-European predecessors.[1] Sections of this book are devoted to examining circumstances in which such lore might have been transmitted and preserved. In fact, extensive evidence attests that cultures regularly adopt significant elements from the mythologies of their predecessors – in particular, with regard to the concept of the *omphalos* or Centre, that focus of existence which was pivotal to archaic cosmologies worldwide. Such considerations will be considered in their appropriate contexts. At this stage, two pertinent instances from the ancient world are worth remark.

---

1   Particularly valuable in this respect is the recent book by the archæologist John Waddell, *Archaeology and Celtic Myth* (Dublin, 2014), who kindly provided the preface to this book. Continuity of cultural elements in societies of differing origin successively occupying the same territory is encountered worldwide. For instance, adverse environmental conditions among coastal tribes of the French Congo led to their gradual extinction and replacement by tribes arriving from the interior. However, the traditions of the indigenous peoples were absorbed by the incomers, in this way becoming preserved by successive generations of immigrant supplanters (Mary H. Kingsley, *Travels in West Africa: Congo Français, Corisco and Cameroons* (London, 1897), p. 401).

If traditions of the high gods of Canaan, El and Baal, associated themselves with venerable mountain peaks all over Syria-Palestine, then it is only to be expected that Mount Zion, the center of Israelite piety from the time of David, would accept traditions common to the [pre-Israelite] religion of Canaan.[2]

Similarly, elements of non-Aryan religion were abs orbed and preserved in the great Indian poetic compendium of Indo-Aryan myth and ritual, the *Rgveda*.[3]

A suggested difficulty in arguing for preservation of lore originating in the Bronze Age or earlier, rests on the fact that the druids, guardians of traditional learning in early Britain, represent a hierarchy of Celtic provenance. For long it was widely accepted that Celtic-speaking immigrants arrived in Britain during the Iron Age: that is to say, some time during the early or middle centuries of the first millennium BC.[4] Since Stonehenge was erected at least two thousand years earlier, it would appear likely that those who built it, and for centuries thereafter conducted rites within its precinct, practised a pre-Indo-European religion, expressed in a lost pre-Indo-European language or languages.

Against this, it has lately been contended that the arrival of the Celts in Britain and Ireland is assignable to a much earlier era than was formerly believed.[5] Declaring that 'There is ... no warranty today for the statement that the first Celtic immigrations to England took place during the Halstatt period in the eighth or seventh century BC', Colin Renfrew argued for a process of what he terms 'cumulative Celticity' over a far more protracted period. The archæological evidence, he proposed, 'implies an Indo-European-speaking population in France and in Britain and in Ireland, and probably in much of Iberia also, by before 4000 BC'.[6] A similar view was advanced by Renfrew's fellow archæologist Marija Gimbutas, who argued that Indo-European (although not necessarily Celtic) speakers could have reached Ireland as early as 3500 BC.[7]

---

2   Richard J. Clifford, *The Cosmic Mountain in Canaan and the Old Testament* (Cambridge, Mass., 1972), p. 140. Jacob's vision in the land of Haran of the ladder reaching from earth to heaven indicates that it was revered as an Omphalos. 'The great antiquity of this city and the remains discovered at the site suggest that Bethel was a cult-center of the Canaanites before it became Israelite. Hence, it is also possible that the ancient Hebrews retained some traditions connected with that particular place' (Luis I. J. Stadelmann, *The Hebrew Conception of the World* (Rome, 1970), p. 151). Cf. R. E. Clements, *God and Temple* (Oxford, 1965), pp. 13–14. The relationship between the Canaanite god El and his Hebrew successor Yahweh is fully explored by Mark S. Smith, *The Origins of Biblical Monotheism: Israel's Polytheistic Background and the Ugaritic Texts* (Oxford, 2001), pp. 135–48.

3   F. B. J. Kuiper, *Aryans in the Rigveda* (Amsterdam, 1991), pp. 15–19. 'The inherited Vedic *culture* ... must for a long time have remained dominant, notwithstanding the foreign influence that made itself felt: a foreign myth could only be adopted by transforming it into an Indra-myth and non-Aryan sorcerers were incorporated and became Vedic *ṛṣis*, authors of a separate collection of hymns' (p. 96). Cf. Asko Parpola, 'From the dialects of Old Indo-Aryan to Proto-Indo-Aryan and Proto-Iranian', in Nicholas Sims-Williams (ed.), *Indo-Iranian Languages and Peoples* (Oxford, 2002), pp. 94–95.

4   E.g. David Greene, 'The Making of Insular Celtic', in *Proceedings of the Second International Congress of Celtic Studies* (Cardiff, 1966), p. 124; Stuart Piggott, *Ancient Europe from the beginnings of Agriculture to Classical Antiquity* (Edinburgh, 1965), pp. 222–23; Anne Ross, *Everyday Life of the Pagan Celts* (London, 1970), pp. 17–18, 24–25; L. Luca Cavalli-Sforza, Paolo Menozzi, and Alberto Piazza, *The History and Geography of Human Genes* (Princeton, 1994), p. 260.

5   Myles Dillon's tentative assignment of Celtic immigration into Britain and Ireland to *c.* 2000 BC (Myles Dillon and Nora Chadwick, *The Celtic Realms* (London, 1967), pp. 4–5) was rejected on linguistic grounds by David Greene ('The Coming of the Celts: The Linguistic Viewpoint', in Gearóid Mac Eoin (ed.), *Proceedings of the Sixth International Congress of Celtic Studies* (Dublin, 1983), pp. 133–37).

6   Colin Renfrew, *Archaeology and Language: The Puzzle of Indo-European Origins* (London, 1987), p. 233–49.

7   Marija Gimbutas, *The Kurgan Culture and the Indo-Europeanization of Europe: Selected Articles from 1952 to 1993* (Washington, 1997), pp. 23, 114, 321, 365. John Waddell also proposed a Bronze Age context for the genesis of Celtic languages and culture in Ireland and Britain ('Celts, Celticisation and the Irish

Yet another distinguished archæologist, Barry Cunliffe, argues for a comparably early date, in his case preferring an oceanic approach route. According to his thesis, proto-Celtic languages became

the lingua franca of the Atlantic community. It could further be argued that the language had developed gradually over the four millennia that maritime contacts had been maintained, perhaps reaching its distinctive form in the Late Bronze Age when communication along the sea lanes was at its most intense, and when many aspects of the elite system, technology, and beliefs had coalesced to create a broadly similar cultural continuum.[8]

On discrete grounds, the Celtic linguist John Koch argues for transmission of an early Celtic language from Tartessus in the south-western Iberian peninsula to Ireland and Britain by sea routes *c*. 1300–*c*. 900 BC.[9]

Clearly, acceptance of a Bronze Age or even Late Neolithic context for the establishment of a Celtic language in Britain would greatly augment the possibility of transmission of very early indigenous lore into the late Iron Age, and thenceforward in continuingly depleted form into the extant literary tradition. However, the hypothesis of importation of a Celtic language or languages into Bronze Age Britain has been subjected to severe criticism, notably by the archæologist and Indo-Europeanist J. P. Mallory, and the Celtic linguist Graham Isaac.[10] So far as I am qualified to judge, the latter appear to have had the better of the controversy.[11] Nonetheless, it is evident that the issue is likely to remain disputed: indeed, it is hard to envisage its ever reaching a definitive conclusion.[12]

In view of this scholarly dissension, I would emphasize that the investigation that follows will be broadly conducted on the cautious premise that a Celtic language (or languages) is likely to have been first introduced into Britain at a period many centuries later than the construction of

---

Bronze Age', in John Waddell and Elizabeth Twohig (ed.), *Ireland in the Bronze Age* (Dublin, 1995), pp. 158–69).

8   Barry Cunliffe, *Facing the Ocean: The Atlantic and its Peoples 8000 BC–AD 1500* (Oxford, 2001), pp. 293–97; idem, 'Tribes and Empires *c*. 1500 BC–AD 500', in Paul Slack and Ryk Ward (ed.), *The Peopling of Britain: The Shaping of a Human Landscape* (Oxford, 2002), pp. 124–26; idem, 'Celticization from the West: The Contribution of Archaeology', in Barry Cunliffe and John T. Koch (ed.), *Celtic from the West: Alternative Perspectives from Archaeology, Genetics, Language and Literature* (Oxford, 2010), pp. 13–38.

9   John T. Koch, 'Paradigm Shift? Interpreting Tartessian as Celtic', in ibid., pp. 208–9; idem, *Tartessian: Celtic in the South-west at the Dawn of History* (Aberystwyth, 2009), pp. 132–42. Koch's hypothesis is criticized by Patrick Sims-Williams, 'Bronze- and Iron-Age Celtic Speakers: What Don't We Know, What Can't We Know, and What Could We Know? Language, Genetics and Archaeology in the Twenty-First Century', *The Antiquaries Journal* (Cambridge, 2012), xcii, p. 431.

10   J. P. Mallory, *In Search of the Indo-Europeans* (London, 1989), pp. 106–7; idem, 'The Indo-Europeanization of Atlantic Europe', in John T. Koch and Barry Cunliffe (ed.), *Celtic from the West 2: Rethinking the Bronze Age and the Arrival of Indo-European in Atlantic Europe* (Oxford, 2013), pp. 28–29, 37; G. R. Isaac, 'The Nature and Origins of the Celtic Languages: Atlantic Seaways, Italo-Celtic and Other Paralinguistic Misapprehensions', *Studia Celtica* (Cardiff, 2004), pp. 49–58; idem, 'The Origins of the Celtic Languages: Language Spread from East to West', in Cunliffe and Koch (ed.), *Celtic from the West*, pp. 153–67.

11   Cf. the valuable review article by Thomas Owen Clancy (*Studia Celtica* (Cardiff, 2013), xlvii, pp. 189–94).

12   Essential reading on this topic is Patrick Sims-Williams's lucid exposition of the largely insuperable problems involved in correlating linguistic, archæological, and genetic aspects of early human migration patterns (*The Antiquaries Journal*, xcii, pp. 427–49).

Stonehenge. The onus therefore lies on me to suggest how archaic lore might have been transmitted from one linguistic culture to another. At the same time, it cannot be too strongly emphasized that the greater part of the enquiry that follows is of necessity concerned with source material of Celtic provenance, coupled with acceptance of the fact that there can be scant *direct* means of assessing how far this literature may have preserved lore originating in pre-Celtic insular societies.

Nevertheless, it is legitimate to stress the intrinsic implausibility of any sort of 'clean break' between the Celtic religio-linguistic matrix and that of its pre-Indo-European predecessor(s). Y-chromosomal and mitochondrial varieties of DNA samplings in Britain and Ireland indicate a strong degree of genetic continuity in their populations from the Late Neolithic and early Bronze Age era.[13] It is consequently likely that disparate languages in the British Isles co-existed over a lengthy period as the Iron Age succeeded to the Bronze Age: a protracted transitional epoch which must have known large-scale local bilingualism, and with it inevitable absorption of at least some of the impressive traditional lore of the indigenous inhabitants, including social and religious beliefs. The majestic presence of colossal megalithic shrines dominating much of the countryside must have served to impress on incoming populations the immutable *rootedness* of indigenous religious beliefs and practices in the landscape they had come to settle and eventually dominate.

Furthermore, incoming Celts, establishing their fiefdoms alongside those of indigenous Bronze-Age tribal rulers, would have been likely on occasion to seek to establish their legitimacy by laying claim to lineal inheritance from the dynasties they had supplanted. In early mediæval Ireland, to provide but one of numerous examples, when the obscure rulers of the territory of Déis Becc in Munster displaced the former Eóganacht kings of Munster,

> the genealogists kitted them [the Déis Becc dynasts] out with a new name, Dál Cais, from an invented pseudo-eponym, Cormac Cas, and new descent from that eponym whom they claimed was brother of Eógan, eponym of the Eóganacht.[14]

Appropriately, a remarkable example of just such a protracted process of cultural interchange is to be found within the British Isles. Despite a relative sparsity of evidence, it seems clear that the language spoken by the Picts in the early mediæval period derived from a non-Indo-European (i.e. pre-Celtic) tongue, which eventually became conflated, or co-existed, with a P-Celtic language similar to, although distinct from, British and Gaulish. Such collaboration was already in existence by the late Iron Age, as place names in Ptolemy's *Geography* attest.[15]

13   Emmeline W. Hill, Mark A. Jobling and Daniel G. Bradley, 'Y-chromosome Variation and Irish Origins', in Colin Renfrew and Katie Boyle (ed.), *Archaeogenetics: DNA and the population prehistory of Europe* (Cambridge, 2000), pp. 203–8; Kim McCone, *The Celtic Question: Modern Constructs and Ancient Realities* (Dublin, 2008), p. 42.

14   Donnchadh Ó Corráin, 'Irish Origin Legends and Genealogy: Recurrent Aetiologies', in Tore Nyberg, Iørn Piø, Preben Meulengracht Sørensen, and Aage Trommer (ed.), *History and Heroic Tale: A Symposium* (Odense, 1985), p. 71.

15   K. H. Jackson, 'The Pictish Language', in F. T. Wainwright (ed.), *The Problem of the Picts* (Edinburgh, 1956), pp. 149–58. Cf. Wilhelm F. H. Nicolaisen, 'Something Old, Something New from the Land of Picts', in Michaela Ofitsch and Christian Zinko (ed.), *Studia Onomastica et Indogermanica: Festschrift für Fritz Lochner von Hüttenbach zum 65. Geburtstag* (Graz, 1995), pp. 138–41. 'Within the period from 500 to 1500 A.D., the initial, unstoppable advance and subsequent retreat of Gaelic in Scotland, as documented by place names, involved interaction with four Indo-European languages and the toponymy that these had created, not to mention the continuing presence of speakers of an unidentified non-Indo-European language or languages. After all, what language did the "Cat" tribes of Sutherland and the "Whale" tribes of Orkney speak?' (W. F. H. Nicolaisen, 'Celtic and Pre-Celtic Place-Name

Further evidence of the pre-Celtic character of Pictish society is indicated by the practice of dynastic matriliny, i.e. while the king must be a male, the royal inheritance passes through a female.[16] Although particular circumstances could result in occasional pragmatic instances of inheritance through a female among the Celtic Britons, matriliny as a system was unknown to the Celts.[17]

The great Celtic scholar Kenneth Jackson's conclusion provides a suggestive analogy to the likely relationship between incoming Celts and their druids, and the indigenous priesthood of Bronze Age Britain:

> If these tentative assumptions are accepted the conclusion would be that a people speaking a separate dialect [from that of Britain south of the Forth] of P-Celtic ... settled in Scotland north of the Firth of Forth ... that they there mingled with an older population of a Bronze Age cultural background whose language was not an Indo-European one; borrowed some of their personal and tribal names; took over their custom of matrilinear succession; *and perhaps even adopted their language to a certain extent, possibly only for religious or ceremonial purposes* [italics inserted], though they retained their own Celtic speech to the end.[18]

Elements in Scotland', in Benjamin T. Hudson and Vickie Ziegler (ed.), *Crossed Paths: Methodological Approaches to the Celtic Aspect of the European Middle Ages* (Lanham, Md., and London, 1991), p. 6). Many of the names and epithets in the earlier sections of the Pictish king-lists are unrecognizable as Celtic, and have consequently long been considered likely to be of pre-Celtic origin (Eoin MacNeill, 'The Language of the Picts', *Yorkshire Celtic Studies* (Leeds, 1938–39), ii, p. 17; Wainwright (ed.), *The Problem of the Picts*, p. 144; *The Antiquaries Journal*, xcii, p. 431).

16   The existence of Pictish matriliny has lately come under attack, although not I believe very persuasively. However, space does not permit adequate examination of the issue here, to which I intend to devote a full discussion elsewhere.

17   Although isolated occasions when a dynasty claimed inheritance through an heiress are recorded (usually when no male heir was available), there exists no trace in Celtic Britain of a matrilineal system per se (Wainwright (ed.), *The Problem of the Picts*, p. 153). An exception has been ascribed to the family of Don in the mediæval Welsh story of *Math uab Mathonwy* (H. M. Chadwick, *Early Scotland: The Picts, the Scots & the Welsh of Southern Scotland* (Cambridge, 1949), pp. 92–93, 94; Nora K. Chadwick, 'Pictish and Celtic Marriage in Early Literary Tradition', *Scottish Gaelic Studies* (Oxford, 1955), viii, pp. 57–67, 87–110). However, it is significant that the protagonists of the tale are unmistakably euhemerized pagan divinities. Indeed, it is not impossible that these myths preserve memories of early contacts between incoming patrilineal Celts and an indigenous population practising a system of matrilineal dynastic inheritance.

18   Wainwright (ed.), *The Problem of the Picts*, pp. 156–57. Jackson's arguments received support from other Celtic scholars (e.g. Myles Dillon and Nora Chadwick, *The Celtic Realms* (London, 1967), p. 72; W. F. H. Nicolaisen, *Scottish Place-Names: Their Study and Significance* (London, 1976), p. 150; Wolfgang Meid, 'Englisch und sein britischer Hintergrund', in Alfred Bammesberger and Alfred Wollmann (ed.), *Britain 400–600: Language and History* (Heidelberg, 1990), pp. 101, 109; Louis Charles Prat, 'Désignation des peuples et pays celtiques', in Gwennolé Le Menn and Jean-Yves Le Moing (ed.), *Bretagne et pays celtiques: langues, histoire, civilisation; mélanges offerts à la mémoire de Léon Fleuriot* (Rennes, 1992), p. 516). Latterly, however, attempts to overturn the argument by Jackson and others for survival of a non-Indo-European language among the Picts acquired a temporary vogue. Thus, it has been declared that 'The ill-founded notion that the Picts, unlike their neighbours, spoke a non-Indo-European language is a present-day myth firmly dispelled by modern research ... although yet to fully permeate popular consciousness' (Sally M. Foster, 'The Picts: Quite the Darkest of the Peoples of Dark Age Britain?', in David Henry (ed.), *the worm the germ and the thorn: Pictish and related studies presented to Isabel Henderson* (Balgavies, 1997), p. 7). The sceptical case has been most fully posed by Katherine Forsyth, *Language in Pictland* (Utrecht, 1997). However, her arguments are roundly rejected by leading Celtic linguists, who broadly accept the survival in some form of a non-Celtic language, on the basis of Pictish place-names, inscriptions, and king-lists. Cf. the review of Forsyth's monograph by Damian McManus in *Cambrian Medieval Celtic Studies* (Aberystwyth, 1999), xxxviii, pp. 108–10; also Graham R. Isaac, 'Scotland',

Naturally, I am not suggesting that a comparable development *necessarily* occurred in the case of early Celtic settlements in Southern Britain. However, the Pictish analogy, which has the virtue of being that found nearest home, indicates the *feasibility* of continuity of traditional lore spanning differing languages and cultures over extensive periods of time. Interestingly, Kim McCone has recently suggested that the earliest names for 'Britons' (**Pritenoi*) and Ireland (*Īweryon-*) may be of pre-Celtic origin.[19]

Turning to another consideration, Mike Parker Pearson draws attention to the fact that evidence of Iron Age human activity connected with megalithic monuments appears markedly scarce, from which he concludes 'that the association of druids with Stonehenge is an entirely recent invention with no basis in prehistoric reality'.[20] Against this, it is likely that religious beliefs focussed on megalithic sites might at times be transmitted in modified form, rather than abruptly abandoned wholesale. For example, changes in ritual practice could have resulted in there being small occasion for deposition of material remains of continuing cultic assemblies at stone circles.[21] The sole authoritative literary account of such an assembly in Britain is found in the early seventh-century Life of Saint Samson of Dol. Travelling through north Cornwall about the middle of the previous century, the Saint came upon a huge crowd (*exercitus*) of pagans participating in rituals focussed on a stone idol (whether this formed part of a larger megalithic complex is unspecified).[22] Since it is likely that the worshippers had foregathered from far and wide, there appears no pressing reason to suppose that they left behind much that is likely to attract the attention of archæologists a millennium and a half later.

Evidence considered in further chapters of this book suggests the survival into early mediæval times of a tradition, recorded in both Britain and Ireland, that rites conducted at the Sacred Centre could be obligatorily cloaked in secrecy, lest they be overheard and frustrated by demonic forces intent on the kingdom's destruction. This precaution would have required those not directly involved in ritual activity to assemble at a discreet distance.[23]

Furthermore, Saint Samson apparently made no attempt to have the site of the pagan mysteries destroyed or shunned, but instead appropriated it to the new religion by inscribing a cross on its principal monolith. In the history of religions, it is indeed rare for a newly introduced faith not to appropriate significant doctrinal and ritual elements from its predecessor. That, after all, is what occurred following the Roman conquest of Britain, when Celtic divinities were assimilated to their Roman counterparts, and again when the English became converted to Christianity.

in Javier de Hoz, Eugenio R. Luján, and Patrick Sims-Williams (ed.), *New Approaches to Celtic Place-Names in Ptolemy's Geography* (Madrid, 2005), pp. 189–214; Oliver Padel, 'Celtic, Pictish and Germanic Onomastics in the work of H. M. Chadwick', in Michael Lapidge (ed.), *H. M. Chadwick and the Study of Anglo-Saxon, Norse and Celtic at Cambridge* (Aberystwyth, 2015), p. 166. Patrick Sims-Williams concludes that, 'Though it is fashionable for scholars to ignore it, a non-Indo-European language does seem to be visible in the inscriptions of Pictland, which have never convincingly been interpreted as Celtic' (*The Antiquaries Journal*, xcii, p. 431).

19   McCone, *The Celtic Question*, pp. 9–11.

20   *Stonehenge: Exploring the Greatest Stone Age Mystery* (London, 2012), p. 179.

21   Cf. Timothey Darvill, 'Ever Increasing Circles: The Sacred Geographies of Stonehenge and its Landscape', in Barry Cunliffe and Colin Renfrew (ed.), *Science and Stonehenge* (Oxford, 1997), p. 193.

22   Pierre Flobert (ed.), *La vie ancienne de saint Samson de Dol* (Paris, 1997), p. 216.

23   'Generally the settlements and the meagre evidence for arable activity were kept at a distance – as at other major Neolithic ceremonial complexes with standing stones, the Iron Age population was avoiding or respecting Stonehenge [at certain stages of its evolution]' (Bowden, Soutar, Field, and Barber, *The Stonehenge Landscape*, p. 78).

It has from time to time been contended that a principal function of Stonehenge was to establish calendrical alignments with heavenly bodies.[24] In early times, accurate predictions of recurring celestial cycles were obtained by means of observations conducted and recorded over extensive periods of time. The celebrated Gaulish Calendar of Coligny, which dates from about AD 200, and whose calculations reflect long centuries of study of the night sky, was surely constructed by druids.[25] Whatever the interpretation of its application, the calendar unquestionably represent several centuries of recording and compilation; the druids were the learned order of Gaul, and the language of the calendar is Gaulish. Any alternative theory surely reflects reluctance to contemplate facts, rather than healthy caution.

Julius Caesar, who enjoyed the uniquely extensive opportunity to establish the facts at close quarters during his years of campaigning in Gaul, reported that the Gaulish druids of his day committed to memory voluminous bodies of poetry, by which means they preserved encyclopædic knowledge of cosmology, astronomy, and other learned lore. He was further informed (presumably by his close contacts among the Gaulish druids) that the original fount of druidic learning lay in Britain. This suggests a belief that significant elements of their archaic lore were not exported across the Channel by Celts from Gaul, but discovered indigenous to Britain.

To what extent was ancient lore preserved in writing?

Bronze Age Britain, for all its artistic, economic, and social achievements, was without doubt an illiterate society. A similarly negative estimate of pre-Roman Iron Age literacy is generally accepted, although in this case the *argumentum ex silentio* is less overwhelming. Even so, if authentic traditions of the construction and early use of Stonehenge were preserved into historical times, it seems that they can only have been transmitted orally throughout much or all of prehistory. The intent of this chapter is to suggest how such traditions *might* have survived over protracted periods of time, i.e. *that the proposition is at least feasible*. After all, many of those academics who reject the possibility of the preservation of ancient lore do so largely on the assumption that it is just that: impossible.

I appreciate that there will be those inclined to eschew an avenue of enquiry, which they would prefer to dismiss from the outset as altogether speculative. However, such donning of a scientific blindfold is unhelpful. Evidence was cited earlier, supporting the likelihood that archaic traditions of Stonehenge survived into the mediæval era. In that case, it is worth considering in what circumstances such extended continuity of transmission might have occurred. For the first two or three millennia of Stonehenge's existence, it must have been transmitted orally. By the later Iron Age, however, there arrives the possibility that traditional lore became in part committed to writing.

In fact, not only is oral transmission comparable as means of preservation of archaic lore to preservation in writing, but the two traditions are closely interrelated. As Marie-Louise Sjoestedt pointed out:

It is chiefly in Ireland that Celtic paganism survived long enough to be committed to writing. And everything tends to suggest that if the oral tradition of Gaul before the

---

24   Cf. C. A. Newham, *The Astronomical Significance of Stonehenge* (Leeds, 1972); John Edwin Wood, *Sun, Moon and Standing Stones* (Oxford, 1978); John North, *Stonehenge: Neolithic Man and the Cosmos* (London, 1996).

25   'Le calendrier de Coligny, celui du lac d'Antre, les diverses inscriptions gauloises ou mixtes trouvées témoignent qu'à partir de ce moment, une partie au moins de la science religieuse des druides est vivante' (Renée Carré, 'Des Julio-Claudiens aux Flaviens, l'enjeu gaulois', in Pierre-Yves Lambert and Georges-Jean Pinault (ed.), *Gaulois et celtique continental* (Geneva, 2007), p. 25).

conquest had been written down and had been preserved to us, it would have revealed a mythological world not very different and certainly not more 'primitive' than that to which the medieval Irish texts give access.[26]

The written source generally possesses the advantage of being less liable to alteration – above all, where prose texts are concerned. I propose to examine the two mediums in reverse order, beginning with the question when written records may plausibly be assumed to have come into use in early Gaul and Britain.

It is likely that some degree of literacy obtained in southern Britain on the eve of the Roman occupation. Gaul had become romanized with remarkable swiftness following its final subjugation by Caesar in 50 BC (Cisalpine Gaul had been absorbed into the Roman polity long before that). Close relations subsisted between Britain and Gaul throughout the century before the conquest of the former by Claudius in 43 AD, when Belgic tribes in south-western Britain maintained close cultural, political, and economic contacts with their compatriots across the Channel.[27]

Caesar records that the male offspring of the Gaulish nobility repaired to the druids for intensive instruction. This probably included writing, since epigraphic evidence from Gaul shows that educated Gauls were capable of employing the Greek or Latin alphabets to record documents and inscriptions in their native tongue. Caesar's account of the superior learning of the British druids suggests that they are unlikely to have lagged behind their continental *confrères* in adopting so useful a practice. This then is the era when it is possible that some at least of their legendary lore could first have been committed to writing.[28]

It was remarked in the previous chapter that identification of the Stone of Scone with the *Lia Fáil* at Tara could have occurred at any time during the early Middle Ages, in view of close connexions with Ireland from the fifth century AD onwards. On the other hand, if Geoffrey of Monmouth's comparable identification of Stonehenge with the stones of Uisneach reflects discrete legends of the two *omphaloi*, the tradition could well have originated in a much earlier era.

---

26 *Gods and Heroes of the Celts* (London, 1949), p. xix. 'There is proof, if proof were needed, that these fundamental resemblances between the données of Welsh and Irish Tales go back to the period of a mythology common to both branches of the Celts' (Cecile O'Rahilly, *Ireland and Wales: Their Historical and Literary Relations* (London, 1924), p. 94). Thomas Charles-Edwards has expressed a similar view to me in conversation.

27 Cf. C. E. Stevens, 'Britain between the Invasions (B.C. 54–A.D. 43)', in W. F. Grimes (ed.), *Aspects of Archaeology in Britain and Beyond: Essays presented to O. G. S. Crawford* (London, 1951), pp. 332–44; Barry Cunliffe, 'Relations between Britain and Gaul in the First Century B.C. and Early First Century A.D.', in Sarah Macready and F. H. Thompson (ed.), *Cross-Channel Trade between Gaul and Britain in the Pre-Roman Iron Age* (London, 1984), pp. 3–23; David Mattingly, *An Imperial Possession: Britain in the Roman Empire, 54 BC–AD 409* (London, 2006), pp. 68–84.

28 That writing was employed by native speakers in a religious context under the Roman occupation is indicated by two inscriptions found at Bath, which bear texts written in a Celtic – possibly British – language (R. S. O. Tomlin (ed.), *Tabellae Svlis: Roman Inscribed Tablets of Tin and Lead from the Sacred Spring at Bath* (Oxford, 1988), pp. 128–29, 133). Cf. idem, 'Was ancient British Celtic ever a written language? Two texts from Roman Bath', *The Bulletin of the Board of Celtic Studies* (Cardiff, 1987), xxxiv, pp. 18–25; Bernard Mees, 'The Celtic Inscriptions of Bath', *Studia Celtica* (Cardiff, 2005), xxxix, pp. 176–81; Alex Mullen, 'Evidence for Written Celtic from Roman Britain: A Linguistic Analysis of *Tabellae Sulis* 14 and 18', ibid. (2007), xli, pp. 31–45; idem, 'Linguistic Evidence for 'Romanization': Continuity and Change in Romano-British Onomastics: A Study of the Epigraphic Record with Particular Reference to Bath', *Britannia* (London, 2007), xxxviii, pp. 35–61.

Occupation of the Salisbury Plain area by the alien Saxon kings of Wessex in the sixth century must effectively have severed links between the Britons of the West and the Stonehenge region.[29] The function of Stonehenge as national *omphalos* appears in consequence to have become forgotten in Wales. The author of the early tenth-century Welsh tale *Cyfranc Lludd a Lleuelys* relates an archaic version of the foundation legend of the Omphalos of Britain, by which time its site had become identified with the late Saxon city of Oxford. Clearly, the original site had dropped out of this line of transmission, although the substitute location suggests that it was understood to lie somewhere in central southern Britain.

It is hard to conceive a more convincing explanation of Geoffrey's effective identification of Stonehenge with Uisneach, than its origin in a belief that the megalithic shrine at the one site had in early times been transferred to the other. At the same time, any suggestion that archaic pagan tradition linked to the megaliths of Stonehenge was known in some form to Geoffrey of Monmouth in the twelfth century AD begs the question how such a tradition might have survived a millennium or more, following its putative final use as focus of cultic ritual.

In his pioneering paper, Stuart Piggott suggested that memories of the extraordinary transfer of the bluestones could have been transmitted for centuries by a priesthood associated with whatever cult was centred on Stonehenge – a tradition of such dramatic interest, and so firmly entrenched, as to have survived into the Christian era. In support of his reconstruction, he cited evidence on the one hand for transmission of pagan lore and practice in early mediæval Wales, and on the other for continuity of burial practices and occupation of British temples from the early Bronze Age into the Iron Age and Roman periods.

There exists no necessary objection to the concept of oral traditions surviving over remarkably long periods of time. Australian aboriginal lore (which was of course oral throughout) accurately preserved a memory of coastal changes occurring some 10,000 years before the time they came to be recorded.[30] The Tlingit of south-eastern Alaska preserved traditions of conflicts occurring *c.* 1150 AD, in a region that became buried beneath a glacier for six or more centuries.[31] Moving nearer home, at Mold in Flintshire, North Wales, there is a cairn known as Bryn yr Ellyllon ('Mound of the Phantom'), which was believed to be haunted by a spectre clad in golden armour, which had been seen to enter it. Eventually the mound was excavated in 1833. After three hundred cartloads of stone had been removed, fragments of a magnificent Bronze Age gold cape were discovered. This suggests that authentic tradition may have survived in the locality over some three thousand years.[32]

---

29   On the other hand, it is worth noting that Cerdic, sixth-century founder of the dynasty of Wessex, bore a British name (H. Munro Chadwick, *The Origin of the English Nation* (Cambridge, 1907), pp. 30–31; Max Förster, *Der Flußname Themse und seine Sippe: Studien zur Anglisierung keltischer Eigennamen und zur Lautchronologie des Altbritischen* (Munich, 1941), pp. 285, 420, 852; David Parsons, 'British *Caratīcos, Old English Cerdic', Cambrian Medieval Celtic Studies* (Aberystwyth, 1997), xxxiii, pp. 1–8). Similarly, the name of his seventh-century descendant Cædwalla derives from British *Cadwallon* (Kenneth Jackson, *Language and History in Early Britain: A Chronological Survey of the Brittonic Languages First to Twelfth Century A.D.* (Edinburgh, 1953), p. 244).

30   Margaret Sharpe and Dorothy Tunbridge, 'Traditions of extinct animals, changing sea-levels and volcanoes among Australian Aboriginals: evidence from linguistic and ethnographic research', in Roger Blench and Matthew Spriggs (ed.), *Archaeology and Language I: Theoretical and methodological orientations* (London, 1997), pp. 346-50.

31   John Waddell, *Archaeology and Celtic myth: an exploration* (Dublin, 2014), p. 26.

32   T. G. E. Powell, 'The Gold Ornament from Mold, Flintshire, North Wales', *Proceedings of the Prehistoric Society* (London, 1953), xix, pp. 161–179; Sir John Morris-Jones, 'Taliesin', *Y Cymmrodor* (London, 1918), xxviii, pp. 1–2; Chris Grooms, *The Giants of Wales: Cewri Cymru* (Lampeter, 1993), p. 137. Doubt has however been cast on the tradition, whose validity there appears no conclusive means of assessing (Hilda Ellis Davidson, *Patterns of Folklore* (Ipswich, 1978), p. 64).

Circumstances in which archaic lore might be transmitted through succeeding ages are similarly suggested by continuity of rites linked to the kingship in early Ireland.

The close association of Celtic royal sites with neolithic burial mounds is a feature which ... argues for a strong continuity within the native Irish tradition. Such megalithic monuments, and many natural hills as well, were regarded as *síde* or Otherworld dwellings (the word is cognate with Latin *sedes*); and the Irish banshee is the Otherworld woman (*ben síde*) – an ancestral goddess keening her princely but mortal descendants.[33]

After citing evidence for continued use of Bronze Age sacred sites into the Iron Age generally, and Stonehenge in particular, Piggott boldly postulated that transmission of traditions of the great sanctuary might plausibly be ascribed to the druids.

And now, at the dawn of the Roman Conquest and of written history, we can no longer escape reference to those elusive figures, obviously by now troubling the reader's mind by their equivocal reputation, the Druids ... such a body of legendary lore as they possessed, such countless verses as they memorized and taught to initiates, is an essential element in the religious continuity we have shown from the archaeological evidence to have existed, and if there were legends of Stonehenge handed down to literate times it is these inheritors of a cult, acknowledged by themselves to be ancient and perhaps containing recognizable Bronze Age elements, who are most likely to have been the medium of its transmission.[34]

The word *druid* is of Celtic origin, being confined in the historical record to Ireland, Britain, and Transalpine Gaul.[35] The absence of any allusion to their order in Celtic lands in southern and eastern Europe may be due to the chance silence of a relatively sparse record. On the other hand, it has been conjectured that Celtic peoples arriving in Gaul and Britain, some time during the middle of the first millennium BC, could have absorbed an older priestly order, whose high antiquity and profound learning impressed incoming Celtic tribes.[36] The term *druid*, which according to some scholars means something like 'wisdom of the wood', is

---

33 Francis John Byrne, *Irish Kings and High-Kings* (London, 1973), p. 20. Similarly, continuity of ritual usage from the neolithic era to the period of Celtic domination is indicated at the primæval capital of Ulster, Eamhain Macha (Navan), as also at Aillinn, the 'capital' of Connacht (Dáithi Ó hÓgáin, *The Sacred Isle: Belief and Religion in Pre-Christian Ireland* (Woodbridge, 1999), pp. 171–72, 179–80).

34 Stuart Piggott, 'The Sources of Geoffrey of Monmouth. II. The Stonehenge Story', *Antiquity: A Quarterly Review of Archæology* (Gloucester, 1941), xv, pp. 314–15. The druids of Gaul appear to have transmitted traditions of great antiquity, for example expressing awareness in the fourth century AD that the ancestors of the Gauls were not indigenous, but originated in lands east of the Rhine (Édouard Galletier, Jacques Fontaine, Guy Sabbah, Marie-Anne Marié, and Laurent Angliviel de la Beaumelle (ed.), *Ammien Marcellin: Histoire* (Paris, 1978-99), i, pp. 135–36).

35 Eoin MacNeill, *Early Irish Laws and Institutions* (Dublin, 1935), pp. 68–69; Xavier Delamarre, *Dictionnaire de la langue gauloise: Une approche linguistique du vieux-celtique continental* (Paris, 2001), pp. 125–26.

36 Sir John Rhŷs, 'Notes on The Coligny Calendar together with an Edition of the Reconstructed Calendar', *The Proceedings of the British Academy* (London, 1910), iv, pp. 8, 35–36; T. Rice Holmes (ed.), *C. Iuli Caesaris Commentarii: Rerum in Gallia Gestarum VII; A. Hirti Commentarius VIII.* (Oxford, 1914), pp. 241–42; Julius Pokorny, 'The Origin of Druidism', *The Smithsonian Report for 1910* (Washington, 1911), pp. 587, 589, 593–97; MacNeill, *Early Irish Laws and Institutions*, pp. 66–67; T. D. Kendrick, *The Druids: A Study in Keltic Prehistory* (London, 1927), pp. 196–211; Adolf Mahr, 'New Aspects and Problems in Irish Prehistory: Presidential Address for 1937', *Proceedings of the Prehistoric Society* (Cambridge, 1937), iii, pp. 417–18; Nora K. Chadwick, *The Druids* (Cardiff, 1966), pp. 15–16; Stuart Piggott, *The Druids* (London, 1968), pp. 184–89; Wood, *Sun, Moon and Standing Stones*, pp. 197, 199.

believed to intimate a conception of the *rootedness* of the ancient cult in the soil of the land.[37] Alternatively, what is perhaps a more likely etymology relates the term to concepts of 'wisdom', in one form or another.[38]

It seems intrinsically likely that Celtic migrations westwards across the Rhine, Alps, and Channel, possibly occurring over a period of centuries and by no means necessarily warlike, absorbed and amalgamated significant aspects of the beliefs and practices of the indigenous inhabitants with whatever religious system the immigrant tribes brought with them.[39] This would more likely than not have resulted in a syncretism of old and new religious beliefs and cultic practices, comparable to that which occurred when the Romans brought their gods to Gaul and Britain. Moreover, it is particularly probable that traditions inhering to megalithic monuments would have been adopted by incoming populations, since of necessity they could bring no relevant information with them. Christianity in early Britain and Ireland in turn acquired much more from druidism than the Church subsequently was overtly willing to acknowledge.[40]

Of late, an influential school of archæology has come to reject the concept of Celtic or other extensive 'invasions', whether in the form of military conquest or large-scale immigration, preferring a model of evolving social, cultural, and linguistic micro-evolution within Britain herself. If correct, this would make continuity of tradition over millennia yet more likely.[41]

It is intrisically probable that the lore of the British druids, which their counterparts in Gaul recognized as *fons et origo* of their own learning, incorporated elements of the cosmology of that ancient race (or races) whom Celtic settlers found in possession of the island. Otherwise, why should the druids of Gaul have acknowledged that the most abstruse and authoritative druidic lore of their order was to be found on the outer periphery of the Celtic world, rather than in its heartland?[42] They were prepared to accept the superiority of this pre-existing body of

---

37   Cf. Pokorny, *Indogermanisches Etymologisches Wörterbuch*, i, p. 215; Calvert Watkins, *The American Heritage Dictionary of Indo-European Roots* (Boston, 1985), p. 12; Thomas V. Gamkrelidze and Vjačeslav V. Ivanov, *Indo-European and the Indo-Europeans: A Reconstruction and Historical Analysis of a Proto-Language and a Proto-Culture* (Berlin and New York, 1995), i, p. 690; Helmut Birkhan, *Kelten: Versuch einer Gesamtdarstellung ihrer Kultur* (Vienna, 1997), p. 898. Ugaritic poetry of the thirteenth or twelfth century BC identified trees and stones as repositories of arcane lore no longer known to men (Mark S. Smith and Wayne T. Pitard (ed.), *The Ugaritic Baal Cycle* (Leiden, 1994–2009), ii, pp. 71, 72, 202–3, 278). It has recently been suggested that the semantic element 'oak' was employed in a metaphorical context (Ranko Matasović, *Etymological Dictionary of Proto-Celtic* (Leiden, 2009), p. 107).

38   '*Dru-wid-*: les deux composés ne se distinguent que par leur second membre, qui appartient à *(h$_2$)w-ei-d-*, l'une des racines de sens général «briller/voir», dans un cas, et dans l'autre à *h$_3$ek^w-*, racine spécifique de la «vision»; toutes deux ont pu signifier «connaître» parce que la vision est le mode priviligié de connaissance dans la pensée indo-européenne' (Françoise Bader, 'Pan', *Revue de Philologie* (Paris, 1989), lxiii, p. 34). Cf. Jan de Vries, *Keltische Religion* (Stuttgart, 1961), pp. 190–91; Bruce Lincoln, 'The Druids and human sacrifice', in Mohammad Ali Jazayery and Werner Winter (ed.), *Languages and Cultures: Studies in Honor of Edgar C. Polomé* (Berlin, 1988), pp. 381, 391; J. Vendryes, E. Bachellery, and P-Y. Lambert, *Lexique étymologique de l'irlandais ancien* (Dublin and Paris, 1959–96), D-203.

39   'Druidism never existed except in Trans-Alpine Gaul, Britain and Ireland. This limitation is a very significant fact, and has suggested that Druidism in our island belonged to an earlier race of inhabitants than the Britons' (Hugh Williams, *Christianity in Early Britain* (Oxford, 1912), p. 45).

40   'Irish hagiography remained to a very large degree unashamedly "pre-Christian" in its themes and, more importantly, in its *dramatis personae*, ninety or more per cent of whom are demonstrably, or implicitly, pagan in origin' (Pádraig Ó Riain, 'Celtic mythology and religion', in Karl Horst Schmidt and Rolf Ködderitzsch (ed.), *Geschichte und Kultur der Kelten: Vorbereitungskonferenz 25.-28. Oktober 1982 in Bonn* (Heidelberg, 1986), pp. 249–50).

41   For a useful exposition of this innovative approach, cf. Simon James, *The Atlantic Celts: Ancient People or Modern Invention?* (London, 1999).

42   Kim McCone has shown convincingly that, contrary to formerly received opinion, Continental *Keltoi* employed the ethnonym as descriptive of Celtic peoples throughout Europe, from Thrace to Spain (*The*

esoteric knowledge, which to exert so impressive an influence must have included much that was extraneous to their own lore. It is clear that the druids of Britain were masters of a substantial body of traditional learning of which their Gaulish counterparts were at once ignorant and were concerned to acquire.

Mediæval Irish literature likewise attests to a tradition that the fount of mystical science was located in Britain. A tract imbued with arcane druidic learning describes a druid novice Néde,[43] who had crossed the sea to study 'divination in Britain', *écsi i nAlbain*. The druidess Fedelm (*Fedelm banfili*) declared to the hosts of Connacht that she had just returned from Britain, whither she resorted in order to acquire prophetic understanding and techniques. The hero Cú Chulainn was directed by the wizard Forgall to obtain perfect knowledge, part-martial and part-magical, from a wise woman Scathach dwelling in the east of Britain.[44]

As Stuart Piggott emphasized, archæological evidence attests to extensive continuity of cult usage at temples, henges, barrows, and other ancient religious sites in Britain, extending from the Neolithic and Bronze Ages to the Late Iron Age.[45] The architectural design of Romano-British temples reflected a modification of pre-Roman British shrines, while the Roman policy of religious tolerance and syncretic amalgamation of Roman ritual and doctrine with indigenous practices and tenets encouraged accomodation of archaic belief-systems within more sophisticated architectural settings.[46]

A classic example of a temple site attesting to unbroken use from the Early Iron Age to the close of the Roman period in the late fourth or early fifth century AD is that at Frilford in Berkshire.[47] Of still greater interest is the temple at Wanborough in Surrey, whose associated artefacts suggest ritual practice ascending to the Bronze Age. Excavations at this Romano-Celtic shrine uncovered uniquely rich 'priestly' regalia, such as might have adorned druid

---

Celtic Question: Modern Constructs and Ancient Realities (Dublin, 2008), pp. 1–8). (The directors of the recent (2015) Celtic exhibition at the British Museum strangely ignored his scholarly study, proclaiming as a received fact the outworn notion that Celtic peoples in early times did not recognize their common Celticity). Caesar divided the peoples of Britain between an aboriginal race dwelling in the interior, and recent Belgic (Gaulish) settlers on the south-east littoral. Clearly, any notion that Belgic emigrants were envisaged as being possessed of greater arcane cosmological lore than the prestigious hierarchy of the druids of Gaul may be dismissed.

43   The text comprises a skilful verbal duel 'de deux druides, ou plutôt de deux filid (ce qui revient au même)', Christian-J. Guyonvarc'h and Françoise Le Roux, *Les Druides* (Rennes, 1986), p. 48.

44   R. I. Best, Osborn Bergin, M. A. O'Brien, and Anne O'Sullivan (ed.), *The Book of Leinster Formerly Lebar na Núachongbála* (Dublin, 1954–83), p. 815; R. I. Best and Osborn Bergin (ed.), *Lebor na Huidre: Book of the Dun Cow* (Dublin, 1929), p. 143; A. G. van Hamel (ed.), *Compert Con Culainn and Other Stories* (Dublin, 1933), p. 46. King Fergna obtained advice from 'Mainchenn, a druid from Britain' (Ulrike Roider (ed.), *De Chophur in Da Muccida* (Innsbruck, 1979), p. 50).

45   Anne Ross, *Pagan Celtic Britain: Studies in Iconography and Tradition* (London, 1967), p. 44; Stuart Piggott, 'Nemeton, Temenos, Bothros: Sanctuaries of the Ancient Celts', in C. F. C. Hawkes, E. M. Jope, and Stuart Piggott (ed.), *I Celti e la Loro Cultura nell'Epoca Pre-Romana e Romana nella Britannia* (Rome, 1978), pp. 50–54; Ann Woodward and Peter Leach, *The Uley Shrines: Excavation of a ritual complex on West Hill, Uley, Gloucestershire: 1977–9* (London, 1993), pp. 303–5.

46   M. J. T. Lewis, *Temples in Roman Britain* (Cambridge, 1966), pp. 9–10; Lorna Watts and Peter Leach, *Henley Wood, Temples and Cemetery Excavations 1962–69 by the late Ernest Greenfield & others* (York, 1996), p. 27.

47   R. G. Collingwood and Ian Richmond, *The Archaeology of Roman Britain* (London, 1969), p. 160; *Britannia: A Journal of Romano-British and Kindred Studies* (London, 1982), xiii, pp. 305–9; Zena Kamash, Chris Gosden, and Gary Lock, 'Continuity and Religious Practices in Roman Britain: The Case of the Rural Religious Complex at Marcham/Frilford, Oxfordshire', ibid. (2010), xli, pp. 95–125; Peter Warry, 'A Possible Mid-Fourth-Century Altar Platform at Marcham/Frilford, Oxfordshire', ibid. (2015), xlvi, pp. 273–79.

hierophants.[48] Another important Romano-Celtic temple at Uley in Gloucestershire, which bears traces of origin in the Neolithic era,[49] stands near a place called Nympsfield, a place-name meaning 'tract of open country belonging to a place called *Nymed*' (a Celtic word for a shrine or holy place), while Uley itself means 'yew-tree glade or clearing'.[50] Both names are redolent of druidic cultic practice.

Barry Cunliffe notes yet another type of setting:

> One further function which developed hillforts may have performed [during the Roman occupation] was that of providing a religious focus of the community. Buildings which might be regarded as temples have now been found, occupying prominent positions, in three forts … The presence of late Romano-Celtic temples within a number of forts surely implies a continuity of religious practice from the pre-invasion period.[51]

One of the most striking instances of continuity in religious practice and maintenance of archaic tradition is provided by the celebrated White Horse at Uffington in Berkshire.[52] Recent archæological investigation has established that 'the figure is at least 2,500 years old, and … it was initially constructed in the early Iron Age or perhaps even the late Bronze Age'.[53] Its survival in broadly unaltered shape to the present day was ensured by the practice of holding regular 'scourings' of the figure, which would otherwise have swiftly vanished beneath encroaching turf.[54] While ascriptions of religious rites to the dramatic figure remain confessedly speculative,[55] it would surely be perverse to suppose that the 'horse' and its regular calendrical scourings reflected *no* religious beliefs, or were unaccompanied by *any* ritual practice.

Despite its modern name, the figure's lack of *membrum virile* proclaims it a mare, which in turn recalls the regal figure of Rhiannon on her white horse gracefully outpacing her human pursuers in the Welsh mediæval tale of *Pwyll Pendeuic Dyuet*. As an unmistakable sovereignty figure, the Uffington image's dramatic location overlooking the broad prospect of the Vale of the White Horse suggests that it could have personified the tutelary deity of whatever pre-Belgic tribe inhabited the Upper Thames region.[56] Alternatively, given the monument's unique character in the British landscape, might it not have represented the age-old ideological concept of the Monarchy of Britain, *Unbeiniaeth Prydain*?[57]

---

48   M. G. O'Connell and Joanna Bird, 'The Roman Temple at Wanborough, excavation 1985–1986', *Surrey Archaeological Collections Relating to the History and Antiquities of the County* (Guildford, 1994), lxxxii, pp. 93–121, 165. Earlier evidence for priestly regalia in Romano-British temples is discussed by Lewis, *Temples in Roman Britain*, pp. 137–38.

49   Woodward and Leach, *The Uley Shrines*, pp. 13–31, 303–5.

50   A. H. Smith, *The Place-Names of Gloucestershire* (Cambridge, 1964–65), ii, pp. 243–44, 253–54.

51   Barry Cunliffe, *Iron Age Communities in Britain: An account of England, Scotland and Wales from the Seventh Century BC until the Roman Conquest* (London, 1991), p. 355.

52   John Waddell, *Archaeology and Celtic Myth* (Dublin, 2014), pp. 124–25, 163.

53   David Miles, Simon Palmer, Gary Lock, Chris Gosden, and Anne Marie Cromarty, *Uffington White Horse and its Landscape: Investigations at White Horse Hill, Uffington, 1989–95, and Tower Hill, Ashbury, 1993–4* (Oxford, 2003), p. 78.

54   Ibid., pp. 61–78; Martin Henig, *Religion in Roman Britain* (London, 1984), p. 39.

55   E.g. John North, *Stonehenge: Neolithic Man and the Cosmos* (London, 1996), pp. 190–96.

56   Barri Jones and David Mattingly, *An Atlas of Roman Britain* (Oxford, 1990), p. 51.

57   The objection that 'it has no rider' (Ronald Hutton, 'Medieval Welsh Literature and Pre-Christian Deities', *Cambrian Medieval Celtic Studies* (Aberystwyth, 2011), lxi, p. 83) is beside the point. It is clear

Be this as it may, preservation of the great chalk figure over a period of millennia attests to the likelihood of perpetuation of concomitant mythological lore and appropriate rituals associated with the divinity.

Megaliths continued to attract worshippers during the early post-Roman period in Britain. An incident in the seventh-century Life of St Samson, to be discussed below in closer detail, describes his arrival before a great crowd of celebrants, gathered about an idol set on a hill in Cornwall. Challenged by the saint, they responded defiantly that they were perfectly within their rights to celebrate the mysteries of their ancestors according to time-honoured practice. When their leader Guedianus was persuaded of the superior efficacy of the Christian god, and agreed to abandon the idolatrous performance, Samson commemorated the occasion by carving a cross on a stone.[58] This incident occurred about the middle of the sixth century AD, and it has been suggested that the 'count' (*comes*) was in reality a pagan priest, i.e. druid.[59]

Cults centred on stones feature regularly in Breton and Welsh hagiography, and rites were believed to have been long practised by witches at megalithic sites.[60] Although we cannot be sure of every case, it seems reasonable to suppose that such rituals generally reflect long-standing usage, rather than random assemblages.

Caesar's reference to Britain as primary fount of druidic lore implies that Celtic immigrants arriving from the Continent encountered an imposing native cult, sustained by a (possibly shamanistic) priesthood.[61] Druids accompanying the settlers could have been sufficiently impressed to evolve over time a syncretism between the indigenous religion, identified with the very soil and rocks of the island, and their own newly imported religious beliefs and practices – which were probably in some respects not dissimilar.

It is likely that the inhabitants of Bronze Age Britain initially encountered by Celtic immigrants spoke a non-Indo-European language. However, it may be assumed that, as with later invaders in historical times, means of mutual communication were established relatively swiftly. As Katherine Forsyth observes,

---

from Rhiannon's bizarre punishment, which obliged her to sit beside a mounting-block 'to offer to guest and stranger to carry them on her back to the court', that the goddess was symbolized by the mare, not its riders (R. L. Thomson (ed.), *Pwyll Pendeuic Dyuet: The First of the Four Branches of the Mabinogi edited from the White Book of Rhydderch with variants from the Red Book of Hergest* (Dublin, 1957), p. 18). Furthermore, the comment that 'only rarely would one allow himself to be carried' suggests that the mare was normally envisaged as unmounted.

58   Pierre Flobert (ed.), *La vie ancienne de saint Samson de Dol* (Paris, 1997), p. 216.

59   Anne E. Lea, 'Lleu Wyllt: an Early British Prototype of the Legend of the Wild Man?', *The Journal of Indo-European Studies* (Washington, 1997), xxv, p. 45. *Comes* may mean 'a worshipper, devotee (of a deity, etc.)' (P. G. W. Glare (ed.), *Oxford Latin Dictionary* (Oxford, 1968–82), p. 459), which would be appropriate to the context of the ceremony described in the *Vita Samsonis*.

60   L. V. Grinsell, 'Witchcraft at some Prehistoric Sites', in Venetia Newall (ed.), *The Witch Figure: Folklore Essays by a group of scholars in England honouring the 75th birthday of Katharine M. Briggs* (London, 1973), pp. 76–77, 79; Bernard Merdrignac, *Recherches sur l'hagiographie armoricaine du VIIème au XVème Siècle* (Saint-Malo, 1985-86), ii, pp. 138–40.

61   An early Bronze Age burial at Upton Lovel, ten miles west of Stonehenge, contains the remains of a man thought from his equipment to have been a shaman (Mike Parker Pearson, *Stonehenge: Exploring the Greatest Stone Age Mystery* (London, 2012), p. 154). On the coast of northern England, a settlement dating from *c.* 8000 BC was found to contain a unique array of 21 sets of antlers with carved eyeholes, which have been plausibly linked to shamanist rituals (J. G. D. Clark, 'Star Carr, a Mesolithic Site in Yorkshire', in R. L. S. Bruce-Mitford (ed.), *Recent Archaeological Excavations in Britain* (London, 1956), pp. 17–19, plate II (a); Brian Hayden, *Shamans Sorcerers and Saints* (Washington, 2003), pp. 149, 151). As I write, archæologists working on the same site have discovered an engraved shale pendant, again thought to have been worn by a shaman (*Daily Mail*, 26 February 2016).

The last pre-Celtic language [of Scotland] was doubtless only the most recent of several linguistic layers, but whatever its nature, it is unlikely to have become extinct within a single generation of the arrival of Celtic. We must therefore imagine a period of bilingualism and co-existence, perhaps with some borrowing in both directions.[62]

In addition, the antiquity of the native language could have served to enhance the prestige of the older faith and its practitioners. Archaic liturgical language is a feature of many religions, such as my own (Russian Orthodox).[63]

One analogy among may be found in the reverence Romans accorded the religion and cultic practices of the Etruscans. The latter were the predominant race in Northern Italy before the rise of Rome, who eventually succumbed to Roman power as it expanded throughout the peninsula. Like the druids, their priesthood was celebrated for the skill and authority of its soothsayers. To the Romans, ever eager to acquire what they deemed valuable from other peoples, the awesome powers of Etruscan *haruspices* appeared unrivalled. As Cicero explained, so superior and authoritative was their *disciplina*, that the Romans adopted wholesale the mantic science and esoteric knowledge of the their predecessors while specialists mastered their non-Indo-European language, and preserved their books for consultation.[64]

The primary appeal of Etruscan religious beliefs to the Romans lay in their perception of the Etruscans as the primæval people par excellence. Their wisdom derived authority from its presumed origin in the soil of Italy.[65] During the late Republic and early Empire the Roman intelligentsia placed high value on 'Etruscan learning', *Etrusca disciplina*.[66]

Romulus was believed to have ploughed a circular furrow around the infant city of Rome 'according to Etruscan religious practice' (*Etrusco rite*). This was the *pomerium*, which marked off the city from the external world, of which the former was its microcosmic simulacrum.[67]

---

62   Katherine Forsyth, *Language in Pictland* (Utrecht, 1997), p. 15. 'It is unlikely that they [the Celts] reached Britain and Ireland through a 100% population replacement, and if the numbers of incoming Celtic-speakers was low, it could be that in most respects they blended into various pre-existing cultures, as often happens with immigrants', (Patrick Sims-Williams, 'Celtic Civilization: Continuity or Coincidence?' Cambrian Medieval Celtic Studies (Aberystwyth, 2012), lxiv, p. 3).

63   Cf. Alderik Blom, 'Linguae sacrae in ancient and medieval sources: An anthropological approach to ritual language', in Alex Mullen and Patrick James (ed.), *Multilingualism in the Graeco-Roman Worlds* (Cambridge, 2012), pp. 124–40.

64   Remo Giomini (ed.), *M. Tvlli Ciceronis Scripta qvae Manservnt Omnia: De Divinatione; De Fato; Timaevs* (Leipzig, 1975), pp. 3, 14, 44, 55. Cf. H. Rackham, W. H. S. Jones, and D. E. Eichholz, (ed.), *Pliny: Natural History* (London, 1938–62), i, pp. 274–80. A convenient collection of references to Etruscan religion by classical authors is to be found in Karl Clemen (ed.), *Fontes Historiae Religionum Primitivarum, Praeindogermanicarum, Indogermanicarum Minus Notarum* (Bonn, 1936), pp. 27–57.

65   'Avant que Rome ne fût, déjà était l'Étrurie. En elle s'incarne la préhistoire de l'Italie et le temps fabuleux des origines… L'Étrurie du passé est la terre mythique des oracles, relayée par Delphes dès que Rome entre dans le temps de l'histoire, ab Vrbe condita …' (Jacqueline Champeaux, 'L'Etrusca disciplina et l'image de l'Étrurie chez Plutarque', in *Les écrivains du deuxième siècle et l'Etrusca disciplina: Actes de la Table-Ronde de Dijon, 9 juin 1995* (Dijon, 1996), p. 62).

66   Elizabeth Rawson, *Intellectual Life in the Late Roman Republic* (Baltimore, 1985), pp. 27–30; N. M. Horsfall, 'Corythus Re-examined', in J. N. Bremmer and N. M. Horsfall, *Roman Myth and Mythography* (London, 1987), pp. 89–104; Roger D. Woodard, *Indo-European Sacred Space: Vedic and Roman Cult* (Urbana and Chicago, 2006), pp. 40–42.

67   This is reflected in its etymology: '*pomērium*, "delimitation" <**po-smēr-yom*, with lengthened grade of **smer-*)' (Edgar C. Polomé, 'Some Reflections on the Vedic Religious Vocabulary', in Dorothy Disterheft, Martin Huld, John Greppin, and Edgar C. Polomé (ed.), *Studies in Honor of Jaan Puhvel* (Washington, 1997), ii, p. 228).

When in due course the bounds of the Roman Empire came to be expanded, the *pomerium* was correspondingy enlarged to reflect the macrocosmic increase.[68]

The Etruscan origin of the *pomerium* was not merely matter for antiquarian recall. Baneful portents throughout Italy in the middle of the first century BC led the pontiffs to summon Etruscan soothsayers to Rome to conduct appropriate prophylactic rites to avert disaster. The most prominent of these *haruspices* was Arruns, a learned Etruscan diviner from Lucca. He presided over complex rituals centred on circumambulation of the sacred boundary (*amburbium*), culminating in the sacrifice of a bull, from whose entrails the seer prognosticated dire consequences for the Roman people.[69]

Romulus was also said to have dug the trench (*mundus*), which Macrobius and others describe as access point to the upper and nether worlds: that is to say, the *omphalos*.[70] The term *mundus*, which appears not to be of Latin origin,[71] has been linked to Etruscan *mutna*, *muni*, 'a subterranean place, tomb'.[72] It was a site of profound ideological significance, which provided a point of intersection for the three cosmic spheres, and a link between sun, moon, earth, and stars.[73]

The most striking instances of Etruscan influence in the conduct of Roman religious rites relate to the Navel (*umbilicus*) of Rome, within the bounds of the *pomerium*. It was possibly this factor that lies behind a remarkable attestation to the enduring prestige of Etruscan divination and haruspication. At the beginning of the fifth century AD, the historians Olympiodorus and Zosimus record that Etruscan seers offered the prefect Pompeianus to protect Rome by launching thunder and lightning against the advancing Gothic army of Alaric.[74] Mantic skills

68 Erich Koestermann (ed.), *P. Cornelii Taciti Libri qvi Svpersvnt: Ab Excessv Divi Avgvsti* (Leipzig, 1960), i, pp. 235–36. Expansion of the *pomerium* in AD 75 may have reflected the conquest of Britain (David J. P. Mason, *Roman Britain and the Roman Navy* (Stroud, 2003), p. 93). For accounts of the *pomerium*, cf. Sir James George Frazer (ed.), *Publii Ovidii Nasonis Fastorum Libri Sex: The Fasti of Ovid* (London, 1929), iv, pp. 380–84; S. R. F. Price, 'The Place of Religion: Rome in the Early Empire', in Alan K. Bowman, Edward Champlin, and Andrew Lintott (ed.), *The Cambridge Ancient History (Second Edition): The Augustan Empire, 43 B.C.–A.D. 69* (Cambridge, 1996), x, pp. 818–20; C. Michael Driessen, 'On the Etymology of Lat. *urbs*', *The Journal of Indo-European Studies* (Washington, 2001), xxix, pp. 41–46; Vassilis Lambrinoudakis and Jean Ch. Balty (ed.), *Thesaurus Cultus et Rituum Antiquorum* (Los Angeles, 2004–6), iv, p. 295.

69 D. R. Shackleton Bailey (ed.), *M. Annaei Lucani De Bello Civili Libri X* (Leipzig, 1988), pp. 21–23. It has been suggested that the rite occurred in BC 46, at the instance of Julius Caesar, then *pontifex maximus* (Robert E. A. Palmer, *The King and the Comitium: A Study of Rome's Oldest Public Document* (Wiesbaden, 1969), pp. 15, 18–20).

70 E. H. Alton, D. E. W. Wormell, and E. Courtney (ed.), *P. Ovidi Nasonis Fastorvm Libri Sex* (Leipzig, 1985), p. 109.

71 Watkins, *The American Heritage Dictionary of Indo-European Roots*, p. 43; Philip Baldi, *The Foundations of Latin* (Berlin, 1999), p. 166.

72 Giuliano Bonfante and Larissa Bonfante, *The Etruscan Language: An Introduction* (Manchester, 1983), p. 144; A. Ernout, A. Meillet, and Jacques André, *Dictionnaire étymologique de la langue latine: Histoire des mots* (Paris, 1994), p. 822. For discussions of the *mundus*, cf. Frazer (ed.), *Publii Ovidii Nasonis Fastorum Libri Sex*, iii, 384–90; Mircea Eliade, *Patterns in Comparative Religion* (London, 1958), pp. 232, 373–74; Georges Dumézil, *Archaic Roman Religion* (Chicago, 1970), pp. 350–53; Lambrinoudakis and Balty (ed.), *Thesaurus Cultus et Rituum Antiquorum*, iv, pp. 282–84.

73 James Willis (ed.), *Ambrosii Theodosii Macrobii: Satvrnalia* (Leipzig, 1963), pp. 76–77; André Le Bœuffle (ed.), *Hygin: L'Astronomie* (Paris, 1983), p. 6.

74 R. C. Blockley (ed.), *The Fragmentary Classicising Historians of the Later Roman Empire: Eunapius, Olympiodorus, Priscus and Malchus* (Liverpool, 1983), ii, p. 160; François Paschoud (ed.), *Zosime: Histoire Nouvelle* (Paris, 1971–89), iii¹, pp. 60–61: cf. the latter editor's valuable note on pp. 275–80. Although Etruscan had apparently declined as a spoken language by the reign of Augustus (Giuliano and Bonfante, *The Etruscan Language*, p. 47; Baldi, *The Foundations of Latin*, p. 161; James Clackson,

possessed by Etruscan *haruspices* included profound understanding of the movements of heavenly bodies.[75]

Similar reverence for occult powers ascribed indigenous races is recorded among other early cultures. In Ireland, the Túatha Dé Danann, who evolved from divine status to being regarded as mortal occupants of the land before the arrival of the ancestors of the Irish, were credited with mastery of magical incantations imbued with supernatural wisdom, enabling them to transform themselves into wolves and witches. This may in part reflect respectful perception of occult powers ascribed the pre-Goidelic inhabitants of Ireland. Mediæval Norsemen correspondingly ascribed enhanced magical powers to their northern neighbours the Saami and Finns, mysterious primæval races dwelling in the icy darkness of the Arctic Circle.[76]

Extensive survival in Britain of megalithic and Bronze Age religious practices and beliefs into the Iron Age, elements of which must surely have been absorbed by incoming Celtic cults, provides the likeliest explanation of the exceptional regard accorded the authority of British druids by their counterparts in Gaul. This is implicit in what Caesar learned from his druid informants in Gaul:

> The *disciplina* [of the druids] is believed to have been discovered (*reperta*) in Britain and thence imported into Gaul, and today diligent students of the matter mostly travel there to study it.

A Dutch Celticist observed that

> Commentators have asked why Caesar did not use the far more natural word 'invented' (*inventa*) instead of 'found' (*reperta*). The answer is that according to druidic belief their wisdom was not really an invention but an element of eternity, found existing at the moment when the first Celtic colonists landed on the British coast.[77]

'Language maintenance and language shift in the Mediterranean world during the Roman Empire', in Mullen and James (ed.), *Multilingualism in the Graeco-Roman Worlds*, pp. 36–38), it survived as an arcane priestly tongue until the fall of the Empire in the West (Nancy Thomson de Grummond, 'Rediscovery', in Larissa Bonfante (ed.), *Etruscan Life and Afterlife: A Handbook of Etruscan Studies* (Detroit, 1986), p. 19; Antonio Udo, 'Des haruspices etrusques dans les *Nuits attiques* d'Aulu-Gelle', in *Les écrivains du deuxième siècle et l'Etrusca disciplina*, p. 119).

75 Rackham, Jones, and Eichholz, (ed.), *Pliny: Natural History*, i, pp. 274–80. The Etruscans specialized in interpretation of natural portents (Giomini (ed.), *M. Tvlli Ciceronis Scripta qvae Manservnt Omnia*, p. 55).

76 A. G. van Hamel (ed.), *Lebor Bretnach: The Irish Version of the Historia Britonum Ascribed to Nennius* (Dublin, 1932), pp. 47–49; Toirdhealbhach Ó Raithbheartaigh (ed.), *Genealogical Tracts I.* (Dublin, 1932), pp. 198, 200; Peter Foote and Humphrey Higgins (tr.), *Olaus Magnus: Historia de Gentibus Septentrionalibus* (London, 1996-98), pp. 18–19. Cf. Hilda Roderick Ellis, *The Road to Hel: A Study of The Conception of the Dead in Old Norse Literature* (Cambridge, 1943), pp. 123–24; Vladimir Shumkin, 'The wizards of Lapland and Saami shamanism', in Juha Pentikäinen (ed.), *Shamanism and Northern Ecology* (Berlin and New York, 1996), pp. 125–33; Clive Tolley, *Shamanism in Norse Myth and Magic* (Helsinki, 2009), i, pp. 61–64. Finnish wizards were much dreaded by the otherwise fearless Norsemen (Bjarni Aðalbjarnarson (ed.), *Heimskringla* (Reykjavik, 1941–51), i, pp. 29, 135). Norsemen also regarded Irish as a language appropriate to incantations (Carolus Plummer (ed.), *Vitae Sanctorum Hiberniae: Partim Hactenvs Ineditae ad Fidem Codicvm Manvscriptorvm Recognovit Prolegominis Notis Indicibvs Instrvxit* (Oxford, 1910), i, p. clx; H. R. Ellis Davidson, 'Hostile Magic in the Icelandic Sagas', in Newall (ed.), *The Witch Figure*, p. 36).

77 A. G. van Hamel, 'Aspects of Celtic Mythology', *The Proceedings of the British Academy* (London, 1935), xx, p. 242.

For such a perception to have appeared so convincing, the most learned of the druids in Britain must have possessed an impressive hoard of insular lore unknown to their colleagues in Gaul. Caesar further explained that in Gaul druid initiates spent up to twenty years memorizing a colossal corpus of learning preserved in verse. This covered an encyclopædic range of topics: cosmology, religion, philosophy, and doubtless more besides. The unique importance of the druidic *disciplina* of Britain is scarcely likely to have have constituted 'more of the same', but rather retention of a substantial authoritative body of archaic mythological lore unknown to their Continental colleagues.[78] The most likely source of such knowledge, distinct from that possessed by the erudite druids of Gaul, was the Bronze Age heritage assimilated by Celts arriving in Britain centuries before the time of Caesar. Moreover, since a static set of beliefs and practices might readily have been co-opted into the repertoire of the Gaulish druids, it must in large part have been the British druids themselves who appeared so impressively original.

The most striking material manifestation of pre-Celtic religious tradition in Britain was without question Stonehenge, whose power to awe and excite enquiry remains undimmed even today, after all direct knowledge of its purpose has seemingly vanished. Nor was the mighty edifice hidden in some remote part of the Island: it dominated the great plain, on which it stood in one of the most accessible and prosperous regions of Southern Britain.

For long, it was widely held that archæological evidence provides scant evidence for continuing use of Stonehenge as a cultic centre in Roman times:

> Only sporadic and occasional activity occurred from the Iron Age to the medieval period. Stonehenge was no longer used as a monument with any specific meaning, but seems to have been considered a suitable location for the occasional burial ... and certainly a place to visit.[79]

Of late, however, accruing evidence indicates extensive occupation of the site during the late Roman period.[80]

It may further be thought improbable that Romano-Britons wholly ignored the mighty religious structure at the heart of *Britannia prima*, when they were in the habit of crossing the Irish Sea to deposit votive offerings at comparably numinous megalithic sites in the sister isle.[81]

There is no means of knowing why its use as a place for great assemblages might have fallen into desuetude, nor is it even certain that this is what occurred. Successive generations might have come to accord it no less reverence, in altered ways. It has been observed of the celebrated White Horse on the Berkshire Downs that

---

78 I agree with Dr Tristram that *disciplina* here implies the entire 'mythology-cum-ideology' practised and inculcated by the druids of Britain (Hildegard L. C. Tristram, 'Early Modes of Insular Expression', in Donnchadh Ó Corráin, Liam Breatnach, and Kim McCone (ed.), *Sages, Saints and Storytellers: Celtic Studies in Honour of Professor James Carney* (Maynooth, 1989), p. 433).

79 Rosamund M. J. Cleal, K. E. Walker, and R. Montague (ed.), *Stonehenge in its landscape: Twentieth-century excavations* (London, 1995), p. 491. Evidence of pre-Roman Iron Age construction has been found at nearby Durrington Walls (G. J. Wainwright and I. H. Longworth, *Durrington Walls: Excavations 1966–1968* (London, 1971), pp. 313–15, 326–28).

80 Timothy Darvill and G. J. Wainwright, 'Stonehenge Excavations 2008', *The Antiquaries Journal* (Cambridge, 2009), lxxxix, pp. 14–15.

81 J. D. Bateson, 'Roman Material from Ireland: A Re-Consideration', *Proceedings of the Royal Irish Academy* (Dublin, 1973), lxxiii, pp. 30–31; George Eogan, 'Prehistoric and Early Historic Culture Change at Brugh na Bóinne', ibid. (Dublin, 1991), xci, p. 118.

use of the Hill during this [Anglo-Saxon] period left little trace … However this general lack of evidence could be interpreted as respect for an ancestral or sacred place perhaps within a landscape that was largely used for pasture.[82]

After all, barely any material evidence survives to record the activities of thousands of participants at the annual fair held on the spot for the scouring of the White Horse, a custom of great antiquity vividly described by Thomas Hughes in the nineteenth century.[83]

Comparative sparsity of material evidence for human presence at Stonehenge, once its successive stages of construction were complete, is open to differing interpretations, none of which may be regarded as conclusive. For example, given the uniquely awesome prestige of the site, it is possible that only an elite grouping was admitted to the inner mysteries.

There are indications that such 'distancing' could have played a part in whatever rituals were practised at Stonehenge. As Professor Parker Pearson notes,

> Stonehenge sits at the centre of an area, up to a mile across, that contains far fewer Bronze Age round barrows than the areas slightly further out from the stone circle. The round barrow cemeteries are concentrated in a wide, doughnut-shaped circle on the skyline around Stonehenge. They sit on the edges of a central, empty 'envelope of visibility' immediately around the stone circle, within which there are less than forty barrows. Since the trial trenches [to the south] were within the envelope of visibility, their emptiness supports the existing evidence that this area closely encircling Stonehenge was deliberately avoided both by Neolithic and Copper Age inhabitants of the area as well as by the Early Bronze Age builders of the round barrows.[84]

Categorical denials by archæologists in the past that druids could have been associated with Stonehenge reflected lack of evidence (but what evidence is there likely to be?), influenced, it is to be suspected, by an understandably critical reaction to the vagaries of modern 'druids' and New Age enthusiasts, who it goes without saying bear no lineal or ideological connexion to the druids of history or prehistory. On the other hand, it was a distinguished Celtic scholar who observed that, given evidence for sanctification of menhirs in later eras,

> it is *a priori* improbable that among the varied manifestations known to us of the religion of the Celts, there are not the remains, more or less perceptible, of earlier cults which the Celts received and incorporated into their own.[85]

---

82   Miles, Palmer, Lock, Gosden, and Cromarty, *Uffington White Horse and its Landscape*, p. 265.

83   *The Scouring of the White Horse; or, the Long Vacation Ramble of a London Clerk* (Cambridge, 1859), pp. 84–101. 'The neighbouring inhabitants have an ancient custom of assembling for this purpose [clearing turf encroaching on the monument], which they term scouring the horse. On these occasions, they are entertained at the expense of the lord of the manor, and keep a kind of rural festival, with various appropriate diversions: the last celebrity of this kind took place in 1780' (Rev. Daniel Lysons and Samuel Lysons, *Magna Britannia; Being A Concise Topographical Account of the Several Counties of Great Britain … Vol. I. – Part II. Containing Berkshire* (London, 1813), p. 391).

84   Mike Parker Pearson, *Stonehenge: Exploring the Greatest Stone Age Mystery* (London, 2012), p. 233.

85   Joseph Vendryes, 'La religion des Celtes', *Mana: Introduction à l'histoire des religions* (Paris, 1948), iii, p. 243. Cf. Dáithí Ó hÓgáin, *The Sacred Isle: Belief and Religion in Pre-Christian Ireland* (Woodbridge, 1999), pp. 40–41; John Waddell, *Archaeology and Celtic Myth* (Dublin, 2014), pp. 15–32. 'In Anglesea they [witches] held their revels near the Druidical stones …' (Marie Trevelyan, *Folk-Lore and Folk-Stories of Wales* (London, 1909), p. 208). 'It is significant that many of the Easter and May Day games and

Stuart Piggott's argument for continuity of tradition and design in early Britain and Ireland, linking earlier rites and beliefs associated with megalithic monuments to Celtic usage and legend surviving into the Christian era, has received subsequent scholarly endorsement.[86] 'It is possible that Stonehenge, at a very advanced date in its long history, may have been the scene of druidic rites,' opined Christopher Hawkes, and the paucity of Roman settlement around Salisbury Plain has been tentatively ascribed to local resistance to alien intrusion into sacred space.[87]

Alternatively, lay participants might have been required to congregate at a respectful distance from esoteric rites practised by hierophants within the sacred shrine. In the mediæval Welsh tale *Cyfranc Lludd a Lleuelys*, which undoubtedly draws on archaic tradition, emphasis is laid on the need for secrecy in respect of rites conducted at the British *omphalos*, lest hostile hosts of the Otherworld eavesdrop on the arcane ritual and frustrate its intent.

Although it is unlikely that it will ever be possible to prove or disprove a druidic connexion with Stonehenge, it is not unreasonable to consider the inherent improbability that British druids ignored so uniquely prominent and accessible a monument, or were so little curious as to have adopted and transmitted *no* traditional lore concerning its origin and purpose – especially in view of the extensive range of cosmological knowledge they are recorded in the first century BC to have preserved.

Certainly, there is nothing intrinsically implausible in the suggestion that traditions linked to megalithic sites were transmitted over a millennium or more from the Bronze Age to the druids of the Iron Age. For a start, such monuments are likely to have retained their numinous aura over prolonged periods of time.

The posited use of prehistoric megaliths for at least some of the stones at Rhynie [in Aberdeenshire] is unlikely to be purely for functional or opportunistic reasons. The decision to reuse pre-existing monuments reveals an attitude towards this resource – that the existing monuments were appropriate for incorporating and remodelling into new practices and meanings. Clarke, following on from the work of Carver (2000), has argued

---

sports were held in ancient ring embankments, at Kirkby in Ireleth the Broomsgill ring, at Eamont near Penrith in King Arthur's Round Table' (Marjorie Rowling, *The Folklore of the Lake District* (London, 1976), p. 119).

86   Stuart Piggott, *Ancient Europe from the beginnings of Agriculture to Classical Antiquity* (Edinburgh, 1965), pp. 232–35; Jan de Vries, *Keltische Religion* (Stuttgart, 1961), p. 196; E. O. James, *The Tree of Life: An Archaeological Study* (Leiden, 1966), pp. 60–63; John Carey, 'Time, Memory, and the Boyne Necropolis', in William Mahon (ed.), *Proceedings of the Harvard Celtic Colloquium* (Cambridge, Mass., 1993), x, pp. 24–36; Gabriel Cooney, 'Sacred and secular neolithic landscapes in Ireland', in David L. Carmichael, Jane Hubert, Brian Reeves, and Audhild Schanche (ed.), *Sacred Sites, Sacred Places* (London, 1994), pp. 39–41; Ó hÓgáin, *The Sacred Isle*, pp. 128–30. 'There is thus a good deal of evidence for veneration of older monuments, specifically mounds, in the Iron Age. These monuments may have been regarded as repositories of spiritual power, perhaps in an unbroken tradition since the time of their construction' (D. M. Waterman, *Excavations at Navan Fort 1961–71* (Belfast, 1997), p. 227).

87   C. F. C. Hawkes, 'Britons, Romans, and Saxons round Salisbury and in Cranborne Chase', *The Archaeological Journal* (London, 1947), civ, p. 32; Stuart Piggott, 'Stonehenge Reviewed', in W. F. Grimes (ed.), *Aspects of Archaeology in Britain and Beyond: Essays presented to O. G. S. Crawford* (London, 1951), p. 292; J. M. de Navarro, 'The Celts in Britain and their Art', in M. P. Charlesworth and M. D. Knowles (ed.), *The Heritage of Early Britain* (London, 1952), p. 68. 'It is amusing to speculate, in view of the vehemence of denials by archaeologists that the Druids had anything to do with Stonehenge, that they very possibly made use of its decaying remains for ceremonies, even though its more subtle features would have long since been forgotten' (Wood, *Sun, Moon and Standing Stones*, p. 199).

that the reuse of prehistoric standing stones is directly linked to a reassertion of existing theological and social identities in the face of new Christian ideology in Pictland.[88]

Piggott concluded his study with a tantalizing suggestion:

In the story of Stonehenge in Geoffrey of Monmouth we may have the only fragment left to us of a native Bronze Age literature – a literature which would be as natural an outcome of a heroic culture such as the Wessex Bronze Age (or that of Mycenae, with which indeed it traded), as are the gold-hilted daggers of the warriors, but so infinitely more perishable.[89]

The nature of such a 'native Bronze Age literature' in general, and archaic traditions associated with Stonehenge in particular, can only be conjectured. Was there epic poetry, comparable perhaps to the Homeric Hymn to Apollo (sixth century BC), which describes the god's foundation of his temple at Delphi, the Omphalos of Greece? It is generally acknowledged that the Welsh story *Cyfranc Lludd a Lleuelys* preserves an enduring memory of the Omphalos of Britain. In its present form, it derives from traditional lore transmitted by the bards.[90] But whence did this significant repository of pagan lore originate, if not from their predecessors, the druids?

Literature of the category envisaged by Piggott would have required oral transmission over two or three millennia. This is far from being implausible, particularly in the case of sacred texts composed in verse. Archaic cultures present examples of oral transmission of enormous bodies of religious lore, not infrequently passed on over centuries, which were eventually committed to writing. Thousands of verses of the Indian *RgVeda* were transmitted by word of mouth for over a millennium, before being transcribed into Sanskrit about 500 BC. In ancient Persia, the entire corpus of Avestan texts was similarly transmitted orally for centuries before being written down.[91] The *Iliad*, which was composed and probably written in the eighth century BC, is believed to have drawn extensively on independent poems treating of the historical siege of Troy in the Late Bronze Age, declaimed by bards over the intervening centuries.[92]

---

88   Meggen Gondek and Gordon Noble, 'Together as One: The Landscape of the Symbol Stones at Rhynie, Aberdeenshire', in Stephen T. Driscoll, Jane Geddes and Mark A. Hall (ed.), *Pictish Progress: New Studies on Northern Britain in the Early Middle Ages* (Leiden, 2011), p. 290; cf. pp. 295–302; Iain Fraser and Stratford Halliday, 'The Early Medieval Landscape of Donside, Aberdeenshire', ibid., pp. 328–30. 'Problems of chronology are not confined solely to the date of the original carving of a monument or its original context but also extend to the various "meanings" it had for the societies that encountered it' (D. Ya. Telegin and J. P. Mallory, *The Anthropomorphic Stelae of the Ukraine: The Early Iconography of the Indo-Europeans* (Washington, 1994), p. 98).

89   *Antiquity*, xv, pp. 305–19.

90   The tale was 'a popular reworking of material which was originally part of the early Welsh pseudo-historical tradition and may have been known in an oral form in the late eleventh century' (Rachel Bromwich (ed.), *Trioedd Ynys Prydein: The Welsh Triads* (Cardiff, 1978), p. xxvii).

91   Calvert Watkins, 'Proto-Indo-European: Comparison and Reconstruction', in Anna Giacalone Ramat and Paolo Ramat (ed.), *The Indo-European Languages* (London and New York, 1998), p. 27; Jost Gippert, 'The Avestan Language and its problems', in Nicholas Sims-Williams (ed.), *Indo-Iranian Languages and Peoples* (Oxford, 2002), p. 166.

92   Barry B. Powell, *Homer and the origin of the Greek alphabet* (Cambridge, 1991), pp. 221–37; John Bennet, 'Homer and the Bronze Age', in Ian Morris and Barry Powell (ed.), *A New Companion to Homer* (Leiden, 1997), pp. 511–34; Joachim Latacz, *Troy and Homer: Towards a Solution of an Old Mystery* (Oxford, 2004), pp. 250–77.

Literary transmission of ancient lore

Thus, any traditions of the function of Stonehenge as national *omphalos*, and still more that of the transfer of the bluestones, must have been transmitted orally for millennia. In addition, it is worth considering the possibility that they could have been committed to writing at a much earlier period than is generally assumed to have been the case.

Although literacy was first established in Western Europe in Latium in the seventh century BC,[93] a century and more passed before its introduction into Gaul. The Greek (Phocean) colony established at Marseilles (Massalia) about the sixth century BC[94] provided the focus for diffusion of writing among the Gauls, who adapted the Greek alphabet for use in their own language. Inscriptions show that the practice was adopted no later than the second century BC:

> Gallo-Greek [i.e. Gaulish texts written in the Greek alphabet] becomes a phenomenon of the late second and first centuries, though we must remember that the earliest attestations can only give a *terminus ante quem* for the creation of the script.[95]

It has at times been assumed that Gaulish writing was broadly confined to use in commercial transactions, funerary inscriptions, and similar practical contexts. This view is however open to doubt. Two factors appear to lie behind the minimalist assessment. In the first place, little material evidence exists to suggest more extensive use of the facility. However, the *argumentum ex silentio* is of dubious value. In Roman Britain the discovery of the famous Vindolanda Tablets unexpectedly demonstrated the existence of what had hitherto been confined to plausible inference: namely, that an extensive body of correspondence was conducted (in Latin) on a daily basis by inhabitants living along Hadrian's Wall, and elsewhere. They included persons belonging to relatively lowly social strata (extending on occasion even to slaves), who might otherwise have been assumed to be illiterate.[96]

We know from a reference by Strabo that the druids were thoroughly familiar with Gallo-Greek writing. In §IV.5. of his *Geography*, he describes how Gauls regularly frequented Massalia (Marseilles), and in consequence became so philhellene as to draw up their legal contracts in Gallo-Greek. In his generally reticent account of the rôle played by the druids of Gaul, Caesar explains that one of their prime functions was to act as judges over tribal and individual crimes, inheritances, and frontier disputes: those failing to accept their judgments being denied access to sacrifices.[97] From this it is clear that druids presided over the legal process at every level, from inter-tribal conflict to crimes perpetrated by private persons. Not only this, but the principal punishment, that of banishment from participation in sacrifices, was a religious sanction over which the druids likewise presided. Indeed, it is hard to see that there existed any judicial

93 Gerhard Meiser, *Historische Laut- und Formenlehre der lateinischen Sprache* (Darmstadt, 1998), p. 2. The earliest epigraphic evidence for Celtic writing is found in Italian inscriptions of the sixth and seventh centuries BC (Karl Horst Schmidt, *Celtic: A Western Indo-European Language?* (Innsbruck, 1996), p. 23; Venceslas Kruta, 'L'épigraphie celtique et son contexte archéologique', in idem (ed.), *Les Celtes et l'écriture* (Paris, 1997), pp. 21–22). An important overview is provided by Javier de Hoz, 'The Mediterranean Frontier of the Celts and the Advent of Celtic Writing', *Cambrian Medieval Celtic Studies* (Aberystwyth, 2007), liii/liv, pp. 1–22.

94 Didier Marcotte (ed.), *Géographes grecs: Ps. – Scymnos : Circuit de la Terre* (Paris, 2000), i, pp. 169–71.

95 Alex Mullen, *Southern Gaul and the Mediterranean: Multilingualism and Multiple Identities in the Iron Age and Roman Periods* (Cambridge, 2013), p. 107); cf. pp. 106–8.

96 Alan K. Bowman and J. David Thomas (ed.), *The Vindolanda Writing-Tablets (Tabulae Vindolandenses II)* (London, 1994), pp. 29–30.

97 Francesco Sbordone (ed.), *Strabonis Geographica* (Rome, 1963–2000), ii, p. 103; Otto Seel (ed.), *C. Ivlii Caesaris Commentarii Rervm Gestarvm: Bellvm Gallicvm* (Leipzig, 1961), p. 184.

function in Gaul that did *not* lie within the druids' province.[98] What is certain is that theirs was without doubt the prevailing rôle. In view of this, given that many of the contracts on which it appears they were called upon to adjudicate were written in Gallo-Greek, is it conceivable that they themselves kept no written records?[99]

A chance allusion by the historian Diodorus Siculus, also writing in the reign of the Emperor Augustus, indicates yet another context for the use of writing in Gaul, in which druids evidently participated. Diodorus was informed that the Celts cast letters onto corpses consigned to funeral pyres, in the belief that the latter could transmit them to dead relatives whom they joined in the Otherworld. He further states that the druids presided over sacrifices,[100] and it is hard to believe that they played no part in so important a ceremony as disposal of the dead (Irish tradition confirms that druids played a leading rôle at funeral rites),[101] nor that the literacy of the Gaulish laity was superior to that of their erudite philosopher-priests. The letters in question were presumably written on combustible material, such as papyrus or wax tablets,[102] since their contents could scarcely have been presumed to reach the Otherworld had they remained intact. If the practice of writing on similarly perishable materials prevailed among the druidic priesthood, that would readily explain the sparse survival of written records.[103]

The assumption that druids made no use of writing for preservation and transmission of their learned lore derives from the seemingly decisive assertion by Julius Caesar that they preserved it exclusively orally: a practice he ascribed to their concern to deny the untutored laity access to sacred doctrines, and further to ensure that druid neophytes sustain their powers of memory. However, it would not be difficult to show that Caesar was for political reasons at pains to suppress the leading

---

98   MacNeill, *Early Irish Laws and Institutions*, pp. 74–75; Chadwick, *The Druids*, pp. 41–42; Guyonvarc'h and Le Roux, *Les Druides*, pp. 77–87. The celebrated Irish druid Sencha invoked authority to adjudicate in a dispute between a powerful tribe and an outsider (R. I. Best and Osborn Bergin (ed.), *Lebor na Huidre: Book of the Dun Cow* (Dublin, 1929), p. 277).

99   Venceslas Kruta observes of the celebrated Botoritta inscription in Spain that, 'while there are still some uncertainties, it seems highly likely that it is a legal text of some sort' (Venceslas Kruta, 'Celtic Writing', in V. Kruta, O. H. Frey, B. Raftery, and M. Szabó (ed.), *The Celts* (London, 1991), p. 494). Indeed, its context appears as much sacral as legal, which accords perfectly with a druidic context. Cf. Javier de Hoz, 'The Botorrita first text. Its epigraphical background', in Wolfgang Meid and Peter Anreiter (ed.), *Die grösseren altkeltischen Sprachdenkmäler: Akten des Kolloquiums Innsbruck, 29. April–3. Mai 1993* (Innsbruck, 1993), pp. 127–28; Wolfgang Meid, *Die erste Botorrita-Inschrift: Interpretation eines keltiberischen Sprachdenkmals* (Innsbruck, 1993), pp. 75–78.

100 J. J. Tierney, 'The Celtic Ethnography of Posidonius', *Proceedings of the Royal Irish Academy* (1960), lx, pp. 227, 228. Cremation was widely practised in Iron Age Gaul (Gerald A. Wait, 'Burial and the Otherworld', in Miranda J. Green (ed.), *The Celtic World* (London, 1995), p. 505; Olivier Büchsenschütz, 'The Celts in France', ibid., p. 558). The early Irish ninth-century Glossary of Cormac records that in pagan times wooden rods bearing occult inscriptions in ogam were interred with the dead (Kuno Meyer, 'Sanas Cormaic', in O. J. Bergin, R. I. Best, Kuno Meyer, and J. G. O'Keefe (ed.), *Anecdota from Irish Manuscripts* (Halle and Dublin, 1907–13), iv, pp. 49–50).

101 Guyonvarc'h and Le Roux, *Les Druides*, pp. 194–99.

102 Writings on wax or papyrus proliferated at Roman shrines (Mary Beard, 'Writing and religion: *Ancient Literacy* and the function of the written word in Roman religion', in J. H. Humphrey (ed.), *Literacy in the Roman world* (Ann Arbor, 1991), pp. 42–44). 'That they [the Celtic Boii of Bohemia] did write is confirmed by the bone frames which originally held wooden tablets coated with wax, along with the many bone and metal styli found in the *oppida* of Stradonice and Závist' (Venceslas Kruta, 'Celtic Writing', in V. Kruta, O. H. Frey, B. Raftery, and M. Szabó (ed.), *The Celts* (London, 1991), p. 494).

103 Tim Cornell provides a persuasive demolition of the minimalist view in the context of early Roman society ('The tyranny of the evidence: a discussion of the possible uses of literacy in Etruria and Latium in the archaic age', in Humphrey (ed.), *Literacy in the Roman world*, pp. 7–33). Evidence for a far wider degree of literacy in Palestine in the time of Christ than was formerly assumed is recapitulated by Alan Millard, *Reading and Writing in the Time of Jesus* (Sheffield, 2001).

rôle played by the druids (with at least one of whose leading figures he maintained cordial relations) throughout the years he spent in Gaul. This protective attitude could well have led him to withhold from Rome knowledge of the existence of druidic archives, any repressive measures against their order being likely to include destruction or confiscation of their records.

A specific instance of Caesar's concern to conceal potentially subversive aspects of the functioning of the druids may suffice here as an example. His assertion of the orality of druidic tradition is prefaced by the categorical statement that 'the druids are wont to be absent from war (*Druides a bello abesse consuerunt*)'. However, this claim is impossible to reconcile with other evidence. Strabo and Diodorus Siculus, writing a generation after Caesar, describe the druids' exercise of absolute authority over issues of peace and war, even to the extent of being empowered to intervene between opposed armies. The independence of the two authors' accounts is confirmed by the fact that, whereas Strabo ascribes the latter function to their authority as arbitrators, Diodorus intimates that it was effected by magical means.[104] The latter version is strikingly borne out by Irish sources,[105] which accord the leading druid Sencha mac Ailill especial power to pacify warring hosts, which was customarily effected by use of a magical wand: 'Sencha arose and shook the branch of peace (*cráeb sída*) over the hosts, so that they were peaceful as if they were sons of one father and one mother.'[106]

In mediæval Ireland and Britain the bishop's crozier inherited powers ascribed its predecessor, the druidic staff. In Ireland a crozier (*bachall*) borne aloft brought victory to an army, while the Welsh St Padarn imposed peace between two armies by means of a wonderful *baculus* named *Cirguen*, which was possessed of a power of enchantment 'such that, if two quarrel, by its means they are reconciled' (*ut, si qui duo discordantes sint, per eius coniurationem pacentur*).[107] In addition, Irish druids were credited with power to separate warring hosts with a magical barrier known as *airbe druad*, 'the druidic fence'.[108] The Irish druid Dubchommar possessed magical power to ensure his king's victory in battle.[109]

---

104 *Proceedings of the Royal Irish Academy*, lx, pp. 228, 241. There is no reason to discount Tacitus's account of druids accompanying a British host on Anglesey in AD 61, who launched magical imprecations against the Roman invading force under Suetonius Paulinus (Erich Koestermann (ed.), *P. Cornelii Taciti Libri qvi Svpersvnt: Ab Excessv Divi Avgvsti* (Leipzig, 1960), i, p. 312).

105 *Senchae*, 'a custodian of tradition, a historian' (E. G. Quin *et al.* (ed.), *Dictionary of the Irish Language: Based mainly on Old and Middle Irish Materials* (Dublin, 1913–76), 'S', col. 176).

106 R. I. Best, Osborn Bergin, M. A. O'Brien, and Anne O'Sullivan (ed.), *The Book of Leinster Formerly Lebar na Núachongbála* (Dublin, 1954–83), p. 416. Cf. ibid., pp. 383, 391, 777; R. I. Best and Osborn Bergin (ed.), *Lebor na Huidre: Book of the Dun Cow* (Dublin, 1929), p. 256; J. Carmichael Watson (ed.), *Mesca Ulad* (Dublin, 1941), pp. 6, 33. Sencha's qualifications for fostering Cú Chulainn correspond to those required of a druid (Christian-J. Guyonvarc'h, 'La conception de Cúchulainn', *Ogam: Tradition celtique* (Rennes, 1965), xvii, p. 386). In the Ossianic tale *Bruiden na hAlmaine* the poet (i.e. druid) Fergus Finnbheoil imposes peace on warring factions (Standish H. O'Grady (ed.), *Silva Gadelica: A Collection of Tales in Irish with Extracts Illustrating Persons and Places* (London, 1892), i, pp. 340–41).

107 William M. Hennessy (ed.), *Chronicum Scotorum: A Chronicle of Irish Affairs, from the Earliest Times to A.D. 1135* (London, 1866), p. 296; Joan Newlon Radner (ed.), *Fragmentary Annals of Ireland* (Dublin, 1978), p. 170; Whitley Stokes (ed.), *Lives of Saints from the Book of Lismore* (Oxford, 1890), pp. 92–93; Charles Plummer (ed.), *Bethada Náem nÉrenn: Lives of Irish Saints* (Oxford, 1922), i, p. 185; Kuno Meyer (ed.), *Betha Colmán maic Lúacháin: Life of Colmán son of Lúachan* (Dublin, 1911), p. 92; A. W. Wade-Evans (ed.), *Vitae Sanctorum Britanniae et Genealogiae* (Cardiff, 1944), p. 256.

108 J. E. Caerwyn Williams, 'Celtic Literature. Origins', in Schmidt and Ködderitzsch (ed.), *Geschichte und Kultur der Kelten*, pp. 136–37. The Irish legal tract *Bretha Nemed toísech* rules that 'a defeat against odds [and] setting territories at war confer status on a druid' (Fergus Kelly, *A Guide to Early Irish Law* (Dublin, 1988), p. 61).

109 M. A. O'Brien, 'The Oldest Account of the Raid of the Collas (circa A.D. 330)', *Ulster Journal of Archaeology* (Belfast, 1939), ii, pp. 172–74.

Diodorus's account of druidic authority on the battlefield clearly drew on authentic Celtic tradition, and refutes Caesar's assertion that the druids played no part in warfare. It is hard not to believe that the claim was further intended to protect cooperative druids of Gaul from official Roman resentment. His related claim that they preserved no written records is similarly implausible, being most likely advanced to protect their sacred writings from expropriation or destruction. As *pontifex maximus* at Rome, Caesar had particular reason to appreciate the value of druidic learning.

Scholars have from time to time remarked the professedly conjectural nature of Caesar's explanation of the druids' exclusive reliance on orality.[110] Nevertheless, there existed no material reason to question this, until a dramatic discovery occurred in southern France in 1897. In that year a peasant, tilling his vineyard near Coligny beside the main highroad from Lyons to Strasburg, uncovered one of the most important Celtic artefacts ever found. Known as the Coligny Calendar, the treasure comprises bronze fragments of a great monthly calendar, designed to establish the dates of recurring annual feast days. It was accompanied by an elegant statue of the Celtic Mars, whose solar function made him an appropriate deity to preside over the divisions of the year.[111]

This chance discovery throws remarkable light on the intellectual capacity and cosmological enquiries of the druids, which were previously known only from passing observations by classical authors. Of these, Julius Caesar alone possessed extensive first-hand knowledge of the matter, principally deriving (it may be assumed) from his prolonged collaboration with the Aeduan druid Diviciacus, a distinguished military commander, skilled orator, friend of Cicero, and occasional habitué of Roman drawing-rooms. Regrettably, however, Caesar provided only a summary account of Gaulish religion and science, which he doubtless considered adequate to satisfy audiences in Italy assembled for annual public readings of his famous *Commentaries*.[112]

The discovery of the Coligny Calendar serves to illustrate the limitations of Caesar's account. It demonstrates beyond expectation the extraordinary extent of druidic 'knowledge of the stars and their motion', as he described it. A recent investigator explains that,

> Utilizing a shifting lunar calendar (itself accurate to 1 day in 521 years) synchronized so that the solstices would follow a recurrent base-6 system of counting marks, Gaulish druids could keep track of solar positions, hundreds of years into the future, to within 1 day in 455 years. In its time, the Coligny calendar plate was by far the most accurate lunar/solar predictor in existence. Europe would await the Renaissance to again achieve such accuracy in astronomical prediction![113]

110 'The validity of Caesar's testimony must be questioned, and in this case he does not cite the authority for his comments, stating explicitly *id mihi duabus de causis instituisse uidentur*' (Mullen, *Southern Gaul and the Mediterranean*, p. 108). 'This motive ... must be estimated as Caesar's conjecture' (Chadwick, *The Druids*, p. 43).

111 Emile Thevenot, *Sur les traces des Mars celtiques (entre Loire et Mont-Blanc)* (Bruges, 1955), pp. 139–40. The Celtic god Nodens is identified with Mars in a number of Romano-British inscriptions (R. E. M. Wheeler and T. V. Wheeler, *Report on the Excavation of the Prehistoric, Roman, and Post-Roman Site in Lydney Park, Gloucestershire* (Oxford, 1932), pp. 100–105; R. G. Collingwood and R. P. Wright (ed.), *The Roman Inscriptions of Britain: I Inscriptions on Stone* (Oxford, 1965), p. 206).

112 T. P. Wiseman, 'The Publication of *De Bello Gallico*', in Kathryn Welch and Anton Powell (ed.), *Julius Caesar as Artful Reporter: The War Commentaries as Political Instruments* (London, 1998), pp. 1–9.

113 Garrett Olmsted, *The Gaulish Calendar: A Reconstruction from the Bronze Fragments from Coligny with an Analysis of its Function as a Highly Accurate Lunar/Solar Predictor as well as an Explanation of its*

Calendar of Coligny
(*c.* AD 200).
(Author's collection)

Whether or not this assessment be accepted *in extenso*, the time scales delineated by the calendar were clearly immense. Designed to reflect the precession of the equinoxes, it provided means of reckoning a Celtic 'Great Year', i.e. a zodiacal cycle of 2,146 years. While its creation and use required profound knowledge of mathematics and astronomy, its purpose was fundamentally religious. Essentially, it reflected the life cycle of divinity, which returned to its beginning after 5,355 years.[114]

Such enormous passages of time become comprehensible in view of the likelihood that many megalithic monuments appear to have been constructed, at least in part, for the purpose of arriving at calculations of such magnitude. Indeed, the *permanence* of monolithic structures may have represented a prime reason for their construction in so colossal and indestructable

Terminology and Development (Bonn, 1992), p. 1. Cf. Stephen C. McCluskey, 'Astronomies and Rituals at the Dawn of the Middle Ages', in Clive L. N. Ruggles and Nicholas J. Saunders (ed.), *Astronomies and Cultures* (Niwot, Colo., 1993), pp. 102–5.

114 Jean-Michel Le Contel and Paul Verdier, *Un calendrier celtique: Le calendrier gaulois de Coligny* (Paris, 1997), pp. 19–22. Archæological evidence in Ireland attests to widespread concern in prehistoric times with the heavenly bodies (Clive Ruggles, 'Astronomy, cosmology, monuments and landscape in prehistoric Ireland', in idem (ed.), *Astronomy, Cosmology and Landscape: Proceedings of the SEAC 98 Meeting, Dublin, Ireland, September 1998* (Bognor Regis, 2001), pp. 51–71; John Waddell, *Archaeology and Celtic myth: an exploration* (Dublin, 2014), pp. 51–52). Prehistoric and primitive methods of recording calendrical phenomena are discussed by Alexander Marshack, *The Roots of Civilization: The Cognitive Beginnings of Man's First Art, Symbol and Notation* (London, 1972), pp. 125–46; R. J. C. Atkinson, 'Ancient Astronomy: Unwritten Evidence', in F. R. Hodson (ed.), *The Place of Astronomy in the Ancient World* (London, 1974), pp. 123–31; Nikolay Konakov, 'Rationality and mythological foundations of calendar symbols of the ancient Komi', in Juha Pentikäinen (ed.), *Shamanism and Northern Ecology* (Berlin and New York, 1996), pp. 135–42; Clive Ruggles, *Astronomy in Prehistoric Britain and Ireland* (Yale, 1999), pp. 79–90.

a medium.[115] To take an exceptional example, the megalithic site at Nabta Playa in the Western Desert of Egypt is thought to have been created for the purpose of astronomical observation and cosmological reckonings some 7,000 years ago.[116]

Clearly, creation of such an outstanding predictive instrument required centuries – even millennia – of observation and recording movements of heavenly bodies. Much of this work must presumably have been undertaken long before the arrival of Celtic tribes in Gaul:

> This calendar with its intercalations is known to us at a very advanced date of its history: in fact it presupposes centuries of astronomical observations, application, contextual placement, and a prolonged process of adjustment. It implies also a system of recording, if not writing, ascending in its origins to 'the mists of time'.[117]

In that case, it appears either that Celts crossing the Rhine into Gaul had been conducting observations of the heavens for a millennium and more in the forests of Germany and Bohemia, bringing with them during their protracted wanderings accurate records of such calculations; or (what is surely more likely) that their druids acquired much of their astronomical knowledge from an indigenous priesthood whom they encountered on their arrival in Gaul.[118] In the same way, the Romans preserved much of the astronomic lore of their predecessors the Etruscans.[119]

There exists no sufficient reason to disbelieve the Gaulish druids' acknowledgment that much of their esoteric knowledge originated in Britain. Just as they expressed awareness that their ancestors had migrated from east of the Rhine, the natural assumption would be that their fellow Celts in Britain had in turn moved on there from Gaul. The explicit account they provided Caesar suggests that the *disciplina* 'discovered' in Britain was (at least in part) the religious system practised by the indigenous people encountered by the forebears of contemporary Celtic Britons at the time of their original settlement.

Reverting to Stonehenge, which is after all indisputably the most extraordinary and sophisticated megalithic temple in Europe, there is nothing intrinsically remarkable in the idea that its priesthood enjoyed unique prestige across much of the Continent from the time of its construction in the late Neolithic period onwards. It will be seen shortly that this is implicit in reports acquired by a well-informed Greek geographer in the fourth century BC, as well as by recent archæological discoveries in the vicinity of Stonehenge.

Making every allowance for the remarkable capacity of highly trained powers of memory obtaining in preliterate societies, it remains hard to envisage the creation of so extraordinarily

---

115 Alignments of the great passage tomb of Knowth in Ireland (third millennium BC) are focussed on the equinoxes (George Eogan, *Knowth and the passage-tombs of Ireland* (London, 1986), pp. 178, 183).

116 Mosalam Shaltout and Juan Antonio Belmonte, 'Introduction: Under Ancient Egyptian Skies', in Mosalam Shaltout and Juan Antonio Belmonte (ed.), *In Search of Cosmic Order: Selected Essays on Egyptian Archaeoastronomy* (Cairo, 2009), pp. 14–16.

117 Paul-Marie Duval and Georges Pinault (ed.), *Recueil des inscriptions gauloises (R.I.G.); Volume III: Les Calendriers (Coligny, Villards d'Héria)* (Paris, 1986), p. 37. 'Plinius's statement implies that the earliest Gaulish calendar originated some 1000 years before the period of the observation he recorded. The earliest of the surviving Gaulish calendrical systems had its origins clearly in the late Bronze Age' (Garrett S. Olmsted, *A Definitive Reconstructed Text of the Coligny Calendar* (Washington, 2001), p. 1).

118 'It is possible that the roots of this [astronomical] knowledge lie in the pre-Celtic European peoples of the Mediterranean …' (Kruta, Frey, Raftery, and Szabó (ed.), *The Celts*, p. 495).

119 H. Rackham, W. H. S. Jones, and D. E. Eichholz, (ed.), *Pliny: Natural History* (London, 1938–62), i, pp. 274–80.

complex and accurate an instrument for recording the movements of celestial bodies as the Coligny Calendar, without assuming its committal to writing *in some form* from a relatively early stage of its evolution.

Other inscribed texts indicate the improbability of supposing the druids of Gaul possessed no means of recording sacred texts in writing. Two inscriptions in particular, those of Larzac and Chamalières, recorded on lead tablets, are highly suggestive. Each constitutes a magical charm, the second invoking the celebrated Celtic gods Maponos and Lugus.[120] Although neither inscription appears to have originated with the druids, it would surely be extraordinary were lesser cults to have encountered no difficulty in recording significant religious matter in writing, while the druids, masters par excellence of esoteric lore, did not. The authors of these inscriptions were heirs to an intricate system of metrical composition,[121] and overall the evidence suggests that

> the earliest inscriptions in Ireland, Britain, Gaul and Iberia were in a linguistic register that one might associate most closely with a priest/druid class that insured the conservatism of the written language.[122]

Altogether, that writing existed as the property of a priestly class in Gaul, as elsewhere, is a possibility not lightly to be dismissed. Many reasons may be imagined why the druids of Gaul might wish to keep their literature secret from outsiders – especially from so aggressively inquisitive a people as the Romans. At the same time,

> It is ... highly likely that the very complexity of the calculations involved in measuring time this way [in the Coligny Calendar] explains why it was committed to writing by a local cult during the period of the Roman Empire.[123]

This consideration applies equally to an earlier stage in the evolution of so sophisticated and complex a record. Overall, it seems likely that at some stage the situation evolved much like early Greek law, which was recorded both orally and in writing, with differing contexts requiring alternative approaches.[124]

Lastly may be considered a passage in the Irish mediæval tale *Baile in Scáil*. When Conn arrives from Tara at the Otherworld house of Lug, the god declaims a lengthy prophecy of those kings of Tara who were yet to reign. However,

---

120 Pierre-Yves Lambert (ed.), *Recueil des inscriptions gauloises (R.I.G.); Volume II, fascicule 2: Textes gallo-romains sur instrumentum* (Paris, 2002), pp. 251–66, 269–80; cf. Wolfgang Meid, *Gaulish Inscriptions* (Budapest, 1992), pp. 38–46. It is suggested that the Chamalières inscription 'conforms to a prayer or incantation such as would be recited during a ritual' (Joseph P. Eska, 'Remarks on linguistic structures in a Gaulish ritual text', in Mark R. V. Southern (ed.), *Indo-European Perspectives* (Washington, 2002), pp. 33–59). Eska however rejects the interpretation of *luge* as *Lug* (ibid. pp. 51–52).

121 Garrett Olmsted, 'The Meter of the Gaulish Inscription from Larzac', *The Journal of Indo-European Studies* (Washington, 1989), xvii, 155–63; idem, 'Gaulish, Celtiberian, and Indo-European Verse, ibid. (1991), xix, pp. 280–82.

122 J. P. Mallory, 'The Indo-Europeanization of Atlantic Europe', in John T. Koch and Barry Cunliffe (ed.), *Celtic from the West 2: Rethinking the Bronze Age and the Arrival of Indo-European in Atlantic Europe* (Oxford, 2013), p. 30.

123 Kruta, Frey, Raftery, and Szabó (ed.), *The Celts*, p. 495.

124 Rosalind Thomas, 'Written in Stone? Liberty, Equality, Orality and the Codification of Law', *Bulletin of the Institute of Classical Studies* (London, 1995), xl, pp. 59–74.

It was difficult then for Cessarn, the poet [*filid*], to memorise that incantation all at once, so he cut it in ogam on four staves of yew, each stave being twenty-four feet long with eight ridges.

Although the poem was composed in the Christian era, while ogam writing is unlikely to have come into existence before the fifth century AD, the motive ascribed to Cessarn probably reflects archaic tradition. The *filid* Cessarn is described as a druid (*druí*),[125] the *filid* having become inheritors of their order in the Christian period.[126] Recourse to writing would in any case be yet more applicable to the druids of Gaul in the late Iron Age, who were familiar with the alphabet adopted from their Greek neighbours.

When writing was first introduced into Britain is unknown. Caesar observed during his visits there that 'by far the most civilized inhabitants are those living in Kent (a purely maritime district), whose way of life differs little from that of the Gauls'.[127]

His allusion is to the Belgic tribes of south-east Britain, who maintained extensive political and economic links with Gaul. It would be strange were their 'way of life' not to have included literacy both among the priestly class and elements of the aristocracy. A passing allusion by Caesar confirms that an educated element among the Belgae dwelling on the Gaulish side of the Channel was able to read.[128] While inscription of British kings' names on tribal coinage may not of itself indicate much, the practice could scarcely have served its purpose unless the coins circulated within a society possessed of some degree of literacy.

Furthermore, it is likely that the druids of Britain achieved literacy long before it extended to political notables. Absence of material evidence signifies little in such a case. As has been seen, for centuries the Romans consulted a wide range of Etruscan books on divination and other occult topics.[129] Although these were greatly prized, a solitary text has survived into modern times, through the chance circumstance of its being written on linen employed to bandage the mummy of a woman in Egypt, where it was preserved by the exceptionally favourable climate.[130]

It has been suggested that 'an archaic dialect of Celtic might have been utilized as a language of culture by the Gaulish calendar priests'. Visits by Gaulish and Irish druids to gain deeper understanding of their craft in Britain might indicate the possibility of a shared sacred tongue – though that, of course, could have been a form of Common Celtic before its separation into Goedelic and Brittonic. Such a (possibly archaic) language might have been employed by the druids,[131] in the same way that Sanskrit came to provide the sacred tongue

---

125   Kevin Murray (ed.), *Baile in Scáil: 'The Phantom's Frenzy'* (Dublin, 2004), pp. 33, 35.

126   Rudolf Thurneysen, *Die irische Helden- und Königsage bis zum siebzehnten Jahrhundert* (Halle, 1921), pp. 66–74.

127   Seel (ed.), *C. Ivlii Caesaris Commentarii Rervm Gestarvm*, p. 138.

128   'Unless he made his interpreter write the letter in Celtic, he evidently had reason to fear that, if it were intercepted, some of the Belgae would be able to read the Latin; in any case that some of them knew how to read' (T. Rice Holmes, *Ancient Britain and the Invasions of Julius Caesar* (Oxford, 1907), p. 266).

129   Georges Dumézil, *Archaic Roman Religion* (Chicago, 1970), pp. 633–72.

130   Bonfante and Bonfante, *The Etruscan Language*, pp. 138–39.

131   Olmsted, *The Gaulish Calendar*, p. 72; Christian-J. Guyonvarc'h, *Le Dialogue des deux sages* (Paris, 1999), p. 115. 'The basic structure of that oral culture [in early Ireland], doubtless druidic in origin like that of Gaul in Caesar's time, is now difficult to discern from the isolated fragments of it that were ultimately congealed in writing. But one can dimly perceive a fascinating amalgam of magic, myth, poetry, law and leechcraft, all of them embodied in formal and deliberately obscure language,

of the Brahmins of India, Arabic the language of the Koran, and Church Slavonic that of the Russian Orthodox liturgy.[132]

The Coligny Calendar was evidently housed in a temple dedicated to Mars, or his Celtic equivalent,[133] whose statue was borne away together with the shattered tablets, under circumstances which can only be guessed.[134] Fragments of another Gaulish calendar were found within a sanctuary precinct not far from Coligny, at Villards d'Héria,[135] and it seems likely that not only calendars, but other written records, were preserved in temples throughout Gaul and Lowland Britain during the Roman occupation.

This brief excursus on the use of writing by druids is emphatically not intended to suggest that traditions were passed down by this medium from the Bronze or Early Iron Age. Nor would it necessarily have provided a more reliable form of transmission, when we recall Caesar's testimony to the vast corpus of oral lore retained by the druids of Gaul in his day. However, it is not impossible that, under the influence of Greeks in Massalia (Marseilles) or Romans in Cisalpine Gaul, the druids caused important records to be inscribed on waxed tablets, bronze plates, or other suitable material, both before and during the Roman occupation of Gaul. The Coligny Calendar confirms that this occurred in a significant specific instance, and attests that such records could be of considerable extent and represent impressive intellectual achievements. If so, this would have ensured that at least some mythological, historical, and cosmological learning was recorded in a medium less susceptible to alteration than that of purely oral tradition, from an earlier date than is generally allowed.

Longevity of oral tradition in early Britain

Another instance of the longevity of traditional lore is provided by evidence for preservation of pre-Roman British historical records over a millennium or more. Compiled in AD 954 or 955, the earliest collection of British royal pedigrees is contained in British Museum Harleian MS 3859. It includes the descent of an otherwise unknown Rhun mab Nwython, whose line is carried back twelve generations to *Caratauc . map . Cinbelin . map . Teuhant* ...[136]

The names of *Caratauc* and his father *Cinbelin* (modern Welsh *Caradawg* and *Cynfelyn*) recall the British king Cunobelinus (Shakespeare's 'radiant Cymbeline'), who ruled the powerful confederation of Catuvellauni and Trinovantes in Southern Britain, and his son Caratacus, who after valiant resistance was defeated in Wales in AD 49 by the Roman general Ostorius Scapula.[137] Preservation of the two names in itself need not amount to much, since the names of the two British kings might have been gleaned at a remove from the works of classical historians.

a "Mandarin" Irish which was understood only by the privileged members of the learned class' (D. A. Binchy, 'Semantic Influence of Latin in the Old Irish Glosses', in John J. O'Meara and Bernd Naumann (ed.), *Latin Script and Letters A.D. 400–900: Festschrift presented to Ludwig Bieler on the occasion of his 70th birthday* (Leiden, 1976), p. 168).

132   Cf. Kees W. Bolle, 'Secrecy in Religion', in idem (ed.), *Secrecy in Religions* (Leiden, 1987), pp. 14–15.

133   Thevenot, *Sur les traces des Mars celtiques*, pp. 139–40; de Vries, *Keltische Religion*, pp. 56–71; Paul-Marie Duval, *Les dieux de la Gaule* (Paris, 1957), pp. 70–72; Le Roux and Guyonvarc'h, *La civilisation celtique*, pp. 134–35.

134   Le Contel and Verdier, *Un calendrier celtique*, p. 31.

135   Duval and Pinault (ed.), *Recueil des inscriptions gauloises*, iii, p. 262.

136   Egerton Phillimore, 'The *Annales Cambriæ* and Old-Welsh Genealogies from *Harleian MS. 3859*', *Y Cymmrodor* (London, 1888), ix, pp. 175–77.

137   Graham Webster, *Rome Against Caratacus: The Roman Campaigns in Britain AD 48–58* (London, 1981), pp. 28–39.

However, the name of Cynfelyn's father falls into a distinct category. Neither Tacitus nor any other Roman historian mentions the father of Cunobelinus, and it was not until the nineteenth century that his identity became known. Coinage of a king Tasciovanus, whose realm appears to have been based on Verulamium (St Albans), was found in increasing numbers. In addition, coins of Cunobelinus describe him as 'son of Tasciovanus', e.g. *CVNOBELINI … TASCIOVANI F[ilivs]*.[138] Gratifyingly, British *Tasciovanus* corresponds on philological grounds to Old Welsh *Teuhant*, the name of the father of *Cinbelin* in the Welsh royal pedigree.[139] Thus, 'there is here material proof that oral tradition in Wales preserved the memory of historical persons of the first century before our era, altogether independently of classical tradition.'[140]

Archaic tradition – whether oral or written – must also lie behind the obscure poem *Gwarchan Cynfelyn* in the Book of Aneirin, which describes Cynfelyn as 'son of Tegfan (*vab tecvann*)' and 'grandson of Cadfan (*wyr catvan*)'. Middle Welsh *Tegfan* corresponds to Old Welsh *Teuhant*, so that once again we find the pre-Roman king Tasciovanus commemorated in Welsh tradition after the passage of a millennium. The poem further mentions Catlew, a name likewise found in the genealogy.[141] Both sources evidently represent the surviving residue of a once rich body of lore.

There are other intriguing names in this Harleian genealogy, which runs in full:

[R]un . map . neithon . map . Caten . map . Caurtam . map . Serguan . map . Letan . map . Catleu . map . Catel . map . decion . map . Cinis scaplaut . map . Louhen . map . Guid gen . map . Caratauc . map . Cinbelin . map . Teuhant … (the line continues with a list of Roman emperors, which was clearly appropriated from another source).

Geoffrey of Monmouth was familiar with a variant version of this genealogy, from which he borrowed the names of three nobles represented as the court of King Arthur: *Run Mapneton, Kinbelin Maptrunat, Cathleus Mapcatel*.[142] *Louhen map Guid gen* in the Harleian genealogy is the former divinity Lleu mab Arianrhod, who is implicitly portrayed as son of Gwydion in

138   R. D. Van Arsdell, *Celtic Coinage of Britain* (London, 1989), pp. 363–84, 421. William Camden recorded a coin 'cum inscriptione TASCIA, & altera parte VER', although without being in a position to appreciate its significance (*Britannia* (London, 1600), p. 356). It is thought likely that, by adding his patronymic, 'Cunobelinus legitimised and reinforced his right to rule through Tasciovanus' (Francis M. Morris, 'Cunobelinus' Bronze Coinage', *Britannia* (2013), xliv, p. 54).

139   John T. Koch, 'Gallo-Brittonic *Tasc(i)ouanos* 'Badger-slayer' and the Reflex of Indo-European *gʷhₗ*', *Journal of Celtic Linguistics* (Cardiff, 1992), i, pp. 101–3; idem, 'Further to Indo-European *gʷh* in Celtic', in Joseph F. Eska, R. Geraint Gruffydd, and Nicolas Jacobs (ed.), *Hispano-Gallo-Brittonica: Essays in honour of Professor D. Ellis Evans on the occasion of his sixty-fifth birthday* (Cardiff, 1995), p. 86. For Tasciovanus's royal title *Rīgon*, cf. John Koch, 'The Loss of Final Syllables and Loss of Declensions in Brittonic', in James E. Doan and Cornelius G. Buttimer (ed.), *Proceedings of the Harvard Celtic Colloquium* (Cambridge, Mass., 1981), i, p. 22.

140   Claude Sterckx, 'De Cassivellaunos à Caswallon', *Studia Celtica* (Cardiff, 1998), xxxii, p. 99. 'The pedigree may represent a genuine line of princes descended from Caratacus' (P. C. Bartrum (ed.), *Early Welsh Genealogical Texts* (Cardiff, 1966), p. 127).

141   Ifor Williams (ed.), *Canu Aneirin* (Cardiff, 1938), pp. 53–55. Cf. Kathryn A. Klar, 'What are the Gwarchanau?', in Brynley F. Roberts (ed.), *Early Welsh Poetry: Studies in the Book of Aneirin* (Aberystwyth, 1988), pp. 97–137. Dr Klar suggested that the poem represents a 'Welsh remnant of Belgic lore' (p. 125).

142   Michael D. Reeve and Neil Wright (ed.), *Geoffrey of Monmouth: The History of the Kings of Britain* (Woodbridge, 2007), p. 211.

the mediæval tale of *Math uab Mathonwy*.[143] In Irish genealogies the god Lug, whose name corresponds to Welsh *Lleu*, similarly features as ancestor of royal dynasties.

Also suggestive are names of Latin derivation, applied to persons whose generational ranking in the pedigree indicates that they lived under the Roman administration of Britain. *Serguan* is *Servandus*, *Decion* looks like *Decianus*, and the epithet of *Cinis scaplaut* is Latin *scapulātus*, 'broad-shouldered'.[144] *Cinis* may be a misreading of *ciuis*, with the common misreading of *n* for *u*: 'Decianus, the broad-shouldered (Roman) citizen'. All in all, it seems that a tenth-century Welsh genealogist possessed access to records of Celtic and Roman Britain, affording authentic glimpses of British history a thousand years before his own day.[145]

The royal genealogies also include names of princes, who (reckoning their generations by the customary thirty years) reigned in the twilight years of the Roman Empire in the West. Again, they not infrequently bear British equivalents of Roman names borne by prominent figures of the period, such as *Custennin* (*Constantinus*), *Gereint* (*Gerontius*), *Patarn* (*Paternus*), and *Tegid* (*Tacitus*).[146] Rachel Bromwich, noting the general reliability of these records, concluded that 'the preservation and codification of these dynastic genealogies was the task of professional genealogists who were attached to the courts of the princes who ruled these dynasties'.[147]

Brief historical allusions attached to such records indicate that their keepers were responsible for preservation of the traditional lore of the realms ruled by their patrons. Glosses are written in both Latin and Old Welsh, bearing appearance of an origin in written records. One such, attached to the pedigree of the dynasty of Strathclyde, with its mixture of Latin and Welsh reads like a reference to a lost written (?) saga.[148]

To what extent such literature was transmitted orally, and how far in writing, can only be conjectured. Writing in the reign of Richard I, Giraldus Cambrensis noted that Welsh bards, singers, and storytellers preserved accurate copies of royal genealogies in old books, written in Welsh.[149] The cultural climate of Roman and early post-Roman Wales must have been at least as conducive to committal of noteworthy material to writing as that of the Plantagenet monarchy.

In Gaul prestigious druidic temples continued in use under Roman rule, if romanized in varying degree. This is evidenced from Coligny and Villards d'Héria (where the druidic

---

143 W. J. Gruffydd, *Math vab Mathonwy: An Inquiry into the Origins and Development of the Fourth Branch of the Mabinogi with the Text and a Translation* (Cardiff, 1928), pp. 197–99.

144 E. Williams B. Nicholson, 'The Dynasty of Cunedag and the 'Harleian Genealogies'', *Y Cymmrodor* (1908), xxi, p. 88.

145 Similarly, the pedigree of the kings of Dyfed contains a section, in which what was originally an account of the establishment of the dynasty by Magnus Maximus in the fourth century AD became misinterpreted at some point as the names of a succession of early rulers (Nikolai Tolstoy, 'Early British History and Chronology', *The Transactions of the Honourable Society of Cymmrodorion: Session 1964* (London, 1964), pp. 261–62). Cf. Thomas D. O'Sullivan, *The De Excidio of Gildas: Its Authenticity and Date* (Leiden, 1978), pp. 104–5.

146 H. M. Chadwick, *Early Scotland: The Picts, the Scots & the Welsh of Southern Scotland* (Cambridge, 1949), p. 150.

147 Rachel Bromwich, 'The Character of the Early Welsh Tradition', in Nora K. Chadwick (ed.), *Studies in Early British History* (Cambridge, 1954), pp. 92–95.

148 *Confer ipse est uero olitauc . dimor . meton . uenditus . est* (*Y Cymmrodor*, ix, p. 173): 'Confer however is from Litauc; he was sold (? he came!) from the Mid-sea', i.e. the Mediterranean Sea' (W. J. Watson, *The History of the Celtic Place-Names of Scotland* (Edinburgh, 1926), p. 102).

149 J. S. Brewer, James F. Dimock, and George F. Warner (ed.), *Giraldi Cambrensis Opera* (London, 1861–91), vi, pp. 167–68.

calendars were discovered)[150] in the south-east, to the Channel coast in the north. Towards the end of the fourth century AD, the orator and poet Ausonius, tutor to the Emperor Gratian, published verses extolling his relatives and friends. Among the former was Attius Patera, who is described as descended from a long line of druids at Bayeux in Armorica (Brittany). There Attius's father Phoebicius had been *aedituus* (custodian) of the temple of Belenos, a Celtic divinity corresponding in Roman eyes to Apollo. Phoebicius (another name for Apollo) was famed for outstanding eloquence and learning: so much so, that he obtained a chair at the prestigious university of Bordeaux (*Burdigallia*).[151] Here we find authoritative evidence that druids could be not merely scholars, but cut distinguished figures in the highly cultured world of late antique Gaul and be recalled with pride as ancestors.[152] It is likely that the temple administered by the erudite Phoebicius housed a library, although whether any of its books included tracts in Gaulish cannot be known.

Pagan revival and druidism in early mediæval Britain

In Britain indications are that paganism flourished with even greater vigour, and to a considerably later date, than in Gaul. The island diocese was more distant from imperial control, and Britain traditionally maintained an independent – at times truculent – attitude towards Rome. As Michael Jones explains,

> Rebellion in Britain naturally takes the form of military revolt, but given local recruitment, the army's long residence in Britain, and the consequent web of ties of patronage, kinship, and marriage, it would be a false distinction to separate the actions of the army in Britain, or the consequences of those actions, from the civilian population or civil government.[153]

These factors led to corresponding survival and resurgence of Celtic culture, paganism, and native aristocratic pride, as Roman authority entered on its final decline.[154] The earliest British historians, Gildas in the sixth century and Nennius in the ninth, understood the history of Roman Britain in crude terms of alien conquest and oppression, which may nonetheless reflect a measure of public perception in historical reality.[155] The name *Cymry*, originally British **kom-brogī* ('fellow-countrymen', subsequently 'Welshmen'), is interpreted as having arisen from this accruing sense of alienation from Rome.[156]

---

150 The specialized knowledge required for creation and use of the Coligny Calendar is most plausibly to be ascribed to the druids (Stephen C. McCluskey, 'Astronomies and Rituals at the Dawn of the Middle Ages', in Clive L. N. Ruggles and Nicholas J. Saunders (ed.), *Astronomies and Cultures* (Niwot, Colo., 1993), pp. 102–4).

151 R. P. H. Green (ed.), *The Works of Ausonius* (Oxford, 1991), pp. 44–46, 50; Altay Coşkun, *Die gens Ausoniana an der Macht: Untersuchungen zu Decimius Magnus Ausonius und seiner Familie* (Oxford, 2002), pp. 112–14.

152 Cf. Emile Bachelier, 'Les Druides en Gaule romaine', *Ogam: Tradition celtique* (Rennes, 1959), xi, pp. 295–306.

153 Michael E. Jones, *The End of Roman Britain* (Ithaca and London, 1996), p. 160.

154 I. LL. Foster and Glyn Daniel (ed.), *Prehistoric and Early Wales* (London, 1965), pp. 178–81; Lewis, *Temples in Roman Britain*, pp. 51–54, 140–44; Ramsay MacMullen, *Enemies of the Roman Order: Treason, Unrest, and Alienation in the Empire* (Cambridge, Mass., 1966), pp. 226–29.

155 Jones, *The End of Roman Britain*, pp. 130–34.

156 Thomas Charles-Edwards, 'Language and Society among the Insular Celts AD 400–1000', in Green (ed.), *The Celtic World*, pp. 710–15.

Specific events likely to have contributed to the attested resurgence of paganism in Britain in the latter part of the fourth century include the pagan revival instituted by the Emperor Julian the Apostate (AD 360–63), and the devastating barbarian invasion of Britain in 367.[157] There is evidence of new construction and extensive restoration of pagan temples in the aftermath of the Roman recovery following the disaster.[158] About this time the imperial authorities instituted or recognized federate tribal kingdoms in western Wales and the Lowlands of Scotland, to whom they delegated authority to protect the province from further attacks by Scots and Picts. This practical measure inevitably strengthened the political autonomy and culture of native kingdoms in the largely unromanized Highland Zone of Britain: a consequence which it doubtless suited Roman military authorities to encourage.[159] Such arrangements closely parallel British policy on the north-west frontier of India in Queen Victoria's day:

> In a nutshell, British imperial policy towards Kashmir in the later nineteenth century was simply the attempt to employ that kingdom as the guardian of the northern frontier, without the hostility, expense and added responsibilities which its annexation would involve.[160]

Given the circumstances, it is is not surprising to find suggestive indications of survival and even resurgence of the druid order in Roman Britain. Indeed, there is no compelling reason to suppose that there ever existed a Roman policy of persecuting or suppressing British druids, save possibly for unrecorded *ad hoc* repressions during the conquest period.[161] On the contrary, writing well after the Roman conquest of Britain, Pliny the Elder (who was born in Cisalpine Gaul) relates that, whereas the druids and their magical practices had been proscribed throughout Gaul by the Emperor Tiberius, in Britain their rites continued to be publicly celebrated on a grandiose scale.[162] Pliny colourfully pictures them as being wafted across the ocean to the distant island, which indicates that the British rituals corresponded to

---

157　Dorothy Watts, *Christians and Pagans in Roman Britain* (London, 1991), pp. 146–49; eadem, *Religion in Late Roman Britain: Forces of Change* (London, 1998), pp. 37–51, 67; W. H. C. Frend, 'Pagans, Christians, and 'the Barbarian Conspiracy' of A.D. 367 in Roman Britain', *Britannia* (1992), xxiii, pp. 121–31; Jones, *The End of Roman Britain*, pp. 180–81.

158　Philip Rahtz and Lorna Watts, 'The End of Roman Temples in the West of Britain', in P. J. Casey (ed.), *The End of Roman Britain: Papers arising from a Conference, Durham 1978* (Oxford, 1979), pp. 183–204. Cf. Philip Rahtz, 'The Roman Temple at Pagans Hill, Chew Stoke, N. Somerset', *Somersetshire Archaeological & Natural History Society: Proceedings during the Year 1951* (Dorchester, 1952), xcvi, pp. 115, 117; Watts and Leach, *Henley Wood*, pp. 25, 143, 147.

159　M. P. Charlesworth, *The Lost Province or the Worth of Britain* (Cardiff, 1949), pp. 26–28; I. A. Richmond, 'Roman and Native in the Fourth Century A.D. and After', in idem (ed.), *Roman and Native in North Britain* (Edinburgh, 1958), pp. 124–25; Graham Webster, *The Cornovii* (Stroud, 1991), pp. 125–26.

160　G. J. Alder, *British India's Northern Frontier 1865–95: A Study in Imperial Policy* (London, 1963), p. 100.

161　Classical allusions to proscription of druidism in the first century AD have been plausibly interpreted as applicable to their 'sanguinary rites', rather than the order itself (Edward Anwyl, *Celtic Religion in Pre-Christian Times* (London, 1906), pp. 54–55; Williams, *Christianity in Early Britain*, p. 50). In contrast Stuart Piggott, declared, 'Druidism as a cult must have been exterminated during the Roman occupation of Britain' ('The Druids in Stonehenge', in Glyn E. Daniel (ed.), *Myth or Legend?* (London, 1955), p. 100), and even so distinguished an authority on British paganism as Anne Ross refers to 'the proscription of the order throughout the empire, in Britain as in Gaul ('Ritual and the Druids' in, in Miranda J Green (ed.), *The Celtic World* (London, 1995), p. 429). It is essential to acccept that there exists *no* evidence for its suppresion in Britain. Even had it been so ordered, it could not have been imposed throughout the remote island, much of which remianed permanently unconquered..

162　Rackham, Jones, and Eichholz (ed.), *Pliny: Natural History*, viii, p. 286. The Roman government of Britain possessed neither reason nor motive to prohibit such displays, save where they involved human sacrifice.

those formerly practised by the druids of Gaul.[163] Piggott, on the unwarranted assumption that druidism in Britain was proscribed by the Romans, sought to dismiss this telling allusion by claiming that 'Pliny was revising his book up to the time of his death in AD 79, but must here refer to a time early or midway in the first century'.[164] His conjecture is however at variance with Pliny's own wording, while his Natural History was in fact compiled between the accession of Vespasian in AD 70 and his own death at the destruction of Pompeii in AD 79.[165]

No adequate reason has been advanced for rejecting Pliny's allusion to British druidism, which he implies was matter of common knowledge in his day.[166] Accordingly, it seems reasonable to accept the measured judgment of Dorothy Watts:

> When Suetonius invaded the sanctuary on Anglesey in AD 60, he slaughtered the Druids and their women prophets. But neither of the accounts of this event ... implies that Druids elsewhere – and as a class – were abolished. It is reasonable to assume that, while their more savage practices would not have been tolerated under a Roman administration, they might have continued in their priestly role... In rural areas where objects such as crowns and sceptres have been found at temple sites (such as Cavenham Heath, Hockwold, and Wanborough) the involvement of Romans in Romano-British cults is unlikely. What is likely is that the priests were also Druids, custodians of the old traditions and secrets... The forces of change were not as strong as those of tradition, and many aspects of the Celtic religion were retained long after the conquerors had departed.[167]

Even in Gaul, as was indicated earlier, it seems that Julius Caesar went to considerable lengths to *protect* the druids of Gaul throughout protracted years of warfare in their country. Due to the relative isolation of Britain, and the eventual collapse of imperial authority at the beginning of the fifth century, Christianity coexisted with paganism as a vigorous but probably minority religion.[168] In contrast, Gaul was by this time largely christianized.[169]

Although there is little evidence for the history of British druids following the departure of the legions, there remain indications that their order continued to flourish in Western Britain. The ninth-century *Historia Brittonum* depicts the fifth-century King Vortigern as consulting his *magi* over the building of a magically-threatened fortress in North Wales. Although it is not always clear whether Latin *magus* be a translation of 'druid', rather than 'wizard' or 'soothsayer', in this case it is likely that the Irish translator of Nennius (like Pliny) accurately rendered *magi*

---

163 'Pliny also had heard of the druids in Britain, but he evidently thought that they had gone to Britain from Gaul' (Nora K. Chadwick, *The Druids* (Cardiff, 1966), p. 15).

164 Piggott, *The Druids*, p. 127.

165 J. Reynolds, 'The Elder Pliny and his Times' in Roger French and Frank Greenaway (ed.), *Science in the Early Roman Empire: Pliny the Elder, his Sources and Influence* (Totowa, NJ, 1986), pp. 7–8.

166 Writers dismissive of the survival of druidism in Britain tend to omit reference to Pliny's statement (e.g. Jean-Louis Brunaux, *Les Druides: Des philosophes chez les Barbares* (Paris, 2006), pp. 47–50; Ronald Hutton, *Blood and Mistletoe: The History of the Druids in Britain* (New Haven and London, 2009), pp. 10–11, 14–15).

167 Watts, *Religion in Late Roman Britain*, p. 136.

168 W. H. C. Frend, 'Religion in Roman Britain in the Fourth Century A.D.', *The Journal of the British Archaeological Association* (London, 1955), xviii, pp. 1–18; Watts, *Christians and Pagans in Roman Britain*, pp. 221, 226–27; eadem, *Religion in Late Roman Britain*, pp. 56–73.

169 Ibid. p. 120.

as 'druids' (*draide*).[170] Earlier in the same history, the *magus* of Ascanius foretells the fate of the wonder-child in his wife's womb: a prophetic feat regularly ascribed to druids in Irish and British sources.[171]

At the least, it may reasonably be assumed that these stories originated in an era when kings maintained and consulted druids on a regular basis. More than a century after Vortigern's day, a British king named Gwallawg, whose kingdom of Elfed lay in what is now south-east Yorkshire, is described in an early (possibly contemporary) praise-poem as being attended by 'a nobleman's host of druids and sorcerers' (*ryfed hael o sywyd sywedyd*).[172] The poem begins with an invocation to God, which (if not interpolated subsequently) suggests that the Christianity espoused by British kings in the heroic age was not incompatible with maintenance of druids. The early Welsh poem *Y Gododdin* mentions a prophet's foretelling a warrior's death in battle. The term employed is again *sywedydd*, 'seer', which in the context suggests 'druid'.[173]

Mediæval Welsh poetry ascribed to the sixth-century bard Talicsin (much of which, although certainly not all, is in fact of considerably later date) contains numerous references to inspired prophets and their utterances. Of the *sywedydd*, Marged Haycock notes in her study of the Book of Taliesin,

> The poetry examples noted here illustrate the range of meaning: 'sage, learned man, instructor', one who has insight and foresight. Some indicate a particular connection with the heavens and celestial bodies, and one at least connects the *sywedyd* with books.[174]

In the poem *Angar Kyfyndawt*, after recapitulating the encyclopædic knowledge of the *sywedydd*, the author declares that 'it has been studied in books' (*Ystyry6yt yn llyfreu*).[175]

This range of knowledge corresponds closely to that accorded the druids by classical authors, and in the poem *Buarth Beird* the archetypal seer Taliesin is made to declare 'I am a druid, I am a craftsman, I am a sage (*syw*)' (*6yf dry6 wyf saer 6yf sy6*) – suggesting that druid, prophet, and

170 Theodor Mommsen (ed.), *Monvmenta Germaniae Historica* (xiii): *Chronica Minora saec. IV. V. VI. VII* (Berlin, 1894), iii, pp. 181–86; A. G. van Hamel (ed.), *Lebor Bretnach*, pp. 56–61. For the correspondence of *magus* and *druid*, cf. J. Rhys, Celtic Britain (London, 1884), pp. 70–71; Plummer (ed.), *Vitae Sanctorum Hiberniae*, i, p. clxii. Pliny translates *druidae* as *magi* (Rackham, Jones, and Eichholz (ed.), Pliny: Natural History, iv, p. 548; viii, p. 216).

171 Mommsen (ed.), *Chronica Minora*, iii, p. 150. Records of druidic prophecies of the glorious career of a hero, heroine, or saint in his mother's womb are legion. Cf. van Hamel (ed.), *Lebor Bretnach*, pp. 15–16; Tomás Ó Cathasaigh (ed.), *The Heroic Biography of Cormac mac Airt* (Dublin, 1977), p. 119; Kuno Meyer (ed.), *Hibernica Minora: Being a Fragment of an Old-Irish Treatise on the Psalter* (Oxford, 1894), p. 50; Standish H. O'Grady (ed.), *Silva Gadelica: A Collection of Tales in Irish with Extracts Illustrating Persons and Places* (London, 1892), i, pp. 74–75; Máirín O Daly (ed.), *Cath Maige Mucrama: The Battle of Mag Mucrama* (Dublin, 1975), p. 64; Kuno Meyer, 'The Expulsion of the Dessi', *Y Cymmrodor* (1901), xiv, p. 108; Vernam Hull (ed.), *Longes mac n-Uislenn: The Exile of the Sons of Uisliu* (New York, 1949), pp. 43–44; Flobert (ed.), *La vie ancienne de saint Samson de Dol*, p. 152; Plummer (ed.), *Vitae Sanctorum Hiberniae*, i, p. 200; R. A. Stewart Macalister (tr.), *The Latin & Irish Lives of Ciaran* (London, 1921), p. 183; W. W. Heist (ed.), *Vitae Sanctorum Hiberniae ex Codice olim Salmanticensi nunc Bruxellensi* (Brussels, 1965), p. 78; Whitley Stokes (ed.), *Lives of Saints from the Book of Lismore* (Oxford, 1890), pp. 35, 57, 84, 119–20; Charles Plummer (ed.), *Bethada Náem nÉrenn: Lives of Irish Saints* (Oxford, 1922), i, pp. 183–184; Kathleen Mulchrone (ed.), *Bethu Phátraic: The Tripartite Life of Patrick* (Dublin, 1939), p. 100.

172 Sir Ifor Williams and J. E. Caerwyn Williams (ed.), *The Poems of Taliesin* (Dublin, 1968), pp. 14, 130.

173 Ifor Williams (ed.), *Canu Aneirin* (Cardiff, 1938), p. 9.

174 Marged Haycock (ed.), *Legendary Poems from the Book of Taliesin* (Aberystwyth, 2007), p. 227.

175 J. Gwenogvryn Evans (ed.), *Facsimile & Text of the Book of Taliesin* (Llanbedrog, 1910), pp. 7, 20, 32.

(poetic) craftsman were regarded as fulfilling complementary rôles. Elsewhere, the expertise of the *sywedydd* in astronomy, a science Caesar recorded as an especial field of learning among the Gaulish druids, is emphasized:

A *sywyon synhwyr. A sewyd amloer*, 'and the wise men of intelligence; and the *sywedydd* and his many moons'.

While *sywedydd* was the word most frequently employed for a seer in the early Middle Ages, other terms correspond more closely to 'druid'. *Dryw*, which has already been noted as synonymous with *syw*, 'sage', was also used for 'prophet'. This relatively rare word derives directly from British and Gaulish 'druid'.[176] Another more frequently used word is *derwydd*, related but not identical to 'druid',[177] meaning 'wise man', 'prophet', 'sage', which is recorded in the mid-ninth century as a term for prophets foretelling the triumph of the Britons over the Saxon invaders. Political prophecy is attested by classical historians as an activity characteristic of the druids, and in one early Welsh mantic poem *derwyddon* is further coupled with *sywedyddion*. The wise men (*magi*) who visited the infant Jesus are termed *derwydon* in a poem on the Nativity, confirming that *derwydd* corresponded to *magus*, the term commonly employed in Latin sources for 'druid'.[178]

The variant nomenclature ascribed to seers and wizards in mediæval Wales probably signifies little. Apart from illuminating references in the early seventh-century *Vita Samsonis*, almost nothing is known of the relationship between druidism and Christianity during what must have been a prolonged period of syncretism, assimilation, and eventual supersession. Mediæval Welsh saints' Lives, which provide virtually all the 'history' recorded on the topic, are largely fictional creations, compiled long after druids had evolved into bards or 'cunning men' (*dewin*), with their orginal rôle largely forgotten.

The eleventh-century Life of St David describes at its outset how a local tyrant in Dyfed, warned by his *magi* that a boy would be born whose power would extend over the realm, attempts to have him murdered.[179] However, scant significance is to be accorded this account, which probably reflects little more than the assumption that an evil druid was the sort of scoundrel likely to resent the advent of a saint.[180]

Although it would be wrong to draw any inference from the dearth of evidence for hostile relationship between druids and Christians, such evidence as does exist suggests that, while there were inevitable frictions, they were far from amounting to endemic strife. The omniscience, prophetic powers, and shape-shifting ability professed by the bards through the

---

176   Ibid., p. 77. For the derivation of *dryw* from British *druῳids, cf. *Geiriadur Prifysgol Cymru: A Dictionary of the Welsh Language (Cardiff, 1950–2002)*, p. 1097; J. Vendryes, E. Bachellery, and P-Y. Lambert, *Lexique étymologique de l'irlandais ancien* (Dublin and Paris, 1959–96), D-202–3.

177   Cf. J. Loth, 'Remarques et additions à la grammaire galloise historique et comparée de John Morris Jones', *Revue Celtique* (Paris, 1915–1916), xxxvi, p. 366; J. Lloyd-Jones, *Geirfa Barddoniaeth Gynnar Gymraeg* (Cardiff, 1931–63), p. 313; Sir Ifor Williams, *Lectures on Early Welsh Poetry* (Dublin, 1944), p. 7; Williams and Bromwich (ed.), *Armes Prydein*, p. 66; Vendryes, Bachellery, and Lambert, *Lexique étymologique de l'irlandais ancien*, D-203.

178   Gwenogvryn Evans (ed.), *Facsimile & Text of the Book of Taliesin*, pp. 18, 27, 32, 47, 74, 76.

179   J. W. James (ed.), *Rhigyfarch's Life of St. David: The Basic Mid Twelfth-Century Latin Text with Introduction, Critical Apparatus and Translation* (Cardiff, 1967), p. 5.

180   Alternatively, the theme may reflect the biblical account of the vindictive rage of Herod, when informed by the visiting *magi* of the imminent birth of one whom he feared would supplant him as king of the Jews: *Tunc Herodes clam vocatis magis diligenter didicit ab eis tempus stellae quae apparuit eis* (Robert Weber (ed.), *Biblia Sacra iuxta Vulgatam Versionem* (Stuttgart, 1969), p. 1528).

fictitious spokesmanship of the pseudo-Taliesin, echo the wide-ranging cosmological claims of their druidic precursors.[181] It is likewise possible that associated mockery of pretensions ascribed to ignorant and lazy monks originated in a patronizing, though by no means necessarily vindictive, attitude earlier adopted by druids at a time when the authority of the Church was burgeoning.

In the lifetime of St Samson, whose *Vita* (see Chapter Nine below) provides uniquely valuable insights into the relationship between druidism and Christianity at the inception of their mutual contact in south-western Britain, the Christian (probably monk) Gildas fulminated against the shameful morals of five contemporary British kings ruling in the west of Britain. The greatest of these was Maelgwn, king of Gwynedd in North Wales. Among charges levelled against him is the king's proclivity for hearkening to his own praises intoned by a rascally crew of *præcones*, in preference to the pious hymns of devout Christians.[182] It has been suggested that Gildas was alluding in characteristically abusive style to the bards, counterparts of the druids, one of whose principal duties was that of lauding their royal patrons in verse.[183]

The denunciation of Maelgwn's *præcones* is accompanied by an excoriation of the king's renunciation of his first wife and ensuing marriage to his nephew's widow. Gildas angrily rejected the legitimacy of this second marriage, which had been vociferously celebrated by *fallaces parasitorum linguae tuorom*, 'the false tongues of thy lackeys'. Professor Charles-Edwards's suggestion that 'they [the *parasiti*] could be identical with the mendacious *praecones* of the previous chapter' seems likely. The term *parasiti* is applied again in a later chapter to deceptive flatterers of kings,[184] and it is unlikely that there existed two distinct categories of court attendants fulfilling the identical rôle.[185]

It is further suggested that the *præcones* of King Maelgwn were a professional caste, rather than a rabble of fawning courtiers.[186] Professor Caerwyn Williams argued that their endorsement of the legitimacy of the king's second marriage implies that they exercised a significant function in relation to that ceremony. Provisions exist in the Welsh laws for the royal bard to receive payment at a king's wedding, a custom which represented a relic of their function in pre-Christian Celtic society, as witnesses to the kindred's giving of the bride to her husband.[187]

181   Sir John Morris-Jones, 'Taliesin', *Y Cymmrodor* (London, 1918), xxviii, pp. 240–53.

182   Mommsen (ed.), *Chronica Minora*, iii, p. 46.

183   Jackson, *Language and History in Early Britain*, p. 117; Rachel Bromwich, 'The Character of the Early Welsh Tradition', in Chadwick (ed.), *Studies in Early British History*, p. 97; J. E. Caerwyn Williams, 'Gildas, Maelgwn and the Bards', in R. R. Davies, R. A. Griffiths, I. G. Jones, and K. O. Morgan (ed.), *Welsh Society and Nationhood: Historical Essays Presented to Glanmor Williams* (Cardiff, 1984), pp. 22–25. Gildas's use of the term is considered a variant form for 'bard' (Patrick Sims-Williams, 'Gildas and Vernacular Poetry', in Michael Lapidge and David Dumville (ed.), *Gildas: New Approaches* (Woodbridge, 1984), p. 175; François Kerlouégan, *Le De Excidio Britanniae de Gildas: Les destinées de la culture latine dans l'île de Bretagne au VIᵉ siècle* (Paris, 1987), pp. 498–99; notes, pp. 174–76). On the other hand, given that Latin *præco* normally means 'buffoon' or 'jester', both the context and Gildas's rebarbative style might suggest that he intended it as dismissive insult rather than descriptive term.

184   Mommsen (ed.), *Chronica Minora*, iii, p. 52.

185   Lapidge and Dumville (ed.), *Gildas: New Approaches*, pp. 175–78; Kerlouégan, *Le De Excidio Britanniae de Gildas*, p. 499; notes, p. 176. A suggestion that Gildas picked up the term *parasiti* for court poets from a reference by Posidonius is most unlikely.

186   Cf. the scoffing *adulatores* of the seventh-century King Ælfwin of Northumbria (Bertram Colgrave (ed.), *The Life of Bishop Wilfrid by Eddius Stephanus* (Cambridge, 1927), p. 50).

187   Aled Rhys Wiliam (ed.), *Llyfr Iorwerth: A Critical Text of the Venedotian Code of Medieval Welsh Law Mainly from BM. Cotton MS. Titus Dii* (Cardiff, 1960, pp. 21–22; Stephen J. Williams and J. Enoch Powell (ed.), *Cyfreithiau Hywel Dda yn ôl Llyfr Blegywryd (Dull Dyfed)* (Cardiff, 1942), p. 25; A. W.

Furthermore, the bard must originally have fulfilled some function for which he received his guerdon. In Vedic India the brahman (priest) was awarded the bridal gown, in return for his recitation of a hymn extolling the divine marriage which provided the paradigm of earthly ceremonies: 'The brahman who knows the Sūryā hymn is alone worthy to receive the bridal gown.'[188] All this suggests that Maelgwn's second wedding was accompanied by pagan rites.[189] Had Christian priests endorsed the unholy union, it is hard to believe that they would not have been denounced by Gildas for their impious collaboration. On the contrary, his wording implies a radical divide between the rite so vociferously upheld by the king's *præcones*, and the usage of the Christian community for which Gildas spoke.

Although Maelgwn professed the Christian faith, even retiring for a time to a monastery, it seems likely that he maintained druids at his court, who fulfilled a rôle which was probably little changed from the pre-Roman Iron Age.

Pagan survivals in sixth-century Britain

Such considerations suggest a considerable degree of survival of Celtic paganism in the Britain of Gildas's day. Superficially, his work conveys the impression that heathen beliefs and practices belonged to the long-distant past of Britain. Since it represents a sustained diatribe against widespread backsliding from the teachings of Christ and the Church, it might be inferred that even a hint of idolatry would have incurred his unrestrained ire. Such, however, does not appear, which may account for the widespread acceptance amongst historians that Celtic Britain in the sixth century AD as a fundamentally Christian country, orthodox in doctrine, and administered by a nationwide hierarchy of bishops and abbots.

However, closer examination of the *De Excidio* suggests a more complex treatment. The brief history of Roman Britain with which Gildas prefixes his work is crudely simplistic and inaccurate. Although he did not profess to be writing a work of history, he was familiar with the works of some late classical historians. Had he chosen, there is no doubt that he could have presented a fuller and more measured picture. However, he was writing polemic and not history, and as generally occurs in such cases he utilized historical evidence as a repository of facts, from which he selected those that supported his ideological edifice.

British paganism he dismissed from the outset. Gildas has nothing to say about its beliefs or practices, save that Britain had once shared 'ancient errors' common to all humanity before the incarnation of Christ. Some decayed temples and statues survived in his day, but only as evidence of long-abandoned superstitious rites. He mentions that mountains, valleys, and rivers were at one time worshipped as divine, but reassures his readers that they had long since reverted to being no more than natural features assigned to grazing and fishing.

However, the archæological record indicates that pagan cults and shrines continued to flourish in Roman Britain, at temples and elsewhere, until the latter part of the fifth century, and

---

Wade-Evans (ed.), *Welsh Medieval Law: Being a Text of the Laws of Howel the Good, Namely the British Museum Harleian MS. 4353 of the 13th Century* (Oxford, 1909), p. 33. Cf. Dafydd Jenkins (tr.), *The Law of Hywel Dda: Law Texts from Medieval Wales Translated and Edited* (Llandysul, 1986), p. 235.

188 Barend A. van Nooten and Gary B. Holland (ed.), *Rig Veda: A Metrically Restored Text with an Introduction and Notes* (Cambridge, Mass., 1994), p. 526.

189 Davies, Griffiths, Jones, and Morgan (ed.), *Welsh Society and Nationhood*, pp. 27–29. Cf. Proinsias Mac Cana, 'An Archaism in Irish Poetic Tradition', *Celtica* (Dublin, 1968), viii, pp. 174–81.

conceivably into the first half of the sixth.[190] Despite this, Gildas was at pains to emphasize that Britain had been a Christian island for several centuries.

Although evidence is sparse for historical events in the fifth and sixth centuries AD, what is known, coupled with intrinsic likelihood, makes it clear that the older religion did not simply vanish in the tidy fashion suggested by Gildas. Professor Frend argued persuasively that the traumatic effect of the great barbarian invasion of AD 367 and its aftermath resulted in a resurgence of British paganism.[191]

After AD 410, the former Roman diocese began to break up into a number of independent kingdoms of varying states of culture and tradition, a process which must further have facilitated considerable disparity of religious practice. At the same time, the fifth and sixth centuries are known as the Age of the Saints, when pioneering holy men preached the faith throughout much of Western Britain. Although almost all extant saints' Lives were composed centuries later, being largely fictitious in character, the names at least of their protagonists appear for the most part authentic, and attest to considerable missionary activity during this epoch. By the same token, this intimates the extent to which much of the island had remained pagan up to that time.

Evidence of the spread of Christianity in what is now south-west England and Wales may further be found in Christian lapidary inscriptions distributed across what is now Wales and the Dumnonian peninsula. The style was thought to have originated in Gaul in the early fifth century, but this is now doubted.[192] Many early saints in Wales and Cornwall were anchorites, who established refuges in locations where they might pray far from the busy sinful world.[193] Others, however, conducted vigorous campaigns to convert the heathen. A vivid glimpse of these disparate courses appears in the earliest and most reliable of British saints' lives, the *Vita Samsonis*. There we learn how the monks of Docco on the Cornish coast barely ventured beyond the confines of their monastery. Meanwhile, St Samson is described as energetically attemping to convert the inhabitants of entire regions to the true faith. His missionary activities in Britain were conducted a decade or so before the middle of the sixth century.

It seems probable that romanized lowland Britain had become at least outwardly Christian by the mid-fifth century. Much Church activity was directed towards combating, not paganism, but the Pelagian heresy whose founder originated in Britain.[194] Bishop Germanus of Auxerre crossed the Channel in AD 429 – possibly also on a subsequent occasion – purportedly in order to restore orthodoxy to the civilized south-east of the island. Whether he instigated a missionary

190 E. A. Thompson, *Saint Germanus of Auxerre and the End of Roman Britain* (Woodbridge, 1984), pp. 17, 32; N. J. Higham, *The English conquest: Gildas and Britain in the fifth century* (Manchester, 1994), p. 79. A dedication, 'perhaps of the late fifth or sixth century', which is interpreted as invocation of a Brittonic pagan deity *Belatucadros*, was found at Castlesteads fort on Hadrian's Wall (R. G. Collingwood and R. P. Wright (ed.), *The Roman Inscriptions of Britain: I Inscriptions on Stone* (Oxford, 1965), p. 734). For Mars Belatucadros, cf. Anne Ross, *Pagan Celtic Britain: Studies in Iconography and Tradition* (London, 1967), pp. 181–82.

191 *Britannia*, xxiii, pp. 121–32. Cf. Charlesworth, *The Lost Province*, p. 24; Jones, *The End of Roman Britain*, pp. 180–81.

192 Jeremy Knight, 'The Early Christian Latin Inscriptions of Britain and Gaul: Chronology and Context', in Nancy Edwards and Alan Lane (ed.), *The Early Church in Wales and the West* (Oxford, 1992), pp. 45–50; Jeremy K. Knight, 'An Inscription from Bavai and the Fifth-Century Christian Epigraphy of Britain', *Britannia* (2010), xli, pp. 283–92.

193 Nora K. Chadwick, *The Age of the Saints in the Early Celtic Church* (London, 1961), pp. 82–87. The earliest literary instances of such retreats in Britain are those related of St Samson himself (Pierre Flobert (ed.), *La vie ancienne de saint Samson de Dol* (Paris, 1997), pp. 178, 206, 220).

194 Thompson, *Saint Germanus of Auxerre and the End of Roman Britain*, pp. 15–25.

movement to 'barbarian' Western Britain about the same time, or whether such a mission arose spontaneously among other Gaulish or British Christians, there is now no means of knowing. What does appear likely is that much of the unromanized highland region in the west continued to be largely pagan throughout much of the fifth and sixth centuries AD.

Gildas's angry verbiage and interminable resort to biblical citations, whether or not entirely apposite to his purpose, have served to occlude evidence of pagan survival. However, one passage in his work throws some light on the contemporary state of religion in western Britain. In the course of his denunciation of five contemporary kings, his conclusion includes these words: 'Let not those wicked men, therefore, be proud of themselves for abstaining from public sacrifice to the gods of the heathen ...'[195]

The natural interpretation of this passage is that the kings in question were little more than nominally Christian. Furthermore, the concession that they avoided public celebration of heathen rites intimates that their discretion was not shared by other kings unnamed by Gildas. The *Vita Samsonis* credibly describes elaborate heathen rites celebrated about this time in Cornwall, and it has already been noted that a generation later the northern king Gwallawg is described in an early poem as surrounded by 'a host of druids and wizards'. In any case, the allusion sits oddly with Gildas's prior assertion that pagan worship had vanished from Britain centuries earlier, when even then it supposedly constituted no more than a form of nebulous nature worship.

The attitude of Gildas towards British paganism was constrained, like so much else in his work, by rigid parameters he imposed on the past and future destiny of his people. In his eyes Britain was a new Israel, whose ancestors dwelt in a Promised Land.[196] He repeatedly makes this identification explicit, and its most overt imagery appears in his account of the martyrdom of St Alban.

The episode, which he mistakenly ascribed to worldwide persecution under the Emperor Diocletian, concerns Roman condemnation of Alban for seeking to protect a fugitive Christian. On his way to execution, the saint by means of prayer created a dry passage across the Thames, through which he led a thousand men while the waters were held back like cliffs on either side. Gildas explicitly likens this episode to the passage of the Ark of the Covenant through the Jordan (Joshua, 3:17), and a parallel with the escape of the Israelites through the Red Sea is likewise unmistakable. Thereafter, according to Gildas, the Britons for all their backslidings remained resolutely Christian.[197] The 'thousand men' whom Alban led to safety through the river (a detail unique to Gildas) stand as forebears of the Britons, whom he envisaged as undergoing in this manner a national rite of baptism.[198]

On the basis of his self-imposed paradigm, 'this sweet concord between Christ, the head, and the members continued', marred at times only by Arianism and other heresies to which the

---

195 *Non sibi scelerati isti, dum non gentium diis perspicue litant, subplaudant* (Mommsen (ed.), *Chronica Minora*, iii, p. 49).

196 Ibid., pp. 31–32. Cf. Robert W. Hanning, *The Vision of History in Early Britain: From Gildas to Geoffrey of Monmouth* (New York, 1966), p. 55; David N. Dumville, 'The Idea of Government in Sub-Roman Britain', in G. Ausenda (ed.), *After Empire: Towards an Ethnology of Europe's Barbarians* (Woodbridge, 1995), p. 185; Karen George, *Gildas's De Excidio Britonum and the Early British Church* (Woodbridge, 2009), pp. 33–34, 54. 'Gildas defined in Britannia a land which embodied its people, the new Israel' (Ian McKee, 'Gildas: Lessons from History', *Cambrian Medieval Celtic Studies* (Aberystwyth, 2006), li, p. 4).

197 Hanning, *The Vision of History in Early Britain*, pp. 52–53.

198 A hymn in the Book of Taliesin bears the title *Marwnad y vil veib*, 'Deathsong of the thousand sons' (Gwenogvryn Evans (ed.), *Facsimile & Text of the Book of Taliesin*, p. 3), whose title appears to have become detached from another (lost) poem (Oliver Davies, *Celtic Christianity in Early Medieval Wales: The Origins of the Welsh Spiritual Tradition* (Cardiff, 1996), p. 170). Could it have been a lament for the thousand 'founding fathers' of Christian Britain?

innate feebleness of the Britons' national character made them at times depressingly susceptible. Any suggestion of paganism coexisting with Christianity in Britain would have violated this ideological concept. The burden of Gildas's message is that the Britons have sinned grievously, but not to the extent that they may not yet be saved by repentance.

In order to sustain this tidy image, Gildas was obliged to effect major restructuring of the history of Roman and post-Roman Britain. Setting aside the extent to which paganism survived in the kingdoms of the five princes denounced in his work, it may be asked why he ignored equally powerful British kingdoms in the North, extending from the Dee to the Forth.[199] It is not unlikely that some at least of their rulers remained, like Gwallawg of Elfed, largely pagan, and hence 'beyond the pale' ideologically, and in consequence (so far as Gildas was concerned) historiographically.

In addition, there was the impressive kingdom of the Picts, whose territory covered most of what is now Scotland north of the Forth, a territory estimated in the early mediæval period at comprising a third of Britain.[200] At the time Gildas wrote the Picts remained resolutely pagan. Although he must have been aware that they were the indigenous inhabitants of the territory they occupied, he elected to misrepresent them as 'a race from across the sea', whose arrival as alien invaders in Britain he describes as having occurred as recently as the time of the departure of the Roman military at the turn of the fourth and fifth centuries AD. Although at one point they are described as overrunning territory as far south as the Roman Wall, he goes on to relate how they were not long afterwards expelled from that region, and subsequently succeeded only in effecting settlements 'in the most remote part of the island' (*in extrema parte insulae*). Gildas's wording intimates that these were little more than bridgeheads, occupied for the purpose of launching piratical raids (*praedas et contritiones nonnumquam facientes*). The reality, which he was plainly concerned to suppress, was that theirs was an extensive, powerful, cultured, and wealthy state, which occupied a large part of Britain – while remaining uncompromisingly pagan.

Much nearer to hand, and yet more difficult to ignore, were the Anglo-Saxon settlements in southern and eastern Britain. The description of their original arrival, first as mercenaries engaged to fight against the northern barbarians, and subsequently as treacherous foes, plays a major part in Gildas's narrative. They are described as having been crushed at the battle of Badon Hill (the victory later ascribed to Arthur) a generation before Gildas's day, after which they had apparently ceased to trouble the Britons.

Although the surviving Saxons remained in possession of a substantial portion of territory occupied before their defeat, Gildas bafflingly provides almost no indication of their status and relationship with the Britons. He merely mentions in passing that a treaty imposed in the aftermath of Badon Hill ensured peace between the two races, and that the intruders retained sufficient autonomy to prevent British pilgrims visiting Christian shrines in or beyond those extensive territories which they occupied. These allusions feature only in passing, so that the invaders might almost be supposed to have vanished from the scene.

---

199 However, the possibility cannot be excluded that Maelgwn's kingdom extended to northern Britain (Eoin MacNeill, 'The Language of the Picts', *Yorkshire Celtic Studies* (Leeds, 1938–39), ii, p. 16). I intend to pursue this question elsewhere.

200 Mommsen (ed.), *Chronica Minora*, iii, p. 154. For a useful survey of Pictish polity before its absorption by the Dalriadic kingdom, cf. Sally Foster, 'The State of Pictland in the Age of Sutton Hoo', in M. O. H. Carver (ed.), *The Age of Sutton Hoo: The Seventh Century in North-Western Europe* (Woodbridge, 1992), pp. 217–34.

Like the Picts, the Saxons continued pagan throughout this period.[201] Here we find another great tract of the island in thrall to heathen power at the time Gildas wrote. During his detailed description of their arrival and wars against the Britons, Gildas applies many disparaging terms to the barbarians, without ever indicating that they were idolaters. It seems that, as with the Picts, he possessed particular motive for ignoring this factor.

All in all, it is hard to avoid concluding that Gildas felt it essential to his depiction of Britain to omit any explicit allusion to the widespread survival of paganism, both within and without 'British' Britain. Of the five kings in western Britain whom he excoriates by name, while he is remorseless in castigating their crimes, he is careful to portray all save one (Constantine of Dumnonia) as professing Christians, while his telltale emphasis on the fact that they did not engage *overtly* in pagan rites hints at other unidentified British rulers who remained resolutely pagan.

Not all leaders of the Church, however, manifested such confidence in the orthodoxy of the native rulers. Fragments of letters by Gildas to a Bishop Finnian in Ireland have survived, one of which recapitulates the former's response to an enquiry concerning the use of excommunication. In the extant excerpt, Gildas provides a succession of instances of exemplary biblical figures, ranging from Noah to Christ, who are depicted as dealing amicably with notorious practitioners of magic and idolatry. In another letter to Finnian, Gildas cites the example of Moses for the undesirability of condemning good princes (*boni principes*) for venial offences.[202] Although Finnian's earlier letter to Gildas has not survived, its burden is implicit in his response. In the eyes of Finnian, Gildas had been overly tolerant in his dealings with prominent pagans in Britain: a policy which the latter in response sought to justify with examples from Holy Writ.

It is likely that the leading laymen whose idolatrous activities implicitly distressed Finnian were the five princes excoriated by Gildas in his *De Excidio*. As has been seen, the latter went out of his way to exonerate them from the charge of openly conducting pagan rites, while at the same time warning them that refusal to obey God could be regarded as a form of idolatry.

Furthermore, Gildas remains oddly silent on the conduct of those unidentified rulers, whether kings or others, who controlled the great swathe of unconquered lowland Britain lying between Wales and Dumnonia in the west on the one hand, and the English settlements in the east on the other. In Ireland, however, it was the western British kings whose activities would have been most familiar. Not only were close communications maintained across the Irish Sea, but the Irish language was widely spoken in Cornwall and south-western Wales at this time. King Voteporix of Dyfed was of Irish descent, and his bilingual Latin and Irish funerary inscription suggests that both languages were spoken at his court.

Gildas's denunciation of the five kings appears as something of an afterthought to his original scheme. It is hard to see why they alone should have been singled out from among numerous other British rulers of his day. The philippic is awkwardly tacked onto his preceding history of Britain. The lengthy denunciation is introduced by an explanation that he had originally intended to conclude his work at this point, 'or indeed earlier' (*vel antea*). The most likely juncture for an earlier conclusion would have been immediately after his dramatic account of the war concluding with the climactic British victory at Badon Hill, and preceding his denunciation of the five kings.

---

201 The extent and effects of Anglo-Saxon heathendom are discussed by Jane Stevenson, 'Christianity in Sixth-and Seventh-Century Southumbria', in ibid., pp. 175–78. Higham suggests that the Saxon invasions provoked a resurgence of paganism among the Britons (*The English conquest*, p. 79).

202 Mommsen (ed.), *Chronica Minora*, iii, pp. 86, 88. Cf. Richard Sharpe, 'Gildas as a Father of the Church', in Michael Lapidge and David Dumville (ed.), *Gildas: New Approaches* (Woodbridge, 1984), pp. 196–98; Michael W. Herren, 'Gildas and Early British Monasticism', in Alfred Bammesberger and Alfred Wollmann (ed.), *Britain 400–600: Language and History* (Heidelberg, 1990), pp. 66–68).

In view of these considerations, it is possible that the polemical attack on the western kings contained in his chapters 28 to 36 reflects Gildas's reaction to Finnian's criticism of his lenient attitude towards the erring princes. In his reply, Gildas defends his treatment of the 'idolaters', the majority of whom he portrays as backsliders, although *not* (as he significantly emphasizes) heathens.

In conclusion, analysis of the *De Excidio* of Gildas suggests these considerations regarding the state of religion in Britain in the early sixth century AD.

1. His concern to depict Britain as an orthodox Christian *patria* led him to withhold reference to pagan cults active in the relatively recent British past, and still more incongruously to suppress any allusion to those extensive tracts of the island which continued uncompromisingly pagan for a generation and more after the time of his writing.

2. He was reproached by Finnian for his overly tolerant attitude towards powerful contemporary 'idolaters', i.e. pagan, or semi-pagan, kings.

3. Although four of the the five Western kings denounced by Gildas for their lax morality were nominally Christian, they continued openly to espouse pagan traditions of their ancestors.

4. In the case of Maelgwn Gwynedd, this extended to the important sphere of royal marriage rites, which guaranteed the legitimacy of the royal succession.

5. Gildas would surely have denounced Christian priests, had they participated in marriage ceremonies flagrantly violating canon law. He did not do so, which suggests that Maelgwn's druids were key participants in the ceremonial.

6. Gildas angrily castigates priests for their obsessive absorption with traditional games and stories. They eagerly listen to 'foolish tales of men of this world' (*ineptas saecularium hominum fabulas*), i.e. legends of the old gods and heroes such as are found in the Four Branches of the *Mabinogi*, and attend what were probably secular (pagan) entertainments dramatizing such themes. Clearly the Church was making uneven headway against the old cultural order.[203] If this be the condition of the clergy, how much more is the laity likely to have been attached to the traditional lore of their country!

7. Finally, it is probable that some priests committed to writing those profane stories to which they were so regrettably attached, as they did in Ireland, and also in Britain at a later period.

Broadly speaking, the religious authority of the druids gradually became replaced by that of the Church, while their rôle as custodians of ancient lore was inherited by the bards. Surviving Welsh mediæval prose and poetry amply confirm that pagan mythology remained an important factor in the bardic repertoire.

More might be adduced to demonstrate a substantial survival of pagan practice among the western and northern Britons in the early mediæval period. Nicholas Higham has suggested some continuance of paganism among Gildas's contemporaries, and argues for a severe decline of the Church in his time. A striking contrast is evident between allusions to paganism in Celtic

---

203 Mommsen (ed.), *Chronica Minora*, iii, p. 62. Cf. Sir Ifor Williams, *Lectures on Early Welsh Poetry* (Dublin, 1944), p. 52; Davies, Griffiths, Jones, and Morgan (ed.), *Welsh Society and Nationhood*, pp. 29–31; Kerlouégan, *Le De Excidio Britanniae de Gildas*, pp. 499–500. The extent to which these traditional stories (*chwedlau*) enraptured much of the priesthood is illustrated by the fact that, more than six centuries after Gildas's day, the same complaint continued levelled against monks enthralled by romantic tales of King Arthur (Roger Sherman Loomis, *Arthurian Tradition & Chrétien de Troyes* (New York, 1949), pp. 17, 22).

literatures and their virtual absence in the Old English equivalent. In early Irish literature pagan survivals are multitudinous, being deeply embedded in the native tradition.[204]

How long and extensively pagan practices, beliefs, or traditions lingered on into the high Middle Ages and beyond is impossible to quantify. While there exists scant evidence for pagan temples surviving beyond the fifth century AD, open-air festivals, such as those celebrating the feast of Lug at harvest time, must have involved many archaic rites and recitations of ancient myths, partially transformed into tales of wonder.

A secret report on the state of religion in North Wales, submitted to the English government about 1600, describes popular gatherings in the region, whose entertainment included tales about Taliesin and Merlin, along with episodes from the lives of early saints.

Upon the Sondaies and hollidaies the multitude of all sortes of men woomen and childerne of everie parishe doe use to meete in sondrie places either one some hill or one the side of some mountaine where their harpers and crowthers singe them songs of the doeings of theire auncestors … Here alsoe doe they spende theire time in hearinge some part of the lives of Thalassyn, Marlin, Beuno, Kybbye, Ieruu, and suche other the intended prophetts and saincts of that cuntrie.[205]

There can be little doubt that such assemblies, for which little other evidence survives, originated in very early times.[206] If they appeared potentially subversive to a government spy at the end of the reign of Elizabeth I, how much more so must they have done in an earlier era, when the Christian faith had as yet to secure its supremacy.

While participants in Tudor times were doubtless professing Christians, this was not always the case. The Welsh Arthurian romance of *Gereint mab Erbin*, composed in the twelfth or thirteenth century, concludes with a dramatic account of its hero's arrival at a strange orchard. To gain entrance he had to penetrate an enchanted mist (*cae nywl*) and a barrier of stakes, all save two of which bore human heads impaled on their points. Among other wonders, a thunderous noise (*twrwf mawr*) heralded the arrival of a truculent warrior, whom however Geraint overpowered. He agreed to spare his adversary's life, on condition 'that this game shall no longer exist here, nor the hedge of mist, nor the magic, nor the enchantment' (*namyn na bo yma uyth y gware hwn, na'r cae nywl, na'r hud na'r lletrith a ry uu*). The cowed warrior submitted, instructing Geraint to blow a horn hanging nearby, which permanently dispelled the wizardry.[207]

Virtually all the details of this incident reflect familiar pagan motifs, from the *twrwf mawr* heralding a malign irruption from the Otherworld to the display of heads and the *cae nywl*, the

204 Higham, *The English conquest*, pp. 55, 65, 77, 75, 79. Cf. Carolus Plummer (ed.), *Vitae Sanctorum Hiberniae: Partim Hactenvs Ineditae ad Fidem Codicvm Manvscriptorvm Recognovit Prolegominis Notis Indicibvs Instrvxit* (Oxford, 1910), i, pp. cxxix–clxxxviii; H. Munro Chadwick and N. Kershaw Chadwick, *The Growth of Literature* (Cambridge, 1932–40), i, pp. 7, 208–9; Tomás Ó Cathasaigh, 'Pagan survivals: the evidence of early Irish narrative', in Próinséas Ní Chatháin and Michael Richter (ed.), *Irland und Europa: Die Kirche im Frühmittelalter* (Stuttgart, 1984), pp. 291–307; Pádraig Ó Riain, 'Celtic Mythology and Religion', in Karl Horst Schmidt and Rolf Ködderitzsch (ed.), *Geschichte und Kultur der Kelten: Vorbereitungskonferenz 25.-28. Oktober 1982 in Bonn* (Heidelberg, 1986), pp. 241–51.

205 Edward Owen, 'An Episode in the History of Clynnog Church', *Y Cymmrodor* (1906), xix, p. 69. Cf. Sir Ifor Williams, 'Hen Chwedlau', *Transactions of the Honourable Society of Cymmrodorion: Sessions 1946–1947* (London, 1948), p. 28.

206 Máire MacNeill showed that the annual fair at Morvah in west Cornwall originated in British pagan festivities corresponding to the Irish pagan festival of Lughnasa (*The Festival of Lughnasa: A Study of the Survival of the Celtic Festival of the Beginning of Harvest* (Oxford, 1962), pp. 382–85).

207 Robert L. Thomson (ed.), *Ystorya Gereint uab Erbin* (Dublin, 1997), pp. 50–54.

latter recalling enchanted mists conjured up by druids, or that which Conn penetrated when approaching the Otherworld palace of Lug in *Baile in Scáil*.[208] While there is little likelihood that pagan shrines continued in use anywhere near approaching the period when the story of *Gereint* was composed, it shows that a lively traditional memory of pre-Christian religious assemblages survived, together with keen appreciation of their incompatibility with the code of a Christian.

Indeed, such open-air cultic sites are likely to have endured much longer than more readily identifiable temple structures. In an earlier era they may have been attended by a priesthood or officiants of some description, who preserved myths and presided over rites associated with sanctified locations. The Omphalos of Ulster was identified with the sanctuary at Emain Macha ('Grove of Macha'). As Tómás Ó Broin explained:

> Emain Macha is a site dedicated to grove worship, and therefore, we expect the earliest Ulster myths, which centre on Emain Macha, to be the product of that ideology. The *Curaid na Craebruaide* [Emain priesthood] are the actors in these myths, and must also be closely bound up with the grove cult, doubtless, the reflex of actual functionaries in the service.[209]

Fragmentary though the evidence is, it can now be seen that there existed many conduits whereby the ancient lore of pre-Roman Britain could have been preserved and transmitted over long centuries into the early Middle Ages. Such 'memories' of a very remote past were capable of surviving radical social, religious and linguistic changes in society.[210]

---

208 Christian-J. Guyonvarc'h and Françoise Le Roux, *Les Druides* (Rennes, 1986), pp. 171–74; Kevin Murray (ed.), *Baile in Scáil: 'The Phantom's Frenzy'* (Dublin, 2004), pp. 33–34.

209 '"Craebruad": The Spurious Tradition', *Éigse: A Journal of Irish Studies* (Dublin, 1973), xv, pp. 103, 112.

210 By the time traditions of the Morvah 'Lughnasa' festival came to be recorded in the second half of the nineteenth century, the language of the celebrants had become entirely transmuted from Cornish into English.

7

Historical Tradition in Mediæval Wales

Geoffrey's Welsh Informants

In the previous chapter, evidence was cited indicating the likelihood of extensive survival of paganism in Britain to a period considerably later than is commonly allowed. Pagan lore endured much longer than pagan belief and practice, as it gradually became modified into forms acceptable (or, at the least, not blatantly offensive) to Church authorities. Thus, the celebrated Four Branches of the *Mabinogi*, which were composed at the beginning of the eleventh century, have long generally been recognized as 'fundamentally the stories of the old Brittonic gods from whom the leading Welsh dynasties claimed descent'.[1]

Although almost all the protagonists of these tales are recognizable as euhemerized pagan deities, it is uncertain how far audiences and readers appreciated this at the time of their composition at the beginning of the eleventh century.[2] However, the author acknowledges their setting in an explicitly pre-Christian era, alludes to a pagan rite of baptism, and ascribes magical potency to appropriate characters.[3] Thus there is nothing untoward in accepting the possibility that some passages at least in Geoffrey of Monmouth's *Historia* similarly originated in archaic lore current in the Wales of his day. Equally, given the predominantly fictive character of his narrative, persuasive reasons are required to substantiate any postulated exception.

Geoffrey was acquainted with at least one contemporary Welsh literary figure, who was well-versed in the early history and literature of his country. At the end of his *Historia*, which concludes with the death of the Welsh King Cadwalader in 689, he commends three distinguished contemporary historians, one Welsh and two English, to abjure writing on the same topic, seeing that they did not possess the book about the British kings which Walter, Archdeacon of Oxford, had obtained for him *ex Britannia*.[4] The two English historians, Henry of Huntingdon and

---

1 Rachel Bromwich (ed.), *Trioedd Ynys Prydein: The Welsh Triads* (Cardiff, 1978), p. lxxxvii.

2 Recognition of pagan divinities may have continued much later than the silence of the evidence appears to suggest. As late as the beginning of the ninth century, the marine deity Manannán mac Lir continued revered by both Irish and Britons: *Scoti [et] Britones eum deum uocauerunt maris, et inde filium maris esse dixerunt* (Kuno Meyer, 'Sanas Cormaic: An Old-Irish Glossary', in O. J. Bergin, R. I. Best, Kuno Meyer, and J. G. O'Keefe (ed.), *Anecdota from Irish Manuscripts* (Halle and Dublin, 1907–13), iv, p. 78).

3 Ifor Williams (ed.), *Pedeir Keinc y Mabinogi* (Cardiff, 1930), pp. xxiii, 150–51; R. L. Thomson (ed.), *Pwyll Pendeuic Dyuet: The First of the Four Branches of the Mabinogi edited from the White Book of Rhydderch with variants from the Red Book of Hergest* (Dublin, 1957), pp. 39–40. Mediæval Irish poets similarly tended to avoid Christian anachronisms (James Carney, 'Two poems from Acallam na Senórach', in James Carney and David Greene (ed.), *Celtic Studies: Essays in memory of Angus Matheson 1912–1962* (London, 1968), p. 24).

4 Reeve and Wright (ed.), *Geoffrey of Monmouth: The History of the Kings of Britain*, p. 281.

William of Malmesbury, appear to have accepted his peremptory injunction with equanimity. Indeed, Henry incorporated a lengthy summary of Geoffrey's work into a fresh edition of his own *Historia Anglorum*, after happening on a copy during a visit to Normandy.[5]

More difficult to deceive, however, was the Welsh historian, Caradog of Llancarfan. While English historians, ignorant of Welsh, could have no pressing reason for requesting to inspect the manuscript of Geoffrey's 'British history', Caradog might well have been expected to be curious. While nothing indicates that Geoffrey enjoyed direct contact with the two English historians, he addresses Caradog as his *contemporaneus*. Although the term could be employed in the sense of 'contemporary',[6] here its alternative meaning 'comrade' appears preferable. Not only is Caradog singled out by this appellation (the other two historians were after all likewise Geoffrey's contemporaries), but in an earlier chapter of his work he declares that it was pressure applied by *contemporanei mei* which induced him to publish the Prophecies of Merlin.[7] This surely implies personal connexion.[8]

Little is known of Caradog of Llancarfan. Geoffrey's words indicate that he was well-versed in Welsh history, but whatever works on that subject he may have composed are now lost. He also wrote the Lives of Saints Gildas and Cadog, and probably those of Illtud and Cyngar.[9]

> Caradoc … was a learned man, and liked to introduce other information or corroborative detail from other sources.[10]

One of the more interesting instances of 'other sources' is the inclusion in his Life of Gildas of a local Glastonbury legend, recounting the story of the abduction of Arthur's Queen Guenevere (*Guennuvar*).[11]

---

5   Diana Greenway (ed.), *Henry, Archdeacon of Huntingdon, Historia Anglorum: The History of the English People* (Oxford, 1996), pp. 558–82. For Henry's discovery of Geoffrey's work (which he warmly recommended as a 'great book'), cf. Margaret Gibson, 'History at Bec in the twelfth century', in R. H. C. Davis and J. M. Wallace-Hadrill (ed.), *The Writing of History in the Middle Ages: Essays Presented to Richard William Southern* (Oxford, 1981), pp. 176–77; Neil Wright, 'The place of Henry of Huntingdon's *Epistola ad Warinum* in the text-history of Geoffrey of Monmouth's *Historia regum Britannie*: a preliminary investigation', in Gillian Jondorf and D. N. Dumville (ed.), *France and the British Isles in the Middle Ages and Renaissance: Essays by Members of Girton College, Cambridge, in Memory of Ruth Morgan* (Woodbridge, 1991), pp. 71–113. Geoffrey's contemporary Geoffrey Gaimar describes how he consulted 'the good book of Oxford which belonged to Archdeacon Walter': *Le bon livere de Oxeford / Ki fust Walter l'arcediaen* (Alexander Bell (ed.), *L'Estoire des Engleis by Geffrei Gaimar* (Oxford, 1960), p. 204). Whatever this book constituted, it cannot have been written *sermone Britannico*, of which it is unlikely Gaimar could have understood a word (ibid., pp. x, liii). 'Gaimar used a complete set of the *Historia* and an Oxford book which may be a second copy of it before 1140' (M. Dominica Legge, 'Master Geoffrey Arthur', in Kenneth Varty (ed.), *An Arthurian Tapestry: essays in memory of Lewis Thorpe* (Cambridge, 1983), p. 24).

6   R. E. Latham and D. R. Howlett (ed.), *Dictionary of Medieval Latin from British Sources* (London, 1975–2013), p. 464.

7   Reeve and Wright (ed.), *Geoffrey of Monmouth: The History of the Kings of Britain*, p. 143.

8   Edmond Faral, *La légende arthurienne - Études et documents* (Paris, 1929), ii, p. 39; Christopher Brooke, 'The Archbishops of St David's, Llandaff and Caerleon-on-Usk', in Nora K. Chadwick (ed.), *Studies in the Early British Church* (Cambridge, 1958), pp. 231–32.

9   Ibid., pp. 228–29, 234–35.

10   Christopher Brooke, 'St Peter of Gloucester and St Cadoc of Llancarfan', in Nora K. Chadwick (ed.), *Celt and Saxon: Studies in the Early British Border* (Cambridge, 1963), p. 310.

11   Theodor Mommsen (ed.), *Monvmenta Germaniae Historica* (xiii): *Chronica Minora saec. IV. V. VI. VII* (Berlin, 1894), iii, p. 109. Cf. Roger Sherman Loomis, *Arthurian Tradition & Chrétien de Troyes*

Caradog was surely sufficiently familiar with the traditional lore of his country to have smelled a rat, had he read (as he surely did) the *Historia Regum Britanniæ*. It is consequently tempting to concur with Lewis Jones, who long ago noted that, in the concluding section of the *Historia Regum Britanniæ*, Geoffrey 'leaves the history of the [subsequent] British kings to Caradoc of Llancarvan, – probably a *protégé* of his who could be let into the secret and be trusted to improve upon it'.[12]

Against this ungenerous suspicion is the fact that subsequent Welsh translators of the *Historia* swallowed it hook, line, and sinker.

Bledri ap Cydifor

We turn now to a second prominent Welsh contemporary, one yet more likely to have provided Geoffrey of Monmouth with relevant information. Bledri ap Cydifor, Prince of Dyfed, was a colourful character who maintained good relations with the Norman settlers of South Wales. In 1115 he was entrusted with the castle of Robert Courtemain at Abercorram.[13] He is described as *latimarius*, interpreter, an office which involved assistance at exchanges between distinguished Welsh potentates and their Anglo-Norman counterparts. Given his illustrious birth, it has been plausibly suggested that Bledri acted as interpreter for King Henry I, who possessed extensive interests in South Wales.[14]

Another magnate of rank and power lofty enough to engage a Welsh aristocrat as adviser and interpreter was the king's illegitimate son, Earl Robert of Gloucester.[15] Robert acquired extensive territory in Deheubarth, in south Wales,[16] where his principal stronghold was Cardiff Castle. He was careful to maintain cordial relations with Welsh princes of the region.[17] They in turn loyally provided him with substantial martial levies, when the earl took to the field after the death of King Henry, acting as his half-sister the Empress Matilda's most potent champion against their cousin King Stephen.[18] The benign rule tactfully exercised by the earl over his Welsh domains, coupled with campaigns waged by his Welsh levies deep inside English territory, led to his featuring in Welsh prophetic poetry ascribed to Myrddin (Merlin) as *mab henri*, 'Son of Henry', the destined deliverer of the Welsh from their English oppressors.[19]

It is not only in his capacity as interpreter that Bledri was likely to have come into personal contact with Earl Robert. The earl was a man of extensive learning, who displayed particular

---

(New York, 1949), pp. 214–22; Bromwich (ed.), *Trioedd Ynys Prydein*, pp. 382–84.

12   W. Lewis Jones, 'Geoffrey of Monmouth', *Transactions of the Honourable Society of Cymmrodorion: Session 1898–1900* (London, 1900), p. 78. The thirteenth-century compiler of *Brut y Tywysogion* designed his chronicle as a sequel to Geoffrey's work (Thomas Jones, *Brut y Tywysogion* (Cardiff, 1953), pp. 4–5). The choncicler clearly accepted it as authentic.

13   Idem (ed.), *Brut y Tywysogion: Peniarth MS. 20* (Cardiff, 1941), p. 66.

14   Constance Bullock-Davies, *Professional Interpreters and the Matter of Britain* (Cardiff, 1966), pp. 10–12.

15   For Robert's career, cf. G. E. C[ockayne]. *et al.* (ed.), *The Complete Peerage: or a History of the House of Lords and all its Members from the Earliest Times* (London, 1910–59), v, pp. 683–86.

16   J. S. Brewer, James F. Dimock, and George F. Warner (ed.), *Giraldi Cambrensis Opera* (London, 1861–91), vi, p. 63.

17   David Crouch, 'The March and the Welsh Kings', in Edmund King (ed.), *The Anarchy of King Stephen's Reign* (Oxford, 1994), pp. 272–73.

18   Greenway (ed.), *Henry, Archdeacon of Huntingdon, Historia Anglorum*, pp. 724–38; K. R. Potter (ed.), *Gesta Stephani: The Deeds of Stephen* (London, 1955), pp. 73–76, 114.

19   William F. Skene (ed.), *The Four Ancient Books of Wales: Containing The Cymric Poems attributed to the Bards of The Sixth Century* (Edinburgh, 1868), i, pp. 209, 223–24, 239, 246; Margaret Enid Griffiths, *Early Vaticination in Welsh with English Parallels* (Cardiff, 1937), pp. 133–34.

interest in the history, factual and legendary (the categories were not altogether distinguished at the time), of early Britain. It was to him that Geoffrey of Monmouth dedicated his *Historia*, extolling him as a patron of rare scholarship and critical judgment. Duke Robert was in turn sufficiently impressed by the work to circulate it among his intellectual friends.[20] Making every allowance for the display of unctuous flattery routinely required of authors addressing their noble patrons, it seems in this instance that Geoffrey's praise was not exaggerated. The sincerity of Earl Robert's interest, coupled with Geoffrey's connexion with Monmouth, makes it not unlikely that the latter on occasion attended the earl's courts at Gloucester, Cardiff, and elsewhere. Bledri ap Cydifor's combined functions as prince of South Wales, popular storyteller, and interpreter to great men, made him similarly apt to be present on such occasions. Altogether, it seems prima facie likely that the two most celebrated contemporary authorities on the legendary history of Britain were personally acquainted.

Like Geoffrey, Bledri possessed a sprightly wit, a cheerful specimen of which was recorded by Giraldus Cambrensis towards the end of the twelfth century.[21] It is widely accepted that this talented and spirited character is one and the same with the figure known from Continental romances as *Breri*, 'who knew the acts and tales of all the kings, of all the nobles who have been in Britain'. A French Arthurian poem, using the form *Bleheris*, describes the troubadour as one 'who was born and reared in Wales ... and who told it [the story of Gauvain, i.e. Gawain] to the count of Poitiers, who loved the story and held it more than any other firmly in memory'.[22]

The count in question is generally taken either for William VII, a celebrated crusader and troubadour, who died in 1127, or his successor William VIII, who died a decade later. It is hard to conceive of a more appropriate source of those tales of early Britain which Geoffrey loved, than the gifted and widely travelled *conteur* (Welsh *cyfarwydd*) Bledri, a prince fluent in Welsh and French, whose rank and talent ensured him a ready welcome at the courts of princes.[23]

There exists a further amusing intimation that Geoffrey and Bledri were acquainted. A list of British kings included in the early part of Geoffrey's book comprises a bald catalogue of regal names culled from Welsh genealogies, interrupted by this unique parenthesis: '*Bledgabred*. He surpassed all singers who had been before him, in singing and in all musical instruments, so that he could be termed the god of jesters.'[24]

---

20 Neil Wright (ed.), *The Historia Regum Britannie of Geoffrey of Monmouth I: Bern, Burgerbibliothek, MS. 568* (Cambridge, 1984), p. 1; Bell (ed.), *L'Estoire des Engleis by Geffrei Gaimar*, pp. 204–5. Shortly before the appearance of Geoffrey's work, William of Malmesbury dedicated his *Gesta Regum* to the Earl of Gloucester, whom he likewise acclaimed for his love of literature and patronage of the liberal arts (R. A. B. Mynors, R. M. Thomson, and M. Winterbottom (ed.), *William of Malmesbury, Gesta Regvm Anglorvm; The History of the English Kings: Volume I* (Oxford, 1998), pp. 10–12, 798).

21 J. S. Brewer, James F. Dimock, and George F. Warner (ed.), *Giraldi Cambrensis Opera* (London, 1861–91), vi, p. 202.

22 Bartina H. Wind (ed.), *Les Fragments du Tristan de Thomas* (Leiden, 1950), p. 143; William Roach, Robert H. Ivy, and Lucien Foulet (ed.), *The Continuations of the Old French Perceval of Chretien de Troyes* (Philadelphia, 1949–83), iv, pp. 539–40.

23 Cf. Pierre Gallais, 'Bleheri, la cour de Poitiers et la diffusion des récits arthuriens sur le continent', *Journal of the International Arthurian Society* (Berlin, 2014), ii, pp. 84–113.

24 *Bledgabred. Hic omnes cantores quos retro aetas habuerat et in modulis et in omnibus musicis instrumentis superabat ita ut deus ioculatorum diceretur* (Reeve and Wright (ed.), *Geoffrey of Monmouth: The History of the Kings of Britain*, p. 67). Cf. Faral, *La légende arthurienne*, ii, p. 142.

The name (which looks like a typical Galfridian mangling of a Welsh personal name)[25] and description are as apt to the famed poet and performer Breri, as they are to his alter ego, the celebrated Welsh wit Bledri ap Cydifor. It seems that Geoffrey impishly inserted the figure of *Bledgabred* into his *History*, under the guise of one of Britain's prehistoric kings. Equally, since he cannot have wished others to detect the frivolous intrusion, the entry was presumably intended for the private amusement of the Welsh prince.

Elsewhere in his *Historia*, Geoffrey includes a further shared joke. This time it is linked to one of the high points of his drama: the conception and birth of Merlin. In Geoffrey's source for the episode, the *Historia Brittonum* of Nennius, the child is discovered at a place called the Plain of Elleti (*campus Elleti*). He explains to Vortigern's emissaries that he has no idea how he came to be conceived, since his mother was a virgin. Geoffrey elaborates this story considerably. According to his adaptation, the boy's mother was daughter to the king of Dyfed, and 'lived in St Peter's Church among the nuns of that city' (*Kaermerdin*). Brought with her son before Vortigern, she explains that she had never cohabited with a man, but was visited at night by what appeared to be a beautiful youth, who subjected her to passionate embraces leading swiftly to the ultimate intimacy. Maugantius (evidently one of the king's druids) explained that the nocturnal visitant was almost certainly an incubus.[26]

The seduction is described with humour, conveying the impression that it afforded the author as much titillating pleasure as we may presume it did his readers. What is striking about this episode in Geoffrey's *Historia* is the particular nature of its setting in an obscure location, which he went out of his way to identify. It is hard not to believe that the intent was mischievous when he decided to relocate the mother of Merlin's erotic encounter to the church of Carmarthen. For in Geoffrey's day St Peter's Church had but recently been built, as anyone with local knowledge must have been aware.[27]

These unusually suggestive details suggest that Geoffrey was familiar with a contemporary scandal, which he wickedly inserted into his book.[28] In the same way, among Merlin's prophecies of the rise and fall of dynasties, Geoffrey introduced reference to a crime of local interest perpetrated in Cornwall during his youth. Oliver Padel has skilfully reconstructed the

---

25   Presumably it was their inability to recognize *Bledgabred* as a Welsh personal name that led mediæval Welsh translators to replace it with the familiar Middle Welsh *Blegywryt* (Henry Lewis (ed.), *Brut Dingestow* (Cardiff, 1942), pp. 43–44; John Rhŷs and J. Gwenogvryn Evans (ed.), *The Text of the Bruts from the Red Book of Hergest* (Oxford, 1890), p. 82; John Jay Parry (ed.), *Brut y Brenhinedd: Cotton Cleopatra Version* (Cambridge, Mass., 1937), p. 63; J. G. Evans, 'Pedigrees from Jesus College MS. 20', *Y Cymmrodor* (1887), viii, p. 90; P. C. Bartrum (ed.), *Early Welsh Genealogical Texts* (Cardiff, 1966), pp. 109, 121). 'On peut se demander si Gaufrei n'a pas confondu deux personnages portant le même nom ou donné à un personnage relativement moderne des traits légendaires … La remarque de Giraldus à propos de son Bledhericus (qui paulo tempora nostra praevenit) conviendrait parfaitement à ce personnage' (J. Loth, *Contributions à l'Étude des Romans de la Table Ronde* (Paris, 1912), pp. 36–37). Cf. Phillimore's discussion in Henry Owen (ed.), *The Description of Pembrokeshire, by George Owen of Henllys, Lord of Kemes* (London, 1892–1936), iii, pp. 213–14.

26   Reeve and Wright (ed.), *Geoffrey of Monmouth: The History of the Kings of Britain*, p. 139. For Tatlock, Geoffrey's naming of the boy who identifies Merlin at Carmarthen as *Dinabutius*, together with Vortigern's mysterious informant *Maugantius* (= *Maucann*) – neither of whom features in the *Historia Brittonum* – 'suggests that he found these two rare names in a source' (J. S. P. Tatlock, *The Legendary History of Britain: Geoffrey of Monmouth's Historia Regum Britanniae and its Early Vernacular Versions* (Berkeley and Los Angeles, 1950), p. 177). The point seems worth consideration. The alternative possibility is that they were Welsh contemporaries known to Geoffrey.

27   Ibid. pp. 67–68.

28   'Nothing is needed to explain Merlin's birth except Nennius *and familiar anecdote, serious or (I fear) roguish* [italics inserted]' (ibid., pp. 173–74). A perceptive guess!

circumstances of this incident, which for reasons no longer apparent was evidently of personal concern to Geoffrey.[29]

Geoffrey's intent becomes clearer still in view of the fact that, at the time he wrote, Bledri ap Cydifor was closely connected with Carmarthen. In 1129–30 he bestowed four carucates of land on Carmarthen Priory. Given his direct association with the church at Carmarthen (it belonged to the priory of which he was benefactor), it is surely likely that the lascivious tale of a virgin violated by a demon in the town church was intended for Bledri's delectation.

In his narrative, Geoffrey added that the prophetic boy's mother was daughter to the king of Dyfed, while Bledri's father Cydifor is described by Welsh chroniclers as 'the man who had been lord over all Dyfed'. As though this were not enough, Cydifor's sister Ellylw bore an illegitimate son to Cadwgan ap Bleddyn, a notorious Don Juan of the day.[30] All this so closely parallels the details of Geoffrey's manifestly tongue-in-cheek account of the birth of a bastard son to the daughter of a king of Dyfed, as to provide a subsidiary explanation for his relocation of Merlin's conception from Nennius's obscure *campus Elleti* to Bledri's favoured town of Carmarthen, *Kaermerdin*.[31] It may also account for Geoffrey's substitution of the name *Myrddin* for the *Ambrosius* of the *Historia Brittonum*.

Bledri's personal accomplishments as raconteur and wit are sufficiently attested. In addition, his birth and upbringing afforded him exceptional access to the ancient lore of his country. He was proud heir to the ancient dynasty of Dyfed, and although extant royal pedigrees of the kingdom appear truncated, there is no compelling reason to doubt his descent from the fifth-century king Tryffin, in whose reign St David was born.[32]

The chief seat of Bledri's father Cydifor lay in the hundred (*cantref*) of Emlyn.[33] The *cantref* is washed on its northern side by the broad sweep of the river Teifi, which at Cenarth races in noisy turbulence down a succession of impressive falls. Here quantities of salmon make their way upstream during their 'running' between spring and autumn. To this day, local fishermen pursue their prey in coracles made from withies framed with untanned leather. It must surely have been here, beside his ancestral home, that Bledri coined his famous jest about the coracle fishers. There are huntsmen, he would say, who bear their horses upon their shoulders, until their quarry comes in view. Then they mount their steeds, and, after catching their prey, lift their mounts upon their shoulders once again, and carry them home.

Bledri's father Cydifor died in 1091, when his sons were old enough to conduct negotiations with a neighbouring prince to ensure the security of their inheritance. As Constance Bullock-Davies suggested:

---

29 O. J. Padel, 'Geoffrey of Monmouth and Cornwall', *Cambridge Medieval Celtic Studies* (Cambridge, 1984), viii, pp. 20–27.

30 *Morgant ap kad'. oellyl o verch gediuor apgollwyn. Y gwr a vv bēndeuic ar holl dyued* (Jones, *Brut y Tywysogion: Peniarth MS. 20*, p. 75).

31 Cf. my paper 'Geoffrey of Monmouth and the Merlin Legend', in Elizabeth Archibald and David F. Johnson (ed.), *Arthurian Literature XXV* (Cambridge, 2008), pp. 17–20.

32 *Rikart ap Mredudd ap Rrydderch ap Bletri ap Kedifor ap Gollwyn ap Gwyn ap Rrydderch ap Elgan wefl hwch ap Kynan ap Arthavad ap Iop ap Dei ap Llywri ap Kynan kylched ap Tryffin varvoc ap Ywain vraisc ap Kyndeyrn vendigaid* (Bartrum (ed.), *Early Welsh Genealogical Texts*, p. 106. Cf. J. Gwenogvryn Evans, *Report on Manuscripts in the Welsh Language* (London, 1898–1902), i, p. 826; A. O. H. Jarman (ed.), *Ymddiddan Myrddin a Thaliesin (O Lyfr Du Caerfyrddin)* (Cardiff, 1951), pp. 27–29.

33 'It is a hilly baren country and nothing considerable in it but the tradition of Cadifor vawr sometime prince of Difot to have lived here; we cannot discover so much as the ruines of any buildings here ...' (Rupert H. Morris (ed.), *Parochialia: Being a Summary of Answers to 'Parochial Queries in Order to a Geographical Dictionary, etc., of Wales' Issued by Edward Lhwyd* (London, 1909–11), iii, pp. 76, 79).

If this same young man returned home [from his stay at the court of Poitiers] before 1116 a fluent French speaker, who would be better calculated to favour the French 'invader' in Carmarthen and better qualified to act as that invader's interpreter? Again, what better place could there have been for the early transmission of Celtic story into French than the hall of Bledhericus in Dyfed, where he could, when he so desired, act as his own *cyfarwydd* and precise translator for the entertainment or convenience of his neighbours and friends, whose minstrels, we may be sure, would have enjoyed his hospitality?[34]

It is further likely that his repertoire of legendary tales and poems owed much to his royal ancestry and patrimony. Welsh national obsession with ancestry remained a byword over the centuries,[35] and doubtless Bledri's court bards and storytellers had enthused him from earliest childhood with the ancient lore of the region, over which his ancestors had ruled with distinction since Roman times.

The *cantref* in which his home was located was particularly rich in exotic legends, originating in Brittonic mythology. It was at Glyn Cuch in Emlyn that Pryderi son of Pwyll, lord of the Otherworld realm of Annwfn, guarded the swine of his foster-father Pendaran Dyfed. He was known as one of the Three Powerful Swineherds of the Island of Britain, 'because no one was able to deceive or compel him'. The triads in which this record appears evidently refer to a tale no longer extant.[36] A fuller account of the story of Pwyll and Pryderi, to which these lost tales clearly bore close connexion, is contained in the First Branch of the *Mabinogi*. At the outset of the story, Pwyll, Lord of Dyfed, set out from his court at Arberth to hunt at Glyn Cuch. On his way he stayed a night at Pen Llwyn Diarwya. Next morning he rode to Glyn Cuch, where he came upon a pack of parti-coloured hounds, whose owner proves to be Arawn, King of Annwfn.[37] Glyn Cuch lies in the *cantref* of Emlyn, as presumably must also Pen Llwyn Diarwya.[38] The obscurity of the latter place name, together with the gratuitous nature of its introduction into the tale, suggests close association of the literary tradition with the locality. At some point the legend of Pwyll and Pryderi had become located in the *cantref* of Emlyn.

I have argued elsewhere that the Four Branches were compiled in Dyfed, during the second decade of the eleventh century.[39] In addition, I suggested that they could have been preserved in the unique library (*llyfrgell*) at Tenby on the south coast, the principal stronghold of Dyfed. The library is described as housing a work or works known as 'The Writings of Britain' (*Ysgrifen Prydein*): an apt enough title for the subject matter of the tales, although this conjecture is more doubtful.[40]

---

34   Bullock-Davies, *Professional Interpreters and the Matter of Britain*, p. 12.

35   J. S. Brewer, James F. Dimock, and George F. Warner (ed.), *Giraldi Cambrensis Opera* (London, 1861–91), vi, p. 200. Cf. Francis Jones, 'An Approach to Welsh Genealogy', *The Transactions of the Honourable Society of Cymmrodorion: Session 1948* (London, 1948), pp. 303–466.

36   Egerton G. B. Phillimore, 'A Fragment from Hengwrt MS. No. 202', *Y Cymmrodor* (1887), vii, p. 131.

37   R. L. Thomson (ed.), *Pwyll Pendeuic Dyuet: The First of the Four Branches of the Mabinogi edited from the White Book of Rhydderch with variants from the Red Book of Hergest* (Dublin, 1957), pp. 1–2.

38   'Penn Llwyn Diarwa (hitherto unlocated) seems to be the fort (SN 2443) above modern Llwynduris' (Andrew Breeze, *The Origins of the Four Branches of the Mabinogi* (Leominster, 2009), pp. 91, 101).

39   Nikolai Tolstoy, *The Oldest British Prose Literature: The Compilation of the Four Branches of the Mabinogi* (Lampeter, 2009).

40   Ibid., pp. 495–543. Thomas Charles-Edwards suggests of *ysgrifen*: 'It may refer to a letter or a charter. The second is the more likely here.' This is on the grounds that '*Ysgrifen* is from Latin *scribendum*, 'what should be written', just as *llên* is from Latin *legendum*, 'what should be read'' (*Wales and the Britons 350–1064* (Oxford, 2013), p. 665). On the other hand, loanwords cannot necessarily be taken

If the Four Branches were composed a century before the time of Bledri, Cydifor ap Gollwyn and his sons must surely have been familiar with them at the end of the same century. In any case, the heirs of the ancient dynasty of Dyfed will have been acquainted with an extensive oral and literary tradition (*hanes, ystyr*), now surviving only in lamentably shattered fragments. Bledri ap Cydifor was not only heir to the royal house of Dyfed, but celebrated at home and abroad as a fount of knowledge relating to the Matter of Britain. In tales and poems chanted or recited before their kings, the household bards of Dyfed must regularly have extolled early ancestors of their dynasty, whose heroic deeds their descendants were invited to emulate.[41]

Plainly, far richer traditions of the ancient monarchy of Dyfed were known to Bledri than have survived the passage of centuries since. He could well have read or heard a version of the story known now by the title *Pwyll Pendeuic Dyuet*. In addition there were related legends now lost. An allusion to one such is preserved in the early poem 'The Spoils of Annwfn' (*Preiddeu Annwfn*), contained in the Book of Taliesin: 'Gwair's prison in Caer Sidi was in order / Throughout the course of the story concerning Pwyll and Pryderi.'[42] Although the allusion to 'Pwyll and Pryderi' suggests a story covering similar matter to that contained in the First Branch of the *Mabinogi*, nothing in the latter overtly corresponds to 'Gwair's prison in Caer Sidi'.

Numerous sagas and poems were undoubtedly recounted at the royal court of Dyfed throughout the early Middle Ages, treating of the heroic past of the dynasty, in which the feats of particular rulers (above all, the euhemerized divinity Pwyll) will have been singled out for glorification. In particular, the two centuries following the withdrawal of Roman rule were traditionally regarded as the heroic age of the Britons of the West and North. In Dyfed, exploits of the kingdom's fifth- and sixth-century rulers such as Aergol, Elgan, and Erbin were extolled in verse composed by court bards half a millennium later. Passing allusions found in extant bardic works imply vastly greater knowledge of heroic and legendary figures of the country's past than has survived the passing of centuries since.[43]

Pwyll and his son Pryderi are treated in the tale of *Pwyll Pendeuic Dyuet* as historical figures, whose exploits in early times had established the bounds of their kingdom. In consequence, an early version of *Pwyll* might have been regarded by the princes and nobles of Dyfed as effectively the foundation charter of the realm.[44] It is further likely that emphasis in *Pwyll* on the *cantref* of Emlyn and its immediate neighbourhood arose from the legend's recitation over centuries at the court of princes who regarded themselves as heirs of Pwyll and Pryderi. Apart from these, the only places in Dyfed located outside this marginal region in the story are *Presseleu* (whose mountain dominates the skyline south of Emlyn) and *Arberth* (today Narberth).

Of these, it is suggested that Arberth also lay in the vicinity of Emlyn. 'Gorsedd Arberth is the prominent mound of Banc-y-Warren, two miles east of Cardigan; nearby Nant Arberth is still

---

to reflect too nicely the semantics of their parent language, and the customary rendering 'writing', 'document', etc., may in this instance be preferable (cf. *Geiriadur Prifysgol Cymru: A Dictionary of the Welsh Language* (Cardiff, 1950–2002), p. 3844; Alexander Falileyev, *Etymological Glossary of Old Welsh* (Tübingen, 2000), p. 141).

41   A. O. H. Jarman (ed.), *Llyfr Du Caerfyrddin gyda Rhagymadrodd Nodiadau Testunol a Geirfa* (Cardiff, 1982) p. 1; Gwenogvryn Evans (ed.), *Facsimile & Text of the Book of Taliesin*, p. 42.

42   Ibid., p. 54.

43   Jarman (ed.), *Ymddiddan Myrddin a Thaliesin*, pp. 17–40.

44   Tolstoy, *The Oldest British Prose Literature*, p. 539.

marked on Ordnance Survey maps,' writes Andrew Breeze. However, although the proximity of Nant Arberth to Glyn Cuch is striking, Sioned Davies notes that 'this does not fit with the geographical details given in the tale'.[45] At the outset of *Pwyll*, Arberth is stated to lie a day's ride from Pen Llwyn Diarwa. Furthermore, an inscribed stone marking the burial place of Voteporix, a powerful sixth-century prince of Dyfed, was erected close to Narberth,[46] indicating association of the dynasty with Arberth.

Whether it be coincidence that a Nant Arberth lay so close to Pen Llwyn Diarwa and Glyn Cuch, or the name came to be applied to the valley in consequence of the story's becoming located in its vicinity, cannot now be known. Either way, it could have influenced the traditional association of Pwyll with the district. Originally, however, the story bears unmistakable indications of its origin in Brittonic mythology. It has long been remarked that the combat between Arawn and Hafgan at a ford on the river Cuch, which marks the frontier between Dyfed and Carmarthen,[47] must originally have taken place on the shadowy divide between this world and the Otherworld realm of Annwfn.[48]

The location of Emlyn as scene of Pwyll's encounters with the kings of the Otherworld probably arose from its status as a principal seat of the rulers of Dyfed. How long this had been the case is unknown, but it was long enough for the setting of the story to have become firmly established in the locality by the time the Four Branches came to be composed at the beginning of the eleventh century. In addition, the Fourth Branch (*Math uab Mathonwy*) identifies nearby Rhuddlan Teifi as a principal seat of Pryderi, legendary founder of Dyfed.[49]

In *Pwyll* and *Manawydan* Arberth features as 'the chief court of Dyfed'. However, it is unlikely that this was ever the case in reality. As W. J. Gruffydd pointed out,

> there is no historical justification for making Arberth the 'chief court' as it is named in *Pwyll*, since it was never the 'chief court' even of the Cantrev of Penfro, much less of the Kingdom of Dyved.[50]

In the *Mabinogi* the *gorsedd* (mound) of Arberth provides a setting for encounters with the supernatural,[51] suggesting that it was a sacral rather than political centre of Dyfed. This further accords with the unmistakably mythical nature of events in *Pwyll*.

---

45   Breeze, *The Origins of the Four Branches of the Mabinogi*, pp. 90–91, 101; Sioned Davies (tr.), *The Mabinogion* (Oxford, 2007), p. 230.

46   R. A. S. Macalister, *Corpus Inscriptionum Insularum Celticarum* (Dublin, 1945–49), i, pp. 342–43; V. E. Nash-Williams, *The Early Christian Monuments of Wales* (Cardiff, 1950), pp. 107, 108. It has been suggested that the VOTEPORIX of the inscription is not the Demetian tyrant *Vortiporius* denounced by Gildas, but 'another member of the same dynasty' (Charles-Edwards, *Wales and the Britons*, p. 175). However, this does not materially affect the present issue.

47   Henry Owen (ed.), *The Description of Pembrokeshire, by George Owen of Henllys, Lord of Kemes* (London, 1892–1936), p. 5.

48   Alwyn Rees and Brinley Rees, *Celtic Heritage: Ancient Tradition in Ireland and Wales* (London, 1961), pp. 178–79. 'It would be right probably to identify them [*Cwn Annwfn* = Hounds of Hades] in the first instance with the pack which Arawn, king of Annwn, is found hunting by Pwyll, king of Dyfed, when the latter happens to meet him in Glyn Cuch in his own realm' (John Rhŷs, *Celtic Folklore: Welsh and Manx* (Oxford, 1901), p. 216). Their combat provides an instance of 'the common Celtic motif of the hero answering a call to aid one party against another in the internal strife of the otherworld' (Proinsias Mac Cana, 'Conservation and Innovation in Early Celtic Literature', *Études Celtiques* (Paris, 1972), viii, p. 78).

49   Ian Hughes (ed.), *Math Uab Mathonwy: Pedwaredd Gainc y Mabinogi* (Aberystwyth, 2000), p. 2.

50   W. J. Gruffydd, *Rhiannon: An Inquiry into the Origins of the First and Third Branches of the Mabinogi* (Cardiff, 1953), p. 18.

51   Thomson (ed.), *Pwyll Pendeuic Dyuet*, pp. 1, 7, 18; Ian Hughes (ed.), *Manawydan Uab Llyr: Trydedd Gainc y Mabinogi* (Cardiff, 2007), pp. 1, 2, 7, 8.

Royal records of early Dyfed

There are indications that written records were preserved at the court of Dyfed from an early date. They could well have come into existence under the Roman occupation. In the late tenth century the powerful Welsh king Owain ap Hywel Dda caused a collection of Welsh royal pedigrees to be assembled. Prominent among these was the dynasty of Dyfed, from whom Owain was descended in the female line, and to whose inheritance he laid claim on grounds of his maternal descent from the country's ancient royal family. The royal pedigree is traced back to what there is reason to believe were authentic rulers living in the fifth and sixth centuries AD.

Their predecessors are represented by a curious mishmash of assorted names, cobbled together at some stage in order to create the primary section of the royal pedigree. This reads as follows:

> *Clotri . map . Gloitguin . map . Nimet . map . dimet . map . Maxim gulecic . map . Protec . map . Protector . map Ebiud . map . Eliud . map . Stater . map . Pincr misser . map . Constans . map . Constantini magni . map . Constantii et helen . luic dauc . que de brittannia exiuit ad crucem xp'I querendam usque ad ierusalem . et inde attulit secum usque adconstantinopolin . et est ibi usque inhodiernum diem.*
>
> [Clodri ap Clydwyn ... and Elen Luyddog, who went out of Britain to search for the cross of Christ as far as Jerusalem, and from there she brought it with her to Constantinople. And it is there to this day.][52]

While the first two names in this list are probably those of historical kings of Dyfed,[53] the remainder manifestly were not. *Maxim Guletic* is Magnus Maximus, a senior Roman military officer, who in AD 383 usurped imperial power in Britain and extended his rule over the Western Roman Empire until his deposition and execution in 388. There is reason to believe that he established client kingdoms in the West of Britain as a protection against barbarian invasions from across the sea, before his departure for the Continent in 385. Although Maximus cannot in reality have been an ancestor of the Dyfed dynasty, his appearance in the pedigree may well reflect an historical connexion.

While the Roman emperors Constantius I (305–6), Constantine the Great (306–37), and Constantius II (337–61), whose names bring up the beginning of the pedigree, cannot have had anything directly to do with the dynasty of Dyfed, each had associations with Britain and could have been inserted into the pedigree at an early date. The names of the three Roman emperors were presumably added to provide appropriately illustrious 'ancestors' for the Roman Maximus. The legend of Helena's discovery of the True Cross is first recorded in the West in AD 395,[54] and the allusion most likely represents a further gloss on the pedigree.

Of the remaining names in the cluster, *protector* denoted a senior Roman military and civil rank. Applicable to distinct contexts, it was used *inter alia* as a title bestowed on barbarian

---

52   *Y Cymmrodor*, ix, pp. 171–72.

53   It has been suggested that Clotri (<*Clotriga*) was a woman (K. D. Pringle, 'The Kings of Demetia', *The Transactions of the Honourable Society of Cymmrodorion: Session 1970* (London, 1971), pp. 71, 72, 75; David Thornton, *Kings, Chronologies, and Genealogies: Studies in the Political History of Early Medieval Ireland and Wales* (Oxford, 2003), p. 143). In fact there can be no doubt that the name is masculine (Patrick Sims-Williams, *The Celtic Inscriptions of Britain: Phonology and Chronology, c. 400–1200* (Oxford, 2003), pp. 32, 147).

54   Jan Willem Drijvers, *Helena Augusta: The Mother of Constantine the Great and the Legend of Her Finding of the True Cross* (Leiden, 1992), pp. 79–93.

chiefs assigned important responsibility on the frontiers. In the winter of 580–81, for example, elaborate arrangements for a treaty negotiation between Roman and Persian ambassadors on the Eastern frontier were entrusted to an officer holding the rank of 'protector of the borders'.[55] It has been seen that a princely Voteporix of Dyfed is described as *protector* on his memorial stone near Arberth, and it seems that the early rulers of Dyfed assumed on an hereditary basis the high Roman rank accorded their predecessor.[56] This reflects the continuing prestige associated with Roman institutions, long after the Empire in the West had collapsed.

Many years ago I suggested that the earliest 'generations' in the Dyfed royal pedigree originated in a brief prose passage, such as are found inserted elsewhere in the Harleian and related genealogies. A compiler at some stage converted this narrative passage into a fragment of the pedigree, by extracting key proper nouns and inserting the word *map*, 'son (of)', between them.[57]

A similar example of such tinkering occurs in another genealogy from the same collection. There a scribe had ineptly inserted *map* at the beginnings of lines, in the course of a similarly creative attempt at asserting a dynasty's fanciful claim to Roman Imperial ancestry. Later, an observant scribe made these telling deletions:

> *map Constantini*
> *magni*
> *map Constantini*
> *map Galerii*
> *map Diocletiani qui per*
> *secutus est xp'ia*
> *nos toto mundo.*[58]

Clearly an earlier compiler or transcriber mistook Latin words for names in the succession of generations. In this case a better-informed editor in due course deleted the intrusive *map*s.

Reverting to the Harleian pedigree of the kings of Dyfed, *Protec* must be a doublet of *Protector*, and may be dismissed accordingly. Nothing is known of *Ebiud* and *Eliud* (assuming them to be distinct names), who may consequently also be omitted from discussion. *Stater map Pincr misser* is intriguing. Given the Romano-British context, we are probably justified in accepting (with minor modifications) suggestions that these words (which correspond to nothing in Welsh) represent Roman titles of rank.[59] *Stater* suggests Latin *stator*, the representative of a provincial governor.[60] Again, *pincr* is surely Latin *pincerna*, 'butler, cup-bearer', with *missr* possibly an abbreviation of *minister*, 'A servant, assistant (esp.

55   μεθορίων προτίκτωρ (R. C. Blockley (ed.), *The History of Menander the Guardsman* (Liverpool, 1985), p. 228). For detailed discussions of the post and rank of *protector*, cf. A. H. M. Jones, *The Later Roman Empire 284–602: A Social Economic and Administrative Survey* (Oxford, 1964), pp. 636–40; John Matthews, *The Roman Empire of Ammianus* (London, 1989), pp. 74–79.

56   Nora K. Chadwick, *Early Brittany* (Cardiff, 1969), p. 185.

57   Nikolai Tolstoy, 'Early British History and Chronology', *The Transactions of the Honourable Society of Cymmrodorion: Session 1964*, pp. 261–62.

58   *Y Cymmrodor*, ix, p. 176. This illustrates the importance of using Phillimore's diplomatic edition of the Harleian annals and genealogies, the erasures being ignored in all other editions. In generation 10 of the pedigrees we find *Cincar braut . map. Bran hen.* Since *braut* means 'brother', the subsequent *map* should likewise be omitted (ibid., p. 174).

59   E. Williams B. Nicholson, 'The Dynasty of Cunedag and the "Harleian Genealogies"', *Y Cymmrodor* (London, 1908), xxi, pp. 80–82; Edmund McClure, *British Place-Names in their Historical Setting* (London, 1910), p. 57.

60   P. G. W. Glare (ed.), *Oxford Latin Dictionary* (Oxford, 1968–82), p. 1815.

one who waits at table)'.[61] Such a post could be one of considerable distinction in the Roman Empire, frequently affording opportunity for enjoyment of close relations with an influential employer. During the lifetime of Maximus, an officer named Hyperechius, a man of good family and education holding the post of *pincerna*, was promoted by the usurper Procopius to high military rank.[62]

Although any attempt to link these terms to historical persons or events must inevitably remain conjectural, it is intriguing to find the panegyrist Pacatus, addressing Maximus's conqueror Theodosius in 388, deriding the fallen usurper as having in former days fulfilled the rôle of waiter in the Emperor's household.[63] The denigration presumably reflects some reality arising from Maximus's close (they shared common Spanish origin, and may have been related)[64] connexion with the Emperor's distinguished father Theodosius the Elder, who with Maximus at his side liberated Britain from barbarian occupation in 368–369.

All this suggests that the genealogy of the kings of Dyfed was originally prefaced by a brief historical account of its establishment, which became clumsily misconstrued as the opening section of the royal pedigree. This record bears every appearance of archaic provenance. Indeed, it is not unlikely that the original version was contemporary with the circumstances which it records.

Pedigrees of the Irish Déisi include an account of a branch of their people who crossed the sea and ruled over Dyfed. The dynasty is described as descending from

Eochaid, son of Artchorp, [who] went over sea with his descendants into the territory of *Demed* [Dyfed], and it is there that his sons and grandsons died. And from them is the race of Crimthann over there, of whom is *Tualador mac Rígin maic Catacuind maic Caittien maic Clotenn maic Næe maic Artuir maic Retheoir maic Congair maic Gartbuir maic Alchoil maic Trestin maic Aeda Brosc maic Corath maic Echach Almuir maic Arttchuirp.*[65]

Setting aside a degree of corruption arising from transliteration of foreign names, these dynasts correspond closely to those found in the Welsh pedigree of the kings of Dyfed. That is, until they arrive at *Guortiper map Aircol map Triphun*, the *Gartbuir maic Alchoil maic Trestin* of the Irish pedigrees. Above that they diverge entirely. In the Welsh version Triphun succeeds his 'father'

---

61   Ibid., pp. 1111, 2283; R. E. Latham and D. R. Howlett (ed.), *Dictionary of Medieval Latin from British Sources* (London, 1975–2013), p. 2283. The abbreviation *missr* < *minister* could reflect a contraction, such as that found in *oma* < *omnia* (W. M. Lindsay, *Early Welsh Script* (Oxford, 1912), p. 42).

62   Édouard Galletier, Jacques Fontaine, Guy Sabbah, Marie-Anne Marié, and Laurent Angliviel de la Beaumelle (ed.), *Ammien Marcellin: Histoire* (Paris, 1978–99), v, p. 87; A. H. M. Jones, J. R. Martindale, and J. Morris, *The Prosopography of the Later Roman Empire* (Cambridge, 1971–92), i, pp. 449–50. Comparison may be made with the great Irish family of Butler, which acquired its surname from Prince John's grant of the high office of Chief Butler (*pincerna*) of Ireland to Theobald Fitz Walter in 1192 (G. E.C[ockayne]. *et al.* (ed.), *The Complete Peerage: or a History of the House of Lords and all its Members from the Earliest Times* (London, 1910–98), ii, pp. 447, 610; A. J. Otway-Ruthven, *A History of Medieval Ireland* (London, 1968), p. 67.

63   *Ille quondam domus tuae neglegentissimus uernula mensularumque seruilium statarius lixa* (Édouard Galletier (ed.), *Panégyriques latins* (Paris, 1949–52), iii, p. 97).

64   Maximus's relationship to the House of Theodosius is discussed by T. S. Mommaerts and D. H. Kelley, 'The Anicii of Gaul and Rome', in John Drinkwater and Hugh Elton (ed.), *Fifth-Century Gaul: a crisis of identity?* (Cambridge, 1992), pp. 118–19; cf. pp. 112–13.

65   Kuno Meyer, 'The Expulsion of the Dessi', *Y Cymmrodor* (1901), xiv, p. 112;. idem, 'The Expulsion of the Déssi', *Ériu* (1907), iii, p. 136; Séamus Pender, 'Two Unpublished Versions of The Expulsion of the Déssi', in idem (ed.), *Féilscríbhinn Torna* (Cork, 1947), pp. 213, 217. Cf. Tomás Ó Cathasaigh, 'The Déisi and Dyfed', *Éigse: A Journal of Irish Studies* (Naas, 1984), xx, pp. 1–33.

Clotri map Clydwyn and the Roman dynasts discussed above, while the Irish version makes Triphun (*Trestin*) son of Corath, son of Eochaid *Allmuir* ('from across the sea').

While this is not the place for a full consideration of the evidence for Irish settlement and conquest in Dyfed in the late Roman period, it is revealing to note the extent to which the names in the pedigrees correspond to the historical situation. The father and grandfather of Guortiper (who lived in the first half of the sixth century) bear names of Latin origin: *Aircol* (< *Agrícóla*) and *Triphun* (< *tribunus*),[66] as might be expected of princes reigning in the late Roman and immediate post-Roman era. Again, in the Irish version Triphun is grandson of the original settler Eochaid, whose *floruit* (reckoning thirty years to a generation) corresponds closely to that of Maximus's period of rule in Britain.

Clearly, the Irish account is to be preferred as an historical record. It corresponds to the circumstances of the Irish settlement in Dyfed, while the equivalent section of the British version is a merely artificial concoction. A likely motive for the fictitious substitution is manifest. As time went by, it became desirable to conceal the fact that the dynasty was descended from barbarian invaders. Furthermore, its princes were now provided with an illustrious ancestor in the person of the great Maximus. Whoever concocted this mélange was not unskilled. Rather than simply invent a suitable ancestry for his master's royal line, he adapted a pre-existing prefatory historical passage into a succession of ancestors of high Roman status.[67]

According to Welsh tradition, the Irish conqueror of South Wales was Clydwyn, the *Gloitguin* of the Harleian genealogy.[68] In light of these considerations, the original version of this prefatory section may be conjecturally reconstructed as follows:

Clotri map Gloitguin, *qui regnauit super* [**Nimet**] **Dimet**, *quem* **Maxim guletic** *fecit* **protector**,
Clodri ap Clydwyn, who ruled over Dyfed, whom Maximus appointed Protector.

Clodri, whose name corresponds equally to Old Irish and Old Welsh *Clutorix*,[69] could if of the former derivation have been the original settler of the dynasty in Britain. The obscurity of the accompanying allusions to the Roman titles *stator* and *pincerna* suggests concern with contemporary factors unlikely to have arisen at a later date.

All this hints at compilation and preservation of written historical records at the court of Dyfed as early as the fourth or fifth century AD. There is nothing inherently implausible in this. As Charles-Edwards has observed:

---

66   Cf. Henry Lewis, *Yr Elfen Ladin yn yr Iaith Gymraeg* (Cardiff, 1943), p. 19; Patrick Sims-Williams, *The Celtic Inscriptions of Britain: Phonology and Chronology, c. 400–1200* (Oxford, 2003), p. 91.

67   It is proposed that the descent from Maxen Gwledig was introduced to 'suit the political aspirations of Owain ap Hywel' (David E. Thornton, 'Orality, literacy and genealogy in early medieval Ireland and Wales', in Huw Pryce (ed.), *Literacy in Medieval Celtic Societies* (Cambridge, 1998), pp. 87–88). For the reasons given here, I am inclined to believe that Maxen was introduced as progenitor of the royal dynasty of Dyfed at a considerably earlier period.

68   *Clytguin. filius Brachan . qui inuasit totam terram Sudgwalliæ* (A.W. Wade-Evans, 'The Brychan Documents', *Y Cymmrodor* (1906), xix, p. 25); *Clytwyn* alias Clitguin *oresgynnaud deheubarth* (ibid., p. 29). *Gloitguin* in the Harleian genealogy is an error for *Cloitguin*, while *Maxim gulecic* should read *guletic* (*gwledig*). The ascription of Brychan as father of Clydwyn is a manifest invention. Brychan was regarded as a prototypical ancestor-figure in the Middle Ages (ibid., pp. 25-27, 29-30; J. S. Brewer, James F. Dimock, and George F. Warner (ed.), Giraldi Cambrensis Opera (London, 1861–91), vi, p. 31).

69   Cf. Damian McManus, *A Guide to Ogam* (Maynooth, 1991), p. 113; Jürgen Uhlich, *Die Morphologie der komponierten Personennamen des Altirischen* (Bonn, 1993), p. 204; Patrick Sims-Williams, *The Celtic Inscriptions of Britain: Phonology and Chronology, c. 400–1200* (Oxford, 2003), p. 147.

One of the most notable features of the [Harleian] genealogies is that three of the pedigrees are traced back to Roman emperors. Nennius contains the earliest version of the origin legend of the British, the story of Brutus … This origin legend was probably fabricated for good political reasons: to establish the kinship of the Britons and the Romans, and therefore, the political respectability of the native British ruling families … It is likely that its origins lie in the Romano-British period, for that is the time when the reasons for composing such a story would be most compelling.

Furthermore,

The whole body of evidence [relating to the Irish settlements in Wales], British and Irish, gives the impression of an old but muddled tradition, not propaganda newly devised on behalf of an intrusive dynasty.[70]

In the fifth century the kingdom of the Demetae probably continued largely pagan, and the earlier influx of a similarly pagan Irish population will have served to reinforce the authority of the druids. In the Life of St Samson, the Saint's grandparents (who lived in the latter part of the fifth century) are described as having been fosterfathers (*altores*) to the kings of their respective countries, Dyfed and Gwent.[71] This function was traditionally fulfilled by the druids. Thus, King Brychan of Brycheiniog was said to have been assigned in infancy to the tutelage of a prophet named Drychan, who was evidently a druid. In the story of *Math uab Mathonwy*, the infant Lleu, afterwards king of Gwynedd, is adopted and educated by the wizard Gwydion, a type of divine druid. In Ireland the daughters of King Loegaire mac Neill were fostered by two of his druids.[72] A druid (*magus*) Broichan at the court of the sixth-century pagan Pictish King Bruide is described as being his royal master's friend and fosterfather (*nutricius*).[73]

That the authority of the druids was accorded high prestige in South Wales at the close of the fifth century, and that they were associated with written literature, is further implicit in the title and function of the *librarius* consulted by Samson's parents before his birth (of whom more below).[74]

All in all, the evidence suggests that written records are likely to have been preserved by druids at the royal court of Dyfed at least throughout the late Roman and post-Roman period, until their functions came gradually to be absorbed into those of clerics and

---

70   *The Transactions of the Honourable Society of Cymmrodorion: Session 1970*, p. 290; Thomas Charles-Edwards, 'Language and Society among the Insular Celts', in Miranda J. Green (ed.), *The Celtic World* (London, 1995), p. 709.

71   Flobert (ed.), *La vie ancienne de saint Samson de Dol*, p. 146.

72   Hughes (ed.), *Math Uab Mathonwy*, p. 8; *Y Cymmrodor*, xix, p. 25; Alan Orr Anderson and Marjorie Ogilvie Anderson (ed.), *Adomnan's Life of Columba* (Edinburgh, 1961), p. 402; John Gwynn (ed.), *Liber Ardmachanus: The Book of Armagh, Edited with Introduction and Appendices* (Dublin, 1913), p. 22; Kathleen Mulchrone (ed.), *Bethu Phátraic: The Tripartite Life of Patrick* (Dublin, 1939), p. 63. 'Comme educateur du futur roi, il [Gwydion] est bien le digne héritier des druides' (Pierre-Yves Lambert, 'Magie et Pouvoir dans la Quatrième Branche du *Mabinogi*', *Studia Celtica* (1994), xxviii, p. 107).

73   Alan Orr Anderson and Marjorie Ogilvie Anderson (ed.), *Adomnan's Life of Columba* (Edinburgh, 1961), p. 402.   King Bruid's wizard Broichan corresponds in name, function, and his opposition to St Columba, to Fraechán, 'who made the druidic 'fence' for Diarmat at the battle of Cúil Dreimne' in 561 (Seán Mac Airt and Gearóid Mac Niocaill (ed.), *The Annals of Ulster (to A.D. 1131)* (Dublin, 1983), i, p. 80). Cf. Anderson and Anderson (ed.), Adomnan's Life of Columba, pp. 84–85.

74   'Le «copiste» est aussi «maître d'école» et même prêtre, I, 6 et Cap. 2; il rappelle surtout les anciens druides par ses dons divinatoires' (Flobert (ed.), *La vie ancienne de saint Samson de Dol*, p. 149).

bards.[75] The evident antiquity of the prefatory passage adapted to the genealogy of the kings of Dyfed suggests that druids could have been concerned *inter alia* with recording royal genealogies and compiling historical notices relating to the dynasty. These are activities specifically ascribed to the bards of his day by Giraldus Cambrensis.[76] Although he lived centuries after the period considered here, it is hard to overestimate how deeply conservative was the culture of the bards, heirs to the druids.

Given that the sacral property of the royal precinct on Preseli Mountain (of which more shortly) appears to have been known to the eleventh-century author of *Pwyll Pendeuic Dyuet*, traditions of the site could have been preserved in writing, following protracted prior oral transmission, from an early date. In the foregoing analysis of the prefatory passage to the Dyfed royal genealogy, one name remains unconsidered. This is the first element of the couplet *Nimet map Dimet*. Its explanation as a misspelt doublet of *Dimet* might appear plausible.[77] After all, *Protec/Protector* and *Ebiud/Eliud* are probably explicable on this account, so why not *Nimet* and *Dimet*? However, an obvious objection is posed by the fact that *nimet* is a real word. Welsh *nyfed* derives through Old Welsh *nimet* from British **nemetā*, 'sanctuary, consecrated precinct'.[78] In view of this, Thomas Charles-Edwards suggests that

> The personal name Nyfed perhaps echoes the Irish use of *nemed*, 'sacred' for a person of high status as well as for a sanctuary. Dyfed is the name of the people transmogrified into the name of a distant ancestor. Nyfed, therefore, was probably chosen simply to rhyme with Dyfed.[79]

This suggestion implicitly assumes that the early names in the Dyfed royal pedigree were adopted at random. However, given indications that they originated in a written record, whose principal names became converted over time into successive generations by the insertion of *map* between them, *nyfed* should perhaps be taken in its normal meaning, which features in British placenames, as well as in cognate Irish and Gaulish forms.[80] Moreover, since *Dyfed* is undoubtedly a topographical name, it seems not unreasonable to take the associated *Nyfed* for another, i.e. 'the *nyfed* (sacred enclosure) of Dyfed'.

The prefatory section of the Welsh versions of the pedigree of the kings of Dyfed appears to have been substituted for their embarrassing descent from a piratical Irish dynasty. Whatever

---

75   The interplay of orality and literacy in the contruction and preservation of early Welsh royal genealogies is discuussed by David Thornton in Pryce (ed.), Literacy in Medieval Celtic Societies, pp. 93–96.

76   *Bardi Kambrenses, et cantores, seu recitatores, genealogiam habent … in libris eorum antiquis et authenticis, sed tamen Kambrice scriptam* (Brewer, Dimock, and Warner (ed.), *Giraldi Cambrensis Opera*, vi, pp. 167–68). The allusion suggests bardic reverence for ancient manuscripts, not only for the information they preserved, but as precious artefacts in their own right.

77   *Y Cymmrodor*, xxi, p. 80.

78   Jackson, *Language and History in Early Britain*, p. 279.

79   Green (ed.), *The Celtic World*, p. 704.

80   A. S. Napier and W. H. Stevenson (ed.), *The Crawford Collection of Early Charters and Documents* (Oxford, 1895), pp. 58–60; W. J. Watson, *The History of the Celtic Place-Names of Scotland* (Edinburgh, 1926), pp. 244–45; Max Förster, *Der Flußname Themse und seine Sippe: Studien zur Anglisierung keltischer Eigennamen und zur Lautchronologie des Altbritischen* (Munich, 1941), pp. 30, 641; Xavier Delamarre, *Dictionnaire de la langue gauloise: Une approche linguistique du vieux-celtique continental* (Paris, 2001), pp. 197–98; Vendryes, Bachellery, and Lambert, *Lexique étymologique de l'irlandais ancien*, N-9; Ranko Matasović, *Etymological Dictionary of Proto-Celtic* (Leiden, 2009), p. 288.

the original formula, its purpose (particularly the claimed link with Maximus) was to graft the royal stock onto a tree of unimpeachable royal legitimacy.

In this context, mention of a sacred enclosure at the outset of a royal genealogy is particularly apposite. As Elizabeth FitzPatrick observes in her survey of mediæval Irish royal inaugurations:

> A recurrent theme running through the adoption of particular sites as inauguration places is the apparently inextricable link between legitimate right to kingship on the one hand and a direct association between the ancestry of the kingship candidate and his inauguration site on the other …
>
> The broad range of inauguration mounds reviewed here suggests that effecting a link between an appointed inauguration site and the eponymous ancestor of a tribal group, a legendary heroic figure or simply an 'ancient' sepulchral/ritual site was seen as imperative to the legitimacy of kingship.[81]

Most of these Irish sites are located on high hills possessing extensive views of the surrounding countryside. Although little is recorded of corresponding Welsh inauguration mounds, it is likely that their kings underwent rites similar to those observed by their Celtic cousins across the Irish Sea. Gildas asserted that fifth-century British kings were anointed 'not by God', but according to some unspecified barbarian procedure.[82]

In the late eleventh century the princes of Dyfed held court within sight of Preseli Mountain, which dominates the horizon south of Emlyn. Clearly, a far richer vein of tradition than that whose sparse strands survive today must have been preserved in the court-house (*llys*) of that peerless preserver and transmitter of the ancient legends of South Wales, Bledri ap Cydifor. Nor is conjecture excessively strained, if we picture the likelihood that royal rites of inauguration and wedding to the maiden sovereignty of the kingdom of Dyfed continued to be fulfilled by Cydifor, 'Prince of all Dyfed', and possibly also his son Bledri. Such, after all, was the practice of contemporary rulers in the sister-island lying within sight of Dyfed across St George's Channel.

It has been seen that Bledri was most likely an acquaintance and informant of Geoffrey of Monmouth. Could Geoffrey's confused account of the foundation of Stonehenge, which appears on independent grounds to derive from archaic tradition, have originated in part or whole with the prince-poet of Dyfed, who it cannot be doubted was profoundly conversant with the archaic lore of Britain? After all, it is unlikely that the author of *Cyfranc Lludd a Lleuelys* was unique among early mediæval *cyfarwyddiaid* in being familiar with traditional lore relating to the British *omphalos*.

Geoffrey's access to local traditions of Stonehenge

The French Arthurian scholar Edmond Faral suggested that Geoffrey could have drawn on local traditions of Stonehenge, which he then embellished with his customary imaginative detail.[83]

81 Elizabeth FitzPatrick, *Royal Inauguration in Gaelic Ireland c. 1100–1600* (Woodbridge, 2004), pp. 68, 97.

82 *Chronica Minora*, iii, p. 37. In contrast, the biblical Samuel was pronounced by God king of a legitimate kingdom (ibid., p. 49).

83 'Geoffroy, peut-être en utilisant certaines traditions locales, mais très certainement en y ajoutant beaucoup du sien, a développé l'histoire de ces vestiges étranges en une simple narration' (Faral, *La légende arthurienne*, ii, pp. 238–39).

Against this view, the American J. S. P. Tatlock scouted any possibility of such protracted survival:

> Modern semi-scientific conjecture as to the actual origin of Stonehenge has no bearing on Geoffrey's account, simply because there is no thinkable channel by which the prehistoric facts could have reached him.[84]

However, this contemptuous dismissal of the possibility of survival of archaic lore appears, as so often in Tatlock's work, excessively sceptical. In the first place, it is clear that an enormous body of oral lore circulated among the largely illiterate population of England in Geoffrey's day. A misleading impression is conveyed by the new humanist historiography of the twelfth century. The greatest historians of the reign of Henry I were at pains to eschew, or at any rate play down, marvellous, exotic, and supernatural factors, in their concern to establish the authentic structure of English history. Thus William of Malmesbury declined to cite 'wild tales' of the great King Arthur, who 'assuredly deserves to be the subject of reliable history rather than of false and visionary fable'. Instead he confined himself to a brief allusion to Arthur's victory at Badon Hill, cited from the *Historia Brittonum* of Nennius.[85]

Praiseworthy though this scholarly attitude is within its confines, what would we not now give to know something of those 'wild tales' and 'false and visionary fables' disdained by twelfth-century historians? While their reticence confers misleading impression of a dearth of legendary lore, there can be no doubt that much they ignored was of great antiquity. The poet Layamon, writing during or shortly after the time of Richard I, made tantalizing allusion to true and false tales recited by minstrels, mocked the plethora of incredible legends of Arthur current in England, and above all rejected 'lies' (folktales or lays) circulating among the 'Britons', i.e. the Welsh, Cornish, and Bretons.[86]

In Wales, knowledge of legends associated with topographical features featured high among the learning required of bards and storytellers, as the catalogues of *Mirabilia* in the *Historia Brittonum*, Stanzas of the Graves (*englynion y beddau*), and Welsh Triads attest in profusion.[87] While some of these traditions appear to be of a speculative character, others are undoubtedly of archaic origin. It will in due course be shown how prehistoric lore connected with the caves of Gower became absorbed into the legend of Saint Illtud, and extensive evidence attests to traditions of Arthur and his companions, often associated with particular geographical regions and natural features.[88] Geoffrey of Monmouth himself alludes to widespread circulation in his day of oral tales of Arthur and his royal predecessors, and it is clear that he was familiar with,

---

84 Tatlock, *The Legendary History of Britain*, p. 40.

85 Mynors, Thomson, and Winterbottom (ed.), *William of Malmesbury, Gesta Regvm Anglorvm*, i, p. 26.

86 G. L. Brook and R. F. Leslie (ed.), *Laȝamon: Brut* (Oxford, 1963–78), pp. 598–601.

87 C. E. Wright, *The Cultivation of Saga in Anglo-Saxon England* (Edinburgh, 1939), pp. 245–49; Ferdinand Lot (ed.), *Nennius et l'Historia Brittonum: Étude critique suivie d'une édition des diverses versions de ce texte* (Paris, 1934), pp. 106–14; Thomas Jones, 'The Black Book of Carmarthen "Stanzas of the Graves"', *The Proceedings of the British Academy* (London, 1967), liii, pp. 97–137; Rachel Bromwich, 'The Welsh Triads', in Roger Sherman Loomis (ed.), *Arthurian Literature in the Middle Ages: A Collaborative History* (Oxford, 1959), pp. 44–51.

88 Faral, *La légende arthurienne*, i, p. 226; Mynors, Thomson, and Winterbottom (ed.), *William of Malmesbury, Gesta Regvm Anglorvm*, i, pp. 26, 520; Antonia Gransden, *Historical Writing in England c. 550 to c. 1307* (London, 1974), p. 213.

and evidently enjoyed, a broad range of traditional lore – although, like his contemporary William of Malmesbury, he made only moderate use of it.[89]

Reference to 'wild tales' and 'false and visionary fables' of Arthur suggests traditions of the larger-than-life Arthur of recorded folklore, who dwelt on mountaintops and battled with giants. However, not all oral tradition was of such an extravagant nature, and it is significant that Geoffrey's sole direct allusion to pre-existing Arthurian lore constitutes his realistic account of Arthur's conflict with Modred, abductor of Queen *Ganhumara*, culminating in the death of the great king on the river Camlan in Cornwall. Geoffrey explains that he obtained his account from Archdeacon Walter:[90] an assertion there is no strong reason to disbelieve. Allusions to the same narrative, clearly independent of Geoffrey, are found in the Welsh triads and other early records. It is generally agreed that there existed early saga material covering the dramatic episode.[91] The point is not the extent to which the story is historical, but that Celtic Arthurian tradition in the early twelfth century included depictions of the hero as a legendary rather than mythical figure.

Geoffrey's account of the erection of Stonehenge provides another instance of his use of independent tradition. Thus, while his description of the Saxons' treacherous slaughter of the Britons is drawn primarily from the *Historia Brittonum*, it includes significant details absent from that source. The massacre of one party by another at a professedly amicable gathering is a widely recorded theme of popular legend – one, moreover, which is known to have been current among Saxons in the early Middle Ages.[92] That the motif commonly represents folklore rather than history is certain, but insufficient attention has been directed towards the consideration that led Geoffrey to locate it at Stonehenge. Although he was undoubtedly given to arbitrary geographical identifications, in this instance there is reason to believe he was not its originator.

The *Historia Brittonum* (which does not identify the site) states that three hundred British nobles perished in the massacre, a number probably reflecting the fact that three hundred represents the traditional number of warriors constituting an early British warband.[93] In Geoffrey's version the figure becomes 460, an oddly specific alteration. However, attention has been drawn to 'the coincidence, that the 460 noble British dead [buried at Stonehenge] neatly matched the 450 or so ancient burial barrows visible in the area round Stonehenge'.[94]

The correspondence is surely too close for coincidence. Geoffrey must have had *some* reason for substituting the figure 460 for the 300 he found in his source. The most likely explanation

---

89   Reeve and Wright (ed.), *Geoffrey of Monmouth: The History of the Kings of Britain*, p. 5.

90   Ibid., pp. 249–53.

91   'Even in the native tradition it would appear that the circumstances of Arthur's death, real or apparent, were the tragic consequences of plotting, dissension at court, and perhaps a nephew's betrayal. There may well have been a *chwedl* (saga) of Camlan ... which was ... an integral part of the Welsh legend of Arthur' (Brynley F. Roberts, 'Culhwch ac Olwen, the Triads, Saints' Lives', in Rachel Bromwich, A. O. H. Jarman, and Brynley F. Roberts (ed.), *The Arthur of the Welsh: The Arthurian Legend in Medieval Welsh Literature* (Cardiff, 1991), p. 81). Geoffrey's allusion to Arthur's removal to the (Otherworld) Isle of Avalon (*in insulam Auallonis*) drew on what was perhaps a distinct tradition of the great King's translation to an Otherworld realm.

92   H. Munro Chadwick, *The Origin of the English Nation* (Cambridge, 1907), p. 42. Cf. 'K811.1. Enemies invited to feast and killed' (Stith Thompson, *Motif-Index of Folk-Literature: A Classification of Narrative Elements in Folktales, Ballads, Myths, Fables, Mediaeval Romances, Exempla, Fabliaux, Jest-Books, and Local Legends* (Bloomington, Indiana, 1955–58), iv, p. 340).

93   Ifor Williams (ed.), *Canu Aneirin* (Cardiff, 1938), pp. liii–lviii.

94   Christopher Chippindale, *Stonehenge Complete* (London, 1983), p. 28.

is that the legendary massacre of the Britons had *already* become associated with Stonehenge, when it would be natural for the surrounding barrows to have been identified as graves of the slaughtered British nobles.

Geoffrey states that the bodies of these illustrious victims were interred in a cemetery (*cimiterium*) beside *mons Ambrii*, the name he accorded the site of Stonehenge.[95] With this may be compared the *cimiterium* supposedly built by St Cadog, at what appears to be the Navel of Britain. It was similarly designed as a place of interment for the bodies of the faithful of all Britain (*totius Britannię*). Lifris explained that this *cimiterium* somehow surrounded Cadog's monastery: *quo fidelium corpora circa templi ambitum sepelirentur*.[96]

A further telling detail added by Geoffrey to the account of the Saxon slaughter in the *Historia Brittonum* is the date of 1 May he assigns to the event. In the Celtic calendar the Calends of May represented a day of peril, when the survival of humanity was threatened by malignant Otherworld forces.[97] Further consideration will be given in due course to the mythological significance of the date in the context of the extermination of the British nobles.

Yet another allusion in Geoffrey's story suggests the existence of independent traditions of Stonehenge and its vicinity. In §§120–125 he describes how the British leader Aurelius, having destroyed the tyrant Vortigern in his Welsh fortress, marched his army to liberate Britain from Saxon oppression. Alarmed by his martial reputation, the invaders' chieftain Hengist withdrew his army to the desolate region in the North lying beyond the river Humber (*trans Hunbrun*), which had suffered devastation during successive invasions by Northern barbarians. There he fortified cities and towns, in preparation for resisting his adversary.

Meanwhile, Aurelius advanced on his track through ravaged countryside. Recovering his courage, Hengist assembled an array of his boldest followers, and prepared to ambush the Britons at a plain called *Maes Beli*. Detecting the trap, Aurelius advanced on the enemy. Before the battle began, Eldol of Gloucester, lone survivor of the massacre at Stonehenge, recounted to Aurelius his experience of that bloody day, in what appears a superfluous duplication of the account already provided.

A hard-fought conflict ensued, in which both sides fought with dogged bravery. Eventually, Hengist found his host giving way, and fled to 'the town of Caer Conan, which is now called Cunungeburg' (*oppidum Kaerconan, quod nunc Cunungeburg appellatur*). The Saxons turned before the walls of the town, where they prepared to make a last stand. A ferocious conflict ensued, in which Eldol performed feats of valour, culminating in the capture of Hengist. With the battle over, and the field won by Aurelius, Eldol avenged the barbarities inflicted by Hengist by cutting off his head. The chivalrous Aurelius then arranged for the body of his brutal adversary to be interred in an earthen mound 'according to pagan practice' (*iussit sepeliri eum et cumulum terrae super corpus pagano more*).[98]

95　Reeve and Wright (ed.), *Geoffrey of Monmouth: The History of the Kings of Britain*, pp. 171, 174.

96　Wade-Evans (ed.), *Vitae Sanctorum Britanniae et Genealogiae*, p. 46. This recalls the *ferta* of the pagan Irish, which is described as a royal burial site surrounded by a circular ditch (John Gwynn (ed.), *Liber Ardmachanus: The Book of Armagh, Edited with Introduction and Appendices* (Dublin, 1913), p. 24).

97　'The unseen world was particularly active on May Eve. The Good People of the Hills were at their revels and humans had to be careful not to disturb or offend them; by watchfulness, ceremony, prayer and charm, all care was taken to safeguard against their machinations, and against the evil magic of human ill-wishers' (Kevin Danaher, 'Irish Folk Tradition and the Celtic Calendar', in Robert O'Driscoll (ed.), *The Celtic Consciousness* (Toronto, 1981), p. 218). I am grateful to Mary O'Hara, the lovely Irish singer (cynosure of my distant days at TCD), for the gift of her presentation copy of this book.

98　Reeve and Wright (ed.), *Geoffrey of Monmouth: The History of the Kings of Britain*, pp. 163–69.

This narrative contains discrepancies suggesting that here, as elsewhere, Geoffrey incorporated earlier source material into his *Historia*. The Welsh name *Maes Beli* is unrecorded in north-east England, whose toponyms are overwhelmingly of Anglian and Scandinavian derivation.[99] In any case, the unanglicized form of the name suggests a Welsh literary source. Hengist's fortifying 'cities and towns' (*ciuitates et oppida*), somehow surviving in a region earlier described as having long been reduced by foreign invasions to an uninhabited wilderness, its every church levelled to the ground, is further inconsistent with the narrative.

Geoffrey was accustomed to despatch the protagonists of his history across the length and breadth of Britain like queens on a chessboard, and it is possible that this section of his narrative was in an earlier account confined within a much more restricted geographical compass. A suggestive hint at the source of the episode is to be found in his account of Hengist's death and burial at the town (*oppida*) of *Cunungeburg*, to which Geoffrey attached the spurious Welsh equivalent *Caer Conan*. This he identified with Conisborough in the West Riding of Yorkshire, whose castle provides the setting for a stirring episode in Sir Walter Scott's *Ivanhoe* (1820).[100]

If, as is not unlikely, Geoffrey's *Cunungeburg* featured in earlier legends of Stonehenge, without specifying its location, it would have been natural for him to identify it with a similarly named stronghold with which he was familiar. For in Geoffrey's day the castle of Conisborough in Yorkshire belonged to the stepfather of his patron Waleran de Meulan.[101]

There are indications that here Geoffrey unwittingly distinguished events, which were originally focussed on Stonehenge. The death of Hengist at the hands of Eldol is not mentioned in any other source, and was presumably either invented or acquired from local tradition, by Geoffrey, who linked it to Eldol's account of the events of the slaughter of Stonehenge.

It has been remarked that the description of Hengist's grave 'shows consciousness of prehistoric mound-burials'.[102] Now, one of the most prominent features of the landscape adjoining Stonehenge is Coneybury Hill, a distinctive monticle surmounted by a henge monument now largely ploughed over.[103] The name Coneybury has been derived from a

---

99   Allen Mawer, *The Place-Names of Northumberland and Durham* (Cambridge, 1920), p. xv; Kenneth Jackson, *Language and History in Early Britain: A Chronological Survey of the Brittonic Languages First to Twelfth Century A.D.* (Edinburgh, 1953), p. 223. 'The total of Celtic names in the North Riding is small' (Gillian Fellows Jensen, 'Place-Names and Settlement in the North Riding of Yorkshire', *Northern History* (Leeds, 1978), xiv, p. 22).

100   Faral, *La légende arthurienne*, ii, p. 237; Henry Lewis (ed.), *Brut Dingestow* (Cardiff, 1942), p. 265. In 1811 Scott wrote to a friend: 'Do you know anything of a striking ancient castle belonging, I think, to the Duke of Leeds, called Coningsburgh? ... I once flew past it on the mail-coach, when its round tower and flying buttresses had a most romantic effect in the morning dawn' (J. G. Lockhart, *Memoirs of the Life of Sir Walter Scott, Bart.* (Edinburgh, 1839–48), iii, p. 371). In 1792 the Hon. John Byng likewise found the castle entrancingly picturesque (C. Bruyn Andrews (ed.), *The Torrington Diaries: Containing the Tours through England and Wales of the Hon. John Byng (later Fifth Viscount Torrington) between the Years 1781 and 1794* (London, 1934–38), iii, p. 27).

101   Tatlock, *The Legendary History of Britain*, p. 21. In reality Conisborough derives from Old English *Cyningstūn*, 'the king's manor' (Eilert Ekwall, *The Concise Oxford Dictionary of English Place-Names* (Oxford, 1936), p. 115). *Caer Conan* 'a tout l'air d'une invention de Geoffroy' (Faral, *La légende arthurienne*, ii, p. 237). Later traditions of Hengist's connexion with Conisborough (e.g. William Camden, *Britannia* (London, 1600), p. 611) doubtless derive from the pervasive influence of the *Historia Regum Britanniæ*.

102   Tatlock, *The Legendary History of Britain*, p. 371.

103   Rosamund M. J. Cleal, K. E. Walker, and R. Montague (ed.), *Stonehenge in its landscape: Twentieth-century excavations* (London, 1995), pp. 37, 38, plate 3.2); Sally Exon, Vince Gaffney, Ann Woodward, and Ron Yorston, *Stonehenge Landscapes: Journeys through real-and-imagined worlds* (Oxford, 2000), p. 75.

combination of Middle English *coni* ('rabbit') and Old English *burg* ('burrow'),[104] indicating that the barrow was colonized by rabbits in the Middle Ages.

A difficulty with this etymology lies in the probability that the region of the barrows must have become densely populated by rabbits from the outset of their earliest arrival, making it unlikely that one barrow in particular should be singled out by this nomenclature.[105] Given the exceptionally impressive nature of the burial mound, combined with its evident relationship to the monument at Stonehenge, it is possible that the name represents folk-interpretation of an original *Cyningesbeorg*, 'king's barrow'. This would surely accord better with early forms such as *le Conynger, le Conyngar*.

That the tomb of Hengist was located at the scene of his infamous action at Stonehenge might further have been suggested by speculative association of *Hengist* with Old English *hencg* ('something hanging, a hinge'), the second element of Stone*henge*.[106]

Chapters 36 to 38 of the *Historia Brittonum*, which contain the legendary account of Vortigern's dealings with Hengist, and are demonstrably of distinct origin from other sections in which the rival leaders feature, spell the Saxon leader's name *Hencgistus*. Elsewhere in the same work he features consistently as *Hengistus* or *Hengist*, the form customarily employed in English sources.[107] Ætiological speculation might readily have posited a link between *Hencgist* and the setting for the massacre reputedly perpetrated at *Stänhengc*, the intrusive *c* possibly reflecting this process. Such confusion could have arisen from a written source locating the grave of Hengist beside Stonehenge in consequence of the false etymology. Unaware of the identity of the Coneybury barrow beside Stonehenge, Geoffrey identified *Cunungeburg* in his source with the impressive castle at distant Conisborough, with whose name he had particular reason to be familiar.[108]

---

104 J. E. B. Gover, Allen Mawer, and F. M. Stenton, *The Place-Names of Wiltshire* (Cambridge, 1939), p. 361; A. H. Smith, *English Place-Name Elements* (Cambridge, 1956) , i, pp. 56, 106. Rabbits were long thought to have been introduced into Britain by the Normans (Colin Matheson, 'The Rabbit and the Hare in Wales', *Antiquity: A Quarterly Review of Archæology* (Gloucester, 1941), xv, pp. 371–72; H. C. Bowen, 'The Celtic Background', in A. L. F. Rivet (ed.), *The Roman Villa in Britain* (London, 1969), p. 21). However, recent excavations at Lynford, near Thetford in Norfolk, have established their presence in Roman Britain.

105 The Stonehenge barrows have long attracted a dense rabbit population (Aubrey Burl and Neil Mortimer (ed.), *Stukeley's 'Stonehenge': An Unpublished Manuscript 1721–1724* (Cambridge, 2005), pp. 36–37).

106 Smith, *English Place-Name Elements*, i, p. 243; Gover, Mawer, and Stenton, *The Place-Names of Wiltshire*, pp. 360–61; Max Förster, *Der Flußname Themse und seine Sippe: Studien zur Anglisierung keltischer Eigennamen und zur Lautchronologie des Altbritischen* (Munich, 1941), p. 326. 'Hengest, whose name later was used to account for the name Stonehenge in the manner usual in local tradition' (Tatlock, *The Legendary History of Britain*, p. 41).

107 Charles Plummer (ed.), *Venerabilis Baedae Historiam Ecclesiasticam Gentis Anglorum; Historiam Abbatum, Epistolam ad Ecgberctum una cum Historia Abbatum Auctore Anonymo* (Oxford, 1896), i, pp. 31, 90; Charles Plummer and John Earle (ed.), *Two Anglo-Saxon Chronicles Parallel: With Supplementary Extracts from the Others; A Revised Text Edited, with Introduction, Notes, Appendices, and Glossary* (Oxford, 1892–99), i, pp. 12–15; A. Campbell (ed.), *The Chronicle of Æthelweard* (London, 1962), pp. 10–11; Fr. Klaeber (ed.), *Beowulf and the Fight at Finnsburg* (Boston, 1950), pp. 41, 43, 246; David N. Dumville, 'The Anglian collection of royal genealogies', *Anglo-Saxon England 5* (Cambridge, 1976), pp. 31, 34, 37; S. R. T. O. d'Ardenne, 'A Neglected Manuscript of British History', in Norman Davis and C. L. Wrenn (ed.), *English and Medieval Studies Presented to J.R.R. Tolkien on the Occasion of his Seventieth Birthday* (London, 1962), p. 93. The form *Hencgistus* appears in the so-called Annals of St Neots (David Dumville and Michael Lapidge (ed.), *The Annals of St Neots with Vita Prima Sancti Neoti* (Cambridge, 1985), p. 6, but given their link with Asser this exception may reflect the influence of the *Historia Brittonum*.

108 Cf. Tatlock, *The Legendary History of Britain*, p. 21.

Moving on, immediately before the defeat and death of Hengist, Geoffrey describes the Saxon chieftain's attempt to destroy the pursuing army of Aurelius by setting up his ambush at *Maes Beli*, which implicitly lay in the vicinity of *Cunengeburg*.[109] Again, this episode reads like an unwitting duplication of the slaughter of the long knives which it follows. In each case the Saxons cunningly seek to massacre the Britons by a deception; in each case it is Hengist who arranges the stratagem; and in each case it is Eldol who wreaks vengeance on the invader. Furthermore, Eldol prefaces the conflict at Maes Beli with a superfluous description of the earlier massacre.

It seems unlikely that there existed an otherwise unrecorded place name *Maes Beli* in the Yorkshire of Geoffrey's day, which suggests rather a Welsh literary source. Beli was a deity in the pagan British pantheon, whose name features prominently in early Welsh literature. Allusions indicate that he formerly reigned over the whole island of Britain and was considered primal ancestor of royal dynasties. The Roman hero of *Breuddwyd Maxen* is said to have conquered the island, driving Beli and his sons into the sea. The implication is that Beli's rule was supplanted by that of a new divinity (Maxen), whereupon he withdrew to become sovereign of an Otherworld realm lying beneath or beyond the ocean. That is to say, Beli became Lord of the Dead.[110]

One of the tenth-century Stanzas of the Graves enquires:

> Whose is the grave on Maes Mawr?
> Proud was his hand on his sword:
> The grave of Beli son of Benlli the Giant.[111]

A Welsh manuscript written in the reign of Charles I contains this legendary account of Beli's death:

> There is a place on the mountain between Iâl and Ystrad Alun above Rhyd y Gyfarthfa that is called *Y Maes Mawr*, the place where was the battle between Meirion ap Tybiawn, and Beli ap Benlli the giant, where Beli ap Benlli was slain, and Meirion placed two standing stones, one at either end of the grave: these were there up to the last forty years.[112]

A process familiar from folklore studies had led to Beli's slayer becoming identified with an heroic character from legendary history,[113] while the originally Otherworld plain *Maes Mawr* became identified in local topography with a particular 'large field or plain' (*maes mawr*).[114] The legend further envisages the site as distinguished by standing stones. Depiction of the

109 Faral, *La légende arthurienne*, ii, p. 236.

110 Rhys, *Lectures on the Origin and Growth of Religion as Illustrated by Celtic Heathendom*, pp. 90–91, 168; Bromwich (ed.), *Trioedd Ynys Prydein*, pp. 281–83.

111 A. O. H. Jarman (ed.), *Llyfr Du Caerfyrddin gyda Rhagymadrodd Nodiadau Testunol a Geirfa* (Cardiff, 1982), p. 44.

112 J. Gwenogvryn Evans, *Report on Manuscripts in the Welsh Language* (London, 1898–1902), i, p. 1078; ii, p. 453.

113 The thirteenth-century poet Bleddyn Fardd alludes to Arthur's warring against Beli's father Benlli (John Morris-Jones and T. H. Parry-Williams (ed.), *Llawysgrif Hendregadredd* (Cardiff, 1933), p. 68).

114 W. J. Gruffydd, *Math vab Mathonwy: An Inquiry into the Origins and Development of the Fourth Branch of the Mabinogi with the Text and a Translation* (Cardiff, 1928), pp. 177–79.

Otherworld as a great plain (*mag mór*) is widely attested in Irish as well as British tradition, suggesting a Common Celtic origin for the conception.[115]

These related factors – the Great Plain as Land of the Dead, its relocation as a terrestrial realm, standing stones marking the resting place of the God of the Dead – bear marked resonances of Stonehenge, surrounded as it is by striking burial mounds in the midst of a fertile plain. *Maes Mawr* and *Maes Beli* could readily have been interchangeable appellations of the British pagan Otherworld. A Welsh translation of Geoffrey of Monmouth's *Historia* actually identifies the site of the massacre of the British nobles at Stonehenge as '*Maes Mawr* in Wales' (i.e. Britain).[116]

Geoffrey's parallel accounts of the Slaughter of the Long Knives and the Saxon ambush and burial of Hengist, with their duplicated versions of Eldol's survival of the massacre, suggest that they originally represented composite elements of a legend attached to Stonehenge. Could it be that the plain about the temple of Stonehenge, focus of a uniquely extended necropolis containing hundreds of burial mounds, was identified in an earlier version of the legend as *Maes Beli*, the Plain of Beli, lord of the illustrous dead?[117]

Reverting to Geoffrey of Monmouth's account of the Slaughter of the Long Knives and its immediate sequel, juxtaposition of his unexplained ascription of the massacre to 1 May (festival of the god Beli), and his effective duplication of the event at a site called *Maes Beli*, the Plain of Beli, is unlikely to be coincidental. In Ireland, and possibly also in Britain, 1 May was Beltane, 'The fire of Bel'.[118] The full relevance of Beli, God of the Dead, to the May-day massacre will be considered in a later chapter. Evidence considered thus far suggests that Geoffrey's source for this section of his *Historia* included the following elements.

1.　There existed a perceived correspondence between the Hill of Uisneach in Ireland and Stonehenge, which led to the belief that stones from the one were transferred to create the other. In reality their rôles were analogous, and, given that the prime function of Uisneach was its status as Omphalos or Centre of Ireland, the story of the transfer is best explained on grounds that Stonehenge in early times fulfilled the same ideological purpose in Britain. That the stones were brought from the far west to Salisbury Plain

---

115　*Ériu*, xii, p. 180; Elizabeth A. Gray (ed.), *Cath Maige Tuired: The Second Battle of Mag Tuired* (Naas, 1982), p. 36; Hans Pieter Atze Oskamp (ed.), *The Voyage of Máel Dúin: A Study in Early Irish Voyage Literature* (Groningen, 1970), pp. 152–58. Cf. also Arthur C. L. Brown, *The Origin of the Grail Legend* (Cambridge, Mass., 1943), p. 437; Jan de Vries, *Keltische Religion* (Stuttgart, 1961), p. 49; Helmut Birkhan, *Kelten: Versuch einer Gesamtdarstellung ihrer Kultur* (Vienna, 1997), p. 534. The Greeks had their Elysian Fields (Ἠλύσιον πεδίον, 'Meadowy Plain'), where the glorious dead dwelt free from discomfort (Helmut van Thiel (ed.), *Homeri Odyssea* (Hildesheim, 1991), p. 55). Cf. Josef Kroll, 'Elysium', in Leo Brandt (ed.), *Arbeitsgemeinschaft für Forschung des Landes Nordrhein-Westfalen* (Cologne, 1953), ii, pp. 7–35; J. P. Mallory and D. Q. Adams (ed.), *Encyclopedia of Indo-European Culture* (Chicago and London, 1997), p. 153). The concept of the Otherworld as rich pasture land is probably of Indo-European origin (Thomas V. Gamkrelidze and Vjačeslav V. Ivanov, *Indo-European and the Indo-Europeans: A Reconstruction and Historical Analysis of a Proto-Language and a Proto-Culture* (Berlin and New York, 1995), pp. 722–23).

116　*Oed y dyd a ossodet duw kalan mei. yny maes maur yngkymre. ylle ygelwit gwedy hynny salisburie* (John Jay Parry (ed.), *Brut y Brenhinedd: Cotton Cleopatra Version* (Cambridge, Mass., 1937), p. 118).

117　Cf. Peniarth MS 50: *Ac yna o gynghor o chedernit y gadó ynys brydein y gwisc ynteu y goron y hun am ben Beli hir . yna tref beli hir y gelwir . gorwynt honno a wastathaa ynys brydein* (Gwenogvryn Evans, *Report on Manuscripts in the Welsh Language*, i, p. 399).

118　'A related figure [to the *Bel* of Beltane] is Welsh *Beli Mawr*, an old progenitor-deity' (H. Wagner, 'Studies in the Origins of Early Celtic Traditions', *Ériu: The Journal of the School of Irish Learning* (Dublin, 1975), xxvi, pp. 16–17).

      may have appeared further confirmed by a lingering tradition preserved in Dyfed of the transportation of bluestones from the royal sanctuary on Preseli Mountain.

2. A slaughter of the Britons occurred at Stonehenge, of which there was but one survivor.

3. This cataclysmic event occurred on 1 May.

4. The British name for the plain on which Stonehenge stands may have been *Maes Beli*, which was also a name for the Land of the Dead. It is hard to conceive of a more appropriate setting for a national necropolis than the uniquely striking monument, set in the midst of an airy plain, and surrounded by noble dead sleeping in hundreds of great barrows.[119]

Identification of the slaughter with a treacherous massacre of British nobles by Saxons represents a secondary accretion, deriving from the legendary history of post-Roman Britain, which incorporated a folklore motif popular in north-west Europe in the early Middle Ages. There are also intimations that Geoffrey's account of Stonehenge drew in part at least on a written source. The most suggestive of these is the misreading of Welsh *Eidol* as *Eldol*, of which more shortly.

The foundation legend of Milan

That legends attached to numinous sites, largely or wholly ignored in literary sources, may linger on in oral tradition for centuries and even millennia is exemplified by a remarkable example from across the Channel. In 1644 John Evelyn visited the town of Bourges in central France, whose inhabitants 'show'd us also a vast tree, which they say stands just in the Center of France'.[120] There can be little doubt that the tradition was exceedingly ancient. Both the name of Bourges and that of the province of Berry, of which it is the capital, derive from the local Gaulish tribal name *Bituriges*, meaning 'People of the King of the World'.[121] The attribute 'King of the World' did not represent any vaunt of political supremacy, but proclaimed the fact that the rulers of the Bituriges were sacral 'kings of the world', their tribal canton being regarded as sacred space set apart from the profane world without.[122]

---

119   For the megalithic complex as necropolis, cf. Jean Leclerc, 'Un phénomè associé au mégalithisme: les sépultures collectives', in Jean Guilaine (ed.), *Mégalithismes de l'Atlantique à l'Ethiopie* (Paris, 1999), pp. 23–40. However, the significance of the Stonehenge barrows as Geoffrey's *cimiterium* rests primarily, not on their original use as burial mounds, but how they had come to be regarded in his day.

120   E. S. de Beer (ed.), *The Diary of John Evelyn* (Oxford, 1955), ii, p. 153.

121   Pokorny, *Indogermanisches Etymologisches Wörterbuch*, i, p. 468; Wolfgang Meid, 'Über *Albiōn, elfydd, Albiorīx* und andere Indikatoren eines keltischen Weltbildes', in Martin J. Ball, James Fife, Erich Poppe, and Jenny Rowland (ed.), *Celtic Linguistics/Ieithyddiaeth Geltaidd; Readings in the Brythonic Languages: Festschrift for T. Arwyn Watkins* (Amsterdam and Philadelphia, 1990), p. 437; Gamkrelidze and Ivanov, *Indo-European and the Indo-Europeans*, i, p. 387; Pierre-Yves Lambert, *La langue gauloise: Description linguistique, commentaire d'inscriptions choisies* (Paris, 1995), p. 36; Xavier Delamarre, *Dictionnaire de la langue gauloise: Une approche linguistique du vieux-celtique continental* (Paris, 2001), pp. 65–6; *The Journal of Indo-European Studies* (Washington, 2003), xxxi, p. 257.

122   Christian-J. Guyonvarc'h, 'Mediolanvm Bitvrigvm: Deux éléments de vocabulaire religieux et de géographie sacrée', *Celticvm I: Actes du Premier Colloque International d'Etudes Gauloises, Celtiques et Protoceltiques; Medolanvm Bitvrigvm MCMLX* (Rennes, 1961), pp. 137–42. For the ideological figure of the 'universal ruler', cf. A. M. Hocart, *Kingship* (Oxford, 1927), p. 10; C. J. Bleeker, *The Sacred Bridge: Researches into the Nature and Structure of Religion* (Leiden, 1963), pp. 220–24; Julia Ching, *Mysticism and Kingship in China: The heart of Chinese wisdom* (Cambridge, 1997), pp. 48–50; Proinsias Mac Cana, *The Cult of the Sacred Centre: Essays on Celtic Ideology* (Dublin, 2011), pp. 87–90; Maxim Fomin, *Instructions for Kings: Secular and Clerical Images of Kingship in Early Ireland and Ancient India* (Heidelberg, 2013), pp. 268–75; John Waddell, *Archaeology and Celtic myth: an exploration* (Dublin, 2014), p. 106.

The philological implication is endorsed by an early section of Livy's history of Rome. Writing in the first century BC, the historian described how in a bygone era the Bituriges were assigned supreme authority among the Celts of Gaul. The tribe enjoyed lavish harvests and an overflowing population under their king Ambigatus. To resolve the latter problem, he despatched his young nephews Segouesus and Bellouesus with vast swarms of the excess population to settle respectively in the Hercynian Forest of Germany, and in Italy. Overcoming seemingly insuperable dangers, Bellouesus succeeded in crossing the perilous barrier of the Alps, and descended into the fertile plain of North Italy, where he founded the city of Milan (*Mediolanum*).[123] The chronological structure of Livy's work indicates that this event was understood to have occurred about 600 BC.

Georges Dumézil has shown that the early section of Livy's history represents euhemerizing transmutation of the mythology of the Roman people into pseudo-historical narrative.[124] The account of Ambigatus and the foundation of Milan falls unmistakably into this category.[125]

The rôle assigned Ambigatus is that of archetypal sovereign, familiar from many Indo-European mythologies. He is the priest-king, residing at the centre of his kingdom, who acts as passive guardian and transmitter of divine kingship. In Ireland his principal counterpart is King Conchobar of the Ulster Cycle, while in Britain the function is fulfilled by Lludd in *Cyfranc Lludd a Lleuelys*. Aged and immobile, Ambigatus like Lludd embodies the monarchical principle, remaining immanent at the heart of his realm.[126] His people's enjoyment of lavish harvests and abundant population, understood by Livy as historical verities, in reality reflects the archaic belief in an indissoluble association between the prosperity of the realm and the rule of a just king.[127]

In his [Conchobar's] reign there was much store of benefits enjoyed by the men of Ulster. There was peace and tranquillity and good fellowship. There were fruits and fatness and harvest of the sea. There was power and law and happy rule (*degflaithius*) during his time among the men of Ulster. There was great dignity and sovereignty (*airechus*) and plenty in the royal house at Emain.[128]

---

123 *Celticvm I*, pp. 165–66.

124 C. Scott Littleton, *The New Comparative Mythology: An Anthropological Assessment of the Theories of Georges Dumézil* (Los Angeles, 1966), pp. 11, 74.

125 Cf. Mac Cana, *The Cult of the Sacred Centre*, pp. 140–42.

126 *Celticvm I*, pp. 167–68.

127 Fomin, *Instructions for Kings*, pp. 43–44, 204.

128 A. G. van Hamel (ed.), *Compert Con Culainn and Other Stories* (Dublin, 1933), p. 20. Cf. Whitley Stokes (ed.), *The Tripartite Life of Patrick, with other Documents Relating to that Saint* (London, 1887), pp. clix–lx; Hocart, *Kingship*, pp. 36–37, 47-57; Maartje Draak, 'Some Aspects of Kingship in Pagan Ireland', in *La Regalità Sacra: Contributi al Tema Dell' VIII Congresso Internazionale di Storia delle Religioni (Roma, Aprile 1955)* (Leiden, 1959), p. 653; Émile Benveniste, *Le vocabulaire des institutions indo-européennes* (Paris, 1969), ii, pp. 26–28; Kim McCone, *Pagan Past and Christian Present in Early Irish Literature* (Naas, 1990), pp. 107–37; M. L. West, *Indo-European Poetry and Myth* (Oxford, 2007), pp. 422–24. Other paradigmatic kings whose reigns brought peace and prosperity to Ireland were Cormac mac Airt and Eochaid mac Erc (Vernam Hull, 'Geanamuin Chormaic', *Ériu* (1952), xvi, p. 84; R. I. Best, Osborn Bergin, M. A. O'Brien, and Anne O'Sullivan (ed.), *The Book of Leinster Formerly Lebar na Núachongbála* (Dublin, 1954–83), pp. 28, 30).

The name *Ambigatus* means 'he who fights on every side',[129] i.e. one who protects his kingdom from a central focus of potency. And, just as Lludd in *Cyfranc Lludd a Lleuelys* looks to his 'brother' Lleuelys to play the active rôle in combating foes from beyond the frontiers, so Ambigatus despatches his 'nephews' to invade and conquer distant territories. Their names are likewise appropriate to their function, *Segouesus* meaning 'Worthy of Victories', and *Bellouesus* 'Strong and Good'.[130] On his arrival in Italy at the head of his swarming host, Bellouesus founds the city of Milan, whose Celtic name *Mediolanum* is a compound of 'centre' and 'full, rich', its etymology and sacral connotation corresponding to those of Meath (< *mide*, 'middle, centre')[131] in Ireland, the province surrounding the Sacred Centre at Uisneach.[132]

While Livy's account is replete with mythological motifs reflecting Roman conceptions of the Augustan period, as an historical event it gains no support from the archæological record. Far from there having been a massive Gaulish invasion of north Italy during the period indicated, evidence attests to the uninterrupted presence of a people known to archæologists as the Golasecca culture, which flourished until long after the purported mass invasion from north of the Alps.

> There is no sign of a break, by which one could conclude the massive immigration of a foreign ('Celtic') ethnic group. It is easy to demonstrate that the Golasecca culture developed from older local roots, which themselves go back to the so-called Fazies Canegrate group of about 1200 BC.[133]

It is clear that Livy incorporated archaic Gaulish myth into his euhemerizing reconstruction of early Roman history.

> One may distinguish without difficulty, in the schema of Gaulish epic, the king-priest, of divine nature, directing with the same felicity the priesthood and war. The schema is likewise mythical: Bellovesus and Segovesus are too close to [the Irish mythic heroes] Cú Chulainn and Conall Cernach not to make one think of the Dioscures [Divine Twins].[134]

Livy originated from Cisalpine Gaul, and it was presumably there that he learned the story of Ambigatus and the foundation of Milan. Analogies in Irish and British tradition suggest that the Gauls had already transformed their mythology into an 'historical' narrative or narratives,

---

129 Delamarre, *Dictionnaire de la langue gauloise*, p. 35.

130 Ibid., pp. 62, 267.

131 Vendryes, Bachellery, and Lambert, *Lexique étymologique de l'irlandais ancien*, M-50.

132 Birkhan, *Kelten*, p. 90.

133 Otto-Herman Frey, 'The Celts in Italy', in Miranda J. Green (ed.), *The Celtic World* (London, 1995), p. 515; Daniele Vitali, 'The Celts in Italy', in V. Kruta, O. H. Frey, B. Raftery, and M. Szabó (ed.), *The Celts* (London, 1991), p. 223; J. P. Mallory and D. Q. Adams (ed.), *Encyclopedia of Indo-European Culture* (Chicago and London, 1997), pp. 233–34. The first Celts to arrive in Italy appeared two centuries after the era Livy assigned to the settlement of Bellouesus (Ludwig Pauli, 'The Alps at the Time of the First Celtic Migrations', ibid., p. 215; Jürgen Uhlich, 'More on the linguistic classification of Lepontic', in Pierre-Yves Lambert and Georges-Jean Pinault (ed.), *Gaulois et celtique continental* (Geneva, 2007), pp. 379–81).

134 *Celticvm I*, pp. 166–70. Cf. Christian-J. Guyonvarc'h and Françoise Le Roux, *Les Druides* (Rennes, 1986), pp. 218–20; Birkhan, *Kelten*, pp. 87, 1005.

before Livy in turn incorporated it into his *History*.[135] Four centuries later, Ammianus Marcellinus learned during a visit to Gaul of indigenous traditions of early migrations and foundations of cities, which probably derived from a mixture of native lore and classical learning.[136]

It is likely that the legendary foundation of Milan by Bellouesus was originally unconnected with the account of the unprecedented wealth of the Bituriges under their king Ambigatus in Central Gaul. Like stories of the foundation of early mediæval kingdoms by descendants of Aeneas or Japhet, European foundation legends were designed to provide their kings and realms with illustrious pedigrees linking them to high antiquity.[137] The foundation legends of Bourges and Milan must originally have been distinct, eventually becoming artificially conjoined by speculative 'history' evolved in a subsequent era. The exodus of a vast proportion of the tribe under pressure of excess population suggests a rationalization of the concept of fruitfulness as characteristic aspect of the benefits conferred on the Bituriges, in consequence of the benign rule of Ambigatus.

But why should the two disparate myths or legends have become associated in this way? The likely answer is that Gauls perceived a striking functional identity between the Centre of Celtic Gaul in the canton of the Bituriges, and that of Cisalpine Gaul at *Mediolanum* (Milan). It would have been characteristic of the compilers of the Gaulish syncretic history (presumably their druids) to recast ideological analogue as historical event. The manner in which the Irish pseudo-historical 'Book of the Takings of Ireland' (*Lebor Gabála Érenn*) became converted from pagan mythology into a 'history' of the earliest settlements of the Green Island illustrates the process. Similarity of the names *Hibernia* (Ireland) and *Iberia* (Spain) facilitated an assumption that the ancestors of the Irish came originally from Spain.[138]

The amalgamation of originally distinct legends of the Sacred Centres of Gaul and Cisalpine Gaul into an historical narrative explaining the creation of the latter as the consequence of a migration of the Bituriges from Gaul to Italy, is closely analogous to Geoffrey of Monmouth's account of the removal of the Irish Navel at Uisneach to Britain in order to create the parallel British Navel at Stonehenge.

Finally, the fact that the tradition of the World Tree at Bourges ('city of the Bituriges') survived into the seventeenth century AD attests to the remarkable tenacity of such traditions. That its legendary association was not (so far as I am aware) recorded before that time demonstrates the extent to which legends of this type may persist for centuries in popular folklore, unrecorded by chroniclers and historians.

---

135   Cf. Thomas F. O'Rahilly, *Early Irish History and Mythology* (Dublin, 1946), pp. 260–85.

136   Galletier, Fontaine, Sabbah, Marié, and de la Beaumelle (ed.), *Ammien Marcellin: Histoire*, i, pp. 135-37. A much earlier classical allusion to oral tradition among the Gauls was noted by Proinsias Mac Cana: 'Now Posidonius, as paraphrased by Athenaeus, did not describe the Gaulish custom [the champion's portion] from his own personal experience – it happened 'in former times' says the text – and therefore the source of his story must have been either *senchas* or story' ('Conservation and Innovation in Early Celtic Literature', *Études Celtiques* (Paris, 1972), xiii, p. 90).

137   Walter Goffart, *Rome's Fall and After* (London, 1989), pp. 133–65.

138   R. Mark Scowcroft, '*Leabhar Gabhála*: Part II: The Growth of the Tradition', *Ériu* (1988), xxxix, pp. 14–15.

8

Celtic Tradition and the Transfer of the Preseli Bluestones

Pwyll, Prince of Dyfed, and the Preseli sanctuary
Geoffrey's seemingly fanciful account of the origin of Stonehenge received a dramatic fillip with the discovery in 1923 that the massive bluestones of Stonehenge originated in the Preseli Mountains of Pembrokeshire.[1] From there, by means of an astounding feat of prehistoric engineering, they were transported in the third millennium BC to Salisbury Plain. In 1941 Stuart Piggott wrote his seminal paper, in which he argued that Geoffrey's account of the bringing of the stones by Merlin and Uther from Ireland was broadly substantiated by this discovery. He concluded:

> Unless then we have in Geoffrey's story an aetiological myth which (again by coincidence) hit on very nearly the true facts, we must examine other possible sources.[2]

Piggott argued that extension of the transportation route beyond Preseli to Ireland reflected a shift arising within the tradition, such as might readily occur over long centuries of transmission. After all, as he observed, the Irish Sea zone comprised a unified cultural and economic region in Neolithic and Bronze Age times.[3]

However, in Chapter Five I argued that a more plausible variant of this hypothesis is indeed explicable in terms of ætiological myth. Ideological parallels associated with the Hill of Uisneach in Meath (whence the stones are described by Geoffrey as being transported) and Stonehenge provide a yet more convincing explanation. The one site was renowned as the traditional Omphalos of Ireland, and the other implicitly as that of Britain. Since no substantial megalithic complex existed at Uisneach in the Middle Ages, that Stonehenge once fulfilled the corresponding function might have appeared to verify a belief that the one had been physically removed to the other. The unique character of Stonehenge among major British megalithic

---

1   R. J. C. Atkinson, *Stonehenge* (London, 1956), p. 36.

2   'The Sources of Geoffrey of Monmouth. II. The Stonehenge Story', *Antiquity: A Quarterly Review of Archæology* (Gloucester, 1941), xv, pp. 305–8.

3   'There is a definite tendency for the shores of the Irish Sea to form a "culture province"' (Sir Cyril Fox, *The Personality of Britain: Its Influence on Inhabitant and Invader in Prehistoric and Early Historic Times* (Cardiff, 1959), p. 44). Cf. H. N. Savory, 'The Later Prehistoric Migrations across the Irish Sea', in Donald Moore (ed.), *The Irish Sea Province in Archaeology and History* (Cardiff, 1970), pp. 38–49.

monuments in being a structure bearing appearance of having been fashioned by men is likely to have provoked speculation in early times regarding its origin.[4]

There remains the question of the significance of Preseli, the numinous quality of whose stones was of such overriding significance to those who accomplished the unequalled feat of their removal to Salisbury Plain. I believe that remarkable evidence, hitherto overlooked in the context, serves to illuminate this aspect.

The first of the four Welsh prose tales known collectively as *Mabinogi* has been accorded the title 'Pwyll Prince of Dyfed' (*Pwyll Pendeuic Dyuet*). In my book *The Oldest British Prose Literature*, I showed that these stories were composed at the beginning of the eleventh century. Regardless of the date, it is generally accepted by Celtic scholars that they contain an extensive substratum of pagan mythological lore.[5]

In the story of *Pwyll*, its eponymous hero weds a beautiful and mysterious lady called Rhiannon, whom he encounters at the fairy mound of Arberth, in Dyfed. Her name derives from British **Rīgantonā*, meaning 'divine queen', i.e. the goddess of the land, to whom legitimate kings were symbolically wed.[6] The common noun *pwyll* means 'wisdom', and it seems likely that the romance ultimately reflects the familiar pagan myth of marriage between an otiose deity, hypostasis of divine understanding,[7] and the earth or sovereignty goddess.[8]

Pwyll and Rhiannon reign prosperously over Dyfed for two years. In the third year, however, growing restless at the queen's failure to produce an heir, the men of Dyfed summon (*dyuynny*) Pwyll to Preseli in Dyfed (*y Bresseleu yn Dyuet*). There they insist on his remarrying, should Rhiannon continue in her failure to bear him a son. Pwyll requests a delay:

> Put this [decision] off for me until the end of the year (*Oedwch a mi hynn hyt ym pen y ulwydyn*). And a year from this time we will arrange to meet (*A blwydyn y'r amser hwnn ni a wnawn yr oet y dyuot y gyt*), and I will accept your decision.

It seems that the issue was required to be resolved where it was raised, i.e. at *Presseleu*. Certainly, there could be no point in making so specific an appointment for the royal court of Arberth, where the king and his nobles must have been assumed to commingle on a daily basis. Evidently

---

4   'In parenthesis I think it not unlikely that the absence of any early medieval records of other stone circles, including Avebury, is due to the fact that they were regarded as natural objects of the countryside, in which by a whim of the Creator the stones stood on end and in some sort of order' (*Antiquity*, xv, p. 308). Cf. Roseanne Schot, 'From cult centre to royal centre: monuments, myths and other revelations at Uisneach', in Roseanne Schot, Conor Newman, and Edel Bhreatnach (ed.), *Landscapes of Cult and Kingship* (Dublin, 2011), p. 97. It has been seen that Henry of Huntingdon took Stonehenge to have been architecturally designed, with gateways set upon gateways.

5   'Il reste acquis définitivement l'image d'un zoomorphisme primitif, littéralement enchâssé dans le christianisme mais dont l'ancienneté n'est plus à démontrer. Cela prouve tout simplement que les récits mythologiques très anciens ont subi un traitement de réécriture et d'adaptation au récit romanesque. C'est ce qui fait le caractère si particulier des quatre branches du Mabinogi et les contes gallois, où l'archaïsme préchrétien du fond contraste violemment avec l'aspect littéraire et christianisé de la forme' (Christian-J. Guyonvarc'h, *Magie, médecine et divination chez les Celtes* (Paris, 1997), p. 144).

6   '**Rīgantonā*, rather than being built on one of the many Celtic words meaning roughly 'queen', is built specifically on the root of *rīx*, the primary and most basic word for the king of the tribe (**toutā*) … **Rīgantonā* is specifically the divine consort of the *rīx*' (John T. Koch, 'A Welsh Window on the Iron Age: Manawydan, Mandubracios', *Cambridge Medieval Celtic Studies* (Cambridge, 1987), xiv, p. 34).

7   Cf. Helmer Ringgren, *Word and Wisdom: Studies in the Hypostatization of Divine Qualities and Functions in the Ancient Near East* (Lund, 1947), pp. 190–93.

8   Kim McCone, *Pagan Past and Christian Present in Early Irish Literature* (Naas, 1990), pp. 112–13.

Preseli was regarded as the appropriate location for resolution of this particular issue. It was there that the nobles of Dyfed required and obtained the king's attendance to resolve the crisis, and implicitly where they would foregather for resolution of the issue. Although emphasis is laid in the Four Branches on a king's requirement to consult with his council on significant issues,[9] it is only in the context of Pwyll's failure to produce an heir that it is required to be held at a particular location remote from the royal court (*prif lys*).

There is a further intimation that this formal gathering at Preseli occurred on a specific calendrical date. On receipt of his nobles' ultimatum, Pwyll replies:

> Postpone this [decision] for me until the end of the year. A year from this time we will arrange to meet, and I will accept your decision.[10]

The pagan Celtic year was divided in two, with winter beginning at *Kalan Gaeaf*, 1 November, and summer at *Kalan Mai*, 1 May.[11] Pwyll's double stipulation that the decision be postponed to 'the end of the year' *and* 'a year hence' suggests that the date envisaged for these successive gatherings was November Eve (*nos Galan Gaeaf*), the close of the Celtic year.[12] By the same token, the original assembly at Preseli must have been held at the preceding *nos Galan Gaeaf*.

November Eve, a crucial division of the year, was regarded as a liminal time of intense danger to humanity, when the portals of the Otherworld gaped wide, and demonic spirits emerged to menace the very existence of mankind.[13] Since a queen's failure to deliver a royal heir likewise threatened the realm with annihilation, November Eve represented the appropriate juncture at which the peril was required to be confronted.

Events relating to Pwyll and his family are separated to a striking degree by intervals of precisely a year. He spends a year to the day in the Otherworld realm of Annwfn; when he first meets Rhiannon, they arrange to wed 'a year from tonight' (*blwydyn y heno*); when Gwawl interrupts their feast, she similarly consents to wed him 'a year from tonight'. Again, in the Third Branch of the *Mabinogi*, *Manawydan mab Llŷr*, Rhiannon's second husband Manawydan and her son Pryderi spend a year living in the wilderness, at the end of which they are abducted to the Otherworld for a further year.

It might be thought that this reflects no more than thematic means of linking successive episodes in the story. Against this, however, it is noteworthy that the feature is absent from the two tales set in North Wales, *Branwen uerch Llŷr* and *Math uab Mathonwy*. Moreover, the treatment in *Pwyll* is distinctive, in that on three occasions an event is arranged a year in advance. Not only this, but at least one of these occasions bears appearance of being linked to the annual calendrical round. Thus, combats between the two Otherworld kings Arawn and

---

9   J. K. Bollard, 'The Role of Myth and Tradition in *The Four Branches of the Mabinogi*', *Cambridge Medieval Celtic Studies* (Cambridge, 1983), vi, pp. 79–80, 83–84.

10 *Oedwch a mi hynn hyt ym pen y ulwydyn. A blwydyn y'r amser hwnn ni a wnawn yr oet y dyuot y gyt* (R. L. Thomson (ed.), *Pwyll Pendeuic Dyuet: The First of the Four Branches of the Mabinogi edited from the White Book of Rhydderch with variants from the Red Book of Hergest* (Dublin, 1957), p. 17). In the Welsh laws, the captain of the royal guard (*penteulu*) is required to stay with the king *hyt em pen e blvydyn*, i.e. after the passage of a year, rather than to the close of the current year (Aled Rhys Wiliam (ed.), *Llyfr Iorwerth: A Critical Text of the Venedotian Code of Medieval Welsh Law Mainly from BM. Cotton MS. Titus Dii* (Cardiff, 1960), p. 5).

11 Alwyn Rees and Brinley Rees, *Celtic Heritage: Ancient Tradition in Ireland and Wales* (London, 1961), pp. 83–94.

12 The pre-Christian year in Britain began on 1 November (T. Gwynn Jones, *Welsh Folklore and Folk-Custom* (London, 1930), p. 146). Although I cannot find this specified in the sources, by the same token the year's end was presumably identified with November Eve, *nos galan gaeaf*.

13 Rees and Rees, *Celtic Heritage*, p. 89.

Hafgan occur on the identical date in successive years.[14] Furthermore, we are told that the night of their conflict was recalled by every inhabitant of Dyfed, suggesting that it was identified in popular tradition with a particular *night* of the year. This again recalls the great annual dividing point: *nos Galan Gaeaf*, 'The *Night* of the Winter Calends'.[15]

Moreover, events separated by a year in *Pwyll* are regularly depicted as occurring at a feast (*gwledd*). It is during a feast that the eponymous hero first encounters the regal Rhiannon, and their marriage is appointed to be held at a further feast a year hence. At that feast her hand is solicited by an importunate suitor Gwawl mab Clud, whom she fobs off by engaging to accept him exactly a year later. When the day arrives, he finds the company feasting, and, after his suit has been evited by deception, Pwyll weds the lady the next evening (i.e. at the same feast). Furthermore, the narrator is at particular pains to identify this feast with its predecessor: 'They went to sit at the tables; and *just as they had sat the year before, each one sat that night.*'

Again, events in *Pwyll* occurring on dates implicitly or explicitly bearing calendrical significance in the pagan Celtic year almost invariably involve intrusion into the terrestrial world by Otherworld characters or events. Pwyll spends precisely a year in the Otherworld (*Annwfn*), returning 'a year from tonight' (*blwydyn y heno*) – when it will be 'the end of the year' (*hyt ym penn y ulwydyn*), i.e. *nos Galan Gaeaf*. When Pwyll proposes to Rhiannon, it is outside his court in Dyfed. However, the marriage takes place a year later at her father's court, in an unnamed land implicitly not located in this world. Finally, it is on the eve of the other liminal festival of the year (*nos Galan Mai*) that Rhiannon's newborn child is abducted by a supernatural power, and substituted for a foal at the court of the terrestrial King Teyrnon.[16]

The feast at which Pwyll first meets Rhiannon lasts three days, recalling the parallel three-day *Samain* feast in Ireland, at which the Young God (Mac Ind Óc) wedded the fairy Caer.[17] When Rhiannon's malevolent Otherworld suitor Gwawl mab Clud makes his unwelcome appearance at her marriage feast with Pwyll, he is tricked into entering *an enchanted bag capable of holding 'all the food and drink of the seven cantrefs'*. Trapped and humiliated, *he is compelled to undertake never to trouble the kingdom of Dyfed again.*[18] The original theme is obscured by the narrator's

---

14 The names of the protagonists suggest the triumph of winter over summer. *Hafgan* means 'summer-white', while in the Stanzas of the Graves Arawn is accorded the patronymic mab *Diwinvin* (A. O. H. Jarman (ed.), *Llyfr Du Caerfyrddin gyda Rhagymadrodd Nodiadau Testunol a Geirfa* (Cardiff, 1982), p. 42), i.e. *Dyfnfyn*, a name suggesting the abyssal underworld of Annwfn (J. Lloyd-Jones, *Geirfa Barddoniaeth Gynnar Gymraeg* (Cardiff, 1931–63), p. 412).

15 Nikolai Tolstoy, *The Oldest British Prose Literature: The Compilation of the Four Branches of the Mabinogi* (Lampeter, 2009), pp. 45–47. 'The grey-clad Arawn, Lord of Annwfn, defeated Hafgan ('Summer White') in what appears to have been a yearly combat …' (Rees and Rees, *Celtic Heritage*, p. 285). The mediæval hunting season began at the Nativity of St John the Baptist, 24 June (Bror Danielsson (ed.), *William Twiti: The Art of Hunting 1327* (Stockholm, 1977), p. 42). However, Arawn's hunting is unrelated to the sporting calendar, his being no terrestrial activity, but that of the supernatural Wild Hunt, whose terrifying course through the night sky took place during winter months (Marie Trevelyan, *Folk-Lore and Folk-Stories of Wales* (London, 1909), pp. 47–54; Roger Sherman Loomis, *Arthurian Tradition & Chrétien de Troyes* (New York, 1949), pp. 46, 132; Michael John Petry, *Herne the Hunter: A Berkshire Legend* (Reading, 1972), p. 83).

16 These dramatic transfers between disparate worlds evoke parallel shifts in the sinister Irish *Samain* story of *Echtra Nerai* (John Carey, 'Sequence and Causation in *Echtra Nerai*', *Ériu: The Journal of the School of Irish Learning* (Dublin, 1988), xxxix, pp. 67–74). Recurrence of supernatural events on successive *Samain* nights occurs also in *Airne Fíngein: Baí ben síde oca acallaim ar gach samain do grés* (Joseph Vendryes (ed.), *Airne Fíngein* (Dublin, 1953), p. 1).

17 Francis Shaw (ed.), *The Dream of Óengus: Aislinge Óenguso* (Dublin, 1934), pp. 61–63.

18 As elsewhere, this indicates a prior version of the story, which the author had not fully incorporated into his literary creation. 'Rhiannon speaks as if she were in Dyfed instead of the unnamed country in

unconvincing attempt to explain it as originating a cruel popular game known as 'Badger in the Bag'. However, this association of an Otherworld intruder, bent on abducting the Maiden Sovereignty of the land, with a magical bag of contrived relevance to the story recalls the Third Oppression (*gormes*) in *Cyfranc Lludd a Lleuelys*. There, a giant enchanter enters the court of Lludd during the night, equipped with *an enchanted hamper capable of holding all the food and drink of the kingdom*, with which he customarily absconds. However, on this occasion he is overpowered by Lludd, *and obliged to undertake never to attempt his robberies again*.

Both stories represent literary adaptations of myths associated with the festival of *nos Galan Gaeaf*, when the demonic forces (*Coraniaid*) of the Otherworld (*Annwfn*) are frustrated, by means of prophylactic rites enacted at a nocturnal feast, from absconding with the wealth of the realm. The hamper or bag capable of abstracting 'all the food and drink' of the realm clearly corresponds to winter dearth, when stock dies and the land becomes unproductive.

Following Pwyll's request to his nobles at Preseli for a year's grace, in which to allow his queen Rhiannon a final chance to beget an heir to the kingdom, the child is born in time on the Calends of May, *Kalan Mai*.[19] Again, the date is significant, since it was the other great festival of the Celtic year, which marked the world's renascence following harsh months of winter darkness and accompanying mortality of humans and livestock. (As the accounts reveal, this escape also presented a moment of extreme danger.) Since the express purpose of the original gathering at Preseli was to ensure the fertility of the queen, whose name Rhiannon ('Divine Queen') and characteristics proclaim her original function as Maiden Sovereignty of the kingdom, it is evident that both place and date bore important religious resonances.[20]

Thus, it appears that the assemblage at Preseli and its abandoned successor were appointed to be held at *nos Galan Gaeaf*, when the survival of the kingship, and hence the country, fell momentarily under dire threat from Otherworld foes. Although winter dearth could not be avoided, prophylactic rites performed at the winter festival ensured that the monarchy and the realm would be restored with the spring. Appropriately, Rhiannon's son was born on 1 May, at the *Kalan Mai*.

The allusion to 'the end of the year' (*hyt ym pen y ulwydyn*) points to the festival of *nos Galan Gaeaf* in Britain, whose corresponding feast in Ireland was that of *Samain*. Celebrated on November Eve (All Hallows' Eve), the festival marked the end of the Celtic old year and beginning of the new, when the cosmos was momentarily split, and demonic beings of the Otherworld afforded opportunity to assail the world of men.[21]

A feature of *Samain* legends was the abduction, or attempted abduction, of a beautiful maiden, who personified the divine figure of the Maiden Sovereignty. On occasion, too, it provided the setting for the wedding of two divine or semi-divine beings.[22] Overall, it was a time

---

which her father's court lies' (Thomson (ed.), *Pwyll Pendeuic Dyuet*, p. 35).

19   Ibid., pp. 16–17.

20   Unfortunately, there is not space here to accord Ronald Hutton's sceptical assessment of Rhiannon as divinity the consideration it deserves ('Medieval Welsh Literature and Pre-Christian Deities', *Cambrian Medieval Celtic Studies* (Aberystwyth, 2011), lxi, pp. 76–84). In any case, the considerations raised here are not addressed in his analysis.

21   'Le rituel royale se situe dans le temps à Samain, à la jonction de la lumière et de l'obscurité. Samain est la fête totale, aussi bien celle du roi qu'on élit que celle du roi qui meurt (de mort naturelle ou accidentelle)' (Françoise Le Roux, '*Recherches sur les éléments rituels de l'élection royale Irlandaise et Celtique*', *Ogam: tradition celtique* (Rennes, 1963), xv, pp. 254–55).

22   Cf. Kuno Meyer, '*Macgnimartha Finn inn so sis*', *Revue Celtique* (Paris, 1882), v, p. 202; A. G. van Hamel (ed.), *Compert Con Culainn and Other Stories* (Dublin, 1933), pp. 60–62; Shaw (ed.), *The Dream of Óengus*, pp. 61–63.

of peril for the king and his kingdom, the potential for destruction of both being symbolized by the threatened abduction of the Maiden Sovereignty. At the same time, there was paradoxically a corresponding aspect of optimism, with lavish consumption of food and drink at a feast guaranteeing the eventual restoration of the world at springtide.[23]

Although descriptions of the winter festival are more fully recorded in Ireland than in Britain, an early Welsh legend establishes the link with the myth of the Maiden Sovereignty with great clarity. The wild tale of *Culhwch ac Olwen* contains many allusions to ancient legends which must otherwise have been lost. Among these is one which has attracted particular attention. Included among a fantastic list of warriors and ladies invoked by Culhwch in his search for the lovely Olwen is Creiddylad, daughter of Lludd Llaw Ereint,

> the most majestic maiden there ever was in the Three Islands of Britain and her Three Adjacent Islands. And for her Gwythyr mab Greidol and Gwyn mab Nudd fight each May-day (*Kalan Mai*) forever until Judgment Day (*dyd brawt*).

Later in the tale we learn more of this recurrent combat. Creiddylad elopes with Gwythyr, only to be abducted by Gwyn ap Nudd on the eve of their marriage. Gwythyr immediately assembles a host but is defeated by Gwyn, who imprisons and cruelly maltreats Gwythyr's leading followers in the North (*y Gogled*). At this Arthur marches to the North, where he obtains the release of the prisoners. He makes peace between the rivals, imposing terms. Creiddylad is to remain unmolested in her father Lludd's house, while Gwyn and Gwythyr are required to fight every May-day from this till Judgment Day, when the victor would obtain the maiden.[24]

This represents no more than a succinct outline of what must once have been an important myth. Fortunately, more is known from other sources, and may also be inferred from the details of this laconic account. Gwyn ap Nudd is described elsewhere in *Culhwch ac Olwen* as possessed of the spirits of the demons of Annwfn, and is elsewhere depicted in a sinister light.[25] Little is known of Gwythyr outside the tale, but the account in *Culhwch* suggests that he was regarded as the legitimate spouse of Creiddylad.

That the battle occurred every May-day suggests calendrical myth. Not only this, but the name *Gwythyr mab Greidawl*, 'Victor son of Scorcher, [provides] not a very inappropriate designation for the summer sun'.[26] Although this explanation has been doubted, it remains likely that the episode derives from a myth of annual combat between forces of summer and winter.[27]

23   Françoise Le Roux and Christian-J. Guyonvarc'h, *Les fêtes celtiques* (Rennes, 1995), pp. 75–76, 77.

24   Bromwich and Simon Evans (ed.), *Culhwch and Olwen*, pp. 13, 35.

25   Ibid., pp. 26–27; cf. pp. 134–35.

26   Rhys, *Lectures on the Origin and Growth of Religion as Illustrated by Celtic Heathendom*, p. 561. *Gwythyr* derives from Latin *Victor* (Patrick Sims-Williams, *The Celtic Inscriptions of Britain: Phonology and Chronology, c. 400–1200* (Oxford, 2003), p. 178), while *greidawl* means 'warm, fervent, hot' (J. Lloyd-Jones, *Geirfa Barddoniaeth Gynnar Gymraeg* (Cardiff, 1931–63), p. 588). 'His attributes may be regarded as the opposite of those of Gwyn, the god of death and darkness, and he was probably a form of the sun-god, the summer sun' (John Rhŷs, *Studies in the Arthurian Legend* (Oxford, 1891), p. 36). However it seems more likely that Gwythyr was originally a divinity associated with fertility and warmth, than the illusory sun-god favoured by much nineteenth-century scholarship.

27   E. K. Chambers, *Arthur of Britain* (London, 1927), p. 74. Idris Foster's reservation is surely overly sceptical: 'It may well be that ... we have a commonplace incident of folklore, and it is better to regard it as such than to probe the abysmal darkness of an abandoned mythology in search of an «explanation»' (Eoin MacNeill and Gerard Murphy (ed.), *Duanaire Finn: The Book of the Lays of Finn* (London and Dublin, 1908–53), iii, p. 201). For ritual contests between summer and winter, cf. E. K. Chambers, *The*

This is not the sole consideration. Firstly, the etymology of the names of Creiddylad and Gwythyr ap Greidawl appears appropriate to their functions in the myth. *Creiddylad* appears to be a compound of *creu*, 'blood', and *dylad*, 'flood, tide, deluge'.[28] This is an apt enough etymology for a figure emblematic of the Maiden Sovereignty, abducted like the Greek Persephone, who preserves the life-force throughout her winter disappearance. For 'blood is the life-giving agent par excellence', the soul-substance which explains the significance of regenerative blood-sacrifices. Among early and primitive peoples, red is the colour of life, corpses and skeletons being daubed with ochre in order to assure the life-spirit of its continuance.[29] In Mithraic ritual sacrificial bull's blood was the stuff of life, while Christians at the Eucharist drink wine as the Blood of Christ.[30]

Alternative semantic terminologies of 'blood' in Indo-European languages indicate an archaic belief in contrasted forms. On the one hand, related words exist for internal blood: that which flows, and contains the vivifying essence of existence. On the other, there is external blood, which coagulates, freezes, and solidifies. This second etymology symbolizes non-life and cessation of existence, i.e. death.[31] The connexion of this conception with that of the Maiden Sovereignty is evident. After being incarcerated for six months of the year by the Lord of the Underworld (*Annwfn*), she is rescued every Calends of May by a divinity associated with heat and light: a process which is re-enacted until the end of time. That she should be called 'Flowing Blood' appropriately signifies her identification with the latent life-force persisting throughout the dead months of winter, which re-emerges as ever fruitful with the spring.

Gwyn ap Nudd, cast as abductor of the Maiden Sovereignty, was popularly envisaged as a swartly sinister divinity, associated with swamps and mountain mists. In contrast, the derivation of his adversary's name from Latin *victor*, together with his patronymic *greidawl* ('warm, fervent, hot'), combine to identify Creuddylad's rescuer Gwythyr as the benign æstival protagonist in the conflict.[32] The myth is explicitly calendrical, and, as Sir John Rhŷs suggested, 'if we had the myth in a more extended form, Gwyn's victory would be found to happen at the beginning of winter.'[33]

Mediaeval Stage (Oxford, 1903), i, pp. 187–88; Kenneth Jackson, *Studies in Early Celtic Nature Poetry* (Cambridge, 1935), pp. 158–59, 162; M. L. West, *Indo-European Poetry and Myth* (Oxford, 2007), p. 237.

28   Andrew Breeze translates the name as 'Rough Torrent' (Richard Coates and Andrew Breeze (ed.), *Celtic Voices English Places: Studies of the Celtic Impact on Place-Names in England* (Stamford, 2000), p. 91). However an early poem contains the form *Creurddilad*, making *Creudilad* the more likely original form (Brynley F. Roberts, 'Rhai o Gerddi Ymddiddan Llyfr Du Caerfyrddin', in Rachel Bromwich and R. Brinley Jones (ed.), *Astudiaethau ar yr Hengerdd* (Cardiff, 1978), pp. 314, 317).

29   Lucien Lévy-Bruhl, *Primitives and the Supernatural* (London, 1936), pp. 265–91; Etienne Patte, *Les Hommes Préhistoriques et La Religion* (Paris, 1960), pp. 62–67 Myra Shackley, *Rocks and Man* (London, 1977), pp. 143–44; Karlene Jones-Bley, 'Red for the Dead', in Dorothy Disterheft, Martin Huld, John Greppin, and Edgar C. Polomé (ed.), *Studies in Honor of Jaan Puhvel* (Washington, 1997), i, pp. 211–20; Vladimir Napolskikh, Anna-Leena Siikala, and Mihály Hoppál (ed.), *Komi Mythology* (Budapest, 2003), pp. 347–49.

30   E. O. James, *Sacrifice and Sacrament* (London, 1962), pp. 27, 60–63, 119, 130, 136-37, 236; Leroy A. Campbell, *Mithraic Iconography and Ideology* (Leiden, 1968), pp. 261–62; Brian Hayden, *Shamans Sorcerers and Saints* (Washington, 2003), pp. 97–99; Stephen Aldhouse-Green, *Paviland Cave and the 'Red Lady': A Definitive Report* (Bristol, 2000), p. 235.

31   Uli Linke, 'Blood as Metaphor in Proto-Indo-European', *The Journal of Indo-European Studies* (Washington, 1985), xiii, pp. 333–43. The Nuer of the Nilotic Sudan fought battles with clubs rather than their prized spears: 'It may be that behind it is the notion that not the same responsibility is felt if the life-blood does not flow as it would from a fatal spear wound – that in a sense the man has not taken the life, that the death happened of itself, as the Nuer would put it … This must mean that blood is thought to have some vitality of its own' (E. E. Evans-Pritchard, *Nuer Religion* (Oxford, 1956), p. 213).

32   Lloyd-Jones, *Geirfa Barddoniaeth Gynnar Gymraeg*, pp. 587–88.

33   Rhys, *Lectures on the Origin and Growth of Religion as Illustrated by Celtic Heathendom*, p. 562.

In the tale of *Pwyll*, Rhiannon's apparent lack of fertility impels the king and nobility of the realm to assemble at a specified spot, evidently chosen for its aptness to the occasion, where measures are undertaken to obviate this deadly threat to the kingdom's perpetuation, and ensure its survival. A stay is granted her until the next Winter Festival, by which time she must either produce an heir, or be compelled to abjure her royal status. Fortunately, in the interval she bears a son, and the future of the realm is assured. Moreover, *the birth of the child is explicitly linked to the Spring Festival, nos Galan Mai*. As if this were not suggestive enough, the baby boy (who proves in the event to be Pwyll's son and heir Pryderi), is initially known as 'Gwri Goldenhair' (*Gwri Wallt Euryn*). One does not have to be a devotee of nineteenth-century solar theories to detect here an evocation, if not of the sun, then of light and heat (*greidawl*) generally.

Thus, behind the euhemerized and romanticized story of *Pwyll*, may be detected a characteristic theme of Brittonic pagan mythology.

1. The King and nobility of Dyfed foregather at an assembly, which is convened in order to ensure the birth of an heir to the kingdom: an event in Celtic societies considered essential for the continuing security, wealth, and fertility of the country.
2. The gathering is appointed for a specified location on Preseli Mountain, again at the annual Winter Festival.
3. A further assembly is arranged to be held 'at the end of the year', 'in a year's time', i.e. the following Winter Festival, *Kalan Gaeaf*.
4. In the event, the Queen bears a son at the time of the Spring Festival (*nos Galan Mai*): a boy whose name 'Gwri Goldenhair' evokes vernal regeneration.
5. Rhiannon's son is said to have been born at the royal court of Arberth. Occasional confusion arises in the story from the author's attempts to reconcile traditions relating to the Otherworld realm of Annwfn, and the earthly kingdom of Dyfed. Since Arberth is explicitly represented as a place where supernatural encounters occur, it may be that Arberth and Preseli represent duplicated aspects of the primal sanctuary of Dyfed.

This is suggested by their respective etymologies.

> The mound of Arberth in the First Branch … was at a place whose name probably meant 'by the grove', prompting speculation that it could have been the site of a sacred oak grove'.[34]

Similarly,

> the early form of the name … *Preseleu* … is a compound of *pres*, a variant of *prys* 'brake, thicket, brushwood' and the pers. name *Seleu* …[35]

---

34 Alfred K. Siewers, 'Writing an Icon of the Land: the *Mabinogi* as a Mystagogy of Landscape', *Peritia: Journal of the Medieval Academy of Ireland* (Turnhout, 2005), xix, p. 222.

35 B. G. Charles, *The Place-Names of Pembrokeshire* (Aberystwyth, 1992), p. 26. Cf. Ifor Williams (ed.), *Pedeir Keinc y Mabinogi* (Cardiff, 1930), pp. 140–41. For *prys* as 'copse' or 'grove', cf. *Geiriadur Prifysgol Cymru: A Dictionary of the Welsh Language* (Cardiff, 1950–2002), p. 2925. *Selyf* is the Welsh version of Solomon, which must have replaced a previous pre-Christian name. Could it have been substituted for *Pwyll*, 'Wisdom'?

Curiously, it seems never to have been enquired why it was necessary for Pwyll's discussions with his nobles to be held far from his court at Arberth, at an uninhabited location among the chill rain-drenched crags of Preseli, on what is implicitly November Eve. It is surely plausible to suppose that *the place in early times possessed a peculiarly numinous faculty: one, moreover, appropriate to the purpose of the conference.* Since the gathering was expressly concerned with procreation of the royal lineage, it may be inferred that there existed a sacral location on Preseli Mountain, whose numen assured the fertility of the dynasty. It looks as though the episode in *Pwyll* reflects an archaic rite, wherein kings of Dyfed repair with their nobles to a sanctified site on Preseli Mountain. The purpose of such gatherings was to ensure the fecundity of the royal line, and by extension (in accordance with widespread belief among early societies) the fertility and welfare of the kingdom as a whole.[36]

In pre-Christian Ireland the most important and best-documented of such rites was that celebrated by the High King at the Feast of Tara, *feis Temro*. *Feis* means literally 'sleeps, spends the night, marries', and refers to

> the symbolical mating of the new king with the local Earth-Goddess, a ἱερος γάμος whose function was to bring fertility to man and beast in his reign. The most celebrated of these royal fertility rites is the so-called 'Feast of Tara' (*feis Temro*), originally a ritual marriage between the new king of Tara and the goddess Medb.[37]

This ceremony was not held, as might be expected, at the outset of a king's reign, but (as three recorded instances in the Irish annals testify) after a varying number of years have passed since his accession. No explanation is provided in the sources for this delay, and Binchy conjectured that

> perhaps the king had first to prove his worth against traditional enemies ... and to enforce his authority over all the subject tribes within the area of his rule. We may take it as certain that the rulers of these tribes attended the 'nuptial feast' in which the symbolical union of king and goddess was externalized.[38]

However, it seems unlikely that subordinate tribes were expected to rise in spontaneous rebellion at the accession of every new dynast. Moreover, a king might be expected to adopt measures to establish his legitimacy before, rather than after, any such outbreak. Given the nature of the rite, is it not preferable to suppose that its prime concern was that of perpetuation of the dynasty? The lack of a royal heir, after all, has throughout history provided a prime source of civil discord. This interpretation appears all but explicit in the Irish story 'The Wooing of Étaín' (*Tochmarc Étaíne*), a version of which was contained in the lost eighth-century compendium

36   Cf. A. M. Hocart, *Kingship* (Oxford, 1927), pp. 99–112; Henri Frankfort, *Kingship and the Gods: A Study of Ancient Near Eastern Religion as the Integration of Society & Nature* (Chicago, 1948), pp. 295–99; Samuel Noah Kramer, *The Sacred Marriage Rite: Aspects of Faith, Myth, and Ritual in Ancient Sumer* (Bloomington, Indiana, 1969), pp. 89–106; Lotte Motz, 'The Sacred Marriage – A study in Norse mythology', in Mohammad Ali Jazayery and Werner Winter (ed.), *Languages and Cultures: Studies in Honor of Edgar C. Polomé* (Berlin, 1988), pp. 449–59.

37   D. A. Binchy, *Celtic and Anglo-Saxon Kingship* (Oxford, 1970), p. 11; idem, 'The Fair of Tailtiu and the Feast of Tara', *Ériu* (1958), xviii, pp. 113–38; James Carney, *Studies in Early Irish Literature and History* (Dublin, 1955), pp. 334–39.

38   *Ériu*, xviii, pp. 137–38.

Cín Dromma Snechtai.[39] In it we read that Eochaid Airem, a year after his accession to the throne of Ireland, sought to hold the *Feis Temro* in order to impose tribute and taxes on his subjects for the next five years. To this, the latter replied that they would not convene the festival for a king who had no queen. Thereupon Eochaid despatched messengers to find the fairest virgin in Ireland, who proved to be Étaín daughter of Étar. She is implicitly portrayed as reincarnation of an earlier Étaín, wife of Midir. The duplication confirms that Eochaid 'is ultimately Midir's double'.[40] The Festival of Tara was duly convened, at which Eochaid and Étaín slept together, i.e. they were married.[41] The assertion that Eochaid proposed to hold the festival in order to raise revenue probably reflects the late unhistorical belief that the *Feis Temro* was primarily a political assembly.[42] In the event, the romance makes no further allusion to this factitious consideration, confirming that originally the ceremony was exclusively concerned with the king's symbolic wedding to the lady who personified the land.

Clearly, the royal consort played an essential rôle at the festival at Tara, focussed as it was on the royal marriage.[43] It was generally believed in early times that heroes and princes were of divine origin, a belief expressed in the recurrent literary motif of the interposition of a god for the father during the night of conception.[44] This myth is famously exemplified by the birth-tale of Arthur, who was conceived when Merlin enabled Uther to substitute himself unrecognized for the husband of his mother Igerna on the night of the great king's conception. There can

---

39   John Carey, 'On the Interrelationships of Some *Cín Dromma Snechtai* Texts', ibid. (1995), xlvi, pp. 89–91. For the date of *Cín Dromma Snechtai*, cf. Rudolf Thurneysen, *Die irische Helden- und Königsage bis zum siebzehnten Jahrhundert* (Halle, 1921), pp. 15–18; Nora White (ed.), *Compert Mongáin and Three Other Early Mongán Tales* (Maynooth, 2006), p. 67. Thomas Charles-Edwards has identified political considerations of the eighth and ninth centuries implicit in the extant text of *Tochmarc Étaíne* ('*Tochmarch Étaíne*: a literal interpretation', in Michael Richter and Jean-Michel Picard (ed.), *Ogma: Essays in Celtic Studies in honour of Próinséas Ní Chatháin* (Dublin, 2002), p. 167).

40   Thomas F. O'Rahilly, *Early Irish History and Mythology* (Dublin, 1946), p. 132. 'Given his role in the story as the figure to whom Étaín properly belongs, and who eventually retakes her from the king, there is a strong case for regarding Midhir as the male-patron of the kingship' (Dáithi Ó hÓgáin, *The Sacred Isle: Belief and Religion in Pre-Christian Ireland* (Woodbridge, 1999) p. 134).

41   Osborn Bergin and R. I. Best, 'Tochmarc Étaíne', *Ériu* (1938), xii, pp. 162–64.

42   Ibid., xviii, p. 138.

43   'Étain is a manifestation of the goddess of sovereignty, for we are told that the men of Ireland would not attend the feast of Tara before Eochaid married her' (Francis John Byrne, *Irish Kings and High-Kings* (London, 1973), p. 61). Cf. O'Rahilly, *Early Irish History and Mythology*, p. 293; Ó hÓgáin, *The Sacred Isle*, p. 134; Richter and Picard (ed.), *Ogma*, pp. 172–73. However the story has become thoroughly euhemerized, and the statement that the men of Ireland would not convene the *feis Temro* 'for a king that had no queen' reads like a traditional aphorism. A pagan Celtic king might have more than one wife at a time, polygamy and concubinage being common among early Welsh and Irish rulers (Theodor Mommsen (ed.), *Monvmenta Germaniae Historica* (xiii): *Chronica Minora saec. IV. V. VI. VII* (Berlin, 1894), iii, 42, 43, 46–47, 191; R. I. Best and Osborn Bergin (ed.), *Lebor na Huidre: Book of the Dun Cow* (Dublin, 1929), p. 133). At the same time it was requisite that a queen be of comparable social standing to the king (Christian-J. Guyonvarc'h, 'La Courtise d'Étain', *Celticvm XV: Actes du Vᵉ Colloque International d'Études Gauloises, Celtiques et Protoceltiques* (Rennes, 1966), p. 304). Could the need for a king to acquire a consort of appropriate rank explain in whole or part the delay between his accession and the holding of the *feis Temro*?

44   Alfred Nutt and Kuno Meyer, *The Celtic Doctrine of Re-birth* (London, 1897), pp. 22–102; Nora K. Chadwick, 'Pictish and Celtic Marriage in Early Literary Tradition', *Scottish Gaelic Studies* (Oxford, 1955), viii, pp. 81–106; Rachel Bromwich (ed.), *Trioedd Ynys Prydein: The Welsh Triads* (Cardiff, 1978), p. 460. The theme features in mythologies worldwide (Edwin Sidney Hartland, *The Legend of Perseus: A Study of Tradition in Story Custom and Belief* (London, 1894–96), i, pp. 71–181; Hocart, *Kingship*, pp. 15, 18–19; Ivan Engnell, *Studies in Divine Kingship in the Ancient Near East* (Uppsala, 1943), pp. 4, 76–78; Frankfort, *Kingship and the Gods*, pp. 159–61, 299–301).

be little doubt that in an earlier version Uther featured as a divinity, who in accordance with widely recorded legend substituted himself for the father on the night of the hero's conception.[45] The motif recurs in Indo-European tradition. In Greek mythology, Zeus fathered Herakles on Alcmene by sleeping with her in the guise of her husband Amphitryon, while the Vedic god Indra adopted the same stratagem to seduce the enticing Ahalyā.[46] Closer to hand are Irish folktale accounts of the conception of the god Lug. The malevolent giant Balor imprisoned his daughter Eithne in an impregnable tower on Tory Island. However (Fin) Mac Kinealy, assisted by a wizard, gains entry and sleeps with the maiden, who subsequently gives birth to 'Lui Lavada' (*Lug lamfáda*).[47] It may also account for the frequently misunderstood theme of *droit de seigneur*, which, regardless of whether or not it occurred in historical reality, ultimately reflects the mythical concept of divine birth.[48]

Reverting to the story of Pwyll's meeting with his nobles at Preseli, parallels with Eochaid's wedding to Étaín at the *feis Temro* are so close as to suggest their representing cognate versions of a Common Celtic theme preserved in Welsh and Irish mythology.

1. The name *Pwyll* means 'wisdom'.
   Midir's name derives from Celtic **Mediros*, which contains the root *med-* (as in Old Irish *midiur*, 'I judge'), bearing parallel semantic significance.[49]
2. When Pwyll first encounters his bride Rhiannon, she is riding an enchanted white steed. Her name indicates that she is the divine Great Queen, of whom a magical horse or mare represented the characteristic attribute.[50]

---

45 Nutt and Meyer, *The Celtic Doctrine of Re-birth*, pp. 22–37; James Douglas Bruce, *The Evolution of Arthurian Romance: From the Beginnings Down to the Year 1300* (Göttingen, 1928), i, p. 135; J. S. P. Tatlock, *The Legendary History of Britain: Geoffrey of Monmouth's Historia Regum Britanniae and its Early Vernacular Versions* (Berkeley and Los Angeles, 1950), pp. 316–19; Alwyn Rees and Brinley Rees, *Celtic Heritage: Ancient Tradition in Ireland and Wales* (London, 1961), p. 222. Uther was renowned in Welsh tradition as a potent magician (Egerton G. B. Phillimore, 'A Fragment from Hengwrt MS. No. 202', *Y Cymmrodor* (London, 1886), vii, pp. 126–27; Rachel Bromwich, 'The Historical Triads: With Special Reference to Peniarth MS. 16', *The Bulletin of the Board of Celtic Studies* (Cardiff, 1946), xii, p. 13; J. Gwenogvryn Evans (ed.), *Facsimile & Text of the Book of Taliesin* (Llanbedrog, 1910), pp. 71–72.

46 R. Merkelbach and M. L. West (ed.), *Fragmenta Hesiodea* (Oxford, 1967), pp. 94–96; Sir James George Frazer (ed.), *Apollodorus: The Library* (London, 1921), i, pp. 172–74; Sukumari Bhattacharji, *The Indian Theogony: A Comparative Study of Indian Mythology from the Vedas to the Puranas* (Cambridge, 1970), p. 272.

47 William Larminie, *West Irish Folk-Tales and Romances* (London, 1893), pp. 1–9; Michael Jeremiah Curtin, *Hero-Tales of Ireland* (London, 1894), pp. 283–88, 297–309; Michael Herity (ed.), *Ordnance Survey Letters Donegal: Letters Containing Information relative to the Antiquities of the County of Donegal Collected during the Progress of the Ordnance Survey in 1835* (Dublin, 2000), pp. 40–44.

48 *Scottish Gaelic Studies*, viii, pp. 98, 107–11; Rees and Rees, *Celtic Heritage*, pp. 227–28; Richard North, *Heathen Gods in Old English Literature* (Cambridge, 1997), pp. 259–64. The *ius primæ noctis* represented a theoretical right of an Irish king, 'en tant que représentant et substitut terrestre du «géniteur universel» (ollathir), cependant il est permis de douter qu'il en ait fait un usage très frequent' (Françoise Le Roux, 'La Courtise d'Étain: Commentaire du texte', *Celticvm XV*, p. 372). Evidence for the practice in reality is tenuous (Sir James George Frazer, *Folk-Lore in the Old Testament: Studies in Comparative Religion Legend and Law* (London, 1918), i, pp. 485–534).

49 'Mider, lord of the síd Otherworld of Brí Léith, whose name (Celt. **Mediros*; root *med-*, as in O. Ir. *midiur*, 'I judge') has probably much the same signification' as *Pwyll*' (O'Rahilly, *Early Irish History and Mythology*, p. 293).

50 W. J. Gruffydd, *Rhiannon: An Inquiry into the Origins of the First and Third Branches of the Mabinogi* (Cardiff, 1953), pp. 103–5. In the Indian *pravargya* sacrifice the mare corresponds to the earth: 'The sacrificer "touches the earth and mutters, 'Thou art Manu's mare'; for this earth is in the shape of a

Étaín bore the epithet *Echraide*, which means 'mounted' or 'horse-riding'.[51]

3. Despite Rhiannon's possession of a supernatural mount, Pwyll manages to ride fast enough to overtake her and declare his love.

Eochaid Airem was correspondingly renowned as a horseman.[52]

4. When Rhiannon removed her veil, Pwyll 'thought that the face of every maiden and every woman he had ever seen was unattractive compared with her face'.

Étaín is described as a maiden 'the dearest and loveliest in Ireland'. In each case, this preternatural beauty corresponds to that of the kingdom, whose sovereignty is personified by the divine or royal bride.[53]

5. Perpetuation of Pwyll's reign is threatened when his queen fails to produce an heir, and his nobles threaten condign action should her barrenness continue.

Midir's people are so concerned with the continuity of his dynasty, that they decline to co-operate with him until he find himself a consort.[54]

6. Pwyll is summoned by his nobles to meet at a designated spot to resolve his bride's apparent infertility.

Midir seeks to convene the traditional Festival of Tara (*feis Temro*), but his nobles boycott the occasion until he obtain an appropriate consort.

7. Pwyll requests his nobles to reconvene a year later to the day, suggesting that both date and place were deemed appropriate to the occasion.[55]

The *feis Temro* was held at Tara, on a calendrical festival, variously identified in the sources as Samain (1 November) or springtide (Easter).[56]

These considerations suggest that the assembly held by Pwyll and his followers at Preseli fulfilled a function comparable to that of the Irish *feis Temro*. Both occasions provided for enactment of rites at a sacred location, centring on the marriage of the king to a consort, who personified the goddess of the land: a ceremonial designed to assure the fertility of the queen, and consequent perpetuation of the dynasty and prosperity of the land.

This may be corroborated by the name of the Welsh assembly-place. As was seen earlier, the first element of *Preseleu* is Welsh *pres* or *prys*, a grove or thicket. However it seems unlikely that any but a few wind-bent scrubs grew on the inhospitable summit of Preseli Mountain, following upland forest clearances in the later Mesolithic era.[57] Given the unique ritual potency implicitly

mare called Manu, and he is her lord Prajāpati, with that mate, his favourite abode, he thus completes him" (A. M. Hocart, *Kingship* (Oxford, 1927), p. 105).

51 E. G. Quin *et al.* (ed.), *Dictionary of the Irish Language: Based mainly on Old and Middle Irish Materials* (Dublin, 1913–76), 'E', col. 31; O'Rahilly, *Early Irish History and Mythology*, p. 293.

52 Edward Gwynn (ed.), *The Metrical Dindshenchas* (Dublin, 1903–35), iii, p. 350.

53 Elsewhere it is confirmed that Étaín's beauty surpassed that of all other women, while her divinity is indicated by her declaration that she was born in a fairy mound (*síd*) (Eleanor Knott (ed.), *Togail Bruidne Da Derga* (Dublin, 1936), pp. 1–2).

54 'The first point to note is that the king's marriage is constantly associated with his consecration ... We gather ... that in Ancient India a king could not be consecrated without a queen' (Hocart, *Kingship*, p. 101).

55 In early India, 'Various rites, duties and observances are said to be performed or undertaken for a year' (J. Gonda, *Prajāpati and the Year* (Amsterdam, 1984), pp. 30–31).

56 *Ériu*, xviii, pp. 127–28.

57 I. G. Simmons, *The Environmental Impact of Later Mesolithic Cultures: The Creation of Moorland Landscape in England and Wales* (Edinburgh, 1996), pp. 225–28.

ascribed the site in *Pwyll*, it is possible that the *pres* of *Presseli* was employed as metonymy for 'sanctuary'. The druids were famously said to worship in forest clearings, and in his *Bellum Civile* Lucan depicts them as conducting fearsome rites within deep groves situated in remote woods (*nemora alta remotis incolitis lucis*). His description of Caesar's siege of Marseilles includes a disturbingly sinister description of the great general's destruction of a sacred grove (*lucus*), where human sacrifices were practised, and even its priest (*sacerdos*) feared to approach the lord of the grove (*dominus luci*), i.e. its presiding deity.[58]

It is likely that Lucan exaggerated the grimmer aspects of his account, in order to exalt Caesar's courage in destroying a site which the local Gauls held sacrosanct. Other classical authors confirm that druids practised their rites in forests and comparably remote spots,[59] possibly reflecting belief in the sacrality of woods and trees.[60]

Appropriation by the Centre

The colossal feat of engineering required to move the Stonehenge bluestones across some two hundred miles from Preseli to Salisbury Plain indicates that they were accorded exceptional spiritual potency at their original site.[61] Otherwise, what can have been the point of so laborious an operation?[62] H. J. Fleure suggested that the bluestones 'were a sacred monument in their original home', concluding that 'a part of Stonehenge had been a sacred monument elsewhere, and was brought to Stonehenge in all probability by sea'.[63] This hypothesis was scouted by Atkinson, who contended that it was Preseli Mountain itself which was regarded as holy.[64] Recent extensive examination of the Preseli region by Pearson and his colleagues leaves it an open question whether or not it was a dismantled monument that was moved to Stonehenge.[65]

These differing suggestions are not incompatible. The mountain dramatically dominates the landscape around, and represents a feature of the landscape singularly appropriate to reverence throughout a broad region. Great ritual importance was attached to extensive mountain views in pagan Irish tradition.[66] The exceptional situation of Preseli Mountain was remarked by a local landowner at the close of the reign of Queen Elizabeth I:

---

58   D. R. Shackleton Bailey (ed.), *M. Annaei Lucani De Bello Civili Libri X* (Leipzig, 1988), pp. 16, 64–66.

59   H. Rackham, W. H. S. Jones, and D. E. Eichholz, (ed.), *Pliny: Natural History* (London, 1938–62), iv, pp. 548–50; A. Silberman (ed.), *Pomponius Mela: Chorographie* (Paris, 1988), pp. 72–73.

60   Christian-J. Guyonvarc'h and Françoise Le Roux, *Les Druides* (Rennes, 1986), pp. 228–31. The druids' increasing resort to remote haunts under the Roman occupation presumably represented a natural precautionary recourse.

61   'Doubtless they had acquired already a sacred significance [at Preseli]' (E. O. James, *The Tree of Life: An Archaeological Study* (Leiden, 1966), p. 62).

62   Mike Parker Pearson, *Stonehenge: Exploring the Greatest Stone Age Mystery* (London, 2012), pp. 274–75.

63   H. J. Fleure, 'Archaeology and Folk Tradition', *The Proceedings of the British Academy* (London, 1932), xvii, p. 379. 'In other words, Stonehenge must once have had a forerunner so sacred that its stones had to be transported and re-erected in the existing sanctuary' (V. Gordon Childe, *Prehistoric Communities of the British Isles* (London, 1940), p. 105. Cf. *Antiquity*, xv, p. 306).

64   Atkinson, *Stonehenge*, pp. 174–75. Subsequent researches bear out Atkinson's conclusion: 'Perhaps Mynydd Preseli was the home of the gods: the Mount Olympus of Neolithic Britain' (Timothy Darvill and Geoff Wainwright, 'Beyond Stonehenge: Carn Menyn Quarry and the origin and date of bluestone extraction in the Preseli Hills of south-west Wales', *Antiquity* (2014), lxxxviii, p. 1112).

65   Pearson, *Stonehenge*, pp. 283–84, 288.

66   Máire MacNeill, *The Festival of Lughnasa: A Study of the Survival of the Celtic Festival of the Beginning of Harvest* (Oxford, 1962), pp. 67, 428; Elizabeth FitzPatrick, *Royal Inauguration in Gaelic Ireland*

Gors Fawr Stone Circle with Preseli Mountain beyond.

From this hill maie be seene all *Penbrokeshire*, and some parte of ix. other shires, vidz. *Carmarthenshire, Cardiganshire, Glamorganshire, Brecknockshire, Montgomery shire, Merioneth shire*, and *Caernarvon shire, Devonshire* and *Somersetshire*, the Iland of *Lundie* and the realme of *Jreland* … allso out of this Mounteine hath manie fine Ryvers their originall and beginninges namelie, *Nevarne, Taf, Clydach, Cledhe, Syvynvey, Gwein, Clydach* againe, and the third *Clydach* w[ch] water most partes of the Countrey … This Mounteine is so highe and farre mounted into the ayre, that when the Countrey about is faire and cleere, the toppe thereof wilbe hidden in a cloude.[67]

This description accords Preseli Mountain three primary characteristics of the Omphalos: its worldwide perspective, its function as source of rivers, and its link to the sky.

The association of physical elevation with sacred transcendence underlies religious thought throughout the world, and is well attested among the Celtic people. The mountain, or even the prominent hilltop, by virtue of its being the spot at which the earth comes nearest the sky, is in some measure a replica of the sacred mountain which touches the sky and which therefore stands, as the Axis Mundi, at the centre of the world.[68]

Writing in the sixth century AD, Gildas alludes to widespread worship of mountains 'upon which the people in their blindness formerly heaped divine honour'.[69] This contemptuous

---

    c. 1100–1600 (Woodbridge, 2004), pp. 131–37).

67   Henry Owen (ed.), *The Description of Pembrokeshire, by George Owen of Henllys, Lord of Kemes* (London, 1892–1936), i, p. 103.

68   Proinsias Mac Cana, 'Placenames and Mythology in Irish Tradition: Places, Pilgrimages and Things', in Gordon W. MacLennan (ed.), *Proceedings of the First North American Congress of Celtic Studies* (Ottawa, 1988), p. 323.

69   Mommsen (ed.), *Chronica Minora*, iii, p. 29.

dismissal appears to have reflected wishful thinking, since evidence attests to continuing veneration of mountains in later times.

Another remarkable tradition is recorded of Tintock, the highest mountain in Lanarkshire. A stone on its summit was believed to be surrounded by a magical mist, within which was to be found a cup from which the visitor was adjured to drink. These details bear striking resonances of the concluding episode of the Welsh romance of *Gereint*; as also an adventure experienced by the hero of the early twelfth-century Anglo-Norman romance of *Fergus* on a 'Black Mountain', probably located in Dumfriesshire.[70]

There are intimations of rituals practised by druids or their female equivalents on mountaintops. The Irish Life of the sixth-century Saint Berach describes his encounter with an enchantress, who repaired with a coven of her followers to a mountain top at Glendalough, where they practised 'druidism, and (magic) craft, and paganism, and diabolical science (*d'imirt draoidhechta, 7 tuaichle, 7 geinntlechta, 7 ealadhan diabail*)'.[71]

Although it is clear that such rites might be performed in the absence of any man-made structure, it is not unlikely that the Stonehenge bluestones comprised a sanctuary of some sort in their original resting place.

It appears that at least two of these stones (150 and 36) had been used previously in another setting, either at the monument or elsewhere, as they have mortice holes which are not necessary in their current setting.

While such work could have been undertaken at an earlier stage in the construction of Stonehenge at its present site, it is equally possible that the stones belonged to an imported structure. Furthermore, there exists no conclusive evidence of their having been dressed beside their present location.[72]

Fortunately, the issue is not of decisive significance in this context. Massive bluestones on Preseli Mountain are found free-standing in consequence of geological evolution, and it would have been possible for a sanctuary to have been established there, requiring little or no modification. It is hard to conceive of its ever becoming possible to decide between this, and the alternative possibility that the stones moved to Stonehenge were regarded as imbued with sacral power in consequence of their connexion with a mountain regarded as peculiarly holy.

In early societies the conquest or absorption of one country by another was frequently symbolically established by sequestration of the most sacred artefacts of the tributary realm, and their reinstatement within the corresponding holy of holies of the victorious power. Thus, in 547 BC the Chinese conqueror of the province of Ch'en was said to have been presented by the defeated ruler with an image of the God of the Soil, and ritual vessels used in the Temple of the Ancestors.

70   J. F. Campbell, *Popular Tales of the West Highlands Orally Collected* (Paisley, 1890–93), iv, p. 320; Wilson Frescoln (ed.), *Guillaume Le Clerc: The Romance of Fergus* (Philadelphia, 1983), pp. 91–98. 'Tintock is Gaelic '*teinteach*, 'place of fire'' (W. J. Watson, *The History of the Celtic Place-Names of Scotland* (Edinburgh, 1926), p. 205).

71   Charles Plummer (ed.), *Bethada Náem nÉrenn: Lives of Irish Saints* (Oxford, 1922), i, p. 30. Cf. Guyonvarc'h and Le Roux, *Les Druides*, p. 147. Ecstatic rapture on mountaintops constituted regular prophetic practice in early Israel (G. W. H. Lampe, *God as Spirit: The Bampton Lectures, 1976* (Oxford, 1977), pp. 51–52).

72   Rosamund M. J. Cleal, K. E. Walker, and R. Montague (ed.), *Stonehenge in its landscape: Twentieth-century excavations* (London, 1995), pp. 29, 398–99; Alex Gibson, *Stonehenge & Timber Circles* (Stroud, 1998), pp. 114, 118–19. That the bluestones were moved at least twice at Stonehenge increases the difficulty of determining whether they were originally dressed elsewhere.

When the invader received these two symbols, the guarantees respectively of sustenance and government, it signified that the entire state had passed into his hands.

Another Chinese ruler would arrange for the plan of a vanquished prince's palace to be copied and recreated within the imperial capital:

In this way he apparently sought to focus and concentrate at his own capital the vital forces that had previously been channelled through rival capitals.

In the twelfth century AD, Jayavarman VII of Cambodia constructed a huge centrally situated temple-mountain, known as the Bàyon, which was surrounded by forty-nine smaller towers representing the provinces of his empire. Each tower housed holy relics symbolizing a particular province, so that all were drawn together into a focus at the centre, where the divine and earthly worlds met.[73]

Similarly, the Romans bore away images of the tutelary deities of cities they conquered, who were invited with much reverence to take up residence in Rome. In the Eternal City the sacred enclosure known as *pomerium* was surrounded by a ditch reputedly ploughed by Romulus, to which handfuls of earth were brought from each Roman district. Thus the enclosure epitomized Roman territory in its entirety. Later, as Rome expanded into a great empire, the *pomerium* was correspondingly increased in size. The *mundus* being a point of access to the Otherworld, component parts of the Empire were symbolically assembled at a point regarded as the centre of the earth ('all roads lead to Rome'), which was divinely sanctioned as a microcosm of the entire world.[74]

In AD 37 Roman annexation of Egypt was marked by removal of an obelisk dedicated to the sun at the temple of Aton in Heliopolis. On its re-erection in Rome, the consul Cornelius Gallus had a Latin text inscribed on it. This imposition of the language of the conqueror on the sacred monument confirmed that the land of Egypt had acquired a new master.[75]

The requirement that a conqueror's absorption of tributary territory be expressed in ideological terms is of great antiquity and extensive record.

---

73   Paul Wheatley, *The Pivot of the Four Quarters: A Preliminary Enquiry into the Origins and Character of the Ancient Chinese City* (Edinburgh, 1971), pp. 431–32. The Qin capital represented 'a microcosm of the Chinese empire on Earth. Each time Qin conquered a Warring State, a replica of that state's palace was built on the northern bank of the Wei River, facing the new palace to the south … Because palaces were seen as the embodiment of states, the Qin could symbolically annex a state by destroying its original palace and rebuilding a "captive" replica in its own capital' (Mark Edward Lewis, *The Early Chinese Empires: Qin and Han* (Cambridge, Mass., 2007), p. 89).

74   Wheatley, *The Pivot of the Four Quarters*, pp. 432–33; Jean Chélini and Henry Branthomme (ed.), *Histoire des pèlerinages non chrétiens: Entre magique et sacré: le chemin des dieux* (Paris, 1987), pp. 147–48. About 205 BC the Romans acquired a stone (probably a meteorite) sacred to the Great Goddess (*Magna Mater*) from Pessinus in Phrygia, which was thereafter preserved in Rome (Arthur Bernard Cook, *Zeus: A Study in Ancient Religion* (Cambridge, 1914–40), iii, pp. 893–98). Before and during battle the Romans employed rituals (*euocatio*) designed to draw their enemies' gods over to their side (John Pairman Brown, *Israel and Hellas* (Berlin, 1995–2001), ii, pp. 242–47). In East Africa, the royal capital of Buganda 'was a microcosm of the kingdom, laid out so that it reflected the administrative order of Buganda as a whole' (Benjamin C. Ray, *Myth, Ritual, and Kingship in Buganda* (Oxford, 1991), p. 203).

75   J. N. Adams, *Bilingualism and the Latin Language* (Cambridge, 2003), pp. 571–72.

Another act of consecration was the transport of ashes from an older altar to the new location, or the use in new foundations of «sacred» elements, ἱερά (ash, implements, decoration, sacrificed material) taken from old sacred places.[76]

In Mexico under the Aztecs, tribute of blood and jewels from every province of the empire was periodically built into the great temple of their capital of Tenochtitlan.[77]

Potent symbolic rites of a similar nature continued to be practised in Ireland and Britain well into the Middle Ages. About 1101 the Munster king Muirchertach ua Briain 'brake down the Stone-house that was in Aileagh' (the great Ulster hillfort capital of Ailech), and brought 'the stones of Ailech' (*clocha Oiligh*) back to his own stronghold of Limerick (*Luimneach*).[78] The ritual significance of this operation may serve to explain the discovery at Navan Fort in Ulster (the *Emain Macha* of the Irish sagas) of a cairn of imported stones encased in a timber building. The care with which this Iron Age structure had been assembled suggested to its excavators that the stones represented an earlier monument which had been transported to Emain Macha.[79]

After his conquest of Wales, Edward I dismantled the slain Welsh king Llywelyn ap Gruffydd's timber hall at Ystumgwern, and transported it four miles northward to the inner ward of his new castle at Harlech. The intent of this action is confirmed by remarkable measures undertaken by the royal conqueror to transfer the holiest relics of Wales and Scotland to London, in order to symbolize the King of England's hegemony over all Britain.[80]

Of these sacred artefacts, the most celebrated is the Stone of Scone, on which Caledonian kings had been crowned since Pictish times. Early accounts refer to the Stone as 'the anchor' (*anchora*) of the Scottish kingdom, and the Moot Hill on which it stood as *collis credulitas*, 'the hill of (religious) faith'.[81] As Nick Aitchison notes in his history of the Stone of Scone: 'These sources express the Stone's symbolic role as the *axis mundi* securing Scone and, indeed, the kingdom of the Scots within the cosmos.'[82]

The Moot Hill at Scone fulfilled a function corresponding to that of the Hill of Uisneach in Ireland. Meath was originally no more than a small area surrounding Uisneach, the *omphalos*

---

76 Vassilis Lambrinoudakis and Jean Ch. Balty (ed.), *Thesaurus Cultus et Rituum Antiquorum* (Los Angeles, 2004–6), iii, p. 339.

77 Eduardo Matos Moctezuma, 'The Templo Mayor of Tenochtitlan: History and Interpretation', in Johanna Broda, David Carrasco, and Eduardo Matos Moctezuma, *The Great Temple of Tenochtitlan: Center and Periphery in the Aztec World* (Berkeley, 1987), pp. 38–39.

78 Denis Murphy (ed.), *The Annals of Clonmacnoise: Being Annals of Ireland from the Earliest Period to A.D. 1408* (Dublin, 1896), p. 46; Rev. L. McKenna (ed.), *ıomarɓáᵹ na ɓƒileaᵭ: The Contention of the Bards* (London, 1918), i, p. 188.

79 D. M. Waterman, *Excavations at Navan Fort 1961–71* (Belfast, 1997), pp. xvi, pp. 37–38, 49, 50-52, 210, 226–27; plates 17–21.

80 G. W. S. Barrow, *Robert Bruce and the Community of the Realm of Scotland* (London, 1965), pp. 102–103; R. R. Davies, *Conquest, Coexistence, and Change: Wales 1063–1415* (Oxford, 1987), pp. 355–56; idem, *The First English Empire: Power and Identities in the British Isles 1093–1343* (Oxford, 2000), pp. 27–28.

81 William F. Skene (ed.), *Chronicles of the Picts, Chronicles of the Scots, and Other Early Memorials of Scottish History* (Edinburgh, 1867), pp. 333; idem (ed.), *Johannis de Fordun Chronica Gentis Scotorum* (Edinburgh, 1871–72), i, p. 23; Marjorie O. Anderson, *Kings and Kingship in Early Scotland* (Edinburgh, 1973), p. 251; Seán Mac Airt and Gearóid Mac Niocaill (ed.), *The Annals of Ulster (to A.D. 1131)* (Dublin, 1983), i, p. 180 . Cf. William F. Skene, *The Coronation Stone* (Edinburgh, 1869), pp. 30–32. *Moot* is presumably either Old English *mōt, gemōt*, or Old Norse *mót*, 'an assembly of people, esp. one concerned with judicial matters' (A. H. Smith, *English Place-Name Elements* (Cambridge, 1956), ii, p. 44; Jan de Vries, *Altnordisches Etymologisches Wörterbuch* (Leiden, 1961), pp. 393–94).

82 Nick Aitchison, *Scotland's Stone of Destiny: Myth, History and Nationhood* (London, 2000), p. 105.

or *axis mundi* of ancient Ireland. The name of the district derives from Celtic **Medion*, meaning 'the middle spot'.[83] This reflects the ideological conception of Ireland as composed of four quarters (Ulster, Connacht, Munster and Leinster), focussed on a Centre (Meath). The Centre was in turn considered a microcosm or epitome of the whole.[84]

According to legend, earth was brought from far and wide to the Moot Hill at Scone, so that it became known as *omnis terra*, 'the whole world'. Mediæval tradition held that the over-liberal Scottish king Malcolm II dispersed his inheritance so profusely as to retain only the Hill of Scone, where Scottish kings seated on their throne dispensed judgment.[85] Since this did not occur in reality, it can only reflect a belief that the Moot Hill epitomized the entire kingdom, with its king ritually stationed at its Centre, from which he dispensed the nation's wealth. Again, the province of Gowrie in which it stood was considered to be the point at which the four provinces of the kingdom of the Southern Picts met.[86] In this mythical palimpsest, the Moot Hill corresponded to Uisneach in Ireland, and Gowrie to Meath. As Pictish culture and society preserved much that was of pre-Indo-European origin, traditions attached to the Moot Hill may have originated in the Bronze Age, or even earlier.

Thus, when Edward I removed the Stone of Scone in 1296 and transported it to London, where it was encased within a wooden throne upon which English monarchs were thenceforth crowned, he invoked the most powerful imagery possible of the subjection of Scotland to English kings. As Aitchison explains:

> Edward's motives were political; he removed the Stone to demonstrate that he was now the overlord of Scotland and that in future the Scots were to have no other kings but Edward and his descendants. Edward believed that without the Stone on which its kings were installed, Scotland had ceased to be an independent sovereign nation, leaving England the dominant and *only* kingdom within the British Isles.[87]

It is in this context that the laborious removal of the Preseli bluestones to Stonehenge may be understood.[88] It can scarcely be doubted that the resources required for erection of the colossal

---

83   O'Rahilly, *Early Irish History and Mythology*, pp. 166, 171; Julius Pokorny, *Indogermanisches Etymologisches Wörterbuch* (Berne, 1959–69), i, pp. 706–7; Xavier Delamarre, *Dictionnaire de la langue gauloise: Une approche linguistique du vieux-celtique continental* (Paris, 2001), p. 188; Roseanne Schot, 'From cult centre to royal centre: monuments, myths and other revelations at Uisneach', in Roseanne Schot, Conor Newman, and Edel Bhreatnach (ed.), *Landscapes of Cult and Kingship* (Dublin, 2011), p. 92.

84   Rees and Rees, *Celtic Heritage*, pp. 118–22. This in turn probably reflected cosmic symbolism: 'the whole is articulated on the number five; the universe is divided into four parts, with at its centre the fifth, highest quarter (zenith), which encompasses the whole: "the heaven is the quarters of space" (*diśo vai svargo lokaḥ*)' (J. C. Heesterman, *The Ancient Indian Royal Consecration: The Rājasūya Described According to the Yajus Texts and Annotated* (The Hague, 1957), p. 104).

85   Thomas Pennant, *A Tour in Scotland and Voyage to the Hebrides. MDCCLXXII. Part II.* (London, 1776), p. 115; Skene (ed.), *Johannis de Fordun Chronica Gentis Scotorum*, i, p. 186. Cf. Aitchison, *Scotland's Stone of Destiny*, p. 106.

86   William F. Skene, *Celtic Scotland: A History of Ancient Alban* (Edinburgh, 1876–80), i, p. 281; Aitchison, *Scotland's Stone of Destiny*, p. 106.

87   Ibid., p. 116. *Et in redeundo per Scone precepit* [Edward] *tolli et Londonias cariari lapidem illum, in quo vt supradictum est reges Scotorum solebant poni loco coronacionis sue, et hoc in signum regni resignati et conquest* (Harry Rothwell (ed.), *The Chronicle of Walter of Guisborough* (London, 1957), p. 281).

88   'A powerful elite, bent on making a monumental religious statement, could have used the relocation of an existing sacred structure as a sign of its own power and as a method of "sanctifying" the "new" monument' (Waterman, *Excavations at Navan Fort 1961–71*, p. 227).

construction work at Stonehenge were those of a powerful monarchy ruling over much or all of the extensive region of southern Britain termed 'Wessex' by prehistorians. Atkinson's conclusion is persuasive:

> I believe, therefore, that Stonehenge itself is evidence of the concentration of political power, for a time at least, in the hands of a single man, who alone could create and maintain the conditions necessary for this great undertaking.[89]

However, given the centuries it took to erect the monument in its successive stages, I suggest that for 'man', should rather be read 'dynasty'.

At the outset of the creation of the sacred complex, a decision was made to bring the bluestones from the extreme western seaboard of Britain, and re-erect them at the sacred site of what was regarded as the Omphalos of Britain at Stonehenge.[90] The mediæval Welsh story of *Pwyll*, which preserves archaic tradition of a sanctuary at Preseli, at which assemblies were held ensuring perpetuation of dynastic rule over the kingdom of Dyfed, suggests the motive for this colossal operation.

Consequently, it is likely that the unequalled feat involved in removing the enormous stones from Dyfed to Salisbury Plain reflects a 'Wessex' domination of south-west Wales, or at any rate some form of subordination of that region to whatever authority controlled southern Britain. In what other circumstance is a Bronze Age ruler of Demetia likely to have submitted to abstraction of the numinous focus of his dynasty's legitimacy and power? The numen of the subordinate region was absorbed into that of the conqueror, so that henceforth all authority, divine and human, became concentrated within the one great shrine at the Centre of Britain. This suggests that it was over four thousand years ago, during the Late Neolithic Era, that the first British monarchy came into existence. By the same token, domination of south-west Wales by the kingdom of 'Wessex' might be regarded as the earliest 'historical' event in British history.

It is hard to envisage any purpose for the colossal operation other than that of absorption at Stonehenge of the generative power of the incorporated stones. We may envisage annual rites performed at the great sanctuary there, whose primary purpose was to preserve and perpetuate a mighty dynasty ruling over Bronze Age Wessex, whose authority extended in some form to the Irish Sea. In view of these considerations, Geoffrey of Monmouth's emphasis on an ideological symbiosis between Stonehenge (*Mons Ambrii*) and the British monarchy may not have been altogether fanciful. It was there that he represents Aurelius as being crowned king and later buried, and there that his successors Uther and Constantine came likewise to be interred.[91]

---

89 Atkinson, *Stonehenge*, p. 165. 'Stonehenge: a rebuilt monument massive and unique, having a majestic dignity and architectural subtlety in the construction and placing of its elements, which in themselves suggest an Authority covering a great part of both Highland and Lowland Britain ...' (Sir Cyril Fox, *Life and Death in the Bronze Age: An Archaeologist's Field-Work* (London, 1959), p. xxv). Massive labour required for the erection of major monuments like Avebury, Stonehenge, and Silbury 'raises the possibility of a political situation more like that of Medieval times, with a super-chief (or king) able to secure labour from his neighbours and lessers' (Colin Burgess, *The Age of Stonehenge* (London, 1980), pp. 171–72). The Britons possessed a term *wortigernos for 'super-chief', which survives in the personal name *Vortigern* (Ifor Williams, 'Hen Chwedlau', *The Transactions of the Honourable Society of Cymmrodorion: Sessions 1946–1947* (London, 1948), p. 57; Kenneth Jackson, 'Varia: II. Gildas and the Names of the British Princes', *Cambridge Medieval Celtic Studies* (Cambridge, 1982), iii, p. 37).

90 'It seems very likely that Stonehenge was a stone circle from its very beginning. From the sizes of the Aubrey Holes it is evident that the stones they once held were small and narrow. This rules out the sarsens, so we're confident that Stonehenge most likely started as a circle of 56 bluestones' (Pearson, *Stonehenge*, p. 193).

91 In Celtic society universal kingship was rooted indissolubly and eternally at the Sacred Centre (Guyonvarc'h and Le Roux, *Les Druides*, pp. 217–26). Indeed, the ideology is characteristic of

9

Maxen the Emperor and the Preseli Sanctuary

The British Emperor

The delightful Welsh mediæval romance of 'The Dream of Maxen Gwledig' (*Breuddwyd Maxen*) is a pseudo-historical compilation, in which late Roman traditional history has been melded with Brittonic myth. Embedded in the latter are remarkable shards of pre-Christian mythology, which can be shown to shed light on the ideology of the *omphalos* or centre, its relationship to the Monarchy of Britain, and even the baffling transfer of the bluestones from Preseli Mountain to Salisbury Plain. Since these considerations have hitherto escaped attention, relevant sections of the story will be examined with particular attention.

The 'historical' element of the romance draws on the career of Magnus Maximus, a distinguished officer of Spanish origin, who held high office in late Roman Britain. It was there that in AD 383 he proclaimed himself Emperor – according to one account, at the insistence of the garrison of the diocese. Two years later he crossed the Channel and invaded Gaul, where he overthrew and killed the reigning Emperor Gratian. Next, he crossed the Alps and occupied Italy, compelling Gratian's brother and co-Emperor Valentinian II to seek asylum in the East. However, the dramatic adventure ended in tragedy, when in 388 Maximus marched on Constantinople, only to be defeated and subsequently executed at Aquileia by the Eastern Emperor Theodosius the Great.[1]

While Roman historians, chroniclers, and imperial panegyrists were unanimous in proclaiming Maximus a treacherous usurper, the indications are that he continued widely popular in Britain. His final overthrow had been distant and dramatic, and, with much of Maximus's army still stationed in Britain and Gaul, it is thought that the victorious Theodosius would have treated the usurper's surviving supporters in the distant island with tactful leniency.[2]

---

monarchical ideology worldwide. The biblical Saul was initiated or confirmed as king at the Israelites' original megalithic shrine at Gilgal (Frank Moore Cross, *Canaanite Myth and Hebrew Epic: Essays in the History of the Religion of Israel* (Cambridge, Mass., 1973), p. 224).

1   For the career of Magnus Maximus cf. A. H. M. Jones, J. R. Martindale, and J. Morris, *The Prosopography of the Later Roman Empire* (Cambridge, 1971–92), i, p. 588; Anthony R. Birley, *The Fasti of Roman Britain* (Oxford, 1981), pp. 346–52; Édouard Galletier, Jacques Fontaine, Guy Sabbah, Marie-Anne Marié, and Laurent Angliviel de la Beaumelle (ed.), *Ammien Marcellin: Histoire* (Paris, 1978–99), vi, pp. 191–92.

2   It is unknown what proportion of the British garrison crossed the Channel with Maximus. However, he can scarcely have entered on so dangerous a military venture without being accompanied by a

Welsh genealogical tradition suggests that, prior to his departure with much of the Roman garrison, Maximus established federate kingdoms along the western periphery of Britain, whose task was to guard against barbarian incursions from Ireland and Pictland (i.e. Scotland north of the Forth).[3] Early Welsh royal pedigrees indicate that the status of Maximus the Emperor (*Maxen Gwledig*) became gradually transformed at an early period from creator of dynasties into their lineal progenitor.[4] This was a natural development, given the hereditary basis of monarchy in the Middle Ages.

Apart from this factor, it seems that little or no knowledge of the historical Maximus was preserved in Welsh bardic lore of the Middle Ages:

> Maxen is more function than hero; he has no real genealogy and his descendants are *ad hoc*, he is not confined to any particular area and he has no firm location, with the consequence that he is free to be utilized by *cyfarwyddiaid* and authors for their own purposes.[5]

The repertoire of the bards was primarily transmitted in oral form, suggesting that insular information on the Maximus of history was largely confined to the written record.[6]

Breuddwyd Maxen Gwledig is preserved in the Welsh mediæval manuscript compendia known as the White Book of Rhydderch (*c.* 1350) and the Red Book of Hergest (*c.* 1382–*c.* 1410), while an earlier fragment is found in the thirteenth-century Peniarth Manuscript 16.[7]

The tale begins with Maxen, the handsomest, wisest, and best of all emperors of Rome, riding out from the city one day to hunt, accompanied by a party of thirty-two vassal kings. Their course took them along the valley of the river which flows past Rome, where they coursed all morning, until the sun stood high in the heavens. By then Maxen had become drowsy, and lay down to take his rest. His attendant kings made a protective roof of their shields to preserve their master from the heat of the sun, and so he slept.

---

substantial body of troops, upon whose loyalty he could rely. Cf. Derek A. Welsby, *The Romano-British Defence of the British Provinces in its Later Phases* (Oxford, 1982), pp. 126–28.

3 M. P. Charlesworth, *The Lost Province or the Worth of Britain* (Cardiff, 1949), pp. 26–28; Leslie Alcock, 'Celtic Archaeology and Art', in Elwyn Davies (ed.), *Celtic Studies in Wales: A Survey* (Cardiff, 1963), p. 36; Sheppard Frere, *Britannia: a history of Roman Britain* (London, 1967), pp. 361–62; Peter Salway, *Roman Britain* (Oxford, 1981), p. 404; Graham Webster, *The Cornovii* (Stroud, 1991), pp. 125–26.

4 Nikolai Tolstoy, 'Early British History and Chronology', *The Transactions of the Honourable Society of Cymmrodorion: Session 1964* (London, 1964), pp. 254–62. Although the precise significance of the rank *gwledig* is uncertain, in the romance it is treated as synonymous with 'emperor': *Maxen Wledic oed amperauder en Ruvein* (Brynley F. Roberts (ed.), *Breudwyt Maxen Wledic* (Dublin, 2005), p. 1).

5 Idem, '*Breuddwyd Maxen Wledig*: Why? When?' in Joseph Falaky Nagy and Leslie Ellen Jones (ed.), *Heroic Poets and Poetic Heroes in Celtic Tradition: A Festschrift for Patrick K. Ford* (Dublin, 2005), p. 305. Cf. Roberts (ed.), *Breudwyt Maxen Wledic*, p. lviii.

6 'It is worth noting … that the Welsh forms of Maximus's name – such as Maxim and Maxen – are likewise unhistorical spelling pronunciations. If the name had survived continuously in spoken Brythonic from the 4th century, the Welsh form would be the unattested *Meisyf (John T. Koch, *Cunedda, Cynan, Cadwallon, Cynddylan: Four Welsh Poems and Britain 383–655* (Aberystwyth, 2013), p. 73). This confirms the name's preservation was largely confined to written records.

7 The texts of *Breuddwyd Maxen* are transcribed in J. Gwenogvryn Evans (ed.), *The White Book Mabinogion: Welsh Tales & Romances Reproduced from the Peniarth Manuscripts* (Pwllheli, 1907), cols. 178–91; John Rhŷs and J. Gwenogvryn Evans (ed.), *The Text of the Mabinogion and other Welsh Tales from the Red Book of Hergest* (Oxford, 1887), pp. 82–92.

While he slept, the Emperor dreamed a dream. It seemed to him that he continued his journey upstream, until he came to the highest mountain in the world. Descending the other side, he saw mighty rivers flowing towards a distant sea. He journeyed across fair and fertile lands, until he arrived at the mouth of the greatest river ever seen, where stood a great city protected by a majestic castle. A fleet lay at anchor in the roads, among which was a vessel of marvellous appearance, glittering from bow to stern in silver and gold. Maxen embarked on board the enchanted ship, passing over a bridge of whalebone which proffered access from the shore.

The ship's sail bent to the breeze, and Maxen crossed sea and ocean, until he came to the fairest island that is in the world. Passing over it from coast to coast, he arrived at the last in a region of towering mountains, steep valleys, and giddy precipices. Beyond, he saw an island set in the sea, facing this craggy land. Hard by uprose a mighty mountain, beneath which flowed a river across a plain until it reached the sea. Beside the mouth of the river stood the most wonderful castle ever glimpsed by man, whose portals lay open before him.

Maxen passed within, where he found himself in a hall whose roof gleamed all of gold, whose walls were bedecked with precious gemstones, and whose doors like its roof were wrought from gold. Golden seats were set about the hall, and silver tables. Before him in his dream, the Emperor saw two handsome splendidly-garbed youths, who were playing at *gwyddbwyll*, upon a board of silver with pieces fashioned from gold. Beside a pillar was stationed a throne of ivory, with two gold eagles upreared upon its back, upon which reclined a venerable silver-haired man. He wore bracelets and rings of gold, a golden torque hung about his neck, and his hair was bound with a golden diadem. Before him was set a *gwyddbwyll*-board, for which he was engaged in carving pieces with a steel file from a golden rod.

Most wonderful of all was a maiden seated on a throne of glowing gold. Brighter than the sun was her beauty: she was dressed in a white silken robe, gilded and bejewelled. She was the fairest sight that ever man beheld, and she rose up before Maxen the Emperor. Then Maxen threw his arms around her, and drew her down so that they sat beside each other upon the golden throne, which provided as much room for the two of them as it had for her alone. And there Maxen and the maiden reclined side by side, his arms around her neck and his cheek resting against her soft cheek, until the whimpering of the hounds and the clashing of shields in the breeze, and the neighing and stamping of the huntsmen's steeds, awoke the Emperor, where he lay sleeping in the sunshine beside the river that runs by Rome.

Maxen arose, and found his whole being filled with yearning for the lovely maiden encountered in the castle of his dream. Returned to his capital, he continued distraught for love of the fair unknown. Finally there came a day when his wise men came to him, and advized him to despatch messengers throughout the world, that they might find her without whose presence the Emperor's existence was as nothing. For a year the messengers travelled about the whole wide world, at the end of which they were no nearer achieving their mission than they had been at the beginning.

Then it was that a shrewd adviser urged Maxen to ride again by the route he had followed, when hunting on the day of his enchanted dream. Arrived at the spot where he had slept, Maxen despatched thirteen messengers to follow the route which he recalled so vividly from his dream. So the messengers ascended that mountain whose summit seemed to touch the sky, followed the course of rivers flowing from the other side as far as the ocean, entered into

---

8   Lady Charlotte Guest (tr.), *The Mabinogion from the Welsh of the Llyfr Coch o Hergest (the Red Book of Hergest) in the Library of Jesus College, Oxford* (London, 1877), p. 443.

Emperor Maxen
before Caer Seint.
(Author's collection)

the magical ship, and passed over to the island of Britain. Across the island they journeyed, until they came at last to the rugged land of Eryri (Snowdonia), beyond which lay the island of Môn (Anglesey) and the peninsula of Arfon. And there, at the mouth of the river Seint, they discovered the fairy castle of Maxen's dream. Passing within, they beheld the youths playing at *gwyddbwyll*, the old man carving gaming-pieces, and the maiden whose beauty held the Emperor in thrall. Then his emissaries enquired whether she would come to Rome to wed their master, or should he come hither to take her for his wife? 'If the Emperor love me, let him seek me here,' was her maidenly reply.

When Maxen was informed of this, he sallied forth with his army until he came to Britain. There he conquered the island from Beli mab Manogan and his sons, driving them into the sea, and passed on until he came to the sea-girt land of Arfon. At Aber Seint he found the castle of his dream, and entering within saw the youths Cynan mab Eudaf and Adeon mab Eudaf playing at *gwyddbwyll*, and their father Eudaf map Caradawg seated on his ivory throne carving pieces for their game. And there, as lovely as she had appeared in his dream, sat the maiden he sought. He threw his arms around her neck, and that night Elen became his bride.

Next day, the new Empress claimed as her marriage portion (*agweddi*) the island of Britain for her father, and required three fortresses to be constructed for her: Caer Seint (Caernarvon), Caer Fyrddin (Carmarthen), and Caerleon. Then Elen caused majestic roads to be constructed between the strongholds of the island. Seven years did Maxen the Emperor remain in Britain with his bride, until a day came when grim tidings were brought to him, where he resided at his castle of Caerleon. A rival had declared himself emperor in Rome, who haughtily challenged Maxen to assert his claim to the throne if he dared. 'If thou comest, and if thou ever comest to Rome,' ran the usurper's taunting message. To which Maximus grimly made response: 'If I come to Rome – and if I come.'[9]

Then Maxen sailed with his host for France, where he conquered all that land, until at last he came before the walls of Rome. For a year he strove in vain to take the mighty city, until

---

9　This pithy exchange appears to reflect a common Celtic literary motif (Kenneth Jackson, 'Four Local Anecdotes from Harris', *Scottish Studies* (Edinburgh, 1959), iii, p. 87).

Elen's brothers brought an army from Britain which stormed the walls and slew the usurper. The grateful Emperor invited Cynan and Adeon to take his army, and conquer for themselves whatever realm they chose in the world. Adeon elected to return to Britain, while Cynan and his followers seized the land of Llydaw (Brittany), where his descendants yet dwell, speaking the tongue of the Britons to the present day.

The story has clearly been refashioned by a professional storyteller (*cyfarwydd*) from disparate sources. It will have been regarded by its hearers as part of the authentic history of early Britain, which was traditionally preserved in an intricate admixture of dramatized legend and history. In the White and Red Book collections it appears next to the tale of the Adventure of Lludd and Lleuelys (*Cyfranc Lludd a Lleuelys*), which recounts how Britain in the primal time was delivered from three supernatural Oppressions (*gormesoedd*). This juxtaposition is probably not fortuitous, and most likely scribes understood both stories to comprise part of their national history (*ystyr*), rather than tales of entertainment (*chwedlau*), such as the later Arthurian romances of *Peredur, Gereint*, and *Owein*, which are included in the same manuscript collections. In Peniarth MS 16, which does not contain *Cyfranc Lludd a Lleuelys, Breuddwyd Maxen* adjoins the Prophecy of Merlin, which was likewise regarded as historical.

It was presumably the author of *Breuddwyd Maxen* who adapted the historical accounts of the career of Maximus contained in the *Historia Brittonum* into a framework for his colourful romance. Doubtless he anticipated the high regard with which his tale would be received at the courts of contemporary kings, some of whom boasted descent from *Maxen Gwledig*.

Geoffrey of Monmouth must have come across a version of the story, which he elaborated in his *History of the Kings of Britain* as an episode in the sober history he claimed to have written. Despite recurrent attempts to detect the influence of Geoffrey behind *Breuddwyd Maxen*,[10] it seems that the Welsh story and that of Geoffrey derive independently from native tradition.[11] As Patrick Sims-Williams observed, the tale represents part of 'the myth of the original monarchy of Britain'.[12]

---

10   Roger Sherman Loomis, *Wales and the Arthurian Legend* (Cardiff, 1956), pp. 5–7, 8. Roy Owen's elaborate reconstruction of the compilation of *Breuddwyd Maxen* suffers from the assumption that literary parallels to its component motifs represent sources, which is generally far from being the case (D. D. R. Owen, *The Evolution of the Grail Legend* (Edinburgh, 1968), pp. 41–49).

11   For the origin of *Breuddwyd Maxen* among the 'learned tales' or 'pseudo-history' of early Britain, cf. Rachel Bromwich, 'The Character of the Early Welsh Tradition', in Nora K. Chadwick (ed.), *Studies in Early British History* (Cambridge, 1954), pp. 126–27, 133–34; eadem, *Celtic Britain* (London, 1963), p. 113. Brynley F. Roberts argues for a date of composition for the romance in the second half of the twelfth century (Roberts (ed.), *Breudwyt Maxen Wledic* (Dublin, 2005), pp. lxxvi–xci; Nagy and Jones (ed.), *Heroic Poets and Poetic Heroes in Celtic Tradition*, pp. 310–14). To me, Geoffrey of Monmouth's account of the reign of 'Maximianus' reads like an attempt to reconcile British traditions of Maxen Gwledig with the semi-historical version contained in §27 of the *Historia Brittonum*. Generally speaking, however, the date of composition of *Breuddwyd Maxen* does not materially affect the issues discussed here, since the author in large part drew upon archaic tradition – and it is that with which I am here primarily concerned.

12   P. P. Sims-Williams, 'Some Functions of Origin Stories in Early Medieval Wales', in Tore Nyberg, Iørn Piø, Preben Meulengracht Sørensen, and Aage Trommer (ed.), *History and Heroic Tale: A Symposium* (Odense, 1985), pp. 106–9. Geoffrey of Monmouth's version is found in Michael D. Reeve and Neil Wright (ed.), *Geoffrey of Monmouth: The History of the Kings of Britain* (Woodbridge, 2007), pp. 99–111. Geoffrey's 'story of the emperor Maximus and his British bride … must be derived ultimately from contact with *cyfarwydd* tradition current in Wales or Brittany' (Rachel Bromwich (ed.), *Trioedd Ynys Prydein: The Welsh Triads* (Cardiff, 1978), p. xcvi; cf. H. Munro Chadwick and N. Kershaw Chadwick, *The Growth of Literature* (Cambridge, 1932–40), i, p. 175). References by Giraldus Cambrensis to *Maximus tyrannus* and the colonization of Brittany derive entirely from his reading of Geoffrey and

Breuddwyd Maxen and the British History

The late John Morris, in his bestselling book *The Age of Arthur*, described the romance of *Breuddwyd Maxen* as 'a straightforward historical narrative, its main facts accurate, their context altogether unknown and misunderstood'.[13] But this is manifestly not the case, since the story reflects historical events only in the loosest way, and Sir John Rhŷs long ago sagely pronounced it essentially mythological in character.[14] Nevertheless, myth may in its own way provide as helpful a tool for interpreting the past as history.[15]

Breuddwyd Maxen originated primarily in a conflation of two distinct sets of sources, embellished with detail taken from native lore and coloured by the author's imaginative rewriting. On the one hand, it drew upon fragments of the essentially timeless myth of the sacral Monarchy of Britain. On the other, it recapitulated and embellished the historical record, as recorded in the *Historia Brittonum*.

> Two strands in the legend appear to be kept apart in the sources – learned, historical information about the Roman Maximus, and native learned speculation about his part in the Breton settlements.[16]

Both strands appear also in the *Historia Brittonum*. In AD 829–30 the North-Welsh monk Nennius compiled his *History of the Britons*, which (if the introductory section of Gildas's polemic be excepted) may boast the title of being the first history of Britain. In his introduction, Nennius bewailed the paucity of surviving materials, emphasizing the industrious extent to which he had pursued records of his country's glorious past, whether from Roman historians, Irish and Saxon records, or the traditional lore of his own people.

Doubt has been cast on the authenticity of this prologue, and the value of Nennius's work as a compendium of much older material similarly disparaged. Even the identity of Nennius as its author has been called in question.[17] As not infrequently occurs, the pendulum appears to have swung overmuch in the direction of scepticism, and Professor Field has shown that there is no compelling reason to discount the authorship of Nennius, nor his explanation of how he assembled his materials.[18]

Nennius's interpretation of his sources led him to believe that seven Roman emperors reigned in Britain, 'but the Romans say there were nine'. At times he found it difficult to reconcile material derived from Roman histories with that handed down in British tradition. This is illustrated by his treatment of Maximus, whom he inadvertently duplicates both as 'the sixth emperor, Maximus' and 'the seventh emperor, Maximianus'.

Gildas (J. S. Brewer, James F. Dimock, and George F. Warner (ed.), *Giraldi Cambrensis Opera* (London, 1861–91), vi, pp. 165–66, 208–9).

13   John Morris, *The Age of Arthur: A History of the British Isles from 350 to 650* (London, 1973), p. 419.

14   John Rhys, *Lectures on the Origin and Growth of Religion as Illustrated by Celtic Heathendom* (London, 1888), pp. 161–68.

15   Cf. Mircea Eliade, *Myth and Reality* (Northampton, 1964), pp. 134–38; Proinsias Mac Cana, *The Cult of the Sacred Centre: Essays on Celtic Ideology* (Dublin, 2011), pp. 1–16.

16   Roberts (ed.), *Breudwyt Maxen Wledic*, p. l.

17   David N. Dumville, 'Nennius' and the *Historia Brittonum*', *Studia Celtica* (Cardiff, 1975-6), x–xi, pp. 78–95.

18   P. J. C. Field, 'Nennius and his History', *Studia Celtica* (Cardiff, 1996), xxx, pp. 159–65.

In §26 *Maximus* is described as the sixth Roman emperor to rule over Britain. In §27 his reign is replicated as the seventh, where he features as *Maximianus*, suggesting a distinct source. In the second passage Maximus is correctly described as departing with the garrison of Britain to overthrow and kill the Emperor Gratian, in consequence of which he obtains the mastery of 'all Europe'. What follows, however, derives from legend. Being unwilling to return his army to their families in Britain, he settled them in an extensive region bounded by the lake on the summit of *Mons Iovis*, a town called *Cant Guic*, and the western hill called *Cruc Ochidient*: 'These are the Britons of Armorica, and they never returned hither up to the present day.'

It was, so we learn, in consequence of their absence that foreign nations (Picts, Scots, and Saxons) were enabled to overrun Britain.

Historically, there is no likelihood that Maximus denuded Britain of troops, since it remained part of the Empire for another twenty years, at the end of which period sufficient forces remained to enable a further usurper, Constantine III, to invade Gaul and proclaim himself Emperor. Nor is it probable that the British settlement in Armorica (hence its subsequent name Brittany) arose in the manner – or even period – recounted. Gildas in the sixth century had asserted that Maximus's army never returned home after his condign defeat. From this unsubstantiated claim derived the plausible, though erroneous, conclusion that the Britons of Armorica were descendants of his host.[19]

Finally, in §29 Nennius returns to the topic with a detailed and this time historically accurate description of events on the Continent preceding Maximus's overthrow of Gratian, his temporary triumph, and his eventual overthrow and execution at the hands of the Emperor Theodosius. Every sentence in this chapter is drawn from the chronicles of Isidore of Seville and Prosper of Aquitaine. It seems likely that §29 represents an afterword, interpolated by Nennius into the initial version of his *History*, which he is known to have completed some thirty years before.[20] This conclusion is based on the following.

1. When Nennius wrote §§26 and 27, he was evidently unaware that Maximus's rule terminated with the brutal finality described in §29.

2. §29 is illogically separated from the preceding accounts of Maximus by §28, which takes the historical narrative beyond his activities to the conclusion of Roman rule in Britain, which is implicitly dated to AD 409.

3. §29 is introduced with the explanatory sentence *Iterum repetendus est sermo de Maximiano tyranno*, 'Once more we revert to the topic of the tyrant Maximianus'. This is scarcely how the author might be expected to have arranged his material, had he been all along in possession of the material cited in §29.

This conclusion is supported by the use made of the *Historia Brittonum* by the author of *Breuddwyd Maxen*. The latter concludes his narrative with Maxen's conquests of Gaul and

---

19 'A very close connection was maintained between the two countries [Britain and Brittany] down well into the Middle Ages, and it is natural that speculation should have been rife in Britain as to the origin of the Britons across the sea. It was an easy deduction to make from the existing facts to conclude that the original Breton colonizers were Maximus's lost soldiers' (Bromwich (ed.), *Trioedd Ynys Prydein*, p. 317).

20 'Fernmail [mentioned as a contemporary in §49] seems to have been reigning *c*. 800. It would seem probable on the whole, therefore, that the reference to Fernmail is due to Nennius himself, and that he wrote a book *c*. 800 or a little after. But a reference in cap. 16 to King Merfyn of Gwynedd, which seems to relate to the year 829 or 830, suggests that the book may have been brought up to date about that time. The reference does not appear to have been in the original version' (Hector Munro Chadwick, 'Vortigern', in Chadwick (ed.), *Studies in Early British History*, pp. 25–26).

Rome, and the killing of the reigning Emperor, with no suggestion of Maxen's ultimate defeat and destruction. That the author's source was the *Historia Brittonum* is evident on other counts. Thus, his assumption that Maximus was Emperor in Rome, and only subsequently came to Britain, derived from Nennius's belief that every Roman emperor ruling in Britain (including Maximus and Maximianus) originated in Rome:

In veteri traditione seniorum nostrorum septem imperatores fuerunt a Romanis in Brittannia.[21]

The reliance of *Breuddwyd Maxen* on the *Historia Brittonum* is further indicated by the identification in the earlier story of the bounds of the territory on which Maximus settled his troops in Gaul. In Nennius's words, they were allotted

multas regiones a stagno quod est super verticem Montis Iovis usque ad civitatem, quae vocatur Cant Guic, et usque ad cumulum occidentalem, id est, Cruc Ochidient.

Mons Iovis is Montjou, a famous mountain sacred to Jupiter and the Celtic god Poeninus, which towers above the Great St Bernard Pass, where the highroad ascends the crest of the Alps.[22] Hard by lies a small lake, which is clearly the *stagnum* mentioned in the *Historia Brittonum*.[23] While this desolate spot never demarcated a frontier within historical times, the particularity of the allusion indicates that the author possessed some knowledge of the locality. Almost certainly, its true significance lay in the fact that the pass comprised one of the principal Alpine routes from Gaul into Italy. *Cant Guic*, the other site Nennius identifies as bounding the British settlement in Gaul, is *Quentowic*, an important trading emporium at Montreuil-sur-Mer near Étaples, on the Channel coast facing Kent.[24] As Lot pointed out, its inclusion in the boundaries of the imaginary Armorican settlement doubtless arose from its being a port used by voyagers travelling from Britain to Rome.[25]

Thus, the selection of these two place names reflects their location along one of the principal routes leading from Britain to Rome, which might readily be envisaged as that taken by Maximus. In reality, the historical Maximus traversed the mountains in 387 by the southerly route, over the Cottian Alps (*Alpibus Cottiis*),[26] and it is most unlikely that the geography of §27 in the *Historia Brittonum* reflects historical circumstances of the late fourth century AD.[27] The Alpine route represented a hazardous experience familiar to many Welsh pilgrims during the

---

21 Ibid., p. 167. The misconception is also implicit in §20, where it is related of Julius Caesar that, of the successive 'British' emperors, he *primus in Brittanniam pervenit et regnum et gentem tenuit* (ibid., p. 163).

22 Francesco Sbordone (ed.), *Strabonis Geographica* (Rome, 1963–2000), ii, p. 162.

23 'The lake here mentioned is thought to be that near the hospice of the great St. Bernard' (Lady Charlotte Guest (tr.), *The Mabinogion from the Welsh of the Llyfr Coch o Hergest (the Red Book of Hergest) in the Library of Jesus College, Oxford* (London, 1877), p. 455).

24 Stéphane Lebecq, 'Communication and exchange in northwest Europe', in Janet Bately and Anton Englert (ed.), *Ohthere's Voyages: A late 9th-century account of voyages along the coasts of Norway and Denmark and its cultural context* (Roskilde, 2007), pp. 171, 175–76.

25 'L'auteur le nomme parce que c'était de son temps le lieu de passage de Bretagne en Gaule (et ensuite en Italie)' (Ferdinand Lot, *Nennius et l'Historia Brittonum: Étude critique suivie d'une édition des diverses versions de ce texte* (Paris, 1934), p. 60).

26 Édouard Galletier (ed.), *Panégyriques latins* (Paris, 1949–52), iii, p. 96.

27 John Morris took the locations listed by Nennius to be the bounds of early Armorica, while Fleuriot related them to the Roman province of Lugdunensis II (*The Age of Arthur*, pp. 250–51; Léon Fleuriot, *Les origines de la Bretagne: L'émigration* (Paris, 1980), pp. 121, 249–51). But *Mons Iovis* (Montjou) never adjoined either region, and it is inherently implausible to suppose that Nennius's account reflects historical reality.

Middle Ages,[28] and the singling out of two of the more noteworthy staging-posts on the journey accounts for application of the toponyms to a discrete context in Nennius's *History*.

While the author of *Breuddwyd Maxen* may likewise have possessed some knowledge of the continental geography of his story,[29] the location of his hero's unexplained ascent on heading north from Italy of 'the highest mountain he had ever seen' (*e menyd uchaf o'r a welsei*) surely reflects Nennius's allusion to Maximus's settlement of British troops beside 'the lake which is on the peak of *Mons Iovis*' (*super verticem Montis Iovis*).

Finally, a curious little detail in *Breuddwyd Maxen* suggests yet another debt to the *Historia Brittonum*. On his arrival at the faery castle in North Wales, Maxen Gwledig encounters a mysterious figure, who is initially described only as a 'grey-haired old man' (*gur gwynllwyt*). Eventually we learn, effectively in an aside, that his name is *Eudaf*. It is likely that he was originally unidentified in an earlier version of the episode. In fact, the name looks like an artificial concoction, originating in misinterpretation of a passage in §27 of the *Historia Brittonum*. There we read that 'the seventh emperor who reigned in Britain was Maximianus' (*Septimus imperator regnavit in Brittannia Maximianus*), i.e. Maximus. After him, 'the eighth was another Severus' (*octavus fuit alius Severus*).[30] Welsh *Eudaf* was frequently treated as corresponding to Latin *Octavius*,[31] and it is possible that misunderstanding of this passage in the *Historia Brittonum* led to the creation of a 'ghost' emperor, *octavus* being taken for the imperial name *Octavius*. Following as the parenthesis does on the account of the usurpation of the regicide Maximianus, could *octavus fuit alius severus* have been misinterpreted as *Octavius fuit alius severus*: 'Octavius was another stern [emperor]'?

Gildas in the sixth century echoed earlier Continental historians' virulent condemnation of Maximus, but by the early ninth Nennius attests to a patriotic tradition according him heroic stature. It is less likely that the latter viewpoint represents a dramatic shift in British public opinion, than that Gildas's derogatory account reflects his personal contemptuous view of his compatriots, whom he castigated as pusillanimous, treacherous, and ungrateful to their Roman rulers, as also the condemnatory attitude of the classical authors he utilized.[32]

The reputation of Maximus continued high in British bardic tradition, although (as has been seen) little was recalled of him save his splendid status as primary monarch and founder of royal dynasties in Britain. When eventually a *cyfarwydd* came to compose the glamorous romance of *Breuddwyd Maxen*, it was to the pages of Nennius's *Historia Brittonum* that he turned for information concerning the martial activities of *Maxen*, as he had become known. From this source derived his misapprehension that he was an indigenous Emperor of Rome, who like his predecessors from Julius Caesar onwards set forth from Rome to conquer Britain. From it, too, he learned how *Maxen* eventually conquered Rome, where he slew the Emperor and reigned in his stead. Finally, Nennius provided the source for his account of the British settlement in Britanny (*Llydaw*).

---

28   Roberts (ed.), *Breudwyt Maxen Wledic*, pp. lxxvii–lxxviii.

29   Ibid., p. lxxvi.

30   Theodor Mommsen (ed.), *Monvmenta Germaniae Historica* (xiii): *Chronica Minora saec. IV. V. VI. VII* (Berlin, 1894), iii, pp. 166–67.

31   Henry Lewis (ed.), *Brut Dingestow* (Cardiff, 1942), pp. 228–29. Welsh *Eudaf* and the cognate Old Breton *Outham* are of Celtic derivation (Eric P. Hamp, 'The Element *–tamo-*', *Études Celtiques* (Paris, 1974), xiv, p. 188).

32   Michael E. Jones, *The End of Roman Britain* (Ithaca and London, 1996), pp. 124–28.

We may have here a hitherto overlooked indication of the date when *Breuddwyd Maxen* was composed. As was shown above, its 'historical' setting clearly derives from §27 of the *Historia Brittonum*. Equally, the author appears to have been ignorant of the content of §29, with its hostile view of the usurper and account of his summary death. This might suggest that *Breuddwyd Maxen* was written *after* Nennius completed his initial draft c. 800, and *before* he added §29 in AD 829. On the other hand, I will present shortly historical considerations pointing to composition about the middle of the following century. This suggests that a copy or copies of the earlier version of the *Historia Brittonum* continued in circulation a century and a half after the work's original completion.

The 'Roman history' of the romance was expanded at some stage by inclusion of an independent tradition that the settlement was effected under the leadership of Cynan, known in Breton tradition as Cynan Meriadoc. In *Breuddwyd Maxen* he features implicitly as brother to Maxen's bride Elen, and is also ascribed a brother Adeon. The eponymous hero of the romance of *Peredur* similarly arrives at the castle of a grey-haired man (*gwr llwyt mawr*), who is accompanied by two youths.[33] There, however, they are unnamed, and it seems likely that their counterparts in *Breuddwyd Maxen* were originally likewise anonymous. The names assigned them by the author would in that case have been bestowed in order to integrate the Breton hero Cynan into the British royal dynasty.

The dream sequence which opens the romance and gives it its title reflects a well-known Celtic dramatic theme. In the early Irish romantic tale of the Dream of Oengus (*Aislinge Óenguso*), its hero dreams of a ravishingly beautiful maiden who appears by his bedside. On awakening, he is consumed by a passion which deprives him of appetite and causes him to relapse into debilitating melancholy. Search is made throughout the length and breadth of Ireland, until eventually she is discovered and united with Oengus.[34] A still closer parallel is found in the Breton Life of St Iudicael, which will be treated more fully below. It is clear that the theme was not original to the story of Maxen, being subsequently assimilated to his tale when it became converted into a romance.

In the Life of St Iudicael and *Breuddwyd Maxen* the dream setting is conjoined to the archaic theme of the wedding of a king to a maiden personifying the sovereignty of the kingdom. William Mahon has shown that the theme of the dream (*aisling*) was utilized in differing contexts, which in early times chiefly constituted the prophetic *aisling* and the love *aisling*.[35] The former category is primarily concerned with perpetuation of the royal dynasty, the beautiful girl of the king's dream or vision being the personification of the sovereignty goddess. In *Baile in Scáil*, King Conn at Tara traverses a mist dividing his realm from that of the Otherworld. There he encounters Lug, the god who presides over the kingship, together with a lovely girl who dispenses the royal ale as each successive dynast is named.

The latter story is understood to represent in its essence 'a symbolic picture of the ceremonial marriage of the high-king with the lady Sovereignty of Ireland'.[36] In this context

33   Glenys Witchard Goetinck (ed.), *Historia Peredur vab Efrawc* (Cardiff, 1976), p. 36.

34   Francis Shaw (ed.), *The Dream of Óengus: Aislinge Óenguso* (Dublin, 1934), pp. 43–64.

35   William J. Mahon, 'The *Aisling* Elegy and the Poet's Appropriation of the Feminine', *Studia Celtica* (Cardiff, 2000), xxxiv, pp. 249–70.

36   Nora K. Chadwick, 'Pictish and Celtic Marriage in Early Literary Tradition', *Scottish Gaelic Studies* (Oxford, 1955), viii, 84–85. Cf. T. F. O'Rahilly, 'On the Origin of the Names Érainn and Ériu', *Ériu: The Journal of the School of Irish Learning, Dublin* (Dublin, 1943), xiv, p. 14; Tomás Ó Cathasaigh, 'Cath Maige Tuired As Exemplary Myth', in Pádraig de Brún, Seán Ó Coileán, and Pádraig Ó Riain (ed.),

the term *baile* ('*vision*; *frenzy, madness* [originally arising out of supernatural revelations]') corresponds to *aisling* ('vision, dream'), as also to *fís* ('A vision (esp. one of symbolic or prophetic import)'.[37] In the case of *Baile in Scáil*, a bardic catalogue treats *fís* and *baile* as synonymous: *Fís Cuind .i. Baile in Scáil*.[38]

It is possible that behind this concept lay actual practice, whereby a king underwent a ritually induced sleep, during which he encountered the sovereignty goddess of the kingdom. In mediæval Ireland storytelling was commonly practised at night, often with the explicit purpose of inducing sleep.[39] An Irish saga records a rite wherein a bull was sacrificed and cooked, after which a man drank of its broth and had 'a spell of truth' chanted over him while he slept:

> Whomever he saw in his sleep would be king, and the sleeper would die were he to utter a falsehood.[40]

The destined king proved to be Conaire Mór, mythical founder of the royal dynasty of Tara. Another account of the royal bull-feast ritual specifies that the 'spell of truth' was delivered by four druids.[41] Had an early legend told of Maxen's accession to the kingship in consequence of a mantic dream, it would have been easy for this in turn to become merged with the literary motif of *aisling*.

Again, it seems that the realm of dreams was regarded as corresponding in some degree to the Otherworld itself.[42] A tale in the Irish Bran cycle represents a druid as projecting his *fís* ('dream' or 'vision') beyond the clouds to a land populated by lovely women, by which is plainly intended the Otherworld.[43] However, the essential point is that Irish and Breton cognate traditions indicate that the motifs of the dream encounter with a beautiful girl and the wedding of the king to the sovereignty goddess are likely to have been combined into a single narrative before the composition of *Breuddwyd Maxen*.

The remaining section of the originally independent prefatory sector of *Breuddwyd Maxen* contains the brief account of Elen's building of national roads, her construction of three cities (the two named ones being in South Wales), and Maxen's ascent of the mountain Y Freni Fawr.

Folia Gadelica: Essays presented by former students to R. A. Breatnach, M.A., M.R.I.A. (Cork, 1983), p. 12; idem, 'The Eponym of Cnogba', *Éigse: A Journal of Irish Studies* (Dublin, 1989), xxiii, pp. 31–32.

37   E. G. Quin *et al.* (ed.), *Dictionary of the Irish Language: Based mainly on Old and Middle Irish Materials* (Dublin, 1913-76), 'A', cols. 247–48; 'B', col. 16; 'C', cols. 152–54.

38   R. I. Best, Osborn Bergin, M.A. O'Brien, and Anne O'Sullivan (ed.), *The Book of Leinster Formerly Lebar na Núachongbála* (Dublin, 1954–83), p. 837.

39   Proinsias Mac Cana, *The Learned Tales of Medieval Ireland* (Dublin, 1980), pp. 13–14.

40   *Fer at-chichead ina chotlad is é bad rí, 7 at-baildis a beóil in tan ad-beiread gaí* (Eleanor Knott (ed.), *Togail Bruidne Da Derga* (Dublin, 1936), p. 4).

41   Myles Dillon (ed.), *Serglige Con Culainn* (Dublin, 1953), p. 9.

42   This touches a philosophical consideration: 'Now Price's suggestion is that we may think of "the next world" as an image world, very like the world of our dreams, but with the additional feature of a more comprehensive and complete correlation of the images involved. The "other" world would, in fact, be a world' (Hywel D. Lewis, *The Self and Immortality* (London, 1973), p. 147).

43   James Carney, 'The Earliest Bran Material', in John J. O'Meara and Bernd Naumann (ed.), *Latin Script and Letters A.D. 400–900: Festschrift presented to Ludwig Bieler on the occasion of his 70th birthday* (Leiden, 1976), pp. 180–81.

It is evident that this section derives from the traditional lore of Dyfed, such as might have been recounted before Bledri ap Cydifor in his hall at Emlyn, beneath the shadow of Preseli Mountain. The statement that the summit of Y Freni Fawr was known thenceforth as 'Maxen's throne' (*cadeir Faxen*) does not mean that the mountain's name was changed (it does not appear that it was),[44] but that its association with the legend of Maxen's ascent was well-known locally.

When was Breuddwyd Maxen composed?

So far as the mythological element in the tale is concerned, the tale's date of composition might be regarded as a broadly irrelevant factor. Nevertheless, the consideration clearly bears *some* significance. Previously unconsidered evidence suggests a date considerably earlier than that which has been generally accepted. This factor applies also to *Cyfranc Lludd a Lleuelys*, which also draws on the mythology of the British *omphalos*.

Most scholars assign composition of *Breuddwyd Maxen* to the thirteenth century, some even as late as the fourteenth.[45] A contributory factor in this late chronology is an assumption that the text betrays the influence of Geoffrey of Monmouth, or the Welsh translations (*Brutiau*) of his work. However, in reality it appears that Geoffrey drew independently on traditions of the legend of Maxen Gwledig, who became a figure of heroic story in Brittany and Wales from an early period.[46]

It seems that the 'Roman history' in *Breuddwyd Maxen* derives from the initial version of the *Historia Brittonum*, compiled by Nennius at the turn of the eighth and ninth centuries. On this basis, the romance could have been composed at almost any time between then and the date of the first manuscript containing the story, i.e. Peniarth MS 16, the relevant section of which was written in the second half of the thirteenth century.[47]

A clue to a more precise date lies in the name of Maximus's bride. The first half of the tenth century saw the rise to power of the celebrated King Hywel Dda, 'the Good'. In 904 the last king of the ancient dynasty of Dyfed, Llywarch ap Hyfeidd, died. His daughter Elen married Hywel, and it was to this alliance that Hywel and his descendants ascribed the legitimacy of their rule over the southern kingdom.[48]

Hywel pursued a policy of close alliance with England, and in 926 the Anglo-Saxon Chronicle records that he made formal submission to the powerful English King Æþelstan.[49] In 942 King

---

44   B. G. Charles, *The Place Names of Pembrokeshire* (Aberystwyth, 1992), p. 381.

45   E. Anwyl, 'The Value of the Mabinogion for the Study of Celtic Religion', in *Transactions of the Third International Congress for the History of Religions* (Oxford, 1908), ii, p. 236; Morgan Watkin, *La civilisation française dans les Mabinogion* (Paris, 1962), pp. 347–49; Roger Sherman Loomis, *Wales and the Arthurian Legend* (Cardiff, 1956), pp. 5–9; Owen, *The Evolution of the Grail Legend*, p. 35; Roberts (ed.), *Breudwyt Maxen Wledic*, pp. lxxxi–lxxxvi.

46   Ifor Williams (ed.), *Breuddwyd Maxen* (Bangor, 1908), p. xxi. Cf. R. L. Thomson (ed.), *Owein or Chwedyl Iarlles y Ffynnawn* (Dublin, 1968), p. lxxviii; Rachel Bromwich, 'The Character of the Early Welsh Tradition', in Chadwick (ed.), *Studies in Early British History*, pp. 108–9, 126–27; Bromwich (ed.), *Trioedd Ynys Prydein*, p. xcvi.

47   Roberts (ed.), *Breudwyt Maxen Wledic*, pp. xi–xii.

48   John Edward Lloyd, *A History of Wales from the Earliest Times to the Edwardian Conquest* (London, 1911), p. 333.

49   Charles Plummer and John Earle (ed.), *Two Anglo-Saxon Chronicles Parallel: With Supplementary Extracts from the Others; A Revised Text Edited, with Introduction, Notes, Appendices, and Glossary* (Oxford, 1892–99), i, p. 107.

Idwal of Gwynedd was killed by the English, when he rose against the suzerainty of Æþelstan's son Eadmund. Hywel profited from this (as also, presumably, from his alliance with Eadmund) to conquer Gwynedd from Idwal's heirs. As Powys also fell at some point to his rule, he attained unique status as ruler of almost all Wales. A monarch of outstanding power and prestige, famed for having compiled a law code for his country, he ruled undisturbed over his expanded realm until his death in 950.[50]

It was presumably following the acquisition of Gwynedd that Hywel's court scribes compiled a collection of pedigrees of British kings. The first in the series traces his paternal descent from the kings of Gwynedd, and the second that of his wife from the royal line of Dyfed.[51] Clearly, the primary purpose of these paired genealogies was to proclaim the legitimacy of Hywel's rule over both North and South Wales.

Whilst his ancestry on both sides appears accurately recorded for some four centuries previously, once they arrive at the immediate post-Roman period (the fifth century AD) they dissolve into a concoction of names, plucked from early records and imaginatively converted into a succession of ancestral figures ascending to the mists of prehistory. On the paternal side Hywel's ancestry is traced to Beli the Great and his wife Anna. Beli Mawr was an important pagan ancestor-deity, while *Anna* has been shown to be a variant form of the name of the Brittonic goddess Don.[52] Such a figure may not have appeared altogether desirable as ancestress of a devout Christian king, and the ingenious court genealogist cautiously identified her (*quam dicunt esse*) as a cousin of the Virgin Mary.

In the present context the ancestry of Hywel's queen is significant. She was daughter and implicitly heiress of Llywarch, last male heir of the kings of Dyfed, the historical section of whose pedigree credibly ascends to the fifth century. Before that appears a cluster of names linked by *map* ('son of'), which according to his wont the compiler abstracted from records available to him, reassembling them into a dynasty of sons succeeding fathers. Prominent among them is the Roman Maximus (*Maxim Guletic*). Several generations further back, the dynasty claimed its ultimate origin from the Emperor Constantius, father of Constantine the Great, and his wife *Helen Luicdauc* ('of the Hosts'), 'who went forth from Britain in search of the cross of Christ as far as Jerusalem, and from there she brought it with her to Constantinople. And it is there to the present day'.[53]

The allusion is to the celebrated legend of the Empress Helena's discovery of the True Cross. Needless to say, her introduction as ancestress of a British royal line is entirely fanciful: indeed, there is no reason to suppose the Empress ever set foot in Britain. That her inclusion was entirely arbitrary is confirmed by the fact that she is placed nine generations before

50 Lloyd, *A History of Wales*, pp. 333–43; David Dumville, 'The 'Six' Sons of Rhodri Mawr: A Problem in Asser's *Life of King Alfred*', *Cambridge Medieval Celtic Studies* (Cambridge, 1982), iv, pp. 5–18; Dafydd Jenkins (tr.), *The Law of Hywel Dda: Law Texts from Medieval Wales Translated and Edited* (Llandysul, 1986), pp. xi–xvii; T. M. Charles-Edwards, *Wales and the Britons 350–1064* (Oxford, 2013), pp. 504–19.

51 The first pedigree in the Harleian collection originally began with Hywel, the name of his son Owain being added subsequently (A. W. Wade-Evans (tr.), *Nennius's 'History of the Britons'* (London, 1938), p. 101).

52 Sir John Rhys, 'President's Address', *Transactions of the Third International Congress for the History of Religions*, ii, pp. 212–13; Chadwick (ed.), *Studies in Early British History*, p. 132; Bromwich (ed.), *Trioedd Ynys Prydein*, p. 282.

53 Egerton G. B. Phillimore, 'The *Annales Cambriæ* and Old-Welsh Genealogies from *Harleian MS. 3859*', *Y Cymmrodor* (London, 1888), ix, pp. 171–72.

Maximus. In reality, Helena died *c.* 328/9,[54] while the historical Maximus met his end two generations later in 388.

Elsewhere Maxen Gwledig was regarded as the ideal figure from the Romano-British past to cite as founder of dynasties.[55] From at least the time Gildas wrote in the sixth century, he was widely understood to have been the last ruler of Roman Britain. There are indications that he established a number of federate kingdoms in western and northern Britain, in order to strengthen the frontier regions against invasion in the absence of those regular troops who followed him to Gaul.

It seems that the added generations of the royal house of Dyfed, which take the line back to the parents of Constantine the Great, reflect a specific concern of that dynasty at the time the Harleian genealogies were assembled. The motive for insertion of the Empress Helena at the head of the pedigree is not far to seek. It was intended to provide an appropriately illustrious progenitrix for Hywel Dda's wife Elen, daughter of King Llywarch of Dyfed. Her death in 928 is recorded in two of the manuscript versions of the early Welsh annals, and it is surely significant that one of them (MS 'B') accords her the Latin name *Helena*.[56] The name *Elen* borne by the tenth-century princess of Dyfed was apparently rare as a Welsh personal name. Who, then, was there more appropriate to select as her primary ancestress than the uniquely pious Empress Helena?[57] The sanctified renown of Helena, mother of Constantine the Great and reputed discoverer of the True Cross, became popular in Wales no later than the tenth century, although at that time she was regarded not as wife of Maximus but his ancestress. The Harleian genealogy which reflects this legend was drawn up shortly after the middle of the tenth century, in the interest of the king of Gwynedd.[58]

In *Breuddwyd Maxen*, the Welsh princess Elen confers Britain as her dowry on the enamoured Emperor Maxen. This element of the romance reflects the age-old myth of the Sovereignty of Britain, whereby the land is personified by a beautiful woman who weds, and so legitimates, a visiting prince. Originally this figure may have borne the name of a Brittonic goddess such as Rhiannon, Arianrhod, or Don. In a Breton version of the legend the corresponding figure is called *Pritella*, presumably a British name, which suggests that the name *Elen* was not original to the Brittonic sovereignty legend.

In fact, the text of *Breuddwyd Maxen* indicates that it was the author himself who first ascribed the name *Elen* to the Maiden Sovereignty figure found in his source. As Brynley Roberts, editor of the story, points out:

---

54 Jan Willem Drijvers, *Helena Augusta: The Mother of Constantine the Great and the Legend of Her Finding of the True Cross* (Leiden, 1992), p. 73.

55 'But famous above all as the reputed founder of dynasties is Maxen Wledic ... who impressed himself on native Welsh tradition as one of heroic stature, whose fame was transmitted to posterity' (Chadwick (ed.), *Studies in Early British History*, p. 94).

56 David N. Dumville (ed.), *Annales Cambriae, A.D. 682–954: Texts A-C in Parallel* (Cambridge, 2002), p. 17.

57 It is curious that, at the other extremity of Christian Europe, the Empress Helena's name was chosen at this time as a personal name by the royal dynasty of Kiev (Christian Raffensperger, *Reimagining Europe: Kievan Rus' in the Medieval World* (Cambridge, Mass., 2012), pp. 156–57).

58 *Y Cymmrodor*, ix, pp. 171–72. The legend of Helena's discovery of the Rood originated in the second half of the fourth century (Drijvers, *Helena Augusta*, pp. 81–93). Cf. Kathleen Hughes, 'The Welsh Latin Chronicles: *Annales Cambriae* and Related Texts', *The Proceedings of the British Academy* (London, 1973), lix, p. 234.

Another innovation for which this author seems responsible is that the name Elen Luyddawg is given to Maxen's wife. Geoffrey of Monmouth did not name Octavius's daughter, and even in the *Breudwyt* the British princess remains un-named in the dream and marriage section of the narrative.[59]

Furthermore, in the version of the story outlined in Jesus College MS 20, the wife of Maxen is named *keindrech verch. Reiden.*[60] *Ceindrech* ('lovely and stronger')[61] is an apt enough name for the Maiden Sovereignty.

If *Breuddwyd Maxen* be detached from its secondary framework of Roman history, there remains a tale whose geographical location is almost entirely confined to South Wales, *Deheubarth*. After her wedding to Maxen, Elen is said to have caused three fortresses to be built in Britain. Although the first was in North Wales, its location remains hazy. We are told that it was in the district of Arfon, but it is not accorded a name, being vaguely described as 'the highest' (or 'the best') castle – implicitly in Britain.

'After that the other two forts were built for her, namely *Caerllion* and *Caerfyrddin*.' Not only are these situated in South Wales, but they are described as sites where Maxen was accustomed to hold court. When he goes hunting, it is from Caerfyrddin (Carmarthen) that he sets out, which was implicitly where he was understood to reside. That a substantial part of the Roman walls of the city were still standing at the end of the twelfth century made it an attractive site for storytellers.[62] Still more explicit is the allusion to Caerleon. It was thither that Maxen's usurping rival at Rome directed his threatening letter, and thence that Maxen despatched his defiant reply.

The abrupt and unexplained introduction of the South Walian interlude into the tale makes little sense,[63] unless it were carried over from archaic tradition sufficiently well-established and widely known not to be ignored. It looks as though Maxen's principal court was originally identified with Caerleon, whose splendid Roman remains inspired Geoffrey of Monmouth to select it as the appropriate city of Britain for King Arthur to stage his coronation.[64]

---

59   Roberts (ed.), *Breudwyt Maxen Wledic*, p. lxiv. The Gwynedd author of the *Historia Brittonum* significantly makes no mention of Elen.

60   Egerton G. B. Phillimore, 'A Fragment from Hengwrt MS. No. 202', *Y Cymmrodor* (1886), viii, p. 84.

61   Stefan Zimmer, 'Die altkymrischen Frauennamen. Ein erster Einblick', in Joseph F. Eska, R. Geraint Gruffydd, and Nicolas Jacobs (ed.), *Hispano-Gallo-Brittonica: Essays in honour of Professor D. Ellis Evans on the occasion of his sixty-fifth birthday* (Cardiff, 1995), p. 323.

62   Brewer, Dimock, and Warner (ed.), *Giraldi Cambrensis Opera*, vi, p. 80.

63   'It is not so immediately apparent, however, why Maxen's bride should have demanded that Caerllion and Caerfyrddin should also be part of her [Elen's] bride-price' (Roberts (ed.), *Breudwyt Maxen Wledic*, p. lxxx).

64   Reeve and Wright (ed.), *Geoffrey of Monmouth: The History of the Kings of Britain*, pp. 209–15; Brewer, Dimock, and Warner (ed.), *Giraldi Cambrensis Opera*, vi, pp. 171–72. Geoffrey ascribes the building of Caerleon to Belinus (Beli), whom Maxen in the Welsh romance overthrew at his conquest of Britain (Reeve and Wright (ed.), *Geoffrey of Monmouth: The History of the Kings of Britain*, p. 59). For Caerleon in the Roman and mediæval eras, cf. Ray Howell, 'Roman Past and Medieval Present: Caerleon as a Focus for Continuity and Conflict in the Middle Ages', *Studia Celtica* (2012), xlvi, pp. 11–21.

Reverting to Hywel Dda, it seems that he continued to regard the South as his principal domain after his acquisition of the throne of Gwynedd, since it was there that he assembled his jurists and other notables from Powys, Gwynedd, and Dyfed, when he issued his famous law code.[65]

Furthermore, reasons will be given shortly for concluding that the original location of Maxen's encounter with the Maiden Sovereignty was the Preseli Mountain Y Freni Fawr, whose summit according to the author of *Breuddwyd Maxen* was identified as 'the seat (or throne) of Maxen'. The evidence suggests that the original setting for Maxen's dream was his otherwise pointless and implausible mountaintop vigil on Y Freni Fawr, and that it was the author of the romance who transposed the site to the imposing Roman ruins at Caernarvon. The selection of prominent Romano-British sites for the setting of his tale reflects its Roman context. They are, however, likely to have been no more original to the story than the other elements of the Roman setting. The mountain Y Freni Fawr therefore belonged to a tradition which identified it as being crowned by the seat or throne of Maxen, where the Emperor was believed to have slept on an occasion so memorable in local lore that the author of the Dream felt obliged to retain it as an incongruous byline in his romance.[66]

Although the description of Maxen's approach to Aber Seint suggests that the author was familiar with the landscape of north-west Wales, this need imply no more than that he had visited Gwynedd.[67] The latter would be likely enough, were *Breuddwyd Maxen* composed, as evidence suggests, to glorify the accession of Hywel Dda to the northern kingdom. An eminent *cyfarwydd* such as the author was most likely to have accompanied his king from court to court as occasion demanded.[68]

It is noteworthy that Maxen's arrival at Caer Seint is preceded in the romance by his conquest of Britain from 'Beli and his sons', whom he is said to have driven into the sea.[69] This fleeting reference appears incongruous, since the tale represents Elen's father Eudaf as ruler of the kingdom. On the other hand, it is entirely apposite to the career of Hywel Dda. After the death of Idwal Foel, king of Gwynedd, in 642, Hywel acted swiftly to occupy the country, when he expelled Idwal's sons from

---

65 Hywel summoned his senior ecclesiastics *hyt y lle a elwir y Ty Gwyn ar Taf yn Dyfet* (Stephen J. Williams and J. Enoch Powell (ed.), *Cyfreithiau Hywel Dda yn ôl Llyfr Blegywryd (Dull Dyfed)* (Cardiff, 1942), p. 1; Aled Rhys Wiliam (ed.), *Llyfr Iorwerth: A Critical Text of the Venedotian Code of Medieval Welsh Law Mainly from BM. Cotton MS. Titus Dii* (Cardiff, 1960), p. 1). The extent of Hywel's responsibility for the legal code bearing his name is discussed by Charles-Edwards, *Wales and the Britons*, pp. 267–73.

66 The wording implies that Maxen's association with the mountain was widely known in pre-existing legendary lore: *ac e gelwir y pebyllua honno er henne hyt hediw Cadeir Vaxen* (Roberts (ed.), *Breudwyt Maxen Wledic*, p. 8).

67 I concur with Thomas Owen Clancy's judgment on the Four Branches: 'The [geographical] details need not be a sign of the location of the author, just of the detailed nature of the material he or she worked on in producing these branches' ('The Needs of Strangers in the Four Branches of the Mabinogi', *Quaestio Insularis: Selected Proceedings of the Cambridge Colloquium in Anglo-Saxon Norse and Celtic* (Cambridge, 2006), vi, p. 5).

68 His enraptured account of the approach to Caernarvon has been taken to suggest that the author was a patriotic *cyfarwydd* of Gwynedd. However, it is excessive to suggest that 'his glowing depiction of the sumptuous details of the castle and its furnishings … reveal an author moved both [by] pride of place and of history' (Nagy and Jones (ed.), *Heroic Poets and Poetic Heroes in Celtic Tradition*, p. 306). The impossibly lavish setting clearly derives from stock descriptions of the sumptuous Otherworld palace.

69 *Ac e goresgynnws er enys y ar Veli vab Manogan, a'e ueibeon, ac a'e gyrrws wynt <ar vor ac>* (Roberts (ed.), *Breudwyt Maxen Wledic*, p. 7). Beli is also implicitly described as king of Britain in the poem *Kein gyfedwch* (Marged Haycock (ed.), *Prophecies from the Book of Taliesin* (Aberystwyth, 2013), p. 100; cf. p. 105).

the kingdom.[70] They claimed descent from the euhemerized deity Beli the Great, whose particular association with Gwynedd caused it to be known as *bro veli*, 'the land of Beli'.[71]

These factors combine to suggest that the legend of Maxen's wedding to a British princess personifying the Sovereignty of the Island originated in South Wales, and was only subsequently partially relocated in Gwynedd by the author of *Breuddwyd Maxen*. It was he, too, who uniquely named the Sovereignty princess *Elen*. All this corresponds closely to significant episodes in the career of Hywel Dda.

Hywel Dda ap Cadell	*Breudwydd Maxen Gwledig*
Hywel asserts descent from Maxen Gwledig.	Maxen Gwledig is Emperor of Rome.
Hywel weds Elen, heiress of Dyfed. He also claims descent from Constantius II and his Empress Helena.	Maxen weds Elen, heiress of Britain. Maxen is a Roman Emperor, implicitly sprung from the imperial dynasty.
Hywel journeys on pilgrimage to Rome and back in 928.	Maxen follows the pilgrim route from Rome to Britain.
Dyfed was Hywel's original patrimony.	Maxen holds court at Caerleon, which is located in early sources in Dyfed.[71]
Hywel occupies Gwynedd, expelling the sons of its King Idwal, descendants of *Beli mawr m. Manogan*.[72]	Maxen occupies Gwynedd, expelling *Beli mab Manogan* and his sons.

These close parallels suggest the years 942–50 as the likely period for composition of *Breuddwyd Maxen*, between Hywel Dda's acquisition of Gwynedd and his death. At the same time, it must once again be emphasized that the date of composition does not materially affect the underlying mythological theme of the romance.

The mythic history

The hunt

The story begins with Maxen's expression of a desire to go hunting. Accompanied by thirty-two kings, he rides out beside the river that flows towards Rome. In his study of the tale, Roy Owen asserted that 'Macsen is presented to us for no obvious reason as a huntsman'.[74] Celtic scholars will however recognize a motif familiar from mediæval Welsh literature and Arthurian romance. The First Branch of the *Mabinogi*, *Pwyll Pendeuic Dyuet*, begins with a hunting

---

70 'Two sons of Idwal, namely Iago and Ieuaf, whom Hywel expelled from the kingdom' (Dumville (ed.), *Annales Cambriae, A.D. 682–954*, p. 17).

71 *Y Cymmrodor*, ix, p. 170; J. Gwenogvryn Evans (ed.), *The Poetry in the Red Book of Hergest* (Llanbedrog, 1911), col. 1405, ll. 28–29. The traditional connexion of Beli with Gwynedd is widely attested (Gruffydd, *Math vab Mathonwy*, pp. 185–6; Haycock (ed.), *Prophecies from the Book of Taliesin*, pp. 48–49).

72 *Kaerusc appellata metropolis Demetiae fuerat; postquam autem Romani uenerunt, praefato nomine deleto uocata est Vrbs Legionum* (Reeve and Wright (ed.), *Geoffrey of Monmouth: The History of the Kings of Britain*, p. 59). In the sixth and seventh centuries, Dyfed extended eastwards as far as Gwent: *de Ventia, prouintia proxima eiusdem Demetie* (Pierre Flobert (ed.), *La vie ancienne de saint Samson de Dol* (Paris, 1997), p. 146).

73 Bartrum (ed.), *Early Welsh Genealogical Texts*, pp. 38–39.

74 Owen, *The Evolution of the Grail Legend*, p. 43; cf. pp. 38–39.

expedition, as does the romance of *Gereint mab Erbin*. In her classic study of the theme, Rachel Bromwich demonstrated that frequently in Celtic tales,

> the intended ruler was set apart from his companions (in the stories he is separated from them in the hunt, either by nightfall or by a magic mist), and would inevitably and in spite of deceptive appearances, come together with the goddess representing his appointed territory.

She further concluded that extant versions represent 'variants of a common Celtic theme which in ultimate origin are as old as the period of the sixth-century Breton settlements'.[75]

The setting of the hunting scene outside Rome represents a secondary development in the story, when the author decided that the story of Maximus, as an Emperor who began his career at Rome, should feature in an appropriately imperial Roman setting. That the episode was depicted in an earlier version as occurring entirely in Britain, is suggested by a brief duplication occurring later in the tale. After Maxen's wedding to Elen, we are abruptly told:

> And one day the Emperor went to hunt at Carmarthen, and he came as far as the summit (*pen*) of Y Freni Fawr. And there the Emperor pitched his tent, and that camping place is called Cadeir Maxen, to this day.[76]

As remarked earlier, this seemingly pointless episode reflects the author's awareness of an earlier version of the legend, in which Maxen's dream was located on the summit of a mountain in Dyfed. A mountaintop was considered an appropriate spot for practice of a mantic seance. In the seventeenth century a tradition was recorded of boulders known as the Bed of Idris (*Gwely Idris*), on the summit of Cader Idris, 'that whoever lies and sleeps on that bed, one of two things will happen to him, either he will be a poet of the best kind, or go entirely demented'.[77]

Poetry and prophecy being commingled in Celtic tradition, the saying clearly reflects the shamanistic frenzy which gripped Welsh bards when declaiming their prophecies.[78] Thus Myrddin (Merlin) acquired prophetic powers when he went mad (*wyllt*), and, according to Geoffrey of Monmouth's *Vita Merlini,* settled by a spring on a mountain summit in the haunted brakes of the Forest of Celyddon.[79]

The unexplained reference to the erection of a tent implies that the purpose of the Emperor's ascent of the hill was to sleep on its summit, where, prior to his reinvention as a Roman emperor, an earlier version of the story set the scene of his Dream. It has been seen that a hunt frequently provided the traditional introductory motif presaging an encounter with the supernatural. The

---

75   Rachel Bromwich, 'Celtic Dynastic Themes and the Breton Lays', *Études Celtiques* (Paris, 1960–61), ix, pp. 453, 467. Cf. Jaan Puhvel, *Comparative Mythology* (Baltimore, 1987), p. 266.

76   *A diwyrnawt yd aeth er amperauder y hely o Gaer Verdin hyt pen e Vreni Vaur a thynnv pebyll eno a oruc er amperauder ac a gelwir y pebyllua honno er henne hyt hediw Cadeir Vaxen* (Roberts (ed.), *Breudwyt Maxen Wledic*, p. 8).

77   Hugh Owen, 'Peniarth MS. 118, Fos. 829–837', *Y Cymmrodor* (London, 1917), xxvii, p. 124.

78   J. S. Brewer, James F. Dimock, and George F. Warner (ed.), *Giraldi Cambrensis Opera* (London, 1861-91), vi, pp. 194–95.

79   Basil Clarke (ed.), *Life of Merlin; Geoffrey of Monmouth: Vita Merlini* (Cardiff, 1973), p. 58. Geoffrey drew extensively on pre-existing Welsh lore for his account of the history of Merlin (Nikolai Tolstoy, 'Geoffrey of Monmouth and the Merlin Legend', in Elizabeth Archibald and David F. Johnson (ed.), *Arthurian Literature XXV* (Cambridge, 2008), pp. 1–42).

redactor relocated the scene of Maxen's dream to the environs of Rome, as befitted a Roman Emperor (the story opens with the words '*Maxen Wledic oed amperauder en Ruvein,* 'Maxen Wledig was Emperor of Rome'). However, he felt obliged to retain the brief and contextually pointless reference to Maxen's ascent and repose upon the mountain in Dyfed, possibly because he respected the integrity of his source, but more importantly in recognition of the fact that a mediæval Welsh audience was likely to be aware of the traditional association of Maxen's dream with the mountain Y Freni Fawr.

The wording of the passage indicates that *the summit* of Y Freni Fawr was understood to be the place where Maxen had his seat or throne, rather than the unlikely contingency of the mountain's having borne two distinct names.

The kings and their shields

The sun rose high in the sky, so that Maxen became drowsy from its intense heat. He lay down to sleep beside the river, while his attendant kings set up their shields upon their spears to shelter him from the sun. As ever, it is important to mark the precise wording of the text:

> This is what his chamberlains did: they made a shelter by raising their shields around him on the shafts of their spears. They placed a gold-chased shield beneath his head and so the Emperor slept.

This episode appears at first glance not a little bizarre. Why did the Emperor not ride out at a time of day more appropriate to the chase? What induced his companions to encumber themselves with shields on a hunting expedition? When compelled to seek shelter from the sun, why should Maxen elect to recline in the open, where he would be exposed to its most burning glare? What was it that suggested to his followers the peculiar device of the shield-shelter? And why did they select so uncomfortable an object as a shield for their sovereign's pillow?

It is unlikely that a skilled storyteller (*cyfarwydd*) would choose deliberately to introduce such a congeries of oddities into his story, and more often than not it is the case that incongruent components represent fossil elements surviving from an earlier recension, disparate sources, or a combination of both. This type of corruption is especially likely to be found where an originally mythological tale has become euhemerized into the type of 'historical' narrative which continued to regale audiences centuries after the introduction of Christianity.

The contrived arrangement, whereby Maxen's vassal kings set up a circle of shields and spears to protect their sovereign from the burning rays of the sun, suggests a ritualistic setting. The Greek geographer Posidonius, writing in the first century BC, describes the placement of a Celtic feast as follows:

> When a large number dine in company they are seated in a circle, with the most important man at the centre, like the leader of the chorus. The host is seated beside him, and then on either side others according to their distinction. Their shieldmen stand behind them, while their spearmen are seated in a circle on the opposite side and feast together like their lords.[80]

---

80   L. Edelstein and I. G. Kidd (ed.), *Posidonius* (Cambridge, 1988–99), i, pp. 84–85.

A Celtic feast was an occasion charged with ritual significance, being regarded as an earthly enactment of the eternal feast attended by heroes in the Otherworld.[81] From Posidonius's account it would seem that the spearmen, who were presumably the principal warriors of the attendant princes, feasted in a separate circle.[82] This however is unclear, and in every other respect the resemblance of this arrangement to that so oddly adopted by Maxen and his companions in *Breuddwyd Maxen* seems too striking to be coincidental. The most important figure at the gathering sits at the centre of a circle formed by his principal subordinates, who in turn are encircled by men bearing shields.

The incongruous use of a gold-chased shield (*tarean eurgrwyder*) for Maxen's pillow recalls the ornamented cosmic shield (*clipeus*) featured widely in imperial iconography of the ancient world. The *clipeus* represented the world, cosmos, or sun:

> Thus, already the Ancient East has seen the world in the image of a circle or *clipeus*, and has placed the cosmocrator, god and king, in its centre.

This belief is also reflected in the ceremonial practice of elevating a monarch on a shield,[83] which may account for its inappropriate use as the emperor's pillow in *Breuddwyd Maxen*.

The number thirty-two ascribed Maxen's attendant kings is likewise suggestive. Early British tradition ascribed Britain twenty-eight cities,[84] while another version made the number thirty-three.[85] The latter figure may correspond to 32 + 1, the additional number frequently representing the focus or embodiment of the remainder.[86] These figures do not derive from any historical or geographical paradigm,[87] and may reflect lunar or astral

---

81   Thomas F. O'Rahilly, *Early Irish History and Mythology* (Dublin, 1946), pp. 121–25; Alwyn Rees and Brinley Rees, *Celtic Heritage: Ancient Tradition in Ireland and Wales* (London, 1961), pp. 147–50.

82   Cf. Michael J. Enright, *Lady with a Mead Cup: Ritual, Prophecy and Lordship in the European Warband from La Tène to the Viking Age* (Dublin, 1996), p. 147.

83   H. P. L'Orange, *Studies on the Iconography of Cosmic Kingship in the Ancient World* (Oslo, 1953), pp. 90–109; idem, 'Expressions of Cosmic Kingship in the Ancient World', in *La Regalità Sacra: Contributi al Tema Dell' VIII Congresso Internazionale di Storia delle Religioni (Roma, Aprile 1955)* (Leiden, 1959), pp. 488–90. The sun is identified as a shield in the Old English poem *Exodus* (George Philip Krapp (ed.), *The Junius Manuscript* (London and New York, 1931), p. 93).

84   Theodor Mommsen (ed.), *Monvmenta Germaniae Historica* (xiii): *Chronica Minora saec. IV. V. VI. VII* (Berlin, 1894), iii, p. 28; Egerton Phillimore, 'The *Annales Cambriæ* and Old-Welsh Genealogies from *Harleian MS. 3859*', (London, 1888), ix, p. 183.

85   *A their prif gaer ar dec ar hugeint* (Egerton G. B. Phillimore, 'A Fragment from Hengwrt MS. No. 202', *Y Cymmrodor* (1886), vii, p. 124; John Rhŷs and J. Gwenogvryn Evans (ed.), *The Text of the Mabinogion and other Welsh Tales from the Red Book of Hergest* (Oxford, 1887), p. 309). Awareness is expressed in the text of the Brut in Jesus MS 61 of a divergence between the figures 28 and 31 [*sic*] (Acton Griscom (ed.), *The Historia Regum Britanniæ of Geoffrey of Monmouth with Contributions to the Study of its Place in Early British History* (London, 1929), pp. 330–31).

86   On occasion early Irish sources ignore Meath, when alluding to the *four* provinces of Ireland. 'Mais, la cinquième étant le centre de chacune des quatre autres, il est normal qu'elle ne soit pas nommé : son existence est implicite …' (Christian-J. Guyonvarc'h and Françoise Le Roux, *Les Druides* (Rennes, 1986), p. 221).

87   'The origin of this list is not at all clear. Plainly it belongs to a Celtic and not to a Roman world: it is neither a list handed down from Roman times, nor the translation of such a list' (F. Haverfield and George Macdonald, *The Roman Occupation of Britain* (Oxford, 1924), p. 289). As Kenneth Jackson explained, 'the compiler knew from Gildas and Bede only so much – that there were traditionally twenty-eight important cities in Britain, not their names, and so he set to work to supply these names from his own sources' ('Nennius and the Twenty-Eight Cities of Britain', *Antiquity: A Quarterly Review of Archæology* (Gloucester, 1938), xii, p. 53).

correspondences to terrestrial sites, such as are known from many early cultures.[88] Thus, the figure 28 suggests lunar mansions (the phases through which the moon cyclically passes).[89] In early China

> These segments of the heavens must … have been thought of as the temporary resting-houses of the sun, moon, and planets, like the tea-houses scattered along the roads on earth; but especially of the moon, the greatest nightly luminary.[90]

The source of the variant figure 33 is less readily explained on this basis, although it may be noted that in early Greece thirty-three constellations were singled out as created by individual gods.[91]

According to Giraldus Cambrensis, Ireland in the twelfth century possessed thirty-two cantreds or districts within its provinces. The province of Meath, which represented an idealized model of the whole island, contained sixteen. In reality, early Ireland may have comprised as many as 150 kingdoms. As with the thirty-three British cities, Giraldus's unrealistically perfect matching numbers correspond to an ideological paradigm, whose origin in a native scholarly source is not hard to detect.[92]

This symbolic pattern of thirty-two kingdoms grouped about a royal centre has left traces in the Irish literary and archæological record. Thus, the early Irish heroic tale 'Bricriu's Feast' (*Fled Bricrenn*) relates how thirty-two Ulster heroes accompanied their High King (*ardríg*) Conchobar to the feast of the mischievous Bricriu, in whose hall they reclined on couches set in cubicles or recesses spaced equidistantly around their sovereign. We are explicitly informed that Bricriu's hall was modelled on the celebrated *Cráebh Ruad* at Emain Macha (Navan Fort) and Tara's mead hall, indicating a common idealized setting for such structures.[93]

This paradigmatic pattern of a company of thirty-two or thirty-three charismatic figures feasting together appears to have been carried over together with other Celtic themes into the Matter of Britain. In the Arthurian romance of *Perlesvaus*, the hero arrives at an obviously Otherworld castle set on an island. Its denizens comprise a company of thirty-three men dressed in white, each of whom appears to be aged thirty-two. They invite Perlesvaus to join them at a separate table, where, following revelation of the castle's mysteries, the young knight is informed that he will achieve his quest and gain the destined throne (*la chaiere*).[94]

---

88 Eric Burrows, 'Some Cosmological Patterns in Babylonian Religion', in S. H. Hooke (ed.), *The Labyrinth: Further Studies in the Relation between Myth and Ritual in the Ancient World* (London, 1935), pp. 63–64.

89 Cf. Vedic *nakṣatra* and Chinese *hsiu* (J. Needham, 'Astronomy in ancient and medieval China', in F. R. Hodson (ed.), *The Place of Astronomy in the Ancient World* (London, 1974), pp. 68–69; O. Neugebauer and D. Pingree (ed.), *The Pañcasiddhāntikā of Varāhamihira* (Copenhagen, 1970–71), i, p. 187).

90 Joseph Needham (ed.), *Science and Civilisation in China* (Cambridge, 1954–), iii, p. 239.

91 Arthur Bernard Cook, *Zeus: A Study in Ancient Religion* (Cambridge, 1914–40), i, pp. 75455.

92 John J. O'Meara, 'Giraldus Cambrensis in Topographia Hibernie: *Text of the First Recension*', *Proceedings of the Royal Irish Academy* (Dublin, 1949), lii, p. 160. A 'cantred' (*trícha cét*) represented the tribal area ruled by a *rí* (Francis John Byrne, *Irish Kings and High-Kings* (London, 1973), p. 270). Byrne's estimate is that 'there were probably no less than 150 kings in the country at any given date between the fifth and twelfth centuries' (ibid., p. 7), while Eoin MacNeill estimated about eighty small states in the historical period (*Early Irish Laws and Institutions* (Dublin, 1935), p. 96). The Book of Rights lists some hundred kingdoms (idem, *Phases of Irish History* (Dublin, 1919), p. 274).

93 R. I. Best and Osborn Bergin (ed.), *Lebor na Huidre: Book of the Dun Cow* (Dublin, 1929), pp. 246, 249, 256.

94 William A. Nitze and T. Atkinson Jenkins (ed.), *Le Haut Livre du Graal: Perlesvaus* (Chicago, 1932–37), i, pp. 387–91. Cf. ibid., ii, pp. 95, 151–56, 339–41; James Douglas Bruce, *The Evolution of Arthurian*

Excavations at Navan Fort, site of the 'capital' of Ulster in the legendary epoch, have revealed the presence of a multi-ring timber structure, whose perimeter was defined by thirty-four post-pairs.[95] From careful comparison of the site with accounts of Otherworld halls (*bruiden*) described in the heroic tales, the archæologist Christopher Lynn observes

> that the size and layout of the multi-ring timber structure accords well enough with the various descriptions of the mythic hostels to suggest that the design of the timber building in site B was inspired in part by the imagined form of the otherworld hostels of the tales.

His considered conclusion is that the elaborate edifice 'was erected primarily as a basis for kingship ceremonial and related activities', and further 'was constructed as a reproduction of the cosmos itself'.[96]

The focus of this monumental building was a gigantic oak post, some 36 feet tall, towering high above its centre.[97] Since this wooden column fulfilled no useful structural function, it is considered to have provided a concrete manifestation of the World Tree or Pillar, which in Irish and other early cosmologies was believed to sustain the universe. Thus, a gigantic oak was said to have stood at the centre of the enclosure of Mac Dá Thó's hostelry, which the hero Fergus mac Roich tore up by the roots.[98] Endrochronological dating indicates that the Emain Macha pillar was fashioned from the trunk of a tree felled during the winter of 95–94 BC. A further remarkable feature of the building is that within a short space of time it came to be destroyed in a manner which can only have been deliberate. The interior was laboriously filled with limestone blocks, after which the timber framework was fired. The remains were then covered over with a thick layer of turfs, after which it became the grassy mound which it remains to this day.[99]

That the structure at Emain Macha was regarded as a replica or manifestation of the Otherworld is further suggested by the fact that one of the names of the Land of Promise in pagan Irish tradition was *Emhain Ablach*, home of the god Manannán mác Lir and birthplace of Lugh.[100] Spacially and temporally every fairy mound (*síd*) comprised a material localization of Otherworld infinity. J. P. Mallory plausibly suggests that the purpose of those who arranged the burning of their great temple at Navan Fort was

Romance: From the Beginnings Down to the Year 1300 (Göttingen, 1928), ii, pp. 16–17; Roger Sherman Loomis, *Arthurian Tradition & Chrétien de Troyes* (New York, 1949), p. 362. 32 chieftains led the Otherworld race of Fomoire, headed by their high king Elatha (Brian Ó Cuív (ed.), *Cath Muighe Tuireadh: The Second Battle of Magh Tuireadh* (Dublin, 1945), pp. 28–29).

95   D. M. Waterman, *Excavations at Navan Fort 1961–71* (Belfast, 1997), pp. 159–71, 224–25. Only half of structure B at Navan Fort has been excavated, on the basis of which the figure of 34 segments represents a plausible inference. Since literary tradition indicates that the typical *bruiden* contained an 'official entrance', it is possible that the temple/hostel originally contained 33 recesses for its real or mythical feasters, the 34th providing a passageway to the Centre.

96   C. J. Lynn, 'Hostels, Heroes and Tale: Further Thoughts on the Navan Mound', *Emania: Bulletin of the Navan Research Group* (Belfast, 1994), xii, pp. 5–20. For conjectural artist's portrayals of the interior and exterior of the original structure at Navan Fort, cf. N. B. Aitchison, *Armagh and the Royal Centres in Early Medieval Ireland: Monuments, Cosmology, and the Past* (Woodbridge, 1994), pp. 86, 88.

97   Waterman, *Excavations at Navan Fort*, pp. xvi, 38–39, 210, 224.

98   *Is and gabais Fergus dóib daur mór ro-boí for lár ind liss assa frēnaib* (Rudolf Thurneysen (ed.), *Scéla Mucce Meic Dathó* (Dublin, 1935), p. 18).

99   Aitchison, *Armagh and the Royal Centres in Early Medieval Ireland*, pp. 82–83.

100 *Baile suthain sith Eamhna* (William F. Skene, *Celtic Scotland: A History of Ancient Alban* (Edinburgh, 1876–80), iii, p. 412); Lilian Duncan, 'Altram Tige Dá Medar', *Ériu* (1932), xi, pp. 188, 196–97.

to take their great temple out of the world of mortal man and move it into the Otherworld. This would mean that they had not brought the great ritual structure to an end – rather, they had preserved it for eternity.[101]

Thus the indications are that an earlier version of the tale of Maxen Gwledig began with a description of the Emperor surrounded by his sub-kings in hierarchical formation, a pattern regularly encountered in early Irish and Welsh literature – not infrequently, as prefatory to an adventure.[102] A number of texts describe the King of Ireland presiding over the Feast of Samain (Hallowe'en) at Tara (itself a magical *mandala*), with his sub-kings and people disposed about him in prescribed hierarchical order. 'On this night of mischief and confusion', wrote the brothers Rees in their seminal work on Celtic mythology,

> the four provincial kings and their people sat four-square around the king of Ireland, symbolizing and asserting the cosmic structure of the state and of society while chaos raged outside.[103]

A Muslim sea atlas of 1551 depicts the sacred stone Ka'ba surrounded by a thirty-two-division 'wind rose'.[104] Another striking example of this paradigmatic pattern is attested in a yet more distant region of the world. Burmese kings were identified with the god Sakka, their courts in their capital cities being regarded as microcosms of Tāvatimsa, divine realm of Sakka. The royal court was arranged as a *mandala*, with the king at the centre, surrounded by his thirty-two lords.[105]

Again, the kingdom of Matarām in Java boasted twenty-eight autonomous principalities. However, it is considered

> rather improbable that we have to interpret it as referring to countries outside central Java. Moreover the above-mentioned passage, plus the information that there are thirty-two high ministers, reflects the cosmogonic background underlying the idea of Javanese kingship. The numbers twenty-eight and thirty-two are certainly symbolic numbers. Twenty-eight is

---

101 J. P. Mallory, *Navan Fort: The Ancient Capital of Ulster* (Belfast, 1985), pp. 19–20. An early Irish hymn envisages the faithful as attaining the *síd* of the King of Heaven (Whitley Stokes and John Strachan (ed.), *Thesaurus Palaeohibernicus: A Collection of Old-Irish Glosses Scholia Prose and Verse* (Cambridge, 1901–3), ii, p. 304; cf. Rolf Baumgarten, 'A Crux in Echtrae Conlai', *Éigse* (1975), xvi, p. 23). Alternatively, Dáithí Ó hÓgáin suggests that 'the destruction may have been a hostile act, and if so could have marked the overthrow of a Bronze Age people at the site by an incoming Celtic group' (*The Sacred Isle: Belief and Religion in Pre-Christian Ireland* (Woodbridge, 1999), p. 172). However, the destruction occurred at a much later period.

102 R. I. Best, 'The Settling of the Manor of Tara', *Ériu* (1910), iv, p. 124; Máirín O Daly, 'A Poem on the Airgialla', ibid. (1952), xvi, pp. 179–80. The tale of *Branwen* opens with a formal portrayal of Bran, seated on the Rock of Harlech, flanked by a patterned hierarchy of family members.

103 Alwyn Rees and Brinley Rees, *Celtic Heritage: Ancient Tradition in Ireland and Wales* (London, 1961), pp. 146–56. Fearing abduction of his bride Étaín by the menacing Otherworld ruler Midir, King Eochaid gathered his chief warriors at Tara in a prophylactic mandala pattern, the court gates being locked, and the principal warriors of Ireland assembled in protective circles around the king and queen, who were positioned 'in the middle of the house', *7 in rí 7 an righan i meadhón an taighe* (Osborn Bergin and R. I. Best, 'Tochmarc Étaíne', *Ériu* (Dublin, 1938), xii, p. 182).

104 J. B. Harley and David Woodward (ed.), *The History of Cartography* (Chicago, 1987–2015), ii, pt. 2, plate 13.

105 Michael Aung-Thwin, 'Heaven, Earth, and the Supernatural World: *Dimensions of the Exemplary Center in Burmese History*', in Bardwell Smith and Holly Baker Reynolds (ed.), *The City as a Sacred Center: Essays on Six Asian Contexts* (Leiden, 1987), pp. 94–95, 99, 100.

4 x 7, which is an interpretation of the seven continents surrounding Jambudvīpa; we have thus seven countries on each side of the four cardinal points of Ho-ling [Java]. And the thirty-two high ministers are the thirty-two deities having their abodes on the Mahāmeru, on the summit of which is found the heaven of Indra, king of the gods.[106]

Such numerical correspondences with Irish and British tradition are unlikely to be coincidental, and an astronomical context conceivably accounts for the near-universality of the theme. A concept of thirty-three skies is widespread in Asiatic shamanist tradition.[107] As with the alternative figures 28 and 33 for the cities of Britain, in Asia the constellations were frequently reckoned at either 28[108] or 33.[109] The setting for Maxen's ritualistic dreaming echoes considerations which are likely to be of cosmic origin.

The heat of the sun

Thus, there is a strong suggestion that the circular disposition of the thirty-two kings around the sleeping Emperor Maxen originally represented a symbolic pattern or protective *mandala*.[110] A further detail in the account of his dreaming serves to confirm its originally ritual context: 'And the sun was high in the sky over his head, and the heat was great, and he fell asleep … And then he had a dream', recounts the storyteller.[111] The Emperor's setting out on a hunting expedition at a time of day which might be anticipated to prove stressful is odd, and it seems likely that the motif of the noontide heat, like those of the hunt and the disposition of the thirty-two kings, derives from archaic ritual practice.

We may also have here further intimation why Maxen positioned himself at the central point of the *mandala*, where he experienced his prophetic dream. In early India it was believed that the Yogic initiate attained a mysterious sun which, 'after having risen in the zenith, he [the Sun] will no more rise or set. He will stand alone in the middle'. The process provided a macroscopic parallel to the microcosmic technique practised within the mind of the Yogi:

> The process of Yoga consists in pursuing the radiant serpent and lifting it from the lowest sphere to the heart, where in union with *praṇar* or life-breath its universal nature is realised, and from it to the top of the skull. It goes out through an opening called the *brahma-randhra*, to which corresponds in the cosmic organism the opening formed by the sun on the top of the vault of the sky.[112]

106 Boechari, 'Some Considerations on the Problem of the Shift of Mataram's Centre of Government from Central to East Java in the 10th Century', in R. B. Smith and W. Watson (ed.), *Early South East Asia: Essays in Archaeology, History and Historical Geography* (Oxford, 1979), p. 478).

107 Mircea Eliade, *Le chamanisme et les techniques archaïques de l'extase* (Paris, 1951), pp. 249, 250–51.

108 Jeffrey F. Meyer, 'Traditional Peking: The Architecture of Conditional Power', in Smith and Reynolds (ed.), *The City as a Sacred Center*, p. 120.

109 Thirty-three Hindu gods dwell in the constellations, *nakṣatra* (Alain Daniélou, *Hindu Polytheism* (London, 1964), pp. 79–84, 97–98). Cf. Jeannine Auboyer, 'Le caractère royal et divin du trône dans l'Inde ancienne', in *La Regalità Sacra*, p. 183. The significance of numbers and numerical congruence in Vedic philosophy is discussed by J. Gonda, *Prajāpati and the Year* (Amsterdam, 1984), pp. 50–53.

110 Proinsias Mac Cana, *The Cult of the Sacred Centre: Essays on Celtic Ideology* (Dublin, 2011), pp. 93–94.

111 *A'r heul oed uchel ar er awyr uch e benn, a'r gwres en uawr ac e doeth kyscu arnaw … Ac ena e gwelei vreudwyt* (Roberts (ed.), *Breudwyt Maxen Wledic*, p. 1).

112 E. A. S. Butterworth, *The Tree at the Navel of the Earth* (Berlin, 1970), pp. 124–28. There existed a widespread belief that the light of the sun at the summer solstice fell perpendicularly on the *axis mundi* (Paul Wheatley, *The Pivot of the Four Quarters: A Preliminary Enquiry into the Origins and Character of*

The sun at its zenith was regarded as a potent manifestation of the sacred Centre of Being in the heavens, just as its terrestrial reflexion the hearth provided the *focus* (Latin 'fireplace') for a royal hall, whose fire at the same time embodied the kingship.[113] The Emperor Julian, in his 'Hymn to King Helios', emphasized the 'middle station' of the sun, that sublime divinity who is 'established midmost among the midmost intellectual gods'.[114]

In Celtic religious iconography and early Irish literature, the sun is regularly represented in the form of a wheel, whose symbolic aptness derives from its physical form, 'with its undertones of sun-rays, movement across the sky, and the surrounding nimbus'. In Christian times, God continued to be invoked as 'the maker of the wheel by which the world is illumined'. T. F. O'Rahilly observed that the Welsh name '*Rhodri*, meaning "king of the wheel (i.e. of the sun)", was evidently in origin a deity-name'.[115] The form of the wheel parallels the sun as centre or focus of the heavens, with its rays radiating from axle to perimeter,[116] and the positioning of Maxen beneath the sun at its zenith at the moment of his dream is unmistakably symbolic.

The heat which overcame Maxen possessed him at the moment when the sun stood above him at its zenith (*A'r heul oed uchel ar er awyr uch e benn*). Similarly, when Odysseus arrived at the isle of the enchantress Circe, he found the sun suspended permanently at the apex of the heavenly vault. As Butterworth pointed out:

> The isle of Circe was not the only place in the world of early Greece where the supreme source of light shone from directly overhead. But if the sun was always in the zenith above the island, it was no ordinary island of the ordinary world, nor was it an ordinary sun: Circe's isle must in some sense have been on the central axis of the universe.

The island where he earlier consorted with Calypso is likewise an *omphalos*.[117]

Furthermore, the excessive heat, which afflicted the Emperor and induced his dream, recalls that 'magical heat' corresponding to the 'inner light' or illumination experienced by shamans of

---

the Ancient Chinese City (Edinburgh, 1971), p. 428). This was said to occur at a column in Jerusalem, so that the city *quae mediterranea et umbilicus terrae dicitur* (P. Geyer, O. Cuntz, A. Francheschini, R. Weber, L. Bieler, J. Fraipont, and F. Glorie (ed.), *Itineraria et Alia Geographica* (Turnholt, 1965), pp. 194–95).

113 Gregory Nagy, *Greek Mythology and Poetics* (Cornell, 1990), pp. 143–80.

114 Wilmer Cave Wright (ed.), *The Works of the Emperor Julian* (London, 1913–23), i, pp. 366, 374–82.

115 John Gwynn (ed.), *Liber Ardmachanus: The Book of Armagh, Edited with Introduction and Appendices* (Dublin, 1913), p. 448; J. A. MacCulloch, *The Religion of the Ancient Celts* (Edinburgh, 1911), p. 271; Miranda Jane Green, *The Wheel as a Cult-Symbol in the Romano-Celtic World With Special Reference to Gaul and Britain* (Brussels, 1984), pp. 296–304; O'Rahilly, *Early Irish History and Mythology*, pp. 304–5, 359; John Waddell, *Archaeology and Celtic myth: an exploration* (Dublin, 2014), pp. 33–55.

116 Hindu temples frequently have huge solar wheels hewn in relief on their plinths (L'Orange, *Studies on the Iconography of Cosmic Kingship in the Ancient World*, p. 57).

117 Butterworth, *The Tree at the Navel of the Earth*, pp. 28–30. Calypso's isle is described by Homer as the ὀμφαλός of the sea, a familiar characteristic of which is its containing four rivers flowing in different directions (Helmut van Thiel (ed.), *Homeri Odyssea* (Hildesheim, 1991), pp. 2, 65). Calypso 'in various respects is the doublet of Kirke', who in turn may have been 'originally a solar power conceived as a "Hawk"' (Arthur Bernard Cook, *Zeus: A Study in Ancient Religion* (Cambridge, 1914–40), i, p. 241), *kirke* being Greek for 'hawk'.

differing cultural traditions, whose effect is attainment of total understanding.[118] Among Finno-Ugric peoples the word for the divinatory trance experienced by their shamans derives from the verbal noun *réj*, meaning 'warmth', the rite being originally practised beside a blazing fire. Similarly, among the Evenki of the Lower Amur in eastern Siberia the word for shamanizing is *jandI*, literally 'to shamanize by the camp-fire'. As Mircea Eliade explained in his classic study of Yoga,

> The technique of 'producing inner heat' is not a tantric innovation. The *Majjhima-nikāya* (I, 244) speaks of the 'heat' obtained by holding the breath, and other Buddhist texts say that the Buddha is 'burning'. The Buddha is 'burning' because he practices asceticism, *tapas* – and we have seen that in India *tapas* is documented from Vedic times, but that the ideology and practices of 'magical sweating' and of creation through autothermy were known from the Indo-European period on; indeed, they belong to an archaic Cultural stage, being attested both in primitive cosmologies and in many shamanisms.[119]

A similar initiatory rite may be reflected in the Norse poem *Grímnismál*. After being held by the giant Geirrøðr for eight nights seated between two blazing fires, the god Óðinn gives utterance to the whole spectrum of cosmological and mythological knowledge.[120]

In Celtic tradition ecstatically induced heat is ascribed to the related quality of heroic or martial frenzy. Arthur's companion Cei possessed with power to preserve objects dry in soaking rain, and his body generated heat sufficient to kindle a fire for his comrades in the most intense cold. Similarly, the Irish hero Cú Chulainn required immersion in a vat of icy water before it was considered safe for him to enter the hall of Cruachan.[121]

All in all, the patterned arrangement of the sleeping Maxen, surrounded by his thirty-two subordinate kings and positioned at the precise centre of the world, suggests that the name of the Roman Emperor became substituted at an earlier stage for that of a divine ruler.[122] The approach to the zenith is not confined to shamanism or yoga, and played a crucial part in the elevation of kings.

118 Mircea Eliade, *Birth and Rebirth: The Religious Meanings of Initiation in Human Culture* (London, 1961), pp. 85–87.

119 Idem, *Yoga: Immortality and Freedom* (New York, 1958), pp. 106–8, 246–47, 330-34, 337, 339. Cf. J. Balász, 'The Hungarian Shaman's Technique of Trance Induction', in V. Diószegi (ed.), *Popular Beliefs and Folklore Tradition in Siberia* (Bloomington and The Hague, 1968), pp. 54–55, 63, 67–73; G. M. Vasilevič, 'The Acquisition of Shamanistic Ability among the Evenki (Tungus)', ibid., pp. 339–40; Butterworth, *The Tree at the Navel of the Earth*, pp. 81-82; Göran Ogén, 'Religious Ecstasy in Classical Sufism', in Nils G. Holm (ed.), *Religious Ecstasy* (Uppsala, 1982), p. 239; Carmen Blacker, *The Catalpa Bow: A Study of Shamanistic Practices in Japan* (London, 1975), pp. 93, 125, 179, 189, 330; Stephen O. Glosecki, *Shamanism and Old English Poetry* (New York, 1989), p. 43.

120 Hans Kuhn and Gustav Neckel (ed.), *Edda: Die Lieder des Codex Regius nebst Verwandten Denkmälern* (Heidelberg, 1962–68), i, pp. 56–68. Cf. David A. H. Evans and Anthony Faulkes (ed.), *Hávamál* (Kendal, 1986–87), p. 33; Carolyne Larrington, '*Vafþrúðnismál* and *Grímnismál*: Cosmic History, Cosmic Geography', in Paul Acker and Carolyne Larrington (ed.), *The Poetic Edda: Essays on Old Norse Mythology* (New York and London, 2002), pp. 59–77.

121 Rachel Bromwich and D. Simon Evans (ed.), *Culhwch and Olwen: An Edition and Study of the Oldest Arthurian Tale* (Cardiff, 1992), p. 14; R. I. Best and Osborn Bergin (ed.), *Lebor na Huidre: Book of the Dun Cow* (Dublin, 1929), p. 264. Cf. Eliade, *Birth and Rebirth*, pp. 84–85.

122 Cf. Mac Cana, *The Cult of the Sacred Centre*, pp. 93–94.

Thus, at the inauguration of Indian kings, a significant rite in the ceremonial involved the monarch's mounting an iron pillar (this recalls the mysterious column beside the Old Man in the faery palace visited by Maxen, discussed below), which has been connected

> with the (later) conception of the throne-pillar of king Vikramāditya which rises with the sun to the zenith and equally descends with the sun to the subterranean abode of the goddess Prabhā … Against this background the raising of the arms of the king may therefore be interpreted as the cosmogonic act of raising the axis mundi; and so we see the king, when receiving the unction, standing erect with raised arms on the throne, as the personification of the cosmic pillar resting on the navel of the earth (the throne) and reaching up to the sky.[123]

This rite was succeeded by that of *Digvyāsthāpanam*, i.e. mounting the quarters of space:

> Through this rite the sacrificer ascends to the zenith: 'from the quarters he goes to the heaven (svarga- loka-)' or 'he 'mounts' the seasons and the year so that all lies beneath him'. At the same time he wins the quarters of space or the seasons, thus mastering the whole of the universe in respect to space as well as to time.[124]

Maxen's succumbing to the heat of the noontide sun reflects rationalization of an earlier tradition, whose significance was no longer understood. Behind the awkwardly contrived episode in the romance lay an allusion to the 'heat' generated by a seer during his mantic trance. This suggests a further consideration. We are told that 'the sun was high in the sky above their heads, and the heat was great', when Maxen decided to recline and sleep. Among the Labours of Herakles, the tenth task assigned the hero was retrieval of the Cattle of Geryon from Erytheia, a mythical island in the Atlantic. Sailing out into the ocean by the Straits of Gibraltar, Herakles began to suffer from the heat of the sun. Angered by this lack of consideration, he threatened the heavenly luminary with his bow. Gratified by the hero's display of courage, the sun bestowed on him the golden bowl in which he (the sun) was accustomed to voyage to his nightly resting place beneath the Western Ocean. Herakles sailed onward in this splendid vessel, achieved the labour, and returned the bowl to the sun.[125]

Butterworth pointed out that the threat uttered by Herakles was no vainglorious boast (the compliance evinced by the sun confirms that), but reflects ascetic practice attested in Vedic India and elsewhere.

> The bow and arrow are common images of the disciplined ecstatic quest of reality. In the *Maitrāyaṇa* (or *Maitri*) *Upaniṣad*, the primal sound *Om* is compared to an arrow, with *manas* (thought, mind) as its point, laid upon the bow of the human body. He who

---

123 J. C. Heesterman, *The Ancient Indian Royal Consecration: The Rājasūya Described According to the Yajus Texts and Annotated* (The Hague, 1957), p. 101.

124 Ibid., p. 104.

125 Sir James George Frazer (ed.), *Apollodorus: The Library* (London, 1921), i, pp. 210–14; Rainer Vollkommer, *Herakles in the Art of Classical Greece* (Oxford, 1988), pp. 14–15. Cf. Frank Brommer, *Heracles: The Twelve Labors of the Hero in Ancient Art and Literature* (New Rochelle, 1986), pp. 41–44. The story has echoes in the golden bowl of the Vedic god Prajāpati, from which emerged his son Puruṣa (Cosmic Man), who bent his bow against his father in order to extract his own divine names (Stella Kramrisch, *The Presence of Śiva* (Princeton, 1981), pp. 100–104).

has practised yoga pierces through the darkness with it to '*Brahman*, who sparkles like a wheel of fire, of the colour of the sun, full of vigour, beyond darkness, that which shines in yonder sun, also in the moon, in the fire, in the lightning. And having seen Him assuredly, one goes to immortality. ...'

The heat which Herakles experienced will have been that realised by *tapas*, 'austerity': he was not a fool, who tried to shoot the sun in the sky because its rays made him over-warm. The heat produced in *tapas* accompanies the attempt to reach the light of ultimate reality. The meanings of Herakles' bow, the sun and the heat felt by the hero are all to be sought in the practice of ecstasy.[126]

The story in its extant form lacks internal logic, a factor which as so often fortuitously provides means of recovering its original significance. Herakles is enabled to reach the island where Geryon pastures his cattle, thanks to the loan of the sun's golden vessel. Yet exaction of the favour was not the motive for his threatening the sun with his bow: we are told simply that the hero was angered at becoming overheated by its burning rays, while the loan of the bowl came as an unanticipated and undemanded favour. In reality, it cannot be supposed that Herakles arrived at the body of water without considering how he might cross the waves to Erytheia. Generation of heat and gaining of access to the sun were prerequisites to his accomplishment of the supernatural quest.

The divinatory technique attributed to Herakles is further illuminated by the widely recorded folktale of the Chain of Arrows, in which a hero hurls darts or shoots arrows skywards, until

one embeds itself in the celestial vault, then another embeds itself exactly in the notch of the first, a third in the second, and so on until they form a long chain of arrows upon which the hero mounts as upon a ladder to heaven.[127]

In a Chinese shamanistic poem the author recalls:

> *I gather my reins and my chariot sweeps aloft.*
> *I take up my long arrow and shoot at the Heavenly Wolf,*
> *Then draw toward me the Dipper and pour out for myself a drink of cassia*
> *And bow in hand plunge into the abyss,*
> *Am lost in mirk and darkness as I start on my journey to the East.*[128]

The sun at its zenith, to which the hero ascends, represents the symbolic focus of the visionary's ecstatic trance.

---

126 Butterworth, *The Tree at the Navel of the Earth*, pp. 133–34.

127 Mircea Eliade, 'Notes on the Symbolism of the Arrow', in Jacob Neusner (ed.), *Religions in Antiquity: Essays in Memory of Erwin Ramsdell Goodenough* (Leiden, 1970), pp. 468–75. Cf. Gudmund Hatt, *Asiatic Influences in American Folklore* (Copenhagen, 1949), pp. 40–48. For specific examples of the myth, cf. Franz Boas (ed.), *Kathlamet Texts* (Washington, 1901), pp. 11–12; idem (ed.), *Tsimshian Texts* (Washington, 1902), p. 88.

128 Arthur Waley, *The Nine Songs: A Study of Shamanism in Ancient China* (London, 1955), pp. 45–46.

The image combines the ecstatic experience of quasi-luminous vision, attained by intense concentration within a precise ascetic discipline, with the conclusion of a process of thought about the nature of reality.

The ultimate purpose of the revelation attained by this means is that of divinely-inspired self-realization.

> This vision illuminates the whole mind and setting the whole soul on fire, draws it up through the body, changing the whole man and transporting him into ultimate Being. Reitzenstein shows that this ultimate state is one in which the man is spoken of as deified.

Finally, it may be considered whether the curious detail of the erect spears set about the sleeping Maxen reflects a comparable concept to that of the arrow-ascent to heaven. Butterworth showed that the lances of the Dioscuri in early Greece represented the 'way up' and the 'way down': 'They are in fact the axis that leads up to heaven and the axis that leads to the underworld.'[129]

The plundering of the cattle of the sun is a theme widely recorded in Indo-European myths of a cattle-stealing god. Burkert sees the quest as originating in earlier shamanist mythology, wherein the shaman resorts to an ecstatic trance, in the course of which he succeeds in replenishing tribal stock from the divine herd belonging to the Master of Animals.[130] In Vedic mythology the sun was identified with a bull, whose cattle were the stars, and tradition held that the route pursued by Herakles in his cattle-raiding expedition was the Milky Way.[131]

> Overall, the depiction of the sun's golden vessel as a boat appears to be a secondary interpretation of a trip that Heracles, who also will experience the shamanic *askesis*, was said to have taken by sailing in the fiery sun's own *depas* or 'drinking cup' ... a utensil that suggests that the voyage is one of intoxication ...[132]

This assessment is surely correct: Herakles gains inspired vision,[133] and ventures forth on his Otherworld expedition, through imbibing an intoxicant from a golden vessel symbolizing the sun, unique source of life and wisdom. This is parallelled in early Irish tradition by the golden cup of Mac Cécht, which cannot be filled by all the waters of the rivers and lakes of Ireland,

---

129 Butterworth, *The Tree at the Navel of the Earth*, pp. 62, 100, 117, 124–28.

130 Walter Burkert, *Structure and History in Greek Mythology and Ritual* (Los Angeles, 1979), pp. 83–94. Cf. Leroy A. Campbell, *Mithraic Iconography and Ideology* (Leiden, 1968), pp. 8–9, 250–52; Denys Page, *Folktales in Homer's Odyssey* (Cambridge, Mass., 1973), pp. 79–83; F. Bader, 'Sémiologie des travaux d'Héraclès', in François Jouan (ed.), *Visages du destin dans les mythologies: Mélanges Jacqueline Duchemin* (Paris, 1983), p. 66; Jarich G. Oosten, *The War of the Gods: The social code in Indo-European mythology* (London, 1985), pp. 109, 111; M. L. West, *Indo-European Poetry and Myth* (Oxford, 2007), pp. 259–62.

131 Cook, *Zeus*, ii, p. 37; Adrian Pârvulescu, 'The Name of the Great Bear', *The Journal of Indo-European Studies* (Washington, 1988), xvi, pp. 97–98.

132 R. Gordon Wasson, Stella Kramrisch, Jonathan Ott, and Carl A. P. Ruck, *Persephone's Quest: Entheogens and the Origins of Religion* (Yale, 1986), p. 171.

133 'Geryon's name is presumably related to γῆρυϲε, γυρύω, which are elevated poetic words for "voice, utter, sing", though cognate with Old Irish *gáir* "shout"' (West, *Indo-European Poetry and Myth*, pp. 260–61).

past which it is borne at dawn, and a sip from whose contents elicits speech from the dead. This goblet represents an obvious icon of the sun.[134]

Reduced to its elemental motifs, the story of the abduction of the Cattle of Geryon by Herakles may be summarized as follows:

1. It is when the sun is at its zenith that the hero generates 'inner heat', i.e. he stations himself at the *axis mundi* and enters into an ecstatic trance, during which all that follows may be supposed to occur.
2. He gains access to the sun by means of his bow and arrows.
3. The sun bestows on him a golden vessel.
4. The vessel provides the vehicle whereby Herakles is enabled to transport himself across the ocean to an Otherworld island in the Western Ocean.[135]

These motifs provide striking parallels to the opening section of *Breuddwyd Maxen*.

1. With the sun implicitly at its zenith, Maxen is overcome by heat, and positions himself at the centre of a circle formed by his thirty-two tributary kings. The adventure which ensues is initially fulfilled within his ensuing dream.
2. Maxen's entourage set their spears in the ground, with their blades pointing skywards.
3. In his ensuing dream he comes upon a wondrous ship, constructed of gold and silver.
4. He is transported in this vessel across the ocean to an Otherworld island in the Ocean, which is only subsequently identified with Britain.

O'Rahilly suggested that the name of an Irish ancestor-deity Írél was ultimately borrowed from that of the Greek *Hēraklēs*. Noting evidence for a widespread cult of Herakles in Gaul, he observed that

It is very likely that the Gauls in taking over the Greek god identified him with their own Lugus (Ir. *Lug*), the god of Light, who was likewise founder of cities, as the many places called Lugdunum (Celt. *Lugudūnon*) testify.[136]

The Celtic god Lug was regarded *inter alia* as a prophet. In the tenth-century *Baile in Scáil* he is represented as foretelling the succession of kings of Tara after Conn of the Hundred Fights. There are other grounds for regarding the figure of Maxen in *Breuddwyd Maxen* as evocative of Lug, and it may be that the misunderstood account of his ecstatic heat reflects traditions associated with that deity, whose name in Britain was represented by the cognate form *Lleu*, the Welsh word for 'light'.

---

134 Eleanor Knott (ed.), *Togail Bruidne Da Derga* (Dublin, 1936), pp. 44–45. Cf. O'Rahilly, *Early Irish History and Mythology*, p. 66.

135 According to Pomponius Mela, Hercules fought with two sons of Neptune, and Rhŷs claimed that 'there can hardly be any mistake as to the two personal names being echoes of Albion and Iverion, Britain and Ireland' ('Notes on the Hunting of Twrch Trwyth', *Transactions of the Honourable Society of Cymmrodorion* (London, 1895), pp. 31–32). However, the restored text reads '*in quo Herculem contra Alebiona et Dercynon, Neptuni liberos, dimicantem, cum tela defecissent*' (A. Silberman (ed.), *Pomponius Mela: Chorographie* (Paris, 1988), p. 55). Nevertheless, given the legendary association with Ocean, Rhŷs's suggestion may be worth noting.

136 T. F. O'Rahilly, 'The Goidels and their Predecessors', *The Proceedings of the British Academy* (London, 1936), pp. 359–60.

Tenth-century Irish
gaming-board.
(Author's collection)

The cosmic board game

The *mandala*-like pattern formed by Maxen and his thirty-two attendant kings suggests in addition the formation assumed by the men (*gwerin*), who are placed about the king (*brenin*) at the centre of the board in the Welsh royal games of *gwyddbwyll* and *tawlbwrdd*.[137] Like chess and other early board games, *gwyddbwyll* and *tawlbwrdd* were originally infused with ritual significance.[138] An account of *tawlbwrdd* and its rules survives in a sixteenth-century Welsh manuscript, which describes the positioning of the pieces at the outset of the game as follows:

> The above board must be played with a king (*brenin*) in the centre and twelve men in the places next to him, and twenty-four lie in wait to capture him. These are placed, six in the centre of every end of the board and in the six central places.[139]

---

137   By strange chance, a relative of the historical Maximus was said to have played at draughts with the emperor Valentinian: a game which served to bring about the downfall of the consul Aetius! (H. B. Dewing (ed.), *Procopius* (London, 1914–40), ii, pp. 39–43).

138   Rees and Rees, *Celtic Heritage*, pp. 154–55. The equivalent game *fidchell* was believed to have been introduced to Ireland by the god Lug (R. A. Stewart Macalister (ed.), *Lebor Gabála Érenn: The Book of the Taking of Ireland* (Dublin, 1938–56), iv, p. 128). Cf. Elizabeth A. Gray (ed.), *Cath Maige Tuired: The Second Battle of Mag Tuired* (Naas, 1982), p. 40.

139   F. R. Lewis, 'Gwerin Ffristial a Thawlbwrdd', *Transactions of the Honourable Society of Cymmrodorion* (London, 1941), pp. 185–205; Eóin MacWhite, 'Early Irish Board Games', *Éigse: A Journal of Irish Studies* (Dublin, 1945), v, pp. 25–35.

The rules provide for a board containing 11 x 11 cells. The tenth-century Irish gaming board from Ireland illustrated below contains 7 x 7 cells, and the number of pieces could correspondingly have differed in earlier times. A similar arrangement, with 32 + 1 pieces and 9 x 9 cells, occurs in the Icelandic game *tablut*.[140]

Although the precise number of pieces and cells in earlier times is unknown, it seems clear that the king was positioned at the centre, with some thirty or more men disposed in a regular pattern about him – an arrangement strikingly similar to the patterned disposal of the sleeping emperor and his subject kings at the outset of *Breuddwyd Maxen*. Moreover, when Maxen awakes from his dream, and the quest for the beautiful queen is re-enacted in reality, he despatches thirteen messengers to find her, i.e. 12 + 1, which again parallels the king in *tawlbwrdd*, with his twelve defensive men. It will be recalled that the comparable board game *gwyddbwyll* features prominently, if mysteriously, among wonders encountered by Maxen in the enchanted castle of his dream.

The opening passages of the Dream of Maxen suggest a ritual model, rationalized by storytellers in a post-pagan era. They parallel moves enshrined in the rules of early board games, as the following table indicates.

Breuddwyd Maxen	*talbwrdd, gwyddbwyll*
The King is established at the Centre, surrounded by 32 kings.	The King is set at the centre of the board, about whom are set 36 (?) men (*gwerin*).
He despatches 13 messengers to discover his goal at Caer Seint.	The King's 12 pieces force a passage to the square he must reach to win.
Caer Seint is situated at the furthest confine of the known world.	The winning square is one of the 'sanctuaries' set at each corner of the board.
Maxen drives the indigenous inhabitants into the sea, and weds the Sovereignty.	He causes his adversaries' pieces to be removed from the board, and gains the stake.

That a Celtic king's marriage to the Maiden Sovereignty might include a ritual board game is instanced in the mediæval Irish tale 'The Wooing of Étaín' (*Tochmarc Étaíne*), whose beautiful heroine personifies the Maiden Sovereignty of Ireland.[142] She is the stake contested by two royal suitors for her hand in a game of *fidchell*, the Irish game corresponding to Welsh *gwyddbwyll*.[143]

A further instance features in an encounter described in the collection of Ossianic tales known as 'The Colloquy of the Ancients', *Acallam na Sénorach*. Caeilte arrives at a palace of women (*lios na mban*), where he meets nine women of the divine race of the Túatha Dé Danann, together with their queen. They engage the hero in successive games of *fidchell*, after each of which they drink a draught

---

140 H. J. R. Murray, *A History of Board games other than Chess* (Oxford, 1952), pp. 63–64.

141 H. O'Neill Hencken, 'A Gaming Board of the Viking Age', *Acta Archaeologica* (Copenhagen, 1933), iv, pp. 85–104. Hencken argued for a Viking origin of the board, but this is disputed.

142 Étaín was believed to be dwelling in the fairy mound of *Síd Nenta* 'in the West', i.e. the Otherworld (Best, Bergin, O'Brien, and O'Sullivan (ed.), *The Book of Leinster*, p. 726).

143 *Ériu*, xii, p. 180. A similar association of gaming and royal union with a female sovereignty figure occurs in the Sanskrit epic *Mahābhārata* (Kim McCone, *Pagan Past and Christian Present in Early Irish Literature* (Naas, 1990), p. 111).

from a vessel of fine mead.[144] Here we encounter two well-attested elements in the Celtic concept of the divine kingship. Nine generations was the traditional number regularly accorded successive dynasties,[145] while a cup of mead was proffered by a Celtic queen, divine or mortal, to her consort at their marriage.[146] The nine women encountered by Caeilte may originally have personified nine mortal queens, while their queen incarnated the Maiden Sovereignty.

In *Breuddwyd Maxen*, the Emperor remains unaware of the location of the Maiden's stronghold, until it comes to be discovered by his messengers. Could *gwyddbwyll* have begun with the king's being obliged in some way to divine which of the four corner spots had been selected by his adversary, as that where the stake was to be won? An unspecified 'trick at each corner of the [*fidchell*] board / even to the extent of changing the chessmen', is mentioned in a mediæval Irish poem.[147]

Finally, it is noteworthy that the sole activity taking place in the Otherworld castle inhabited by Elen is the mysterious Old Man's construction of men (*gwerin*) for the *gwyddbwyll* game being played throughout Maxen's visit. Were we enabled to peer over the shoulders of the two players, later identified as Cynan and Adeon, I suspect we might witness a succession of moves paralleling those which led the love-lorn Emperor to the portals of the enchanted fortress Caer Seint. The game played in the Otherworld palace established and perpetuated the monarchy of Britain, of which Maxen was regarded as founder.

No players are mentioned in the opening account of Maxen's dream, and as Cynan was originally unconnected to the story of Maxen, with Adeon a 'ghost' figure, it may be suspected that Maxen himself was originally one of the players. Was the similarly unidentified Old Man his adversary, with Elen as the stake?

The cosmic mountain

The symbolism of the sun at its zenith, and the positioning of the imperial visionary at the mid-point of the royal circle, are by no means the sole indications in *Breuddwyd Maxen* that the Emperor's dream was originally located at the Centre of the Earth. At the outset of the tale we are told that he pursued the bank of the river (i.e. the Tiber) beside which he was sleeping, until he came to 'the highest mountain in the world', whose summit seemed to touch the sky. Instead of skirting its base, he

---

144   Standish H. O'Grady (ed.), *Silva Gadelica: A Collection of Tales in Irish with Extracts Illustrating Persons and Places* (London, 1892), i, p. 227.

145   Medb represents the Irish Sovereignty figure, which explains why 'that woman, Medb Lethderg, cohabited with nine kings of Ireland' (Toirdhealbhach Ó Raithbheartaigh (ed.), *Genealogical Tracts I.* (Dublin, 1932), p. 148). 'Though there were nine of lineage / Between a good son and sovereignty / The right course in fair justice / Is to make him king on the instant' (ibid., p. 31). 'Feidelm Noichruthach, daughter of Conchobar; for ninefold her shape, each shape more lovely than the others', wed nine successive kings of Ulster (Maigréad Ní C. Dobbs, 'Agallamh Leborchaim', *Études Celtiques* (Paris, 1949), v, p. 155): 'Fedelm of the nine shapes, daughter of Conchobar – nine shapes she could display, and each shape more lovely than the other' (Best and Bergin (ed.), *Lebor na Huidre*, p. 256), i.e. she personified the Maiden Sovereignty in nine successive incarnations. A dynasty of nine kings called Eochaid ruled over Ailech (Edward Gwynn (ed.), *The Metrical Dindshenchas* (Dublin, 1903–35), iv, pp. 116–18), while another line of nine kings and nine queens rests in the cemetery of Cell Chorbbáin (pp. 340–42). The concept may be of Indo-European origin, being paralleled in Germanic cosmology (Thomas D. Hill, 'Woden as "Ninth Father": Numerical Patterning in Some Old English Royal Genealogies', in Daniel G. Calder and T. Craig Christy (ed.), *Germania: Comparative Studies in the Old Germanic Languages and Literature* (Woodbridge, 1988), pp. 161–74).

146   R. Mark Scowcroft, 'Abstract Narrative in Ireland', *Ériu* (1995), xlvi, pp. 130–37.

147   J. G. O'Keefe, 'A Portrait', in Osborn Bergin and Carl Marstrander (ed.), *Miscellany Presented to Kuno Meyer by Some of his Friends and Pupils on the Occasion of his Appointment to the Chair of Celtic Philology in the University of Berlin* (Halle, 1912), p. 246.

made his way to the top and descended the other side. Crossing a plain lying beyond, he arrived at the mouth of a mighty river, where he embarked for Britain.

These directions would have appeared familiar to contemporary Welshmen. As Sir Ifor Williams observed, 'The geographical features in the Dream are readily recognised!'[148] Throughout the Middle Ages Welshmen were accustomed to travelling on pilgrimage to Rome, and the crossing to Italy not infrequently required a passage of the Alps by the Mont Cenis pass.[149] However, it is clear that the description reflects something other than straightforward geographical itinerary. It would be a mistake to take the reference to the mountain attained by Maxen as synecdoche for a mountain pass. The description is precise. After ascending the river (Tiber) to its source, Maxen

> came to the highest mountain he had ever seen, and he thought the mountain was as high as the sky. And when he came over (*dros*) the mountain he saw that he was travelling along level plains …

The emphasis is on the mountain, and its proximity to the sky. No reader could fail to take this as meaning anything other than that Maxen gained its summit, before descending to the broad plain beyond. This episode is duplicated in the description of the subsequent journey undertaken by his messengers, when they ascend a second towering peak on their arrival in Wales. Once again, it is emphasized that the top of the mountain touched the sky. From its summit they glimpse the lands beyond spread out as though on a map:

> And as they crossed over that mountain they saw great level plains and broad rivers flowing through them. And then they said, 'look', they said: 'the land our lord saw!'

The summit provided a vantage point from which the vast expanse of country below could be surveyed. Thus, the mountain ascent is no mere geographical detail, but represents an intrinsic element of the story, whose significance is not far to seek.

As everything about the journey to Caer Seint and the remarkable scene within its halls suggests, the Dream represents a journey to the Otherworld, to which the mountain 'which reached the sky' (*e menyd en gyuwch a'r awyr*) afforded access. Beyond it Maxen found himself among the fairest and most level lands man ever saw (*gwladoed gwastat tecaf o'r a welsei den eryoet o'r parth arall e'r menyd*). This echoes descriptions of the Happy Otherworld as a flowery plain,[150] while the gorgeous dwelling where Maxen discovers his maiden mistress is unmistakably an Otherworld palace.

The concept of the World Centre or *omphalos* as a holy mountain features in many early cosmologies. At times it is identified with a geographical pinnacle, at others a purely mythical peak. In China Mount Kunlun was regarded as the central axis of the universe; in India and

---

148 Williams (ed.), *Breuddwyd Maxen*, p. 21. The 'highest mountain in the world' was presumably the *Mons Iovis* of the *Historia Brittonum*, which was believed to mark the south-eastern limit of the region settled by the British troops of Maximianus (Mommsen (ed.), *Chronica Minora*, iii, p. 166). It may also have been the mountain known locally as 'the column of the sun' (*solis columna*), which was believed to be the source of the Rhone (*Rhodanus*) (Dietrich Stichtenoth (ed.), *Rufus Festus Avienus: Ora Maritima* (Darmstadt, 1968), p. 48).

149 Roberts (ed.), *Breudwyt Maxen Wledic*, pp. lxxvii–lxxviii.

150 Cf. Séamus Mac Mathúna (ed.), *Immram Brain: Bran's Journey to the Land of the Women* (Tübingen, 1975), pp. 39–40.

among many of the peoples of Central Asia and Mongolia it was the cosmic Mount Meru in the North; in Java it appears to have been identified with Mount Penanggungan.[151] The mountain Himingbjörg ('heaven mountain') of Norse mythology ascended to the misty skirt of heaven, to which access was gained by means of the rainbow bridge *Bifröst*.[152] Wales was divided into four provinces, with the lofty mountain Pumlumon ('five peaks') as Centre.[153]

In biblical Israel differing mountains were at various times identified as the *omphalos* or centre of the world: Mount Sinai, Mount Gerizim, Mount Zion. Several of the more remarkable events in the life of Jesus occur on mountains. Mount Tabor, traditionally the scene of the Transfiguration, derives its name from Hebrew *ṭabbūr*, 'navel', and the mountain where the Devil tempted Jesus was implicitly a World Mountain:

> The high mountain from the vantage point of which the whole world can be viewed bears some resemblance to the cosmic mountain of apocalyptic literature – i.e. the mountain which is the centre and high point of the earth.[154]

Thus the text of *Breuddwyd Maxen* unwittingly confirms that the Emperor's dream was originally envisaged as being induced at the Sacred Centre, where the Vedic *brahman*, like his shamanic counterparts, positioned himself as support and connexion of the three cosmic regions, heaven, earth, and the underworld. This symbolic juncture provides a focus and representation of all that exists, a perfect equilibrium between opposed cosmic forces, and unification of the microcosmic self with the macrocosmic universe.[155]

The parenthetical explanation in *Breuddwyd Maxen* that its eponymous hero 'came to the highest mountain he had ever seen, *and he was sure that the mountain was as high as the sky*' (*e menyd en gyuwch a'r awyr*), confirms that the peak he ascended was the cosmic mountain, traditionally envisaged as both *omphalos* and support of the sky.[156] In the story the mountain is implicitly located in the Alps, as might be expected in the course of an overland journey from Rome to Britain. Furthermore, it possesses its counterpart at the Emperor's destination in

---

151 Kiyohiko Munakata, *Sacred Mountains in Chinese Art* (Urbana and Chicago, 1991), pp. 9–12, 28, 33, 43, 80; Alain Daniélou, *Hindu Polytheism* (London, 1964), pp. 144–45; Eliade, *Le chamanisme et les techniques archaïques de l'extase*, pp. 241–44; Smith and Watson (ed.), *Early South East Asia*, p. 478.

152 Anthony Faulkes (ed.), *Snorri Sturluson: Edda; Prologue and Gylfaginning* (Oxford, 1982), pp. 20, 25–26.

153 Rees and Rees, *Celtic Heritage*, pp. 175–76.

154 Terence L. Donaldson, *Jesus on the Mountain: A Study in Matthean Theology* (Sheffield, 1985), pp. 31–42, 72–79, 87–104; Vincent Mora, *La symbolique de la création dans l'évangile de Matthieu* (Paris, 1991), pp. 19–124; Michel Aubineau, 'Une homélie grecque inédite sur la Transfiguration', *Analecta Bollandiana* (Brussels, 1967), lxxxv, p. 423; Hooke (ed.), *The Labyrinth*, pp. 51–52; Richard J. Clifford, *The Cosmic Mountain in Canaan and the Old Testament* (Cambridge, Mass., 1972), pp. 135, 183. For a stylized image of Mount Meru, with circular base and encircling dragon, cf. Dorothy C. Wong, 'The Mapping of Sacred Space: Images of Buddhist Cosmographies in Medieval China', in Philippe Forêt and Andreas Kaplony (ed.), *The Journey of Maps and Images on the Silk Road* (Leiden, 2008), p. 59.

155 Cf. Eliade, *Yoga*, pp. 115–17; idem, *Occultism, Witchcraft, and Cultural Fashions: Essays in Comparative Religions* (Chicago, 1976), pp. 18–22; idem, *The Quest: History and Meaning in Religion* (Chicago, 1969), pp. 140–41; Jamsheed Kairshasp Choksy, 'Purity and Pollution in Zoroastrianism', *The Mankind Quarterly* (Washington, 1986), xxvii, pp. 187–88; Leonard Charles Feldstein, *Homo Quaerens: The Seeker and the Sought; Method Become Ontology* (New York, 1978), pp. 82–83; idem, *The Dance of Being: Man's Labyrinthine Rhythms; The Natural Ground of the Human* (New York, 1979), pp. 129–30.

156 'And they brought me to a place of dark storm-clouds and to a mountain whose summit reached to heaven. And I saw the places of the luminaries and the chambers of the stars and of thunder-peals, to the uttermost reaches …' (Matthew Black (tr.), *The Book of Enoch or I Enoch: A New English Edition* (Leiden, 1985), p. 35).

Wales. Arrived in his dream at a mountainous region (subsequently identified as Arfon), he sees an island (Anglesey) in the sea opposite:

> and between him and the island he saw a land whose plain was as long as its sea, whose forest was as long as its mountain. And *from the mountain* [italics inserted] he saw a river flowing across the land, making for the sea, and at the mouth of the river he saw the fairest great castle that anyone had ever seen …

When Maxen's messengers make the same journey, we are told that they crossed Britain 'until they saw Eryri', i.e. the massif of Snowdonia. Clearly Snowdon itself is the mountain ascended by Maxen during his dream visit. He paused on its summit, from which he viewed Arfon and Anglesey spread below him. This represents an obvious duplication of his ascent of the Alpine peak. In each case the Emperor gratuitously ascends an uniquely lofty mountain, from whose peak he gazes over a broad expanse of level countryside towards his destination.

It seems likely, therefore, that in an earlier version Maxen (or rather the Brittonic god whom he has replaced in the Welsh romance) originally ascended but one mountain, which in turn bears unmistakable indications of being the *omphalos*. Not only are we told in each case that its summit reached the sky, but from the initial Alpine peak Maxen 'saw great broad rivers from the mountain to the sea' (*a phrif avonyd mawr a welei o'r menyd hyt y mor*).[157] Again, when Maxen ascends the second mountain (i.e. Snowdon), 'from that mountain he saw a river flowing across the land, making for the sea' (*ac o'r menyd hwnnw avon a welei en redec ar draus e wlat en kyrchu e mor*).[158] A prime characteristic of the *omphalos* mountain is that it constitutes a miraculous source of rivers.[159] *Originally, then, the hero was depicted as ascending the World Mountain* (Omphalos), *which was identified with Snowdon*. Furthermore, as will be seen, the same consideration must apply to his otherwise unaccountable subsequent ascent of the mountain Y Freni Fawr in Dyfed.

The Roman setting of Maxen's hunt and dream represents a literary construct, originating from the assertion in the *Historia Brittonum* that the seven (alternatively nine) Roman emperors who ruled Britain came thither from Rome (*fuerant a Romanis in Brittannia*). Given that this 'historical' context represents a manifestly secondary stage of the story's evolution, there can be little doubt that the original mountain climbed by Maxen lay in Britain. To what has already been observed, we may add that the inconsequential nature of Maxen's ascent of the Welsh mountain suggests an *interpretatio difficilior*, to which preference should be accorded. Geographically speaking, Snowdon lies nowhere near any route a traveller approaching Caernarvon from the Continent might have been expected to take.

The river of life

As was pointed out earlier, the dream-journey of Maxen in *Breuddwyd Maxen* reflects a remarkable degree of geographical verisimilitude. At the same time, it includes a striking incongruity which has escaped the attention of modern scholars, no less than it did that of the mediæval redactor. At the story's inception, Maxen and his attendants are described as riding forth from the capital of his empire, until they 'came to the valley of the river that flowed down

---

157   Roberts (ed.), *Breudwyt Maxen Wledic*, p. 1.

158   Ibid., p. 2.

159   Butterworth, *The Tree at the Navel of the Earth*, pp. 8, 53.

to Rome' (*ac a doethant e deffrynt er avon a digwyd y Ryvein*). This could imply that they traced the course of the Tiber *upstream*, an inference confirmed by the sequel, in which the dreaming Maxen follows the river to its source (*hyt e blaen*), which the author located in the Alps.

However, when Maxen later comes to retrace his tracks in order to indicate to his messengers the direction in which they should extend their search for the maiden of his dream, he explains: 'And I walked *west* in the direction of the source of the river' (*ac yg kyveirit blaen er avon e tu a'r gorllewin e kerdwn*). It seems unlikely that an author who was clearly well-informed about the geography of Italy and Germany believed that the Tiber rose west of Rome, or that a journey westwards from the city could have brought his hero to the Alps.

The likely explanation of this egregious error is, yet again, that the Roman setting of this section of the story represents a late secondary stage in transmission of the story. Furthermore, the relocation is unlikely to have occurred unless an earlier version had failed to specify the geographical location. Everything indicates that the original setting of the adventure lay in its entirety in Britain. The ideological basis underlying the romance is that of the establishment of the Monarchy of Britain, and (by implication) legitimation of dynasties tracing their ancestry to Maxen Gwledig. The motifs of hunt and dream provide the matrix within which the story is generated, and their location in geographical space and historical time arose from subsequent pseudo-historical rationalization of what is ultimately a mythical narrative.

Thus, the river and sky-soaring mountain from whose breast it flows represent features which were originally cosmological in conception. Just as the cloud-capped peak ascended by Maxen in his vision suggests the World Mountain of shamanist and other early cosmologies, so the stream pouring from it reflects the related conception of the River of Life. The twelve great rivers of Ireland were believed to flow from the island's Navel at Uisneach.[160] Sacred mountains around the world were sources of rivers and rain-bearing clouds, and from the Mountain at the Centre cosmic streams emerge from the Otherworld, whose waters are imbued with prophetic potency. In early China seekers after enlightenment ascended the Yellow River to its well head on the mythical Mount Kunlun, where they sought life-supporting water flowing from the sacred mountain. In Siberia the shaman's ecstatic journey likewise took him the length of a great river coursing down from the summit of the World Mountain, which afforded a waterway leading to the Otherworld. A Tungus shaman's song tells of his perilous ascent of eight precipitous waterfalls, in which he is assisted by attendant birds and fish. Finally he arrives

> *There where the sharp peak* [*stands*]
> *In the very middle of the earth.*

In Celtic and Arthurian tradition wells and springs were similarly believed to provide access to chthonic enlightenment, being regarded as entrances to the Otherworld.[161] In Geoffrey of

---

160 Nora White (ed.), *Compert Mongáin and Three Other Early Mongán Tales* (Maynooth, 2006), p. 77.

161 Waley, *The Nine Songs*, p. 47; Munakata, *Sacred Mountains in Chinese Art*, pp. 4, 31–32, 42, 73, 99; G. M. Vasilevich, 'Early Concepts about the Universe among the Evenks (Materials)', in Henry N. Michael (ed.), *Studies in Siberian Shamanism* (Toronto, 1963), pp. 57–59, 72–73, 76; A. F. Anisimov, 'The Shaman's Tent of the Evenks and the Origin of the Shamanistic Rite', ibid., pp. 98, 112–13; idem, 'Cosmological Concepts of the Peoples of the North', ibid., pp. 188, 190, 192, 202–6; G. M. Vasilevič, 'Shamanistic Songs of the Evenki (Tungus)', in V. Diószegi (ed.), *Popular Beliefs and Folklore Tradition in Siberia* (Bloomington and The Hague, 1968), pp. 352–58; A. G. van Hamel, 'Aspects of Celtic Mythology', *The Proceedings of the British Academy* (London, 1934), xx, p. 246.

Monmouth's *Vita Merlini*, the inspired prophet utters his mantic verses seated beside a spring on the summit of a high mountain.[162]

That the geographical setting of *Breuddwyd Maxen* could not logically have required its hero's ascent of the highest mountain in the world en route from Italy to Britain, suggests that the episode derived from an independent source, integrated with only partial success into the storyteller's plot. The motifs of the sun at its zenith, the heat with which the Emperor became imbued at the outset of his vision, his mandala-like positioning in the midst of his thirty-two kings, and his ascent of what is evidently the World Mountain by way of the River of Life, together represent complementary aspects of what is essentially a single cosmological theme. It may in consequence be supposed that an earlier version of the story depicted Maxen's gaining access to the Otherworld palace of the beautiful goddess of the land, by means of divinatory techniques reflecting widely attested shamanistic ritual practice.

The enchanted ship

Arrived in his dream at the mouth of 'the largest river ever seen', Maxen discovers a wonderful ship, of which 'one plank was of gold, and he saw that the other was of silver' (*e neill ystyllen a welei ef yn eureit a'r llall en areanneit*). Although the story does not explicitly state as much, the impression conveyed is that of an unmanned vessel, wafted by a magical force to its destination. This represents a recurrent theme in Celtic and Arthurian literature. In the mediæval Irish story 'The Adventure of Conle' (*Echtra Condla*), Conle the Red is lured away to the Otherworld by a lone beautiful maiden in a ship of glass. A similarly unmanned boat conveyed Saint Brendan through a heavy mist to the Land of the Saints, while the infant bard Taliesin floated in a leather coracle for forty years, before fetching up against King Gwyddno's magical weir at Aber Conwy.[163] The heroes of Arthurian romance frequently encounter magical self-propelling ships.[164]

The concept of Britain as a palimpsest of the Otherworld, to which the souls of the dead were ferried, is attested as early as the sixth century AD. The Byzantine historian Procopius, who obtained his information from a Frankish embassy visiting Constantinople, learned that along the Frankish coast of the Channel lay a number of fishing villages. The inhabitants at night were from time to time summoned by a mysterious knocking sound, accompanied by a muffled voice instructing them to convey assembled corpses in special boats across the sea to *Brittia*. The voyage occupied one hour instead of the normal twenty-four, while on their return the vessels skimmed the waves. On gaining the coast of *Brittia*, the sailors were hailed by a mysterious voice naming each newly-arrived corpse, together with those of their ancestors.[165]

---

162 *Fons erat in summo ciuiusdam vertice montis* (Basil Clarke (ed.), *Life of Merlin; Geoffrey of Monmouth: Vita Merlini* (Cardiff, 1973), p. 58).

163 Kim McCone (ed.), *Echtrae Chonnlai and the Beginnings of Vernacular Narrative Writing in Ireland* (Maynooth, 2000), p. 123; Charles Plummer (ed.), *Bethada Náem nÉrenn: Lives of Irish Saints* (Oxford, 1922), i, p. 49; Patrick K. Ford (ed.), *Ystoria Taliesin* (Cardiff, 1992), p. 68.

164 Anita Guerreau-Jalabert, *Index des motifs narratifs dans les romans arthuriens français en vers (XIIᵉ-XIIIᵉ Siècles)* (Geneva, 1992), pp. 41, 48, 79.

165 Dewing (ed.), *Procopius*, v, pp. 266–70. A variant version of the legend, apparently of independent provenance, is given by the Lombard historian Paulus Diaconus (G. Waitz (ed.), *Pauli Historia Langobardorum* (Hanover, 1878), pp. 198–99).

Lastly, the superfluous detail of the whalebone gangplank, by means of which Maxen enters the waiting vessel, suggests the possibility that an earlier version included the familiar theme of a perilous bridge affording access to the Otherworld, which only the initiate or hero may traverse.[166]

The faery palace

After crossing sea and ocean, Maxen 'saw he had come to the loveliest island in the world' (*ef a welei y dyuot y enys decaf o'r byt*). The wording suggests that Britain is envisaged as a terrestrial manifestation of the Otherworld, a perception which receives further emphasis as the tale evolves. Awaking from his dream, Maxen despatches messengers to discover the island stronghold, where dwelt the maiden without whose love he found he might experience no peace of mind.

> Then the messengers travelled until the end of a year, wandering about the world, seeking news about the dream. But when they came back at the end of the year, they had no more news than they did the day they set out.

Clearly, the Britain of Maxen's Dream was not to be found in this world.

Disembarked on the island (only in a subsequent passage is it identified as Britain), Maxen in his dream journeys onward until he arrives at a gorgeous dwelling by the sea. Beside a river-mouth, beyond a land of broad plain and forest, lies a magnificent palace, with roof and doors made of gold, and walls of precious jewels. The furniture is similarly fashioned from gold and silver, and its inhabitants are resplendently garbed in gorgeous raiment and lavish jewellery.

When Maxen subsequently visits the palace of his dream in reality, it is identified with *Caer Seint*, i.e. the Roman fortress of Caernarvon (*Segontium*) in North Wales. However, it is evident that this identification with a specific geographical location represents a further secondary element in the evolution of the story. The selection of Caernarvon arose from the recasting of the story as an episode in Romano-British history. The dream palace is unmistakably the resplendent mansion of the Otherworld. That it was originally unconnected with Caernarvon is indicated not only by the internal evidence of *Breuddwyd Maxen* but by descriptions of similarly splendid dwellings in other early Welsh stories, where the context unequivocally denotes a supernatural palace.

It is not hard to identify convergent factors leading to identification of the Otherworld palace with Caernarvon. The ruined Roman fortress impressed itself on mediæval Welshmen as the site of a structure of exceptional magnificence and wealth. Its walls then stood considerably higher than they appear today. Apart from inevitable dilapidation arising over the passage of time, much material was removed for the construction of Edward I's nearby magnificent castle in 1283–87.[167]

---

166 Cf. E. H. Ruck, *An Index of Themes and Motifs in Twelfth-Century French Arthurian Poetry* (Cambridge, 1991), p. 170; Guerreau-Jalabert, *Index des motifs narratifs dans les romans arthuriens français en vers*, p. 381; Stith Thompson, *Motif-Index of Folk-Literature: A Classification of Narrative Elements in Folktales, Ballads, Myths, Fables, Mediaeval Romances, Exempla, Fabliaux, Jest-Books, and Local Legends* (Bloomington, Indiana, 1955–58), ii, p. 459 = E481.2.1; E481.2.1.1; E481.2.1.2; iii, pp. 26–27 = F152; Ørnulf Hodne, *The Types of the Norwegian Folktale* (Oslo, 1984), pp. 106–7; Lowry Charles Wimberly, *Folklore in the English & Scottish Ballads* (Chicago, 1928), pp. 110–16. An excellent overview of this theme is provided by C. J. Bleeker, *The Sacred Bridge: Researches into the Nature and Structure of Religion* (Leiden, 1963), pp. 180–90.

167 R. E. Mortimer Wheeler, 'Segontium and the Roman Occupation of Wales', *Y Cymmrodor* (London, 1923), xxxiii, p. 94. Despite this, the ruins continued impressive for centuries to come: 'Huic freto SEGONTIVM vrbs cuius meminit Antoninus superimposita erat, cuius murorum religuias nonnullas

In the early Middle Ages, the ruined buildings remained sufficiently impressive to be evoked by Geoffrey of Monmouth's Merlin as epitomizing British national pride and hope:

> *Urbs Sigeni et turres et magna palatia plangent*
> *Diruta donec eant ad pristina predia Cambri.*
> The town of Segontium, with its towers and great palaces will be torn down,
> And the Welsh will mourn them until they recover their ancient patrimony.[168]

In the ninth century the fortress was reputed an inexhaustible source of Roman gold and silver coins 'seeded' by the Emperor Constantine II. It was presumably its reputation for fabulous wealth that led Geoffrey to make Rodarchus present Merlin with 'gold and glittering gems and cups wrought by Wayland in the town of Segontium'.[169] Its fabled profusion of riches, combined with the impressive remains of the fortress, made it an ideal site for elevation to the status of Otherworld palace. Thus, when Pwyll, Prince of Dyfed, exchanges places with Arawn, king of the Otherworld realm of Annwfn, he arrives at a glittering court, of which the narrator explains, 'And of all the courts he had seen in the world, this was the court best provided with food and drink and gold vessels and princely jewels.'

Such brimming splendour represents a characteristic feature of the Otherworld palace.[170] Saint Collen found the stronghold of the divinity Gwyn mab Nudd on the summit of the Glastonbury Tor to be 'the fairest castle that he had ever seen' (*a welai y kastell teka ar a welsai*). In 'The Knight of the Fountain' (*Chwedyl Iarlles y Ffynnawn*), Cynon and subsequently Owain travel from Arthur's court to visit a castle far from the inhabited world, which is set by a river in 'the fairest valley in the world'. Like those visited by Maxen and Pwyll, the stronghold's wealth and luxury prove beyond compare. Further similarities lie in the fact that Pwyll, like Maxen, sits next to the queen of the castle, with whom he sleeps that night; and that Maxen, Pwyll, and Cynon alike find the respective halls presided over by a mysterious anonymous host. Finally, both *Breuddwyd Maxen* and *Historia Peredur vab Efrawc* contain the motif of the two gallant youths, who in the first tale are found playing at *gwyddbwyll*, and in the second shooting at or with their dagger-hilts.[171]

It was traditional in Celtic societies for the Otherworld to be ascribed terrestrial locations, further to their original in another dimension.[172] R. S. Loomis suggested that a variant of the story of the hero's visit to the castle inhabited by the Maiden Sovereignty was known to

vidimus iuxta Ecclesiolam in S. Publicij honorem constructam' (William Camden, *Britannia* (London, 1600), p. 596). For the building of Edward I's castle at Caernarvon, cf. J. Goronwy Edwards, 'Edward I's Castle-Building in Wales' *The Proceedings of the British Academy* (London, 1944), xxxii, pp. 43-52.

168   Clarke (ed.), *Life of Merlin*, p. 84.

169   *Aurum gemmasque micantes / pocula que sculpsit Guielandus in urbe Sigeni* (ibid., p. 64).

170   In Irish literature one may compare the lavish splendours of the *bruidne* of Ailill and Medb at Mag Crúachan (Wolfgang Meid (ed.), *Táin Bó Fraích* (Dublin, 1967), pp. 3–5), and the spacious hall of Lug with its golden roof-tree (Kevin Murray (ed.), *Baile in Scáil: 'The Phantom's Frenzy'* (Dublin, 2004), p. 34).

171   R. L. Thomson (ed.), *Pwyll Pendeuic Dyuet: The First of the Four Branches of the Mabinogi edited from the White Book of Rhydderch with variants from the Red Book of Hergest* (Dublin, 1957), p. 4; S. Baring-Gould and John Fisher, *The Lives of the British Saints: The Saints of Wales and Cornwall and such Irish Saints as have Dedications in Britain* (London, 1907–13), iv, p. 377; R. L. Thomson (ed.), *Owein or Chwedyl Iarlles y Ffynnawn* (Dublin, 1968), pp. 2–4, 10–11; Glenys Witchard Goetinck (ed.), *Historia Peredur vab Efrawc* (Cardiff, 1976), pp. 36–37.

172   'In pagan Ireland every district of importance tended to have its own *síd* or hill within which the Otherworld was believed to be located; nevertheless there was in Celtic belief but one Otherworld, despite the fact that so many locations were assigned to it' (O'Rahilly, *Early Irish History and Mythology*, p. 290).

the twelfth-century French poet Chrétien de Troyes, in whose *Le Conte del Graal* it features as the Castle of Ladies visited by Gauvain. The theme appears also to have been familiar to Marie de France, since it resembles an episode in her lay *Guingomar*. Thus, the magnificent palace visited by Maxen was originally no terrestrial stronghold but, as Loomis termed it, 'a faery dwelling'.[173] The fact that Caernarvon currently lay ruined and uninhabited made it the more readily evoked as a marvellous palace inhabited by legendary luminaries in a bygone era.

However, the Otherworld identity of *Caer Segeint* was plainly unknown to the North Welsh compiler of the early ninth-century *Historia Brittonum*, which contains the earliest literary allusion to the stronghold. In his chronological epitome of Roman emperors traditionally held to have ruled over Britain, Nennius states that

> The fifth was Constantine, son of Constantine the Great, and there [in Britain] he dies, and his tomb is shown beside the city which is called *Cair Segeint*, as writing shows which is on the stone of his burial-mound. And he sowed three seeds, that is, of gold, silver, and bronze, in the pavement of the aforesaid city, so that no poor person might ever dwell therein, and it is called by another name *Minmanton*.[174]

In reality, there exists no likelihood that the younger Constantine ever visited Britain. Born at Arles in 317, after a brief period as Caesar in the West he was slain in battle at the age of twenty-three by his brother Constantius II at Aquileia.[175] It has been conjectured that an inscription commemorating a less illustrious dignitary of the same name was known at Caernarvon in the early middle ages, leading to the mistaken belief that it marked an imperial grave.[176] That a tomb reputed to be his existed is clear, but the legend is perhaps more credibly accounted for by the large number of coins of Constantine I and his son recovered in modern times from the site, which were doubtless found in much greater profusion during the early Middle Ages.[177]

Neither of the variant accounts of the reign of Maximus in the *Historia Brittonum* makes any reference to his association with *Caer Segeint*, which suggests that, at the time of its composition (AD 829/30) by an author who was a native of Gwynedd familiar with legends of Segontium, Maximus's association with the site had yet to come into being.

The ruins of Segontium were known as *Caer Custennyn* ('Fortress of Constantine') at the end of the eleventh century, when the Latin Life of Gruffydd ap Cynan (*c.* 1140) describes Hugh, Earl of Chester, as building a castle *in Arvon in antiqua urbe Constantini imperatoris filii Constantii Magni*.[178] Such allusions as exist suggest that this stronghold was regarded as one of the principal courts of the early kings of Gwynedd, without suggestion of any supernatural connotation. In

173   Keith Busby (ed.), *Chrétien de Troyes: Le Roman de Perceval ou Le Conte du Graal* (Tübingen, 1993), pp. 307–58; Alfred Ewert (ed.), *Marie de France: Lais* (Oxford, 1947), pp. 6–8. Cf. Roger Sherman Loomis, *Arthurian Tradition & Chrétien de Troyes* (New York, 1949), pp. 445–47, 458–59; idem, *Wales and the Arthurian Legend* (Cardiff, 1956), p. 9.

174   Mommsen (ed.), *Chronica Minora*, iii, p. 166.

175   Jones, Martindale, and Morris, *The Prosopography of the Later Roman Empire*, i, p. 223.

176   Lot (ed.), *Nennius et l'Historia Brittonum*, pp. 59–60; Edmond Faral, *La légende arthurienne - Études et documents* (Paris, 1929), i, p. 212; M. P. Charlesworth, *The Lost Province or the Worth of Britain* (Cardiff, 1949), p. 28.

177   P. J. Casey and J. L. Davies, with J. Evans, *Excavations at Segontium (Caernarfon) Roman Fort, 1975–1979* (London, 1993), pp. 142–51, 153.

178   Paul Russell (ed.), *Vita Griffini Filii Conani: The Medieval Latin Life of Gruffudd ap Cynan* (Cardiff, 2005), p. 72. Cf. Williams (ed.), *Breuddwyd Maxen*, pp. xviii–xix.

the early eleventh-century story of *Branwen*, *Kaer Seint yn Aruon* is identified as a royal court of the king of Gwynedd, and in the Life of St Beuno the Saint visits Hywel Dda's seventh-century forebear Cadwallon ap Cadfan at *kaer yn aruon*.[179]

Evidently, association of Maximus with Caernarvon did not belong to the indigenous lore of mediæval Gwynedd, nor is there any indication that it was regarded locally as an enchanted castle. Its reputation as source of unceasing wealth arose from the fact that it was exceptionally rich in deposits of Roman coinage.

In fact, it is clear that the opening section of *Breuddwyd Maxen* was originally located in Dyfed, where the faery palace was believed to be situated on top of the mountain Y Freni Fawr. The *sole* location in the romance linked by name to Maxen lies in Dyfed, and it is clear from the wording that the spot was *already* known as his seat (*Cadeir Faxen*) at the time of writing. This reflects his transformation over the centuries into a demi-god, as occurred in the case of Arthur, who was popularly believed to occupy a similar throne (*cathedra Arthuri*) on the inaccessible summit of a mountain in Brycheiniog.[180]

Subsequently, a *cyfarwydd* familiar with the *Historia Brittonum* of Nennius relocated his opening episode in what he took to be the more appropriate setting of Rome and its environs. When Maxen arrives in Britain, the author located his encounter with the lovely Elen at what he considered the correspondingly appropriate Romano-British setting of Segontium.

The author's identification of the Roman fortress of Segontium (*Caer Seint*) as the faery palace where Maxen discovers the lovely Elen was suggested by his reading of the *Historia Brittonum*, which unmistakably provided his source for the 'historical' career of Maxen Gwledig. §26 of that work contains its first reference to Maximus, who is declared to have been the sixth Roman emperor to reign over Britain. The preceding chapter §25 describes the reign of the fifth emperor, his predecessor Constantine:

> *Quintus Constantinus Constantini magni filius fuit et ibi moritur et sepulcrum illius monstratur iuxta urbem, quae vocatur Cair Segeint, ut litterae, quae sunt in lapide tumuli, ostendunt. Et ipse seminavit tria semina, id est auri argenti, aerisque, in pavimento supradictae civitatis, ut nullus pauper in ea habitaret umquam …*
>
> The fifth was Constantine, son of Constantine the Great, and there [in Britain] he dies and his tomb is shown near the city which is called *Cair Segeint*, as letters, which are on the stone of his grave, declare. And he sowed three seeds, that is of gold, silver, and bronze in the pavement of the aforesaid city so that no poor person might ever dwell in it …

Caer Seint is the sole residence of a Roman emperor in Britain to be identified in Nennius's work, and in consequence the author of *Breuddwyd Maxen* might naturally have taken it for the permanent residence of Romano-British emperors, of whom the most prominent was Constantine's successor Maximus.[181] Then again, its supernatural profusion of inexhaustible

---

179 Thomson (ed.), *Branwen uerch Lyr*, p. 9; J. Morris Jones and John Rhŷs (ed.), *The Elucidarium and Other Tracts in Welsh from Llyvyr Agkyr Llandewivrevi, A.D. 1346 (Jesus College MS. 119)* (Oxford, 1894), p. 123.

180 J. S. Brewer, James F. Dimock, and George F. Warner (ed.), *Giraldi Cambrensis Opera* (London, 1861–91), vi, p. 36.

181 'The genealogies reveal that Maxen and Constantine were already being associated with each other and it would have been easy for a Gwynedd author to choose to locate his retelling of the Maxen legend in Caernarfon' (Nagy and Jones (ed.), *Heroic Poets and Poetic Heroes in Celtic Tradition*, p. 307).

wealth not only singled it out among the twenty-eight cities of Britain, but suggested it as the gorgeous palace where Maxen weds the maiden sovereignty in *Breuddwyd Maxen*.

On the basis of the foregoing considerations, evolution of the legend of Maxen Gwledig may be seen to have pursued something approaching the following pattern.

1. From an early epoch, not later than the beginning of the ninth century and probably much earlier, Maximus had come to be regarded as an heroic native Romano-British monarch, who led the hosts of Britain to victory on the Continent, where they overthrew the reigning Emperor and established their own sovereign on the imperial throne.

2. As such, he provided an appropriate ancestor-figure for powerful royal lineages of Western Britain, where from an early stage he was adopted by genealogists as progenitor of several dynasties ruling strategic kingdoms in that region. His attraction arose from the belief that he was the last Roman ruler of Britain, descent from whom conferred combined Roman and British legitimacy on those who proclaimed themselves his successors.[182] This belief reflected a degree of historical reality. It was probably the rôle played by the historical Maximus in establishing federate kingdoms on the frontiers of the Roman diocese of Britain that subsequently led to his transformation from founder to ancestor of royal dynasties.

3. Such a monarch would naturally be presumed to have wed the Maiden Sovereignty of Britain, royal union with the mother-goddess being 'perhaps the most important element in the druid cosmogonic mythology'.[183] The goddess bore different names at various times and places, while each mortal queen was regarded as her incarnation.

4. In the second half of the tenth century, the kings of Gwynedd traced their paternal ancestry from Beli the Great, primal ancestor-deity of the Britons, whose name the legendary history declared that Britain bore before the island became known as *Ynys Prydein*. Hywel's queen Elen was a princess of Dyfed, who claimed descent through Maximus from Constantine and Helen. In contrast, the royal house of Gwynedd made no dynastic claim to inheritance from Maxen or Elen.[184]

5. That a princess of Dyfed was christened Elen towards the end of the ninth century suggests that stories of her putative ancestress the Empress Helena were already being recited at her father King Llywarch's court.

6. In the romance Maxen is represented as conquering Britain from Beli and his sons, the previous rulers of Britain, who were traditionally associated with Gwynedd. Evidently Maxen was originally regarded as an intruder, albeit a beneficent one, in North Welsh tradition.

---

182 Chadwick (ed.), *Studies in Early British History*, p. 94; Bromwich (ed.), *Trioedd Ynys Prydein*, p. 452.

183 J. E. Caerwyn Williams, 'Celtic literature. Origins', in Karl Horst Schmidt and Rolf Ködderitzsch (ed.), *Geschichte und Kultur der Kelten: Vorbereitungskonferenz 25.-28. Oktober 1982 in Bonn* (Heidelberg, 1986), pp. 140–41. The concept is of Indo-European origin: 'In the same way Penelope, although not a lady of Ithaka, could with her hand bestow the sovereignty of Ithaka' (A. M. Hocart, *Kingship* (Oxford, 1927), p. 103).

184 At a later date a series of collateral descents were advanced to exalt the ancestry of Rhodri Mawr of Gwynedd, which included descent in the female line from *Maxen wledic* (J. G. Evans, 'Pedigrees from Jesus College MS. 20', *Y Cymmrodor* (1887), viii, p. 87). However, this was unrelated to the inheritance of Gwynedd, and is ignored in the Harleian collection, which was compiled in the interest of Hywel Dda.

7. It has been seen that a likely occasion for transference of the setting of the legend from Dyfed to Gwynedd was the reign of Hywel of Gwynedd, *c.* 942–50 AD. The fact that the impressive site of the Roman fortress at Caernarfon had long been a ruin served to account for the fact that the gorgeous palace of the tale was no longer in existence.

8. Early legend identified *Caer Seint* (*Segontium*) as the palace where a foreign ruler might be expected to claim as his bride the heiress to the British monarchy. In *Branwen verch Llŷr*, Branwen is wooed and won by Matholwch, King of Ireland. One of her father's principal courts was at Caer Seint, and it was there that he received her appeal for rescue from maltreatment at her husband's hands, and wrathfully summoned the armed hosts of Britain. In striking congruence, Matholwch is described as arriving at Caer Seint in a fleet of *thirteen ships* to claim Branwen as his bride, while Maxen in *Breuddwyd Maxen* despatches *thirteen messengers* across the sea to Caer Seint to make the same proposal to Elen.[185] According to the fourteenth-century Welsh bard Justus Llwyd, the wedding of Branwen occurred in the Palace of Maxen (*llys Maxen*), by which was presumably intended Caer Seint.[186]

Inside the Faery Palace

The cosmic board game

The sole activity depicted as occurring in the Otherworld castle inhabited by Elen is a mysterious game of *gwyddbwyll*. Given that Maxen's entry into the enchanted castle and wedding to Elen confer upon him the kingship of Britain, it is noteworthy that a ritual game of dice played an integral part in the enthronement of Hindu kings in early India.[187]

The scene greeting Maxen as he enters the palace at Caer Seint conveys the impression of imagery frozen in time. There are the two youths forever playing at the board game *gwyddbwyll*; the noble patriarch seated impassively on his eagle-throne, the unexplained column upreared beside him; his silent occupation, carving *gwyddbwyll*-pieces from a gold bar; and the peerlessly beautiful maiden, seated on a chair of red gold. It is surely significant that all these factors represent primary components of the myth of kingship in Celtic society.

Evidence attests to the fact that the related Welsh and Irish board games (*gwyddbwyll, fidchell*) reflect a cosmic paradigm. Both names bear essentially the same meaning. *Gwyddbwyll* is a compound of *gwydd + pwyll*, 'wood-intelligence, wood-sense, wood of meditation'. Similarly, Irish *fidchell* derives from *fid + ciall*, 'wood-intelligence'.[188] Although the rules of neither game are preserved in full, enough is known to justify our envisaging the king established at the centre, surrounded by his warriors, while his adversaries congregate menacingly around the perimeter. The board represents a *mandala*, wherein the king must constantly be sustained against his destructive adversaries. In Vedic India,

185 Derick S. Thomson (ed.), *Branwen uerch Lyr: The Second of the Four Branches of the Mabinogi edited from the White Book of Rhydderch with variants from the Red Book of Hergest and from Peniarth 6* (Dublin, 1961), p. 1.

186 *Hi adoeth yn noeth o neithaʊr vranwen. hyt yn llys vaxen nyt lles vocsach* (Gwenogvryn Evans (ed.), *The Poetry in the Red Book of Hergest*, col. 1365, ll. 39–41).

187 Heesterman, *The Ancient Indian Royal Consecration*, 143–57. Cf. Titus Burckhardt, *Mirror of the Intellect: Essays on Traditional Science & Sacred Art* (Cambridge, 1987), pp. 142–48.

188 *Geiriadur Prifysgol Cymru*, p. 1754; E. G. Quin *et al.* (ed.), *Dictionary of the Irish Language: Based mainly on Old and Middle Irish Materials* (Dublin, 1913–76), 'F', col. 128.

The combat which takes place in the game of chess thus represents, in its most universal meaning, the combat of the *devas* with the *asûras*, of the 'gods' with the 'titans', or of the 'angels' with the 'demons', all other meanings of the game deriving from this one.[189]

Cosmic implications recur in connexion with early board games worldwide. A Chinese account of the game *go*, compiled in the fifth century BC, explains that

The board must be square, and represents the laws of the earth. The lines must be straight like the divine virtues. There are black and white stones, divided like *yin* and *yang* [the two balanced forces of the cosmos]. Their arrangements on a board is like a model of the heavens.

The centre point provided the polar focus around which the four quarters (representing the four seasons) revolved. Games were played on mountaintops, traditionally sites of the Centre of the world.[190]

The concept of the heavens as a macrocosmic gaming-table was invoked by the eighth-century Irish poet Blathmac:

He [God] owns the extent that he marks out of the seven heavens about the kingly seat; it is his hand that has strewn in them the gaming-board (*fidchell*) of beautiful stars.[191]

The druids were famed for their knowledge of the heavenly bodies.[192] Given the indebtedness of the Irish bardic tradition to its pagan precursor, it is likely that the poet's metaphor reflects druidic cosmology.

Tantalizing allusions in Irish mediæval literature attest to the cosmic implications of these venerable board games. Thus, the *brandub* board was identified with Ireland herself, with Tara as its 'centre'. Who holds that square is legitimate owner of the board. Four other squares are identified with the four great provincial capitals, which the king is urged to occupy.[193]

The corresponding British board game, *gwyddbwyll*, evidently bore similar cosmic application. In the Life of Saint Cadog, Arthur, together with his traditional companions Cai and Bedwyr, is discovered playing at *alea* on the hill of Boch Rhiw Carn.[194] Although *alea* has been translated

---

189   Burckhardt, *Mirror of the Intellect,* pp. 143. Cf. Rees and Rees, *Celtic Heritage,* pp. 154–56, 391; Reidar Th. Christiansen, *Studies in Irish and Scandinavian Folktales* (Copenhagen, 1959), p. 218; Ursula Dronke (ed.), *The Poetic Edda: Volume II Mythological Poems* (Oxford, 1997), pp. 119–21.

190   John Fairbairn, 'Go in China', in I. L. Finkel (ed.), *Ancient Board Games in perspective: Papers from the 1990 British Museum colloquium* (London, 2007), p. 134; Joseph Needham (ed.), *Science and Civilisation in China* (Cambridge, 1954-), iv (part 1), pp. 318–34; Edward H. Schafer, *The Vermilion Bird: T'ang Images of the South* (Berkeley, 1967), p. 143; idem, *Pacing the Void: T'ang Approaches to the Stars* (Berkeley, 1977), pp. 79–80, 81; Munakata, *Sacred Mountains in Chinese Art,* pp. 30, 104. During a visit to Korea in 1988, I was privileged to witness two shamans playing a traditional board game (*patok?*) in their mountaintop temple.

191   James Carney (ed.), *The Poems of Blathmac Son of Cú Brettan; Together with the Irish Gospel of Thomas and a Poem on the Virgin Mary* (Dublin, 1964), p. 64.

192   Guyonvarc'h and Le Roux, *Les Druides,* pp. 59-60; Fergus Kelly, 'The beliefs and mythology of the early Irish, with special reference to the cosmos', in Clive Ruggles (ed.), *Astronomy, Cosmology and Landscape: Proceedings of the SEAC 98 Meeting, Dublin, Ireland, September 1998* (Bognor Regis, 2001), pp. 169–70.

193   *Éigse,* v, p. 30.

194   A. W. Wade-Evans (ed.), *Vitae Sanctorum Britanniae et Genealogiae* (Cardiff, 1944), pp. 26.

as 'dice', it more frequently denotes a board game.[195] As a mortal king, Arthur is unlikely to have found a hilltop the most convenient place to enjoy such a diversion, but nothing could be more appropriate to his acquired divine status than that he be envisaged as playing *gwyddbwyll* on a ritually appropriate elevation. The divinized Arthur was popularly believed to reside on mountain summits, such as Cadeir Arthur in Brycheiniog. In *Culhwch ac Olwen* he is discovered seated with Bedwyr on the top of Pumlumon, in 'the greatest wind in the world'.[196] Pumlumon's central position in Wales, coupled with the fact that four rivers sprang from its flanks, points to its being the Omphalos of Wales.[197]

The etymology of *gwyddbwyll* is cognate with that of 'druid', the latter word being generally interpreted as 'wisdom of the wood'.[198] The 'wood' is normally understood as referring to a tree or trees, but conceivably intimates mastery of the wooden *gwyddbwyll* board, where the player's skill at conducting the game sustained cosmic equilibrium at a microcosmic level. In the Welsh mediæval romance of *Breuddwyd Rhonabwy*, a game of *gwyddbwyll* played between Arthur and his adversary Owain echoes the larger battle being fought nearby between Arthur's men and Owain's ravens, and appears to prefigure the former's celebrated victory at Badon.[199]

The pieces in *gwyddbwyll* are termed in Welsh *gwerin*, which also means 'people, folk, nation', just as Irish *fidchell* pieces are termed *fer*, 'man'.[200] That they personified humanity is further suggested by the Welsh tradition of remarkable *gwyddbwyll* games, wherein the pieces play without human intervention.[201] That the *fidchell* board represented the earth, and its pieces mankind, is again suggested by a thirteenth-century Irish poet's metaphor: 'the world before we were sent abroad into it was an empty board without pieces' (*'na chlár fholamh gan fhoirinn*).[202] (In parenthesis, it is intriguing to note the extent to which modern cosmologists cite the rules of chess as analogous to laws governing the cosmos.)[203]

---

195 R. E. Latham and D. R. Howlett (ed.), *Dictionary of Medieval Latin from British Sources* (London, 1975–2013), p. 60; Murray, *A History of Board games other than Chess*, pp. 31, 56, 57.

196 Brewer, Dimock, and Warner (ed.), *Giraldi Cambrensis Opera*, vi, p. 36; Bromwich and Simon Evans (ed.), *Culhwch and Olwen*, pp. 34–35.

197 John Rhŷs, *Celtic Folklore: Welsh and Manx* (Oxford, 1901), pp. 391–92; Rees and Rees, *Celtic Heritage*, pp. 175–76; Mac Cana, *The Cult of the Sacred Centre*, pp. 205–6.

198 Françoise Bader, 'Pan', *Revue de Philologie* (Paris, 1989), lxiii, p. 34; Thomas V. Gamkrelidze and Vjačeslav V. Ivanov, *Indo-European and the Indo-Europeans: A Reconstruction and Historical Analysis of a Proto-Language and a Proto-Culture* (Berlin and New York, 1995), i, p. 690; Helmut Birkhan, *Kelten: Versuch einer Gesamtdarstellung ihrer Kultur* (Vienna, 1997), p. 898; J. P. Mallory and D. Q. Adams (ed.), *Encyclopedia of Indo-European Culture* (Chicago and London, 1997), p. 598; Xavier Delamarre, *Dictionnaire de la langue gauloise: Une approche linguistique du vieux-celtique continental* (Paris, 2001), pp. 125–26.

199 Melville Richards (ed.), *Breudwyt Ronabwy: Allan o'r Llyfr Coch o Hergest* (Cardiff, 1948), pp. 12–18. Irish tradition likewise records a combat between men playing at *fidchell* and predatory ravens (O'Grady (ed.), *Silva Gadelica*, i, pp. 220-21). Could this association have anything to do with the fact that *brandub*, the name of another Irish board game, means 'black raven'? (J. Vendryes, E. Bachellery, and P-Y. Lambert, *Lexique étymologique de l'irlandais ancien* (Dublin and Paris, 1959–96), B-78). It is curious that 'foot-soldiers' in chess are termed 'rooks' (Tony Hunt (ed.), *Les Gius Partiz des Eschez: Two Anglo-Norman Chess Treatises* (London, 1985), pp. 48–49).

200 *Geiriadur Prifysgol Cymru*, p. 1643; Quin *et al.* (ed.) *Dictionary of the Irish Language*, 'F', cols. 81–82.

201 Eurys I. Rowlands, 'Y Tri Thlwys ar Ddeg', *Llên Cymru* (Cardiff, 1958) v, p. 36; Goetinck (ed.), *Historia Peredur vab Efrawc*, pp. 66–67.

202 N. J. A. Williams (ed.), *The Poems of Giolla Brighde Mac Con Midhe* (Dublin, 1980), p. 226.

203 John Polkinghorne, *The Faith of a Physicist: Reflections of a Bottom-Up Thinker* (Princeton, 1994), p. 169; Martin Rees, *Before the Beginning: Our Universe and Others* (London, 1997), p. 176.

We have seen how the reconstructed elaborate rite which induced the dream that enabled Maxen to attain the faery palace is imbued with analogies applicable to Celtic board games. When the hero enters the enchanted stronghold, the first thing he sees is a game of *gwyddbwyll* in play, with an old man carving pieces (*gwerin*, men) for an empty board set before him. The two games, one implicit without the castle, the other explicit within, are surely interrelated.

The Old Man

The venerable figure seated on an ivory throne plays an oddly ambivalent rôle in the story. His sole occupation is that of carving *gwyddbwyll* pieces, to be deployed on a *gwyddbwyll* board set before him. He plays no active part in the narrative, and the impression is conveyed that he remains on his throne throughout.

It looks as though he originally bore no name, since it is presented in the tale effectively as an afterthought. Subsequently, when adapting the native legend to the contrived Roman setting of *Breuddwyd Maxen*, the redactor understood him to be Maxen's predecessor as ruler of Britain, and bestowed on him the name *Eudaf*, which as has been seen probably originated in misunderstanding of the numeral *octavus* in Nennius's *Historia Brittonum*.

Next in the story, Elen claims and is granted as part of her maiden fee (*agwedi*) the island of Britain for her father from sea to sea. There is some confusion here, which further betrays the author's difficulty in handling his source. If the old man were not already ruler of Britain prior to the arrival of Maxen, then who was? Furthermore, he plays no part in ensuing dramatic events, in which Maxen acts as de facto sovereign of the island.

Everything about the old man – the dignified splendour of his appearance, his glorious palace and ivory throne, his paternity of Elen, the kingdom's heiress – indicates that he was indeed king of Britain. Furthermore, Elen's insistence that he be accorded rule over the island – rule which in the event he apparently does not exercise – makes it clear that he remains throughout king in some guise, even after Maxen takes control of the country.

This otiose figure bears every appearance of representing a concept familiar to Celtic mythology, ultimately originating in Indo-European tradition. There exist distinct Indo-European terminologies for 'king, lord, god'. The first category, $*h_2ns$- or $*h_2ans$-, applies to the '(symbolic) generator (of his subjects)', while the second, $*h_3r\bar{e}\hat{g}$-, contains the active implications 'rule, ruler, regulate'.[204]

The concept of the passive royal guarantor of stability and order, paired with the active ruler who leads in war and government, repeatedly recurs in Celtic mythology. The most striking example is that of the Irish gods Núadu and Lugh in Ireland, and their Welsh counterparts Lludd and Lleu(elys) in Britain. The relationship is also found in the story of *Pwyll Pendeuic Dyuet*. There Pwyll (whose name means 'wisdom') withdraws to the Otherworld, leaving his son Pryderi to govern the kingdom of Dyfed in peace and war. That Pwyll originally dwelt permanently in the Otherworld realm of Annwfn is confirmed by his alternative appellation *Pwyll Penn Annwfn*, 'Pwyll, Head of Annwfn'.[205]

The inert state of the otiose ruler is emphasized by his apparent inability to propagate an heir. Yet, at the same time he must beget the vigorous ruling monarch! This mythological

204 Calvert Watkins, *How to Kill a Dragon: Aspects of Indo-European Poetics* (New York and Oxford, 1995), pp. 8–9. Cf. M. L. West, *Indo-European Poetry and Myth* (Oxford, 2007), pp. 411–12; Maxim Fomin, *Instructions for Kings: Secular and Clerical Images of Kingship in Early Ireland and Ancient India* (Heidelberg, 2013), pp. 336–38.

205 W. J. Gruffydd, *Rhiannon: An Inquiry into the Origins of the First and Third Branches of the Mabinogi* (Cardiff, 1953), p. 40.

paradox is rationalized by various 'explanations' found in legends and romances. Thus Pwyll encounters difficulty in producing an heir by his queen, and when eventually she does give birth the baby is mysteriously abducted, to be discovered and brought up at the court of an earthly king and queen. Uther Pendragon, who was originally a godhead, can only beget Arthur by impregnating a noblewoman, to whom he appears in the semblance of her husband, and as suddenly departs.

Another close parallel, almost certainly of Celtic derivation, features in the history of the Holy Grail, as recounted in the romance of *Perceval* by Chrétien de Troyes. The Fisher King dwells apart from men in his enchanted castle. He is effectively identified with the father of the youthful hero Perceval, each of whom, after being rendered impotent by a spear-thrust in the groin, dwells apart from the world of men in the heart of a great forest – characteristic location of the measureless eternity of the Otherworld.[206] In fact, the Fisher King presents what is perhaps the closest parallel to the Old Man of *Caer Seint*. Each remains seated and effectively immobile within an enchanted palace, where he receives the young and vigorous heir to the kingdom. He is king, but does not rule, his active function being assigned to the dynamic young warrior.

The status of the otiose monarch or deity (most of the protagonists of these stories being originally gods) has been well described by Georges Dumézil:

> Germanic and Indian facts which have recently been collated suggest that the Indo-Europeans were acquainted with a celestial god who was not and could not himself be either king or father, but who guaranteed the continuity of births and provided for the succession of kings. He was a variety of 'primordial god' or 'framing god' (the first to appear and last to disappear), whose slow rhythm – the slowness of the world's history – was felt to be in sharp contrast with the brevity of generations and of kingdoms.[207]

The otiose god is also the creator god, who, after his initial act of bringing the world into existence, relapses into a state of latent potency.[208] His function accounts for the Old Man of Caer Seint's carving (chess)men, *gwerin*, from a golden bar. They are presumably intended in due course to participate in the shifting fortunes of the *gwyddbwyll* board: a game in which he himself would play no direct part. Thus time is born out of eternity.

The Hall Pillar

Next there is the hall-column, at whose foot the Old Man is seated on his ivory throne. Its mention appears entirely gratuitous, but there can be little doubt that this was originally the world-pillar, which in early cosmologies was understood to sustain the sky, linking earth and heaven. The Saxons in early mediæval Germany worshipped an enormous wooden pillar, 'called

---

206 Wimberly, *Folklore in the English & Scottish Ballads*, pp. 122–27.

207 Georges Dumézil, *Archaic Roman Religion* (Chicago, 1970), p. 409. Cf. Françoise Le Roux, 'La Courtise d'Etain: Commentaire du texte', *Celticvm XV: Actes du Vᵉ Colloque International d'Études Gauloises, Celtiques et Protoceltiques* (Rennes, 1966), pp. 372–73.

208 The concept extends well beyond Indo-European tradition. The M'pongwe, Igalwa, and Ajumba 'have, as is constant among the Bantu races of South-West Africa, a great god – the creator, a god who has made all things, and who now no longer takes any interest in the things he has created. Their name for this god is Anyambie ... This god, unlike other forms of the creating god in fetish, has a viceroy or minister he has created, and to whom he leaves the government of affairs. This god is Mbuiri or Ombwiri ...'. (Mary H. Kingsley, *Travels in West Africa: Congo Français, Corisco and Cameroons* (London, 1897), p. 228: cf. pp. 228–29).

in their language *Irminsul*, which in Latin is said to be the universal column which sustains all things' (*eum lingua Irminsul appellantes, quod Latine dicitur universalis columpna, quasi sustinens omnia*).[209] The name *Irminsul* means something like '(divine) universal pillar', and corresponds mythologically to the World Tree Yggdrasil in Norse mythology.[210] Similar sky-supports are found in other cosmologies.[211] Gaulish 'Jupiter columns' are believed to reflect the same concept among the Continental Celts, while Irish tradition records that a 'single column' was erected at the sacred centre Tara by the mythical King Cormac mac Airt. A provision in the Welsh laws that a king in his hall should be seated 'next to the column' (*yn nessaw y'r colouyn*) may reflect this archaic paradigm.[212]

King, throne, and column are regularly associated in ancient cosmologies as emblematic of the Sacred Centre, Navel of the earth. In Vedic India and early Israel the royal throne was identified with the Navel.[213] This was because universal kingship was believed to have been established eternally at the Sacred Centre.[214]

The Matchless Maiden

As has been seen, a familiar literary motif in Celtic Britain and Ireland is that of the hero who dreams of a beautiful maiden, falls helplessly in love, and seeks everywhere until he finds her. The theme (*aisling*) is more fully attested in Irish literature than Welsh, the heroine being frequently a fairy.[215] Behind one strand of this theme lies that of the mortal prince who seeks out and weds an Otherworld queen who personifies the sovereignty of the land – a myth fundamental to pagan Celtic cosmology. So entrenched was this concept, that its most magnificent flowering occurred as late as the seventeenth and eighteenth centuries, when Jacobite poets lamented in pathetic terms the fate of the beautiful Fair One (Ireland or Scotland), whose rightful husband (the legitimate Stuart king) had been exiled and deprived of his bride and inheritance by a squalid foreign usurper.[216]

209 Werner Trillmich and Rudolf Buchner (ed.), *Quellen des 9. und 11. Jahrhunderts zur Geschichte der Hamburgischen Kirche und des Reiches* (Darmstadt, 1961), pp. 170–72.

210 H. Munro Chadwick, *The Origin of the English Nation* (Cambridge, 1907), pp. 226–30; Cook, *Zeus*, ii, pp. 50–57; iii, pp. 1116–17; Jan de Vries, *Altgermanische Religionsgeschichte* (Berlin, 1956–57), ii, pp. 387–89; G. Turville-Petre, 'Thurstable', in Norman Davis and C. L. Wrenn (ed.), *English and Medieval Studies Presented to J.R.R. Tolkien on the Occasion of his Seventieth Birthday* (London, 1962), pp. 241–49.

211 Clive Tolley, *Shamanism in Norse Myth and Magic* (Helsinki, 2009), i, pp. 272–91.

212 Arthur Bernard Cook, *Zeus: A Study in Ancient Religion* (Cambridge, 1914–40), ii, pp. 57–100; Pierre Lambrechts, *Contributions à l'étude des divinités celtiques* (Bruges, 1942), pp. 81–99; Jan de Vries, *Keltische Religion* (Stuttgart, 1961), pp. 31–34; Miranda Jane Green, *The Wheel as a Cult-Symbol in the Romano-Celtic World With Special Reference to Gaul and Britain* (Brussels, 1984), pp. 173–74; Ruth Lehmann (ed.), *Fled Dúin na nGéd* (Dublin, 1964), p. 2; Wiliam (ed.), *Llyfr Iorwerth*, p. 3. Cf. Tolley, *Shamanism in Norse Myth and Magic*, i, p. 279.

213 Jeannine Auboyer, 'Le caractère royal et divin du trône dans l'Inde ancienne', in *La Regalità Sacra: Contributi al Tema Dell' VIII Congresso Internazionale di Storia delle Religioni (Roma, Aprile 1955)* (Leiden, 1959), pp. 182–83; Heesterman, *The Ancient Indian Royal Consecration*, pp. 101, 141–42, 147-50; A. J. Wensinck, *The Ideas of the Western Semites Concerning the Navel of the Earth* (Amsterdam, 1916), pp. 54–58.

214 Le Roux and Guyonvarc'h, *Les Druides*, pp. 217–26.

215 Chadwick (ed.), *Studies in Early British History*, p. 108; J. E. Caerwyn Williams and Patrick K. Ford, *The Irish Literary Tradition* (Cardiff, 1992), pp. 218–20.

216 T. F. O'Rahilly, 'On the Origin of the Names Érainn and Ériu', *Ériu* (1943), xiv, pp. 20–21; Schmidt and Ködderitzsch (ed.), *Geschichte und Kultur der Kelten*, p. 144; Benjamin T. Hudson, *Prophecy of Berchán: Irish and Scottish High-Kings of the Early Middle Ages* (Westport, Conn., 1996), pp. 7–8; Murray G. H. Pittock, *Poetry and Jacobite Politics in Eighteenth-Century Britain and Ireland* (Cambridge, 1994),

The lovely Elen wedded by Maxen in the Welsh romance unmistakably personifies the Maiden Sovereignty of Britain, and the 'Dream' sprang from this familiar *genre*. However *Breuddwyd Maxen* includes elements which the author failed to understand when adapting his source, which show that the theme was originally richer than appears in the extant literary setting of the motif.

Maxen and Cadeir Faxen

Following his marriage at Caernarvon to Elen of the Hosts, heiress of Britain, the setting of Maxen's tale is without explanation abruptly tranferred to South Wales. In the course of a day's hunting, he (again, unaccountably) ascends the summit of a mountain, where he sets up camp:

> And one day the Emperor went to hunt from Carmarthen to the summit of Y Freni Fawr (*hyt pen e Vreni Vaur*), and there the Emperor pitched his tent, and that encampment is named to this day *Cadeir Faxen* ('the Seat or Throne of Maxen').[217]

It has already been noted that this seemingly pointless digression replicates Maxen's ascent of the Alpine mountain, at the outset of his journey to Britain. On each occasion his discovery of the Maiden Sovereignty in the faery castle is prefaced by a hunt, and in each the author conveys awareness that Maxen ascended a mountain, evidently without understanding why. Clearly, the two occasions represent duplicate versions of a single original. Since the Roman 'historical' setting represents a secondary development of the legend, it would appear that in an earlier version the mountain ascended by Maxen at his approach to the Otherworld castle was Y Freni Fawr.

The incongruous reference to his camping on the mountaintop (was he accustomed to carry a tent when hunting?) suggests that at some stage the figure of Maxen had become substituted for a demi-god. In the romance of *Branwen* the giant Bran is housed in a tent, since he cannot fit within a house: "They were not in a house, but in tents, for Bendigeidfran had never been contained in a house."[218] The implication being that, as a divinity, his person could not be confined within a material structure.[219]

Representation of the firmament or cosmos as a tent reflects a belief in the Otherworld as unconfined by walls or roof: a concept likely to be more archaic than its rationalizing depiction

---

pp. 5, 45, 187–201. When circumstances demanded, the rôles might be reversed, as when Prince Charles Edward is invoked as the beautiful curly-haired Morag with whom the poet longs to be reunited (John Lorne Campbell (ed.), *Highland Songs of the Forty-Five* (Edinburgh, 1933), pp. 144–48). Roy Owen's explanation seems to me mistaken, when he described *Breuddwyd Maxen* as 'A Celtic dream-legend subjected to some form of rationalisation when it was taken over by the French or indeed by the Anglo-Normans' (D. D. R. Owen, *The Evolution of the Grail Legend* (Edinburgh, 1968), pp. 78–80). I cannot detect any trace of French influence in the story.

217   Roberts (ed.), *Breudwyt Maxen Wledic*, p. 8.

218   Derick S. Thomson (ed.), *Branwen uerch Lyr: The Second of the Four Branches of the Mabinogi edited from the White Book of Rhydderch with variants from the Red Book of Hergest and from Peniarth 6* (Dublin, 1961), pp. 3, 12.

219   'That he was a deity in origin is clear from the fact that he is constantly described as being so huge that no house could ever contain him' (Anne Ross, *Pagan Celtic Britain: Studies in Iconography and Tradition* (London, 1967), p. 252). Cf. Bromwich (ed.), *Trioedd Ynys Prydein*, p. 284. 'Celtic religion was essentially aniconic and atectonic. The Celts worshipped the ubiquitous invisible forces of nature in the open air ...' (M. J. T. Lewis, *Temples in Roman Britain* (Cambridge, 1966), p. 4). 'Celtic holy places did not necessarily need a building' (Martin Henig, *Religion in Roman Britain* (London, 1984), p. 21). Cf. further Jane Webster, 'Sanctuaries and Sacred Places', in Miranda J. Green (ed.), *The Celtic World* (London, 1995), p. 448.

as a gorgeous palace. Recognition that God cannot be contained within a building features in the Old Testament, e.g. I *Kings* 8.27. Both the Hebrew Yahweh and his predecessor the Ugaritic El were envisaged as dwelling in tents, and tent-shrines were erected for their worship.[220] A festival tent bearing cosmic decorations on its roof representing the sky, which covered an entire assembly, was erected at the Greek *omphalos* site at Delphi, while Germanic peoples similarly shared a concept of the sky as a sail or tent.[221]

We find this motif all but explicit in the famous episode in the ninth-century *Historia Brittonum*, when the marvellous child Ambrosius reveals the mystery of the fighting dragons to Vortigern's druids. After digging in the king's fortress, a pond is discovered. 'What is in the pond?' asks the prophetic boy. Two vessels appear: 'what is in the closed vessels?' Between them lies a tent, which when unfolded provides the arena for the contest of two mysterious creatures (*vermes*) which it contains. The boy explains the significance of their conflict, adding the telling words, 'The tent is a symbolic image of your kingdom' (*Regni tui figura tentorium est*).[222] The version of this episode found in *Cyfranc Lludd a Lleuelys* has the 'dragons' rising into the æther (*yn yr awyr*) in the course of their struggle, which is likely to be closer still to the original conception. Siberian and other shamans customarily regard the curved roof of a tent as a model of the sky.[223]

It is clear that Nennius did not fully understand this curious episode, which he sought to explain in terms of the political situation in the fifth century AD. The inconsequential nature of Maxen's mountain ascent at Preseli betrays the fact that it derived from a source independent of the main narrative of *Breuddwyd Maxen*. Maxen's unexplained sojourn in a tent on the summit of a mountain suggests that the Emperor's name became substituted during the early mediæval period for that of a Brittonic divinity, whether Lleu or another.[224] Application of the name *Cadeir Faxen* to the summit of the mountain Y Freni Fawr occurs only in the tale of Maxen's Dream, where the wording confirms that the belief that it was the setting of Maxen's tent and sleep was

---

220 Mark S. Smith (ed.), *The Ugaritic Baal Cycle* (Leiden, 1994), i, pp. 188–9, 231–32. In early Canaan the god 'Ēl dwelt in a tent, frequently envisaged as situated on a mountaintop (Frank Moore Cross, *Canaanite Myth and Hebrew Epic: Essays in the History of the Religion of Israel* (Cambridge, Mass., 1973), pp. 36, 39, 42–43, 55, 72–73, 125; Clifford, *The Cosmic Mountain in Canaan and the Old Testament*, pp. 123–31). The concept applied likewise to his divine successor:'Yahweh is known in Judah. / In Israel, great is his name. / His tent was in Salem, / And his dwelling, in Zion' (ibid., p. 151).

221 Arthur Bernard Cook, *Zeus: A Study in Ancient Religion* (Cambridge, 1914–40), ii, p. 178; Roberta Frank, 'What Kind of Poetry is *Exodus*?', in Daniel G. Calder and T. Craig Christy (ed.), *Germania: Comparative Studies in the Old Germanic Languages and Literature* (Woodbridge, 1988), pp. 193–95).

222 Mommsen (ed.), *Chronica Minora*, iii, pp. 184–85.

223 Ivar Paulson, 'Die Religionen der nordasiatischen (sibirischen) Völker', in Ivar Paulson, Åke Hultkrantz, and Karl Jettmar, *Die Religionen Nordeurasiens und der amerikanischen Arktis* (Stuttgart, 1962), p. 28; Mihály Hoppál, 'Hungarian Mythology and Folklore', in Mihály Hoppál and Juha Pentikäinen (ed.), *Uralic Mythology and Folklore* (Budapest, 1989), p. 149; Anna-Leena Siikala and Mihály Hoppál, *Studies on Shamanism* (Budapest, 1992), p. 44; Åke Hultkrantz, 'A new look at the world pillar in Arctic and sub-Arctic religions', in Juha Pentikäinen (ed.), *Shamanism and Northern Ecology* (Berlin and New York, 1996), p. 37.

224 That Maxen was originally a deity was first suggested by Sir John Rhŷs (*Lectures on the Origin and Growth of Religion as Illustrated by Celtic Heathendom* (London, 1888), pp. 161–68; idem, *Studies in the Arthurian Legend* (Oxford, 1891), pp. 110–11, 162). 'The similarity of the Welsh tale, *Breuddwydd Macsen*, to *Aislinge Oenguso* leads one to suspect that Macsen Wledig replaced *Maccan (?)' (Eóin MacWhite, 'Problems of Irish Archaeology and Celtic Philology', *Zeitschrift für celtische Philologie* (Tübingen, 1955), xxv, p. 23). *Maccan óc has in turn been identified with Brittonic Maponos (Heinrich Wagner, 'Studies in the Origins of Early Celtic Civilisation', *Zeitschrift für celtische Philologie* (Tübingen, 1971), xxxi, p. 25).

sufficiently well-established in the traditional lore of Dyfed for the author to feel obliged to insert it (somewhat incongruously) into his narrative.

Further indication that Maxen's adventure was originally located in South Wales is provided by the author's casual allusion to his holding court at Caerleon. It was thither that the Roman emperor despatched his messenger to Maxen, indicating that it was regarded as the citadel where Maxen was customarily resident.[225] Independent early tradition, as has been seen, consistently claimed Maxen Gwledig as a ruler in South Wales. Although *Breuddwyd Maxen* makes him wed a princess of North Wales, no such assertion was advanced by genealogists or bards on behalf of the royal house of Gwynedd.

These considerations combine to suggest that the palace where Maxen wed Elen was originally located on the summit of Y Freni Fawr in Dyfed.[226] Prior to this allusion, Maxen's encounter with the beautiful Elen in her faery palace is twice prefaced by his seemingly superfluous ascent of a lofty mountain peak. The implication must surely be that, in an earlier version, the setting for Elen's supernatural palace was envisaged as the summit of a mountain. Furthermore, the gratuitous nature of the brief account of Maxen's ascent of Y Freni Fawr, coupled with the implication that he rested there in an Otherworld dwelling (tent), indicates that it provided the original setting for Maxen's Dream. Reasons have been given for regarding the Gwynedd setting of the romance as a secondary development, consciousness of which led to the author's preservation of the Dyfed location at Y Freni Fawr. The author's wording indicates popular awareness of the latter mountain as the location of Maxen's Throne, which doubtless explains why the author felt impelled to mention the traditional site – albeit incongruously.

A legend of a faery palace located on the summit of Y Freni Fawr survived as late as the nineteenth century. A local story told of a shepherd boy, who grazed his flock on the slopes of a nearby hill, Y Freni Fach. Glancing up at the peak of Y Freni Fawr, to check whether the fog mantling its top presaged good or bad weather, he glimpsed a troop of fairy folk (*Tylwyth Teg*) dancing there merrily to the strains of a harp. Filled with curiosity, he ascended the sister-mountain and drew near to the supernatural revellers. They proved to be diminutive but beautifully dressed maidens and gallants gambolling happily about the cromlech crowning the summit of Y Freni Fawr. Approaching closer still, the youth entered a ring, wherein stood a fabulously beautiful fairy palace, where every delicacy of food and wine was provided for regalement of the inhabitants. Sadly, on drinking from a forbidden well, the palace and all vanished from his sight, and he stood shivering in the night air, alone on the mountain on the very spot where he first entered the ring.[227]

This account bears striking resemblance to Saint Collen's ascent of the Glastonbury Tor, where he encountered a similarly jocund and splendidly garbed company, presided over by Gwyn ap Nudd, lord of the Otherworld realm of Annwfn. In accordance with the requirements of hagiography, the Saint caused the deity, his palace, and followers to vanish, so that he, like the shepherd boy on Y Freni Fawr, found himself alone among green mounds skirting the hilltop.[228]

225 Roberts (ed.), *Breudwyt Maxen Wledic*, p. 9.

226 'The union of Zeus with Hera was likewise referred to by the Greeks to a variety of mountaintops' (Cook, *Zeus*, i, pp. 154–57).

227 Wirt Sikes, *British Goblins: Welsh Folk-Lore, Fairy Mythology, Legends and Traditions*. (London, 1880), pp. 82–84.

228 Baring-Gould and Fisher, *The Lives of the British Saints*, iv, pp. 377–78.

Thus, converging evidence suggests that Maxen's encounter with the Maiden Sovranty was at an earlier stage of the evolving tradition located on the summit of Y Freni Fawr. The mountain is the easternmost height of the range of Preseli Mountain, which also provided the setting for Pwyll's conference with his nobles after his marriage to Rhiannon. The two encounters present suggestive parallels. In each case the protagonist is a king, in whose person may be detected a euhemerized deity.[229] In each case the purpose of the encounter is to ensure the continuing welfare of the kingdom. In the case of Pwyll, perpetuation of the dynasty through procreation of a royal heir is what lies at stake. In the case of Maxen, his marriage to the goddess of the land (of whom Pwyll's Rhiannon is another manifestation) guarantees its future security, prosperity, and (implicitly) royal progeny.[230]

Thus, converging evidence identifies Preseli Mountain as imbued with numinous potency, specifically associated with the well-being of the monarchy of Britain, upon which the security of the island was anchored.

The royal sanctuary of Dyfed

Dual association of Maxen with a mountain and foundation of a dynasty is further suggested by the celebrated ninth-century inscription on the Pillar of Eliseg in North Wales. This contains a brief account of the kings of Powys, which ascribes the origin of their dynasty to the marriage of a progenitor to a daughter of Maximus. The surviving words of an adjacent fragmentary passage are 'mountain' (*mons*), 'kingdom' (*monarchia*), and 'Maximus of Britain' (*Maximus Brittanniae*).[231] The only mountain with which Maxen is associated is Y Freni Fawr, and it is tempting to infer that this section linked his establishment of the kingdom to that mountain.

Y Freni Fawr, which supported the Seat or Throne of Maximus, is one of the hills of the Preseli massif in east Pembrokeshire. The name *Presseleu* probably denoted in early times, as now, the entire range of Preseli Mountains. In *Culhwch ac Olwen*, Arthur is described as arriving at *Presseleu* accompanied by 'the forces of the world', which suggests a more extensive area than a solitary peak.[232]

The primary section of the tenth-century Dyfed royal pedigree in the earliest version (Harleian MS 3859) reads:

> *Gloitguin . map . Nimet . map . dimet . map . Maxim gulecic . map . Protec . map . Protector …*

---

229 Rhŷs, *Studies in the Arthurian Legend*, pp. 110–11, 162.

230 Towards the conclusion of *Breuddwyd Maxen* the Emperor abruptly vanishes from the story, without having begotten a lineal heir. However, the Old Welsh royal genealogies show that he was traditionally regarded as founder of dynasties.

231 V. E. Nash-Williams, *The Early Christian Monuments of Wales* (Cardiff, 1950), p. 123.

232 Bromwich and Simon Evans (ed.), *Culhwch and Olwen*, p. 38. B. G. Charles suggested that 'from the context of the Welsh language source (Mabinogion) it is clear that the name was originally applied to a particular place not to the range of hills later called Presely. The name seems to have spread to cover the whole mountain range' (*The Place-Names of Pembrokeshire*, p. 26). This follows Phillimore's suggestion in Henry Owen (ed.), *The Description of Pembrokeshire, by George Owen of Henllys, Lord of Kemes* (London, 1892–1936), p. 448. However, Owen himself, writing at the close of Elizabeth I's reign, firmly asserts the contrary: 'this name *Percelly* is a *genus* as *Coteswalde* is in *Gloucestershire*, diuerse particuler places therin havinge speciall and proper names'(p. 104). Owen's ancestors had been lords of Cemais, which included much of Preseli Mountain, for centuries, and he must have been familiar with early traditions of the locality (ibid., pp. vi–x, 447–92). Giraldus Cambrensis mentions a wealthy man who dwelt on the northern slope of Preseli Mountain: *a boreali montium de Presseleu latere mansionem habens* (Brewer, Dimock, and Warner (ed.), *Giraldi Cambrensis Opera*, vi, p. 111). The reference seems appropriate to the Mountain as a whole, rather than one of its upland peaks.

Gloitguin is the Old Welsh form of Middle Welsh *Clydwyn*.[233] Clydwyn is the earliest likely historical figure (apart from Maximus) to feature in the line. An early record describes him as 'Clydwyn, son of Brychan, who conquered the whole region of South Wales'.[234] Whatever the nature of this otherwise unrecorded event, the implication is that he was was regarded as a founder of the dynasty. Several pedigrees in the Harleian MS begin with a brief prefatory historical notice, and this is what we appear to have here in garbled form.

Assuming the names contained in this notice to be those of successive rulers of Dyfed, the genealogist converted them into generations by interposing a succession of '*maps*' ('son of'). In view of indications that the historical Maximus established a number of federate rulers on the western fringes of Britain, before his departure for the Continent in AD 385, the original notice may conjecturally be read as follows:

Gloitguin [*rex*] *Nimet* [*in*] *Dimet* [*quem*] *Maxim Guletic* [*fecit*] *Protector*:
Clydwyn, king of the Sanctuary in (or of) Dyfed, whom Maximus the *Gwledig* made Protector.

As noted earlier, *protector* was a senior Roman military rank, whose duties could include responsibility for administering a frontier region.

On this assumption, Clydwyn may be envisaged as having established his rule with a characteristic double claim to legitimacy: inauguration at the traditional royal sanctuary of Dyfed, combined with authority granted by the Roman ruler of Britain. Similarly, the inscription on the pillar of Eliseg claimed descent for the kings of Powys, both from the native British king Vortigern and 'king' Maximus.

Given the early claim of the kings of Dyfed to descend from Maximus, it may be surmised that the sacred precinct (*nimet*) of Dyfed (*Dimet*), associated with Maxen in their royal pedigree, was one and the same with the Throne of Maxen (*Cadeir Faxen*). Was this also the assembly-place on *Presseleu*, where Pwyll Prince of Dyfed convened with his nobles to ensure the generation and perpetuation of the royal house, of which he was similarly the legendary founder?[235]

There exists another possible early allusion to the royal sanctuary of Dyfed. The poem *Trawsganu Cynan Garwyn* in the Book of Taliesin extols an historical sixth-century king of Powys in characteristically hyperbolical terms. Scholars are divided as to whether it represents a genuine sixth-century effusion (possibly by the poet Taliesin), or a later (tenth-century?) propaganda piece couched in imitation of such a work.[236] The argument is broadly grounded in

---

233 Jackson, *Language and History in Early Britain*, p. 388.

234 *Clytguin. filius Brachan . qui inuasit totam terram Sudgwalliæ* (A. W. Wade-Evans, 'The Brychan Documents', *Y Cymmrodor* (1906), xix, p. 25); *Clytwyn* alias Clitguin *oresgynnaud deheubarth*, 'the conqueror of Deheubarth' (p. 29).

235 In the ancient Near East, establishment of a sanctuary 'can be considered an essential element of kingship' (Joachim Becker, *Messianic Expectation in the Old Testament* (Philadelphia, 1980), p. 19); cf. pp. 22–23.

236 Sir John Morris-Jones, 'Taliesin', *Y Cymmrodor* (1918), xxviii, pp. 133–34, 199–202; I. LL. Foster and Glyn Daniel (ed.), *Prehistoric and Early Wales* (London, 1965), pp. 228–30; Sir Ifor Williams and J. E. Caerwyn Williams (ed.), *The Poems of Taliesin* (Dublin, 1968), pp. xxviii–xxxv; 16–28; Jenny Rowland, *Early Welsh Saga Poetry: A Study and Edition of the Englynion* (Cambridge, 1990), pp. 182–83; John T. Koch (ed.), *The Gododdin of Aneirin: Text and Context from Dark-Age North Britain* (Cardiff, 1997), p. lxxxvii; Graham R. Isaac, '*Trawsganu Kynan Garwyn mab Brochuael*: a Tenth-Century Political Poem', *Zeitschrift für celtische Philologie* (Tübingen, 1999), li, pp. 173–85. I have suggested fresh reasons for

historical considerations, but fortunately the dating is only tangentially relevant to the present issue.

Cataloguing Cynan's victories over his neighbours, the poet refers to a triumph in Dyfed: 'A battle at the Hill of Dyfed (*kat yg cruc dymet*). Aergol breaking into a run.'

Since Aergol was an historical king of Dyfed who lived a generation before Cynan, it has been suggested, either that the allusion is to 'the descendants of Aergol', or that Aergol 'was unable to rest in his grave because the men of Powys were defeating the men of Dyfed, his land, and that in Dyfed itself'. However, association of an ancestral Aergol's distress over a foreign victory at the Hill of Dyfed suggests an alternative explanation. Welsh *crug* may mean 'hillock, tumulus, cairn', but its appearance in West Country place names as synonymous with 'hill', together with literary allusions, indicates that it might bear application to larger eminences.[237]

Now, the 'Hill of Dyfed' would make little sense were it applicable to any eminence in the country. It must surely have signified '*the* Hill of Dyfed', i.e. Preseli Mountain (*Mynydd Presseli*), the sole eminence of note in the kingdom. This may also explain the allusion to an earlier king of Dyfed, rather than a contemporary of Cynan of Powys. Aergol was remembered as 'a good king' by Gildas, who wrote a generation after his day. This, and the fact that *Aircol* is the Old Welsh rendering of Latin *Agricola*, suggests that he was among those early dynasts who founded their realms in the immediate post-Roman period.[238]

It would be easy to understand the allusion to the dead Aergol's imagined distress at the arrival of an enemy host on Preseli Mountain, were it the sacred site where successive kings of Dyfed were inaugurated, and which (as the purpose of the royal assemblage on *Presseleu* in *Pwyll Pendeuic Dyuet* indicates) was imbued with *mana* ensuring the continuity of their dynasty.[239]

Finally, it may be remarked that infliction of a sacreligious assault on a sacred spot conferring royal potency on the kings of Dyfed would be in keeping with Celtic practice. Thus, the sacred

---

inferring a sixth-century original of the poem (Nikolai Tolstoy, 'Cadell and the Cadelling', *Studia Celtica* (Cardiff, 2012), xlvi, pp. 81–83). This argument has been reinforced by John T. Koch, *Cunedda, Cynan, Cadwallon, Cynddylan: Four Welsh Poems and Britain 383–655* (Aberystwyth, 2013), pp. 105–51, T. M. Charles-Edwards, *Wales and the Britons 350–1064* (Oxford, 2013), p. 16, and Patrick Sims-Williams, 'Powys and Early Welsh Poetry', *Cambrian Medieval Celtic Studies* (Aberystwyth, 2014), lxvii, pp. 38–41).

237   J. E. B. Gover, Allen Mawer, and F. M. Stenton, *The Place-Names of Devon* (Cambridge, 1931–32), p. 638; A. H. Smith, *The Place-Names of Gloucestershire* (Cambridge, 1964–65), ii, pp. 115–16; A. D. Mills, *The Place-Names of Dorset* (Cambridge, 1977–), ii, pp. 268, 275; J. Lloyd-Jones, *Geirfa Barddoniaeth Gynnar Gymraeg* (Cardiff, 1931–63), p. 180. The Irish cognate *crúach* signifies equally 'hill' or 'mountain' (Quin et al. (ed.), *Dictionary of the Irish Language*, 'C', col. 554).

238   'Evidently his family was Romanised enough to adopt Roman names, like so many of their British neighbours and some of the Irish' (Jackson, *Language and History in Early Britain*, p. 170). Aergol's epithet *llawhir*, 'of the long hand' (J. Gwenogvryn Evans and John Rhŷs (ed.), *The Text of the Book of Llan Dâv Reproduced from the Gwysaney Manuscript* (Oxford, 1893), p. 125; Gwenogvryn Evans (ed.), *The Poetry in the Red Book of Hergest*, col. 1384, 24), suggests a ruler who expanded his territory. The Stanzas of the Graves declare that 'the grave of Aergol is in Dyfed' (A.O.H. Jarman (ed.), *Llyfr Du Caerfyrddin gyda Rhagymadrodd Nodiadau Testunol a Geirfa* (Cardiff, 1982), p. 44). Was it needless to specify the site more precisely, because it was so well-known?

239   A comparable instance of symbolic desecration of an enemy kingdom's centre (it being identified with the kingdom as a whole) is recorded in the Irish annals. In 770 Donnchadh mac Domnall of the Uí Néill defeated the men of Leinster in battle, after which he and his army 'remained for three days in Ráith Alinne and burnt all the borderlands of the Leinstermen with fire'. Ráith Alinne (Knockaulin in County Kildare) 'was identified … with the kingdom of Leinster, in the same way that other Iron-Age sites were identified with powerful kingdoms' (T. M. Charles-Edwards (tr.), *The Chronicle of Ireland* (Liverpool, 2006), i, p. 237).

trees (*bile*) of rival realms were regularly destroyed by victorious Irish kings.[240] In the words of Proinsias Mac Cana, such actions 'had the obvious aim of slighting the royal prestige of dangerous opponents through violating certain of its traditional attributes'.[241] In 988 Brian Boru marched his army into Meath and temporarily occupied Uisneach.[242] Since the site was of no conceivable strategic value, the move was clearly intended as a symbolic challenge to Mael Sechnaill's high kingship of Ireland.

The Pillar at the Centre of the Earth

The archaic core of *Breuddwyd Maxen* comprises a legendary dramatization of the British myth of kingship, focussed on the Sacred Centre of the island. The antiquity of the tradition is unsurprising, given the centrality of the monarchical institution to Celtic society. Professedly Christian kings in Gildas's day observed pre-Christian traditions which shocked churchmen like himself, but remained too deeply grounded in national consciousness for their proscription to be effective.

It was probably on authentic historical grounds that Maximus was regarded in early genealogical tradition as having established the royal dynasty of Dyfed, while his restricted connexion with Gwynedd almost certainly originated exclusively with *Breuddwyd Maxen*. It has been seen that the account in that romance of his ascent of a lofty peak in the impressive Preseli range[243] replicates his prior ascents of the Alpine and Snowdonian heights, both being described as reaching to the sky. The comment that the mountain summit had become known as the throne of Maxen (*cadeir Vaxen*), an appellation implicitly antedating composition of *Breuddwyd Maxen*, suggests that it was in fact the original location of Maxen's encounter with the Maiden Sovereignty. Its abrupt and gratuitous appearance in the narrative, together with characteristic accompanying motifs of the introductory hunt and the mountaintop tent in which Maxen sleeps, combine to confirm this conclusion. Moreover, there can be little doubt that the Gwynedd setting of the story represents a secondary stage in the tradition, arising from the author's decision to recast it in a Romano-British historical context, focussed on the impressive remains of the Roman fortress at Caernarvon.

At the same time, the story intimates that Gwynedd possessed its own Sacred Centre. Each of the major kingdoms of Ireland possessed such a Centre:

> The provincial capitals of Ireland had many features in common with those of the centre. Almost without exception they stood on hills, or at least on artificial mounds. They were burial places, a feature which they share with churches, rather than with the palaces, of

---

240 Mac Cana, *The Cult of the Sacred Centre*, pp. 77–79. The Tree of Tortu and Yew of Ross sprouted in the night that Conn, the primal king of Ireland, was born (Kenneth Jackson (ed.), *Cath Maighe Léna* (Dublin, 1938), p. 51).

241 In 980 the kingdom of Dal-Cais was plundered by Maelsechlainn, who then felled the tree of Magh Adhair, whose successor was wrecked in 1049 by Aedh Ua Conchobhair (William M. Hennessy (ed.), *Chronicum Scotorum: A Chronicle of Irish Affairs, from the Earliest Times to A.D. 1135* (London, 1866), pp. 228, 278; David Comyn and Rev. Patrick S. Dinneen (ed.), *The History of Ireland by Geoffrey Keating, D.D.* (London, 1902–14), iii, p. 246. Cf. Maigréad Ni C. Dobbs, 'Nínine Écess', *Études Celtiques* (Paris, 1949), v, p. 151; Proinsias Mac Cana, 'Aspects of the Theme of King and Goddess in Irish Literature', ibid. (1958), viii, p. 63.

242 Seán Mac Airt (ed.), *The Annals of Inisfallen (MS. Rawlinson B. 503)* (Dublin, 1951), p. 166.

243 'This hill is seene from farre, especiallie from the East partes of the Countery and serveth as a marke to guide the waie to strangers that have occcasion to theis partes' (Owen (ed.), *The Description of Pembrokeshire*, i, p. 106).

Dinas Emrys from the mountain slope above. (Courtesy Flickr Rory Francis)

our own time. Like churches, too, they were dedicated to the memory of founders, who were in most cases believed to be buried in them.[244]

Cyfranc Lludd a Lleuelys describes how the euhemerized divinities Lludd and Lleuelys established the Centre of Britain by means of transverse measurements of the island of Britain. In the story the spot has become identified with the late-Saxon town of Oxford, which however must have replaced the original site in Southern Britain, which was by then evidently forgotten. On his brother's advice, Lludd transferred the talismanic 'dragons' discovered there for safety 'to the strongest place' (*yn y lle kadarnhaf*) in the kingdom. Lludd accordingly buried them in a *kist vaen* (stone chest) 'in the safest place' (*yn y lle diogelaf*) he could find. This proved to be in Snowdonia (*yn Eryri*). 'After that', the storyteller noted, 'the place was called *Dinas Emreis*.'[245]

No reason is given for adoption of the name Dinas Emrys, which suggests that it was that by which the site was already known. The belief that the dragons contained in a stone at the site had been transferred thither from the exact centre of Britain, as recounted in *Cyfranc Lludd a Lleuelys*, was most likely due to awareness of characteristic parallel legends attached to each *omphalos*.

After describing Maxen's marriage with the beautiful Maiden Sovereignty in her Otherworld palace at *Aber Seint*, *Breuddwyd Maxen* explains that Elen requested the following as her maiden fee (*agweddi*): 'three principal castles to be built for her in three places of her choice in the island of Britain. And she chose that the highest castle be built for her in Arfon.'[246]

---

244 Rees and Rees, *Celtic Heritage*, pp. 166–67.

245 Brynley F. Roberts (ed.), *Cyfranc Lludd a Llefelys* (Dublin, 1975), pp. 4, 5.

246 *A gwneithur teir prif gaer idi hitheu en e tri lle a dewissei en enys Brydein. Ac ena y dewissaud wneuthur e gaer uchaf en Arvon idi* (Roberts (ed.), *Breuddwyd Maxen*, p. 8).

The expression used to describe the chief castle built by Elen is *e caer uchaf yn Arvon*. *Uchaf* means either 'highest', or 'best, greatest, chief'.[247] The context clearly indicates the former sense, since the castle at Aber Seint (Caernarfon) where Maxen first encountered her is described as 'a mighty castle, the fairest that anyone had ever seen' (*a welei prifgaer decaf o'r a welsei den eryoet*), i.e. 'the best'.[248] So superlative an appearance could scarcely be surpassed by another, nor would there have been much point in attempting the feat. It may also be questioned why Elen required another castle, when she already dwelt in a glittering palace of such unparalleled splendour.

Again, *uchaf* as a place name element almost invariably denotes 'higher, highest, above'. The expression 'the *highest* (or 'best') stronghold in Arfon' (*y caer uchaf yn Arvon*) recalls the setting of Dinas Emrys in *Cyfranc Lludd a Lleuelys*, which is described as 'the *strongest* place' (*y lle kadarnhaf*) and 'the *securest* place' (*y lle diogelaf*) 'in your kingdom' (*y'th gyfoeth*), i.e. Britain.[249] We may compare the selection by Vortigern's druids of a suitable spot on which to erect a citadel where he might find safety. The fortress subsequently known as Dinas Emrys is described as 'a place which would be *securest* from barbarian foes for all time' (*quia tutissima a barbaris gentibus in aeternum erit*).[250] These repeated superlatives suggest that scholars, who on discrete grounds identified 'the highest fort in Arfon' with Dinas Emrys, were probably right.[251]

The striking setting of Dinas Emrys in Nant Gwynant makes it singularly apt to the description *y caer uchaf yn Arvon*. In the early nineteenth century, Sir Richard Colt Hoare was struck by the fact that 'no situation could have been found better calculated for retirement or defence, as it fills up nearly the whole valley, and the steepness of its sides renders it very difficult of access'.[252]

The palace where Maxen first found his lovely Elen in the story is clearly to be identified with the impressive remains of the Roman fortress at Segontium. That only its ruins remained at the time of writing made its former status as a faery castle the more credible. If my tenth-century dating of *Breuddwyd Maxen* be accepted, it was at the time the sole fortress in the vicinity, in which case Elen's 'new' stronghold must be looked for elsewhere. Preferring a later date of composition, Brynley Roberts suggested that the subsequent erection of a Norman *castellum* close to the site led the author to make 'the change in name [from *Caer Aber Seint*] to Caernarfon, from a simple location marker to a reflection of status'.[253] But the story implies that the new *caer* was at least as grand as the bejewelled golden palace at *Aber Seint*, where Maxen

---

247 *Geiriadur Prifysgol Cymru*, p. 3692.

248 Roberts (ed.), *Breuddwyd Maxen*, p. 78.

249 *Y caer uchaf* corresponds semantically to the Celtic toponym **Ouksamā*, 'the highest (or very high) place' (cf. Juan Luis García Alonso, 'Celtic and Pre-Celtic Indo-European Place-Names in the Territory of the Arevaci as defined by Ptolemy', in Ronald Black, William Gillies, Roibeard Ó Maolalaigh, and D. W. Harding (ed.), *Celtic Connections: Proceedings of the 10th International Congress of Celtic Studies* (Phantassie, East Linton, 1999–2005), ii, pp. 91–92; Peter Anreiter and Ulrike Roider, 'Quelques noms de lieux d'origine celtique dans les Alpes orientales (particulièrement en Autriche)', in Pierre-Yves Lambert and Georges-Jean Pinault (ed.), *Gaulois et celtique continental* (Geneva, 2007), pp. 116–17). *Uxama* (Osma) in Spain is associated in an inscription with the family of the god Lug (José Vives (ed.), *Inscripciones Latinas de la España Romana* (Barcelona, 1971), p. 98). Cf. Gruffydd, *Math vab Mathonwy*, pp. 237–38.

250 Roberts (ed.), *Cyfranc Lludd a Llefelys*, pp. 4, 5; Mommsen (ed.), *Chronica Minora*, iii, pp. 181–82.

251 Rhys, *Lectures on the Origin and Growth of Religion as Illustrated by Celtic Heathendom*, p. 161; Williams (ed.), *Breuddwyd Maxen*, p. 25.

252 Sir Richard Colt Hoare (tr.), *The Itinerary of Archbishop Baldwin through Wales, A.D. MCLXXXVIII. By Giraldus de Barri* (London, 1806), p. 126. Wendy Davies notes similarly that 'this rocky outcrop dominates both the valley and all passage through it' (*Wales in the Early Middle Ages* (Leicester, 1982), p. 24).

253 Roberts (ed.), *Breuddwyd Maxen*, pp. lxxvii–ix, 40–42.

had discovered Elen. A modest Norman motte-and-bailey – one, moreover, whose recent origin must have been familiar to all – was decidedly inappropriate for the centuries-old majestic former residence of a Roman empress.

What I suggest happened is something on the follow lines. At a late stage in the evolution of the story of *Breuddwyd Maxen* (I have argued for its original composition in the tenth century, but that need not be significant here), a *cyfarwydd* adapted a native version of the sovereignty legend into a romantic history of the popular figure of Magnus Maximus (*Maxen Gwledig*). His reading of the *Historia Brittonum* led him to assume that Maxen arrived from Rome, in consequence of which the original tale became enshrined in the framework of Romano-British history. This in turn led to identification of an originally Otherworld palace with the celebrated ruins of the Roman fortress of Segontium (*Cair Segeint*) in North Wales. As the original tale (or tales) was probably fairly widely known, its integration into a Roman setting could not escape some duplication. Elen's 'highest castle … in Arfon' was absorbed into the narrative by making it her 'second home' (the first in the history of Wales?). The indications are that by this was intended Dinas Emrys.

The wording of the *Historia Brittonum* envisages Dinas Emrys as located *on* a mountain. Since the rocky outcrop on which it stands lies at the base of Snowdon, it is presumably that mountain to which reference is made. Both this, and the allusion to the mountain climbed by Maxen as he came to Aber Saint, suggest that in mythical terms the deity whose name had come to be supplanted by that of Maxen was envisaged as enthroned on the peak of Snowdon, while his temple lay at its base, i.e. Dinas Emrys. In the same way,

> Among the Canaanites, the high god was thought to dwell in a temple or tent on the holy mountain. The earthly temple of the deity [below] was considered a copy of the heavenly temple on the mountain.[254]

The temple at Jerusalem was in early times identified with Mount Zaphon, the highest mountain in Syria. In Ugaritic mythology, the latter was 'believed to be a world-mountain, reaching up to the height of heaven, so that Baal's domain was really cosmic in extent'.[255]

The Maxen of *Breuddwyd Maxen* must originally have been a divinity, whose wedding to the terrestrial sovereignty figure constitutes a typical sacred marriage, *hieros gamos*. The otherwise inexplicable detail of his diverging from his way to ascend the summit of Snowdon, before his appearance in the glorious palace where he weds the Maiden Sovereignty, suggests a god descending from his mountaintop throne to his temple below.

In early cosmologies there existed a close association, amounting essentially to identification, between the mountain residence of the deity and his temple beneath. As Eliade explained,

254 Clifford, *The Cosmic Mountain in Canaan and the Old Testament*, p. 177; cf. pp. 177–78; Mark S. Smith, *The Origins of Biblical Monotheism: Israel's Polytheistic Background and the Ugaritic Texts* (Oxford, 2001), pp. 169–70. Cf. Eric Burrows, 'Some Cosmological Patterns in Babylonian Religion, in S. H. Hooke (ed.), *The Labyrinth: Further Studies in the Relation between Myth and Ritual in the Ancient World* (London, 1935), pp. 53–55. Again, comparison may be made with the dispute over the relative holiness of Mount Gerizim and the Temple Mount in Jerusalem (Isaac Kalimi, 'Zion or Gerizim? The Asssociation of Abraham and the *Aqeda* with Zion/Gerizim in Jewish and Samaritan Sources', in Meir Lubetski, Claire Gottlieb, and Sharon Keller (ed.), *Boundaries of the Ancient Near Eastern World: A Tribute to Cyrus H. Gordon* (Sheffield, 1998), pp. 442–57).

255 R. E. Clements, *God and Temple* (Oxford, 1965), pp, 4–9, 72; Clifford, *The Cosmic Mountain in Canaan and the Old Testament*, pp. 131–60. For the Norse concept of the cosmic mountain as support of heaven, cf. Tolley, *Shamanism in Norse Myth and Magic* , i, pp. 293–94.

To take all the facts in a single broad view, one may say that the symbolism in question [i.e. that of the Centre] expresses itself in three connected and complementary things:

1. The 'sacred mountain' where heaven and earth meet, stands at the centre of the world;
2. Every residence or palace, and by extension, every sacred town and royal residence, is assimilated to a 'sacred mountain' and thus becomes a 'centre';
3. The temple or sacred city, in turn, as the place through which the Axis Mundi passes, is held to be a point of junction between heaven, earth and hell.[256]

Local tradition in Snowdonia associated a legendary son of Maxen with Dinas Emrys and the nearby valley of Nant Gwynant, while the poet Rhys Goch Eryri refers to the district around Dinas Emrys as 'the land of the son of Maxen' (*tir mab Macsen*).[257]

Drawing attention to the images of two eagles (*delw deu eryr*), which in *Breuddwyd Maxen* are described as ornamenting the Old Man's throne in Caer Seint, Brynley Roberts remarks that 'this detail may have been included to hint at the association of the dream-maiden's castle, as yet unlocated, with Eryri (Snowdonia), popularly derived from *eryr*, 'eagle'.[258] The Welsh name for Snowdon itself is Yr Wyddfa, from *gwyddfa*, 'throne': a term corresponding to *gorsedd*, in the context indicating the seat of a divinity.[259] It was believed that Arthur (implicitly in his rôle as demi-god) resided on the summit of a mountain in Brecon called *Cadeir Arthur*, 'Arthur's Throne'. The concept of an eagle perched on a mountaintop throne is further suggested by Giraldus's account of a fabulous eagle, which was believed every fifth year to prognosticate war from the topmost peak of Snowdon.[260]

It was probably the author of *Breuddwyd Maxen* who identified the Otherworld palace inhabited by Elen and her father with the stately ruins of Segontium. Equally, indications are that the Otherworld palace was originally located on the cloud-mantled peak of Snowdon. If so, the palace where Maxen encountered Elen, and 'the highest fort built for her in Arfon', were originally one and the same.

---

256 Mircea Eliade, *Patterns in Comparative Religion* (London, 1958), p. 375. Ascription of celestial counterparts to terrestrial sanctuaries is further discussed by Eliade in his *Le mythe de l'éternel retour: Archétypes et répétition* (Paris, 1949), pp. 21–29.

257 T. Gwynn Jones, *Welsh Folklore and Folk-Custom* (London, 1930), p. 80; Henry Lewis, Thomas Roberts, and Ifor Williams (ed.), *Cywyddau Iolo Goch ac Eraill* (Cardiff, 1937), p. 172; Bromwich (ed.), *Trioedd Ynys Prydein*, pp. 478–79, 560.

258 Roberts (ed.), *Breuddwyd Maxen*, p. 24. Cf. J. Lloyd-Jones, 'or, eryr, dygyfor, Eryri', *The Bulletin of the Board of Celtic Studies* (Cardiff, 1928), iv, pp. 140–41.

259 *Geiriadur Prifysgol Cymru*, p. 1755; Williams and Caerwyn Williams (ed.), *The Poems of Taliesin*, pp. 61–62. Several mountains in Greece were believed to be, or sustain, the throne of Zeus (Cook, *Zeus*, i, pp. 124–48). For the concept of mountain as seat of divinity in Semitic and Indo-European tradition, cf. Saul Levin, *Semitic and Indo-European: The Principal Etymologies with Observations on Afro-Asiatic* (Amsterdam and Philadelphia, 1995), pp. 143–45). In Japan, 'The deity we must therefore imagine as dwelling at the top of the mountain, to which at some previous time, lured by the inviting shapes of the conical summit and the trees, he has descended from an even higher point in the sky' (Blacker, *The Catalpa Bow*, pp. 80–81).

260 Brewer, Dimock, and Warner (ed.), *Giraldi Cambrensis Opera*, vi, pp. 36, 136. A subsequent king of Gwynedd, Maelgwn, is represented in legend as enthroned on a 'white throne of waxen wings' (*cadeyr wen o adanet cuyredyc*) (Morfydd E. Owen, 'Royal Propaganda Stories from the Law-Texts', in T. M. Charles-Edwards, Morfydd E. Owen, and Paul Russell (ed.), *The Welsh King and his Court* (Cardiff, 2000), p. 251). Eagles sent by Zeus were closely associated with the Greek *omphalos* at Delphi (Cook, *Zeus*, ii, pp. 179–87).

The transfer of mythological symbols of the *omphalos* from Oxford to Dinas Emrys is explained if the latter site be understood to have been the traditional Centre of Gwynedd. The connexion with the umbilical Centre is suggested by a further curious passage from *Breuddwyd Maxen*. After describing Elen's construction of 'the highest fort in Arfon', together with others at Carmarthen and Caerleon, the story continues:

> Elen decided to build great roads from each fort to the other across the Island of Britain. Because of that they are called *Ffyrdd Elen Luyddog* ('the Roads of Elen of the Hosts'), since she came from the Island of Britain, and the men of the Island of Britain would never have assembled those large armies for anyone but her.

The wording indicates that the forts in question are not just the three identified strongholds built by Elen in Wales, but those of Britain generally. Highways, revealed by a goddess, and stretching the length and breadth of the country, suggest the mythological paradigm of those eternal roads, whose axis is the *omphalos* of the land. Elen's rôle as creator of roads is paralleled in Ireland by the prophetic maiden Rothníam, who emerges from a fairy mound (*síd*) to reveal *inter alia* the five chief roads of Ireland (*coicc primroid Erenn*) radiating from Tara, which appeared that *Samain* night.[261]

The name of *Rothníam* (= 'wheel' + 'beauty, lustre') recalls that of the British goddess Arianrhod ('silver wheel'), mother of Lleu (Lug) in Welsh tradition. The 'wheel' in turn evokes the *omphalos* of the kingdom, with its roads radiating to the periphery. A relief on the Gundestrup Cauldron depicts the bust of a goddess flanked by two wheels.[262]

In another Irish mediæval tale, *Togail Bruidne Da Derga*, the number of roads meeting at Tara is given as four.[263] The variation may reflects a distinction between the Five Great Roads featuring in the physical landscape of early Ireland,[264] and the 'cosmological model used in *TBDD* [which] depicts the four roads radiating from Tara in four cardinal directions …'[265] Thus there existed a dual conception of the early Irish road system, which narrators were not always successful in reconciling.

It is likely that the name *Elen* in *Breuddwyd Maxen* has replaced (or been adapted from) that of a Celtic goddess. Sir John Rhŷs recorded a folklore tradition from the neighbourhood of Dinas Emrys, which told of three sisters who escaped the drowning of their city in Cardigan

261 Joseph Vendryes (ed.), *Airne Fíngein* (Dublin, 1953), pp. 9–11; R. I. Best, Osborn Bergin, M.A. O'Brien, and Anne O'Sullivan (ed.), *The Book of Leinster Formerly Lebar na Núachongbála* (Dublin, 1954–83), iii, pp. 672–75.

262 Flemming Kaul, *Gundestrupkedlen: Baggrund og billedverden* (Copenhagen, 1991), p. 25). Cf. Miranda Jane Green, *The Wheel as a Cult-Symbol in the Romano-Celtic World With Special Reference to Gaul and Britain* (Brussels, 1984), p. 172.

263 Eleanor Knott (ed.), *Togail Bruidne Da Derga* (Dublin, 1936), p. 5.

264 Colm O Lochlainn, 'Roadways in Ancient Ireland', in John Ryan (ed.), *Féilsgríbinn Eóin Mhic Néill* (Dublin, 1940), pp. 471–73. A section of what may have been the ancient road linking the Navel of Ireland at Uisneach to the provincial 'capital' of Connacht at Cruachain has been excavated near Corlea (Helmut Birkhan, *Kelten/Celts: Bilder ihrer Kultur/Images of their Culture* (Vienna, 1999), p. 285).

265 Grigory Bondarenko, 'Roads and Knowledge' in Togail Bruidne Da Derga', in Jacqueline Borsje, Ann Dooley, Séamus Mac Mathúna, and Gregory Toner (ed.), *Celtic Cosmology: Perspectives from Ireland and Scotland* (Toronto, 2014), p. 193.

Bay. He suggested that they were sisters of the goddess Arianrhod, whose stronghold stood on the coast. One of them was called *Elan*, whom he identified with Maxen's *Elen*.[266]

The association of Elen with roads evidently preceded composition of *Breuddwyd Maxen*. As Brynley Roberts emphasized, 'it was the inclusion of Sarn Elen (Luyddawg) within this section that led to the name Elen (Luyddawg) being given to Maxen's wife almost as an afterthought'.[267]

The explanation of the construction of roads, which serves scant narrative purpose, suggests that the author was unaware how the roads came to be associated with Elen, nor what was the significance of her epithet.

> Elen decided to build great roads from each town (*caer*) to the other across the Island of Britain. On account of that they are called the Roads of Elen of the Hosts, *since she came from the Island of Britain, and the men of the Island of Britain would never have assembled those large armies for anyone but her.*

The italicized passage appears disconnected, providing no rational explanation of Elen's sobriquet, and may be set aside as a confused exegetical gloss. Evidently the author had no idea why the princess was known as *lluydog*, and consequently ventured this lame attempt at an explanation.[268] Given that nothing in the tale suggests that Elen commanded armies, could it be that her epithet was originally *llwyddog*, 'prosperous', 'conferring prosperity'? She was after all originally the sovereignty goddess, one of whose salient characteristics was abundance of wealth, combined with lavish munificence.[269]

The strong likelihood is that Maxen is likely to have been originally a Brittonic divinity, for whose name that of the exemplary Roman ruler came to be substituted. Opinions may differ as to the identity of the putative god, but his arrival as vigorous 'rescuer' of the Monarchy of Britain during the otiose reign of 'Eudaf' suggests that he was Lleu (Lug), who in similar circumstances came to the aid of the passive Lludd. The latter's 'measuring' of Britain in *Cyfranc Lludd a Lleuelys* from each cardinal point to establish its Centre corresponds to the discovery of the four great roads of Ireland focussed on the Sacred Centre at Uisneach.

This interpretation accords with the mythopœic paradigm. The god (Lludd/Núadu) is the paternal deity, 'immobile mover', 'inactive but instigating'.

> The [otiose] god does not shift in person, but he is the centre from which all derives, and to which all returns.[270]

With the arrival of the dynamic young hero Lleu/Lug, the rule of the king comes into active effect over his people. *Breuddwyd Maxen Gwledig* provides a classic example of the ideology of

---

266 John Rhŷs, *Celtic Folklore: Welsh and Manx* (Oxford, 1901), pp. 208–9. For the site of Caer Aranrhod, cf. F. J. North, *Sunken Cities: Some legends of the coast and lakes of Wales* (Cardiff, 1957), pp. 213–33.

267 Roberts (ed.), *Breudwyt Maxen Wledic*, p. lxi.

268 When Maxen besieges Rome, he is represented as accompanied by his wife Elen Luyddog, without any suggestion that she played a part in the command structure. Shortly after their arrival they are joined by a fresh host (*llu*) from Britain. Although it proves to be commanded by her brothers Cynan and Adeon, it is emphasized that its arrival was unanticipated by Elen (ibid., p. 9). Were she traditionally renowned as a leader of hosts, this episode would have provided opportunity for the author to provide a satisfactory explanation of her sobriquet.

269 O'Rahilly, *Early Irish History and Mythology*, p. 305.

270 *Celticvm XV*, pp. 372–73.

the dual kingship: Eudaf seated and silent beside the world pillar, creating men (*gwerin*), while the martial hero Maxen arrives (like Lleu) from across the sea (i.e. from the Otherworld), to extend Eudaf's rule from coast to coast across Britain. What more symbolic manifestation of this psychic outflow from the Centre could there be, than extension of roads from the hub of the island to its extremities? At the same time, Eudaf's baffling retention of legitimate authority over Britain confirms his continuing function as passive sustainer of the sovereignty.

These considerations combine to suggest that Elen's 'highest fort in Arfon' reflects *omphalos* ideology. Certainly, the towering height of Snowdon provides a fitting site for the mythic concept. As the sinologist Paul Wheatley observed: 'This feeling that an *omphalos* should be raised as near the heavens as possible seems to have been an almost universal concept in the traditional world.'[271] (Among the early Israelites, Mount Sinai was regarded as a cosmic mountain: 'the contact point between heaven and earth where the Torah came to earth.')[272]

Moving on, Elen's building of the 'highest' fortress is followed by this curious sentence:

> And soil from Rome was brought there, so that it would be healthier for the emperor to sleep and sit and walk around.

This reads like a motif retained, rather than invented, by the storyteller. Since there can be little doubt that the Roman setting of *Breuddwyd Maxen* was its author's artificial construction, it seems that we should look for the original source in a native British context.

The Roman setting of Maxen's Dream patently represents a secondary development, and it also appears that its original setting was the height of Y Freni Fawr on Preseli Mountain in Dyfed. Accordingly, it was presumably from there that, in an earlier version, soil was carried to 'the highest fortress'. This is precisely what might be expected, were it at one time believed that the Gwynedd *omphalos* (whether Snowdon or Dinas Emrys) was ideologically linked to its Dyfed counterpart on Preseli Mountain. In the same way, *Cyfranc Lludd a Lleuelys* provides a story designed to account for the fact that mythical themes attached to the national Omphalos of Britain (erroneously relocated at Oxford) correspond to those associated with Dinas Emrys in Gwynedd.

The passage accords with the belief that provincial *omphaloi* are symbiotically linked to the central *omphalos* of the entire realm. The link may be established by transportation of earth, or other symbolically appropriate material, from one to the other. To quote Paul Wheatley again:

> This central axis of the universe, of the kingdom, the city, or the temple could be moved to a more propitious site or duplicated whenever circumstances rendered this desirable, for it was an attribute of existential rather than of geometrical space.

Conquered holy places might be symbolically removed to the victor's Centre. Thus,

> At his investiture a [Chinese] noble carried a clod of earth from that side of the sacred altar facing the direction in which his benefice lay to the capital of his territory, where it formed the nucleus of his own altar to the God of the Soil.[273]

---

271 Wheatley, *The Pivot of the Four Quarters*, p. 429.

272 Donaldson, *Jesus on the Mountain*, pp. 31–35, 72–73; Frank Moore Cross, *Canaanite Myth and Hebrew Epic: Essays in the History of the Religion of Israel* (Cambridge, Mass., 1973), pp. 163–69.

273 Wheatley, *The Pivot of the Four Quarters*, pp. 417–18, 431–32, 435.

That this widely attested belief existed also in the British Isles is suggested by a curious account of the 'heart of Fál' springing out of the Stone of Destiny at Tara and depositing itself at the alternative cult site of Tailtiu. John Carey questions whether this may not reflect the transfer of part of the stone in order to establish the ritual transfer of power from the sanctuary of Tara to Tailtiu.[274]

It seems that folk custom retained a lingering reflexion of the concept. As Marie Trevelyan (Emma Mary Thomas) learned at the end of the nineteenth century,

> It was formerly customary with farmers, upon changing farms, to take some earth from the place they were leaving to the new home. This earth was strewn here and there among the gardens, orchards, and lands 'for luck'.[275]

The custom doubtless derived from a belief that spiritual continuity was assured by a symbolic transfer of the old farm to the new. The same concept, this time on a macrocosmic scale, explains a Pictish legend associated with their Sacred Centre at the Moot Hill beside Scone, which 'relates, that the hill in question was called *omnis terra*, being composed of earth brought here by gentlemen out of every country they had travelled in'.[276]

On the presumption that Y Freni Fawr was the original setting for Maxen's dream, it will have been from there that an earlier version of the tale described its soil as being transported to 'the highest point' in Arfon. The purpose was to convey a form of *mana* from the Sacred Centre of Dyfed to that of Gwynedd. In historical terms, such a transfer could well have represented a symbolic accompaniment to Hywel Dda of Dyfed's annexation of Gwynedd.

This analysis of the romance of *Breuddwyd Maxen* posits two basic conclusions. First, Maxen's encounter with the Maiden Sovereignty was originally located on Y Freni Fawr, the principal height of Preseli Mountain. It is also on Preseli that the story of *Pwyll Pendeuic Dyuet* locates the Dyfed ruler's assemblage, convened there to ensure perpetuation of the national

---

274 'Tara and the Supernatural', in Edel Bhreatnach (ed.), *The Kingship and Landscape of Tara* (Dublin, 2005), pp. 39–40.

275 Marie Trevelyan, *Folk-Lore and Folk-Stories of Wales* (London, 1909), p. 43. Similar beliefs, establishing a connexion between the old house and the new, were known in the Irish countryside (Seán Ó Súilleabháin, *A Handbook of Irish Folklore* (Wexford, 1942), p. 15). Thorolfr Mostrarskegg brought earth from Thor's temple at his home in Norway to his new settlement in Iceland (Forrest S. Scott (ed.), *Eyrbyggja Saga: The Vellum Tradition* (Copenhagen, 2003), pp. 10–11). Fijian islanders constructed mounds on which they built their temples, which were considered centres of tribal existence. When obliged to shift in consequence of endemic warfare, 'they carried away some of the sacred soil with them to their new home, where they used it to build up a new mound, or rather "to shape it" as they expressed it' (A. M. Hocart, *Kingship* (Oxford, 1927), p. 183; cf. pp. 183–86). When King Makoko placed his country in the Congo region under protection of the French, 'The treaty was ratified on a day appointed, in the presence of all the vassal chiefs of Makoko. On its completion the grand fetish master put a little earth in a box and presented it to M. de Brazza, saying, "Take this earth and carry it to the great chief of the whites. It will remind him that we belong to him."' (Mary H. Kingsley, *Travels in West Africa: Congo Français, Corisco and Cameroons* (London, 1897), p. 360). Among some Siberian peoples, 'the eldest son, when setting out for a long journey somewhere, took ashes and embers from the family hearth. He did the same also when after wedding he left his parents to move into a tent of his own' (V. A. Tugolukov, 'Some Aspects of the Beliefs of the Tungus (Evenki and Evens)', in V. Diószegi and M. Hoppál (ed.), *Shamanism in Siberia* (Budapest, 1978), p. 419). Again, 'When the historic [Maori] canoes landed in New Zealand, the new arrivals deposited their sacred stones (*kura*, or *mauri-kohatu*) in the forests to preserve the *hau* of the birding-grounds, that is their power of productiveness' (James Cowan, *The Maori: Yesterday and To-day* (Auckland, 1930), p. 59). With these rites may be compared the folk belief that a man standing on earth brought from his country of origin is considered as being still there (Thompson, *Motif-Index of Folk-Literature*, iv, p. 80 = J1161.3).

276 Thomas Pennant, *A Tour in Scotland and Voyage to the Hebrides. MDCCLXXII. Part II.* (London, 1776), p. 115.

dynasty. Maxen's visit to Elen was conducted with the same purpose: his wedding to the Maiden Sovereignty legitimated his succession to the kingship, and assured his function as progenitor of the British royal line. Although the latter factor is not asserted in the romance, it may be considered implicit in view of his rôle in early royal genealogies as founder of royal lines: in particular, that of Dyfed, the great kingdom dominated by Preseli Mountain.

Likewise, it was from Preseli that the famous bluestones were transported, with immense labour, to be re-erected at the site of Stonehenge. The likeliest explanation of that astounding operation was that a powerful Bronze Age ruler of the 'Wessex' region was concerned to absorb the *mana* of the Demetian Navel into that of Southern (or conceivably all) Britain. This transfer reflects at a spectacular level the same ideological motive as that inherent in bearing earth from 'Rome' (for which read Y Freni Fawr) to the Sacred Centre of Gwynedd.

Breuddwyd Maxen Gwledig contains suggestive details of the mythology of the *omphalos*. While cast in the form of a romance, the motifs of the marriage of the king to the Maiden Sovereignty, the otiose deity (the Old Man) beside the World Pillar, the ritual game of *gwyddbwyll* – all culminating in the accession of a dynamic new king – represent significant themes from pagan ideology. The mediæval romance preserves hints of archaic rituals, which comparative evidence suggests are likely to have been enacted by British kings in very early times.

Lastly may be considered independent evidence, which strikingly confirms that the account of Maxen's encounter in *Breuddwyd Maxen* with the Maiden Sovereignty at the Centre reflects archaic myth, which (as as has been shown) the author adapted to his 'history' of Maximus the Roman Emperor.

The Breton Life of Saint Iudicael was composed in the early decades of the eleventh century. The extant text is Latin, but there are indications that it derives from an earlier version written, in part or whole, in Breton. While clearly independent of *Breuddwyd Maxen*, it includes elements closely echoing the central motifs of Maxen's reception in the mountain palace.

> One night, Iudael, a most noble king, then yet of but youthful years, weary after hunting, slept … In a dream he saw a most lofty mountain standing in the midst of his realm of Brittany, i.e. at its navel, which was difficult to reach by way of a stony track. And there, at the summit of that mountain (*in cacumine montus ipsius*), he saw himself seated in an ivory chair. And within his view there was a wondrous huge post in the form of a round column, secured by its roots in the ground, its mighty branches reaching the sky, and its straight shaft reaching from the earth up to the heavens. [A lengthy passage follows, extolling the gilded glories of the pillar] …
>
> And just then, he saw next to him the daughter of his subject Ausoc. She was named Pritell, a lovely girl,[277] as yet unknown by man [i.e. she was a virgin]. Turning to look at her, he said, 'Girl, what are you doing here?'
>
> She answered him: 'My king Iudael, in some manner it has been fore-ordained by our Maker that you and I should come to this place, and that the custody of this ornamental pillar should be handed on for a time from no man in the world but yourself to no woman but myself, and that after that it be passed on from no woman but myself to no man but yourself'.

---

277 Andrew Breeze suggests to me that 'Breton Pritella would presumably mean 'she who is small and beautiful, well-shaped little one', on the basis of Welsh pryd, 'shape'', and that it 'is better described as a latinization of OB rather than OB pure'. Cf. his 'Two Ancient Names: *Britanni* and *Londinium*', *Eos: Commentarii Societatis Philologae Polonorum* (Warsaw, 2014), ci, pp. 313–14.

And after these words were said, the heavens closed. And in the morning, Iudael awoke from his dream and rose.

Marvelling at his vision, Iudael sent a messenger to the celebrated seer *Taliosinus* (the Welsh bard Taliesin), who expounded the dream as follows:

'The dream that I hear is marvellous, and it signifies and proclaims a wonder. It concerns your good and noble lord Iudael as he sits and reigns in his kingdom. And from the daughter of Ausoc he will have a better and far more capable son to reign on earth and in heaven, from whom, by God's gift, will descend the strongest sons of the entire race of the Bretons: from these men will arise royal counts and heavenly priests ...'

The prophecy is fulfilled. King Iudael weds the virgin beauty of his dream, who in due course gives birth to the exemplary St Iudicael. A verse celebrates the wonderful fertility and wealth of the land of Brittany, which are implicitly consequences of the conception.

As John Koch comments,

Readers of early Celtic prose tales will recognize in the foregoing elements of a dynastic foundation legend or the so-called 'Celtic sovereignty myth', involving a *hieros gamos* or 'sacred marriage', in which the king is joined with a woman who symbolizes his land.[278]

Close parallels with *Breuddwyd Maxen Gwledig* are plainly recognizable. At the same time, it is evident that neither account derives from the other, but rather from a common theme grounded in early Brittonic tradition, either originating from the time of the Breton settlements in the fifth or sixth century AD, or the Old Breton period (ninth to eleventh century).[279] The Roman framework of *Breuddwyd Maxen* is entirely missing from the tale in the Breton Saint's Life, providing further confirmation that this element represents authorial invention – the charismatic Roman Emperor Maximus having been substituted for what was originally a divine or royal figure in autochthonous tradition.

The Breton version of the king's encounter with the Maiden Sovereignty follows the archaic paradigm more closely and explicitly than does the Welsh story of Maxen. Iudael, like Maxen, experiences his dream while resting after hunting. His encounter with the beautiful virgin takes place on top of a mountain, corresponding to Maxen's parallel meeting, which I have given reasons for being originally located on the Preseli Mountain Y Freni Fawr. This further confirms that it, and not Caer Seint (which lies almost at sea level), was the original setting of his experience.

Emphasis on the lofty mountain's 'standing in the middle of his realm of Brittany, i.e. at its navel' (*in medio sue regionis Britannie, id est, in umbilico*), fulfils the archaic requirement that

278 John T. Koch, '*De sancto Iudicaelo rege historia* and Its Implications for the Welsh Taliesin', in Nagy and Jones (ed.), *Heroic Poets and Poetic Heroes in Celtic Tradition*, pp. 248-52. Cf. Bernard Merdrignac, *Recherches sur l'hagiographie armoricaine du VIIème au XVème Siècle* (Saint-Malo, 1985–86), ii, pp. 38–40; Caroline Brett, 'Breton Latin Literature as Evidence for Literature in the Vernacular, A.D. 800–1300', in *Cambridge Medieval Celtic Studies* (Cambridge, 1989), xviii, pp. 17–18; Léon Fleuriot, *Les origines de la Bretagne: L'émigration* (Paris, 1980), p. 280.

279 Proinsias Mac Cana, *The Cult of the Sacred Centre: Essays on Celtic Ideology* (Dublin, 2011), pp. 161–71.

the king's wedding with the sovereignty take place at the *omphalos* of his kingdom. Iudael seats himself on an ivory chair found at the summit, recalling both the ivory throne of the old man in *Breuddwyd Maxen*, and the early identification of Y Freni Fawr as *cadeir Vaxen*, the Throne of Maxen.

The huge pillar, which in *Breuddwyd Maxen* receives only glancing mention, features in the Breton tale as an unmistakable World Pillar, sustaining the sky at the centre of the earth.[280] Again, the virgin is closely associated with the Pillar, which recalls *inter alia* the belief among peoples of northern Siberia that a shaman gains access to the *dunne mushun*, mistress of the clan land, by penetrating under the roots of the sacred clan-tree, in order to enter her enchanted dwelling.[281]

Finally, we learn that king Iudael's marriage to the maiden at the World Pillar will bring forth a line of mighty kings to rule over the land of the Bretons. (The perpetually virgin priestess (*Pythía*) of the Greek *omphalos* at Delphi was likewise reputed to be the bride of its presiding divinity Apollo).[282] Concomitantly, the country will experience rich harvests and fructify lavishly: both primary indications of true kingship.[283] The Life of Saint Iudicael illustrates and endorses the originally cosmic character of *Breuddwyd Maxen*.

Lleu and Maxen

In the first section of *Breuddwyd Maxen*, Maxen enacts the part of a divinity, whom he replaced when the originally mythical tale became contrivedly embedded within a framework derived from Nennius's version of Romano-British history. The god in question was probably Lleu, the Lugus of Gaul and Lug of Ireland. In addition, it can be seen that Maxen's activities in Britain bear marked resemblances to those of Lleu(elys) in *Cyfranc Lludd a Lleuelys*.

Cyfranc Lludd a Lleuelys	*Breuddwyd Maxen*
Lleu(elys) crosses the sea to Britain.	Maxen crosses the sea to Britain.
He measures the island and discovers its exact Centre.	He arrives at a site, whose column and throne indicate it to be the Centre of Britain. The roads of Britain radiate from the site.
Lludd, King of Britain is a *roi fainéant*, who maintains the dignity of his office but is unable to act against his country's foes without the assistance of Lleu(elys).	The King of Britain (at first unnamed, later identified as Eudaf) is a *roi fainéant*, who maintains the dignity of his office while remaining a passive figure uninvolved in the affairs of the kingdom.

---

280 In Hindu cosmology, 'The tall central tower of the temple, the *shikhara*, may represent the cosmic mountain, Mount Meru' (John McKim Malville and John M. Fritz, 'Cosmos and Kings at Vijayanagara', in Clive L. N. Ruggles and Nicholas J. Saunders (ed.), *Astronomies and Cultures* (Niwot, Colo., 1993), p. 146).

281 A. F. Anisimov, 'Cosmological Concepts of the Peoples of the North', in Henry N. Michael (ed.), *Studies in Siberian Shamanism* (Toronto, 1963), p. 177. Cf. Mircea Eliade, *Le chamanisme et les techniques archaïques de l'extase* (Paris, 1951), pp. 79–88.

282 Cook, *Zeus*, ii, pp. 2010.

283 Fomin, *Instructions for Kings*, pp. 204–7.

The island is threatened by the sinister Otherworld race *Coraniaid*, whose destruction is instigated by Lleu(elys).	The leader of the *Coraniaid* is elsewhere identified as Caswallawn, son of Beli. Maxen drives the tribe of Beli (*meibion Beli*), i.e. the Coraniaid, into the sea.
The invaders dispelled, Lludd resumes his reign over Britain.	Although Maxen assumes control of Britain, repudiating the threatening demands of the Roman Emperor, Eudaf unaccountably remains king.

Breuddwyd Maxen provides rare insights into the ideology of the Sacred Centre in Brittonic mythology. In addition, it confirms that Preseli Mountain was in early times accounted the *omphalos* of south-west Wales, from which the *mana* of the Demetian site was transferred to the Omphalos of Gwynedd.

10

A Christianized Myth of the Sacred Centre: The Life of St Illtud

The British cosmogony

Although it is known that the druids engaged in extensive cosmological studies, it has been asserted that 'Celtic tradition has preserved no native story of the creation of the world and of man'.[1] This is not entirely true,[2] and I hope to show that what amounts to a British pagan cosmogonic treatise has in fact survived, after lying concealed as a palimpsest for centuries beneath a veneer of Christianity. In addition, the disguised myth throws further light on the mythological function of the Centre of Britain.

The text in question was compiled nine centuries ago. Although familiar to Welsh ecclesiastical historians, it has retained many of its secrets to the present day. Nine centuries is of course recent in terms of the age of Stonehenge, and postdates the conversion of Britain to Christianity by some four or five centuries. Nevertheless, there are indications that this source reflects traditions of remarkable antiquity, which shed unexpected light on the belief-system of Celtic peoples settled in Britain centuries before Caesar came and conquered – and even, it may be, preserving elements of the cosmology of those Bronze Age peoples whom the Celts themselves superseded and absorbed.[3]

Welsh Saints' Lives

The curious traveller in Wales is swiftly made aware of the enormous number of saints to whom Welsh churches are dedicated. The place name element *Llan-*, prefixed to the name of a saint, normally indicates a parish church.[4] While some evoke celebrated figures from the wider Christian tradition, such as the Virgin Mary and Archangel Michael, the overwhelming majority

---

1   Alwyn Rees and Brinley Rees, *Celtic Heritage: Ancient Tradition in Ireland and Wales* (London, 1961), p. 95.

2   'We can be virtually certain on comparative grounds that the Irish had a native mythology of the beginnings of the actual world, and indeed this has not been entirely erased' (Proinsias Mac Cana, 'Conservation and Innovation in Early Celtic Literature', *Études Celtiques* (Paris, 1972), viii, p. 99).

3   'They [the Celts in Britain and Ireland] were conquerors ... of long-established and usually advanced cultures and not colonists of virgin lands: one must therefore assume significant cultural admixture' (Donnchadh Ó Corráin, 'Law and Society – principles of classification', in Karl Horst Schmidt and Rolf Ködderitzsch (ed.), *Geschichte und Kultur der Kelten: Vorbereitungskonferenz 25.-28. Oktober 1982 in Bonn* (Heidelberg, 1986), p. 234).

4   Elwyn Davies, *Rhestr o Enwau Lleoedd: A Gazetteer of Welsh Place-Names* (Cardiff, 1957), pp. 56–67.

commemorates native saints. A comprehensive list of some 360 Welsh parishes accounts for almost as many dedications to the 'primitive saints of Wales'.[5] While the national Saint David (Welsh *Dewi Sant*) is a familiar figure to many, of the great majority of his fellow saints little or nothing survives beyond the bare names, together with occasional snatches of traditional lore of dubious historical value.[6] Some of these revered figures never in fact existed, their names and attached legends having evolved in the Middle Ages as a result of ætiological speculation.[7]

Mediæval Welsh proliferation of saints includes the modest figure of 20,000 believed to lie interred on the little island of Bardsey in the Irish Sea.[8] Who were these venerated figures and whence derived their claim to sanctity? Only a handful are accorded biographies preserved in mediæval manuscripts, and even these have for the most part been shown by scholars to represent little more than imaginative fiction. The Age of the Saints lay principally in the fifth and sixth centuries AD, while almost all their Lives were compiled by professional hagiographers more than half a millennium later.

A prominent example, the Life of Saint Illtud (*Vita Sancti Iltuti*), was written in the early decades of the twelfth century. The Saint is described as founder of the monastery of Llantwit Major in South Wales, with whose topography and traditions his biographer displays close familiarity. The latter has been identified as Caradog of Llancarfan, the contemporary of Geoffrey of Monmouth, with whom he was probably acquainted.[9] Caradog was a professional hagiographer, who wrote lives of several important saints. Hugh Williams was doubtless correct in envisaging the *Vita Iltuti* as 'evidently a *legenda*, a kind of memorial sermon read in church during the service on the saint's day ...'.[10] There are internal indications in the *Vita* of access to earlier sources, which the author probably found in the library of Llantwit Major. One episode features also in the early ninth-century *Historia Brittonum* of Nennius, suggesting that 'both authors drew on an earlier, subsequently lost, Life of St Illtud'.[11]

---

5   Rice Rees, *An Essay on the Welsh Saints or the Primitive Christians Usually Considered to Have Been the Founders of Churches in Wales* (London, 1836), pp. 323–58; A. W. Wade-Evans, 'Parochiale Wallicum', *Y Cymmrodor* (London, 1910), xxii, pp. 119–22.

6   'We should accept ... that most Brittonic saints cannot be placed in history as real figures or made the subject of biography. For most we possess only a name that appears to be a personal name rather than some other kind of word, and is linked with one or more places. Even the records of names and places begin well after the times when the persons concerned must have lived', Nicholas Orme, *The Saints of Cornwall* (Oxford, 2000), p. 19). Cf. O. J. Padel, *A Popular Dictionary of Cornish Place-Names* (Penzance, 1988), pp. 19–25.

7   Imaginary saints are also to be found in Brittany: cf. René Largillière, *Six saints de la région de Plestin: Saint Haran, saint Karé, saint Tuder, saint Nérin, saint Kémo, saint Kirio* (Rennes, 1922), pp. 85–92.

8   The 20,000 saints of Bardsey are commemorated by two fifteenth-century poets, Hywel ab Dafydd and Thomas Celli (S. Baring-Gould and John Fisher, *The Lives of the British Saints: The Saints of Wales and Cornwall and such Irish Saints as have Dedications in Britain* (London, 1907–13), iv, pp. 436–38). It is to be suspected that their inflated number reflects the island's prior rôle as a pagan realm of the dead, corresponding to *Tech Duinn* off the west coast of Ireland. The island of Aran was similarly believed to be the resting place of an untold number of holy men and saints (Carolus Plummer (ed.), *Vitae Sanctorum Hiberniae: Partim Hactenvs Ineditae ad Fidem Codicvm Manvscriptorvm Recognovit Prolegominis Notis Indicibvs Instrvxit* (Oxford, 1910), i, p. 208).

9   Christopher Brooke, 'The Archbishops of St David's, Llandaff and Caerleon-on-Usk', in Nora K. Chadwick (ed.), *Studies in the Early British Church* (Cambridge, 1958), pp. 228, 234–35. Cf. Gilbert H. Doble, *Saint Iltut* (Cardiff, 1944), pp. 27–28, 31.

10   Hugh Williams, *Christianity in Early Britain* (Oxford, 1912), p. 320.

11   David N. Dumville, *Saint David of Wales* (Cambridge, 2001), pp. 8–9.

Illtud's birth and parentage

The Life of Illtud begins with an account, characteristic of Celtic hagiography, of the Saint's aristocratic ancestry and birth. We learn that his father *Bicanus* was born in Brittany of a long line of princely rulers, where he became a distinguished soldier. His mother *Rieingulid*, daughter to *Amlawdd*, king of Britain, crossed the Channel to wed *Bicanus*. In due course she fulfilled her husband's ardent desire by giving birth to a fine boy, on whom was bestowed the name *Iltutus*. The infant displayed precocious mastery of learning, and on arrival at the appropriate age correspondingly excelled in military proficiency.

While Celtic saints were expected to be of noble birth, which many doubtless were, the account of Illtud's ancestry and early career is unique, both in the emphasis it lays on his father's martial qualities and on his own early career as a professional soldier. However, this section of his biography cannot reflect historical reality. It has been observed that 'it is hardly likely in the conditions of the sixth century that a great teacher should have graduated as a soldier'.[12] Although he became traditionally known as *Illtud Varchawg*, 'Illtud the soldier', the epithet is not recorded in any early source, and almost certainly reflects the account given in the Life, which would have been read aloud or paraphrased in parish churches dedicated to the Saint at his festival on 6 November.[13]

There are, however, indications that the author drew for his biography on an early source or sources, which either he or a predecessor did not understand and consequently misinterpreted.[14] The names of Illtud's father, mother, and maternal grandfather bear resonances of pre-Christian British mythology which are too marked to be ignored.

Illtud's father is described as 'Bicanus, a most famous soldier', *Bicanus miles famosissimus*. The name is unique to the Life of Illtud, and there is reason to believe that it arose from the author's misunderstanding of his source.

In due course I shall adduce evidence attesting to the widespread belief in early Britain and Ireland that a woman's impregnation was brought about by ingestion of a minute embryonic creature issuing directly or indirectly from her husband or lover. In one of the most graphic accounts, the Irish hero Cú Chulainn's mother Dechtine conceives her son by the god Lug, through momentarily swallowing an unspecified *míl bec*, 'tiny creature'.[15]

---

12   Christopher Brooke, 'St Peter of Gloucester and St Cadoc of Llancarfan', in Nora K. Chadwick (ed.), *Celt and Saxon: Studies in the Early British Border* (Cambridge, 1963), p. 304.

13   In the early seventeenth century the Cornish antiquary Nicholas Roscarrock describes Illtud as 'cosyn unto Kyng Arthur & a secular knight, that forsoke all yᵉ worldly pompe & was a religyous man', while in Queen Anne's reign the rector of Llanilltud near Dolgelley reported that 'About Illtud they mention nothing save that he was Illtud the Knight': *Am Elhdyd nis krybwylhant am dano amgen nag Elhdyd Varchog* (Baring-Gould and Fisher, *The Lives of the British Saints*, iii, pp. 314–15, 317; Rupert H. Morris (ed.), *Parochialia: Being a Summary of Answers to "Parochial Queries in Order to a Geographical Dictionary, etc., of Wales" Issued by Edward Lhwyd* (London, 1909–11), i, p. 1). Allusions in mediæval Welsh poetry to Illtud's martial career add nothing of value to the information contained in his Life (Elissa R. Henken, *Traditions of the Welsh Saints* (Cambridge, 1987), pp. 108–10).

14   The hagiographer lays exceptional emphasis on the legality of the marriage between Illtud's parents. Canon Doble conjectured that this arose from a desire to distance Illtud from scandalous circumstances attending conceptions of other saints (Doble, *Saint Iltut*, p. 15). The allusion is presumably to the frequency with which they are described as being born of an unwed virgin – not infrequently in consequence of rape. In fact, the regularity with which the motif features in saints' Lives suggests that it was regarded as effectively a prerequisite for sanctity (Elissa R. Henken, *The Welsh Saints: A Study in Patterned Lives* (Cambridge, 1991), p. 24).

15   That the Irish *míl* represented a creature so tiny that it could inadvertently be swallowed is intimated by an Irish charm cited in an Anglo-Saxon leech-book (J. H. C. Grattan and Charles Singer, *Anglo-Saxon Magic and Medicine: Illustrated Specially from the Semi-Pagan Text 'Lacnunga'* (Oxford, 1952), p. 107).

An episode in the story of *Math uab Mathonwy* shows that this concept also featured in Welsh tradition. When the virgin Arianrhod (originally a deity) visits the wizard Gwydion, she leaves behind 'a small something' (*y ryw bethan*), which in due course grows up to become the hero (originally god) Lleu. The Welsh version has been more rationalized than its Irish counterpart. While the Irish version recognizes the minuscule entity as an animate creature instrumental in bringing about pregnancy, the Welsh author apparently did not comprehend the underlying significance of the 'small something'. In fact, in each case the context indicates that the similarly named Irish *míl bec* and Welsh *rhyw bethan* correspond in representing the spiritualized seed or embryo, which in Indo-European tradition was understood to be the cerebro-spinal stuff of life transferred in sexual congress from a man to a woman.

The Old Welsh equivalent of Irish *míl bec* would be the cognate form *mil* ('animal, beast, creature') + *bichan* ('small, minute').[16] Finding reference in an earlier version of Illtud's birth-tale to the part played by a mysterious *mil bychan*, the mediæval hagiographer might readily have misinterpreted it as '*Bychan* the soldier (*mil*)'.[17] Such a misapprehension would be the more understandable if (as is likely in respect of a saint) Illtud was originally accounted son of a virgin. In light of these considerations, I suggest that the unique name and rank of *Bicanus miles* arose from misinterpretation of an earlier account of Illtud's miraculous conception. This in turn led to the hagiographer's account of the saint's pursuing the improbable course of a military career. As has been seen, no early source suggests that Illtud was ever a soldier. On the contrary, the oldest account, contained in the seventh-century Life of St Samson, states categorically that he was by birth (heredity) a magician, i.e. a druid. We learn further from the same source that he was ordained a priest in early youth by St Germanus.[18]

In Caradog's *Vita Iltuti* the conception and birth of Illtud are represented as taking place in *Letavia*, a latinization of *Llydaw*. This is the Welsh name for Brittany, which the hagiographer took for the land of his nativity. At the same time, Brittany was traditionally identified in early Britain and Ireland as a transmarine location of the Otherworld,[19] and it was probably in this

16   *Geiriadur Prifysgol Cymru: A Dictionary of the Welsh Language* (Cardiff, 1950–2002), p. 2455. In Gaulish the noun is *milo-*, '(little) animal' (Xavier Delamarre, *Dictionnaire de la langue gauloise: Une approche linguistique du vieux-celtique continental* (Paris, 2001), p. 192), while Irish *míl¹* is likewise 'animal en général, surtout animal de petit taille' (J. Vendryes, E. Bachellery, and P-Y. Lambert, *Lexique étymologique de l'irlandais ancien* (Dublin and Paris, 1959–96), M-51). The word in all three Celtic languages derives from the Indo-European root *mēlo-, smēlo-* (Julius Pokorny, *Indogermanisches Etymologisches Wörterbuch* (Berne, 1959–69), i, p. 724; Ranko Matasović, *Etymological Dictionary of Proto-Celtic* (Leiden, 2009), pp. 271–72). Welsh *bychan*, 'small', derives from Old Welsh *bichan* (J. Morris Jones, *A Welsh Grammar: Historical and Comparative* (Oxford, 1913), p. 156; Alexander Falileyev, *Etymological Glossary of Old Welsh* (Tübingen, 2000), p. 15; Patrick Sims-Williams, *The Celtic Inscriptions of Britain: Phonology and Chronology, c. 400–1200* (Oxford, 2003), p. 137).

17   *Bychan* could have been mistaken for a personal name, given its similarity to the royal *Brychan*. Welsh *mil-* ('soldier') is a borrowing from Latin *mīles* (Henry Lewis, *Yr Elfen Ladin yn yr Iaith Gymraeg* (Cardiff, 1943), p. 8), as is also Irish *míl²* (E. G. Quin *et al.* (ed.), *Dictionary of the Irish Language: Based mainly on Old and Middle Irish Materials* (Dublin, 1913-76), 'M', cols. 135–36). Andrew Breeze draws my attention to Canon Doble's postulated identification of *Bicanus* with the OW personal name *biguan* found in the Book of Llandaff (J. Gwenogvryn Evans and John Rhŷs (ed.), *The Text of the Book of Llan Dâv Reproduced from the Gwysaney Manuscript* (Oxford, 1893), p. 219). However, the correspondence is hard to justify on phonological grounds, and reflects no more than Doble's presumption that *Bicanus* was a proper noun.

18   *Germanus ordinauerat eum in sua iuuentute presbiterum* (Pierre Flobert (ed.), *La vie ancienne de saint Samson de Dol* (Paris, 1997), p. 156).

19   John Rhys, *Lectures on the Origin and Growth of Religion as Illustrated by Celtic Heathendom* (London, 1888), p. 168; Christian J. Guyonvarc'h, 'Celtique commun *Letavia*, gaulois *LETAVIS*, irlandais *Letha*;

sense that it featured in a prior version of the legend of Illtud. Nowhere in the earlier account of the Saint is there any suggestion of his originating from the Continent.[20]

This is not the only indication that the birth-tale of Illtud derives from a myth of the British pagan theogony. His mother is called *Rieingulid*, which the hagiographer translates *regina pudica*, 'modest queen': a compound of Welsh *rhiein*, 'queen', and *gwlydd*, 'gentle, kindly, modest'.[21] However, the rôle assigned Rieingulid in the Life of St Illtud suggests rather that she represents a figure pre-eminent in Celtic mythology, the Maiden Sovereignty. She was the beautiful and ever-virginal divine personification of the land of Britain, whose geographical features are almost all feminine in Welsh, and whose flowery landscape was likened by Gildas in the sixth century to 'a chosen bride adorned with various jewels'.[22]

Could it be that the original name of Illtud's mother was *Rieingulad*, 'Queen of the Land' (*gwlad*, 'land, country'), and that *gwlydd* represents either a simple misreading arising during transcription, or (as an extended passage in the Life extolling her meek and chaste disposition suggests) modification into a compound personal name appropriate to the pious mother of a saint?[23] In favour of this suggestion is the nomenclature associated with the comparable birth of St Cadog in the *Vita Cadoci*. He is described as being born to a princess named *Guladus* (< *gwlad*).[24]

la porte de l'Autre Monde', *Ogam: Tradition Celtique* (Rennes, 1967), xix, pp. 490–94; idem, *Magie, médecine et divination chez les Celtes* (Paris, 1997), pp. 315–16. Could the identification have been influenced also by Latin *lethaeus*, 'of or belonging to Lethe', i.e. Death? (R. E. Latham and D. R. Howlett (ed.), *Dictionary of Medieval Latin from British Sources* (London, 1975–2013), p. 1587).

20	'It is noteworthy that there is no indication in this Breton Life [*Vita Samsonis*], that Illtud himself was a Breton' (Arthur Wade-Evans, *Welsh Christian Origins* (Oxford, 1934), p. 133). Could it be that the putative ancestor of the Goidels in Ireland, *Míl Espáine*, likewise originated in misunderstanding of the germinative soul-creature, *míl*? Spain (*Espáin*), like Brittany, was traditionally regarded as a location of the Otherworld (Rhys, *Lectures on the Origin and Growth of Religion as Illustrated by Celtic Heathendom*, pp. 90–91; Françoise Le Roux, 'La mort de Cúchulainn', *Ogam* (1966), xviii, p. 386; Marie-Thérèse Brouland, *Le Substrat celtique du lai breton anglais Sir Orfeo* (Paris, 1990), p. 147). The god Lug was fostered by Tailtiu, daughter of *Magmóir ri Espáine* (Elizabeth A. Gray (ed.), *Cath Maige Tuired: The Second Battle of Mag Tuired* (Naas, 1982), p. 38), *Mag Mór* being the Great Plain of the Otherworld (Helmut Birkhan, *Kelten: Versuch einer Gesamtdarstellung ihrer Kultur* (Vienna, 1997), p. 534).

21	Cf. the note by Henry Lewis in Doble, *Saint Iltut*, p. 33.

22	Mommsen (ed.), *Chronica Minora*, iii, p. 28; Morris-Jones, *A Welsh Grammar*, 225–26; Proinsias Mac Cana, 'Placenames and Mythology in Irish Tradition: Places, Pilgrimages and Things', in Gordon W. MacLennan (ed.), *Proceedings of the First North American Congress of Celtic Studies* (Ottawa, 1988), pp. 338–39; Françoise Le Roux and Christian-J. Guyonvarc'h, *La civilisation celtique* (Rennes, 1990), p. 73. In the druidic 'Colloquy of the Two Sages' we find the statement *Ar adnacht i mbrú a mathar .i. i talmain*, 'he has been buried in his mother's womb, i.e. in the earth' (R. I. Best, Osborn Bergin, M. A. O'Brien, and Anne O'Sullivan (ed.), *The Book of Leinster Formerly Lebar na Núachongbála* (Dublin, 1954–83), p. 825). The concept of the land as goddess was widespread among Indo-European cultures (M. L. West, *Indo-European Poetry and Myth* (Oxford, 2007), pp. 414–17). 'The idea of Ireland as a woman wedded to her rightful king persisted all through the centuries' (T. F. O'Rahilly, 'On the Origin of the Names Érainn and Ériu', *Ériu: The Journal of the School of Irish Learning* (Dublin, 1943), xiv, p. 17: cf. pp. 14–21).

23	'*Rieingulid*, like *Trynihid*, is probably a made-up name' (Doble, *Saint Iltut*, p. 33).

24	A. W. Wade-Evans (ed.), *Vitae Sanctorum Britanniae et Genealogiae* (Cardiff, 1944), p. 24. *Gwladus* means "Landesherrin'(?)' (Stefan Zimmer, 'Die altkymrischen Frauennamen. Ein erster Einblick' in Joseph F. Eska, R. Geraint Gruffydd, and Nicolas Jacobs (ed.), *Hispano-Gallo-Brittonica: Essays in honour of Professor D. Ellis Evans on the occasion of his sixty-fifth birthday* (Cardiff, 1995), p. 323). Cf. J. Lloyd-Jones, *Geirfa Barddoniaeth Gynnar Gymraeg* (Cardiff, 1931–63), p. 690). Andrew Breeze reminds me of the name *Gwladus* in this context.

If so, Illtud's mother is to be identified with the Maiden Sovereignty figure depicted in the First Branch of the *Mabinogi*. Should the emendation *Rhieingulad* be accepted, the name becomes all but synonymous with that of *Rhiannon* (< *Rīgantonā*, 'Great Queen').

Moving on, the father of *Rieingulid* in the Life of Saint Illtud is *Anblaud, Britannie regis*: '*Anlawdd*, king of Britain'. Little is recorded of him in Welsh traditional lore.[25] He has been described as 'a shadowy figure whose daughters are the mothers of heroes, his only role in extant Welsh texts, and a device which allows heroes like Culhwch, Gorau and St Illtud to be Arthur's cousins'. Anlawdd's nebulous nature led one scholar to suggest that he 'seems to be a function rather than a person. He is an "empty" character who is never given a narrative context but who exists merely so that his daughters may be the mothers of heroes.'[26] In Welsh genealogies he features as *Amlawdd Gwledig*, 'Amlawdd the Sovereign', the first element (*gwlad*) of his title combining the meanings of 'country' and 'authority, kingship'.[27]

Thus *Anlawdd* appears originally to have constituted no more than a generic appellation for a divine ancestor-figure, whose function is indicated by his name. The prefix *an* is an intensive, while the second element has been interpreted as *blawdd*, 'great tumult, confusion'.[28] However, it is hard to envisage how such a term might have appeared appropriate for an ancestor figure, and a more apt interpretation is suggested by the word *blawd*, 'flour'. In Indo-European mythology the brain was held to be both lodging place of the human spirit and source of semen, which in turn was understood to be passed down the marrow of the spine, and so through sexual congress into the mother's womb. Close analogy was also drawn between the human head as source of fertility, and the head or ear of corn.[29] Just as flour represents grain brought to culinary fruition, semen contains an embryonic form of human life 'cooked' in the womb.[30] It looks as

25 *Gorlois yarll Kernyv, ac Eigyr uerch Amlavd Wledic y wreic* (Henry Lewis (ed.), *Brut Dingestow* (Cardiff, 1942), p. 136).

26 Brynley F. Roberts, '*Culhwch ac Olwen*, the Triads, Saints' Lives', in Rachel Bromwich, A. O. H. Jarman, and Brynley F. Roberts (ed.), *The Arthur of the Welsh: The Arthurian Legend in Medieval Welsh Literature* (Cardiff, 1991), p. 94; idem, 'Geoffrey of Monmouth, *Historia Regum Britanniae* and *Brut y Brenhinedd*', ibid., p. 111. Cf. Lewis (ed.), *Brut Dingestow*, pp. 266–67; Rachel Bromwich (ed.), *Trioedd Ynys Prydein: The Welsh Triads* (Cardiff, 1978), pp. 365–66; Rachel Bromwich and D. Simon Evans (ed.), *Culhwch and Olwen: An Edition and Study of the Oldest Arthurian Tale* (Cardiff, 1992), pp. 44–45.

27 J. G. Evans, 'Pedigrees from Jesus College MS. 20', *Y Cymmrodor* (1887), viii, p. 85; Bromwich (ed.), *Trioedd Ynys Prydein*, p. 239; P. C. Bartrum (ed.), *Early Welsh Genealogical Texts* (Cardiff, 1966), pp. 39, 61, 93. For *gwledig*, cf. P.-Y. Lambert, '"Tribunal" *et* "praetorium" *en vieux-breton*', *The Bulletin of the Board of Celtic Studies* (Cardiff, 1987), xxxiv, pp. 120–21.

28 Bromwich (ed.), *Trioedd Ynys Prydein*, p. 366; Bromwich and Simon Evans (ed.), *Culhwch and Olwen*, pp. 44–45. An earlier suggestion that *Anblawdd* represents Norse *Olafr* is unlikely (Idris LL. Foster, 'The Irish Influence on Some Welsh Personal Names', in Rev. John Ryan (ed.), *Féilsgríbinn Eóin Mhic Néill* (Dublin, 1940), pp. 29–30).

29 Richard Broxton Onians, *The Origins of European Thought about the Body, the Mind the Soul, the World Time, and Fate: New Interpretations of Greek, Roman and kindred evidence also of some basic Jewish and Christian beliefs* (Cambridge, 1954), pp. 105–22.

30 The Hippocratic text 'On the Nature of the Child' draws the analogy between early ripening of semen and bread being baked in an oven (Helen King, 'Making a Man: Becoming Human in Early Greek Medicine', in G. R. Dunstan (ed.), *The Human Embryo: Aristotle and the Arabic and European Traditions* (Exeter, 1990), pp. 14–15). Similarly, 'In the *Dream Book* of Artemidorus, an important source for ancient imagery, a hearth (*hestia*) and a baking-oven can represent women, because they receive things which produce life. Dreaming of seeing fire in a hearth means that your wife will become pregnant' (ibid., p. 16). Galen likewise emphasized the part played by heat in generation (Phillip de Lacy (ed.), *Galeni De Semine* (Berlin, 1992), p. 186).

though *Anlawdd* personified the divine matrix of procreativity, from which kings, heroes, and saints originated.[31]

The significance of 'flour' in this context is further indicated by an allusion in the early eleventh-century Welsh tale *Branwen uerch Llŷr*. The second part describes an invasion of Ireland by an army led by Bran, king of Britain. Reduced to seeking terms, the Irish invite Bran and his followers to confer in a huge house. There they plan a treacherous ambush, concealing armed warriors in bags hanging from especially constructed pegs on the pillars of the great hall. The plot is frustrated by Efnisien, one of Bran's relatives, who enters the hall beforehand and promptly espies the obtrusive bags – a contingency so predictable that one wonders how the Irish failed to anticipate it. Efnisien asks a Irishman standing by what the nearest bag contains. 'Flour, friend' (*blawt, eneit*), replies the other.[32] However the Welsh prince, feeling the shape of a human head, pinches his fingers through its skull until they meet in the brain.

After killing all two hundred of the enemy in this exemplary fashion, Efnisien chants this curious verse:

> *Yssit yn y boly hwnn amryw ulawt,*
> *Keimeit, kynniuyeit, diskynneit yn trin,*
> *Rac kydwyr cadbarawt.*
> There is in this bag a different flour,
> Champions, warriors, attackers in battle,
> Against soldiers ready for war.[33]

The four tales of the *Mabinogi*, of which *Branwen* is the second, include a number of such verses, in the metre known as *englyn*. It has been shown that these *englynion* are older than the tales, having been co-opted by the author into his stories. That he was not always fully apprised of their true context and meaning is indicated by unexplained anomalies, which a purely creative author would have been unlikely to perpetrate. Fortunately, these provide clues affording invaluable glimpses of the nature of his sources, a consideration materially applicable to the *englyn* in question.

1. The overly ingenious manner in which the Irish prepare their ambush appears all but designed to invite discovery:

    And the Irish devised a stratagem: they fixed a peg on each side of the hundred pillars that were in the hall, and hung a hide bag on each peg with an armed warrior inside each one.

---

31   The name of the Irish heroine Gráinne has been plausibly derived from *gráinne*, 'grain' (Thomas F. O'Rahilly, *Early Irish History and Mythology* (Dublin, 1946), p. 302). She is at the same time an obvious hypostasis of the Sovranty Goddess (Jan de Vries, *Keltische Religion* (Stuttgart, 1961), p. 242), while an alternative meaning 'ugly' is incompatible with her unique loveliness (Nessa Ní Shéaghdha (ed.), *Tóruigheacht Dhiarmada agus Ghráinne: The Pursuit of Diarmaid and Gráinne* (Dublin, 1967), p. 2.

32   The primary meaning of *eneit* is 'soul', which was also employed in the sense of 'friend'. However in view of the particular circumstances, could the Irishman's reply originally have signified 'flour-soul'?

33   Derick S. Thomson (ed.), *Branwen uerch Lyr: The Second of the Four Branches of the Mabinogi edited from the White Book of Rhydderch with variants from the Red Book of Hergest and from Peniarth 6* (Dublin, 1961), pp. 12-13.

What can have been the point of this peculiar arrangement? Would it not have been simpler for the warriors to station themselves outside the doorways, in shadowy corners of the hall, or immediately behind each column? Must not the novel spectacle of ten score man-sized hanging bags inevitably attract the attention of Bran and his following, as indeed it excited the suspicion of Efnisien the moment he entered the hall? The attack could only prove fully effective if properly synchronized, but how were men trussed within bags to know when the decisive moment had arrived, or to act when it did? The story makes no mention of any signal, and even were one to be given, each warrior would have to spend time cutting his way out of the bag in which he was confined. A subsequent allusion reveals that the Britons attending the banquet were armed. How could so clumsy and readily detectable a scheme be expected to succeed? These difficulties are compounded by the unexplained decision to suspend the assassins from two hundred especially constructed pegs!

2. Why did the Irishman who informed Efnisien that the bags contained flour not utter a word of warning to his fellow countrymen, as the Welshman moved from one to another of the two hundred suspended sacks, methodically killing their occupants? And why did the Irish attendant fail to reveal their slaughter to his king and following, as they entered the hall shortly afterwards?[34]

3. Efnisien's method of eliminating the menace appears as eccentric as it is implausible. That he slew them by feeling for their heads and crushing their skulls is bizarre. Why not stab them swiftly with his sword? Of his final victim we are told that even the fact that he was wearing a helmet did not prevent Efnisien's fingers from meeting in the centre of his brain.

The talented author of *Branwen* is unlikely to have been so inept as to concoct so incoherent and implausible an account from nothing, and the most plausible explanation is that here, as elsewhere, he sought to make sense of a source he did not understand. Although scholars have puzzled over this bewildering episode, hitherto no persuasive explanation has been proposed.[35] A treacherous ambush conducted at a feast attended by rival parties represents a fairly commonplace theme of folklore and history. However in *Branwen* it is the attendant anomalies which are of primary significance: a factor which becomes evident when they are considered separately.

I believe that the explanation lies in the author's failure to understand and coherently adapt the source material to his creative narrative. The *englyn* makes it clear that it contained reference to warriors in bags, who are obscurely described as constituting 'a different flour' or 'form of flour' (*Yssit yn y boly hwnn amryw ulawt*). The writer adapted his source into a version of the familiar 'ambush at the feast' theme – with the distinctive factor of its eccentric failure.

---

34 Patrick Ford argued that the Irishman in question was one of those inside the bags, but I do not see how this can be reconciled with the context. Why would Efnisien speak to a sack; and, if he did so, is it likely that even a stage Irishman would be so naïf as to claim from within that he was 'a form of flour'? (Patrick K. Ford, 'Branwen: A Study of the Celtic Affinities', *Studia Celtica* (Cardiff, 1987/8), xxii/xxiii, pp. 34–35).

35 Mac Cana's argument that it was adapted from the Irish tale *Cath Belaig Dúin Bolg* was rejected by the editor of *Branwen* on the grounds that it 'is ingenious, but does not carry conviction' (Proinsias Mac Cana, *Branwen Daughter of Llŷr: A Study of the Irish Affinities and of the Composition of the Second Branch of the Mabinogi* (Cardiff, 1958), pp. 65–70; Thomson (ed.), *Branwen uerch Lyr*, p. 36). Kenneth Jackson drew attention to international stories of ingenious ambushes, such as those effected by the Trojan Horse and Ali Baba, but similarly ignored the unique imponderables of the Welsh tale (*The International Popular Tale and Early Welsh Tradition* (Cardiff, 1961), pp. 101–102).

Further light is shed by the sequel. A violent dispute breaks out in the banqueting hall, provoking ferocious conflict between the rival parties. Although dreadful mutual slaughter results, the outcome is left oddly obscure, being confined to the enigmatic statement that 'from that came such victory as the men of the Island of the Mighty [i.e. Britain] gained, and their [the Britons] only victory was the escape of seven men'. We are left ignorant of the fate of the Irishmen in the hall, and nothing further is related of their king Matholwch, who had prior to this juncture played a major part in the story. However, after an interlude it is inconsequentially noted that 'in Ireland none was left alive, save five pregnant women'. Setting aside the fact that there is no suggestion that every Irishman in the hall was slain, how could a localized conflict, however sanguinary, have depopulated the entire island?

The storytellers of mediæval Wales were not concerned with writing fiction in the sense that it is understood in the modern world. Their task was to retell the archaic lore of the land, in particular stories of gods and goddesses, kings and queens, heroes and heroines of former times. The authenticity of these stories was not in question, being a fundamental part of the history (*hanes*) of early Britain, as it was understood in native tradition, and the artist's rôle was to 'renew' them by reinterpretation of their often disjointed subject matter, embellishment of their language, and other literary improvements.[36] The genius of the unknown author of the Four Branches of the *Mabinogi* (the stories of 'Pwyll, Prince of Dyfed', 'Branwen Daughter of Llŷr', 'Manawydan Son of Llŷr', and 'Math Son of Mathonwy') is displayed by his imposition of rational structure on obscure or confused material available to him, conferring colour and character on personalities who in some cases may originally have been little more than evocative names, and enriching his narrative with lively dialogue.

The process of reconciling and adapting early material, whether poetry or prose, bore scant resemblance to the critical approach of the modern historian or literary scholar. The vast corpus of traditional lore circulating in early mediæval Wales was regarded as comprising an essentially truthful account of the glorious past, and the structure imposed upon it by the author of the *Mabinogi* was intended to make coherent sense, as well as an artistic whole, of a disparate body of traditional tales, verses, and snatches of lore largely detached from their original contexts. The most obvious of these are the three sets of verses (*englynion*), ten triads, proverbs, and other floating citations scattered throughout the text, together with occasional comments and glosses alluding to matters known to the author.

Of course, these skilfully composed stories should primarily be read as the superb literature they are. From the historian's point of view, however, their fascination lies in unique glimpses they provide of an earlier rich body of myth and legend, which would otherwise be all but entirely lost. While each section of the narrative requires particular consideration, it is the points where the content appears incongruous or incomprehensible that invite closest examination. Every scholar who has subjected the work to analysis is agreed that the author was a master of his profession, who melded his assembled materials with exquisite skill into a magnificent composite whole.[37] It is a reasonable premise that such an artist would be unlikely to perpetrate

36 'It would be a mistake to draw a firm line between historical and mythical *gormesoedd*; as we have seen, there was no clear distinction between history and myth' (P. P. Sims-Williams, 'Some Functions of Origin Stories in Early Medieval Wales', in Tore Nyberg, Iørn Piø, Preben Meulengracht Sørensen, and Aage Trommer (ed.), *History and Heroic Tale: A Symposium* (Odense, 1985), p. 106).

37 'What is striking in *The Mabinogi* is the consummate skill with which the author adapts these materials, creating a revitalized myth infused with a vision and a moral code to meet the contemporary needs of his audience, a myth in terms of which it could examine and evaluate its own society. This is, of course, one of the recognized roles of mythology. It is also an important function of a work of literature, and

grave lapses of logic through slipshod inattention, and one may safely proceed from the broad presumption that those that occur (and they are many) are likely to have arisen from the respect with which he treated the venerable body of literature from which he wrought his masterpiece. This, together with the likelihood that many among his audience or readership were familiar with much of this lore, meant that he was constrained to operate on the basis of self-imposed reluctance to tamper with his source material any more than appeared requisite to his purpose.

Bearing these considerations in mind, we may return to anomalies in the description of the Irishmens' ambush in *Branwen*. A leather bag containing an armed warrior hangs on each side of a large column. A hostile figure pinches each bag, killing its inmate. This done, he cites a verse declaring that every bag contained 'a form (or variant) of flour', which he equates with 'champions' and 'warriors'. It does not require a Freudian mystagogue to detect what lies behind all this. The imagery of erect columns with bags hanging on either side is telling enough, even without their explicit etymological implications. The Welsh word for scrotum is *ceillgwd*, a compound of *caill*, 'testicle', and *cwd*, 'bag', while *cwd* alone may also mean 'scrotum'.[38] Similarly, Latin *columna*, 'column', could signify 'penis',[39] as is likely to have been the case with its Welsh derivative *colofn*.

The hundred columns of the hall in which the Irish and Welsh hosts meet in *Branwen* represent obvious literary exaggeration. According to the Welsh laws a king's house contained a hypothetical (although presumably broadly accurate) six columns: a factor with which the author of *Branwen* will have been personally familiar. In the hierarchical setting portrayed by the mediæval law codes, the king's principal heir (*edling*) is seated on the opposite side of the fire, 'and next to him the judge, between him and the column (*yrydaw a'r golofyn*)'.[40] Where this evidently special column stood in a real hall is unclear, but the early romances confirm that kings were associated with prominent pillars. In *Breuddwyd Maxen* the emperor journeys in his sleep to a fairy palace, where 'at the base of the pillar in the hall he saw a hoary-headed man seated in a chair of ivory'. The old man wears a diadem, and is clearly a king. He and his column are further alluded to in the story, and the fact that the reference is left unexplained suggests the traditional association in royal ideology between king and column.[41]

In the romance of *Peredur* (whose hero corresponds to the Perceval of Arthurian romance) a mysterious uncle puts the budding hero to the test by presenting him with a sword which he must strike against a column of iron standing in his hall. This episode in turn recalls the Norse hero Sigurd's withdrawal of a sword set by the god Óðinn in a magical tree called *barnstokk* growing in

---

The Mabinogi is both myth and literature' (J. K. Bollard, 'The Role of Myth and Tradition in *The Four Branches of the Mabinogi*', *Cambridge Medieval Celtic Studies* (Cambridge, 1983), vi, p. 86).

38   *Geiriadur Prifysgol Cymru*, pp. 452, 635. Cf. Latin *scrotum*, 'bag' (J. N. Adams, *The Latin Sexual Vocabulary* (London, 1982), pp. 74–76).

39   Ibid., pp. 16–17. *Palus*, 'pole', was also employed with obscene connotation (pp. 16, 23–24).

40   Aled Rhys Wiliam (ed.), *Llyfr Iorwerth: A Critical Text of the Venedotian Code of Medieval Welsh Law Mainly from BM. Cotton MS. Titus Dii* (Cardiff, 1960), p. 91; Stephen J. Williams and J. Enoch Powell (ed.), *Cyfreithiau Hywel Dda yn ôl Llyfr Blegywryd (Dull Dyfed)* (Cardiff, 1942), p. 4). Similarly the physician sits 'at the foot of the column': *medyd ymon y kolovyn* (Wiliam (ed.), *Llyfr Iorwerth*, p. 3). An *englyn* in the Urien cycle describes a host's merriment about 'this pillar', the setting apparently being a festive hall: *Yr ysǒffǒl hǒnn arhǒnn draǒ: mǒy gordyfnassei amdanaǒ* (J. Gwenogvryn Evans (ed.), *The Poetry in the Red Book of Hergest* (Llanbedrog, 1911), col. 1041, ll. 3637).

41   Calvert Watkins, 'Some Celtic Phrasal Echoes', in A. T. E. Matonis and Daniel F. Melia (ed.), *Celtic Language, Celtic Culture: A Festschrift for Eric P. Hamp* (Van Nuys, California, 1990), pp. 52–55; Derick Thomson, 'The Seventeenth-Century Crucible of Scottish Gaelic Poetry', *Studia Celtica* (Cardiff, 1991/92), xxvi/xxvii, p. 157.

the centre of King Volsung's hall.[42] The anvil, or stone, from which Arthur drew his enchanted sword, may also have originated in the World Pillar.[43] In Celtic societies kings were frequently identified, or closely associated, with trees, and their 'inauguration often took place at the tribal sacred tree'.[44] This symbolism is exemplified in Greek legend by the marital bed of Odysseus, the bedpost of which he had fashioned out of a huge olive tree, whose roots remained growing in the ground.[45]

In view of these considerations, it is hard to avoid concluding that the sacks hanging on each side of the pillars in the great hall in *Branwen* represent testicles.[46] Each contains potential to produce an armed warrior, and by squeezing them in turn within his vice-like grip Efnisien aborts Ireland's matrix of armed men. This in turn provides a rational explanation of the mysterious depopulation of Ireland, which features without explanation at the conclusion of the tale. Male generative potency in Ireland is intercepted by a malignant power, but the future of the race is assured by the fact that five women (implicitly one for each province of Ireland) fortuitously happen to be pregnant at the critical moment.

Thus far the evidence, to which I would postulate a final conclusion. The annihilation of the entire population of Ireland, followed by its regeneration in the form of five ancestral males emerging from a womb-like cave, suggests the myth of the periodical destruction and rebirth of mankind.[47] This resurrection was held in various cosmologies to occur at the Centre or *omphalos* of the land, which in Ireland was in early times the Hill of Uisneach. Given the belief that Uisneach constituted the focus of the five provinces of Ireland, it would have been natural to suppose that the five founding mothers of the land originated there. The land itself was regarded as feminine, and it was on the Hill of Uisneach that Conle was approached by an Otherworld woman, who invited him to a delightful land wherein dwelt none but women and maidens.[48] It is likely that the woman was the Maiden Sovereignty of Ireland, and that her Happy Otherworld was originally located within the hill itself. It was believed to be hollow, and to contain a gorgeous palace where time stood still.

The columns ranged around the Irish hall are of unmistakably phallic character. A malign being crushes the warriors of Ireland lodged in paired bags, where they are identified in

---

42   Örnólfur Thorsson (ed.), *Völsunga saga og Ragnars saga loðbrókar* (Reykjavík, 1985), pp. 12–14.

43   A hollow tree stood in the hall of king Aðils, within which he was enabled to escape his foes by means of magical enchantments (D. Slay (ed.), *Hrólfs Saga Kraka* (Copenhagen, 1960), p. 97).

44   Whitley Stokes and John Strachan (ed.), *Thesaurus Palaeohibernicus: A Collection of Old-Irish Glosses Scholia Prose and Verse* (Cambridge, 1901–3), ii, p. 295; Edward Gwynn (ed.), *The Metrical Dindshenchas* (Dublin, 1903–35), iv, p. 440; Standish H. O'Grady (ed.), *Silva Gadelica: A Collection of Tales in Irish with Extracts Illustrating Persons and Places* (London, 1892), i, p. 77; Charles Plummer (ed.), *Bethada Náem nÉrenn: Lives of Irish Saints* (Oxford, 1922), i, p. 324; idem (ed.), *Vitae Sanctorum Hiberniae*, i, p. 253. Cf. ibid., i, p. civ; James Hogan, 'The Ua Briain Kingship in Telach Óc', in John Ryan (ed.), *Féilsgríbinn Eóin Mhic Néill* (Dublin, 1940), p. 419.

45   Titus Burckhardt, *Mirror of the Intellect: Essays on Traditional Science & Sacred Art* (Cambridge, 1987), pp. 162–63.

46   Professor Ford suggests that 'The fully armed warriors hiding out in the bags hanging on the pegs are, as it were, by metonymy, in wombs' (*Studia Celtica*, xxii/xxiii, p. 36). While *boly croen* could mean 'wombs', this interpretation fails to account for their contrived hanging *in pairs* on pegs on either side of each of the hundred pillars.

47   It may well be that the episodes in *Branwen* of the battle of the meal-bag hall, and the subsequent emergence of the five Irish founding fathers from the maternal cave are of distinct provenance. Nevertheless, it seems the author recognized their affinity as related traditions of the cataclysmic end and reappearance of mankind.

48   Kim McCone (ed.), *Echtrae Chonnlai and the Beginnings of Vernacular Narrative Writing in Ireland* (Maynooth, 2000), p. 121–23.

the *englyn* as '*a form of flour*', i.e. the seminal life-force. This destructive action is followed immediately by the slaughter of the entire population of the land. We seem to have here dual versions of the periodic extermination of the inhabitants of Ireland, of which the first appears the more primitive.

The 'columns' (*colouyn*) in the story are envisaged as the wooden pillars of an Irish hall contemporary with the story's composition in the early eleventh century. However, their phallic nature suggests the possibility that in an earlier version of the story the assembly was envisaged as occurring within a megalithic structure. If so, they were originally stone menhirs imbued with procreative power ensuring the continuance of mankind. This in turn recalls the circular stone circles of megalithic times, from which the strange story of Efnisien and the scrotum-bags may ultimately have originated. (It will be argued in Chapter Eighteen that this was a prime function of the pillars of Stonehenge). The *mana* contained within the stones ensured the births of successive generations of humanity, until the close of a recurrent cycle when a destructive force intervened to abort the process. Sexual potency inhering to stones recalls the phallic herms of ancient Greece, which afforded protection to their communities. The common practice of breaking off the stone phallus of a herm presumably represented a mischievous assault on its protective power – comparable to the squeezing of the bags in the Welsh tale.[49]

Instances are adduced below of the widespread tradition in early Ireland and Britain of sexual potency ascribed to stones. In particular, the mothers of saints and heroes are frequently described as giving birth to their offspring on flagstones.[50] This practice attests to a belief in a unique form of *mana* contained within the stone, which quickened the mother's womb. The description in *Branwen* of Efnisien's slaughter of the warriors of Ireland concealed in bags suggests a rationalization of the reverse side of the medal. By pinching the 'form of flour' in the bags hanging from the columns he aborts the warriors' birth. In an earlier version, we may picture the destruction of mankind by a malignant being (*efnisien*, 'angry, hostile'),[51] which extinguishes the élan vital preserved within the columns.

Reasons were given earlier for associating the original story of the destruction and resurrection of the Irish race with the *omphalos* of the land at Uisneach. Again, given the ideological identification of Uisneach and Stonehenge, may we not envisage a similar belief associated with the mighty monoliths on Salisbury Plain? Geoffrey's location of Stonehenge as site of the slaughter of all the Britons save a single survivor indicates a parallel conception of cyclical immolation. In his version, the figure of the historical pagan Hengist came to be substituted for that of a malignant wizard, comparable to the midnight intruder who fought with Lludd in *Cyrànc Lludd a Lleuelys*; while his murderous followers have replaced the destructive

49   Mircea Eliade, *Patterns in Comparative Religion* (London, 1958), pp. 233–35; Walter Burkert, *Structure and History in Greek Mythology and Ritual* (Berkeley and Los Angeles, 1979), pp. 39–41; John Pairman Brown, *Israel and Hellas* (Berlin, 1995–2001), ii, pp. 131–32.

50   It seems likely that these recumbent stones represent a modification introduced under the influence of Christian literature, in which maidens simply lie on the slab at childbirth. In the Life of Saint David, two stones rise up at the time of his mother Nonnita's virgin conception. Nine months later, at the moment of her birth-pangs, she is said to have gripped a stone on which she leaned so tightly as to leave the imprint of her fingers on its surface (J. W. James (ed.), *Rhigyfarch's Life of St. David: The Basic Mid Twelfth-Century Latin Text with Introduction, Critical Apparatus and Translation* (Cardiff, 1967), pp. 4, 5). The allusion is presumably to a pillar bearing an ogam inscription, and it may be significant that all three stones associated with the maiden's impregnation and conception were originally represented as standing upright.

51   J. Lloyd-Jones, *Geirfa Barddoniaeth Gynnar Gymraeg* (Cardiff, 1931–63), p. 445.

Coraniaid.[52] Similarly, Efnisien's rôle in *Branwen* corresponds to that ascribed Hengist in the Welsh tale utilized by Nennius.

The birth of Taliesin

A mediæval Welsh legend of the birth of the poet Taliesin recounts how the witch Ceridwen engaged in furious pursuit of Gwion Bach, a lad who had stolen three precious drops of the potion of magical inspiration which spilled from her shattered cauldron. During his flight Gwion transformed himself into the shape of a hare, whereupon Ceridwen became a greyhound. After further shape-shifting escapes, the child concealed himself in the form of a grain of wheat in a great pile of winnowed wheat in a barn. The diabolical Ceridwen promptly became a black hen and swallowed Gwion into her womb (*croth*). There she bore him for nine months, when he was reborn as a human baby. Finding herself unwilling to slay her own child, she placed him in a coracle or leather bag (*korwgyl ne vol kroen*), which she set afloat in a lake. Eventually the bag was cast ashore, when the precocious infant revealed himself to be the inspired poet and prophet Taliesin.[53]

The poem entitled *Angar kyfyndawt* ('Hostile Alliance') in the *Book of Taliesin*, which reflects an earlier version of the tale, makes Taliesin declare:

> *I was a sheaf of corn.*
> *Ground meal of the farmers;*
> *I was corn in the furrow,*
> *I grew on the hill.*
> *He who sowed me harvested me,*
> *I am placed in an oven;*
> *I am dropped from his hand*
> *While he was roasting me.*
> *A hen swallowed me,*
> *With red claws, a crested foe;*
> *I remained nine nights*
> *Retained in her crop.*
> *I matured,*
> *I was the drink before a gwledig* [Lord],
> *I was dead, I was alive.*[54]

From this it appears that Taliesin's transformations passed through the entire process of being sown as grain, harvested, dried, and baked into bread of possibly sacred nature. The two concepts of the embryo as grain of corn gestating in a hen's crop as a womb, and that of the grain of corn being grown, harvested, and baked from flour into bread, are run so as to work in tandem. Of

---

52   In the same way the malevolent Irish mythical race *Fomoire* (who fulfil a rôle comparable to that of the Welsh *Coraniaid*) became identified with marauding Vikings from the Hebrides (Proinsias Mac Cana, 'The Influence of the Vikings on Celtic Literature', in Brian Ó Cuív (ed.), *The Impact of the Scandinavian Invasions on the Celtic-speaking Peoples c. 800–1100 A.D.* (Dublin, 1975), pp. 94–95; Elizabeth A. Gray, 'Cath Maige Tuired : Myth and Structure', *Éigse: A Journal of Irish Studies* (Naas, 1982), xix, pp. 16–17; Donnchadh Ó Corráin, 'The Vikings in Scotland and Ireland in the Ninth Century', *Peritia: Journal of the Medieval Academy of Ireland* (Turnhout, 1998), xii, pp. 310–13.

53   Patrick K. Ford (ed.), *Ystoria Taliesin* (Cardiff, 1992), p. 67.

54   J. Gwenogvryn Evans (ed.), *Facsimile & Text of the Book of Taliesin* (Llanbedrog, 1910), pp. 22–23.

the two, the concept of successive transmutations of grain as a mythical representation of the recurring life cycle of mankind is likely to be the more archaic.

As Patrick Ford, editor of the prose story, noted: 'Like Taliesin, the Irishmen [in *Branwen*] are enclosed in skin bags; the difference is that while Taliesin emerges newborn from his *bol croen*, the Irish all die inside theirs.'[55] Thus Taliesin's birth is successful, frustrating his mother's murderous intentions, while the Irishmen in *Branwen* are aborted. The themes reflect opposed facets of the same theme.

The motif of the shape-shifting pursuit, during which pursued and pursuer change themselves into a series of matched predators and prey, is recorded as a folklore theme as far afield as Ireland and Central Asia.[56] Although like many folklore stories it reflects aspects of early belief-systems, as a folktale its appeal lay primarily in its ingenuity and humour.[57] In contrast, analogies between the recurring life-cycles of grain and mankind play a major rôle in many early mythologies. In Homeric Greece and elsewhere barley-groats were identified with the marrow of men and 'the more solid part of the cerebro-spinal life-substance', i.e. that which constitutes the embryo transmitted from the male parent into the female's womb. Ears of wheat featured at the heart of the Phrygian and Eleusinian Mysteries, while in Egypt the semen of Osiris was identified with grain, ritually ingested by his votaries. In Central America the gods were held to have made man of maize: Mayan myth emphasized the newly born child's psychic union and identity with the cereal.[58]

In *Angar kyfyndawt* Taliesin declares:

> He who sowed me harvested me,
> I am placed in an oven;
> I am dropped from his hand
> While he was roasting me.

The myth and accompanying rite of 'drying' a body by fire in order to provide a passage to resurrection is attested in the ancient Near East, and it may have been reflected in a belief which the geographer Strabo ascribed to the druids: 'They assert (and others with them) that souls and the universe are indestructible, although fire or water may at times prevail.'[59]

The tale of Taliesin reflects a familiar mythological metaphor, in which the sexual act is envisaged as analogous to milling or grinding,[60] while the mother's womb corresponds to an oven, within which seed is baked and transformed into bread, the staff of life. It is likely, too, that analogy was drawn between flour borne in sacks from the mill to be kneaded and

---

55   Ford (ed.), *Ystoria Taliesin*, p. 96.

56   Jeremiah Curtin, *Myths and Folk-Lore of Ireland* (London, 1890), pp. 152–56; Nora K. Chadwick and Victor Zhirmunsky, *Oral Epics of Central Asia* (Cambridge, 1969), pp. 153–55.

57   This is well illustrated by T. H. White's entertaining treatment of Madam Mim's conflict with Merlin in *The Sword in the Stone*.

58   Onians, *The Origins of European Thought about the Body, the Mind the Soul, the World Time, and Fate*, pp. 222, 228, 229, 274, 279; George E. Mylonas, *Eleusis and the Eleusinian Mysteries* (Princeton, 1962), pp. 275–76, 305–306; E. A. Wallis Budge, *Osiris and the Egyptian Resurrection* (London, 1911), i, p. 80; J. Eric S. Thompson, *Maya History and Religion* (Norman, Okla., 1970), pp. 282–84. Cf. Stith Thompson, *Motif-Index of Folk-Literature: A Classification of Narrative Elements in Folktales, Ballads, Myths, Fables, Mediaeval Romances, Exempla, Fabliaux, Jest-Books, and Local Legends* (Bloomington, Indiana, 1955–58), v, p. 392 = T511.8.4).

59   Francesco Sbordone (ed.), *Strabonis Geographica* (Rome, 1963–2000), ii, p. 145. Cf. Onians, *The Origins of European Thought about the Body, the Mind the Soul, the World Time, and Fate*, pp. 283–85.

60   Cf. the obscene application of Latin *molo* (Adams, *The Latin Sexual Vocabulary*, pp. 152–53).

baked, and semen contained in the male scrotum which is transferred to the female womb for procreation.[61]

Wheat was employed in early Celtic societies as exemplar or metaphor for gifted intelligence, or the parallel faculty of holiness (i.e. perfection). Thus, an exceptionally talented British poet in the sixth century AD was described as 'Cian, who is known as "Wheat of Song"' (*Cian qui uocatur Gueinth Guaut*); while an early ninth-century Irish martyrology declared that 'the saints are God's wheat'.[62] Saint Illtud is recorded in his Life as having established agriculture among his people, and to have constructed three barns in Brittany from which corn or wheat was miraculously transported across the sea to save them during a time of dearth.[63] The significance of this might be discounted on grounds that miraculous provision of food is not infrequently ascribed to saints,[64] but for the fact that among salient qualities ascribed to Illtud was that of culture hero. Moreover, it has been seen that Brittany in the Life of Illtud generally stands for the Otherworld, ultimate source of the *élan vital*.

Illtud's father Anlawdd features in tradition as a prototypical ancestor figure, and it can I believe now be seen why it is preferable to take the principal element of his name as *blawd*, 'flour', rather than the inexplicable *blawdd*, 'tumult'.

To recapitulate: evidence suggests that the account of the Saint's parentage and birth in the Life of Illtud reflects an archaic account of the human birth-process. *Anlawdd* ('especial flour') is the original generative matter from which life is maturated. From it emerges the primal woman *rhieingulad* ('queen of the country'), who personifies the (feminine) landscape. She in turn is impregnated by *bicanus miles*, the embryo envisaged in early Celtic mythology as a tiny creature: in Welsh, *mil bychan* or *y rhyw bethan*. That this process originally represented divine conception is confirmed by its being located in the Otherworld, *Letavia*. Illtud is described in the Life of St Samson as 'the wisest of druids' (*magicus sagacissimus*), and I believe we have here preserved, under thin disguise, a uniquely explicit glimpse into an important aspect of the cosmogony of the British druids.

Saint Illtud

The earliest account of St Illtud features in the Life of St Samson, which was composed in the early seventh century, while drawing extensively on earlier testimony of sixth-century origin. Its narrative derives in part from elements of pagan cosmology, suggesting that pre-Christian rites and beliefs continued to flourish in the sixth century AD. Although Britain was undergoing a continuing process of conversion to Christianity, many heathen traditions and tenets were preserved by Welsh bards and storytellers, which in this way became absorbed into Christian literature.

In Samson's *Vita* the Saint begins his career by being sent to study at the school of Illtud (*Eltutus*), 'the famous master of the Britons'. Of him we are told that 'by birth he was a most wise magician, having knowledge of the future', who presided over a splendid monastery. He was an inspired prophet, who among other prognostications foretold his own death, and the

61   It was believed in early Egypt that the generative seed of man was nurtured within the mother's womb (J. Gwyn Griffiths (ed.), *Plutarch's De Iside et Osiride* (Cambridge, 1970), pp. 514–15).

62   Sir John Morris-Jones, 'Taliesin', *Y Cymmrodor* (London, 1918), xxviii, frontispiece; Whitley Stokes (ed.), *Félire Óengusso Céli Dé. The Martyrology of Oengus the Culdee* (London, 1905), p. 187.

63   Wade-Evans (ed.), *Vitae Sanctorum Britanniae et Genealogiae*, pp. 208, 226–28.

64   Henken, *The Welsh Saints: A Study in Patterned Lives*, pp. 74–79.

departure of his soul in the form of an eagle.[65] This last episode represents a well-attested pagan belief, being notably recounted of the euhemerized divinity Lleu, in the Fourth Branch of the *Mabinogi*.[66] In view of these allusions, it has been suggested that Illtud was a druid, at a time of syncretism between traditional paganism and the emergent power of Christianity.[67] A major social function of the druids was maintenance of schools, where they transmitted their lore to youthful neophytes,[68] and the *monasterium* at which Illtud was enrolled may have been such a college, which was in the process of becoming adapted to the requirements of the new religion.

Once again, etymology may serve to illuminate Illtud's original rôle. His hagiographer explains his name *Iltutus* as Latin '*ille*, he, who is *tutus*, safe from every fault'. This is clearly fanciful. The early form of the name, *Eltut(us)*, is a compound, whose prefix *el-* denotes 'many, numerous',[69] while *tud* means 'tribe or people'.[70] Given that the opening section of the Life of Saint Illtud reflects a mythological paradigm of divine birth, Eltut may be envisaged as a primal ancestor figure, the First Man: '(lord or father of) many tribes or peoples'. His mother Rieingulad, 'Earth Queen', was created in the Otherworld (*Letavia*) from *Anlawd*, the primal yeast or dough constituting the life-potential of matter. She was then impregnated, implicitly by a divinity, and generated the seminal life force (*mil bychan*) within her womb.

Another version of the myth features in yet more transparent guise in the Fourth Branch of the *Mabinogi, Math uab Mathonwy*. The leading characters of the story are unmistakably euhemerized divinities. Arianrhod, whose name means 'Silver Wheel' (i.e. the moon), arrives at the court of Gwydion, whose name means 'born from a tree'.[71] At her departure, Arianrhod pauses on the threshold, where she leaves behind 'a small something' (*y ryw bethan*). Gwydion snatches it up, and in due course it becomes the infant Lleu, i.e. the god Lug.[72] The mother's peculiar stance in the doorway at the moment of her delivery corresponds to the liminal setting of a birth in this world of a child

---

65 Flobert (ed.), *La vie ancienne de saint Samson de Dol*, pp. 156, 158–60. 'Thus naturally the eagle becomes in the imagery of the East a symbol of the flight of the soul towards the stars, of the resurrection of the dead, of apotheosis: the eagle is not only *theophorus* but also *psychophorus*' (H. P. L'Orange, *Studies on the Iconography of Cosmic Kingship in the Ancient World* (Oslo, 1953), p. 69). Cf. pp. 69–72.

66 Ian Hughes (ed.), *Math Uab Mathonwy: Pedwaredd Gainc y Mabinogi* (Aberystwyth, 2000), pp. 14, 15–16. For evidence of Celtic belief in bird-souls, cf. P. L. Henry, *The Early English and Celtic Lyric* (London, 1966), pp. 26–27, 48–49, 134–49, 205–6.

67 Rev. Thomas Taylor (tr.), *The Life of St. Samson of Dol* (London, 1925), p. 14; Wade-Evans, *Welsh Christian Origins*, pp. 133, 211.

68 Otto Seel (ed.), *C. Ivlii Caesaris Commentarii Rervm Gestarvm: Bellvm Gallicvm* (Leipzig, 1961), pp. 185–86; A. Silberman (ed.), *Pomponius Mela: Chorographie* (Paris, 1988), pp. 72–73; R. I. Best and Osborn Bergin (ed.), *Lebor na Huidre: Book of the Dun Cow* (Dublin, 1929), p. 158; R. I. Best, Osborn Bergin, M.A. O'Brien, and Anne O'Sullivan (ed.), *The Book of Leinster Formerly Lebar na Núachongbála* (Dublin, 1954–83), pp. 287, 816; Plummer (ed.), *Vitae Sanctorum Hiberniae*, ii, p. 111.

69 D. Simon Evans (ed.), *The Welsh Life of St David* (Cardiff, 1988), p. 43.

70 *Geiriadur Prifysgol Cymru*, pp. 1203, 3651; Sir John Rhŷs, 'Gleanings in the Italian Field of Celtic Epigraphy', *The Proceedings of the British Academy* (London, 1914), vi, pp. 329–31; Max Förster, *Der Flußname Themse und seine Sippe: Studien zur Anglisierung keltischer Eigennamen und zur Lautchronologie des Altbritischen* (Munich, 1941), p. 805. Irish *iltúatha* means 'many peoples' (Quin *et al.* (ed.), *Dictionary of the Irish Language*, 'I', col. 59), while the form *Illtud* suggests Irish usage (Pádraig Ó Riain, *The Making of a Saint: Finbarr of Cork 600–1200* (Dublin, 1997), p. 11).

71 Joseph Vendryes, 'La religion des Celtes', *Mana: Introduction à l'histoire des religions* (Paris, 1948), iii, p. 281. 'In Celtic, the word for "priest, druid" is formed on the ancient Indo-European word for "tree": OIr. *drúi* "druid", Gaul. *Druides*, pl. *Druidae*' (Thomas V. Gamkrelidze and Vjačeslav V. Ivanov, *Indo-European and the Indo-Europeans: A Reconstruction and Historical Analysis of a Proto-Language and a Proto-Culture* (Berlin and New York, 1995), i, p. 690).

72 Hughes (ed.), *Math Uab Mathonwy*, p. 8.

conceived in the Otherworld.[73] The *mil bychan* which implicitly became Illtud, and the *rhyw bethan* which was the embryo of Lleu, are all but synonymous.

As Kim McCone has written,

> Itself a, or even the, supremely liminal event, the birth of a hero(ine) destined to cross and recross all manner of thresholds, is particularly prone to be enhanced by further liminal associations ...[74]

In Ireland Lug was regarded as ancestor deity of royal dynasties, and there are indications that his counterpart Lleu in Wales fulfilled a parallel function.[75] Given close parallels between the birth-tales of Lleu and Illtud, could the latter's name originally have been an epithet of Lleu: *El-tud*, 'progenitor of many tribes'? The Irish ancestor deity was Eochaid *Ollathair* ('All-father'), while the Norse god Óðinn was likewise called Alfǫðr (All-father'), 'because he is father of gods, men, and all things'.[76] Further parallels between Illtud and Lleu will discussed presently.

The feast at Medgarth

We come now to a dramatic episode in Illtud's Life, linking him to the myth of the Sacred Centre, and so arguably to Stonehenge. On attaining maturity, he crossed the sea from Brittany and sought service at the court of his cousin King Arthur, the glories of whose court and martial fame had attracted him from afar. However, after an unaccountably brief period of service with that paradigmatic ruler, he transferred his services to a minor princeling in Glamorgan named *Poulentus* (Paul). It has been

---

73   For parallel examples of conceptions or births at the perimeters of buildings, cf. Theodor Mommsen (ed.), *Monvmenta Germaniae Historica* (xiii): *Chronica Minora saec. IV. V. VI. VII* (Berlin, 1894), iii, p. 108; James (ed.), *Rhigyfarch's Life of St. David*, p. 4; Whitley Stokes (ed.), *Lives of Saints from the Book of Lismore* (Oxford, 1890), p. 36. St Brigid is described as being born at the entrance to a house, and in the Scottish Highlands rituals in her honour were performed on doorsteps (Séamas Ó Catháin, *The Festival of Brigit: Celtic Goddess and Holy Woman* (Dublin, 1995), pp. 36–37). Doorways provided archetypal liminal locations, belonging neither to one world nor another (cf. Jeremiah Curtin, *Hero-Tales of Ireland* (London, 1894), p. 171). The Norwegian Lapps knew a goddess Uksakka, whose name derives from *uks/uksa*, 'door' or 'door-opening'. Her function was to determine the sex of a mother's unborn baby (Rafael Karsten, *The Religion of the Samek: Ancient Beliefs and Cults of the Scandinavian and Finnish Lapps* (Leiden, 1955), p. 41). In northern Siberia, 'If the childbirth was in the dwelling house, the woman usually gave birth on the threshold of a dwelling room' (Vladimir Napolskikh, Anna-Leena Siikala, and Mihály Hoppál (ed.), *Komi Mythology* (Budapest, 2003), p. 147).

74   Kim McCone, *Pagan Past and Christian Present in Early Irish Literature* (Naas, 1990), p. 189. Cf. pp. 189–90, 193–94.

75   Eoin MacNeill, *Celtic Ireland* (Dublin, 1921), p. 47; Eoin MacNeill and Gerard Murphy (ed.), *Duanaire Finn: The Book of the Lays of Finn* (London and Dublin, 1908–53), iii, pp. 206–8; Pádraig Ó Riain, 'Celtic mythology and religion', in Karl Horst Schmidt and Rolf Ködderitzsch (ed.), *Geschichte und Kultur der Kelten: Vorbereitungskonferenz 25.-28. Oktober 1982 in Bonn* (Heidelberg, 1986), pp. 249–51; Francis John Byrne, *Irish Kings and High-Kings* (London, 1973), p. 68. Lug's Welsh counterpart Lleu features as an ancestor-figure in the Harleian genealogies, and the conclusion of *Math uab Mathonwy* may be taken to imply that he was regarded as primal ancestor of the kingdom of Gwynedd. Graham Isaac points out that there is no reason to suppose that Lleu did not in due course produce an heir and enjoy a successful reign, which would have provided a fitting conclusion to *Math uab Mathonwy* (*Studi Celtici* (Alessandria, 2002), i, pp. 276–77). 'The cycle ends in effect with Gwynedd (under Lleu's restored reign) seeming to represent a new hope for integration of the Otherworld of native British tradition with the microcosm of Wales' (Alfred K. Siewers, 'Writing an Icon of the Land: the Mabinogi as a Mystagogy of Landscape', *Peritia* (2005), xix, p. 209). Lleu's epithet *hen* ('old') in the Harleian pedigree indicates a primary ancestor (Patrick K. Ford (ed.), *The Poetry of Llywarch Hen* (Los Angeles, 1974), pp. 25–32).

76   Osborn Bergin and R. I. Best, 'Tochmarc Étaíne', *Ériu: The Journal of the School of Irish Learning* (Dublin, 1938), xii, p. 142; Anthony Faulkes (ed.), *Snorri Sturluson: Edda; Prologue and Gylfaginning* (Oxford, 1982), p. 13.

observed that 'Illtud's visit [to Arthur] is unmotivated' in the narrative, while equally no indication is provided why the knight so swiftly abandoned his desire to serve the great king.[77]

It is likely that originally Illtud undertook military service under Arthur alone, while his transfer to the court of *Poulentus* reflects the Saint's association with St Cadog of Nantcarfan, whose abbey foundation lay in the district of Penychen, described by the hagiographer as ruled by the obscure petty ruler *Poulentus*. The source of the latter name will be suggested shortly. Welsh saints' lives customarily present Arthur in a negative light,[78] making it likely that the monarch's appearance in the Life of Illtud as the munificent warrior-king of secular legend reflects prior tradition, rather than hagiographical stock-in-trade.

One day the courtiers of King Poulentus, who included Illtud, sallied forth to hunt in the countryside near Cadog's monastery, whither they despatched an arrogant demand to the Abbot for food. Cadog complied, but as punishment for their sacreligious offence the warband was suddenly swallowed up by the earth. Illtud alone survived, through the fortunate chance of his becoming separated from his companions while pursuing birds with a hawk. Overawed by his miraculous escape, he repaired to Cadog, from whom he begged forgiveness. The Saint urged him to abandon his earthly status and become a monk. Illtud eagerly complied, and, after obtaining permission from his king, retired to a rural solitude, accompanied by his wife Trynihid and personal attendants.[79]

This condign punishment of the royal hunting party is also described in the Life of St Cadog, written by Lifris, Abbot of Nantcarfan, in the latter part of the eleventh century.[80] The Life of Illtud is later, having been compiled by Caradog of Llancarfan or another (anonymous) writer in the third or fourth decade of the following century. There can be little doubt that Caradog borrowed the principal elements of the motif of the miraculous engulphment from Lifris's earlier account.[81]

The version in the Life of St Cadog provides a verbose account of the disappearance of the impious picnickers, making no mention however of Illtud's fortunate escape. This features in an ensuing section (clearly originating in duplication of source material), which recounts how the warband of 'Poul surnamed Pennichen' (the Poulentus king of Penychen in the Life of Illtud) sallied forth to go hawking. Arrived at a place called *Medgarth*, they insisted that Cadog provide them with fifty loaves of bread, a cask of mead, and a fat grazing sow. A curious detail records that the party 'lay down in the form of a circle surrounding it [the feast], and the pig being cut in pieces to be roasted, they carefully prepared dinner'.

When the banquet was ready, the feasters awaited the arrival of Illtud, captain of the guard, without whom they would not dine. However, on his arrival the ground suddenly opened up

---

77   Brynley F. Roberts, '*Culhwch ac Olwen*, the Triads, Saints' Lives', in Bromwich, Jarman, and Roberts (ed.), *The Arthur of the Welsh*, p. 82.

78   Cf. J. S. P. Tatlock, *The Legendary History of Britain: Geoffrey of Monmouth's Historia Regum Britanniae and its Early Vernacular Versions* (Berkeley and Los Angeles, 1950), pp. 183–94; O. J. Padel, *Arthur in Medieval Welsh Tradition* (Cardiff, 2000), pp. 37–47. The shabby image assigned Arthur by Welsh hagiographers probably arose from a desire to wean audiences from attachment to profane tales of the great king. In the 1140s Ailred of Rievaulx lamented that novices in his abbey wept more over 'fictitious tales of someone (I don't know who) called Arthur (*fabulis quae vulgo de nescio quo finguntur Arcturo*) than over pious books', and went on to denounce such stories as 'fables and lies' (Antonia Gransden, *Historical Writing in England c. 550 to c. 1307* (London, 1974), p. 213).

79   Wade-Evans (ed.), *Vitae Sanctorum Britanniae et Genealogiae*, pp. 196–98.

80   J. S. P. Tatlock, 'The Dates of the Arthurian Saints' Legends', *Speculum: A Journal of Mediaeval Studies* (Cambridge, Mass., 1939), xiv, pp. 345–49; Chadwick (ed.), *Celt and Saxon*, pp. 283–310.

81   Doble, *Saint Iltut*, pp. 31, 34.

and swallowed them into the abyss. Illtud, who alone was preserved by his late appearance, observed both the disappearance of the prince and his companions and the miraculous preservation of their comestibles, which were transferred unharmed to a neighbouring hillock. As in his own Life, he was sufficiently overawed by what he had witnessed to repair to Cadog and become enrolled as a monk. Finally, Cadog retrieved the miraculously preserved feasters' food and drink, with which he fed poor people corresponding in number to the rapacious feasters of King Poul.[82]

The first of the two accounts in the Life of Cadog contains a significant allusion absent from the Life of Illtud. After describing the disappearance of the truculent king and his followers beneath the earth, the author Lifris mentions that 'the trench (*fossa*) in which they were swallowed up can still be seen by passers by, remaining open still as testimony to the event'. Evidently an oral tradition had become attached to a striking fissure in the vicinity, identified by Lifris as setting of the dramatic episode. Folktales of this sort generally comprise a brief account of a dramatic incident associated with a particular feature of the landscape, to which the names of historical or legendary protagonists had subsequently become attached. In the case of Illtud, it is likely that a local tale of a king and his followers swallowed up in the ground during a feast had by the eleventh century become converted to the hackneyed theme of a dramatic clash between the most celebrated local saint and a tyrannical prince of the region.

A succession of circumstantial details suggest once again that the legend represents rationalization of pagan myth into 'historical' legend.

1. The site of the royal feast was at Medgarth, 'in the middle of a plain' (*in campi meditullium*). There was a court and township called Medgarth among the estates of the abbey of Nantcarfan,[83] whose site remains unknown. *Medgarth* means 'middle enclosure', an apt appellation for any farm steading set in a median location.[84] At the same time, it may also signify the Sacred Centre of Celtic and Indo-European cosmologies.[85] That it was 'in the middle of a plain' suggests the latter interpretation.   .
    Numerous place names in the Celtic world called *Mediolanum*, 'Middle Plain',[86]

---

82   Wade-Evans (ed.), *Vitae Sanctorum Britanniae et Genealogiae*, pp. 58–60, 62–64.

83   Ibid., p. 120.

84   Welsh *garth* derives from Celtic **gorto-*, 'fence, enclosure, pen' (Matasović, *Etymological Dictionary of Proto-Celtic*, pp. 164–65), and thence from Indo-European **ghórdos* or **ghórtos* (J. P. Mallory and D. Q. Adams, *The Oxford Introduction to Proto-Indo-European and the Proto-Indo-European World* (Oxford, 2006), p. 221). 'Miðgarðr in [Norse] mythology was the world of people, created by gods, a fortress protecting men from attack by the giants. But in actual Scandinavian topography this word was … used as a name for farmsteads and settlements' (A. J. Gurevich, *Categories of Medieval Culture* (London, 1985), p. 49).

85   The name of the province of Meath, in which lay the Sacred Centre of Ireland at Uisneach, derives from Celtic **Medion*, 'the middle spot' (Thomas F. O'Rahilly, *Early Irish History and Mythology* (Dublin, 1946), p. 166). 'The semantic development from "middle" to "tree, forest" points clearly to the original association of **medʰyo-* "middle" with the center of the tree symbolizing the world' (Thomas V. Gamkrelidze and Vjačeslav V. Ivanov, *Indo-European and the Indo-Europeans: A Reconstruction and Historical Analysis of a Proto-Language and a Proto-Culture* (Berlin and New York, 1995), pp. 405–6, 647–48). Cf. Julius Pokorny, *Indogermanisches Etymologisches Wörterbuch* (Berne, 1959–69), i, p. 442; Patrick Sims-Williams, 'The Celtic Languages', in Anna Giacalone Ramat and Paolo Ramat (ed.), *The Indo-European Languages* (London and New York, 1998), p. 354.

86   '… -lanon a, comme dans le composé similaire *Medio-nemeton* en GB, une connotation religieuse ou mythique qui nous échappe (± 'accomplissement, plénitude')' (Xavier Delamarre, *Dictionnaire de la*

attest to the concept of the Sacred Centre, or *omphalos*, Navel of the Land, where the realms of mortals and immortals meet.[87] While there is no landscape feature that might plausibly be termed a plain in the vicinity of Llantwit Major, the Otherworld is regularly represented in early Welsh and Irish sources as a great plain: *maes mawr*, *mag mór*.[88]

2. We are told that Poul's party 'lay down in the form of a circle' during their feast. The impression is conveyed that Lifris found this oddly gratuitous detail in his source. Participants at a picnic enjoyed in the open air might more naturally be assumed to sit or lie haphazardly at spots convenient about the fire, and the formal pattern appears contrived and superfluous. It is possible that it reflects a ritualistic distribution. It was seen earlier, in the discussion of the story of 'The Dream of Maxen', that participants in the eternal banquet enjoyed in the Celtic Otherworld were believed to assemble in a circle, where they dined on pork. The concept of a ritual meal conducted within a round conceivably arose from a tradition reflecting gatherings at circular temples, enclosures, and other megalithic monuments of the Neolithic and Bronze Ages.[89]

This paradigmatic pattern features most famously in British legend. The motif of a king seated with his companions in a circle immediately recalls King Arthur and his Round Table. The first mention of the latter (*la Reonde Table*) appears in the Norman Wace's verse history of Britain, known as the *Brut*, which was completed by 1155.[90] Half a century later, Layamon compiled an English version, which recounted how rivalry at his board led Arthur to have a Round Table constructed in Cornwall, whose qualities were that it could seat *sixtene hondred and mo*, all on an equality, and accompanied Arthur wherever he went. The last detail recalls the Arthur of the early romances, who is often portrayed as remaining unmoved at the

langue gauloise: Une approche linguistique du vieux-celtique continental (Paris, 2001), p. 166). Cf. Pierre-Yves Lambert, *La langue gauloise: Description linguistique, commentaire d'inscriptions choisies* (Paris, 1995), pp. 43, 141.

87   For *mediolanum* cf. Christian-J. Guyonvarc'h, 'Mediolanum Bitvrigvm: Deux éléments de vocabulaire religieux et de géographie sacrée', *Celticvm I: Actes du Premier Colloque International d'Etudes Gauloises, Celtiques et Protoceltiques* (Rennes, 1961), pp. 142–61; François Falc'hun, *Les noms de lieux celtiques* (Rennes, 1966), pp. 71–90; J. P. Mallory and D. Q. Adams (ed.), *Encyclopedia of Indo-European Culture* (Chicago and London, 1997), pp. 205–6; Alexander Falileyev, Ashwin E. Gohil and Naomi Ward, *Dictionary of Continental Place-Names: A Celtic Companion to the Barrington Atlas of the Greek and Roman World* (Aberystwyth, 2010), pp. 159–60.

88   R. L. Thomson (ed.), *Owein or Chwedyl Iarlles y Ffynnawn* (Dublin, 1968), p. 2; *Ériu*, xii, p. 180; Elizabeth A. Gray (ed.), *Cath Maige Tuired: The Second Battle of Mag Tuired* (Naas, 1982), p. 36; Hans Pieter Atze Oskamp (ed.), *The Voyage of Máel Dúin: A Study in Early Irish Voyage Literature* (Groningen, 1970), pp. 152–58.

89   'In the British Isles, circular embanked enclosures, sometimes containing rings of upright stones or wooden posts, can only be interpreted as open-air temples or sanctuaries, comparable to the embanked circles and rings of carved wooden posts of the North American Indians', Stuart Piggott, *Ancient Europe from the beginnings of Agriculture to Classical Antiquity* (Edinburgh, 1965), p. 115). Cf. N. B. Aitchison, *Armagh and the Royal Centres in Early Medieval Ireland: Monuments, Cosmology, and the Past* (Woodbridge, 1994), pp. 74–99; D. M. Waterman, *Excavations at Navan Fort 1961–71* (Belfast, 1997), pp. 218–24. Literature on the subject is profuse. The significance of the 'magic circle' in early cosmogonies, etc., is discussed by Mircea Eliade, *Patterns in Comparative Religion* (London, 1958), p. 371. Semantic implications of the verb 'go round' (hence 'wheel', 'circle') in Semitic and Indo-European languages are discussed by Saul Levin, *Semitic and Indo-European: The Principal Etymologies with Observations on Afro-Asiatic* (Amsterdam and Philadelphia, 1995), p. 272.

90   I. D. O. Arnold and M. M. Pelan (ed.), *La partie arthurienne du Roman de Brut: (Extrait du manuscrit B.N. fr. 794)* (Paris, 1962), pp. 74, 156.

fulcrum of his great table, attended by a vast company.[91] The Round Table was famed far and wide among the Britons (i.e. Welsh, Cornish, and Bretons), who recounted many tales concerning it. Doubtless both authors drew on minstrels' recitations, and Layamon's allusion to the Table's Cornish origin suggests that enduring Celtic enclave as one of the principal regions where such tales originated.[92]

It has been suggested that the Round Table existed as a material artefact,[93] but there can be little doubt that it was in reality purely legendary in conception. Early tradition told of Arthur's withdrawal to the Otherworld realm of Avalon (Welsh *Ynys Afallach*, the Isle of Apples), and a folklore belief that he lived on with his knights in a cave is attested the length and breadth of Britain, and as far afield as Italy.[94] That his feast took place in the Underworld is further indicated by the traditional belief in Caernarvonshire that the oily appearance of water emerging from a spring was caused by animal fat borne from Arthur's kitchen.[95] This reflects the widespread conviction that his feast took place within a hollow hill, a traditional location of the Otherworld generally, and Arthur's court in particular.

The originally divine nature of Arthur's Round Table is further indicated by the number of knights assembled about it. Just as Bricriu's hall contained twelve couches for warriors surrounding the raised couch on which their host reclined, so Arthur's and the Grail Feasts were assigned twelve knights each.[96] Although the number is occasionally linked in the romances to the twelve apostles, the numeral twelve was as firmly rooted in Celtic indigenous numerological tradition as in biblical.[97] The eighth-century Irish legal tract *Críth Gablach* assigns a king twelve

---

91   Cf. John V. Fleming, 'The Round Table in Literature and Legend', in Martin Biddle, *King Arthur's Round Table: An archaeological investigation* (Woodbridge, 2000), pp. 5–30.

92   G. L. Brook and R. F. Leslie (ed.), *Laʒamon: Brut* (Oxford, 1963–78), ii, pp. 594–601.

93   It has been suggested that the Round Table represented 'a vague memory of the great Roman amphitheatre' at Caerleon (J. Pokorny, 'Miscellanea Celtica', *Celtica* (Dublin, 1956), iii, p. 307).

94   John S. Stuart Glennie, *Arthurian Localities; their Historical Origin, Chief Country, and Fingalian Relations* (Edinburgh, 1869), pp. 66–67; Sir John Rhŷs, *Studies in the Arthurian Legend* (Oxford, 1891), p. 18; Edwin Sidney Hartland, *The Science of Fairy Tales. An Inquiry into Fairy Mythology* (London, 1891), pp. 207–9, 211-12; John Rhŷs, *Celtic Folklore: Welsh and Manx* (Oxford, 1901), pp. 457–58, 461–64, 468, 473, 477; Marie Trevelyan, *Folk-Lore and Folk-Stories of Wales* (London, 1909), pp. 135–37; E. K. Chambers, *Arthur of Britain* (London, 1927), pp. 221–27; Arthur C. L. Brown, *The Origin of the Grail Legend* (Cambridge, Mass., 1943), pp. 63–65; T. Gwynn Jones, *Welsh Folklore and Folk-Custom* (London, 1930), pp. 88–89; Ceridwen Lloyd-Morgan, 'From Ynys Wydrin to Glasynbir: Glastonbury in Welsh Vernacular Tradition', in Lesley Abrams and James P. Carley (ed.), *The Archaeology and History of Glastonbury Abbey: Essays in Honour of the Ninetieth Birthday of C. A. Ralegh Radford* (Cambridge, 1991), pp. 312, 315.

95   Gwynn Jones, *Welsh Folklore and Folk Custom*, p. 113. 'The Arthur of romance has succeeded to the attributes of the Hero (the Welsh Lleu, Ir. Lug), and the feast over which he presides, like Finn's feast at Almu, is ultimately, as could be demonstrated, the Otherworld-Feast, from the lordship of which the god had been deposed' (O'Rahilly, *Early Irish History and Mythology*, pp. 526–27. Cf. idem, 'Buchet the Herdsman', *Ériu* (1952), xvi, p. 20).

96   Richard O'Gorman (ed.), *Robert de Boron, Joseph d'Arimathie: A Critical Edition of the Verse and Prose Versions* (Toronto, 1995), pp. 250–54; William A. Nitze and T. Atkinson Jenkins (ed.), *Le Haut Livre du Graal: Perlesvaus* (Chicago, 1932–37), i, p. 118; cf. ii, p. 266; Albert Pauphilet (ed.), *La Queste del Saint Graal: Roman du XIIIe siècle* (Paris, 1923), pp. 266–71. Arthur's knight Bohort was rewarded by King Brangoire (a version of the name of the god Bran, who is closely associated with Arthur in Welsh tradition) by being seated with twelve knights at a table, where he was served by the king's daughter (Alexandre Micha (ed.), *Lancelot: Roman en prose du XIIIe siècle* (1978–83), ii, p. 176). Cf. Roger Sherman Loomis, *Arthurian Tradition & Chrétien de Troyes* (New York, 1949), pp. 63–64, 174, 245–46, 386.

97   The number twelve bore sacral significance in Indo-European tradition (Gamkrelidze and Ivanov, *Indo-European and the Indo-Europeans*, i, p. 752). The twelve gods of Greece, Rome, the Hittites, and Egypt originally presided over the months of the year (Charlotte R. Long, *The Twelve Gods of Greece*

men in his retinue, and the twelve rivers of Ireland were believed to flow from the island's Sacred Centre at Uisneach.[98] Arthur himself is described in the ninth-century *Historia Brittonum* as gaining twelve victories over the Saxons, the number being artificially inflated by locating four at one site. In Irish and other early lore the bear, an animal closely associated with Arthur owing to identification of his name with Welsh *arth*, 'bear', was held to possess the strength of twelve men.[99] Furthermore, Gervase of Tilbury, who compiled his *Otia Imperiala* in the second decade of the thirteenth century, refers to Arthur's institution of the Round Table on a magical island in Cornwall, together with a fellowship of twelve knights.[100] His allusions appear to derive from insular tradition, most likely Cornish.

Returning to the Life of Illtud, the inconsequential nature of the Saint's brief stay at the court of Arthur, and his apparently unmotivated transfer to that of Poul Penychen, was remarked earlier. It seems likely that his attendance on Arthur was originally the sole occasion of his military service. This is emphasized by the circular disposition of the feasters at Medgarth, which corresponds to the traditional arrangement at Arthur's court. The incongruities may be reconciled on the assumption that the story of Illtud's dual military service originated in a single account of his attendance at the Otherworld Feast.[101]

Poulentus is described as subruler of the district (*cantref*) of Penychen in Glywysing. He is identical with *Poul Penychen*, who plays the same rôle vis-à-vis the saint in the Life of Cadog. *Poul* (clearly the original name) is a mysterious character. Nothing is known of him save what appears in the Lives of Cadog and Illtud, where he features as an incongruously obscure figure for a chieftain whose court implicitly rivals that of Arthur. It is unlikely that he enjoyed any historical existence. It is hard to envisage what led Lifris to introduce the name – unless, that is, it featured in his source as a sufficiently significant figure in the legend of Illtud to invite inclusion in the *Vita Cadoci*.

This indeed appears the likeliest explanation. The story of the impious feasters who disappear beneath the earth became attached to Medgarth, a spot situated in the district of Penychen. At one point Lifris duplicates the episode of the wicked king and his followers swallowed up by the earth, renaming him on this occasion *Sawyl Penuchel*,[102] a name featuring in the early pedigrees of a North British royal dynasty.[103] It looks as though Lifris, seeking to identify 'Poul Penychen', ransacked the genealogies, where he happened on a fairly similar name. The epithet *Penuchel* ('High Head') appeared sufficiently close to *Penychen* to suggest identity, especially when

---

and Rome (Leiden, 1987), pp. 144–86). For the significance of the number twelve in the Bible, cf. John MacQueen, *Numerology: Theory and outline history of a literary mode* (Edinburgh, 1985), pp. 15–16.

98   D. A. Binchy (ed.), *Críth Gablach* (Dublin, 1941), pp. 18, 23; R. I. Best and Osborn Bergin (ed.), *Lebor na Huidre: Book of the Dun Cow* (Dublin, 1929), p. 337. The significance of the number twelve in Celtic tradition is emphasized by the brothers Rees (*Celtic Heritage*, pp. 150–54).

99   Ó Catháin, *The Festival of Brigit*, pp. 124–25.

100 S. E. Banks and J. W. Binns (ed.), *Gervase of Tilbury: Otia Imperialia; Recreation for an Emperor* (Oxford, 2002), p. 424; cf. p. 310.

101 James Douglas Bruce suggested that the legend of King Arthur's Round Table originated in accounts of Celtic feasting, such as that recorded by Posidonius (*The Evolution of Arthurian Romance: From the Beginnings Down to the Year 1300* (Göttingen, 1928), i, p. 87).

102 Wade-Evans (ed.), *Vitae Sanctorum Britanniae et Genealogiae*, pp. 58–60.

103 Egerton Phillimore, 'The *Annales Cambriæ* and Old-Welsh Genealogies', *Y Cymmrodor* (1888), ix, p. 179; Wade-Evans (ed.), *Vitae Sanctorum Britanniae et Genealogiae*, p. 320; P. C. Bartrum (ed.), *Early Welsh Genealogical Texts* (Cardiff, 1966), pp. 56, 69, 73; Bromwich (ed.), *Trioedd Ynys Prydein*, pp. 41, 238.

coupled with *Sawyl*. Although *Sawyl* is in reality the Welsh form of *Samuel*,[104] an ecclesiastical author might have taken it for *Saul*, the original name of the biblical Paul (from which Old Welsh *Poul* derives).[105]

Now, the name *Poul* in the context of Lifris's story takes on especial relevance. The seemingly banal story of the miraculous punishment of him and his men suggests another archaic motif deriving from pagan Celtic mythology. The hero Eltut passes over as sole survivor from the Otherworld feast presided over by *Poul* into this world, where he becomes father of tribes, protector and fecundator of his country. This appropriately occurs at the Centre of the land (*Medgarth*), traditional birthplace of the founder of a fresh cycle of mankind.

Poul, Lord of the Otherworld Feast, recalls the similar sounding *Pwyll* of mediæval Welsh story. Eponymous protagonist of the tale *Pwyll Pendefig Dyfed* ('Pwyll Prince of Dyfed'), he is there described as withdrawing to the subterranean Otherworld of *Annwfn*, a name meaning 'bottomless' or 'immensely deep'.[106] There he became known as Pwyll, Head of Annwfn (*Pwyll Penn Annwuyn*), and an early Welsh poem mentions *peir pen annwfyn*, 'the Cauldron of the Head of Annwfn'. That is, the cauldron of the Otherworld Feast, over which Pwyll presided.[107]

Welsh *pwyll* means 'wisdom, judgment', which finds a correspondence in the name of the Irish god-king *Conn*, 'head'.[108] There is also marked resemblance between Pwyll as disembodied Head of the Otherworld, and Bran in the associated tale of *Branwen*. After being wounded in the thigh (a euphemism for emasculation), Bran arranges for his decapitated Head to be present at the Otherworld Feast on the Isle of Gwales.[109] These figures in turn recall the Fisher King of the Grail romances, who is likewise wounded in the groin and remains sedentary in a magical

---

104 Kenneth Jackson, *Language and History in Early Britain: A Chronological Survey of the Brittonic Languages First to Twelfth Century A.D.* (Edinburgh, 1953), p. 415; Sims-Williams, *The Celtic Inscriptions of Britain*, pp. 143, 196.

105 Cf. Baring-Gould and Fisher, *The Lives of the British Saints*, iii, p. 306; J. Loth, 'Remarques et additions à la grammaire galloise historique et comparée de John Morris Jones', *Revue Celtique* (Paris, 1915–16), xxxvi, p. 152.

106 J. Morris Jones, *A Welsh Grammar: Historical and Comparative* (Oxford, 1913), p. 160; *Mana*, iii, p. 308; Thomson (ed.), *Pwyll Pendeuic Dyuet*, pp. 25–26. Heinrich Wagner interpreted the name as 'immensely deep', comparing it with Akkadian *apsu* and Greek àbyssos ('Studies in the Origins of Early Celtic Traditions', *Ériu* (1975), xxvi, pp. 7, 9–10). The terminology reflects a concept of cosmic dualism between the bright supraterrestrial world and its counterpart, the dark Underworld (Wolfgang Meid, 'Über *Albiōn, elfydd, Albiorīx* und andere Indikatoren eines keltischen Weltbildes', in Martin J. Ball, James Fife, Erich Poppe, and Jenny Rowland (ed.), *Celtic Linguistics/Ieithyddiaeth Geltaidd; Readings in the Brythonic Languages: Festschrift for T. Arwyn Watkins* (Amsterdam and Philadelphia, 1990), p. 436).

107 Thomson (ed.), *Pwyll Pendeuic Dyuet*, p. 7; J. Gwenogvryn Evans (ed.), *Facsimile & Text of the Book of Taliesin* (Llanbedrog, 1910), p. 54.

108 O'Rahilly, *Early Irish History and Mythology*, pp. 281–83; Heinrich Wagner, 'Studies in the Origins of Early Celtic Civilisation', *Zeitschrift für celtische Philologie* (Tübingen, 1971), xxxi, p. 56; Matasović, *Etymological Dictionary of Proto-Celtic*, p. 179.

109 The cult of the sapient head may ultimately be of shamanistic origin. In §IV.26, Herodotus describes how the Central Asian Issedones preserved the head of a dead father, which was stripped to the skull and gilded, after which it was preserved as a sacred relic, being brought out once a year to be honoured with sacrifice (Haiim B. Rosén (ed.), *Herodoti Historiae* (Leipzig, 1987-97), i, p. 367). Cf. J. D. P. Bolton, *Aristeas of Proconnessus* (Oxford, 1962), pp. 76–78. In Norse mythology, Óðinn preserved Mímir's head with herbs, spoke spells over it, and learned from it many hidden things (Bjarni Aðalbjarnarson (ed.), *Heimskringla* (Reykjavik, 1941–51), i, pp. 13, 18). The name *Mímir* derives from Indo-European *(s)mer-*, meaning 'to meditate, recall, remember' (Pokorny, *Indogermanisches Etymologisches Wörterbuch*, i, p. 969).

castle, where he maintains a marvellous feast eventually attended by his destined successor, the young hero Perceval.[110]

Behind these mythological figures lies the archaic concept of an otiose deity, immanent in the cosmos, source and sustainer of all that exists. In time humanity is destined to be saved by a vibrant young god, who renews the world by initiating a fresh cycle of humanity. A version of this myth evidently underlies the Life of Illtud, obscured only by an element of confusion arising from the author's rationalizing relocation in this world of events which were originally set in the Otherworld. Thus Arthur, whose Roman name (*Artorius*) betrays the relative lateness of his substitution for a Celtic deity, is portrayed as a king of Britain, whose service Illtud inconsequentially abandons for that of the obscure kinglet Poul(entus). In an earlier pagan version, Illtud may be envisaged as eventually emerging from the Otherworld realm ruled by Pwyll-Arthur (each being traditionally envisaged as host of the Otherworld Feast), to pursue an heroic career on earth. As in customary fashion the story became euhemerized, it appears that the divinity *Pwyll penn Annwuyn* became recast as a local mortal princeling, *Poul pendefig Pennychen* — Penychen being as we know a sub-district (*commot*) of the kingdom of Glywysing, where Illtud's monastery is located.[111]

Further considerations are similarly suggestive. In the *Vita Cadoci*, Poul and his followers are described as engaging in a hawking party, from whose immolation Illtud alone escapes. No explanation is given for his survival, but in the *Vita Iltuti* it is accounted for by his temporarily absenting himself while exercising his hawk. One of Arthur's two principal companions in British tradition was his nephew Gwalchmai (the Gawain of Continental romance), whose name means 'Hawk of the Plain'.[112] Given the unmistakably mythological characteristics of Gwalchmai in the sources, it is tempting to identify the plain in question with that of the Otherworld. A name for the Irish Otherworld was *Mag Meld*, the 'fair plain', which was characterized by an abundance of flowers.[113] King Conn at Tara discovered the hall of the god Lug set in a great plain, and in early Welsh romance Culhwch and his companions 'went forth until they came to a wide, open plain, where they saw a fort, the most splendid in the world'. It was a magical stronghold, which was clearly located in the Otherworld.[114]

The image of a man of exceptional gifts, who through association with a hawk becomes lone survivor of a cataclysm located at the Centre (*Medgarth*) which engulphs everyone around him, has a remarkable echo in Irish mythology. Ireland, it was believed, had been populated by five successive races, each of which came to be destroyed by natural disaster. One man alone survived these cyclical cataclysms. Túan mac Cairell was a shape-shifter, who transformed

---

110   Cf. Jean-Michel Picard, 'The Strange Death of Guaire Mac Áedán', in Donnchadh Ó Corráin, Liam Breatnach, and Kim McCone (ed.), *Sages, Saints and Storytellers: Celtic Studies in Honour of Professor James Carney* (Maynooth, 1989), p. 369.

111   J. Gwenogvryn Evans, 'Extracts from Hengwrt MS. 34', *Y Cymmrodor* (1888), ix, p. 331.

112   Ernst Windisch, *Das Keltische Brittannien bis zu Kaiser Arthur* (Leipzig, 1912), p. 172; Jackson, *Language and History in Early Britain*, p. 449; Bromwich (ed.), *Trioedd Ynys Prydein*, pp. 369, 552; *The Welsh History Review* (Cardiff, 1963), p. 85; Bromwich and Simon Evans (ed.), *Culhwch and Olwen*, p. 105.

113   Séamus Mac Mathúna (ed.), *Immram Brain: Bran's Journey to the Land of the Women* (Tübingen, 1975), pp. 39–40; Hans P. A. Oskamp, 'Echtra Condla', *Études Celtiques* (Paris, 1974), xiv, 221–25; Myles Dillon (ed.), *Serglige Con Culainn* (Dublin, 1953), pp. 5–6. Indo-European peoples envisaged the Otherworld as a fertile pasture land (Gamkrelidze and Ivanov, *Indo-European and the Indo-Europeans*, i, pp. 722–23).

114   Kevin Murray (ed.), *Baile in Scáil: 'The Phantom's Frenzy'* (Dublin, 2004), p. 34; Bromwich and Simon Evans (ed.), *Culhwch and Olwen*, p. 15. In the latter tale, 'The *gorsedd* (or *crug*), "knoll, mound", has close analogies with the Irish *síd* or Otherworld-hill' (*Ériu*, xvi, p. 11; cf. Ifor Williams (ed.), *Pedeir Keinc y Mabinogi* (Cardiff, 1930), p. 121).

himself into animal and bird forms enabling him to surmount untold perils. The most striking form he adopted was that of a great hawk, in which guise he 'outlived all the peoples who had settled in the land of Ireland'. From being wretched and plagued by fear he became inspired, acquired knowledge of all things, and survived generations of men throughout a span of ages.[115]

In early Irish society birds were widely regarded as souls or soul-carriers.[116] In Britain, the pagan god Lleu and the Christian Illtud were believed to have departed this life in eagle guise.[117] The curious circumstance of Illtud's survival at Medgarth suggests a version of this motif, comparable to that found in the Irish story of Túan mac Cairell. Illtud alone survived the cataclysm, hovering above the earth's collapse in the form of a hawk: a mythic theme rationalized by the hagiographer into the adventure of a falconer.

The sudden disappearance into the ground of all the feasters apart from Illtud suggests a swallowing up into the maw of death, i.e. they passed from this world into the subterranean Otherworld of *Annwfn*. The mention by Illtud's hagiographer that the hole into which they vanished remained visible in his day suggests a pre-existing legend, which had become attached to a natural feature locally identified as a point of access to the Otherworld. As the brothers Rees observed:

> At the centre [of many cosmologies] there is a shaft which is the mouth of the nether regions into which the waters of the Deluge flowed, a hole in the ground like the Roman *mundus* into which the spirits of the dead depart, or an oracular cave as at Delphi.[118]

Any cleft in the earth could be taken for an entrance to *Annwfn*, the 'bottomless' Otherworld. Dafydd ap Gwilym describes a fox disappearing into its subterranean lair as dwelling 'deep down in *Annwfn*'.[119]

A chasm in the district of Penychen was believed to provide access to Arthur's eternal Round Table feast. According to local Somerset legend, his traditional stronghold at Cadbury was hollow, with an iron gate providing access to the interior.[120] An explanation of the Penychen legend compatible with the accounts preserved in the Lives of Cadog and Illtud may be posited on the following lines. At the conclusion of a cosmic cycle, the race of men passes into the Otherworld, where they participate in the eternal feast at Arthur's Round Table. (The figure of Arthur has implicitly replaced that of the Otherworld divinity Pwyll – hence the duplication.) This annihilation must have brought about the extinction of humanity on earth, but for the escape of a solitary survivor in the form of a hawk, who ensures mankind's continuing survival.

115 John Carey, 'Scél Túain meic Chairill', *Ériu* (1984), xxxv, p. 102.

116 Cf. Alexander Heggarty Krappe, *Balor With the Evil Eye: Studies in Celtic and French Literature* (Columbia, 1927), pp. 93–103; Marina Smyth, *Understanding the Universe in Seventh-Century Ireland* (Woodbridge, 1996), p. 73.

117 Hughes (ed.), *Math Uab Mathonwy*, p. 14; Flobert (ed.), *La vie ancienne de saint Samson de Dol*, p. 158.

118 Rees and Rees, *Celtic Heritage*, p. 159. Cf. Eliade, *Patterns in Comparative Religion*, pp. 232, 373–74.

119 Rachel Bromwich (ed.), *Dafydd ap Gwilym: A Selection of Poems* (Llandysul, 1982), p. 91. The poem *Angar Kyvyndawt* contrasts 'in Annwfn below the earth, in air above the earth': *yn annόfyn ygorόyth. yn awyr uch eluŷd* (J. Gwenogvryn Evans (ed.), *Facsimile & Text of the Book of Taliesin* (Llanbedrog, 1910), p. 20).

120 Rev. J. A. Bennett, 'Camelot', *The Proceedings of the Somersetshire Archæological and Natural History Society* (Taunton, 1890), xxxvi, pp. 2–5. For caves as entrances to the Otherworld, cf. Theo Brown, *The Fate of the Dead: A Study in Folk-Eschatology in the West Country After the Reformation* (Cambridge, 1979), pp. 69–71.

That Illtud was regarded as an universal progenitor is suggested by his name, '(Father of) Many Tribes'.

In addition, the account of his parentage suggests an archaic conception of the manner in which human beings are generated in the Otherworld (*Letavia*). A tiny sperm-creature (*míl bychan, rhyw bethan*), is transmitted from the primæval Father into the womb of the Earth Queen (*Rhiein-gulad*). These events are linked to the *medgarth*, or 'Middle Enclosure' of the land, originally the island of Britain, which in local legend became attached to a natural chasm popularly believed to provide access to the Otherworld. Like a fly in amber, the Life of Saint Illtud preserves a remarkably explicit version of the cosmic pagan myth of primæval birth and regeneration, traditionally centred on the *omphalos* of the land, *medgarth*.

The concluding passage of this episode in the Life of Illtud describes how the food and drink from the feast were miraculously removed to a nearby hillock, after which St Cadog put them to Christian use by distributing them to the poor. One could hardly seek a clearer intimation of the hagiographer's appropriation of a pagan legend to exalt the Church. Yet more significant is his emphasis on the fact that the food and drink (mead and pork) remained uncorrupted (*intemerata atque intacta constiterunt*). A characteristic of the Otherworld feast is that its comestibles continue eternally replenished.[121]

The pagan cosmogony of Britain

All these considerations suggest that the principal elements in the Medgarth episode of the *Vita Iluti* originated in a cosmogonic myth attached to the Omphalos of Britain. In the beginning was the First Man, who was conceived by the goddess of the land (the Maiden Sovereignty) in the Otherworld. He alone survives the universal cataclysm, hovering above the void in the guise of a hawk.

The fortuitous survival of this pagan cosmogony is owing to its having been assigned a local habitation in South Wales, at a spot bearing the seemingly apt name Medgarth. The originally distinct legend of the engulphed feasters was interpolated by the hagiographer Lifris into his Life of St Cadog. A generation later, Caradog of Llancarfan similarly inserted the tale into his Life of St Illtud. His was evidently a discrete version of the legend, since it preserves the archaic element rationalized as Illtud's escape with his hawk. This suggests that Caradog did not borrow (at least, not entirely) the motif from Lifris, but possessed independent knowledge of the theme.

In this way, an originally cosmological myth became attached to a local place name in the district of Penychen, Medgarth, meaning 'Middle Farmstead' or 'Middle Enclosure'. A not uncommon toponym,[122] it could equally stand for the Omphalos of Britain, focus of British

---

121 Thomas F. O'Rahilly, *Early Irish History and Mythology* (Dublin, 1946), pp. 121–22. The Irish inexhaustible cauldron, *caire ainsicean*, provided food without limit at successive banquets (Ruth Lehmann (ed.), *Fled Dúin na nGéd* (Dublin, 1964), p. 16). In Valhöll the Norse heroes feasted on the flesh of the boar Sæhrímnir, which was cooked each day and made whole again each evening (Faulkes (ed.), *Snorri Sturluson: Edda*, p. 32). From the poem *Grímnismál* we learn that a goat browsing on the World-Tree Yggdrasil provided a cask of clear mead which never ran dry (Hans Kuhn and Gustav Neckel (ed.), *Edda: Die Lieder des Codex Regius nebst Verwandten Denkmälern* (Heidelberg, 1962–68), i, p. 62).

122 Cf. O. J. Padel, *Cornish Place-Name Elements* (Cambridge, 1985), pp. 158–59. The Middle Farm is a placename in Wenvoe, Glamorgan (Gwynedd O. Pierce, *The Place-Names of Dinas Powys Hundred* (Cardiff, 1968), p. 315). OE *middel* is similarly found in place-name compounds (A. H. Smith, *English Place-Name Elements* (Cambridge, 1956), ii, p. 40; Anton Fägersten, *The Place-Names of Dorset* (Uppsala, 1933), pp. 130, 200; Helge Kökeritz, *The Place-Names of the Isle of Wight* (Uppsala, 1940), p. 129: etc.). *Middelham* in Roxburghshire is 'quite obviously means "the middle village"' (W. F. H. Nicolaisen, *Scottish Place-Names: Their Study and Significance* (London, 1976), p. 22).

mythology, which accounts for the transference of a national myth to an obscure spot bearing a name corresponding to that of the *omphalos*.

In *Cyfranc Lludd a Lleuelys*, the Centre of the island is established by Lleuelys's measurement of Britain by length and breadth, the spot where the lines crossed being established as the central point, *y pwynt perued*. It is a little surprising that neither *pwynt* nor *perfedd* is of Celtic derivation. *Perfedd* is a borrowing from Latin *permedius*, 'middle', being presumably adopted during the Roman occupation of Britain. *Pwynt* is an English loanword, which must accordingly have been absorbed into Welsh at an even later date.[123] Nevertheless, given the archaic antecedents of the pagan legend, it is evident that in an earlier era the Centre must have been known by terminology of purely Celtic derivation. Was it *medgarth*, 'the central enclosure', a compound evoking the widely distributed Celtic placename *mediolanum*?

The banishment of Trynihid

The *Vita Iltuti* provides further previously hidden glimpses of pre-Christian mythology. After his escape from the annihilation visited on the retinue of Poulentus, Illtud received a blessing from Saint Cadog, and undertook thenceforward to pursue a life dedicated to the service of God. That night an angel appeared to him in a dream, instructing him among other things to set aside his wife *Trynihid*, and adopt a life of chastity. He awoke, and, pondering these instructions, asked his wife to rise and check the welfare of their horses (an odd reaction, surely?). The moon happening to be shining brightly, this she was able to do. She left their couch completely naked, with her hair hanging loose. On her return the wind blew it aside, revealing her nudity to her husband. Newly committed to the rigorous life of a hermit, when she sought to return to their bed Illtud harshly told the unfortunate woman to depart forthwith.

She meekly accepted this rough treatment. Fortunately, 'she liked mountain solitude' and withdrew to a neighbouring eminence, on which she built an oratory and devoted herself to a life of chastity and prayer. One day she revisited her husband, whom she found worn and ragged from the life of privation to which he had committed himself. This 'improper visit' led to her being struck blind on the spot. However, the Saint successfully prayed to God to heal her. Sadly, her face was no longer so lovely as it had been, being disfigured by pallor and unsightly spots.[124]

This unfeeling rejection of a wife, as loyal as she was pious and beautiful, has provoked sharp criticism at the hands of Illtud's modern biographers. One dismissed the erotic incident as a 'diseased fancy' of the hagiographer, which was 'entirely his own idea'.[125] Such a moral judgment is understandable, only if the episode be taken *au pied de la lettre*. However, even by the sometimes eccentric standards of mediæval hagiography, the episode appears gratuitously unpleasant and irrational. Why was it necessary to inspect the horses in the middle of the night, particularly when we learn that they were supervised by grooms (*custodes*)? Why should the lady go out into the cold entirely naked, when her clothes presumably lay beside the bed? Why the superfluous detail of her hair entirely covering her body, until it was blown aside by the wind? And why should temporary blindness cause her complexion to be permanently blemished in the manner so particularly described? God had pardoned her fault, which was in any case so

---

123 Ifor Williams (ed.), *Cyfranc Lludd a Llevelys* (Bangor, 1910), p. 27; Förster, *Der Flußname Themse und seine Sippe*, pp. 625, 664, 854; Lewis, *Yr Elfen Ladin yn yr Iaith Gymraeg*, p. 44.

124 Wade-Evans (ed.), *Vitae Sanctorum Britanniae et Genealogiae*, pp. 198–200, 216–18.

125 Baring-Gould and Fisher, *The Lives of the British Saints*, iii, pp. 307, 310; Doble, *Saint Iltut*, p. 34. Canon Doble condemned 'the repulsive stories of Iltut's treatment of his wife, which he has invented' (ibid., p. 28).

venial as to appear incomprehensible. Her nakedness was exposed purely in consequence of her husband's instruction, and when she returned she promptly responded to his reproach by vowing herself to chastity, and attempted no further conjugal intercourse with him.

Closer examination suggests that once again Lifris is seeking to make sense of an episode whose real meaning had over time become obscured. Since Trynihid was evidently in the habit of sleeping naked, what provoked Illtud's otherwise unaccountable revulsion was the sight of her nude body *exposed by bright moonlight*. There are in fact striking indications that the lady was a personification of the moon.

1. Her nudity is associated with moonlight for a reason unexplained by, and perhaps unknown to, the hagiographer. Given indications that she was originally a moon-goddess, it is significant that Romans were prohibited from observing Trynihid's divine counterpart Diana bathing.[126]

2. The exposure of her pure, pale flesh in consequence of the wind's blowing aside her hair evokes emergence of the moon from behind clouds. In early times clouds were widely envisaged as a veil concealing the moon's face from observers.[127]

3. Particular emphasis is laid on Trynihid's chastity, *femina castissima*. The Roman moon goddess Diana was likewise famously virginal, *dea virgo*.[128]

4. Trynihid 'liked mountain solitude' and founded an oratory upon a hill. Diana was widely worshipped on mountains, possibly because the moon appears to pass close to their summits.[129]

5. The pallor and accompanying spots which unaccountably mar Trynihid's beautiful face recall craters and other geological formations disfiguring the moon's wan surface. The Greek geographer Hecatæus, describing a northern island widely identified with Britain, states that her inhabitants studied lunar natural features similar to those found on earth.[130]

These considerations suggest that the Trynihid episode in the Life of Illtud originated in pagan lunar mythology. In a celebrated passage, Pliny describes the importance to the druids of the moon's phases for establishing the dates of their most important sacrifices.[131] In France a traditional rite persisted up to a late period of ascending a hill on St John's Eve in order to ensure resolution of the lunar and solar solstices.[132]

Although her rôle in the Life of Illtud suggests that Trynihid was originally a lunar goddess, her name is not found in any other source, nor has it been assigned a satisfactory

---

126   E. H. Alton, D. E. W. Wormell, and E. Courtney (ed.), *P. Ovidi Nasonis Fastorvm Libri Sex* (Leipzig, 1985), p. 108.

127   Sophie Lunais, *Recherches sur la lune, I: Les auteurs latins de la fin des guerres puniques à la fin du règne des Antonins* (Leiden, 1979), p. 100.

128   Georges Dumézil, *Archaic Roman Religion* (Chicago, 1970), p. 408.

129   Lunais, *Recherches sur la lune, I*, pp. 116–17.

130   C. H. Oldfather (ed.), *Diodorus of Sicily* (London, 1933–67), ii, p. 40.

131   H. Rackham, W. H. S. Jones, and D. E. Eichholz, (ed.), *Pliny: Natural History* (London, 1938–62), iv, pp. 548–50.

132   Claude Gaignebet and Jean-Dominique Lajoux, *Art profane et religion populaire au Moyen Age* (Paris, 1985), p. 70. Hilltop shrines were once common in Britain (Brown, *The Fate of the Dead*, pp. 68–70).

etymology.[133] One possibility is that *Trynihid* represents an orthographical misreading of *Ar(i)
anrhod*, the euhemerized Celtic goddess who plays a significant rôle in the prose tale *Math
uab Mathonwy*, and is mentioned in other Middle Welsh sources.[134] It is likely that she was
originally a moon goddess, or at any rate associated with the moon, since her name derives
from a compound of Middle Welsh *ariant*, 'silver', and *rot*, 'wheel'.[135] The Old Welsh form of
the goddess's name (*argant*) is preserved by the English poet Layamon, who describes how the
mortally wounded Arthur was taken by queen *Argante* to her transmarine realm of *Aualun*
(Avalon).[136] A comparable name *Eurolwen* ('golden wheel') probably reflects solar imagery,
while *Arianrhod* ('silver wheel') corresponds to the moon, envisaged as a wheel in Norse and
Greek literature.[137]

In *Math uab Mathonwy* Arianrhod dwells in a sea-girt fortress on the Welsh coast, inhabited
only by women. However, that she originally dwelt in a celestial realm is suggested by popular
ascription of her stronghold to the constellation Corona Borealis. Furthermore, the Welsh Triads
allude to her bearing sons by *Lliaws mab Nwyfre*, whose name means 'Multitude son of Sky'.[138]
We may have here the detritus of a British version of the widespread myth, wherein the male
sky-god (the sun) begets the human race on the feminine moon, which was widely regarded as
a reservoir of souls.[139]

Correspondence was noted earlier between the birth-tales of Illtud and Lleu. In addition,
both figures are described as departing this world in the guise of an eagle. *Illtud* means 'one who

---

133 Wade-Evans suggested that the placename Llantriddyd preserves the name of Trynihid (*Welsh Christian
     Origins*, p. 134; cf. Doble, *Saint Iltut*, pp. 38–39). However, the identification is untenable on philological
     grounds (Pierce, *The Place-Names of Dinas Powys Hundred*, pp. 123–24).

134 For references to Ari(i)anrhod, cf. Ifor Williams (ed.), *Pedeir Keinc y Mabinogi* (Cardiff, 1930),
     pp. 269–70; Hughes (ed.), *Math Uab Mathonwy*, pp. xxiii–xxvii.

135 'Arianrhod, "silver wheel"' (O'Rahilly, *Early Irish History and Mythology*, pp. 304). Cf. John Rhys,
     Lectures on the Origin and Growth of Religion as Illustrated by Celtic Heathendom (London, 1888),
     p. 284; Jan de Vries, *Keltische Religion* (Stuttgart, 1961), p. 134; John T. Koch, 'A Swallowed Onomastic
     Tale in Cath Maige Mucrama?', in John Carey, John T. Koch, and Pierre-Yves Lambert (ed.), *Ildánach
     Ildírech: A Festschrift for Proinsias MacCana* (Andover and Aberystwyth, 1999), p. 74. MW *arian(t)* <
     Celtic *arganto (Alexander Falileyev, *Etymological Glossary of Old Welsh* (Tübingen, 2000), p. 11).

136 Brook and Leslie (ed.), *Laȝamon: Brut*, ii, p. 750.

137 O'Rahilly, *Early Irish History and Mythology*, pp. 304–5; Françoise Bader, *La langue des dieux, ou
     l'hermétisme des poètes indo-européens* (Pisa, 1989), pp. 240–44. Rachel Bromwich suggested that the
     correct form could be *aran*, 'round, compact' (*Trioedd Ynys Prydein*, pp. 278–79), but even ignoring
     the early form recorded by Layamon, 'round wheel' seems an improbable oxymoron. Little is recorded
     of pre-Christian British knowledge of the heavenly bodies, but the pagan Irish in the seventh century
     AD envisaged the sun as a wheel (John Gwynn (ed.), *Liber Ardmachanus: The Book of Armagh, Edited
     with Introduction and Appendices* (Dublin, 1913), p. 448).

138 Rhŷs, *Celtic Folklore*, p. 645; Rachel Bromwich, 'The Historical Triads: With Special Reference to
     Peniarth MS. 16', *The Bulletin of the Board of Celtic Studies* (Cardiff, 1946), xii, p, 14; John Rhŷs and
     J. Gwenogvryn Evans (ed.), *The Text of the Mabinogion and other Welsh Tales from the Red Book of
     Hergest* (Oxford, 1887), p. 298. For Lliaws cf. J. Loth, 'Remarques et additions à la grammaire galloise
     historique et comparée de John Morris Jones', *Revue Celtique* (Paris, 1915–16), xxxvi, pp. 384–385. On
     the other hand, this might represent no more than popular speculation, deriving from the tradition
     that Arianrhod's realm was not of this world.

139 Y. Vernière, 'La lune, réservoir des âmes', in François Jouan (ed.), *Mort et fécondité dans les mythologies:
     Actes du Colloque de Poitiers 13–14 Mai 1983* (Paris, 1986), pp. 101–8. Indo-European myth envisaged
     the masculine sun as married to the feminine moon (Gamkrelidze and Ivanov, *Indo-European and the
     Indo-Europeans*, i, p. 591). According to Plutarch, the Egyptians called 'the moon (the Selene) the mother of
     the world and they believe her nature to be both male and female since she is filled and made pregnant
     by the sun, while she herself in turn projects and disseminates procreative elements in the air' (J. Gwyn
     Griffiths (ed.), *Plutarch's De Iside et Osiride* (Cambridge, 1970), p. 186; cf. pp. 462–64).

'Rhiannon and
Pwyll at Narberth'.
(Author's collection)

had many tribes', while Lleu's mother Arianrhod wed *Lliaws*, whose name means 'multitude'. Nor do these parallels constitute the sole indications that the Life of Illtud represents a palimpsest of that of the god Lleu.

It is possible that there existed an association, even amounting to identity, between Arianrhod in the Fourth Branch of the *Mabinogi*, and Rhiannon in the First. Each was originally a sovereignty goddess, Mother of the primal king. Each has her son removed or withheld at birth, who is then fostered by a putative father. Each son grows into a Wonder Child, who suffers a tragic epiphany.[140] Rhiannon manifests equine characteristics similar to (though not necessarily implying identification with) those of the Mare Goddess (Epona) of the Celts, and her first appearance on a white mare gliding serenely by, immune to pursuit by earthly beings, further evokes an image of the moon sailing scatheless through the night sky. Likewise, the name *Arianrhod* ('Silver Wheel') suggests an appellation of the moon. Illtud's wife Trynihid is implicitly identified with the moon, as well as being gratuitously associated with horses in the same episode.

Illtud as cosmocrator

Succeeding chapters of the *Vita Iltuti* include accounts of events in Illtud's life, which if taken individually might appear no more than conventional hagiographical motifs, but in the context of the Life as a whole convey the impression of a paradigmatic mythological biography, focussed on the Centre.

Having withdrawn to a wilderness, Illtud provides refuge for a hunted stag, which he speedily domesticates and employs in drawing carts. The wasteland occupied by the Saint belongs to a truculent King Meirchiaun, who had left it uncultivated in order to provide game for hunting. Illtud allays the monarch's ire by miraculously supplying him with fish, wine, and mead. Falling asleep after gorging his fill, the king is advised by an angel in a dream to permit Illtud and his followers to remain undisturbed in his forest. 'His protection will be inviolable with kings and

---

140 Proinsias Mac Cana, *The Mabinogi* (Cardiff, 1992), p. 129; Pierre-Yves Lambert, '*Magie et Pouvoir dans la Quatrième Branche du* Mabinogi', *Studia Celtica* (Cardiff, 1994), xxviii, p. 98.

Cernunnos deity on the Gundestrup Cauldron (*c.* 200 BC). (Author's collection)

with princes in this kingdom,' explains the heavenly visitor, 'kings and princes will heed his instruction, subject peoples will abide by his counsel.'[141] On waking, Meirchiaun promptly cedes the region to the Saint, observing that none exists in the land more fertile. Illtud gathers a team of industrious labourers, who toil and till until the valley becomes as wonderfully productive as it had previously been barren, while its formerly impoverished inhabitants are provided with ample sustenance.

The blot on this prosperous landscape comprises a succession of destructive sea floods, which threaten to inundate the entire valley. Thrice the Saint constructs elaborate earthworks to hold the tides at bay, but they continue as often destroyed by the breakers. It seems that the peaceful settlement is doomed, until an angel advises Illtud in a dream to proceed to the water's edge, and brandish his staff or crozier (*baculus*) against the angry main. He does so, when sure enough the sea obediently withdraws behind the line indicated by the Saint.[142] The land thus reclaimed proves wonderfully fertile both for cultivation and grazing. That autumn, when the time came to harvest the crops, a huge flock of birds appeared and began devouring the monks' precious grain. However, they in turn were miraculously induced to abandon their depredations, and the harvest was saved.

A familiar figure from early mythologies may be recognized here: that of the culture hero, who at the outset of time on earth (*in illo tempore*) fecundates the untamed wilderness, establishing its prosperity for future generations of mankind.[143]

1.   Taming and control of wild animals recurs in saints' lives, normally as a commonplace miracle. At the same time the motif has roots in much more archaic tradition. As Elissa Henken explains:

---

141 This encomium is strikingly similar to that accorded Samson by the *librarius*.

142 This recalls one of the primary qualities ascribed to the Centre, its immunity to flooding (Eliade, *Patterns in Comparative Religion*, pp. 233, 375, 376).

143 Stith Thompson, *The Folktale* (New York, 1946), pp. 310–17; idem, *Motif-Index of Folk-Literature: A Classification of Narrative Elements in Folktales, Ballads, Myths, Fables, Mediaeval Romances, Exempla, Fabliaux, Jest-Books, and Local Legends* (Bloomington, Indiana, 1955–58), i, pp. 122–25.

The saints' mastery over animals is another aspect of their supernatural control of nature. The saints appear as lords to whom the animals rush for protection and whom they gladly serve. In this, they are firmly based in Celtic tradition with its antlered gods of the Cernunnos type, attended by all manner of beasts, and found depicted on the Gundestrup cauldron as well as reflected in Owein's dark man in the woods.[144]

The surrounding circumstances of this section in Illtud's Life suggest that such a figure lies behind the pious tamer of the stag. Prominent in many primitive cultures is the divinity known to anthropologists as the Master of Animals. Societies engaged in a hunter-gatherer existence revere him as a supernatural figure, who controls the wilderness and all wild creatures inhabiting it. His function is that of protector of game and helper of mankind, whom it is necessary for men to propitiate in order to ensure continuance of their prey.[145]

2. King Meirchiaun is an anomalous figure in the context. As Canon Doble observed:

> In c. 8 we are introduced to King Meirchiaun, without a word of explanation as to who he was or what had become of Poulentus. The reason must be that our author has now turned from the *Vita Cadoci* to the local traditions of Llantwit.[146]

At the outset we learn that Meirchiaun was surnamed *Uesanus*, meaning 'wild' or 'frenzied'. On what grounds he bore the epithet is unexplained, although it was clearly considered significant. On a couple of occasions he expresses hostility towards Illtud, but his loutish behaviour reflects no more than what was expected in hagiography of a secular ruler's truculent attitude towards a holy man. Moreover, the incidents are unconvincingly motivated, and appear at least in part arbitrarily contrived to explain Meirchiaun's epithet.

3. At his first appearance, we are told that the king had designated the region where Illtud settled as a wasteland in order to preserve it for hunting. This seems a feeble explanation, given the confined area occupied by the saint and his companions. It looks as though local legend identified Meirchiaun with the wilderness, of which he was protector. His epithet *Uesanus* recalls the Welsh Merlin, *Myrddin*, who retired to the wilderness, where he dwelt with stags and wolves, and whose epithet *Wyllt* likewise means 'wild'. There are other resemblances. Meirchiaun seeks to capture a stag from Illtud. Myrddin 'became a Man of the Woods (*silvester homo*), as if dedicated to the woods', settled by a spring on a mountain summit, where he observed the woodland and wild beasts, and rode on a stag at the head of a herd of deer, driving them as a shepherd does sheep.[147]

---

144 Henken, *The Welsh Saints: A Study in Patterned Lives*, p. 80.

145 Åke Hultkrantz, 'The Owner of the Animals in the Religion of the North American Indians', in idem (ed.), *The Supernatural Owners of Nature: Nordic symposium on the religious conceptions of ruling spirits (genii loci, genii speciei) and allied concepts* (Uppsala, 1961), pp. 53–64; Olof Petterson, 'The Spirits of the Woods: Outlines of a Study of the Ideas about Forest Guardians in African Mythology and Folklore', ibid., pp. 101–11; Ivar Paulson, 'Die Religionen der nordasiatischen (sibirischen) Völker', in Ivar Paulson, Åke Hultkrantz, and Karl Jettmar, *Die Religionen Nordeurasiens und der amerikanischen Arktis* (Stuttgart, 1962), pp. 38–64.

146 Doble, *Saint Iltut*, p. 35.

147 Basil Clarke (ed.), *Life of Merlin; Geoffrey of Monmouth: Vita Merlini* (Cardiff, 1973), pp. 56, 58, 74–76. In the French Merlin romances Merlin is discovered in rough garments herding beasts in Northumberland

In the twelfth century local written sources now lost described Saint Illtud's possession of a mare, which was covered by a stag and gave birth to a swift creature with the front of a horse and rear of a deer.[148] Could this hybrid creature reflect a legend of Illtud's employment of a stag as a steed?

In this section of the Life, both Illtud and Meirchiaun markedly resemble the Celtic god of the wild, Cernunnos, whose

> closest link is with the particular emblem of the stag, who accompanies him and whose antlers he borrows... The boundary between humankind and the animal world is blurred and even dissolved, and Cernunnos' image is that of a true blend of man and beast.[149]

It seems that Illtud, who features as a Christianized lord of the wilderness, is treated as having displaced a Celtic divinity. *Meirchiaun* derives from Latin *Marciānus*,[150] and consequently cannot have been the original name of the supplanted deity, which must have been of Celtic derivation. Near Illtud's foundation at Llantwit Major lay a fortress known as *Caer Meirchiaun*,[151] from which Lifris could have appropriated the name for that of the Lord of the Forest dispossessed by Illtud.[152]

Could the name *Meirchiaun* have become substituted for that of *Myrddin*, in view of unpalatable druidic connotations assigned the deranged prophet?[154] The North Welsh poet Gwilym Ddu associates *Meirchyawn* and Myrddin.[155]

4. A significant aspect of the Meirchiaun episode lies in the prophecy that Illtud's 'protection will be inviolable with kings and with princes in this kingdom' (*inuiolabilis erit eius protectio a regibus et a principus in hoc regno*), and 'kings and princes will heed his instruction, subject peoples will abide by his counsel' (*reges et principes parebunt suo documento; subiecti populares adherebunt consilio*). This phraseology echoes the likely etymology of Illtud's name, 'one who possesses many tribes'. The Saint's authority is assigned to the whole of Britain (*per totam Britannia*), which is described as a realm containing many kingdoms and principalities. It is further foretold that 'he will be a refuge and a support, like a pillar

(Alexandre Micha (ed.), *Robert de Boron: Merlin, Roman du XIIIᵉ siècle* (Geneva, 1979), pp. 128–32; Gaston Paris and Jacob Ulrich (ed.), *Merlin: Roman en prose du XIIIᵉ siècle* (Paris, 1886), i, pp. 65–66; H. Oskar Sommer (ed.), *Le Roman de Merlin or the Early History of King Arthur: Faithfully Edited from the French MS. Add. 10292 in the British Museum (About A.D. 1316)* (London, 1894), pp. 37–38, 40. The tradition of Merlin's riding a stag was also known in Wales (Bromwich (ed.), *Trioedd Ynys Prydein*, p. 473).

148 The tradition of Illtud's taming of the stag was preserved in Brycheiniog at the end of the twelfth century (J. S. Brewer, James F. Dimock, and George F. Warner (ed.), *Giraldi Cambrensis Opera* (London, 1861–91), vi, p. 28).

149 Miranda Green, *Symbol and Image in Celtic Religious Art* (London, 1989), p. 96; cf. pp. 95–96.

150 Sims-Williams, *The Celtic Inscriptions of Britain*, p. 10.

151 *Castellum regis Meirchiauni* (Wade-Evans (ed.), *Vitae Sanctorum Britanniae et Genealogiae*, p. 232).

152 Doble, *Saint Iltut*, p. 35.

153 Flemming Kaul, *Gundestrupkedlen: Baggrund og billedverden* (Copenhagen, 1991), p. 21.

154 The prophetic poem *Armes Prydein*, composed in Wales about the middle of the tenth century, associates Myrddin with the druids: *Dysgogan awen ... Dysgogan Myrdin*, 'the *awen* [prophetic inspiration] foretells ... Myrddin foretells', *Dysgogan derwydon meint a deruyd*, 'druids foretell all that will happen' (Sir Ifor Williams and Rachel Bromwich (ed.), *Armes Prydein: The Prophecy of Britain From the Book of Taliesin* (Dublin, 1972), pp. 2, 12).

155 Gwenogvryn Evans (ed.), *The Poetry in the Red Book of Hergest*, col. 1229, ll. 37–38.

supporting a standing house'. It is normally secular heroes and kings to whom this simile or metaphor is accorded. Thus a hero of the Old North was known as Pabo *Post Prydein*, 'Pabo, Pillar of Britain'.[156] As has been seen, pillar and king were closely associated.

5. Illtud is granted a uniquely fertile (*nulla fertilior per patriam*) parish, with ideal crops and perfect climate, from which he feeds his own large household and a hundred poor people daily. The ascription to a saint of an exceptionally productive piece of land recurs in Welsh and Irish hagiography, as also in secular saga. The implications are clearly brought out in the Third Branch of the *Mabinogi*, the tale of *Manawydan uab Llŷr*. At the conclusion of the story, Manawydan brings wheat from abroad to Arberth in his realm of Dyfed. The land having previously been reduced by a malevolent wizard to a wasteland, Manawydan survives initially by catching fish and wild animals. Next he tills the soil and plants three fields which produce 'the best wheat in the world'.

This is fiction, but the myth underlying the episode is a familiar one. The mound of Arberth, the 'capital' of Dyfed, is a spot providing access to the Otherworld, where encounters with supernatural beings regularly occur. It was probably an *omphalos*, or Sacred Centre, one of whose characteristics is that of linking this world to the Other.[157] The *omphalos* was also, as has been seen, the spot where the world was created, whence its wealth originated, and from which it is constantly replenished. From this sprang the myth of a sacred garden, orchard, or field enjoying supernatural fertility and temperate climate, which functioned as microcosm and fount of the wealth of the land. In Ireland a hill near Cashel was known as 'the garden of Ireland', 'in consequence of a belief that every plant which grows in Ireland is to be found upon it'.[158] The classic instance of this belief is the Garden of Eden, which enjoyed perpetual summer and unfailing plenitude of crops and animals. It contained a well, whence four rivers flowed towards the four cardinal points, indicating its focal location at the centre of the world.[159]

---

156 The concept of the hero as pillar is of Indo-European origin (Calvert Watkins, 'Some Celtic Phrasal Echoes', in A. T. E. Matonis and Daniel F. Melia (ed.), *Celtic Language, Celtic Culture: A Festschrift for Eric P. Hamp* (Van Nuys, CA., 1990), pp. 52–55).

157 A. J. Wensinck, *The Ideas of the Western Semites Concerning the Navel of the Earth* (Amsterdam, 1916), pp. 58–59.

158 T. Crofton Croker, *Fairy Legends and Traditions of the South of Ireland: The New Series* (London, 1828), p. 258.

159 For Irish traditions of the Garden of Eden, cf. David Greene, Fergus Kelly, and Brian O. Murdoch (ed.), *The Irish Adam and Eve Story from Saltair na Rann* (Dublin, 1976), i, pp. 18–24; R. A. Stewart Macalister (ed.), *Lebor Gabála Érenn: The Book of the Taking of Ireland* (Dublin, 1938–56), i, pp. 56, 58, 196. For the biblical Eden, cf. Claus Westermann, *Genesis 1-11: A Commentary* (London, 1984), pp. 207–11. In mediæval cartography 'the four rivers of paradise – Tigris, Euphrates, Pishon, and Gihon – are usually shown on *mappae mundi* as fanning out from the location of paradise in a simple, stylized fashion, they were also represented as real rivers: the Tigris, Euphrates, Ganges, and Indus, as on the "Jerome" map of Palestine' (J. B. Harley and David Woodward (ed.), *The History of Cartography* (Chicago, 1987–2015), i, p. 328). The Biblical Hebrew 'word Eden (*ēden*) means "fertility, abundance, luxuriance" … Eden may be thought then to be the terrestrial sacred mountain fertilized by the storm-god and in this sense a "garden"' (Mark S. Smith, *The Origins of Biblical Monotheism: Israel's Polytheistic Background and the Ugaritic Texts* (Oxford, 2001), p. 293). The Garden of Eden and the Jerusalem Temple were associated reflexions of the cosmic centre (ibid., pp. 169, 171). For the Garden of Eden as primary Centre of generation, cf. also Richard J. Clifford, *The Cosmic Mountain in Canaan and the Old Testament* (Cambridge, Mass., 1972), pp. 98–103. At Eleusis in Greece, the sacred plain of Rarian 'was the first to be sown and first to produce crops, and it is accordingly their custom to take the sacrificial barley and make cakes for the sacrifices out of its produce' (Maria-Helena Rocha-Pereira (ed.), *Pavsaniae Graeciae Descriptio* (Leipzig, 1973–81), i, pp. 88–89). During the winter, while Proserpine was confined

The Welsh triads allude to two such exemplary enclosures: the Wheat Field in Gwent (*maes gỗenith yg went*), where the supernatural sow Henwen bought forth a grain of wheat and a bee (emblems of natural wealth in Celtic tradition); and Llonyon in Pembrokeshire (*llonyon ym penỗro*), where she went on to deliver grains of barley and wheat.[160]

The most explicit account features in the Life of St Cadog, described earlier, which provided a material source for the *Vita Iltuti*. There we read that Cadog sowed grain in a fertile field known as *Eruguenn*, or 'holy meadow' – and nowhere else. This suggests the ever-renewed source of the country's prosperity.

A subsequent passage in the Life throws valuable light on this matter. Following an intervening visit to Ireland (an obvious interpolation), Cadog returns to find his homeland suffering from severe famine. After praying he is visited by a mouse, which brings him a grain of corn in its mouth. After several such visits, the saint follows his little helper, who leads him to a mound beneath which he finds an exceptionally beautiful subterranean structure, built in earlier days. It proves to be filled with good wheat, which Cadog distributes among the suffering population.

It has been suggested that the underground granary was part of a long-abandoned Roman building.[161] However, the story cannot be taken literally. Roman granaries were for obvious reason built above ground, in order to be cool, airy, and dry.[162] Damp would have made the grain unusable after a single Welsh winter: besides, the burden of the tale is that mice enjoyed free access to the cellar! Nevertheless, the tale must have originated in something. While the motif of the helpful mouse bears appearance of folklore derivation, a magnificent subterranean store of imperishable grain which feeds an entire region is surely another facet of the Otherworld source of crops grown within Cadog's sacred acre. This further reflects the myth of an underground realm (i.e. Otherworld cave), where grain is retained throughout the winter, until in spring it sprouts at a single sanctified spot, whence the crops of the entire realm derive their fertility.

In his *Vita Cadoci*, Lifris makes the relationship between the two accounts clear through a revealing slip. Concluding the episode of the underground grainstore, he explains that the king of the region gave Cadog 'the part of that field in which the wheat was found'.[163] It will be recalled that the wheat was *not* found in a field, but in an underground chamber beneath a mound, and it appears that the author

in the underworld, the Rarian Plain lay barren, to be fructified on her reappearance with the spring (N. J. Richardson (ed.), *The Homeric Hymn to Demeter* (Oxford, 1974), p. 132).

160 *The Bulletin of the Board of Celtic Studies*, xii, p. 13; Egerton G. B. Phillimore, 'A Fragment from Hengwrt MS. No. 202', *Y Cymmrodor* (1886), vii, pp. 131–32. Cf. Marged Haycock (ed.), *Prophecies from the Book of Taliesin* (Aberystwyth, 2013), pp. 116–17.

161 Baring-Gould and Fisher, *The Lives of the British Saints*, ii, p. 18.

162 Robert H. Rodgers (ed.), *Palladii Rvtilii Tavri Aemiliani Viri Inlvstris: Opvs Agricvltvrae de Veteniraria Medicina de Insitione* (Leipzig, 1975), pp. 22–23.

163 *Qui partem agri illius, in quo triticum repertum est, qui Lannspitit nuncupatur, uiro Dei donaui*t (Wade-Evans (ed.), *Vitae Sanctorum Britanniae et Genealogiae*, pp. 44–50).

has rationalized an earlier version, in which the saint's miraculous harvests were understood to originate in the Underworld.[164]

In an early Welsh poem Myrddin (Merlin) laments in his wilderness exile:

> The fields are my barn, my corn is not plenteous.
> My summer store does not sustain me.[165]

While 'barn' (*ysgybor*) may have been intended metaphorically, it is possible that the poet was invoking the mythical concept of corn's originating in a subterranean granary.

6. Next we come to Illtud's miraculous repulsion of the sea. At first he constructed a massive dyke of earth and stones, which was however broken down thrice by the onrush of the waters. Then an angel advised him in a dream to drive them back by the power of his staff. This proved successful: never again did the sea exceed its accepted bounds, and the land reclaimed proved exceptionally fertile for crops and kine.

This theme was found by the Saint's biographer Lifris in the Life of St Paul Aurelian, composed by Wrmonoc towards the end of the ninth century. It also occurs in the eleventh-century Life of St Gildas, written by a monk of Ruys in Brittany. The latter version does not include the Saint's use of his staff to drive back the waves (he relies on prayer alone). However, it is clear that in the original conception the staff played an essential part. It, or what purported to be it, was long preserved in South Wales. Local tradition recalled that Illtud gave his disciple Baglan

> a staff (the head whereof, being of brasse, was preserved till of late years, a sacred relick, wch had wonderfull effects upon the sick, &c.) and bid that he should let that guide him till he should come to a place where he found a tree that bore three sortes of fruite, and there erect a church for him selfe.[166]

Although St Baglan was accorded a place among the Welsh saints, his name in fact arose from a misunderstanding of Welsh *bagl*, 'crozier'.[167] Still, the story attests to the high regard paid to Illtud's staff in ensuing centuries.

---

164 An Irish folklore tale recounts how grain is preserved by the fairies in holes beneath rocks (Máire MacNeill, *The Festival of Lughnasa: A Study of the Survival of the Celtic Festival of the Beginning of Harvest* (Oxford, 1962), p. 585). Among the Maya of Central America, 'There is a predominant belief that corn was first produced from a sacred cave with the help of the rain gods' (Karen Bassie-Sweet, *At the Edge of the World: Caves and Late Classic Maya World View* (Norman and London, 1996), p. 12; cf. pp. 68, 110, 151–52, 210; J. Eric S. Thompson, *Maya History and Religion* (Norman, Okla., 1970), pp. 284–85).

165 A. O. H. Jarman (ed.), *Llyfr Du Caerfyrddin gyda Rhagymadrodd Nodiadau Testunol a Geirfa* (Cardiff, 1982), p. 35.

166 Ch. Cuissard, 'Vie de Saint Pol de Léon', *Revue Celtique* (Paris, 1883), v, pp. 422–23; Mommsen (ed.), *Chronica Minora*, iii, pp. 92–93; Morris (ed.), *Parochialia*, iii, p. 27.

167 Welsh *bagl* derives from Latin *baculus* (Lewis, *Yr Elfen Ladin yn yr Iaith Gymraeg*, p. 18), as does the cognate Irish *bachall* (J. Vendryes, E. Bachellery, and P-Y. Lambert, *Lexique étymologique de l'irlandais ancien* (Dublin and Paris, 1959–96), B-3).

It has been observed that 'the crosier, which serves as the saint's instrument of wonder-working [is] … the hagiographical equivalent of a magic wand'.[168] The croziers of British and Irish bishops were credited with astonishing powers, owing little to Christian doctrine.[169] Not infrequently British bishops created springs or wells by driving their staves into the ground (as did Illtud when reclaiming the sea-strand). That of St Padarn possessed peculiarly beneficial power. Standing between two hostile armies, he imposed peace by means of his wonderful *baculus* named *Cirguen*: 'for such is the virtue of that staff that if two quarrel, by its means they are reconciled'.[170] This is precisely the power ascribed the Wand of Peace (*cráeb sída*) wielded by Sencha mac Ailill, chief druid of Ulster, with which he regularly quelled squabbles between the irascible warriors of his day, together with their shrill dames.[171] The point does not need to be laboured further, the evidence being so extensive. It is manifest that the staff or crozier (*baculus*) of the abbot or bishop had acquired all the powers of the druid's enchanted staff.[172]

It has already been seen to what extent the figure of Illtud presented in his Life reflects that of a divinity, rather than a magician. Actually, there need be no incompatability, since Celtic mythology knew of a Divine Druid whose powers were invoked by the druids.[173] In Welsh tradition this figure is most clearly manifested by Math uab Mathonwy, who in the tale of that name features as a powerful magician able to hear every whisper borne on the wind. He also possesses a magic wand (*hutlath*), with which he punishes his nephews by transforming them into successive animal shapes, constructs a lovely young woman from flowers, and brings to life the primal poet Taliesin.[174] Thus Math's wand was endowed at once with punitive and creative powers.

The divine druid in Ireland was the Dagda, whose name means 'the Good God'. Like Illtud, he was credited with controlling the crops.[175] His staff of life (*an lorg mór*) possessed opposed powers similar to those of Math's wand, whose rough end brought nine men to life while the

---

168 Henken, *Traditions of the Welsh Saints*, p. 111. The Irish St Colman drove back a river with his *baculus* (Carolus Plummer (ed.), *Vitae Sanctorum Hiberniae: Partim Hactenvs Ineditae ad Fidem Codicvm Manvscriptorvm Recognovit Prolegominis Notis Indicibvs Instrvxit* (Oxford, 1910), i, p. 267), while Declan's *bachall* repelled a sea flood (ibid., ii, pp. 43–44; Rev. P. Power (ed.), *Life of St. Declan of Ardmore and Life of St. Mochuda of Lismore* (London, 1914), p. 30). In Britain, Saints Samson and Gwynllyw created springs with their croziers, as did Saint Senán in Ireland (Pierre Flobert (ed.), *La vie ancienne de saint Samson de Dol* (Paris, 1997), p. 206; Wade-Evans (ed.), *Vitae Sanctorum Britanniae et Genealogiae*, p. 180; Whitley Stokes (ed.), *Lives of Saints from the Book of Lismore* (Oxford, 1890), p. 65).

169 The magical production of water by Moses, when he struck the rock in Horeb with his rod, is the most celebrated instance of a familiar international motif (Sir James George Frazer, *Folk-Lore in the Old Testament: Studies in Comparative Religion Legend and Law* (London, 1918), iii, pp. 463–64; Ferdinand Jozef Maria de Waele, *The Magic Staff or Rod in Graeco-Italian Antiquity* (Ghent, 1927), pp. 88–89; Thompson, *Motif-Index of Folk-Literature*, ii, p. 268 = D1549.5).

170 Wade-Evans (ed.), *Vitae Sanctorum Britanniae et Genealogiae*, p. 256. Cf. the important note in Rachel Bromwich (ed.), *The Beginnings of Welsh Poetry: Studies by Sir Ifor Williams, D.Litt., LL.D., F.B.A.* (Cardiff, 1980), pp. 183–85.

171 Best, Bergin, O'Brien, and O'Sullivan (ed.), *The Book of Leinster*, ii, p. 416; iv, p. 777; Best and Bergin (ed.), *Lebor na Huidre*, p. 256; J. Carmichael Watson (ed.), *Mesca Ulad* (Dublin, 1941), p. 6.

172 A wide range of examples was adduced by Plummer (ed.), *Vitae Sanctorum Hiberniae*, i, pp. clxxiv–clxxvi.

173 A full discussion of '*le dieu-druide*' is given by Christian-J. Guyonvarc'h and Françoise Le Roux, *Les Druides* (Rennes, 1986), pp. 335–40.

174 Hughes (ed.), *Math Uab Mathonwy*, pp. 1, 5–7, 11–12; Gwenogvryn Evans (ed.), *Facsimile & Text of the Book of Taliesin*, pp. 26, 68. For Math's functions, cf. Georges Dumézil, 'La quatrième branche du Mabinogi et la théologie des trois fonctions', in Proinsias Mac Cana and Michel Meslin (ed.), *Rencontres de religions: Actes du colloque du Collège des Irlandais tenu sous les auspices de l'Académie Royale Irlandaise* (Juin 1981) (Paris, 1986), pp. 26–28.

175 *Ériu*, xii, p. 142; Best, Bergin, O'Brien, and O'Sullivan (ed.), *The Book of Leinster*, p. 1120.

smooth slew nine.[176] To the druids of the gods of Ireland (*Túatha Dé Danann*) he declared: 'The power which you boast, I will wield it all myself.' He was said to have acquired his superior knowledge (*éolas*) from Bodb, king of the fairy mound (*síd*) of Munster, and whenever occasion required had recourse to his unique 'knowledge and learning' (*fhessa 7 fhireolais*) and 'wizardry and occult knowledge' (*draidecht 7 d' fhisidecht*).[177]

Like Thor in Scandinavian mythology, the Dagda was a god of boundaries, using his colossal club to demarcate frontiers between kingdoms and hacking marks of guidance with his axe on tree-trunks.[178] His club or staff acted on occasion as a formidable weapon, and one such incident provides a striking parallel with Illtud's repulsion of the sea with his staff. A dreadful sea-monster known as *muir-selche*, dwelling beneath an enchanted sea (*muir druídechta*), possessed power to suck an armoured man down into the bottom of its treasure-bag (*istadbuilc*). The Dagda rid mankind of the menace by crushing it with his 'staff of fury' (*lorg anfaid*), uttering at the same time magical incantations which drove it and the magical sea back together.[179]

The monster must originally have personified the ocean, just as its bag represented the abyssal depths where the drowned dead are garnered. As Jacqueline Borsje observes in her study of water monsters in early Irish tradition: 'in a wider sense it is the sea (either this magic one or the sea in general) that exacts tribute from humanity, sucking people into its depths.'[180] Similarly, in early Israel Yahweh was represented as crushing the dragon of the sea, after which he 'placed the sand as the boundary for the sea, a perpetual barrier which it cannot pass; it may toss, though not prevail, its waves may roar, but cannot pass over it'.[181]

All this suggests that when Illtud drove back the sea through the power of his magic staff, setting a bound to its destructive realm, and defining for all time a region of abundant fertility where he and his followers could dwell in contentment, he fulfilled the function of a benevolent deity (*Dagda*, 'Good God') at the outset of creation. The name *Eltut*, combined with telling allusions at the beginning of Illtud's Life, suggests a primal ancestor divinity. It is interesting that the Irish ancestor-deity Dagda bore another name, whose epithet bears much the same meaning.

---

176   Watson (ed.), *Mesca Ulad*, pp. 27–28; Osborn Bergin, 'How the Dagda got his Magic Staff', in *Medieval Studies in Memory of Gertrude Schoepperle Loomis* (Paris and New York, 1927), pp. 402–404.

177   Elizabeth A. Gray (ed.), *Cath Maige Tuired: The Second Battle of Mag Tuired* (Naas, 1982), p. 44; Francis Shaw (ed.), *The Dream of Óengus: Aislinge Óenguso* (Dublin, 1934), p. 50; *Medieval Studies in Memory of Gertrude Schoepperle Loomis*, pp. 402, 404.

178   Gray (ed.), *Cath Maige Tuired*, pp. 46, 48–50.

179   A. G. van Hamel (ed.), *Compert Con Culainn and Other Stories* (Dublin, 1933), pp. 35–36; Edward Gwynn (ed.), *The Metrical Dindshenchas* (Dublin, 1903–35), iv, p. 294. During his visit to the Shetland Isles in 1814, Sir Walter Scott learned from local fishermen 'of a kraken or some monstrous fish being seen off Scalloway ... They pretended [i.e. asserted] that the suction, when they came within a certain distance, was so great as to endanger their boats.' The creature was patently not a whale, 'as whales are the intimate acquaintance of all Zetland sailors' (J. G. Lockhart, *Memoirs of the Life of Sir Walter Scott, Bart.* (Edinburgh, 1839–48), iv, pp. 216–17).

180   Jacqueline Borsje, *From Chaos to Enemy: Encounters with Monsters in Early Irish Texts. An Investigation Related to the Process of Christianization and the concept of Evil* (Turnhout, 1996), pp. 45–48.

181   John Day, *God's Conflict with the dragon and the sea: Echoes of a Canaanite myth in the Old Testament* (Cambridge, 1985), pp. 1–61.

There was a famous king of Ireland of the race of the Túatha Dé, Eochaid Ollathair his name. He was also named the Dagda.

Ollathair means 'great father', i.e. 'ancestor', and his dwelling place was the Omphalos of Ireland:

> Uisneach of Meath in the centre of Ireland (*a medon Erenn*) ... was Eochaid's house, Ireland stretching equally far from it on every side, to south and north, to east and west.[182]

It was at *Medgarth*, the 'Median Enclosure', that Illtud survived the engulphing of the fifty 'Round Table' revellers of King Poulentus. Like Illtud too, the Dagda was associated with the Otherworld perpetual feast.

> From Murias was brought the Dagda's cauldron (*coiri an Dagdai*). No company ever went away from it unsatisfied.

He consumed a gargantuan meal from the king of the Fomoire's cauldron: 'His belly was as big as a house cauldron, and the Fomoire laughed at it.' His tub flowed during the incoming tide, but became dry at the ebb, i.e. it was of cosmic proportions.[183]

The parallels appear too many and close to be fortuitous. The semantic correspondence of *Eltut* to *Ollathair* echoes the possibility that *Eltut* was originally the epithet of the British ancestor deity. It will be recalled that Illtud's rôle at Medgarth was originally that of sole survivor of the eschatological cataclysm, whose function is to restore the human race at the outset of each successive cosmic cycle. Another of the Dagda's alternative names was *Athgen mBethai*, 'rebirth of the world'.[184]

Parallels have been noted between between Illtud, Meirchiaun, and Myrddin (Merlin) as Lords of the Forest. There exist also functions in common between Illtud and Myrddin as protectors of Britain. An archaic Welsh triad, 'The Names of the Island of Britain', states that the first name borne by the island was *Clas Merdin*, 'Myrddin's Precinct'.[185] While one would like to know more of this tantalizing allusion, it suggests a tradition that the island of Britain was believed originally to have lain under the protection of Myrddin, presumably acting as its tutelary divinity. The term *clas* ('precinct, enclosure') intimates that it was he who defined and protected the coastal bounds

182 *Ériu*, xii, pp. 142, 144; Macalister (ed.), *Lebor Gabála Érenn*, iv, pp. 152–54. For *ollathair*, cf. Vendryes, Bachellery, and Lambert, *Lexique étymologique de l'irlandais ancien*, p. O-21. The epithet is paralleled in Norse mythology by Óðinn's sobriquet *Alfǫðr*, 'All-Father', i.e. father of gods and men (Faulkes (ed.), *Snorri Sturluson: Edda*, p. 13). Cf. Jan de Vries, *Altgermanische Religionsgeschichte* (Berlin, 1956–57), ii, pp. 84–86; E. O. G. Turville-Petre, *Myth and Religion of the North: The Religion of Ancient Scandinavia* (London, 1964), pp. 55–56.

183 Gray (ed.), *Cath Maige Tuired*, pp. 24, 46; Macalister (ed.), *Lebor Gabála Érenn*, iv, p. 106; Best, Bergin, O'Brien, and O'Sullivan (ed.), *The Book of Leinster*, p. 700. 'Being owner of the inexhaustible cauldron, he was lord of the Otherworld Feast ... The gluttony attributed to him is but a later development of the same idea ... It was easy to imagine one who presided at a perpetual feast as possessing an insatiable appetite' (O'Rahilly, *Early Irish History and Mythology*, p. 469).

184 Gray (ed.), *Cath Maige Tuired*, p. 48. Cf. eadem, 'Cath Maige Tuired: Myth and Structure', *Éigse* (Naas, 1983), xix, p. 241.

185 *Y Cymmrodor*, vii, p. 124; Rhŷs and Gwenogvryn Evans (ed.), *The Text of the Mabinogion and other Welsh Tales from the Red Book of Hergest*, p. 309. For the antiquity of the tradition enshrined in *Enweu Ynys Brydein*, cf. Bromwich (ed.), *Trioedd Ynys Prydein*, pp. cxxiii–cxxvii; Brynley F. Roberts, 'Geoffrey of Monmouth and Welsh Historical Tradition', *Nottingham Mediaeval Studies* (Nottingham, 1976), xx, p. 34.

of the island of Britain.[186] Finally, a Breton legend associates Merlin with a staff endowed with power to slay or resuscitate. This recalls the Dagda's club, with which the god could kill the living and revive the dead, and which he employed also to demarcate the frontiers of kingdoms.[187]

The divinity and the saint

This is the appropriate juncture to confront a difficulty which may already have struck the reader. If, as I believe has been shown in the course of this chapter, the *Vita Iltuti* be in large part a thinly disguised adaptation of the myth of a Celtic deity, how is this to be reconciled with the story of Illtud contained in the earlier *Vita Samsonis*? There Eltutus, who acted as tutor to the youthful Samson, features as a partially christianized *mortal* druid, who combined the rôle with that of abbot, at a time when the two religions appear to have cohabited on relatively equable terms.

The provenance of the *Vita Samsonis* is such that its contents may broadly be accepted as authentic history. Among salient episodes in this early account of the career of Eltutus, we learn that he was ordained by St Germanus of Auxerre,[188] presided over a splendid monastery (which clearly existed, since it was subsequently visited by the author of the *Vita*), and assisted at the ordination of Samson by bishop Dubricius. In phraseology echoing that of the *Vita Samsonis*, Gildas extols the tutor of King Maelgwn of Gwynedd as 'the refined teacher of almost the whole of Britain', a description widely regarded as alluding to Illtud.[189] Clearly Eltutus was an historical figure: a partially christianized druid – but one who cannot at the same time have been a god. Yet the protagonist of the later *Vita Iltuti* has, I believe, been shown to be a euhemerized divinity! How is the apparent discrepancy to be reconciled?

There exists a wide disparity between the figures depicted in the two sources. In contrast to the Illtud of the *Vita Iltuti*, Eltutus in the *Vita Samsonis* is not said to have been born in Brittany, did not serve as a soldier, had no recorded connexion with King Arthur, was not married, and did not die in Brittany. A likely conclusion is that Caradog of Llancarfan constructed his narrative from a distinct source: one which contained the myth of a pagan deity, whom he transformed into a Christian saint.

I have suggested the possibility that *Eltut* was an epithet borne by the god Lleu, in his capacity as ancestor deity. Could an early sixth-century druid have borne the same name? It may be that *Eltut* was the name or sobriquet of the god over whose sanctuary the druid-abbot Eltutus presided, whose name he acquired as his votary. This, after all, is precisely what occurred in the fourth century at the temple dedicated to the Celtic god Belenus, on the opposite side of the Channel at Bayeux. Belenus being equated with Apollo in Roman eyes, the guardians of his shrine adopted names reflecting the association. Attius *Patera* sook his second name from that of the followers of Apollo, his father and brother were known as *Phoebus* (the alternative name for Apollo), and the name of his son *Delphidius*

---

186 'In this Triad, which must be the echo of an ancient notion, the pellucid walls confining Merlin become, by a touch of the pencil of the mythic muse, co-extensive with the utmost limits of our island home' (Rhys, *Lectures on the Origin and Growth of Religion as Illustrated by Celtic Heathendom*, p. 168).

187 Claude Sterckx, *Les mutilations des ennemis chez les celtes préchrétiens* (Paris, 2005), pp. 122–25.

188 Chronology does not permit Illtud to have been ordained by Germanus (Nora K. Chadwick, 'The Lost Literature of Celtic Scotland', *Scottish Gaelic Studies* (Oxford, 1953), vii, p. 137). It has been suggested that there was a distinct fifth-century Saint Garmon in Powys, whom Nennius confused with the celebrated Gaulish bishop (David N. Dumville, 'Sub-Roman Britain: History and Legend', *History: The Journal of the Historical Society* (London, 1977), lxii, p. 186), but this seems doubtful. Cf. my article 'Cadell and the Cadelling of Powys', *Studia Celtica* (Cardiff, 2012), xlvi, pp. 74–75, where the point is endorsed by T. M. Charles-Edwards, *Wales and the Britons 350–1064* (Oxford, 2013), pp. 442–43.

189 Williams, *Christianity in Early Britain*, p. 317; John Edward Lloyd, *A History of Wales from the Earliest Times to the Edwardian Conquest* (London, 1911), p. 145; John Morris, *The Age of Arthur: A History of the British Isles from 350 to 650* (London, 1973), p. 205).

derived from the famous temple of Apollo at Delphi.[190] The aristocrat Ausonius, who had been tutor to the Emperor Gratian and attained senatorial and consular rank, was clearly proud of this druidic connexion.[191]

The druid dynasty of Bayeux was thoroughly romanized (as was Gaul generally by this time), and it is unlikely that Gaulish was spoken among educated people when Ausonius came to extol the fine qualities of the temple priesthood.[192] In marked contrast, British and Irish were languages of everyday speech in south-west Wales in the sixth century AD. Only churchmen, kings, and some of the greater aristocracy are likely to have spoken Latin, and then only in appropriate contexts and with varying degrees of fluency.[193] On the assumption that the druids of Britain followed practices similar to those of their brethren just across the Channel, there is nothing implausible in the concept of a British druid presiding over a sanctuary, who adopted the name or epithet of the god to whom his temple was dedicated.

Eltut, it is true, is not the name of a known Celtic deity. However, its apparent meaning '(father of) many peoples' suggests an epithet, whose counterpart is attested among neighbouring peoples, Celtic and Germanic. As has been seen, the Irish god Dagda was known also as Eochaid *Ollathair*, 'Eochaid the Great Father' or 'Universal Progenitor'.[194] Caesar informs us that 'the Gauls all assert their descent from *Dis pater* and say that it is the druidic belief'.[195] In the Norse pantheon, Óðinn was called *Alfǫðr* ('All-Father') 'because he is father of gods, men, and all things'.[196] His Anglo-Saxon counterpart Woden was described by Bede as progenitor of royal dynasties.[197]

---

190 R. P. H. Green (ed.), *The Works of Ausonius* (Oxford, 1991), pp. 44–46, 50. It has been suggested that the name of *Arborius*, uncle to Ausonius, may further reflect a druidic connexion, druids being famous frequenters of groves (Altay Coşkun, *Die gens Ausoniana an der Macht: Untersuchungen zu Decimius Magnus Ausonius und seiner Familie* (Oxford, 2002), p. 113).

191 Hagith Sivan, *Ausonius of Bordeaux: Genesis of a Gallic Aristocracy* (London, 1993), p. 55. 'The entire picture of a Gaulish god Belenus, equated with Apollo, and his temple-priest and two succeeding generations of the priest's family all bearing names of Delphic associations, all famous for their eloquence and claiming descent from a backward druidical stock of remote western Gaul, is as convincing as it is picturesque, a welcome glimpse of a Gaulish god and his attendant priest in the twilight of Gaulish heathendom' (Myles Dillon and Nora Chadwick, *The Celtic Realms* (London, 1967), p. 142).

192 'The ancient *Continental Celtic* languages … were all dead by AD 500 and mostly much earlier' (Patrick Sims-Williams, 'The Celtic Languages', in Anna Giacalone Ramat and Paolo Ramat (ed.), *The Indo-European Languages* (London and New York, 1998), p. 345). However, the evidence is insufficient to judge for certain when Gaulish finally succumbed to Latin as a spoken language (James Clackson, 'Language maintenance and language shift in the Mediterranean world during the Roman Empire', in Mullen and James (ed.), *Multilingualism in the Graeco-Roman Worlds* (Cambridge, 2012), pp. 42–45).

193 Thomas Charles-Edwards, 'Language and Society among the Insular Celts AD 400–1000', in Miranda J. Green (ed.), *The Celtic World* (London, 1995), pp. 703–36.

194 O'Rahilly, *Early Irish History and Mythology*, p. 58; Christian-J. Guyonvarc'h, 'La Courtise d'Étain', *Celticvm XV: Actes du Vᵉ Colloque International d'Études Gauloises, Celtiques et Protoceltiques* (Rennes, 1966), p. 372; Vendryes, Bachellery, and Lambert, *Lexique étymologique de l'irlandais ancien*, O-21.

195 Seel (ed.), *C. Ivlii Caesaris Commentarii Rervm Gestarvm: Bellvm Gallicvm*, p. 188.

196 Faulkes (ed.), *Snorri Sturluson: Edda*, p. 13.

197 Charles Plummer (ed.), *Venerabilis Baedae Historiam Ecclesiasticam Gentis Anglorum; Historiam Abbatum, Epistolam ad Ecgberctum una cum Historia Abbatum Auctore Anonymo* (Oxford, 1896), i, p. 32. As divine ancestor of English dynasties, Woden was envisaged as 'transmitting his divine breath to his Anglo-Saxon scions' (S. R. T. O. d'Ardenne, 'A Neglected Manuscript of British History', in Norman Davis and C. L. Wrenn (ed.), *English and Medieval Studies Presented to J. R. R. Tolkien on the Occasion of his Seventieth Birthday* (London, 1962), pp. 88–93. Cf. William A. Chaney, *The Cult of Kingship in Anglo-Saxon England: The Transition from Paganism to Christianity* (Manchester, 1970), pp. 28–33.

It has been observed that, 'Irish hagiography remained to a very large degree unashamedly "pre-Christian" in its themes and, more importantly, in its *dramatis personae*, ninety or more per cent of whom are demonstrably, or implicitly, pagan in origin.'[198]

In Ireland a druid might likewise receive the name of a god. Thus, the chief prophet of Ireland (*prímfáith na hÉirenn*), Bec mac Dé, whose name means 'Bec, son of (a) god', foretold the glorious career of St Brendan, and revealed the soul of a dead child in a princess's womb to be in heaven.[199]

The man in the cave

We come now to the final episode in the Life of Illtud that appears to throw light on the pagan mythology of Celtic Britain. The truculent King Meirchion, angered by divine retribution inflicted on his unjust steward, gathered his soldiers and set out with the purpose of killing Illtud, and wreaking destruction on his monastery and fellow monks. At the approach of the hostile host the saint fled, until he arrived at the bank of the River Ewenny, where he discovered a hidden cave. There he secluded himself for a year and three days, using a stone for his bed, and sustained by a sufficiency of food provided by the grace of heaven.

Meanwhile the people of the country searched high and low for their benefactor and spiritual protector.

He was diligently searched for in woods and in forests and in the retreats of deep valleys, and was not found after painstaking searches.

Plaintive prayers for his recovery were raised to heaven, in which rich and poor alike extolled his deeds and virtues. They concluded with this curiously well-informed asseveration:

If he survives in this world, he is retained in a subterranean prison (*in carcare subterraneo*).
If he be dead, may he live, as we hope, in eternal repose.

The suggestion appears to be that Illtud was understood to have withdrawn to the Otherworld, which in early Welsh tradition could be envisaged as a prison (*carchar*).[200] Arianrhod, mother of Lleu, was said to have presided over one, which must have been located in the Otherworld, or conceivably constituted the Otherworld itself.[201] As has been seen, the Otherworld realm of Annwfn was situated beneath the earth.

Eventually Illtud was enticed back to his community by the sweet clangour of a bell belonging to Saint David. On emerging from his secret recess, he was hailed by the people as their protector from every hardship and danger.

---

198 Padraig Ó Riain, 'Celtic mythology and religion', in Karl Horst Schmidt and Rolf Ködderitzsch (ed.), *Geschichte und Kultur der Kelten: Vorbereitungskonferenz 25.-28. Oktober 1982 in Bonn* (Heidelberg, 1986), pp. 249–50. Cf. Plummer (ed.), *Vitae Sanctorum Hiberniae*, i, pp. cxxix–clxxxviii.

199 Stokes (ed.), *Lives of Saints from the Book of Lismore*, p. 100; Plummer (ed.), *Vitae Sanctorum Hiberniae*, ii, p. 138.

200 Egerton G. B. Phillimore, 'A Fragment from Hengwrt MS. No. 202', *Y Cymmrodor*, vii, p. 130; Gwenogvryn Evans (ed.), *Facsimile & Text of the Book of Taliesin*, p. 54; Hughes (ed.), *Manawydan Uab Llyr*, p. 11; Bromwich and Simon Evans (ed.), *Culhwch and Olwen*, p. 33.

201 *Myui a vum ar vann krog mewn karchar Arianrhod*: 'I was thrice in the prison of Arianrhod' (Ford (ed.), *Ystoria Taliesin*, p. 77).

Before we were sad, now we are happy and safe from every adversity and peril. We fear none, save God who is worthy of fear in this refuge. No one will dare to harm us under so potent a rule. Kings and princes will obey the virtuous chief (*princeps*); this place [or monastery, *locus*] will be first among the places of this region. Our joys lay hidden in a secret cave; they do not spread throughout our borders without past sorrow. That cave was not dark but full of light, for while Illtud was dwelling there, it did not cease shining with angelic splendour.

Unfortunately, all was not well, for Meirchion's wrath was provoked anew by the condign punishment of another of his stewards, who suffered for his misdeeds by being sucked down into a swamp. Once again the king armed his brutal followers, and sallied forth with the intention of ridding himself once and for all of the troublesome abbot. Fortunately, divine justice caught up with him just in time, when he too disappeared beneath the slimy surface of a well-placed bog.

Meanwhile, Illtud found his life of piety and prayer increasingly disturbed by devout multitudes who paid him court, and withdrew (this time voluntarily) to a cave called *Lingarthica*. There he remained for three years, sustained as before by divine providence. Then one day there occurred a remarkable event. A boat approached across the sea, guided by two pious men, and disembarked at the mouth of the cave. Illtud welcomed his visitors, who delivered into his custody the corpse of an exceptionally holy man. The name of the deceased was revealed to Illtud, with the rider that it must never be disclosed. The two men then re-entered their boat and departed as mysteriously as they had arrived. What followed is a little confused, and best given in the words of the hagiographer:

> These things accomplished, he took the body and the altar which had been above the form (*facies*) of the very holy man, and buried it honourably in the cave, the altar being suspended over the buried body as it had been before by the divine will, through which many miracles were effected through its sanctity.[202]

It will be seen that this history includes a succession of curiosities:

1. Illtud's initial flight to the cave by the Ewenny appears uncharacteristically cowardly for a saint. Although Meirchion vows to wreak condign vengeance on his fellow monks and abbey, Illtud leaves them to their fate without any attempt to protect them.
2. Despite this, the king fails to fulfil his violent threat. Monks and monastery survive unscathed, no explanation being afforded for the tyrant's quiescence.
3. Illtud's flight appears needless, since the entire population laments his absence and seeks his restitution, undaunted by their sovereign's rage against the pious exile.

Some of these incongruities may be explained as arising from duplication. Twice divine vengeance disposes of a malevolent steward of King Meirchion, who has been troubling Illtud; twice the saint finds refuge in a cave; and twice he returns to sustain his rapturous flock. The two stewards are manifestly fictional, their names being created by the hagiographer (or a predecessor) from ordinary words. That of the first, *Cyblim*, is the Welsh adjective *cyflym*, 'quick, quick-witted, acute'.

---

202 Wade-Evans (ed.), *Vitae Sanctorum Britanniae et Genealogiae*, pp. 218–26.

The second, *Cefygyd*, is *cyfygydd*, a figurative term for a warrior.[203] Neither word is recorded elsewhere as a proper noun. The savage rage of King Meirchion must also have been a fabrication designed to explain Illtud's retreats, which it is clear were in both cases originally voluntary.

Of Illtud's successive retirements, the first appears to be a duplication of the second. While no one has been able to discover an appropriate cave on the banks of the Ewenny, whose placid stream and gentle pastures make such a feature unlikely, the second retreat is attested in a much earlier source. In his early ninth-century *Historia Brittonum*, Nennius describes a miraculous altar in Gower suspended by God's power, in a place called *Loyngarth*. He goes on to recount how Saint Iltutus, praying there in a cave, was visited by two men in a ship, bearing the body of a holy man with an altar 'above his face'. The visitants explain that the holy man had requested that the body be taken to Iltutus, in order that they might inter him. In addition, they emphasize that on no account should his name ever be revealed. After the burial the men sail away, while Iltutus builds a church about the body and altar, the latter remaining 'to this day' suspended by the will of God.[204]

It is apparent that the author of the Life of Illtud borrowed his account from an independent source utilized by both authors. The episode is clumsily slotted into the Life, and bears every appearance of interpolation. As Canon Doble pointed out:

In c. 23 [the succeeding chapter] we are suddenly transported back to Llantwit, without any attempt being made to take the saint with us, and a topographical legend about two stones in the neighbourhood is given.[205]

The story of the sanctified corpse in the cave is intriguing. Although Celtic saints were capable of effecting miracles of every description, the mysterious hanging altar remains singularly enigmatic. Although Nennius does not appear to have seen it himself, despite having visited the district, he records two miracles associated with the altar. An unnamed prince is said to have tested its miraculous suspension by passing a rod over its surface, for which offence he died within the month. Another who peered beneath it was promptly blinded, and was likewise dead before a month was out. It seems that Nennius obtained these accounts from natives of the district, although without having visited the spot himself – a likely enough contingency, in view of its inaccessibility.

A curious factor in the description is the assertion that Illtud built a church 'around the body of the holy man and around the altar'. Caradog was clearly puzzled by the description, and confined himself to stating that the holy man and altar were within the cave. Did Nennius understand that the saint somehow constructed a church within the cave? He appears to have been confused by reports he had obtained, when he came to recount the marvels of the neighbourhood.

Loyngarth is the Old Welsh form of Ystym *Llwynarth*, a name anglicized as Oystermouth, at Mumbles Head in South Wales, the first element of which derives from Welsh *ystum*, 'a turn, a turning, a bend'.[206] *Llwynarth* was a district, and *ystym llwynarth* is included in an Elizabethan

203 J. Lloyd-Jones, *Geirfa Barddoniaeth Gynnar Gymraeg* (Cardiff, 1931–63), p. 219.

204 Mommsen (ed.), *Chronica Minora*, iii, pp. 215–16.

205 Doble, *Saint Iltut*, p. 40. Dumville suggests that the hagiographer and Nennius drew on a lost early life of Illtud (David N. Dumville, *Saint David of Wales* (Cambridge, 2001), pp. 8–9).

206 T. J. Morgan and D. Ellis Evans, 'Place-Names', in W. G. King and R. E. Takel (ed.), *The Scientific Survey of Swansea and its Region* (Swansea, 1971), p. 199.

Hound's Hole cave.

list of Welsh *commots* and *cantrefs*.[207] Ten miles west of Oystermouth the church of Oxwich is dedicated to St Illtud, while the magnificent cliffs to south and west contain a number of remarkable caves. One of these was presumably that occupied by Illtud, and it is possible that Nennius or his informants conflated the legend of the burial in the cave with Illtud's foundation church at nearby Oxwich.

Extraordinary though it may seem, not only is Illtud's cave identifiable, but the miraculous 'altar' remains intact at the present day! The south coast of the Gower peninsula contains a number of deep caverns running into the base of a narrow peninsula called Yellow Top. One of these, Hound's Hole, is set at the very edge of the Bristol Channel, being generally accessible only at low tide. It is approached through a confined entrance and penetrates deep into the rock. Its most striking feature is a protuberance of calcareous tufa, known to geologists as a travertine, suspended from the ceiling above the heart of the subterranean chamber. Viewed by the flickering light of pine torch or oil lamp, it might well have provoked awe and wonder in the minds of those who in early times were bold enough to penetrate the gloomy chasm.[208]

If the striking travertine in the Hound's Hole cave provides a likely candidate for the hanging altar protected by Illtud, what of the body of the mysterious 'holy man'? Close by Hound's Hole is a larger cave called Goat's Hole, where in 1823 the geologist William Buckland discovered bones from a skeleton, tinctured red with ochre and buried in sediment on the floor of the cave. The dye had probably been applied to the body or clothing at the time of death. It was long assumed that the bones were those of a female, who became known as the 'Red Lady' of Paviland. However subsequent research has established that the body was that of an active male

---

207 J. Gwenogvryn Evans, *Report on Manuscripts in the Welsh Language* (London, 1898–1902), i, p. 919.

208 Stephen Aldhouse-Green, *Paviland Cave and the 'Red Lady': A Definitive Report* (Bristol, 2000), pp. 10–14. Cf. *The Antiquaries Journal* (Cambridge, 2012), xcii, pp. 461–62.

in his mid-twenties.[209] The burial took place some 26,000 years ago, during the early Upper Palæolithic era, making it the oldest ritual interment yet discovered in Britain.

There are indications that the cave was regarded as possessed of exceptional sanctity over a period of five to eight thousand years, until about 19,000 BC. As a recent authoritative survey reports,

> What we can say is that the corpse was that of a person of high status, a status possibly gained through membership of an important lineage, social or familial group. Moreover, the last rites – in that they must have constituted a minor theatrical event – would have resembled the liturgy of a shamanic performance, and may plausibly have been presided over by a shaman.
>
> I have identified Goat's Hole, Paviland, as a possible *locus consecratus*, with the cave, or the hill which contained it, viewed as a sacred site. Caves were boundary-crossing places where shamans or medicine men may have experienced altered states of consciousness. In the context of an oscillating climatic showdown as the last glacial maximum approached – and the likelihood that human presence in Britain was episodic in consequence – sacred sites may have been the objects of special visits, even pilgrimage.[210]

The Goat's Hole cavern most likely continued as a resort of especial sanctity in later periods. As has been seen, Celtic Britons nurtured a belief in caves as points of access to, or locations of, the Otherworld. Particularly familiar is the legend of Arthur and his knights sleeping in a subterranean hall, whence one day they will emerge to save Britain in her hour of peril.[211] The Arthur of this folklore tradition was plainly a divinity in origin, and there are intimations that he at some point supplanted, or became identified with, the Celtic god Bran, one of their primary functions being that of guide of men's souls in their passage to the Otherworld.[212]

In AD 83–84, at a gathering at Delphi, the Greek writer Plutarch met a learned grammarian called Demetrius, who explained that he was on his way home to Tarsus, after a visit to Britain. He was an expert on oracles, and Plutarch calls him 'a holy man', possibly a pagan priest. He had been despatched to Britain by the Emperor Domitian to explore and report on the nearest of 'many scattered uninhabited islands off Britain, some of them named after *daimones* or heroes'. He visited one such island, which was inhabited only by a few holy men (druids?). Not long after his arrival there occurred a terrible storm, attended by howling gales and enormous waterspouts. The islanders explained these as signs attendant on the death of a Great One.

> There was one island, they told him, where Kronos lay asleep, imprisoned and guarded by Briareos: sleep was the bond devized to bind him, and there were many *daimones* with him as servants and attendants.[213]

---

209 Aldhouse-Green, *Paviland Cave and the 'Red Lady'*, pp. 145–47.

210 Ibid., pp. 245–46.

211 John Rhŷs, *Celtic Folklore: Welsh and Manx* (Oxford, 1901), pp. 456–97.

212 Alexander H. Krappe, 'Arturus Cosmocrator', *Speculum: A Journal of Mediaeval Studies* (Cambridge, Mass., 1945), xx, pp. 412–14. 'The Arthur who dug up Bran's head seems to regard himself as his successor and heir', Arthur C. L. Brown, *The Origin of the Grail Legend* (Cambridge, Mass., 1943), p. 303.

213 W. Sieveking and Hans Gärtner (ed.), *Plvtarchvs Pythici Dialogi* (Stuttgart and Leipzig, 1997), pp. 81–82.

The Emperor's curiosity had focussed on newly conquered Britain, since the Isles of the Blessed where Kronos ruled were believed to lie somewhere out in the Atlantic. According to Hesiod, Zeus released Kronos from his bonds to rule the Isles of the Blessed 'along the shore of deep swirling Ocean'. Various accounts attest to a belief in early times that Kronos ruled a realm situated somewhere beyond the shores of the Atlantic.[214]

This belief is reflected by references in the poem *Ora Maritima*, compiled by the late Roman poet Rufus Festus Avienus, which drew on a Massiliot voyagers' guide (*periplus*) dating from the fifth century BC. We learn that five days' sail from the Pillars of Hercules (Straits of Gibraltar) lay two islands sacred to Kronos's Roman counterpart Saturn.

> After this there is an ocean island rich in grass and sacred to Saturn. But there is such potent force in the island that if anyone sails up to it, the sea around the island is stirred, the island itself is shaken, and all the salt water, roaring loudly, splashes up although the rest of the sea is as quiet as a swamp.

A neighbouring island was also dedicated to Saturn.[215]

These Atlantic islands sacred to Saturn, with their sudden miraculous storms, are sufficiently reminiscent of Demetrius's account of the island of Kronos as to suggest the same legend, and confirm the antiquity of the myth in the West.

Further details of the mission of Demetrius in Britain were provided by the remarkable discovery in 1840 of two bronze plates at York, bearing inscriptions in Greek. The first reads: 'To the deities of the governor's headquarters Scribonius Demetrius (set this up),' and the second: 'To Ocean and Tethys Demetrius (set this up).'[216] At the time of Demetrius's visit (AD 82), the Roman governor Agricola was engaged in extensive preparations for an invasion of Ireland.[217] The second inscription recalls another erected by Alexander the Great to commemorate his conquests in the East, and it appears that the vainglorious Domitian envisaged the forthcoming conquest (which never took place) as complementary to those of the Macedonian world conqueror. Just as Alexander took with him scientists to record discoveries in his newly gained territories and beyond,[218] so Domitian sent a learned Greek to discover whether he could not locate the fabled Islands of the Blest.[219]

The York inscriptions suggest that Agricola authorized the assistance Demetrius required – presumably a ship and escort. However, Demetrius told Plutarch that he learned of the island

---

214 M. L. West (ed.), *Hesiod: Works & Days* (Oxford, 1978), pp. 102–103, 193–96; Rackham, Jones, and Eichholz, (ed.), *Pliny: Natural History*, ii, p. 488; Sbordone (ed.), *Strabonis Geographica*, ii, p. 79. There was a *kronion* (temple of Kronos) on an island near Cadiz (Maria Eugenia Aubet, *The Phoenicians and the West: Politics, colonies and trade* (Cambridge, 1993), pp. 229–30). Nearly two centuries before Domitian, the rebel Roman leader Sertorius had contemplated sailing from Spain to the Blessed Isles (C. F. Konrad, *Plutarch's Sertorius: A Historical Commentary* (Chapel Hill and London, 1994), pp. 109–10).

215 Dietrich Stichtenoth (ed.), *Rufus Festus Avienus: Ora Maritima* (Darmstadt, 1968), p. 24.

216 A. R. Dufty (ed.), *Ebvracvm: Roman York* (Leicester, 1962), p. 133; R. G. Collingwood and R. P. Wright (ed.), *The Roman Inscriptions of Britain: I Inscriptions on Stone* (Oxford, 1965), p. 222.

217 Giovanni Forni (ed.), *Taciti De Vita Iulii Agricolae* (Rome, 1962), pp. 178–82.

218 O. A. W. Dilke, *Greek and Roman Maps* (London, 1985), pp. 29, 59–60, 70, 134–35.

219 Jonathan Wooding suggests that Demetrius's voyage 'might have had a religious as well as military intent in exploration' (*The Location of the Promised Land in Hiberno-Latin Literature*, in Jacqueline Borsje, Ann Dooley, Séamus Mac Mathúna, and Gregory Toner (ed.), *Celtic Cosmology: Perspectives from Ireland and Scotland* (Toronto, 2014), p. 94).

where Kronos slept only by report, and the absence of any indication of its whereabouts in the account he gave Plutarch suggests the possibility that his informants withheld its precise location.

The imprisonment of Kronos by Briareos was widely interpreted in antiquity as a seasonal myth. The Greek writer Theopompus, who was born on the island of Chios *c.* 480 BC, wrote that

those who live in the west view the winter as Kronos and give it this name, while summer they name Aphrodite, and spring Persephone; and they believe that everything has been created from the union of Kronos and Aphrodite. The Phrygians believe that the god sleeps in winter and is awake in summer, and with Bacchic frenzy they celebrate in the one season his being lulled to sleep and in the other his being aroused. The Paphlagonians declare that he is fettered and imprisoned during the winter, but that in the spring he moves and is freed again.[220]

Kronos was associated with stormy, violent weather, while at the same time being connected with the fertility of grain, which he guarded during the dark, dormant season of the year.[221]

The Romans named their corresponding deity Saturn, whose virgin daughter Vesta released underground grain at the behest of Jove. On 15 December, at the festival of *Consualia*, Romans prayed to Saturn for permission to take grain from barns for sowing and eating.[222] Saturn was revered as the god of sowing, who bore a sickle as his symbol and was invoked by the tribe of the Salii at the time of sowing.[223]

While it would be rash to identify the Paviland peninsula with the island or islands sacred to Kronos-Saturn (the legend may have been no more than that, or there may have been several geographical habitations ascribed to the god), the resemblances are remarkable. There are indications that the so-called Paviland 'Red Lady' was regarded over millennia as sleeping in expectation of a salvificatory awakening. Martin West has remarked on parallels between Kronos and 'other rulers of golden eras: Yima, Alexander, Arthur, Holger Dansk, Barbarossa. They are still alive in some hidden place, and perhaps some day they and the happy times will return.'[224]

The awakening is envisaged as occurring either at the end of time, or on a perennial basis, the year being a microcosmic representation of eternity. Kronos and Saturn guarded subterranean grain in anticipation of its release with the spring growth. Just so Illtud, who concealed himself in a cave in Gower, was credited with miraculous release of corn to his grateful people. Attention has been drawn to the implications of his discovery of an underground granary, and a subsequent passage in the Life duplicates this in yet more transparent manner.

---

220 J. Gwyn Griffiths (ed.), *Plutarch's De Iside et Osiride* (Cambridge, 1970), p. 227.

221 Arthur Bernard Cook, *Zeus: A Study in Ancient Religion* (Cambridge, 1914–40), ii, p. 1289. 'Kronos represents the germination of seeds in autumn and winter … It is a time of rest and winter sleep … The time of Kronos is a time in which, after a close and sultry late summer, everything starts to breathe again as the first rains fall, so that all kinds of seeds germinate and the grass of the field regains its green colour' (A. P. Bos, *Cosmic and Meta-Cosmic Theology in Aristotle's Lost Dialogues* (Leiden, 1989), p. 11; cf. pp. 10–13).

222 Alton, Wormell, and Courtney (ed.), *P. Ovidi Nasonis Fastorvm Libri Sex*, pp. 149–50. Cf. Robert Turcan, *The Gods of Ancient Rome: Religion in Everyday Life from Archaic to Imperial Times* (Edinburgh, 2000), p. 81. The *Consualia* is thought to have been originally part of Saturn's own feast of *Saturnalia*, which began two days later (Georges Dumézil, *Archaic Roman Religion* (Chicago, 1970), p. 277).

223 Sir James George Frazer (ed.), *Publii Ovidii Nasonis Fastorum Libri Sex: The Fasti of Ovid* (London, 1929), ii, p. 122; iii, p. 68; iv, p. 111. 'Saturnus, an agricultural *numen* of sowing, took the part of primeval Cronos' (John Ferguson, *The Religions of the Roman Empire* (London, 1970), p. 211).

224 West (ed.), *Hesiod: Works & Days*, p. 195.

Towards the close of his life, we are told that Illtud visited Mont Saint Michel (*ecclesia sancti Michaelis*) in Brittany (*Letavia*). In Britain he owned three barns full of corn (*tri horrea frumenti plena*). This he ordered to be thrashed, stored in his granaries (*in granariis reponeretur*), and reserved against his return to Wales. A famine suddenly breaking out in Brittany, Illtud caused his corn to be miraculously transferred thither, feeding the entire region. Despite the pleas of the grateful inhabitants, he returned to Britain. However, not long afterwards he recrossed the sea, and came to die at the monastery of Dol, where he was interred.[225]

There is some confusion in this account. Mont Saint Michel lies in Normandy, not Brittany, and the monastery was not founded until well over a century after Illtud's time. All early evidence indicates that he was understood to have been buried at Llantwit in Wales. As Canon Doble pointed out:

> It is difficult to understand why in this chapter he [the hagiographer] brings Iltut back from Brittany to Wales only to send him back immediately to die there. Our author's language in this chapter is half-hearted and hesitating. It looks as if, when he wrote c. 15, he thought that Samson and Iltut were both buried at Llantwit.[226]

Plainly, much of this confusion arose from the author's erroneous belief that Illtud was born in Brittany, which is described as his patrimony (*hereditas*). In fact, as was shown earlier, in early mediæval Wales Brittany (*Letavia*) featured as a terrestrial location of the Otherworld, and it is clear that this is what was intended by the author's source. It looks as though the Saint was at one time envisaged as being born in *Letavia*, whither he repaired at his death, i.e. his origin lay in the Otherworld, to which he returned once his earthly span was completed.

The cave where Illtud was believed to reside during his absence from Britain appears in an earlier stage of the tradition to have been that in the Gower. Just as traditions of the national *omphalos* accrued in the *Vita Iltuti* to a local *Medgarth*, so the cave to which Illtud made seasonal withdrawals was provided with a duplicated local site near his monastery at Llantwit. Moreover, since the *Medgarth* episode in the Lives of Cadog and Illtud derived from an earlier account of Illtud's escape from the Otherworld over a chasm in the earth, so the legend of the Gower cave could have drawn upon a variant aspect of the same cosmological tradition.

The mortal St Illtud, i.e. the Eltut of the *Vita Samsonis*, is credibly described as dying in his monastery of Llantwit.[227] In the *Historia Brittonum*, he is said to have withdrawn to a cave in the Gower. It has been seen that he was there visited by two men, who brought with them the body of 'a most holy man', with an unexplained altar floating in the air above him, at whose burial they requested the Saint to assist. After adjuring Illtud never to reveal the name of the corpse (which they had not vouchsafed anyway!), the strangers departed as mysteriously as they had arrived. Illtud built a church to accord with their request, in which the body was preserved, with the altar miraculously suspended beside it from that day forward.

The explanation of this confused account seems to be as follows. The dead holy man is surely Illtud himself, who could not be named, since the hagiographer understood his real grave to be at Llantwit. The 'hanging altar' was at one time believed to be Illtud's own tomb, which was identified with the remarkable travertine hanging from the roof of the Hound's Hole Cave.

---

225 Wade-Evans (ed.), *Vitae Sanctorum Britanniae et Genealogiae*, pp. 226–28.

226 *Saint Iltut*, pp. 40–42.

227 Ibid., p. 41.

However, when the mortal and immortal Illtuds became merged in hagiographical tradition, it was not possible to situate the Saint's final resting place in the Gower, since he was understood to be interred at Llantwit. Thus, the mysterious episode related in the *Historia Brittonum* was adapted to accommodate itself to distinct traditions: those at Llantwit relating to the saint, and the far older myth of the Gower cave, which belonged to the pagan world of the druids and their unknown predecessors.

Hound's Hole Cave is singularly apt for the resting place of a divinity conceived in the Otherworld, who crosses the margin between eternity and temporality. Within the cave the sleeping god remains apart from mankind and the world. Meanwhile, the waves' ceaseless roar at its threshold declare the proximity of the unfathomed ocean, archetypal image of eternity. In the words of an Irish druid, there is 'wealth from the sea, i.e. measureless is this sea of knowledge'.[228]

By happy coincidence, the Hound's Hole Cave was it seems believed to be the refuge where the First Man, like the Irish Tuan who also lurked in a cave, awaited his reappearance, while the contiguous Paviland Cave contained the material bones of the earliest man yet discovered in Britain. However, it is likely that for millennia the remains were revered as those of a deity, whose salient characteristics corresponded sufficiently to become identified after long millennia with those of the Romano-Greek god Kronos.

Finally, the arrival in a boat of a Kronos-like figure at the Hound's Hole Cave recalls the legendary reception of his counterpart Saturn at Rome, where he disembarked after arriving by sea.[229]

Illtud as harvest deity

This interpretation may also account for Illtud's confusing voyages to and fro across the Channel, in the course of his providing corn in national emergencies. The wonderful store of grain hoarded in three barns, transferred to granaries, and miraculously transported across the sea, was believed to have originated in *Letavia*, i.e. the Otherworld. In reality, the famine occurred in South Wales, when Illtud like Saturn responded to his people's plea by releasing the subterranean grain. Fortunately, the text preserves direct allusion to the mythical tradition, when we are told that the grain fed the the inhabitants of Brittany, 'and moreover, sowed its cultivated lands' (*et insuper agriculturas seminauit*). The saint's granaries represent a rationalization of the Otherworld source of natural wealth, from which fields are seasonally fructified and barns filled.

It has been suggested that this episode was inspired by the passage in the Life of Saint Cadog alluded to earlier, where a mouse reveals an underground grain store which relieves the poor of the country.[230] However, although the fundamental concept (a mythical explanation of the origin of crops) is the same, the details are so different as rather to suggest variant versions of the same myth, utilized independently by the two hagiographers. The author's confused understanding of his source indicates that he did not merely copy or invent the incident.

228 Best, Bergin, O'Brien, and O'Sullivan (ed.), *The Book of Leinster*, p. 820. The ocean was regarded by the Celts as source of inspirational and material fruitfulness (H. Wagner, 'Studies in the Origins of Early Celtic Traditions', *Ériu* (1975), xxvi, pp. 1–10). For the symbolism of the sea in early cosmologies, cf. C. J. Bleeker, *The Rainbow: A Collection of Studies in the Science of Religion* (Leiden, 1975), pp. 174–80.

229 Frazer (ed.), *Publii Ovidii Nasonis Fastorum Libri Sex*, ii, pp. 121–22.

230 Wade-Evans, *Welsh Christian Origins*, p. 135; Doble, *Saint Iltut*, p. 42.

It may be significant that Illtud, the supernatural provider of grain, was commemorated in mediæval Wales on 6 November,[231] shortly before the time of year when Romans implored their harvest god to release grain from granaries (i.e. the divine store lodged beneath the earth).

Before leaving this episode, it is worth reverting to the first of the two accounts of Illtud's cavern retreats, that implausibly located by the River Ewenny. During his disappearance, the distraught people of the locality voice a grievous lament, which the author of the Life cites in direct speech. Who will now protect and guard us? He gave freely and continuously of his bounty, assisting the destitute and sufferers. 'Unceasingly he sowed apostolic teachings, multiplying the seed a hundredfold.' 'If he is surviving in this world, he is confined in a subterranean prison. If he be dead, may he live, as we hope, in eternal rest.' After his return, which the Saint acknowledged could not have been brought about save by divine intervention, his people give voice to an ecstatic pæan, in which they extol the restoration of order, justice, and piety throughout the land.

> Our joys lay hidden in a secret cave; they do not spread throughout our borders without past grief. That cave was not dark but full of light, for while Illtud inhabited it, it did not cease to shine with angelic splendour.

These passages bear the impression of derivation from an older source. They recall too the 'grieving the likes of which I have never seen' expressed at the imprisonment of the divine son Mabon in *Caer Loyw*, the Otherworld 'Shining City'; the anguished search of Gwydion for his nephew Lleu in *Math uab Mathonwy*; and Arthur's expedition to liberate the chained prisoner Gweir from Caer Sidi.[232] In early Greece it was common for divinities to be 'reduced to mortal rank' over a passage of time, and 'given a home beneath the earth, each in a definite place in Greek territory, near living men, and able to help them'.[233] This transformation echoed shamanistic beliefs regarding gods or heroes who withdraw to caverns, before returning rejuvenated to resume their beneficent work for men on earth.[234]

A striking parallel is found in the Hittite myth of Telepinus, son of the storm-god, whose departure afflicted the world with famine and privation. Urged by his fellow divinities, the storm-god sent messengers to find his son. He at first declined to return, with the consequence that springs ceased to flow, houses collapsed in ruin, and cattle died in the fields. Gods and men uttered plaintive pleas for Telepinus to return, and restore prosperity to the land. Eventually he relented in face of their supplicatory hymns.

> Telepinus came home to his house and cared (again) for his land. The mist let go of the windows, the smoke let go of the house. The altars were set right for the gods, the hearth

231 Silas M. Harris, 'The Kalendar of the *Vitae Sanctorum Wallensium* (B.M. Cotton MS., Vespasian A.xiv)', *Journal of the Historical Society of the Church in Wales* (Cardiff, 1953), iii, p. 52; Wade-Evans (ed.), *Vitae Sanctorum Britanniae et Genealogiae*, p. 228. Cf. Baring-Gould and Fisher, *The Lives of the British Saints*, iii, p. 317.

232 Bromwich and Simon Evans (ed.), *Culhwch and Olwen*, p. 33; Hughes (ed.), *Math Uab Mathonwy*, pp. 14–15; Gwenogvryn Evans (ed.), *Facsimile & Text of the Book of Taliesin*, pp. 54–56.

233 Erwin Rohde, *Psyche: The Cult of Souls and Belief in Immortality among the Greeks* (London, 1925), p. 102; cf. pp. 88–114.

234 Julian H. Steward, 'Panatübiji' an Owens Valley Paiute', *Bulletin of the Smithsonian Institution Bureau of American Ethnology* (Washington, 1938), cxix, p. 187; Robert M. Torrance, *The Spiritual Quest: Transcendence in Myth, Religion, and Science* (Berkeley and Los Angeles, 1994), pp. 204–205.

let go of the log. He let the sheep go to the fold, he let the cattle go to the pen. The mother tended her child, the ewe tended her lamb, the cow tended her calf. Also Telepinus tended the king and the queen and provided them with enduring life and vigour.[235]

The name *Telepinus* has been derived from an Indo-European word for 'mole', evoking the god's withdrawal beneath the surface of the earth.[236] He was understood to possess a storehouse, from which he brought wine to serve the gods assembled on their mountain.[237] This recalls Illtud's subterranean barns and granaries, from which he relieved the dearth afflicting his country. The fear lest Telepinus fail to return from his self-imposed exile was such, that daily prayers were uttered pleading with him to return and ensure the livelihood of the people.

Whether thou art in heaven above among the gods, noble Telepinus; whether gone to the sea or to the mountains to roam; whether gone to war to the country of the enemy – now let the sweet and soothing cedar essence lure thee! Come home into thy temple! Here I am entreating thee with sacrificial loaves and libations, allow thyself to be lured forth![238]

As Mircea Eliade remarked, the myth also bears striking resemblances to the Wasteland of the Grail romances, when the emasculated Grail King withdraws to his Otherworld castle, leaving his kingdom desolate. There he is sought out by the youthful hero (Perceval), whose destiny is to restore the afflicted kingdom.[239] Could the anguished pleas ascribed the sorrowful people in Illtud's Life at his disappearance, and the rapturous thanksgiving for his return from the cave, reflect pagan hymns addressed to the deity, upon whose benevolent presence the prosperity of the kingdom depended?

Again, one is reminded of Apollo's departure from Delphi to the wintry land of the Hyperboreans, where he remained for a year. The Delphians composed a pæan and song imploring his return, while the poet Alcaeus hymned a plea which enticed the god back at midsummer, when once again the land became fruitful.[240]

These possibilities are further suggested by the fact that the hagiographer does not appear to have understood the implications of the prayers he cites. Could this ostensibly Christian source have preserved a dim memory of a fragment of pagan ritual, relating to the cosmology of the Sacred Centre (*Medgarth*) in early Britain?

---

235 James B. Pritchard (ed.), *Ancient Near Eastern Texts Relating to the Old Testament* (Princeton, 1969), pp. 126–28. Cf. Arvid S. Kapelrud, *Baal in the Ras Shamra Texts* (Copenhagen, 1952), pp. 38–39, 131, 134; Joseph Fontenrose, *Python: A Study of Delphic Myth and its Origins* (Berkeley and Los Angeles, 1959), p. 129; E. O. James, *The Worship of the Sky-God: A Comparative Study in Semitic and Indo-European Religion* (London, 1963), pp. 37–38; Walter Burkert, *Structure and History in Greek Mythology and Ritual* (Berkeley and Los Angeles, 1979), pp. 123–25; Smith, *The Origins of Biblical Monotheism*, pp. 121–22; Bernhard Maier, 'Maponos und Telipinu: zu einer Theorie W. J. Gruffydds', in Bernhard Maier, Stefan Zimmer, and Christiane Batke (ed.), *150 Jahre »Mabinogion« - Deutsch-Walische Kulturbeziehungen* (Tübingen, 2001), pp. 79–90; Gregory McMahon, 'Cultural Boundaries in Hittite Ritual', in Gary Beckman, Richard Beal and Gregory McMahon (ed.), *Hittite Studies in Honor of Harry A. Hoffner Jr. on the Occasion of His 65th Birthday* (Winona Lake, Ind., 2003), pp. 270–71.

236 Gamkrelidze and Ivanov, *Indo-European and the Indo-Europeans*, i, p. 450.

237 Pritchard (ed.), *Ancient Near Eastern Texts Relating to the Old Testament*, p. 358.

238 Ibid., pp. 396–97.

239 Mircea Eliade, *A History of Religious Ideas* (London, 1979), i, p. 142.

240 Denys Page, *Sappho and Alcaeus: An Introduction to the Study of Ancient Lesbian Poetry* (Oxford, 1955), p. 245.

The subterranean god

Another legend similar to that of Illtud is attached to the figure of Merlin, who is represented in mediæval romances as enticed into a cave or rock by spells he had revealed to an enchantress. As a Scottish prophet eerily pronounced: 'A wykede womane ... has closede him in a cragge of cornwales coste.'[241]

However he was not dead, and was able to address passers-by from within his place of incarceration.[242]

Like much else in Arthurian romance, this episode appears to have been adapted from Celtic legend. According to Welsh tradition, Myrddin (the Welsh form of *Merlin*) assumed custody of the Thirteen Treasures of the Island of Britain, and withdrew with them to the *Ty Gwydr*, or House of Glass.[243] In time this unmistakably Otherworld haven became identified with the island of Bardsey in the Irish Sea.[244] Myrddin, like Illtud, was regarded as Protector of Britain. Like Illtud, he was Lord of the Wilderness. Again, like Illtud he was associated with the Omphalos of Britain, in Merlin's case identified by Geoffrey of Monmouth with Stonehenge, and in Illtud's with a local aptly-named *Medgarth*. Whether or not the two figures be ultimately one and the same, an ideological connexion is evident.[245]

Returning to the body of the 'Red Lady' preserved in the Goat's Hole cave at Paviland, a significant associated find comprised a large number of fragments of ivory rods. It is suggested that they represent either ornaments or magical wands.[246] However, given the 'special ancestral status' of the body indicated by the evidence, another possibility is that their function was that of 'soul-rods'. In pagan Ireland there existed a custom of measuring corpses with a rod named *fé*, which was inscribed with pagan charms in ogam script, and placed beside the body in the grave.[247]

The opening section of the Life of Illtud contains a veiled account of the Celtic doctrine of the transmission of the soul at conception. That his name means 'one who possessed many tribes' suggests the Illtud-figure was originally regarded as primal ancestor of the British people. Correspondingly, the ivory wands in the Paviland Cave may have been 'soul-rods'. Precisely why they were laid beside the body in the cave can only be conjectured. If they were placed there in

---

241 Gaston Paris and Jacob Ulrich (ed.), *Merlin: Roman en prose du XIII*ᵉ *siècle* (Paris, 1886), ii, pp. 191–99; James A. H. Murray (ed.), *The Romance and Prophecies of Thomas of Erceldoune* (London, 1875), p. xxxii; H. Oskar Sommer (ed.), *Le Roman de Merlin or the Early History of King Arthur: Faithfully Edited from the French MS. Add. 10292 in the British Museum (About A.D. 1316)* (London, 1894), pp. 452, 483–84; Elspeth Kennedy (ed.), *Lancelot do Lac: The Non-Cyclic Old French Prose Romance* (Oxford, 1980), i, pp. 23–24; Alexandre Micha (ed.), *Lancelot: Roman en prose du XIII*ᵉ *siècle* (1978–83), vii, pp. 41–43.

242 Sommer (ed.), *Le Roman de Merlin*, pp. 493–94.

243 Gwenogvryn Evans, *Report on Manuscripts in the Welsh Language*, i, p. 911.

244 Bromwich (ed.), *Trioedd Ynys Prydein*, p. cxxxiii, 474, 560; Ceridwen Lloyd-Morgan, 'Narratives and Non-Narratives: Aspects of Welsh Arthurian Tradition', in eadem (ed.), *Arthurian Literature XXI: Celtic Arthurian Material* (Cambridge, 2004), p. 131.

245 It may be that Illtud bore direct association with Stonehenge. Geoffrey provides Eldol with a brother Eldad, bishop of Gloucester (*Eldadus Claudiocestrensis episcopus, frater Eldol*), who presides over the interment of British nobles slain at the site of Stonehenge (Reeve and Wright (ed.), *Geoffrey of Monmouth: The History of the Kings of Britain*, pp. 135, 169). It has been suggested that this otherwise unknown ecclesiastic is to be identified with Illtud (Gilbert H. Doble, *Saint Iltut* (Cardiff, 1944), p. 49).

246 Aldhouse-Green, *Paviland Cave and the 'Red Lady'*, pp. 116–17, 118–19, 233.

247 Kuno Meyer (ed.), 'Sanas Cormaic: An Old-Irish Glossary Compiled by Cormac Úa Cuilennáin', in O. J. Bergin, R. I. Best, Kuno Meyer, and J. G. O'Keefe (ed.), *Anecdota from Irish Manuscripts* (Halle and Dublin, 1907-13), iv, pp. 49–50. For the possible find of such a rod in a grave near the Boyne, cf. Conor Newman, 'The sacral landscape of Tara: a preliminary exploration', in Roseanne Schot, Conor Newman, and Edel Bhreatnach (ed.), *Landscapes of Cult and Kingship* (Dublin, 2011), pp. 30–31.

a single batch, did they symbolize the multiplying generations of his descendants? Or were they deposited individually by devotees, seeking to link their souls to the figure from whom all mankind claimed descent?

The painting of the body in the Goat's Hole Cave with ochre was designed to ensure immortality for the being who 'slept' there. Red, being the colour of blood, was widely ascribed in early cultures to life and health.[248] The millennia during which his body continued (as the archæological evidence indicates) a focus of cultic visits suggests that his presence was regarded as providing material benefits to his people. By implication, his death represented no more than a sleep. Indeed, the body in the cave appears to have attracted pilgrimages from devotees over a colossal span of years. It would be good to know, for example, what drew those visitors to this remote spot, who offered or mislaid coins of the British usurper Carausius (AD 286–93) and the Roman emperor Constantius II (337–61).[249] Did Demetrius the grammarian scramble along the tideline of the Paviland peninsula, and enter the murky chasm in the cliff, in the days when Domitian ruled the Empire?

However, it is the story of Illtud's reception and interment of a holy man of mysterious provenance in a Gower cave which most strikingly suggests a remarkable, although by no means incredible, survival of myth and associated rituals concerning a potent being confined in a cave by the margin of the sea. In ancient Greece, those in search of enlightenment underwent various rituals before entering a darkened cave, where they were vouchsafed knowledge of the future by the resident hero.

> In fact, the method of *Incubation*, or temple-sleep, by which Amphiaraos (like many other daimones and Heroes) was questioned, was based on the assumption that the daimon, which was only visible indeed to mortal eyes in the higher state achieved by the soul in dreams, had his permanent dwelling at the seat of his oracle.[250]

The confused account in the *Historia Brittonum* suggests that originally Illtud and the sanctified being in the cave were one and the same. As the pagan myth coalesced with the career of the historical St Illtud, the burial place of this composite figure was assigned to the Saint's foundation monastery of Llantwit. Hence arose the artificial distinction between Illtud and the holy man, which may also account for the peculiar instruction of those mysterious men who brought the body to the cave:

> You must not reveal his name to anyone! (*et nomen eius non reveles ullo homini*).

It might appear at this point that my investigation has strayed somewhat from Stonehenge. In fact, I have sought to show that the Life of Saint Illtud represents a thinly veiled adaptation of pagan myths associated with the Celtic concept of the Sacred Centre. In his original guise as divinity, Illtud was primæval ancestor of the British people, sole survivor of those cycles of destruction and rebirth which the Celts believed the world to be regularly subjected.

---

248 J. Gwyn Griffiths, 'The Symbolism of Red in Egyptian Religion', in J. Bergman, K. Drynjeff, and H. Ringgren (ed.), *Ex orbe religionum: studia Geo Widengren* (Leiden, 1972), pp. 208–16.

249 Aldhouse-Green, *Paviland Cave and the 'Red Lady'*, pp. 20, 24.

250 Rohde, *Psyche*, p. 92. Initiates spent thrice nine days consulting Zeus in a cave on Mount Ida (ibid., p. 96). Pausanias records a vivid account of his own visit to the subterranean oracle of Trophonios (Rocha-Pereira (ed.), *Pavsaniae Graeciae Descriptio*, iii, pp. 77–80).

He emerged as survivor of the cataclysm, reborn like the Irish Fintán in the form of a hawk from the Otherworld, where the divine figures of Arthur or Pwyll presided over the eternal feast in the Underworld realm of *Annwfn*. The geographical point at which the New Man emerged into this world was a real or suppositious chasm, providing access to the subterranean Otherworld, located at a spot known as *Medgarth*, 'the Middle Enclosure'. This name led to its identification with the Omphalos of Britain, from which the British people sprang at the beginning of the current age.

Saint's Life and pagan myth

Analysis of the *Vita Iltuti* throws light from such varied angles on the myth of the Brittonic *omphalos*, that it may assist to provide a tentative reconstruction of its sources.

Illtud the druid

Illtud (*Eltutus*) lived in what is now South Wales during the first half of the sixth century AD. Heir to a line of hereditary druids, he was famed throughout Britain for his mastery of the characteristic druidic powers of prophecy and magic.[251]

Illtud the abbot

While our earliest source (the *Vita Samsonis*) is disarmingly frank about Illtud's pagan antecedents and authority, he features primarily as abbot of a magnificent monastery. It is likely that this originated as a druidic college or temple, like the temple of Belenus at Bayeux, just across the Channel, and that presided over by the *librarius* consulted by the parents of Saint Samson. Conversion of heathen temples into Christian churches represented regular practice at this time throughout the Roman Empire.[252] Plummer observed that 'it is quite possible that some at least of the schools and monasteries of Ireland were direct successors of these ancient druidic institutions'.[253] In Gaul, Saint Martin built churches at the sites of heathen temples he destroyed, very likely making use of the original structures, confining his activity to ridding them of overtly pagan symbolism. Archæological evidence indicates that surviving temples in post-Roman Britain were regularly adapted to Christian use.[254]

While late saints' Lives often recount stereotypical conflicts between saint and druid, evidence suggests that in early times the two religions tended to coexist – or even coalesce – amicably.

---

251 *Genereque magicus sagacissimus et futurorum praescius* (Flobert (ed.), *La vie ancienne de saint Samson de Dol*, p. 156). Druids frequently belonged to hereditary dynasties (Plummer (ed.), *Vitae Sanctorum Hiberniae*, i, p. clix; Guyonvarc'h and Le Roux, *Les Druides*, p. 54).

252 Ramsay MacMullen, *Christianity and Paganism in the Fourth to Eighth Centuries* (New Haven and London, 1997), p. 133; F. R. Trombley, *Hellenic Religion and Christianization C. 370–529* (Leiden, 1993–94), i, pp. 98–147, 330. A Christian memorial was erected within the temple of Apollo at Daphne, thus effectively annexing it to the new religion (Alan Wardman, 'Pagan Priesthoods in the Later Empire', in Martin Henig and Anthony King (ed.), *Pagan Gods and Shrines of the Roman Empire* (Oxford, 1986), p. 257). In early Anglo-Saxon England heathen temples were regularly converted into Christian churches (William A. Chaney, *The Cult of Kingship in Anglo-Saxon England: The Transition from Paganism to Christianity* (Manchester, 1970), pp. 73–77).

253 Plummer (ed.), *Vitae Sanctorum Hiberniae*, i, pp. clxiv–v; Cf. Richard North, *Heathen Gods in Old English Literature* (Cambridge, 1997), pp. 83–85.

254 C. Halm (ed.), *Sulpicii Severi: Libri qui Supersunt* (Vienna, 1866), i, p. 123. Cf. K. R. Dark, *Civitas to Kingdom: British Political Continuity 300–800* (Leicester, 1994), pp. 60, 68; W. J. Wedlake, *The Excavation of the Shrine of Apollo at Nettleton, Wiltshire, 1956-1971* (Dorking, 1982), pp. 104-5; Ann Woodward and Peter Leach, *The Uley Shrines: Excavation of a ritual complex on West Hill, Uley, Gloucestershire: 1977–9* (London, 1993), p. 321.

Given their priestly prestige, inspired learning, aristocratic status, and immense political influence, druids must have appeared ideal candidates for high ecclesiastical office. There is no reason to suppose that such 'conversion' presented any insurmountable difficulty. Saint Patrick is said to have invited the chief druid of Leinster, Dubthach maccu Lugair, to nominate a suitable candidate as bishop of his kingdom. Dubthach selected a young druid named Fíacc Fínd, who became its first bishop.[255]

Illtud and Lleu

As a druid, Illtud was a votary of the great Celtic god Lug, Welsh *Lleu*. The name *Eltut* means 'of many tribes', appropriate epithet for a celebrated ancestor-deity. In some way Illtud appears to have been identified with the god he served. His soul departed at his death in the form of an eagle, a transmogrification undergone by Lleu in the Welsh mediæval story *Math uab Mathonwy*.

Conversion of the insular Celts may well have been facilitated by striking resemblances of their native god Lleu to Christ. In *Math uab Mathonwy* Lleu is born of a virgin, and grows into an astonishingly precocious child. Ultimately, however, he comes to a tragic end. Betrayed by a treacherous foe, he is mortally wounded by a spear-thrust in the side. Hanging in his death-throes from a tree, he is miraculously resuscitated by his father Gwydion, who features as a type of divine druid. Restored to life, Lleu brings peace and justice to his kingdom. At the same time, there is no doubt that his story derives from native Celtic tradition, owing nothing to the Gospel story of Christ.[256]

Similarly, the account in the Norse poem *Hávamál* of Óðinn's ritualistic hanging on the World Tree evinces close resemblances to the British and biblical divine sacrifices, while being likewise of demonstrably independent origin. As a distinguished scholar of Norse myth has remarked,

> While we cannot preclude the possibility of Christian influence on the scene described in the *Hávamál*, when we analyse the lines, we realize that nearly every element in the Norse myth can be explained as a part of pagan tradition, and even of the cult of Óðinn …

The sacrifice of Óðinn to himself may thus be seen as the highest conceivable form of sacrifice, in fact so high that, like many a religious mystery, it surpasses our comprehension. It is the sacrifice, not of king to god, but of god to god, of such a kind as is related in Scripture of the sacrifice of Christ.[257]

---

255 Gwynn (ed.), *Liber Ardmachanus*, pp. 8–9, 353–6; Whitley Stokes and John Strachan (ed.), *Thesaurus Palaeohibernicus: A Collection of Old-Irish Glosses Scholia Prose and Verse* (Cambridge, 1901–3), ii, p. 307. The dramatic account of the visit of the two druids to Tara represents later hagiographical invention (Kim McCone, 'Dubthach Maccu Lugair and a Matter of Life and Death in the Pseudo-Historical Prologue to the *Senchas Már*', *Peritia: Journal of the Medieval Academy of Ireland* (Galway, 1986), v, pp. 1–35). Nevertheless, there is no compelling reason to doubt Fiacc's druidic origin. Such conversions were probably of frequent occurrence, as the prestige of Roman Christianity increased in the land.

256 Allusion to the circumstances of Lleu's death has been detected in the early North British poem *Gododdin*: 'In this light, I take *eryr Gwyδyen* 'Gwydyon's eagle' to be a reference to the Fourth Branch's account of Lleu's transformation to an eagle' (John T. Koch (ed.), *The Gododdin of Aneirin: Text and Context from Dark-Age North Britain* (Cardiff, 1997), p. 160). Despite detailed parallels with the crucifixion of Christ, that of Lleu clearly derives from indigenous tradition (Anne Ross, *Pagan Celtic Britain: Studies in Iconography and Tradition* (London, 1967), p. 34; Proinsias Mac Cana, *Celtic Mythology* (London, 1970), p. 29).

257 E. O. G. Turville-Petre, *Myth and Religion of the North: The Religion of Ancient Scandinavia* (London, 1964), pp. 43, 48. Cf. Richard North, *Heathen Gods in Old English Literature* (Cambridge, 1997), pp. 83–85.

11

The Hyperborean Temple

An early Greek account of Stonehenge?
It cannot be emphasized too strongly that Geoffrey of Monmouth's account of the removal of the stones of Uisneach in Ireland to Salisbury Plain reflects ideological, rather than physical, correspondence between the two sites. Uisneach was renowned in Irish tradition as the Centre of Ireland, and a tradition that Stonehenge fulfilled the same function in early Britain provides the most plausible explanation of the effective identification (the stones of Stonehenge = those formerly at Uisneach) of the two sites in Geoffrey's narrative. It will be recalled that Merlin is significantly portrayed as requiring the stones to be re-erected on exactly the same pattern they constituted at their site of origin. In addition, it will shortly be seen in Chapter Twelve that the early Welsh story *Cyfranc Lludd a Lleuelys* explicitly confirms that traditions of the Omphalos of Britain continued current in the Middle Ages.

Other evidence intimates that Stonehenge was the original *omphalos*. An historiographical void covers the early millennia of the monument's existence, the first explicit allusion being that of Henry of Huntingdon, written not long before AD 1135. However, there exists a remarkable description of what may well have been Stonehenge, compiled a millennium and a half before Geoffrey's day. In the first century BC, the geographer Diodorus of Sicily recorded this oft-cited description of a Northern temple:

> Hecataeus and certain others say that in the regions beyond the land of the Celts there lies in the ocean an island no smaller than Sicily.

This island was situated in the North, being inhabited by a people known as Hyperboreans. Its exceptional fertility and temperate climate resulted in dual annual harvests, and it was considered particularly holy as the birthplace of Leto, mother of Apollo. In consequence 'the inhabitants are looked upon as priests of Apollo' and 'daily praise this god continuously in song and honour him exceedingly'.

> And there is also on this island both a magnificent sacred precinct of Apollo and a notable temple (τέμενός τε 'Απόλλωνος μεγαλοπρεπὲς καὶ ναὸν ἀξιόλογον), which is adorned with many votive offerings and is spherical in shape (σφαιροειδῆ τῷ σχήματι).

There was in addition a city (πόλις), implicitly situated nearby, which was likewise sacred to the god.[1] Most inhabitants of the island were players of the cithara, who plied their instruments continuously in the temple, while singing hymns glorifying the deeds of the god. They spoke a Hyperborean (i.e. Northern) language peculiar to themselves, despite which they had enjoyed warm relations with the Athenians and Delians since ancient times. From time to time Greeks visited the island, leaving behind costly votive offerings inscribed in their own tongue.

The proximity of the moon to the northern island facilitated observation of the lunar landscape.[2] Apollo visited the island every nineteenth year, when the stars returned to their original place in the heavens. There he played and danced continuously each night from the vernal equinox until the rising of the Pleiades, in this way 'expressing his delight in his exploits'. The kings of the island's city and the guardians of the sacred precinct succeeded on an hereditary basis, being known as *Boreadae*, 'descendants of Boreas'.[3]

Diodorus explained that he derived his information from writings of the Ionian philosopher Hecataeus of Abdera (a city on the Aegean coast of Thrace), who lived towards the end of the fourth century BC, as well as from other unidentified authors.[4] Comparison of the Hyperborean island to Sicily was probably influenced as much by their respective shapes as by their size. Julius Caesar was informed that Britain was triangular in its proportions, and classical authors regularly noted the same of the coastline of Sicily.[5]

If, as must surely be the case, the 'island no smaller than Sicily' off the coast of Gaul (*Celtica*) is Britain, then it is hard not to infer that the great temple was Stonehenge.[6] The description 'spherical' (σφαιροειδής) recalls the temple of Vesta at Rome. That temple was likewise described as perfectly round, corresponding to the spherical shape of the earth, and its fire epitomized that which was believed to burn beneath the earth. Both its circularity and sacred hearth (*focus*) marked it out as central alike to the world and the universe.[7] These factors,

---

1   Could this be the settlement at Durrington Walls beside Stonehenge, the most extensively populated Neolithic settlement discovered in Britain? The account provided by Hecataeus suggests that the 'city' was associated with the temple, while 'we can conclude that the Durrington Walls village was the hub of a network that stretched across southern Britain to provide supplies to feed an army-sized population possibly bringing some animals from as far away as Scotland' (Mike Parker Pearson, *Stonehenge: Exploring the Greatest Stone Age Mystery* (London, 2012), p. 121). Although the 'town' was in use only from *c.* 2600 to 2300 BC (ibid., pp. 117–18), traditions of this extraordinary metropolis might well have remained current centuries later.

2   Aubrey Burl suggests that this detail is only applicable to a site considerably further north (Pearson, *Stonehenge*, p. 353). However, given that the claimed proximity of the moon does not accord with reality, it is likely that the description indicates no more than that the site was associated with lunar observation.

3   C. H. Oldfather (ed.), *Diodorus of Sicily* (London, 1933–67), ii, pp. 36–40.

4   Cf. J. D. P. Bolton, *Aristeas of Proconnessus* (Oxford, 1962), p. 24.

5   Britannia 'ends in a corner with two opposed angles comprising a triangle, and completely similar to Sicily' (A. Silberman (ed.), *Pomponius Mela: Chorographie* (Paris, 1988), p. 81). Cf. Otto Seel (ed.), *C. Ivlii Caesaris Commentarii Rervm Gestarvm: Bellvm Gallicvm* (Leipzig, 1961), p. 137; Francesco Sbordone (ed.), *Strabonis Geographica* (Rome, 1963–2000), ii, pp. 148–49; H. Rackham, W. H. S. Jones, and D. E. Eichholz, (ed.), *Pliny: Natural History* (London, 1938–62), ii, pp. 62, 64.

6   'At least we can say that Diodorus had heard some report of a striking circular northern temple; and since there was then no better example in existence than Stonehenge, one may cautiously treat his as the first potential reference to that monument, albeit very oblique', John North, *Stonehenge: Neolithic Man and the Cosmos* (London, 1996), p. 395. Cf. John Rhys, *Lectures on the Origin and Growth of Religion as Illustrated by Celtic Heathendom* (London, 1888), pp. 194–95.

7   E. H. Alton, D. E. W. Wormell, and E. Courtney (ed.), *P. Ovidi Nasonis Fastorvm Libri Sex* (Leipzig, 1985), pp. 145–48. If Stonehenge were regarded as a microcosmic representation of the cosmos, it could have been understood as a sphere in symbolic terms, comparable to the archaic Greek conception of

combined with the likelihood that Apollo's temple in Britain was regarded as complementary to that at Delphi, suggest that the circular British temple was likewise considered the *omphalos* of the island.

The reference to the inhabitants' concern with the moon, and their use of a nineteen-year calendar, indicates that they employed a lunar calendar, which Hecataeus identified with the Greeks' Metonic system. That the druids employed a lunar calendar is reported by Pliny.[8] Hecataeus's reference to the inhabitants' concern with the appearance of the moon, whose features appear exceptionally clear in the northern latitude, together with its position in relation to the stars, could at least in part reflect the practice in early societies of recording phases of the moon in order to maintain an accurate calendar.[9]

The precision of the details supplied by Hecataeus, which provide as credible a depiction of Britain as might be expected from a Greek of his era, stand in marked contrast to other early references to the land of the Hyperboreans, whose extreme vagueness is indicated by the Thracian etymology of their name: 'those living on the far side (of the mountains) of the North.'[10] In reality the Hyperboreans were a purely mythical race.[11] A century before Hecataeus, the Boeotian poet Pindar told how they bestowed on Herakles the olive wreath used as the prize of Olympic victory, and pronounced the road to their land impossible to discover by land or sea, save on one occasion by the legendary hero Perseus.[12] Herodotus similarly learned that not even northern peoples like the Scythians and Issedones knew anything of the Hyperborean homeland.[13]

The account of the triangular island off the coast of Celtica is characterized by the precision of its geography, and its remarkably specific account of the religious beliefs and practices of the Hyperboreans. In no other source are they associated with the Celts,[14] an island, or the ocean. In

the sky as 'a solid hemisphere like a bowl' (G. S. Kirk and J. E. Raven, *The Presocratic Philosophers: A Critical History with a Selection of Texts* (Cambridge, 1957), p. 10).

8   Rackham, Jones, and Eichholz, (ed.), *Pliny: Natural History*, iv, p. 548.

9   Cf. Yigal Bloch, 'Middle Assyrian Lunar Calendar and Chronology', in Jonathan Ben-Dov, Wayne Horowitz, and John M. Steele (ed.), *Living the Lunar Calendar* (Oxford, 2012), p. 43. 'In traditional non-Western societies, moon-sighting is always embedded in a social and cultural context' (Stanislaw Iwaniszewski, 'Telling Time with the Moon: An American Overview', in ibid., p. 313).

10   Thomas V. Gamkrelidze and Vjačeslav V. Ivanov, *Indo-European and the Indo-Europeans: A Reconstruction and Historical Analysis of a Proto-Language and a Proto-Culture* (Berlin and New York, 1995), i, pp. 574, 585; Hjalmar Frisk, *Griechisches Etymologisches Wörterbuch* (Heidelberg, 1954–72), ii, p. 967; Pierre Chantraine, *Dictionnaire étymologique de la langue grecque: Histoire des mots; avec un Supplément sous la direction de: Alain Blanc, Charles de Lamberterie, Jean-Louis Perpillou* (Paris, 1999), pp. 1157–58.

11   Cf. James S. Romm, *The Edges of the Earth in Ancient Thought: Geography, Exploration, and Fiction* (Princeton, 1992), pp. 60–67; Robert L. Fowler (ed.), *Early Greek Mythography* (Oxford, 2000-2013), ii, pp. 606–7.

12   Bruno Snell (ed.), *Pindari Carmina cvm Fragmentis* (Leipzig, 1964), i, pp. 14, 113–14; Ian Rutherford, *Pindar's Paeans: A Reading of the Fragments with a Survey of the Genre* (Oxford, 2001), pp. 209–13.

13   Haiim B. Rosén (ed.), *Herodoti Historiae* (Leipzig, 1987–97), i, p. 370. 'In other words, the country and its inhabitants belong to mythical geography' (Mircea Eliade, *A History of Religious Ideas* (London, 1979), i, p. 269). Cf. Denys Page, *Sappho and Alcaeus: An Introduction to the Study of Ancient Lesbian Poetry* (Oxford, 1955), pp. 250–52.

14   Heraclidus Pontus identified the Celts who sacked Rome as Hyperboreans, but this probably represents no more than loose use of the term in the sense of 'Northern' (Philip P. Freeman, 'The Earliest Greek Sources on the Celts', *Études Celtiques* (Paris, 1996), xxxii, pp. 27, 34.

all other Greek references they are located on the edge of the Eurasian land mass in the vicinity of the Arctic Ocean, north of the equally mythical snow-covered Rhipaean Mountains.[15]

Hecataeus's account implies that the Hyperboreans dwelt *solely* in the triangular island beyond Celtica, suggesting that it was he who speculatively identified its inhabitants with the fabulous northern race. Evidently he was ignorant of the true name of the island and its inhabitants, who, he asserts, spoke a language unique to themselves, i.e. distinct from that of the Celts of northern Gaul. All in all, it seems Hecataeus's description of the island must be treated as distinct from the legendary Hyperboreans of the North. His account conveys every appearance of authenticity, and may well have been based on accounts brought back by visitors to the great circular shrine. Recent archæological discoveries in the Stonehenge region indicate that pilgrims did indeed travel from far afield in southern Europe to visit the uniquely prestigious sacred precinct from very early times.[16] The assertion by Hecataeus's informants that the islanders spoke a language unique to themselves conceivably reflects the presence of a surviving Bronze Age population.

The costly votive offerings deposited by Greek visitors to their shrine may have included amber. Herodotus describes how offerings wrapped in wheat-straw were brought from the land of the Hyperboreans through Scythia to the Adriatic, and thence to Delos and other Greek cities. In earlier times the Hyperboreans had travelled the entire journey, but latterly the traffic had become undertaken by middlemen. It is thought that the unspecified commodity, which was evidently precious and fragile, was amber from the Baltic.[17] Archæological evidence shows that extensive trade in this luxury product was conducted in the Bronze Age between the Mediterranean and the 'Wessex culture' of Southern Britain.[18]

It is possible that Hecataeus acquired information from accounts by the Massaliot explorer Pytheas.[19] It may well have been Pytheas, the first mariner known to have circumnavigated

---

15   M. Cary and E. H. Warmington, *The Ancient Explorers* (London, 1929), pp. 198 99.

16   Apollonius of Rhodes recounts how Apollo passed over from Lycia to the land of the Hyperboreans. When in due course the Argonauts arrive at an island hallowed by his presence, they build an altar and sacrifice to him in hope of safe return. Around the burning sacrifice they set up a broad dancing-ring (χορός). Next they erect a temple to Concord (ὁμόνοια), which survives 'to the present time' (Hermann Fränkel (ed.), *Apollonii Rhodii Argonavtica* (Oxford, 1961), pp. 86–87). The 'dancing-ring' tantalizingly recalls the *chorea gigantum* of Geoffrey of Monmouth: it would be tempting but unprovable to suppose that Apollonius had heard travellers' tales of the Hyperborean island known to Hecataeus.

17   Rosén (ed.), *Herodoti Historiae*, i, pp. 370–72. Cf. Arthur Bernard Cook, *Zeus: A Study in Ancient Religion* (Cambridge, 1914–40), ii, p. 498. The route described is not the most direct, but significantly reflects that employed in the amber trade, which was conducted by way of the Adriatic (Peter Gelling and Hilda Ellis Davidson, *The Chariot of the Sun and other Rites and Symbols of the Northern Bronze Age* (London, 1969), pp. 120–21). Pausanias records a different route from that described by Herodotus (Maria-Helena Rocha-Pereira (ed.), *Pavsaniae Graeciae Descriptio* (Leipzig, 1973–81), i, p. 73): for an explanation of the divergence, cf. J. G. Frazer, *Pausanias's Description of Greece* (London, 1898), ii, pp. 405–6.

18   Stuart Piggott, *Ancient Europe from the beginnings of Agriculture to Classical Antiquity* (Edinburgh, 1965), pp. 137–38, 161; Jacques Briard, *The Bronze Age in Barbarian Europe: From the Megaliths to the Celts* (London, 1979), pp. 68, 80; Anthony F. Harding, 'British Amber Spacer-Plate Necklaces and their Relatives in Gold and Stone', in Curt W. Beck and Jan Bouzek (ed.), *Amber in Archæology: Proceedings of the Second International Conference on Amber in Archaeology, Lilice 1990* (Prague, 1993), pp. 53–58; Stephen Shennan, 'Amber and its Value in the British Bronze Age', ibid., pp. 59–66; Helen Hughes-Brock, 'Amber in the Late Bronze Age: Some Problems and Perspectives', ibid., pp. 219–29. For a list of amber finds in the Stonehenge vicinity, cf. Sally Exon, Vince Gaffney, Ann Woodward, and Ron Yorston, *Stonehenge Landscapes: Journeys through real-and-imagined worlds* (Oxford, 2000), p. 118).

19   'Nor do I see any objection to the old idea that Stonehenge was the original of the famous temple of Apollo in the land of the Hyperboreans, the stories of which were based in the first instance most likely

Britain, who first noted her triangular shape and compared Britain with Sicily.[20] He is said to have explored Britain's interior,[21] and the description of the circular temple could reflect information acquired by the voyager during his disembarkations on the British coast.[22]

The belief that Apollo migrated between Delos and the Hyperorean island could reflect perceived similarities between the Greek Apollo and the presiding divinity of the northern island.[23] Apollonius Rhodius cites an instance of the Celts preserving their own version of a myth of the Hyperborean Apollo.[24] The god in the Celtic pantheon who most closely resembled Apollo is Lugus (Irish *Lug*, Welsh *Lleu*). The parallels are remarkable. The respective Greek and Celtic gods are alike represented as precocious, eternally youthful, virile, and radiant. Apollo was famed as an archer, and his Welsh counterpart Lleu bore the epithet *llawgyffes*, 'of the sure (or skilful) hand', reflecting his unerring skill in casting missiles.[25] It was common practice in early Greece and Rome for foreign deities to be identified with corresponding figures from their own pantheons.

Apollo was associated with ravens. He assumed the guise of one when guiding his followers to Libya; the shamanistic seer Aristeas accompanied him in the form of a raven; he employed ravens as messengers.[26] Lugus is likewise closely associated with the bird: indeed, it has been contended

on the journal of Pytheas' travels' (Rhys, *Lectures on the Origin and Growth of Religion as Illustrated by Celtic Heathendom*, p. 194).

20   Oldfather (ed.), *Diodorus of Sicily*, iii, p. 152. It is likely that Diodorus's measurements of Britain derive from Pytheas (D. Stichtenoth, *Pytheas von Marseille: Über das Weltmeer* (Cologne, 1959), p. 75; C. F. C. Hawkes, *Pytheas: Europe and the Greek Explorers* (Oxford, 1975), p. 38; Christina Horst Roseman (ed.), *Pytheas of Massalia: On the Ocean* (Chicago, 1994), p. 20).

21   Hans Joachim Mette (ed.), *Pytheas von Massalia* (Berlin, 1952), p. 26. Dicks accepted the reality of his exploration of the interior of Britain (D. R. Dicks (ed.), *The Geographical Fragments of Hipparchus* (London, 1960), p. 179). That Strabo does not mention the northern temple of Apollo does not prove anything either way, given that he 'probably discarded much of the information that Eratosthenes obtained from Pytheas' (Duane W. Roller (ed.), *Eratosthenes' Geography* (Princeton and Oxford, 2010), p. 18; cf. pp. 128–29). In particular, 'Strabo placed within the realm of fabricated geography details that Eratosthenes found reliable, most notably the data from Pytheas of Massalia' (ibid., p. 22).

22   Diodorus, who may here be citing Pytheas, notes that the inhabitants of *Belerium* (Land's End) were civilized people, who maintained continual contact with travelling merchants (Oldfather (ed.), *Diodorus of Sicily*, iii, p. 156).

23   Cf. E. R. Dodds, *The Greeks and the Irrational* (Berkeley, 1951), pp. 161–62; Christian-J. Guyonvarc'h and Françoise Le Roux, *Les Druides* (Rennes, 1986), p. 309.

24   Fränkel (ed.), *Apollonii Rhodii Argonavtica*, p. 194. Herodotus (§V.7) records that the nobility of Thrace focussed worship on Hermes (Haiim B. Rosén (ed.), *Herodoti Historiae* (Leipzig, 1987–97), ii, p. 4). Hermes corresponds to Roman Mercurius and Celtic Lugus (Henrich Wagner, 'The Origin of the Celts in the Light of Linguistic Geography', *Transactions of the Philological Society* (Oxford, 1969), lxviii, p. 245; idem, 'Studies in the Origins of Early Celtic Civilisation', *Zeitschrift für celtische Philologie* (Tübingen, 1971), xxxi, p. 21). It is consequently reasonable to assume Thracian familiarity with pan-Celtic lore of Lug-Mercurius.

25   Ian Hughes (ed.), *Math Uab Mathonwy: Pedwaredd Gainc y Mabinogi* (Aberystwyth, 2000), p. 8. Apollo *Citharoedus* ('the Harper') is equated with the Celtic god Maponos (Proinsias MacCana, 'Celtic Religion and Mythology', in V. Kruta, O. H. Frey, B. Raftery, and M. Szabó (ed.), *The Celts* (London, 1991), p. 601). Maponos, as Divine Son, in turn corresponds closely to Lugus (Nikolai Tolstoy, *The Quest for Merlin* (London, 1985), pp. 205–6, 211; Pierre-Yves Lambert, 'Magie et Pouvoir dans la Quatrième Branche du *Mabinogi*', *Studia Celtica* (Cardiff, 1994), xxviii, p. 98).

26   Rosén (ed.), *Herodoti Historiae*, i, p. 362; Frederick Williams (ed.), *Callimachus: Hymn to Apollo* (Oxford, 1978), p. 11; Peter K. Marshall (ed.), *Hygini Fabvlae* (Stuttgart and Leipzig, 1993), p. 169; André Le Bœuffle (ed.), *Hygin: L'Astronomie* (Paris, 1983), p. 81; Sir James George Frazer (ed.), *Apollodorus: The Library* (London, 1921), ii, p. 14; W. R. Paton et al. (ed.), *Plvtarchi Moralia* (Leipzig, 1953–78), ii, p. 379C.

that his name derives from a word signifying 'raven'.[27] Legend told that, when the Gaulish city of Lugdunum (Lyons) was founded, selection of the site was confirmed by the appearance of a flock of ravens.[28] Lugus/Mercurius is frequently portrayed in Gaulish iconography with an attendant raven or ravens.[29] A mediæval Irish poem describes him as accompanied by ravens and crows. In addition, there are striking parallels between Lug and the Norse god Óðinn, whose two raven messengers perched on his shoulders, whispering information in his ears.[30]

Although Lug is well-known as a Celtic god, in Britain at least his cult may have absorbed significant elements of pre-Celtic mythology. In the mediæval Welsh tale of *Math uab Mathonwy*, inheritance within the dynasty to which Lleu (= Lug) is heir has been shown to reflect the non-Celtic practice of matriliny.

> The whole picture of this legendary North Welsh family suggests a matrilinear succession, matrilocal in character, with probably marriage within the first degree ... The whole story is, of course, pure legend; but the underlying social implications are certainly ancient. It should be noted that these features are not found in the other stories of the *Mabinogion*.[31]

When Apollo was born on Delos, his heroic precocity became immediately apparent from his breaking free of the white cloth in which he had been bound. He arose, demanded his lyre and bow, and began walking. The baby Lleu in *Math uab Mathonwy* likewise flung aside the sheet in which he was wrapped, and before he was two walked to a nearby court. In next to no time he had learned to ride, and was begging for horses and weapons.[32]

Again, Apollo was a herdsman whose influence over the cows, goats and ewes he tended caused them to bear twins, and ensured prodigious production of milk.[33] In Wales the god Lleu, in the pious guise of St Lleudad ('Father Lleu'), was said to have possessed a miraculous cow which was a source of unstinted milk. In Ireland, Lug's mother Ethne subsisted on a permanent supply of milk, provided by a magical cow brought from India by the gods Manannán and Aengus to Brug na Bóinne, which was drawn into a silken spancel and mether of gold. A similarly fecund cow was kept by Manannán in the Otherworld realm of Emhain Ablach, while Ethne's life alternated between Bruig na Bóinne and Emhain Ablach, where she milked both cows. Irish folklore legends of Lug's upbringing associate him with a wondrous cow called Glas Gavlen, which was at once the sole cow in Ireland and a stupendous milk-producer. In

27   Antonio Tovar, 'The God Lugus in Spain', *The Bulletin of the Board of Celtic Studies* (Cardiff, 1982), xxix, p. 593; *Zeitschrift für celtische Philologie*, xxxi, pp. 19–24; Mallory and Adams (ed.), *Encyclopedia of Indo-European Culture*, p. 142.

28   Joannes Zwicker (ed.), *Fontes Historiae Religionis Celticae* (Bonn, 1934–36), p. 92.

29   Jan de Vries, *Keltische Religion* (Stuttgart, 1961), pp. 50–51; Anne Ross, *Pagan Celtic Britain: Studies in Iconography and Tradition* (London, 1967), pp. 249–50; Helmut Birkhan, *Kelten: Versuch einer Gesamtdarstellung ihrer Kultur* (Vienna, 1997), pp. 722–23.

30   Kuno Meyer (ed.), 'The Colloquy between Fintan and the Hawk of Achill', in O. J. Bergin, R. I. Best, Kuno Meyer, and J. G. O'Keefe (ed.), *Anecdota from Irish Manuscripts* (Halle and Dublin, 1907-13), i, p. 31; Ross, *Pagan Celtic Britain*, p. 252.

31   Nora K. Chadwick, 'Pictish and Celtic Marriage in Early Literary Tradition', *Scottish Gaelic Studies* (Oxford, 1955), viii, pp. 87–89.

32   Filippo Càssola (ed.), *Inni Omerici* (Milan, 1975), p. 116; Hughes (ed.), *Math Uab Mathonwy*, pp. 8, 10. The parallel appears to have been first remarked by Rhys, *Lectures on the Origin and Growth of Religion as Illustrated by Celtic Heathendom*, pp. 383–84.

33   Càssola (ed.), *Inni Omerici*, pp. 180–218; Williams (ed.), *Callimachus: Hymn to Apollo*, p. 11; Frazer (ed.), *Apollodorus: The Library*, i, p. 90; ii, pp. 18–20.

another legend, Lug creates magical kine by means of druidry (*do druidhecht Loga Lāmfota*), whose milk made from transmuted bog water kills the tyrant Bres.[34]

Both Apollo and Lug were pastoral deities, bringing fecundity to cattle. The Lesbian poet Alcaeus, who lived at the turn of the seventh and sixth centuries BC, addressed a hymn to Apollo. In it he described how the god was instructed by Zeus to make his way to Delphi, but instead travelled in a swan-drawn chariot to the land of the Hyperboreans. There he remained for a year, until the dulcet strains of Alcaeus's lyre drew him to the happy Delphians. It was now high summer, and in recognition of the deity's presence the country grew warm and glowing, nightingales sang melodiously, swallows and cicadas chanted, and rushing streams and rivers glinted like silver – all on account of the happy arrival of Apollo. This rôle gained Apollo the title νόμιος, 'the pastoral (god)'.[35]

Among many parallels between Apollo and Lug, the most striking lies in each god's mastery of multifarious arts and skills. Pindar and Callimachus extol Phoebus Apollo as archer and poet, prophet, healer, shepherd, founder of cities, at once eternally young and protector of the young.[36] Similarly, Lug was ascribed the epithet *samildánach*, 'very gifted, skilled, accomplished, having many skills or accomplishments', i.e. 'the god who can do everything', and had cities and forts named after him.[37]

In 'The Battle of Mag Tuired', when Lug makes his first arrival at the court of Núadu at Tara, he is challenged by the royal porter: 'What art do you practice? For no one without an art enters Tara.' To Lug's response that he is a builder, the porter retorts that they already have a builder. As the youthful newcomer proffers further claims to specific skills, to each the porter rejoins that it is already possessed by a specialist at Tara. So the exchanges continue, until Lug resolves the issue by demanding:

Ask the king whether he has one man who possesses all these arts: if he has, I will be unable to enter Tara.[38]

On this being reported to the king, Lug is ordered to be admitted, 'for a man like that has never before come into this fortress'. In this way Lug entered the court, and established himself among the gods of the Túatha Dé Danann.

---

34   Elissa R. Henken, *Traditions of the Welsh Saints* (Cambridge, 1987), pp. 171–72; W. J. Gruffydd, *Math vab Mathonwy: An Inquiry into the Origins and Development of the Fourth Branch of the Mabinogi with the Text and a Translation* (Cardiff, 1928), p. 183; Lilian Duncan, 'Altram Tige Dá Medar', *Ériu: The Journal of the School of Irish Learning* (Dublin, 1932), xi, pp. 194–98; William Larminie, *West Irish Folk-Tales and Romances* (London, 1893), pp. 4–8; Jeremiah Curtin, *Hero-Tales of Ireland* (London, 1894), pp. 283–88, 297–98, 302–4, 305, 308–11; Edward Gwynn (ed.), *The Metrical Dindshenchas* (Dublin, 1903-35), iii, 218–22; R. A. Stewart Macalister (ed.), *Lebor Gabála Érenn: The Book of the Taking of Ireland* (Dublin, 1938–56), iv, pp. 148, 228. Cf. further John Leavitt, 'The Cow of Plenty in Indo-Iranian and Celtic Myth', in Karlene Jones-Bley, Martin E. Huld, and Angela della Volpe (ed.), *Proceedings of the Eleventh Annual UCLA Indo-European Conference: Los Angeles June 4–5, 1999* (Washington, 2000), pp. 209–24.

35   Williams (ed.), *Callimachus: Hymn to Apollo*, p. 11; Denys Page, *Sappho and Alcaeus: An Introduction to the Study of Ancient Lesbian Poetry* (Oxford, 1955), p. 245. 'Alcaeus saw in Apollo not only the lawgiver and the source of divination and poesy, but also the pastoral god, creator of the "Golden Summer", protector of flocks and herds, of trees and flowers and harvests; the god of husbandry' (ibid., p. 248).

36   Snell (ed.), *Pindari Carmina*, i, p. 95; Williams (ed.), *Callimachus: Hymn to Apollo*, p. 10.

37   *Transactions of the Philological Society*, lxviii, p. 247.

38   Elizabeth A. Gray (ed.), *Cath Maige Tuired: The Second Battle of Mag Tuired* (Naas, 1982), pp. 38–40.

Perhaps most significant in the context of Hecataeus's account of the British temple is the fact that in early Welsh tradition it was Lleu (*Lleuelys*) – that is to say, Lug in his Welsh form – who discovered the Omphalos of Britain, while Apollo established its Greek counterpart at Delphi.

Hyperborean Apollo and Celtic Lug

In Greece, according to Hecataeus, the grey barren months of winter are marked by Apollo's absence in the chill North, while his annual reappearance at high summer brings warmth, fertility, and joy to his people.[39] Among the Celts of Western Europe three-day harvest festivals were held at the beginning of August to celebrate the reappearance of the god Lug. In Ireland the festival was Lughnasa, 'the Assembly of Lug'. As the ninth-century Glossary of Cormac explained:

> *Lugnasad*, i.e. the assembly of Lugh son of Ethle, i.e. an assembly held by him at the beginning of harvest each year at the coming of *Lugnasad*.[40]

The assembly brought 'corn and milk in every homestead, peace and fine weather on its account', and peace reigned throughout the land.[41]

Living in a Greek frontier town on the border of Thrace, Hecataeus was well placed to acquire reliable information about Greek and Celtic mythology. Words and names from both languages are found in Thracian. The Thracians possessed their own cult of Apollo, whose epithet κυρμιλῃνός is of Celtic derivation.[42] The first element in the epithet, Proto-Celtic *kormi-, 'beer', recalls the 'red ale' distributed by the Maiden Sovereignty in the presence of Lug to Ireland's destined kings.[43] That a cult of Lug existed among the Thracians is confirmed by the placename Λουκουνάντα, 'Valley of Lugus'. This name possesses its exact counterpart in North Wales, in Nantlle ('Valley of Lleu'), a locality associated with traditions of the Welsh Lugus.[44]

A significant aspect of the respective myths of Apollo and Lug is that each features as a 'visitor'. Emphasis is laid at the outset of the Homeric Hymn to Apollo on the dramatic nature of his arrival in Olympus. The gods tremble and rise from their seats, as he enters and bends his bright bow. His mother Leto takes it, and leads him to a vacant chair (θρόνος), where Zeus welcomes him as his son and presents him with nectar in a golden cup. The King of Gods drinks to his son, being followed by the other gods in their seats.[45]

In *Cath Maige Tuired* the young Lug achieves a similarly dramatic debut. His arrival at the court of Núadu, king of the divine race of the Túatha Dé Danann, is described in glowing terms. Like Apollo,

39 For the legendary associations of Apollo, Delos, and the Hyperboreans, cf. Romm, *The Edges of the Earth in Ancient Thought*, pp. 60–67.

40 Kuno Meyer, 'Sanas Cormaic: An Old-Irish Glossary', in O. J. Bergin, R. I. Best, Kuno Meyer, and J. G. O'Keefe (ed.), *Anecdota from Irish Manuscripts* (Halle and Dublin, 1907–13), iv, pp. 66–67.

41 R. I. Best, Osborn Bergin, M. A. O'Brien, and Anne O'Sullivan (ed.), *The Book of Leinster Formerly Lebar na Núachongbála* (Dublin, 1954–83), p. 949. Cf. Máire MacNeill, *The Festival of Lughnasa: A Study of the Survival of the Celtic Festival of the Beginning of Harvest* (Oxford, 1962).

42 Vladimir E. Orel, 'Thracian and Celtic', *The Bulletin of the Board of Celtic Studies* (Cardiff, 1987), xxxiv, p. 3.

43 Kevin Murray (ed.), *Baile in Scáil: 'The Phantom's Frenzy'* (Dublin, 2004), pp. 34–35.

44 Patrick Sims-Williams, *Ancient Celtic Place-Names in Europe and Asia Minor* (Oxford, 2006), p. 93; *The Bulletin of the Board of Celtic Studies*, xxxiv, p. 5; Ifor Williams (ed.), *Pedeir Keinc y Mabinogi* (Cardiff, 1930), p. 291.

45 Càssola (ed.), *Inni Omerici*, p. 106.

he is 'a handsome, athletic young warrior'. After surmounting a succession of test questions designed to establish his fitness to enter the royal hall, he is admitted and seats himself in 'the seat of the sage' (*suide súad*), 'because he was a sage in every art'. Later, like Apollo, he excels at marksmanship, despatching a slingshot neatly through the eye of the leader of the oppressive Fomoire.[46]

The Seat of the Sage recalls not only the 'throne' which awaits Apollo on Olympus, but also the Siege Perilous at King Arthur's Round Table, which remained vacant until the arrival of the destined Grail knight, the youthful Perceval.[47] The motif may ultimately be of shamanic origin. It has been suggested that the earliest version of the Finnish epic *Kalevala* contained an episode in which the shamanist chieftain Lemminkäinen arrives at remote Päivolä, where he

> demands a seat at the back of the room, a place of honor. In the battle which ensues with the Master of Päivolä, either with weapons or words, Lemminkäinen eventually emerges victorious to sit at the place meant for a sage. At issue here is a chanting competition between shamans.[48]

In his account of the triangular island in the North, Hecataeus explains that the Hyperborean Apollo was honoured there principally in a splendid sacred precinct (*temenos*) and spherical (circular?) temple. It is unclear whether they were distinct shrines, or whether the *temenos* surrounded the round temple. If, as seems probable, it was the latter, the reference could be to the ditch and bank encircling Stonehenge, which demarcated the boundary between sacred centre and surrounding profane space.

Thus, it can be seen that the Apollo of Greek legend corresponds at almost every point to the Celtic deity Lug. Possibly Hecataeus had learned from an account by Pytheas, or amber-merchants plying their trade in northern waters, of cultic beliefs associated with a uniquely splendid circular temple. This was associated with the seasonal appearances of a deity, whose attributes corresponded closely to those of Apollo. The deity was clearly Lugus, whose realm in insular Celtic tradition was believed to inhere within a megalith. This pillar-stone was associated with the legitimation of successive national dynasts, of whom Lugus was regarded as ancestor and protector.

At the time when the principal structures of Stonehenge were being erected in the Late Neolithic and Bronze Ages, Britain is likely to have been inhabited by a pre-Celtic population. How far a cult of Lug at the national *omphalos* represented an intrusive culture, and to what extent it became absorbed into an earlier, comparable mythical paradigm, can only be matter for conjecture. The Gaels of Ireland believed that their ancestors were enabled to occupy the island in return for agreeing to assign it the names of its three indigenous goddesses, Banba, Fótla, and Ériu.[49] When the arrogant Donn declared that they looked only to their own gods and strength, he was sharply informed that neither he nor his descendants could have any share in the island. Although these exchanges are of course legendary, they suggest a paradigmatic expectancy that security may only be gained by formal acknowledgment of earlier native deities. Indeed, the early Irish did not believe that the gods of pre-Goidelic Ireland were destroyed, but held that they remained present beneath the ground, dwelling in elf-mounds under the sway of the marine deity Mannanán mac Lir.[50]

46　Gray (ed.), *Cath Maige Tuired*, pp. 38–40, 60.

47　Sir John Rhŷs, *Studies in the Arthurian Legend* (Oxford, 1891), pp. 26–28.

48　Juha Y. Pentikäinen, *Kalevala Mythology* (Bloomington and Indianapolis, 1989), p. 36.

49　R. I. Best, Osborn Bergin, M. A. O'Brien, and Anne O'Sullivan (ed.), *The Book of Leinster Formerly Lebar na Núachongbála* (Dublin, 1954–83), p. 50.

50　Lilian Duncan, 'Altram Tige Dá Medar', *Ériu: The Journal of the School of Irish Learning* (Dublin, 1932), xi, pp. 187–88.

Recently, John T. Koch has proposed

that Celtic speech had reached Ireland [and Britain] primarily through the agency of the peripatetic professional classes (*aes dáno* 'people of skill', to use the Old Irish term …), rather than a conquering warrior aristocracy. I also suggested that the key chronological horizon had been the Late Bronze Age, or about 1200–600 BC in calendar years … I continue to see the extratribal professional/artisan class(es) as key figures in this process … with the pan-Celtic god, the outsider Lugus … as the divine genius of their class.[51]

Long-term continuity of religious tradition, spanning differing cultures and creeds, is generally more likely than not. For example, the Finnish word *pyhä*, 'sacred', has been shown to ascend to the Bronze Age (*c.* 1000 BC), where it originated as a Germanic loan from the adjective **wiha-*.[52] Another Finnish term *hiisi*, 'sacral place' or 'place of sacrifice', appears equally archaic in its usage as a toponym.[53]

In Britain linguistic evidence indicates that the Pictish language originally conflated a pre-Indo-European stratum with a *p*-Celtic language similar to Cumbric or British.[54] It is consequently likely that there occurred a protracted period in the Scottish Highlands during which Celtic immigrants maintained linguistic contacts with an indigenous Bronze Age population. Linguistic interchange inevitably tends to be accompanied by a degree of mutual absorption of cultural conceptions and traditions. Again, the Pictish dynastic system of matrilineal succession bears every appearance of originating in a pre-Celtic culture. As attested in historical times, it was a system ideally suited to facilitate assimilation at royal and aristocratic social levels between old and new cultures, a period of coexistence very likely subsisting over a period of millennia.

Hecataeus of Abdera and the Northern shrine of Apollo

In his description of the great circular temple on the triangular island off the coast of *Celtica* (Gaul), Hecataeus alludes to its apparent proximity to the moon, and the consequent ability of the inhabitants to distinguish natural features on its surface. Evidently, concern with lunar observation played a significant part in rites associated with the shrine, while evidence for lunar alignments is claimed for

---

51   John T. Koch, 'Paradigm Shift? Interpreting Tartessian as Celtic', in Barry Cunliffe and John T. Koch (ed.), *Celtic from the West: Alternative Perspectives from Archaeology, Genetics, Language and Literature* (Oxford, 2010), p. 209. 'Druidism and the cult of Lugus come to mind as things that might have spread after the [Celtic] languages spread' (Patrick Sims-Williams, 'Celtic Civilization: Continuity or Coincidence?', *Cambrian Medieval Celtic Studies* (Aberystwyth, 2012), lxiv, p. 42).

52   Thomas A. Idinopulos and Edward A. Yonan (ed.), *The Sacred and its Scholars: Comparative Methodologies for the Study of Primary Religious Data* (Leiden, 1996), pp. 44–47.

53   Ibid., pp. 47–52; Mauno Koski, 'A Finnic Holy Word and its Subsequent History', in Tore Ahlbäck (ed.), *Old Norse and Finnish Religions and Cultic Place-Names* (Åbo, 1990), pp. 404–40.

54   K. H. Jackson, 'The Pictish Language', in F. T. Wainwright (ed.), *The Problem of the Picts* (Edinburgh, 1956), pp. 129–66; W. F. H. Nicolaisen, *Scottish Place-Names: Their Study and Significance* (London, 1976), pp. 173–91; idem, 'Celtic and Pre-Celtic Place-Name Elements in Scotland', in Benjamin T. Hudson and Vickie Ziegler (ed.), *Crossed Paths: Methodological Approaches to the Celtic Aspect of the European Middle Ages* (Lanham, Md., and London, 1991), pp. 1–10; Wilhelm F. H. Nicolaisen, 'Something Old, Something New from the Land of Picts', in Michaela Ofitsch and Christian Zinko (ed.), *Studia Onomastica et Indogermanica: Festschrift für Fritz Lochner von Hüttenbach zum 65. Geburtstag* (Graz, 1995), pp. 137–42. This conclusion has of late been disputed by non-linguists, but remains espoused by leading Celtic scholars.

Stonehenge.[55] According to Hecataeus, the Apollonian deity visits the northern island every nineteen years, when the stars return to their previous course – a phenomenon known to the Greeks as 'the year of Meton'.[56] On his appearance the god dances joyfully and plays on the lyre (cithara), from the vernal equinox to the rising of the Pleiades in spring.

As has been seen, the Celtic god approximating to Greek Apollo is Lugus, known in Ireland as *Lug*, and in Wales *Lleu*. The Irish tale 'The Second Battle of Mag Tuired' describes his decisive intervention in a cataclysmic battle between the gods of Ireland (*Túatha Dé Danann*, 'the Tribes of the Goddess Dana') and a sinister race of Otherworld invaders called the *Fomoire*. Scholars are agreed that, although euhemerized into a conflict between rival hosts occurring in an earlier historical era, the story represents an invaluable source for Irish pagan mythology.

The most important rôle in the drama is played by Lug *Samildánach* ('of many skills'), who saves the Túatha Dé Danann from defeat at the hands of their destructive foes. Núadu, king of the Túatha Dé, is holding a great feast at Tara, when the gallant young stranger presents himself at the gate. Protracted interrogation and tests proving his supremacy in all skills culminate with his playing the harp so beautifully that the king and his courtiers are entranced into sleep, weeping, and rejoicing. At Núadu's invitation the stranger takes his throne for thirteen days. After a year's preparation, Lug leads the hosts of Ireland against the Fomoire, who are resoundingly defeated at Mag Tuired on the feast of *Samain* (1 November).[57]

It has been seen that parallels between this account and Hecataeus's description of Apollo's visit to the Hyperborean sanctuary are striking.

1. Lug, master of every art, corresponds in divine attributes to Apollo, who *inter alia* presided over singers and harpers.[58]

2. Núadu's feast at Tara, at which Lug first manifests himself, represents a mythological paradigm of the celebrated Feast of Tara (*feis Temro*). While Irish legendary accounts associate it with the season of *Samain*, Binchy suggested that in reality it is likely to have occurred 'at seed-time', i.e. spring.[59]

---

55 For discussions of the question, cf. John Edwin Wood, *Sun, Moon and Standing Stones* (Oxford, 1978), pp. 100–101; John North, *Stonehenge: Neolithic Man and the Cosmos* (London, 1996), pp. 25, 221–27, 480–89, 544; Mike Parker Pearson, *Stonehenge: Exploring the Greatest Stone Age Mystery* (London, 2012), pp. 44, 45–49. 'There *was* lunar symbolism in Stonehenge 1 and 2, and there are hints that some of it may have carried through to Stonehenge 3', Clive Ruggles, 'Astronomy and Stonehenge', in Barry Cunliffe and Colin Renfrew (ed.), *Science and Stonehenge* (Oxford, 1997), p. 225; cf. pp. 207, 214–20; C. A. Newham, *The Astronomical Significance of Stonehenge* (Leeds, 1972), pp. 12–14.

56 O. Neugebauer, *The Exact Sciences in Antiquity* (Providence, RI, 1957), p. 8; Alan E. Samuel, *Greek and Roman Chronology: Calendars and Years in Classical Antiquity* (Munich, 1972), pp. 44–49; Wood, *Sun, Moon and Standing Stones*, pp. 70–76.

57 Gray (ed.), *Cath Maige Tuired*, pp. 38–42.

58 M. L. West (ed.), *Hesiod: Theogony* (Oxford, 1966), p. 115; Gray (ed.), *Cath Maige Tuired*, p. 94. Apollo in Romano-British inscriptions is equated with the Celtic deity Maponos, 'the Divine Son'. Dedications invoking *APOLLO MAPONUS* have been found at Ribchester and Corbridge (R. G. Collingwood and R. P. Wright (ed.), *The Roman Inscriptions of Britain: I Inscriptions on Stone* (Oxford, 1965), pp. 194–95, 368), while *MAPONUS APOLLO* features also at Corbridge (p. 369). For a distribution map of dedications to the Celtic Apollo in Britain, cf. Barri Jones and David Mattingly, *An Atlas of Roman Britain* (Oxford, 1990), p. 278. The legends of Mabon and Lleu (the Welsh Lug) are correspondingly 'related stories, handed down to us in a fragmentary form which leaves it impossible to ascertain in what way they were related to one another' (Rhys, *Lectures on the Origin and Growth of Religion as Illustrated by Celtic Heathendom*, p. 404).

59 D. A. Binchy, 'The Fair of Tailtiu and the Feast of Tara', *Ériu* (1958), xviii, pp. 134–35.

Hecataeus declares that Apollo appeared among the Hyperboreans at the time of the vernal equinox.

3. On being permitted to enter Tara, Lug's supremacy in all arts and skills so impressed the company of the gods as to entitle him to occupy 'the seat of the sage' (*suide súad*). (In a comparable episode of the archaic Irish druidic dialogue 'The Conversation of the Two Sages' (*Immacallam in dá Thuarad*), the neophyte Néde deceitfully gains the place of chief *ollamh* of Ireland,[60] seating himself on the *ollamh's* throne (*cathair ollaman*), where he dons a robe of office ornamented with a covering of birds' feathers. A cloak of birds' plumage was a favoured ritual garb of the Siberian shaman).[61]

According to the Homeric Hymn to Apollo, the gods on Olympus trembled at the young god's first entry among them, whereupon he was led to a vacant seat where Zeus welcomed him as his son.[62]

4. Lug gains acceptance among the gods of Ireland with a virtuoso performance on the harp.

Apollo celebrates his stay among the Hyperboreans by playing continuously on the lyre, and 'expressing his delight in his exploits'. This recalls the bards of Gaul, whom the Roman historian Ammianus Marcellinus described in the fourth century AD as 'singing to the accompaniment of the lyre heroic verses commemorating distinguished men'.[63]

5. Lug occupies Núadu's throne for thirteen days. While the number may reflect an intercalary period of twelve days (= thirteen nights) inserted in the Celtic calendar to reconcile lunar and solar years,[64] in the context of the story it is clear that Lug acted as substitute king throughout the summer.

Apollo's visit to the Hyperboreans takes place in accordance with a nineteen-year cycle designed to rectify the disparity between lunar and solar years.

6. The calendar of the druids was based on lunar reckoning.[65]

Hecataeus prefaces his account of the calendrical significance of Apollo's visit with a reference to the Hyperboreans' attentive observation of the moon.

60 'An ollav is many things to a king or prince, but I would say that he is most significantly the shadow of a high-ranking pagan priest or druid' (James Carney, *The Irish Bardic Poet: A study in the relationship of Poet and Patron as exemplified in the persons of the poet, Eochaidh Ó hEoghusa (O'Hussey) and his various patrons, mainly members of the Maguire family of Fermanagh* (Dublin, 1967), pp. 7–8).

61 Best, Bergin, O'Brien, and O'Sullivan (ed.), *The Book of Leinster*, pp. 815–16; Åke Hultkrantz, 'Ecological and Phenomenonological Aspects of Shamanism', in V. Diószegi and M. Hoppál (ed.), *Shamanism in Siberia* (Budapest, 1978), pp. 33, 36; E. A. Alekseenko, 'Categories of the Ket Shamans', ibid., p. 256; G. N. Gračeva, 'A Ngasan Shaman Costume', ibid., p. 317. Cf. N. Kershaw Chadwick, *Poetry & Prophecy* (Cambridge, 1942), plate 2.

62 Càssola (ed.), *Inni Omerici*, p. 106. The chair (θρόνος) on which Apollo takes his seat is distinguished by its being vacant, and it appears that ἑδράων is used for those occupied by the other gods.

63 Édouard Galletier, Jacques Fontaine, Guy Sabbah, Marie-Anne Marié, and Laurent Angliviel de la Beaumelle (ed.), *Ammien Marcellin: Histoire* (Paris, 1978-99), i, p. 136.

64 T. Gwynn Jones, *Welsh Folklore and Folk-Custom* (London, 1930), pp. 145–46, 166, 238; Alwyn Rees and Brinley Rees, *Celtic Heritage: Ancient Tradition in Ireland and Wales* (London, 1961), p. 93; Claude Gaignebet and Jean-Dominique Lajoux, *Art profane et religion populaire au Moyen Age* (Paris, 1985), p. 64; Jean-Michel Le Contel and Paul Verdier, *Un calendrier celtique: Le calendrier gaulois de Coligny* (Paris, 1997), p. 17.

65 Rackham, Jones, and Eichholz (ed.), *Pliny: Natural History*, iv, p. 548.

All this suggests that Hecataeus's description of the apotheosis of Apollo in the Hyperborean island was based on accounts of the god Lug, brought from Britain to Greece, either by travellers (such as merchants), or pilgrims to the Northern holy site. In the Welsh tale *Math uab Mathonwy*, Lleu (who corresponds to Irish Lug) dies in the autumn[66] and is implicitly resurrected in the spring, suggesting a deity credited with cyclical summer appearances.

Apollo's dancing while playing the lyre, and Lug's proficiency with the harp, may again reflect shamanistic ritual.

> In Finno-Ugric popular literature we find the echo of journeys by mediums accomplished by the hero-shaman or by his assistant spirits in animal form along a river in search of a medicine to restore life. In the Udmurt area the shaman candidate, under the guidance of the God of the Sky, Inmar, during his own initiation had to go to the bank of a very large river and dance or leap on [to?] the strings of a lyre.[67]

The Greek poet Alcaeus, writing about the turn of the seventh and sixth centuries BC, composed a Hymn to Apollo which supplies further details of the god's relations with the Hyperboreans. Zeus equipped the newborn Apollo with a golden lyre and despatched him to Delphi in a chariot drawn by swans. Instead, he flew to the land of the Hyperboreans. Distraught by his absence, the Delphians composed songs and performed rites imploring him to join them. After a year Apollo responded and arrived in his swan-drawn chariot to general jubilation at Delphi. The pæan of Alcaeus was designed to induce the divinity to bestow his beneficent presence on Delphi and exalt his subsequent arrival. With his return glorious summer bathed the whole land in sunshine.[68]

A clay model found at Dupljaja in Serbia represents a divinity borne in a three-wheeled chariot, with a bird perched on its front, drawn by two larger birds whose bodies merge back into it. The floor of the chariot is marked with a sun symbol, on top of which stands a a male figure in a long robe who must be regarded as an anthropomorphic representation of the sun. As Peter Gelling and Hilda Ellis Davidson pointed out, these details reflect descriptions of the Northern Apollo: 'The phrase [of Alcaeus] "swans were the chariot" describes most admirably the Dupljaja model: they did not simply draw the chariot – they constituted it.'[69]

The legend of a Northern Apollo could have arisen from long-term contacts established from the Bronze Age onwards along trade routes between Northern Europe and Greece, which made the Greeks aware of a British deity whose attributes corresponded so closely to those of their own Apollo as to suggest identity.[70] As a solar divinity Apollo was understood to absent himself

---

66   The season of Lleu's death is indicated by its occurrence at a time when swine were turned out into the forest to eat acorns, i.e. the late autumnal pannage (Ian Hughes (ed.), *Math Uab Mathonwy: Pedwaredd Gainc y Mabinogi* (Aberystwyth, 2000), pp. 14–15).

67   Carla Corradi Musi, *Shamanism from East to West* (Budapest, 1997), p. 7.

68   Although the poem itself has not survived, it was paraphrased in prose by the sophist Himerius (Page, *Sappho and Alcaeus*, pp. 244–52).

69   Gelling and Davidson, *The Chariot of the Sun*, pp. 119–20.

70   This explanation appears more likely than that the cult of Apollo originated in Northern Europe, as suggested by Rendel Harris in *The Ascent of Olympus* (Manchester, 1917), pp. 48–53, and Alexander Haggerty Krappe (*The Science of Folk-Lore* (London, 1930), p. 326). However, shamanistic attributes of the Northern god could have influenced the Greek conception of Apollo: 'the origins of this god are to be looked for in northern Europe: he is associated with a northern product, amber, and with a northern

each winter, and accounts of the cult of a Hyperborean counterpart at a magnificent shrine in Britain could have accounted for these seasonal disappearances.

The primary attribute of Delphi was that of *omphalos*, or Navel of the world. The site was held to have been determined by the flight of eagles or swans from opposite ends of the earth, whose point of convergence established the spot where the shrine of Apollo came to be built at Delphi.[71] Accordingly, it is not unlikely that the great circular temple, at which was celebrated the parallel cult of the divinity dwelling in the triangular Hyperborean island (Britain), correspondingly enclosed the insular Navel.

Evidence unearthed in recent years by archæologists substantiates the intrinsic likelihood that Stonehenge excited awe across much of Europe from a very early period. At Boscombe Down, two and a half miles south-east of Stonehenge, the skeleton of a man aged between thirty-five and forty-five was discovered in 2002. His burial is dated to *c*. 2480–2340 BC. Wrist guards found among his possessions have led to his being nicknamed the 'Amesbury Archer', and artefacts deposited with the body indicate that he was a man of some wealth. Chemical analysis of tooth enamel shows that he probably came from the western Alps, making his way to Britain either down the Rhine, or overland across Gaul.[72] Other burials in the same area attest to the fact that people travelled great distances across Europe to visit Stonehenge in the third millennium BC.[73]

A further startling discovery was made at Boscombe Down, where the grave of a boy aged about fourteen or fifteen was uncovered. A valuable amber necklace was interred with him, the burial being dated to about 1550 BC. Analysis of a sliver of one of his teeth proves that he originated from a region yet more distant than that which saw the birth of the 'Amesbury Archer'. His native home lay somewhere in the vicinity of the Mediterranean, possibly Iberia (Spain).

Given his age, it is likely that this youth came to Britain as member of a family group. Of the proximity of these graves to Stonehenge, Andrew Fitzpatrick of Wessex Archaeology observes:

> Stonehenge would have been well known across Europe ... They [the group including the boy] may have come to trade but visited Stonehenge along the way. It would have been an awesome sight. It would have been one of the greatest temples of its time.[74]

bird, the whooper swan; and his "ancient garden" lies at the back of the north wind ... It would seem that the Greeks, hearing of him from missionaries like Abaris, identified him with their own Apollo' (E. R. Dodds, *The Greeks and the Irrational* (Berkeley, 1951), pp. 161–62; cf. pp. 141, 144; Mircea Eliade, *Le chamanisme et les techniques archaïques de l'extase* (Paris, 1951), pp. 349–50).

71   Francesco Sbordone (ed.), *Strabonis Geographica* (Rome, 1963–2000), iii, p. 366; W. Sieveking and Hans Gärtner (ed.), *Plvtarchvs Pythici Dialogi* (Stuttgart and Leipzig, 1997), p. 59. Cf. Jane Ellen Harrison, *Themis: A Study of the Social Origins of Greek Religion* (Cambridge, 1912), pp. 396–98, 404–406; Cook, *Zeus*, ii, pp. 168–93.

72   A. P. Fitzpatrick, *The Amesbury Archer and the Boscombe Bowmen* (Salisbury, 2011), pp. 230–34; idem, ''The Arrival of the Bell Beaker Set in Britain and Ireland', in John T. Koch and Barry Cunliffe (ed.), *Celtic from the West 2: Rethinking the Bronze Age and the Arrival of Indo-European in Atlantic Europe* (Oxford, 2013), pp. 47–55.

73   Barry Cunliffe, 'Celticization from the West: The Contribution of Archaeology', in Cunliffe and Koch (ed.), *Celtic from the West*, pp. 29–31.

74   Richard Alleyne, 'Buried at Stonehenge: boy with the amber necklace', *The Daily Telegraph*, 29 September 2010. Cf. Fitzpatrick, *The Amesbury Archer and the Boscombe Bowmen*, pp. 191–94, 203–7.

This dramatic new evidence substantiates the intrinsic likelihood that Stonehenge was famed throughout Europe over a period of millennia. When Celtic peoples arrived in Britain they are consequently unlikely to have stumbled unadvised upon the temple. They must have been long aware of the great shrine by repute: indeed, many had repaired to it on pilgrimage long before any substantial Celtic settlement took place.[75] The prime motive for visiting the sanctuary will have been primarily religious – although it could be that travellers were also drawn by a great fair associated with religious rituals conducted at the site, such as occurred at similar festivals in Ireland.

Of all people likely to visit the monument in order to gain understanding of its numinous functions, who more so than the wisest men of Gaul, those whose prime concern was acquisition of cosmic lore? Here, inexorably, we return to the druids. As Caesar learned from them,

> It is understood that this branch of study [*disciplina*, the learning of the druids] originated in Britain, and was transferred from there to Gaul, and at the present time diligent students of the matter for the most part travel there to study it.[76]

Here we have reliable record of the respect which the druids accorded the indigenous cosmology of Britain. It would be extraordinary had well-informed people in Gaul *not* been aware of Stonehenge, during an era of Continent-wide trade and travel. Of these, the learned geographer and historian Hecataeus of Abdera, living on the edge of the Celtic world, was as likely as any to have acquired such knowledge.

---

75   Paul-Marie Duval comments on the account by Hecataeus that 'ce culte, de nature solaire, est sans doute antérieur aux Celtes' (*Les dieux de la Gaule* (Paris, 1957), p. 11).

76   *Disciplina in Britannia reperta atque inde in Galliam translata existimatur, et nunc qui diligentius eam rem cognoscere volunt, plerumque illo discendi causa proficiscuntur* (Seel (ed.), C. Ivlii Caesaris Commentarii Rervm Gestarvm: Bellvm Gallicvm, p. 185).

12

The Conversation of Lludd and Lleuelys

Cyfranc Lludd a Lleuelys

Among mediæval Welsh prose tales, 'The Encounter of Lludd and Lleuelys' (*Cyfranc Lludd a Lleuelys*) is of especial interest in studies of British pagan mythology. Closely related versions of the text are preserved in the two great mediæval Welsh manuscript compendia, the White Book of Rhydderch and the Red Book of Hergest.[1] Although the story is short and readily summarised, it repays detailed examination in view of its unique account of the mythical origins of the British *omphalos*. Indeed, as the sole early source to make explicit allusion to the national Centre, as well as providing a tantalizing account of its significance, it is arguably pre-eminent among texts relevant to the present study.

Beli the Great, King of Britain, had three sons: Lludd, Caswallawn, and Nynniaw. In an evident attempt to reconcile variant traditions, the writer promptly adds: 'And according to the story (*A herwyd y kyuarwydyt*), his fourth son was Lleuelys.' After Beli's death his eldest son Lludd succeeded him as king, who rebuilt the city of London in splendid fashion and proved a paragon of heroic valour and courtly generosity[2] – qualities most likely deriving from native Welsh traditions of Lludd as the archetypal divine ruler. Lleuelys being his favourite brother, Lludd arranged for him to be married to the heiress of the king of France, whose realm he in due course inherited and ruled well and wisely.

However, after a time three dreadful Oppressions (*gormesoedd*) assailed the island of Britain. The First was the invasion of a people called Coraniaid,[3] whose knowledge (*gwybot*) was so great that any word spoken throughout the land, however quiet, was borne to them upon the wind. Thus, they remained inviolate from harm. The Second was decidedly more menacing. Every May-day Eve (*nos Kalan Mei*) a ghastly shriek was heard throughout the land, which so pierced the hearts of men and terrified them that they lost their complexion and their strength, women miscarried, sons and daughters lost their senses, and all beasts, forests, land, and waters became

---

1   The White Book version is incomplete, and the only mediaeval text which preserves the tale in its entirety is the Red Book of Hergest (J. Gwenogvryn Evans (ed.), *The White Book Mabinogion: Welsh Tales & Romances Reproduced from the Peniarth Manuscripts* (Pwllheli, 1907), p. 96; John Rhŷs and J. Gwenogvryn Evans (ed.), *The Text of the Mabinogion and other Welsh Tales from the Red Book of Hergest* (Oxford, 1887), pp. 93-99). Professor Roberts reproduces a version by the sixteenth-century Welsh antiquary Ellis Gruffydd, who most likely drew upon North Welsh oral tradition (Brynley F. Roberts (ed.), *Cyfranc Lludd a Llefelys* (Dublin, 1975), pp. 17–22).

2   Like the rest of the opening section, the reference originates with Geoffrey of Monmouth, who speculatively derived *London* from *Lud*: *Vnde nominata fuit postmodum Kaerlud et deinde per commutationem nominis Kaerlundein* (Michael D. Reeve and Neil Wright (ed.), *Geoffrey of Monmouth: The History of the Kings of Britain* (Woodbridge, 2007), p. 67).

3   The form *Coraniaid* represents a late development (Ifor Williams (ed.), *Cyfranc Lludd a Llevelys* (Bangor, 1910), p. xii).

barren. The Third Oppression was as sinister as it was mysterious. Some unknown power succeeded in abstracting undetected all stores of food and drink from the royal courts (*yn llyssoed y brenhin*), so that there was nothing left to consume beyond what could be devoured on the first night.

As the storyteller observes, the fact that the nature of the second and third Oppressions remained obscure made them seemingly impossible to avert. Unable to obtain relief from the devastation which these arcane scourges inflicted upon the land, Lludd convened his nobles and requested their advice. Their counsel was unanimous: Lludd should consult with his brother Lleuelys, king of France, who was reputed the wisest of men.[4]

They accordingly prepared a fleet 'in secrecy and silence' (*yn dirgel ac yn distaw*), and sailed towards France. Meanwhile Lleuelys, learning of his brother's approach, advanced with a fleet of his own, so that they met in the midst of the sea. There the brothers embraced and conferred. Lleuelys had already divined the purpose of his brother's mission. On being informed of the eavesdropping by the ubiquitous Coraniaid, he arranged the construction of a long bronze horn through which he and his brother might commune in secret. But when one spoke, only disjointed, unintelligible speech was heard by the other. Lleuelys perceived the source of the mischief to be a devil (*kythreul*) concealed in the horn, whom he expelled by means of wine.

This enabled Lleuelys to advise his brother in secrecy how to rid himself of the Three Oppressions. He explained to Lludd that he would present him with 'creatures' (*pryuet*, modern Welsh *pryfed*), some of which he should crush and dissolve in water, while preserving the remainder for future contingencies. The nature of these *pryfed* remains unexplained in the tale. After performing this distillation, the king must summon both his people and the Coraniaid to a meeting, on the pretext of making peace between them. Once assembled, he should sprinkle them with the solution. The liquid possessed a property enabling it to distinguish between native Britons and alien Coraniaid, leaving the former unharmed while poisoning the latter.

Next, Lleuelys explained how to counter the other two Oppressions. He revealed the second *gormes* to be a native dragon, who was being savagely attacked by a rival of foreign extraction. The scream which caused dire devastation throughout the land emanated from the British dragon. The only means of countering the menace was to measure the island from end to end and side to side. Once the exact centre (*y pwynt perued*) had in this way been established, a hole must be dug on the spot. A vatful of the best mead should be placed within the hole, and covered with a brocaded cloth.

After this Lludd was to lie in wait, when he would witness the two dragons fighting in the form of dreadful animals. After a time their ferocious struggle would ascend to the air above, until they fell back exhausted in the shape of young pigs onto the cloth, so sinking down into the vat (*kerwyn*). Once trapped inside the vessel, they would consume the mead and fall asleep. The moment that occurred, Lludd must wrap them in the cloth mantle, place them within a stone chest, and bury it in the ground 'in the strongest place you can find in your kingdom'. So long as they were preserved at that spot, so long would the alien Oppressions be kept at bay.

All that remained for consideration was the Third Oppression, which caused the disappearance of all comestibles prepared in the king's courts. Lleuelys revealed the author of these depredations to be a powerful wizard (*gwr lleturithawc kadarn*), who employed his enchantments to place the court in thrall to a magical sleep, which enabled him to abduct all royal food, drink, and other

---

4   The Irish Lug, who corresponds to British Lleu, was accounted a redoubtable wizard (Elizabeth A. Gray (ed.), *Cath Maige Tuired: The Second Battle of Mag Tuired* (Naas, 1982), p. 40; R. A. Stewart Macalister (ed.), *Lebor Gabála Érenn: The Book of the Taking of Ireland* (Dublin, 1938–56), iv, p. 148).

The Fighting Dragons at the Centre of Britain.[5]

provisions. In order to frustrate the menace, Lludd must stand guard over his banquets and feasts, preventing himself from succumbing to the sorcerer's spells by stationing himself beside a vat of cold water, within which he should immerse himself whenever he sensed drowsiness coming near to overcoming him.

Lludd returned home to Britain, in order to put his brother's instructions into effect. First, he summoned all his subjects, together with their foes, to an assembly. There he sprinkled over them the distillation compounded from the *pryfed*, as prescribed by Lleuelys. As his brother had foretold, the Coraniaid were immediately destroyed, leaving the unscathed Britons henceforth immune from their Oppression.

Next, in accordance with his brother's further instruction, Lludd measured Britain by its length and breadth, which determined its centre to lie at Oxford (*Rytychen*). There he effected the stipulated preparations, maintaining vigil all night. In the still hours the fighting dragons made their appearance, precisely as his brother had said they would. Battling furiously, their struggle raged as they ascended into the upper air. Eventually wearied of their strife, they collapsed onto the sheet, dragging it with them to the bottom of the vat. There they guzzled the

5   Lady Charlotte Guest (tr.), *The Mabinogion from the Welsh of the Llyfr Coch o Hergest (the Red Book of Hergest) in the Library of Jesus College, Oxford* (London, 1877), p. 466.

mead and succumbed to sleep.[6] Swiftly wrapping them in the cloth, Lludd bore them off to the safest place he could find. This lay in the remote fastness of mountainous Snowdonia (*Eryri*), where he deposited the vat and its dangerous contents within a stone chest. The site, formerly known as *Dinas Ffaraon Dandde* ('The Fortress of Fiery Pharaoh'), was thenceforth called *Dinas Emrys*. In this way, the scream which had spread terror and disaster throughout Lludd's kingdom ceased.

Finally Lludd prepared a great feast. When it was ready, he stood guard with the vat of cold water beside him, just as his brother had prescribed. About the third watch of the night, the air was filled with entrancing sleep-inducing music, whose magical harmony all but overpowered him. But the moment he felt himself being overcome by drowsiness, Lludd sprang into the water to revive himself, just as his brother had instructed. Before long a heavily armed giant appeared, bearing a basket. To the astonishment of Lludd, the grim enchanter thrust all the food and drink prepared for the banquet into his basket and turned to depart with the plunder. The king at once sprang forward, shouting 'Stop! Stop!' (*Arho! Arho!*), challenging the stranger to turn and fight. A mortal combat ensued, so fiercely contested that sparks flew from their clashing blades. After a desperate conflict, Lludd succeeded in overcoming the intruder, forcing him to the ground. The giant sorcerer begged for mercy, which Lludd granted him only after he had sworn to restore all he had stolen, and undertook never again to harass his kingdom.

It was in this way that Lludd preserved Britain from the Three Oppressions which had assailed its land and people, and ruled over the island in prosperity until the end of his days.

Brynley F. Roberts, the most recent editor of *Cyfranc Lludd a Lleuelys*, explains its origins as follows. A prophetic poem contained in the Book of Taliesin, whose language and orthography indicate a date of composition prior to the close of the eleventh century, associates Lludd and Lleuelys with an invasion of Britain by a mysterious race from across the sea. This and other more oblique references suggest that the extant story represents a popular reworking of material which was originally part of the early Welsh pseudo-historical tradition and may have been known in an oral form in the late eleventh century.[7]

Many of the Welsh translations of Geoffrey of Monmouth's *History of the Kings of Britain*, known as *Brutiau*, include a more compact version of the adventure of Lludd and Lleuelys, inserted at what was considered to be the appropriate juncture of King Lud's renaming of London as *Kaer Lud*. Evidently, the originator of the interpolation assumed that Geoffrey had overlooked an important piece of Welsh 'history', too celebrated to ignore, and took it upon himself to rectify the omission.[8]

'At some stage', concludes Professor Roberts, 'this version of the tale, together with its setting ... is abstracted and becomes the literary version of the story of Lludd and Llefelys',

---

6   There is a discrepancy here, suggesting that the storyteller was perplexed by the account of the 'dragons'. In his advice to Lludd, Lleuelys described how they would turn into piglets at their descent. However, in the event this detail is omitted.

7   Roberts (ed.), *Cyfranc Lludd a Llefelys*, pp. xvii–xviii, xxviii–xxix.

8   J. J. Parry, 'The Welsh Texts of Geoffrey of Monmouth's *Historia*', *Speculum: A Journal of Mediaeval Studies* (Cambridge, Mass., 1930), v, p. 430; Brynley F. Roberts, 'Geoffrey of Monmouth, *Historia Regum Britanniae* and *Brut y Brenhinedd*', in Rachel Bromwich, A. O. H. Jarman, and Brynley F. Roberts (ed.), *The Arthur of the Welsh: The Arthurian Legend in Medieval Welsh Literature* (Cardiff, 1991), p. 112. A text of the *Brut* version is contained in John Jay Parry (ed.), *Brut y Brenhinedd: Cotton Cleopatra Version* (Cambridge, Mass., 1937), pp. 64–70, and a translation of another in Acton Griscom (ed.), *The Historia Regum Britanniæ of Geoffrey of Monmouth with Contributions to the Study of its Place in Early British History* (London, 1929), pp. 301–5.

i.e. that summarized above from the text in the Red Book of Hergest. While Roberts accepts that the original oral version most likely continued in circulation after the appearance of the *Brut* version, he concludes that

> a hypothetical oral *Cyfranc Lludd a Llefelys* does not seem to have directly influenced the 'literary' tale. In its new guise, the tale is expanded, not so much by the addition of new material, but by elaborating statements made in the Brut version.[9]

Roberts's explanation for the tale's original introduction into the *Brut* is convincing. However, although it is clear that he was right in asserting that the *Brut* version provided the basis of *Cyfranc Lludd a Llefelys*,[10] it appears that the author of the latter was familiar with another version. At the outset, he explains that Beli the Great had three sons, Lludd, Caswallawn, and Nyniaw, adding that 'according to the story, Lleuelys was a fourth son' (*A herwyd y kyuarwydyt, petweryd mab idaw uu Lleuelis*). Reference to 'the story' (*y cyfarwyddyd*) has been taken for an allusion to an independent Welsh version.[11] In fact, it is the *Brutiau* that include Lleuelys among the sons of Beli, indicating that the cited 'story' was that found in the *Brut* version. Nevertheless, the parenthesis suggests that the author was familiar with another version in which Lleuelys was *not* accounted a son of Beli. Another manuscript of the *Brut* goes out of its way to explain that, while Beli's first three sons were children by his wedded wife, Lleuelys was born to a mistress (*a llevelys oi gariadwraic i kowsai*). This suggests that this author too was concerned to reconcile divergent traditions of Lleuelys's paternity. Similarly, Ellis Gruffydd, an early sixteenth-century Welsh chronicler, who possessed access to much traditional lore now lost, describes Lleuelys (*Lywelus*) as a fellow monarch to Lludd, without any suggestion of blood relationship.[12]

Some of minor variations between the versions could reflect the influence of a version other than the *Brut*, while a glossed passage concerning the alternative name of Dinas Emrys must reflect either that or another native source.

The fourteenth-century Book of Taliesin contains two obscurely worded prophetic poems, entitled respectively 'The Great Praise of Lludd' and 'The Great Discussion of Lludd'. The latter contains a reference to *ymarwar llud a llefelis*, 'the discussion of Lludd and Llefelys', a title synonymous with that of *Cyfranc Lludd a Lleuelys*.[13] As Brynley Roberts noted, 'it is possible that the *Cyfranc*, under the name *Ymarwar Lludd a Llefelys* and presumably in an oral form, was known late in the eleventh century.'[14] Again, allusion in the Welsh Triads to 'the Dragons which

---

9　Roberts (ed.), *Cyfranc Lludd a Llefelys*, p. xxx.

10　It is clear on linguistic grounds that the 'mabinogion' and *Brut* versions derive from the same archetype, (ibid., pp. xxiii–xxiv, xxxi.)

11　'This introductory phrase – 'and according to the storytellers', in the Welsh translation of the *History* – refers to the fact that the author is taking the tale from native Welsh tradition and is supplementing Geoffrey's account' (Sioned Davies (tr.), *The Mabinogion* (Oxford, 2007), p. 252).

12　Parry (ed.), *Brut y Brenhinedd: Cotton Cleopatra Version*, p. 64; Roberts (ed.), *Cyfranc Lludd a Llefelys*, p. 18.

13　J. Gwenogvryn Evans (ed.), *Facsimile & Text of the Book of Taliesin* (Llanbedrog, 1910), pp. 78–79. Geoffrey of Monmouth alludes to a great quarrel (*maxima contencio*) between Lud and his brother Nennius (Reeve and Wright (ed.), *Geoffrey of Monmouth: The History of the Kings of Britain*, p. 31). *Contencio* could be a translation of *cyfranc*, in which case it may confirm the prior existence of a version of the extant tale – though it is hard to explain the substitution of *Nennius* for *Lud*.

14　Roberts (ed.), *Cyfranc Lludd a Llefelys*, p. xx. Cf. Margred Haycock (ed.), *Prophecies from the Book of Taliesin* (Aberystwyth, 2013), pp. 176–77.

Lludd son of Beli buried in Dinas Emrys in Eryri' indicate that this episode had become part of the traditional repertoire of the bards.[15]

The fact that independent Welsh versions of the story of the Three Scourges were evidently known to the author of *Cyfranc Lludd a Llefelys*, while the variant details in that tale are so minor, suggests that the *Brut* version tallied closely with other traditional accounts of the same legend.

Moving on, it is possible that a clue to the date of composition of *Cyfranc Lludd a Lleuelys* has escaped attention, which if correct confirms that the tale was in existence prior to Geoffrey of Monmouth's work. It is generally accepted that the first element of the name *Lleuelys* derives from the name of the Welsh god Lleu,[16] an account of whose birth, death, and resurrection is recounted in *Math uab Mathonwy*, the last of the Four Branches of the *Mabinogi*. The story is patently that of an euhemerized deity, a function further to be inferred from other references in early Welsh literature, and still more from parallel rôles played by the Irish counterparts of Lludd and Lleuelys, Núadu and Lug, in the story of the Battle of Mag Tuired.[17] The name *Lleu* is cognate both with that of the Gaulish god Lugus, and his Irish counterpart Lug.[18]

Scholars have encountered difficulty in explaining the otherwise unrecorded form *Lleuelys*. Sir John Rhŷs conjectured that the second element represents *esles* or *–eslis*, 'defence, protection', only to abandon the suggestion in favour of the personal name *Elis* used as a compound.[19] However, neither hypothesis has gained any scholarly support, and Brynley Roberts declared in 1975 that 'The name *Llefelys* has not been satisfactorily explained', which is where the problem appears to have been left.[20]

Welsh god and French king

However, commentators overlooked W. J. Gruffydd's earlier conclusion that 'the name *Llevelys* is clearly based on a scribal misreading of *Leueeis*, the Norman-French form of Louis'.[21] The suggestion appears prima facie plausible, and is supported by evidence extending beyond the obvious etymological resemblance. Gruffydd presumably had in mind the fact that Lleuelys is described as king of France, a country whose name had at some stage become substituted for

---

15   *The Bulletin of the Board of Celtic Studies*, xii, p. 14; Rhŷs and Gwenogvryn Evans (ed.), *The Text of the Mabinogion and other Welsh Tales from the Red Book of Hergest*, p. 300. As neither extant version states that it was Lludd who interred the dragons, this may suggest yet another variant of the tradition. Another triad tells how Lludd's son Afarwy treacherously summoned Caesar to Britain (ibid., p. 298), but this story derives from the Bruts (Bromwich (ed.), *Trioedd Ynys Prydein*, pp. 134–35).

16   Georges Dumézil, *Mythe et Épopée* (Paris, 1968–73), i, p. 613; Patrick K. Ford (tr.), *The Mabinogi and other Medieval Welsh Tales* (Berkeley, 1977), p. 112; P. P. Sims-Williams, 'Some Functions of Origin Stories in Early Medieval Wales', in Tore Nyberg, Iørn Piø, Preben Meulengracht Sørensen, and Aage Trommer (ed.), *History and Heroic Tale: A Symposium* (Odense, 1985), p. 125; Jaan Puhvel, *Comparative Mythology* (Baltimore, 1987), p. 179.

17   Cf. Françoise le Roux, 'Le dieu-roi NODONS/NUADA', *Celticvm VI: Actes du Troisième Colloque International d'Études Gauloises, Celtiques et Protoceltiques* (Rennes, 1963), pp. 450–53; Proinsias Mac Cana, *The Mabinogi* (Cardiff, 1992), pp. 77–78.

18   Kenneth Jackson, *Language and History in Early Britain: A Chronological Survey of the Brittonic Languages First to Twelfth Century A.D.* (Edinburgh, 1953), p. 441.

19   Sir John Rhŷs, 'All around the Wrekin', *Y Cymmrodor* (London, 1908), xxi, pp. 54–55; idem, 'Notes on The Coligny Calendar together with an Edition of the Reconstructed Calendar', *The Proceedings of the British Academy* (London, 1910), iv, pp. 252–53.

20   Roberts (ed.), *Cyfranc Lludd a Llefelys*, p. xx. According to Geoffrey of Monmouth the father of Heli (= Beli) was *Cligueillus*, which looks like a phonetic rendering of *Lleuelys* (Reeve and Wright (ed.), *Geoffrey of Monmouth: The History of the Kings of Britain*, p. 67).

21   W. J. Gruffydd, *Folklore and Myth in the Mabinogion* (Cardiff, 1958), p. 20.

that of the transmarine (or subaqueous) Otherworld realm, where Lleu dwelt in the original legend.[22] Similar transformations are regularly encountered in early Irish and Welsh literature, where tales of purely mythical origin have become euhemerized as 'history'. Consequently, adaptation of the Welsh name *Lleu* into a close approximation of French *Louis* would appear a likely enough development, in view of the celebrity of successive Carolingian and Capetian kings bearing that name. The dual modifications of Lleu's kingdom into France, and his name into an otherwise unknown Welsh form markedly similar in pronunciation and orthography to *Louis*, is unlikely to have arisen by chance. A mediæval *cyfarwydd* (storyteller) could readily have taken *Lleu brenhin Ffreinc* for the familiar combination of 'Louis King of France', leading at some point to a trifling spelling 'correction', effected by addition of a suffix approximating to the second syllable of *Louis*.

Louis features in mediæval French sources in variant forms, such as *Loois, Lowis, Liwes, Loëwis,* and *Loeis*.[23] A Welshman in the early mediæval period, taking the native name *Lou* (as *Lleu* was spelt in Old Welsh)[24] for a Cymric version of French *Loeis*, might well have concocted a disyllabic hybrid such as *Leu-wys* or *Leu-ues*.[25] In early Welsh manuscripts the letter *u* stood indifferently for the vowel *u* and spirant *v*,[26] and the awkward juxtaposition of two letters *u* could make *f* (which replaced *v*) a likely preference for a scribe faced with a name otherwise unknown to Welsh nomenclature. Gruffydd's 'scribal misreading' probably occurred at this secondary stage, after *Lleu* had become transformed into a Welsh approximation of *Louis*.[27]

The story of Lleu and Lleuelys, in its extant form, is treated as an episode in early British history (hence its adoption into the *Brutiau*), rather than what it really was: an historicized fragment of pre-Christian mythology. Originally Lleu came from the Otherworld, and once converted into the ruler of an earthly kingdom it was natural to identify it with neighbouring France.[28] In this way, the resemblance of *Lleu* (OW *Lou*) to *Louis*, a name popular with French kings since the early ninth century, would have borne obvious resonance.

---

22 'Llefelys, qui n'est autre que Lleu, l'équivalent du dieu Lugh –, le roi de Gaule – autrement dit d'un «autre monde» outremer' (Claude Sterckx, *Mythologie du monde celte* (Paris, 2009), p. 201).

23 Alexander Bell (ed.), *L'Estoire des Engleis by Geffrei Gaimar* (Oxford, 1960), pp. 105, 106; Jeanne Wathelet-Willem (ed.), *Recherches sur la chanson de Guillaume: Etudes accompagnées d'une édition* (Paris, 1975), ii, p. 1224; W. N. Bolderston (ed.), *La vie de Saint Remi: Poème du XIIIe siècle par Richier* (London, 1912), p. 354. The name had evolved from Frankish *Hloðawig* into Old French *Chloevis*. As the initial aspirate weakened it gradually disappeared, resulting in Old French *Loewis*, etc. (M. K. Pope, *From Latin to Modern French with Especial Consideration of Anglo-Norman: Phonology and Morphology* (Manchester, 1934), p. 227).

24 Egerton Phillimore, 'The *Annales Cambriæ* and Old-Welsh Genealogies from *Harleian MS. 3859*', *Y Cymmrodor* (London, 1888), ix, p. 176.

25 Final *–s* continued to be sounded in Old French (Pope, *From Latin to Modern French*, p. 222).

26 'The Middle Welsh letter form Ⴍ ... can stand for *w, f,* or *u* in the present-day Welsh alphabet' (John T. Koch, *Cunedda, Cynan, Cadwallon, Cynddylan: Four Welsh Poems and Britain 383–655* (Aberystwyth, 2013), p. 19). Cf. John Strachan, *An Introduction to Early Welsh* (Manchester, 1909), p. 3.

27 The intrusive final *-l-* of *Lleuelys* could have been introduced to assist in mastering the proliferation of vowels in *Loeis*, or alternatively have arisen from a misreading of *i* as *l*.

28 The Celtic Otherworld was frequently envisaged as lying beyond or beneath water (Christian-J. Guyonvarc'h and Françoise Le Roux, *Les Druides* (Rennes, 1986), pp. 315–22). In Indo-European cosmology water represented the boundary between the living and the dead (Thomas V. Gamkrelidze and Vjačeslav V. Ivanov, *Indo-European and the Indo-Europeans: A Reconstruction and Historical Analysis of a Proto-Language and a Proto-Culture* (Berlin and New York, 1995), i, p. 724).

The name *Lleuelys* is first attested in a Welsh poem which has been assigned to the eleventh century.[29] The last Louis to have ruled France before then was Louis V (967–87), whose sobriquet *le fainéant* suggests the unmemorable character of his reign. However, his predecessor Louis IV (921–54) made a considerable impact on the history of his time, while a remarkable episode in his early life might readily have led a Welsh bard to identify him with the national hero and former divinity Lleu.

In 923 King Charles the Simple of France was overthrown and imprisoned by his rebellious nobles. However, his son Louis (*Ludouicus*) escaped with his English mother Eadgifu to the court of her brother Æþelstan, king of the English. Louis brought with him a large fleet, which his uncle assisted Æþe to maintain. After thirteen years' hospitable exile in England, Louis recrossed the Channel at the behest of a powerful faction of French magnates, and ascended his father's throne. His long years of exile caused Louis IV (as he now became) to become known as *Louis d'Outremer*, 'Louis from over the Sea'.[30]

In *Cyfranc Lludd a Lleuelys*, Lleuelys King of France (*Leuelis brenhin Freinc*) sails 'with an enormous fleet' (*llynghes gantaw diruawr*) – a factor entirely superfluous to the context of the story (it is absent from the *Brut* version) – from his own country to advise his ally the King of Britain, with which he returns home across the sea. We may well have here the original model for the transformation of the British god *Lleu* into a French king *Louis*, thus further accounting for the otherwise unaccountable hybrid form *Lleuelys*.

Many instances are recorded of the introduction of anachronistic historical figures into the timeless world of early Welsh legend,[31] and it is likely enough that the dramatic career of 'Louis from over the Sea' attracted contemporary public interest in Wales, where parallels between Louis's name and history and those of the Welsh Lleu, who likewise came from 'abroad',[32] might well have invited speculative comparison in the decades that followed.

If so, this provides a *terminus ante quem* of c. 940 for composition of *Cyfranc Lludd a Lleuelys* in its extant form. Although the adventurous career of Louis d'Outremer was momentous in its

---

29 *Ymarwar llud bychan.* This poem contains the sole mediæval instance of the form *Llefelys*: *kyn ymarwar llud a llefelis* (J. Gwenogvryn Evans (ed.), *Facsimile & Text of the Book of Taliesin* (Llanbedrog, 1910), pp. 78–79). However, the intrusive consonant is absent from the twelfth-century poet Llywelyn Fardd's citation of the same poem: *val ymarwar llut a lleuelys* (John Morris-Jones and T. H. Parry-Williams (ed.), *Llawysgrif Hendregadredd* (Cardiff, 1933), p. 208; J. Gwenogvryn Evans (ed.), *Poetry by Medieval Welsh Bards* (Llanbedrog, 1926), p. 329). For the composition of this poem, cf. Margaret Enid Griffiths, *Early Vaticination in Welsh with English Parallels* (Cardiff, 1937), pp. 127–28; Rachel Bromwich (ed.), *Trioedd Ynys Prydein: The Welsh Triads* (Cardiff, 1978), p. 425; Roberts (ed.), *Cyfranc Lludd a Llefelys*, p. xx. 'The metre here is classical Cyhydedd Naw Ban, very much as in [the tenth-century] Armes Prydein, with regular 5+4 patterning and much internal rhyme' (Haycock (ed.), *Prophecies from the Book of Taliesin*, p. 177).

30 Georg Waitz (ed.), *Richeri Historiarum Libri IIII.* (Hanover, 1877), pp. 39–42; Elisabeth M. C. van Houts (ed.), *The Gesta Normannorum Ducum of William of Jumièges, Orderic Vitalis, and Robert of Torigni* (Oxford, 1992–95), i, pp. 72, 74, 80–84.

31 Thus Alan Fyrgan, Duke of Brittany from 1084 to 1119, features in a triad as a confederate of King Arthur at the sixth-century battle of Camlan (Bromwich (ed.), *Trioedd Ynys Prydein*, pp. 270–71), while William the Conqueror participates in Arthur's pursuit of the fabulous boar Twrch Trwyth! (Rachel Bromwich and D. Simon Evans (ed.), *Culhwch and Olwen: An Edition and Study of the Oldest Arthurian Tale* (Cardiff, 1992), pp. 11, 27, 39).

32 In *Math uab Mathonwy*, Lleu's mother Arianrhod dwells in a Castle of Maidens accessible by sea. As St Lleudad, he continued protector in perpetuity of the monastery and 'treasures' (*anlloet*) of the island of Enlli (John Morris-Jones and T. H. Parry-Williams (ed.), *Llawysgrif Hendregadredd* (Cardiff, 1933), pp. 42–48). Lleu's grave was traditionally located beneath the sea (A. O. H. Jarman (ed.), *Llyfr Du Caerfyrddin gyda Rhagymadrodd Nodiadau Testunol a Geirfa* (Cardiff, 1982), p. 40).

day, it was not one to which a later writer in Britain was likely to revert. The English and Welsh annals contain no record of his exile in England, memory of which could have been largely effaced by the devastating effect of Viking invasions which tore the kingdom apart following the death of Louis's protector Æþelstan in 939.

Reasons were earlier given for believing that the other 'historical' Welsh *cyfarwyddyd*, 'The Dream of Maxen Gwledig' (*Breuddwyd Maxen Wledic*), was compiled during the reign of Hywel Dda, king of North and South Wales, following his conquest of Gwynedd in 942–50. In 926 Hywel made formal submission to Æþelstan at Hereford, when he might well have met the exiled Louis d'Outremer in his train.[33]

In fact, the two tales are likely to have been linked in historiographical terms, as the concept was understood in mediæval Wales. While *Cyfranc Lludd a Lleuelys* describes the invasion of Britain in a primal era by the Coraniaid, *Breuddwyd Maxen* makes Maxen's rule in Britain begin with his expulsion of a comparably hostile race into the sea.[34] Thus, the first tale recounted events in Britain under what was believed to have been the unified monarchy of pre-Roman times, and the second the epic career of the most celebrated Roman ruler of Britain.

It is possible that a further trace of this decisive stage in the evolution of *Cyfranc Lludd a Lleuelys* is to be found in the *Historia Regum Britanniæ* of Geoffrey of Monmouth. The generally fictional character of his work is well-known, as also his occasional inclusion of scraps of earlier authentic lore, which he pressed into service of what may be regarded as Britain's first historical novel.[35]

In his Book XI, the Oxford scholar describes an invasion of Britain by *Gormundus*, 'king of the Africans', a people whom the author incongruously locates in Ireland (*Saxones iuerunt propter Gurmundum regem Affricanorum in Hiberniam*). Invited by the perfidious Saxons, the African monarch descends upon Britain with an innumerable host of barbarian followers, who wreak devastation so appalling as to leave her towns unpopulated and fields waste throughout the country from sea to sea (*a mari usque ad mare*). No sooner has Gormundus gained this prize, at what may be presumed to have been considerable cost and effort, than he unaccountably delivers his conquests over to the Saxons and abruptly vanishes from the tale.[36]

The episode is plainly fictitious,[37] but it seems not unlikely that Geoffrey based his imaginative tale on a Welsh account of an Oppression (*gormes*), such as those which feature in *Cyfranc Lludd a Lleuelys*. The lack of any logical explanation for the temporary stay of the Africans in Ireland suggests that Geoffrey's source told of an invasion of Britain by a black (i.e. Otherworld) race from beyond the Irish Sea. Like France, Ireland was traditionally identified by the Welsh with the Otherworld, and the story of *Branwen uerch Llŷr* contains an episode concerning a strange people from Ireland, whose progeny migrate to Britain and spread secretly throughout the land,

33   R. A. B. Mynors, R. M. Thomson, and M. Winterbottom (ed.), *William of Malmesbury, Gesta Regvm Anglorvm; The History of the English Kings: Volume I* (Oxford, 1998), i, pp. 214–16.

34   The term 'sons (*meibion*) of Beli' probably denotes a tribe or people. The *filii Liethan* described in the *Historia Brittonum* as settling in Britain correspond to the Irish tribal grouping Uí Liatháin.

35   'A writer of fiction up to a point, a hoaxer perhaps, he was also a very learned man, and this was the age of monastic forgeries' (M. Dominica Legge, 'Master Geoffrey Arthur', in Kenneth Varty (ed.), *An Arthurian Tapestry: essays in memory of Lewis Thorpe* (Cambridge, 1983), p. 26).

36   Reeve and Wright (ed.), *Geoffrey of Monmouth: The History of the Kings of Britain*, pp. 257–59.

37   For a wholly unconvincing argument that Geoffrey based the invasion of Gormund on historical events, cf. E. Williams B. Nicolson, 'The Vandals in Wessex and the Battle of Deorham', *Y Cymmrodor* (London, 1906), xix, pp. 5–17. It is however possible that Geoffrey confused the dark invaders with the Danish settlers in Ireland, who were known as *dubgenti*, 'black gentiles' (Henry Lewis (ed.), *Brut Dingestow* (Cardiff, 1942), p. 277).

arming themselves with exceptional (i.e. magical) weapons, for the evident purpose of seizing control of the kingdom. Bran's account of this sinister immigration indicates awareness that the horde was conspiring to supplant his rule over Britain, and narrative logic identifies the infiltrators with the sinister Caswallawn and his followers, who are found at the close of the tale to have overrun the kingdom.[38] A triad states that it was in the time of Caswallawn that the *gormes* of the Coraniaid originated in Arabia, land of legendary 'black' men.[39]

Again, the wholesale devastation wrought by Gormund's hordes throughout Britain makes little sense as it stands, since he arrives at the invitation of the Saxons for the purpose of assisting them to acquire the very wealth he is represented as wantonly destroying. Nor does it appear reasonable that so brutal a conqueror would meekly have abandoned his hard-won conquests for no consideration to the Saxons, who at the time occupied an obscure corner of the kingdom, having played a subordinate part in his strenuous campaigning. Finally, Geoffrey might surely have explained whether – let alone whither – Gormund and his colossal host of Africans departed the country, once their barbaric ravages were completed.

It is evident that Geoffrey arbitrarily introduced at this juncture a story he had heard of an oppression (*gormes*), manifesting itself in the guise of a swart race sweeping out of the Western Ocean to ravage Britain, following which it vanished as mysteriously as it had appeared. Possibly, too, his (presumably Welsh) source connected this black enchantment with the underhand conquests of the English, an association found also in the triad cited above.

This interlude in turn includes a further apparently irrelevant detail. In the midst of his campaigning, we are told that Gormund was visited by Isembard, nephew of King Louis of France (*Isembardus, nepos Lodouici regis Francorum*), who begged the invader's assistance in reclaiming his lawful inheritance, which Louis had allegedly usurped. Nothing more is related of this visit, whose outcome remains unresolved. The allusion derives from a French *chanson de geste* entitled *Gormond et Isembard*, none of whose romantic plot however bears any relevance to the events described in Geoffrey's *Historia*.[40] This bald and arbitrary interruption, which is all it amounts to, must nevertheless have been introduced for a reason.

It is possible that the apparently pointless 'Gormund' section derived from a garbled version of the story of Lludd and Lleuelys, which in turn throws further light on the evolution of the name *Lleuelys*. Geoffrey of Monmouth's account of Gormund's invasion describes an Oppression of Britain by an alien race, whose 'African' origin is reminiscent of the Arabian provenance ascribed the Coraniaid in the triad. In the midst of this devastation, Britain is visited by a young prince, nephew to King Louis of France. It would be entirely in keeping with Geoffrey's approach to his sources were he to have conflated a Welsh tale of a *gormes*, centring upon a visit to Britain by a 'Louis' from France, with the well-known romance of *Gormond et Isembard*,[41] in which a French King Louis also plays a significant role. If so, Geoffrey's story provides corroborative evidence for the identification of *Lleu(elys)* in *Cyfranc Lludd a Lleuelys* with a *Louis* of France.

---

38   Cf. Nikolai Tolstoy, *The Oldest British Prose Literature: The Compilation of the Four Branches of the Mabinogi* (Lampeter, 2009), pp. 333–51.

39   Rachel Bromwich, 'The Historical Triads: With Special Reference to Peniarth MS. 16', *The Bulletin of the Board of Celtic Studies* (Cardiff, 1946), xii, p. 14.

40   Edmond Faral, *La Légende Arthurienne - Études et Documents* (Paris, 1929), ii, pp. 312–13; J. S. P. Tatlock, *The Legendary History of Britain: Geoffrey of Monmouth's Historia Regum Britanniae and its Early Vernacular Versions* (Berkeley and Los Angeles, 1950), pp. 135–38. Geoffrey must surely have known, as did his contemporary Gaimar, how remote was the story of Gormund in time and space from sixth-century Britain (Alexander Bell (ed.), *L'Estoire des Engleis by Geffrei Gaimar* (Oxford, 1960), pp. 103–8; cf. pp. 247–48).

41   Could mention of a *gormes* have prompted Geoffrey's invocation of the popular tale of Gormund?

Overall, there seems good reason to regard *Cyfranc Lludd a Lleuelys* as deriving from a *cyfarwyddyd* compiled by an unknown Welsh author about the middle of the tenth century, which in turn represented the retelling of a mythical narrative whose ultimate origins are to be sought in the darkness of prehistory.

The 'triple' scourges

Cyfranc Lludd a Lleuelys is unique among British sources in providing a detailed legendary account of the umbilical Centre of Britain. Parallel themes found in the Irish tale *Cath Maige Tuired* serve in part to illuminate some of its obscurer elements. Brynley Roberts remarked that

> The authors of 'native' Welsh tales design their stories upon essentially simple patterns which reflect structures already existing in oral narrative. *Cyfranc Lludd a Lleuelys* is an extended triad.[42]

Indeed, it could in a sense be described as a triple triad. Firstly, the three Oppressions (*teir gormesoedd*) are enumerated; next, Lleuelys interprets their significance; finally, Lludd acts on his brother's advice to nullify each menace in succession.

The concept of a triplicity of dire threats to the well-being or survival of a people is recorded among Indo-European peoples as far afield as Ireland and India.[43] An inscription authorized by the Persian king Darius contained a prayer to the god Ahuramazda for protection of his realm against three potent threats: *dušiyārā* (failed harvest), *hainā* (hostile army), and *draugā* (lying). Together they spell devastation for the entire community. Dearth and blight ruin the farmers on whom the economy depends, invaders menace the warrior class, and lying threatens the priestly caste, whose responsibility is to sustain cosmic truth and equilibrium.[44] In §413 of Plato's Republic, Socrates lists triple scourges of theft, spells, and violence as causes of deviation from truth.[45]

However, it looks as though this triadic pattern was imposed at a secondary stage on the matter of *Cyfranc Lludd a Lleuelys*, which originally constituted a narrative focused around a unitary theme. For it is apparent from the story itself that the Three Oppressions (*gormesoedd*) are but facets of a single *gormes*.

1. The Coraniaid possess occult power of overhearing any conversation throughout the island, which preserves them from harm.

   The same faculty is accorded the wizard Math in *Math uab Mathonwy*, as also the fairies in Welsh folklore tradition.[46] In neither of these cases is there any suggestion that

---

42 Brynley F. Roberts, 'Where Were the Four Branches of the Mabinogi Written?', in Joseph Falaky Nagy (ed.), *The Individual in Celtic Literatures* (Dublin, 2001), p. 64.

43 Cf. Whitley Stokes and John Strachan (ed.), *Thesaurus Palaeohibernicus: A Collection of Old-Irish Glosses Scholia Prose and Verse* (Cambridge, 1901–3), ii, p. 256. Triplicity of cosmic disasters in Irish tradition is discussed by Séamus Mac Mathúna, 'The Irish Cosmos Revisited: Further Lexical Perspectives', in Jacqueline Borsje, Ann Dooley, Séamus Mac Mathúna, and Gregory Toner (ed.), *Celtic Cosmology: Perspectives from Ireland and Scotland* (Toronto, 2014), pp. 12–15.

44 Émile Benveniste, *Le vocabulaire des institutions indo-européennes* (Paris, 1969), i, pp. 288–89; ii, p. 27; Georges Dumézil, *Mythe et Épopée* (Paris, 1968–1973), i, pp. 615–23; iii, pp. 353–54; idem, *Les dieux souverains des Indo-Européens* (Paris, 1986), pp. 223–24; Puhvel, *Comparative Mythology*, pp. 179–80.

45 S. R. Slings (ed.), *Platonis Rempvblicam* (Oxford, 2003), pp. 125–26.

46 Ian Hughes (ed.), *Manawydan Uab Llyr: Trydedd Gainc y Mabinogi* (Cardiff, 2007), pp. 1, 4; John Rhŷs, *Celtic Folklore: Welsh and Manx* (Oxford, 1901), pp. 195–96, 674. It has been suggested that the Coraniaid of early

this supernatural faculty, being fundamentally defensive, was deployed for destructive purpose. While the Coraniaid were regarded as a race of alien oppressors (*gormes*), it seems that in *Cyfranc Lludd a Lleuelys* their supernatural power of hearing has become artificially distinguished as an Oppression in its own right.

The comment 'because of that, no harm could be done to them' appears insufficient reason to regard the power of eavesdropping per se as a *gormes*. The author appears conscious of the deficiency, since he adds this laboured 'explanation':

> And nevertheless the first *gormes* was plain and clear, but no one knew the meaning of the other two *gormes*, and on account of that there was more hope of deliverance from the first than there was of the second or third.

2. The May-day scream, which ruins the prosperity and fertility of Britain and her inhabitants, is in contrast unquestionably destructive.

   Nonetheless, the explanation remains confusing. The scream proves to be uttered by the British dragon during the conflict with its alien counterpart. But why should its cry prove so destructive *to its own people*? Since neither creature is seen to gain the victory, why is it only the British dragon that shrieks?[47] And why does the solution to this menace lie in burying the dragons securely in a stone chest? Should not the foreign dragon be expelled from the land – as indeed it eventually will be, according to the earlier account of the same event in the *Historia Brittonum*?

3. The third *gormes*, which abstracts all food and drink from every courthouse in Britain, is in practical terms identical in effect to the second. Each brings about the reduction of the island to an unproductive wasteland, the king's courts (*llyssoedd y brenhin*) representing an obvious synecdoche for Britain herself.

   This last *gormes* is closely paralleled in *Manawydan uab Llŷr*, when a terrible noise (*twrwf*) heralds the mysterious reduction of Dyfed to an untamed wilderness. The symbolic function of the royal courts appears similarly indicated, when it is stated that all buildings had vanished, save for the court houses (*tei y llys*), which stood unoccupied by man and beast.[48]

It appears that the structure of the triple scourges in *Cyfranc Lludd a Lleuelys* was artificially imposed on what was at an earlier stage a single *gormes*. The first is not presented as a scourge at all but a useful attribute (*cyneddf*) of the Coraniaid, which might assist in protecting them from reprisals on the part of those they threatened. The armed wizard of the third *gormes*, who similarly caused the royal comestibles to vanish, was presumably envisaged as their king. In *Manawydan* the ruler of the Coraniaid is identified as Caswallawn, seems however unlikely to have been the original name. The opening sentence of *Cyfranc Lludd a Lleuelys* lists Caswallawn

---

tradition were originals of what were 'now regarded as mischievous fairies' (J. A. MacCulloch, *The Religion of the Ancient Celts* (Edinburgh, 1911), p. 114). In the Norse *Gylfaginning* the god Heimdallr is said to possess hearing so sharp that he can hear grass growing on earth and wool on sheep (Anthony Faulkes (ed.), *Snorri Sturluson: Edda; Prologue and Gylfaginning* (Oxford, 1982), p. 25).

47   A *Brut* version seeks to correct the anomaly by ascribing the British dragon's scream to anger (Parry (ed.), *Brut y Brenhinedd*, p. 67).

48   Hughes (ed.), *Manawydan Uab Llyr*, pp. 2–3; In the Norse *Gylfaginning* the god Heimdallr is said to possess hearing so sharp that he can hear grass growing on earth and wool on sheep (Anthony Faulkes (ed.), *Snorri Sturluson: Edda; Prologue and Gylfaginning* (Oxford, 1982), p. 25).

as a younger brother of Lludd, but he is not alluded to further. From this it could have been inferred that he was the unnamed armed magician who, as the third *gormes*, plundered the royal courts. All this bears out Professor Mac Cana's suggestion that 'it may even be that they [the Coraniaid] were once the sole or the central oppression in the original narrative from which the extant text is derived'.[49]

At some stage, therefore, the story had become recast as a triad. In addition, an attempt was made to explain and rationalize its originally magical character in order to recast it as a dramatic episode from British history, as it features in its extant form. Thus the scream, which in an earlier version was probably understood to emanate from the subterranean realm of Annwfn, was transferred to the afflicted native dragon.

Furthermore, the struggle between Lludd and the giant intruder, which is represented as a fierce sword-fight, must originally have been depicted as a duel between rival enchanters employing magical arts, such as occurs in the concluding section of *Manawydan mab Llŷr*. Lleuelys actually describes the destructive raptor as 'a powerful enchanter (*gwr lleturithawc*) ... Through his magic and enchantment (*y hut a leturith*)' he puts everyone to sleep, and plunders the royal courts. These attributes of his original function as malignant wizard have survived the process of euhemerization, whereby he was transformed into a dangerous armed robber.

The divine king and the druid

It has been suggested that, as a work of literature, *Cyfranc Lludd a Lleuelys* compares unfavourably with the celebrated Four Branches of the *Mabinogi*. Brynley Roberts comments:

> *Cyfranc Lludd a Llefelys* does not have the descriptive quality or the attention to detail which heightens the effect of wonder or the natural realism which is a feature of other native tales. It is written in a flat, neutral style where the direct yet suggestive conciseness of the other tales has given way to baldness and factual expression. There is here an almost complete lack of dialogue, no attention to character, and no attempt to involve the reader in the action or to dwell upon the wonder of the three *gormesoedd*.[50]

Nevertheless, despite its unadorned presentation, the story may exert peculiar fascination on a receptive reader. The matter-of-fact narration of the sinister threats, and the mysterious manner in which they come to be repelled, is related in tantalizingly laconic terms. The solutions provided by Lleuelys are as enigmatic as the menaces they are designed to frustrate. Why, for example, was it necessary for the brothers to use a horn to communicate their plans in secret, when the Coraniaid were able neither to detect Lludd's covert disembarkation from Britain, nor overhear his preliminary discussion with Lleuelys, before the latter introduced the precautionary device of the bronze speaking-tube? Who or what was the obstructive devil concealed in the horn, and what if any his connexion to the Coraniaid? What was the especial power of wine, that alone afforded means of removing the menace? Most baffling of all, what exactly were the *pryfed*, which when dissolved in water provided magical means of distinguishing between the Britons and the malevolent Coraniaid?

Yet again, why did the British dragon's scream bring ruination upon the country it personified, rather than a cry uttered by the alien aggressor? What was the relevance of the strange details

---

49   Proinsias Mac Cana, *The Mabinogi* (Cardiff, 1992), pp. 77–78.
50   Roberts (ed.), *Cyfranc Lludd a Llefelys*, p. xxviii.

of the dragons' battle, and the means adopted for their entrapment? Why the need for removing them to North Wales for interment? Who was the giant enchanter that deprived feasters throughout Britain of all their food and drink? Might Lludd not have found more convenient means of preventing himself from falling asleep than plunging himself into a vat of cold water? Overall, the events bear a strangely dreamlike quality, and occur in a world which seems only partially bounded by time and space.

Lludd's third adventure appears particularly uncanny. The ill-boding visitation and combat take place in the deep of night, in some lonely unidentified royal hall. Strange music, of unknown origin, resounds eerily in the crepuscular stillness. Although it is the inhabitants of Britain who are subjected to the alien Oppressions, an image is conjured of a solitary Lludd, fulfilling his soteriological rôle in a shadowy stronghold, occupied by himself and his wizard adversary alone. The overall impression conveyed is one, not of mystification indulged for its own sake, but of a narrative so abbreviated and rationalized at the hands of successive mediæval scribes or narrators as to have become no longer fully understood.

There can be little question but that the story of Lludd and Lleuelys derives almost in its entirety from native Welsh tradition, and may indeed be regarded as falling into the same category as the Four Branches.[51] The only detectable alien elements are such minor modifications as adaptation of the name *Lleu* to that of French *Louis*, identification of the Centre of Britain with the late Saxon town of Oxford, and the scribe's use of a scattering of Norman French loan-words. While the latter are unlikely to have been absorbed into the Welsh language before the middle of the eleventh century, they provide no safe means of dating the story's original composition. As foreign words entered the vocabulary of the Welsh people, so they became absorbed into narrative tradition (whether oral or written) during a process of recitation and redaction extending over many generations, well before the story's eventual preservation in extant manuscript versions.[52]

Although the tale was probably regarded as historical by its narrator, it is evident that its origins lie in the pre-Christian traditional lore of the British people. The names of its protagonists, the theme of the triple Oppressions, and the Discovery of the Fighting 'Dragons' are attested elsewhere in early Welsh literature, all being recognizable as motifs rooted in Celtic pagan cosmology.

The names of *Lludd* and *Lleuelys* are those of prominent deities belonging to the British heathen pantheon. This in itself suffices to show that the story originally concerned the exploits of divine beings, who evolved after the establishment of Christianity into figures believed to have lived in the distant historical past. As Sir John Morris-Jones observed: 'Words generally

---

51 'The reason ... for the difference between *Cyfranc Lludd a Llefelys* and the other tales is that the author deliberately tailored it to suit the general style of his translation of the *Brut*; I suggest that, far from being an amateur story-teller of middling competence, he was, rather, a highly skilled one with an acute sense of stylistic difference, his main concern being to create a seamless garment rather than a purple patch. If that is correct, *Cyfranc Lludd a Llefelys* deserves to be treated on the same footing as the other tales as regards date, rather than to be passed by in silence, and we are justified in appealing to it when asking whether some of the other tales might not equally belong to the same period' (Iestyn Daniel, 'The date, origin, and authorship of 'The Mabinogion' in the light of *Ymborth yr enaid*', *The Journal of Celtic Studies* (Turnhout, 2004), iv, p. 124); cf. pp. 123–24, 138–39.

52 Morgan Watkin, *La civilisation française dans les Mabinogion* (Paris, 1962), pp. 349–52; idem, 'The Chronology of the White Book of Rhydderch on the Basis of its Old French Graphical Phenomena', *The National Library of Wales Journal* (Aberystwyth, (1964), xiii, pp. 349–52. Cf. also comments by T. M. Charles-Edwards, 'The Date of the Four Branches of the Mabinogi', *The Transactions of the Honourable Society of Cymmrodorion: Session 1970* (London, 1971), pp. 265–66; Tolstoy, *The Oldest British Prose Literature*, pp. 29–38.

persist only in association with ideas; and it is inconceivable that British names of British gods could have survived except in traditions concerning them.'[53]

Thus, the starting point for investigation lies in consideration of the *dramatis personæ* of the story.

Cyfranc Lludd a Lleuelys begins in characteristically laconic fashion with the statement that Beli Mawr ('Beli the Great'), son of Mynogan, reigned over Britain until his death. Beli Mawr features in early Welsh tradition as primal ruler of Britain and archetypal ancestor of royal dynasties.[54] The sons of Beli are named at the outset of the story as Lludd, Caswallawn, Ninniaw, and 'according to the story, his fourth son was Lleuelys'. The list is revealing. The names of the father and his first three sons are drawn from the principal Welsh translations of Geoffrey's *Historia Regum Britanniæ*, which state that Beli Mawr had three sons, Llud, Caswallawn, and Nynnyaw, while making no mention of Lleuelys.[55] This bears out the independent existence of a version of *Cyfranc Lludd a Lleuelys*, which specifies that 'according to the story' (*herwyd y kyuarwydyt*), i.e. the source of the *Cyfranc*, Llcuelys was an additional son of Beli.

The status of the *Historia Regum Britanniæ* (in mediæval Wales and its Welsh translations) was such that no one seriously challenged its authority.[56] All that could be done was to attempt reconciliation of the authentic indigenous tradition to Geoffrey's concocted history.[57] The opening passage of *Cyfranc Lludd a Lleuelys* is all that reflects the influence of Geoffrey's *Historia*, from which the names of Caswallawn and Ninniaw were omitted. In any case they play no part in the story, the protagonists of which being (as its title declares) Lludd and Lleuelys.

It appears that originally Lludd and Lleuelys bore no blood relationship to one another. The first was a (divine) ruler who embodied the abstract principle of kingship, while the second was an omniscient (divine) magician, to whose arcane wisdom (*gwybot*) the realm looked for protection and survival. As the mysteries which underlie the story are unravelled, it becomes apparent that its two protagonists stand for paired archetypal figures lying at the heart of Celtic mythology: the King and the Druid.[58]

Allusions to Lludd in early Welsh literature are relatively rare. Some have already been cited above. The tenth-century 'Stanzas of the Graves' include among resting places of legendary British heroes that of an otherwise unknown Taflogau son of Lludd.[59]

The name of Ludgate Hill, site of St Paul's cathedral, was asserted by Geoffrey of Monmouth to derive from King Lud, whose name he appropriated as founder of London: *Saxonice uero Ludesgate*

---

53 Sir John Morris-Jones, 'Taliesin', *Y Cymmrodor* (London, 1918), xxviii, p. 240.

54 Roberts (ed.), *Cyfranc Lludd a Llefelys*, pp. xii–xiii.

55 *Beli Mavr … deu ugein mlyned y bu urenhin yn enys Prydein. Ac y hvnnv y bu tri meib, Llud, a Chaswallavn, a Nynnyav* (Lewis (ed.), *Brut Dingestow*, p. 44; John Rhŷs and J. Gwenogvryn Evans (ed.), *The Text of the Mabinogion and other Welsh Tales from the Red Book of Hergest* (Oxford, 1887), p. 82). Caswallawn and Lludd are singled out from 'seven sons of Beli' in a prophetic poem antedating Geoffrey's work: '*Seith meib o veli dyrchafyssyn. kaswallaon allud achestudyn*' (Gwenogvryn Evans (ed.), *Facsimile & Text of the Book of Taliesin*, p. 70). Identification by name of 'sons' of Beli may however have originated in misinterpretation of the term *meibion Beli* as 'sons of Beli', rather than 'descendants' (i.e. race) of the Otherworld despot.

56 The oft-repeated assertion that the HRB was rejected as authentic history by Giraldus Cambrensis rests on a misunderstanding (Nikolai Tolstoy, 'Geoffrey of Monmouth and the Merlin Legend', in Elizabeth Archibald and David F. Johnson (ed.), *Arthurian Literature XXV* (Cambridge, 2008), pp. 27–33).

57 Cf. Patrick Sims-Williams, *Rhai Addasiadau Cymraeg Canol o Sieffre o Fynwy* (Aberystwyth, 2011).

58 Guyonvarc'h and Le Roux, *Les Druides*, pp. 107–20.

59 Jarman (ed.), *Llyfr Du Caerfyrddin*, p. 42.

nuncupatur; while he further ascribed that of Billingsgate to Belinus: *Belinesgata*.[60] That two of the ancient gates of the capital should have borne names so similar to those of prominent British deities might appear suggestive, but for the fact that one at least is of Old English derivation.[61]

Our knowledge of Lludd would be scant indeed, but for two revealing references to *Lludd Llaw Ereint*, 'Lludd of the Silver Hand', in the mediæval Welsh prose tale *Culhwch ac Olwen*.[62] Were it not for this record of his epithet, the standing of Lludd in British mythology must have remained obscure. More than a century ago, Sir John Rhŷs noted that the epithet of 'Lludd of the Silver Hand' corresponds to that of the Irish god Núadu Airgetlám, 'Núadu of the Silver Hand', and suggested that the original form of *Lludd* must accordingly have been *Nudd*, having evolved into *Lludd* from alliterative attraction of the epithet *Llawereint*. The logic of this view has led to broad scholarly acceptance.[63] A divinity Nodens or Nodons, whose British name corresponding to later Welsh *Nudd*, is recorded in Romano-British inscriptions located as far apart as Lancashire and the coast of the Bristol Channel. They attest to his status as an important god in the pre-Christian era, who was associated or identified with the Roman Mars.[64] The southern site is that of the

---

60   Reeve and Wright (ed.), *Geoffrey of Monmouth: The History of the Kings of Britain*, pp. 59, 67.

61   Cf. John Rhŷs, *Celtic Folklore: Welsh and Manx* (Oxford, 1901), p. 448; Williams (ed.), *Cyfranc Lludd a Llevelys*, pp. x–xi. Old English *ludgaet* means 'postern' (J. D. Pheifer (ed.), *Old English Glosses in the Épinal-Erfurt Glossary* (Oxford, 1974), p. 40). Jackson appears to suggest that the name might nevertheless reflect awareness of Lludd's legendary foundation of London: 'The derivation of *London* from *Lludd* is of course erroneous, though it gained currency in England early; whence *Ludgate*, etc' (Kenneth Hurlstone Jackson, *A Celtic Miscellany: Translations from the Celtic Literatures* (London, 1951), p. 342). This is not impossible, since OE *ludgaet* might have originated from a celebrated gate at London, in the same way that the Russian common noun вокзалъ, 'railway station', derives from English *Vauxhall*. An OE element *lud-* does not appear to be recorded elsewhere, nor is a suggested Icelandic derivation very convincing (F. Holthausen, *Altenglisches Etymologisches Wörterbuch* (Heidelberg, 1934), p. 207).

62   Rachel Bromwich and D. Simon Evans (ed.), *Culhwch and Olwen: An Edition and Study of the Oldest Arthurian Tale* (Cardiff, 1992), pp. 13, 33.

63   John Rhys, *Lectures on the Origin and Growth of Religion as Illustrated by Celtic Heathendom* (London, 1888), p. 125; Ifor Williams (ed.), *Cyfranc Lludd a Llevelys* (Bangor, 1910), p. 11; W. J. Gruffydd, *Math vab Mathonwy: An Inquiry into the Origins and Development of the Fourth Branch of the Mabinogi with the Text and a Translation* (Cardiff, 1928), p. 77; Rev. John Ryan (ed.), *Féilsgríbinn Eóin Mhic Néill* (Dublin, 1940), p. 34; Nora K. Chadwick, 'Intellectual Contacts between Britain and Gaul in the Fifth Century', in *Studies in Early British History* (Cambridge, 1954), p. 197; Thomas F. O'Rahilly, *Early Irish History and Mythology* (Dublin, 1946), p. 496. A dissentient view was expressed by A. G. van Hamel ('Aspects of Celtic Mythology', *The Proceedings of the British Academy* (London, 1934), xx, p. 235). Cf. however the discussion by Jan de Vries, with its telling conclusion that 'the motif of the silver hand is far too specific to appear in two places without any connexion', (*Keltische Religion* (Stuttgart, 1961), pp. 103–104). An alternative (to me, equally plausible) explanation of the anomalous form Lludd is that of Georges Dumézil: 'il est (avec un ll- initial au lieu du n- attendu, peut-être par assonance avec Llevelis?)' (*Mythe et Épopée*, i, p. 613).

64   R. G. Collingwood and R. P. Wright (ed.), *The Roman Inscriptions of Britain: I Inscriptions on Stone* (Oxford, 1965), pp. 104–105, 206. The related personal name N[V]DINTI is found on a sixth-century inscription in Carmarthenshire (V. E. Nash-Williams, *The Early Christian Monuments of Wales* (Cardiff, 1950), p. 109; cf. Kenneth Jackson, *Language and History in Early Britain: A Chronological Survey of the Brittonic Languages First to Twelfth Century A.D.* (Edinburgh, 1953), p. 619). At Yarrowkirk in Stirlingshire another inscription of about the same era bears the name NVD[OGEN]I (R. A. S. Macalister, *Corpus Inscriptionum Insularum Celticarum* (Dublin, 1945–49), i, p. 493). *Nudogeni* would mean 'Born of (the god) Nudos', but an alternative reading NVDI has been suggested (Charles Thomas, 'The Early Christian Inscriptions of Southern Scotland', *Glasgow Archaeological Journal* (Glasgow, 1991–92), xvii, pp. 3–4). The name *Nudd* was borne by other early Welsh kings (P. C. Bartrum (ed.), *Early Welsh Genealogical Texts* (Cardiff, 1966), pp. 57, 69, 73, 86), whereas that of *Lludd* is confined to the scanty allusions to the former god cited above.

great Romano-British temple of Lydney, which was dedicated to Nodens. The similarity of the first element of the place name to *Lludd* is in this case too great to be coincidental.[65]

Further correlation between Irish Núadu and Welsh Nudd is indicated in early Irish literature, where Núadu features as a prominent ancestor (generally grandfather) of the celebrated Fenian hero Fionn Mac Cumhaill, while Welsh tradition knew a deity *Gwyn mab* (son of) *Nudd*. The cognate *Fionn* and *Gwyn* derive from a Common Celtic proper noun **Windos*, 'the White (i.e. Blessed, Holy) One'.[66]

Identity of name alone can provide no certain guide to the antiquity of related Irish and Welsh traditions, since borrowing from one language to the other might have occurred at any time in prehistory. Inter-cultural transference might similarly be held to account for further correspondences, such as the common renown of Fionn and Gwyn as superlative huntsmen.[67] However, evidence indicates that the paired figures were deeply rooted in their respective cultures.

The Battle of Mag Tuired

The first step towards understanding the mythological implications of *Cyfranc Lludd a Lleuelys* lies in establishing the distinctive rôles played by the story's two protagonists.

---

65 John Carey, 'Nodons in Britain and Ireland', *Zeitschrift für celtische Philologie* (Tübingen, 1984), xl, p. 18; John T. Koch, 'A Welsh Window on the Iron Age: Manawydan, Mandubracios', *Cambridge Medieval Celtic Studies* (Cambridge, 1987), xiv, p. 41. An alternative suggestion is 'sailor's island', from Old English *lida*, 'sailor' and *ēg*, 'island' (Eilert Ekwall, *The Concise Oxford Dictionary of English Place-Names* (Oxford, 1936), p. 294; A. H. Smith, *The Place-Names of Gloucestershire* (Cambridge, 1964–65), iii, pp. 257–58). Although the philological expertise of the latter two scholars was exemplary, their judgment appears in this instance a little contrary. The ruins of the great temple on the hill at Lydney must have presented a striking spectacle when the Hwicce first settled the region: a thousand years later they still survived to a height of three feet (R. E. M. Wheeler and T. V. Wheeler, *Report on the Excavation of the Prehistoric, Roman, and Post-Roman Site in Lydney Park, Gloucestershire* (Oxford, 1932), p. 1). The Wye marked the frontier between Welsh and English for centuries, resulting in much local intermingling of the two races (Margaret Gelling, *The West Midlands in the Early Middle Ages* (Leicester, 1992), pp. 114–17). Further to the striking coincidence of name, it is reasonable to suppose that lingering legends of the god Lludd, dwelling in his great palace overlooking the Severn estuary, would have become known to local English inhabitants, with adoption of the site's indigenous name the likely outcome. Comparison may be made with the Old English name of the Wrekin (*Wrocen*), site of a comparably important shrine of the god Lug, which was borrowed about the same time from British (*Dinlleu*) *Gwrygon*, '(fortress of Lleu) the divine man or hero' (Jackson, *Language and History in Early Britain*, pp. 388, 557, 601–602; John T. Koch, 'Gleanings from the *Gododdin* and other Early Welsh Texts', *The Bulletin of the Board of Celtic Studies* (Cardiff, 1991), xxxviii, pp. 112–13). Any assimilation of *Lydney* to Old English *lida* need reflect nothing more than the widely attested Anglo-Saxon tendency towards 'folk-perversion of earlier Celtic names' (Allen Mawer, *Place-Names and History* (Liverpool and London, 1922), pp. 14–15). On the other hand, it is intriguing to speculate whether association of the first element of *Lyd*ney with Old English 'sailor' could also have been influenced by the function of the divinity Nodens, whose name indicates close association with the sea (H. Wagner, 'Studies in Early Celtic Traditions', *Ériu* (Dublin, 1975), xxvi, p. 8; William Sayers, "*Mani Maidi an Nem* …": Ringing Changes on a Cosmic Motif', ibid., (1986), xxxvii, p. 117; Puhvel, *Comparative Mythology*, p. 180).

66 Stefan Zimmer, 'Die altkymrischen Frauennamen. Ein erster Einblick', in Joseph F. Eska, R. Geraint Gruffydd, and Nicolas Jacobs (ed.), *Hispano-Gallo-Brittonica: Essays in honour of Professor D. Ellis Evans on the occasion of his sixty-fifth birthday* (Cardiff, 1995), p. 322; Matasović, *Etymological Dictionary of Proto-Celtic*, p. 423. Heinrich Wagner preferred a derivation from an Indo-European present-stem **u-i-n-d-*, 'finds out, discovers': 'An original meaning "he who finds out, knows" suits perfectly the figure of *Find* in Irish tradition, who has been described as a *warrior-hunter-seer*' ('Studies in the Origins of Early Celtic Civilisation', *Zeitschrift für Celtische Philologie* (1971), xxxi, p. 23).

67 Cf. Eoin MacNeill and Gerard Murphy (ed.), *Duanaire Finn: The Book of the Lays of Finn* (London and Dublin, 1908–53), iii, pp. 198–204; Joseph Falaky Nagy, *The Wisdom of the Outlaw: The Boyhood Deeds of Finn in Gaelic Narrative Tradition* (Los Angeles, 1985), p. 236; Dáithí Ó hÓgáin, *Fionn mac Cumhaill: Images of the Gaelic Hero* (Dublin, 1988), p. 16.

One of the clearest indications that the relationship between the Irish gods Núadu and Lug on the one hand, and their Welsh counterparts Lludd and Lleu on the other, derives from common Celtic mythology lies in telling parallels between the Welsh story of Lludd and Lleuelys and the Irish mythological tale 'The (Second) Battle of Mag Tuired' (*Cath Maige Tuired*). Lludd's Irish counterpart Núadu features prominently in this early Irish tale, which recounts events culminating in a cataclysmic war between rival races disputing sovereignty over the land of Ireland. They are its legitimate occupants, the *Túatha Dé Danann* ('Peoples of the Goddess Danu'), and a sinister transmarine race of invaders known as *Fomoire*.

Although location of the battle at Moytirra in Connacht is centuries old, it cannot have been original to the site. In fact the Battle of Mag Tuired is altogether unhistorical, being derived from archaic pagan myth, which in time became transformed into an historical battle waged between rival races in early times.

Mediæval Ireland's men of learning, the *filid*, constructed from the cherished myths and legends of pagan times an elaborate history of their country, painstakingly synchronized with what was known of world history from classical literature and the Bible. The story of *Cath Maige Tuired* was appropriated in this way by the *filid* (scholars), who incorporated it in abbreviated form into their colossal work of syncretic history, the 'Book of the Takings of Ireland', *Lebor Gabála Érenn*. Although the text includes much in the way of magical enchantments, together with warriors and witches possessed of supernatural powers, it is essentially depicted as a sequence of historical events. (At one point in the text it is noted that 'the battle of Mag Tuired and the destruction of Troy took place at the same time'.)[68]

The extent of this elaborate process of euhemerization becomes manifest when comparison is made with the cognate Welsh tale of *Cyfranc Lludd a Lleuelys*. Save for its 'historical' introduction and the concluding sword-fight between Lludd and the midnight enchanter, every aspect of the Welsh tale involves magic and the supernatural. The Welsh never developed their own 'Book of Takings', beyond the modest attempt by Nennius in the ninth century to compile a history of Britain based on scanty available sources.[69] Three centuries later Geoffrey of Monmouth concocted his own brilliant version, which proved so universally popular as effectively to preclude further Cymric initiative in that direction. At the same time, he appears to have rejected the unmistakably supernatural tale of Lludd and Lleuelys as too patently unhistorical for inclusion.

Despite the extensive process of historicization to which it was subjected, *Cath Maige Tuired* retains many original elements of what must once have been a significant narrative in Common Celtic mythology.[70] That the story existed in something like its present state as early as the ninth century is indicated by its implicit identification of the Otherworld race of Fomoire with the

---

68 Gray (ed.), *Cath Maige Tuired*, p. 40.

69 There may have been a British 'Book of Conquests', since lost, which is however unlikely to have been much more extensive than the extant *Historia Brittonum* (Peter C. Bartrum, 'Was there a British 'Book of Conquests'?', *The Bulletin of the Board of Celtic Studies* (Cardiff, 1968), xxiii, pp. 1–5).

70 'In the tale of Lludd and Llefelys ... one of these *gormesoedd* is a race called Coraniaid, clearly supernatural beings, and we may have here the remnants of a truly mythological story, similar to the Irish tale of the battle of Mag Tuired, which recounted the winning or the defence of Britain against Otherworld enemies' (Brynley F. Roberts, 'Geoffrey of Monmouth and Welsh Historical Tradition', *Nottingham Mediaeval Studies* (Cambridge, 1976), xx, p. 33). Cf. Rhys, *Lectures on the Origin and Growth of Religion as Illustrated by Celtic Heathendom*, p. 610; Alwyn Rees and Brinley Rees, *Celtic Heritage: Ancient Tradition in Ireland and Wales* (London, 1961), pp. 46–47; *Celticvm VI*, pp. 450–53; Roberts (ed.), *Cyfranc Lludd a Llefelys*, pp. xix, xxxiii; Patrick K. Ford (tr.), *The Mabinogi and other Medieval Welsh Tales* (Berkeley, 1977), pp. 111–12; Mac Cana, *The Mabinogi*, pp. 77–78.

Vikings, whose destructive raiding aroused apocalyptic fears in Ireland.[71] However, this does not account for location of the battle at Moytirra, near Lough Arrow in County Sligo, since neither the site nor its surrounding region appears to bear any significance for the Viking Age.[72]

Thomas Charles-Edwards has suggested that dynastic wars in north-east Connacht in the seventh or early eighth century provide a context for identification of the battle-site, and that "'The Second Battle of Mag Tuired" could well have been written at a local church such as Senchue'.[73] While not impossible, it is difficult to envisage why a minor provincial conflict should have become identified with the great eschatological war of Irish mythology. Moreover, a bloody historical battle at Moytirra at that time might surely be expected to have featured in the annals.[74]

Moytirra lies in a region of barren hills and uncultivated peatbogs, whose landscape has changed little since megalithic times.[75] A local historian of the nineteenth century found the ambience of the locality mysterious, even sinister.

> In appearance the plateau of Moytura is one of the most unattractive in Ireland – sombre, weird, and barren. Dull, however, as it looks, it commands a varied and picturesque prospect: all round, the mountains of Leitrim and Sligo; to the south, the rich and cultivated tract of *Tir Tuathal*; at various points, the lakes of Lough Bo, Lough na Suil, Lough Skean, Lough Ce, and Lough Arrow; and on the west, the sunny, smiling slopes of Hollybrook, backed up by the historic Dunaveeragh.[76]

The remote rock-strewn tableland provides an evocative setting for Ireland's 'last dim weird battle in the west'. Moytirra lies at the heart of a desolate wilderness of lakes and mountains. Peculiar to the site are multitudinous boulders crowded upon the hill and scattered about the surrounding slopes. Hosts of grim monoliths stand gathered about either side of the steep road, by which the visitor ascends from Ballindoon to the summit of the elevated plain. On gaining the height, he finds himself standing amidst a confused array of colossal grey boulders, ranged in ranks and columns about the windy plain. Large numbers stand erect, after withstanding relentless buffetings from wild gales and torrential downpours over thousands of Atlantic winters.[77]

A likely reason for selection of this boulder-strewn plain is suggested by the name of the tale. An upland district, remote from the haunts of men, provided appropriate location for a

---

71 Proinsias Mac Cana, 'The Influence of the Vikings on Celtic Literature', in Brian Ó Cuív (ed.), *The Impact of the Scandinavian Invasions on the Celtic-speaking Peoples c. 800–1100 A.D.* (Dublin, 1975), p. 94. A version of the story was current no later than the beginning of the ninth century, when it was cited by Bishop Cormac in his Glossary (Kuno Meyer, 'Sanas Cormaic', in O. J. Bergin, R. I. Best, Kuno Meyer, and J. G. O'Keefe (ed.), *Anecdota from Irish Manuscripts* (Halle and Dublin, 1907-13), iv, p. 83).

72 O'Rahilly showed that the two Battles of Moytura represent duplication of the same event, and that the traditional site in County Sligo was envisaged as the location of both battles (*Early Irish History and Mythology*, pp. 388–90).

73 T. M. Charles-Edwards, *Early Christian Ireland* (Cambridge, 2000), p. 41.

74 A skirmish by the site in 1398 'is the only battle at Magh Tuireadh (after the Second Battle of Magh Tuireadh, at least) recorded in the annals before 1422' (Mícheál Hoyne, 'The Political Context of Cath Muighe Tuireadh, the Early Modern Irish Version of the Second Battle of Magh Tuireadh', *Ériu* (2013), lxiii, p. 105).

75 E. R. Norman and J. K. St Joseph, *The Early Development of Irish Society: The Evidence of Aerial Photography* (Cambridge, 1969), p. 14.

76 Archdeacon T. O'Rorke, *The History of Sligo: Town and County* (Dublin, 1889), ii, p. 269.

77 Ibid., ii, pp. 260–63. Cf. Eugene O'Curry, *Lectures on the Manuscript Materials of Ancient Irish History* (Dublin, 1861), pp. 245–50.

supernatural conflict.[78] *Mag Tuired* means 'Plain of Pillars'.[79] Such a name was appropriate to an impressive megalithic site, and is not unique to Moytirra.[80] The massive standing stones could readily have given rise to a belief that they originated in a deadly struggle between supernatural adversaries. A plain in Gaul near the Rhône contained such an array of huge boulders, which were believed to have been supplied by Jupiter to Hercules, when the latter ran out of arrows during a battle with the sons of Neptune. The place bore the name *Campi Lapidei*, which recalls that of *Mag Tuired*.[81] Alternatively, given archaic identification of 'pillar' and 'hero',[82] the serried ranks of menhirs might have been taken for an awesome assembly of petrified warriors.[83]

Brian Ó Cuív suggested that 'it is quite possible that an Irish storyteller may have deliberately chosen such an impressive site for a tale, which, after all, must have been composed for a noble audience'.[84] It can scarcely be doubted that what made Moytirra not only 'impressive', but appropriate to the setting of the story, was the awe-inspiring array of monoliths assembled at the wild spot.

> The dews drop slowly and dreams gather: unknown spears
> Suddenly hurtle before my dream-awakened eyes,
> And then the clash of fallen horsemen and the cries
> Of unknown perishing armies beat about my ears.
>
> We who still labour by the cromlech on the shore,
> The grey cairn on the hill, when day sinks drowned in dew,
> Being weary of the world's empires, bow down to you,
> Master of the still stars and of the flaming door.[85]

Earlier, similarities were noted between the Welsh tale *Cyfranc Lludd a Lleuelys* and the Irish story of the Battle of Magh Tuireadh (*Cath Maige Tuired*). As the brothers Rees noted,

---

78 The *Gigantomachy* of Hesiod was assigned such a geographical location on a plain below Mount Othrys (M. L. West (ed.), *Hesiod: Theogony* (Oxford, 1966), p. 340).

79 *Tuir* bears related meanings of 'pillar' and 'chief' (Quin *et al.* (ed.), *Dictionary of the Irish Language*, 'T', col. 366; MacNeill and Murphy (ed.), *Duanaire Finn*, iii, p. 338; J. Vendryes, E. Bachellery, and P-Y. Lambert, *Lexique étymologique de l'irlandais ancien* (Dublin and Paris, 1959–96), T-173). Dáithi Ó hÓgáin envisages the battle as originally fought over a cosmic pillar in the sea: 'Among the changes, the setting has been brought to land and, probably from a confusion due to the word *tuir*, the action is situated at Magh Tuireadh (Moytirra in Co. Sligo)' (*The Sacred Isle: Belief and Religion in Pre-Christian Ireland* (Woodbridge, 1999), p. 144).

80 There was another Magh Tuireadh, near Cong in County Mayo (Edmund Hogan, S. J., *Onomasticon Goedelicum: Locorum et Tribuum Hiberniae et Scotiae; An Index, with Identifications, to the Gaelic Names of Places and Tribes* (Dublin, 1910), p. 532).

81 A. Silberman (ed.), *Pomponius Mela: Chorographie* (Paris, 1988), p. 55: H. Rackham, W. H. S. Jones, and D. E. Eichholz, (ed.), *Pliny: Natural History* (London, 1938-62), ii, p. 28; Francesco Sbordone (ed.), *Strabonis Geographica* (Rome, 1963–2000), ii, pp. 105–9.

82 Calvert Watkins, 'Some Celtic Phrasal Echoes', in A. T. E. Matonis and Daniel F. Melia (ed.), *Celtic Language, Celtic Culture: A Festschrift for Eric P. Hamp* (Van Nuys, CA, 1990), pp. 52–55.

83 The concept is widely recorded: cf. W. G. Wood-Martin, *Traces of the Elder Faiths of Ireland: A Folklore Sketch; A Handbook of Irish Pre-Christian Traditions* (London, 1902), ii, pp. 209–21.

84 Brian Ó Cuív, 'Cath Maige Tuired', in Myles Dillon (ed.), *Irish Sagas* (Dublin, 1959), p. 37.

85 'The Valley of the Black Pig' (Richard J. Finneran (ed.), *W. B. Yeats: The Poems; A New Edition* (London, 1983), pp. 65–66.

The three plagues that befall Britain in the short tale called 'Lludd and Llefelys' bear certain resemblances to ... the despoiling of Tuatha Dé Danann by the Fomoire ... It will be remembered that Nuadu, King of Tuatha Dé Danann, yields his throne to Lug, the sage, in order to be delivered from the bondage of the Fomoire. In this Welsh story, Lludd the king of Britain, whose name is probably the equivalent of *Nuadu*, rids the Island of three plagues by following the instructions of his wise brother Llefelys ... After the dragons have been buried, they ensure that no plague shall enter the Island. This safeguard, together with the giant's promise that he will restore the losses he has inflicted, and never repeat them, and that he himself will become the liegeman of Lludd, recalls the conditions which ... Lug, after the battle of Mag Tuired, demands of Loch and of Bres [the defeated chiefs of the Fomoire].[86]

There is also the striking correspondence between the epithets borne by Lludd and Núadu.

Lludd occurs elsewhere as Lludd Llaw Ereint, 'Lludd of the Silver Hand, or Arm', and his obvious counterpart in Irish is the divine Nuadha Airgedlámh, who corresponds to him in name and epithet and whose kingdom is saved from the Fomhoire by the intervention of the god Lugh, just as Lludd's kingdom is saved by the intervention of Llefelys.[87]

To these parallels may be added association of the opening of both narratives with 1 May, the date of the Celtic spring festival (*Kalan Mai*). At the same time, it is clear from their distinct approaches to what is clearly a common theme that neither tale borrowed from the other, but rather descend from a Common Celtic original.[88]

The events recounted in *Cath Maige Tuired* were incorporated in abbreviated form into the sprawling compendium of early Irish pseudo history known as the 'Book of the Takings of Ireland' (*Lebor Gabála Érenn*). There is also a version of *Cath Maige Tuired*, which describes an earlier battle of the same name, in which the adversaries of the Túatha Dé Danann are the Fir Bolg, rather than the Fomoire. It is evident, however, that the so-called First and Second Battles of Moytura represent variant versions of a common legendary tradition.[89]

Parallels between *Cath Maige Tuired* and *Cyfranc Lludd a Lleuelys* are unmistakable. First, there is the nihilistic character of the malevolent race of Fomoire, corresponding to that of the Coraniaid in the Welsh tale.[90] Before becoming euhemerized as a race of barbaric invaders of Ireland, the Fomoire personified forces of chaos and darkness, bent on expropriation and destruction of their enlightened opponents the Túatha Dé Danann, the divine race revered by the pagan Irish. The division between the adversaries is not entirely clear-cut, however, since leaders on both sides are interrelated.

The 'history' (*senchas*) recounts how, after defeating their predecessors the Fir Bolg at the First Battle of Magh Tuireadh, the Túatha Dé took possession of Ireland. During the victory, the latter's king Núadu lost his hand, hacked off by Srend mac Sengainn. Subsequently it was replaced by a working silver substitute contrived by Dían Cécht, physician to the Túatha Dé.

86   Alwyn Rees and Brinley Rees, *Celtic Heritage: Ancient Tradition in Ireland and Wales* (London, 1961), p. 46. 'The Irish tale to which our story ['Lludd and Lleuelys'] bears a striking resemblance is "The Second Battle of Mag Tuiredh"' (Patrick K. Ford (tr.), *The Mabinogi and other Medieval Welsh Tales* (Berkeley, 1977), p. 111).

87   Mac Cana, *The Mabinogi*, p. 78.

88   'L'histoire [Cyfranc Lludd a Lleuelys] ... ressemble à maint égard à celle du CMT' (Françoise Le Roux, 'Le dieu-roi Nodons/Nuada', *Celticvm VI: Actes du Troisième Colloque International d'Études Gauloises, Celtiques et Protoceltiques* (Rennes, 1963), p. 451). 'Les convergences assez maigres seraient donc l'indice d'un fonds commun, infiniment plus lointain que la date de cristillisation des légendes' (p. 453).

89   Christian-J. Guyonvarc'h (tr.), *Textes mythologiques irlandais I* (Rennes, 1980), i, p. 40).

90   Sterckx, *Mythologie du monde celte*, p. 203.

Unfortunately, this disfigurement was held by the women of the Túatha Dé to render Núadu unfit for kingship.[91] Accordingly he was replaced by Eochu Bres, a prince of mixed parentage, whose father was king of the Fomoire, and his mother Ériu (the native name for Ireland), a princess of the Túatha Dé.

However Bres proved considerably more inadequate a ruler than his predecessor. His hospitality was so niggardly that the Túatha Dé found their knives were not greased by him (i.e. they received no meat at his board), their breath did not smell of ale, they enjoyed none of the professional entertainment to which they were accustomed, and their fighting ability declined. Blight descended upon the land of Ireland, and the Túatha Dé in desperation imposed rigorous conditions upon Bres, in return for his guarantee that he would abdicate after seven years. Bres, deceitfully playing for time, persuaded his kinsfolk the Fomoire, together with ferocious allies assembled from as far abroad as the Hebrides and Norway, to intervene and ensure his uninterrupted enjoyment of the kingship.

Meanwhile, the Túatha Dé restored Núadu to the throne, who celebrated his restoration with a great feast at Tara. One momentous day there appeared before the gate of the glorious citadel a dashing young warrior, who responded to the gatekeeper's customary interrogation by informing him that his name was Lug, who bore the nickname samildánach, 'many-skilled'. Questioned as to what arts he might contribute to the court at Tara, he declared himself pre-eminent in every skill, from magical to martial. Núadu accordingly ordered him to be admitted to their company.

So impressive was Lug's catalogue of his powers, that he was requested to assist in saving the Túatha Dé from the oppression of the Fomoire. It was agreed that he should occupy the throne of Núadu for the space of thirteen days. Extensive preparations, military and magical, were undertaken for the coming conflict, and Lug himself was provided with enchanted weapons forged by the three gods of Danu. The cosmic nature of the conflict becomes apparent at a secret conference of the Túatha Dé attended by Lug and the druids of Ireland, at which the samildánach received assurance that the cause of the Túatha Dé would be sustained by the mountains and lakes of Ireland, as well as destructive showers of rain binding their urine within the bodies of the men and horses of the Fomoire.

Finally, the moment arrived when the opposed forces became joined in battle. Lug's life was considered so precious that his comrades consigned him to the care of his nine foster fathers. After he had addressed the leaders of the Túatha Dé in turn, exacting from each an account of his peculiar skill, battle broke and raged with unparalleled ferocity. No sooner had the slaughter begun, than Lug escaped from his guardians and launched a potent spell against the Fomoire. At first matters appeared to be going badly for the lawful rulers of Ireland. The champion of the Túatha Dé, Ogma, fell fighting in single combat with Indech, a gigantic leader of the Fomoire. Núadu too was slain by Balor, king of the Fomoire, who was Lug's maternal grandfather. Balor possessed a malevolent eye, whose deadly power destroyed all upon whom he levelled his gaze.

---

91 For the magical implications, cf. Tomás Ó Cathasaigh, 'Pagan survivals: the evidence of early Irish narrative', in Próinséas Ní Chatháin and Michael Richter (ed.), *Irland und Europa: Die Kirche im Frühmittelalter* (Stuttgart, 1984), pp. 303–7. The account of Núadu's dismemberment arose from misunderstanding of an early laudatory epithet 'silver hand or arm' (Stefan Zimmer, 'The making of myth: Old Irish Airgatlám, Welsh Llaw ereint, Caledonian Ἀργεντοκόξος', in Michael Richter and Jean-Michel Picard (ed.), *Ogma: Essays in Celtic Studies in honour of Próinséas Ní Chatháin* (Dublin, 2002), pp. 295–97).

Eventually Lug saved the day, driving Balor's eye through the back of his head with a stone hurled from his sling.

Thanks to Lug the battle was won, with a countless host of Fomoire slaughtered. He spared Bres, who was compelled to reveal charms ensuring that Ireland was plentifully provided with milk and crops. In this way was the lawful rule of the Túatha Dé Danann restored, their magical harp and sword recovered, and their abducted cattle returned to graze the green pastures of Ireland in safety. The story however ends on an ambivalent note. The baleful witch-goddess Morrígan declares a reign of prosperity over all the land of Ireland, only to continue with a versified prophecy foretelling the world's ending in physical, moral, and cosmic turmoil.[92]

Just as Lludd and Lleuelys possess their Irish equivalents in Núadu and Lug, so too the rival divine races disputing the sovereignty of Ireland, the Peoples of the Goddess Danu or Ana (*Túatha Dé Danann*) and the Fomoire, have their parallels in Welsh tradition.

Paired Celtic divine rulers: Núadu/Nudd and Lug/Lleu

The respective functions of the corresponding Irish and Welsh paired deities Núadu/ Nudd(Lludd) and Lug/Lleu(elys), the first conceptualizing the royal distributer and guarantor of wealth and prosperity for the community, and the second a youthful outsider, saviour of the gods, and embodiment of all their attributes and powers, reflect archaic Celtic tradition. Allowing for exceptions, where there is reason to infer cross-cultural borrowing in relatively recent historical times, the correspondence of names and epithets between the Irish and Welsh gods broadly reflects a common mythological substratum shared by the earliest ancestors of insular Celtic peoples settled on opposite sides of the Irish Sea.[93]

It is possible to explore further into the darkness of prehistory, in search of the origins and explanation of the strange tale of the Encounter of Lludd and Lleuelys. The Celtic languages represent an important branch of the Indo-European parent-tongue, which in turn was spoken some five millennia ago by a people whose original homeland remains a topic of hotly debated scholarly dispute, being identified with regions ranging as far afield as the Caucasus, southern Russia and the Balkans.[94] Just as the lost parent language can be recreated from elements common to its descendants, similarly much of its technology, social organization, and religious beliefs have been painstakingly reconstructed by scholars in the fields of philology, archæology, and comparative religion.

Particularly striking are parallels between Vedic religious literature in India, written in Sanskrit and composed (probably in the Punjab) in its surviving form some two and a half

---

92   Gray (ed.), *Cath Maige Tuired*, pp. 24–72; Brian Ó Cuív (ed.), *Cath Muighe Tuireadh: The Second Battle of Magh Tuireadh* (Dublin, 1945), pp. 18–57.

93   Cf. Patrick K. Ford, 'Branwen: A Study of the Celtic Affinities', *Studia Celtica* (Cardiff, 1987/8), xxii/ xxiii, p. 39; Patrick Sims-Williams, 'Some Celtic Otherworld Terms', in A. T. E. Matonis and Daniel F. Melia (ed.), *Celtic Language, Celtic Culture: A Festschrift for Eric P. Hamp* (Van Nuys, California, 1990), pp. 57–60.

94   Helpful surveys of problems inherent in identifying the original Indo-European homeland are provided by Winfred P. Lehmann, *Die Gegenwärtige Richtung der Indogermanistischen Forschung* (Budapest, 1992), pp. 25–43; J. P. Mallory and D. Q. Adams, *The Oxford Introduction to Proto-Indo-European and the Proto-Indo-European World* (Oxford, 2006), pp. 443–63.

thousand years ago,[95] and the pagan mythology of the Celts, preserved in prose and verse committed to writing after Ireland and Britain became converted to Christianity in the early Middle Ages. This remarkable survival of traditional institutions and beliefs, separated by continents and seas over a period of thousands of years, is probably not due to chance, but to what Myles Dillon termed 'the discovery that what is old is likely to survive on the periphery of an area ...' Among both Celts and Hindus, their respective priestly classes of druids and brahmins preserved to an impressive extent common Indo-European rites and beliefs. The fact that much of this lore was recapitulated in verse ensured its continuing transmission in largely uncorrupted form.[96]

In the Hindu pantheon two powerful gods, Mitra and Varuna, are regularly linked, performing paired functions. Mitra is the mighty protector of his people, god of pure achievements, whose nature reflects that of the sun, guardian of contracts and friendships. Above all, 'the essential characteristic of Mitra is truth'. Mitra 'puts things right', he is 'the dispenser of active benevolence par excellence', 'he protects the honest and orderly relations which render social life possible. He is the enemy of quarrels, of violence, the guide toward right action.' The Avestan Mithra of the early Iranians is a ubiquitous god of contracts, who as Saviour of the World brings completion to religion and salvation to his followers.[97]

Varuna, on the other hand,

represents the inner reality of things, higher truth (*rta*), and order in their transcendent aspects, beyond the understanding of man. His absolute power is felt during the night and in all that is mysterious, while man-made laws, represented by Mitra, rule the day.[98]

The complementary relationship between these two inseparable deities was further explained by Jan Gonda as follows:

It would ... appear to me that the Mitra of the Vedic texts – who 'does not possess any individuality on the physical side' – rather is the god who, while maintaining the *rta* – that untranslatable term which may be approximately described as the supreme and fundamental order-and-reality conditioning the normal and right, natural and true structure of cosmos, ritual and human conduct – puts things right, regulates the contracts between men and the divine powers, and exhibits benevolence and active interest. Whereas Varuna, the representative of the static aspects of kingship, is a guardian of that *rta*, his companion and complement Mitra, being no less concerned with it and no less its promoter, is rather its maintainer, the one who keeps its manifestations in the right condition, who redresses

---

95   Yves Bonnefoy and Wendy Doniger (ed.), *Mythologies: A Restructured Translation of Dictionnaire des mythologies et des religions des sociétés traditionelles et du monde antique* (Chicago, 1991), p. 799. For the Aryan settlement in north-west India, cf. Asko Parpola, 'Aryan Languages, Archeological Cultures, and Sinkiang: Where Did Proto-Iranian Come into Being, and How Did It Spread?', in Victor H. Mair (ed.), *The Bronze Age and Early Iron Age Peoples of Eastern Central Asia* (Philadelphia, 1998), pp. 125–26.

96   Myles Dillon, 'The Archaism of Irish Tradition', *The Proceedings of the British Academy* (London, 1947), xxxiii, pp. 246–47; idem, *Celt and Hindu* (Dublin, 1973), p. 4. Heinrich Wagner suggested that the tradition may even derive from pre-Indo-European tradition (*Zeitschrift für celtische Philologie*, xxxi, p. 42).

97   Alain Daniélou, *Hindu Polytheism* (London, 1964), pp. 115–16; Sukumari Bhattacharji, *The Indian Theogony: A comparative Study of Indian Mythology from the Vedas to the Puranas* (Cambridge, 1970), pp. 221–23; Ilya Gershevitch (ed.), *The Avestan Hymn to Mithra* (Cambridge, 1959), pp. 26–44; Leroy A. Campbell, *Mithraic Iconography and Ideology* (Leiden, 1968), pp. 226, 261, 293, 329, 390.

98   Daniélou, *Hindu Polytheism*, p. 118; cf. pp. 118–21.

if something has gone wrong, who adjusts, restores, appeases, stabilizes, the god also who unites men. It is interesting to notice, while Varuṇa is characterized as *satyadharman* 'the one whose principle of stability and normal conduct is in harmony with truth and reality'... Mitra is in the same formula said to be *suśeva*, i.e. 'the kindly one'. The poet of ṚV. 7, 82, 5, after stating that Indra and Varuṇa had made all the created things of this world, says that it was Mitra who honoured Varuṇa by his state of peace and safety ... Mitra's co-operation is needed for the sake of peace, stabilization and maintenance of order.[99]

It was customary to regard the two divinities as inseparable. In Gonda's words, 'the pair of gods represents in a complementary way the two-sided aspect of the idea they stand for.' This 'idea' was that of twin stabilizing powers sustaining the cosmos, each operating with a beneficent intention requiring the balance of the other in order to ensure maintenance of universal equilibrium throughout the cosmos. What those powers respectively represented has been well expressed by Georges Dumézil:

> Mitra is 'our world', concerned with the earth and its different environments, concerned with everything with which man has a close relationship; Varuṇa is concerned with the rest of the world, especially the sky, and also with the 'great expanses of water', the ocean; scaled down to the limits and the needs of an individual society, their relationship remains the same, the 'close' being everything within the society, the 'distant' being everything outside, everything unfamiliar ... Mitra has an affinity with the day, with light, with white (or red); Varuṇa's affinity is with the night, with darkness, everything unfamiliar.[100]

Both gods were invoked during consecrations of Indian kings at the critical moment when the king received the unction, standing erect at sunrise with raised arms upon the throne 'as the personification of the cosmic pillar resting on the navel of the earth (the throne) and reaching up to the sky'.[101] The king, who at once incarnated divinity and acted as the womb of his people, was sustained by the dual powers who in themselves and through him maintained that quality of Truth (*ṛta*) which permeates the cosmos, providing it with order.

Mircea Eliade traced a worldwide mythological pattern, whereby the original Creator, god of the sky, gradually recedes in men's consciousness, becoming eventually a remote *deus otiosus*, concerned intermittently, or barely at all, with his creation. The principal focus of worship then develops into an all-powerful deity who is a 'more concrete, more dynamic, more fertile divinity or religious force'. Thus the Sumerian sky-god Anu came to be replaced by the virile dragon-slaying Marduk, Varuṇa became sky-god in lieu of Dyaus in India, and Zeus supplanted Kronos and Ouranos. A similar pattern has emerged among many so-called primitive peoples, particularly in Africa.[102]

99   J. Gonda, *The Vedic God Mitra* (Leiden, 1972), pp. 109–10.

100 Ibid., p. 40; Georges Dumézil, 'The Vedic Mitra: a résumé of theses and references', *The Journal of Mithraic Studies* (London, 1976), i, pp. 26–35.

101 J. C. Heesterman, *The Ancient Indian Royal Consecration: The Rājasūya Described According to the Yajus Texts and Annotated* (The Hague, 1957), pp. 101–102.

102 Mircea Eliade, *Patterns in Comparative Religion* (London, 1958), pp. 38–123. Heinrich Wagner further noted that 'the so-called "ellyptic" dual of the type *Mitrā* i.e. "Mitra- and Varuna-" ... seems to have Sumerian and Semitic parallels' ('Studies in the Origins of Early Celtic Traditions', *Ériu* (1975), xxvi, p. 8). The correspondence between Marduk's assumption of military leadership in place of Anu, and Lug's effective supersession of

It can be seen how close is the parallel between the Hindu divine pair Mitra-Varuṇa, and that of the insular Celts represented by Lug/Lleu and Núadu/Nudd. The latter represents the 'older' deity, he who sustains heaven and earth, and who peopled the latter with the human race. Humanity inevitably develops life and impetus of its own, becoming distanced from divinity. Divinity does not disappear, but recedes into the framework of the cosmos: the earth, the great waters of the deep, the unattainable dome of the sky. However, through the institution of kingship, human society remains structured as a microcosm of the divine order. The king provides the focus of his people, personifying divinity, which is concealed from human perception, and linking humanity with divinity. In early Britain and Ireland this relationship was projected in mythology onto the reign of Núadu/Nudd, who represented idealized concepts of kingship, legality, and cosmic/human hierarchical order.

The Irish Lug, like his British counterpart Lleu, was an eternally youthful warrior-god, whose intervention within historical time ensures the survival of a humanity perennially menaced by destructive forces of chaos, over which divinity had established material and spiritual order. It was Lug who intervened at the battle of Magh Tuired to save the gods from destruction at the hands of the dark legions of the Fomoire, and he who arrived to protect his heroic son Cú Chulainn when he stood alone as champion of the beleaguered kingdom of the Ulaidh (Ulster).[103] Here the British version of the myth preserves a significantly archaic element, whereby Lug's counterpart Lleu saves Lludd's kingdom by means of exclusively magical, rather than military, skills. This must represent the more archaic setting.

Evidence indicates that among the Celts and other peoples there existed in early times such a system of dual concept of kingship, providing a paradigm of divine dualism. Philology further confirms the great antiquity of the separation of 'passive' and 'active' aspects of divinity and monarchy. Linguists have distinguished terminology in Indo-European languages, preserving distinct words for 'king, lord, god': the one signifying 'beget, engender, produce', and the other 'rule, ruler, regulate'.[104] In mediæval Ireland it was believed that the armies of the king of Tara were in early times led in battle by a martial substitute (*tuarcnid flatha*), while the monarch himself remained secure within his sacred capital.[105]

The reverse side of the medal to these benign attributes was provided in Ireland by Bres mac Elatha, whose conduct offended every canon of lawful sovereignty. His hospitality was grudging and parsimonious, he maintained none of the skilled artists whose performances exalt a king's household with display of divinely-inspired craftsmanship, and none of the great princes of the kingdom (i.e. the gods of the Túatha Dé Danann) was seen at court, save the Dagda and Ogma mac Étaín, who were assigned demeaning tasks. As if these impious derogations from his royal duties were insufficient to demonstrate the illegitimacy of his rule, he secretly invited the inveterate foes of Ireland, the Fomoire, to invade the kingdom. Every one of these shortcomings offended against the ideological bases of sovereignty, as they were understood in early Irish

Núadu in *Cath Maige Tuired*, is certainly striking (cf. Thorkild Jacobsen, *Toward the Image of Tammuz and Other Essays on Mesopotamian History and Culture* (Cambridge, Mass., 1970), pp. 164–67).

103 R. I. Best, Osborn Bergin, M. A. O'Brien, and Anne O'Sullivan (ed.), *The Book of Leinster Formerly Lebar na Núachongbála* (Dublin, 1954–83), p. 324.

104 *Zeitschrift für Celtische Philologie*, xxxi, pp. 25–26; Francis John Byrne, *Irish Kings and High-Kings* (London, 1973), p. 23; Calvert Watkins, *How to Kill a Dragon: Aspects of Indo-European Poetics* (New York and Oxford, 1995), pp. 8–9.

105 M. A. O'Brien, 'The Oldest Account of the Raid of the Collas (circa A.D. 330)', *Ulster Journal of Archaeology* (Belfast, 1939), ii, p. 172).

society. Just as the reign of Núadu provided a paradigm of right rule, so that of Bres supplied its negative counterpart.[106]

Bres is described as having been illicitly conceived upon a woman of the divine Túatha Dé by Elatha, a prince of the Fomoire. Since the kings of Ireland were at once earthly counterparts of divinity, and frequently descended from one of the principal gods of the Celtic pantheon, it may be that this relationship implies that kings who proved inadequate to their exalted office were held to be no true descendants of Lug or Núadu, but tainted by influx of Fomorian blood.

Again, it is possible that, in an earlier conception, the reigns of Núadu and Bres alternated on a regular basis, representing light and dark, good and evil, positive and negative aspects of the royal function. This polarity features in other mythologies. In early Greece, for example, the Arcadian god Lykos ('daylight') is succeeded by his brother Nyktimos ('darkness').[107] The first Battle of Mag Tuired established the priority and legitimacy of the Túatha Dé Danann. Thereafter, up to the time of the second Battle of Mag Tuired, an impasse or equal balance of power subsisted between coexisting divine and diabolical hierarchies, right rule and misrule, order and chaos.

As their respective genealogies reveal, 'the distinction between the Tuatha and the Fomoire is blurred', and it has been suggested in consequence that 'there is at bottom no real distinction' between the Túatha Dé and Fomoire.[108] Both forces represent aspects of the original creation from the void, an originally formless mass imbued with potential for development of good and bad entities alike.

Núadu was not himself the creator god, that demiurge whose act of creation was inspired by no purpose extending beyond its own achievement. From the demiurge emanated divine power, whose beneficent function was to ensure that the created world assumed and preserved an existence imbued with meaning and purpose. In order that his purpose might be achieved, the beneficent deity becomes incarnated in the institution of kingship, the royal function being analogous to that of a terrestrial god:

Society considered him [the king] much more as a maintainer of equipoise ('un équilibrateur') or a distributor of wealth than as the wielder of civil and military authority. It is to him that the revenues and tribute of vassals and subject or allied peoples are rendered, and it is from him that there emanate gifts, perquisites, benefactions.

Should he prove a good king, his quality will be manifested by the outcome:

The archetype of the Celtic sovereign is the one whose good administration and remarkable good fortune permit him to give without reckoning, without meanness

---

106 Elizabeth A. Gray, 'Cath Maige Tuired: Myth and Structure', *Éigse* (Naas, 1982), xix, pp. 12–15. The noun *bres* signifies here 'uproar, din, conflict' (Françoise Le Roux, 'La Mort de Cúchulainn: Commentaire du texte', *Ogam* (1966), xviii, p. 378; J. Vendryes, E. Bachellery, and P-Y. Lambert, *Lexique étymologique de l'irlandais ancien* (Dublin and Paris, 1959–96), B-85). Was *Bres* originally an hypostasis of primæval chaos?

107 Arthur Bernard Cook, *Zeus: A Study in Ancient Religion* (Cambridge, 1914–40), i, pp. 65, 734–39. Cf. Jaan Puhvel, 'The Warrior at Stake', in Edgar Polomé (ed.), *Homage to Georges Dumézil* (Washington, 1982), pp. 29–30.

108 Rees and Rees, *Celtic Heritage*, pp. 39–40; O'Rahilly, *Early Irish History and Mythology*, pp. 482–83, 524. Genealogies of the rival races are tabulated by Jarich G. Oosten, *The War of the Gods: The Social Code in Indo-European Mythology* (London, 1985), pp. 126–29.

or denial. Under the reign of a good king abundance is universal: the earth is fruitful, animals are fertile, justice is accessible and benign, military victory assured.

This was if he followed the paradigm established by Núadu. Equally, however, his reign might prove to be modelled on that of the Fomorian Bres:

> The bad king is he who burdens his subjects with dues and taxes without affording them anything in return: under his reign the earth is sterile, animals refuse to give birth, justice is iniquitous and vexatious, military defeat inevitable.

For an Irish king to be successful it was not requisite to display intrepid vigour and resourceful initiative – rather the reverse. He must observe a host of obligations and instructions, and model himself upon heroic kings of the past, whose patterned lives provide a paradigm for all time. Above all, the king must take scrupulous care to observe magical interdictions known as *geisi* (Welsh *tynged*), which hedged his life about with prohibitions against a host of actions, some of a general character, and others bizarrely specific. Broadly speaking, the purpose of *geisi* was twofold. First, they represented means whereby the druids imposed quasi-legal constraints on kings. Second, they were intended to preclude them from re-enacting baneful events of the distant past, which had brought disaster upon earlier dynasts. In mediæval literature the motif almost invariably involves a king's inadvertent violation of his *geis*, generally with fatal consequences.[109] The overall implication is that human existence is circumscribed by a host of imperceptible dangers, which only the most minute attention to prescribed ritual may obviate.

In a word, the functions of a Celtic king were primarily magical and ritual, since human society represents a microcosm of the divine. The capacity of mankind satisfactorily to order its transitory existence is circumscribed to so great an extent by the immutable constraints of mortality, combined with a material cosmos potentially indifferent to his fate, that his sole hope lies in adjusting the pattern of terrestrial existence to that of the divine order sustaining the universe.

Hence the hostile forces in the Welsh story threatening Lludd's kingdom, and the prophylactic countermeasures revealed by his brother Lleuelys, are fundamentally magical in character. Although the story in its surviving form has been restructured as an episode in British history, it is essentially a myth of twin divinities, whose distinctive functions serve to ensure the preservation of cosmic order and balance, so accounting for the infusion and maintenance of human existence and social order within the framework of eternity.

To recapitulate, parallels between the Welsh *Cyfranc Lludd a Lleuelys* and the Irish story of *The Battle of Mag Tuired* are as follows.

1. The names of the principal protagonists, *Lludd* (= *Núadu*) and *Lleu* (= *Lug*), derive from Common Celtic originals, whose respective passive and active functions likewise correspond.
2. In each case the kingdom is threatened with destruction by a malign alien race.

---

109 Maartje Draak, 'Some Aspects of Kingship in Pagan Ireland', in *La Regalità Sacra: Contributi al Tema Dell' VIII Congresso Internazionale di Storia delle Religioni (Roma, Aprile 1955)* (Leiden, 1959), pp. 662–63; Françoise Le Roux and Christian-J. Guyonvarc'h, *La civilisation celtique* (Rennes, 1990), p. 71.

3. The reigning king proving incapable of protecting his country, a talented and energetic outsider intervenes to save it.

Correspondences between *Cyfranc Lludd a Lleuelys* and *Cath Maige Tuired* suggest a common origin in earlier Celtic mythology. While the magical aspect is more pervasive in the former, in both cases it is clear that the battle against cosmic forces of destruction (Coraniaid, Fomoire) is waged essentially by means of occult rites and arcane enchantments.

It will not have escaped attention that there is one important distinction between the respective rôles of the paired divinities Lludd/Núadu and Lleu/Lug in the Welsh and Irish versions of the victory of the gods over the Coraniad/Fomoire. The contrasted functions of the divinities have become reversed in the case of the Welsh pair, with Lleu personifying the passive wisdom of the 'withdrawn' sovereign, and Lludd personifying the active warrior. It is clear that the allocation of attributes is correctly represented in the Irish saga, and somehow became partially reversed in the Welsh tale.

The explanation for this incongruous switch is I believe evident. As the introductory passage in *Cyfranc Lludd a Lleuelys* makes clear, the story in its extant form had become absorbed into the Welsh versions of Geoffrey of Monmouth's imaginative *History of the Kings of Britain*. In the latter, *Lud* is portrayed as a powerful sovereign, who rebuilt London to such grandiose extent as to cause it to be renamed *Kaerlud*. An independent tradition, presumably of Welsh origin, which was circulating in Geoffrey's day, added to this the assertion that Lud was an exceptionally active monarch, who conquered many islands of the sea.[110] Clearly, it would have appeared incongruous had his character been transformed into that of a *roi fainéant*, who left the dangerous work of fighting to the outsider Lleu. Accordingly, the interpolator of the story of Lludd and Lleuelys into the *Brut* appears to have 'corrected' the kings' rôles in this respect, in order to make them accord with the supposedly authoritative narrative of the *Historia Regum Britanniæ*.

The secret conference between Lludd and Lleuelys

Although the parallels between *Cath Maige Tuired* and *Cyfranc Lludd a Lleuelys* have frequently been remarked, a significant factor appears to have been overlooked. In the Welsh story, Lludd's apparently insurmountable problem in countering the threat posed by the Three Oppressions (*gormesoedd*) arises from the fact that the hostile race of Coraniaid possesses the occult faculty of being able to overhear every whisper borne on the wind. This frustrated Lludd's capacity to devise counter-measures undetected. However, when he came to confer with his brother Lleuelys, the latter arranged for the construction of a bronze horn, possessed of a magical property which prevented their conversation from being overheard by any outsider.[111]

In the Irish story, Lug withdraws on the eve of battle with the gods of the Túatha Dé Danann to a place called Grellach Dollaid. There they spend a year in secret conference, 'so that Grellach Dollaid is called the *Amrún* of the Men of the Goddess [Danu]' (*Amhrún Fer nDéa*). *Amrún* is a compound of the noun *rún*, 'secret', with the intensive prefix *an-*, 'great, very'. Evidently the

---

110   *Belinus frater Cassibellani regis et erat filius Luid fortissimi regis qui multas insulas maris bellis occupauerat* (Diana Greenway (ed.), *Henry, Archdeacon of Huntingdon, Historia Anglorum: The History of the English People* (Oxford, 1996), p. 32).

111   Roberts (ed.), *Cyfranc Lludd a Llefelys*, p. 3.

site was charged with an arcane property which denied the Fomoire means of eavesdropping on the discussion.[112]

Grellach Dollaid has been identified with a spot named Grallagh Greenan, near Lower Iveagh.[113] However, the parenthesis 'so that Grellach Dollaid is called the *Amrún* of the Men of the Goddess' suggests that the geographical identification originated in a gloss assigning a location to *Amhrún Fer nDéa*. In *Tochmarc Emire* ('The Wooing of Emer'), Cú Chulainn travels to meet his lovely Emer by way of a series of what are clearly Otherworld locations, one of which is named *amrún fer ndéa*.[114] This suggests that the secret conference at which Lug and the Túatha Dé Danann concerted measures for the destruction of the Fomoire was originally to be found on the marges of the Otherworld.

The parallel with the Welsh story is clear. In each case, on the eve of battle against the country's assailants, the god Lug concerts magical measures designed to effect their overthrow, in circumstances of exceptional secrecy ensuring their concealment from the ubiquitous foe. The consultation of the paired gods is conducted at sea, midway between Britain and France. As France in this context stands for the Otherworld, it seems that originally the Welsh tradition, like the Irish, located the encounter on the frontier between this world and the Other.

Here, it is the Welsh version of the event which can be seen to have shed its originally magical propensities, which have become rationalized into a purely material precaution (use of the long horn). That this is what occurred is further indicated by inconsistencies in the narrative. The precise wording of the passage is telling:

> And when Lludd told his brother the reason for his mission, Lleuelys said that he already knew why he had come to these lands. Then they took joint council as to how they could conduct their discussion differently, in order that the wind might not carry their speech and the Coraniaid discover what they said. And then Lleuelys caused a long bronze horn (*corn hir o euyd*) to be made, and they talked through the horn …

The conference implicitly occurs during the brothers' meeting on shipboard in the midst of the English Channel, concluding as it does with the words, 'And then Lludd returned again to his own country' (*Ac yna yd ymchoeles Llud dracheuyn y wlat*). The ingenious precaution instituted by Lleuelys to prevent the Coraniaid from intercepting the conference is curious, being unparalleled elsewhere in Welsh and Irish literature. The fact that three manuscripts of the early Llanstephan MS 1 *Brut* version of the story omit this factor suggests that it likewise puzzled mediæval audiences.[115]

Obvious incongruities suggest themselves. Since Lleu was already apprised of Lludd's predicament, why did he not bring the horn with him from the outset? Were there facilities on

---

112   Gray (ed.), *Cath Maige Tuired*, p. 42; Edward Gwynn (ed.), *The Metrical Dindshenchas* (Dublin, 1903–35), iv, p. 302.

113   Gray (ed.), *Cath Maige Tuired*, p. 95. *Grellach Dolluid* is named as a spot to which Cú Chulainn withdrew during his combat with Fergus mac Róich (John Strachan and J. G. O'Keefe (ed.), *The Táin Bó Cúailnge from the Yellow Book of Lecan with Variant Readings from the Lebor na Huidre* (Dublin, 1912), p. 77; R. I. Best and Osborn Bergin (ed.), *Lebor na Huidre: Book of the Dun Cow* (Dublin, 1929), p. 206). Again, it was at Grellach Dolluid that Cú Chulainn held his tryst with the Irish war-goddess Mórrígan (Johan Corthals (ed.), *'Táin Bó Regamna' und 'Táin Bó Flidais'* (Hamburg, 1979), pp. 68–69).

114   A. G. van Hamel (ed.), *Compert Con Culainn and Other Stories* (Dublin, 1933), p. 26.

115   Roberts (ed.), *Cyfranc Lludd a Llefelys*, p. 11.

board ship for construction of such an instrument? Why does the author emphasize its being 'a *long* bronze horn' (*corn hir o euyd*), when one of normal size might be considered more apt for the purpose?

It looks as though the horn was introduced at some stage of the story's transmission as rationalization of an earlier version, in which king and god encrypted their conversation by means of a mysterious precaution no longer understood. That the horn was 'long' may reflect a literalistic intimation of the cosmic gulf dividing the worlds of gods and men. In a similar situation, the Norse god Thor struggled in vain to drain the giant Útgarðaloki's horn, which the latter then revealed to be connected to the ocean. Despite Thor's apparent failure, it was found that his herculean effort had brought the tidal ebb and flow into existence.

> Thor looked at the horn, and it did not seem all that big, although *it was rather long* (*Þórr lítr á hornit, ok sýnist ekki mikit ok er þó heldr langt*).

Plainly, the horn, whose contents must formerly have represented a microcosmic counterpart of the sea, was accorded exceptional length in a rationalizing attempt to account for the link between the two.[116]

It has been seen that identification of Lleuelys's homeland with France represents a relocation of what was originally the Otherworld, which was frequently conceived as being separated from this by water.[117] In *Cath Maige Tuired*, it is evident that Lug has arrived from the Otherworld, when he first requests entry to the court of Núadu at Tara. He declares himself to be foster son of Tailtiu (a pagan goddess), daughter of *Magmór rí Espáine*. Both *Mag Mór* ('the great plain') and *Espáin* (Spain) are attested locations of the Irish pagan Otherworld.[118]

It might be thought inconsistent that Lleuelys should travel from the Otherworld to meet Lludd, who was after all himself also a deity (Nudd). However, in the story Lludd has been recast as an historical king of Britain under the influence of Geoffrey of Monmouth's account of the reign of 'king' Lud. Similarly, when the Irish story *Baile in Scáil* describes Conn's visit to the palace of Lug, Conn is depicted as king of Tara, while Lug is unmistakably a god dwelling in an Otherworld palace. Yet Conn, like Lludd, was originally a god.[119]

The 'devil' in the horn

Next may be considered associated details, which are unique to the Welsh account of the consultation between king and god:

---

116 Anthony Faulkes (ed.), *Snorri Sturluson: Edda; Prologue and Gylfaginning* (Oxford, 1982), pp. 40–41, 43. A comparable belief is recorded of the Irish god Dagda, whose *drochta* (tub) leaked during incoming tides, and ceased doing so at their ebb (Best, Bergin, O'Brien, and O'Sullivan (ed.), *The Book of Leinster*, p. 700).

117 Lowry Charles Wimberly, *Folklore in the English & Scottish Ballads* (Chicago, 1928), pp. 108–110.

118 W. J. Gruffydd, *Math vab Mathonwy: An Inquiry into the Origins and Development of the Fourth Branch of the Mabinogi with the Text and a Translation* (Cardiff, 1928), pp. 177, 178.

119 'Here Conn is merely king of Tara, and as a mortal he no longer possesses the power of seeing into the future; hence it is necessary to transport him to the Otherworld in order that the future may be revealed to him' (Thomas F. O'Rahilly, *Early Irish History and Mythology* (Dublin, 1946), p. 283).

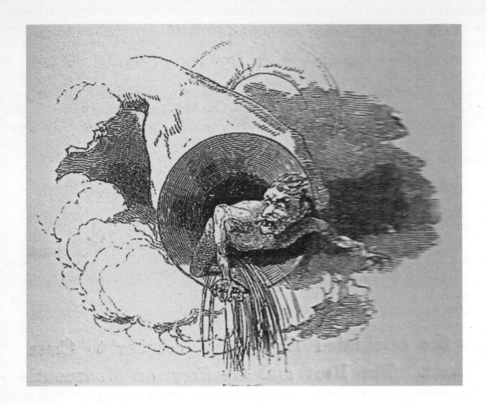

Fanciful impression of the devil in the horn.[121]

> But whatever speech one of them uttered through the horn, only odious (*atcas*), contrary
> (*gwrthwyneb*) speech was heard by the other. When Lleuelys saw that, and that a demon
> (*kythreul*) was obstructing them and creating turmoil in the horn (*ac yn teruyscu trwy y
> corn*), he had wine poured into the horn to cleanse it. By virtue of the wine (*y gwin*), the
> demon was driven out.[120]

There are three component elements to this episode.

1. Their conversation was initially unintelligible.
2. This proved to be caused by a devil concealed in the horn.
3. The obstruction was removed by pouring wine into the pipe.

It is possible that the author understood this curious little episode little better than
modern scholars, none of whom appears to have attempted an explanation. It is best to
consider the three elements independently, before assessing what sense may be made of the
composite text.

The requirement that the conference be conducted in secret corresponds to the episode in
Cath Maige Tuired, in which, on the eve of battle against the Fomoire, Lug and the druids of the

---

120 Roberts (ed.), *Cyfranc Lludd a Llefelys*, p. 3.

Túatha Dé Danann hold the secret conference called *Amhrún Fer nDéa*. In the text it has become located at an obscure location in the Irish countryside. However, the term *amrún* suggests that originally there obtained a supernatural factor, which protected the gods' discussion from being overheard by their adversaries.

In *Cyfranc Lludd a Lleuelys*, parallel means of maintaining the secrecy of mutual communications is provided by the material device of the long bronze horn, which conveys appearance of being a rationalization of an earlier occult recourse. However, nothing corresponding to the 'devil' is to be found in *Cath Maige Tuired*. In fact, his intrusion appears odd, not to say unaccountable. Brynley Roberts expressed a bafflement likely to have have been shared by readers in earlier centuries:

> There is, however, no suggestion in the *Cyfranc* that the Coranieid are dwarfs, unless it is presumed that one of their number was the 'devil' in the horn, and this is not explicit, even if the episode was part of the original tale.[122]

In fact, the devil is effectively disqualified from being one of the Coraniaid. It was entirely contrary to their interest to *prevent* the conspirators' speech from being understood, when their magical power was employed for the specific purpose of overhearing, and so frustrating, their adversaries' hostile intentions.

No other instance of this motif appear to be known. Brynley Roberts's concluding clause suggests his suspicion that the devil may not have been 'part of the original tale'. The explanation implied by the anonymous author, namely, that a devil covertly obtruded himself into the horn for the peevish purpose of distorting speech, is unconvincing. How had he managed to creep in unperceived? Who was he? By what method did he succeed in perverting the brothers' speech? What was his motive for so doing? That the nuisance is so readily overcome deprives the incident of dramatic effect.

Bearing these factors in mind, the passage describing the obstruction which initially prevented communication between him and Lleuelys is illuminating.

> But whatever speech one of them uttered through the horn, only odious (*atcas*), contrary (*gwrthwyneb*) speech was heard by the other. When Lleuelys saw that, and that a devil (*kythreul*) was obstructing them and creating turmoil in the horn (*ac yn teruyscu trwy y corn*) …

The repetitive terminology used to emphasize the brothers' frustrating inability to communicate (*atcas, gwrthwyneb, teruyscu*) is striking, and suggests an explanation for the unsatisfactory intrusion. The word used for the supernatural saboteur is *cythraul*, 'devil, demon', which derives from Latin *contrārius*. The same word gave rise to the Welsh adjective *cythrol*, 'adverse, contrary, hostile'.[123] Might it be that, in an earlier recension of the tale, this plethora of near-synonymous terms descriptive of confusion included the further apt term *cythrol*, which

---

121 Lady Charlotte Guest (tr.), *The Mabinogion from the Welsh of the Llyfr Coch o Hergest (the Red Book of Hergest) in the Library of Jesus College, Oxford* (London, 1877), p. 465. Interestingly, the artist shows the horn as emanating from outer space, rather than shared by two kings on board a ship.

122 Roberts (ed.), *Cyfranc Lludd a Llefelys*, p. xxxii.

123 *Geiriadur Prifysgol Cymru*, p. 826.

became subsequently misunderstood or misread as *cythraul*?[124] Such a modification could have occurred, either through simple error, or deliberately in order to account for the otherwise inexplicable obstruction to communication experienced by the protagonists of the tale.

A plausible explanation of the brothers' mutual incomprehensibility – one which requires no unaccountably intrusive 'devil' – is further suggested by the respective parts played by the protagonists. It has already been seen that, while the wise Lleuelys retains traits indicative of his earlier *divine* status, Lludd is recast as a fallible *mortal* king of Britain. Comparing further *Cyfranc Lludd a Lleuelys* with the Irish tale, *Baile in Scáil*, we find that the latter story likewise casts Lug (Welsh *Lleu*) in his authentic rôle of deity, while King Conn of Tara is the terrestrial ruler who seeks his aid. Although originally a divinity, Conn likewise became converted into a mortal ruler.

This distinction suggests a reason why king and god might initially have encountered an insurmountable barrier to mutual converse. There existed a widespread belief in early societies that gods speak a language distinct from that of humans. In the Icelandic *Alvíssmál*, the poet recapitulates alternative words used by paired categories of mortals and immortals,[125] as do Homer and other early Greek authors. Comparable distinction was drawn in Ireland between the language of poets (*berla filid*), who were ascribed access to the gods, and the speech of men.[126] Citing the arcane druidic tract 'The Colloquy of the Two Sages' (*Immacallam in dá Thuarad*), the author of the prologue to the legal code *Senchas Már* commented: 'Dark was the speech which the poets spoke in that case, and the judgement which they gave was not clear to the princes.'[127]

This belief in distinct languages ascribed gods and men, widespread in early societies, has been comprehensively studied by Calvert Watkins and Françoise Bader.[128]

The Irish grammatical tract *Auraicept na n-Éces* and other mediæval sources indicate that the concept of distinct languages of gods and men existed in early Ireland.[129] Stefan Zimmer has recently shown that the Irish Life of Saint Brigid (*Bethu Brigte*) accords the Saint a peculiar style of direct speech, which he identifies as a characteristic retained from her prior status as pagan goddess.[130] This factor probably accounts for the belief that Welsh fairies were believed to speak

124 Two manuscripts of the *Brutiau* employ the abstract noun *cythreulaeth* ('devilry, fiendishness') to describe the obstruction: *Ac adnabot o Lewelis ryûynet* **cythreûliaeth** *yn y corn. Ac o rinwedd y gwin mynet* **cythreûliaeth** *or corn* (Roberts (ed.), *Cyfranc Lludd a Llefelys*, p. 11). It seems unlikely they would have ignored the colourful 'devil', had they been apprized of his existence.

125 Hans Kuhn and Gustav Neckel (ed.), *Edda: Die Lieder des Codex Regius nebst Verwandten Denkmälern* (Heidelberg, 1962–68), i, pp. 81–86; West (ed.), *Hesiod: Theogony*, pp. 386–88.

126 Christian-J. Guyonvarc'h, *Le Dialogue des deux sages* (Paris, 1999), pp. 20–21.

127 John Carey, 'An Edition of the Pseudo-Historical Prologue to the '*Senchas Már*', *Ériu* (1994), xlv, p. 19. A similar instance, involving the bafflement of a student (*gilla*) when addressed in the *berla filid* by a seer (*éices*), is recorded in the early ninth-century Glossary of Cormac (Bergin, Best, Meyer, and O'Keefe (ed.), *Anecdota from Irish Manuscripts*, iv, pp. 69–70).

128 Calvert Watkins, 'Language of Gods and Language of Men: Remarks on Some Indo-European Metalinguistic Traditions', in Jaan Puhvel (ed.), *Myth and Law among the Indo-Europeans: Studies in Indo-European Comparative Mythology* (Berkeley and Los Angeles, 1970), pp. 1–17; Françoise Bader, *La langue des dieux, ou l'hermétisme des poètes indo-européens* (Pisa, 1989), pp. 189–272.

129 Puhvel (ed.), *Myth and Law among the Indo-Europeans*, pp. 8–16.

130 Stefan Zimmer, 'Weiblich? Heilig? Göttlich? Zur Diktion der Hl. Brigid', in Gabriele Uelsberg, Michael Schmauder, and Stefan Zimmer (ed.), *Kelten am Rhein: Akten des dreizehnten Internationalen Keltologiekongresses* (Mainz am Rhein, 2009), ii, pp. 319–27.

a language distinct from that of mankind. This was described in the twelfth century by Giraldus Cambrensis: a belief that survived into the nineteenth in folklore tradition.[131]

The same author describes a category of Welsh prophets, known as *awenyddion*. Their vaticinations were declaimed while in a state of inspired frenzy, and appeared incoherent to those who witnessed them. Once the mantic fit had passed, they retained no recollection of what they had uttered. Visions and dreams were the source of their inspiration. The alien tongue in which their prophecies were uttered probably corresponded to the *berla filid* of Irish bards.[132]

It is possible that the epithet *Lletieith* ('half-speech') borne by the British sea-god Llŷr reflects his use of divine speech,[133] the ocean being regarded as source of wisdom, and the murmur of its waves an expression of divine utterance.[134] Similarly, Cían, father of the god Lug, bore the alternative name scál balb ('stammering spirit'), which was 'doubtless with reference to his foreign tongue'.[135] Also analogous is the widely-held conception, recorded on both sides of the Irish Sea, that the inhabitants of the Otherworld (i.e. the dead) cannot converse with mortals.[136] The Welsh poem *Preiddeu Annwfn* ('The Spoils of Annwfn') declares that it was 'difficult' to hold speech (*anhaᴐd ymadraᴐd*) with the watchman of an Otherworld stronghold.[137] This suggests a problem with mutual understanding, rather than an insurmountable wall of silence.

This widespread belief in distinct divine and human languages is likely to have existed among the pagan Celts of Gaul, and hence their cousins in Britain, given close relations between the druids of both nations attested by Caesar. Describing Gaulish society in the first century BC, Diodorus Siculus wrote:

> They have also certain philosophers (φιλόσοφοί) and theologians (θεολόγοι), whom they term druids (δρουίδας) … Their custom is that no one should offer sacrifice without a philosopher (φιλόσοφος); for they say that thanks should be offered to the gods by those skilled in the divine nature, on the assumption that they were people who can speak their language, and through them likewise they hold that benefits should be asked.[138]

The assertion that the druids 'were people who can speak their [the gods'] language' might be taken to mean no more than that they were professionally qualified to communicate with the gods. However, in view of widespread evidence for ascription of differing tongues to gods and humans, it is likely that druidic learning included understanding of the divine language.

The largest Romano-British pagan temple yet discovered is situated at Lydney in Gloucestershire, overlooking the Severn estuary. Inscriptions attest to its dedication to the

---

131   J. S. Brewer, James F. Dimock, and George F. Warner (ed.), *Giraldi Cambrensis Opera* (London, 1861–91), vi, pp. 77–78; John Rhŷs, *Celtic Folklore: Welsh and Manx* (Oxford, 1901), pp. 269–79, 660.

132   Brewer, Dimock, and Warner (ed.), *Giraldi Cambrensis Opera*, vi, pp. 194–95.

133   Rachel Bromwich (ed.), *Trioedd Ynys Prydein: The Welsh Triads* (Cardiff, 1978), p. 427.

134   Joseph Falaky Nagy, *The Wisdom of the Outlaw: The Boyhood Deeds of Finn in Gaelic Narrative Tradition* (Los Angeles, 1985), pp. 162–63.

135   *Cían mac Déin Checht .i. Scál Balb ainm aile dó* (Best, Bergin, O'Brien, and O'Sullivan (ed.), *The Book of Leinster*, i, p. 34). Cf. Myles Dillon and Nora Chadwick, *The Celtic Realms* (London, 1967), p. 143.

136   Arthur C. L. Brown, *The Origin of the Grail Legend* (Cambridge, Mass., 1943), pp. 127–28; O'Rahilly, *Early Irish History and Mythology*, p. 493; Proinsias Mac Cana, *Celtic Mythology* (London, 1970), p. 129.

137   Gwenogvryn Evans (ed.), *Facsimile & Text of the Book of Taliesin*, p. 55.

138   J. J. Tierney, 'The Celtic Ethnography of Posidonius', *Proceedings of the Royal Irish Academy* (Dublin, 1960), lx, p. 228 = p. 251. 'The Druids in Diodorus are 'philosophers and theologians', 'skilled in the divine nature' and able to communicate with the gods' (Stuart Piggott, *The Druids* (London, 1968), p. 119).

British god Nodens, whose name evolved into Welsh *Nudd*, the Lludd of *Cyfranc Lludd a Lleuelys*. On the floor of the main temple building was discovered this large and handsome mosaic inscription:

D[eo] M[arti] N[odonti] T[itvs] FLAVIVS SENILIS PR[aepositvs] REL[igionis] EX STIPIBVS POS‹S›VIT | O[pitu]LANTE [...] VICTORINO INTERPI[e]TIANTE.
To the god Mars Nodens, Titus Flavius Senilis, superintendent of the cult, from the offerings had this laid, with the assistance of Victorinus, interpreter.[139]

The office of Victorinus was initially explained by R. G. Collingwood as that of official interpreter to the Roman fleet based in the Bristol Channel. Subsequently, R. P. Wright more convincingly accounted for his rôle as that of 'interpreter of dreams'. This reflects the fact that the temple functioned, in part at least, as a place of incubation, where visitors sought revelations from dreams.[140] (It may incidentally be wondered whether the *interpres* was not a druid, as was probably the *librarius* who interpreted the dream of St Samson's mother in similar circumstances a century or so later.)

The mosaic inscription is interrupted by a prominent circular entry point, which provided access to a clay funnel descending into the earth below. This was evidently designed to provide means of pouring libations to the god.[141] This suggests that a primary duty of the *interpres* was that of facilitating communication between visiting votaries and the presiding deity.[142]

The corresponding functionary at Greek oracular cult shrines was the *prophetes* (προφάτας): 'one who speaks for a god and interprets his will to man', an 'interpreter, expounder of the μάντις [seer]'.[143] Much is known of his rôle, which may throw some light on the part played by the less well-documented Lydney *interpres*. At Delphi, for example,

The *Prophetes*, who had already received the enquirer's question in verbal or written form, put it to the Pythia [priestess], and conveyed the answer back. Whether the enquirer himself could hear distinctly what the Pythia said is never stated, for our authorities draw no distinction between the answer as spoken by her and as conveyed by the *Prophetes*, and yet it is clear that he was responsible for reducing it to form. The references to the Pythia's voice often imply that she did not speak in ordinary tones, but cried or shouted. This circumstance would be quite consistent with a trance state. One may suppose, too, that her replies may have been confused and incoherent. It was the business, then, of the *Prophetes* to make sense from them and to reproduce them in verse.[144]

---

139 R. E. M. Wheeler and T. V. Wheeler, *Report on the Excavation of the Prehistoric, Roman, and Post-Roman Site in Lydney Park, Gloucestershire* (Oxford, 1932), pp. 102–4, plate XIX; S. S. Frere and R. S. O. Tomlin (ed.), *The Roman Inscriptions of Britain: Volume II Instrumentum Domesticum; Fascicule 4* (Stroud, 1992), p. 84.

140 *Britannia* (London, 1985), xvi, pp. 248–49. Cf. Wheeler and Wheeler, *Report on the Excavation of the Prehistoric, Roman, and Post-Roman Site in Lydney Park*, pp. 49–52; M. J. T. Lewis, *Temples in Roman Britain* (Cambridge, 1966), p. 89. For incubation among the Celts, cf. Fernand Benoit, *Le symbolisme dans les sanctuaires de la Gaule* (Brussels, 1970), pp. 23–24, 61–62, 103; Bernhard Maier, *Die Religion der Kelten: Götter – Mythen – Weltbild* (Munich, 2001), p. 130.

141 Ibid., p. 28.

142 *Interpres*, 'an interpreter (of omens, oracles, dreams, etc.)', P. G. W. Glare (ed.), *Oxford Latin Dictionary* (Oxford, 1968–82), p. 947.

143 Henry George Liddell and Robert Scott, *A Greek-English Lexicon* (Oxford, 1940), p. 1540.

144 H. W. Parke, *Greek Oracles* (London, 1967), p. 84. Cf. Joseph Fontenrose, *Python: A Study of Delphic Myth and its Origins* (Berkeley and Los Angeles, 1959), pp. 218–19.

The *prophetes* is represented in the sources as delivering a translation of the Pythia's response in Greek verse (usually hexameters),[145] her utterances being declaimed in a language unintelligible to the lay visitor. Although it is not expressly stated that she employed the language of the gods, it is reasonable to assume that such was the case. After all, her function was not to speak in her own person, but as the mouth of Apollo, who like his fellow Olympians was known to speak a tongue distinct from that of men. In fact, he was more likely than most Greek gods to have spoken an alien language, since he was held to be an outsider originating among the Hyperboreans of the North, whom Diodorus Siculus (citing Hecataeus of Abdera) records possessed a language peculiar to themselves.[146]

It seems likely, therefore, that Victorinus, the *interpres* at Lydney, fulfilled a function comparable to that of the *prophetes* at Delphi. He it was, presumably, who poured the libation into the funnel of the mosaic pavement of the temple, as an offering to the presiding deity Nodens. Having obtained the goodwill of the god in the accustomed manner, he expounded the god's response to the pilgrim's enquiry, presumably rendered into Latin or British.

Finally, this ritual artefact in the Lydney temple recalls the 'long horn', which enabled Lludd to communicate with the former divinity Lleuelys in *Cyfranc Lludd a Lleuelys*. Whereas in the Brut versions of the tale the instrument is termed simply *cor hir*, 'long horn', in the storyteller's version it becomes 'a long bronze horn' (*corn hir o euyd*). It is possible that his reflects no more than a storyteller's embroidery. Equally, it conceivably represents an attempt to rationalize what is certainly a puzzling factor in the exchange. While *corn hir* could refer to a musical instrument or drinking vessel, it may also signify a long shaft, as found in the Anglesey placename Corn Hir, 'Long Chimney'.[147] Could this have been the means of communication between god and king in an earlier version of the story?

Purgation by wine

Next, it may be enquired whence derived the peculiar detail of the pouring of wine through the horn to ensure expulsion of the 'devil'? I can discover no instance of wine being employed for the purpose described, i.e. purgation of an evil spirit from a vessel.[148] On the other hand, its very incongruity suggests that it was present in the story in an earlier form. That there existed an obstruction to communication at the outset seems clear, and for the story to proceed as it does, some means for its removal must also have been included. Had another method of effecting its disposal been described, there could be no reason to replace it with the puzzling purgative wine.

In fact, removal of the incongruous 'devil' suggests an answer. What remains is a king who, unable to converse freely with a deity, pours wine into a funnel: an action which facilitates communication without further hindrance. In this context, the wine could have originated in a

---

145 E. R. Dodds, *The Greeks and the Irrational* (Berkeley and Los Angeles, 1951), pp. 92–93; H. W. Parke and D. E. W. Wormell, *The Delphic Oracle* (Oxford, 1956), i, pp. 30–34.

146 C. H. Oldfather (ed.), *Diodorus of Sicily* (London, 1933–67), ii, p. 38. For the Hyperborean origin of Apollo, cf. Arthur Bernard Cook, *Zeus: A Study in Ancient Religion* (Cambridge, 1914–40), ii, pp. 459–65; Dodds, *The Greeks and the Irrational*, pp. 141, 161–62.

147 Gwilym T. Jones and Tomos Roberts, *Enwau Lleoedd Môn* (Bangor, 1996), p. 36.

148 The mediæval ballad of *King Arthur and the King of Cornwall* describes a horn that cannot be sounded until a powder 'blent' with 'warme sweet milke' be poured into it (John W. Hales and Frederick J. Furnivall (ed.), *Bishop Percy's Folio Manuscript. Ballads and Romances* (London, 1867–68), i, p. 373). This however bears scant resemblance to the account in *Cyfranc Lludd a Lleuelys*, where the horn is not one intended to be sounded; nor in the ballad is it suggested that it was inhabited by any sort of demon. The ballad recipe is evidently a form of simple charm.

libation to the deity, whose acceptance of the offering ensures his receptive beneficence. Such a rite recurs in religious ceremonies throughout the ancient world.[149] Thus, we have on the one hand a story recounting how communication is established between Lleuelys in the Otherworld and the British royal divinity Lludd, in consequence of wine being poured through a funnel connecting the two. On the other, there was a funnel in the temple of Nodens (> *Nudd/Lludd*), whose purpose was to channel libations establishing contact between a mortal interlocutor and the temple deity.

It was not unusual for temples to be provided with channels sunk in earth or rock, into which sacrificial liquid was poured to a god residing in the nether world. It was comparison with similar funnels at temples at Pesch (Rhineland) and the Bakcheion at Athens that led the excavators of Lydney to the conclusion that 'it was presumably used for carrying libations into the earth'.

The foregoing considerations serve to explain apparently untoward circumstances attendant on the conversation through the horn recounted in *Cyfranc Lludd a Lleuelys*. Originally Lleuelys was a divinity (Lug), dwelling in the Otherworld. In time his realm became identified with France, the Celtic Otherworld being frequently envisaged as lying beyond or beneath the sea. (In this case, as has been seen, the choice was further influenced by the assumption that *Lleu* was a Welsh version of the French royal name *Louis*.) At the same time, Lludd, who was likewise originally a divinity, had become converted into an historical king of Britain, who succeeded his father Beli on the throne and rebuilt London.[150] The brothers' consultation in the Channel, midway between their respective kingdoms, represents further rationalization of an encounter which, at a prior stage in the story's evolution, took place at a liminal juncture where the earthly kingdom of Lludd adjoined the Otherworld realm of Lleu(elys).[151]

---

149 Cf. Benveniste, *Le vocabulaire des institutions indo-européennes*, ii, pp. 209–21; Walter Burkert, *Structure and History in Greek Mythology and Ritual* (Berkeley and Los Angeles, 1979), pp. 41–43; idem, *Greek Religion* (Cambridge, Mass., 1985), pp. 35–36, 70–73; Leslie Kurke, 'Pouring Prayers: A Formula of IE Sacral Poetry', *The Journal of Indo-European Studies* (Washington, 1989), xvii, pp. 113–25; Vassilis Lambrinoudakis and Jean Ch. Balty (ed.), *Thesaurus Cultus et Rituum Antiquorum* (Los Angeles, 2004-6), i, pp. 237–53; plates 56–62.

150 Henry of Huntingdon's account of Beli, Caswallawn and Lludd as successive kings of Britain indicates that their absorption into the British pseudo-historical tradition predates Geoffrey of Monmouth's work (Roberts (ed.), *Cyfranc Lludd a Lefelys*, pp. xiii–xv).

151 In *Baile in Scáil*, Conn encounters Lug in an enchanted mist just beyond the rampart of his stronghold at Tara.

13

The Three Oppressions of the Island of Britain

The calendrical framework of the Three Oppressions

Although *Cyfranc Lludd a Lleuelys* describes how Britain was afflicted by three Oppressions (*teir gormes*), it has been seen that originally there were but two – possibly one. The expansion of two *gormes* into three arose in consequence of the familiar Celtic practice of classifying themes in triadic groupings.[1] The supernatural power of hearing possessed by the Coraniaid cannot of itself have represented a *gormes*, since it bears no intimation of having inflicted any harm on the population of Britain. It became converted into a *gormes* when the tale became artificially recast in the traditional format of a triad of scourges.[2] At the same time, the Coraniaid were presumably present in an earlier version, given their sinister rôle in Welsh tradition as supernatural oppressors of Britain.

It is noteworthy that both true Oppressions (the lethal scream and the theft of comestibles from the royal courts) are specified as occurring *at night*. The first was heard each May Eve, while the second took place 'about the third watch of the night' (*am y tryded wylua o'r nos*). Not only this, but they were clearly envisaged as occurring *every year*. We are told that the first was heard every May Eve (*pob nos Kalan Mei*), while the third implicitly occurred *on a particular night of each year*, since the king was enabled to anticipate the event when adopting precautions his brother prescribed for its frustration.

While the Calends of May represented a festival of hope marking the beginning of summer in the Celtic calendar, both it and its eve were paradoxically characterized also as an occasion of fear, when malevolent hosts from the Otherworld menaced the survival of Britain and her people. That May Eve was a date associated with danger to the kingdom, in the event narrowly averted, is evinced by an episode in the First Branch of the *Mabinogi*, *Pwyll Pendeuic Dyuet*. Teyrnon king of Gwent, possessed a mare, more lovely than any horse or mare in his kingdom. Every May Eve (note the significant recurrence of the event) she was delivered of a colt, which as promptly disappeared. Eventually, when the anniversary once again came round, Teyrnon decided to maintain nocturnal watch. He had the mare brought into the house and watched while she gave birth to a magnificent foal. At that instant a terrible claw darted through the window and seized the foal by the mane.

---

1   Rachel Bromwich (ed.), *Trioedd Ynys Prydein: The Welsh Triads* (Cardiff, 1978), pp. lxiii–xiv.

2   Saint Beuno countered *teir gormes*, which implicitly threatened dearth of food and drink (Elissa R. Henken, *Traditions of the Welsh Saints* (Cambridge, 1987), pp. 82–83).

Teyrnon promptly hacked off the sinister visitant's arm at the elbow with his sword. At the same moment an eldritch shriek (*twrwf a diskyr*) pierced the night air. Dashing outside in pursuit, he swiftly recalled that he had left the door open, and returned in haste. There, beside the door, he discovered swaddled in a mantle of brocaded silk a baby boy of exceptional growth. Teyrnon and his queen adopted the child, who subsequently proved to be son of the Otherworld lord Pwyll and his queen Rhiannon, who named him Pryderi.[3]

The personal names are significant. *Rhiannon* derives from British **Rīgantonā*, 'Great Queen' (i.e. the sovereignty goddess),[4] while *Teyrnon* is from **Tigernonos*, 'the Great King'.[5] Unfortunately, this has led to much speculative discussion of Rhiannon and Teyrnon as paired divinities: the supreme God and Goddess of the Brittonic pantheon. This is incompatible with the text, which is the sole source in which the two figures appear together. The story unequivocally depicts Rhiannon as possessed of the attributes of a goddess, while Teyrnon is the mortal ruler of an earthly realm: 'At that time, Teyrnon Twrf Liant was lord over Gwent Is Coed [a principality in what is now Monmouthshire], and he was the best man in the world.' As Jessica Hemming emphasizes: 'There is no reason to suppose, from the story as we have it, that Teyrnon had any divine attributes.'[6] He was not, as is sometimes implied, the husband of Rhiannon. Teyrnon is wedded to a mortal queen, who though unnamed plays a minor but nonetheless significant part in the tale. Rhiannon's husband is explicitly identified as Pwyll, who was like her a deity ('Pwyll, Head of the Underworld'), while Gwri (later Pryderi) is expressly stated to have been their son.

The etymology of Teyrnon's name, 'the Great King', together with his description as 'the best man in the world' identify him as an exemplary (possibly archetypal) *earthly* monarch, whose supposititious child is the product of a parturition occurring in the Otherworld.

The unexplained association of the nativity of Gwri/Pryderi with that of a colt recalls the birth-tale of the Irish hero Cú Chulainn, in which two colts are born in the same moment as the Irish hero.[7] While the link between the births is left unexplained, it most likely reflects the close association found in Celtic and Indo-European traditions between horse/mare and king/queen.[8]

---

3   R. L. Thomson (ed.), *Pwyll Pendeuic Dyuet: The First of the Four Branches of the Mabinogi edited from the White Book of Rhydderch with variants from the Red Book of Hergest* (Dublin, 1957), pp. 18–19.

4   John T. Koch, 'A Welsh Window on the Iron Age: Manawydan, Mandubracios', *Cambridge Medieval Celtic Studies* (Cambridge, 1987), xiv, p. 34; Stefan Zimmer, 'Die altkymrischen Frauennamen. Ein erster Einblick', in Joseph F. Eska, R. Geraint Gruffydd, and Nicolas Jacobs (ed.), *Hispano-Gallo-Brittonica: Essays in honour of Professor D. Ellis Evans on the occasion of his sixty-fifth birthday* (Cardiff, 1995), pp. 324–25.

5   W. J. Gruffydd, *Rhiannon: An Inquiry into the Origins of the First and Third Branches of the Mabinogi* (Cardiff, 1953), pp. 99–100; Eric P. Hamp, 'Mabinogi', *The Transactions of the Honourable Society of Cymmrodorion: Sessions 1974 and 1975* (London, 1975), pp. 245, 248.

6   'Ancient Tradition or Authorial Invention? The "Mythological" Names in the Four Branches', in Joseph Falaky Nagy (ed.), *Myth in Celtic Literatures* (Dublin, 2007), p. 89.

7   A. G. van Hamel (ed.), *Compert Con Culainn and Other Stories* (Dublin, 1933), pp. 4–5. Cf. Françoise Le Roux, 'La Conception de Cúchulainn', *Ogam: Tradition Celtique* (Rennes, 1965), xvii, pp. 406–8.

8   Cf. Wolfgang Meid, 'The Indo-Europeanization of Old European Concepts', *The Journal of Indo-European Studies* (Washington, 1989), xvii, pp. 297–307; Edgar C. Polomé, 'Das Pferd in der Religion der eurasischen Völker', in Bernhard Hänsel and Stefan Zimmer (ed.), *Die Indogermanen und das Pferd: Akten des Internationalen interdisziplinären Kolloquiums Freie Universität Berlin, 1.-3. Juli 1992* (Budapest, 1994), pp. 48–49; Helmut Birkhan, *Kelten: Versuch einer Gesamtdarstellung ihrer Kultur* (Vienna, 1997), pp. 541–44. Rhiannon is first encountered by Pwyll riding a white mare, which led some scholars to identify her with the Celtic horse-goddess Epona (Gruffydd, *Rhiannon*, pp. 103–5; Paul-Marie Duval, *Les dieux de la Gaule* (Paris, 1957), p. 47).

In *Pwyll*, the terrible hand and claw represent an intrusive folklore motif.[9] Setting that aside, we are left with what is effectively an attempted abduction of a royal heir by a malignant Otherworld figure on May Eve, and the infant's rescue by the king. Given the fact that kings in Celtic societies personified the enduring fruitfulness and security of the land, an obvious parallel exists between the episode in *Pwyll*, and the second *gormes* in *Cyfranc Lludd a Lleuelys*, which afflicted the land with universal dearth. Each is prefaced by that uncanny clamour (*twrwf a diskyr, diaspat*) which customarily heralded a hostile Otherworld irruption in early Welsh tradition; each threatens the continuing well-being of the kingdom; and each recurs on May Eve.

Furthermore, each is eventuated by royal intervention, likewise effected on May Eve. In *Pwyll*, King Teyrnon frustrates the intruder's assault by means of physical violence. However, this aspect represents a later stage in the tale's evolution, when what must earlier have been a magical contest was replaced by the folklore theme of a child's attempted abduction by hand or claw, frustrated by the king's trusty blade. The element of enchantment is retained in *Cyfranc Lludd a Lleuelys*, despite being confused by the author's pardonable difficulty in understanding the significance of the sprinkling of the *pryfed*-impregnated water.

That the third *gormes* is represented as occurring on a comparable night of peril, when the wealth of the kingdom is again threatened with destruction at the hands of an Otherworld power, points to its occurrence at November Eve, *nos Galan Gaeaf*. This was the famous night when the gates of the Otherworld were opened wide, disgorging its infernal denizens to wreak destruction on the world of men.

If, as the story relates, this universal blight occurred *every* May Eve and (implicitly) *every* November Eve, it follows that it was effectively countered on each date annually. Appropriate prophylactic measures had been imparted to Lludd (the king) by Lleuelys (the god) in the primal time, which were thereafter put into effect by the king at annual festivals commemorating the two original theophanies.

The 'first' gormes: the Coraniaid

Why the Coraniaid constituted an Oppression is left unexplained in *Cyfranc Lludd a Lleuelys*, since allusion is made only to their supernatural power of hearing, which protected them from any hostile move by those who opposed them. The purely defensive nature of this faculty (*kynedyf*) provides insufficient grounds for their being considered a *gormes*.[10] Nevertheless, it seems that the threat posed to the island of Britain by the Coraniaid was matter of common knowledge among mediæval Welsh bards. A triad records

> *Teir gormes a doeth yr enys hon. Ac nyt aeth ur un drachevyn. Un onadunt kywda6t y corranyeit. A doethant eman yn oes caswalla6n m. beli. Ac o avia pan hanoedynt.*
>
> Three Oppressions that came to this Island ... One of them (was) the people of the Coraniaid, who came here in the time of Caswallawn mab Beli. And they came from Arabia.[11]

---

9   George Lyman Kittredge, 'Arthur and Gorlagon', *Studies and Notes in Philology and Literature* (Boston, 1903), viii, pp. 222–45, 275; Alexander Heggarty Krappe, *Balor With the Evil Eye: Studies in Celtic and French Literature* (Columbia, 1927), pp. 88–89; Kenneth Jackson, *The International Popular Tale and Early Welsh Tradition* (Cardiff, 1961), pp. 90, 91–95.

10   Math uab Mathonwy is ascribed this power, which he implicitly employs in a purely defensive capacity (Ian Hughes (ed.), *Math Uab Mathonwy: Pedwaredd Gainc y Mabinogi* (Aberystwyth, 2000), p. 1).

11   Rachel Bromwich, 'The Historical Triads: With Special Reference to Peniarth MS. 16', *The Bulletin of the Board of Celtic Studies* (Cardiff, 1946), xii, p. 14.

It is unclear how the Coraniaid came to be associated with Caswallawn.[12] It may be that the story catalogued in this triad originated an erroneous belief that he was ruler of the alien *gormes*. In *Branwen uerch Llŷr* and *Manawydan uab Llŷr* it is reported that the followers of the evil wizard Caswallawn ap Beli overran Britain during the absence of her king Bran in Ireland. When Pryderi proposes killing some of Caswallawn's subjects, Manawydan dissuades him with the warning that Caswallawn and his men would learn of the deed, and exact revenge.[13] This suggests a supernatural auditory power, enabling the oppressor and his followers to effect retribution in the event of their being attacked. This of course is precisely the quality accorded the Coraniaid in *Cyfranc Lludd a Lleuelys*. Given their association with Caswallawn in the triad, the 'followers' to whom Manawydan makes reference must surely have been the Coraniaid. All this confirms that their *gormes* represented a theme once familiar in Welsh mythological lore.[14]

The author of *Cyfranc Lludd a Lleuelys* was evidently puzzled to account for their rôle. Although described as a *gormes* dangerous to the Britons, in the event nothing is related of any harm they might have inflicted. All we learn is that they had arrived from another land to settle in Britain, that they could overhear every conversation borne to them on the wind, and that it was consequently (why?) requisite to destroy them utterly. To achieve this charitable end, they were required to be invited to an assembly with the Britons on pretext of arranging peace between the parties, where they would be selectively annihilated by means of a mysterious potion.

The mode of collecting the Coraniaid together suggests rationalization of a factor obscure to the author. Since the alien crew had no reason to believe themselves threatened, why should they feel drawn to the proposed peace conference? Why, when gathered together, were the rival races implicitly to be intermingled rather than assembled (as might naturally be expected) in separate bodies? How was the lethal showerbath to be deployed undetected by the Coraniaid? The lustration plainly puzzled the author. He appears to have had no idea what the *pryfed* were, nor why the water in which they were distilled should prove fatal to the foe, while sparing the indigenous inhabitants.

Cyfranc Lludd a Lleuelys retains an archaic element in the tradition which is elsewhere missing. Whereas in *Pwyll* the Otherworld raptor is personified as a single monstrous intruder, in *Cyfranc Lludd a Lleuelys* the threat is posed by a numberless swarm, identifiable only by means of a magical prophylactic (lustration by charged water). It is clear that the supernatural

---

12   'Caswallawn is made up of *cas*, "hateful," + *Galam*' (Arthur C. L. Brown, *The Origin of the Grail Legend* (Cambridge, Mass., 1943), p. 389). Although the etymology is untenable (Pierre-Yves Lambert, *La langue gauloise: Description linguistique, commentaire d'inscriptions choisies* (Paris, 1995), p. 193), it is not impossible that *cass*- evoked the epithet 'hateful', so influencing association of Caswallawn with the hostile Coraniaid.

13   Ian Hughes (ed.), *Manawydan Uab Llyr: Trydedd Gainc y Mabinogi* (Cardiff, 2007), p. 4.

14   It has been thought that the Coraniaid are further to be identified with the mischief-making *Korrigan* (plural *Korriganed*) of Breton folklore (cf. Vicomte Hersart de la Villemarqué (ed.), *Barzaz Breiz: Chants Populaires de la Bretagne* (Paris, 1867), pp. li-lix). The latter's baleful qualities included concern to inflict widespread suffering on mankind (Walter Yeeling Evans Wentz, *The Fairy-Faith in Celtic Countries: Its Psychological Origin and Nature* (Rennes, 1909), p. 110), and a capacity ten times greater than that of humans for gorging comestibles (Donatien Laurent, *Aux sources du Barzaz-Breiz: La mémoire d'un peuple* (Douarnenez, 1989), p. 88). A Korrigan uttered an uncannily terrifying scream from the deep (Anatole le Braz, *La légende de la mort chez les Bretons armoricains* (Paris, 1928), i, p. 404). These attributes bear obvious similarity to those ascribed the Coraniaid in Welsh tradition.

Coranaid, who arrived from an unidentified land and succeeded in infesting the entire island of Britain, represented an elemental threat to the kingdom's well-being.

Although described as a 'people' (*kenedyl*), the impression conveyed in the narrative is that of a malevolent swarming, invisible to the eye, which could only be countered by magical means. An early ninth-century Irish prayer implores protection against fog-borne demons (*ar demnaib na céo*). Paradigmatic threats posed by such ubiquitous supernatural foes of mankind ranged from foreign invasions and wars to plagues, fires, and famines.[15] The nebulous character of these eerie adversaries is well expressed in an Old English protective charm 'against the mighty terror that is hateful to everyone, against the evil thing that invades the land'.[16]

The author of *Cyfranc Lludd a Lleuelys* was plainly puzzled by the nature of the menace posed by the Coraniaid. He begins by explaining that their power of overhearing every conversation in the land protected them from harm – a purely defensive attribute. After describing the very real threats to the kingdom's well-being posed by the second and third *gormesoedd*, the author returns to the first:

[*Ac eyssoes kyhoed oed ac amlwg er ormes kyntaf,*] *a'r dwy ormes ereill nyt oed neb a wyppei pa ystyr oed uddunt, ac wrth hynny mwy gobeith oed kaffel gwaret o'r gyntaf noc oed o'r eil neu o'r dryded.*
[And nevertheless the first *gormes* was evident and plain,] but no one knew the cause of the other two *gormes*, and for that reason there was more hope of getting rid of the first than there was of the second or the third.[17]

This begs the question how the presence of the Coraniaid ever became known to the Britons, given the emphasis on their preternatural power of hearing, which enabled them to infest much of Britain undetected. Overall, it must again be emphasized that originally there were only two *gormesoedd*, each of which constituted a mysterious nocturnal annihilation of the wealth of the kingdom. The Coraniaid were it seems authors of both depredations (which in turn represent variants of the same threat), and over time their supernatural auditory power became separated into a distinct *gormes*. Hence arose the odd consideration that the first *gormes* in the story does not amount to an oppression at all: the Coraniaid had arrived in Britain, where their supernatural power of hearing protected *them* from oppression by *others*!

As has been seen, these anomalies must have arisen in consequence of the restructuring of the *gormesoedd* into a triad. The first is in reality not a *gormes* but a *cynneddf* ('innate quality'), while the second and third represent successive manifestations of the same menace: the attempted annihilation of the wealth of the kingdom of Britain every May Eve, and a repetition of this dire danger on a subsequent night, which can only have been November Eve.

---

15 Whitley Stokes and John Strachan (ed.), *Thesaurus Palaeohibernicus: A Collection of Old-Irish Glosses Scholia Prose and Verse* (Cambridge, 1901–3), ii, p. 256; Gerard Murphy (ed.), *Early Irish Lyrics: Eighth to Twelfth Century* (Oxford, 1956), p. 26; R. I. Best, Osborn Bergin, M.A. O'Brien, and Anne O'Sullivan (ed.), *The Book of Leinster Formerly Lebar na Núachongbála* (Dublin, 1954–83), p. 1619. St Brendan was prevented from landing at a harbour by swarms of black-faced devils and leprechauns (Whitley Stokes (ed.), *Lives of Saints from the Book of Lismore* (Oxford, 1890), p. 112).

16 *Wið þane grymma gryre, / wið þane micela egsa þe bið eghwam lað* (Elliott van Kirk Dobbie (ed.), *The Anglo-Saxon Minor Poems* (New York, 1942), p. 127).

17 The clause in square brackets is omitted in the Red Book of Hergest text, being supplied from Llanstephan MS 1 (Brynley F. Roberts (ed.), *Cyfranc Lludd a Llefelys* (Dublin, 1975), p. 10). The parenthesis is suggestive of bafflement on the part of the author of the extant text.

The charged water

The threat posed by the Coraniaid is inadequately accounted for, unless it be understood that it was they who were responsible for the plagues which follow. Yet more obscure are the measures expounded by Lleuelys to effect their extermination.

> And after their speech was unobstructed, Lleuelys told his brother that he would give him some *pryfed* and that he should keep some of them alive for breeding, in case by chance that sort of *gormes* came a second time, but he should take some others of the *pryfed* and crush them in water, and that he declared would be good for destroying the race of the Coraniaid. That is to say, after he returned home to his realm, he should summon all the people together, his people and the race of the Coraniaid, to one meeting on pretence of making peace between them, and when they were all together, he should take the charged water and pour it over one and all, and he averred that the water would poison the race of the Coraniaid and would not kill and would not harm anyone of his own race …
>
> And then Lludd returned again to his country and without delay he summoned every single one of his own people and the Coraniaid. And as Lleuelys had taught him, he crushed the *pryfed* in the water and poured it over one and all. And immediately all the Coraniaid were in this way destroyed without hurt to any of the Britons.[18]

At the inception of modern Celtic studies, Sir John Rhŷs declared himself bewildered by the nature of the 'charged water' (*dwuyr rinweddawl*), confessing that 'I do not profess to understand the story about the water'.[19] Nearly a century later Professor Brynley Roberts acknowledged similar bafflement, venturing only that 'I know of no parallel to the story of the insects crushed in water, but a possible comparison is the exorcizing of fairies by sprinkling holy water'.[20]

A solution to the mystery lies in recognizing that the episode comprises two distinct elements: (i) the lustration which distinguishes and destroys the Coraniaid; (ii) preservation of the *pryfed* provided by Lleuelys, whose function appears to have been as opaque to the author of *Cyfranc Lludd a Lleuelys* as it is likely to be to a modern reader.

For the first, use of lustration to destroy malign beings is a rite familiar from Welsh tradition. A striking parallel to the destruction of the Coraniaid features in the Life of St Collen. The saint, whose name means 'hazel', was probably originally a member of the Brittonic pantheon.[21] The Life tells us that he dwelt in a cave of the Glastonbury Tor (*i vynydd glassymbyri*). Invited one day to confer with the pagan deity Gwyn ap Nudd on its summit, he arrived to find the ruler of the Otherworld (*brenin Anwn*) seated on a golden throne, surrounded by a merry throng of his followers. The indignant saint flung holy water (*dwr bendiged*) from a sprinkler (*siobo*) over them, causing the king, his company, and their *castell* to vanish utterly, leaving behind only those grassy banks that remain visible to the present day.[22]

---

18   Ibid., pp. 3, 4.

19   *Lectures on the Origin and Growth of Religion as Illustrated by Celtic Heathendom* (London, 1888), p. 606.

20   *Cyfranc Lludd a Llefelys*, p. xxxiii.

21   A supernatural being named Coll mab Collfrewy acted as guardian to the travelling sow Henwen, who conferred cultural benefits on various localities in Cornwall and Wales (*The Bulletin of the Board of Celtic Studies*, xii, p. 13).

22   S. Baring-Gould and John Fisher, *The Lives of the British Saints: The Saints of Wales and Cornwall and such Irish Saints as have Dedications in Britain* (London, 1907–13), iv, pp. 377–78.

In Ireland, St Patrick banished demons from the pagan Fianna by sprinkling holy water over them with an aspergillum (*deiséad*), when they were driven in their myriads to the marginal regions of Ireland. Thus the blessed water *of itself* distinguished the demons whom the saint detected swarming among humankind. In the Scottish Highlands and Islands, sprinkling with water heated over a fresh fire cured plague and murrain.[23] In Wales, the poet Dafydd ap Gwilym fancifully likened mist and rain to 'a tin sieve that was rusting' (*Rhidyll ystaen yn rhydu*), a metaphor suggesting moisture from the heavens dispensed as though from a sprinkler.[24]

None of these examples includes the motif of the mysterious 'creatures' dissolved in water, as featured in *Cyfranc Lludd a Lleuelys*. This suggests that the (holy) water and *pryfed* were originally distinct elements: a conclusion which is implicit in the storyteller's evident bewilderment. The early Tudor poet Lewys Môn, alluding to the same legend, treats the 'charged water' as conventional holy water (*dŵr-swyn*), omitting reference to the bewildering *pryfed*.[25] Since holy water *tout court* sufficed for destruction or expulsion of demons, it is tempting to infer that the account of the *pryfed* was incorporated from another strand of the tradition. In fact, it will be shown shortly that the two 'dragons' at the Centre, regarding whose nature the author was self-evidently confused, were originally *pryfed*, with the meaning of 'soul-creatures'.

Returning to the relevant passage in *Cyfranc Lludd a Lleuelys*, it appears not unlikely that the account of the *pryfed* (here italicized) constitutes an interpolation:

And after their speech was unobstructed, Lleuelys told his brother,
  [*namely, that he would give him some pryfed and that he should keep some of them alive for breeding, lest by chance that sort of gormes came a second time, but he should take some others of the pryfed and crush them in water, and that he declared would be good for destroying the race of the Coraniaid.*]
  after he returned home to his realm, that he should summon all the people together, his people and the race of the Coraniaid, to one meeting on pretence of making peace between them, and when they were all together, he should take the charged water and sprinkle it over one and all, and he averred that the water would poison the race of the Coraniaid and would not kill and would not harm anyone of his own race.

The curious stipulation that some *pryfed* be retained for breeding is omitted from the ensuing account of Lludd's fulfilment of the instruction, and from the *Brut* versions of the tale in its entirety. Yet it is at once too specific and too cryptic not to reflect an authentic fragment of tradition. (It is also the passage which suggests most strongly that the author of *Cyfranc Lludd a Lleuelys* possessed access to a variant version of the tale). Although the full implications of this puzzling passage will become apparent only after examination of the motif of the supposititious 'dragons', it will help to flag some conclusions in advance.

23 Myles Dillon (ed.), *Stories from the Acallam* (Dublin, 1970), p. 3; M. Martin, *A Description of the Western Islands of Scotland* (London, 1703), p. 113.

24 Rachel Bromwich (ed.), *Dafydd ap Gwilym: A Selection of Poems* (Llandysul, 1982), p. 133. The widespread concept of rain as water poured through a holed vessel or sieve is discussed in detail by Arthur Bernard Cook, *Zeus: A Study in Ancient Religion* (Cambridge, 1914–40), iii, pp. 338–54.

25 Eurys I. Rowlands (ed.), *Gwaith Lewys Môn* (Cardiff, 1975), p. 254. 'Lewis Môn ... uses "dŵr swyn", the usual expression for holy water, in describing Lludd's action', Roberts (ed.), *Cyfranc Lludd a Llefelys*, p. xxxiii.

1. Since a prime attribute of holy water was its destruction of demons, introduction of a further element (*pryfed* crushed in the water) appears superfluous.

2. The term employed for the water deadly to the Coraniaid is *y dwuyr rinwedawl*. The adjective *rinwedawl* means 'efficacious', 'possessing virtue or power', i.e. the holy water of itself sufficed to destroy maleficent entities.[26]

3. Distillation of a distinct ingredient, so far as I am aware, features nowhere else in Celtic or comparable lore of lustrations.

4. It will shortly be seen that the 'dragons' of the third *gormes* were originally *pryfed*. Since it was their preservation in water (*Historia Brittonum*) or mead (*Cyfranc Lludd a Lleuelys*) that assured the security of the kingdom, it is clear that the function of the 'dragons' and the *pryfed* kept for breeding is essentially the same.

5. The rambling and partially incoherent italicized passage is stylistically uncharacteristic of the tale, which is elsewhere marked by a commendably terse and lucid approach.[27]

6. The explanation that some *pryfed* should be kept for reproduction, *lest the gormes of the Coraniaid recur*, is incompatible with the ensuing assertion that 'immediately *all* the Coraniaid were in this way destroyed' (*Ac an diannot y diffeithawd holl giwtawt y Coranneit*). Clearly, they were *not* expected to return.

7. On the other hand, the correspondence of *pryfed* to Irish *cruim*, in the sense of minute soul-creatures, suggests a rational explanation for the curious provision that Lludd 'should keep some of them alive for breeding' (*a gadu rei onadunt yn vyw y hiliaw*).

The concept of a *pryf*, or minute creature, passing into a mother's womb as the agent of procreation, survived in Welsh folklore: 'in Wales it is still said of a pregnant girl that she has swallowed an insect (*pry'*) or a spider (*corryn*).'[28]

However, confusion occasionally arose from the widespread usage of *pryf* as a term of broad context, classifying entities ranging from 'small animal' to 'creature' – often with the connotation of something sinister and supernatural.

The Welsh Laws catalogue beaver, marten, and stoat (*llostlydan, a beleu, a charlwng*) as *tri phryf* to which a king is entitled, from which the collars of his garments are made.[29] Elsewhere the term is used of insignificant creatures, such as sea-worms or reptiles.[30] Not infrequently it bears an uncanny suggestion, as when a plague-bearing cloud is termed a *pryf*. Equally sinister are an unspecified 'hateful *pryf* from the stronghold of Satan' (*pryf atkas goris kayr Satnas*), and

---

26 Williams (ed.), *Cyfranc Lludd a Llevelys*, p. 46; Roberts (ed.), *Cyfranc Lludd a Llefelys*, p. 12.

27 'The *Cyfranc* takes its place unobtrusively in the Brut because of its factual tone and unimaginative expression' (ibid., p. xxix).

28 Alwyn Rees and Brinley Rees, *Celtic Heritage: Ancient Tradition in Ireland and Wales* (London, 1961), p. 228. Among the Kamchadal people of Kamchatka, 'A woman who wished to become pregnant had to eat spiders' (M. A. Czaplicka, *Aboriginal Siberia: A Study in Social Anthropology* (Oxford, 1914), p. 129). Similarly, with the Gonds of central India a 'fish or insect is eaten in the belief that it will be thus reborn as a child' (Sir James George Frazer, *Adonis, Attis, Osiris: Studies in the History of Oriental Religion* (London, 1914), i, pp. 95–96). Cf. Rees and Rees, *Celtic Heritage*, p. 404.

29 Melville Richards (ed.), *Cyfreithiau Hywel Dda o Lawysgrif Coleg yr Iesu Rhydychen LVII* (Cardiff, 1957), pp. 37, 106; A. W. Wade-Evans (ed.), *Welsh Medieval Law: Being a Text of the Laws of Howel the Good, Namely the British Museum Harleian MS. 4353 of the 13th Century* (Oxford, 1909), p. 131; Hywel D. Emanuel (ed.), *The Latin Texts of the Welsh Laws* (Cardiff, 1967), pp. 126, 250, 500.

30 *Edrich de poen imy gan mor pryued* (A. O. H. Jarman (ed.), *Llyfr Du Caerfyrddin gyda Rhagymadrodd Nodiadau Testunol a Geirfa* (Cardiff, 1982), p. 55); *pysgod a nouiantt / gwenin a velantt / pryued a ymlusgantt* (Patrick K. Ford (ed.), *Ystoria Taliesin* (Cardiff, 1992), p. 81).

uncanny *pryfed* whose baleful presence is comparable to that of the Hounds of Night (*cŵn y nos*). In a Welsh version of the Grail legend, Peredur encounters an exotic white animal (*aniueil gwynn*), little larger than a hare, from whose belly emerge *pryfet* like tiny dogs, which tear it to pieces.[31]

All this goes to show that the precise meaning of *pryfed* is largely only to be determined from the context, although some degree of consistency may be detected in the varied usage. Generally speaking, the imagery evoked is of minute entities, crawling or creeping, and often of Otherworld provenance. In Welsh folk tradition the soul was conceived as a black lizard (*madfall ḋu*), capable of departing and returning to the body.[32] In earlier times this tiny supernatural creature might well have been termed a *pryf*: in the Middle Ages the salamander was classified among *pryfed*.[33]

The associated facets (vessel, mead, cloth cover) in *Cyfranc Lludd a Lleuelys* indicate that these *pryfed* bear a sense close to that of the cognate Irish word *cruim*: that 'fly' or 'worm', which germinates within a princess's womb. In the Irish tales, the *cruim*, or soul-creature, is preserved in vessels of mead or water. These in turn are covered by a (frequently ornate) cloth, through which the *cruim* is strained when imbibed by a designated princess.

The earliest account of the 'dragons', contained in the *Historia Brittonum*, provides further evidence substantiating the hypothesis that the silken 'covering' was originally a curtain or screen. It is described as 'a folded tent, as he had said' (*tentorium complicatum, sicut dixerat*). As the prophetic child Ambrosius goes on to explain, 'the tent is a representation of your kingdom' (*regni tui figura tentorium est*). 'The kingdom' being a synecdoche for the world, the 'tent' separated creation from the limitless space of eternity in the sky above. In shamanistic cosmology, the roof of the tent stands for the night sky, whose stars feature as rents admitting light through its leather covering.[34] Conversely, in Hungarian mythology the sky was envisaged as covering the world 'like a tent; holes in it are the stars'.[35]

Nennius's version of the story echoes that of *Cyfranc Lludd a Lleuelys* in another significant respect. He tells us that the two sleeping 'worms' (*duo [dormientes] vermes*) are to be found in the exact centre of the tent, *in medio tentorii*. This corresponds to their discovery at the Centre of Britain (*y pwynt perued*, i.e. the *omphalos*) in *Cyfranc Lludd a Lleuelys*, and confirms that the tent was a microcosmic simulacrum of Britain herself.

Overall, it seems that the tradition evolved on the following lines:

31 Sir Ifor Williams, 'Hen Chwedlau', *The Transactions of the Honourable Society of Cymmrodorion: Sessions 1946–47* (London, 1948), p. 57; Bromwich (ed.), *Dafydd ab Gwilym*, p. 148; Rev. Robert Williams (ed.), *Selections from the Hengwrt MSS. Preserved in the Peniarth Library* (London, 1876–92), i, p. 319.

32 John Rhŷs, *Celtic Folklore: Welsh and Manx* (Oxford, 1901), pp. 603–4; T. Gwynn Jones, *Welsh Folklore and Folk-Custom* (London, 1930), p. 202.

33 J. Morris Jones and John Rhŷs (ed.), *The Elucidarium and Other Tracts in Welsh from Llyvyr Agkyr Llandewivrevi, A.D. 1346 (Jesus College MS. 119)* (Oxford, 1894), p. 168.

34 Ivar Paulson, 'Die Religionen der nordasiatischen (sibirischen) Völker', in Ivar Paulson, Åke Hultkrantz, and Karl Jettmar, *Die Religionen Nordeurasiens und der amerikanischen Arktis* (Stuttgart, 1962), p. 28; G. M. Vasilevich, 'Early Concepts about the Universe among the Evenks (Materials)', in Henry N. Michael (ed.), *Studies in Siberian Shamanism* (Toronto, 1963), p. 47; Åke Hultkrantz, 'A new look at the world pillar in Arctic and sub-Arctic religions', in Juha Pentikäinen (ed.), *Shamanism and Northern Ecology* (Berlin and New York, 1996), p. 37. The early Semites likewise envisaged the sky as a tent (A. J. Wensinck, *The Ideas of the Western Semites Concerning the Navel of the Earth* (Amsterdam, 1916), pp. 44–45).

35 Mihály Hoppál, 'Hungarian Mythology: Notes to Reconstruction', in Mihály Hoppál and Juha Pentikäinen (ed.), *Uralic Mythology and Folklore* (Budapest, 1989), p. 149.

1. The *pryfed* were tiny soul-creatures, contained in mead-filled vessels, covered in cloth, and believed to be preserved at the Centre of Britain.
2. Over time, probably under the influence of Christianity, the nature of the *pryfed* became obscure. The cleric Nennius speculatively identified them with warring dragons found in the biblical Book of Esther (*vide infra*), which he in turn converted into personifications of the rival races of English and Welsh.
3. When holy water was required to be sprinkled over the malicious hosts of the Coraniaid, it was assumed to be that contained in the vessels holding the *pryfed*. It would have been easy to assume that their mysterious distillation in water was designed to ensure its prophylactic potency.

So far as the Centre is concerned, that upon which the myth is focussed in the *Historia Brittonum* is implicitly the Omphalos of Gwynedd, rather than that of Britain. On the other hand, it is significant that the outcome of the struggle between the Fighting Dragons will determine the fate of Britain as a whole. In fact, there can be little doubt that in this respect *Cyfranc Lludd a Lleuelys* preserves the more archaic version, with the primary *omphalos* located at the Centre of Britain. The geographical transfer may reflect pragmatic recognition that *Britannia* had become confined more or less permanently to the West, in consequence of the establishment of the English kingdoms. As Proinsias Mac Cana observed,

> In such a context it is not inconceivable that the removal of the contending dragons from Oxford to Snowdonia should be viewed as a reflex, direct or indirect, of just such a change of focus within Welsh or British mythic history.[36]

This may be indicated by Lleuelys's unexplained requirement that the dragons be removed to the strongest place (*yn y lle kadarnhaf*) in the kingdom. Oxford was no longer safe, whereas inaccessibly mountainous Gwynedd was. Equally, the transfer might at the time have been regarded as a temporary expedient. The *Historia Brittonum* was composed in AD 829/30, when King Ecgberht of Wessex was triumphantly extending his rule over much of England. During the summer following Nennius's completion of his work, the English king invaded North Wales and (according to English sources) compelled their kings' submission to his rule.[37] However, such things had happened before, when the indomitable Britons of the West repeatedly recovered their independence. At this time much of Western Britain remained in British hands, from the Severn Sea to the River Forth. The child Ambrosius's interpretation of the fighting dragons foretells the eventual expulsion of the English, and a century later the prophetic poem *Armes Prydein* could confidently asserted that the British peoples, from Brittany to the Forth,

---

36   Proinsias Mac Cana, *The Cult of the Sacred Centre: Essays on Celtic Ideology* (Dublin, 2011), p. 205. It was from about the time of the composition of *Cyfranc Lludd a Lleuelys* that the permanence of the Saxon conquest of England became grudgingly acknowledged by the Britons. For example, in 1022 an annalist modified Llywelyn ap Seisyll's claim to be *vrenhin holl brydein* to *vrenhin yr holl vrutanied* (Thomas Jones (ed.), *Brut y Tywysogion: Peniarth MS. 20* (Cardiff, 1941), p. 15). Thus, the king of Gwynedd's traditional claim to be 'King of all Britain' is modified to his being 'king of all the Britons', i.e. the Welsh. In fact, with the contraction of 'British' Britain in Saxon times, virtually the whole insular tradition became redefined within the bounds of Wales (Proinsias Mac Cana, 'Conservation and Innovation in Early Celtic Literature', *Études Celtiques* (Paris, 1972), viii, pp. 114–15).

37   Charles Plummer and John Earle (ed.), *Two Anglo-Saxon Chronicles Parallel: With Supplementary Extracts from the Others; A Revised Text Edited, with Introduction, Notes, Appendices, and Glossary* (Oxford, 1892–99), i, pp. 60–63.

in alliance with the Vikings of Ireland, would reconquer the whole of the island, in accordance with prophecies uttered by Myrddin (Merlin) and the druids.[38]

The likelihood that Gwynedd possessed its own umbilical Centre is suggested by another prophetic poem, where reference is made to 'Gwynedd from her outer border to her centre (*perued*)'.[39] All in all, it seems reasonable to assume that Gwynedd, like other British kingdoms, possessed its own independent provincial centre with its own localized mythological tradition. Rites and beliefs associated with provincial *omphaloi* are likely to have corresponded to those attached to the umbilical centre of Britain. Ensurance that they continued accurately to replicate rituals conducted at the national *omphalos* could have been a prime motive for regular convergence, noted by Julius Caesar, of the druids of Gaul on the Centre located in the territory of the Carnutes.

The Sacred Centre of Dyfed at Arberth was affected by a mysterious shriek, similar to that emanating from the Centre of Britain in *Cyfranc Lludd a Lleuelys*, which likewise reduced the kingdom to a wasteland. Again, it was seen in Chapter Ten how legends associated with the British *omphalos* became identified with a spot in South Wales fortuitously bearing the apt name *Medgarth*, 'Middle Enclosure'.

Kalan Mai in British folk tradition

It is not only mythological tradition that preserves the tradition of a springtide saining lustration in early Britain. Traditional rites and folklore traditions may preserve elements of archaic lore as old as, or older than, literary sources.[40] The combination of themes in *Cyfranc Lludd a Lleuelys* recalls beliefs and practices associated with the *Kalan Mai* in British folk tradition. It will be recalled that the horrific scream

> was heard every May-day eve about every hearth in the Island of Britain, and it pierced people's hearts and terrified them so much that men lost their colour and their strength, and women miscarried, and young men and maidens lost their senses, and all animals and trees and the earth and the waters were left barren.

Here we are presented with a classic description of the Wasteland, a theme familiar from Celtic and Arthurian legend. Moreover, it includes two significant related factors: the scourge is inflicted on May-eve, and its accompanying scream is heard 'about every hearth'. In Celtic

---

38   I have given reasons for supposing that *Armes Prydein* was composed in AD 941 (Nikolai Tolstoy, 'When and where was *Armes Prydein* composed?', *Studia Celtica* (Cardiff, 2008), xlii, pp. 145–49). In the reign of Richard I, and still later, belief in the eventual British reconquest of Britain continued vigorously entertained throughout Wales (J. S. Brewer, James F. Dimock, and George F. Warner (ed.), *Giraldi Cambrensis Opera* (London, 1861–91), vi, pp. 215–16, 227; Patrick K. Ford (ed.), *Ystoria Taliesin* (Cardiff, 1992), p. 86).

39   Gwenogvryn Evans (ed.), *Facsimile & Text of the Book of Taliesin*, p. 71. The name of the *kymōt perued* in Ceredigion identifies another *omphalos* site in Wales (John Rhŷs and J. Gwenogvryn Evans (ed.), *The Text of the Mabinogion and other Welsh Tales from the Red Book of Hergest* (Oxford, 1887), p. 410; J. Gwenogvryn Evans, *Report on Manuscripts in the Welsh Language* (London, 1898–1902), i, p. 953). The commot Perfedd lies on the western slope of Pumlumon, which, as source of three principal rivers of Wales, was once an *omphalos* (Rees and Rees, *Celtic Heritage*, p. 175).

40   O. J. Padel, 'The Nature Of Arthur', *Cambrian Medieval Celtic Studies* (Aberystwyth, 1994), xxvii, pp. 19–31; Sara Graça da Silva and Jamshid J. Tehrani, 'Comparative phylogenetic analyses uncover the ancient roots of Indo-European folktales', *Royal Society Open Science* (London, 2016). I am indebted to Professor John Waddell for drawing my attention to the latter study.

Britain, May-day was the festival of St Bridget, whose principal rite was the damping down of hearths, and their rekindling with fire brought from a central neid-fire.

To understand the full significance of this ritual, it is needful to recall the extent to which winter in early societies was identified with death.

The conceptual link between the dying body and winter probably made sense in light of what could be empirically observed in the case of vegetative growth. In winter, most plants inevitably pass through a season of saplessness, of rest and apparent death. In many parts of the Indo-European world, this period coincides with the onset of frost and cold. When the outside temperature drops and all liquids begin to freeze, when water can become solid ice or rain may turn to snow, then also the sap of plants ceases to flow. As in winter the fluids and the sap of plants, so in death the flow of blood subsides and blood turns cold and solid. Perhaps the icy cold of winter was assumed to have the same effects on the liquids of the body as on the fluids of plants.[41]

In many mythologies, gods such as the Greek Kronos are depicted as enduring a death-like sleep throughout the winter.[42]

On this basis, one might expect the coming of spring to have been celebrated as a time of unalloyed joy and pleasurable expectation. So it largely was, but in early Britain and Ireland it was also a time of melancholy reflexion. Not only was winter envisaged in mythopœic terms as a sleep of death, but in stark reality it was indeed a period of mortality, particularly among the old and infirm. Stock, too, on which mankind depended for survival, became sorely depleted in number by the coming of spring.[43]

An anonymous Welsh poet of the Middle Ages greets the beginning of summer as a time for grievous lamentation, as he reflects on the number of his friends who have passed away that winter. The melancholy cry of the cuckoo sounds a painful echo, as in another poem whose author grieved that a friend who had heard it in happier days would not do so again.[44] Its effect was singularly poignant in Welsh ears, *cw* (pronounced *coo*) being the interrogative 'where?'. 'The monotonous, persistent question *cw-cw-* "Where? Where?" rang in their ears, and saddened their hearts', as folk mourned those who had succumbed to the bitter season.[45]

---

41 Uli Linke, 'Blood as Metaphor in Proto-Indo-European', *The Journal of Indo-European Studies* (Washington, 1985), xiii, p. 340. Cf. pp. 340–42.

42 Sir James George Frazer, *Adonis, Attis, Osiris: Studies in the History of Oriental Religion* (London, 1914), ii, p. 41.

43 In 1739 an Irish writer urged the necessity 'to increase the quantity of our Hay in *Ireland*, the Scarcity of which often falls heavy on our poor, and sweeps away thousands of our weak cattle in *March* and *April*' (A. T. Lucas, *Cattle in Ancient Ireland* (Kilkenny, 1989), p. 38). Cf. p. 33.

44 A. O. H. Jarman (ed.), *Llyfr Du Caerfyrddin gyda Rhagymadrodd Nodiadau Testunol a Geirfa* (Cardiff, 1982), p. 15; J. Gwenogvryn Evans (ed.), *The Poetry in the Red Book of Hergest* (Llanbedrog, 1911), p. 10. Such plaintive vernal reflexions may also owe much to 'the organic connection of man with nature characteristic of Welsh poems such as this' (P. L. Henry, *The Early English and Celtic Lyric* (London, 1966), p. 81). An Irish poem on the travails of old age pitifully laments entrance into the 'winter of age which overwhelms everyone' (Donncha Ó hAodha, 'The Lament of the Old Woman of Beare', in Donnchadh Ó Corráin, Liam Breatnach, and Kim McCone (ed.), *Sages, Saints and Storytellers: Celtic Studies in Honour of Professor James Carney* (Maynooth, 1989), p. 313).

45 Sir Ifor Williams, *Lectures on Early Welsh Poetry* (Dublin, 1944), p. 13; Henry, *The Early English and Celtic Lyric*, p. 74. Cf. Kenneth Jackson, *Studies in Early Celtic Nature Poetry* (Cambridge, 1935), p. 179.

May-day was a time of fear as well as hope. The purpose of rites conducted that day was to ensure survival after emergence from sickness, death, cold, darkness, and all other ills associated with winter, while at the same time welcoming renewal brought by the benign world of summer. Cattle were driven between fires, domestic animals sacrificed, and wild creatures killed on suspicion of being shape-shifting sorceresses. Elaborate precautions were adopted to frustrate the maleficent designs of witches, demons, and elves, and ritual combats were staged in which the forces of summer overcame those of winter.[46]

The early ninth-century Irish Glossary of Cormac, in connexion with the Beltane (May-day) festival, records 'two fires which druids used to make through spells (or with great spells), and they used to bring the cattle to those fires against the murrains of each year'.[47]

In the seventeenth century a Highland writer recorded that malefactors in the Hebrides were formerly burned between two fires, from which arose the proverb '*he is between two Fires of Bel*, which in their Language they express thus. *Edir da hin Veaul or Bel*'.[48]

It is to be suspected that ritual passing *between* fires symbolized passage *through* a purging fire. A May-day custom of burning sheep could further reflect a belief that stock possessed by demons succumbed to fire,[49] while those that were not survived the conflagration.

It was also believed in former times that the bon-fires lighted in May or Midsummer protected the lands from sorcery, so that good crops would follow.

Not only were stock and crops tested in this way, but humans also. In Wales, young men bounded across fires, at considerable risk of personal injury.[50]

It can be seen that the purpose of such rites, particularly those associated with the ubiquitous bonfires, was the simultaneous destruction of demonic forces of the Otherworld and protection of a select remainder. Gorse, too, was burned at May-day, in order to destroy witches and other unchancy beings.[51] The practice intimates that swarming forces of evil lurked all around, imperceptible to the human eye, being eradicable only through a general conflagration. Until Teyrnon laid especial watch, he was baffled to know how his favoured colt came to disappear, nor was Manawydan initially aware of the identity of the rapacious swarm which robbed him of his wheat.

The concept of a purging springtide fire receives legendary expression in the early ninth-century Tripartite Life of St Patrick. Among miracles recounted of the saint's attendance at the Feast of Tara (which, as was seen earlier, was probably held in the spring) is one which occurred in an especially constructed house, half of dry wood and half of fresh. Patrick's companion Benen was ensconced in the dry section, where he wore the druid Lucat Móel's coat (*tunach in drúad*). Meanwhile, the druid entered the fresh section, garbed in Patrick's chasuble (*casal*). The

---

46 Rhŷs, *Celtic Folklore*, pp. 305–10; Trevelyan, *Folk-Lore and Folk-Stories of Wales*, pp. 25–26; Jonathan Ceredig Davies, *Folk-Lore of West and Mid-Wales* (Aberystwyth, 1911), pp.74–76; Máire MacNeill, *The Festival of Lughnasa: A Study of the Survival of the Celtic Festival of the Beginning of Harvest* (Oxford, 1962), p. 380; Rees and Rees, *Celtic Heritage*, pp. 91–92, 286–90.

47 Kuno Meyer, 'Sanas Cormaic', in O. J. Bergin, R. I. Best, Kuno Meyer, and J. G. O'Keefe (ed.), *Anecdota from Irish Manuscripts* (Halle and Dublin, 1907-13), iv, p. 12.

48 M. Martin, *A Description of the Western Islands of Scotland* (London, 1703), p. 105.

49 Rhŷs, *Celtic Folklore*, pp. 307–8; E. K. Chambers, *The Mediaeval Stage* (Oxford, 1903), i, p. 140.

50 Ceredig Davies, *Folk-Lore of West and Mid-Wales*, p. 76.

51 Rhŷs, *Celtic Folklore*, p. 309.

dwelling was then barred and put to the flames. When they had died down, it was discovered that the pagan druid and his half of the house had been consumed by the fire, while sparing the chasuble in which he was clad. Meanwhile the Christian Benen survived, his druidic coat alone being burned to ashes.[52]

This purgative factor associated with the spring festival is enshrined in British traditional lore. Attention was drawn earlier to the dramatic episode of the treacherous slaughter of British nobles at Stonehenge by Hengist's ferocious Saxons. All the Britons were slain save one, the valiant Eldol. Geoffrey's prime source for his account of the event was the ninth-century *Historia Brittonum*, to which he added the telling detail that the massacre was perpetrated on 1 May, *kalendis Maii*.[53] I have argued that the name *Eldol* (which is otherwise unknown to Welsh onomastics) originated in misreading of a loanword *eidol*, 'soul', and that the story originated in a myth of cyclical destruction of the human race during the winter of the earth, survival of the species being assured by the escape of a single man (originally a soul-bearer). The theme is found also in Irish tradition, which records the destruction of thousands of Partholon's people by plague on the Kalends of May (Beltane), of whom one man (Tuán) alone survived to perpetuate the Irish race.[54]

A version of this tradition is also found in Arthurian romance. The *Suite Merlin* describes the youthful Arthur's unwitting incest with his sister. Merlin subsequently warns him that their offspring is destined to inflict great harm on the realm. Questioned further by Arthur, he reveals that the child will be born in Britain on 1 May: *Saches qu'il naistera le premier jour de may et ou royaume de Logres*. In order to destroy the unidentifiable 'evil child' *Mordrès* (Mordred), Arthur arranges for all children born that day to be embarked at sea in an unmanned boat.[55] In the event they are rescued (Mordred's survival being essential to the Arthurian tragedy), but given the explicit coincidence of the event with the Calends of May it is likely that this episode represents a confused retelling of the myth of springtide destruction and the predestined *survival* of a lone individual.

The concept of May-day as a liminal juncture, when a privileged survivor slips from the world of death and darkness into that of life and light, may account for a further rite practised that day. The Wrekin, in Shropshire on the Welsh border, is an impressive hill site, whose Welsh name was *Dinlle Gwrygon*, 'fortress of Lleu the divine man/hero'.[56] At the Wrekin Wakes, celebrated on the first Sunday in May, girls used to

> scramble down the steep face of the cliff and squeeze through a natural cleft in the rock called the Needle's Eye, and believed to have been formed when the rocks were rent at the Crucifixion; should she look back during the task, she will never be married.[57]

---

52   Kathleen Mulchrone (ed.), *Bethu Phátraic: The Tripartite Life of Patrick* (Dublin, 1939), pp. 35–36.

53   Reeve and Wright (ed.), *Geoffrey of Monmouth: The History of the Kings of Britain*, pp. 133–37.

54   Best, Bergin, O'Brien, and O'Sullivan (ed.), *The Book of Leinster*, pp. 16, 19.

55   Gaston Paris and Jacob Ulrich (ed.), *Merlin: Roman en prose du XIIIᵉ siècle* (Paris, 1886), i, pp. 154, 158, 203–11.

56   John T. Koch, 'Gallo-Brittonic *Tasc(i)ouanos* 'Badger-slayer' and the Reflex of Indo-European g^wh^1', *Journal of Celtic Linguistics* (Cardiff, 1992), i, pp. 109–10.

57   Sir John Rhys, 'All around the Wrekin', *Y Cymmrodor* (London, 1908), xxi, p. 2.

It may be that, in earlier times, the pilgrims undertook a ritual journey, from which not all were believed to emerge, as they passed from one sphere of existence to another. It was popularly believed that a door in a rock provided access to the realm of the fairies each May-day.[58]

Among numerous precious fragments of originally pagan lore preserved in the mediæval story of *Culhwch ac Olwen* is the tale of Gwyn and Gwythyr, which clearly reflects seasonal myth. Every Kalends of May until the day of judgment (*pob dyw kalan Mei uyth hyt dyt brawt*) they fight for the hand of beautiful Creiddylad, by whom is clearly intended the Maiden Sovereignty of the island. Emphasis is implicitly laid on her perpetual chastity, in addition to which she is pictured as retaining in perpetuity her pristine youth and beauty.[59]

The identity of the rivals for her hand is also illuminating. Gwyn mab Nudd appears elsewhere in *Culhwch* as an expert huntsman, and a malevolent one at that: 'God has put the spirit of the devils of Annwfn in him, lest the world be destroyed; he will not be spared thence.'[60] Later tradition made him leader of the Wild Hunt, guiding the souls of the dead across the night sky. This function is possibly alluded to in an early poem, which describes his hound Dormach as pursuing its course through the heavens.[61]

The poet Dafydd ap Gwilym identified fog advancing across the hills as 'high towers belonging to the tribe of Gwyn, the province of the wind', and declared he could hear the hounds of Gwyn baying within the obscurity.[62] Finally, it may be noted that Gwyn confined the followers of his rival Gwythyr 'in the North (*Y Gogledd*)'. Geographically this was a region broadly corresponding to the present Lowlands of Scotland beyond Hadrian's Wall, but for the Celts 'north' also bore dark connotations comparable to those evoked by Latin *sinister*.[63]

The sixth-century Byzantine historian Procopius received a report from Britain that the island was divided by a wall (clearly that of Hadrian), the land beyond which was given over to a lifeless wilderness inhabited by 'countless snakes and serpents and every other kind of wild creature'. Men and animals entering this pestilential region suffered instantaneous death.[64] Procopius questioned whether this might not reflect myth rather than fact, and he was clearly right to do so. His description befits a Land of the Dead, and an early Welsh poem alludes to the shades of men slain in battle flitting from the vicinity of the Roman Wall northwards to the desolate wilderness of the Forest of Celyddon.[65]

---

58   Idem, *Celtic Folklore*, pp. 20–21.

59   Krappe, *Balor With the Evil Eye*, p. 151.

60   Bromwich and Simon Evans (ed.), *Culhwch and Olwen*, pp. 26–27.

61   T. Gwynn Jones, *Welsh Folklore and Folk-Custom* (London, 1930), p. 203; Jarman (ed.), *Llyfr Du Caerfyrddin*, p. 72. 'He appears in *Kulhwch* as a devilish huntsman … His dog, Dormach, is referred to, and the difficult line in 14c may refer to the wild hunt in the sky' (Jenny Rowland, *Early Welsh Saga Poetry: A Study and Edition of the Englynion* (Cambridge, 1990), p. 244). For the Wild Hunt in Celtic tradition, cf. Wolfgang Meid, 'Über Albiōn, elfydd, Albiorīx und andere Indikatoren eines keltischen Weltbildes', in Martin J. Ball, James Fife, Erich Poppe, and Jenny Rowland (ed.), *Celtic Linguistics/Ieithyddiaeth Geltaidd; Readings in the Brythonic Languages: Festschrift for T. Arwyn Watkins* (Amsterdam and Philadelphia, 1990), p. 437.

62   Rachel Bromwich (ed.), *Dafydd ap Gwilym: A Selection of Poems* (Llandysul, 1982), pp. 133, 135.

63   Gray (ed.), *Cath Maige Tuired*, p. 74. The Welsh word *gogledd*, 'north', is a compound of *cledd*, 'left' (J. Morris Jones, *A Welsh Grammar: Historical and Comparative* (Oxford, 1913), p. 156).

64   H. B. Dewing (ed.), *Procopius* (London, 1914–40), v, pp. 264–66.

65   A. O. H. Jarman (ed.), *Ymddiddan Myrddin a Thaliesin (O Lyfr Du Caerfyrddin)* (Cardiff, 1951), p. 58. Cf. Rhys, *Lectures on the Origin and Growth of Religion as Illustrated by Celtic Heathendom*, p. 153.

There must surely be a connexion between the conflict of Gwyn ap Nudd and Gwythyr ap Greidawl, fought every year on 1 May, and ritual battles heralding the arrival of spring waged on the same date at Lleu's stronghold of Dinlle Gwrygon. Could *gwythyr* and *greidawl* have been originally epithets of Lleu? Nantlle ('Valley of Lleu') in Snowdonia provides the setting for Lleu's death in the tale *Math uab Mathonwy*, where tradition told also of a dazzling monster 'Gold-bristle', who was hunted and killed there. These allusions suggest a solar function (though not identity) for Lleu.[66]

In the myth of the abduction of Creiddylad we encounter further reflexion of the fear that spring may not return, unless appropriate prophylactic rites be enacted at the vernal festival. In the Battle of Gwyn and Gwythyr, Creiddylad embodies the potent figure of the Maiden Sovereignty, that lovely virgin goddess who personifies the land of Britain, whom the cruel god of winter fogs bears away, like Persephone in Greek myth, to his realm of darkness and death.

In *Cyfranc Lludd a Lleuelys* a lustration is performed every Calends of May, whose function is to distinguish and destroy baneful Otherworld forces throughout the land while preserving humanity unharmed. This closely parallels May-day rites practised in Britain and Ireland, whose purpose is effectively identical, viz. rigorous purgation of demonic elements (invisible agents of disease, etc.), which simultaneously promotes the survival of a chosen few among kin and kine.

There might appear to be a distinction between purgation by water in the first instance, and by fire in the second. However, although fire may have been regarded as the more efficacious element for destroying witches and demons,[67] there is evidence for widespread use of water for a similar purpose. Washing in May dew was believed to cure affected parts of the body, as well as improve the complexion of young girls, i.e. it preserved fair skin, while banishing blemishes.

> The fair maid who, the first of May,
> Goes to the fields at break of day
> And washes in dew from the hawthorn tree,
> Will ever after handsome be.[68]

Of particular interest is the fact that lustrations were performed on May-day, with the purpose of punishing anyone who failed to act appropriately to repel witches.

> On May day, the boys of many towns and villages in Cornwall and Devon used to parade the streets and exercise what they considered their right to throw water over those they met who were not wearing hawthorn [a prophylactic against witches] in their hats or button-holes. The boys used all sorts of containers for the water,

---

66   Ibid., pp. 404–5. In the Irish tale *Oidhe Chloinne Tuireann* Lugh's radiant face is all but identified with the rising sun (Seán Ua Ceallaiġ (ed.), *Trí Truaġa na Scéaluiḋeaċta* (Dublin, 1927), pp. 13–14).

67   In West Cornwall, fire was employed by 'the most noted conjurers' for extirpation of malignant fairies harming farmers' cattle (William Bottrell, *Stories and Folk-Lore of West Cornwall* (Penzance, 1870–80), ii, pp. 75–76).

68   Rhŷs, *Celtic Folklore*, pp. 308–9; Robert Latham and William Matthews (ed.), *The Diary of Samuel Pepys* (London, 1970–83), viii, p. 240; ix, pp. 549, 551; Christina Hole, *English Custom & Usage* (London, 1941), p. 69; A. R. Wright and T. E. Lones, *British Calendar Customs* (London, 1936–40), ii, pp. 205–7.

e.g. cans, buckets, or cows' horns. The day, 1st May, was called Dippy-day and sometimes Ducking-day.[69]

In *Cyfranc Lludd a Lleuelys*, the imagery conveyed is of a towering Lludd, sprinkling his 'charged' water from on high over serried ranks of Britons and Coraniaid. It is to be suspected that watering rituals corresponded with an analogous belief that spring showers were endowed with fertilizing power, while leaving waste those tracts of earth which remained barren. Their regenerating effect was evocatively noted by the Rev. Francis Kilvert on May-day 1875:

> When I rose and looked out this morning the ground was damp with soft and blessed rain. The weather was warm and showery. All the morning, the tender dripping rain whispered rustling in the trees with a showery mist and the grass could almost be heard to grow.[70]

The second gormes: the deadly scream

It has been seen that the first *gormes* (the arrival of the Coraniaid in Britain) was originally not a *gormes* at all, but a facet of the succeeding *gormesoedd*, for which the Coraniaid were implicitly also responsible. In the second *gormes*, the degradation of Britain into a wasteland is heralded by a ghastly shriek. This recalls the concluding section of *Manawydan mab Llŷr*, which recounts the destruction of the eponymous hero's exemplary wheatfields.

> He went to keep watch over the [third] field. And while he was doing so towards midnight, he heard the loudest noise in the world (*nachaf twryf mhwyaf yn y byt*); he watched. There came a huge host of mice (*Llyma eliwlu y byd o lygot*) – they could neither be counted nor measured.[71]

This immeasurable swarm of hitherto invisible predatory rodents, whose devastation at first remained inexplicable to Manawydan, recalls the irruption of the sinister Coraniaid in *Cyfranc Lludd a Lleuelys*. Each is accompanied by a hideous night-time wail.

In Welsh tradition the Otherworld scream generally features as herald, rather than cause, of supernatural assaults against humanity. Geoffrey of Monmouth describes Arthur's visit to Loch Lomond, where every year a flock of eagles 'used to gather to mark with loud and concerted cries any marvel about to occur in the kingdom'.[72] This account is repeated in Welsh in the Brut Dingestow, and other versions add details clearly deriving from native lore. The Red Book of Hergest *Brut* notes that the eagles' gathering took place every May-day (*pop kalan mei*), while the Cotton Cleopatra version specifies that their prophetic cry portended

---

69   Ibid., pp. 240–41; Chambers, *The Mediaeval Stage*, i, p. 122.

70   William Plomer (ed.), *Kilvert's Diary: Selections from the Diary of the Rev. Francis Kilvert* (London, 1977), iii, p. 179.

71   Hughes (ed.), *Manawydan Uab Llyr*, p. 8. The 'mice' represent rationalization of an originally Otherworld destructive power, just as did locusts in the ancient Near East (Alfred Haldar, *The Notion of the Desert in Sumero-Accadian and West-Semitic Religions* (Uppsala, 1950), pp. 56-63).

72   *Quae singulis annis conuenientes prodigium quod in regno uenturum esset celso clamore communiter edito notificabant* (Michael D. Reeve and Neil Wright (ed.), *Geoffrey of Monmouth: The History of the Kings of Britain* (Woodbridge, 2007), p. 201).

'an oppression of another country which is coming to that kingdom' (*gormes arall wlat yr deyrnas honno*).[73]

This indicates a British tradition of a dire scream heard every May-day, which presaged a *gormes* threatening imminent destruction to the kingdom. Although the wording of the passage in the Cotton Cleopatra *Brut* is a little unclear, it presumably means that the 'kingdom' (*yr deyrnas*) – i.e. Britain is menaced by an Oppression from another country (*gormes arall wlat*).[74] This echoes the portrayal of the Coraniaid in *Cyfranc Lludd a Lleuelys* as a race (*cenedyl*) hostile to the Britons.

The abduction of King Teyrnon's foal every May Eve was also accompanied by an eerie shriek (*twrwf mawr*).[75] Once again, there is no suggestion that the latter represented a *gormes* in its own right: it heralded the imminent onslaught. Again, the non-lethal nature of the comparable Scream from the Otherworld (*diasbad uwch Annwfn*) in the Welsh laws serves to confirm that the *diaspat* in *Cyfranc Lludd a Lleuelys* was originally an accompaniment to the *gormes* in question, rather than constituting a *gormes* in itself.

All this confirms that the first and second *gormesoedd* in *Cyfranc Lludd a Lleuelys* originally featured as dual aspects of a single episode, which became separated when the legend was converted into a triad. Thus, it was originally the Coraniaid who were authors of the destruction of Britain's fertility and wealth. Their supernatural power of hearing protected them from destruction, enabling them to threaten Britain with national annihilation every May Eve, while their assault was heralded by a fearsome cry. In the event, this dire threat to the survival of the Britons was overcome by a lustration, which proved lethal to the destructive invaders while preserving the native inhabitants.

We are told that the second *gormes* was a scream heard every May Eve (*nos Kalan Mai*) about every hearth in the island of Britain, and it pierced people's hearts and terrified them so much that men lost their complexion and their strength, women miscarried, young men and maidens lost their senses, and all animals and trees and the earth and the waters were left barren.

Lleuelys's explanation of this terrible scourge appears beside the point. He tells his brother that a foreign dragon is battling with a British one, which utters the horrible scream. No indication is given why it should have such a devastating effect on the kingdom; nor why it should be the British dragon alone that screams, when neither is described as being the loser in the struggle; nor why it should be its anguished or angry cry that inflicts disaster on its own people; nor why the conflict recurs every May-day. Logically, the remedy for the affliction lay in the British dragon's defeat of its alien adversary, but in the event there is no intimation of victory or defeat on either side.

It seems indisputable that the author was perplexed as to the nature of the scream. During their consultation prior to the event, Lleuelys assured Lludd that, so long as the dragons continue safely confined, 'no *gormes* shall arrive in the Island of Britain from anywhere else'. However, this assurance conflicts with the ensuing sentence expounding the nature of the third *gormes* – which occurs *subsequent* to the dragons' interment. Again, when Lludd on his return to Britain witnesses the dragons' combat, there is no suggestion of a scream uttered during

---

73 Henry Lewis (ed.), *Brut Dingestow* (Cardiff, 1942), p. 150; John Rhŷs and J. Gwenogvryn Evans (ed.), *The Text of the Bruts from the Red Book of Hergest* (Oxford, 1890), p. 192; John Jay Parry (ed.), *Brut y Brenhinedd: Cotton Cleopatra Version* (Cambridge, Mass., 1937), p. 161.

74 The sentence makes more sense if *hwnnw* be taken as a mistake for *hwnn*, 'this'.

75 R. L. Thomson (ed.), *Pwyll Pendeuic Dyuet: The First of the Four Branches of the Mabinogi edited from the White Book of Rhydderch with variants from the Red Book of Hergest* (Dublin, 1957), p. 19.

their struggle. Only after the event we are informed that 'and so ceased the terrible scream that was in the land'. As though these inconsistencies were not enough, Lludd's prior explanation relates that the dragons will turn into piglets when they collapse exhausted into the vat. In the event, however, there is no mention of this strange transmogrification, and they remain dragons throughout!

It is evident that the author of *Cyfranc Lludd a Lleuelys* understood neither the nature of the May-day scream, nor its relationship to the legend of the fighting dragons. The likeliest explanation is that, while the successive motifs – the deadly scream, the 'dragons', and their removal from the Centre to Gwynedd – undoubtedly derive from traditional lore, their explanation in the tale largely represents authorial speculation.

The momentary transformation of the dragons in the first instance into piglets appears too incongruous to have been simply invented. In fact, it will be seen shortly that the 'dragons' entered the story in consequence of the creatures' speculative identification with biblical dragons in Nennius's earlier account of the event. Originally the paired creatures were, as Nennius himself makes clear, Latin *vermes*, i.e. indeterminate minute creatures: in Welsh, *pryfed*. It is likely that the intrusive 'piglets' reflect an earlier attempt to interpret this obscure term. Moreover, it will further be shown shortly that another early Welsh tale misinterprets *pryfed* as 'pigs'.

Terrifying screams are widely attested in Welsh and Irish tradition, their context being not infrequently similar to that provided by the scream (*diaspat*) in *Cyfranc Lludd a Lleuelys*. The flooding of the realm of Cantre'r Gwaelod, recounted in an early poem in the Black Book of Carmarthen, was heralded by a ghastly shriek. Among early literary sources, only in *Culhwch ac Olwen* do we encounter the cry as *cause* of the ensuing destruction. On his arrival at the court of Arthur, Culhwch declares that, if he be not admitted, he will utter three destructive cries across the length of Britain, causing all pregnant women at court to miscarry, while the remainder would never conceive. However, the baneful consequences are so close to those found in *Cyfranc Lludd a Lleuelys*, that a similar misinterpretation of the shriek as cause, rather than accompaniment, of the disaster may be suspected to lie behind the extant account.[76]

A close parallel to the devastating consequence of the scream in *Cyfranc Lludd a Lleuelys* features in the story of *Manawydan uab Llŷr*. Manawydan and his stepson Pryderi foregather on the Hill (*gorsedd*, which may mean equally 'hill' or 'throne') of Arberth, a sacred centre of the kingdom of Dyfed. All at once they find themselves enveloped in a blanket of mist, whose descent is accompanied by an uncanny outcry (*twrwf*). When eventually the sky clears, the pair find themselves gazing over a desolate wasteland, void of human habitation, domestic animals, and cultivated land.[77]

A similar encounter occurs in Arthurian romance. When Perceval arrives at Arthur's court, he boldly seats himself on a vacant stone chair at the Round Table, which Arthur warns him is reserved for the best knight in the world. Immediately the stone cracks apart, and a fearful cry (*braist*) arises, of such unspeakable anguish that everyone present believed

---

76   Rachel Bromwich and D. Simon Evans (ed.), *Culhwch and Olwen: An Edition and Study of the Oldest Arthurian Tale* (Cardiff, 1992), pp. 4–5; Jarman (ed.), *Llyfr Du Caerfyrddin*, pp. 80–81.

77   Hughes (ed.), *Manawydan Uab Llyr*, pp. 2–3.

the world was falling into the abyss (*abisme*).[78] Meanwhile all around was enveloped in impenetrable darkness.[79]

Comparably frightening screams feature in Irish tradition. The 'Book of Conquests of Ireland' (*Lebor Gabála Érenn*) refers to 'three demon voices in Ireland after plunder, to wit, whistling and outcry and groaning'. At the first Battle of Magh Tuiread, 'the furies, monsters and wizards of judgement cried so loud that their voices could be heard among rocks and waterfalls and in caverns of the earth. It was like the hideous screams of the last days of torment, when the human race departs the earth.' Suibhne Geilt and his British counterpart Ealladhan were driven to madness and wilderness exile by three shouts of malediction uttered by opposed armies in battle. A folktale told of cattle aborted by an eerie yell emanating from the decapitated head of a giant.[80]

The uncanny premonitory scream is not confined to insular Celtic tradition. In Arabia, Islamic legend told of a similarly dreadful cry called ṣayḥaḥ, which heralded the total destruction of the Thamūd people:

> There came upon them a *scream* from heaven, in which there was the sound of every thunderbolt and the voice of every thing on earth that has a voice, and it cut through their hearts in their breasts, and they all perished, young and old.[81]

The baneful scream in mediæval Welsh law

In *Cyfranc Lludd a Lleuelys*, the scream is said to have reduced Britain every May Eve to the characteristic ills of a Wasteland. To counter its effect, Lleuelys recommends prophylactic rites that will obviate any repetition of this disaster. These were presumably conducted at the time of the event, *nos Kalan Mai*. But what was the significance of that eerie shriek, which it has been seen the author erroneously interpreted as cause, rather than accompaniment, of the *gormes*?

Light is thrown on the mystery by a curious provision of mediæval Welsh law, whereby ownership of immovable property was associated with the household hearth.

> The fire on the hearth appears to symbolize the right to inhabit house and land which was enjoyed by the father and passes to the son. *Dadannudd* [the legal term] is used also, however, for simple possession of house and land and for the legal action by which a man may claim land which either he himself or his father had possessed.

---

78   This recalls the ill-boding *diasbad uwch Annwfn* of the Welsh laws, where *Annwfn* literally signifies 'abyssal'.

79   William Roach (ed.), *The Didot Perceval: According to the Manuscripts of Modena and Paris* (Philadelphia, 1941), pp. 149–50.

80   R. A. Stewart Macalister (ed.), *Lebor Gabála Érenn: The Book of the Taking of Ireland* (Dublin, 1938–56), iv, pp. 132, 158, 196; J. Fraser, 'The First Battle of Moytura', *Ériu: The Journal of the School of Irish Learning, Dublin* (1915), viii, p. 44; J. G. O'Keeffe (ed.), *Buile Śuibhne* (Dublin, 1931), pp. 7, 54; Jeremiah Curtin, *Myths and Folk-Lore of Ireland* (London, 1890), p. 201.

81   Jaroslav Stetkevych, *Muhammad and the Golden Bough: Reconstructing Arabian Myth* (Bloomington and Indianapolis, 1996), pp. 78–82, 139–40. The dangerous outcome of an unearthly shriek is recorded at a very early date. In a Sumerian version of the epic of Gilgamesh, the hero advises his comrade Enkidu, on his proposing a descent to the Underworld, to obey the tabus of that unearthly realm, or 'the outcry of the nether world will seize you!' Despite this, Enkidu rashly violates every one, upon which 'the outcry of the nether world seized him' (A. R. George (ed.), *The Babylonian Gilgamesh Epic* (Oxford, 2003), pp. 771–72).

Parallels with rites associated with the Beltane (1 May) fire are striking, and it is clear that legal provisions concerned with inheritance and claims to property ultimately reflect (as is often the case with Celtic legal provisions) a mythological paradigm.

Lighting a fire on a hearth symbolized primary evidence of ownership. In the event of a disputed claim, the absent proprietor was required to establish that the defendant was an intruder, or *gormes* – the same term as that used in connexion with the deadly scream *over every hearth* in *Cyfranc Lludd a Lleuelys*. Furthermore, judgment was delivered either on the ninth day after *Kalan Mai*, or following the winter festival of *Kalan Gaeaf*. Kindling the hearth represented the 'irreducible core' of measures required to establish ownership.[82]

A further curious provision of Welsh law envisages a menacing challenge to inheritance, when ownership attains the ninth generation of a family. Variations and obscurities occur in the legal texts, but the essential provision seems to be that 'the ninth man is the last surviving member of a kindred which has all died out except for him'. Quite why a family of landholders should be faced with finding their title revocable after eight generations is not explained, nor is it easy to envisage any practical circumstance which might invoke application of such a law. For a start, it would have been difficult to establish the degree of succession after an interval of nearly three centuries, when another legal ruling affirms that no one can be sure of his descent after more than *seven* generations. And in what plausible circumstances might the ninth heir in succession be expected to abandon his holding, or otherwise permit a carpet-bagging intruder to establish himself in his stead? No instance is recorded of an attempt at such a displacement in actual practice. Indeed, it is difficult to envisage its implementation, particularly in view of the fact that the law makes no provision for enforcement, which must inevitably have been required in order to effect so arbitrary a transfer of well-established ownership. Nor does the law contain any provision entitling one intruder rather than another to assert his claim to replace the ninth-generation landholder. Finally, if, as is implied, the intruder possessed legal justification for his action, could the hereditary landowner really have re-established his right purely in consequence of a peculiar shriek?

It seems inescapable that this strangely conceived supersession in the ninth generation reflects a mythological underpinning of the law of inheritance, rather than its implausible, impractical, and unrecorded application in royal courts. This becomes yet clearer when a further aspect is considered. The wording of the legal texts is unclear, nor are they entirely consistent with each other. According to some of the oldest manuscripts of the Welsh laws:

> If the ninth person comes to ask for land, his ownership is extinguished, and he gives a shriek (*dyaspat*) because he is passing from owner to non-owner (*o pryodaur en ampryodar*). And then the law hears that shriek and gives him an allowance: that is to say, as much as each one of their number who are seated against him. And that is called *dyaspat uuch Annuuen*, and though that shriek be uttered subsequently, it will never be

82   T. M. Charles-Edwards, 'Welsh *diffoddi, difa* and Irish *do-bádi* and *do-ba*', *The Bulletin of the Board of Celtic Studies* (Cardiff, 1969), xxiii, pp. 210–13; idem, *Early Irish and Welsh Kinship* (Oxford, 1993), pp. 211–15, 274–303. May-day was the occasion of servants' changing their employment, renewal of leases, &c (Lady Wilde, *Ancient Legends, Mystic Charms, and Superstitions of Ireland. With Sketches of the Irish Past* (London, 1888), p. 114; Marie Trevelyan, *Folk-Lore and Folk-Stories of Wales* (London, 1909), p. 26). In mid-nineteenth-century Ireland, 'A curious custom is practised at the May and November fairs namely that of servants coming to them [farmers]' (Anne O'Dowd, 'Rabbles and Runaways, Church Gates and Street Corners', in Alan Gailey and Dáithí Ó hÓgáin (ed.), *Gold Under the Furze: Studies in Folk Tradition Presented to Caoimhín Ó Danachair* (Dublin, 1982), p. 167). The same custom obtained in Wales (John Rhŷs, *Celtic Folklore: Welsh and Manx* (Oxford, 1901), pp. 211–12).

heard. And others say that the ninth person is not entitled to give that shriek but that he has passed from owner to non-owner.[83]

If the modern reader find this baffling, it does not appear that authors of mediæval Welsh law codes understood it any better. Setting aside the confusing preamble, why was the strange cry called 'the shriek louder than (or over) *Annwfn*'? Annwfn was the abyssal Otherworld of the pagan Britons. Attempts appear to have been made to rationalize this element, one code emending it to a 'cry over the lost spot (*diaspat u6ch aduan*)', uttered in order to obtain admission. Others refer to it as a 'weak cry', possibly alluding to the pitiable predicament of the excluded heir.[84]

Overall, the reference to the Otherworld is clearly to be preferred. The supernatural aspect is supported by the account mentioned earlier of Culhwch's arrival at King Arthur's court, at the outset of *Culhwch ac Olwen*. As has been seen, when Arthur's porter denies him entrance to his master's feast, Culhwch threatens to raise those three shrieks (*teir diaspat*), which would be heard at both extremities of Britain and across the sea in Ireland, and cause all women in Arthur's court to miscarry or become sterile. Although the passage is satirical, it echoes the dire effect ascribed the scream in *Cyfranc Lludd a Lleuelys* too closely not to derive from archaic tradition.

Fundamental elements of this bizarre legal provision may be summarized as follows.

1. The fire burning on the ancestral hearth is identified with continuity of family ownership. Correspondingly, ritual covering and uncovering of the live ember among the ashes before the fireback stone (*pentanfaen*) provide primary proof of landholding.[85] Survival of the ember through continuous banking up and rekindling of the fire symbolizes survival of the familial soul-substance through successive generations.

2. A crisis of ownership was envisaged as recurring with every ninth generation of a family, when the heir was liable to find himself deprived of his inheritance. This cannot reflect anything likely to have occurred in reality, and clearly puzzled the authors of the legal codes.

3. The deprivation was accompanied by a mysterious Otherworld shriek, for which the jurisconsults again found themselves unable to account satisfactorily.

Striking similarities may be observed between the legal allusion to the *diasbad uwch Annwfn* and the eerie scream in *Cyfranc Lludd a Lleuelys*.

1. In both accounts, the scream is of supernatural origin.
2. In both, its destructive effect is specifically associated with householders' hearths.

---

83 Wiliam (ed.), *Llyfr Iorwerth*, pp. 55–56; J. Gwenogvryn Evans (ed.), *Facsimile of the Chirk Codex of The Welsh Laws* (Llanbedrog, 1909), p. 61).

84 Wade-Evans (ed.), *Welsh Medieval Law*, pp. 315–16; Emanuel (ed.), *The Latin Texts of the Welsh Laws*, p. 133; cf. pp. 256, 501–2. *A honno a elwyr dyaspat uchawn* (Dafydd Jenkins (ed.), *Llyfr Colan: Y Gyfraith Gymreig un ôl Hanner Cyntaf Llawysgrif Peniarth 30* (Cardiff, 1963), p. 35). Cf. the illuminating discussion by Charles-Edwards, *Early Irish and Welsh Kinship*, pp. 403–6.

85 Williams and Powell (ed.), *Cyfreithiau Hywel Dda yn ôl Llyfr Blegywryd*, p. 118. Cf. Frederic Seebohm, *The Tribal System in Wales: Being Part of an Inquiry into the Structure and Methods of Tribal Society* (London, 1904), pp. 82–84.

3. In *Cyfranc Lludd a Lleuelys* the sinister *diasbad* accompanies extinction of wealth, manifested by barrenness among women and sterility throughout nature. In the Welsh laws the *diaspat uwch Annwfn* heralds extinction of a family line and landholding, amounting effectively to microcosmic application of the wasteland theme in *Cyfranc Lludd a Lleuelys*.

Celtic law in Britain and Ireland preserved much that was of exceedingly venerable origin. As Binchy observed: 'Irish law preserves in semi-fossilized condition many primitive 'Indo-European' institutions of which only faint traces survive in other legal systems derived from the same source.'

Comparative studies have shown that the legal systems of Indo-European societies are grounded in the concept of an unchanging cosmic order established by the gods. The law's affinity to the natural order is most strikingly exemplified by the institution of divine kingship, which among other requirements hedged a ruler about with innumerable taboos and other magical provisions, maintenance of which was essential for ensuring peace, prosperity, and social order throughout the kingdom. For untold centuries before it became enshrined in writing, Celtic law was codified and transmitted orally in verse by the druids, and subsequently (in Ireland) the *filid*. As the early Irish law code *Senchas Már* expressed it, law had been preserved by 'the joint memory of the ancients, the transmission from one ear to another, the chanting of the poets'.[86]

Accordingly, legendary allusions and anecdotes abound in Celtic legal codes. Their function was to adduce timeless precedents from mythical eras, which established the sanctity of legal provisions for all time. An illuminating example in the Welsh codes stipulates compensation for specific crimes committed against the queen, viz. violating her protection, striking her, or snatching something from her hand.[87] The second and third provisions proscribe rare – indeed, unlikely – offences, and are trivial compared with other conceivable affronts. In reality they reflect, not potential mishaps which might actually occur, but a central myth of the sacral kingship.

Since the queen incarnated the divine Maiden Sovereignty, her abduction by an Otherworld *gormes* posed the direst threat to the kingdom which she personified. An example of such ravishment is found in a legendary episode contained in the Life of St Gildas, where a lawless King Melvas kidnaps Queen *Guennuvar* (Guinevere) for the space of a year, until eventually she is recovered by King Arthur.[88] Other versions of this outrage modify the kidnapping to a

---

86 The literature on the subject is vast: cf. D. A. Binchy, 'The Linguistic and Historical Value of the Irish Law Tracts' *The Proceedings of the British Academy* (London, 1943), xxix, pp. 195–227; Myles Dillon, 'The Archaism of Irish Tradition', ibid. (1947), xxxiii, pp. 245–64; idem, 'The Taboos of the Kings of Ireland', *Proceedings of the Royal Irish Academy* (Dublin, 1951), liv, pp. 1–36; Émile Benveniste, *Le vocabulaire des institutions indo-européennes* (Paris, 1969), ii, pp. 99–105.

87 Williams and Powell (ed.), *Cyfreithiau Hywel Dda yn ôl Llyfr Blegywryd*, p. 4; Wiliam (ed.), *Llyfr Iorwerth*, p. 2.

88 Theodor Mommsen (ed.), *Monvmenta Germaniae Historica* (xiii): *Chronica Minora saec. IV. V. VI. VII* (Berlin, 1894), iii, p. 109. In a French romance Melwas features as *Moloas … li sires de l'Isle de Voirre*, 'Melwas, lord of the Isle of Glass', a locality described in terms unmistakably characteristic of the Celtic Otherworld (Mario Roques (ed.), *Erec et Enide* (Paris, 1955), p. 58). The reading *Voirre* in MS R (ibid., p. 241) is clearly to be preferred. A variant version of the Queen's abduction features in the Arthurian romance of *Durmart* (Joseph Gildea (ed.), *Durmart le Galois: Roman Arthurien du Treizième Siècle* (Villanova, Pa., 1965–66), i, pp. 110–11): cf. Roger Sherman Loomis, *Arthurian Tradition & Chrétien de Troyes* (New York, 1949), p. 78.

degrading assault in the royal court. In one of the Triads, the villainous Medrawd (Mordred) drags Gwenhwyfar from her throne and strikes her. (In another, the insult is effected by one Gwenhwyfach – probably a doublet of *Gwenhwyfar.*) Similarly, the eponymous heroine of *Branwen*, who stands likewise for the Maiden Sovereignty, is removed to Ireland by its king, where she is inexplicably subjected to a daily slap by the royal butcher. In the romance of *Peredur* an intruder knight snatches Gwenhwyfar's goblet, pours drink over her face and breast, and strikes her a great blow (*bonclust*) in the face.[89] Here we find close parallels to the insults for which protection is provided in the Welsh laws.

As O'Rahilly pointed out, it is clear that the theft of Gwenhwyfar's cup originally signified abduction of the queen herself.[90] In view of this, it is difficult not to conclude that provisions in Welsh law for preserving the queen from irritating insults reflected the legendary fate of Gwenhwyfar, divine prototype of the queenship. Rather than poor manners at the dinner-table, putative maltreatment of the queen originally represented a paradigm of her abduction.

In the case of the scream over Annwfn, the household hearth provides a microcosmic representation of the kingdom as a whole. In effect, the scream heralded the extinction of one cycle of humanity and its replacement by another.[91] In Welsh law the critical moment for inheritance of a landholding arrived with the ninth generation. Such a recurrent crisis can scarcely have occurred in reality, and unmistakably suggests a mythological scheme.[92]

While the precise source and nature of the terrifying scream experienced by the people of Britain in the time of Lludd and Lleuelys remains mysterious, it appears that originally it portended extinction of the royal line on completion of the paradigmatic cycle of nine generations, and the effective reduction of Britain to a wasteland. However, the story shows how the disaster could be averted by performance of prescribed rites. It is surely these that lie behind the recommendations Lleuelys urges on Lludd, to which I now turn.

The fighting 'dragons'

In *Cyfranc Lludd a Lleuelys* the scream is heard every May Eve, when it afflicts Britain with universal dearth and sterility. It emanates from the Centre of the kingdom, where it proves to be uttered by a dragon personifying the British people, which is being assailed by a foreign dragon. Prior existence of this theme is attested by its appearance in the early ninth-century *Historia Brittonum*.

---

89   Egerton G. B. Phillimore, 'A Fragment from Hengwrt MS. No. 202', *Y Cymmrodor* (1887), vii, p. 123; Derick S. Thomson (ed.), *Branwen uerch Lyr: The Second of the Four Branches of the Mabinogi edited from the White Book of Rhydderch with variants from the Red Book of Hergest and from Peniarth 6* (Dublin, 1961), pp. 8, 18; Glenys Witchard Goetinck (ed.), *Historia Peredur vab Efrawc* (Cardiff, 1976), p. 11.

90   T. F. O'Rahilly, 'On the Origin of the Names Érainn and Ériu', *Ériu* (1943), xiv, p. 7.

91   'Among the Turco-Mongolian people, to destroy the hearth, or to put out the hearth-fire, was a common metaphor for the destruction of one's yurt, the extermination of the whole family and bringing the family line to an end' (Igor de Rachewiltz, *The Secret History of the Mongols: A Mongolian Epic Chronicle of the Thirteenth Century* (Leiden, 2006-13), p. 367; cf. p. 381).

92   I have discussed the ideological concept of dynastic descent to the ninth generation, with its accompanying danger of extinction of the line, in my article 'Cadell and the Cadelling of Powys', *Studia Celtica* (Cardiff, 2012), xlvi, pp. 71–74.

It has been seen that the uncanny scream represents a theme familiar to Welsh tradition – so much so, that it became encapsulated in mediæval Welsh law. It was not destructive per se, but emanated from the Otherworld as premonitory warning or accompaniment of the imminent destruction of a dynasty or realm. Its variant titles in the legal codes suggest that its import was no longer fully understood. It seems that this incomprehension was shared by the author of *Cyfranc Lludd a Lleuelys*, and the confused accounts of the fighting dragons both in his work and the earlier *Historia Brittonum* suggest that the scream and 'dragons' originated in what were ultimately distinct traditions.

There is reason to believe that the paired 'creatures' originally represented elemental entities, the obscurity of whose nature led to Nennius's identification of them in the more comprehensible and exalted guise of biblical warring dragons. That their precise nature was far from clear to the authors of both texts is indicated by their confused terminology. In the earlier *Historia Brittonum* version of the story, the prophetic child Ambrosius initially terms the creatures *vermes*, which he then explains as 'dragons': 'the two *vermes* are two dragons' (*duo vermes duo dracones sunt*). The respective wording of the parallel accounts unmistakably indicates, firstly, that Latin *vermes* is a translation of Welsh *pryfed*;[93] and, secondly, confirms that the explanatory 'dragon' element represents an authorial gloss by Nennius himself.

Both Latin *vermis* and Welsh *pryf* lack semantic precision, being generally employed as amorphous terms for minuscule creatures such as worms or ants, as also small beasts.[94] Nennius's wording that 'the two *vermes* are two dragons' betrays the fact that it was in reality obscure to him just what were the *vermes*. Furthermore, the evident need for an explanation strengthens the likelihood that the original term was *pryfed* (a term of indeterminate meaning), rather than specific creatures, such as the 'badgers' favoured by Sir Ifor Williams.[95]

Similar linguistic disarray reigns throughout the version of the discovery of the 'creatures' in *Cyfranc Lludd a Lleuelys*. First, the anonymous author tells us that the dragons fought 'in the shape of monstrous animals' (*Ac yna ti a wely y dreigeu yn ymlad yn rith aruthter aniueileit*). Since dragons are themselves 'monstrous animals', this confirms the author's bewilderment in handling his source. Next, they rise into the air 'in the shape of dragons' (*yn rith dreigau yn yr arwyr*). But since we were told at the outset that they *are* dragons, what can this qualification be intended to signify? The implication, surely, is that initially they were *not* dragons, but mysterious 'monstrous animals'. Finally, in the course of two short sentences, they manifest themselves without explanation 'in the form of two little pigs' (*yn rith deu barchell*).

As has been seen, the destructive scream originated in authentic Celtic tradition, where however it is nowhere associated with dragons. The author's description betrays the contrived nature of his exegesis. Since emphasis is laid on the indecisive nature of their combat, why is it only the British dragon that screams during the fighting? Why should its cry inflict annihilation

---

93 Cf. Williams (ed.), *Cyfranc Lludd a Llevelys*, pp. xvii–xix; *The Transactions of the Honourable Society of Cymmrodorion: Sessions 1946–1947*, pp. 56–57; Bromwich (ed.), *Trioedd Ynys Prydein*, pp. 93–95.

94 For the comparative etymology of *vermis*, incorporating creeping, frequently tiny, reptiles or insects, cf. Julius Pokorny, *Indogermanisches Etymologisches Wörterbuch* (Berne, 1959–69), i, p. 1152; Thomas V. Gamkrelidze and Vjačeslav V. Ivanov, *Indo-European and the Indo-Europeans: A Reconstruction and Historical Analysis of a Proto-Language and a Proto-Culture* (Berlin and New York, 1995), i, pp. 191–92, 445; J. P. Mallory and D. Q. Adams (ed.), *Encyclopedia of Indo-European Culture* (Chicago and London, 1997), pp. 24, 649–50.

95 *The Transactions of the Honourable Society of Cymmrodorion: Sessions 1946–1947*, pp. 56–57.

on its own people? Why should a shriek of anguish or rage bring about so universally devastating an affliction? And why is there no mention of the scream during the fight, when in due course Lludd fulfils his brother's instructions for bringing the dragons to book?

These attempts in the parallel narratives to explain what their authors plainly found inexplicable confirm that their disparate versions reflect awkward attempts to interpret archaic tradition. Setting aside for the moment the scream, and discounting Nennius's speculative interpretation of *vermes* as fighting dragons, we are left with something on the following lines. At the Centre of Britain two *vermes/pryfed* are lodged beneath the ground. There, within a chest, they lie wrapped in a folded tent (*tentorium complicatum*) or sheet of brocaded silk (*llenn o pali*), submerged within or beside a vessel (*uas, cerwyn*) containing mead.

The wording of the *Historia Brittonum* indicates that the paired creatures were originally *vermes*, Old Welsh *pryuet*. There can be no question but that it was Nennius himself who concocted 'the explanation placed in the mouth of the prophetic child Ambrosius'. He identified them with biblical dragons, which he reinterpreted as personifications of the warring Welsh and Saxon races: an explanation apt to his 'historical' interpretation of the legend as an episode in fifth-century British history. The origin of this interpretation was convincingly identified a century ago by the German scholar Paul Feuerherd, in an important paper since almost entirely overlooked. In the biblical Book of Esther (Vulgate version), Mordecai experiences a prophetic dream. He sees the earth convulsed with tremors below and above its surface, whereupon two fighting dragons appear, whose cry portends mortal conflict between the Jews and their oppressors.

> *Et ecce, duo dracones magni, paratique contra se in proelium.*
>
> *Ad quorum clamorem cunctae concitatae sunt nationes, ut pugnarent contra gentem iustorum.*

As a cleric, Nennius will have been thoroughly familiar with the text of the Bible, which in turn represented the obviously appropriate source from which to quarry an explanation of the prophetic imagery of the *vermes/pryfed*.[96]

Latin *uermis* means 'a worm, maggot, or other small creature', alternatively 'serpent'. The diminutive *uermiculus* was employed of an earthworm or grub, both words being generally applicable to tiny, usually limbless, creatures.[97] Sir Ifor Williams, while accepting the unmistakable implication of the text that the creatures were originally *vermes*, interpreted them as 'badgers'.[98]

---

96   Paul Feuerherd, *Geoffrey of Monmouth und das Alte Testament mit Berücksichtigung der Historia Britonum des Nennius* (Halle, 1915), pp. 69–79, 95. Early insular ecclesiastics were naturally familiar with the Book of Esther (D. R. Howlett, *British Books in Biblical Style* (Dublin, 1997), p.150). Furthermore, the biblical *clamor* recalls the *diaspad* heralding the discovery of the paired dragons in *Cyfranc Lludd a Lleuelys*. It is noteworthy that, 'From Chapter 21 onward, Gildas makes frequent reference to Old Testament prophecies which are fulfilled in British events' (Robert W. Hanning, *The Vision of History in Early Britain: From Gildas to Geoffrey of Monmouth* (New York, 1966), p. 55). Nennius in turn was familiar with the work of Gildas: '*Historia Brittonum* can in many respects be understood as a commentary on Gildas's *De excidio Britanniae*' (John T. Koch, '*De sancto Iudicaelo rege historia* and Its Implications for the Welsh Taliesin', in Joseph Falaky Nagy and Leslie Ellen Jones (ed.), *Heroic Poets and Poetic Heroes in Celtic Tradition: A Festschrift for Patrick K. Ford* (Dublin, 2005), p. 261).

97   P. G. W. Glare (ed.), *Oxford Latin Dictionary* (Oxford, 1968–82), p. 2037; R. E. Latham and D. R . Howlett (ed.), *Dictionary of Medieval Latin from British Sources* (London, 1975–2013), p. 3639; François Kerlouégan, *Le De Excidio Britanniae de Gildas: Les destinées de la culture latine dans l'île de Bretagne au VIᵉ siècle* (Paris, 1987), p. 264.

98   Williams (ed.), *Cyfranc Lludd a Llevelys*, pp. xvii–xix; Ifor Williams, 'Hen Chwedlau', *The Transactions of the Honourable Society of Cymmrodorion: Sessions 1946–1947* (London, 1948), pp. 56–57. It was presumably the

This, though, seems the less likely rendering. It was, after all, Nennius himself who translated the story into Latin. It also seems likely that he obtained the story from oral transmission. Had he understood *vermis* to mean badger (*melis*), would he not have rendered it as such?

Plainly, neither Nennius nor presumably his informant understood precisely what was intended by the term *uermis*. That they did not indicates that the original Welsh term *pryf* was used in its generic sense of 'larva, maggot, worm' – often with supernatural connotations. The descriptive term *aruthter* ('monstrosity') employed in *Cyfranc Lludd a Lleuelys* bears a similar implication. As will now be shown, this interpretation is borne out by allusions in related sources.

Despite the popularity of dragons in Irish legend,[99] the translator of the Irish version of the *Historia Brittonum* ignored Nennius's scriptural interpretation of the *uermes* as dragons, instead identifying the fighting creatures as *cruim*, i.e. 'worms' or 'maggots': *cruim* being both the cognate form of Welsh *pryf* (Brittonic *prem*),[100] and regular Irish translation of *uermis*.[101] The translator's omission of the 'dragons' explanation in the original text suggests, either that he possessed independent knowledge of the tradition, or that the 'dragons' were absent from the version he used. In any event, incongruous though the rendering might appear, there is reason to believe that something on the lines of 'two maggots' (*da cruim*) represents the original concept.

An early Irish story preserves a version of this theme, which goes far towards clarifying incongruities contained in the two British tales. 'The Wandering of the Two Swineherds' (*De Cophur in dá Muccida*) contains archaic features indicative of pre-Christian origin.[102] The relevant section of the story runs as follows. (Two versions have been preserved, but I am here concerned only to single out the pertinent motifs).

Two shape-shifting swineherds, Friuch and Rucht, were friends versed in the lore of paganism (*suithe ngentlechta*), and also shape-shifters. Provoked into a dispute, they spent two years as quarrelsome ravens fighting together, before reverting to human guise. After further mutual strife, they 'assume the shape of water creatures, i.e. the shape of two water-worms (or 'insects')'[103] (*ndelbaib míl n-uiscci .i. hi richt dā dorbui*). One went into the spring of Garad in Connacht, and the other into that of the river Cronn in Cuailnge (Ulster).

One day queen Medb of Connacht came to wash her face in the first spring, bearing with her a small bronze vessel (*lestur*), in which to wash her hands. As she dipped it into the water, the tiny

fact that Feuerherd's monograph was published in Germany during the Great War that led to Williams's unawareness of its existence when writing shortly after the conflict. The Welsh scholar's high reputation in turn led subsequent scholars to continue writing in ignorance of the German writer's identification of the source of Nennius's 'dragons.' Cf. Rachel Bromwich (ed.), *Trioedd Ynys Prydein: The Welsh Triads* (Cardiff, 1978), p. 93).

99   J. F. Campbell, *The Celtic Dragon Myth* (Edinburgh, 1911), pp. xviii–xxvii; Tom Peete Cross, *Motif-Index of Early Irish Literature* (Bloomington, Ind., 1952), pp. 48–50. Cf. Rev. James MacDougall, *Folk Tales & Fairy Lore in Gaelic and English Collected from Oral Tradition* (Edinburgh, 1910), pp. 96–99. *Prem iaram isin chombreic is cruim isi[n] gäidilg* (Kuno Meyer, 'Sanas Cormaic: An Old-Irish Glossary Compiled by Cormac Úa Cuilennáin', in O. J. Bergin, R. I. Best, Kuno Meyer, and J. G. O'Keefe (ed.), *Anecdota from Irish Manuscripts* (Halle and Dublin, 1907–13), iv, p. 19).

100 'Celt. *kwrimis* (: W *pryf*) > OIr. *cruim* 'worm" (Patrick Sims-Williams, 'Indo-European *gʷʰ* in Celtic, 1894–1994', in Joseph F. Eska, R. Geraint Gruffydd, and Nicolas Jacobs (ed.), *Hispano-Gallo-Brittonica: Essays in honour of Professor D. Ellis Evans on the occasion of his sixty-fifth birthday* (Cardiff, 1995), p. 202) Cf. Ranko Matasović, *Etymological Dictionary of Proto-Celtic* (Leiden, 2009), pp. 181–82.

101 A. G. van Hamel (ed.), *Lebor Bretnach: The Irish Version of the Historia Britonum Ascribed to Nennius* (Dublin, 1932), pp. 59–60.

102 Rudolf Thurneysen, *Die irische Helden- und Königsage bis zum siebzehnten Jahrhundert* (Halle, 1921), pp. 276–84.

103 *Dorb*, 'small insect or worm (esp. one that lives in water, opp. to cruim *earth-worm*)' (E. G. Quin *et al.* (ed.), *Dictionary of the Irish Language: Based mainly on Old and Middle Irish Materials* (Dublin, 1913-76), 'D', col. 353); ? < 'petit insecte ailé' (J. Vendryes, E. Bachellery, and P-Y. Lambert, *Lexique étymologique de l'irlandais ancien* (Dublin and Paris, 1959–96), D-174).

creature slipped into it. Momentarily lost in admiration of its lovely colours (a likely indication of its supernatural character), Medb became suddenly aware that the water had vanished, leaving the minute entity alone in the empty vessel. She enquired whether it could foretell her future, once she had gained the sovereignty of Connacht. The worm (or insect) obligingly advised her to marry king Ailill, who afterwards became her consort, and returned to the spring.

One day, a certain Fiachna mac Daire came to the second spring. There he discovered another *míl*, or tiny creature, whose advice similarly enabled him to gain wealth and prosperity. It further explained that one of Fiachna's cows would drink him, while one of Medb's would do the same by his rival. So it happened, after which the creatures resumed their fighting, as before in successive transformations. The two manuscript versions of the story vary the catalogue of shapeshifting forms adopted by the rivals, the Book of Leinster version stating that they became in turn two stags, two champions, two ghosts, and two dragons (*da draic*). Finally, 'they dropped from the air, and were two water-worms' (*dofuittet díb línaib assind aér comtar dí dorbbi*).[104]

Parallels are unmistakable between this story, and the accounts of the Fighting Dragons found in the *Historia Brittonum* and *Cyfranc Lludd a Lleuelys*. They include the following:

1. The two swineherds recall the incongruous two small pigs (*deu barchell*), into which the dragons are said to become momentarily transformed in *Cyfranc Lludd a Lleuelys*. (*Pryfed* also 'become' pigs in *Math uab Mathonwy* – a factor which will be examined shortly).
2. Several of the swineherds' fights take place in the air, as *do those of* the British 'dragons'.
3. The *vermes* of the *Historia Brittonum* are discovered in a pool *(stagnum)*, while the creatures in *De Cophur in dá Muccida* inhabit springs.
4. Queen Medb discovers her creature in a vessel (*lestar*) she brings to the well. The 'dragons' in Nennius's version are found inside 'two vessels' (*duo vasa*).[105]

The curious detail, found in all these versions, of the creatures' ascent into the upper air, is explained by a passage in the Irish mythological tale *Tochmarc Étaíne*. Transformed by the witch Fuamnach into a cruim floating in a pool, Étaín becomes in turn a purple fly (*cuil corcrai*), which arises from the water.[106]

This is not the place to pursue the precise relationship between the Irish and British versions of the battling shape-shifters. The pagan character of the Irish story, together with its archaic language, indicates a date of composition not later than the ninth century.[107] Reference to the creatures as dragons suggests some interchange between the respective stories. At the same time, the British and Irish versions differ in major respects, suggesting a distinct origin deriving from Common Celtic pagan mythology.

The present issue here is that of identifying the strange fighting creatures. One thing is clear: when these stories assumed their extant forms, their authors were puzzled how to interpret them. In the *Historia Brittonum* considerable confusion is evinced concerning the trappings of the display: the pond, the pavement, the two vessels, the folded tent. It is hard not to conclude

---

104 Best, Bergin, O'Brien, and O'Sullivan (ed.), *The Book of Leinster*, pp. 1121–22; Ulrike Roider (ed.), *De Chophur in Da Muccida* (Innsbruck, 1979), pp. 24–58.

105 The Irish word *lestar*, 'vessel', was synonymous with Latin *uas*, 'vessel': '.i. uás · *lestar*' (Whitley Stokes and John Strachan (ed.), *Thesaurus Palaeohibernicus: A Collection of Old-Irish Glosses Scholia Prose and Verse* (Cambridge, 1901–1903), ii, p. 119).

106 Osborn Bergin and R. I. Best, 'Tochmarc Étaíne', *Ériu* (Dublin, 1938), xii, p. 152.

107 Thurneysen, *Die irische Helden- und Königsage*, p. 278; Roider (ed.), *De Chophur in Da Muccida*, p. 19.

that this collection of items bore a significance which by the ninth century was no longer understood. It is clear too from the text itself that the interpretation of *vermes* as dragons represents a conjectural gloss, which Nennius placed in the mouth of the prophetic child. This speculative rendering originated in his familiarity with the dream episode in the Book of Esther, which he applied to his innovative setting of the originally mythical tale in the context of the British-Saxon wars of the fifth century AD.

The episode in *Cyfranc Lludd a Lleuelys* likewise contains motifs in common with the *Historia Brittonum*, which include the vessel in which the 'dragons' are held, the piece of cloth in which they are wrapped, their submersion in a liquid (water or mead), and their subterranean location. Finally, their common retention at a uniquely safe spot, identified by a figure possessed of mantic powers (Lleuelys, Ambrosius), ensures the security of the island of Britain.

Together with the parallel Irish tale, all three versions betray bewilderment over the nature of the paired creatures, the significance of the vessel or vessels in which they were contained, the function of the cloth covering, and the relevance of the story to the sovereignty of the land. However, comparison with a further related theme in mediæval Irish literature provides a key to resolving the mystery. This is the birth-tale of the Ulster hero Conchobor (*Compert Conchobair*).

One day the maiden Nes was wandering in a wilderness, when she came upon a lovely pool. Discarding her clothes, she entered the water and bathed. All at once the druid Cathbad appeared and compelled her to become his wife. One night at home Cathbad became thirsty. Nes searched in vain throughout their fortress for a beverage. Accordingly, she repaired to the river Conchobor, where she strained water into a cup through her veil, and brought it to Cathbad. He ordered a candle to be brought, which enabled him to espy two worms in the water (i.e. they were imperceptible to normal view). Drawing his sword, Cathbad compelled Nes to drink the water. She drank twice, swallowing a worm with each gulp, and promptly became pregnant – according to some because of the worms, according to others being impregnated by her lover Fachtna Fáthach. When her time came, Nes returned to the river Conchobor, where she was delivered of a baby boy on an adjacent flagstone. The child, who was born with a worm in each hand, received the name of the river. He tumbled into the water, whence he was rescued by Cathbad.[108]

It is clear that ingestion of the 'worms' induced pregnancy, while the alternative explanation that Nes was impregnated by a lover represents no more than rationalization of the original motif, which was by then no longer fully understood (or considered proper) when the tale came to be retold in Christian times.

Parallels with *De Cophur in dá Muccida* are striking. Like Medb, Nes goes to the river bearing a vessel. There she accidentally swallows the two worms in water, a theme distanced in the story of the Two Swineherds, where the worm is imbibed by Medb's cow, instead of the queen herself. The curious motif of the veil, through which Medb drinks the worms,[109] recalls the mysterious cloth in which the dragons are wrapped in the British tales.

Other stories throw yet further light on the theme of the two worms. Evidently the names of the heroine and her son could be variously assigned, since virtually the same tale is told of the druid Cathbad's daughter Finnchaím. She proved infertile, whereupon a druid uttered spells over a well. The maiden then

---

108 Kuno Meyer (ed.), 'Irish miscellanies: Anecdota from the Stowe MS. n° 992', *Revue Celtique* (Paris, 1883), vi, p. 173–186.

109 A natural expectation would be that the veil should *retain* the worms. That it was introduced to *permit* them to pass into Medb's mouth suggests a distinct consideration.

drank a draught out of the well, and with the draught she swallowed a worm (*dorb*), and the worm was in the hand of the boy as he lay in his mother's womb, and it pierced the hand and consumed it.

The child grew up to become the hero Conall Cernach.[110]

Other stories tell of maidens who become pregnant while bathing, while omitting the element of inseminatory worms. Queen Mugain thrice drank water blessed by saints Finnian and Áed, in consequence of which she dramatically gave birth successively to a lamb, a salmon, and the future King Áed Sláne. Becnat, mother of Saint Fínán, was impregnated by an amorous salmon while bathing in Loch Lein. (This mildly salacious tale is modified in another version, in which she merely dreams of becoming impregnated by the fish). It looks as though a fish has become substituted for the mysterious 'worm' of earlier mythic versions. In a rather more squalid anecdote, an over-excited robber, spying on the virgin Cred while she washed her hands in a well, was unable to prevent himself from ejaculating. His sperm landed on some cress, which the girl unhappily ate, in consequence of which she conceived the future Saint Báthíne. Again, this essentially pagan tale is rendered decent in a sanitized version, wherein conception follows from eating watercress blessed by a saint.[111]

Water was widely understood to possess fecundating power, particularly when under the control of a druid.[112] Parallel beliefs are found widespread across the world, suggesting an origin in very early times. In Eliade's words,

> Principle of what is formless and potential, basis of every cosmic manifestation, container of all seeds, water symbolizes the primal substance from which all forms come and to which they will return either by their own regression or in a cataclysm. It existed at the beginning and returns at the end of every cosmic or historic cycle; it will always exist, though never alone, for water is always germinative, containing the potentiality of all forms in their unbroken unity … Immersion in water symbolizes a return to the pre-formal, a total regeneration, a new birth, for immersion means a dissolution of forms, a reintegration into the formlessness of pre-existence; and emerging from the water is a repetition of the act of creation in which form was first expressed. Every contact with

110   Sharon Arbuthnott (ed.), *Cóir Anmann: A Late Middle Irish Treatise on Personal Names* (Dublin, 2005–7), i, p. 87; ii, pp. 69–70.

111   Ibid., ii, pp. 37–38; Best and Bergin (ed.), *Lebor na Huidre*, p. 134; Whitley Stokes (ed.), *Félire Óengusso Céli Dé. The Martyrology of Oengus the Culdee* (London, 1905), pp. 112, 134–36; idem (ed.), *Lives of Saints from the Book of Lismore* (Oxford, 1890), p. 142; W. W. Heist (ed.), *Vitae Sanctorum Hiberniae ex Codice olim Salmanticensi nunc Bruxellensi* (Brussels, 1965), p. 153. The mermaid Bec, daughter of Cain, who startlingly gave birth to twenty-two children after a trout squirted spawn into her mouth while she was sleeping under water, is presumably the same as Becnat, mother of Saint Fínán (Simon Rodway, 'Mermaids, Leprechauns, and Fomorians: A Middle Irish Account of the Descendants of Cain', *Cambrian Medieval Celtic Studies* (Aberystwyth, 2010), lix, p. 2). A Sanskrit tale, similar to that of the impregnation of Becnat, relates the uncanny experience of an Indian princess who bathed in the Ganges. The motif recurs in the *Mahabharata*, and a similar mishap is related of the Peruvian goddess Cavillaca (Edwin Sidney Hartland, *The Legend of Perseus: A Study of Tradition in Story Custom and Belief* (London, 1894–96), i, pp. 94, 118–20).

112   J. A. MacCulloch, *The Religion of the Ancient Celts* (Edinburgh, 1911), p. 196; Christian-J. Guyonvarc'h and Françoise Le Roux, *Les Druides* (Rennes, 1986), pp. 126, 163–64.

water implies regeneration: first, because dissolution is succeeded by a 'new birth', and then because immersion fertilizes, increases the potential of life and of creation.[113]

Accounts of women impregnated by entering water, or drinking an object or creature in water, are widely recorded.[114] The Dinka of the Nilotic Sudan believed in 'the impregnation of a barren woman by a Power of the river'. In Hellenistic times the Nile was believed to fecundate men's semen in intercourse. In England, so late as the seventeenth century, ingestion of a fish was popularly believed to influence pregnancy. The garrulous John Aubrey recorded of George Abbot, Archbishop of Canterbury:

> His mother, with child of him [Abbot's father], longed for a jack [small pike], and dream't that if shee could eate a jack, her son should be a great man. The next morning, goeing to the river … with her payle, to take up some water, a good jack came into her payle. Which she eat up, all, her selfe. This is generally received for a trueth.[115]

A remarkably explicit portrayal of the Irish pre-Christian myth of procreation features in the story of 'The Wooing of Étaín' (*Tochmarc Étaíne*), discussed earlier. Midir's marriage to the lovely Étaín provokes the jealousy of his first wife Fuamnach (concubinage being lawful in early Ireland), a powerful and malignant witch, who acquired her magical arts from a druid named Bresal. A year after their wedding, Midir and Étaín paid a visit to the enchantress, who proved unctuously welcoming. She led Étaín into her bedroom, where she invited the maiden to seat herself on a chair in the middle of the room. Then Fuamnach struck her with her magic wand, turning her into a pool in the middle of the house. At this, the witch departed to the druid's home. Midir also 'left the house to the water into which Étaín had turned'.

Next, 'the heat of the fire and the air and the heaving of the ground heated the water so that the pool that was in the middle of the house turned into a maggot (*cruim*), and after that the *cruim* became a purple fly (*cuil corcrai*)' of surpassing beauty. In this form Étaín came to Midir, who recognized her and cherished her above all mortal women. Discovering what had occurred, the vengeful Fuamnach conjured up a wind of enchantment, which blew Étaín away, condemning her to float on breezes above the ocean.

Eventually Étaín returned to Ireland. But once again the evil Fuamnach expelled her with a magical wind, so that she was tossed about (again as a fly) in the air above Ireland for a further seven years. Finally, she landed on the roof of a house in Ulster. Inside, she tumbled into a golden beaker from which the wife of Étar was drinking. The woman drank her down, so that Étaín was conceived in her womb.

---

113 Mircea Eliade, *Patterns in Comparative Religion* (London, 1958), pp. 188–89; cf. pp. 189–93. For numerous further examples of belief in the fecundating power of water, cf. Hartland, *The Legend of Perseus*, i, pp. 105–22; Richard Broxton Onians, *The Origins of European Thought about the Body, the Mind the Soul, the World Time, and Fate: New Interpretations of Greek, Roman and kindred evidence also of some basic Jewish and Christian beliefs* (Cambridge, 1954), pp. 118, 229–33, 473–74.

114 Hartland, *The Legend of Perseus*, i, pp. 133–35.

115 Godfrey Lienhardt, *Divinity and Experience: The Religion of the Dinka* (Oxford, 1961), pp. 40, 142–43, 172; Karl Preisendanz (ed.), *Papyri Graecae Magicae: Die Griechischen Zauberpapyri* (Stuttgart, 1973–74), i, p. 4; Andrew Clark (ed.), *'Brief Lives,' chiefly of Contemporaries, set down by John Aubrey, between the Years 1669 & 1696* (Oxford, 1898), i, p. 24. The Irish shapeshifter Túan mac Cairell was reborn after being devoured as a fish by Cairell's queen (John Carey, 'Scél Túin meic Chairill', *Ériu* (Dublin, 1984), xxxv, p. 102).

She was called Étaín daughter of Étar. Now it was a thousand and twelve years from the first begetting of Étaín by Ailill until her last begetting by Étar.[116]

Thus, not only was it assumed that she was daughter of Étar, but the wording suggests that in some way she actually *was* his daughter.

This strange series of events was subjected to illuminating analysis by the French Celticist Françoise Le Roux. She showed that, by transforming Étaín into a pool of water, the most elemental of substances, Fuamnach 'returns her to the supreme principle from which all emanates'. Next, she becomes a 'worm': actually, a chrysalis, crude manifestation of physical existence before the advent of spirituality. Gradually, she is transformed into a butterfly (or dragonfly?), i.e. transmutation into the pure beauty of spirituality.[117] Finally, when she falls into the goblet of Étar's wife, she resumes the form of an imperceptible 'worm' ingested in liquid, that germinative life-force which generates the birth of a hero.

Tochmarc Étaíne retains a half-understood version of the cosmic myth of cyclical renewal, evidently more archaic than those preserved in the stories of Fintán mac Bochra and Tuán mac Cairell. The latter survive perennial cataclysms by being transformed into animal, bird, or fish. In the case of Étaín, she grows from an imperceptible substance, immersed within the boundless waters of eternity, into a winged insect, an aery spirit skimming above sea and land. Next, she is immersed in liquor imbibed by the wife of Étar. The 'golden beaker' in which she is found at a feast must originally have contained mead rather than water, and the fact that the child conceived in consequence was believed to be the daughter of the imbiber's husband confirms that the *cruim*, or soul-creature, was so minute as to be imperceptible.

The text may even preserve an echo of the story's original cosmic setting, when we learn that Étaín's rebirth as a *cruim* was prefaced by 'the heat of the fire and the air and the heaving of the ground [which] heated the water' in which she was miraculously reincarnated. The elements combine to create a new earth out of the dissolution of its predecessor.

We are further told that 'it was a thousand and twelve years from the first begetting of Étaín by Ailill until her last begetting by Étar', a figure intended to convey a generational succession of rebirths over untold centuries.[118] Étaín is unmistakably a personification of the sovereignty goddess: a perpetual virgin, incarnated as mortal consort of successive kings and heroes.[119]

When turned into water, she is described as being seated 'on a chair in the middle of the house' (*isin cathair for lar an taigi*). The significance of the setting is further emphasized, when we learn that 'the pool that was in the middle of the house turned into a worm' (*lind ro baí for lar in tighi*). This emphasis on the centre suggests that the divine birth-process is envisaged as

---

116 *Ériu*, xii, pp. 152–56.

117 In Irish and Cornish folklore, the soul was identified with a butterfly or moth (Rhŷs, *Celtic Folklore*, p. 612).

118 *Celticvm XV*, pp. 355–73.

119 'Étaín is a manifestation of the goddess of sovereignty, for we are told that the men of Ireland would not attend the feast of Tara before Eochaid married her' (Francis John Byrne, *Irish Kings and High-Kings* (London, 1973), p. 61). Cf. Thomas F. O'Rahilly, *Early Irish History and Mythology* (Dublin, 1946), p. 293; T. M. Charles-Edwards, '*Tochmarc Étaíne*: a literal interpretation', in Michael Richter and Jean-Michel Picard (ed.), *Ogma: Essays in Celtic Studies in honour of Próinséas Ní Chatháin* (Dublin, 2002), pp. 172-73).

occurring at the *omphalos*, that sacred spot from which it was traditionally held that mankind emerged at the beginning of recurrent epochs. The conversion of the pool into a worm is a little hard to envisage, and may reflect misunderstanding of an earlier version, in which the microcosmic 'worm' floated in the generative waters of the primæval flood – like the infant Taliesin in his skin bag.

It is likely that this sophisticated explanation of the birth-process belonged to learned lore transmitted by the druids. Caesar, who was exceptionally well-informed concerning their order, described how they taught that souls (*animae*) do not perish with death, but are transmitted to another body.[120] This refined doctrine became partially rationalized into realization of the invisible soul-substance as a tangible creature, described as a grub, worm, or snake, i.e. a minuscule entity of indeterminate *genus*.[121]

Anne Ross has drawn attention to the iconography of Celtic and Germanic snake-goddesses:

> Single goddesses are interesting in that they appear not only with snakes of normal type, but, on occasions, with the Celtic iconographic hybrid, the ram-horned or ram-headed snake, which seems to have come into being through an attempt to combine the imagery of the ram (a fertility motif) with the chthonic emblem of the snake.

A pertinent instance in Britain manifests component elements of the myth:

> One British goddess from Ilkley in Yorkshire stands grasping two snakes in her hands … her snakes are rigid, zigzag shapes. It is possible that we have a name for this goddess: she may be Verbeia the goddess of the river Wharfe in Ilkley, where an altar to her was set up; indeed, the form of the snakes themselves may represent rippling water.[122]

Here we encounter combined imagery of the sovereignty goddess, paired snakes, fertility, and water. The fact that Verbeia holds two snakes recalls the birth-tale of Conchobar discussed above. In the story of *Math uab Mathonwy*, the virgin Arianrhod bears twin boys in succession. The first, a sturdy yellow-haired child, is baptized Dylan and inexplicably takes to the sea:

> And there and then, as soon as he came to the sea, he took on the sea's nature (*annyan y mor a gauas*) and swam as well as the best fish in the sea. Because of that he was called Dylan Eil Ton – no wave ever broke under him.

120 Otto Seel (ed.), *C. Ivlii Caesaris Commentarii Rervm Gestarvm: Bellvm Gallicvm* (Leipzig, 1961), p. 186.

121 The *psyche* was envisaged in Greek tradition in the guise of a snake (Onians, *The Origins of European Thought about the Body, the Mind the Soul, the World Time, and Fate*, pp. 122, 129, 159, 206–7, 249; Jan Bremmer, *The Early Greek Concept of the Soul* (Princeton, 1983), pp. 80–81, 127).

122 Anne Ross, *Pagan Celtic Britain: Studies in Iconography and Tradition* (London, 1967), plate 68a; Miranda Green, *Symbol and Image in Celtic Religious Art* (London, 1989), pp. 25–26. Cf. Helmut Birkhan, *Kelten: Versuch einer Gesamtdarstellung ihrer Kultur* (Vienna, 1997), p. 1076. The Ilkley inscription is reproduced in R. G. Collingwood and R. P. Wright (ed.), *The Roman Inscriptions of Britain: I Inscriptions on Stone* (Oxford, 1965), pp. 212–13. The name of the goddess may be perpetuated in that of the river (Eilert Ekwall, *English River-Names* (Oxford, 1928), p. 455).

It has been contended that he became a seal,[123] but if so that must represent a secondary interpretation. What the text tells us is that he was not a fish (nor implicitly any other sea-creature), but became absorbed as an element of the boundless ocean.[124] His name means 'Dylan, Son of the Wave', and it is with waves that he is particularly associated. (Welsh *dylan* means 'sea' or 'wave', which was evidently taken for a proper noun before the composition of *Math uab Mathonwy*). A rhetorical question in the Book of Taliesin enquires, 'Why is the roar of the sea fierce against the shore? It is avenging Dylan.' Again, the Stanzas of the Graves record that 'where the wave makes a noise, the grave of Dylan is at Llan Beuno'.[125]

According to Welsh and Irish tradition, the sea rolls against the shore in continual successions of nine waves, of which the ninth was widely accorded especial potency.[126] As the brothers Rees explained:

> The ninth wave is the greatest, but it comes from the outermost limits of the cosmos. What lies beyond the bounds of the cosmos is, in a sense, inferior to it, but it is also the source of all things.[127]

This made the ninth wave a bearer of wisdom from the wellspring of eternity. A prophetic poem ascribed to Merlin (Myrddin) makes him declare: 'And I prophesy before the ninth wave.'[128]

The ninth wave was also endowed with sexual potency. The pseudo-Taliesin poet declared: 'As for creation, I was created from nine forms of elements … from water of the ninth wave.'[129] Welsh tradition told of 'a mermaid, bearing the name of Gwenhidwy ['White Phantom'], whose sheep were the waves and … the ninth wave was the ram'.[130] Ram and goat are familiar symbols of male sexual vigour in early cosmologies and folklore tradition, and a semantic connexion has been traced in several languages between the words for 'goat', 'sea, waves', and 'sexual potency'.[131] The phallic significance of the ram is reflected in Celtic mythology by the widespread iconographic motif of the ram-headed serpent.[132]

---

123 Sarah Larratt Keefer, 'The lost tale of Dylan in the Fourth Branch of *The Mabinogi*', *Studia Celtica* (Cardiff, 1989/90), xxiv/xxv, pp. 26–37.

124 *Celticvm XV*, p. 357.

125 J. Gwenogvryn Evans (ed.), *Facsimile & Text of the Book of Taliesin* (Llanbedrog, 1910), p. 27; Jarman (ed.), *Llyfr Du Caerfyrddin*, p. 36; Patrick K. Ford (ed.), *Ystoria Taliesin* (Cardiff, 1992), p. 136.

126 Best, Bergin, O'Brien, and O'Sullivan (ed.), *The Book of Leinster*, p. 51; David Comyn and Rev. Patrick S. Dinneen (ed.), *The History of Ireland by Geoffrey Keating, D.D.* (London, 1902–14), ii, pp. 85–86; J. H. Bernard and R. Atkinson (ed.), *The Irish Liber Hymnorum* (London, 1898), i, p. 25; Fergus Kelly, *Early Irish Farming: a study based mainly on the law-texts of the 7th and 8th centuries AD* (Dublin, 1997), pp. 569–70; Trevelyan, *Folk-Lore and Folk-Stories of Wales*, p. 1.

127 Rees and Rees, *Celtic Heritage*, p. 204. A variant of this belief was evidently known to Mrs Thrale (a Welsh lady), who condemned as 'a great Mistake that every tenth Wave is bigger then the rest … I have watched the Sea for hours at Brighthelmstone, and never could make it come right to the Notion either in calm or rough Weather' (Katharine C. Balderston (ed.), *Thraliana: The Diary of Mrs. Hester Lynch Thrale (Later Mrs. Piozzi) 1776–1809* (Oxford, 1951), p. 370).

128 Jarman (ed.), *Llyfr Du Caerfyrddin*, p. 29.

129 Gwenogvryn Evans (ed.), *Facsimile & Text of the Book of Taliesin*, p. 25.

130 T. Gwynn Jones, *Welsh Folklore and Folk-Custom* (London, 1930), p. 75.

131 Françoise Bader, *La langue des dieux, ou l'hermétisme des poètes indo-européens* (Pisa, 1989), pp. 130, 197–98.

132 Ross, *Pagan Celtic Britain*, pp. 342–45.

In Norse mythology the god Heimdallr, whose name is associated with a poetic name for 'ram' (*heimdali*), is described as a ram, born at the world's edge, the son of nine mothers, who were nine waves of the ocean.[133] He was the divine ancestor of humanity, an exalted, otiose deity, distinguished from all the other gods.[134] This recalls the belief in renewal of the world by successive cycles of nine generations, discussed above on pages **211–212**, while the sexual symbolism of the ram-headed god who renews the cycle is too evident to require elaboration.

The pseudo-Taliesin poet declares that 'I am frail and small on the frothy surface of Dylan's sea', and that he subsists 'in the water as foam'. This suggests an archaic version of the account of the infant Taliesin's being borne across the sea in a leather bag or coracle, which Patrick Ford interprets as a symbol of the womb.[135] It also evokes the widespread identification of foam with seminal fluid, a concept famously attested in the myth of Aphrodite, the first element of whose name is probably ἀφρός, 'foam',[136] and who was generated from spume at the edge of the sea.[137]

Reverting to the story of the twin birth of Dylan and Lleu, it will be recalled that in *Math uab Mathonwy* Lleu was conceived as 'a small something' (*y ryw bethan*), which was incubated by his father, the wizard Gwydion. It was further seen that Welsh *rhyw bethan* corresponds to Irish *míl bec*, that tiny 'creature' which passes into the female womb, to be conceived in due course as an infant child.

It is tempting to regard this twin birth-tale as reflecting dual aspects of an interrelated theme in Celtic mythology.[138] First, Arianrhod gives birth to Dylan, when she steps over Gwydion's wand. Next, she lets fall the embryo of Lleu, while preparing to depart through Gwydion's doorway. In each case delivery takes place at a liminal juncture. Gwydion's chamber is plainly a rationalization

133 Jan de Vries, *Altgermanische Religionsgeschichte* (Berlin, 1956–57), ii, pp. 238–44; Georges Dumézil, 'Remarques comparatives sur le dieu scandinave Heimdallr', *Études Celtiques* (Paris, 1959), viii, pp. 269–72; Jan de Vries, *Altnordisches Etymologisches Wörterbuch* (Leiden, 1961), p. 219; Clive Tolley, *Shamanism in Norse Myth and Magic* (Helsinki, 2009), i, pp. 369–405.

134 R. L. M. Derolez, *Les dieux et la religion des Germains* (Paris, 1962), pp. 134–39; Richard North, *Heathen Gods in Old English Literature* (Cambridge, 1997), pp. 280–87.

135 Gwenogvryn Evans (ed.), *Facsimile & Text of the Book of Taliesin*, p. 23; Ford (ed.), *Ystoria Taliesin*, p. 96. On the Polynesian island of Tikopia, birth ceremonies included 'appeals for *manu* to a particular ancestor or deity whom the family regard as likely to be interested. Then he is asked to present the child in the normal position to make birth easy, and to expedite labour by bringing on the flooding. This is referred to here as "the twice-breaking wave"; other formulae refer to a larger succession of waves' (Raymond Firth, *Tikopia Ritual and Belief* (London, 1967), p. 41).

136 Paul Friedrich, *The Meaning of Aphrodite* (Chicago, 1978), pp. 201–202; Michael Janda, 'The Religion of the Indo-Europeans', in Karlene Jones-Bley, Martin E. Huld, Angela della Volpe, and Miriam Robbins Dexter (ed.), *Proceedings of the Seventeenth Annual UCLA Indo-European Conference: Los Angeles October 27-28, 2005* (Washington, 2006), p. 7. An alternative suggestion that the identification with ἀφρός represents popular etymology need not materially alter its significance in the present context (Pierre Chantraine, *Dictionnaire étymologique de la langue grecque: Histoire des mots; avec un Supplément sous la direction de: Alain Blanc, Charles de Lamberterie, Jean-Louis Perpillou* (Paris, 1999), p. 148). Cf. Hjalmar Frisk, *Griechisches Etymologisches Wörterbuch* (Heidelberg, 1954–72), i, p. 197.

137 Foam formed around the castrated testicles of Ouranos, from which Aphrodite was born (M. L. West (ed.), *Hesiod: Theogony* (Oxford, 1966), p. 119). 'The Greeks apparently looked upon foam as one manifestation of the sky-god's seed' (Cook, *Zeus*, iii, pp. 273–76). Cf. Giulia Sissa, *Greek Virginity* (Cambridge, Mass., 1990), pp. 31, 188; Hartland, *The Legend of Perseus*, i, p. 134; Miriam Robbins Dexter, 'Born of the Foam: Goddesses of River and Sea in the "Kingship in Heaven Myth"', in Dorothy Disterheft, Martin Huld, John Greppin, and Edgar C. Polomé (ed.), *Studies in Honor of Jaan Puhvel* (Washington, 1997), ii, pp. 83–102.

138 'The whole story of the birth is so confused that we cannot very well separate the histories of the twins' (W. J. Gruffydd, *Math vab Mathonwy: An Inquiry into the Origins and Development of the Fourth Branch of the Mabinogi with the Text and a Translation* (Cardiff, 1928), p. 136).

of what was in an earlier version a cosmic dwelling. What amounts to the conception of Dylan in a wave of the sea represents the birth-process in a cosmic dimension. In *Math uab Mathonwy* his virgin mother Arianrhod is described as dwelling in a castle where sea and land meet,[139] and as moon-goddess ('Silver Wheel') she may be expected to have controlled the tides.[140] From this it may inferred that her delivery was originally envisaged as taking place in an archetypally liminal context on the sea-shore: the borderline between the material and the eternal. Dylan, who does not bear a theonym, is the seed or embryo borne across ocean (i.e. from the Otherworld) by a (ninth?) wave (*dylan*) to land. Next, the *rhyw bethan*, 'small entity', evolves into the god Lleu. It will be recalled that, in *Cyfranc Lludd a Lleuelys*, Lleuelys (i.e. Lleu) also comes from across the sea to join his brother Lludd, king of Britain.

The story of the births of Arianrhod's twin sons derives from archaic tradition, reflected also in the twin ram-headed serpents borne by goddesses in British and Gaulish iconography. As was seen, small paired creatures feature in Nennius's account of the paired *vermes* found at Dinas Emrys, as well as in early Irish birth-tales. In 'The Conception of Conchobar' (*Compert Conchobair*), described earlier in another context, we learn that the hero's mother Nes went to the River Conchobor. There she strained water through her veil into a cup, returning with it to the druid Cathbad, who demanded that a candle be brought to examine its content. Two worms became visible in the liquid (*Is ann batar dá dhuirb isin uisci*). The druid forced Nes to drink them down, which she did with a gulp for each. Nine months later she gave birth to the infant Conchobar, on a flagstone beside the river bearing his name. At the moment of parturition he was discovered to be holding a worm in each hand. He tumbled into the river, to be rescued by Cathbad.

These paired worms clearly represent what may be termed 'soul-creatures', and it was surely such a birth-tale that underlies the elaborated and partially rationalized story of the parallel births of Dylan and Lleu. The druid Cathbad's presiding over the twin births in the Irish tale corresponds to the rôle of the divine druid Gwydion in *Math uab Mathonwy*. Also common to both is the association of water with conception and birth. Particularly intriguing is the detail that Nes strained the water bearing the two worms through her veil into the cup. No explanation is given for this curious detail, which has not to my knowledge been discussed by scholars. However, it is one of several clues that serve to explain the pagan Celtic myth of parturition.

Association of a cloth covering with a birth-tale recurs in several Irish and Welsh versions. That it comprised an archaic component of the myth is confirmed by unconvincing attempts to account for its presence. Thus, we learn of the baby Cormac mac Airt that a vessel (*muide*) of yew was constructed about him, with a purple cloak placed on top, 'in order that the hands of the people greeting the boy might not reach him, lest he be crushed'.[141] This explanation makes no sense in the context of the episode, where mother and child are depicted as dwelling in an unpopulated wilderness. The exegetical parenthesis represents an attempt to explain a motif which was no longer understood. Setting aside the suspect rationalization, why should the

139 In the twelfth century AD it was believed that *Argante* (an Old Welsh form of *Arianrhod*) ruled over Avalon, a land lying beyond the sea, and implicitly a realm of the dead (G. L. Brook and R. F. Leslie (ed.), *Laʒamon: Brut* (Oxford, 1963–78), ii, p. 750).

140 The link between phases of the moon and tidal ebb and flow was fully understood in the ancient world (Hans Joachim Mette (ed.), *Pytheas von Massalia* (Berlin, 1952), p. 17; L. Edelstein and I. G. Kidd (ed.), *Posidonius* (Cambridge, 1988-99), i, pp. 190–99); H. Rackham, W. H. S. Jones, and D. E. Eichholz, (ed.), *Pliny: Natural History* (London, 1938–62), i, p. 346).

141 Tomás Ó Cathasaigh (ed.), *The Heroic Biography of Cormac mac Airt* (Dublin, 1977), p. 122; Máirín O Daly (ed.), *Cath Maige Mucrama: The Battle of Mag Mucrama* (Dublin, 1975), p. 70.

infant have been placed in a vessel, and what was the purpose of the cloak, which after all might have suffocated him? Attempts have been made to explain the vessel as some more appropriate receptacle, but they remain unsatisfactory, both on the principle of *lectio difficilior*, and the inappropriate nature of the suggested analogies.[142] After all, the noun *muide*, derived from Latin *modius*, signifies 'a vessel for holding liquids'.[143]

A likely explanation is that his source, which the author plainly failed to understand, recounted how the 'worm' (i.e. embryo) of the future hero was contained in a cup or other vessel, covered by a cloth, as occurs in *Compert Conchobair*. This would explain Gwydion's peculiar treatment of the embryo or soul-creature (*y ryw bethan*), which grew up to be the wonder-child Lleu. On its being dropped by Arianrhod, we are told that, before anyone could see it, Gwydion wrapped a covering or veil of silk (*llenn o bali*) around it, and hid it in a small chest (*cist*). Why it was required to be treated in this oddly elaborate fashion is unexplained. The Irish analogy suggests that originally the 'small thing' was preserved within a receptacle covered by a silken cloth.

We appear to have travelled some way from the two 'dragons' discovered by Lludd and Lleu at the Centre of Britain. However, reconsideration of that episode will clarify the digression. Lludd dug a hole in the ground, into which he placed a vat full of the best mead possible, and laid a covering of silk (*llenn o pali*) on top of it. In due course the dragons appear and begin fighting, after which they sink exhausted onto the cover, which they drag down with them to the base of the vat. There they drink the mead and fall asleep, after which Lludd wraps the cloth around them and hides them in a stone chest (*kist vaen*).

The resemblance to the birth-tale of Lleu, who (under the name of *Lleuelys*) expounds the mystery to Lludd, is sufficiently telling to require little emphasis. The two amorphous entities are contained in a receptacle, which to have contained mead must originally have been a vat or drinking vessel. They are wrapped in a covering of silk, again without reason given. Subsequently, like the embryo Lleu in *Math uab Mathonwy*, they are placed in a chest.

The Irish birth-tales of Conchobar and Cormac on the one hand, and the Welsh accounts of Lleu's birth and the entrapment of the dragons on the other, suggest an explanation reconcilable in terms of what was originally a common tradition. The two 'dragons' (i.e. *vermes*, as rendered in Latin in the *Historia Brittonum* version) are the two 'worms' ingested by Nes. The vat filled with mead is the drinking vessel which contained them, and the silken cover the veil through which they were strained.[144]

The mead in the vat in the British tale is likely to represent an archaic element, mead being the sacramental drink par excellence, and also the name borne by the Irish sovereignty goddess *Medb*, whose name means 'mead'.[145] It was she who proffered a cup of mead to each lawful king of Ireland

---

142 Ó Cathasaigh (ed.), *The Heroic Biography of Cormac mac Airt*, pp. 53–54; O Daly (ed.), *Cath Maige Mucrama*, p. 124.

143 Quin et al. (ed.), *Dictionary of the Irish Language*, 'M', col. 184; Vendryes, Bachellery, and Lambert, *Lexique étymologique de l'irlandais ancien*, M-71.

144 A helpful discussion of some of these issues, together with Indo-European parallels, is provided by Angelique Gulermovich Epstein, 'Miscarriages and Miraculous Births in Indo-European Tradition', *The Journal of Indo-European Studies* (Washington, 1994), xxii, pp. 151–63.

145 'The very name Medb (<*Medʰw-ā) is a feminine derivative of *mid* "mead" (<*medʰu) and must once have signified something like "mead-woman"' (Kim McCone, *Pagan Past and Christian Present in Early Irish Literature* (Naas, 1990), p. 109; cf. pp. 109–10, 120). Cf. also Wolfgang Meid, 'Der mythologische Hintergrund der Irischen Sage', in Miriam Robbins Dexter and Edgar C. Polomé (ed.), *Varia on the Indo-European Past: Papers in Memory of Marija Gimbutas* (Washington, 1997), p. 250.

in succession.[146] In 'The Phantom's Frenzy' (*Baile in Scáil*), a young girl personifying the sovereignty dispenses ale from a cup to successive kings of Ireland from the primal ruler Conn onwards. This ritual is performed under instruction of the god Lug, Irish counterpart of Welsh Lleu.[147] The story clearly evolved from the myth of Sovereignty, whereby the birth of successive kings results from a union in the Otherworld between Lug and the Maiden Sovereignty, the generative element being passed from one to the other in a goblet of mead. This event in the divine world was replicated on earth at royal inaugurations, with the queen presenting the goblet to the king.[148]

In the Irish tale 'The Conception of Cú Chulainn' (*Compert Con Culainn*), the maiden Deichtine enters a mysterious house. Passing through a door (a characteristically symbolic representation of the point of access between the material world and the Otherworld),[149] she encounters a nameless woman in her final birth-pains. This mysterious female bears a boy in Deichtine's presence, while outside a mare gives birth to twin foals, who become the boy's companions. Deichtine adopts the child, and returns to the capital of Ulster at Emain Macha. Sadly, the boy dies while still an infant.

In her grief at the child's death, Deichtine requests a drink, which is brought to her in a copper vessel. As she approaches her lips to the cup, a *míl bec* (tiny creature) springs from the liquid into her mouth, and after two or three attempts is absorbed by her breath. That night she is visited by the god Lug mac Eithne, who reveals that she is pregnant by him, that it was his son whom she had raised, he who entered her throat (from the goblet), and his the son that now lies within her womb. Thus, it is evident that the woman Deichtine found in the house was a mortal counterpart of herself.

Afterwards she weds a mortal, Sualtam mac Roech. Ashamed at lying with a man when pregnant, on going to bed

> she rejected a second time that which was within her bosom and recovered her virginity. She then went to her husband. She swiftly became pregnant again, and gave birth to a child called Setanta.

That is, he was the destined hero Cú Chulainn.[150]

The story is complicated by other factors (there are two manuscript versions), but essential elements of this section comprise the following: (i) Deichtine conceives a son by the god Lug in the Otherworld, who dies in infancy; (ii) at the court of Emain Macha she is impregnated by a

---

146   *Celticvm XV*, pp. 339–50.

147   Kevin Murray (ed.), *Baile in Scáil: 'The Phantom's Frenzy'* (Dublin, 2004), p. 34.

148   Michael J. Enright, *Lady with a Mead Cup: Ritual, Prophecy and Lordship in the European Warband from La Tène to the Viking Age* (Dublin, 1996).

149   Egress from the Otherworld hall on the island of Gwales was provided by three doors, one of which afforded access to this world (Derick S. Thomson (ed.), *Branwen uerch Lyr: The Second of the Four Branches of the Mabinogi edited from the White Book of Rhydderch with variants from the Red Book of Hergest and from Peniarth 6* (Dublin, 1961), p. 16). For other examples of doors leading to Fairyland or the Otherworld, cf. Nora White (ed.), *Compert Mongáin and Three Other Early Mongán Tales* (Maynooth, 2006), p. 272; J. F. Campbell (ed.), *Leabhar na Feinne: Heroic Gaelic Ballads Collected in Scotland Chiefly from 1512 to 1871* (London, 1872), p. 198; Rhŷs, *Celtic Folklore*, pp. 20–22; Alexander Carmichael (ed.), *Carmina Gadelica: Hymns and Incantations with Illustrative Notes on Words, Rites, and Customs, Dying and Obsolete: Orally Collected in the Highlands and Islands of Scotland* (Edinburgh, 1900–71), ii, pp. 22, 23; Charles Plummer (ed.), *Bethada Náem nÉrenn: Lives of Irish Saints* (Oxford, 1922), i, p. 71. The Turkic peoples of the Altai-Sayan mountains believe that entrance to the Otherworld is provided by a door in a rock or cave (Maria M. Tátar, 'Mythology as an areal problem in the Altai-Sayan area: the sacred holes and caves', in Pentikäinen (ed.), *Shamanism and Northern Ecology*, pp. 269–70, 272).

150   A. G. van Hamel (ed.), *Compert Con Culainn and Other Stories* (Dublin, 1933), p. 5.

minute soul-creature, which again proves to derive from Lug; (iii) she weds the mortal Sualtam, rejects the embryo, and recovers her virginity; (iv) she gives birth to Cú Chulainn, who is in reality an incarnation of Lug.

Allowing for complexities inevitably accruing over centuries of transmission, essentials of the theme appear as follows.

1. Deichtine personifies the maiden sovereignty of Ireland, who, despite giving birth to successive kings and heroes, remains eternally a virgin. (Her name is thought to derive from the adjective *decht*, 'pure, refined').[151]

2. As we are oddly told that she rejected 'a second time that which was in her bosom', it looks as though her offspring by Lug was dropped, like Arianrhod's second infant, in the form of a 'small thing'.

3. She weds a mortal nobleman, giving birth to the hero Cú Chulainn.

4. In reality, the father is Lug, who as a divinity passes between the Otherworld and the terrestrial realm. He entered her womb in the form of a tiny entity, *míl bec*.

5. Deichtine recovers (i.e. retains) her virginity.

All this suggests that an earlier version described how Deichtine's pregnancy in the Otherworld was paralleled by one in this.[152] In each case the real father was Lug, while in the earthly case the putative father was the mortal Sualtam. The Otherworld birth was aborted, since the gods are eternal, and mortal births consequently cannot take place in their realm.

This section of *Compert Con Culainn* is futher illuminated by parallels found in the Welsh story *Pwyll Pendeuic Dyuet*.[153] Pwyll (whose name means 'wisdom') moves with facility between his earthly kingdom of Dyfed, and the Otherworld realm of Annwfn. While in Annwfn he sleeps with the queen of that land, without however entering into sexual relations, i.e. she remains a virgin. Returned to Dyfed, he weds Rhiannon, whose name (< *Rīgantonā*, 'divine queen') and attributes proclaim her the sovereignty goddess.[154] After Pwyll has repaired to Preseli Mountain, implicitly an appropriately sanctified spot in Dyfed, she bears him a son, who however vanishes the same night. The scene shifts abruptly to the court of a king named Teyrnon ('Lord'), in the kingdom of Gwent to the east. He possesses the finest mare in the realm, which bears a foal every May Eve. On this occasion, however, the foal is removed by a mysterious claw, and in its place Teyrnon discovers a baby wrapped in a silken cloth (*llen o bali*). Teyrnon brings the boy up as his own, and later takes him to the court of Pwyll, where he is identified as Rhiannon's vanished son.

---

151   Vendryes, Bachellery, and Lambert, *Lexique étymologique de l'irlandais ancien*, D-39-40.

152   This pagan Celtic myth of conception finds a parallel in Lapp shamanistic belief. 'The principal function of [the supreme deity] Radien ... is to bring down the human soul into the mother's womb. This takes place through the mediation of the goddess Maderakka who, in her turn, will add a body to the soul so that a complete embryo comes into existence' (Rafael Karsten, *The Religion of the Samek: Ancient Beliefs and Cults of the Scandinavian and Finnish Lapps* (Leiden, 1955), p. 47; cf. p. 56). Among Australian aborigines, it was widely believed that divine 'spirit children' pass into a pregnant mother's womb (Ronald M. Berndt, *Australian Aboriginal Religion* (Leiden, 1974), v, pp. 10–11).

153   Cf. the illuminating discussion by Françoise Le Roux, 'La conception de Cúchulainn: Commentaire du texte', *Ogam: Tradition celtique* (Rennes, 1965), xvii, pp. 406–10.

154   Eric P. Hamp, 'Mabinogi', *The Transactions of the Honourable Society of Cymmrodorion: Sessions 1974 and 1975* (London, 1975), p. 245; John T. Koch, 'A Welsh Window on the Iron Age: Manawydan, Mandubracios', *Cambridge Medieval Celtic Studies* (Cambridge, 1987), xiv, p. 34.

Common elements in the Irish and Welsh stories are apparent. A goddess conceives a child in the Otherworld, who dies or disappears, 'thus failing to make the direct transition from the fully supernatural to the fully human realm'.[155] What is effectively the same child appears in a mortal household at the identical moment. Meanwhile a foal (or foals) is likewise born at the same time. The child grows up to become a princely hero.

Yet again, the motif recurs in a brief passage in the mediæval Welsh tale *Culhwch ac Olwen*, a repository of allusions to the old mythology. The hero Culhwch is directed to discover 'Mabon mab Modron, who was stolen from between his mother and the wall when only three nights old'.[156] Since *Mabon mab Modron* means 'Divine Son of Divine Mother', these names effectively correspond to the goddess Rhiannon and her abducted son Pryderi. Like the door through which Deichtine passes at her first conception, the unexplained wall beside which Mabon was parted from his mother symbolizes the barrier dividing this world from eternity.

These accounts, confused as they have become in greater or lesser degree, originate in the mythology of royal or heroic births. While kings and heroes possess mortal fathers, in reality their mothers are impregnated by a deity, who was generally understood to be the god Lug. This was accounted for by a simultaneous conception occurring in the Otherworld, where the goddess's parturition is confined to delivery of the minuscule 'soul-creature', i.e. that vivifying particle which is transmitted from the father to the mother during sexual congress: in Irish *cruim, míl bec*; in Welsh *pryf, rhyw bethan*. The soul-creature slips from the Otherworld into that of mortal men, where it enters a maiden's womb.

This mythical paradigm probably accounts for the incidence of dual 'soul-creatures', such as the paired minute worms in the birth-tale of Conchobar (*Compert Conchobair*). It may also be reflected in Welsh folklore tradition:

> In some parts of the Principality there was formerly a tradition that every farm-house had two snakes, a male and a female. They never appeared until just before the death of the master or mistress of the house; then the snakes died.[157]

It is a pity that Marie Trevelyan did not provide the Welsh term for these 'snakes'. As household 'soul-creatures', were they *pryfed*? As has been seen, the term covers a wide range of small beings, ranging from actual snakes to minuscule worms and maggots, real or mythical.[158]

Snakes in primitive cultures are widely believed to enjoy a sympathetic relationship with man. Often they are encouraged to live in houses alongside the family.

> The Montols [of Northern Nigeria] believe that at the birth of every individual of their race, male and female, one of these snakes, of the same sex, is also born. If the snake be killed, his human partner in life dies also and at the same time. If the wife of a compound-owner gives birth to a son, shortly after the interesting event, the snake of the establishment will be seen with a young one of corresponding sex. From the moment of

155   McCone, *Pagan Past and Christian Present*, p. 198.
156   Bromwich and Simon Evans (ed.), *Culhwch and Olwen*, p. 31.
157   Trevelyan, *Folk-Lore and Folk-Stories of Wales*, p. 174.
158   *Geiriadur Prifysgol Cymru: A Dictionary of the Welsh Language* (Cardiff, 1950–2002), pp. 2919–21.

birth, these two, the snake and the man, share a life of common duration, and the measure of the one is the measure of the other.

Similarly, among the Zulus the hut-snake was the alter ego of one of its human inhabitants. A scar on a snake corresponded to one borne by a man, while a man with one eye was matched by a nearby serpent similarly afflicted.[159]

In the Nilotic Sudan,

> among the Western Twij Dinka, one of the emblems of [the divinity] Flesh is a small and harmless red snake, and Rek Dinka have told me that Flesh will sometimes manifest itself to masters of the fishing-spear (in a dream?) as a tiny newborn child of a light red colour, lighter than any Dinka child is even at birth. To dream of a small red snake, or a red newborn child, is counted as a good omen. One man told me that Flesh manifested itself in a dream as a red baby coming out of the river, a clear association of ideas with the divinity Flesh with the origin of the first master of the fishing-spear in the river, and that recurrent theme of Dinka thought, the impregnation of a barren woman by a Power of the river.[160]

Here again we encounter the combination of the small snake with human birth and insemination from immersion in water.

In conclusion, I would draw attention to Jeremy Narby's intriguing investigation, in which he associates the twin serpents of shamanistic belief with the DNA double helix.[161] His argument would surely be fortified by analogy with Celtic soul creatures, which are frequently envisaged as paired dragons or serpents.[162]

The Gundestrup Cauldron

Returning to Celtic tradition, it has been seen that the mythical Irish King Conchobar's mother Nes conceived him by drinking two minute worms from a cup. When her son was born, he was discovered holding a worm in each hand. This recalls imagery on a plate of the celebrated Gundestrup cauldron. One of the most striking artefacts of the Celtic world, it contains images in relief of motifs largely, if not wholly, deriving from Celtic mythology.

---

159 J. G. Frazer, *Balder the Beautiful: The Fire-Festivals of Europe and the Doctrine of the External Soul* (London, 1913), ii, pp. 209–10; The Rev. Canon Callaway, *The Religious System of the Amazulu. Izinyanga Zokubula; or, Divination, as Existing among the Amazulu, in their own Words, with a Translation into English, and Notes* (London, 1870), pp. 196–200. Among the Greeks, the snake was regarded as a soul animal, linked to the house or grave of the departed (Bremmer, *The Early Greek Concept of the Soul,* pp. 80–81), while in Germany many homes likewise contained beneficent house snakes (Jakob Grimm, *Germanic Mythology* (Washington, 1997), p. 82).

160 Lienhardt, *Divinity and Experience*, pp. 142–43.

161 Jeremy Narby, *The Cosmic Serpent, DNA and the origins of Knowledge* (London, 1998).

162 Paired dragons recur as elemental beings in cosmologies worldwide (Ivar Paulson, 'Die Religionen der nordasiatischen (sibirischen) Völker', in Ivar Paulson, Åke Hultkrantz, and Karl Jettmar, *Die Religionen Nordeurasiens und der amerikanischen Arktis* (Stuttgart, 1962), p. 38; Kaj Birket-Smith, 'Studies in Circumpacific Culture Relations: IV. The Double-Headed Serpent', *Historisk-filosofiske Meddelelser* (Copenhagen, 1973), xlvii, pp. 1–14; Terence DuQuesne, 'Raising the Serpent Power: some parallels between Egyptian religion and Indian Tantra' in idem (ed.), *Hermes Aegyptiacus: Egyptological Studies for BH Stricker* (Oxford, 1995), pp. 53–68).

Discovered in Denmark in 1891, it is believed to date from the last century or so BC.[163] Its origin has long been the subject of considerable debate. It has been suggested from iconographic parallels that the cauldron was the work of a craftsman belonging to a Celtic people (the Triballoi) in Thrace.[164]

Alternatively, Garrett Olmsted argued that comparisons with motifs on Gaulish coinage and other artefacts indicate the cauldron's origin in Gaul, somewhere between the rivers Loire and Somme. More specifically, he suggested that the cauldron was constructed at the town of Cenabum, now Orléans.[165] At the time the cauldron is believed to have been made, Cenabum was the major entrepôt for trade in Gaul. It represented a major point of intersection, possessing a key bridge across the Loire, about halfway along the river's navigable length.[166]

The conjecture bears suggestive connotations. Cenabum was the principal town of the tribe of the Carnutes, being probably the place where Caesar describes the druids of Gaul as convening on a fixed date each year to confer on religious questions, and judge cases in their courts.[167] The location was regarded as centre of all Gaul, i.e. its *omphalos*.[168] Of the name of the town,

> The element *cen-* … represents the IE. root *ken-* 'to spring from, to issue from', which in turn derives from an Indo-European verb *k̇en-*, meaning 'give birth'. The root also provided the basis for *k̇en(t^h-)*, 'clan, tribe, collectivity'.[169]

This recalls one of the primary attributes of the *omphalos*, namely, that it was the place where the country and its people ultimately originated.[170]

The internal baseplate of the Gundestrup Cauldron bears a magnificent bas-relief in silver of a dying bull, with an armed warrior and hound beside it.[171] Now, it is a well-attested fact that bull-sacrifice was one of the principal rites employed at the inauguration of Celtic kings in Ireland and Gaul.[172] In addition to indications that Cenabum was the place where the Cauldron

---

163 Flemming Kaul, 'The Gundestrup Cauldron', in V. Kruta, O. H. Frey, B. Raftery, and M. Szabó (ed.), *The Celts* (London, 1991), p. 538.

164 Flemming Kaul, 'The History of the Find', in Doris Edel (ed.), *Thracian Tales on the Gundestrup Cauldron* (Amsterdam, 1991), pp. 7–42.

165 Garrett S. Olmsted, *The Gundestrup Cauldron: Its Archaeological Context, the Style and Iconography of its Portrayed Motifs, and their Narration of a Gaulish Version of Táin Bó Cúailnge* (Brussels, 1979), pp. 100–102.

166 Seel (ed.), *C. Ivlii Caesaris Commentarii: Bellum Gallicum*, pp. 208, 214–15; Francesco Sbordone (ed.), *Strabonis Geographica* (Rome, 1963–2000), ii, p. 128.

167 Seel (ed.), *C. Ivlii Caesaris Commentarii Rervm Gestarvm: Bellvm Gallicvm*, pp. 183–85.

168 Bernhard Maier, *Die Religion der Kelten: Götter – Mythen – Weltbild* (Munich, 2001), p. 58. 'Centre géographique de la Gaule, Cénabum en était un foyer religieux important, ce qui explique l'afflux d'éléments non indigènes' (Germaine Aujac, François Lasserre, and Raoul Baladié (ed.), *Strabon: Géographie* (Paris, 1966-89), ii, p. 148).

169 D. Ellis Evans, *Gaulish Personal Names: A Study of some Continental Celtic Formations* (Oxford, 1967), pp. 175–77; Gamkrelidze and Ivanov, *Indo-European and the Indo-Europeans*, p. 652.

170 On the other hand, Pierre-Yves Lambert believes the name may not be of Celtic derivation ('The place names of *Lugdunensis* [Λουγδουνησία] (Ptolemy II 8]', in Javier de Hoz, Eugenio R. Luján, and Patrick Sims-Williams (ed.), *New Approaches to Celtic Place-Names in Ptolemy's Geography* (Madrid, 2005), pp. 242–43).

171 Flemming Kaul, *Gundestrupkedlen: Baggrund og billedverden* (Copenhagen, 1991), p. 26.

172 Eleanor Knott (ed.), *Togail Bruidne Da Derga* (Dublin, 1936), p. 4; Myles Dillon (ed.), *Serglige Con Culainn* (Dublin, 1953), pp. 8–9. Cf. Françoise Le Roux, 'Recherches sur les éléments rituels de l'élection royale Irlandaise et Celtique', *Ogam* (1963), xv, pp. 245–53; Proinsias Mac Cana, 'Conservation and

Plate of the Gundestrup Cauldron. (Author's collection)

originated, the pictorial reliefs on the latter suggest that it was closely associated with portentous rituals conducted at a Sacred Centre. However, in the present context the geographical provenance of the cauldron remains a secondary issue.[173]

Another plate depicts a procession of warriors bearing a huge tree, as each of their company is in turn immersed in a cauldron by a deity. This must represent the World Tree, *Yggdrasil* in Norse mythology, which was believed to stand at the earth's centre, providing a link between earth and heaven.[174] It also symbolized the divine kingship. After wedding the Norwegian king Hálfdan the Black, his queen Ragnhild dreamed she held a thorn which grew swiftly into a giant tree, whose branches covered all Norway and beyond.[175]

Innovation in Early Celtic Literature', *Études Celtiques* (Paris, 1972), xiii, pp. 91–94; Francis John Byrne, *Irish Kings and High-Kings* (London, 1973), pp. 17–20.

173 'This controversial cult-vessel … may have been manufactured in Thrace in the third or fourth century BC. But despite its provenance and its possible origins, the cauldron may well have been a Celtic liturgical object. Some of the images fashioned in repoussé on its inner and outer plates – the antlered deity, the wheel-god and the ram-horned serpent for instance – are too idiosyncratic to belong other than to the Celtic world' (Green, *Symbol and Image in Celtic Religious Art* , p. 8).

174 Kaul, *Gundestrupkedlen*, p. 23. Cf. Green, *Symbol and Image in Celtic Religious Art*, p. 155.

175 Bjarni Aðalbjarnarson (ed.), *Heimskringla* (Reykjavik, 1941–51), i, p. 90. Cf. Georgia Dunham Kelchner, *Dreams in Old Norse Literature and their Affinities in Folklore* (Cambridge, 1935), p. 56; King Diarmaid mac Cerbaill dreamed of such a tree growing over Tara, which he identified with himself (Standish H.

Three further plates portray an impressive god grasping on either side of his head two young warriors holding hounds, another holding two stags by their back legs, while a third is embossed with a deity gripping two mythical beasts by their necks.[176]

Given the significance of the cauldron in Celtic mythology as a receptacle of rebirth, together with a vivid depiction on the Gundestrup cauldron of the rite in practice, it is possible that these exotic reptiles (whether hippocamps or dragons) provide a stylized depiction of two such 'worms' as were grasped by the newly born Irish king Conchobar. In Indo-European languages the terminology of 'serpent', 'snake', 'worm', 'dragon', and 'insect' is broadly interchangeable.[177] In a ritual context, such as that which the Gundestrup Cauldron provides, exotic serpentine beasts could have been considered more appropriate than insignificant worms.

Finally, might the curious two-headed creature beneath the godhead, resting its twin heads against two recumbent men on either side of the image, portray the concept of twin births occurring simultaneously in the Otherworld and on earth, separated by an arc representing the curved expanse of ocean/time?

The paired 'dragons' at the British omphalos
It can now be seen that in pagan Celtic Ireland and Britain the concept of divine procreation included the following factors.

1. The divinely engendered 'seed' was envisaged as a minute creature, originally of indeterminate form. Of Deichtine's inhalation of the creature (*míl bec*) in the goblet, which brought about the conception of Cú Chulainn, Françoise Le Roux observed:

   > The general sense of the passage is that the animal was so light, so tiny, that Deichtine's breath was sufficient to cause her to swallow it, without even imbibing the liquid … One will compare the motif of the 'fly' in *Tochmarc Étaíne*, before the rebirth of the goddess.[178]

2. In some instances the liquid contained in the drinking-vessel is left unspecified. However, in view of the fact that that the event frequently takes place at a feast or other social occasion, it is unlikely to have been water. An important rite at royal inaugurations was the queen's presentation of a goblet of mead to the legitimate king, while the sovereignty goddess of Ireland bore the name *Medb*, 'mead'.

3. Evidence suggests that the soul-creature's being filtered through a veil or other cloth covering, when imbibed with the liquid, reflects the concept of a cloth as emblematic of the barrier set between eternity and temporality, through which the embryo must emerge for divinity to become incarnated in humanity. This may also be reflected by the cloth's significance being enhanced by emphasis on its exceptional quality.

O'Grady (ed.), *Silva Gadelica: A Collection of Tales in Irish with Extracts Illustrating Persons and Places* (London, 1892), i, p. 77).

176 Kaul, *Gundestrupkedlen*, pp. 28, 29, 31.

177 Calvert Watkins, *How to Kill a Dragon: Aspects of Indo-European Poetics* (New York and Oxford, 1995), pp. 519–24.

178 *Ogam*, xvii, pp. 373–74.

This also accounts for the fact that the goddess is frequently depicted wearing a veil in Celtic and other mythologies. Rhiannon wears one when wooed by Pwyll,[179] while the *llenllein* worn by Enid in the romance of *Gereint mab Erbin* may likewise have mantled her face.[180] Saint Brigid in Ireland, originally a high goddess, is associated with a veil presented to her by a character called Mac Caille, which means 'Son of the Veil'.[181]

In the *Odyssey*, the goddesses Calypso and Circe don a veil at the moment of Odysseus's departure from their Otherworld isles. The name Calypso (Καλυψώ) means 'veiled one', or 'covered one'.[182]

Thus the veil borne by the euhemerized Celtic sovereignty goddess indicates her divine status vis-à-vis mankind. It also evokes her hymeneal purity: no matter how often she consorts with mortal kings, she remains inviolate in the Otherworld, i.e. 'behind the veil'. The concept appears to be of Indo-European origin, if not older. In the Hittite laws, veiling an adulterous wife reaffirms her marriage, i.e. the slate is symbolically wiped clean.[183]

4. Originally, it seems that in appropriate contexts the cloth or veil was envisaged as a curtain dividing this world from that of eternity. Thus the Welsh word *llen* (Irish *lenn*) may equally denote material or metaphorical cloth. A common meaning is that of a 'figurative veil or curtain (dividing, e.g., this world from the next)'.[184]

Similarly, 'mantles of invisibility' preserved Otherworld figures from observation in this world. When the malign wizard Caswallawn in *Branwen* inflicts indiscriminate slaughter on the inhabitants of Britain, he is described as wearing a 'magic cloak', *llen hut*, and as killing his victims with a sword, which was all of him that was visible to mortal eyes.[185] As he seems to have personified a plague-demon, it may be surmised that in an earlier version his blows were directed against mortal men from behind an enchanted curtain or screen, which concealed his Otherworld persona from his activity in the physical world.

---

179 Thomson (ed.), *Pwyll Pendeuic Dyuet*, pp. 10–11. The Gaulish horse-goddess Epona is represented as veiled in Gaulish sculpture (*Britannia: A Journal of Romano-British & Kindred Studies* (London, 1995), xxvi, p. 305).

180 Robert L. Thomson (ed.), *Ystorya Gereint uab Erbin* (Dublin, 1997), p. 12.

181 John Gwynn (ed.), *Liber Ardmachanus: The Book of Armagh, Edited with Introduction and Appendices* (Dublin, 1913), p. 21; Whitley Stokes (ed.), *Félire Óengusso Céli Dé. The Martyrology of Oengus the Culdee* (London, 1905), p. 66 J. H. Bernard and R. Atkinson (ed.), *The Irish Liber Hymnorum* (London, 1898), i, 114; Donncha Ó hAodha (ed.), *Bethu Brigte* (Dublin, 1978), p. 6. Cf. further Máirín Ní Dhonnchadha, 'Caillech and Other Terms for Veiled Women in Medieval Irish Texts', *Éigse: A Journal of Irish Studies* (Dublin, 1994–5), xxviii, pp. 71–96.

182 Helmut van Thiel (ed.), *Homeri Odyssea* (Hildesheim, 1991), pp. 70, 142; Frisk, *Griechisches Etymologisches Wörterbuch*, i, pp. 768–69.

183 Harry Angier Hoffner, Jr. (ed.), *The Laws of the Hittites: A Critical Edition* (Leiden, 1997), p. 157; cf. p. 226. For the association of a maiden's veil with virginity in Greek mythology and wedding practice, cf. Sissa, *Greek Virginity*, pp. 94–97, while 'in Rome virginity evoked the image of a veil' (p. 175). The moon, which was regarded as a reservoir of souls, impregnated by the sun (Y. Vernière, 'La lune, réservoir des âmes', in François Jouan (ed.), *Mort et fécondité dans les mythologies: Actes du Colloque de Poitiers 13-14 Mai 1983* (Paris, 1986), 101–8), was believed to be veiled (Sophie Lunais, *Recherches sur la lune, I: Les auteurs latins de la fin des guerres puniques à la fin du règne des Antonins* (Leiden, 1979), p. 100).

184 *Geiriadur Prifysgol Cymru*, p. 2151.

185 Thomson (ed.), *Branwen uerch Lyr*, p. 16.

Again, following King Arthur's translation from an historical figure into a deity, he was said to own 'the Mantle in Cornwall: whoever was under it could not be seen, and he would see everyone'.[186]

The supernatural barrier provided by the curtain or veil separating the divine from the earthly realm is strikingly manifested by the magnificent curtain in the Temple of Solomon at Jerusalem, which divided *hekal* (the earth) from *debir* (the heavens):

> The veil represented the boundary between the visible world and the invisible, between time and eternity. Actions performed within the veil were not of this world but were part of the heavenly liturgy. Those who passed through the veil were the mediators, divine and human, who functioned in both worlds …[187]

5. Twin parallel figures in British mythology are Gwri Gwallt Euron in *Pwyll Pendeuic Dyuet*, and Lleu mab Arianrhod in *Math uab Mathonwy*. Each is child of a goddess, born into this world as putative son of an earthly father. Each infant is decribed as being wrapped in cloth of fine silk (*llenn o bali*). No reason is given for this detail, which contrasts with the almost total absence of references to characters' raiment throughout the Four Branches of the *Mabinogi* (the other significant exception being that of Rhiannon's veil). The extraneous nature of this detail is emphasized in the case of Gwri, when it is explained that he was also wrapped in swaddling-clothes. The baby Lleu cast his *llenn* aside, as he struggled to break free (i.e. into the world of mortals).

Sense may be made of all these references to veils, mantles, and bed-coverings, if it be understood that originally the newly born son of a deity was envisaged as emerging through a supernatural barrier, which separated spiritual conception in the Otherworld from carnal parturition on earth. During centuries of transmission of the stories in a Christian milieu, the original significance of the *llenn o bali* became confused and eventually forgotten. However, earlier emphasis laid on the significance of the silken cloth ensured its retention in subsequent literary adaptations. No longer able to comprehend its function, mediæval storytellers conceived it as a costly covering or bedspread.

Here we may return to the fighting 'dragons' in *Cyfranc Lludd a Lleuelys*. It will be recalled that Lludd instructs his brother to prepare a vat of the best mead that can be made (*kerwyneit o'r med goreu a aller y wneuthur*), placing a cloth of brocaded silk over the top of the vat. Two creatures in the form of monstrous beasts (*yn rith aruthter aniueileit*), i.e. beings not of the natural world, begin fighting, rising into the air in the shape of dragons. Eventually they fall back onto the sheet in the form of two little pigs (*deu barchell*), making the sheet sink down with them, until it lies at the bottom of the vat. They consume the mead, and fall asleep.

Successive elements of the Celtic myth of divine conception may be detected in this account. Two creatures of ambivalent nature are found in a vessel of mead, covered by a silken cloth, through which they emerge and return. The incongruously shifting terminology betrays the fact that the author is ignorant what creatures they are. Nennius's tale of the revelation of the boy Ambrosius is inserted into an account of warfare in the time of Vortigern between Britons

---

186 Eurys I. Rowlands, 'Y Tri Thlwys a Ddeg', *Llên Cymru* (Cardiff, 1958), v, pp. 36, 37, 39, 40, 45.

187 Margaret Barker, *The Gate of Heaven: The History and Symbolism of the Temple in Jerusalem* (London, 1991), p. 105; cf. pp. 104–32.

and English, in whose military arrays dragon standards were traditional.[188] Evoking the dragons of Mordecai's dream in the Book of Esther, which bore comparable symbolic significance, Nennius interpreted the baffling *pryfed* of his source (which he translated as *vermes*) as martial dragons, symbolizing the warring Britons and Saxons. Their combat, a factor absent from the mythological schema, further betrays the artificiality of this interpretation.

In *Cyfranc Lludd a Lleuelys* the dragons' conflict is contrived to account for the originally independent motif of the mysterious scream. The inhabitants of Britain were made aware of the battle by a terrible, destructive shriek issuing from the British dragon. It was shown earlier that this scream reflects that described in the Welsh Laws as the 'Scream of Annwfn' (*diaspat Annwfn*), which heralded the extinction of a family line after a cycle of nine generations, and its replacement by another. Originally it cannot have emanated from the 'dragons', the contrived nature of whose introduction into the legend is demonstrable.

The significance of these convergent motifs should by now be clear. The Scream intimates the end of a cycle of humanity, traditionally reckoned at a paradigmatic nine generations. Accompanying cosmic annihilation is emphasized by the fact that the land becomes desolate and unproductive, and women miscarry. In the story this appalling disaster all but occurs, being averted only by intervention of the divine saviour Lleu(elys) at the time of the festival of *Kalan Mai*, which celebrated the close of winter and opening of spring. Although the events of the myth take place in the primal time, citation of the calendrical date suggests they were re-enacted every *Kalan Mai*.

Lleu's Irish counterpart Lug was traditionally accounted supernatural father of mortal kings, as well as progenitor of royal dynasties, and there are indications that he fulfilled the same functions in early mediæval Wales. The original myth told of the cyclical extinction of humanity, and its regeneration through intervention of the god Lleu. The theophany occurred at the Centre of Britain, traditionally conceived as the point where the land and its inhabitants originated, and focus of its wealth and cosmic equilibrium, and site of ceremonies ensuring perpetuation of the divinely ordained Monarchy of Britain. There a rite of rebirth took place. Two minuscule creatures embodying the seed of life are discovered in a mead-vessel, covered by a silk cloth.

The cloth was in reality a symbolic screen, dividing the Otherworld from the realm of mortals, who were believed to have been originally brought into existence at the *omphalos*. Originally invisible, the tiny soul-creatures (*pryfed*) pass through barriers of time and space, generating a fresh race of mankind: in this instance, the British people. Finally, it is the discovery and secure disposal of the *pryfed* which averts universal dearth, and potential extinction of the British race. *Cyfranc Lludd a Lleuelys* places us in the fortunate position of obtaining a glimpse of this archaic myth of cosmic renewal. Moreover, details of the

---

188 Dragon standards were regularly employed by the Roman army (Édouard Galletier, Jacques Fontaine, Guy Sabbah, Marie-Anne Marié, and Laurent Angliviel de la Beaumelle (ed.), *Ammien Marcellin: Histoire* (Paris, 1978–99), i, pp. 165, 182; M. D. Reeve (ed.), *Vegetius: Epitoma Rei Militaris* (Oxford, 2004), p. 72; John Barrie Hall (ed.), *Clavdii Clavdiani Carmina* (Leipzig, 1985), pp. 38, 44; W. B. Anderson (ed.), *Sidonius: Poems and Letters* (London, 1936–65), i, p. 96; W. M. Lindsay (ed.), *Isidori Hispalensis Episcopi Etymologiarvm sive Originvm: Libri XX* (Oxford, 1911), §XVIII.iii.3). Not only is it intrinsically likely that they were borne by military units stationed in Britain, but it was probably during this period that Latin *dracō* was borrowed as Welsh *dreic* (cf. Kenneth Jackson, *Language and History in Early Britain: A Chronological Survey of the Brittonic Languages First to Twelfth Century A.D.* (Edinburgh, 1953), p. 303). English hosts also appear to have borne dragon banners from an early period (William A. Chaney, *The Cult of Kingship in Anglo-Saxon England: The Transition from Paganism to Christianity* (Manchester, 1970), pp. 37–38). In the Bayeux Tapestry a mounted warrior who appears to be a Saxon bears a shield adorned with a dragon emblem (David M. Wilson (ed.), *The Bayeux Tapestry* (London, 1985), plate 70).

description suggests the likelihood of accompanying ritual activity, lacking which myth must remain functionally sterile.

Gwydion's 'swine' and the Centre of Gwynedd

Another early story provides additional glimpses of the ideology of the Centre, this time preserved in North Wales. A curious episode in *Math uab Mathonwy*, the Fourth Branch of the *Mabinogi*, tells how the wizard Gwydion, together with his brother Gilfaethwy, abducted the swine of Pryderi in the South. Since the precise terminology, easily obscured in translation, is so revealing, I include the Welsh wording where relevant.

At the outset of the episode, Gwydion explains to Math, king of Gwynedd:

'I have heard that some kind of *pryfed* that have never been in this island before (*y ryw* ***bryuet*** *ni doeth y'r ynys honn eiroet*) have come to the South.' 'What are they called?' asked Math. '***Hobeu***, Lord.' 'What sort of animals are they?' 'Small animals (***aniueileit*** ***bychein***), whose meat is better than beef. They are small; and they change names (*Bychein ynt wynteu; ac y maent yn symudaw enweu*); they are called pigs (***moch***) now.' 'Who owns them?' 'Pryderi son of Pwyll – they were sent to him from Annwfn by Arawn king of Annwfn.' (And up to the present time they preserve that name in the word for a side of pork: half a *hob* (*enw hwnnw hanner hwch, hanner hob*).

Gwydion and Gilvaethwy accordingly travel disguised as bards to the stronghold of Pryderi at Rhuddlan Teifi in Ceredigion, where they obtain the creatures by means of enchantment and deception.

During their return with their booty to Gwynedd, they halt along the way at a succession of places, whose names contain the element *moch*, 'pig'. Meanwhile Pryderi musters his forces, and advances hotfoot in pursuit of the raiders.

'Men,' said Gwydion, 'we will march these animals (*aniueileit*) into the strongest place of Gwynedd (*kedernit Gwynet*), for they are assembling their hosts behind us.' So they [Gwydion and Gilfaethwy] arrived at the highest township of Arllechwedd, and made a pen for the pigs there, and on that account the township was called Creuwryon' (*Sef y kyrchyssant y dref uchaf o Arllechwoed, ac yno gwneuthur creu y'r moch, ac o'r achaws hwnnw y dodet Creuwryon ar y dref*). And after making a pen (*creu*) for the pigs, they sought Math vab Mathonwy in Caer Dathal. And when they arrived there, the country was being rallied. 'What news here?' said Gwydion. 'Pryderi is assembling twenty-one cantrefs [districts] to come after you,' they replied. 'It is odd how slowly you have come.' 'Where are the animals (*aniueileit*) you went after?' said Math. 'They have made a pen for them in the other cantref below,' said Gwydion.[189]

There are striking parallels between this episode, and the account of the dragons in *Cyfranc Lludd a Lleuelys*. There is the same perplexity over the nature of the creatures, their contrived identification as pigs, and the description of the place where they are to be held as the securest spot in Gwynedd. In *Cyfranc Lludd a Lleuelys* the shift from dragons to pigs and back again

---

189 Ian Hughes (ed.), *Math Uab Mathonwy: Pedwaredd Gainc y Mabinogi* (Aberystwyth, 2000), pp. 2–4.

provides the most incongruous aspect of the metamorphoses witnessed by Lludd at the Centre, while I believe at the same time supplying the key to resolving the mystery.

In *Math uab Mathonwy* the creatures are at first termed *pryfed*, a word of indeterminate meaning, ranging as has been seen from 'insect' to 'larva, maggot, worm', 'reptile, serpent, snake, dragon', or '(small) wild animal, beast, creature, quarry, vermin'. We learn that these *pryfed* originally emanated from the Otherworld realm of Annwfn, ruled by Arawn. He transferred them to Dyfed, which in the stories of *Pwyll Pendeuic Dyuet* and *Math uab Mathonwy* features as an earthly counterpart of Annwfn.[190] Gwydion's initial bafflement over their identity appears to reflect that of the author, who makes Math enquire what they are called, despite his having just been told. '*Hobeu*' is the reply. The term evidently meant nothing to Math, who enquires yet again: 'what sort of animals are they?' 'Small animals (*aniueileit bychein*)' responds Gwydion, 'whose meat is better than beef. They are small; and they change names (*Bychein ynt wynteu; ac y maent yn symudaw enweu*)'. Finally, he declares that 'they are now called pigs (*moch*)'.

W. J. Gruffydd was surely right in detecting here a succession of at least two explanatory glosses, although he did not attempt to explain their origin.[191] It is evident that successive transcribers could make neither head nor tail of the 'small animals'. A careful reading suggests that, in an earlier version, the creatures abducted by the raiders from Gwynedd were simply named *pryfed*, which it is emphasized had never before been seen in Britain.[192] A subsequent copyist sought to clarify this for puzzled readers by explaining that *pryfed* meant 'small animals' – as indeed it may do. However, 'small animals' being both imprecise and little more than a tautologous term for *pryfed*, readers were presumably left little the wiser. Another glossator appears to have struggled further, explaining that they were *hobeu*. Although *hob* is recorded in the sixteenth century as synonymous with *hwch*, 'pig', the continuing confusion and pointless parenthetical gloss (half a *hob* = half a pig, a flitch)[193] make it evident that, for whatever reason, the word *hobeu* was not in general use at the time *Math uab Mathonwy* was compiled.

The first point to note is that the 'explanation' that *pryfed* means 'pigs' is plainly incompatible with the narrative itself, which recounts how *pryfed* first arrived in Britain during the era depicted in the Fourth Branch of the *Mabinogi*. However, in the Second Branch, *Branwen uerch Lyr*, swineherds in Ireland are depicted pasturing their pigs on seaweed, and the Third (*Manawydan uab Lyr*) describes a dramatic encounter with a wild boar. Finally, in *Math uab Mathonwy* itself, shortly after his abduction of *pryfed* from the South, Gwydion is punished by Math, who turns him into a 'wood sow' (*moch coet*). Later, Gwydion visits a swineherd, and sets off in search of one of the latter's sows in a neighbouring wood. These allusions make it abundantly clear that the author of the Four Branches and his readers were fully aware that pigs domesticated and wild had long been native to Britain at the period in which the stories are set.

All this indicates that an earlier version simply related that Gwydion introduced *pryfed* from Annwfn to Gwynedd. What they were, and why they were brought, the author of *Math uab Mathonwy* evidently had no notion. Stopping-places bearing the place name element *moch* were only introduced into the tale *after* an earlier redactor or glossator came to interpret *pryfed* as 'pigs'. The reason for this odd explanation is unimportant in the context. One possibility is that

190   Sir John Morris-Jones, 'Taliesin', *Y Cymmrodor* (London, 1918), xxviii, p. 237.

191   Gruffydd, *Math vab Mathonwy*, p. 42.

192   In Gwydion's initial account, everything that follows his initial allusion to the mysterious *pryfed* bears appearance of originating in a succession of explanatory glosses.

193   *Geiriadur Prifysgol Cymru*, p. 1880. Cf. Ifor Williams (ed.), *Pedeir Keinc y Mabinogi* (Cardiff, 1930), p. 256.

at some point a redactor sought to explain the *pryfed* (the term clearly original to the episode) in the sense (recorded elsewhere) of 'small animals', *aniueileit bychein*. The rationalizing context of their theft in *Math uab Mathonwy* required them to be of value to humans, which could in turn explain their identification as pigs.

This in turn recalls the 'weird creatures' (*aruthter aniueileit*), which in *Cyfranc Lludd a Lleuelys* (omitting their erroneous identification as dragons) so oddly become piglets (*parchell*) enclosed in a vat of mead, enclosed by a valuable silk cover. All this suggests that the *pryfed* of *Math uab Mathonwy* correspond to the 'strange animals' (*aruthter aniueileit*) of *Cyfranc Lludd a Lleuelys*, and consequently likewise to the precursors of the latter, the *vermes* of the *Historia Brittonum*. The confusion arose from the forgotten esoteric significance of *pryfed*, in its originally supernatural sense.

Returning to the story, Gwydion tells his fellow-robber Gilvaethwy:

'We will make for the fastness of Gwynedd (*kedernit Gwyned*) with these animals; there is a mustering on our track'. The place they made for was the highest *tref* [settlement] in Arllechwedd, and there they constructed a sty for the swine (*creu y moch*), and for that reason the *tref* was called Creuwyryon.

Creuwyryon, or *Creuwyrion*, was identified by Sir John Rhŷs with Corwrion, a farm two miles from the coast south of Bangor.[194] In fact, there can be no doubt that, in common with all other localities named in this section of *Math uab Mathonwy*, the identification represents ætiological speculation by its author. Just as the reivers' resting places on their journey home from Dyfed were selected on the basis of the common placename element *moch*, 'pig', so Corwrion was chosen in the belief that its prefix *cor* corresponded to *creu*, 'pigsty'.

The explanatory parenthesis in the text reads like exegetical comment by the author, which is probably the case:

They reached the highest township of Arllechwedd, and made a pen for the pigs there, and for that reason the township was called Creuwryon.[195]

Furthermore, the location of Rhŷs's Corwrion in no way corresponds to Gwydion's allusion to 'the highest habitation in Arllechwedd', as the place where the pigs were to be penned. Much of Arllechwedd is indeed wild and mountainous, but Corwrion is located a mere three hundred feet above sea level, with nothing about its surroundings to suggest the natural stronghold of the story. If the reference to Arllechwedd be discounted as an interpolation arising from the episode's interpretative location at Corwrion, the place where the *pryfed* were secured will originally have been 'the strongest part of Gwynedd' (*yg kedernit Gwyned*), whither Gwydion had declared his intention of driving the swine. The description echoes that found in the *Historia Brittonum*, where the securest spot in Britain is identified by Vortigern's druids as being 'in the mountains of Snowdon' (*in montibus Hereri*). Similarly, on the advice of Lleuelys, Lludd removes the fighting dragons to 'the safest place he could find in Snowdonia (*Eryri*)' (*yn y lle diogelaf a gauas yn Eryri*), which proves to be Dinas Emrys on Snowdon's southern flank.[196]

---

194 Rhŷs, *Celtic Folklore*, pp. 69–70. Cf. Williams (ed.), *Pedeir Keinc y Mabinogi*, p. 260.

195 *Sef y kyrchyssant y dref uchaf o Arllechwoed, ac yno gwneuthur creu y'r moch, ac o'r achaws hwnnw y dodet Creuwryon ar y dref* (Hughes (ed.), *Math Uab Mathonwy*, p. 3).

196 In 1114 the men of Gwynedd withdrew before an overwhelming onslaught by the army of Henry I to the mountains of Eryri, as 'the wildest and safest place to which to retreat': *hyd ymynyded eryri kanys*

On this basis, it seems that an earlier version of the story described how Gwydion brought *pryfed* from *Annwfn* (the Otherworld) to a secure spot in Snowdonia, identified as *Creuwyrion*. Now, although *creu* indeed means 'sty', it may also bear more general application, such as 'enclosure', 'place of defence', or 'stockade'. Its Irish cognate *cró* is likewise a 'term of wide application, the basic meaning being *enclosure, enclosed space, fold, pen*'.[197] The second element in the placename, *wyrion*, is the plural of ŵyr, 'grandson, grandchild, descendant'. In the Welsh Laws *wyrion*, 'descendants', corresponds to Latin *progenies*, 'lineage'.[198]

The significance of the wizard Gwydion's bringing *pryfed* from the Otherworld to a place called 'Enclosure of the Progeny' should now be apparent. Essentially, it replicates his subsequent rôle in harbouring that 'small something' (*y ryw bethan*) at the foot of his *gwely* ('lineage'), which in due course grows into the ancestor-deity Lleu. In each case Gwydion introduces the seed of the embryonic human race from the Otherworld into Britain. Pryderi's *pryfed* originate in Dyfed, which here corresponds to Annwfn, while the *rhyw bethan* emerges from behind a silken sheet or curtain (*llenn o bali*), which has been shown to symbolize the barrier dividing the respective worlds of gods and men.

This pagan myth of parturition is introduced a third time into *Math uab Mathonwy*, in the account of the death and resurrection of Lleu. Reduced to its essentials, the episode occurs as follows. When Lleu comes of age, he is the most handsome youth ever seen. Math and Gwydion then create a wife for him by magic, from wild flowers. She is correspondingly the loveliest of maidens, named *Blodeuedd*, 'Flowery', or 'Formed from Flowers'.[199] However, she proves as false as she is fair, entering into an adulterous intrigue with a passing huntsman.

Lleu's wife and her lover conspire together, and the latter treacherously slays Lleu with a poisoned spear, 'which hit him in his side (*ystlys*), so that the shaft stuck out of him but the head remained inside'. The stricken hero flies off in the guise of an eagle, uttering a terrible scream. News of the tragedy reaches Gwydion, who sets off in search of his son. After a prolonged search through Gwynedd and Powys, Gwydion arrives at the house of a landowner (*aillt*)[200] at Maenawr Pennarth. There the swineherd of the household explains how their sow leaves its sty (*creu*) every day for an unknown destination. Next morning, Gwydion follows her upriver to a valley called Nantlle.

There the sow halts beneath a tree, where she begins to graze. Approaching, Gwydion finds her devouring 'worms and rotten flesh' dropping from a bedraggled eagle perched on top of the tree. Gwydion recognizes the eagle as Lleu and utters three verses (*englynion*) which entice it down into

---

ynyalaf adiogelaf lle oed hw̄nw y ffo ydaw (Thomas Jones (ed.), *Brut y Tywysogion: Peniarth MS. 20* (Cardiff, 1941), p. 59).

197   Ifor Williams (ed.), *Canu Aneirin* (Cardiff, 1938), p. 143; *Geiriadur Prifysgol Cymru*, p. 582; O. J. Padel, *Cornish Place-Name Elements* (Cambridge, 1985), p. 73; Quin *et al.* (ed.) *Dictionary of the Irish Language*, 'C', cols. 536–67; Vendryes, Bachellery, and Lambert, *Lexique étymologique de l'irlandais ancien*, C-240.

198   *Geiriadur.Prifysgol Cymru*, p. 3745; T. M. Charles-Edwards, *Early Irish and Welsh Kinship* (Oxford, 1993), p. 229. 'As to *wyryon* or *wyrion*, made into *wrion* in Corwrion according to the modern habit, it would seem to be no other word than the usual plural of *wyr*, a grandson, formerly also any descendant in the direct line. If so, the name of an ancestor must have originally followed …' (Rhŷs, *Celtic Folklore*, p. 70).

199   Stefan Zimmer, 'Die altkymrischen Frauennamen. Ein erster Einblick', in Joseph F. Eska, R. Geraint Gruffydd, and Nicolas Jacobs (ed.), *Hispano-Gallo-Brittonica: Essays in honour of Professor D. Ellis Evans on the occasion of his sixty-fifth birthday* (Cardiff, 1995), p. 323.

200   'The simple word *aillt* meant a client in the early poem, *Y Gododdin*, one "mead-reared" in the hall of a king, but by the twelfth century could be equated with a villein, one of several examples from the language of early Welsh society of terms moving down the ladder of status' (T. M. Charles-Edwards, *Wales and the Britons 350–1064* (Oxford, 2013), p. 299).

his lap. With a touch of his magic wand (*hutlath*), the wizard conjures Lleu back to life. However, the young man's body is pitifully wasted, and it takes physicians a year to restore him to health. After Lleu has exacted revenge on his would-be murderer, the story concludes with this fairytale ending:

> Then Llew Llaw Gyffes [Lleu of the Skilful Hand] took possession for a second time of the land, and ruled over it prosperously. And according to the lore, he was lord after that over Gwynedd.[201]

A number of points emerge from this section of the story, which together indicate its underlying stratum of myth.

1. Lleu's assassin hurls a spear at him, which strikes him 'in his side (*ystlys*), so that the shaft stuck out of him but the head remained inside' (*neita y paladyr ohonaw, a thrigyaw y penn yndaw*).

   It looks as though *ystlys* is employed here as a euphemism for the sexual organ.[202] In *Culhwch ac Olwen*, Culhwch's unpleasant stepmother lays this fate upon him: 'I will swear a destiny that your *ystlys* shall not strike against a woman till you get Olwen daughter of Yspaddaden Penkawr.'[203] The spearhead which remains embedded in the victim's wound further recalls the Fisher King in Wolfram's *Parzival*, who 'was wounded by a poisoned lance so grievously that he never recovered'. It pierced his scrotum, so that 'he bore the lance-head away with him in his body'.[204]

2. Lleu survives his death, being resurrected in the form of an eagle. This recalls the survival of the cosmic cataclysm by St Illtud and Fintán mac Bochra, each of whom survives immolation by hovering over the abyss in the guise of a hawk.

3. The maggoty 'worms' dropping from the eagle are called *pryfed*, i.e. the soul-bearers.

   In shamanistic cosmologies, human souls are envisaged as originating as birds clustered on the branches of the World Tree.[205]

4. The tree, in whose topmost branches Gwydion discovers the eagle, is endowed with qualities suggestive of the World Tree, which stands at the centre of the world, linking earth and heaven.[206]

5. Gwydion sings Lleu onto his lap (*arfet*); he lands on Gwydion's knee (*glin*), who strikes him with his magic wand (*hudlath*) and restores him to his own shape.

---

201 Hughes (ed.), *Math Uab Mathonwy*, pp. 11–17.

202 '*Latus* ('side') is often vaguely suggestive of the male genitalia' (J. N. Adams, *The Latin Sexual Vocabulary* (London, 1982), p. 49).

203 Bromwich and Simon Evans (ed.), *Culhwch ac Olwen*, p. 2. A Latin poem seeking divine protection from sexual temptation pleads for help in keeping devilish desires from the author's 'flank' (*costa*) (David Howlett, 'Seven Studies in Seventh-Century Texts', *Peritia: Journal of the Medieval Academy of Ireland* (Turnhout, 1996), x, p. 25). Cf. also Adams, *The Latin Sexual Vocabulary*, pp. 50–51.

204 Karl Lachmann and Bernd Schirok (ed.), *Wolfram von Eschenbach: Parzival* (Berlin, 1999), pp. 245–47.

205 Mircea Eliade, *Le chamanisme et les techniques archaïques de l'extase* (Paris, 1951), p. 245; A. V. Smoljak, 'Some Notions of the Human Soul among the Nanais', in V. Diószegi and M. Hoppál (ed.), *Shamanism in Siberia* (Budapest, 1978), pp. 439–41; Carla Corradi Musi, *Shamanism from East to West* (Budapest, 1997), pp. 94–95.

206 Heinrich Wagner, 'Studies in the Origins of Early Celtic Civilisation', *Zeitschrift für celtische Philologie* (Tübingen, 1971), xxxi, pp. 35–36. 'These englynion may be part of a description of the Other World' (Gruffydd, *Math vab Mathonwy*, p. 44).

Further euphemisms are here detectable. While Welsh *arffed* may be 'groin' or 'lap', another meaning is 'private parts' or 'pudenda'.[207] Similarly, the knee was widely employed in Indo-European tradition as a euphemism or analogy for 'penis'.[208]

Gwydion's rôle in resuscitating his son recalls that of the Irish creator-god, the Dagda, who similarly possessed a magic staff with which he recalled to life his son Cermait, who was slain by Lug (the Irish counterpart of Lleu). Its peculiar power was to kill nine men with its rough end, and bring nine to life with its gentle one.[209] The number presumably reflects Celtic belief in the passage of humanity through successive nine-generational cycles, with the Dagda ('the Good God') as creator divinity presiding over the process.

The story of the birth, death, and resurrection of Lleu in *Math uab Mathonwy* became extensively modified during the process of its conversion into a tragic romance. At the same time, that it retains an intrinsic core of myth is unmistakable. Through a mixture of deception, ingenuity, and magic, Gwydion succeeds in extracting *pryfed* from the Otherworld, which he brings to the 'highest' place of Gwynedd at a location known as *creuwryon*. What *pryfed* were was no longer understood. An alternative explanation of their transformation into pigs to that advanced earlier is that it represents a guess on the part of the redactor, based on the grounds that *Creuwryon* contains the element *creu*, 'pigsty'. The Otherworld realm of Annwfn had become identified with the kingdom of Dyfed,[210] and the route pursued by the stolen 'swine' was linked to placenames containing the common toponymic element *moch*, 'pig'. Their final destination was *Creuwryon*, which was located at 'the highest place' (*y dref uchaf*) in 'the fastness of Gwynedd' (*kedernit Gwynet*). This spot a glossator mistakenly identified with an obscure farmstead in Arllechwedd fortuitously named *Creuwryon*, one meaning of *creu* being 'pigsty'.

The secondary nature of this identification is indicated by the fact that Creuwryon in Arllechwedd is neither in a high place, nor does it lie within the fastness of Gwynedd, i.e. Snowdonia. The contrived character of the redactor's interpretation is further betrayed by the fact that at this point of *Math uab Mathonwy* the precious 'pigs' inexplicably vanish from the story![211]

---

207 *Geiriadur Prifysgol Cymru*, p. 196. Cf. Latin *gremium*: 'The word literally denoted the lap. In this case a word for an adjacent area (as distinct from an adjacent part of the body) was transferred to the genitalia' (Adams, *The Latin Sexual Vocabulary*, p. 92).

208 Claude Sterckx, 'Les Têtes Coupées et le Graal', *Studia Celtica* (1985/1986), xx/xxi, p. 27; Jean-Michel Picard, 'The Strange Death of Guaire Mac Áedáin', in Donnchadh Ó Corráin, Liam Breatnach, and Kim McCone (ed.), *Sages, Saints and Storytellers: Celtic Studies in Honour of Professor James Carney* (Maynooth, 1989), pp. 368–69, 374; Claude Sterckx, *Les mutilations des ennemis chez les celtes préchrétiens* (Paris, 2005), pp. 143–44; Onians, *The Origins of European Thought about the Body, the Mind the Soul, the World Time, and Fate*, pp. 174–86, 491.

209 Osborn Bergin, 'How the Dagda got his Magic Staff', in *Medieval Studies in Memory of Gertrude Schoepperle Loomis* (Paris and New York, 1927), pp. 402–6; J. Carmichael Watson (ed.), *Mesca Ulad* (Dublin, 1941), pp. 27–28.

210 Rees and Rees, *Celtic Heritage*, pp. 178–79. 'Such was the Welsh story of Enchantments of Britain, as the romancers were wont to call them, a story so well known to the Welsh bards of the 14th century in its connection with Dyfed, that D. ab Gwilym repeatedly calls the south-west of Wales the Land of Illusion and the Realm of Glamour' (Sir John Rhŷs, *Studies in the Arthurian Legend* (Oxford, 1891), p. 291).

211 Could the introduction of swine into the story have been influenced by the attested association of the divinity Lugus/Mercurius with a pig? Cf. Claude Sterckx, 'Sucellos et Valéria Luperca', in John Carey, John T. Koch, and Pierre-Yves Lambert (ed.), *Ildánach Ildírech: A Festschrift for Proinsias MacCana* (Andover and Aberystwyth, 1999), pp. 255–59.

While the original nature of the author's material has become confused by introduction of extraneous legendary and folktale motifs, it seems that underlying the central section of *Math uab Mathonwy* is a concealed depiction of the conception and birth of Lleu, the 'First Man' common to many mythologies.[212] *Pryfed*, or soul-creatures, are brought from Annwfn (i.e. the Otherworld) to a designated 'enclosure of the ancestors' (*creuwyrion*) in this world.

It was seen earlier that, when the boy comes of age, the two divine wizards Math and Gwydion create for him a wife from wildflowers, whom they name *Blodeuedd*, 'Flowery' or 'Form of Flowers'. That night the young couple's wedding-feast is celebrated, and immediately afterwards Lleu is granted as his patrimony 'the best *cantref* (district) that a young man can have'. Here again we encounter an instance of thinly disguised pagan myth. The maiden created from flowers is the Maiden Sovereignty of the land. Gildas, writing in the sixth century, describes how 'the flowers of divers colours on these [the hills of Britain], trodden by human feet, gave them the semblance of a fair picture, like a chosen bride adorned with various jewels'.[213] The imagery suggests the archaic concept of the land as a maiden, lavishly adorned for union with her legitimate spouse. Furthermore, 'the best *cantref*' suggests sacred space around the *omphalos*, source of fecundity and wealth.

The familiar theme of the abduction of the Maiden Sovereignty has become converted into a romantic account of Blodeuedd's adulterous betrayal of her husband with the adventurer *Gronw Pebyr*, 'Gronw the Radiant',[214] shortly after her marriage to Lleu. It is not only his epithet that indicates Gronw to have been a denizen of the Otherworld. It is doubly implicit that his fatal first encounter with Blodeuedd occurs at a liminal juncture, i.e. the borderline between the terrestrial world and the supernatural Otherworld. For we are told that 'as night approached, he came past the gate of the fort' (*a'r nos yn nessai, ef a doeth heb porth y llys*):[215] that is, their encounters occurred *at twilight* (between day and night), and *beside the entrance* (neither within, nor without).

In addition, Gronw's riding at dusk at the head of a hunt in pursuit of a stag recalls the Leader of the Wild Hunt, a familiar figure from Celtic and other mythologies, who careers with his pack across the night sky in pursuit of the souls of the departed.[216] In British mythology he was the demonic Gwyn ap Nudd, whose aid was essential to hunting the enchanted boar Twrch Trwyth. He was accompanied by a spectral hound named Dormach, who coursed the sky beside him.[217]

---

212 Cf. Arthur Christensen, *Les types du premier homme et du premier roi dans l'histoire légendaire de Iraniens* (Stockholm, 1917–34), i, pp. 31–41.

213 Mommsen (ed.), *Chronica Minora*, iii, p. 28.

214 Williams (ed.), *Pedeir Keinc y Mabinogi*, p. 286.

215 Hughes (ed.), *Math Uab Mathonwy*, p. 12.

216 William Henderson, *Notes on the Folk Lore of the Northern Counties of England and the Borders* (London, 1866), pp. 97–106; Gwynn Jones, *Welsh Folklore and Folk-Custom*, pp. 202–3; Michael John Petry, *Herne the Hunter: A Berkshire Legend* (Reading, 1972), pp. 43–61; Hans Peter Duerr, *Dreamtime: Concerning the Boundary between Wilderness and Civilization* (Oxford, 1985), pp. 36–39; Pierre Bouet, 'La "Mesnie Hellequin" dans l'Historia Ecclesiastica d'Orderic Vital', in Danièle Conso, Nicole Fick, and Bruno Poulle (ed.), *Mélanges François Kerlouégan* (Paris, 1994), pp. 61–78.

217 Bromwich and Simon Evans (ed.), *Culhwch and Olwen*, pp. 26-27; Jarman (ed.), *Llyfr Du Caerfyrddin*, p. 72. Cf. Gwynn Jones, *Welsh Folklore and Folk-Custom*, p. 203; John Carey, 'Nodons in Britain and Ireland', *Zeitschrift für celtische Philologie* (1984), xl, p. 15; Jenny Rowland, *Early Welsh Saga Poetry: A Study and Edition of the Englynion* (Cambridge, 1990), p. 244. Idris Foster's suggestion that Dormach 'may have been originally the name of Gwynn's horse' seems an unnecessary modification (Eoin MacNeill and Gerard Murphy (ed.), *Duanaire Finn: The Book of the Lays of Finn* (London and Dublin, 1908-53), iii, p. 202).

Significantly, it was Gwyn ap Nudd who abducted beautiful Creuddylad, on the eve of her marriage to Gwythyr. She is described as 'the most majestic maiden there ever was in the Three Islands of Britain and her Three Adjacent Islands' – another obvious Sovereignty figure. Thereafter Gwyn and Gwythyr fight for her every May-day (*Kalan Mai*) until the Day of Judgment (*dyd brawt*).[218] It looks as though Creuddylad was envisaged as disappearing with Gwyn every winter, rejoining Gwythyr ('Victor', i.e. Lleu) for the summer months. All this, as recounted earlier, recalls the familiar Greek myth of Persephone.[219]

The name *G(w)ronw(y)* corresponds to Welsh *gwron*, 'hero' (British **Wiro-wonos*),[220] which, together with his epithet 'Radiant Hero', evokes the ambivalent status of Otherworld figures. This sinister huntsman corresponds to the divine hunter Gwyn ap Nudd, abductor of another personification of the Maiden Sovranty.

At Blodeuedd's instigation, Gronw slays Lleu with an enchanted spear, whereupon the latter's spirit or soul flies off in the form of an eagle. His putative father Gwydion sets out in search of him. After much wandering, he arrives at the house of a peasant at *Maenawr Bennardd* (Pennarth). There Gwydion overhears a conversation between the peasant and his swineherd, in which the latter explains that every morning when their sow is released, she vanishes for the day to an unknown destination. Gwydion, who seemingly understands what this portends, contrives to be present next morning when the sow is released. He follows in her track, until she arrives at a valley which the author explains 'is now known as Nantlleu', i.e. 'Valley of Lleu'.

There the sow halts under an oak tree and begins feeding. Approaching, Gwydion discovers that she is eating rotten flesh and maggots. Looking up, he espies an eagle in the topmost branches: 'And when the eagle shakes himself, the worms and rotten flesh fall from him and the sow eats them.' At this, 'he (Gwydion) senses that the eagle is Lleu', and chants three verses of the metre known as *englynion*.

Like other *englynion* in the *Mabinogi*, the poetry is older than the prose within which it is embedded.[221] Being also less readily altered than prose, verse can be valuable for preserving an earlier source, which at times the author evidently did not fully understand.[222] Thus, although the setting of the scene is recognizable in terms of the topography of Gwynedd, it is plain that the oak belongs in the Otherworld: 'Rain does not wet it, heat no further melts it.'[223] It was

---

218 Bromwich and Simon Evans (ed.), *Culhwch and Olwen*, p. 35.

219 Yves Bonnefoy and Wendy Doniger (ed.), *Mythologies: A Restructured Translation of Dictionnaire des mythologies et des religions des sociétés traditionelles et du monde antique* (Chicago, 1991), pp. 452–56.

220 John T. Koch, 'Further to Indo-European **g^{wh}* in Celtic', in Eska, Gruffydd, and Jacobs (ed.), *Hispano-Gallo-Brittonica*, p. 84; Patrick Sims-Williams, 'Indo-European **g^{wh}* in Celtic, 1894–1994', ibid., pp. 205–6.

221 'The three *englynion* sung by Gwydion could, and very probably did, exist before the final redactor got to work' (T. M. Charles-Edwards, 'The Date of the Four Branches of the Mabinogi', *The Transactions of the Honourable Society of Cymmrodorion: Session 1970* (London, 1971), p. 265).

222 'Verse, as the characteristic medium of the learned priest-poet, was the ideal vehicle for sacred or canonical lore: genealogy, senchas and other constituents of tribal tradition which were supposed to be transmitted intact from verbal or substantial change ...' (Proinsias Mac Cana, 'Notes on the Combination of Prose and Verse in Early Irish Narrative', in Stephen N. Tranter and Hildegard L. C. Tristram (ed.), *Early Irish Literature - Media and Communication* (Tübingen, 1989), p. 131).

223 Remarkable parallels exist between the death of Lleu and that of the Norse god Óðinn, who sacrificed himself by hanging from a tree (MacCana, *Celtic Mythology*, p. 29; E. O. G. Turville-Petre, *Myth and Religion of the North: The Religion of Ancient Scandinavia* (London, 1964), pp. 42–43; Ross, *Pagan Celtic Britain*, p. 34). These myths are in turn paralleled to equally striking extent by circumstances attendant on the Crucifixion of Christ (Nikolai Tolstoy, *The Quest for Merlin* (London, 1985), pp. 175–82).

probably the author of *Math uab Mathonwy* who first located the mythical account of Lleu's death in a valley bearing his name.

As Gwydion sings, the eagle descends the branches by degrees, until it lands on his knee. The wizard strikes him with his magic wand, upon which he resumes his human form, albeit sadly emaciated.[224] The extent to which the death and recovery of Lleu appear charged with imagery of sexual impotence and regeneration is striking. The first verse of the *englynion* reads:

> An oak grows between two veils [or lakes],
> Very dark is the sky and the valley.
> Unless I speak untruly
> It is because of Lleu's *oulodeu*.[225]

Some scholars have sought to emend *oulodeu* to *blodau*, 'flowers', which however makes no sense in the context. Others prefer *aelodau*, whose usual meaning 'limbs' is no more helpful.[226] The sense of the verse requires that Lleu's *oulodeu* bring darkness (*gorddufrych*) upon the landscape. This probably reflects the dire state in which Lleu manifested himself, both as the decrepit eagle and the near-skeleton he appears when restored to human form. The intimations are that Lleu's disappearance from the earth in eagle guise coincided with the onset of winter dearth and deprivation.

Now, while *aelodau* generally means 'limbs', it could also signify 'testicles'. Thus, in 1116 the host of Owain ap Cadwgan vowed to maim the followers of his adversary Gruffudd ap Rhys by 'cutting off their members' (*dorri y aelodeu*), i.e. castrating them.[227] It has been seen that Lleu's receipt of the fatal wound in his 'side' (*ystlys*) is likely to represent a euphemism for the groin. Bearing in mind the familiar correlation in early times between royal virility and the fertility of the realm, it seems likely that winter dearth was explained in mythological terms by Lleu's temporary 'death' and emasculation.

This interpretation makes sense of the *englyn*, wherein darkness enshrouding the land is brought about in some way by the condition of Lleu's *aelodau*. Further confirmation appears in the final verse and its aftermath. Gwydion conjures Lleu onto what is usually translated as his 'lap', *arffed*. However, *arffed* represents yet another euphemism for 'groin' or 'private parts'. That this was the original meaning here is further suggested by the statement that Lleu 'dropped down onto Gwydion's knee (*glin*)'. In Indo-European cultures the knee is closely linked etymologically and semantically to the generative (Latin *genus*, 'knee') organ.[228]

This imagery suggests that originally Gwydion's magical generative powers were employed to restore Lleu's virility. It may further be conjectured that his restoration was linked to the beginning of the Celtic summer at the May-day festival, when the earth recovers its fertility after the prolonged 'death' of winter. Local tradition at Nantlle and elsewhere associated Lleu

---

224 Hughes (ed.), *Math Uab Mathonwy*, pp. 14–16.

225 *Oulodeu lleổ* is the reading in both manuscripts (Gwenogvryn Evans (ed.), *The White Book Mabinogion*, p. 54; Rhŷs and Gwenogvryn Evans (ed.), *The Text of the Mabinogion and other Welsh Tales from the Red Book of Hergest*, p. 78).

226 Cf. Gruffydd, *Math vab Mathonwy*, pp. 36, 341; Williams (ed.), *Pedeir Keinc y Mabinogi*, pp. 292–93; Patrick K. Ford (tr.), *The Mabinogi and other Medieval Welsh Tales* (Berkeley, 1977), p. 107; Hughes (ed.), *Math Uab Mathonwy*, p. 69; Davies (tr.), *The Mabinogion*, p. 62. Timothy Lewis's derivation remains unconvincing (*Mabinogi Cymru* (Aberystwyth, 1931), pp. 159–61).

227 Jones (ed.), *Brut y Tywysogion: Peniarth MS. 20*, p. 73.

228 Onians, *The Origins of European Thought*, pp. 174–86, 491.

with the sun. While not a sun-god, it appears that he was closely linked to summer warmth and light (Welsh *lleu*). A local tradition of his betrayal and death assigns him the name *Huan*, Welsh for 'sun'.[229]

From this it may be inferred that a pagan myth of Lleu, euhemerized in *Math uab Mathonwy*, described (i) his wedding to the Maiden Sovereignty of Britain; (ii) her abduction, and his 'death' at the hands of his sinister Otherworld adversary, the Lord of the (winter) Wasteland; (iii) his resuscitation with the beginning of summer, weak and wasted; his magical restoration to pristine vigour and beauty; and the overthrow of his saturnine rival.

Although not expressly specified, the season of Lleu's disappearance in eagle guise is implicit in the narrative of *Math uab Mathonwy*. A mediæval audience would at once have recognized that the swineherd's daily release of his master's sow to seek food in an upland valley reflected the traditional practice of pannage. In September, October, and November, swine were driven into woods and forests, where they consumed nuts and acorns falling as leaves turned yellow.[230] 'A fair calm season is autumn … Sweet acorns in high woods … Hazelnuts of finest crop fall from great ancient trees of forts,' as an Irish poet sang.[231] In mediæval Ireland maturity of mast was particularly associated with the festival of Samain.[232]

Many Indo-European cultures accorded close correlation between the acorn (Latin *glāns*) and the gland of the human penis, with corresponding connotation of fertility, and there are indications that this identification existed in Celtic mythological tradition.[233] Again, this concept is implicit in the account of the death of Lleu in *Math uab Mathonwy*. Small objects dropping from an oak tree to be devoured by a grazing sow naturally suggest acorns. Yet we are told that they fell in fact from the emaciated eagle in its topmost branches, which led the author to interpret them as 'rotting flesh and maggots'.

Clearly the nature of these objects perplexed the author, who provided distinct terminology for the 'maggots'. At first, they are *cynrhon*, which indeed means 'maggot', and afterwards *pryfed*. *Pryfed* may mean 'maggot' or 'worm', but, as has been seen, it is also the term for the minuscule soul-creature passing from man to woman at conception. It is the latter concept which seems apt to the context of Lleu's death and resurrection. (The 'rotting flesh' was probably added to account for the otherwise incomprehensible 'maggots'.)[234]

---

229 Rhys, *Lectures on the Origin and Growth of Religion as Illustrated by Celtic Heathendom*, pp. 404–5; Gruffydd, *Math vab Mathonwy*, pp. 198–99.

230 Pigs were agisted in royal demesne woods from 14 September until about 11 November (G. J. Turner (ed.), *Select Pleas of the Forest* (London, 1901), p. xxvi; Helen E. Boulton (ed.), *The Sherwood Forest Book* (Nottingham, 1965), pp. 61, 65). For references to pannage in the Welsh legal codes, cf. Williams and Powell (ed.), *Cyfreithiau Hywel Dda yn ôl Llyfr Blegywryd*, pp. 93–94; Melville Richards (ed.), *Cyfreithiau Hywel Dda o Lawysgrif Coleg yr Iesu Rhydychen LVII* (Cardiff, 1957), p. 82; Wiliam (ed.), *Llyfr Iorwerth*, pp. 86–87. The practice is alluded to in the earliest British penitentials (Ludwig Bieler (ed.), *The Irish Penitentials* (Dublin, 1963), pp. 140, 152).

231 Best, Bergin, O'Brien, and O'Sullivan (ed.), *The Book of Leinster*, pp. 436-37. Cf. Kelly, *Early Irish Farming*, pp. 83–84.

232 O'Grady (ed.), *Silva Gadelica*, i, p. 319.

233 Paul Friedrich, *Proto-Indo-European Trees: The Arboreal System of a Prehistoric People* (Chicago, 1970), pp. 131–32; Ernout, Meillet, and André, *Dictionnaire étymologique de la langue latine*, p. 276; Séamas Ó Catháin, *The Festival of Brigit: Celtic Goddess and Holy Woman* (Dublin, 1995), pp. 72–73, 86; Mallory and Adams (ed.), *Encyclopedia of Indo-European Culture*, p. 408; Martin Huld, 'Albanian *gögel* and Indo-European "acorns"', *The Journal of Indo-European Studies* (Washington, 2007), xxxv, pp. 121–28.

234 In Norse mythology dwarves were believed to have acquired life as maggots or small worms (*maðkar*), generated in the flesh of the primal giant Ymir (Anthony Faulkes (ed.), *Snorri Sturluson: Edda; Prologue and Gylfaginning* (Oxford, 1982), p. 15). Cf. Jan de Vries, *Altnordisches Etymologisches Wörterbuch* (Leiden, 1961), p. 374.

'November' in *Les très riches heures du duc de Berry,*
c. 1412–1416.

Earlier in the story, Gwydion employs his powers of wizardry to abduct *pryfed* from the Otherworld realm of Annwfn (identified with Dyfed), which he transfers to a secure place in Gwynedd, called *creuwyrion. Creuwyrion* means 'enclosure of the descendants' – a highly appropriate term for the mythical spot where humanity originated at the beginning of cyclical time. However, since *creu* may also mean 'pigsty', the puzzled author inferred that the mysterious *pryfed* were swine.

The second verse of the *englynion* uttered by Gwydion makes it clear that the oak (a tree pre-eminently sacred to the druids, whose name may mean something like 'wisdom of the oak')[235] on which Lleu hung was a location of the Otherworld. The name Gwydion (Old Welsh Guidgen < *Vidugenos) means 'wood-born'.[236] Thus this episode essentially replicates Gwydion's earlier obtention of life-bearing *pryfed* from the Otherworld realm of *Annwfn.*

Again, dire mortality and winter 'death', with but few survivors left to revive the species, is symbolized by Lleu's initial reappearance as 'nothing but skin and bone'. (In shamanist cultures, the skeleton was regarded as permanent hereditary guarantee of the perpetuation of life, flesh being taken for the discardable maternal inheritance.)[237] In *Math*, Lleu's cure is ascribed to local doctors, but originally it must have been effected by Gwydion's magic, just as his rescue from the treetop was brought about by his incantation.

235　Bader, *La langue des dieux,* pp. 77–85; Helmut Birkhan, *Kelten: Versuch einer Gesamtdarstellung ihrer Kultur* (Vienna, 1997), p. 898; Xavier Delamarre, *Dictionnaire de la langue gauloise: Une approche linguistique du vieux-celtique continental* (Paris, 2001), pp. 125–26.

236　Joseph Vendryes, 'La religion des Celtes', *Mana: Introduction à l'histoire des religions* (Paris, 1948), iii, p. 281.

237　Roberte Hamayon, *La chasse à l'âme: Esquisse d'une théorie du chamanisme sibérien* (Nanterre, 1990), pp. 103–4, 233, 240, 355, 665-67, 767, 770.

It was natural that acorns, possibly in view of their sexual connotation, were regarded as a manifestation or symbolical representation of *pryfed*. Falling from trees at the beginning of winter, they lie inert in the earth until the spring, when they germinate into seedling oaks. However, most are devoured by swine, so that only a chosen few survive the season of privation to propagate the species in the spring. A conception of this sort must lie behind a curious folk belief: 'In Cardiganshire and Carmarthenshire, it is believed that if nuts will be numerous, many children will be born that year.'[238]

At Hallow-e'en (*Nos Galan-gaeaf*), the opening night of winter, Welsh folklore told of a frightening black sow which seized upon folk who failed to make their escape with sufficient swiftness. A popular verse, recorded by Sir John Rhŷs in the nineteenth century, evoked

> A cutty black sow
> On every stile,
> Spinning and carding
> Each November-eve.

The stile represents another archetypal liminal juncture, dividing the Otherworld from that of mortals. We learn further that, at the same season,

> people would cast stones or pebbles into the fire, and sometimes walnuts or hazel-nuts. When these were shot out by the heat, or if the nuts burst, the younger folk ran aside, fearing the 'goblin black-tailed sow' would come and drive them into the fire.

Next day the people came to search for the stones or nuts they had flung into the fire:

> To find them indicated good luck during the next twelve months and the contrary was an omen of misfortune and even of death.[239]

This folk-custom combines all the principal elements of the myth of the death and resuscitation of Lleu: the symbolic representation of individuals by nuts; the swallowing of a sizeable number by an Otherworld sow; association of the sow both with darkness and night, together with liminal contexts (November-eve, the stile); occurrence of the event at the advent of winter; assurance of a happy future to a fortunate few survivors.

Although the myth of Lleu unmistakably originates in indigenous paganism, it bears obvious parallels to the Passion of Christ. Gwydion, the creator-god, brings mankind into existence from a prior state of non-being. Perennially threatened by cosmic annihilation, the species is saved by the sacrificial death on a tree and resurrection of his Son, divine personification of mankind.[240]

Originally, 'the highest place' (*y dref uchaf*), to which the *pryfed* were brought from Annwfn, would have been a descriptive term for that sacred point from which the population of Britain

---

238 Jonathan Ceredig Davies, *Folk-Lore of West and Mid-Wales* (Aberystwyth, 1911), p. 221.

239 Rhys, *Lectures on the Origin and Growth of Religion as Illustrated by Celtic Heathendom*, pp. 515–17; Trevelyan, *Folk-Lore and Folk-Stories of Wales*, p. 255; J. A. MacCulloch, *The Religion of the Ancient Celts* (Edinburgh, 1911), pp. 261–62; Gwynn Jones, *Welsh Folklore and Folk-Custom*, p. 47; Trefor M. Owen, *Welsh Folk Customs* (Cardiff, 1974), pp. 123–24. The Black Sow features in other European folklore traditions (Carla Corradi-Musi, 'Finno-Ugric Shamanism and European Magic', in Mihály Hoppál and Juha Pentikäinen (ed.), *Uralic Mythology and Folklore* (Budapest, 1989), p. 243).

240 Nikolai Tolstoy, *The Quest for Merlin* (London, 1985), pp. 175–82.

emerged at the Beginning. It was also known as *Creuwyrion*, 'Enclosure of the Descendants'. Earlier, I considered the possibility that 'the highest place' was originally envisaged as the peak of Snowdon.

In early times a close correlation obtained between the concepts of World Tree and Cosmic Mountain.[241] Was the sacrificial death and resurrection of Lleu originally envisaged as occurring on the summit of Snowdon? In *Math uab Mathonwy* Lleu appears as an eagle in the topmost branches of what is clearly the World Tree, located between two lakes. In mediæval Wales, tradition told of a wonderful eagle (*aquila fabulosa*) dwelling in the mountains of Snowdonia, which sharpened its beak on a particular stone pierced with a hole at an especially significant sacred festival. In addition, the two lakes immediately below the peak were believed to be endowed with miraculous properties.[242] At the conclusion of *Math uab Mathonwy*, Lleu hurls a spear at his adversary Gronw, penetrating a stone which the latter had placed before himself.[243]

As myths of divinities, associated with the cloud-capped summit of Snowdon,[244] became euhemerized into legends of heroic figures from the pre-Roman mythical past, so it would have been natural in time for them to become linked to sites in adjacent regions more appropriate to human habitation. In this way the Sacred Centre of Gwynedd could have become transferred over time from the peak of Snowdon to the distinctive eminence of Dinas Emrys at its base. A century later *Cyfranc Lludd a Lleuelys* described how the Centre of Britain was effectively transferred from Oxford to Dinas Emrys. As the powerful kingdom of Gwynedd possessed its own archaic Centre (it has been seen that an early prophetic poem in the Book of Taliesin alludes to 'Gwynedd from her furthest border to her centre (*perued*)'), this 'move' may have been based (at least in part) on a misconception that parallel traditions of the *omphalos* meant that the one had actually been transferred to the other – as in the case of the legendary transportation of the stones of Uisneach to Stonehenge, and that of the coronation stone of the Picts from Tara to Scone.

Relocation of the Centre from an original celestial mountain to a temple enshrining the concept represented widespread practice in the ancient world.

The mountain, because it is the meeting place of heaven and earth, is situated at the centre of the world, and is of course the highest place of the earth. That is why so many sacred places – "holy places", temples, palaces, holy towns – are likened to "mountains"

241 Gamkrelidze and Ivanov, *Indo-European and the Indo-Europeans*, i, p. 574. 'The world tree is often believed to grow on the world mountain' (Clive Tolley, *Shamanism in Norse Myth and Magic* (Helsinki, 2009), i, p. 292).

242 J. S. Brewer, James F. Dimock, and George F. Warner (ed.), *Giraldi Cambrensis Opera* (London, 1861–91), vi, pp. 135–36. This eagle may be one and the same as the Eagle of Gwernabwy, the oldest creature in the world, which pecked at the stars from its mountaintop eyrie (Bromwich and Simon Evans (ed.), *Culhwch and Olwen*, p. 33). The mountain is implicitly the highest in the world.

243 Hughes (ed.), *Math Uab Mathonwy*, p. 17.

244 In early times, when it is unlikely that many possessed leisure or inclination to ascend the inhospitable peak of Snowdon, a splendid palace of its god might readily have been imagined enshrouded among clouds. In nineteenth-century Greece, villagers living in the vicinity of Mount Olympus believed that on its peak there stood 'a mysterious palace adorned with columns of white marble, adding that these had been seen long ago by a shepherd, but that they would not be seen now-a-days' (Cook, *Zeus*, i, p. 114). From British folklore accounts, we learn similarly that such mountain-top palaces might come and go.

and are themselves made "centres", become in some magic way part of the summit of the cosmic hill.[245]

The original structure at Dinas Emrys on the lower slope of Snowdon was constructed in the fifth century AD. Subsequently a large cistern was dug within its ramparts, beside which was built a remarkable circular stone platform, some seventeen feet in diameter, 'about half of which rested on the peaty filling of the cistern'.[246] This so closely resembles the setting in the *Historia Brittonum* of the discovery of the dragons by Vortigern and his assembled druids at Dinas Emrys, as to suggest a link between the two. The excavators of the site suggested that

> the very fact that a cistern should have been dug on the site of a dwelling, presumably to water animals on Dinas Emrys, suggests a profound change in the nature of the occupation of the whole site, from a permanent settlement to a temporary refuge to which animals were brought in time of danger.[247]

Against this interpretation, it may be observed that the cistern appears to be a unique construction, which would be strange had its usage represented regular agricultural practice. Could it be that it was created, together with the adjacent platform, for the specific purpose of conducting rituals associated with the Centre?[248] There is evidence of 'abominable rites' (in the eyes of the Christian Church) conducted before assembled multitudes in early mediæval Britain. Furthermore, it may be questioned whether Dinas Emrys, with its modest defences,[249] was ever designed as an effective military stronghold.[250] However that may be, it is hard to believe that the Centre of Gwynedd was located at a purely secular site, possessed of no sacral associations.

Naturally, no dragons were ever housed within the cistern, and it will be recalled that they did not in any case comprise part of the original legend, having entered it only in consequence of Nennius's misinterpretation of Latin *vermes* (i.e. Welsh *pryfed*) as 'dragons' – a fallacy derived from Mordechai's dream in the Book of Esther. In *Cyfranc Lludd a Lleuelys*, Lleuelys explains that *pryfed* must be dissolved in water, and sprinkled over the people gathered at an 'assembly' (*dadleu*). Were lustrations practised on the platform beside the cistern at Dinas Emrys?

Lustrations are associated with the Greek Navel at Delphi.[251] They also fulfilled an important rite (*abhiseka*) at the inauguration of kings in Vedic India. The king in turn conducted annual royal lustration (*nīrājāna*) of horses and arms, which expelled demons, warded off disease, and ensured plenty:

---

245 Mircea Eliade, *Patterns in Comparative Religion* (London, 1958), p. 100. Cf. Richard J. Clifford, *The Cosmic Mountain in Canaan and the Old Testament* (Cambridge, Mass., 1972), pp. 177–81.

246 H. N. Savory, 'Excavations at Dinas Emrys, Beddgelert (Caern.), 1954–56', *Archaeologia Cambrensis* (Cardiff, 1960), cix, pp. 46–48.

247 Ibid., p. 44.

248 A considerable body of evidence attests to the creation in early times of purely ritual wells and cisterns (John Waddell, *Archaeology and Celtic myth: an exploration* (Dublin, 2014), pp. 68–69).

249 *Archaeologia Cambrensis*, cix, p. 51.

250 Cf. Professor Waddell's comments on the 'hillfort' of Rathgall in Ireland (*Archaeology and Celtic myth*, p. 146).

251 Vassilis Lambrinoudakis and Jean Ch. Balty (ed.), *Thesaurus Cultus et Rituum Antiquorum* (Los Angeles, 2004-6), iii, pp. 27–28.

If this ceremony takes place every year all diseases in the kingdom are destroyed, the enemies will be defeated and there will be plenty of food.[252]

The account of the arrival in Gwynedd of *pryfed* brought from the Otherworld, their concentration at *Creuwyrion*, and their function in the myth of Lleu hanging on the Tree, illuminates not only the significance of the Centre of Gwynedd, but also its macrocosmic counterpart, the Omphalos of Britain at Stonehenge. This correlation is further suggested by the transfer of the Preseli bluestones from the local Centre of south-west Wales (Dyfed) to the site of Stonehenge, together with the inference from *Cyfranc Lludd a Lleuelys* that rites occurring at the Sacred Centre of Britain were so similar to those practised at Dinas Emrys, as to give rise to the idea that they had been transferred from the one to the other.

The third gormes: the giant wizard

In *Cyfranc Lludd a Lleuelys* the overthrow of all three *gormesoedd* is implicitly achieved by magical, rather than martial means. The invisible Coraniaid are purged from among the British people by means of a lustration, and the securing of the two 'dragons' found at the Centre nullifies the deadly effect of the springtide scream. While the midnight irruption of the raider of the royal victuals at Lludd's court is countered in single combat, it is evident that this represents superficial rationalization of what was originally a supernatural conflict. Thus, the intruder is described as a powerful *magician* (*gwr lleturithawc kadarn*), and his appearance is heralded by music of mysterious potency – in Celtic tradition a characteristic intimation of proximity to the Otherworld.[253]

The author appears throughout to be describing rites whose purport had long become forgotten. His own attempts to explain them (the unaccountable devil in the horn, pigs that turn into dragons, and a wizard who relies exclusively on his sword) appear half-hearted and unconvincing. The final conflict is plainly incompatible with the prior assertion that its *gormes* involved the ravaging of *all* provisions from *every* courthouse in Britain, *even up to a year's supply* (further intimation of the tale's calendrical base): a feat clearly beyond the capacity of a single raider armed with a sword! The explanation lies in the hamper borne by the intruder, which we are told was large enough to contain all the comestibles in the king's courts.

A similarly expansive receptacle features in the tale of *Pwyll Pendeuic Dyuet*. Pwyll's wedding-feast is interrupted by a truculent visitant, Gwawl ap Clud, who demands the hand of Pwyll's bride Rhiannon, together with all 'the preparations and provisions that are here'. Rhiannon proffers Pwyll an inexhaustible 'little bag' (*cot uechan*), which could take 'all the food and drink in these seven cantrefs'. At the same time, she suggests means of deceiving Gwawl. An appointment is arranged for him to return 'a year from tonight' to claim her hand. After the year is up, Gwawl arrives at their feast. However, he is tricked into entering Rhiannon's bag, after which he is beaten by Pwyll and his men. It was in this way, so we are told, that there arose the

---

252 J. Gonda, *Ancient Indian Kingship from the Religious Point of View* (Leiden, 1966), pp. 71–72, 87–89, 93–96.

253 Séamus Mac Mathúna (ed.), *Immram Brain: Bran's Journey to the Land of the Women* (Tübingen, 1975), pp. 33, 34, 35, 36, 37. The Birds of Rhiannon sing before Bran's Head at the Otherworld feast in Harlech (Thomson (ed.), *Branwen uerch Lyr*, p. 15). 'Music is sometimes a lure to the land of the dead' (Arthur C. L. Brown, *The Origin of the Grail Legend* (Cambridge, Mass., 1943), p. 271). Cf Lowry Charles Wimberly, *Folklore in the English & Scottish Ballads* (Chicago, 1928), p. 293.

game of 'Badger-in-the-Bag'. A contrite Gwawl is released on promising compliance with strict conditions ensuring his future good behaviour.[254]

Some folkloric and dramatic modifications have been introduced by the author of *Pwyll*. However, it is not difficult to detect that behind these lies a tale of an aggressive intruder, intent on abduction of Rhiannon and the wealth of the realm. Originally the unfillable bag must have belonged to Gwawl, in which he intended to remove 'all the food and drink in these seven cantrefs'. Given also that his intended prize Rhiannon personified the sovereignty of the land, it can be seen that Gwawl fulfilled the same function as the giant wizard in *Cyfranc Lludd a Lleuelys*. The malign character of Gwawl is further emphasized in the sequel to Pwyll, *Manawydan mab Llŷr*, where a disguised wizard named Llwyd uab Cil Coed reveals himself to be cousin to Gwawl, and his would-be avenger. Since Llwyd transforms Dyfed into a wasteland and ravages Manawydan's harvests,[255] it can be seen that this pretty pair (who may originally have been one and the same) were leaders of a destructive Otherworld race corresponding to the Coraniaid.

The concept of an universal predator bearing a bag of cosmic proportions, capable of absorbing the wealth of an entire kingdom, may account for the Irish mythological race known as Fir Bolg, 'Men of the Bags (or Bag)'. They appear to be identical with the sinister Fomoire, who contested mastery of Ireland with the benign Túatha Dé. The Fir Bolg are represented as the latter's adversaries in the First Battle of Mag Tuired. Following their defeat at the hands of Lug and the gods of Ireland, they migrate under the leadership of their king Umor to Arran, Islay, Rathlin, and Man.[256] Not only does the First Battle of Mag Tuired read like a duplicate of the Second,[257] but we learn that it was exiled survivors of the Fir Bolg who brought the Fomoire to Ireland.[258]

All this suggests that Sir John Rhŷs was right in arguing that Fir Bolg was 'one of the names of the Fomori', that their Bags were employed for carrying off the agricultural wealth of Ireland, and that the same consideration applies to the hamper or basket (*cawell*) in which the giant sorcerer of *Cyfranc Lludd a Lleuelys* bore away the wealth of the island of Britain. The ruler who frustrated the depredation was in each case the same: Núadu in Ireland, and his counterpart Lludd (= *Nudd*) in Britain.[259] Again, Lludd's ally Lleu in the Welsh tale is accounted grandson of Don, while his counterpart Lug in the Irish version belongs to the *Túatha Dé Danann*, 'the People of the Goddess Don'.[260]

These considerations suggest that the bag borne by the giant wizard overcome by Lludd in *Cyfranc Lludd a Lleuelys* corresponded to that from which the Fir Bolg took their name, and that, just as Fir Bolg and Fomoire were interchangeable in Irish tradition, the Man of the Hamper

254 R. L. Thomson (ed.), *Pwyll Pendeuic Dyuet: The First of the Four Branches of the Mabinogi edited from the White Book of Rhydderch with variants from the Red Book of Hergest* (Dublin, 1957), pp. 12–15.

255 Ian Hughes (ed.), *Manawydan Uab Llyr: Trydedd Gainc y Mabinogi* (Cardiff, 2007), pp. 9–11.

256 Mommsen (ed.), *Chronica Minora*, iii, p. 156; A. G. van Hamel (ed.), *Lebor Bretnach: The Irish Version of the Historia Britonum Ascribed to Nennius* (Dublin, 1932), p. 23; Gray (ed.), *Cath Maige Tuired*, p. 26.

257 'The story of the first battle of Mag Tuired was in existence before that of the second, to which it served as a model' (O'Rahilly, *Early Irish History and Mythology*, p. 388).

258 Best, Bergin, O'Brien, and O'Sullivan (ed.), *The Book of Leinster*, pp. 646-49; Macalister (ed.), *Lebor Gabála Érenn*, iv, pp. 10, 22, 34; Toirdhealbhach Ó Raithbheartaigh (ed.), *Genealogical Tracts I.* (Dublin, 1932), pp. 101–2.

259 Sir John Rhŷs, 'Notes on The Coligny Calendar together with an Edition of the Reconstructed Calendar', *The Proceedings of the British Academy* (London, 1910), iv, pp. 251–54.

260 MacNeill and Murphy (ed.), *Duanaire Finn*, iii, pp. 208–10.

in the British account was leader or personification of the comparably rapacious Coraniaid. In addition, the indications are that his annual ravaging of Britain occurred at or about *nos Galan Gaeaf* (All Hallows Eve). This likelihood is confirmed by the Irish cognate version of the myth, in which the assault takes place at *Samhain* (1 November).

The archaic provenance of the final *gormes* in *Cyfranc Lludd a Lleuelys* is again confirmed by the appearance of almost every element in an episode of the Irish text *Agallamh na Senórach* ('The Colloquy of the Ancients'), an encyclopædic collection of stories concerning the legendary hero Fionn mac Cumhaill and his warband, the *Fíanna*. Each year at the festival of *Samhain*, Conn, the archetypal king of Ireland, holds court in his great hall at Tara. At the time of the tale, the stronghold had long lain at the mercy of a predatory being called Aillén mac Midhna. For twenty-three years he had appeared before Conn's hall each *Samhain*, when he would lull the court to sleep with fairy music, and commit the citadel to flames. None could resist the music's spell: even women in their birth-pangs and sorely wounded warriors forgot their pain and slumbered.

On this occasion, however, the youthful Fionn unexpectedly arrived at the court house and seated himself among the banqueters. He was welcomed by the king, who placed his horn in the lad's hand. Next, Conn arose, and appealed to the company to provide one among them who would preserve Tara from the perennially destructive visit of Aillén. All remained silent, conscious of their inability to resist the intruder's spell, until Fionn arose and undertook to fulfil the task.

At this, one of Conn's warriors named Fiacha mac Conga proffered him a spear possessed of especial potency, explaining that, the moment he heard the insidious sound of the fairy music, he should apply its point to a sensitive part of his body. By this means he would stay awake. Sure enough, when the fiend appeared, Fionn pricked himself and remained vigilant. When Aillén discharged his customary blast of fire from his mouth at the citadel, Fionn deflected it with his cloak, pursued the startled wizard to his fairy mound, and flung his spear with deadly effect through the marauder's back. The young hero then decapitated the fallen aggressor and returned to Tara, where he triumphantly mounted the head on a pole.[261]

Aillén is a diminutive of *Ailill*, which is in turn a cognate form of Welsh *ellyll*, 'phantom, demon'.[262] As O'Rahilly explained, 'Finn's victory over Aillén means that he deposed the lord of the festive otherworld …'.[263] Aillén's patronymic mac Midna is also suggestive. The name *Midnu* (genitive *Midna*) is a compound of *mid-*, 'mid-, middle' + *-gnó(e)*, 'beautiful, renowned',[264] indicating association with the Sacred Centre at Tara. In *Agallamh na Senórach*, Fionn is described as mounting the head of the slain Aillén on a pole. Another source describes how the fallen aggressor was interred under a stone (*cloch*) at Tara, erected by Fionn.[265] Evidently, there existed a stone at Tara associated with Aillén. His patronymic

261 O'Grady (ed.), *Silva Gadelica*, i, pp. 130–32; Nessa Ní Shéaghdha (ed.), *Agallamh na Seanórach* (Dublin 1942–45), i, pp. 186–97; Kuno Meyer (ed.), *Fianaigecht: Being a Collection of Hitherto Inedited Irish Poems and Tales Relating to Finn and his Fiana, with an English Translation* (Dublin, 1910), p. 46.

262 O'Rahilly, *Early Irish History and Mythology*, p. 300; M. A. O'Brien, 'Etymologies and Notes', *Celtica* (Dublin, 1956), iii, p. 182; Dáithí Ó hÓgáin, *The Sacred Isle: Belief and Religion in Pre-Christian Ireland* (Woodbridge, 1999), pp. 181–82.

263 O'Rahilly, *Early Irish History and Mythology*, p. 279.

264 Jürgen Uhlich, *Die Morphologie der komponierten Personennamen des Altirischen* (Bonn, 1993), pp. 278–79.

265 MacNeill and Murphy (ed.), *Duanaire Finn*, ii, p. 80.

Midnu, suggests that this powerful wizard launched an assault on the kingship of Ireland at its Sacred Centre, only to be slain by the liberating hero Fionn.[266]

Fionn mac Cumhaill entered Irish legend at a relatively late date, when he acquired many of the characteristics of the god Lug. In O'Rahilly's words, 'Finn is ultimately the divine Hero, Lug or Lugaid, just like Cúchulainn'.[267] Dáithi Ó hÓgáin has suggested that the account of his overthrow of the fire-breathing Aillén derives from Lug's slaying of the giant Balor, who was possessed of a destructive single eye.[268] At the same time, Fionn's overthrow of Aillén includes details, such as the deployment of enchanted music to induce sleep in the feasters at Tara, together with the hero's ingenious means of resisting it, which reflect a tradition closer in significant respects to the parallel Welsh version contained in *Cyfranc Lludd a Lleuelys*.[269]

Reasons were given earlier for inferring that it was Lleu, rather than Lludd, who originally overcame the nocturnal enchanter in *Cyfranc Lludd a Lleuelys*. In the Irish versions of the story the Otherworld tyrant is overthrown, not by the passive Núadu (whose name and character correspond to those of the British Lludd), but by the dynamic young hero Lug (Lleu). The extant Welsh text presents as a lively sword-fight what must originally have been a conflict involving weaponry of occult potency. This transformation presumably occurred at a relatively late stage, when the myth, otherwise so evident in the tale, came to be incorporated into the legendary history of Britain.

It can be seen that the adventure of Fionn mac Cumhaill at Tara closely complements the third *gormes* in *Cyfranc Lludd a Lleuelys*.

1. The King of the realm is assailed in his palace by a demon possessed of destructive supernatural power.
2. The attack takes place at *Samhain*, which is the likely occasion of the visitation of the supernatural marauder in *Cyfranc Lludd a Lleuelys*.
3. An enterprizing visitor undertakes the King's salvation.
4. In the Irish version he is Fionn, who was probably substituted for Lug in an earlier version. Similarly, in the Welsh tale it is likely that (as in *Cath Maige Tuired*) the victory was originally gained by Lleu (< *Lug*), who intervened to save the passive Lludd (< *Nudd*).
5. Hitherto the wizard's assault had proved successful through his use of enchanted music, which irresistibly lulls to sleep all who hear it.
6. On this occasion, however, a precautionary measure is adopted to ensure that the solitary watcher remain awake.
7. The wizard is consequently frustrated in his aggressive attempt, being slain or overpowered.

---

266 The grave of Midnu was at Tara (Edward Gwynn (ed.), *The Metrical Dindshenchas* (Dublin, 1903–35), i, p. 18).

267 *Early Irish History and Mythology*, p. 277. Fionn 'may in fact be an allonymous saga version of Lug' (Jaan Puhvel, *Comparative Mythology* (Baltimore, 1987), p. 187).

268 Ó hÓgáin, *The Sacred Isle*, pp. 9–10, 14–15. Cf. the detailed discussion by Gerard Murphy, in MacNeill and Murphy (ed.), *Duanaire Finn*, iii, pp. lxx–lxxxv.

269 'The soporific effect of enchanted music is no less strikingly instanced in balladry' (Wimberly, *Folklore in the English & Scottish Ballads*, p. 297).

8. In the Welsh story, Lludd converses with Lleuelys through an enchanted horn. In the Irish tale, Conn places his horn in Fionn's hand, and holds another while he conducts the ensuing discussion.

The Welsh tale preserves a form of words indicating that the assault on Lludd's palace originally corresponded to a ravaging of the entire kingdom, with the supernatural foe plundering the comestibles in *every one of* the king's courts (*yn llyssoedd y brenhin*). The same consideration applies to Tara, in the context of the adventure of Fionn at Conn's court:

> To the extent that Tara was, more than any other place, identified with the kingship of Ireland, it would be only natural to see any attack on the stability and order which that kingship existed to protect as being an attack on Tara and its ruler. Or, to express the same concept in more concrete terms, Tara could be taken to represent Ireland as a whole.[270]

The consideration of *pars pro toto* applies likewise to the Welsh version of the story. For the giant wizard's raid on Lludd's palace to have been simultaneously effective in every court of the realm suggests that the Welsh king's court likewise constituted the Omphalos of Britain, an attack on which represented an assault on the realm as a whole. This is in keeping with what is in any case intrinsically likely, viz. that *all* the *gormesoedd* catalogued in *Cyfranc Lludd a Lleuelys* were focussed on the Centre of Britain.

The sole material distinction between the Welsh and Irish stories lies in the fact that, whereas in the former it is the king (Lludd) who finally overpowers the spectral intruder, in the Irish version the victory is achieved on his behalf by the youthful warrior Fionn. However, their respective functions suggest that, in an earlier version of the Welsh version of the legend, Lleu not merely proffered advice to Lludd but himself undertook the successive measures requisite for defeating the enemies of the inactive king. In *Math uab Mathonwy* Lleu is described as evincing precocious desire for horses and weaponry, being supremely skilful (*llawgyffes*), and casting dart or spear with daunting accuracy.[271] Lludd, in contrast, is nowhere identified as a warrior in *Cyfranc Lludd a Lleuelys*, and prior to the intervention of Lleuelys proved impotent to resist the supernatural scourges of his kingdom.

Similarly, in *Cath Maige Tuired* it is the daring young warrior Lug who arrives at court and slays Núadu's remorseless foe Balor. Balor in turn bears strong resemblance to Aillén in the tale of Fionn. While Aillén discharges a lethal jet of flame from his mouth, Balor possesses a malignant power of the eye, which destroys whatever it gazes upon.

Just as the indications are that all events described in *Cyfranc Lludd a Lleuelys* originally occurred at the Omphalos of Britain, so it is likely that those of *Cath Maige Tuired* were likewise centred on Tara. In each case, too, it looks as though the conflict with the aggressive foe, whether Coraniaid or Fomoire, was originally waged exclusively by magical means. Over time, and with Christian disapproval of any recognition of the old gods per se, the divine protagonists became increasingly euhemerized into kings of rival races, and the struggle was transmuted into a war waged with physical weapons across tracts of the Irish landscape. This is suggested also by parallels between *Cath Maige Tuired* and *Baile in Scáil*. In the latter story, Conn mounts guard on the rampart of Tara, to ensure that Ireland be not overwhelmed by fairies or Fomoire (*fir ˙sithi*

---

270 John Carey, 'Tara and the Supernatural', in Edel Bhreatnach (ed.), *The Kingship and Landscape of Tara* (Dublin, 2005), p. 35.

271 Hughes (ed.), *Math Uab Mathonwy*, pp. 10, 17.

uel Fomoiri). Thus, Ireland as a whole is preserved by a prophylactic rite conducted at its Centre. Again, as in other versions of the myth, the situation is essentially saved by Lug, whose prophetic catalogue of royal dynasts guarantees the integrity of the kingdom for future generations.[272]

Although the Irish stories depict Conn as holding court in Tara, it is likely that the original setting was the primary Omphalos of Ireland, the Hill of Uisneach. In *Airne Fíngein*, Conn surveys Ireland on every side from from the central vantage point of Uisneach in Meath.[273] It was probably in consequence of emphasis laid by the Christian Church on Tara as seat of the converted monarchy, that the royal site came largely to supplant the archaic *omphalos* at Uisneach.[274]

There are in fact indications that the primary setting for the Battle of Mag Tuired was originally Uisneach. In 'The Death of the Children of Tuireann', King Núadu travels from Tara to the Hill of Uisneach, in order to pay a weighty tribute extorted annually by the rapacious Fomoire. There he is met by Lug of the Long Hand (*Lugh Lámhfhada*). Shortly afterwards, a large ugly troop of envoys arrives from the Fomoire. Lug angrily declares his intention of killing them, and sets about doing so, leaving only nine alive to bear his defiant challenge to their king Balar.[275] Thus it seems probable that the eschatological Battle of Mag Tuired (at which Lug slew Balor, king of the Fomoire) was originally located at Uisneach, appropriate setting for a national conflict of cosmic dimensions. Elsewhere, we read that Lug was mortally wounded at Uisneach and plunged to his death in nearby Lough Lugborta. Another version has him slain at Uisneach itself.[276]

A great stone (*kist uaen*), identified by Lleu(elys), is the sole material object of note implicitly associated with the British Centre in *Cyfranc Lludd a Lleuelys*. In *Cath Maige Tuired*, Lug is challenged on his arrival by Ogma, who flings a gigantic flagstone (*márlícc*) beyond the boundary of Tara. Lug hurls it back, 'so that it lay in the centre of the royal hall (*for lár an ríghthighi*)'. The episode appears intended to explain the origin of the celebrated stone *Fál*.[277] In *Baile in Scáil*, as Conn approaches the rampart of Tara to protect the site from the depredations of the Fomoire, he steps onto this enchanted monolith, whose significance is explained by his druids. In each case, an impressive menhir is the principal or sole specified feature of the Sacred Centre. In all three instances, the stone is associated directly or implicitly with Lleu/Lug, and in two of them the stone is associated with a supernatural scream.

The description of the enchanted stone *Fál* in *Baile in Scáil* is particularly revealing.

> *Fál* (i.e. under a rock, i.e. a rock under a king) ... is the name of the stone and *Inis Fáil* is its place of origin, and it was placed in Tara of *Tír Fáil*.

272 Murray (ed.), *Baile in Scáil*, p. 33.

273 Vendryes (ed.), *Airne Fíngein*, p. 23.

274 Cf. Byrne, *Irish Kings and High-Kings*, pp. 48–69; Charles Doherty, 'Kingship in Early Ireland', in Bhreatnach (ed.), *The Kingship and Landscape of Tara*, pp. 3–31.

275 Seán Ua Ceallaiġ (ed.), *Trí Truaġa na Scéaluiđeaċta* (Dublin, 1927), pp. 6–7.

276 Gwynn (ed.), *The Metrical Dindshenchas*, iv, p. 278; Macalister (ed.), *Lebor Gabála Érenn*, iv, p. 184.

277 'La pierre dont il s'agit, dans ce paragraphe à la rédaction si maladroite, est la Pierre de Fal, à la fois symbole de souveraineté et propriété indivise de tous les dieux. Il est charactéristique qu'elle soit confiée à la garde d'Ogma, à la fois dieu de la guerre et spécialiste de la magie, c'est-à-dire le plus capable d'en assurer la protection. Le sens de ce passage est ici qu'Ogme, par ressentiment (ou jalousie?) contre Lug, brise et déplace la pierre de la Souveraineté, mais que Lug s'empare de la souveraineté complète sur Tara et toute l'Irelande en restaurant la pierre et en la remettant en place' (Christian-J. Guyonvarc'h, *Magie, médecine et divination chez les Celtes* (Paris, 1997), p. 65).

Inis Fáil ('Island of Fál') and *Tír Fáil* ('Land of Fál') are alternative names for Ireland.[278] In O'Rahilly's words, 'The ordinary meaning of Ir. *fál* is "hedge, fence". Its Welsh counterpart is *gwawl*, "wall" (Celt. **vālo-*). The fundamental idea of these words is "a circle" or 'a circular surround".'

This semantic identification of stone, rampart, and country indicates that the space enclosed by the rampart is a microcosm of the land of Ireland as a whole. Conn's mounting watch and ward on the rampart of Tara against the malign hosts of the Fomoire corresponds to ritual protection of the entire island, from sea to sea.

Next, Conn is surrounded by a mist, through which he crosses a plain until he reaches the glorious House of Lug. It is clear that he has passed into the Otherworld, which is frequently described in Irish and Welsh sources as lying concealed beyond a magical mist.[279] This is confirmed by what follows. In his palace, the god Lug prognosticates before Conn the succession of royal dynasts whose rule will follow his. Already, when Conn stepped on the *Lia Fáil*, his druid had explained that the shrieks it uttered correspond to the number of his descendants destined to rule over Ireland. The two episodes complement each other. Evidence has already been adduced, suggesting that Lug was on occasion envisaged as dwelling within a rock.

In *Cyfranc Lludd a Lleuelys*, the scream associated with a stone located at the national Centre is explained by Lleu (Lug) to Lludd (Núadu/Conn) as arising from a ceaseless struggle between rival dragons personifying Britain and her alien oppressor[280] – implicitly, the Coraniaid (Irish Fomoire). In each case the future of the kingdom is revealed by a scream or screams linked to a massive stone.

Overall, the Irish and Welsh legendary accounts of their respective *omphaloi* confirm that properties fundamental to the insular Celtic ideology of the Centre include the following.

1. The Navel is a microcosm of the Kingdom, where ritual activities are conducted at the most important calendrical festivals, which exert corresponding effect over the entirety of the realm.[281]

2. The *omphalos* is focussed on, or identified with, a huge menhir. In 'The Settling of the Manor of Tara', Fintán mac Bochra (a type of the First Man) assembles the nobles of Ireland at Uisnech, where he erects a pillar-stone of five ridges, one for each of the five divisions of Ireland.[282]

3. The *omphalos* stone affords privileged persons access to the Otherworld. Similarly, in early Israel,

---

278 Quin *et al.* (ed.), *Dictionary of the Irish Language*, 'F', cols. 36–37.

279 R. I. Best and Osborn Bergin (ed.), *Lebor na Huidre: Book of the Dun Cow* (Dublin, 1929), p. 258; Charles Plummer (ed.), *Bethada Náem nÉrenn: Lives of Irish Saints* (Oxford, 1922), i, p. 49; O'Grady (ed.), *Silva Gadelica*, i, p. 354; Hughes (ed.), *Manawydan Uab Llyr*, pp. 2, 6; Thomson (ed.), *Ystorya Gereint uab Erbin*, pp. 50–54.

280 Relocation of the imprisoned 'dragons' at Dinas Emrys in Gwynedd represents a secondary development in the story. From this it may be inferred that the *cistvaen* within which the 'dragons' were confined at Dinas Emrys was originally located at the umbilical Centre of Britain.

281 In *Cyfranc Lludd a Lleuelys*, 'the properties of this particular place allowed the king to overcome the *gormes* which was causing (among other things) the total failure of the fecundity of his realm' (John T. Koch, 'A Welsh Window on the Iron Age: Manawydan, Mandubracios', *Cambridge Medieval Celtic Studies* (Cambridge, 1987), xiv, p. 48).

282 R. I. Best, 'The Settling of the Manor of Tara', *Ériu* (1910), iv, p. 152.

The stone upon which Jacob slept [at Bethel] was not only the "House of God"; it was also the place where, by means of the angels' ladder, communication took place between heaven and earth.[283]

4. The stone is identified with the god Lug, who is either embodied by it, or envisaged as dwelling within it. In Mircea Eliade's words,

   Stone is no 'petrified spirit', but a concrete representation, a provisional or symbolic 'habitat' of that spirit.[284]

5. In *Cath Maige Tuired*, Lug is described as flinging an enormous monolith into the royal hall at Tara, which thereafter lies at its centre (*for lár an ríghthighi*). Thus, the palladium at the heart of the kingdom is envisaged as a mighty stone, originally erected by Lug.
6. Beyond the menhir's encircling rampart, demonic forces of destruction (Fomoire, Coraniaid) foregather at the two great night-time festivals of the Celtic year (May Eve and November Eve) to reduce the world to the chaotic wasteland it was before being brought into ordered existence by the gods. Ritual acts performed in association with the pillar-stone, if conducted with meticulous attention to traditional practice, ensure that the forces of darkness are subjugated and repelled.
7. These rites were expounded in the primal era by Lug, before the sovereignty god known variously as Núadu, Conn, and Lludd.

The focus on a single menhir as irreducible core of the kingdom lies at the heart of the myth, while there are indications that it was further envisaged as hub of a megalithic complex. In *Cath Maige Tuired*, Ogma hurls the great stone (*márlícc*) beyond the bound of Tara, whereon Lug returns it to the middle of the royal hall. There follows the curious detail, whereby Lug additionally replaced the piece which the stone had broken from the side of the hall, so that it was mended again.

This in turn recalls the action of the wonder child Ambrosius in the *Historia Brittonum*, who expounded to Vortigern mysteries designed to preserve his royal fortress from nightly ruination by unseen foes (Coraniaid).[285] In Geoffrey of Monmouth's partially derivative version, Merlin comes to the aid of Aurelius, implementing measures to ensure that the monument at Stonehenge be protected from a mysterious force preventing its construction. Claude Sterckx evokes parallels between Merlin and Fintán mac Bochra, the primal man who erected the *omphalos* stone at Uisneach.[286] There exists also close correspondence between significant aspects of the legends of Merlin and Lug.[287]

In the *Historia Brittonum* version of the Collapsing Castle motif, the king's concern is to protect timber and stones assembled to build his fortalice from nightly disappearance at the hands of unseen foes. However, when the boy Ambrosius arrives, this aspect is ignored, and

283 Mircea Eliade, *Patterns in Comparative Religion* (London, 1958), p. 231. '... the imagery may well be that of the worshippers ascending and descending the stairs of a Mesopotamian ziqqurat; but, if so, the point of the narrative is not that Ur or Harran or Babylon is the Gate of Heaven but that the Gate of Heaven is found in the land of Israel' (Eric Burrows, 'Some Cosmological Patterns in Babylonian Religion', in S. H. Hooke (ed.), *The Labyrinth: Further Studies in the Relation between Myth and Ritual in the Ancient World* (London, 1935), p. 53).

284 Eliade, *Patterns in Comparative Religion*, p. 219.

285 Could this reflect the belief that the assault of the hosts of the Otherworld traditionally occurred on a particular *night* – that of *Nos Galan Gaeaf*?

286 Claude Sterckx, *Les dieux protéens des celtes et des indo-européans* (Brussels, 1994), pp. 53–54.

287 Tolstoy, *The Quest for Merlin*, pp. 174–75.

focus is directed exclusively onto 'closed vases' enclosing paired dragons – contrasted details, indicating an origin in discrete legendary sources. The discovery is in this respect more credibly represented in the parallel account in *Cyfranc Lludd a Lleuelys* as a single stone embodying the mystery.

Stonehenge was erected during the late Neolithic and Bronze Ages, while Lugus and Nudos are Celtic divinities associated with the British and Irish Iron Ages. However, myth and ritual attached to prominent megalithic structures were frequently absorbed and modified by incoming cultures. Indeed, pre-existing myth and ritual were very likely accepted as intrinsic elements inhering to such numinous monuments, the god of the sanctuary being believed to dwell within the holy stone.[288] An early ninth-century Irish source records that pagans worshipped a particular stone, the chief idol of the North (Ulster), from which a demon (i.e. heathen god) used to speak.[289]

Such continuities within successive cultures are recorded worldwide. In early Israel, Yahweh the god of Israel absorbed, not only salient attributes, but the very name of the Bronze Age Canaanite god 'Ēl.[290] The sacred stone Bethel (*Bêt-ʾēl*), on which Jacob dreamed of the ladder providing access to heaven, was accorded the name of the pre-Yahwist deity, the site having clearly been an important shrine of 'Ēl in Canaan.[291]

While this is not the place to extend the comparison, it may be noted how widespread are many of the fundamental mythical beliefs nurtured by mankind. One of the most important rites of the Hebrews occurred at the spring festival, when the Ark of the Covenant was triumphantly paraded to the sanctuary of Gilgal. Twelve stones stood there, representing the twelve tribes of Israel. The Ark itself was preserved in a tent-shrine, an ancient tradition subsequently revived by King David at Jerusalem.[292]

The account in the *Historia Brittonum* of the discovery of the arcanum at the heart of Vortigern's enchanted citadel, whose confusion betrays the author's inability fully to understand his source, describes it as two 'vases', between which was a folded tent (*tentorium*), which in turn contained two creatures which proved to be 'dragons'. The child Emrys explained the tent to the king as an image of his kingdom, thus affirming that what passed within the fortress was of cosmic proportions.

Again, when King David headed the procession which brought the Ark into Jerusalem at the spring festival, he danced in ecstasy before it, a rite doubtless according with archaic (shamanistic?) practice. This recalls Hecataeus of Abdera's description of the great temple in Britain, where the visiting Apollo is engaged in dancing continuously from the spring equinox until harvest time.

---

288 Sir James George Frazer, *Folk-Lore in the Old Testament: Studies in Comparative Religion Legend and Law* (London, 1918), ii, pp. 58–77; C. G. Jung, *Alchemical Studies* (London, 1968), pp. 97–101.

289 Whitley Stokes (ed.), *Félire Óengusso Céli Dé. The Martyrology of Oengus the Culdee* (London, 1905), p. 186.

290 David Noel Freeman, *Pottery, Poetry, and Prophecy: Studies in Early Hebrew Poetry* (Winona Lake, Ind., 1980), pp. 85–90.

291 Mircea Eliade, *Patterns in Comparative Religion* (London, 1958), pp. 229–31; Clifford, *The Cosmic Mountain in Canaan and the Old Testament*, pp. 103–7; Frank Moore Cross, *Canaanite Myth and Hebrew Epic: Essays in the History of the Religion of Israel* (Cambridge, Mass., 1973), pp. 44–75; Mark S. Smith, *The Origins of Biblical Monotheism: Israel's Polytheistic Background and the Ugaritic Texts* (Oxford, 2001), pp. 135–45.

292 Cross, *Canaanite Myth and Hebrew Epic*, pp. 103–5, 231. For the nature of the Ark of the Covenant cf. Barker, *The Gate of Heaven*, pp. 138–41.

Such myths reflect the association of stone with eternity.

The hardness, ruggedness, and permanence of matter was in itself a hierophany in the religious consciousness of the primitive. And nothing was more direct and autonomous in the completeness of its strength, nothing more noble or more awe-inspiring, than a majestic rock, or boldly-standing block of granite. Above all, stone *is*. It always remains itself, and exists of itself; and more important still, it *strikes*. Before he even takes it up to strike, man finds in it an obstacle – if not to his body, at least to his gaze – and ascertains its hardness, its roughness, its power. Rock shows him something that transcends the precariousness of his humanity: an absolute mode of being. Its strength, its motionlessness, its size and its strange outlines are none of them human; they indicate the presence of something that fascinates, terrifies, attracts and threatens, all at once. In its grandeur, its hardness, its shape and its colour, man is faced with a reality and a force that belong to some world other than the profane world of which he is himself a part.[293]

---

293 Eliade, *Patterns in Comparative Religion*, p. 216.

14

Pagan Survival in the Early Middle Ages

The wizard of the north and the conception of Saint Samson

I have sought to demonstrate that a substantial body of pagan Celtic mythology survives as a palimpsest preserved in early Welsh secular and hagiographical literature. What remains uncertain is *how* these precious shards of mythography managed to survive into the Christian Middle Ages. While discussion of avenues of transmission must of necessity remain in large part speculative, it seems nevertheless worthwhile to investigate historical circumstances in which transmission could have taken place. At the least, I hope to show that survival of pagan lore into the early mediæval period is *feasible* – to such an extent, that in large degree the onus lies with the entrenched sceptic to demonstrate the contrary.

It is curious to what extent that handful of sceptics which rules out of court the very possibility of traces of ancient pre-Christian belief systems being discoverable in mediæval sources frequently evinces little serious interest in – or at times even knowledge of – the early literatures of Wales and Ireland. Perhaps they should heed the advice of Sherlock Holmes, which he proffered to a worldly-wise police inspector:

> Breadth of view, my dear Mr Mac, is one of the essentials of our profession. The inter-play of ideas and the oblique uses of knowledge are often of extraordinary interest.[1]

This chapter is concerned with the Life of the sixth-century St Samson of Dol, a biography which is generally accepted to have drawn upon broadly authentic contemporary and near-contemporary sources. This *Vita* throws a uniquely instructive light on the survival of Celtic paganism in south-western Britain at the outset of the Middle Ages, with particular reference to a major local cult of the god Lleu (Lugus). This late flourishing of pre-Christian religious beliefs also illumines the historical context for preservation of archaic lore in early Welsh mediæval literature.

Mediæval hagiographers occasionally identify their heroes' adversaries as malignant druids, but in fact it is well-known that more often than not the saints' lives represent a mélange of pious fictions, the great majority having been composed centuries after the events they describe. However, the Life of St Samson (*Vita Samsoni*), is exceptional, both for its early date of composition and its general intimations of authenticity.

Samson was born in South Wales, and later migrated to Brittany, where he founded the bishopric of Dol about the middle of the sixth century AD. Since he is recorded to have attended

---

1   *The Valley of Fear.*

the Council of Paris in 561 or 562, he was presumably born about the first decade of the sixth century.[2] The preface to his earliest biography explains that its anonymous author, writing at Dol in Brittany, derived his information from the testimony of an aged man, a cousin of the saint who became a pious deacon at a religious house founded by Samson 'beyond the sea', i.e. in Cornwall or Wales. This patriarch spoke with authority, since he had also enjoyed extensive opportunity to consult his uncle Henoc, another cousin of Samson, who had in turn obtained valuable further information from the saint's mother. In addition, the hagiographer's venerable informant furnished him with written accounts earlier brought to Brittany.[3]

The *Vita Samsonis* presents a striking contrast to the general run of mediæval lives of early British saints, composed centuries after the era in which their subjects lived, and comprising for the most part fantastic admixtures of pious miracles, folklore motifs, ætiological anecdotes, speculative etymology, and other familiar stock-in-trade of the genre. Their authors were often professional hagiographers, for whom it represented acceptable procedure to replicate in an individual saint's biography miraculous and other hackneyed motifs characterizing saints' lives generally.[4] The Life of Samson in contrast appears for the most part inherently credible, and consistent with what is known of sixth-century history, literature, and language.[5] The author's approach may fairly be compared with that of two other great hagiographers of the age, Adomnan and Bede.

The *Vita* is in consequence generally accepted as the work of an author who drew upon authoritative oral and literary sources, utilizing them with considerable care in a scrupulous attempt to reconstruct their protagonist's career. The chronology implicit in the introduction suggests that the author wrote within a few decades of the saint's death, probably during the opening years of the seventh century.[6] After a quarter of a century, Patrick Sims-Williams's

---

2   *Samson subscripsi et consensi in nomine Christi* (Charles de Clercq (ed.), *Concilia Galliae A. 511 – A. 695* (Turnhout, 1963), p. 210). For an interpretation of the preface, and the date of the Council, cf. Pierre Flobert, 'Le témoignage du rédacteur de la Vie Ancienne de Saint Samson sur sa date relative', in Gwennolé Le Menn and Jean-Yves Le Moing (ed.), *Bretagne et pays celtiques: langues, histoire, civilisation; mélanges offerts à la mémoire de Léon Fleuriot* (Rennes, 1992), pp. 163–65.

3   Pierre Flobert (ed.), *La vie ancienne de saint Samson de Dol* (Paris, 1997), pp. 140–42. Cf. François Kerlouégan, 'Les Vies De Saints Bretons Les Plus Anciennes Dans Leur Rapports Avec Les Iles Brittaniques', in Michael W. Herren (ed.), *Insular Latin Studies: Papers on Latin Texts and Manuscripts of the British Isles* (Toronto, 1981), pp. 200–202.

4   Elissa R. Henken, *The Welsh Saints: A Study in Patterned Lives* (Cambridge, 1991), pp. 1–14.

5   The language of the *Vita Samsonis* is consistent with the author's being a countryman of Gildas and contemporary of Gregory of Tours, both major clerical writers of the sixth century (F. Duine, *Questions d'hagiographie et vie de S. Samson* (Paris, 1914), p. 16; Arthur W. Wade-Evans, *Welsh Christian Origins* (Oxford, 1934), p. 45; Bernard Merdrignac, *Recherches sur l'hagiographie armoricaine du VIIème au XVème Siècle* (Saint-Malo, 1985–86), i, pp. 45–51).

6   J. Loth, 'La vie la plus ancienne de Saint Samson de Dol d'après des travaux récents: remarques et additions', *Revue Celtique* (Paris, 1914), xxxv, pp. 269–300; Duine, *Questions d'hagiographie et vie de S. Samson*, pp. 16, 66; Wade-Evans, *Welsh Christian Origins*, p. 205; Kenneth Jackson, *Language and History in Early Britain: A Chronological Survey of the Brittonic Languages First to Twelfth Century A.D.* (Edinburgh, 1953), p. 40; Kathleen Hughes, 'Synodus II S. Patricii', in John J. O'Meara and Bernd Naumann (ed.), *Latin Script and Letters A.D. 400–900: Festschrift presented to Ludwig Bieler on the occasion of his 70th birthday* (Leiden, 1976), p. 145; Susan M. Pearce, *The Kingdom of Dumnonia: Studies in History and Tradition in South-Western Britain A.D. 350–1150* (Padstow, 1978), pp. 188–89; Wendy Davies, *Wales in the Early Middle Ages* (Leicester, 1982), p. 215; Pierre Flobert, 'La vie ancienne de saint Samson et l'histoire', *Études Celtiques* (Paris, 1992), xxix, pp. 183–89. Charles Thomas's reconstruction of the biographical tradition is preferable to that of Flobert (Charles Thomas, *And Shall These Mute Stones Speak?: Post-Roman Inscriptions in Western Britain* (Cardiff, 1994), pp. 223–26, 247–48; Pierre Flobert, 'Le témoignage du rédacteur de la vie ancienne de saint Samson sur sa date relative', in Gwennolé Le

observation remains effectively unchallenged: 'Jackson dates the earliest Breton Latin saint's Life, the *Vita Samsonis*, to the early seventh century, and this much-discussed date has never been convincingly disproved.'[7]

The part played by Samson's mother Anna in providing information available to the hagiographer adds an exceptional aura of authenticity to the opening account of the saint's parentage and birth. Moreover, the author was in general not reliant upon isolated anecdotal report, but conversed at leisure in the still calm of his Breton monastery with the well-informed and evidently garrulous old deacon, with whom he further listened to readings of written material brought across the sea from Britain.[8]

Samson's father Amon, who came from the powerful kingdom of Dyfed (*Demetia*) in south-west Wales, appears either to have remained or reverted to being a pagan, until converted by his son in later life. Significantly, both Amon and his younger brother Umbraphel bore names of Celtic derivation, whereas Samson's mother Anna and her sister Afrella, who came from the wealthy Romanized kingdom of Gwent bordering Dyfed to the east in what is now Monmouthshire, were in the second case certainly, the first possibly, baptized with Christian names of Latin origin.[9] Both their fathers were of noble blood, who acted as fosterfathers to the heirs of their respective sovereigns – an office traditionally assigned to the druids.

Some years passed after the marriage of Anna, without any sign of her conceiving a child. The deprivation was particularly distressing, in view of the fact that her younger sister Afrella had borne three healthy sons during this period. Anna and her husband Amon prayed and fasted, but without effect. Eventually, however, there came a day when they attended church on a feast-day. When the service was over, an animated discussion broke out among the congregation concerning a certain *librarius* who dwelt in a distant land to the north (*in longinquam terram aquilonis habitante*). It appeared that he was a man possessed of powerful mantic gifts, who attracted crowds of enquirers from many of the kingdoms (*a multis provinciis*) of Britain,[10] seeking to profit from his inspired knowledge, which in the experience of those who had made the visit invariably proved accurate. Many present resolved without delay to have recourse to

---

Menn and Jean-Yves Le Moing (ed.), *Bretagne et pays celtiques: langues, histoire, civilisation; mélanges offerts à la mémoire de Léon Fleuriot* (Rennes, 1992), pp. 161–66). In any case Flobert's argument that the *Vita Samsonis Ia* was compiled *c.* 700 does not (as he is himself at pains to emphasize) materially affect the value of the text as an historical source. Moreover, a significant indication appears to have been overlooked by the sceptics. §15 opens with the words *Nam non longe post, dubio adhuc anno,* the allusion being to Samson's ordination (Flobert (ed.), *La vie ancienne de saint Samson de Dol*, p. 170). This can only mean 'Furthermore, not long after (I cannot recall what year up to now) ...' That the writer *might* have remembered the precise year suggests he wrote sufficiently close to the event (i.e. within the span of a lifetime), that he could be expected to have known it. The wording is inconsistent with any suggestion that he lived a century or more after the death of Samson.

7   'Dating the Transition to Neo-Brittonic: Phonology and History, 400–600', in Alfred Bammesberger and Alfred Wollmann (ed.), *Britain 400–600: Language and History* (Heidelberg, 1990), p. 222. Dumville has expressed a sceptical view, but I believe has yet to argue his case (David N. Dumville, *Saint Patrick, A.D. 493–1993* (Woodbridge, 1993), p. 141).

8   The author of the written source used by the author of the *Vita Samsonis* was attached to a British monastery (probably in Cornwall), which serves to explain the primary concern of the *Vita* with Samson's antecedents in Britain (B. Merdrignac, 'La première Vie de saint Samson: Étude chronologique', *Stvdia Monastica* (Barcelona, 1988), xxx, pp. 244–51). The source was based largely on the testimony of Samson's mother (pp. 271–72).

9   *Revue Celtique*, xxxv, pp. 282–85. Loth tentatively suggested *Afrella* as a brittonicized rendering of *Aurelia*.

10 The author designates the kingdoms of Dyfed and Brittany as *provinciae*, as also possibly Cornwall (cf. Duine, *Questions d'hagiographie et vie de S. Samson*, p. 62).

this wonderful seer. Amon and Anna, who had particular reason to seek help, accompanied the throng in their long and arduous journey.

It was not until the end of the third day that the cavalcade arrived at the place where the prophet had his abode. There they found him seated in the midst of an immense throng of pilgrims, advising individuals on their particular concerns. When it came to their turn, Amon threw himself on his knees before the *librarius*, and prepared to implore him to consider their distressing predicament. Before he could begin, however, the seer interrupted him to say that he knew full well why they were there. Was not his wife barren, and did she not require aid? Let Amon present the sanctuary with a silver rod equal in length to his wife, and God would reward him with offspring. Overwhelmed with joy, Amon promised to bestow three such rods upon the diviner.

Impressed by his evident intelligence and sincerity, the Master (*magister*)[11] invited the couple to recover from their arduous journey by taking a night's rest in his guest-chamber (*hospitium*). While she lay sleeping, Anna dreamed that she was visited by an angel, who told her that her womb was now blessed with fertility, in consequence of which she was destined to give birth to a son who would become a high priest (*summus sacerdos*), whom she should christen Samson. Next morning, her heavenly visitant assured her, the Master would grant her proof of the truth of her vision.

When Anna awoke, she told her husband of the glad tidings. Even as they rejoiced together and made ready to depart, the Master appeared at their door in a state of exultation. Evidently fully apprised of what had passed in Anna's dream, he declared that she was indeed destined to bear a son, who would in time become a high priest such as Britain had never known before. He should be called *Samson*, and handed over at the proper time to be instructed in scholarly learning (*cum disciplinis discendis*). Overjoyed by the news, Amon and Anna returned home, where in due course the child whose glorious destiny the seer had prognosticated was born.[12]

It was suggested by Robert Fawtier, compiler of the first scholarly edition of the *Vita Samsonis*, that 'the story of his mother's sterility is a simple borrowing from the story of Anna, mother of the Virgin Mary', who according to an apocryphal gospel was vouchsafed divine assurance of progeny long after passing the normal age for childbirth.[13] To this Joseph Loth rejoined that the name *Anna* is independently attested in Celtic onomastics, noting further that the author of the *Vita Samsonis* expressly states that Samson's mother was apprehensive that she might be sterile, *not* because her age was excessively advanced, but on account of some physiological deficiency spared her sister (*non pro ætatis sed naturæ inæqualitate cum sua sorore*). Furthermore Samson's birth was followed by those of five brothers and a sister.[14] Early Welsh and Irish law provided that a girl became nubile at the age of fourteen.[15] Thus Anna need have been no more than

---

11   *Magister*, 'master of disciples' (Thomas A. Kelly (ed.), *Sancti Ambrosii Liber de Consolatione Valentiniani: A Text with a Translation, Introduction and Commentary* (Washington, 1940), p. 274). It is tempting to wonder whether an original *magus* may have been replaced by the more acceptable *magister*.

12   Flobert (ed.), *La vie ancienne de saint Samson de Dol*, pp. 148–54.

13   Robert Fawtier (ed.), *La vie de Saint Samson: Essai de critique hagiographique* (Paris, 1912), p. 36; cf. Duine, *Questions d'hagiographie et vie de S. Samson*, p. 29. The 'gospel' in question was the second-century *Protevangelium* of James (J.K. Elliott (tr.), *The Apocryphal New Testament: A Collection of Apocryphal Christian Literature in an English Translation* (Oxford, 1993), pp. 57–59.

14   *Revue Celtique*, xxxv, pp. 281–82.

15   Aled Rhys Wiliam (ed.), *Llyfr Iorwerth: A Critical Text of the Venedotian Code of Medieval Welsh Law Mainly from BM. Cotton MS. Titus Dii* (Cardiff, 1960), p. 32; Kathleen Mulchrone, 'The Rights and Duties of Women with Regard to the Education of their Children', in D. A. Binchy (ed.), *Studies in Early Irish Law* (Dublin, 1936), pp. 188, 189. In mediæval Ireland it was customary for the elder daughter to

twenty when she began to despair of bearing a child, her distress being exacerbated by her younger sister's prior marriage and easy first delivery.

The likely explanation is that the name chosen reflected the fact that the birth of the biblical Samson was similarly tardy, being moreover likewise prefigured by an annunciation. His mother Manoah remained barren, until in response to her prayers an angel appeared before her, who announced that she would give birth to one who would begin the deliverance of Israel from the Philistines (Judges, xiii). The hagiographer's allusion to St Samson's name as 'not inappropriate' (*nomine non immerito*) confirms that the *librarius* had the Old Testament Samson in mind when urging the name upon the saint's mother. That no further attempt is made in the *Vita* to emphasize the parallel suggests that the resemblance was simply noted, rather than appropriated by the hagiographer from the Book of Judges.[16]

Use of names from the Old Testament was quite common in early Wales.[17] As an additional factor, might the pugnacious Samson have been selected as a compromise between the mother's Christianity and the father's attachment to the heroic code of their pagan forebears? A generation later Gildas looked for pious allegory to the biblical Samson's most spectacular feat, when he identified the pillars of the temple of Dagon destroyed by Samson as the twin indulgences of soul and flesh.[18]

Apart from this, the *mise-en-scène* of Samson's conception in the early *Vita* bears only the most superficial Christian colouring, consisting as it does of nothing more than ascription of Anna's conception to the will of Almighty God, *Deus omnipotens*. Loth's comment on the significant absence of any extravagant circumstance in the story of Anna's conception is telling:

> We have there, it seems to me, a striking proof of the truthfulness of the hagiographer; the event is disproportionate to the extravagances of the commentary: the hagiographer provides us with both the true story and the legendary.[19]

The account of Anna's concern at her failure to conceive and her visit to the *librarius* is entirely credible, derived as it surely was from her own recollection, and those of relatives who knew her well. In its essentials the episode reflects practices and tenets of British paganism, on which it sheds a fascinatingly authoritative light.

The persistence of pagan belief and practice as depicted in the *Vita Samsonis* is particularly striking, and further indicative of an early date of composition. In later Welsh saints' lives the hero is customarily depicted as overpowering a succession of malicious demons and truculent heathen despots, pantomime villains for the most part, whose regular humiliations provide rungs on the ladder of the hero's ascent to beatification. Their authors clearly possessed no direct

---

wed before the younger (Standish H. O'Grady (ed.), *Silva Gadelica: A Collection of Tales in Irish with Extracts Illustrating Persons and Places* (London, 1892), i, p. 359).

16   Robert Weber (ed.), *Biblia Sacra iuxta Vulgatam Versionem* (Stuttgart, 1969), i, pp. 343–44. Frazer described the career of the biblical Samson with relish as 'that of an utterly selfish and unscrupulous adventurer, swayed by gusts of fitful passion and indifferent to everything but the gratification of his momentary whims' (Sir James George Frazer, *Folk-Lore in the Old Testament: Studies in Comparative Religion Legend and Law* (London, 1918), ii, p. 481).

17   Sir Ifor Williams and Rachel Bromwich (ed.), *Armes Prydein: The Prophecy of Britain From the Book of Taliesin* (Dublin, 1972), p. xxvii.

18   Theodor Mommsen (ed.), *Monvmenta Germaniae Historica* (xiii): *Chronica Minora saec. IV. V. VI. VII* (Berlin, 1894), iii, p. 66.

19   *Revue Celtique*, xxxv, pp. 281–83.

knowledge of paganism, which had expired as a living religion centuries before their day.[20] The *Vita Samsonis*, in contrast, is (especially in its earlier section) imbued with an atmosphere where heathen practices and concepts flourish as an accepted part of everyday life. At the same time, the relationship between evangelizing Christianity and the older faith, which it was in the early stages of superseding, is depicted as remarkably equable.[21]

The narrative provides several indications that the *librarius* was a pagan prophet. While the Latin word means no more than 'clerk' or 'book-keeper', its Welsh derivative *llyfrawr* (plural *llyfrorion*) acquired the meaning 'soothsayer, sorcerer, magician'.[22] Allusions in early Welsh verse show that *llyfrorion* possessed ability to penetrate the veil of the future, and enjoyed omniscient understanding of cosmology.[23] Both powers represent characteristic attributes of the druids. The term *llyfrawr* was probably synonymous with 'druid', suggesting that much of the lore of the order was preserved in books. Whether or not they employed writing before the arrival of the Romans, it is implausible to suppose that they did not become literate during the long centuries of Roman rule in Britain.[24]

Writing in Ireland in the seventh century, St Patrick's biographer Muirchu describes a contest between the saint and the druids of King Loegaire at Tara, during which the king vainly required the druids to test their books against Patrick's by casting them into water.[25] While the episode is unlikely to be historical, it shows at least that within a couple of generations or so of their replacement by bards and *filid* Irish druids were reputed to have owned books. A passage in the epic tale *Táin Bó Cúalnge* ('The Cattle-raid of Cooley') associates druids with reading (from ogam script), and a suggestive if enigmatic link may be found in the word *Drvvides* ('druids') inscribed, together with accompanying ogam inscription, on a pillar-stone at Killeen Cormac in County Kildare.[26] Whether or not Irish druids possessed knowledge of writing, the likelihood that their British counterparts did so is clearly considerable, in the context of the highly literate culture of Roman and post-Roman Britain.

---

20 Cf. Kenneth Jackson, 'The Sources for the Life of St Kentigern', in Nora K. Chadwick (ed.), *Studies in the Early British Church* (Cambridge, 1958), p. 321.

21 Such evidence as exists suggests that in Britain and Ireland the pre-Christian religion and its mythology were superseded and in part absorbed by the new religion almost without a struggle. Cf. Carolus Plummer (ed.), *Vitae Sanctorum Hiberniae: Partim Hactenvs Ineditae ad Fidem Codicvm Manvscriptorvm Recognovit Prolegominis Notis Indicibvs Instrvxit* (Oxford, 1910), i, pp. cxxix–xxxiii.

22 Henry Lewis, *Yr Elfen Ladin yn yr Iaith Gymraeg* (Cardiff, 1943), p. 41; *Geiriadur Prifysgol Cymru: A Dictionary of the Welsh Language* (Cardiff, 1950–2002), p. 2257; Wade-Evans, *Welsh Christian Origins*, pp. 208–9; Williams and Bromwich (ed.), *Armes Prydein*, pp. xxvi, 15, 70–71.

23 Williams and Bromwich (ed.), *Armes Prydein*, p. 14; J. Gwenogvryn Evans (ed.), *Facsimile & Text of the Book of Taliesin* (Llanbedrog, 1910), p. 20.

24 'The *llyfrawr* appears to be a popular seer ... The word, however, derives from the Latin *librarius*, and the semantic shift suggests an earlier close connection between book-learning and the *llyfrawr*' (Patrick Sims-Williams, 'Gildas and Vernacular Poetry', in Michael Lapidge and David Dumville (ed.), *Gildas: New Approaches* (Woodbridge, 1984), p. 172).

25 John Gwynn (ed.), *Liber Ardmachanus: The Book of Armagh, Edited with Introduction and Appendices* (Dublin, 1913), p. 9.

26 R. A. S. Macalister, 'The "Druuides" Inscription at Killeen Cormac, Co. Kildare', *Proceedings of the Royal Irish Academy* (Dublin, 1914), xxxii, pp. 227–38; idem, *Corpus Inscriptionum Insularum Celticarum* (Dublin, 1945–49), i, pp. 22–24. Cf. Ifor Williams in *The Transactions of the Honourable Society of Cymmrodorion: Sessions 1943 and 1944* (London, 1946), pp. 153–54; Damian McManus, *A Guide to Ogam* (Maynooth, 1991), p. 61. This intriguing inscription is ignored by Ronald Hutton in his dismissal of the possible connexion of Irish druids with ogam script (*Blood and Mistletoe: The History of the Druids in Britain* (New Haven and London, 2009), pp. 44–46).

Reverting to the *librarius* of the *Vita Samsonis*, it is noteworthy that, while quotations of direct speech ascribed to him include innocuous references to Almighty God (possibly owing more to Anna's reporting than reality), there is no allusion to any Christian rite accompanying the session.

A poem replete with pagan allusions, preserved in the Red Book of Hergest, refers to Gwydion and his son Lleu as skilled enchanters, *keluydyon*, who are further compared or identified with practioners of the occult arts termed *lyfyryon*.[27] From the context it appears that both categories of magician were credited with omniscience, just as the *librarius* consulted by Anna and Amon 'was sought out by many kingdoms, because all who resorted to him held whatever he told them to be proven true for certain'. *Llyfrorion* are also mentioned in the tenth-century Welsh prophetic poem *Armes Prydein Vawr*, 'The Great Prophecy of Britain', whose auditors are cautioned not to seek out a *llyfrawr* or greedy poet but to adhere to the Great Prophecy for understanding of what the future held in store. This confirms that the *llyfrorion* claimed prophetic powers.

Evidently the *librarius* consulted by Samson's parents was a forebear of the *llyfrorion* of later centuries. He is ascribed mastery of every topic on which he might be consulted, and accurately predicts future events. In Celtic cosmology little or no distinction was drawn between the natural and occult sciences, and initiates were held to possess penetrating understanding of matters physical and metaphysical.[28] Julius Caesar reported that the druids 'possessed much knowledge of the stars and their movement, of the size of the cosmos and the earth, of natural philosophy, and of the functions and powers of the immortal gods, which they discuss and pass down to their students'.[29]

This ideological base is reflected in etymology. The Irish word *fis* signifies equally 'investigation, knowledge' and 'revelation, occult knowledge', connotations to be found in its Welsh cognates *gwybod*, *gwŷdd*.[30] The etymology reflects the archaic conception of learned knowledge as lore originating in the Otherworld, and accessible only to practitioners proficient in mantic arts.

In an early Irish poem, a druid explains the source of his inspired wisdom. His *fis*, he said, had ascended into the high clouds, whence it perceived a well inhabited by bejewelled Otherworld women. James Carney, editor of the poem, described this experience as a 'curious shamanistic visionary procedure'.[31] A comparable concept may be detected in early Welsh literature. The Welsh word *cyfarwydd* contains the element *gwŷdd*, meaning either 'store of knowledge' or 'storyteller'. The mediæval Welsh Arthurian tale *Culhwch ac Olwen* recounts adventures encountered by the young hero Culhwch in his search for the beautiful Olwen. Arrived at Arthur's court, he requests the king's assistance. Arthur willingly despatches scouts who search his realm for the space of a year without avail. Arthur then assigns selected companions to assist the young noble in his quest. They include Cynddylig Cyfarwydd, of whom the storyteller declares: 'He was as good a guide in lands he had never seen as in those he had.'[32] This was not the nonsensical boast it might appear. Arthur's realm (that is to say, the terrestrial world) had

---

27   J. Gwenogvryn Evans (ed.), *The Poetry in the Red Book of Hergest* (Llanbedrog, 1911), p. 20.

28   Plummer (ed.), *Vitae Sanctorum Hiberniae*, i, p. clxi; *Y Cymmrodor*, xxviii, pp. 241–48; Marged Haycock, '"Preiddeu Annwn" and the Figure of Taliesin', *Studia Celtica* (Cardiff, 1983–84), xviii–xix, pp. 56–58.

29   Otto Seel (ed.), *C. Ivlii Caesaris Commentarii Rervm Gestarvm: Bellvm Gallicvm* (Leipzig, 1961), p. 186.

30   Quin *et al.* (ed.) *Contributions to a Dictionary of the Irish Language*, 'F', pp. 152–53; *Geiriadur Prifysgol Cymru*, pp. 1745, 1754; Pokorny, *Indogermanisches Etymologisches Wörterbuch*, i, pp. 1124–27.

31   James Carney, 'The Earliest Bran Material', in John J. O'Meara and Bernd Naumann (ed.), *Latin Script and Letters A.D. 400–900: Festschrift presented to Ludwig Bieler on the occasion of his 70th birthday* (Leiden, 1976), pp. 181, 184–85.

32   Rachel Bromwich and D. Simon Evans (ed.), *Culhwch and Olwen: An Edition and Study of the Oldest Arthurian Tale* (Cardiff, 1992), p. 15.

been scoured for a year to no avail. The ensuing expedition bears indications of having been originally set in the Otherworld. It appears that what the author (who was, after all, himself a *cyfarwydd*) meant, or his source reflected, was that Cynddilig's knowledge (*gwŷdd*) made him as familiar with the Otherworld as he was with this.

The peculiar talent ascribed Cynddilig in the old story aptly illustrates the arcane nature of knowledge in early Celtic society. It was not that wisdom comprised understanding both of matters material and spiritual, but rather that it was a society whose world-view acknowledged no insuperable distinction between the sacred and the profane, the cosmos in its entirety being imbued with sacrality.[33]

The description of the *librarius* consulted by Samson's parents suggests this faculty of omniscience. Those who flocked 'from many kingdoms' to consult him did so from multifarious motives, and it was generally understood that he was able to provide an answer to whatever question was put to him. The sole instance of his knowledge preserved in the *Vita* relates to what we would today term 'the sacred': matters which no empirical approach might elucidate. These were the foretelling of the conception of a male child, and the glorious destiny which awaited him.

The circumstances of the reception of Samson's parents by the *librarius* are further characteristic of Celtic heathendom. On their arrival he immediately foretells a glorious future for the child destined to be engendered in Anna's womb. A recurrent theme in mediæval Irish literature is that of the druid who pronounces the destiny of a child while yet in the womb.[34]

Again, the silver rod precisely the height of Amon's wife, which the *librarius* requests as meed of his assistance, is a motif of pagan origin featuring in the story of *Branwen*, and enshrined in mediæval Welsh law. A gold or silver rod of the same height as the king is prescribed in the codes as compensation for an insult to himself or his queen, as well as for rapes of virgins, who came directly under the king's protection.[35] These provisions are related to the well-known Celtic tradition of the mating of the king with the country.[36]

---

33 Françoise Le Roux and Christian-J. Guyonvarc'h, *La civilisation celtique* (Rennes, 1990), pp. 145–47.

34 Mommsen (ed.), *Chronica Minora*, iii, p. 150; Kuno Meyer (ed.), *Hibernica Minora: Being a Fragment of an Old-Irish Treatise on the Psalter* (Oxford, 1894), p. 50; A. G. van Hamel (ed.), *Lebor Bretnach: The Irish Version of the Historia Britonum Ascribed to Nennius* (Dublin, 1932), pp. 15–16; Vernam Hull, "The Conception of Conchobar", in J. Fraser, P. Grosjean, and J. G. O'Keeffe (ed.), *Irish Texts* (London, 1931–34), iv, pp. 8–9; Máirín O Daly (ed.), *Cath Maige Mucrama: The Battle of Mag Mucrama* (Dublin, 1975), p. 64; Whitley Stokes (ed.), *Lives of Saints from the Book of Lismore* (Oxford, 1890), pp. 183, 204, 231; Charles Plummer (ed.), *Bethada Náem nÉrenn: Lives of Irish Saints* (Oxford, 1922), i, p. 192; Kuno Meyer, 'The Expulsion of the Dessi', *Y Cymmrodor* (London, 1901), xiv, p. 108; O'Grady (ed.), *Silva Gadelica*, i, pp. 74–75; Vernam Hull (ed.), *Longes mac n-Uislenn: The Exile of the Sons of Uisliu* (New York, 1949), pp. 43–44; Kathleen Mulchrone (ed.), *Bethu Phátraic: The Tripartite Life of Patrick* (Dublin, 1939), p. 100. Cf. Plummer (ed.), *Vitae Sanctorum Hiberniae*, i, clxii; Tom Peete Cross, *Motif-Index of Early Irish Literature* (Bloomington, Ind., 1952), p. 394 (M311); Dorothy Ann Bray, *A List of Motifs in the Lives of the Early Irish Saints* (Helsinki, 1992), p. 115.

35 Derick S. Thomson (ed.), *Branwen uerch Lyr: The Second of the Four Branches of the Mabinogi edited from the White Book of Rhydderch with variants from the Red Book of Hergest and from Peniarth 6* (Dublin, 1961), pp. 4–5; Aled Rhys Wiliam (ed.), *Llyfr Iorwerth: A Critical Text of the Venedotian Code of Medieval Welsh Law Mainly from BM. Cotton MS. Titus Dii* (Cardiff, 1960), pp. 2, 73; Stephen J. Williams and J. Enoch Powell (ed.), *Cyfreithiau Hywel Dda yn ôl Llyfr Blegywryd (Dull Dyfed)* (Cardiff, 1942), pp. 3, 43–44; A. W. Wade-Evans (ed.), *Welsh Medieval Law: Being a Text of the Laws of Howel the Good, Namely the British Museum Harleian MS. 4353 of the 13th Century* (Oxford, 1909), pp. 2–3; Hywel D. Emanuel (ed.), *The Latin Texts of the Welsh Laws* (Cardiff, 1967), pp. 110, 194, 224, 243, 277, 317, 338, 436, 470, 473.

36 Robin Chapman Stacey, 'King, Queen, and *Edling* in the Laws of Court', in T. M. Charles-Edwards, Morfydd E. Owen, and Paul Russell (ed.), *The Welsh King and his Court* (Cardiff, 2000), pp. 35–37; Morfydd E. Owen, 'Shame and Reparation; Woman's Place in the Kin', in Dafydd Jenkins and Morfydd E. Owen (ed.), *The Welsh Law of Women: Studies presented to Professor Daniel A. Binchy on his eightieth*

It will be recalled that the description of the encounter with the *librarius* was most likely obtained by Samson's hagiographer from his mother Anna, a devout Christian who was doubtless concerned to avoid any imputation of pagan associations. Furthermore, her account makes it clear that her husband Amon was the driving force behind the visit. It was he who rejoiced outside the church and arranged the journey, while Anna meekly agreed to accompany him. On their arrival, it was again Amon who fell on his knees before the *librarius* and begged his help. And it was Amon who joyfully offered to confer three silver rods on their host, when only one was requested. Anna interpreted her overwhelming desire for conception as having been answered by her (Christian) God, despite the suspect circumstances.

It is likely that such differing perceptions were facilitated by a relative absence during this early period of any entrenched antagonism between the old and new religions.[37] The assessment of an astute nineteenth-century scholar, Alfred Nutt, of the ambivalent circumstances of their convergence, with particular respect to the motif of the virgin birth, is as applicable to fifth-century Britain as it is to early mediæval Ireland. The passage is worth quoting in full, not least because I am unaware of any comparable discussion of the topic possessed of such clarity and plausibility.

> Nor, indeed, does the history of Ireland record any such persistent and conscious struggle between the old and new, the native and foreign faiths, as is known to have been waged in the [Germanic] North. And yet, seeing that association with the members of the pagan Irish pantheon, the Tuatha De Danann, is characteristic of the re-birth scheme, opportunity was afforded, had such been desired, for trumping the Christian ace by the elaboration of an Irish divine virgin-born being, who could be successfully opposed to the foreign deity. The entire absence of even the faintest attempt in this direction is to my mind proof conclusive that pagan Ireland did not borrow directly and deliberately from the incoming creed. Again, the confused, fragmentary nature of the traditions themselves, the evident effort revealed by the texts to rationalize or discard the features of the re-birth scheme, point in the same direction. It is only what might fairly be expected from our knowledge of the introduction of Christianity into Ireland, a task achieved with far greater tenderness than elsewhere for the existing native beliefs, with far greater accommodation to the social organisation of the race to be converted. Whether the shamrock incident actually occurred or not, the story certainly yields a glimpse of the methods by which Christian dogma was recommended to the native theologian. Is it too much to assert that the first Christian missionaries would probably appeal to the existence of birth-stories, such as those told of Cuchulinn or Conall, as evidence for the miraculous birth of Christ? Later, when the faith was firmly established, a different feeling would undoubtedly form itself; stories in any way parallel with the great mystery of Christianity would come to wear an uncanny aspect; unconsciously they would tend to be minimised, to be replaced by other versions. The orthodox Irish monk-antiquary of the tenth-eleventh centuries

---

birthday 3 June 1980 (Cardiff, 1980), pp. 49–50; Ifor Williams (ed.), *Pedeir Keinc y Mabinogi* (Cardiff, 1930), pp. 175–76; Thomson (ed.), *Branwen uerch Lyr*, pp. 25–26; Elissa R. Henken, *Traditions of the Welsh Saints* (Cambridge, 1987), pp. 115–16.

37   The sole suggestion of any confrontation between the old and new religions in St Patrick's writings comprises a glancing allusion to insults received at the hands of unbelievers: *ab incredulis contumelias perferre* (Ludwig Bieler (ed.), *Libri Epistolarum Sancti Patricii Episcopi* (Dublin, 1952), i, p. 77). Even this may reflect little more than conventional cliché (cf. Bieler's comment in ibid., ii, p. 167). In marked contrast, the Saint's largely legendary early biographies are stacked with bruising encounters between him and his heathen adversaries.

would doubtless regard such stories much in the same way as does the orthodox believer of today stories of virgin-birth in the sacred records of other than the Christian religion; his attitude would be the same – the least said the soonest mended. To this unconscious glossing, rationalising, eliminating attitude on the part of the class to which, materially, we owe the preservation of Irish mythic romance, I attribute the features characterising the texts in which the re-birth scheme is embodied.[38]

Overall, the significance of the description of Samson's parents' visit to the *librarius* lies in the fact that it provides the closest we have to an authoritative account of a British druid. It attests to the respect he was accorded in the early Christian period and the mantic powers at his disposal, together with rites accompanying their deployment. From the account, which derives at a close remove from St Samson's mother, it may be inferred: (i) the wizard's primary function was that of inspired prophet; (ii) incubation was a customary practice for visitors seeking enlightenment; (iii) the mage practised in an established centre, famed abroad, and hence probably of no very recent foundation; (iv) this centre possessed facilities adequate to administering to the wants of large numbers of visiting pilgrims at any one time. All this suggests that the *librarius* functioned in a flourishing heathen temple complex, which as late as *c.* AD 500 continued to attract crowds of neophytes from across much of *Britannia*.

Here we may pause to consider the inviting possibility that the shrine presided over by the *librarius* was the uniquely magnificent Romano-British temple at Lydney, dramatically situated on a ridge overlooking the Severn Sea. Its construction is reliably dated by coin-evidence to the late fourth century AD, and inscriptions record that it was dedicated to the Brittonic god Nudos, the Nudd or Lludd of early Welsh tradition. There are indications of its survival in use at least to the latter part of the fifth century, when Samson's parents consulted the *librarius*. Although the extent of this late survival is difficult to establish with certainty, the most recent excavators of the site cautiously accepted Sir Mortimer Wheeler's conclusion in his pioneering report:

> The reduction of Wheeler's chronology to one more in conformity with comparable sites elsewhere does not of itself prove that Lydney did not have a function in the period down to, or even beyond, the occupation of the Forest of Dean region by Saxons. An inability to recognize a distinctive post-Roman material culture is a characteristic element of early post Roman studies.[39]

Factors making it tempting to identify the Lydney temple with the sanctuary presided over by the *librarius* visited by the parents of St Samson towards the end of the fifth century include the following.

---

38 Alfred Nutt and Kuno Meyer, *The Celtic Doctrine of Re-birth* (London, 1897), pp. 100–101. Early Irish saints were heirs to, coexisted with, and appropriated the powers of the druids (Charles Plummer (ed.), *Bethada Náem nÉrenn: Lives of Irish Saints* (Oxford, 1922), ii, p. 361).

39 P. J. Casey and B. Hoffmann, 'Excavations at the Roman Temple in Lydney Park, Gloucestershire in 1980 and 1981', *The Antiquaries Journal* (Salisbury, 1999), lxxix, p. 115. Cf. R. E. M. Wheeler and T. V. Wheeler, *Report on the Excavation of the Prehistoric, Roman, and Post-Roman Site in Lydney Park, Gloucestershire* (Oxford, 1932), pp. 22–23, 60–63, 127–29; T. C. Lethbridge, *Herdsmen & Hermits: Celtic Seafarers in the Northern Seas* (Cambridge, 1950), p. 87. The difficulty of determining any sort of reliable *terminus ante quem* for late Romano-British temples is emphasized by Philip Rahtz, 'Pagan and Christian by the Severn Sea', in Lesley Abrams and James P. Carley (ed.), *The Archaeology and History of Glastonbury Abbey: Essays in Honour of the Ninetieth Birthday of C. A. Ralegh Radford* (Cambridge, 1991), pp. 7–8, 16–17.

'Reconstruction of the temple-settlement'. (Author's collection)

1. The sanctuary was visited by huge crowds, who travelled from far and wide to consult the seer.

   The Lydney temple is unique in Britain for its size and splendour.

2. Instead of answering Anna's enquiry on their arrival, the *librarius* directs his visitors to spend the night in a 'guest house' (*hospitium* > Welsh *yspytty*),[40] where Anna experiences her prophetic dream.

   Excavations at Lydney have revealed the existence of a magnificent long building, divided into cubicles. This is thought to have been 'an "abaton", used perhaps to supplement the "chapels" in the temple itself for the purpose of that temple-sleep through which the healing-god and his priesthood were wont to work.[41]

3. The *librarius* expounds the meaning of Anna's dream.

   A mosaic inscription at Lydney records the presence of a dignitary bearing the title of *interpres*, i.e. an interpreter of dreams.

---

40   Henry Lewis, *Yr Elfen Ladin yn yr Iaith Gymraeg* (Cardiff, 1943), p. 43; Rachel Bromwich and D. Simon Evans (ed.), *Culhwch and Olwen: An Edition and Study of the Oldest Arthurian Tale* (Cardiff, 1992), p. 55.

41   Wheeler and Wheeler, *Report on the Excavation of the Prehistoric, Roman, and Post-Roman Site in Lydney Park*, pp. 49–52; M. J. T. Lewis, *Temples in Roman Britain* (Cambridge, 1966), p. 89; *The Antiquaries Journal*, lxxix, pp. 84, 89–95.

An objection to this identification might arise from the assertion that the *librarius* dwelt three days' journey away, in the far north (*in longinquam terram aquilonis*). At first sight, this could appear incompatible with the geographical setting implicit in this section of the *Vita*. However, arrival 'on the third day' is an expression employed several times in the *Vita*, and implies no more than a journey of some duration.[42] If the three days' journey be discounted, Lydney appears a likely enough location for the great shrine presided over by the *librarius*. The royal residence of Amon's homeland of Gwent was traditionally located at Caerwent,[43] from which Lydney lies some distance to the north-east.

Eltut the druid

The *Vita Samsonis* provides a further account of a partially Christianized druid, such as may be presumed to have existed during a protracted syncretic transitional period following the introduction of Christianity. The *librarius* concluded his elucidation of Anna's dream with a blessing, together with an instruction to deliver the boy at the appropriate time to be properly educated (*trades eum disciplinis discendis*). The child Samson was in due course taken by his parents to be schooled at 'the splendid monastery' of *Eltutus*, i.e. St Illtud. Illtud's qualifications are catalogued in detail:

> *Ille vero Eltutus de totis Scripturis veteris scilicet ac novi Testamenti et omnis philosophiæ generis, metricæ scilicet ac rhetoricæ, grammaticæque et arithmeticæ, et omnium artium philosophiæ omnium Britannorum compertissimus erat, genereque magicus sagacissimus et futurorum præscius ...*[44]

This Eltutus was of all the Britons the most accomplished in all the Scriptures, that is to say the Old and New Testaments, and in philosophy of every kind, namely of geometry, rhetoric, grammar, and arithmetic, and of all the arts of thaumaturgy; and by birth [i.e. heredity] he was a supremely wise magician, having knowledge of the future.

Thus Illtud is portrayed in the *Vita Samsonis* both as a Christian and as master and practitioner of arts, which the Church eventually came to regard with aversion. Christian saints, like their biblical predecessors, were customarily ascribed prophetic powers, but the appellation *magicus sagacissimus* can only be read in a pagan context.[45] The native terms for 'druid' in early British and Irish sources are regularly translated into Latin as *magus* or *magicus*, and *vice versa*.[46] Although some of the terminology of the specialist skills with which Illtud is credited derives

---

42 Flobert (ed.), *La vie ancienne de saint Samson de Dol*, pp. 150, 188, 196. Three days was the statutory delay allowed for a journey within a *cantref*: *Oet arwassaf yn vn gymh6t neu yn vn cantref tri dieu* (Morfydd E. Owen, 'The Cyfnerth Text', in T. M. Charles-Edwards, Morfydd E. Owen and D. B. Walters (ed.), *Lawyers and Laymen: Studies in the History of Law presented to Professor Dafydd Jenkins on his seventy-fifth birthday* (Cardiff, 1986), p. 194).

43 H. Idris Bell (ed.), *Vita Sancti Tathei and Buched Seint y Katrin: Re-edited, after Rees, from the MSS. in the British Museum* (Bangor, 1909), pp. 4–5.

44 Flobert (ed.), *La vie ancienne de saint Samson de Dol*, p. 156.

45 'The use of the term *magicus* is reminiscent enough of the druidic world for a number of scribes to correct it to *magnificus*' (Oliver Davies, *Celtic Christianity in Early Medieval Wales: The Origins of the Welsh Spiritual Tradition* (Cardiff, 1996), p. 13).

46 Mommsen (ed.), *Chronica Minora*, iii, pp. 150, 181–86; van Hamel (ed.), *Lebor Bretnach*, pp. 15–16, 53–61; John Gwynn (ed.), *Liber Ardmachanus: The Book of Armagh, Edited with an Introduction and Appendices* (Dublin, 1913), pp. 3, 22, 24, 28, 30; Wade-Evans appears to have been first to suggest that Illtud was originally a druid (*Welsh Christian Origins*, pp. 133, 211). However, we may note the query: 'Was he a Druid by birth or descent?' (Rev.

from the Roman curriculum of higher education, in the main they denote occult arts ascribed to sorcerers. Thus *mathematica* in the context must mean 'magic'.[47] In the second section of the *Vita Samsonis* the Saint learns that a certain deacon is attended by an evil spirit, in the guise of a black boy. Falling direly ill, the possessed man confessed in his agony that he had from childhood been trained in the magical arts, *philosophiae machinatione*, another term employed to describe Illtud's occult powers.[48]

The *curriculum vitæ* ascribed the partially Christianized druid Eltutus attests to the fact that he was profoundly literate. Since we learn in addition that his druidical office was hereditary, this provides striking confirmation of the likelihood that druids, during and after the Roman occupation, were (as might naturally be expected) generally literate.

Close parallels are to be found between the anonymous *librarius* to whom the parents of Samson repaired in their desperation, and St Illtud who was subsequently entrusted with the boy's education. Each is famed throughout the land for his omniscience; each is a renowned prophet; each predicts the coming greatness of Samson in strikingly similar phraseology; and each outwardly professes the Christian faith, despite backgrounds and *modi operandi* bearing unmistakable intimations of paganism. In the next chapter it will be shown that the sections of the later mediæval life of St Illtud essentially represents a hitherto undetected Christian palimpsest erected on the foundations of a pagan saga. It is plain that the hagiographer regarded these two numinous figures as fulfilling analogous functions. The *librarius* being an infallible prophet, his injunction to Anna to deliver Samson to be educated at the appropriate time suggests that he had in mind a renowned *confrère* to whom in the event Samson's parents resorted.[49]

The setting of the story of St Samson provides unique glimpses of the establishment of Christianity in Britain, whose full implications have been generally overlooked. In the fifth century it seems that much of western Britain continued largely pagan, while the Romano-British church represented a vigorous minority religion. A century later, Gildas describes a Britain in which Christianity is at least officially accepted as the religion of kings and people. In fact, as I have sought to show in Chapter Five *supra*, for ideological reasons he deliberately occluded widespread continuance of paganism in the Britain of his day.

At the same time, lapidary inscriptions and burials distributed across south-western England and Wales indicate the spread of Christianity in western Britain, although widescale conversion does not appear to have made much headway before the turn of the fifth and sixth centuries

---

Thomas Taylor (tr.), *The Life of St. Samson of Dol* (London, 1925), p. 14). Moreover, the librarius 'rappelle surtout les anciens druides par ses dons divinatoires' (Flobert (ed.), *La vie ancienne de saint Samson de Dol*, p. 149).

47   Duine, *Questions d'hagiographie et vie de S. Samson*, pp. 59, 61. Eltut is ascribed 'la totalité des arts libéraux et la métrique, ce qui ne l'empêche pas d'être magicien et devin (cf. i, 2–3, le librarius)' (Flobert (ed.), *La vie ancienne de saint Samson de Dol*, p. 157). 'Such cultural fusion is exactly what one would have expected on *a priori* grounds to have been characteristic of this region at this time' (E. G. Bowen, *The Settlements of the Celtic Saints in Wales* (Cardiff, 1956), p. 45).

48   Fawtier (ed.), *La Vie de Saint Samson*, 164. Bernard Merdrignac defines *philosophia* here as 'la maîtrise de la science profane, avec les risques que cela implique' (Le Menn and Le Moing (ed.), *Bretagne et pays celtiques*, pp. 174–75). In the Later Roman Empire the term *philosophus* was widely employed for magicians and astrologers (Ramsay MacMullen, *Enemies of the Roman Order: Treason, Unrest, and Alienation in the Empire* (Cambridge, Mass., 1966), pp. 320–21). For the folklore theme of the demon as black man, cf. Merdrignac, *Recherches sur l'hagiographie armoricaine du VIIème au XVème siècle*, ii, p. 152.

49   'The instruction by an older mantic person' was characteristic of the childhood and upbringing of seers in early Ireland and Wales (N. Kershaw Chadwick, *Poetry & Prophecy* (Cambridge, 1942), p. 54).

AD. However, this distribution of inscribed memorial stones with predominantly Christian connotations indicates frustratingly little. Not only are they difficult to date within a century or more,[50] but the fact that lapidary inscriptions (a) commemorate no more than a tiny minority of the population, and (b) are Christian in character, inevitably presents an unbalanced impression of the influence of the new religion.[51]

The only contemporary evidence of the state of Christianity in south-western Britain in St Samson's day suggests that its influence remained slight and precarious. Gildas, writing *c.* 540, begins his catalogue of contemporary royal criminals with Constantine of Dumnonia, whose realm extended across modern Cornwall and Devonshire. It is suggested that his principal stronghold lay at Tintagel,[52] the wealthiest and most substantial royal fortress in south-western Britain, which was located on the coast of the region of Trigg where (as we shall see) Samson attended a major pagan festival.

While the other four targets of Gildas's vitriolic attack, kings reigning in what is now Wales, are charged with multifarious heinous sins and crimes, Constantine alone is excoriated for engaging in a violent attack on the church itself. Two young princes (dangerous Christian heirs?), seeking refuge from his wrath in a monastery, were murdered by the king, who had sacreligiously disguised himself as an abbot in order to obtain entry and slaughter the youths before the altar. He is further indicted for frequent acts of adultery, and ridding himself of his lawful wife – crimes which the king may not have regarded as such, since they could represent licit practice among pagan British rulers. Although Henry VIII and Oliver Cromwell sufficiently attest to the fact that a professed Christian may prove a brutal tyrant, Gildas declares that Constantine had effectively apostacized, reverting to repudiation of Christian belief (*incredulitas*),[53] which his indignant critic equated with ignorance (*insipientia*) – presumably of Christian principles and conduct.

That Western Britain was far from having been fully converted to Christianity in the early sixth century AD is further indicated in revealing detail by the *Vita Samsonis* itself. Equally striking is the light it throws on the manner in which conversion is recorded to have been effected. Pagans are not struck down by fire from heaven, swallowed up by swamps, or abruptly incapacitated by debilitating sickness, as is customarily the case in later mediæval hagiography. In the *Vita Samsonis* professing pagans are drawn to profess the new faith on becoming persuaded of its superior credibility and efficacy, and the narrative broadly confirms that the switch from the old religion to the new was widely accomplished without untoward ill-feeling or strife. Of course, the process is very unlikely to have been uniform, and Proinsias Mac Cana perceived traces of a tradition of hostility between Christians and druids during the early period of conversion in Ireland.[54]

---

50   'It is clear that no stone can be dated more precisely than to within one or two centuries' (Elisabeth Okasha, *Corpus of Early Christian Inscribed Stones of South-west Britain* (Leicester, 1993), p. 57).

51   Charles Thomas, *Christian Celts: Messages & Images* (Stroud, 1998), pp. 62, 82–100.

52   Ken Dark, *Britain and the End of the Roman Empire* (Stroud, 2000), p. 155.

53   'Incredulitas, "1 a lack of belief, disbelief, doubt; b (spec.) lack of Christian belief"' (R. E. Latham and D. R. Howlett (ed.), *Dictionary of Medieval Latin from British Sources* (London, 1975–2013), p. 1312).

54   'Christianisme et paganisme dans l'Irlande ancienne', in Proinsias Mac Cana and Michel Meslin (ed.), *Rencontres de religions: Actes du colloque du Collège des Irlandais tenu sous les auspices de l'Académie Royale Irlandaise* (Juin 1981) (Paris, 1986), pp. 59–62. However, Mac Cana went on to document the considerable degree of syncretism which obtained in the ensuing period (pp. 64–65), and judiciously concluded by observing 'le fait que la transition du paganisme au christianisme ait été dans l'ensemble pacifique; elle ne s'est pas faite sans acrimonie, mais elle se passa pratiquement sans violence' (p. 71).

A pagan realm in sixth-century Britain

Chapters 45 to 51 of the *Vita Samsonis* describe the saint's activities in Cornwall, where he spent a summer during his journey from Wales to Brittany. The account of his career in the peninsula is readily summarized. After crossing the Severn estuary, he arrived outside a monastery called Docco.[55] Declaring his desire to confer with a sage (*sapiens*) among them, the monks deputed the wisest of their company to confer with him beyond the bounds of the monastery. He proved to be one *Viniauus* (Winiaw), a divinely inspired prophet, who enquired the saint's destination. Seating himself beside Samson, Winiaw politely declined his visitor's request to stay in the monastery, on the pretext that he might disapprove the current lax state of its brethren. He concluded by urging the saint to provide some outward sign of the power of the Lord over the country (*patria*), before crossing the sea to Europe.

Samson, sensing that the Holy Spirit was speaking through his interlocutor, departed with his companions. One day, as they traversed a region called *Tricurius* (Trigg), they came upon a great crowd of people conducting dramatic rituals before a stone idol. Samson having miraculously restored to life a youth who falls from his horse, they and their leader Count Guedianus (*comes Vedianus*) are persuaded to renounce their pagan practices, and accept baptism at the hands of the saint. Samson then carved a cross on a standing stone, which the author of the Life had personally examined during a visit to the spot.[56]

Next, the British leader informed Samson that beyond an adjacent river the neighbourhood was being rendered uninhabitable by the ravages of a venomous serpent, who dwelt in a cave. The Saint boldly entered its subterranean lair, whereupon the reptile coiled upon itself and bit its own tail. Without further ado, Samson slipped off his belt, looped it round the reptile's neck, and slung the creature from a nearby hill (rather a complicated method of disposal, it may be thought). After this the Saint constructed a monastery not far from the cave, where he installed his father Amon as abbot. Finally, Samson led his party to the coast, where they embarked for Brittany.[57]

---

55   In the parish of St Kew, near Padstow (Gilbert H. Doble, *The Saints of Cornwall* (Chatham and Oxford, 1960–70), pp. 105–8).

56   In the ensuing chapter, Samson is said to have persuaded the worshippers to destroy their idol. However, it is possible that its 'destruction' was rhetorical, and that the idol was the menhir on which Samson carved the cross attesting to the triumph of Christianity over paganism.

57   Flobert (ed.), *La vie ancienne de saint Samson de Dol*, pp. 210–22. It has been suggested that Samson followed the transpeninsular route from Padstow to Fowey (for which see William Copeland Borlase, *The Age of the Saints: A Monograph of Early Christianity in Cornwall with the Legends of the Cornish Saints* (Truro, 1893), pp. 62–65; *Revue Celtique*, xxxv, pp. 290–92; E. G. Bowen, *Saints, Seaways and Settlements in the Celtic Lands* (Cardiff, 1969), pp. 24, 95, 168). This however is based on the hagiographer's assumption that Samson crossed from sea to sea virtually without interlude. In fact, he has clearly telescoped events fairly drastically, given that Samson arrived in Cornwall shortly after Easter, and attended a Cornish pagan festival, which as will be seen probably occurred at the beginning of August. After that, he passed time as an eremite in a cave, and completed construction of a monastery, before eventually departing for Europe – presumably that autumn, or the next spring. Baring-Gould's colourful description of Samson's itinerary from coast to coast is based on the misconception that the journey ensued immediately on his disembarkation in Cornwall (S. Baring-Gould and John Fisher, *The Lives of the British Saints: The Saints of Wales and Cornwall and such Irish Saints as have Dedications in Britain* (London, 1907–13), iv, pp. 156–57). Since nothing in the *Vita* suggests that Samson intended from the outset to extend his journey to Brittany, there may be something in Fawtier's preference for a more direct voyage from south Wales across the Severn estuary, with the saint's party disembarking at Samson's Bay near Ilfracombe, and eventually departing for Dol from the south coast of Devonshire (*La vie de Saint Samson*, pp. 5961).

Canon Doble, historian of the Cornish saints, observed that 'this section describing Samson's passage through Cornwall is perhaps the most interesting in the whole *Vita*'.[58] It is generally accepted as being grounded in historical reality, not least because one of the author's declared sources was Henoc, whom Samson had appointed deacon during his stay in Cornwall, and who dwelt there for decades thereafter.[59] Moreover, the author himself travelled to at least one of the sites of Samson's exploits in Cornwall, where he profited from local information.

The broad impression conveyed by the Cornish section of the *Vita Samsonis* is of a land given over almost entirely to paganism. Christian activity appears confined to two isolated locations: the monastery of Docco at Padstow, which is in any case described as altogether inactive, and another founded by Samson himself at the place where he encountered the idolaters of Trigg.[60] The most vividly recounted episode is the scene of pagan worship, which attracted a vast crowd (*exercitus*) of celebrants. This picture conveyed of a predominantly heathen land is substantiated by further consideration of the Cornish interlude in Samson's career.

Particularly intriguing is the initial episode, when Samson and his party on disembarking in Cornwall arrive at the monastery of Saint Docco. Approaching its gates, Samson invited the monks to send out a wise man from among them to speak with him. In response they despatch their wisest, '*Winiau* by name, who was also called by them in the British language *Lleu*' (*Viniauum nomine, qui et ipse britannica lingua cum illis lux vocitabatur*) – Latin *lux*, 'light', being *lleu* in Welsh.

Samson and Winiau entered into a convoluted colloquy, their moral and intellectual equality being emphasized by their sitting beside each other. Samson began by requesting a brief sojourn for his party before they continued on their journey. However, *sanctus Vinniauus* (as he is suddenly described) politely declined Samson's request for hospitality, on the bizarre grounds that the monks had relapsed so direly into their former practices (*in nostris prioribus institutis laxamur*), that the presence among them of one so markedly virtuous must prove insufferable.

This peculiar pretext is wholly incompatible with the requirement of monasteries in the early insular Church to provide hospitality for travellers.[61] Indeed, if *sanctus Vinniauus* is to be identified (as scholars are inclined to think)[62] with a contemporary Irish St Finnian, a penitential compiled by the latter specifically requires monastic houses to be scrupulous in extending generous welcome to pilgrims, hospitality being enjoined by God Himself.[63]

What is to be made of this peculiar exchange? What precisely were those previous practices (*nostri priores institutiones*), to which the recalcitrant brethren had reverted? The allusion suggests a condition more drastic and specific than mere temporary relapse from the monastic

---

58 Doble, *The Saints of Cornwall*, v, p. 89.

59 Bernard Merdrignac, 'Henoc, les *Philosophi* et Pental: remarques sur la *Vita Ia Samsonis*', in Le Menn and Jean-Yves Le Moing (ed.), *Bretagne et pays celtiques*, pp. 167–80.

60 Thomas, *And Shall These Mute Stones Speak?*, pp. 233–34, 305, 306.

61 Carolus Plummer (ed.), *Vitae Sanctorum Hiberniae: Partim Hactenvs Ineditae ad Fidem Codicvm Manvscriptorvm Recognovit Prolegominis Notis Indicibvs Instrvxit* (Oxford, 1910), i, pp. cxiii–xiv; Rev. John Ryan, *Irish Monasticism: Origins and Early Development* (London, 1931), pp. 318–21.

62 David N. Dumville, 'Gildas and Uinniau', in Michael Lapidge and David Dumville (ed.), *Gildas: New Approaches* (Woodbridge, 1984), pp. 207–14. 'He [Finnian] would most economically be seen as a British bishop who became associated with (and perhaps an important figure in) the mission in Ireland in the sixth century' (ibid., p. 214). Cf. also Pádraig Ó Riain, 'Finnian or Winniau?', in Próinséas Ní Chatháin and Michael Richter (ed.), *Irland und Europa: Die Kirche im Frühmittelalter* (Stuttgart, 1984), pp. 52–57.

63 *Et in domibus nostris suscipiendi sunt peregrini, sicut preceptum est a Domino* (Ludwig Bieler (ed.), *The Irish Penitentials* (Dublin, 1963), p. 86).

ideal. Given other indications that Cornwall remained largely pagan at this time, might the brethren have reverted to heathenism? It has been seen that the school (*scola*) of the hereditary druid (*magicus*) Eltutus, at which Samson was educated in Christian doctrine, most likely originated as a druidic college, much of whose pagan practices continued. The ultimate triumph of Dark Age Christianity, following an extended evolutionary process of which scant evidence survives, makes it tempting to assume an inexorably teleological progress. In reality, there must have been any number of occasions when communities reverted in whole or part to the old religion, of which Samson's encounter in Cornwall may represent a prime example. It has been widely assumed that the monks of Docco were simply failing in their Christian duties. However the assumption is neither in accord with the burden of the text, nor the logic of the event. If monastic discipline had simply become lax, why did Winiau not request Bishop Samson's assistance in recalling the brothers to their duty? The explanation that their failings might embarrass the vigorously proselytizing saint is unconvincing, and suggests a clumsy attempt by the author to explain an episode he did not understand.

The content of §46 of Samson's *Vita* is particularly obscure and confusing. First may be taken the rank and name of the sage who conferred with the saint in the hinterland beyond its bounds. Lynette Olson points out that 'the *Docco* episode is intriguingly original in Celtic hagiography … Iuniauus [Winiau] being described as "the wisest" without being designated by the title of abbot or by any other monastic office or ecclesiastical order'.[64] At the time, an Irish *sapiens* enjoyed no office within a given church or monastery.[65] Did the monastery possess no abbot, the obvious figure to confer with their distinguished visitor and make the decision whether or not to admit him? This is emphasized by the fact that it is incongruously the monks (*fratres*) who despatch one among them to confer with Samson. The honorific prefix of the delegate, *sanctus Vinniauus*, reads like a parenthesis in the midst of his reported colloquy with Samson. Yet again, it would have been unusual, to say the least, to find a saint holding an indeterminate or subordinate situation in a monastery.

The author himself appears markedly confused. His introductory description terms Samson's interlocutor 'the wisest amongst them [the *fratres* of the monastery], *Winiau* by name, who was also termed by them "light" in the British language' (*Viniauum nomine, qui et ipse britannica lingua cum illis lux vocitabatur*). But, given that *Winiau* is itself a British name, what can have been the purpose of 'explaining' it by another? It has been suggested that *lux* is a translation of the first element of *Winiau*, since *Win-* represents British **uindos* (> Welsh *gwynn*, 'white').[66] But that can scarcely be the case, given that the meanings are *not* the same, while *win-* is in any case an adjective and *lux* a noun. Furthermore, since the first language of the author of the Life was British,[67] it is hard to envisage the purpose intended by providing an incorrect 'translation' of one British word by another. Nowhere else in the *Vita* can its author be found engaging in so superfluous and incomprehensible an exercise.

In fact, the obvious meaning the passage must surely have conveyed to a contemporary reader or auditor makes its interpretation clear. The 'wisest man' (*sapientissimus*) in the monastery is

---

64   Lynette Olson, *Early Monasteries in Cornwall* (Woodbridge, 1989), pp. 14–16.

65   T. M. Charles-Edwards, *Early Christian Ireland* (Cambridge, 2000), pp. 264–67.

66   Fawtier (ed.), *La vie de Saint Samson*, p. 61; *Revue Celtique*, xxxv, p. 295. 'Indication précieuse : l'hagiographe sait le breton et l'étymologie de Winiau n'est pas fausse (bret. gwenn, «blanc; lumineux; heureux; béni»' (Flobert (ed.), *La vie ancienne de saint Samson de Dol*, p. 214).

67   T. M. Charles-Edwards, *Wales and the Britons 350–1064* (Oxford, 2013), p. 625. Cf. *Revue Celtique*, xxxv, p. 299.

described as '*Winiau* by name, who was called by them 'light' in the British language'. Among scholars, Wade-Evans came closest to understanding the implication: 'He was apparently a *magicus*, druid, like Illtud, or a *librarius*. His name [*Winiau*] would yield in modern Welsh Iniaw or Inio, and his appellation Lleu.'[68]

However, if by 'appellation' Wade-Evans meant 'sobriquet', this conveys a misleading impression, since the wording indicates that the two names were regarded as of equally valid application, i.e. *Winiau = Lleu*. Given that the Welsh word for 'light' is *lleu*, any early seventh-century Briton on either side of the Channel would surely have identified a gifted seer named Lleu with *Lleu mab Gwydion* (Old Welsh *Lou map Guidgen*), best-known of the gods of the Celtic pantheon, both in the British Isles and on the Continent. In the *Vita Samsonis*, Winiau-Lleu is described as 'divinely inspired, and knowing much concerning the future' (*Erat namque ille diuinitus inspiratus et multorum de futuris conscius*). Lleu was similarly renowned in Welsh tradition as an enchanter familiar with 'the books' (of magic), i.e. he was a (divine) *librarius*, like the *magister* who foretold Samson's pre-eminent greatness. The gift of prophecy was a salient characteristic of Lleu's Irish counterpart Lug.[69] The Welsh for *sapiens* ('wise man') is *doethwr*, which in the context suggests 'wizard' or 'diviner'. Finally, as will be shown shortly, the *Vita Samsonis* provides yet more explicit indication of the mysterious sage's identification with the Brittonic deity.

The author cannot have intended *Lleu* as a translation of *Winiau*, since that is what it plainly is not. Nor was he bizarrely seeking to identify two disparate *names* as one: he evidently understood that one *figure* corresponded to the other. He is scarcely likely to have identified a British cleric with a pagan god (Lug being as celebrated in Gaul as he was in Britain),[70] whereas the reverse process could have appeared desirable. His confusion over Winiau's status and honorific appellations suggests that the readily recognizable *Lleu* was already present as

---

68   Wade-Evans, *Welsh Christian Origins*, p. 224. The depiction of Winiau as both *sapientissimus* and an inspired prophet closely echoes that of the Christianized druid Eltut, who was at once a *magicus sagacissimus et futurorum præscius* (Flobert (ed.), *La vie ancienne de saint Samson de Dol*, p. 156).

69   *Neuleu ag6ydyon . a uuant geluydyon . neu awdant lyfyryon* (Gwenogvryn Evans (ed.), *The Poetry in the Red Book of Hergest*, col. 1054, ll. 16–17. In *Baile in Scáil*, Lug is the prophet *par excellence*, who foretells the future rulers of Tara.

70   Antonio Tovar, 'The God Lugus in Spain', *The Bulletin of the Board of Celtic Studies* (Cardiff, 1982), xxix, pp. 593–94. 'Par la nombre des documents qui attestent son culte, Mercure paraît bien être le plus grand dieu de Gaule romaine' (Paul-Marie Duval, *Les dieux de la Gaule* (Paris, 1957), p. 67; cf. idem, 'Problèmes des rapports entre la religion gauloise et la religion romaine', in Proinsias Mac Cana and Michel Meslin (ed.), *Rencontres de religions: Actes du colloque du Collège des Irlandais tenu sous les auspices de l'Académie Royale Irlandaise* (Juin 1981) (Paris, 1986), pp. 48–49). Cf. Proinsias Mac Cana, 'Placenames and Mythology in Irish Tradition: Places, Pilgrimages and Things', in Gordon W. MacLennan (ed.), *Proceedings of the First North American Congress of Celtic Studies* (Ottawa, 1988), p. 323. In Roman Gaul, Lugus was equated with Mercurius, above all in inscriptions; but it is likely that his indigenous name remained widely employed in common parlance, incantations, and the like – as also in place names. Festivals corresponding to Lughnasa were widely celebrated in France (Máire MacNeill, *The Festival of Lughnasa: A Study of the Survival of the Celtic Festival of the Beginning of Harvest* (Oxford, 1962), pp. 385–91; Sir John Rhŷs, 'Notes on The Coligny Calendar together with an Edition of the Reconstructed Calendar', *The Proceedings of the British Academy* (London, 1910), iv, p. 236). 'Rivros [in the Coligny Calendar] could be, therefore, another name or by-name of the all-knowing Gaulish Mercurius/Lugu-, comparable with Skr. ṛbhu- "crafty, skilful" ... and perhaps also with Greek Ὀρφεύςε the name of the divine (Thracian?) singer' (Heinrich Wagner, 'Studies in the Origins of Early Celtic Civilisation', *Zeitschrift für celtische Philologie* (Tübingen, 1971), xxxi, pp. 28–29). Lug's festival at Lugdunum (Lyons) was likewise celebrated at harvest time (Stephen C. McCluskey, 'Astronomies and Rituals at the Dawn of the Middle Ages', in Clive L.N. Ruggles and Nicholas J. Saunders (ed.), *Astronomies and Cultures* (Niwot, Colo., 1993), pp. 105–9).

the name of Samson's interlocutor in the author's source. Accordingly, he identified him with what some undeclared consideration suggested to him to be an appropriately distinguished ecclesiastic of the day.

Vinniauus is the British form of Irish *Finnian* and *Finbarr*,[71] which has led historians to identify the mysterious wise man from Docco with one or other of three celebrated sixth-century Irish saints of that name. Bishop Findbarr (*sanctus Vinniavus*) was a venerable scholar who had instructed St Columba before his departure for Iona in AD 563.[72] St Finnian of Clonard was an impressive figure in the contemporary Irish Church, known also by the Brittonic form of his name, *Winiau* (it is generally considered that he was British by birth). His death from plague is recorded in AD 549.[73] Finally, there is Findbarr of Moville (Mag mBili in Ulster), who died in AD 579.[74]

Persuasive arguments have been advanced for regarding all or some of these ecclesiastics as having been originally one and the same – both with each other, and also to a Finnian (*Vennianus auctor*) who corresponded with Gildas in Britain, and was author of a surviving penitential.[75] All this broadly accords with the chronology of St Samson's visit to Cornwall, which probably occurred about 520–30.

The monastic scholar who wrote the *Vita Samsonis* was apparently familiar with the writings of Gildas,[76] which include the correspondence conducted with Finnian. Fragments of Gildas's responses have been preserved, which were circulated as the primary guide to monastic discipline.

These fragments are not ecclesiastical legislation; they belong to a letter of counsel from one man to another, Gildas to 'Vinnian'. They survive because they were quoted as providing authoritative guidance, and so acquired something of the status of legislation … The surviving fragments form the most important source which we possess concerning monastic practice in the Celtic Churches in the sixth century … Certainly [Gildas's] Fragments 1 & 7 concern the subjects of disputes arising from a desire for stricter monastic observance. One may plausibly see the fragments as treating various aspects of the one single argument, with a little allowance for a certain diffuseness of construction and the loss of much of the discussion. On this assumption, it will be seen that fragments 4 and 5 deal with precisely the subject mentioned by Columbanus.[77]

---

71 '*Uinniau*, if we remove the Latin inflexion, is a British name – it could belong to any of the neo-Brittonic languages – a hypocoristic form built on the first element *Uind*- (> *Uinn*-) with the specialist suffix **iawos*' (David N. Dumville, 'Gildas and Uinniau', in Michael Lapidge and David Dumville (ed.), *Gildas: New Approaches* (Woodbridge, 1984), p. 209). 'The Brittonic origins of the Irish form of the pet name are not in dispute' (Pádraig Ó Riain, 'Finnio and Winniau: A Return to the Subject', in John Carey, John T. Koch, and Pierre-Yves Lambert (ed.), *Ildánach Ildírech: A Festschrift for Proinsias MacCana* (Andover and Aberystwyth, 1999), p. 189).

72 Alan Orr Anderson and Marjorie Ogilvie Anderson (ed.), *Adomnan's Life of Columba* (Edinburgh, 1961), pp. 196, 324–26, 470.

73 Seán Mac Airt and Gearóid Mac Niocaill (ed.), *The Annals of Ulster (to A.D. 1131)* (Dublin, 1983), i, p. 76.

74 Ibid., p. 90.

75 Pádraig Ó Riain, 'Finnian or Winniau?', in Próinséas Ní Chatháin and Michael Richter (ed.), *Irland und Europa: Die Kirche im Frühmittelalter* (Stuttgart, 1984), pp. 52–57; Richard Sharpe, 'Gildas as a Father of the Church', in Lapidge and Dumville (ed.), *Gildas: New Approaches*, p. 198; Dumville in ibid., pp. 207–14; Pádraig Ó Riain, *The Making of a Saint: Finbarr of Cork 600–1200* (Dublin, 1997), pp. 5–6; T. M. Charles-Edwards, *Early Christian Ireland* (Cambridge, 2000), pp. 292–93.

76 'L'hagiographe a probablement lu Gildas' (Flobert (ed.), *La vie ancienne de saint Samson de Dol*, p. 99).

77 Lapidge and Dumville (ed.), *Gildas: New Approaches*, pp. 197–98. The fragmentary text of Gildas's letters to Finnian is to be found in Theodor Mommsen (ed.), *Monvmenta Germaniae Historica* (xiii): *Chronica Minora saec. IV. V. VI. VII* (Berlin, 1894), iii, pp. 86–88.

The influence of Gildas's writing on Samson's perception of his duties was marked:

> Its [*Vita Samsonis*] strong emphasis on the ascetic life in contrast to the worldliness of the established churches and prelates of Samson's time provides an interesting parallel to the reform-movement centred on Gildas … Much of Samson's career could be seen as illustrating the trend advocated by Gildas.[78]

In one of his letters, Finnian (*Vennianus auctor*) enquires of Gildas what should be done about monks who, impelled by (excessive) monastic enthusiam (*fervore monachorum*) to seek a more perfect life, relapse or depart to the wilderness: *aut laxantur aut ad deserta fugiunt*. Although Gildas's response to this failing is not preserved, he was in general averse to over-rigorous displays of piety.

It is possible that the author of the Life of St Samson mistook Gildas's allusion to monks who relapse (*laxantur*) or desert their monasteries in his letter to *sanctus Vennianus* as referring to the oddly wayward monks of Docco. In §§66–68 of his *De Excidio* (a work also likely to have been known to Samson), Gildas denounces *sacerdotes* and *clerici* who abandon their calling to wallow in sin. Prominent among their failings was a besotted attendance at public 'games' and recitations of a distinctly pagan character.[79] The charges might have been taken as applicable to the backsliding monks of that place, among whom the hagiographer might have interpreted Gildas's correspondent *Vennianus* as an unavailing objector.

This advances one explanation of the equivocal status and conduct of the mysterious *sapiens* at Docco, but unfortunately remains only a possibility.

Moving on, I suspect that the author's unconvincing reason for so pointedly setting the meeting of Samson and his interlocutor *beyond* the monastery's perimeter originated in the fact that Samson had in reality little or nothing to do with the site, his activities being confined to the pagan hinterland without.

The broad picture which emerges of the Dumnonian peninsula encountered by Samson provides a striking contrast between the dubiously Christian enclave in the 'monastery' at Docco, and the vast horde (*exercitus*) of worshippers gathered at the pagan assembly in the neighbouring region (*pagus*) of Trigg. Comparable festivals of the god Lug in Ireland were attended in some cases by the inhabitants of more than one petty kingdom (*tuath*).[80] The destructive serpent overcome by Samson is said with unusual specificity to have ravaged *two* regions (*duos pagos*), suggesting symbolically that a neighbouring province was likewise given over to paganism. This gloomy picture accords with Gildas's description of the contemporary Dumnonian king Constantine as an inveterate apostate foe of the Church.

It is likely that the second region tyrannized by the heathen serpent was that of Pydar, to the west of Trigg. The serpent is described as living in a cave beyond a river, which was conceivably the Camel, which divides Pydar from Trigg. The 'monastery' at Docco, situated as it was beside the estuary of the Camel, would in that case have lain at the heart of the pagan realm, whose 'capital' was most likely nearby Tintagel.

---

78   Lapidge and Dumville (ed.), *Gildas: New Approaches*, p. 199.

79   G. S. M. Walker (ed.), *Sancti Columbani Opera* (Dublin, 1957), p. 8; Mommsen (ed.), *Chronica Minora*, iii, 62–64.

80   MacNeill, *The Festival of Lughnasa*, p. 427.

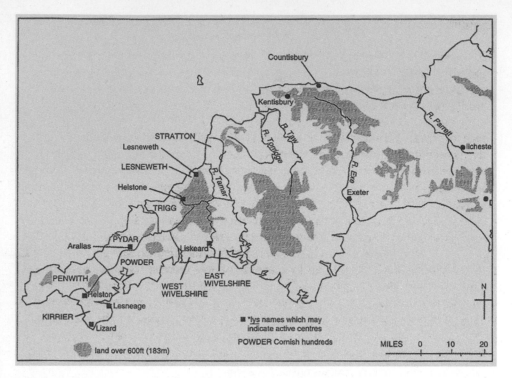

Dark-Age Dumnonia, showing bounds of Trigg and Pydar divided by the river Camel. (Author's collection)

Although much remains obscure, overall it seems likely that the figure of *Winiau* in the *Vita Samsonis* was abstracted from a distinct context, and became conflated with the popular deity Lleu. It need not be thought that there is anything incongruous in the author's envisaging a dialogue between the saint and a pagan deity. When St Martin of Tours was engaged in evangelizing his pagan countrymen in Gaul in the previous century, his biographer recorded this rueful recollection: 'As for demons, as each one came to him, he would denounce it by its own name. From Mercury he had to endure particular hostility. Jove, he used to say, was brutish and obtuse.'[81]

By this, Martin meant that he found the multi-talented and attractive figure of Mercury hard to discredit in the minds of the heathen, while the largely otiose Jove appeared in contrast ponderous and unengaging. Thus, Martin treated pagan gods as figures with whom he might contend at a personal level, and acknowledged Mercury to be a formidable adversary, worthy even of grudging respect.[82] *Mercurius* was of course the Roman *interpretatio* of the revered Celtic god Lugus (British *Lleu*).

---

81   *Iam uero daemones, prout ad eum quisque uenisset, suis nominibus increpabat. Mercurium maxime patiebatur infestum, Iouem brutum adque hebetem esse dicebat* (C. Halm (ed.), *Sulpicii Severi: Libri qui Supersunt* (Vienna, 1866), p. 196).

82   Elsewhere we learn that the Devil on numerous occasions manifested himself to St Martin, in the guise of the Celtic divinities Jove (*Nudos*), Mercury (*Lugus*), and Minerva (*Brigantia*) (Jacques Fontaine (ed.), *Sulpice Sévère: Vie de Saint Martin* (Paris, 1967–69), p. 300). It is evident that these were not delusory images from a pagan past, but potent adversaries in the flesh. I believe the learned editor of the *Vita* to have been mistaken in seeking the origin of Martin's diabolical confrontations in classical and ecclesiastical sources (ibid., pp. 963–81). The encounters are located in the Gaulish countryside, whose popular divinities were surely known by their indigenous names.

Heathen deities were rarely dismissed as imaginary beings by mediæval Christians. Rather, it was believed that they survived in degenerate form as demons, fairies, or wizards. Thus, the former gods of Ireland, the *Túatha Dé Danann*, were believed to be dwelling beneath the earth, or if remaining above ground to have become witches, werewolves, and the like.[83] An incident in St Samson's biography shows that this perception obtained in post-Roman Britain.

Prior to his departure from Wales, Samson was crossing a huge forest, when he encountered a murderous witch of horrific appearance. Before suffering a condign death in consequence of the saint's intervention, she explained to him that she was a sorceress (*theomacha*), one of nine sisters who haunted the wood.[84] It might be thought that the episode reflects nothing more than a folkloric encounter, but for the fact that nine fell sisters living in south-east Wales (the Forest of Dean?) are recorded as figures of local legend. In the romance of *Peredur mab Efrawg* they feature as the Nine Witches of nearby Gloucester (*naw gwidon … Gwidonot Kaer Loyw ynt*).[85]

The company of nine witches represents a troop of erstwhile goddesses.[86] What exactly occurred at Samson's encounter in the forest cannot be known, but the general authenticity of the Life suggests that it reflects some material event, if in distorted form. It is possible that the account emanated from the saint's deacon, who, being pursued by the witch, fainted in terror, and was eventually resuscitated by a 'kiss of life' applied by Samson. In that case, the story ultimately reflects the deacon's version of the event, he being represented as too overcome to witness Samson's discomfiture of the terrifying hag. Indeed, he might likewise have been the venerable deacon, a cousin of Samson, who is cited as one of the writer's principal sources in the prologue to the *Vita*.[87] In that case, the account of the witch's death in consequence of Samson's prayer could reflect a confused memory or tradition of (i) the deacon's memorable terror when passing through eerie thickets popularly believed to be haunted by a ghastly figure in a scarlet cloak, bearing a bloodstained trident; (ii) what he learned subsequently of the saint's exorcism of the terrifying goddess.

Finally, we come to a further striking intimation that §46 of the *Vita Samsonis* reflects confused interpretation of a legendary confrontation of St Samson with the god Lleu during his stay in Dumnonia. The amicable *Lux* concludes his peroration to Samson with these words:

> But you, while pursuing your peaceful journey, must before crossing over to Europe demonstrate at least once that the authority of God is manifested by you in this country (*uirtus Domini manifestetur in ista patria*), before you become physically separated from us.

It would be flying in the face of hagiographical convention were a demand of this nature to be uttered without its becoming in due course fulfilled. In fact, this is precisely what does occur. It will be seen shortly that the pagan festival attended by Samson, briefly described above, was most likely the Celtic harvest festival of Lug (Irish *Lughnasa*). Although it is implausible to

83 J. Carmichael Watson (ed.), Mesca Ulad (Dublin, 1941), p. 1; Lilian Duncan, 'Altram Tige Dá Medar', *Ériu* (Dublin, 1932), xi, pp. 187–88; Toirdhealbhach Ó Raithbheartaigh (ed.), *Genealogical Tracts I.* (Dublin, 1932), pp. 198, 200.

84 Flobert (ed.), *La vie ancienne de saint Samson de Dol*, pp. 184–86.

85 Glenys Witchard Goetinck (ed.), *Historia Peredur vab Efrawc* (Cardiff, 1976), pp. 29–30. In Geoffrey of Monmouth's Life of Merlin, the wounded King Arthur is taken for healing to the Island of Apples (*Ynys Afallach*), where he is tended by the prophetess and shapeshifter Morgen, who is one of nine sisters (Basil Clarke (ed.), *Life of Merlin; Geoffrey of Monmouth: Vita Merlini* (Cardiff, 1973), pp. 100–102).

86 Anne Ross, *Pagan Celtic Britain: Studies in Iconography and Tradition* (London, 1967), pp. 227–28.

87 Flobert (ed.), *La vie ancienne de saint Samson de Dol*, pp. 140–42.

suppose that Samson succeeded in permanently suppressing so time-honoured and popular a celebration during the course of a single visit, hagiographical convention demanded that he should be represented as having done so.

The occasion of his triumph was his resuscitation of the youth apparently killed on falling from his horse during the ceremony. This miracle, we are told, 'enabled the authority of God to be publicly displayed' (*continuo adest uirtus Dei publice ostensa*). The allusion confirms that this climactic miracle was regarded as fulfilment of the pledge enjoined on the saint by 'Lux', following the former's arrival in Cornwall. Again, Samson's inscription of a cross on the monolith was very likely intended as a concrete manifestation of the requested 'sign'.[88]

The author was aware that Samson did not, for a reason unconvincingly explained in the *Vita*, visit the monastery of Docco. Beyond the bounds of the monastery, he encountered an inspired prophet, who bore a British name corresponding to Latin *lux*, 'light'. The inadequate pretext for holding the conference outside the monastery suggests that the area of influence presided over by the intrusive *Lux* lay in the pagan world beyond its bounds, *in ista patria*, i.e. Cornwall, or (more likely) the entire south-western peninsula of Dumnonia.

Overall, it is clear that the figures of *Winiau* and *Lux* were originally as distinct as are their names. That of the former appears to have been introduced by the author of the *Vita* in the course of an awkward attempt to explain why Samson failed to obtain collaboration in his mission from the monastery at Docco. Beyond its bounds, it appears that paganism prevailed across the greater part of Dumnonia, its principal manifestation being the momentous gathering in honour of the god Lug, to which I now turn. The curious provision for Samson's acceptance of *Lux* as a figure of equal status with himself, their amicable converse, and the saint's fulfilment at the festival of Lug of *Lux*'s injunction to provide a signal mark of God's triumph in the region – all these point to an attempt by the author to explain an accomodation between Christian saint and pagan deity, when the former is claimed by his hagiographer to have effected a token victory over the latter.

At the same time, in one respect the hagiographer's version of events probably represents polite fiction, since neither time allowed, nor does intrinsic likelihood suggest, that Samson converted at least two entire provinces to Christianity during his brief visit. The latter occurred some time during the first half of the sixth century,[89] and Charles Thomas has noted the scant impact of Christianity at that time: 'before about 600 there may have been very few' Christian sites in the south-west. 'In AD 500, Cornwall was barely Christian', and before 700 there were neither territorial bishoprics, large land-owning monasteries, nor 'the emergence of a system of pastoral care applicable beyond individual clans and estates'.[90]

These perplexing aspects of Samson's activities in Cornwall could reflect a tradition of the saint's explanation of a potentially embarrassingly pragmatic policy characterizing this episode in his career. No reason is given in the Life for Samson's failure to remain and proselytize Cornwall, nor for his corresponding decision to transfer his mission to distant Brittany.[91] Continuing prevalance of active paganism (possibly sustained by the murderous apostate king

---

88   Ibid., pp. 215, 216.

89   'Since Samson is by now implicitly in his thirties, the date may be around 520–30' (Thomas, *And Shall These Mute Stones Speak?*, p. 229).

90   Ibid., pp. 233–34, 305, 306.

91   The prophecy of Eltut may safely be ignored, when he acclaimed the infant Samson as future supreme priest of the Britons, 'on both sides of the sea' (*citra utraque mare*). Not only is the vaticination *ex post facto*, but it remains unclear whether the sea in question was the Severn Sea or the Channel. When Samson comes to leave Wales, he arrives *citra Habrinum mare*.

Constantine of Dumnonia) provides the likeliest explanation why Samson abandoned any attempt at large-scale evangelization of Cornwall, instead extending his journey with a maritime crossing to Brittany, which in contrast was outwardly at least a Christian realm.[92]

The attractive portrait of *Lux* (*Lleu*) suggests that Samson found him a charismatic figure. A comparably sympathetic image of Lleu characterizes his Christ-like portrayal in the Welsh tale of *Math uab Mathonwy*.[93] The account of the exchange between Samson and *Lux* is appropriate to the condition of Cornwall in the early decades of the sixth century, when the greater part of the peninsula may be envisaged as continuing resolutely pagan, being given over to the cult of Lleu. This reconstruction is confirmed by what ensues in the *Vita Samsonis*.

His 'conference' with *Lux* concluded, Samson drove off with his cavalcade to gain the Channel coast, in order to cross over to Europe while the season permitted. The next two chapters of the Life recount a dramatic interruption to the author's account of the journey (undoubtedly greatly curtailed in the narrative).

> Now, one day, when he was passing through a region called *Tricurius*, he heard on his left (to be precise), men who (in the manner of the rite of the Bacchantes) worshipped a certain temple by means of a worthless play (*quoddam fanum per imaginarium ludum adorantes*); and, making a sign to his monks to stand still and pray silently to God, while he descended from his carriage; and, standing watching those who worshipped the idol, he saw before them, on top of a certain high hill, an atrocious idol standing. (I too have been on that hill, where I adored and touched with my hand the sign of the cross which Saint Samson carved with an iron instrument on a standing stone). When Saint Samson saw this, he made towards them in haste, taking with him only two monks, and politely asked them not to revere an idol while neglecting God who made all things; their chief Guedianus meanwhile standing at their head. And when they pleaded in extenuation that it was not wrong to celebrate the mysteries of their ancestors with a play, some being enraged, others contemptuous, but not a few of superior intelligence exhorting him to depart, the power of God was displayed before them. For a certain youth, driving horses along a course, fell from a certain swift horse to the ground, and, breaking his neck in his fall, lay almost lifeless from his tumble.

Samson declared before the lamenting multitude that he would resuscitate the victim, on condition they agree to destroy their idol and cease their profane worship. After two hours of prayer over the apparent corpse, the Saint's orisons achieved their purpose. The young man arose, and the grateful worshippers, headed by *Guedianus*, knelt before Samson and afterwards destroyed the idol. Could it be that this particular episode reflects the climactic conclusion of a mystery play (*ludus*), with a participant enacting the leading rôle of *Gwydion*, in a dramatic rendering of the resuscitation of the youthful Lleu as recounted at the conclusion of *Math uab Mathonwy*? It would be a natural development, following hagiographical convention, to

---

92 The angel who visited Samson in a dream on the eve of his departure from Wales enjoined him to fulfil his destiny as a pilgrim *ultra mare*, 'beyond the sea'. When Samson comes to leave Wales, he arrives *citra Habrinum mare*. This being the sea which he then crosses, a natural interpretation of the injunction indicates the Dumnonian peninsula as the saint's intended destination (Flobert (ed.), *La vie ancienne de saint Samson de Dol*, p. 212).

93 Remarkable parallels between the birth and upbringing of Christ and Lleu were noted by Alwyn D. Rees, 'Modern Evaluations of Celtic Narrative Tradition', in *Proceedings of the Second International Congress of Celtic Studies* (Cardiff, 1966), p. 60).

substitute the Christian saint (Samson) for the original pagan protagonist responsible for the miraculous healing.[94]

Astounded by this feat, the pragmatic Guedianus induced his followers to accept baptism at the hands of the saint. Next, he implored Samson to rid the land of a destructive dragon or serpent menacing the district. Headed by the young man whose life Samson had saved (was Lleu the original protagonist of this incident?), the crowd repaired to the cave where the ravening reptile was skulking. Stricken with fear, the creature with insensate passion bit its own tail! Without further ado, the saint whipped off his belt, slipped it round the beast's neck, and tossed it to its death from a nearby height.[95] The first part of this section of the narrative, the conversion of Guedianus and his followers, is generally accepted by historians as a description of an authentic historical event. His slaying of the serpent tends in contrast to be dismissed as a stock hagiographical miracle, lacking any historical basis, beyond being possibly based on a local dragon-slaying legend.[96]

Tricurius, where the heathen 'play' occurred, is Trigg, a large administrative district of north-east Cornwall.[97] That the Saint's intervention effected a permanent halt to an ancestral ritual attracting the inhabitants of the entire region appears intrinsically implausible, and smacks of standard hagiographical repertoire. Is it likely that Samson, in the course of his summer's passage across the peninsula (to which he never returned), should have been in a position to put a lasting end to a great provincial festival of this antiquity and importance? Only had he remained in Cornwall and continued his ministry might such an outcome be considered plausible.

In reality many of the great pagan annual festivals of Ireland and Wales continued to be celebrated in the guise of popular fairs as late as the nineteenth century. It is clear that this is what also occurred in Cornwall. As Christianity prevailed over the old religion, the overtly pagan nature of local heathen rites became gradually modified into annual gatherings centred on recounting legends, re-enactments of the deeds of past heroes, giants, and monsters, and other such bucolic jollities.[98]

At Morvah in the extreme west of Cornwall, where the native language, whose isolation served to preserve local lore, survived until a late date,[99] a fair attended by the greater part of the local inhabitants was celebrated every first Sunday in August until the latter part of the nineteenth century. The focus of this popular occasion was a group of menhirs at a spot known as the Giant's Field. A highlight of the revelry was the recitation (presumably by professional storytellers) of lengthy tales, the principal hero of which was one Jack the Tinkard, who overcame a local giant living on a hill. The annual fair was understood to commemorate the original assembly established by Jack, who

> cleared and cultivated large tracks [tracts?] of the lower lands, which, until then, were overgrown with thickets of brambles, hazel, and oak. In breaking up the ground they

---

94   'Long and intimate duels with the local sorcerer were almost *de rigueur* in the life of a successful saint. Sometimes one senses that the one is a doublet, rather than an enemy, of the other' (Peter Brown, *Authority and the Sacred: Aspects of the Christianisation of the Roman World* (Cambridge, 1995), p. 67). Cf. pp. 67–68.

95   Flobert (ed.), *La vie ancienne de saint Samson de Dol*, pp. 216–20.

96   Cf. Duine, *Questions d'hagiographie et vie de S. Samson*, p. 30; Doble, *The Saints of Cornwall*, v, pp. 91-93; Thomas, *And Shall These Mute Stones Speak?*, p. 230.

97   Susan Pearce, *South-western Britain in the Early Middle Ages* (London, 2004), pp. 253–54.

98   At the parallel August Calends festival of Carmun in Ireland, entertainment included horse-racing, fairs, and feats; tales of Finn and the Fíanna, sieges, raids, and wooings; pipes, fiddlers, and minstrels (R. I. Best, Osborn Bergin, M. A. O'Brien, and Anne O'Sullivan (ed.), *The Book of Leinster Formerly Lebar na Núachongbála* (Dublin, 1954–83), p. 850).

99   Martyn F. Wakelin, *Language and history in Cornwall* (Leicester, 1975), p. 92.

found no end of tin, which they piled up around their dwelling-place and covered over with the turf and furze-ricks, that it mightn't be stolen.[100]

Máire MacNeill, in her classic study of the Irish festival of Lughnasa, showed that this Cornish celebration was originally its British counterpart, being the annual harvest gathering in honour of the god Lug. The parallels are unmistakable. On both sides of the Irish Sea the festival was held on the first Sunday in August. In each case the rites were conducted on a hill, being frequently focussed on a stone or stones. The character of Jack the Tinkeard bears marked similarity to that of Lug, in whose honour the Irish festival was held. Jack was portrayed as progenitor of the multitudes assembled for the feast. He was also 'master of skills and ingenuity', a skilled archer and harpist, a culture hero who cleared the primæval wilderness, ensuring wealth for humanity. Finally, he slew an oppressive giant, who was swallowed up by the earth within his own hill.[101] These parallels between the Cornish and Irish Lughnasa festivals on the one hand, and the rites practised by Guedianus and his followers in the *Vita Samsonis* on the other, attest to the potency of the cult of Lug in Cornwall at the time of Samson's visit, as also to the enduring survival of celebrations of his festival.[102]

Tradition told also of Jack's beautiful bride Genevra, who was abducted by a giant wizard. Jack however made use of his bowmanship to vanquish the wicked raptor and recover his winsome consort.[103] *Genevra* is the Cornish form of *Gwenhwyfar*, i.e. Arthur's queen Guinevere, who was likewise carried off by a sinister Otherworld potentate, before being recovered by her lawful spouse.[104] Arthur, whose originally historical persona became over time transformed into that of a god,[105] appears from this to have replaced Lleu (Lug), whose bride Blodeuedd was carried off by the nocturnal huntsman Gronwy Pefr.[106]

When Samson arrived, he discovered the participants worshipping an abominable idol in the form of a standing stone, erected on the summit of a hill. According to Máire MacNeill's reconstruction of attendant rites at the Lughnasa festival, they included 'an installation of a head on top of the hill and a triumphing over it by an actor impersonating Lugh'.[107] The episode of the young man miraculously resuscitated by Samson echoes a further characteristic of the festival of Lug. During the Saint's visit, 'a certain youth, driving horses along a course (*equos in cursu dirigens*), fell from a certain swift horse to the ground'. Horse-racing was similarly a prominent feature of the Irish Lughnasa and Cornish Morvah fair festivals, while Lleu himself was famed in legend as a horseman.[108]

---

100 Robert Hunt, *Popular Romances of the West of England; or, The Drolls, Traditions, and Superstitions of Old Cornwall* (London, 1865), i, pp. 53–55; William Bottrell, *Stories and Folk-Lore of West Cornwall* (Penzance, 1870–80), i, p. 40.

101 MacNeill, *The Festival of Lughnasa*, pp. 381–85.

102 I first suggested that the rites presided over by Guedianus represented the festival of Lug in my *The Quest for Merlin* (London, 1985), pp. 91–94.

103 Bottrell, *Stories and Folk-Lore of West Cornwall*, i, pp. 34–37.

104 Sir John Rhŷs, *Studies in the Arthurian Legend* (Oxford, 1891), pp. 49–70.

105 Arthur C. L. Brown, *The Origin of the Grail Legend* (Cambridge, Mass., 1943), p. 304.

106 It is likely that an earlier version of the tale preserved in *Math uab Mathonwy* saw Blodeuedd restored (i.e. the Maiden Sovereignty) to Lleu. For close parallels between the birth-tales of Arthur and Lug, cf. *supra*, p. 72. It may be that Tintagel was originally regarded as the stronghold of Arianrhod and birth-place of Lug (Lleu).

107 MacNeill, *The Festival of Lughnasa*, p. 426.

108 Ibid., pp. 143, 254, 305, 319, 326, 328–29, 338, 341, 344–45, 619, 624. Lleu was celebrated for his horsemanship (Ian Hughes (ed.), *Math Uab Mathonwy: Pedwaredd Gainc y Mabinogi* (Aberystwyth, 2000), p. 10), and possessed a steed Melyngan, who coursed like a seagull (J. Gwenogvryn Evans (ed.), *Facsimile & Text of the Book of Taliesin* (Llanbedrog, 1910), pp. 26–27, 48; John Rhŷs and J. Gwenogvryn Evans (ed.), *The Text of the Mabinogion and other Welsh Tales from the Red Book of Hergest* (Oxford, 1887), p. 306. Cf. Rachel Bromwich, 'The Triads of the Horses', in Sioned Davies and Nerys Ann Jones (ed.), *The Horse in Celtic Culture: Medieval Welsh Perspectives* (Cardiff, 1997), pp. 112–13.

Participants in the festival attended by Samson protested that there could be nothing wrong in their celebrating 'the mysteries of their ancestors in a play' (*mathematicam eorum parentum in ludo seruare*). Their leader (*comes*), with whom Samson converses, is named *Guedianus*. It would be natural to suppose that the principal figure at the rites played a leading part in the dramatic representation of the god's achievement: in which case, it would have been entirely appropriate for him to have assumed that of Gwydion, father of Lleu.[109] All this suggests that Samson may, through misunderstanding of his reported activities in Cornwall, have subsequently become believed to have encountered both Lleu and Gwydion during his stay in heathen Cornwall. The coincidence of the paired names *Lux* (Lleu) and *Guedianus* (Gwydion) in the Cornish episode of the *Vita Samsonis* is undoubtedly striking.

The festival at Morvah cannot have been that interrupted by Samson. His biographer states that the latter was held in the region of Trigg, which was bounded by the rivers Camel and Tamar. His account most likely originated with Samson's cousin Henoc, who had joined him shortly after the confrontation with Guedianus and his followers, and consequently rests on good authority. Probably each of the major districts of Cornwall had its own festival of Lleu on 1 August, that of Penwith being celebrated at Morvah, and that of Trigg on the unidentified hill visited by Samson.

It appears that Samson's biographer conflated disparate traditions of the saint's encounter with the prevailing deity of the land. On the one hand, he found *Lleu* an engaging personality: intelligent, wise, and possessed of mantic powers. This beneficent attitude recalls the comparably sympathetic account of Lleu contained in the mediæval story of *Math uab Mathonwy*. There, the infant hero, born of a virgin, proves preternaturally precocious. He subsequently suffers a cruel end, being slain by a foe who thrusts a spear into his side. However, he is not dead: his mutilated body is brought down from the tree in which it is discovered, he is resurrected, and lives on as protector of his people. It would not have been difficult to convert such a narrative into a Christian miracle play!

That there is nothing anachronistic about Samson's association with a pagan festival, with its attendant dramatic mysteries, is confirmed by Gildas's denunciation about the same time of the participation of lax contemporary clerics in 'public games' (*ludicra*), which very likely included pagan or semi-pagan dramas.[110]

To recapitulate: on landing in Cornwall, the saint found the laodicean monks of the isolated monastery of Docco relapsed into their former semi-pagan condition. Beyond its perimeter, paganism flourished throughout the countryside, untouched by the new religion, and focussed

---

109 'This episode in the *Vita* [*Samsonis*] seems to preserve the memory of Gwydion as a pagan priest and to confirm the pre-Christian ascription of the tale' (Anne E. Lea, 'Lleu Wyllt: an Early British Prototype of the Legend of the Wild Man?', *The Journal of Indo-European Studies* (Washington, 1997), xxv, p. 45). As early at the tenth century, Lleu features in Welsh tradition as 'son of Gwydion' (Egerton Phillimore, 'The *Annales Cambriæ* and Old-Welsh Genealogies from *Harleian MS.* 3859', *Y Cymmrodor* (London, 1888), ix, p. 176), while the saga of Gwydion and Lleu enshrined in *Math uab Mathonwy* preserves what is clearly a relationship enshrined in archaic tradition. A link between Gwydion and Samson is independently suggested by a Welsh genealogy in Peniarth MS 181, which portrays them as brothers: *Plant Don o arvon = gwydion, ssamsson, amaethon* ... (J. Gwenogvryn Evans, *Report on Manuscripts in the Welsh Language* (London, 1898–1902), i, p. 1004). It is unlikely that the genealogist inferred this connexion from the extant Lives of Samson. The *comes Vedianus* of the Breton *Vita* appears as *Gedianus* in the Welsh version (J. Gwenogvryn Evans and John Rhŷs (ed.), *The Text of the Book of Llan Dâv Reproduced from the Gwysaney Manuscript* (Oxford, 1893), pp. 19–20). Nothing suggests that genealogists were in the habit of consulting the Book of Llandaff, and neither the context nor form of the name is likely to have suggested the familiar figure of Gwydion.

110 Mommsen (ed.), *Chronica Minora*, iii, p. 62.

on the charismatic figure of the god Lleu. By the time of the compilation of Samson's Life at the beginning of the seventh century, Cornwall had become widely converted to Christianity. Finding allusions to the heathen god Lleu equivocal and mysterious, the Breton hagiographer appears confusedly to have identified him with *Winiaw*, the British name of the Irish Finnian who corresponded with Gildas over problems relating to recalcitrant monks. Striking parallels between the life of Lleu, as it appears in *Math uab Mathonwy*, and that of Christ in the Gospels, may account for the author's sympathetic portrayal of this charismatic pagan divinity.

That Samson happened on the pagan rites by chance while crossing Cornwall must surely represent a simplification of the actual event. It may rather be surmised that, having become aware of the precarious situation of Christianity in the peninsula, he and his followers decided to attend the festival at the appointed time, with a view to protesting at so overtly pagan a celebration.[111] That he was entirely successful may be questioned, and it is possible that his intervention extended little further than his carving of a cross on the idol, as described in the *Vita*. That symbolic gesture might even have been intended to signify a degree of syncretism between the two religions of the country, rather than outright rejection or supersession of the ancient faith.

The World Serpent

The concluding episode of Samson's activities at the pagan festival of Trigg sheds further light on its intent. Samson's suppression of what appears to have been a Cornish pagan harvest festival concludes with his victory over a destructive serpent living in a nearby cave. The two events are closely associated. Not only is the saint informed of the oppressive creature while attending the festival, but he is accompanied to its lair by the entire crowd of celebrants. Curiously, they are led, not by Guedianus, but by the unnamed youth who fell from his steed and was resuscitated by Samson. Was he was the character acting the part of Lleu, who in *Math uab Mathonwy* 'dies', to be restored to life by Gwydion's spells?

The saint's overpowering of the serpent has been generally dismissed as a hackneyed folktale. However, it contains a curious detail absent from such legend: a detail indicating that it represents yet another theme associated with Lughnasa festivals in Ireland, wherein St Patrick or another heroic figure was believed to have destroyed or bound a malignant serpent.[112]

We read that Samson lassooed the Cornish serpent *with his linen girdle*, and flung it from a height – possibly that on which stood the monolith worshipped by the celebrants. This feat, which might suggest the screen exploits of Roy Rogers, in fact echoes a theme familiar from Celtic tradition. In the first place, it is repeated by Samson on his arrival in Brittany, where he collars another destructive serpent with his cloak (*palliolum*).[113] In the early Irish saga *Táin*

---

111 The *Vita* begins the description of Samson's confrontation with the pagan worshippers as follows: *Quadam autem die, cum per quendam pagum quem Tricurium uocant deambularet, audiuit, ut uerum esset, in sinistra parte de eo,* heathen celebrants enacting their rites. This has consistently been taken literally, as signifying that 'one day, as he was walking through a certain district which they call *Tricurius,* he heard, to be precise, on his left hand …' A depiction of the saint's chance stumbling on the crowd of revellers appears implausible, while the emphasis laid on their being on the saint's left-hand side is likewise appears incongruous. However, Latin *sinister* may mean equally 'left' or 'north', as is also implicit in the Welsh word *gogledd* (J. Loth, 'Remarques à *l'Historia Brittonum* dite de Nennius', *Revue Celtique* (Paris, 1932), xlix, pp. 160–61). Again, Latin *pars* corresponds to Welsh *parth,* 'area, region' (*Geiriadur Prifysgol Cymru: A Dictionary of the Welsh Language* (Cardiff, 1950–2002), p. 2694). Thus the likeliest meaning of the passage is that Samson received reports of the festival, *which took place in the northern part of Trigg.*

112 MacNeill, *The Festival of Lughnasa,* pp. 146, 147, 154, 200, 505.

113 Flobert (ed.), *La vie ancienne de saint Samson de Dol,* p. 230.

Bó Fraích, a serpent is overcome when it darts into the hero Conall Cernach's belt (*criss*). The precise magical function of the belt is left unclear, suggesting that the author drew on a native tradition he did not understand, rather than (as has been claimed) borrowing from the *Vita Samsonis*.[114] Again, in the early ninth century St Senán is described as binding a sea-monster to the coast of Inis Cathaig, while a tradition in the Scottish Highlands told of Fingal's subjugation of a ferocious hound by means of his stepmother's magic belt *Con-taod*.[115]

Control of a serpent by means of an enchanted belt, whose application perplexed the ninth-century author of *Táin Bó Fraích*, probably derived from shamanist tradition. Finnish shamans wore an ornamented belt ascribed exceptional magical powers, which was associated with the divine sage Väinämöinen. A further link connected the belt with serpents: 'A snake's tail is a bit of Väinämöinen's belt', ran a popular saying.[116] Did the belt stand for a protective serpent, encircling the shaman or warrior?

This may also serve to explain a secondary motif, passed over by commentators. When Samson arrives before its cave, the serpent rises up and bites its tale 'in anger'. This might seem an endearingly peevish reaction, until we recall the earth-encircling snake or dragon Ouroboros, featured in many mythologies, of which the most familiar exemplar is the world-serpent *Miðgarðsormr* of Norse mythology, which encircles the ocean while biting its tail.[117]

Although the Old Testament Leviathan (Irish *Lebedán*) was familiar to the Christian Irish in the Middle Ages,[118] it was commonly as the biblical monster of the deep, rather than the

---

114   Wolfgang Meid (ed.), *Táin Bó Fraích* (Dublin, 1967), p. 15. James Carney contended that 'There can be little doubt but that this incident in the life of St. Samson is the source of the corresponding incident in TBF' (*Studies in Early Irish Literature and History* (Dublin, 1955), p. 124). In fact there is much room for doubt: cf. Anne Ross, *Pagan Celtic Britain: Studies in Iconography and Tradition* (London, 1967), pp. 347–48; Wolfgang Meid (ed.), *Die Romanze von Froech und Findabair: Táin Bó Froích* (Innsbruck, 1970), pp. 219–20; Dewi Wyn Evans, 'The Learned Borrowings from *Táin Bó Fraích*', in Michael Richter and Jean-Michel Picard (ed.), *Ogma: Essays in Celtic Studies in honour of Próinséas Ní Chatháin* (Dublin, 2002), pp. 186–87.

115   Whitley Stokes (ed.), *Félire Óengusso Céli Dé. The Martyrology of Oengus the Culdee* (London, 1905), p. 90; Paul Grosjean, 'Trois pièces sur S. Senán', *Analecta Bollandiana* (Brussels, 1948), lxvi, p. 217; J. F. Campbell (ed.), *Leabhar na Feinne: Heroic Gaelic Ballads Collected in Scotland Chiefly from 1512 to 1871* (London, 1872), pp. 153, 154.

116   Martti Haavio, *Väinämöinen: Eternal Sage* (Helsinki, 1952), pp. 213–14. In §I.iii of Saxo's History, the mythical Danish king Skyoldus binds a giant bear with his belt (*cingulo*), and delivers it to his companions to slay (J. Olrik, H. Ræder, and Franz Blatt (ed.), *Saxonis Gesta Danorum* (Copenhagen, 1931–57), i, p. 11).

117   Cf. Bernard Merdrignac, 'Une course en char dans l'hagiographie bretonne? Saint Samson contre la *Theomacha*', in John Carey, Máire Herbert, and Pádraig Ó Riain (ed.), *Studies in Irish Hagiography: Saints and Scholars* (Dublin, 2001), pp. 152–55. The *Miðgarðsormr* in Norse mythology twists in giant rage and stirs the seas (Hans Kuhn and Gustav Neckel (ed.), *Edda: Die Lieder des Codex Regius nebst Verwandten Denkmälern* (Heidelberg, 1962–68), i, pp. 11, 13, 14). Originally Óðinn flung the serpent into the deep, where it lies in the encircling ocean biting its tail (Anthony Faulkes (ed.), *Snorri Sturluson: Edda; Prologue and Gylfaginning* (Oxford, 1982), p. 27).

118   Whitley Stokes and John Strachan (ed.), *Thesaurus Palaeohibernicus: A Collection of Old-Irish Glosses Scholia Prose and Verse* (Cambridge, 1901–3), i, pp. 316, 412; J. G. O'Keefe, 'Poem on the Observance of Sunday', *Ériu: The Journal of the Irish School of Learning, Dublin* (Dublin, 1907), iii, p. 145; James Carney (ed.), *The Poems of Blathmac Son of Cú Brettan; Together with the Irish Gospel of Thomas and a Poem on the Virgin Mary* (Dublin, 1964), p. 82; Robert Atkinson (ed.), *The Passions and the Homilies from Leabhar Breac: Text, Translation, and Commentary* (Dublin, 1887), p. 219; R. I. Best, 'The Adventures of Art son of Conn, and the Courtship of Delbchæm', *Ériu*, iii, p. 156. A mediæval saga describes *Leuidan* as encircling the globe and lashing its tail to overthrow the earth (Eleanor Knott (ed.), *Togail Bruidne Da Derga* (Dublin, 1936), p. 15). While it is possible that the biblical name has here become attached to a native monster, the source is too late to be relevant to composition of the *Vita Samsonis*.

encircling World Serpent biting its tail. The earliest Christian allusion to the dragon biting its own tail is by Isidore of Seville in his *Etymologiæ*, who interpreted it as an image of the recurring year.[119] However, nothing suggests that the author of the *Vita Samsonis* consulted Isidore. Samson himself died long before the Spanish scholar compiled his work, while every consideration indicates that the Saint's biographer relied on native sources for the narrative content of his *Vita*.

Furthermore, the concept is sufficiently embedded in Indo-European, Celtic and other mythologies to suggest the existence of an indigenous insular Celtic World Serpent, corresponding to those recorded in other early cultures.[120] In the Scottish Highlands the earth-encircling snake was known as *Cirein Cròin*, an 'immense sea-animal' which 'was originally a whirlpool, or the sea-snake of the Edda, that encircled the entire world'.[121]

Partially obscured allusions are found in the mediæval Voyage of Saint Brendan. At one point the saint and his companions disembark at what they take for an island. On landing, they ignite a camp fire, whereupon the 'island' begins to writhe violently. Escaping in their ship, Brendan discovers that they had inadvertently landed on the back of an enormous fish. 'He is always trying to bring his tail to meet his head, but he cannot,' explained the Saint; 'He bears the name *Jasconius*.'[122] Plainly this 'fish' was the tail-biting World Serpent, and the fact that it is ascribed an Irish name (< *iasc*, 'fish'), rather than Leviathan (*Lebedán*), suggests the mythical monster's indigenous provenance.[123]

---

119 *Sic enim apud Aegyptios indicabatur ante inventas litteras picto dracone caudam suam mordente, quia in se recurrit* (W. M. Lindsay (ed.), *Isidori Hispalensis Episcopi Etymologiarvm sive Originvm: Libri XX* (Oxford, 1911), §V.36). Cf. Myles Dillon, *Early Irish Literature* (Chicago, 1948), p. 29.

120 'On the whole, the evidence suggests that serpents, ram-headed, crested, aquatic, were of very considerable importance in the mythologies of both the European and the insular Celts ...' (Anne Ross, *Pagan Celtic Britain: Studies in Iconography and Tradition* (London, 1967), p. 348).

121 John Gregorson Campbell, *Superstitions of the Highlands & Islands of Scotland Collected entirely from Oral Sources* (Glasgow, 1900), p. 220. For a possible Cymric parallel, cf. Sir John Rhŷs, *Studies in the Arthurian Legend* (Oxford, 1891), p. 157.

122 Carl Selmer (ed.), *Navigatio Sancti Brendani Abbatis from Early Manuscripts* (Notre Dame, Indiana, 1959), pp. 20–21. A cryptic allusion to 'the wall of beasts (*míl*) that surrounds *Iasconn*', generated by the (world-) river Boyne, occurs in Joan Newlon Radner (ed.), *Fragmentary Annals of Ireland* (Dublin, 1978), p. 4. The text of the *Navigatio* is thought to date from the eighth century (Jonathan M. Wooding, 'Fasting flesh and the body in the St Brendan dossier', in Jane Cartwright (ed.), *Celtic Hagiography and Saints' Cults* (Cardiff, 2003), p. 162). Cf. Jacqueline Borsje, *From Chaos to Enemy: Encounters with Monsters in Early Irish Texts. An Investigation Related to the Process of Christianization and the concept of Evil* (Turnhout, 1996), pp. 125–29; Clara Strijbosch, *The Seafaring Saint: Sources and Analogues of the Twelfth-Century Voyage of Saint Brendan* (Dublin, 2000), pp. 195–300. 'What the tail-biting monster [in *Navigatio Brendani*] represents is the world-surrounding Cosmic Ocean' (Joseph Campbell, 'Indian Reflections on the Castle of the Grail', in Robert O'Driscoll (ed.), *The Celtic Consciousness* (Toronto, 1981), p. 6).

123 The dragon or world-serpent, in many instances represented as biting its own tail, is widely attested in cultures outside biblical tradition (Stith Thompson, *Motif-Index of Folk-Literature: A Classification of Narrative Elements in Folktales, Ballads, Myths, Fables, Mediaeval Romances, Exempla, Fabliaux, Jest-Books, and Local Legends* (Bloomington, Indiana, 1955–58), i, p. 369 = B61; Arthur Bernard Cook, *Zeus: A Study in Ancient Religion* (Cambridge, 1914–40), i, p. 192; Richard Broxton Onians, *The Origins of European Thought about the Body, the Mind the Soul, the World Time, and Fate: New Interpretations of Greek, Roman and kindred evidence also of some basic Jewish and Christian beliefs* (Cambridge, 1954), pp. 247–53; Joseph Fontenrose, *Python: A Study of Delphic Myth and its Origins* (Berkeley and Los Angeles, 1959), p. 523; Leroy A. Campbell, *Mithraic Iconography and Ideology* (Leiden, 1968), p. 350; Roger Beck, 'Interpreting the Ponza Zodiac: II', *Journal of Mithraic Studies* (London, 1978), ii, pp. 141–42; Hans Dieter Betz, *The Greek Magical Papyri in Translation: Including the Demotic Spells* (Chicago,

Later in the same work the hagiographer returns to the theme. One day the voyagers found the water so clear they could see the ocean floor. There they espied a vast quantity of fish: 'From their enormous number they appeared like an encircled city, with their heads placed to their tails where they lay.'[124]

The significance of the motif of the fish biting their own tails is obvious. This dual approach to the theme, of whose significance the writer was evidently unaware, suggests distinct sources for each underlying allusion to the World Serpent.[125]

In Hebrew mythology the cosmic serpent was envisaged as enclosing all creation. By breaking him, God created form and matter on earth. The dragon represents primæval chaos, while his death brings time and order into being.[126] The Irish festival of Lughnasa and its British counterparts celebrated the annual harvest as a rebirth of the land, which included the slaying of a malign serpent by a pagan deity, who was eventually replaced by St Patrick. Thus, the serpent-slaying incident in the *Vita Samsonis* may well reflect confused memory of a myth re-enacted at the ceremony, with the Saint in customary manner substituted for the pagan saviour god.[127]

The unusual (in Celtic sources) motif of the serpent's biting its own tail in the *Vita Samsonis* is emphasized by its prior occurrence at the Saint's overpowering of a Welsh serpent. On that occasion, at the Saint's exhortation,

The serpent, both hearing and scenting him, twisted its head to where its tail was with a ferocious hissing and foaming ... [overcome by the Saint, it] gathered itself up into a ball, as it gnawed its tail with its savage teeth. [Condemned to die,] the serpent stood on its tail, and raising its head aloft, and absurdly making a bow (*arx*) of itself, cast forth all its venom and was dead.[128]

1986), i, p. 337; Roger Beck, *Planetary Gods and Planetary Orders in the Mysteries of Mithras* (Leiden, 1988), p. 55; Samson Eitrem, 'Dreams and Divination in Magical Ritual', in Christopher A. Faraone and Dirk Obbink (ed.), *Magika Hiera: Ancient Greek Magic and Religion* (Oxford, 1991), p. 180; Brita Polttila, 'The Cosmology of Finnish Shamanistic Folk Poetry', in Mihály Hoppál and Juha Pentikäinen (ed.), *Northern Religions and Shamanism* (Budapest, 1992), pp. 170–71; László Kákosy, 'Ouroboros on Magical Healing Statues', in Terence DuQuesne (ed.), *Hermes Aegyptiacus: Egyptological studies for BH Stricker* (Oxford, 1995), pp. 123–29; Calvert Watkins, *How to Kill a Dragon: Aspects of Indo-European Poetics* (New York and Oxford, 1995), pp. 460–63). 'In a Central Asian Turkic tale the dragon twines round the world mountain several times, and hence by implication round the world (OTŠIRVANI), like the Norse serpent Miðgarðsormr' (Clive Tolley, *Shamanism in Norse Myth and Magic* (Helsinki, 2009), p. 341). 'The biblical Leviathan came to be understood as a monster coiled round the earth, presumably by conflation with a non-biblical myth of separate origin' (M. L. West, *Indo-European Poetry and Myth* (Oxford, 2007), p. 348. Muslim traditions of the World Serpent apparently derive from Hebrew cosmogony (A. J. Wensinck, *The Ideas of the Western Semites Concerning the Navel of the Earth* (Amsterdam, 1916), pp. 58–62).

124   Selmer (ed.), *Navigatio Sancti Brendani*, pp. 56–57.

125   Borsje, *From Chaos to Enemy*, p. 35.

126   Biblical references to the multi-headed Leviathan are discussed by Mary K. Wakeman, *God's Battle with the Monster: A Study in Biblical Imagery* (Leiden, 1973), pp. 62–68.

127   'The main burden of these [Lughnasa] legends is the victory of Christianity over Paganism and they are specifically connected with the sites and origins of the assemblies' (MacNeill, *The Festival of Lughnasa*, p. 83).

128   Flobert (ed.), *La vie ancienne de saint Samson de Dol*, pp. 194–96.

It seems, Samson was envisaged as the Christian champion, who overthrew the old religion symbolized by the encircling World Serpent.[129]

In an earlier version of the *ludus* at the Trigg festival, the ferocious reptile could have been dramatically represented being confined underground by Samson, within the hill crowned by the megalith, which at every Calends of August provided a focus of worship for the populations of Trigg and Pydar. In view of the frequency of accounts of serpents overthrown and bound by the liberating hero at Lughnasad festivals, Máire MacNeill conjectured that pagan rites associated with the festival included a play representing the incarceration of a serpent in a hole or cavern beneath the hill.[130] The serpents overcome by Samson in Cornwall and Brittany are both represented as dwelling in caves, which probably reflects a rationalization of subterranean dwellings.

The account of Samson's sojourn in Cornwall in the early part of the sixth century AD provides a unique glimpse of a land continuing broadly pagan in its beliefs and rituals. By the time the *Vita Samsonis* came to be written at the beginning of the seventh century, sustained Christian missionary campaigns had brought about extensive conversion of the region. However, the Saint's Life suggests that pagan traditions had been not so much rejected, as absorbed by the new religion. Ancient festivals continued to be celebrated by the populace, either without overt veneration of pagan deities, or through their replacement by Christian or folk heroes. Their myths were recounted as legendary tales (such as those lying behind the Four Branches of the *Mabinogi*, or related at Morvah Fair), and integrated into the Lives of early saints, in particular those of Samson and Illtud.[131]

St Samson's exploits in Cornwall attest to the fact that paganism retained a strong hold over south-western Britain as late as the sixth century AD. Nor should it be thought that this was a backward region, isolated from other kingdoms in Britain. Ken Dark has shown that Dumnonia remained in many respects extensively Romanized throughout this period.[132] Samson's encounter with 'Guedianus' attests to the widely recorded association of calendrical rites and accompanying legends with megalithic monuments. Finally, these indications of pagan survival into the early Middle Ages suggest avenues whereby Geoffrey of Monmouth's account of the construction of Stonehenge might have drawn on the lore of pre-Christian Britain.

---

129 The symbolism of this episode is discussed by Bernard Merdrignac in his *Récherches sur l'hagiographie armoricaine*, ii, p. 97; Carey, Herbert, and Ó Riain (ed.), *Saints and Scholars*, pp. 152–55.

130 *The Festival of Lughnasa*, p. 426.

131 In the twelfth century the populace living around Traprain Law in Lothian preserved a tradition that the local St Kentigern was born of a virgin – a motif likely to have been transposed from his grandfather *Leudonus*, i.e. Lleu, son of the virgin goddess Arianrhod. The sparsity of allusions in mediæval historiography to popular preservation of overtly pagan legends is explained by the hagiographer's contemptuous dismissal of the rustics' belief as 'stupid and ignorant': ... *quia populus stultus et insipiens, in diocesi Sancti Kentegerni degens, ipsum de virgine conceptum, et natum adhuc astruere non veretur* (Alexander Penrose Forbes (ed.), *Lives of S. Ninian and S. Kentigern. Compiled in the Twelfth Century* (Edinburgh, 1874), p. 163).

132 *Britain and the End of the Roman Empire*, pp. 150–70.

15

The Omphalos of Britain

The British Omphalos

That Britain once possessed its own *omphalos*, comparable to those of Ireland and Gaul, can scarcely be disputed. The mythical circumstances of its coming into being are described in the early tenth-century Welsh tale of *Cyfranc Lludd a Lleuelys*, examined earlier in chapters Twelve and Thirteen. "When you get home," Lleuelys advised his brother Lludd after their discussion in mid-Channel, 'have the Island measured, its length and breadth, and where you discover the exact centre, have that place dug up...' Some time after that Lludd had the length and breadth of the island measured, and the central point was found to be in Oxford.[1]

Here we have a uniquely unequivocal allusion to the British *omphalos*, traditional Sacred Centre of the island. There can be no doubt that the description reflects archaic lore. Ireland's *omphalos* was located at Uisneach, and that of the Gauls at a site in the territory of the Carnutes, which was probably Orleans (*Cenabum*). Britain must likewise have possessed her own Centre, of which *Cyfranc Lludd a Lleuelys* fortunately preserves this remarkable account.[2]

Plainly, Oxford cannot have been the original site of the *omphalos* of Celtic Britain. Its Welsh name *Rhydychen* is not of Brittonic derivation, but a translation of Old English *Oxenford*.[3] The *burh* of Oxford was founded at the Hincksey crossing, either in the latter part of Alfred the Great's reign, or more probably that of his successor Edward the Elder at the beginning of the tenth century.[4] It goes without saying that the authentic location of the *omphalos* will have been established in British tradition long before that time.

Welsh understanding of English geography was sufficiently accurate in the Middle Ages, and it seems unlikely that the British *omphalos* would have been located so far south without some basis in tradition. From a purely geographical perspective, the central spot should lie somewhere in the central Midlands. As Richmond (a Welshman!) declares in Shakespeare's *Richard III* (V, 2):

1 Roberts (ed.), *Cyfranc Lludd a Llefelys*, pp. 4–5.
2 John T. Koch, 'A Welsh Window on the Iron Age: Manawydan, Mandubracios', *Cambridge Medieval Celtic Studies* (Cambridge, 1987), xiv, pp. 47–49.
3 Margaret Gelling and Doris Mary Stenton, *The Place-Names of Oxfordshire* (Cambridge, 1953–54), p. 19.
4 Anne Dodd, 'Synthesis and Discussion', in eadem (ed.), *Oxford Before the University: The Late Saxon and Norman Archaeology of the Thames Crossing, the Defences and the Town* (Oxford, 2003), pp. 19–21, 31–32.

> this foul swine [King Richard]
> Lies now even in the centre of this isle,
> Near to the town of Leicester, as we learn:
> From Tamworth thither is but one day's march.[5]

While it will probably never be known for certain how Oxford came to be substituted for the original site of the *omphalos*, it is likely that its late adoption reflected the city's importance from the beginning of the tenth century, when it was regarded as one of the two principal towns of Wessex (the other being London).[6] At the same time, there is no suggestion in the Welsh story of there being any habitable structure where the dragons are discovered. The monolith within which they come to be sealed is the sole landmark associated with 'the central point' (*y pwynt perued*) of the island of Britain.[7]

When the Fighting Dragons are eventually subdued, Lludd fulfils his brother's instruction, removing them to Dinas Emrys in Snowdonia, where he 'hid them in a stone chest (*kist uaen*)'. As has already been shown, the selection of Dinas Emrys as an alternative to the *pwynt perued* of Britain probably arose from the fact that the former was the *pwynt perued* of Gwynedd, provincial *omphaloi* having undoubtedly existed in addition to the great national Navel.[8] This is further suggested by the fact that a century earlier in the *Historia Brittonum* the entirety of the episode of the discovery of the dragons is located at Dinas Emrys.[9] In *Cyfranc Lludd a Lleuelys* the 'dragons' are lodged within the stone chest *after* their transfer to Dinas Emrys. However, as the transfer represents an obviously secondary stage in the story's evolution, it seems reasonable to infer that their confinement within the stone was originally associated with the *pwynt perued* of all Britain.

It seems too that the 'dragons' were originally envisaged as being lodged throughout within the *kist uaen*, or 'stone chest'.[10] Given the contrived nature of the British legend's transfer to North Wales, it is likely that retention of the 'dragons' (originally *vermes*, or *pryfed*) within a

---

5   A tradition (it is not known how old) places the centre of England at the village of Meriden, lying not far from Leicester and Market Bosworth. It was to this that Shakespeare evidently alluded.

6   Charles Plummer and John Earle (ed.), *Two Anglo-Saxon Chronicles Parallel: With Supplementary Extracts from the Others; A Revised Text Edited, with Introduction, Notes, Appendices, and Glossary* (Oxford, 1892–99), i, pp. 95, 97. In 924 Ælfweard son of king Eadweard died at Oxford (ibid., p. 105).

7   In the early eleventh-century romances of *Branwen* and *Manawydan*, towns (Hereford, a neighbouring unnamed town, and London) are realistically portrayed as places of habitation.

8   Ireland likewise possessed her provincial centres. Thus, the primæval seer Fintán declared that he had imbibed 'over the navel of Ulster', ós imlind Usnig (R. I. Best, 'The Settling of the Manor of Tara', *Ériu: The Journal of the School of Irish Learning* (Dublin, 1910), iv, p. 150), while a flagstone at Cashel marked the Omphalos of Munster (Alwyn Rees and Brinley Rees, *Celtic Heritage: Ancient Tradition in Ireland and Wales* (London, 1961), pp. 186–87). The fine carved Turoe stone in Co. Galway surely represents another *omphalos* (Helmut Birkhan, *Kelten/Celts: Bilder ihrer Kultur/Images of their Culture* (Vienna, 1999), p. 186). The Greeks similarly possessed local *omphaloi* distinct from the celebrated Navel at Delphi (J. G. Frazer, *Pausanias's Description of Greece* (London, 1898), v, pp. 318–20; Hans-Volkmar Herrmann, *Omphalos* (Münster, 1959), pp. 60–69; Luis I.J. Stadelmann, *The Hebrew Conception of the World* (Rome, 1970), p. 150).

9   'La souveraineté est là où est la pierre, et si la pierre est transportée ailleurs, la souveraineté la suit' (Christian-J. Guyonvarc'h (tr.), *Textes mythologiques irlandais I* (Rennes, 1980), i, p. 90).

10   Not infrequently in popular belief, a giant or hero lies beneath, or within, a large stone: *Rhiw vath o Gromlech ne gist vaen wrth vaes mynnan lhe kladhwyd mynan gawr*, 'There is a sort of a Tomb or stone chest by Maes Mynnan where Mynan a giant was buried' (Rupert H. Morris (ed.), *Parochialia: Being a Summary of Answers to "Parochial Queries in Order to a Geographical Dictionary, etc., of Wales" Issued by Edward Lhwyd* (London, 1909–11), i, p. 69). Cf. Chris Grooms, *The Giants of Wales: Cewri Cymru* (Lampeter, 1993), pp. 205–6. On kistvaens generally, see further [John Humffreys Parry (ed.)], *The*

stone provided a salient motif in the mythology of the British *omphalos*. Thus, dual physical characteristics of the British Centre described in *Cyfranc Lludd a Lleuelys* are:

1. It lay somewhere in central southern England, at a site which by the time of the tale's composition had become forgotten in Wales. It was relocated at Oxford, probably in consequence of the town's contemporary importance, combined with its geographical location at the heart of southern England.
2. Its palladium was a substantial menhir[11], imbued with supernatural potency. The Irish *omphalos* at Uisneach was similarly focussed on the Stone of Uisneach (*lic an Uisnech*), which marked the median point where every province met.[12]

The sacred hearth and the omphalos

A further detail in *Cyfranc Lludd a Lleuelys* illumines the significance of the destructive shriek in the context of Celtic tradition. We are told that it 'was heard every May-day above every hearth in the Island of Britain'. But what is the significance of its effect being focussed on 'every hearth', when we learn at the same time that it was so universal that 'all animals and trees and the earth and the waters were left barren'?

The explanation lies in the remarkable symbolism accorded the hearth (and hearthstone) as Centre (*omphalos*), both in Celtic and Indo-European tradition, and archaic cosmologies worldwide.[13] The Greek goddess Hestia derives her name from ἑστία, 'hearth', a word etymologically linked to 'altar' (on which sacred fires burned). The related term ἐσχάρα likewise signifies alike 'hearth' and 'altar', as well as 'external female genitals'.[14]

Cambro-Briton (London, 1820–22), iii, p. 471. The concept of the 'stone coffer' suggests rationalization of an entity earlier envisaged as dwelling within a rock.

11   'Bearing in mind what we learn from Lia Fail and some of the traditions preserved in France, we have good reason to identify these "centres" with omphalic stones. In the village of Amancy (district of La Roche), for instance, there can be found – proof positive of the "centre" – a "Middle-of-the-World Stone". The Pierre Chevetta in the Moutiers district has never been covered by floods, which seems to be a faint echo of the "centre" that the deluge could never engulf' (Mircea Eliade, *Patterns in Comparative Religion* (London, 1958), p. 233). Stone *omphaloi* in France are discussed by Françoise Le Roux, 'Le *Celticvm* d'Ambigatus et l'*Omphalos* gaulois: La royauté suprême des *Bituriges*', *Celticvm I: Actes du Premier Colloque International d'Etudes Gauloises, Celtiques et Protoceltiques; Medolanvm Bitvrigvm MCMLX* (Rennes, 1961), pp. 182–84.

12   John Gwynn (ed.), *Liber Ardmachanus: The Book of Armagh, Edited with Introduction and Appendices* (Dublin, 1913), p. 21; John J. O'Meara, 'Giraldus Cambrensis in Topographia Hibernie: *Text of the First Recension'*, *Proceedings of the Royal Irish Academy* (Dublin, 1949), lii, p. 159; R. A. Stewart Macalister (ed.), *Lebor Gabála Érenn: The Book of the Taking of Ireland* (Dublin, 1938–56), iv, p. 74; David Comyn and Rev. Patrick S. Dinneen (ed.), *The History of Ireland by Geoffrey Keating, D.D.* (London, 1902–14), i, p. 110.

13   For the Indo-European cult of the hearth, and its function as tribal and world *omphalos*, cf. Angela Della Volpe, 'From the Hearth to the Creation of Boundaries', *The Journal of Indo-European Studies* (Washington, 1990), xviii, pp. 157–84; eadem, 'On Indo-European Ceremonial and Socio-Political Elements Underlying the Origin of Formal Boundaries', *The Journal of Indo-European Studies* (1992), xx, pp. 84–98.

14   Hjalmar Frisk, *Griechisches Etymologisches Wörterbuch* (Heidelberg, 1954–72), i, pp. 576–77; John Chadwick, *Lexicographica Graeca: Contributions to the lexicography of Ancient Greek* (Oxford, 1996), pp. 111–15; Pierre Chantraine, *Dictionnaire* étymologique de la langue grecque: Histoire des mots; avec un Supplément sous la direction de: Alain Blanc, Charles de Lamberterie, Jean-Louis Perpillou (Paris, 1999), p. 379.

The cult of the Roman goddess Vesta, mythological and etymological counterpart of Greek Hestia,[15] was literally focussed (Latin *focus*, 'hearth') on a perpetual fire burning in her temple. The goddess was a virgin, and her fire was tended by the celebrated Vestal Virgins. The temple was round, corresponding to the spherical shape of the earth, and its fire epitomized that which was believed to burn beneath the earth. No images were created of the goddess, since she was at once guardian of the holy flame (*flammæ custos*) and its personification within her temple.[16]

The cult of Vesta was intimately linked to that of the Roman kingship, and Rome herself. Her temple was believed to have been founded by the legendary prototypical priest-king Numa, while the monarchy embodied the principle of sacred fire. A colourful legend related how Servius Tullius, who was regarded as exemplary First King of the dynasty, was conceived in consequence of his mother's becoming impregnated by a male sexual organ arising from the ashes of the royal hearth. Flames blazed about the infant heir's head as he slept, signalling his divine origin.[17]

Belief in the procreative power of the blazing hearth is widespread. The Evenk people of Siberia believe that souls inhabit a dwelling called *omiruk*, 'receptacle of souls'.

> When the time comes for a new kinsman to be born, the soul *omi* leaves the *omiruk* and from the upper world of the universe, as the Evenks say, *kharandu bururen*, 'falls into the tent, into the hearth' where lives the mythical mistress of the fire, *togo mushun*, venerated as the guardian of the souls of kinsmen. From this mythical mistress of the clan hearth and, at the same time, the guardian of the souls of kinsmen, the *omi* passes into a woman's womb, initiating a new generation of kinsmen.[18]

Identification of kings with fire is characteristic also of Celtic cosmology. A sixth-century North British king was extolled as *aryal flam*, 'the spirit of flame, or fire', while an earlier Irish ruler was described as 'Niall mac Diarmaid, the red flame'.[19] The king as personification of the sun appears to reflect association with the celestial source of fire, rather than his identification as a sun-god. An aura of divine flame or light is described as issuing from the heads of kings and royal heroes in Indo-European and other cultures.[20] The greatest of North British princes in the

15 Émile Boisacq, *Dictionnaire étymologique de la langue grecque: étudiée dans ses rapports avec les autres langues indo-européennes* (Heidelberg and Paris, 1916), p. 290; A. Ernout, A. Meillet, and Jacques André, *Dictionnaire étymologique de la langue latine: Histoire des mots* (Paris, 1994), p. 729; J. P. Mallory and D. Q. Adams (ed.), *Encyclopedia of Indo-European Culture* (Chicago and London, 1997), pp. 203, 281; M. L. West, *Indo-European Poetry and Myth* (Oxford, 2007), pp. 144–45.

16 E. H. Alton, D. E. W. Wormell, and E. Courtney (ed.), *P. Ovidi Nasonis Fastorvm Libri Sex* (Leipzig, 1985), pp. 145–48.

17 Ibid., p. 157; H. Rackham, W. H. S. Jones, and D. E. Eichholz, (ed.), *Pliny: Natural History* (London, 1938–62), x, p. 160.

18 A. F. Anisimov, 'Cosmological concepts of the Peoples of the North', in Henry N. Michael (ed.), *Studies in Siberian Shamanism* (Toronto, 1963), p. 204; cf. p. 97. At the royal township of Buganda, a powerful African kingdom beside Lake Victoria, 'Outside the palace gates, on the left side, was the royal hearth (*Ggombolola*); its constantly burning flame signified that the king was alive and well' (Benjamin C. Ray, *Myth, Ritual, and Kingship in Buganda* (Oxford, 1991), p. 136; cf. p. 140).

19 Ifor Williams (ed.), *Canu Aneirin* (Cardiff, 1938), p. 38; R. I. Best, Osborn Bergin, M. A. O'Brien, and Anne O'Sullivan (ed.), *The Book of Leinster Formerly Lebar na Núachongbála* (Dublin, 1954–83), p. 805. A formidable Northumbrian ruler waging war against the Britons of the North was identified in early Welsh heroic poetry by the sobriquet *fflamddwyn*, 'flamebearer' (Sir John Morris-Jones, 'Taliesin', *Y Cymmrodor* (London, 1918), xxviii, p. 154).

20 A. M. Hocart, *Kingship* (Oxford, 1927), p. 27; Jaan Puhvel, 'Greek ΑΝΑΞ', *Zeitschrift für vergleichende Sprachforschung auf dem Gebiete der Indogermanischen Sprachen* (Göttingen, 1956), lxxiii, pp. 202–22;

post-Roman heroic age, Urien Rheged, was likened to 'a flaming wheel across the world', while the Welsh name *Rhodri* means 'king of the wheel' – probably with reference to the sun.[21] In the Welsh Laws, the king is described as sitting with the sun behind him when administering justice, while Irish kings and Highland chiefs were likened to the sun.[22]

In light of extensive evidence, Sir James Frazer concluded, 'it is natural to infer that in old days the Common Hearth with its perpetual fire was originally the hearth of the king, and consequently what we incorrectly call the temple of Vesta was of old the King's house.'[23]

This archaic belief is likewise entrenched in mediæval Welsh social practice. Seating in a royal hall reflected hierarchical order, and the symbolic implication of the Welsh legal provision for the king and his heir (*edlyng, gwrthrych*) to sit facing each other across the burning hearth is unmistakable.[24]

Finally, there was a powerful sexual element in the ideology of the hearth and eternal fire of Vesta. The names *Hestia* and *Vesta* derive from an Indo-European root **w-es-*, 'stay, dwell, spend the night'. Another cognate derivative is the Irish term *feis(s)* or *fess* (< Celtic **westā*), meaning 'spending the night, sleeping', particularly with the implication of sleeping with another person, i.e. enjoying sexual congress.[25] The 'perpetual' fire on the hearth in Vesta's temple was rekindled annually on 1 March by means of a fire-drill, a process whose implicit identification with the sexual act is recorded in differing cultures around the world.[26] Again, in Indo-European tradition the life-soul was envisaged as fire in the cerebro-spinal 'marrow', passing into the female organ during impregnation.[27] A regular theme in Irish saints' Lives is that of a holy man conceived by fire or flame.[28]

Elena Cassin, *La splendeur divine: Introduction à l'étude de la mentalité mésopotamienne* (Paris, 1968), pp. 65–69; Enrico Campanile, 'Meaning and prehistory of OIr. *lúan láith*', in Mohammad Ali Jazayery and Werner Winter (ed.), *Languages and Cultures: Studies in Honor of Edgar C. Polomé* (Berlin, 1988), pp. 89–95.

21 Sir Ifor Williams and J. E. Caerwyn Williams (ed.), *The Poems of Taliesin* (Dublin, 1968), p. 10; Thomas F. O'Rahilly, *Early Irish History and Mythology* (Dublin, 1946), p. 359. The Celtic Jupiter bears a wheel (Arthur Bernard Cook, *Zeus: A Study in Ancient Religion* (Cambridge, 1914-40), i, pp. 288–90; Isabelle Fauduet, *Les temples de tradition celtique en Gaule romaine* (Paris, 1993), p. 101).

22 A. W. Wade-Evans, 'Peniarth MS. 37. Fol. 61A-Fol. 76B', *Y Cymmrodor* (1904), xvii, p. 142; M. A. O'Brien (ed.), *Corpus Genealogiarum Hiberniae* (Dublin, 1962), i, p. 71; Caomhín Breatnach (ed.), *Patronage, Politics and Prose: Ceasacht Inghine Guile; Sgéala Muice Meic Dhá Thó; Oidheadh Chuinn Chéadchathaigh* (Maynooth, 1996), p. 98; Rev. Alexander Cameron, *Reliquiæ Celticæ: Texts, Papers, and Studies in Gaelic Literature and Philology* (Inverness, 1894), ii, p. 264.

23 Sir James George Frazer (ed.), *Publii Ovidii Nasonis Fastorum Libri Sex: The Fasti of Ovid* (London, 1929), iv, p. 182; cf. pp. 180–82.

24 Stephen J. Williams and J. Enoch Powell (ed.), *Cyfreithiau Hywel Dda yn ôl Llyfr Blegywryd (Dull Dyfed)* (Cardiff, 1942), p. 4; A. W. Wade-Evans (ed.), *Welsh Medieval Law: Being a Text of the Laws of Howel the Good, Namely the British Museum Harleian MS. 4353 of the 13th Century* (Oxford, 1909), p. 4; Hywel D. Emanuel (ed.), *The Latin Texts of the Welsh Laws* (Cardiff, 1967), pp. 110, 194, 277, 318, 437.

25 Julius Pokorny, *Indogermanisches Etymologisches Wörterbuch* (Berne, 1959–69), i, p. 1170; Frisk, *Griechisches Etymologisches Wörterbuch*, i, pp. 576–77; E. G. Quin *et al.* (ed.), *Dictionary of the Irish Language: Based mainly on Old and Middle Irish Materials* (Dublin, 1913–76), 'F', col. 67; Ranko Matasović, *Etymological Dictionary of Proto-Celtic* (Leiden, 2009), pp. 417–18.

26 Frazer (ed.), *Publii Ovidii Nasonis Fastorum Libri Sex*, iii, pp. 38–41; iv, pp. 208–11.

27 Richard Broxton Onians, *The Origins of European Thought about the Body, the Mind the Soul, the World Time, and Fate: New Interpretations of Greek, Roman and kindred evidence also of some basic Jewish and Christian beliefs* (Cambridge, 1954), pp. 149–58.

28 Carolus Plummer (ed.), *Vitae Sanctorum Hiberniae: Partim Hactenvs Ineditae ad Fidem Codicvm Manvscriptorvm Recognovit Prolegominis Notis Indicibvs Instrvxit* (Oxford, 1910), i, pp. cxxxvii, clviii.

A striking parallel to the Roman goddess Vesta is found in Celtic Ireland. Whilst evidence indicates that Saint Brigid lived from AD 439 to 524, and founded her celebrated church at Kildare,[29] many hagiographical miracles and other activities ascribed to her originate in myths of a powerful pagan divinity of the same name. Brigid herself was closely associated with fire. An early hymnographer addressed her as 'Brigid ever excellent woman, golden sparkling flame', while a gloss describes a fiery column blazing from her head to the roof-tree.[30]

The twelfth-century Norman-Welsh writer Giraldus Cambrensis, who spent two years in Ireland after Henry II's conquest, provides a remarkable account of Saint Brigid's sanctuary at Kildare in Leinster. He tells us that an inextiguishable fire was tended there by nineteen nuns. Each guarded the holy place in turn, and on the twentieth night they invoked Brigid, who protected the fire unseen throughout the hours of darkness. No matter how much wood was burned, the ashes never increased. The sanctuary was surrounded by a circular fence or hedge of withies, which no male might safely cross: a taboo proved (so Giraldus was informed) by the sorry fate of two ruffianly Norman soldiers who sought to violate it. The nuns were prohibited from blowing on the fire with their mouths, which they fanned with bellows or winnowing forks. Nearby fields known as 'Brigid's meadows' were ascribed miraculous fertility.[31]

This intriguing story has attracted scholarly interest for more than a century. It has been widely accepted as the description of an actual rite of great antiquity, which continued in practice up to the end of the twelfth century, if not later. In Sir James Frazer's words,

> Now, at Kildare in Ireland the nuns of St. Brigit tended a perpetual fire down to the suppression of the monasteries under Henry VIII; and we can hardly doubt that in doing so they merely kept up, under a Christian name, an ancient pagan worship of Brigit in her character of a fire-goddess or patroness of smiths ... To me the nuns of St. Brigid seem to be most probably the successors of a Celtic order of Vestals.[32]

Despite the scholarly consensus, I find this interpretation implausible. Perpetual fires are indeed recorded at mediæval Irish monasteries,[33] one of which was said to be maintained at Kildare.[34] However, the latter does not appear to have been regarded as anything out of the ordinary, and

---

29 Daniel McCarthy, 'The Chronology of St Brigid of Kildare', *Peritia: Journal of the Medieval Academy of Ireland* (Turnhout, 2000), xiv, pp. 255–81; Dorothy Ann Bray, 'Ireland's Other Apostle: Cogitosus' St Brigit', *Cambrian Medieval Celtic Studies* (Aberystwyth, 2010), lviii, pp. 55–70.

30 Whitley Stokes and John Strachan (ed.), *Thesaurus Palaeohibernicus: A Collection of Old-Irish Glosses Scholia Prose and Verse* (Cambridge, 1901–3), ii, pp. 325, 329.

31 *Proceedings of the Royal Irish Academy*, lii, pp. 150–51, 154.

32 Sir James George Frazer, *The Magic Art and the Evolution of Kings* (London, 1911), ii, pp. 240, 241; idem, *Lectures on the Early History of the Kingship* (London, 1905), pp. 223–26. Cf. J. A. MacCulloch, *The Religion of the Ancient Celts* (Edinburgh, 1911), pp. 68–69; Anne Ross, *Pagan Celtic Britain: Studies in Iconography and Tradition* (London, 1967), pp. 360, 361; Kim McCone, *Pagan Past and Christian Present in Early Irish Literature* (Naas, 1990), p. 164.

33 Standish H. O'Grady (ed.), *Silva Gadelica: A Collection of Tales in Irish with Extracts Illustrating Persons and Places* (London, 1892), i, pp. 14, 42; Charles Plummer (ed.), *Bethada Náem nÉrenn: Lives of Irish Saints* (Oxford, 1922), i, pp. 25, 110, 234.

34 Plummer (ed.), *Vitae Sanctorum Hiberniae*, i, pp. cxl–xli. In 1220 Henry of London, Archbishop of Dublin, is said to have ordered the Kildare fire to be extinguished (S. Baring-Gould and John Fisher, *The Lives of the British Saints: The Saints of Wales and Cornwall and such Irish Saints as have Dedications in Britain* (London, 1907–13), i, p. 266).

receives no mention in the Latin and Irish Lives of St Brigid, despite their repeated emphasis on her association with fire. Although her fame was exceeded only by that of St Patrick, mediæval Irish literature affords no hint of the remarkable ceremonial which so struck the imagination of Giraldus. The earliest Life of Brigid, written in Latin by Cogitosus in the seventh century, contains a detailed description of the abbey of Kildare and its associated legends, without however including any reference to the remarkable ritual, nor the sanctuary where it purportedly occurred. Yet the hagiographer's accuracy and technical expertise in architecture have excited the admiration of modern historians.[35]

It is implausible to suppose that Brigid's hagiographers ignored so dramatic a rite, given their exhaustive concern to record miraculous aspects of her career and cult. In fact, a careful reading of Giraldus's account suggests that his description of the fire ritual at Kildare originated from disparate sources.

1. He begins by recording a widespread belief that Brigid's fire at Kildare was inextinguishable (*ignis Brigide, quem inextinguibilem dicunt*).

2. To this he adds an implicit correction: it is *not* in fact inextinguishable (*non quod extingui non possit, sed quia tam solicite, tam accurate*). As mentioned above, there existed report of a perpetual fire burning at Kildare, which like its counterparts in other monasteries required no maintenance. Indeed, that was what was miraculous about them. Giraldus himself, however, had heard a distinct, more colourful, version, which he proceeds to describe. The fire is sustained by a select group of nuns and holy women (*moniales et sancte mulieres*), who devote themselves to its preservation. Without their attendance, the holy fire would languish and fail.

It is uncertain whether Giraldus ever visited Kildare.[36] Certainly, it is hard to credit his witnessing so exotic a ceremony, which is nowhere else recorded, and equally hard to envisage occurring in practice. The likely explanation is that the ceremonial he describes reflects myth rather than ritual. In the same way, his colourful account of the inaugural ritual of the kings of Tyrconnell is generally thought to reflect archaic lore, rather than current practice. With regard to the latter account, Proinsias Mac Cana noted

> That the rite was then obsolete in his time is indicated by other accounts of roughly contemporary inauguration, and one can only conclude that it reached Giraldus as an item of *seanchas*, or oral tradition, which remains wholly unattested elsewhere.[37]

---

35 Daniel McCarthy, 'Topographical Characteristics of the *Vita Prima* and *Vita Cogitosi Sanctae Brigitae*', *Studia Celtica* (Cardiff, 2001), xxxv, pp. 259–61.

36 It might be thought that the beautifully illuminated book kept at Kildare which so impressed Giraldus attests to a visit. However, there is no indication of the length of his stay (assuming it occurred), nor the extent to which he was enabled to inspect the monastery and its environs. Furthermore, it is not impossible that he inspected the book elsewhere.

37 Proinsias Mac Cana, 'Mythology and the Oral Tradition', in Miranda J. Green (ed.), *The Celtic World* (London, 1995), p. 784. Cf. Françoise Le Roux, 'Recherches sur les éléments rituels de l'élection royale irlandaise et celtique', *Ogam: Tradition celtique* (Rennes, 1963), xv, pp. 126–35; Francis John Byrne, *Irish Kings and High-Kings* (London, 1973), pp. 17–20; Bart Jaski, *Early Irish Kingship and Succession* (Dublin, 2000), p. 59; Charles Doherty, 'Kingship in Early Ireland', in Edel Bhreatnach (ed.), *The Kingship and Landscape of Tara* (Dublin, 2005), pp. 18–19; Ronald Hutton, 'Medieval Welsh Literature and Pre-Christian Deities', *Cambrian Medieval Celtic Studies* (Aberystwyth, 2011), lxi, pp. 80–81.

Implications of the foregoing evidence may be summarized as follows.

1. Brigid's fire is described as surrounded by a circular fence or hedge, implying that it lay under an open sky. Maintenance of the rites described must have proved wholly impractical for any length of time under an Irish climate. The description evokes rather the site of an ancient sanctuary, concerning which wonderful tales were told, rather than a structure erected within a monastic complex. Again, it must be emphasized that Cogitosus makes no allusion to such an enclosure in his detailed account of the monastery at Kildare.

2. The goddess Brigid was closely associated with fire.[38]

3. While no other record in the British Isles of a concourse of women tending a sacred fire is known, Giraldus's description bears marked similarity to an allusion in the early Welsh poem *Preiddeu Annwfn*, 'The Spoils of the Otherworld'. There reference is made to a divine cauldron 'kindled by the breath of nine maidens'.[39] Nine maidens recur in different guises in Celtic mythology. We read of the Munster king Ruad who slept successively with nine Otherworld women beneath the sea; a queen and her nine foster-sisters who cross over the sea; when the famed voyager Bran visited the Island of Women, he found thrice nine couches awaiting him and his followers; Queen Morgan, who bore away the dying Arthur to the Otherworld of Annwfn, was accompanied by nine sisters; nine witches were slain by the Arthurian hero Cai on the uplands of Ystafngwn; a wicked king of Leinster confined the princess Dairine in a forest refuge, together with her nine foster-sisters; nine sisters of the divine race of the Túatha Dé Danann dwelt in an Otherworld stronghold, called 'the palace of women' (*Lis na mban*). Fairies in the Scottish Highlands operated through nine ages.[40]

    The nine Otherworld maidens of *Preiddeu Annwfn* are paralleled by nine chaste shape-shifting divinatory priestesses (*Gallizenae*) of a Gaulish god, who are described in the first century AD as practicing occult arts on the island of Sena at the mouth of the Loire.[41]

---

38   Jan de Vries, *Keltische Religion* (Stuttgart, 1961), pp. 78–79; McCone, *Pagan Past and Christian Present*, pp. 164–65.

39   J. Gwenogvryn Evans (ed.), *Facsimile & Text of the Book of Taliesin* (Llanbedrog, 1910), p. 55.

40   A. G. van Hamel (ed.), *Compert Con Culainn and Other Stories* (Dublin, 1933), pp. 39–41; 39–41; Edward Gwynn (ed.), *The Metrical Dindshenchas* (Dublin, 1903–35), ii, p. 28; Séamus Mac Mathúna (ed.), *Immram Brain: Bran's Journey to the Land of the Women* (Tübingen, 1975), pp. 111–13; A. O. H. Jarman (ed.), *Llyfr Du Caerfyrddin gyda Rhagymadrodd Nodiadau Testunol a Geirfa* (Cardiff, 1982), p. 69; Basil Clarke (ed.), *Life of Merlin; Geoffrey of Monmouth: Vita Merlini* (Cardiff, 1973), p. 100; O'Grady (ed.), *Silva Gadelica*, i, pp. 182–83, 189–90, 226–27; Alexander Carmichael (ed.), *Carmina Gadelica: Hymns and Incantations with Illustrative Notes on Words, Rites, and Customs, Dying and Obsolete: Orally Collected in the Highlands and Islands of Scotland* (Edinburgh, 1900–71), ii, p. 334.

41   A. Silberman (ed.), *Pomponius Mela: Chorographie* (Paris, 1988), p. 81. *Gallizenae* is explained as 'Gaulish girls' (Bernhardt Maier, 'Gaulish *Genā* 'Girl; Unmarried Woman'? A note on Pomponius Mela, *De Chorographia* III 48', *Studia Celtica* (1997), xxxi, p. 280). Another classical source explains that no men were allowed on the island, and describes how the maidens crossed to the mainland to cohabit with their husbands (L. Edelstein and I. G. Kidd (ed.), *Posidonius* (Cambridge, 1988–99), i, pp. 239–40). This looks like a rationalization of their virginity. 'I see no reason to reject the suggestion that they are an early literary reflex of the inhabitants of the otherworld Land of Women, and in particular of the thrice nine women who welcomed the voyagers in *Immram Brain*' (Proinsias Mac Cana, 'The Sinless Otherworld of *Immram Brain*', *Ériu: The Journal of the School of Irish Learning* (Dublin, 1976), xxvii, p. 112). Cf. Christian-J. Guyonvarc'h, *Magie, médecine et divination chez les Celtes* (Paris, 1997), pp. 323–25.

It is possible that Giraldus, who presumably acquired his account of Brigid's fire from an oral source, mistook 'nine' for 'nineteen'.

4. The curious detail of Brigid's being supernumary to the vigil of her handmaidens recalls the extent to which 'Irish literature abounds with "companies of nine". In a number of cases, it is made clear that the nine comprise a leader and eight others', an abstraction arising from 'the concept of the additional unit as the unifying or superior factor'.[42]

5. In view of these considerations, I suggest that the myth was originally attached, not to Kildare (*Cell dara*), but to the similar-sounding and relatively obscure Killare (*Cell áir*).[43] Killare lies a couple of miles from the Sacred Centre of Ireland at Uisneach, which unlike Kildare was closely associated with an impressive fire legend. The name *Uisneach* is believed to derive from **us-tin-āko-*, 'place of hearth, or of cinders', and an account of the wizard Mide (whose name derives from that of Meath, the central province in which Uisneach is situated) tells of his kindling a mystic fire which blazed over the four quarters of Ireland, *tar cethri hairde hÉrend*. The druids complained of the smoke, whereupon he cut off their tongues and interred them at the site.[44]

Foundation of the monastery of Killare was ascribed to a bishop Áed, who bore Brigid's name as patronymic,[45] and whose monastery at Killare contained buildings dedicated to her. Áed means 'fire', and it is likely that the supposed saint was originally 'a christianized pagan fire deity'.[46]

6. The natural site for an eternal fire of the High Goddess was Uisneach, the Omphalos of Ireland. The concept of a central vivifying fire is common to many cosmologies.[47]

---

42   Rees and Rees, *Celtic Heritage*, pp. 193, 201–4. Cf. John MacQueen, *Numerology: Theory and outline history of a literary mode* (Edinburgh, 1985), pp. 29–30; Miranda Green, *Symbol and Image in Celtic Religious Art* (London, 1989), p. 169.

43   A lone manuscript of Giraldus's *Topographia Hibernie* reads *Kildaria* for *Killarao* (*Proceedings of the Royal Irish Academy*, lii, p. 143). Confusion of the two toponyms occurs also in the *Vita Sancti Tigernaci*, where the Saint is said to have been baptized by St Brigid *in Kyllarensi monasterio* (Plummer (ed.), *Vitae Sanctorum Hiberniae*, ii, p. 266). In fact, this was an error for Kildare: *in Kelldarensi monasterio* (W. W. Heist (ed.), *Vitae Sanctorum Hiberniae ex Codice olim Salmanticensi nunc Bruxellensi* (Brussels, 1965), p. 111).

44   J. Vendryes, E. Bachellery, and P-Y. Lambert, *Lexique étymologique de l'irlandais ancien* (Dublin and Paris, 1959–96), U-22; Best, Bergin, O'Brien, and O'Sullivan (ed.), *The Book of Leinster*, pp. 941–42; O'Grady (ed.), *Silva Gadelica*, ii, p. 475. For the unique significance of fires at Uisneach, cf. Rees and Rees, *Celtic Heritage*, pp. 156–57, 159, 162–63; Philippe Jouët, 'La parole dans la civilisation celtique: mythes et figures', in Venceslas Kruta (ed.), *Les Celtes et l'écriture* (Paris, 1997), pp. 77–78. 'A series of fragmentary constructions, and an ash layer indicating a series of fires' were discovered during excavations at Uisneach (Bernard Wailes, 'The Irish "Royal Sites" in History and Archaeology', *Cambridge Medieval Celtic Studies* (Cambridge, 1982), iii, p. 18). 'The date at which these events took place (the late Iron Age) makes it quite conceivable that collective memory of such practices informed the tradition preserved in early literature that Uisneach was a place of assembly, associated, among other things, with a fire-cult' (Roseanne Schot, 'From cult centre to royal centre: monuments, myths and other revelations at Uisneach', in Roseanne Schot, Conor Newman, and Edel Bhreatnach (ed.), *Landscapes of Cult and Kingship* (Dublin, 2011), p. 105.

45   *Aed mac Bricc .i. ó Chill áir i Mide* (Whitley Stokes (ed.), *Félire Óengusso Céli Dé. The Martyrology of Oengus the Culdee* (London, 1905), p. 240).

46   McCone, *Pagan Past and Christian Present*, pp. 165–66. Áed is characterized by solar attributes (Thomas F. O'Rahilly, *Early Irish History and Mythology*, p. 472). Could *Aed mac Bricc* represent a ghost figure concocted from áed Brigte, 'Brigid's fire'.

47   For the Central Fire in Orphic cosmology, cf. Peter Kingsley, *Ancient Philosophy, Mystery, and Magic: Empedocles and Pythagorean Tradition* (Oxford, 1995), pp. 172–94. The city of Istakhr in Fars 'was the ideological heart of the [Persian] empire, since the temple of the dynasty's fire – the coronation place of many Sasanian rulers – was situated there' (B. A. Livitsky, Zhang Guang-da, and R. Shabani Samghabadi (ed.), *History of civilizations of Central Asia; Volume III The crossroads of civilizations: A.D. 250 to 750* (Paris,

The hearth of Vesta was literally the *focus* of Rome, and a perpetual fire at Apollo's temple at Delphi, the Omphalos of Greece, burned beside its famous Navel-stone. Like the eternal fire of Vesta at Rome, the hearth at Delphi was tended by a select group of chaste women, while the temple itself appropriately lay under the protection of the goddess Hestia ('hearth').[48]

7. Given evidence for a significant fire-cult at Uisneach, it may be that the celebrated Stone of Uisneach (*lic an Uisnech*) was once regarded as hearthstone of the site. The cult of Brigid was closely associated with hearths,[49] and sacred fire was envisaged as immanent in hearthstones. Saint Ciaran reignited a perpetual fire at Saighir, which had been maliciously quenched, by conjuring fire from a stone he carried into the monastery.[50]

8. The Irish High Goddess's especial connexion with the hearth may reflect the widespread belief that fire was originally controlled by a woman, whose secret men prized from her with difficulty. Frazer conjectured that the conception arose from the earliest means of making fire, the fire-drill, which generates heat and flame within the hole in the wood into which it is inserted. A corresponding belief held that fire reposed latent within the wood.[51]

9. The existence of a perpetual fire at the Centre is well-attested in early Greek cosmology, together with a close association, extending to identity, of hearth and *omphalos*.

> There is ... evidence that the Greeks in fact associated the sacred hearth with the navel (ὄμφαλος), particularly in that the hearth can be seen as rooted in the earth, just as the umbilical cord (another meaning of ὄμφαλος) roots the embryo in the womb.[52]

10. Just as the *omphalos* was the Centre from which all creation emanates, so the hearth or stove played a uniquely procreative rôle. The sexual connotation of the hearth of Vesta in Rome has already been noted. The Lappish birth-goddess Sarakka 'was associated with the fire-place in the hut', and the Khanty of Siberia envisaged the stove as a vulva or womb, and in the Hindu *Upanishad* 'The woman's lap is equated with the altar ... her vulva with the altar fire'.[53] With regard to the cult of St Brigid, it was believed in the Scottish Highlands that the mark of a club detected in the ashes of her hearth foretold

1996), p. 42). Religions worldwide have treated the interrelated concepts of hearth, altar, and sun as nurturing *foci* of the world, and means of access to God (Joseph Campbell, *The Hero with a Thousand Faces* (Princeton, 1972), pp. 42–3; Brian Hayden, *Shamans Sorcerers and Saints* (Washington, 2003), pp. 79–80).

48 Frazer, *Pausanias's Description of Greece*, v, pp. 351–52; H. W. Parke and D. E. W. Wormell, *The Delphic Oracle* (Oxford, 1956), i, pp. 35–36; Filippo Càssola (ed.), *Inni Omerici* (Milan, 1975), p. 398.

49 Séamas Ó Catháin, *The Festival of Brigit: Celtic Goddess and Holy Woman* (Dublin, 1995), pp. 53–56.

50 O'Grady (ed.), *Silva Gadelica*, i, pp. 14–15; Plummer (ed.), *Bethada Náem nÉrenn*, i, p. 111.

51 Sir James George Frazer, *Myths of the Origin of Fire* (London, 1930), pp. 5, 15, 18, 23–28, 31–32, 42–45, 90–92, 131–34, 220–21; V. I. Vasiljev, 'Animistic Notions of the Enets and the Yenisei Nenets', in V. Diószegi and M. Hoppál (ed.), *Shamanism in Siberia* (Budapest, 1978), pp. 435, 436. It was frequently a goddess who bestowed fire on mankind (Freerk C. Kamma (ed.), *Religious Texts of the Oral Tradition from Western New Guinea* (Leiden, 1975–78), i, pp. 90–94, 96–99).

52 Carl A. Huffman, *Philolaus of Croton: Pythagorean and Presocratic* (Cambridge, 1993), p. 197; cf. pp. 41–42, 197, 226–27, 237–38, 243–46, 320–21.

53 Olof Petterson, *Jabmek and Jabmeaimo: A Comparative Study of the Dead and the Realm of the Dead in Lappish Religion* (Lund, 1957), p. 31; Vladimir Napolskikh, Anna-Leena Siikala, and Mihály Hoppál (ed.), *Khanty Mythology* (Budapest, 2006), pp. 241–42; Margaret Stutley, *Ancient Indian Magic and Folklore: An Introduction* (London, 1980), p. 50.

a fruitful year.[54] This mysterious unseen club recalls the phallic manifestation in the hearth of Vesta.

Thus, while a perpetual fire was maintained at Kildare, as at other abbeys, the indications are that Giraldus misinterpreted a *myth* of the goddess Brigid's hearth associated with *Killare*, as descriptive of a wholly improbable contemporary *ritual* practised at St Brigid's famous abbey of *Kildare*. He was acquainted with traditions of Uisneach, being aware that a stone on the hill was regarded as Omphalos of Ireland.

Giraldus took his account of Merlin's transfer of the *chorea gygantum* from Geoffrey of Monmouth's History. He evidently failed to recognize Geoffrey's *Killaraus mons* as denoting Killare. He repeated Geoffrey's identification (*in monte de Killarao*) when recounting Merlin's removal of the giants' stones, but elsewhere when mentioning Killare he spells it *Kilair*, evincing no awareness that it was the original site of the celebrated Giants' Dance.[55] Thus the likelihood is that the sacred fire of Brigid, with its attendant nineteen virgins, was likewise originally associated with *Killare* (i.e. Uisneach). A pardonable error led Giraldus into the erroneous assumption, unrecorded in any Irish source, that it was located at the Saint's celebrated monastery at *Kildare*.

Giraldus's account of Brigid's fire could well have originated in traditions preserved in the vicinity of Uisneach. It was probably during his visit to Ireland in 1183 that he came to know Hugh de Lacy, on whom Henry II settled the principality of Meath in feu.[56] De Lacy built several castles, one of which was at Killare. Among the Anglo-Norman nobility he was remarkable for espousing a conciliatory policy towards the native Irish, and three years before his acquaintance with Giraldus he had married a daughter of Ruaidrí Ua Conchobair, king of Connacht.[57] Consequently, he is more likely than most of his *confrères* among Ireland's Norman overlords to have taken an interest in the native lore of the land.

Giraldus could have acquired knowledge of Uisneach and its traditions from Hugh de Lacy himself, or from members of his entourage (which may well have included household bards following in the train of his Irish princess), who enjoyed opportunity to obtain information from the Irish inhabitants of Killare – including monks from the local monastery of St Áed. By the twelfth century, Kildare had been established for more than half a millennium as centre of the cult of St Brigid, and it would be understandable if, in this instance, legendary lore of the goddess Brigid's holy fire at Uisneach/Killare were to have become confused with the perpetual fire maintained at St Brigid's monastery at Kildare.

There are indications that a parallel cult existed in Celtic Britain. *Brigid* means 'the high goddess' or 'the exalted one', the British goddess Brigantia (*Deae Victoriae Brigantiae*) invoked on Roman inscriptions beside Hadrian's Wall.[58] Under the Roman ægis she became assimilated

---

54   M. Martin, *A Description of the Western Islands of Scotland* (London, 1703), p. 119.

55   'Giraldus himself recognized no connection between the stone [at Uisneach] and the Giants' Choir … To me, however, the two stories appear to have been originally one, the error having arisen from the place-names Killare and Kildare' (John Rhys, *Lectures on the Origin and Growth of Religion as Illustrated by Celtic Heathendom* (London, 1888), pp. 192–93).

56   A. J. Otway-Ruthven, *A History of Medieval Ireland* (London, 1968), pp. 52, 53, 61, 181. Giraldus's lively description of de Lacy's appearance suggests personal acquaintance with the baron (A. B. Scott and F. X. Martin (ed.), *Expugnatio Hibernica: The Conquest of Ireland by Giraldus Cambrensis* (Dublin, 1978), p. 190).

57   Ibid., pp. 192, 194, 338.

58   O'Rahilly, *Early Irish History and Mythology*, p. 38; Calvert Watkins, 'Italo-Celtic Revisited', in Henrik Birnbaum and Jaan Puhvel (ed.), *Ancient Indo-European Dialects: Proceedings of the Conference on Indo-*

as the Celtic goddess Minerva mentioned by Caesar, and as *Sul Minerva* presided over the celebrated hot baths at Bath (*Aquæ Sulis*). *Sul* (< *sūli-*) means 'sun', an attribute recalling the Irish Brigid's attested association with fire.[59]

The realm in the rock

In the Welsh mediæval story *Culhwch and Olwen*, its hero Culhwch, accompanied by the pick of Arthur's warriors, arrives 'at a great plain, and they could see a fort, the greatest fort in the world'. The owner of this unmistakably Otherworld stronghold is Custennin the Herdsman, a skin-clad giant who rules over an untamed wilderness, grazed only by his flock of sheep. He is recognizable as a figure familiar from shamanistic mythology discussed earlier in the context of the Life of St Illtud, the Lord of Animals, who presides over forest and tundra as guardian of wild beasts.[60] *Custennin* derives from Latin *Constantīnus*,[61] which clearly cannot have been the Brittonic deity's original name. A clue to the latter is provided by the sixth-century king Constantine of Cornwall, who is accorded in early genealogies the epithet *gorneu*.[62] While this means 'Cornish',[63] it might easily have been mistaken – particularly when featured in isolation (as in the genealogies) – for Welsh *cornawc*, 'horned'.[64] The notion of a horned monarch in turn recalls the Celtic divine Lord of the Animals: the antlered god Cernunnos, whose name means 'the Horned God'.[65]

When the party entered Custennin's castle they were welcomed by his wife, who 'opened a coffer at the far end of the hearthstone (*pentan*), and from it emerged a youth with yellow curly hair'. Their hostess explained that he was the sole survivor of her twenty-three sons, the remainder having been slain by her malevolent brother-in-law, the giant Ysbyddaden. The lad joins Culhwch and his companions, and, in consequence of valuable aid lent them in a subsequent adventure, receives from them the name *Goreu*, 'best'. At the conclusion of the tale, Goreu decapitates Ysbaddaden and impales his head on the courtyard post, after which 'he took possession of his fort and his country'.[66] The unexplained confinement of the youth in the

European Linguistics Held at the University of California, Los Angeles April 25–27, 1963 (Berkeley, 1966), p. 40; Anne Ross, *Pagan Celtic Britain: Studies in Iconography and Tradition* (London, 1967), pp. 360–62). Stephan Zimmer has shown that passages of the saint's direct speech cited in *Bethu Brigte* contain archaic Indo-European indications of her original nature as a powerful pagan goddess ('Weiblich? Heilig? Göttlich?', in Gabriele Uelsberg, Michael Schmauder, and Stefan Zimmer (ed.), *Kelten am Rhein: Akten des dreizehnten Internationalen Keltologiekongresses* (Mainz am Rhein, 2009), ii, pp. 319–27).

59 Ernst Windisch, *Das Keltische Brittannien bis zu Kaiser Arthur* (Leipzig, 1912), p. 97; Kim McCone, *Pagan Past and Christian Present in Early Irish Literature* (Naas, 1990), pp. 161–65; Matasović, *Etymological Dictionary of Proto-Celtic*, p. 324.

60 Åke Hultkrantz (ed.), *The Supernatural Owners of Nature: Nordic symposium on the religious conceptions of ruling spirits (genii loci, genii speciei) and allied concepts* (Uppsala, 1961).

61 Henry Lewis, *Yr Elfen Ladin yn yr Iaith Gymraeg* (Cardiff, 1943), p. 4.

62 P. C. Bartrum (ed.), *Early Welsh Genealogical Texts* (Cardiff, 1966), pp. 58, 65.

63 'Corneu means "of Cornwall"' (Kenneth Jackson, *Language and History in Early Britain: A Chronological Survey of the Brittonic Languages First to Twelfth Century A.D.* (Edinburgh, 1953), p. 708).

64 Cf. Middle Welsh *kythreul corna6c*, 'horned devil' (J. Gwenogvryn Evans (ed.), *The Poetry in the Red Book of Hergest* (Llanbedrog, 1911), col. 1161, 34).

65 '**ker-h₂-*, dans gaul. *Cernunnos* dieu 'Cornu', dérivé d'un nom de la "corne"' (Françoise Bader, 'Fonctions des Allitérations', in Edgar C. Polomé and Carol F. Justus (ed.), *Language Change and Typological Variation: In Honor of Winfred P. Lehmann on the Occasion of His 83rd Birthday* (Washington, 1999), i, pp. 309–10). Cf. Xavier Delamarre, *Dictionnaire de la langue gauloise: Une approche linguistique du vieux-celtique continental* (Paris, 2001), p. 91.

66 Bromwich and Simon Evans (ed.), *Culhwch and Olwen*, pp. 17–18, 30, 42.

coffer, together with the odd parenthesis that it lay 'at the far end of the hearthstone', look like a rationalization of an earlier version in which *he emerged from the hearthstone itself*.

This colourful incident bears appearance of a significant theme in pre-Christian mythology. Successive rulers die, until after a stipulated number of generations the dynasty becomes extinct. The land reverts to an untilled wasteland, presided over by the Lord of Beasts. However the royal heir (progenitor of a fresh dynasty) emerges from the royal hearthstone to reinstitute the kingship. The interpretation of the young prince's name as *goreu* ('best') is artificially contrived: 'a fanciful onomastic explanation is once more given for a personal name whose composition was either misunderstood by the redactor, or he was making a deliberate pun upon it.'[67]

The story of the 'birth' of Goreu in *Culhwch ac Olwen* recalls an episode in another early Welsh tale, discussed earlier in a different context. In *Math uab Mathonwy*, the Fourth Branch of the *Mabinogi*, the maiden Arianrhod steps over the wizard Math's magic wand (*hutlath*), and gives birth to Dylan.[68] The infant instantly takes to the sea in the guise of what was apparently understood to be a seal, and is subsequently slain by his uncle Gofannon. This part of the episode manifests a correspondence between the British goddess Arianrhod ('Silver Wheel') and the Irish goddess Brigid. For the latter (under the alternative form *Bríg*) was not only pre-eminent as a virgin, but possessed a son called Rúadán, who was both associated with seals and killed by Goibniu, Irish counterpart of the Welsh smith-god Gofannon.[69]

Returning to Arianrhod: on hearing her offspring's cry she made for the door, where as she passed through she left 'a small something' (*y ryw bethan*). Before anybody looked, Gwydion wrapped a sheet of silk around it, and hid it in a chest 'under the foot of his bed'. Some time later his fellow-wizard Math heard a cry, and discovered within the chest a child, who was eventually named Lleu by his mother Arianrhod.[70]

Once again we encounter a barely disguised fragment of British pagan mythology. Math, with his wand of enchantment, epitomizes the Divine Druid.[71] Arianrhod, who declares herself a maiden and dwells in a sea-girt stronghold inhabited only by women, is likewise an obvious personification of the Maiden Sovereignty. Her curious stance in the doorway, when she drops

---

67 Ibid., p. 140. This explanation appears preferable to the interpretation by John Mac Queen, 'Goreu son of Custennin', *Études Celtiques* (Paris, 1958), viii, pp. 154–63. Later in the story, the giant oddly volunteers that 'the time has come to take away my life', whereupon Goreu obligingly cuts off his head and mounts it in the castle courtyard. This may represent a further rationalization, this time of the well-known myth of an otiose deity presiding over the Otherworld in the form of a severed head (Claude Sterckx, 'Les Têtes Coupées et le Graal', *Studia Celtica* (1985–1986), xx/xxi, pp. 1–42; Michael J. Enright, *The Sutton Hoo Sceptre and the Roots of Celtic Kingship Theory* (Dublin, 2006), pp. 94–95).

68 'It is clear that the wand is credited with phallic power' (Edwin Sidney Hartland, *The Legend of Perseus: A Study of Tradition in Story Custom and Belief* (London, 1894-96), i, p. 128).

69 Elizabeth A. Gray (ed.), *Cath Maige Tuired: The Second Battle of Mag Tuired* (Naas, 1982), p. 56. Rúadán possessed thirty blue horses from the sea, which had been transformed by St Brendan from seals (Plummer (ed.), *Vitae Sanctorum Hiberniae*, ii, p. 248; idem (ed.), *Bethada Náem nÉrenn*, i, pp. 88–89; O'Grady (ed.), *Silva Gadelica*, i, pp. 67–68). Connlaed bishop of Kildare, Brigid's chief artisan, was known as 'Seal-head': *Ronncenn nomen eius prius* (Stokes (ed.), *Félire Óengusso Céli Dé*, p. 128; cf. Stokes and Strachan (ed.), *Thesaurus Palaeohibernicus*, ii, p. 347). For a further link between Brigid and seals, cf. Whitley Stokes (ed.), *Lives of Saints from the Book of Lismore* (Oxford, 1890), p. 49. Goibniu and Gofannon are discussed by Gerard Murphy in Eoin MacNeill and Gerard Murphy (ed.), *Duanaire Finn: The Book of the Lays of Finn* (London and Dublin, 1908-53), iii, pp. lxxxiii–iv; Hughes (ed.), *Math uab Mathonwy*, pp. xxviii–ix.

70 Ibid., pp. 7–8.

71 'Le dieu-druide' (Christian-J. Guyonvarc'h and Françoise Le Roux, *Les Druides* (Rennes, 1986), pp. 335–40).

the 'small something' (*y ryw bethan*) – presumably an embryo – represents a liminal situation between this world and the Other.

Viewed in this light, the curious action adopted by Gwydion of placing the 'small something' in a chest (*cist*) at the foot of his bed (*gwely*) suggests yet another feature of British mythology. Lleu, like his Irish counterpart Lug, was regarded as divine or semi-divine ancestor of royal dynasties. In a tenth-century royal genealogy, he appears under the name and patronymic *Louhen map Guid gen.* i.e. 'Lleu *hên*, son of Gwydion'.[72] The adjective *hên*, 'old', in this context signifies 'primal ancestor'.[73]

In Welsh law the word *gwely* passed by semantic evolution from 'bed' to 'marriage bed', and so through 'married couple *qua* ancestors or parents' to 'the land held by the segment of a lineage (or occasionally the whole lineage)'.[74] The provision that Gwydion place the embryo in its container 'under the foot' (*is traed*) of the *gwely* appears at first sight odd. However, if *gwely* be accorded its legal meaning of 'marriage bed' and/or 'ancestral married couple', and *traed* its alternative meaning of 'base, pedestal, foundation', the significance of the episode becomes manifest.

The 'small thing' in the chest represents the germinal source of a princely lineage. When this account is compared with the story of the 'birth' of Goreu in a chest 'beside' a hearthstone, the concept becomes clearer still. Originally Goreu was born, like the Etruscan king Servius Tullius, from the hearthstone itself, the *cist* or chest from which he appeared representing a rationalization of the hearthstone. Added to this is the fact that standing stones are at times termed in Welsh *kistvaen*, 'stone chest', probably under the influence of an archaic belief that menhirs could act as receptacles.[75] Receptacles of what? A concept widespread in early societies held that men were born from trees or rocks struck by divine lightning. In ancient Israel twelve megaliths were identified with the twelve tribes of the land, which they implicitly embodied.[76]

The belief that lightning fecundated the rock was accompanied by a complementary understanding that its fire remained immanent within the rock, where it germinated the embryo. The *kistvaen* probably reflects a rationalization, whereby the stone was understood to be an ark, within which an embryo or other living creature might be confined. Thus, in *Cyfranc Lludd a Lleuelys* the fighting 'dragons' are confined within a *kistvaen*, or stone chest. It is probable that in an earlier version they (or rather, the *vermes* they had come to replace) were understood to be immured within a solid rock.

The birth-tale of Goreu reflects the concept of the birth of the founder of a new dynasty from a hearthstone, as does that of Lleu in *Math uab Mathonwy*. That in an earlier version it was a hearthstone accords with well-established mythical pattern, confirmed by a further

---

72 Egerton Phillimore, 'The *Annales Cambriæ* and Old-Welsh Genealogies from *Harleian MS.* 3859', *Y Cymmrodor* (1888), ix, p. 176. Above *Louhen* in the pedigree appears a list of Roman emperors, which represents an obviously 'learned' intrusion.

73 Patrick K. Ford (ed.), *The Poetry of Llywarch Hen* (Los Angeles, 1974), pp. 25–32.

74 T. M. Charles-Edwards, *Early Irish and Welsh Kinship* (Oxford, 1993), pp. 226–56.

75 At Eastyn near Wrexham, Lhuyd was informed of the remains of a Roman bath constructed of 'square bricks Fo mendiodh kymydogion gwedi kael y gîst-vaen' (Rupert H. Morris (ed.), *Parochialia: Being a Summary of Answers to "Parochial Queries in Order to a Geographical Dictionary, etc., of Wales" Issued by Edward Lhwyd* (London, 1909–11), i, p. 97).

76 Nagy, *Greek Mythology and Poetics*, pp. 181–201; Calvert Watkins, *How to Kill a Dragon: Aspects of Indo-European Poetics* (New York and Oxford, 1995), pp. 161–64; John Pairman Brown, *Israel and Hellas* (Berlin, 1995–2001), ii, pp. 205–206. A useful bibliography of the birth of men and gods from rocks is provided by Mircea Eliade, *Forgerons et alchimistes* (Paris, 1956), p. 191.

motif in traditional lore. A character named variously Mabon mab Modron and Mabon mab Mellt features in *Culhwch ac Olwen* and other early Welsh literary sources. In fact Mabon is but another name for Lleu. Like Lleu, Mabon is described as son of a goddess, born under peculiar circumstances, and removed at birth from his mother. In view of the close parallels, *Mabon mab Modron*, 'Divine Son, son of Divine Mother', looks like a descriptive term for Lleu mab Arianrhod. Indeed, they are all but identified in an early verse mentioning 'the grave on Nantlle's height ... Mabon son of Mydron the swift',[77] since *Nantlle*, a beautiful valley in Snowdonia, means 'Valley of Lleu'. *Mabon mab Mellt* is surely a doublet of Mabon mab Modron,[78] whose name 'Divine Son, son of Lightning' further recalls the widespread myth of the god or hero born in consequence of divine lightning striking a tree or rock, imbuing it with creative fire.[79]

It was widely believed in early times that the realm of the dead lay within a large rock or rocky hill, access to which was gained by means of a narrow cleft or crevice.[80] Entering such a passage could represent an initiatory rite, the neophyte being symbolically reborn by passing from one world to the other.[81]

Lleu, Illtud, and the world in the stone

Here may be noted illuminating parallels between the Life of St Illtud examined in Chapter Ten, and the account of the birth of Lleu in *Math uab Mathonwy*. I have suggested that much of the Life of Illtud represents a thinly-disguised retelling of pagan myth, focussed on the Omphalos (*medgarth*) of Britain.

1. Lleu is *inter alia* an ancestor deity.
   The name *Illtud* apparently means '(Father of) many peoples'.
2. The mother of Lleu is the virgin goddess Arianrhod, whose name means 'Silver Wheel'. This is surely an allusion to the moon,[82] whose pale beauty and correlation with the

77 Thomas Jones, 'The Black Book of Carmarthen 'Stanzas of the Graves', *The Proceedings of the British Academy* (London, 1967), liii, p. 136.

78 Ross, *Pagan Celtic Britain*, pp. 208–209; Bromwich and Simon Evans (ed.), *Culhwch and Olwen*, p. 152.

79 Claude Sterckx, 'Les Têtes Coupées et le Graal' (Cardiff, 1985/1986), *Studia Celtica*, xx/xxi, p. 19.

80 King Svegdir entered a rock in east Sweden as big as a house, where Óðinn dwelt, from which he (Svegdir) never emerged (Bjarni Aðalbjarnarson (ed.), *Heimskringla* (Reykjavik, 1941–51), i, pp. 27–28). Among Siberian peoples, 'Sometimes a hero or a mythical being can enter the world of the dead by entering a rock' (Maria M. Tátar, 'Mythology as an areal problem in the Altai-Sayan area: the sacred holes and caves', in Juha Pentikäinen (ed.), *Shamanism and Northern Ecology* (Berlin and New York, 1996), p. 269).

81 Jeremiah Curtin, *Myths and Folk-Lore of Ireland* (London, 1890), pp. 194–95, 197, 199; Lowry Charles Wimberly, *Folklore in the English & Scottish Ballads* (Chicago, 1928), pp. 126–34; Bronislaw Malinowski, *The Foundation of Faith and Morals: An Anthropological Analysis of Primitive Beliefs and Conduct with Special Reference to the Fundamental Problems of Religion and Ethics* (Oxford, 1936), p. 15; Mircea Eliade, *Birth and Rebirth: The Religious Meanings of Initiation in Human Culture* (London, 1961), pp. 52, 58, 61, 64–66; E. O. G. Turville-Petre, *Myth and Religion of the North: The Religion of Ancient Scandinavia* (London, 1964), pp. 55, 63–64; Carmen Blacker, *The Catalpa Bow: A Study of Shamanistic Practices in Japan* (London, 1975), pp. 71–72; Anna-Leena Siikala, *The Rite Technique of the Siberian Shaman* (Helsinki, 1978), p. 291.

82 O'Rahilly, *Early Irish History and Mythology*, p. 304; de Vries, *Keltische Religion*, p. 134. For the widespread concept of the moon as wheel, cf. Françoise Bader, *La langue des dieux, ou l'hermétisme des poètes indo-européens* (Pisa, 1989), pp. 240–44.

menstrual cycle led to her being regarded as a veiled and virginal goddess, wife of the sun.[83] By similar analogy, the moon was regarded as vessel of creation and repository of souls.[84]

In the *Vita Iltuti*, Illtud's wife Trynihid is made to live apart from her 'husband', emphasis being laid on her chastity. She is all but identified with the moon, and dwells far off in an oratory upon a mountaintop. In view of these considerations, it is tempting to regard the otherwise unrecorded and apparently meaningless name *Trynihid* as an orthographical corruption of *Arianrhod*, with initial 'A' mistaken for 'T'. Trynihid's virginity could have misled the hagiographer into discounting her rôle as mother,[85] converting her instead into a wife who, for a highly implausible motive (her husband espies her naked at night!), dwells apart as a chaste votary.

3. Lleu begins life as 'a small something' (*y ryw bethan*), which was presumably an embryo or 'soul-bearer'.

Illtud's father is called *Bicanus miles*, interpreted by the hagiographer as 'Bicanus the soldier'. However, this more likely represents a ghost name originating in misunderstanding of *mil bychan*: that same 'small creature' which, according to insular Celtic belief, fecundated a mother's womb.

4. The *rhyw bethan*, placed by Math inside a stone (chest), grows into a gifted youth, who in due course becomes redemptive ruler of his country, and putative ancestor of the tribe (*gwely*).

Illtud, spurred by an unsaintly fit of abject cowardice in face of persecution, conceals himself in a cave, where he lies on a stone for over a year. Eventually he is persuaded by the people of the country to return among them, to be hailed as supreme above all kings and princes. This looks like a cosmological birth-tale or creation legend, preceded as it is by the account of King Meirchion the Wild reigning over a wasteland inhabited by savage beasts. Similarly, the realm to which Goreu succeeds as ruler on emerging from his hearthstone had previously been untamed forest, under the sway of the skin-clad herdsman Custennin. Both Meirchion and Custennin correspond to the shamanist Lord of the Animals, who features in Continental Celtic iconography as the horned god Cernunnos.

5. Mabon mab Modron, counterpart of Lleu, 'was stolen from between his mother and the wall when only three nights old'.[86]

Illtud remains in his womb-like cave for the curious 'space of one year and for the space of three days and nights in addition'. The repetitive phraseology suggests that the year was added to an original ritualistic three days and nights – possibly in order to magnify the term of Illtud's endurance.

---

83   H. Rackham, W. H. S. Jones, and D. E. Eichholz, (ed.), *Pliny: Natural History* (London, 1938–62), i, pp. 348–50; Sophie Lunais, *Recherches sur la lune, I: Les auteurs latins de la fin des guerres puniques à la fin du règne des Antonins* (Leiden, 1979), pp. 75–76, 100, 127; Thomas V. Gamkrelidze and Vjačeslav V. Ivanov, *Indo-European and the Indo-Europeans: A Reconstruction and Historical Analysis of a Proto-Language and a Proto-Culture* (Berlin and New York, 1995), p. 591.

84   Stella Kramrisch, *The Presence of Śiva* (Princeton, 1981), pp. 38–39; Y. Vernière, 'La Lune, réservoir des âmes', in François Jouan (ed.), *Mort et fécondité dans les mythologies: Actes du Colloque de Poitiers 13–14 Mai 1983* (Paris, 1986), pp. 101–108.

85   Mothers of saints are frequently portrayed as virgins, their impregnation being often accounted for by rape (Elissa R. Henken, *The Welsh Saints: A Study in Patterned Lives* (Cambridge, 1991), p. 24).

86   Bromwich and Simon Evans (ed.), *Culhwch and Olwen*, p. 33.

There are further indications of Lleu's association with a sacred rock. In the earliest recension of the Welsh battle-poem *Y Gododdin*, mention is made of *Llech leutu tut leudvre*, 'the rock of Lleu's tribe'.[87] Evidently this was the talisman of a tribe which revered Lleu with particular devotion. The setting for the poem is the Scottish Lowlands, known in the early mediæval period as *Lleuddiniawn* (afterwards Lothian). The name means 'the Country of Lugu-dūnon, i.e. of the Fort of [the God] Lugus'.[88]

The earlier Life of the sixth-century St Kentigern describes a King Leudonus, from whom *Leudonia* (i.e. *Lleuddiniawn*) takes its name. Like Lleu in *Math uab Mathonwy* and Lug in Irish tradition, Leudonus is slain by a javelin-cast. His followers then erect a carved stone in his memory standing on top of another larger boulder near a hill called *Dumpelder*.[89] Dumpelder is the striking hill of Traprain Law, lying about twenty miles east of Edinburgh, which in Roman and early post-Roman times was the principal fortress of the powerful tribe of the Votadini. At the time of composition of the Life of Kentigern, a stone evidently stood not far from Traprain Law, possibly bearing an inscription believed to commemorate 'Leudonus', i.e. the god Lleu, euhemerized in the *Vita* as a royal nation-founder.

Clearly, not every holy rock was regarded as representing a hearthstone. Equally, it seems likely that this was the case with Lleu. The idea of a baby emerging from a hearthstone could have appeared implausible once the myth evolved into legend, but fortunately this element survives in lightly adapted form in the description of the 'birth' of Goreu in *Culhwch ac Olwen*.

The purpose of this digression is to suggest that the widely attested myth associated with a sacred stone at the heart of the kingdom was known in early Britain, as in early Ireland. The strange story of Goreu in *Culhwch ac Olwen* originated in an account of the birth of the First Man or First King from the sacred hearthstone of the realm. The parallel birth-tales of Lleu and Illtud provide more elaborate versions of the same myth.

The festival of Brigid

Just as the cosmic hearth stood as divine focus of the realm, so the hearthstone of a home provided a microcosmic duplication of that focus. Belief systems comparable to that of the Irish high goddess Brigid are ancient and widespread.

> Totemism, and conceptions [such as?] that of the mythical ancestral mother, as a supernatural protectress of the clan and of its household, the mistress of the fire, the eternal fire, as the centre and the symbol of the community of the clan, are very ancient ideas. We can assume that they go back to a period which may be called 'Early Matriarchal Society', or in terms of archaeology, the 'Aurignacian Period'.

In Manchuria, 'in the eyes of the Amur Ulchi the common fire was the first and foremost sign of fellowship in the clan. Within the fire dwelt the 'mistress of the fire', *poza-mama*.[90]

---

87 John T. Koch (ed.), *The Gododdin of Aneirin: Text and Context from Dark-Age North Britain* (Cardiff, 1997), p. 2. Professor Koch dates composition of the earliest recension to the seventh century (p. lxxi).

88 Ibid., p. 131.

89 Alexander Penrose Forbes (ed.), *Lives of S. Ninian and S. Kentigern. Compiled in the Twelfth Century* (Edinburgh, 1874), pp. 245–46, 249.

90 O. Nahadil, 'Mother Cult in Siberia', in V. Diószegi (ed.), *Popular Beliefs and Folklore Tradition in Siberia* (Bloomington and The Hague, 1968), pp. 459–77. The hypothesis of a matriarchal stage in the evolution

The seventh-century Life of St Patrick by Muirchú describes how the Saint and his followers arrived at Tara at Eastertide, just as King Loegaire mac Níall was celebrating the country's pagan fire festival. Associated with this rite was a custom that anyone in Ireland who ventured to light his fire before that of the king should suffer death. A contest ensued between the king's druids and the Christian missionaries, victory being predictably gained by the latter.[91] It is thought that 'Muirchu has distorted genuine traditions of the Beltaine fire-ritual celebrated on the first of May by placing this feast at Tara rather than Uisnech and making it coincide with the Christian Easter'.[92]

In addition the legal prohibition on anyone's lighting a fire before the royal fire reflects misunderstanding, or rationalization, of the belief that every fire in Ireland derived from the fire ignited on the Hill of Uisneach, at the feast of Beltane. As popular practice in Ireland and Scotland attests, household fires were extinguished and reignited at Beltane. The Patrician account reflects a myth of country-wide reignited fires emanating from a fire blazing at the Centre. That this central fire was the hearth or altar of the high goddess Brigid could not of course be intimated by the seventh-century hagiographer, particularly once Brigid had become venerated as the pre-eminent female Christian saint of Ireland.

The custom survived until a late date in the Scottish Highlands.

The people of North Uist extinguished their own fires and generated a purification fire at Sail Dharaich, Sollas. The fire was produced from an oak log by rapidly boring with an augur. This was accomplished by the exertions of '*naoi naoinear ciad ginealach mac*' – the nine nines of first-begotten sons. From the neid-fire produced on the knoll the people of the parish obtained fire for their dwellings. Many cults and ceremonies were observed on the occasion, cults and ceremonies in which Pagan and Christian beliefs intermingled. 'Sail Dharaich,' Oak Log, obtained its name from the log of oak for the neid-fire being there. A fragment of this log riddled with augur holes marks a grave in 'Cladh Sgealoir,' the burying ground of Sgealoir in the neighbourhood.

Like the sacred fire of Vesta at Rome, the neid-fire was rekindled with a fire-drill – a rite whose sexual connotation was noted earlier. The rite of lighting the neid-fire (*tein eigin*) at Beltane on a hill, from which fire was taken to the hearths of the neighbourhood, perpetuated at a local level the pre-Christian belief that rekindled fires at Beltane originated in Brigid's sacred fire at the Centre of the land.[93]

All this serves to confirm the high antiquity of the Celtic vernal fire-festival throughout Western Europe and beyond:

---

of prehistoric man has however been long discredited.

91 John Gwynn (ed.), *Liber Ardmachanus: The Book of Armagh, Edited with Introduction and Appendices* (Dublin, 1913), pp. 6–8; Kathleen Mulchrone (ed.), *Bethu Phátraic: The Tripartite Life of Patrick* (Dublin, 1939), p. 25–30.

92 Francis John Byrne, *Irish Kings and High-Kings* (London, 1973), pp. 64–65. Cf. Ludwig Bieler (ed.), *The Patrician Texts in the Book of Armagh* (Dublin, 1979), p. 203.

93 Alexander Carmichael (ed.), *Carmina Gadelica: Hymns and Incantations with Illustrative Notes on Words, Rites, and Customs, Dying and Obsolete: Orally Collected in the Highlands and Islands of Scotland* (Edinburgh, 1900–71), i, pp. 167–91; ii, pp. 367–71. Cf. Martin, *A Description of the Western Islands of Scotland*, p. 105; J. G. Frazer, *Balder the Beautiful: The Fire-Festivals of Europe and the Doctrine of the External Soul* (London, 1913), i, pp. 146–60; Seán Ó Súilleabháin, *A Handbook of Irish Folklore* (Wexford, 1942), pp. 79, 324–26, 333–39; Françoise Le Roux and Christian-J. Guyonvarc'h, *Les fêtes celtiques* (Rennes, 1995), pp. 108–11.

When we reflect on the close relation between the Latin and Celtic peoples, as attested by the affinity of their languages, we may allow ourselves to conjecture that the annual renewal of the fire at Rome on the first of March was genetically connected with the annual renewal of the fire in Scotland and Ireland on the first day of May and the last day of October respectively.[94]

Such calendrical rites are widely recorded in Wales.[95] Although evidence for Beltane fires in England is sparse in comparison, references to *Beltancu* payments in the north-east suggest that the tradition survived locally, despite supersession of the Brittonic tongue by English.[96] Besides, it would be implausible to suppose that Britain, with her attested devotion to Minerva (*Brigantia*), did not prior to the Anglo-Saxon conquest celebrate a springtide fire-festival comparable to those of Ireland and Gaul. On the analogy of Ireland, one would expect there to have existed in pre-Christian Britain a central fire of the goddess Brigantia, together with corresponding rites performed each spring at every hearth in the island. Following the Roman occupation, it seems the rite was 'tamed', being relocated from its original site to the splendid Roman temple of Sul Minerva built at Bath.

A unique allusion is found in the *Collectanea Rerum Memorabilium* of the Roman writer Caius Julius Solinus, who lived towards the end of the second century AD. After mentioning the existence of numerous hot springs in Britain, he continues: 'Over these springs the divinity of Minerva presides, and in her temple the perpetual fires never whiten into ash, but when the flame declines it turns into rocky lumps.'[97] The temple is clearly that of Sul Minerva at Bath, and the 'rocky lumps' are plausibly taken for coal from the nearby Mendip mines.[98]

While coals may well have burned on or beside the altar of Minerva, one is left wondering how it was possible to be ignorant of the fact that burned coals turn into ash.[99] Both the writer's description and Giraldus's statement that the ashes of Brigid's similarly perpetual fire never increased suggest confusion arising from hearsay accounts, [100] rather than eyewitness testimony. Moreover, given close functional similarity between the two rites, it is hard not to believe that they are describing parallel phenomena. Precise interpretation remains uncertain, but the similarities are so close between the Irish high goddess Brigid and the goddess Brigantia in Gaul and Britain, whom the Romans knew as Minerva, as to indicate

---

94   Sir James George Frazer (ed.), *Publii Ovidii Nasonis Fastorum Libri Sex: The Fasti of Ovid* (London, 1929), iii, p. 39.

95   Marie Trevelyan, *Folk-Lore and Folk-Stories of Wales* (London, 1909), pp. 22–24; Jonathan Ceredig Davies, *Folk-Lore of West and Mid-Wales* (Aberystwyth, 1911), p. 76.

96   Beltane fires continued in Gloucestershire into the late eighteenth century (Thomas Pennant, *A Tour in Scotland; MDCCLXIX* (London, 1776), p. 111).

97   Joannes Zwicker (ed.), *Fontes Historiae Religionis Celticae* (Bonn, 1934–36), v, p. 90.

98   Sheppard Frere, *Britannia: A History of Roman Britain* (London, 1967), p. 297.

99   It would be pleasing, though speculative, to identify the author with the Solinus who invoked Minerva's punishment of the thief who stole his clothes while he was taking the baths (R. S. O. Tomlin (ed.), *Tabellae Svlis: Roman Inscribed Tablets of Tin and Lead from the Sacred Spring at Bath* (Oxford, 1988), p. 150).

100 *Et cum tanta lignorum strues tanto in tempore sit hic consumpta, nunquam tamen cinis excreuit* (*Proceedings of the Royal Irish Academy*, lii, p. 150).

their ultimate identity. There are also obvious similarities with the perpetual fire at the hearth of the goddess Vesta in Rome.[101]

There exists no evidence for significant settlement at Bath before the foundation of the Roman town of *Aquæ Sulis*, and it is likely that the imperial authorities followed the familiar pattern of *Romanitas*, transferring (and thus co-opting) the cult from its original site to a magnificent temple of their own construction. That is what probably occurred in Gaul, when the sacred centre in the territory of the Carnutes, presided over by the druids, was relocated by Augustus at distant Lyons (*Lugdunum*), in safely Romanized Southern Gaul.[102]

The native Celtic goddess Brigantia must have been revered in Britain long before the arrival of the Romans, together with her perpetual fire at the holy site from which it was transferred by the Roman authorities after the occupation. In Ireland the perpetual fire of Brigid was associated with the national *omphalos* at Uisneach, while the fire of Vesta in Rome burned at the centre of the Roman world. It would be natural to expect, therefore, that the original site of the principal hearth of the British Minerva was located at the Omphalos of Britain.

101　de Vries, *Keltische Religion*, pp. 78–80.

102　J. F. Drinkwater, 'Lugdunum: 'Natural Capital' of Gaul?', *Britannia: A Journal of Romano-British and Kindred Studies* (London, 1974), vi, pp. 139–40.

16

The Destruction and Renewal
of the World

Cyclical renewal in Celtic mythology

The survival of Illtud in the guise of a hawk at *Medgarth* ('middle enclosure'), together with the corresponding association of his Irish avian counterpart, Fintán mac Bochra, with the Irish *omphalos* at the stone of Uisneach, provide exemplary representations of the myth of cyclical renewal. They include the immolation of mankind, the survival at the Centre of a solitary select individual, and the inception of a fresh cycle of humanity with his return. This concept is implicit in the uniquely explicit account of the British *omphalos* preserved in *Cyfranc Lludd a Lleuelys*, where we learn that the uncanny scream brought about universal mortality and dearth every May-day Eve (*pob nos Kalan Mei*). For the disaster to occur *every* year implies that there was a corresponding annual resuscitation. In fact, it is clear that the essential purpose of the story is to recapitulate the mythical underpinnings of rituals to be performed each year, which if correctly implemented anticipate and obviate the threatened cataclysm.

Writing in the reign of the Emperor Augustus,[1] the Greek geographer and historian Strabo reported that 'the druids ... say that men's souls, and also the universe, are indestructible, although both fire and water will at some time or other prevail over them'.[2] This suggests that the souls of men, being immortal, regularly re-emerge after a succession of universal cataclysms ('fire and water'). The doctrine is also implicit in the Roman poet Lucan's rhetorical address to the druids: 'If you sing of certainties, death is the centre of continuous life.' That is to say, intervals of death punctuate the extended life of mankind.[3]

---

1   G. W. Bowersock, *Augustus and the Greek World* (Oxford, 1965), pp. 126–29, 132–33; Katherine Clarke, 'In Search of the Author of Strabo's *Geography*', *The Journal of Roman Studies* (London, 1997), lxxxvii, pp. 92–110).

2   Francesco Sbordone (ed.), *Strabonis Geographica* (Rome, 1963–2000), ii, p. 145. 'Nous voyons un peu mieux ce que les druides ont voulu dire ... quand ils ont prophétisé que, à la fin du monde, régneront seuls le « feu et l'eau » ..., annonce d'un apocalyptique retour aux sources de l'existence' (Françoise Le Roux, 'La courtise d'Etain', *Celticvm XV: Actes du Vᵉ Colloque International d'Études Gauloises, Celtiques et Protoceltiques* (Rennes, 1966), pp. 338–39). The theme of universal destruction by fire and water recurs in many eschatologies (A. J. Wensinck, 'The Semitic New Year and the Origin of Eschatology', *Acta Orientalia* (Oslo, 1923), i, pp. 188–89).

3   D. R. Shackleton Bailey (ed.), *M. Annaei Lucani De Bello Civili Libri X* (Leipzig, 1988), p. 16. The Gaulish Calendar of Coligny has been interpreted as reflecting the life cycle of divinity, which reverts to its beginning after 5355 years (Jean-Michel Le Contel and Paul Verdier, *Un calendrier celtique: Le calendrier gaulois de Coligny* (Paris, 1997), p. 20).

The concept of cyclical renewals of the earth and humanity features in Irish mythology. The most explicit examples are those of the legendary sages Fintán mac Bochra and Tuán mac Cairell. Fintán had lived since before the Flood, surviving it and successive cataclysms which periodically overwhelmed Ireland. By means of shape-shifting powers which transformed him successively into a salmon, an eagle, a hawk, he was enabled to survive in the ocean or sky beyond the desolated earth. During such intervals he remained 'alone in Ireland'. These periodic natural disasters feature as lacunae separating the pseudo-historical five settlements of Ireland, which Fintán's longevity enables him to describe from the beginning.[4]

Fintán is closely associated with Ireland's two Sacred Centres, Tara and Uisneach, whose parallel functions caused them to be likened to paired kidneys in a beast. On his first arrival at Tara, he is accompanied by a retinue

> of eighteen companies, i.e. nine before him and nine behind. And there was not one among them who was not of the seed of Fintán – sons, grandsons and descendants of his was that host.

By this it is implied that he was at once primary descendant and ancestor of the Irish, while his appearance at Tara and subsequently at Uisneach reflects the concept of the destruction and rebirth of the human race at the *omphalos* of the realm.

The number nine is frequently employed in magical contexts, but here the fact that Fintán's forebears and descendants are implicitly divided into bodies of nine appears to reflect the widely recorded belief that dynasties endure for spans of nine generations. The impression conveyed is that of a divine ancestor, a Celtic Adam who reappears at the Centre after each successive destruction of the earth, where he regenerates the human race. The mother of Fintán is called *Bóchra* or *Bóchna* ('Ocean'), while her father's name *Bith* means 'World'.[5] Again, we catch a glimpse of pre-Christian cosmological myth, in which the deity – offspring of a marine mother, who is in turn daughter of a terrestrial grandfather – survives in a watery Otherworld in the shape of a fish or as a bird hovering above the waves, during successive intervals of the world's disappearance beneath the waters. Appropriately, the flood bears Fintán to a refuge called *Tul Tuindi*, a compound meaning 'on the summit of the wave'.[6]

He is said to have married a sister of Lug at *Magh Ráin*, 'a name for the sea'.[7] There may be an element of identification between the two figures, since in *Cath Maige Tuired* Lug, like Fintán, arrives at Tara as renewer of the kingship. In *Math uab Mathonwy*, Lug's Welsh counterpart Lleu succeeds his apparently impotent predecessor Math, reigning after him wisely and well over the

---

4   Kuno Meyer (ed.), 'The Colloquy between Fintan and the Hawk of Achill', in O. J. Bergin, R. I. Best, Kuno Meyer, and J. G. O'Keefe (ed.), *Anecdota from Irish Manuscripts* (Halle and Dublin, 1907–13), i, pp. 24–39; R. I. Best, 'The Settling of the Manor of Tara', *Ériu: The Journal of the School of Irish Learning* (London, 1910), iv, pp. 128–60; R. I. Best, Osborn Bergin, M. A. O'Brien, and Anne O'Sullivan (ed.), *The Book of Leinster Formerly Lebar na Núachongbála* (Dublin, 1954–83), pp. 13–14, 32–33; Joseph Vendryes (ed.), *Airne Fíngein* (Dublin, 1953), pp. 5–7; R. A. Stewart Macalister (ed.), *Lebor Gabála Érenn: The Book of the Taking of Ireland* (Dublin, 1938–56), ii, p. 188.

5   Cf. Venceslas Kruta (ed.), *Les Celtes et l'écriture* (Paris, 1997), pp. 85–86; Claude Sterckx, *Les dieux protéens des celtes et des indo-européans* (Brussels, 1994), pp. 21–29.

6   Vendryes (ed.), *Airne Fíngein*, p. 38.

7   Edmund Hogan, S. J., *Onomasticon Goedelicum: Locorum et Tribuum Hiberniae et Scotiae; An Index, with Identifications, to the Gaelic Names of Places and Tribes* (Dublin, 1910), p. 529.

kingdom. That there existed a British version of the legend is suggested by parallels between the legends of Fintán and Myrddin (Merlin).[8]

A related legend is that of Tuán mac Cairell (*Scél Tuáin meic Chairill*), which includes further revealing details.[9] Like Fintán, Tuán was sole survivor of successive extinctions of the human race in Ireland. In consequence he was similarly enabled to provide eyewitness accounts of the five settlements of the island.[10] According to Tuán, Ireland was first occupied 1,002 years after the Flood by the son of Agnoman and his following. Eventually they were all destroyed by a plague lasting a week. 'Then', recalled Tuán,

> I was fleeing from refuge to refuge and from cliff to cliff, protecting myself from wolves. Ireland was empty for thirty-two years. Age came upon me at last, and I could no longer travel. I was in cliffs and wildernesses, and I had caves of my own.

A new race of people arrived, whom the seer observed from his rocky refuges. One night while asleep he became a wild stag, and thereafter roamed Ireland at the head of a herd of stags. Fresh transformations occurred with successive invasions, as they came in turn to be extinguished. On each occasion, Tuán was the sole survivor, becoming in turn a wild boar, hawk, and fresh-water salmon. In this last guise he barely survived attempts by fishermen and hawks to catch him. Eventually, he was caught and taken to the court of King Cairell. There he was cooked and eaten by the king's wife, so that he entered her womb. In due course he was born as a human baby, prophesied, and in extreme old age (as Christian convention required) baptized by St Patrick.[11]

The story of Tuán combines motifs found elsewhere in early Irish literature. Knowledge of history is explained by the existence of a preternaturally ancient seer, whose participation in past events enables him subsequently to place them on record.[12] Oisín and Caoilte survive their fellow Fenian heroes for centuries, when they recount their exploits to St Patrick.[13] This reflects a familiar mode of hallowing a pagan tale by according it respectability through the blessing of St Patrick. Similarly, the Ulster epic *Táin Bó Cúailnge* was discovered centuries after the events

---

8   Sterckx, *Les dieux protéens des celtes et des indo-européens*, pp. 53–54.

9   The tales of Tuán and Fintán appeared so similar as to lead on occasion to their protagonists' identification (R. A. Stewart Macalister (ed.), *Lebor Gabála Érenn: The Book of the Taking of Ireland* (Dublin, 1938–56), iii, pp. 22, 42; v, p. 224). Elsewhere, the antediluvian survivor who recounts Ireland's history to St Patrick is named *Ruan*, which is presumably a mistake for *Tuán* (John J. O'Meara, 'Giraldus Cambrensis in Topographia Hibernie: *Text of the First Recension'*, *Proceedings of the Royal Irish Academy* (Dublin, 1949), lii, pp. 157–58; David Comyn and Rev. Patrick S. Dinneen (ed.), *The History of Ireland by Geoffrey Keating, D.D.* (London, 1902–14), i, p. 154). In the early ninth-century Glossary of Cormac the lone survivor of the great plague (*duinebad mōr*) is unnamed (Kuno Meyer (ed.), *Sanas Cormaic*', in Bergin, Best, Meyer, and O'Keefe (ed.), iv, pp. 107–8).

10   It is likely that the two themes were originally distinct: (i) annual survival after winter of a solitary representative of the human race; (ii) his function as memorialist of past events, which he is uniquely empowered to recall.

11   Kuno Meyer, 'Mitteilungen aus irischen Handschriften', *Zeitschrift für celtische Philologie* (Halle, 1901), iii, p. 31; John Carey, 'Scél Tuáin meic Chairill', *Ériu* (1984), xxxv, pp. 101–2. For discussions of the text, cf. Alfred Nutt and Kuno Meyer, *The Celtic Doctrine of Re-birth* (London, 1897), ii, pp. 76–82; Christian-J. Guyonvarc'h (tr.), *Textes mythologiques irlandais I* (Rennes, 1980), i, pp. 153–56; *Ériu*, xxxv, pp. 93–100; Kim McCone, *Pagan Past and Christian Present in Early Irish Literature* (Naas, 1990), pp. 75–77.

12   This recalls the Greek myth of Tiresias, whose life Zeus extended for seven generations, conferring on him prophetic knowledge of past, present, and future (Luc Brisson, *Le mythe de Tirésias: Essai d'analyse structurale* (Leiden, 1976), pp. 43–45).

13   Standish H. O'Grady (ed.), *Silva Gadelica: A Collection of Tales in Irish with Extracts Illustrating Persons and Places* (London, 1892), i, pp. 94–95.

it describes, when a poet conjured forth from his grave pillar the hero Fergus mac Róig, a participant in the great cattle raid: 'Fergus then related the whole *Táin* to him, as it happened, from start to finish.'[14]

Tuán's periodic transformation into fish, fowl and animal guise is clearly distinct from this theme, as is the repeated destruction of the inhabitants of Ireland. Each repopulation of Ireland is preceded by a lengthy period when the land is understood to have lain waste, being inhabited only by wild beasts. This must reflect a belief that the appearance of man on earth was preceded by that of animals. This presumption, widespread in early societies, conflicts with biblical tradition, in which the beasts of the field are created after Adam.

Significant in the present context is the theme of recurrent natural disasters depopulating the world, with a single survivor embodying humanity as a whole during lengthy intervening periods, when the earth lies wild and desolate. Tuán's refuges under water as a salmon, in the air as a hawk, and in caves as a boar reflect the concept of an essence of humanity (élan vital) surviving latent within the elements (water, air, earth) until the time arrives for the rebirth of humanity.

The transformation of Fintán and Tuán into hawks during the periods of void intervening between historic cycles recalls the story of Illtud, discussed in Chapter Ten. In an earlier version, the saint became a hawk when his companions were swallowed up by the earth, which enabled him to pass from the earthly realm of Arthur to that of the Glamorganshire princeling *Poul Pennychen*, i.e. Pwyll Pen Annwfn, lord of the Otherworld.

Although the corpus of Welsh traditional lore is markedly sparser than the Irish, it nonetheless preserves lingering intimations of the existence of a belief corresponding to that of the Irish. In *Math uab Mathonwy*, the haughty maiden Arianrhod lays a malign destiny (*tynged*) on her infant son Lleu: 'And I will swear a destiny on him ... that he have never a wife from the race that is on earth now.'[15]

As W. J. Gruffydd commented, perhaps the reference to the 'race that is on earth at this time' pre-supposes a belief that the earth was populated by successive races, differing from each other.[16]

The story of *Branwen* relates how, after mutual slaughter of Britons and Irish in the Meal-bag Hall and the return home of a handful of British survivors, Ireland was depopulated 'save for five pregnant women in a cave in the wastes of Ireland'. In due course they bore five sons who mated incestuously with their mothers, in this way becoming ancestors of the inhabitants of the five provinces of Ireland.[17] While the episode appears to be of Irish origin, its appearance in *Branwen* confirms that the theme was also known in Wales.

---

14   Best, Bergin, O'Brien, and O'Sullivan (ed.), *The Book of Leinster*, p. 1119. Cf. Kevin Murray, 'The Finding of the '*Táin*', *Cambrian Medieval Celtic Studies* (Aberystwyth, 2001), xli, pp. 17–23.

15   *A mi a dynghaf dynghet idaw ... na chaffo wreic uyth, o'r genedyl yssyd ar y dayar honn yr awr honn* (Ian Hughes (ed.), *Manawydan Uab Llyr: Trydedd Gainc y Mabinogi* (Cardiff, 2007), p. 11).

16   W. J. Gruffydd, *Math vab Mathonwy: An Inquiry into the Origins and Development of the Fourth Branch of the Mabinogi with the Text and a Translation* (Cardiff, 1928), p. 251. The same belief appears implicit in the ancient Owl of Cwm Cawlwyd's assertion that the wooded valley in which he dwelt had been destroyed by a race of men (*kenedlaeth y dynyon*). Two successive woods grew up after intervals, suggesting epochs of human habitation interrupted by interludes of silvan desolation (Rachel Bromwich and D. Simon Evans (ed.), *Culhwch and Olwen: An Edition and Study of the Oldest Arthurian Tale* (Cardiff, 1992), p. 32).

17   Derick S. Thomson (ed.), *Branwen uerch Lyr: The Second of the Four Branches of the Mabinogi edited from the White Book of Rhydderch with variants from the Red Book of Hergest and from Peniarth 6* (Dublin, 1961), p. 17. Cf. Cecile O'Rahilly, *Ireland and Wales: Their Historical and Literary Relations*

This anecdote is jocular, conveying appearance of having been 'turned round' in Wales as a scoff at the 'bare-bottomed Irish'. Behind it lies a genuine cosmological tradition of the conclusion of one age and succession of another. Five husbandless women giving birth in the bowels of the earth suggests that, in archaic myth, the ancestors of a renewed race of men were conceived within the (feminine) earth. Again, this recalls the hibernation of the primal ancestor Illtud, '(father of) many tribes)', in a cave.

The eschatological concept of a destructive internecine conflict survived variously by three or seven men, accrued to traditions in Britain of the historical battles of Camlann, Arderydd, and Catraeth, all of which were fought in the sixth century AD. Allusions in early Welsh poetry indicate that these traditionally bloody battles became identified with cosmic annihilation, from which but one or a handful of men escaped. Thus the poet Gruffudd ab yr Ynad Coch, in his elegy on the great Welsh king Llywelyn ap Gruffudd, includes 'many an agonized wail, as at the battle of Camlann' among manifestations of the coming end of the world. Myrddin (Merlin) similarly declares, 'Since the battle of Arderydd, I care not if the sky were to fall, and the sea to overflow' – elemental catastrophes characteristic of the world's ending. At the same time, emphasis on the survival of select individuals implies that, despite the devastating slaughter, perpetuation of the human race is assured.[18]

The legend of Merlin (Myrddin) is particularly apt to the Irish context. Driven insane by the destructive slaughter of Arderydd, he flees to the Forest of Celyddon. There he dwells alone in the wilderness under bitter wintry conditions, becoming closely associated (at times effectively identified) with stags, wolves, and boars.[19]

It is a curious and surely significant fact that the three archetypal British poets (*cynfeirdd*), Myrddin, Taliesin, and Aneirin are each represented as sole survivor of a savagely destructive battle.[20] In addition, Aneirin obscurely depicts himself as confined in a subterranean prison (i.e. cave).[21] This recalls the fact that the two great survivors of the recurring universal cataclysm in Ireland, Fintán and Tuán, were likewise poets. Although these Welsh examples have become largely rationalized and historicized, enough remains of the eschatological theme of destruction and eventual re-emergence to indicate the existence of a myth comparable to instances preserved in more explicit and detailed form in mediæval Irish literature.

(London, 1924), p. 111; Proinsias Mac Cana, *Branwen Daughter of Llŷr: A Study of the Irish Affinities and of the Composition of the Second Branch of the Mabinogi* (Cardiff, 1958), pp. 32–37.

18 Gwenogvryn Evans (ed.), *The Poetry in the Red Book of Hergest*, col. 1417; A. O. H. Jarman (ed.), *Llyfr Du Caerfyrddin gyda Rhagymadrodd Nodiadau Testunol a Geirfa* (Cardiff, 1982), p. 35. Cf. W. J. Gruffydd, 'The Mabinogion', *The Transactions of the Honourable Society of Cymmrodorion: Session 1912–1913* (London, 1913), pp. 38–39; Rachel Bromwich (ed.), *Trioedd Ynys Prydein: The Welsh Triads* (Cardiff, 1978), pp. 160–62, 208–10.

19 Ibid., pp. 469–72. Comparison of battle fury to the sky falling (i.e. cosmic annihilation) was rooted in Celtic tradition (Kenneth Hurlstone Jackson, *The Oldest Irish Tradition: A Window on the Iron Age* (Cambridge, 1964), pp. 13, 31–32; Philip P. Freeman, 'The Earliest Greek Sources on the Celts', *Études Celtiques* (Paris, 1996), xxxii, pp. 32, 37, 43–44. Myrddin's plaint appears to have been overlooked in this context.

20 *The Transactions of the Honourable Society of Cymmrodorion: Session 1912–1913*, p. 56.

21 Angelique Gulermovich Epstein, 'Miscarriages and Miraculous Births in Indo-European Tradition', *The Journal of Indo-European Studies* (Washington, 1994), xxii, p. 156. Patrick K. Ford envisaged Aneirin's confinement as evoking the 'dark place' in which a Welsh or Irish poet sought inspiration for his œuvre ('The Death of Aneirin', *The Bulletin of the Board of Celtic Studies* (Cardiff, 1987), xviii, pp. 41–50).

The concept of history as a series of recurring cycles is found worldwide, and has been comprehensively examined by Mircea Eliade.[22] It is well-attested in Indo-European societies, together with the accompanying theme of periodic destruction of the earth by fire or water.[23] In Vedic India,

> In the history of creation, one day and night of the Immense Being is called a *kalpa*. This day is divided into fourteen parts. One Manu rules over each of these parts, which are called *manvantaras* (reign of a Manu). Each *manvantara* lasts two and a half equinoxial processions, that is, 4,320,000 human years. There are thus fourteen Manus in a *kalpa*, and for the rule of each Manu a different set of the seven sages, different gods, a different Indra, and different avatars appear.[24]

Temporality is born and dies repeatedly throughout eternity:

> The Godhead also destroys the universe, or rather reabsorbs it after having brought it forth. And this occurs both eternally, beyond time – this is the spanda vibration – and cyclically, throughout the recurring cosmic periods of time, the kalpas.[25]

The Calendar of Coligny in Celtic Gaul was designed (presumably by druids) to reflect a similar schema, whereby the life cycle of divinity returns to its beginning after a protracted period.[26] In early Greece, Orphic teaching held that 'only Zeus, the divine aspect of the cosmos as a whole, was eternal, periodically consuming the rest and regenerating them out of himself'.[27]

In Norse mythology the destruction of the world (*Ragnarök*) is heralded by a cruelly savage winter (*fimbulvetr*). However, a man and woman called Líf and Lífðrasir ('Life' and 'Persistent Life')[28] survive *fimbulvetr* by hiding in Hoddmímir's wood, where after universal destruction they raise up a fresh race of men. The implication seems to be that this process is repeated forever.[29]

The concept is found in societies outside Indo-European tradition. In the early Near East, the New Year festival commemorated successive destructions of the earth and its recovery, intervals in creation being marked by flood and dearth.[30] In the distant Americas, the Maya performed rituals representing the symbolic destruction and reconstruction of the world, which was periodically destroyed and recreated by the gods. It was largely for this reason that their

22   Mircea Eliade, *Le mythe de l'éternel retour: Archétypes et répétition* (Paris, 1949), pp. 167–94.

23   Georges Dumézil, *Mythe et Épopée* (Paris, 1968–73), i, pp. 208–57; Christophe Vielle, *Le mytho-cycle héroïque dans l'aire indo-européenne: Correspondances et transformations helléno-aryennes* (Louvain, 1996), pp. 156–58).

24   Alain Daniélou, *Hindu Polytheism* (London, 1964), pp. 326–27. The names of the fourteen Manus and fourteen *manvantaras* are given on pp. 318–19, 327.

25   André Padoux, *Vāc: The Concept of the Word in Selected Hindu Tantras* (New York, 1990), p. 422.

26   Le Contel and Verdier, *Un calendrier celtique*, p. 20.

27   M.L. West, *The Orphic Poems* (Oxford, 1983), p. 113.

28   Jan de Vries, *Altnordisches Etymologisches Wörterbuch* (Leiden, 1961), p. 355.

29   Hans Kuhn (ed.), *Edda: Die Lieder des Codex Regius nebst Verwandten Denkmälern* (Heidelberg, 1962–68), i, pp. 10–14; Anthony Faulkes (ed.), *Snorri Sturluson: Edda; Prologue and Gylfaginning* (Oxford, 1982), pp. 48–53; Tim William Machan (ed.), *Vafþrúðnismál* (Cambridge, 1988), p. 67.

30   *Acta Orientalia*, i, pp. 166–73.

elaborate calendrical system was devised, which calculated the date of the impending universal catastrophe, while structuring and maintaining social institutions. Sacred texts recorded and illustrated these cosmic destructions and re-creations, and it was to ensure that the rebirth of the world duly occurred that rites and beliefs relating to its protection and renewal played so important a part in the Maya priestly cosmology.[31]

The Salmon of Llyn Llyw

Of the various shape-shifting forms adopted by Fintán mac Bóchra and Tuán mac Cairell during those protracted intervals when the world continued desolate and uninhabited, the salmon appears to have been the most significant. Fintán survived the Flood and existed for half a millennium as a salmon, re-emerging in that guise every springtide. In a poem ascribed to him extolling Ireland's Sacred Centre at Tara, the poet and prophet describes himself as 'a salmon not of one stream'.[32] It was also in salmon guise that Tuán was caught and cooked, and eaten by King Cairell's queen. In consequence he was reborn as a seer possessed of universal knowledge. The supernatural sagacity ascribed the salmon in these transformations recalls the Salmon of Linn Feic, a pool in the sacred river Boyne. There it was caught by the hero Fionn mac Cumhaill, who after cooking it acquired the gift of wisdom.[33]

The sacred salmon of Ireland have their counterpart in Welsh legend, in the shape of the Salmon of Llyn Llyw.[34] In the story of *Culhwch ac Olwen*, before he can obtain a series of prescribed Wonders, Arthur is advised that he must first seek out Mabon mab Modron. However, Mabon cannot be found without first discovering his cousin Eidoel mab Aer. Arthur and his host arrive 'at the outer wall of Gliui's fortress, in the place where Eidoel lay in prison' (*hyt yn rackaer Gliui yn y lle yd oed Eidoel yg karchar*). Gliui at first pleads to be left in peace, but eventually agrees to release Eidoel. Arthur then instructs Eidoel, Gwrhyr *Gwalstoed Ieithoedd* ('the Interpreter'), Cai, and Bedwyr to undertake the liberation of Mabon.

They are guided on their way by successive birds and animals, each more ancient than its predecessor, whose explanations Gwrhyr translates to his comrades. Finally, they encounter the Salmon of Llyn Llyw, a pool in the Severn estuary. He explains that he is borne upriver with every flood-tide, until he comes to

> the bend in the wall of Caerloyw' (*hyt ymach mur Kaer Loyw*). He offers to take 'one of you ... on my two shoulders'. And the ones who went on the Salmon's shoulders were Cai and Gwrhyr Gwastad Ieithoedd.

In this way they arrive below the wall of Caer Loyw, beyond which they hear Mabon mab Modron bemoaning his pitiable lot. They then return to Arthur with the news, who promptly orders an assault on the fortress. Meanwhile Cai and Bedwyr sail thither on the

---

31   Karen Bassie-Sweet, *At the Edge of the World: Caves and Late Classic Maya World View* (Norman and London, 1996), pp. 3–4, 9, 33–40, 112, 132–47.

32   Edward Gwynn (ed.), *The Metrical Dindshenchas* (Dublin, 1903–35), i, p. 4. The wise salmon of the Boyne 'is identified with the all-knowing Fintan' (Thomas F. O'Rahilly, *Early Irish History and Mythology* (Dublin, 1946), p. 319).

33   Kuno Meyer, '*Macgnimartha Finn inn so sis*', *Revue Celtique* (Paris, 1882), v, p. 201; John Gregorson Campbell, *The Fians; or, Stories, Poems, & Traditions of Fionn and his Warrior Band* (London, 1891), pp. 19–20, 26–27.

34   John Rhys, *Lectures on the Origin and Growth of Religion as Illustrated by Celtic Heathendom* (London, 1888), pp. 554–55; O'Rahilly, *Early Irish History and Mythology*, p. 319.

'The Salmon of Llyn Llyw approaches Caer Loyw'. [36]

Salmon's back. Arrived at Caer Loyw, Cai breaks through the wall, and bears Mabon on his shoulders back to Arthur.[35]

As is not infrequently the case with the earliest Welsh tales, the narrative contains anomalies and incongruities reflecting authorial attempts to impose consistency and sense on his sources. This process was not always entirely successful, with the rewarding consequence for the modern scholar that surviving textual discrepancies may on occasion be shown to intimate something of what was contained in material no longer extant, which the author adapted to his own requirement.

With regard to the adventure of the Salmon of Llyn Llyw, it is evident that the successive rescues of Eidoel and Mabon represent duplicated versions of a single original. No reason is given why the rescue of Mabon should be dependent on that of Eidoel. Plainly, the paired episodes were closely linked, but in precisely what manner remained obscure to the author. The

35 Bromwich and Simon Evans (ed.), *Culhwch and Olwen*, pp. 31–33.

36 Lady Charlotte Guest (tr.), *The Mabinogion from the Welsh of the Llyfr Coch o Hergest (the Red Book of Hergest) in the Library of Jesus College, Oxford* (London, 1877), p. 259.

name of *Gliui*, owner of the fortress in which Eidoel is imprisoned, is an eponym abstracted from the Old Welsh name of the city of Gloucester (*Cair Gloui* or *Gliui*),[37] where Mabon was likewise confined. In the latter case the city is given the Middle Welsh version of its name, *Caer Loyw*: further intimation that the author drew upon variant versions of what was ultimately the same legend.

Although the Salmon offers to take 'one of you' on his shoulders to Caer Loyw, in the event *two* travel with him. They are identified as Cai and Bedwyr, but since the rescue of Eidoel is a stipulated prerequisite to that of Mabon, it seems likely that it was originally Eidoel who travelled on the Salmon's back. This is confirmed by the fact that his three companions represent likely supernumaries. Gwrhyr 'the Interpreter' is an artificial character introduced to enable Mabon's rescuers to converse with animals and birds, while Cai and Bedwyr (Kay and Bedivere of the Arthurian romances) are Arthur's stock companions in early Welsh literature. Furthermore, Eidoel inexplicably disappears from the narrative at this point. Since it is specifically he who is required for Mabon's rescue, it seems that Eidoel and Mabon were originally one and the same figure.[38]

The Romano-British placename *Glevum* derives from the British word for 'light', 'bright', meaning 'bright place, bright town'.[39] This probably evoked the splendid appearance of the important Roman walled town of Gloucester, situated on the edge of 'Wild Wales'.[40] The name could in turn have led to its becoming identified or confused with the Otherworld glass fortress familiar from early Welsh and Irish tradition,[41] whose pellucid walls symbolized the invisible barrier separating this world from the Other.[42]

In early Irish mythology, as the ancestors of the Irish sailed towards their new homeland, they encountered 'a glass tower (*turrim vitream*) in the midst of the sea, and they used to see persons on the tower and tried to speak to them, and never did they reply'. This was clearly a Tower of the Dead, whose inhabitants were traditionally unable to converse with the living. In Welsh legend Myrddin (Merlin) is represented as withdrawing into a House of Glass (*Tŷ Gwydr*), where he preserved the Thirteen Treasures (i.e. talismans) of the island of Britain. Yet more apt to the account in *Culhwch* is a verse in the early Welsh poem *Preiddeu Annwfn*, 'The Spoils of the Otherworld'. There Arthur is represented as leading an expedition to the Otherworld, in order to rescue a prisoner whose lamentable cries, like those of Mabon in *Culhwch*, are heard afar off. During their journey, Arthur and his

---

37   Ibid., p. 141.

38   Cf. W. J. Gruffydd, *Rhiannon: An Inquiry into the Origins of the First and Third Branches of the Mabinogi* (Cardiff, 1953), p. 97.

39   A. L. F. Rivet and Colin Smith, *The Place-Names of Roman Britain* (London, 1979), pp. 368–69. For the derivation and development of Welsh *gloyw*, 'bright', cf. J. Morris Jones, *A Welsh Grammar: Historical and Comparative* (Oxford, 1913), p. 130; Alexander Falileyev, *Etymological Glossary of Old Welsh* (Tübingen, 2000), p. 62.

40   The hero of the Arthurian romance of *Owein* visited a clearly Otherworld 'shining' (*llywychedic*) fortress (R. L. Thomson (ed.), *Owein or Chwedyl Iarlles y Ffynnawn* (Dublin, 1968), p. 2). In Ireland, Tara was known as the 'gleaming fort', *cathir glan* (Best, Bergin, O'Brien, and O'Sullivan (ed.), *The Book of Leinster*, p. 113).

41   Roger Sherman Loomis, *Arthurian Tradition & Chrétien de Troyes* (New York, 1949), pp. 89, 456.

42   Time being suspended in immortality, man undergoes the illusion of attaining the Otherworld in which he is in reality already immersed (Christian-J. Guyonvarc'h and Françoise Le Roux, *Les Druides* (Rennes, 1986), p. 288).

men arrive at 'the Glass Fort' (*Caer Wydyr*), with whose six thousand (i.e. multitudinous) inhabitants they are mysteriously inhibited from conversing.[43]

Clearly, it is in the context of an Otherworld stronghold that *Caer Loyw* features as the site of Mabon's imprisonment in *Culhwch ac Olwen*. Mabon mab Modron ('Son, son of Mother') is an important figure in pagan Celtic mythology. He is the Divine Son, who is identified with Christ in a mediæval Welsh poem.[44] In *Culhwch ac Olwen* he is described as having been 'stolen from between his mother and the wall when only three nights old' (*a ducpwyt yn teir nossic ody rwng y vam a'r paret*).[45] Thus, in this tradition he was abducted as a newborn infant and held in the Otherworld (the 'Shining City' of *Caer Loyw*), until the moment arrived for his delivery and restoration to this world. This recalls the abduction of Mabon's *alter ego* Lleu in *Math uab Mathonwy*, who vanished over the winter in eagle guise to reappear in the spring.

Again, the motif recalls the birth of Pryderi in the story of *Pwyll*, the First Branch of the *Mabinogi*. On the same night that his mother Rhiannon gave birth, the child mysteriously vanishes. Meanwhile, in a distant kingdom a baby is discovered in equally singular circumstances in the stable of King Teyrnon. He is named Gwri Goldenhair (*Gwri Wallt Euryn*), but as he grows his resemblance to Rhiannon's husband Pwyll becomes so striking that Teyrnon takes him to Pwyll's court. There it is realized that he is Rhiannon's child. He is renamed Pryderi, and brought up as Pwyll's heir.[46]

There can be little doubt that this legendary tale reflects a pagan myth of the birth of the Divine Son (Gwri-Mabon) to the Divine Queen (Rhiannon < *Rigantona*). In *Culhwch* Arthur is associated with *Mabon mab Mellt* ('Mabon son of Lightning') and *Gware Gwallt Eurin* ('Gware Golden Hair'), who appear to be one and the same figure.[47] The name *Gwri* (of which *Gware* is probably an orthographic variant) reflects Brittonic *Wironos, 'the divine man, hero'.[48]

Concern here is with the motif of the abduction of the infant deity. His disappearance at birth in one kingdom, and simultaneous appearance in another, reflects transposition between the Otherworld and that of mortal men, which is what might be expected of the Christ-like figure of Mabon, 'the Divine Son'. The unexplained allusion in *Culhwch* to his having been 'stolen from between his mother and the wall' recalls an element of the birth-tale of Lleu in *Math uab Mathonwy*, a figure corresponding to that of Mabon. The goddess Arianrhod comes to the court of Gwydion, where she lets fall a small object *in the doorway*. This was the embryo of the infant Lleu, who grows up under the care of his putative father Gwydion.[49]

As was observed earlier, the doorway represents a liminal point of access between this world and the Other. Thus, the strange allusion to the abduction of Rhiannon's baby son beside an unexplained wall originated in misunderstanding of his passage through the supernatural

---

43   Theodor Mommsen (ed.), *Monvmenta Germaniae Historica* (xiii): *Chronica Minora saec. IV. V. VI. VII* (Berlin, 1894), iii, p. 155; Eurys I. Rowlands, 'Y Tri Thlws ar Ddeg', *Llên Cymru* (Cardiff, 1958), v, pp. 52–53; J. Gwenogvryn Evans (ed.), *Facsimile & Text of the Book of Taliesin* (Llanbedrog, 1910), p. 55.

44   Ibid., p. 47.

45   Bromwich and Simon Evans (ed.), *Culhwch and Olwen*, p. 31.

46   R. L. Thomson (ed.), *Pwyll Pendeuic Dyuet: The First of the Four Branches of the Mabinogi edited from the White Book of Rhydderch with variants from the Red Book of Hergest* (Dublin, 1957), pp. 17–18, 20–22.

47   Bromwich and Simon Evans (ed.), *Culhwch and Olwen*, p. 36.

48   John T. Koch, 'Gleanings from the *Gododdin* and other Early Welsh Texts', *The Bulletin of the Board of Celtic Studies* (Cardiff, 1991), xxxviii, pp. 112–13.

49   Ian Hughes (ed.), *Manawydan Uab Llyr: Trydedd Gainc y Mabinogi* (Cardiff, 2007), p. 8.

barrier dividing the celestial court of Rhiannon from Teyrnon's terrestrial hall in Gwent. This could also account for the curious emphasis in *Culhwch* on the manner in which the rescuers of Eidoel/Mabon initially arrive at 'Gliui's outer wall' and 'the bend in the wall of Caerloyw', rather than entering the city itself.

The function of the myth, which in *Pwyll, Math*, and *Culhwch* becomes an inadequately explained transfer of the infant hero from his mother's Otherworld realm to that of an earthly potentate, was to account for a divine Virgin Birth. The Wonder Child is conceived in the Otherworld, and born in this. In *Math* it is unmistakably the divine embryo which is transferred, and it is likely that this was originally the case with the birth-tales in *Pwyll* and *Culhwch*.[50]

Thus the adventure of the Salmon of Llyn Llyw at Caer Loyw represents a garbled retelling of pagan myth.[51] Originally the divine embryo or soul-creature is required to be 'rescued' from the Otherworld, in order that the Divine Son may be born on earth. That this was accomplished through an abduction possibly reflects the fact that parturition is a moment of peril to a mother, frequently requiring outside intervention for its accomplishment.

The pagan Celtic doctrine of Incarnation

Other considerations support this interpretation. First, there is the intriguing figure of the Salmon of Llyn Llyw. It is he who plays the central part in the extraction of Mabon from the Shining City, in order to restore him to the retinue of King Arthur. In his introductory explanation, the Salmon recounts how the Eagle of Gwernabwy extracted 'fifty tridents from his back', implicitly thrust into him by predatory fishermen. He further explains that he travels upriver to Caer Loyw 'with every tide'.

The gratuitous reference to the Salmon's savage wounding by fishermen's weapons recalls the parallel Irish account of Tuán mac Cairell, who explained that, during his time spent as a salmon,

> I escaped from every peril: from the hands of fishermen ... and the spears of fishers (*a gaaíb iascaire*), so that the wounds of them are in me.

Again, the ascent of the Salmon of Llyn Llyw 'with every tide' (*gan bob llanw*) echoes Fintán mac Bóchra's becoming a salmon 'in every spring' (*hi richt égne ar gach n-úarán*). The primary river inhabited by Fintán as a salmon was the Boyne, one of the two holiest rivers of Ireland. In Britain the corresponding sacred stream was the Severn,[52] home of the Salmon of Llyn Llyw. Furthermore, in each case the holy salmon dwells in a pool of the river.

Tuán and Fintán were transformed into salmon, in order to survive cataclysmic floods engulfing the earth. They embodied the soul-matter, which is preserved and transmitted to fresh races of men as each cycle of the world dies and revives. This concept is paralleled on a macrocosmic level by the belief of the early Irish that every individual possesses a fish of life

---

50   This process is made all but explicit in accounts of the birth of the Irish hero Cú Chulainn (A. G. van Hamel (ed.), *Compert Con Culainn and Other Stories* (Dublin, 1933), pp. 3–8). Cf. the enlightening analyses by Christian-J. Guyonvarc'h and Françoise Le Roux, 'La conception de Cúchulainn', *Ogam: Tradition celtique* (Rennes, 1965), xvii, pp. 363–410.

51   'L'épisode ... de Mabon ab Modron avec son saumon nous mène en plein préhistorique' (J. Loth, *Contributions à l'Étude des Romans de la Table Ronde* (Paris, 1912), p. 50).

52   R. I. Best, Osborn Bergin, M. A. O'Brien, and Anne O'Sullivan (ed.), *The Book of Leinster Formerly Lebar na Núachongbála* (Dublin, 1954–83), p. 860.

(*an t-éasc*), which was understood to circulate within the blood. Also known as the 'salmon of life' (*an bradán beatha*), it was regarded as transmitter of the life force from generation to generation.[53] In the Irish romance of 'The Pursuit of Diarmaid and Gráinne', when Gráinne meets Diarmaid her salmon of life is described as nearly popping out of her mouth in her excitement at seeing her lover.[54]

The regular journey made by the Salmon of Llyn Llyw up the holy river Severn to the Shining City of Caer Loyw suggests a macrocosmic image of the human life-cycle, in which the 'salmon of life' repeatedly voyages between divine inception in the oceanic Otherworld to birth in this world, and eventual return to the realm of eternity. The relationship of this concept to the myth of Mabon mab Modron, with which it is associated in *Culhwch*, should now be obvious.

Originally, it seems, Mabon mab Modron was the liberated prisoner. His name and myth are well-attested in pagan Celtic tradition, in contrast to Eidoel, who features uniquely as Mabon's *alter ego* in *Culhwch*. But where did the alternative name *Eidoel* originate? Given telling indications that the episode of *Culhwch* in which he features reflects the Celtic doctrine of the soul, a likely explanation is that it represents a learned borrowing, either from Latin īdōlum, *eidōlon*, or from the original Greek *eidolon* (εἴδωλον), 'the soul' or 'shade of the departed'.[55] In the *Odyssey*, Odysseus encounters the εἴδωλον of his dead mother; reference is made to 'the asphodel meadows where the ghosts (ψυχαί) dwell, the spectres (εἴδωλα) of those who have died'; while the εἴδωλον of Herakles languishes in Hades, as he himself feasts with the gods on Olympus. Pindar alludes to 'an image of life' (αἰῶνος εἴδωλον), which survives corporeal death.[56]

Any borrowing of īdōlum into British with the meaning 'soul' must have occurred at an early date, since following the introduction of Christianity the word took on the biblical meaning of a pagan

53 Bo Almqvist, 'Fylgyor, livsfjärilar och livsfiskar: Några bidrag till isländsk-irisk själstro', in Ailbhe Ó Corráin (ed.), *Proceedings of the Third Symposium of Societas Celtologica Nordica held in Oslo 1-2 November 1991* (Uppsala, 1994), pp. 132–34, 137–39. A parallel belief is recorded in Iceland (ibid., pp. 139–40). Cf. Seán Ó Súilleabháin, *A Handbook of Irish Folklore* (Wexford, 1942), p. 178. In Brittany on 1 April villagers invoked 'le «peskik avril, petit poisson d'avril»' (L.-F. Sauvé, '*Formulettes et traditions diverses de la Basse-Bretagne*', *Revue Celtique*, v, p. 189). The French expression *poisson d'avril* corresponds to 'April Fool' in English, but evidently had an older meaning.

54 Nessa Ní Shéaghdha (ed.), *Tóruigheacht Dhiarmada agus Ghráinne: The Pursuit of Diarmaid and Gráinne* (Dublin, 1967), p. 28.

55 Hjalmar Frisk, *Griechisches Etymologisches Wörterbuch* (Heidelberg, 1954–72), i, p. 452.

56 Helmut van Thiel (ed.), *Homeri Odyssea* (Hildesheim, 1991), pp. 146, 160; Bruno Snell (ed.), *Pindari Carmina cvm Fragmentis* (Leipzig, 1964), ii, p. 111. 'On death the ψυχή escapes from the boy, now merely dead matter; the soul, which made life possible, lives on in Hades as an εἴδωλον, with the outward form of the human body which it had once imbued with life. Thus Odysseus had recognized the ψυχή of his mother, and indeed assumed that the ψυχή was his mother' (Alfred Heubeck, Stephanie West, J. B. Hainsworth, and Arie Hoekstra, *A Commentary on Homer's Odyssey* (Oxford, 1988–92), ii, p. 90); cf. p. 114. Cf. further Jan Bremmer, *The Early Greek Concept of the Soul* (Princeton, 1983), pp. 78–80, 81, 83; Michael Clarke, *Flesh and Spirit in the Songs of Homer: A Study of Words and Myths* (Oxford, 1999), pp. 195–205.

statue or image.[57] It is likely, therefore, that it was introduced into Britain during the Roman occupation, which saw much syncretism between British and Roman religious practice and terminology.[58]

That *Eidoel* derives from *eīdōlon* is suggested by a further passage in the episode in *Culhwch ac Olwen*. Following Arthur's successful plea for the delivery of Eidoel mab Aer from Caer Gliui, there comes this curious exchange:

> His men said to Arthur, 'Lord, go home. You cannot go with your army to seek **a thing so small as this** (*Ny elly di uynet a'th lu y geissaw peth mor uan a'r rei hynn*)'.

Arthur does not respond to this urging, which remains unexplained and unpursued. The context indicates that the allusion is to the prisoner (*carcharawr*) Eidoel. But since he has just been liberated, what is the point of the protest? More significantly, what was the 'small thing' which his followers pronounced too trivial to justify Arthur's quest? This odd description is scarcely appropriate to the warrior Eidoel.

However, given that *Eidoel* appears to have been originally a shade or spirit surviving in the Otherworld, who was reborn as the Adamite progenitor of mankind at the conclusion of cosmic winter, one is reminded once again of the account of the birth of Lleu in *Math uab Mathonwy*. There the virgin Arianrhod leaves 'a small something' (*y ryw bethan*) with Gwydion ap Don, which after incubation becomes the infant Wonder Child Lleu. The 'small something' was clearly an embryo soul-creature generated in the Otherworld, as Arianrhod's liminal stance in Gwydion's doorway indicates.[59] The descriptive term also evokes the *míl bec*, that 'tiny creature', which grew into the divinely-conceived Irish hero Cú Chulainn.

The incongruous disappearance of Eidoel from the narrative in *Culhwch* has been noted, following his release from the castle of Gliui. Although it is earlier asserted that the liberation of Mabon is dependent on that of Eidoel, in the event the latter figure plays no part in the exploit. At the same time, the context suggests that the Salmon's offer to take one man on his shoulders to seek out Mabon at Caer Loyw was originally directed at Eidoel. All these anomalies are effectively reconciled, if it be understood that the Salmon was originally the migratory soul-spirit, *which was also known by the loanword Eidoel* (i.e. the soul), which passes at regular intervals ('with every tide') between this world and the Otherworld stronghold of *Caer Gliui*. At another level, an earlier version could have related the myth of the birth of Mabon, which is significantly alluded to when the necessity for rescuing (i.e. facilitating the birth of) Mabon is first expounded in *Culhwch*.

---

57 A. Ernout, A. Meillet, and Jacques André, *Dictionnaire étymologique de la langue latine: Histoire des mots* (Paris, 1994), p. 306. Ídol ab idolo, idos [εἶδος] *isin grēic, forma isin laitin. Unde idolum .i. delba 7 arracht[a] inna [n]dūlæ dognītis in geinti* (Bergin, Best, Meyer, and O'Keefe (ed.), *Anecdota from Irish Manuscripts* (Halle and Dublin, 1907-13), iv, p. 63). The earliest insular usage of biblical idolum (i.e. pagan image) is found in St Patrick's *Confessio* (Ludwig Bieler (ed.), *Libri Epistolarum Sancti Patricii Episcopi* (Dublin, 1952), i, p.78).

58 Cf. Christian-J. Guyonvarc'h, 'Notes d'étymologie et de lexicographie gauloises et celtiques XXXII', *Ogam* (1969), xxi, pp. 315–30. Traces may have survived of the older meaning. The seventeenth-century lexicographer John Davies identified Welsh *ellyll* ('ghost, spirit') with '**idolum**, *spectrum, lemures, larvae*' (*Dictionarium Duplex Brittanico Latinum* (London, 1632)). 'Idolum, Delu, lhŷn, eilyn, ʒaydhelu. *An image, an idol; also a false imagination*' (Edward Lhuyd, *Archæologia Britannica, Giving some Account Additional to what has been hitherto Publish'd, of the Languages, Histories and Customs Of the Original Inhabitants of Great Britain* (Oxford, 1707), p. 67).

59 Hughes (ed.), *Math Uab Mathonwy*, p. 8. Cf. Claude Stercckx, 'Les Têtes Coupées et le Graal', *Studia Celtica* (Cardiff, 1985–1986), xx/xxi, p. 26.

17

The Collapsing Castle and the Sacred Centre

Geoffrey's adaptation of Nennius

Consideration was paid earlier to Geoffrey of Monmouth's account of the treacherous massacre of British nobles by Hengist's Saxons. The besotted British tyrant Vortigern agreed with the Saxon warlord to bring a delegation to confer with him and his followers at the forthcoming Calends of May (*kalendis Maii*), on Salisbury Plain (*in pago Ambrii*). The treacherous barbarian arranged for his followers to secrete knives about their persons, with which at a prearranged signal they were to slaughter the hapless Britons. The ruse proved successful: despite a valiant resistance, 460 unarmed Britons fell. Apart from Vortigern, whom Hengist held fast by his cloak, there was but one survivor. This was a doughty Briton named Eldol, Earl of Gloucester (*consul Claudiocestriae uocabulo Eldol*), who grabbed a stake he found lying to hand, slew seventy of the enemy, and escaped to his own city. The victims were subsequently given Christian burial by St Eldad (*beatus Eldadus*) at a spot near Salisbury, Hengist occupied virtually all of what is now England and Wales, while the pusillanimous Vortigern sought a haven in the rugged mountains of North Wales. After the tyrant's death, his successor Aurelius arranged for Merlin and Uther Pendragon to bring the Giants' Dance from Ireland, and erect it as a memorial to the fallen *in monte Ambrii*.[1]

Geoffrey's principal source for this episode was the *Historia Brittonum*, compiled by the North Welsh monk Nennius in the early ninth century. While his story follows much the same pattern as that subsequently recounted by Geoffrey, the latter adds details not found in the former. Neither the date nor place of the massacre is specified in Nennius's version, which also makes no mention of Eldol and Eldad, nor any allusion to the erection of Stonehenge as a memorial to the tragedy.[2]

While Geoffrey coloured the event with his customary dramatic embroidery, reasons were given in Chapter Four for concluding that he drew on independent traditional lore attached to Stonehenge. As a day commemorative of near-universal slaughter, the Calends of May accords with British tradition, as does an implicit association with *Maes Beli*, a likely name for the pagan

---

1   Michael D. Reeve and Neil Wright (ed.), *Geoffrey of Monmouth: The History of the Kings of Britain* (Woodbridge, 2007), pp. 135–37, 171–74. The *pagus Ambrii* is presumably Salisbury Plain, and the *mons Ambrii* that gentle hill on which the stones from Ireland were erected.

2   Theodor Mommsen (ed.), *Monvmenta Germaniae Historica* (xiii): *Chronica Minora saec. IV. V. VI. VII* (Berlin, 1894), iii, pp. 189–90.

realm of the dead. Geoffrey further altered Nennius's figure of 300 British nobles interred on the spot to 460: a figure broadly corresponding to the number of prehistoric burial mounds clustered in the plain around Stonehenge. Finally, he locates the burial of Hengist beneath a barrow called *Cunengeburg*, which surely represents an allusion to Coneybury Hill, the most striking henge monument in the immediate vicinity of Stonehenge.

Before drawing the threads together, two further episodes in Geoffrey's *Historia* repay consideration.

1. §§106–108. On Vortigern's withdrawal to Wales, his druids advise him to build a fortress beside Snowdon. However, no matter how much work is accomplished during the day, the structure is mysteriously cast down at night. The druids advise the king to sacrifice a fatherless child, whose blood sprinkled on the stones will prevent its further destruction. Messengers eventually find the infant Merlin, who is brought before Vortigern, and only avoids being sacrificed by revealing the mystery of the two *vermes* concealed within the foundations of the building.

2. §§128–30. After expelling the Saxons and killing Hengist, Vortigern's heroic successor Aurelius Ambrosius decides to erect an appropriately magnificent memorial to the victims of the slaughter on Salisbury Plain. However, although we have just learned that his carpenters and masons industriously restored cathedrals and churches the length and breadth of Britain, they now unaccountably declare themselves incapable of the task. The Archbishop of Caerleon then explains to the king that the man capable of fulfilling it is Merlin. Aurelius despatches messengers in search of the prophet, who eventually discover him and bring him before the king. Merlin explains that the solution is to transfer the stones of the Giants' Dance from Ireland. The operation proves successful, and the stones stand secure upon the spot for all eternity (*stabunt in aeternum*).

Similarities between Geoffrey's account of Vortigern's collapsing castle, and that of the subsequent erection of Stonehenge, are so close as to suggest that they represent divergent versions of a common legendary corpus. The following motifs are common to both episodes.

1. A unique building is planned, but is prevented by a mysterious power from being completed.
2. The king is told that this seemingly insuperable obstacle can be overcome by inviting Merlin to provide a solution.
3. Merlin initially proves hard to trace, but is eventually tracked down.
4. His retreat lies in South Wales.[3]
5. His mantic perception enables him to frustrate the destructive occult force, and the structure is successfully erected.

This further confirms that Geoffrey drew on more than one early legend of Stonehenge.

---

3   In the case of the Stonehenge episode, *in nationem Gewisseorum*, a region erroneously located by Geoffrey in South Wales (J. S. P. Tatlock, *The Legendary History of Britain: Geoffrey of Monmouth's Historia Regum Britanniae and its Early Vernacular Versions* (Berkeley and Los Angeles, 1950), pp. 74–75).

Merlin Ambrosius

In the *Historia Brittonum* the Fatherless Boy brought to Vortigern's castle is called *Ambrosius*. While Geoffrey in other respects follows the earlier account fairly closely, he calls the prophetic boy *Merlin*, and in consequence locates his home at Carmarthen, the Welsh name for which is *Caerfyrddin*, which he took for 'the fortress of Myrddin'. The prophet Merlin (Welsh *Myrddin*) was a potent figure in Welsh tradition long before Geoffrey compiled his work.[4] Geoffrey reconciles the apparent discrepancy in names by describing the youthful seer as 'Merlin, who was also called Ambrosius', *Ambrosius Merlinus*.[5]

It might be supposed that Geoffrey introduced this conjuncture in order to justify an arbitrary substitution of Merlin for Ambrosius. But that appears not to be the case, since a Welsh poem dating from well over a century before Geoffrey's day invokes a wizard named *Merddin Emrys*.[6] Sir John Rhŷs commented:

> In order to approach the original conception our course is clear: we must give all the attributes of Emrys and the Merlins to one Merlin Emrys; but this is only theoretically clear, as the process is disturbed by the historical element introduced in the person of Aurelius Ambrosius, who may possibly be regarded as in a sense responsible for some of the chief difficulties in our way, looked at from a mythological point of view.[7]

Graham Isaac has presented a persuasive case for treating the Welsh name *Myrddin* as a compound proper noun **Myrddyn*, meaning 'ghost, spirit, wraith' (*ellyll*) + *dyn*, 'man'. His patronymic *Morfryn*, found in early Welsh verse, may be interpreted as 'mountain spirit' – an apt enough appellation, given Myrddin's association in early poetry with *gwyllion y mynydd* ('mountain spectres').[8]

The pre-Galfridian Myrddin saga depicts the seer as driven to frenzy during the bloody battle of Arderydd near Carlisle, from which he flees north to the forest of Celyddon, where he dwells among mountain ghosts. This suggests a symbolic representation of withdrawal to the Otherworld. As early as the sixth century AD, the wilderness beyond Hadrian's Wall was regarded in Britain as a land inhabited by the dead.[9] The realm of the departed was frequently conceived as a wintry northern wilderness.[10] In the Welsh prophetic poem *Hoianau*, Myrddin is described as spending the nights of his exile in the Coed Celyddon, immersed in snow up to his hips and icicles in his hair. It is the season when the the earth has become barren:

---

4   Nikolai Tolstoy, 'Geoffrey of Monmouth and the Merlin Legend', in Elizabeth Archibald and David F. Johnson (ed.), *Arthurian Literature XXV* (Cambridge, 2008), pp. 1–42.

5   Reeve and Wright (ed.), *Geoffrey of Monmouth: The History of the Kings of Britain*, p. 141.

6   Thomas Jones, 'The Black Book of Carmarthen "Stanzas of the Graves"', *The Proceedings of the British Academy* (London, 1967), liii, p. 136. Jones considered the *englynion* in Peniarth MS 98 (one of which contains the mention of *Merddin Emrys*) to be 'at least as old as those in the Black Book' (p. 99), and that the *englynion y beddau* as a whole were composed 'probably as early as the ninth or tenth century' (p. 100).

7   John Rhys, *Lectures on the Origin and Growth of Religion as Illustrated by Celtic Heathendom* (London, 1888), p. 152.

8   Graham R. Isaac, 'Myrddin, Proffwyd Diwedd y Byd: Ystyriaethau Newydd ar Ddatblygiad ei Chwedl', *Llên Cymru* (Cardiff, 2001), xxiv, pp. 13–23.

9   H. B. Dewing (ed.), *Procopius* (London, 1914–40), v, pp. 264–66.

10   Lowry Charles Wimberly, *Folklore in the English & Scottish Ballads* (Chicago, 1928), pp. 136–38, 413.

> The meadows are my barn, my corn is not plenteous.
> My summer store does not sustain me.[11]

Myrddin's patronymic *Morfryn*, 'mountain spirit', possibly reflects the tradition that he underwent a species of living death within a rock. The romantic story of the enchanter Merlin's enticement into a tomb by the sensual Ninien or Vivien may likewise have originated in a legend of his withdrawal into a rock, or mountain. Variously described as a stone, or stone chamber, in the heart of a forest, it was a magical place of incarceration, the key to which was known to the seer's beautiful seductress.[12]

In Continental Arthurian romance the site was variously located in the forests of Brochéliande and Darnantes, in Brittany. In Britain a tradition located it in Cornwall:

> And merwelus merlyne is wastede away
> Wyth A wykede womane – woo mycht sho be! –
> Scho has closede him in a cragge of cornwales coste,

as a Middle English poem delightfully puts it. A Merlin's Rock is recorded at Mousehole in Cornwall, which may reflect this legend.[13]

Whilst exaggerated claims by earlier scholars have provoked justified scepticism regarding wilder assertions of the Celtic origins of Arthurian romance, the incarceration of Merlin appears to justify the hypothesis in a specific instance.[14] In the first place, the name of Merlin's seductive nemesis, which appears variously in the French romances as *Niniene* and *Viviane*, was shown by Professor Jarman to have originated in a misunderstanding of Welsh *hwimleian*. This word, meaning '(prophetic) wild man', features in Welsh vaticinatory verse ascribed to Myrddin, and came to be misinterpreted (still in a Welsh context) as (a) feminine, and (b) a proper noun.[15]

Secondly, Merlin's final resting place in Continental romances, described variously as a stone tomb, chamber, and even *la plus bele tour del monde*, bears every indication of representing a refinement on the Celtic concept of the Otherworld realm located within a rock or mountain. That the motif existed in Welsh tradition is indicated by Myrddin's withdrawal among mountain

11   A. O. H. Jarman (ed.), *Llyfr Du Caerfyrddin gyda Rhagymadrodd Nodiadau Testunol a Geirfa* (Cardiff, 1982), pp. 29–35. One stanza exceptionally declares that 'the thorns are flowering, the mountainside is green, the earth is beautiful'. However, the poem as a whole is characterized by images of deprivation and suffering, and this passage reads like an intrusive snatch of nature poetry.

12   Gaston Paris and Jacob Ulrich (ed.), *Merlin: Roman en prose du XIIIᵉ siècle* (Paris, 1886), ii, pp. 191–99; H. Oskar Sommer (ed.), *Le Roman de Merlin or the Early History of King Arthur: Faithfully Edited from the French MS. Add. 10292 in the British Museum (About A.D. 1316)* (London, 1894), pp. 483–84; Elspeth Kennedy (ed.), *Lancelot do Lac: The Non-Cyclic Old French Prose Romance* (Oxford, 1980), i, pp. 23–24; Alexandre Micha (ed.), *Lancelot: Roman en prose du XIIIᵉ siècle* (1978–83), vii, pp. 41–43; Lucy Allen Paton, *Les Prophecies de Merlin: Edited from MS. 593 in the Bibliothèque Municipale of Rennes* (New York, 1926), i, pp. 487–88; Eugène Vinaver (ed.), *The Works of Sir Thomas Malory* (Oxford, 1948), p. 126.

13   James A. H. Murray (ed.), *The Romance and Prophecies of Thomas of Erceldoune* (London, 1875), p. xxxii; Robert Hunt, *Popular Romances of the West of England; or, The Drolls, Traditions, and Superstitions of Old Cornwall* (London, 1865), i, p. 198.

14   Cf. Lawrence E. Eson, 'Merlin's Last Cry: Ritual Burial and Rebirth of the Poet in Celtic and Norse Tradition', *Zeitschrift für celtische Philologie* (Tübingen, 2006), lv, pp. 180–200.

15   A. O. H. Jarman, 'A Note on the Possible Welsh Derivation of *Viviane*', in R. H. Spencer (ed.), *Gallica: Essays presented to J. Heywood Thomas by colleagues, pupils and friends* (Cardiff, 1969), pp. 1–12. For the treatment of Viviane in the Continental romances, cf. Paul Zumthor, *Merlin le Prophète: Un thème de la littérature polémique de l'historiographie et des romans* (Lausanne, 1943), pp. 240–60.

shades (*gwyllion*), as also by a prophetic poem entitled *Gwasgargerdd Fyrddin yn y bedd*, 'The Diffused Song of Myrddin in the Grave'. This poem, which dates from the early decades of the twelfth century,[16] is too early to have been influenced by Continental romance literature. In French Arthurian romances, Merlin is described as speaking to mortals from his tomb,[17] which recalls the theme employed in the Welsh poem.

In Celtic tradition the Otherworld is frequently located within a rock or mountain. Cadbury Castle, the Dark Age hillfort in Somerset traditionally associated with King Arthur, was reputedly hollow: a belief no doubt originating in the concept of the King's residence within a subterranean hall.[18] Location of the Otherworld inside a hill or mountain is likely to be autochthonous, whilst being also widely attested in shamanistic cosmologies.[19]

Further to Merlin's entombment, he is described as uttering a cry (*brais*) from his place of incarceration, which was heard throughout all Britain (*Logres*), wreaking marvels which the author regrettably fails to specify. A similar scream was heard when Perceval seated himself on the Siege Perilous, which brought such darkness upon the land that it was impossible to see beyond a league. At the same time, a mysterious voice pronounced that the enchantment would not be lifted from the land of Britain until the Fisher King had been asked the appropriate question concerning the Grail. This destructive scream is also found in the German romance of *Lanzelet*, in the context of an uncanny swamp which, three days before the summer solstice, utters a shriek heralding general mortality of beasts.[20] Allusions in French Arthurian romances indicate that a *Conte del Brait*, now unfortunately lost, described Merlin's sad end and final cry.[21]

This shriek or similarly baneful sound, frequently prefacing or accompanying a disastrous affliction on the land, is almost certainly of Celtic origin. The usual Welsh terms are *diaspat* and *twrwf*, among whose most striking instances are the mysterious outcry wreaking mortality on

16   *Arthurian Literature XXV*, pp. 35–36.

17   Sommer (ed.), *Le Roman de Merlin*, pp. 493–94.

18   John Rhys, 'Welsh Fairy Tales', *Y Cymmrodor* (London, 1883), vi, pp. 184–86; Rev. J. A. Bennett, 'Camelot', *The Proceedings of the Somersetshire Archæological and Natural History Society* (Taunton, 1890), xxxvi, pp. 2–3; Wimberly, *Folklore in the English & Scottish Ballads*, pp. 132–34; Seán Ó hEochaidh, Máire Mac Neill, and Séamas Ó Catháin (ed.), *Síscéalta ó Thír Chonaill: Fairy Legends from Donegal* (Dublin, 1977), pp. 38, 40, 60, 62, 64, 70, 76, 78, 172–78, 220–22; Theo Brown, *The Fate of the Dead: A Study in Folk-Eschatology in the West Country After the Reformation* (Cambridge, 1979), p. 70; Marie-Thérèse Brouland, *Le Substrat celtique du lai breton anglais Sir Orfeo* (Paris, 1990), pp. 208–19.

19   Reidar Th. Christiansen, *The Dead and the Living* (Oslo, 1946), pp. 88-93; Olof Petterson, *Jabmek and Jabmeaimo: A Comparative Study of the Dead and the Realm of the Dead in Lappish Religion* (Lund, 1957), p. 173; Carmen Blacker, 'Initiation in the Shugendo: The Passage through the Ten States of Existence', in C.J. Bleeker (ed.), *Initiation: Contributions to the Theme of the Study-Conference of the International Association for the History of Religions Held at Strasburg, September 17th to 22nd 1964* (Leiden, 1965), pp. 97-99; eadem, *The Catalpa Bow: A Study of Shamanistic Practices in Japan* (London, 1975), pp. 80-84. In *Eyrbyggja Saga* Thorstein's shepherd sees the north side of the mountain Helga Fell opened, revealing Thorstein feasting within among a joyous company. It transpires that he had just died from drowning (Forrest S. Scott (ed.), *Eyrbyggja Saga: The Vellum Tradition* (Copenhagen, 2003), p. 30).

20   Paris and Ulrich (ed.), *Merlin*, ii, p. 198; William Roach (ed.), *The Didot Perceval: According to the Manuscripts of Modena and Paris* (Philadelphia, 1941), pp. 149-51; Florian Kragl (ed.), *Ulrich von Zatzikhoven: Lanzelet* (Berlin, 2006), i, p. 396.

21   James Douglas Bruce, *The Evolution of Arthurian Romance: From the Beginnings Down to the Year 1300* (Göttingen, 1928), i, pp. 480-82; F.C. Johnson, 'An Edinburgh Prose Tristan: the 'Bret'', *The Modern Language Review* (Cambridge, 1933), xxviii, pp. 456-64; Fanni Bogdanow, *The Romance of the Grail: A Study of the Structure and Genesis of a Thirteenth-Century Arthurian Romance* (Manchester, 1966), pp. 51-54, 55, 67-68, 85.

men and beasts and dearth of crops in *Cyfranc Lludd a Lleuelys*, and the noise like thunder which similarly heralded the reduction of prosperous Dyfed into a Wasteland in *Manawydan uab Llŷr*.

An early Welsh triad records that Britain was first known as *Clas Myrddin*: 'The first Name which this Island bore, before it was taken or settled: *Clas Myrddin*,' i.e. 'Myrddin's Precinct, or Enclosure.'[22] The word *clas*, in Welsh and Irish, means 'earthen rampart', a synecdoche for enclosed space surrounded by a ditch and earth wall. The word derives from Celtic **klado-s*, 'what is dug'.[23] The context suggests an archaic conception of balance between microcosm and macrocosm. The island is envisaged in terms of a fortified enclosure. Here Sir John Rhŷs's comment is suggestive:

> In this Triad, which must be the echo of an ancient notion, the pellucid walls confining Merlin become, by a touch of the pencil of the mythic muse, co-extensive with the utmost limits of our island home.[24]

Merlin's association with ritual activities conducted at the Omphalos of Britain, whether Dinas Emrys or Stonehenge, suggests the possibility that the name *Clas Myrddin* was also applicable to the central precinct, whose bounds differentiated between sacred space at the Centre, and profane space without. When Lludd and Lleuelys measure Britain to establish its exact centre, they find that 'the properties of this particular place allowed the king to overcome the *gormes* which was causing (among other things) the total failure of the fecundity of his realm'.[25] That is to say, the Centre fulfilled its characteristic function of a microcosm of the land of Britain. In Chapter Thirteen, I sought to demonstrate that Oxford in *Cyfranc Lludd a Lleuelys* represents a mediæval substitution for Stonehenge, the original Centre (*pwynt perued*) of Britain.

Some years ago, in my book *The Quest for Merlin*, I endorsed the suggestion that Myrddin (Merlin) was one of the *cynfeirdd*, the primary bards of Britain who flourished in the sixth century. Graham Isaac's interpretation of the seer's name as **Myrddyn*, 'ghost, spirit, wraith', suggests that it may also have been employed as a generic appellation. His sudden appearances and disappearances suggest a being possessed of supernatural qualities. In addition, the key rôle ascribed him in ensuring the deposition of Vortigern, the conception of Arthur, and the establishment of Stonehenge as burial-place of kings, suggests a druidic or brahman-like figure, central to the ideology of sacral kingship: the 'Divine Druid'.[26] It seems likely that the figure of

---

22   *Kyntaf hen6 a uu ar yr ynys hon. kynnoe chael nae chyuanhedu: glas merdin* (Egerton G. B. Phillimore, 'A Fragment from Hengwrt MS. No. 202', *Y Cymmrodor* (London, 1887), vii, p. 124; John Rhŷs and J. Gwenogvryn Evans (ed.), *The Text of the Mabinogion and other Welsh Tales from the Red Book of Hergest* (Oxford, 1887), p. 309).

23   J. Lloyd-Jones, *Geirfa Barddoniaeth Gynnar Gymraeg* (Cardiff, 1931–63), p. 143; E. G. Quin *et al.* (ed.), *Dictionary of the Irish Language: Based mainly on Old and Middle Irish Materials* (Dublin, 1913–76), 'C', cols. 222–23. Cf. Eric P. Hamp, '*Clas*: Lucus a non lucendo', in Kathryn A. Klar, Eve E. Sweetser, and Claire Thomas (ed.), *A Celtic Florilegium: Studies in Memory of Brendan O Hehir* (Andover, Mass., 1996), pp. 40–42.

24   Rhys, *Lectures on the Origin and Growth of Religion as Illustrated by Celtic Heathendom*, p. 168.

25   John T. Koch, 'A Welsh Window on the Iron Age: Manawydan, Mandubracios', *Cambridge Medieval Celtic Studies* (Cambridge, 1987), xiv, p. 48. 'The central point of the island is represented as the cockpit in which is enacted the crucial struggle between cosmic order and its antithesis and the knowledge of it enables the king to secure his kingdom against the supernatural power of the *gormes* that threatens the vigour of its men and the fertility of its land and its womenfolk' (Proinsias Mac Cana, *The Cult of the Sacred Centre: Essays on Celtic Ideology* (Dublin, 2011), p. 199).

26   Guyonvarc'h and Le Roux, *Les Druides*, pp. 335–40; Françoise Le Roux and Christian-J. Guyonvarc'h, *Les fêtes celtiques* (Rennes, 1995), p. 174.

Merlin represents a composite of interwoven strands of early history and legend, together with a substratum of archaic myth.

In Ireland the mythical King Conaire is described as being raised to the kingship by spectres (*siabrai*), and later deposed by them when he violated taboos fundamental to maintenance of the institution.[27] Similarly, the name of another mythical Irish King Ailill is cognate with Welsh *ellyll*, 'phantom' or 'spirit'. It has been suggested that 'Ailill was originally another term for the figure of the father-deity presiding over the institution of kingship'.[28] That the figure of Merlin fulfilled some such function in early Britain is consistent with the traditional relationship of king and druid in early Celtic society.[29]

The child sacrifice and the fighting creatures

In Geoffrey of Monmouth's *Historia Regum Britanniæ* the name of Merlin has replaced that of the prophetic child Ambrosius who features in the *Historia Brittonum* of Nennius. As has already been noted, the two names were linked before Geoffrey wrote. The Stanzas of the Graves (*englynion y beddau*) include this verse:

> Bedd ann ap lleian ymnewais fynydd,
> lluagor llew Ymrais,
> Prif ddewin Merddin Emrys.
> The grave of the nun's misfortune on Newais mountain
> Causing gaps in a host, lion of Emrais;
> Chief diviner, Myrddin Emrys.

The *englynion y beddau* in Peniarth MS 98, which contain this verse, are 'at least as old as those in the Black Book [of Carmarthen]', which were composed 'probably as early as the ninth or tenth century'.[30] The Welsh word *dewin*, which derives from Latin *divinus*, 'diviner, prophet',[31] at times retained its original meaning, at others the looser sense of 'sage' or 'sorcerer'. The insinuation (if it be so) that Myrddin was son of a nun (i.e. a virgin) intimates that his paternity was unknown, i.e. he was born of a divine father and mortal mother.[32]

---

27 Lucius Gwynn, 'De Síl Chonairi Móir', *Ériu: The Journal of the School of Irish Learning* (Dublin, 1912), vi, p. 136; Eleanor Knott (ed.), *Togail Bruidne Da Derga* (Dublin, 1936), p. 8.

28 Dáithi Ó hÓgáin, *The Sacred Isle: Belief and Religion in Pre-Christian Ireland* (Woodbridge, 1999), pp. 181–82.

29 Guyonvarc'h and Le Roux, *Les Druides*, pp. 107–20.

30 *The Proceedings of the British Academy*, liii, pp. 99, 100, 136; Geoffrey himself describes the seer as *Merlinus, qui et Ambrosius dicitur* (Reeve and Wright (ed.), *Geoffrey of Monmouth: The History of the Kings of Britain*, p. 141). The term *anap y lleian* is explained by Patrick Sims-Williams, 'anfab² 'illegitimate child': a ghost-word', *The Bulletin of the Board of Celtic Studies* (Cardiff, 1978), xxviii, pp. 90–93.

31 Henry Lewis, *Yr Elfen Ladin yn yr Iaith Gymraeg* (Cardiff, 1943), p. 9; Stefan Zimmer, 'Dating the loanwords: Latin suffixes in Welsh (and their Celtic congeners)', in Alfred Bammesberger and Alfred Wollmann (ed.), *Britain 400–600: Language and History* (Heidelberg, 1990), p. 277. Myrddin was already famed as a prophet in the early tenth century (Sir Ifor Williams and Rachel Bromwich (ed.), *Armes Prydein: The Prophecy of Britain From the Book of Taliesin* (Dublin, 1972), p. 2).

32 It is unclear whether 'the nun's misfortune' reflects a birth-tale of Myrddin Emrys, or an independent tale. Although Geoffrey of Monmouth's account of Merlin's parentage is evidently his own invention, the virgin birth motif is applied in the *Historia Brittonum* to Ambrosius (= Emrys). The theme is a familiar one. The mother of St David was a virgin named *Nonnita* (cf. Latin *nonn*, 'nun'), who was ravished by a king named *Sanctus* ('Holy One') on the occasion of her son's conception, but otherwise

The story of Ambrosius and Vortigern contained in §§40–42 of the *Historia Brittonum* originated in a saga distinct from the remainder of Nennius's work. §38 describes how Hengist assured Vortigern that he could count on his Saxons as allies against 'any man or any nation' (*non timebis te superari ab ullo homine neque ab ulla gente*). §39 interrupts the narrative to recount a contention between Vortigern and St Germanus, which concludes with the tyrant's flight when he is cursed and condemned by the Saint and council of the Britons: *maledictus est et damnatus a sancto Germano et omni Brittonum concilio.*[33]

§40 begins with Vortigern summoning his druids (*magi*), in order to seek their advice as to what he should do. They counsel him to withdraw to the remotest part of his kingdom, where he would find a fortified citadel (*arcem munitam invenies*) in which he might be safe from the nation he had invited into the kingdom (i.e. the Saxons). Their intent was to kill him and conquer the entirety of his realm. Accordingly, the king and his druids traverse many regions, before eventually arriving among the mountains of *Heriri* (Snowdonia) in Gwynedd. There the king finds a site on one of the mountains, suitable for construction of a fortress. His druids concur with the choice, advising him to 'make a citadel in this place, for it will be most safe from barbaric nations forever'.

The contradictions embedded in this section of the *Historia Brittonum* are self-evident. In §39 the adversaries who compel Vortigern's withdrawal are his British compatriots, with no indication of a Saxon presence in Britain. From acting as his trusty allies against the Picts and Scots in the preceding §38, in §§40–42 the Saxons incongruously appear on the point of conquering the entire island of Britain. In §43, however, they have reverted to occupying no more than a toe-hold in eastern Kent, where they wage a losing campaign against Vortigern's son Vortimer.

The Snowdonian episode's incompatability with the preceding and succeeding chapters is unmistakable, and the story of the Fatherless Boy and the Fighting Dragons must be of independent provenance.[34] As H. M. Chadwick noted over a century ago,

> §§40-42 seem to form a distinct episode. Guorthigirnus appears here as a heathen, and though there is a reference to the invaders, they are not called *Saxones*, as elsewhere, but *gens Anglorum*.[35]

As a native of Gwynedd, Nennius was well-placed to have heard the story recited, whether in his monastery (at Bangor?), or at the court of King Merfyn Frych. He records visits he paid to other

---

remained chaste (J. W. James (ed.), *Rhigyfarch's Life of St. David: The Basic Mid Twelfth-Century Latin Text with Introduction, Critical Apparatus and Translation* (Cardiff, 1967), pp. 3–4). In the Latin *Vita* her name appears only once, following which she is identified simply as *mater*. In the Welsh Life she is introduced as *lleian* ('nun'), with the (glossed?) parenthetical explanation *enw a lleian oed Nonn*: 'the name of the nun was Nun' (!) (D. Simon Evans (ed.), *The Welsh Life of St David* (Cardiff, 1988), p. 2). Thereafter she is twice called Nonn, but overall it looks as though she was originally an unidentified virgin.

33 Mommsen (ed.), *Chronica Minora*, iii, pp. 180–81.

34 Edmond Faral, *La légende arthurienne - Études et documents* (Paris, 1929), i, 113–14. The story is clearly of Welsh provenance: Sir Ifor Williams likened its use of dramatic dialogue to that employed in *Manawydan uab Llŷr* ('Hen Chwedlau', *The Transactions of the Honourable Society of Cymmrodorion: Sessions 1946-1947* (London, 1948), p. 50).

35 H. Munro Chadwick, *The Origin of the English Nation* (Cambridge, 1907), p. 39. Cf. Edmond Faral, *La légende arthurienne - Études et documents* (Paris, 1929), i, pp. 113–14.

sites in Wales, in order to inspect local supernatural phenomena.[36] Given that Gwynedd was his homeland, it seems not unlikely that he journeyed to the historic site of the prophetic encounter. His description of the cistern at Dinas Emrys conceivably indicates personal observation,[37] although he could of course have heard recitations of *chwedlau* associated with Dinas Emrys at any time and place. It is stories such as this to which Nennius refers in his preface as 'the tradition of our elders' (*ex traditione ueterum nostrorum*), which he distinguishes from his literary sources.[38]

In his account of Vortigern and the child Ambrosius, Nennius conflates two motifs that must originally have been distinct. First, there is the belief in human sacrifice as an efficacious rite conducted to ensure the sustaining of a structure. In early times this was on occasion actually practised,[39] and survives as a theme in Celtic literature.[40] Both aspects are recorded in numerous cultures around the world.[41] It is suggested that they reflect the concept of a divine being sacrificed at the beginning of time, whose body became converted into natural features of the earth. Each foundation sacrifice undertaken thereafter was believed to perpetuate the original sacrifice, so ensuring the stability of the structure with which it was associated.[42]

Although local Centres were regarded as microcosmic *omphaloi*, the rite of sacrifice and its accompanying myth were primarily linked to the *omphalos* of the country, which stood for that of the whole world. Thus, Golgotha was regarded as Centre of the earth, where it was held that Christ's blood sprinkled on Adam's skull buried beneath Him redeemed the First Man.[43] The legend of Romulus's slaughter of his brother Remus on completion of the wall around

---

36   Mommsen (ed.), *Chronica Minora*, iii, pp. 216, 218.

37   'The 'pavement over a pool' of the *Historia Brittonum* would seem to have a real existence and the author was referring to a recognized feature on the hilltop of Dinas Emrys' (Brynley F. Roberts (ed.), *Cyfranc Lludd a Llefelys* (Dublin, 1975), p. xxxviii). Cf. H. N. Savory, 'Excavations at Dinas Emrys, Beddgelert (Caern.), 1954–56', *Archaeologia Cambrensis* (Cardiff, 1960), cix, p. 56.

38   Rachel Bromwich (ed.), *The Beginnings of Welsh Poetry: Studies by Sir Ifor Williams, D.Litt., LL.D., F.B.A.* (Cardiff, 1980), p. 72, 'On trouve à la base de ce chapitre une légende topographique' (Ferdinand Lot, *Nennius et l'Historia Brittonum: Étude critique suivie d'une edition des diverses versions de ce texte* (Paris, 1934), p. 178). David Dumville aptly termed the saga 'the folkloristic … 'dinnshenchas' of Dinas Emrys' ('The Historical Value of the *Historia Brittonum*', *Arthurian Literature* (Cambridge, 1986), vi, pp. 20, 23).

39   Whitley Stokes (ed.), *Lives of Saints from the Book of Lismore* (Oxford, 1890), p. 30; Kuno Meyer (ed.), 'Sanas Cormaic: An Old-Irish Glossary', in O. J. Bergin, R. I. Best, Kuno Meyer, and J. G. O'Keefe (ed.), *Anecdota from Irish Manuscripts* (Halle and Dublin, 1907–13), iv, p. 42; R. I. Best, Osborn Bergin, M. A. O'Brien, and Anne O'Sullivan (ed.), *The Book of Leinster Formerly Lebar na Núachongbála* (Dublin, 1954–83), pp. 1051–52. Cf. Lot (ed.), *Nennius et l'Historia Brittonum*, pp. 89–90; Guyonvarc'h and Le Roux, *Les Druides*, pp. 70–74.

40   Donald Atkinson, *The Roman-British Site on Lowbury Hill in Berkshire* (Reading, 1916), pp. vii–viii, 7–11, plate IIIA; Sir Ian Richmond, *Hod Hill* (London, 1968), ii, p. 16, plates 6, 7A; Leslie Alcock, ''Excavations at South Cadbury Castle, 1969', *The Antiquaries Journal* (London, 1970), l, pp. 16–17, 23–24; John C. Barrett, P. W. M. Freeman, and Ann Woodward, *Cadbury Castle Somerset: The later prehistoric and early historic archaeology* (London, 2000), pp. 67–69. 'The general character of the burial suggested that it was a dedicatory sacrifice intended to bless the later rampart' (Leslie Alcock, '*By South Cadbury is that Camelot …*': The Excavation of Cadbury Castle 1966-1970 (Aylesbury, 1972), p. 103, plate 31).

41   S. Baring-Gould, *Strange Survivals: Some Chapters in the History of Man* (London, 1892), pp. 1–35; S. R. Driver, *Modern Research as illustrating the Bible* (London, 1909), pp. 69–72; Sir James George Frazer, *Taboo and the Perils of the Soul* (London, 1911), pp. 90–91; Alexander Heggarty Krappe, *Balor With the Evil Eye: Studies in Celtic and French Literature* (Columbia, 1927), pp. 65–81; Myles Dillon, 'The Archaism of Irish Tradition', *The Proceedings of the British Academy* (London, 1947), xxxiii, pp. 256–59.

42   A. M. Hocart, *Kingship* (Oxford, 1927), pp. 192–95; Mircea Eliade, *Forgerons et alchimistes* (Paris, 1956), pp. 31–33; J. Gonda, *Prajāpati and the Year* (Amsterdam, 1984), p. 85; Jaan Puhvel, *Comparative Mythology* (Baltimore, 1987), pp. 284–90.

43   Mircea Eliade, *Patterns in Comparative Religion* (London, 1958), p. 375.

newly founded Rome is believed to reflect a myth of foundation sacrifice. In Britain, the burial of St Odran in order to sustain St Columba's church at Iona reflects the unique sanctity of the island. Its concentration of royal burials is explained by a prophecy that Iona would alone survive the final flood at the world's end.[44]

Not far from Stonehenge lies the intriguing site known as Woodhenge. Postholes indicate it to have been a massive wooden circular structure erected in the third millennium BC.[45] At an early stage of excavation a remarkable discovery occurred at the site.

> Though much simpler and ruder in its design and lay-out than Stonehenge, Woodhenge shows many points of resemblance to it, one of the most striking being that the only burial was in a grave occupying the same relative position to the rings that the "altar" stone does to the circles at Stonehenge.

The burial was that of a young child, about three years of age, whose skull had apparently been cleft before burial, thus suggesting that the burial was in the nature of a dedicatory or sacrificial act.[46]

This conclusion has recently been challenged on grounds that 'the skull could have collapsed naturally along the bone's sutures under the pressure of earth from above, rather than being damaged by a deliberate blow'. It is also suggested 'that the child was not buried here by the Neolithic builders but was added in the Early Bronze Age, when the wooden monument would have been decayed ruins'.[47] Neither objection can be regarded as conclusive. Since the bones were destroyed by enemy bombing in the Second World War, any attempt to refute Mrs Cunnington's conclusions (and those of her experienced doctor husband) must remain speculative. Moreover, given extensive evidence for child sacrifice as means of ensuring the permanence of a building, coupled with the fact that the Woodhenge interment is the only one found at the site, it is hard not to suppose that the burial was intended for some especial purpose appropriate to such an exceptional structure.

The find has been linked to a comparable one at Stonehenge.

In 1926, Hawley discovered a burial at the centre of Stonehenge. This had been badly disturbed by earlier riflings but the pit lay along the major NE-SW axis of the monument

---

44   Thomas Pennant, *A Tour in Scotland and Voyage to the Hebrides. MDCCLXXII. Part I.* (London, 1776), pp. 284–85; Alexander Carmichael (ed.), *Carmina Gadelica: Hymns and Incantations with Illustrative Notes on Words, Rites, and Customs, Dying and Obsolete: Orally Collected in the Highlands and Islands of Scotland* (Edinburgh, 1900–71), ii, p. 348. Cf. Aidan MacDonald, 'Aspects of the Monastic Landscape in Adomnán's Life of Columba', in John Carey, Máire Herbert, and Pádraig Ó Riain (ed.), *Studies in Irish Hagiography: Saints and Scholars* (Dublin, 2001), pp. 15–30. Belief in the destruction of mankind by an universal flood seven years before the Day of Judgment is recorded by Tírechán in seventh-century Ireland (John Gwynn (ed.), *Liber Ardmachanus: The Book of Armagh, Edited with Introduction and Appendices* (Dublin, 1913), p. 30). Cf. Richard Irvine Best and Hugh Jackson Lawlor (ed.), *The Martyrology of Tallaght: from the Book of Leinster and MS. 5100-4 in the Royal Library, Brussels* (London, 1931), p. 96.

45   R. J. C. Atkinson, *Stonehenge* (London, 1956), p. 176; Alex Gibson, *Stonehenge & Timber Circles* (Stroud, 1998), pp. 100–104.

46   M. E. Cunnington, *An Introduction to the Archæology of Wiltshire from the Earliest Times to the Pagan Saxons* (Devizes, 1934), p. 61. Cf. V. Gordon Childe, *Prehistoric Communities of the British Isles* (London, 1940), p. 108; Atkinson, *Stonehenge*, pp. 170–71; Gibson, *Stonehenge & Timber Circles*, pp. 95–96. A fragment of a child's skull and associated bones were found at Uisneach, the corresponding Irish *omphalos* (Roseanne Schot, 'From cult centre to royal centre: monuments, myths and other revelations at Uisneach', in Roseanne Schot, Conor Newman, and Edel Bhreatnach (ed.), *Landscapes of Cult and Kingship* (Dublin, 2011), p. 105).

47   Mike Parker Pearson, *Stonehenge: Exploring the Greatest Stone Age Mystery* (London, 2012), p. 85.

and was marked by a post. This recalls the child sacrifice at Woodhenge, marked by a cairn in the centre of the monument and aligned on the main axis. The Stonehenge burial cannot be dated, but the multiple postholes, the central axially aligned burial, and the abundant animal remains do suggest a closer parallel with Woodhenge than has hitherto been admitted.[48]

That human sacrifice occurred at Stonehenge is more surely attested by another deposition. In this case, the remains are clearly datable to the Bronze Age, and show that the victim was killed by being shot with flint-headed arrows.[49] The method is of considerable interest, since the Roman geographer Strabo relates that a method of sacrifice employed by the druids involved shooting their victim with arrows.[50] While it is unlikely that there were druids identifiable as such at Stonehenge during the Bronze Age, as with other religions there was a marked tendency among the Celts to incorporate archaic artefacts for ritual purposes.[51]

No trace of human sacrifice was found during the excavation of Dinas Emrys. It may well be that the theme of the sacrificial victim in the *Historia Brittonum* became attached to the site in a purely legendary context. In the *Historia Brittonum* the distinct legends of the Fatherless Boy and the Fighting Dragons are awkwardly linked, and must originally have constituted independent traditions attached to Dinas Emrys. The more archaic version found in *Cyfranc Lludd a Lleuelys* has nothing to say about the need for human sacrifice. Furthermore, this aspect peters out unsatisfactorily in Nennius's version. In the event, the boy is *not* sacrificed as had been required, for which no good reason is given. Instead, he expounds the mystery of the Fighting Dragons. That this exposes the druids' ignorance is scarcely sufficient reason for their proposal to be abandoned, and in the event Vortigern is unaccountably reduced to meekly obeying the child's injunction that he depart and seek refuge elsewhere. In fact, Vortigern's departure to another fortress in north Wales reflects no more than the author's awareness of a site named *Nant Gwrtheyrn* ('Valley of Vortigern') in the peninsula of Lleyn. The site of a stronghold in the valley, associated in later tradition with Vortigern, was very likely the *Cair Guorthigirn* known to Nennius.[52]

§41 of the *Historia Brittonum* relates how the king's messengers scoured the country until they discovered a boy with the requisite qualification at *campus Elleti*, in the region of Glywysing (*in regione, quae vocatur Gleguissing*). This principality lay in south Wales, but the *campus Elleti* has eluded identification. It is possible that the site was originally to be found in the Otherworld, or

48   Gibson, *Stonehenge & Timber Circles*, p. 117.

49   Rosamund M. J. Cleal, K. E. Walker, and R. Montague (ed.), *Stonehenge in its landscape: Twentieth-century excavations* (London, 1995), p. 456; Barry Cunliffe and Colin Renfrew (ed.), *Science and Stonehenge* (Oxford, 1997), p. 29; Gibson, *Stonehenge & Timber Circles*, pp. 94–95.

50   Francesco Sbordone (ed.), *Strabonis Geographica* (Rome, 1963–2000), ii, p. 146.

51   Stuart Piggott instanced 'the golden sickle for the cutting of the mistletoe, which Fox has plausibly equated with one of gilded bronze in the Late Bronze Age style' ('The Sources of Geoffrey of Monmouth II. The Stonehenge Story', *Antiquity: A Quarterly Review of Archaeology* (Gloucester, 1941), xv, p. 315). In *Culhwch ac Olwen*, the giant Ysbaddaden hurls three poisoned stone (-headed) spears at Culhwch and his companions (Rachel Bromwich and D. Simon Evans (ed.), *Culhwch and Olwen: An Edition and Study of the Oldest Arthurian Tale* (Cardiff, 1992), pp. 19–21). Cf. Inger Zachrisson, 'Can Grave Customs be Taken over by One Ethnic Group from Another?', in Mihály Hoppál and Juha Pentikäinen (ed.), *Northern Religions and Shamanism* (Budapest, 1992), p. 12; John Pairman Brown, *Israel and Hellas* (Berlin, 1995–2001), ii, pp. 219–20, 241–42. However, it is not wholly certain that the body found at Stonehenge was that of a sacrificial victim: for alternative possibilities, cf. Pearson, *Stonehenge*, pp. 195–96.

52   Melville Richards, 'Nennius's 'Regio Guunnessi'', *Caernarvonshire Historical Society: Transactions* (Caernarvon, 1963), xxiv, pp. 21–27.

at a terrestrial location possessed of Otherworld connotations. The boy's mysterious birth and precocious mantic gifts indicate an essentially supernatural figure. Interesting parallels are to be found in the Irish tale 'The Adventures of Art son of Conn' (*Echtra Airt meic Cuind*).[53]

Conn, king of Ireland, banishes his son Art from Tara and Ireland for the space of a year. When the time passes without provision of corn or milk throughout Ireland, Conn summons his druids to account for the dearth. They explain that it is caused by the sinfulness of Conn's wife, a beautiful Otherworld maiden named Becuma. The sole cure, they continue, is for the son of a sinless couple to be brought to Ireland, where he should be slain before Tara, and his blood mingled with the soil of Tara. Leaving Art to rule in his place, Conn accordingly sets forth in search of the sinless boy. Setting sail from Benn Edair (the Hill of Howth), he reaches the Land of Promise (*Tir Tairrngaire*). The island and its royal hall are filled with wonders, confirming its identification with the Happy Otherworld. There Conn meets Segda Saerlabraid, the youthful son of its king and queen. He explains to the royal couple that he has come in search of the son of a sinless couple. To this the king responds that, in accordance with the custom of the fairy realm, he and the queen slept together but once, on the occasion of Segda's conception. (This looks like a rationalization of the bride's original rôle as a virgin). They reluctantly agree to permit their son to journey with Art to Tara.

On his return, Conn's druids advise him to slay the youth, and sprinkle his blood over the afflicted earth and produce. At this point, a woman arrives, bringing a cow which she offers as a substitute sacrifice. At the same time, she challenges the druids to declare what is contained in two bags borne by the beast. To this they confess their bafflement. After the cow is killed and its blood poured over the soil of Ireland and the doors of Tara, the woman requires the bags to be opened. They prove to contain two birds, one with one leg, and one with twelve. They fight with each other, and to the surprise of the onlookers the one-legged bird proves the victor. Explaining that the twelve-legged bird represents the king's druids, the woman urges Conn to have them hanged. It is not stated whether this in fact occurs. After vainly urging the king to put aside his wife, the woman departs with Segda, who is revealed to be her son.[54]

While the (literally) lame anecdote of the fighting birds may reflect the battling *cruim* found in the Irish translation of the *Historia Brittonum*, in other respects the story bears every appearance of being original.[55] Where the British tale is at pains to rationalize the child's lack of a father, the Irish version more authentically assigns him a supernatural origin.

The version of the discovery of the battling 'dragons' contained in *Cyfranc Lludd a Lleuelys* contains no hint of child sacrifice. The incongruous manner in which the latter motif is integrated into Nennius's story suggests that he found it independently attached to the site of

---

53　Faral, *La légende arthurienne*, i, p. 117; Lot, *Nennius et l'Historia Brittonum*, pp. 89-90; Guyonvarc'h and Le Roux, *Les Druides*, pp. 70–74.

54　R. I. Best, 'The Adventures of Art son of Conn, and the Courtship of Delbchæm', *Ériu* (1907), iii, pp. 154–62. The story is listed in early mediæval catalogues (Proinsias Mac Cana, *The Learned Tales of Medieval Ireland* (Dublin, 1980), p. 53).

55　Dáithi Ó hÓgáin's suggestion that the episode as a whole represents a borrowing from the Irish *Historia Brittonum* seems excessive (*The Sacred Isle: Belief and Religion in Pre-Christian Ireland* (Woodbridge, 1999), p. 48). Myles Dillon suggested a common Indo-European motif ('The Archaism of Irish Tradition', *The Proceedings of the British Academy* (London, 1947), xxxiii, pp. 257–59). The theme recurs on so widespread a basis as possibly to derive from an even earlier stratum of myth. Kim McCone preferred a borrowing from the infant Jesus's demonstration of precocious wisdom in the temple (*Pagan Past and Christian Present in Early Irish Literature* (Naas, 1990), pp. 17–18). However, this ignores the close parallels with *Cyfranc Lludd a Lleuelys*.

Dinas Emrys and awkwardly sought to integrate it into the discrete theme of the prophetic exegesis of the mystery of the 'dragons' (*vermes*).

It is evident from the confused wording of the *Historia Brittonum* that the prophetic child was unnamed in Nennius's source. Great emphasis is laid on the fact that, in accordance with the druids' requirement, he should have no father. His mother's declaration that she was a virgin, never having known a man, qualified him for the druids' purpose. Throughout the ensuing dialogue between him and the king, he is referred to simply as 'the boy' (*puer*). At its conclusion, the boy firmly insists that Vortigern depart forthwith:

> *tu tamen de ista arce vade … et ego hic manebo.* **Et rex adolescentem dixit: quo nomine vocaris? Ille respondit: Ambrosius vocor, id est, Embreis Guletic ipse videbatur. Et rex dixit: de qua progenie ortus es? At ille: unus est pater meus de consulibus Romanicae gentis.** *et arcem dedit illi …*
>
> 'Nevertheless, go from this citadel … and I will remain here'. **And the king said to the boy, 'by what name are you called?' He replied, 'I am called Ambrosius', that is, he was seen to be** *Embreis Guletic*. **And the king said, 'of what stock are you come?' And he: 'one of the consuls of the Roman nation is my father'.** And he gave him the citadel …

The passage in bold represents an unmistakable gloss, almost certainly added by Nennius himself. It will be recalled that the boy's qualification for becoming a sacrificial victim rested expressly on his *not* having a father – but now he proudly declares his father's name and ancestry![56] But how could he conceivably have known them, when his own mother had declared her ignorance of his paternity? Consistency is restored only if this gloss be removed.

The name and ancestry claimed by the boy raise further telling points. After declaring himself to be 'Ambrosius', Nennius explains 'that is, he was seen to be *Embreis Guletic*'. There must have been a reason for Nennius to introduce this implausible identification with the celebrated fifth-century Romano-British commander Ambrosius, the most likely being that the stronghold was *already* known as *Dinas Emrys*.[57] Having identified the eponymous *Emrys* of Dinas Emrys with the Ambrosius Aurelianus of Gildas, it would be natural to to identify his similarly unnamed adversary in the topographical legend with his infamous enemy Vortigern.

Vortigern's unsatisfactorily explained bestowal of the fortress on Ambrosius is manifestly designed to account for the name *Dinas Emrys*:

> Though the name of the stronghold is not given, the author implies that it is the hill fort near Beddgelert called Dinas Emrys, by the boy's final words, 'ego hic manebo', followed by his name, Embreis Guletic.[58]

It is not difficult to detect the essential purpose of the interpolated passage. The stronghold bore the name *Dinas Emrys* when Nennius adapted the lore of the site to his *History*. The author of *Cyfranc Lludd a Llefelys*, which generally provides a more archaic version of the

---

56   This recalls Captain Mainwaring's response to the German officer's insistence on Private Pike's revealing his name!

57   Brynley F. Roberts (ed.), *Cyfranc Lludd a Llefelys* (Dublin, 1975), p. xxxiv.

58   Roberts (ed.), *Cyfranc Lludd a Llefelys*, p. xxxiv.

legend, evidently knew nothing of the figure whose name the site bore, merely stating without explanation that 'After that this place was called *Dinas Emreis*'.[59]

As an historicizing Christian historian, Nennius more than once interprets pagan myth as sober history. From Gildas he knew of Ambrosius as a patriotic Romano-British leader, while independent Welsh tradition identified him as the leading adversary of Vortigern.[60] It would be natural for Nennius to identify a local fortress apparently bearing his name as the stronghold of Ambrosius, and he accordingly adapted legendary lore attached to the site into that part of his historical narrative which the episode interrupts.[61] Historically, however, it is wholly improbable that either British leader had anything to do with the remote hillfort. Their activities belonged to the south and east of Britain.[62]

Elsewhere in the *Historia* Vortigern is implicitly depicted as a Christian king, who attends a synod of the British Church where he submits to condemnation by St Germanus. One of his sons is adopted by the saint, who becomes in due course canonized and founder of a monastery. In the Dinas Emrys episode, however, the context is altogether pagan and magical. When the king is at a loss what to do, like Conn in *Eachtra Airt meic Cuind* he turns to his druids for advice. They recommend his withdrawal to a stronghold of their choosing, their function in this respect presumably deriving from skill in geomancy. In Ireland the druids of King Eochaidh Feidhlioch similarly direct the king to a site in Connacht they adjudge appropriate for construction of a fortress.[63]

Nothing in the *Historia* preceding or following the Dinas Emrys interlude suggests that the Saxons threatened to 'seize all the regions which you have loved, together with the whole of your nation after your death'. Isolated in his castle, assailed each night by a destructive unseen foe, the threat to Vortigern is unmistakably posed by adversaries not of this world. They irresistibly recall the Otherworld race of the Coraniaid in the corresponding account in *Cyfranc Lludd a Lleuelys*, who could overhear every conversation in Britain, and whose presence was so pervasive that they were indistinguishable from the native inhabitants of the island. Furthermore, reduction of the king's realm to a single stronghold surviving among an overwhelming tide of foes recalls the *omphalos*, which was traditionally regarded as surviving the cataclysmic Flood.[64]

---

59   Ibid., p. 5.

60   §31. *Guorthigirnus regnavit in Brittannia et dum ipse regnabat, urgebatur a metu Pictorum Scottorumque et a Romanico impetu nec non et a timore Ambrosii* (Mommsen (ed.), *Chronica Minora*, iii, p. 171).

61   'I venture to charge Nennius with blending the half druidical boy of miraculous origin with the historical prince' (F. Liebermann, 'Nennius: The Author of the *Historia Brittonum*', in A. G. Little and F. M. Powicke (ed.), *Essays in Medieval History Presented to Thomas Frederick Tout* (Manchester, 1925), p. 40). I have shown that the similarly extended account of the foundation of the kingdom of Powys in §§32–35 was adapted to a local legend attached to the hillfort of Moel Fenlli (Nikolai Tolstoy, 'Cadell and the Cadelling of Powys', *Studia Celtica* (Cardiff, 2012), xlvi, pp. 59–83).

62   Vortigern 'is perhaps best seen as an overlord of some sort, who had a general control over military matters for the territories of a group of southern *ciuitates*' (David N. Dumville, 'Sub-Roman Britain: History and Legend', *History: The Journal of The Historical Association* (London, 1977), lxii, p. 185).

63   David Comyn and Rev. Patrick S. Dinneen (ed.), *The History of Ireland by Geoffrey Keating, D.D.* (London, 1902–14), ii, p. 186.

64   The Iban of Borneo believe that in the primæval age a great flood covered the earth, save for a single peak on which perched a solitary survivor called Dayan Racha. Impregnated by a fragment when rubbing sticks together while making fire, she gave birth to Simpang-Impang, First Man of the Iban people (Erik Jensen, *The Iban and their Religion* (Oxford, 1974), pp. 76–78).

Before and after the Dinas Emrys saga recounted in §§40–42, Vortigern's resistance to Saxon aggression is conducted by purely political and military means. §§43 and 44 describe the hard-fought war in which Vortigern's son Vortimer drives the Saxons back to the Isle of Thanet, while in §45 the king summons a council of his nobles to determine his response to a Saxon peace overture.[65]

To recapitulate: it is clear that Nennius sought with difficulty to meld two distinct traditions linked to Dinas Emrys.

1. The widely recorded theme of the child foundation sacrifice. In this, as in most other versions of the legend, the victim was unnamed.
2. The revelation of the prophetic 'dragons', whose significance is expounded by a visitor possessed of mantic powers. Such a figure is likely to have borne a name, which Nennius understood to be that attached to the fortress.

As historian of fifth-century Britain, Nennius identified the eponym of Dinas *Emrys* with the Romano-British warlord *Ambrosius*. Since the *Historia Brittonum* elsewhere portrays Ambrosius as the principal rival of Vortigern, logic dictated that the latter be identified with the pagan tyrant intent on immolating the British hero. As the ruler traditionally held responsible for admitting the hated Saxons into the country, Vortigern bore an unsavoury reputation in British tradition. In the Triads he is condemned as one of the 'Three Dishonoured Men … and the second is Gwrtheyrn the Meagre, who first gave land to the Saxons in this Island, and was the first to enter into an alliance with them', while the tenth-century poem *Armes Prydein* excoriates the Saxons as 'scavengers' (*kechmyn*) of Gwrtheyrn Gwynedd.[66]

The motif of the foundation sacrifice was originally distinct from the discovery of the fighting 'dragons', although both became attached to the site of Dinas Emrys. In the words of Professor Mac Cana, 'here the episode of the dragons is joined to the motif of the foundation sacrifice (aborted in this instance through the precocious wisdom of the intended victim).'[67]

If we set aside the first, originally unrelated, motif, and omit the despised name of Vortigern as speculative identification, the king in the Dinas Emrys saga appears in a quite different light. His kingdom all but overwhelmed by dark forces of the Otherworld, he finds himself impotent to protect his sole surviving stronghold, which stands as a microcosm of the realm. Eventually, a brilliant young saviour appears, whose occult power enables him to deflect the threat by resolving the *mysterium*.

Omitting the distinct theme of the foundation sacrifice, and deprived of the baleful name of Vortigern, the beleaguered king at Dinas Emrys fulfils the classic function of a *deus otiosus*.

Germanic and Indian facts which have recently been collated suggest that the Indo-Europeans were acquainted with a celestial god who was not and could not himself be either king or father, but who guaranteed the continuity of births and provided for the succession of kings. He was a variety of 'primordial god' or 'framing god' (the first to appear and last to disappear), whose

---

65   *Guorthegirnus cum suis maioribus natu consilium fecerunt et scrutati sunt, quid facerent* (Mommsen (ed.), *Chronica Minora*, iii, p. 189).

66   John Rhŷs and J. Gwenogvryn Evans (ed.), *The Text of the Mabinogion and other Welsh Tales from the Red Book of Hergest* (Oxford, 1887), pp. 298–99; Sir Ifor Williams and Rachel Bromwich (ed.), *Armes Prydein: The Prophecy of Britain From the Book of Taliesin* (Dublin, 1972), p. 4.

67   Proinsias Mac Cana, *The Cult of the Sacred Centre: Essays on Celtic Ideology* (Dublin, 2011), p. 199.

slow rhythm – the slowness of the world's history – was felt to be in sharp contrast with the brevity of generations and of kingdoms.[68]

The balancing counterpart of this sovereignty god is a young and vigorous divinity, who seizes the initiative, actively intervening to protect the realm from external threats. Such paired divine figures are found across the Indo-European world. In India, 'Varuna … personifies the static aspects of dominion', while 'Indra, the god of energetic action … may be regarded as the representative of the dynamic aspects of leadership'.[69] When St Martin was preaching the Gospel in fourth-century Gaul, he declared himself constantly under attack from the Gaulish god Mercury (the Roman name for the native Celtic deity *Lugus*, Welsh *Lleu*), but found his colleague Jupiter pedestrian and unintelligent.[70]

Detachment of the motif of the foundation sacrifice from that of the prophetic youth and the fighting dragons likewise shows the correspondence of the original version of the latter story to that found in *Cyfranc Lludd a Lleuelys* to be much closer than has hitherto been appreciated. Now it can be seen that the youth in the *Historia Brittonum* fulfilled the rôle of prophetic magician *tout simple*. Like Lleuelys, he arrives at the moment of crisis to save Britain and her beleaguered king from annihilation at the hands of their unseen enemies. In each case the ensuing contest is waged at the *omphalos* of the island, of which it is the microcosm. The *Historia Brittonum* version confirms that the battle against the demonic enemy is conducted at the umbilical Centre (*in medio tentorii*), the rest of the country having succumbed to its ubiquitous foes.

In *Cyfranc Lludd a Lleuelys*, Lleuelys arrives across the sea from France, which in the context stands for the Otherworld.[71] Likewise, the wise youth 'Emrys', who expounds the mystery of the *vermes* before 'Vortigern', must in an earlier version have originated in the Otherworld. That his home lay in South Wales reads like Nennius's own interpretation. The origin of the *campum Elleti, qui est in regione, quae vocatur Gleguissing* remains mysterious. A *campus Elleti* is unknown to Welsh topography. A boundary site near Llantwit Major mentioned in the Book of Llandaff is called *palus Elleti*, but a swamp appears an unlikely spot for the wise child's domicile.[72]

The nineteenth-century Irish scholar James Henthorn Todd suggested that confusion could have arisen over the territorial name *Gleguissing*, the Old Welsh form of the province of Glywysing in south Wales: 'That plain was not indeed *in regione Glewysing*, but it was in the *regio Gewisseorum* or in *Gewissing*, the territory of the West Saxon kings, descended from Gewiss.'

68   Georges Dumézil, *Archaic Roman Religion* (Chicago, 1970), p. 409. 'Le dieu père impersonnel, qui est le moteur immobile, est inactif, mais agissant … Le dieu ne se déplace en personne, mais il est le centre dont tout vient et où tout retourne. La vie et la mort sont produites toutes deux par un pouvoir unique en son essence, mais double dans sa manifestation', so ensuring the succession of births and deaths, and royal reigns (Françoise Le Roux, 'La courtise d'Etain', *Celticvm XV: Actes du Ve Colloque International d'Études Gauloises, Celtiques et Protoceltiques* (Rennes, 1966), pp. 372–3).

69   J. Gonda, 'The Sacred Character of Ancient Indian Kingship', in *La Regalità Sacra: Contributi al Tema Dell' VIII Congresso Internazionale di Storia delle Religioni (Roma, Aprile 1955)* (Leiden, 1959), p. 174–75. Cf. Paul Thieme, 'Mitra and Aryaman', *Transactions of the Connecticut Academy of Arts and Sciences* (New Haven, 1957), xli, pp. 59–71; J. Gonda, *The Vedic God Mitra* (Leiden, 1972), pp. 18–36; Georges Dumézil, *Les dieux souverains des Indo-Européens* (Paris, 1986), pp. 55–85.

70   C. Halm (ed.), *Sulpicii Severi: Libri qui Supersunt* (Vienna, 1866), p. 196.

71   Christian J. Guyonvarc'h, 'Notes d'Étymologie et de Lexicographie gauloises et celtiques XXVIII', *Ogam: Tradition Celtique* (Rennes, 1967), xix, pp. 490–94; Guyonvarc'h and Le Roux, *Les Druides*, pp. 309–10.

72   J. Gwenogvryn Evans and John Rhŷs (ed.), *The Text of the Book of Llan Dâv Reproduced from the Gwysaney Manuscript* (Oxford, 1893), p. 148.

He went on to conjecture that the plain (*campus*, Welsh *maes*) in question was Salisbury Plain, which from the mid-sixth century AD lay at the heart of the kingdom of the Gewissæ of Wessex.[73]

All this is tantalizingly suggestive. The author of *Cyfranc Lludd a Lleuelys* located the geographical setting for the encounter with the Fighting Dragons in central southern Britain, i.e. Wessex. Moreover, Welsh writers did indeed evince confusion, arising from similarity of nomenclature, between Old English *Gewissæ* and the South Walian principality of *Ewias*.[74] As Todd suggested, similar confusion could have arisen between *Gewissæ* and *Gleguissing* – especially had the Old Welsh territorial suffix *-ing* been attached to *Gewissæ*.

Todd's suggestion is strengthened further by Geoffrey's account of Merlin's appearance prior to the restoration of Stonehenge. Here the emissaries discover his dwelling-place in the land of the Gewissæ, at the spring of Galahes: *inuenerunt eum in natione Gewisseorum ad fontem Galahes, quem fuerat solitus frequentare.*[75] Since this episode represents an obvious duplication of the discovery of Merlin's previous place of origin,[76] whence he was brought to protect Vortigern's castle from supernatural delapidation, *Gewissæ* conceivably represents the original location. For this account is clearly to be preferred to the earlier discovery of Merlin at Caerfyrddin in Glywysing, an identification arising from Geoffrey's misinterpretation of *Caerfyrddin* as 'the city of Myrddin (Merlin)'.

The toponym *Galahes* seems oddly specific, and conceivably designated an actual spring on or near Salisbury Plain, in the territory of the *Gewissæ*.[77] It is surely likely that Geoffrey of Monmouth considered Stonehenge worth visiting. Its dramatic description by his contemporary historian Henry of Huntingdon might be expected to have whetted his insatiable curiosity and delight in marvels. We have seen that he was apprised of a tradition associated with Coneybury Hill beside Stonehenge, as also that there were an estimated 460 burial mounds in the vicinity, while evidence suggests that he collected local folklore accounts of the erection of the monument itself.[78] However, I am not suggesting that the figure of Merlin featured in such lore, since it has been seen that it was Geoffrey himself who introduced him into the story. Rather, it points to the

73   James Henthorn Todd (ed.), *leabhar breathnach annso sis: The Irish Version of the Historia Brittonum of Nennius* (Dublin, 1848), pp. xxv–xxvi.

74   Considerable confusion existed between *Euwas*, *Iwys*, and *Gynoys* (*recte Gyuoys*) (Thomas Jones (tr.), *Brut y Tywysogion or the Chronicle of the Princes: Peniarth MS. 20 Version* (Cardiff, 1952), p. 139). 'The similarity of the name of the district of *Ewias* … caused the Welsh to believe that it was the same place as the home of the Gewissi in later times. For as regards sound, *Ewias* certainly came a good deal closer to *Gewissi* than did either *Gwent* or *Gwennwys*!' (Sir Ifor Williams and Rachel Bromwich (ed.), *Armes Prydein: The Prophecy of Britain From the Book of Taliesin* (Dublin, 1972), p. xxxiii).

75   Reeve and Wright (ed.), *Geoffrey of Monmouth: The History of the Kings of Britain*, p. 171. The *fons* or *ualles* of Galahes is mentioned in the *Prophetiæ Merlini*, without intimation of locality (ibid., pp 153, 155).

76   'On voit l'étrangeté de la situation quand, devant les pierres de Stonehenge, Merlin est mis en présence du roi Aurèle, du même qu'il avait été mis précédemment en présence du roi Vortegirn' (Faral, *La légende arthurienne*, ii, p. 243).

77   There is a place called Gallow Hayes in East and West Grimstead, some miles south of Stonehenge (J. E. B. Gover, Allen Mawer, and F. M. Stenton, *The Place-Names of Wiltshire* (Cambridge, 1939), pp. 379–80). A possible derivation is from OE *geolu*, 'yellow' + **hæs*, 'brushwood' (A.H. Smith, *English Place-Name Elements* (Cambridge, 1956), i, pp. 200, 218). But there can be no certain means of identifying the spot now, nor of determining whether *Galahes* be of English or Brittonic derivation.

78   'Il se peut qu'à l'origine de ce récit il y ait eu quelque tradition populaire relative au monument mégalithique de Stonehenge près de Salisbury' (Paul Zumthor, *Merlin le Prophète: Un thème de la littérature polémique de l'historiographie et des romans* (Lausanne, 1943), p. 32).

possibility that Geoffrey's awareness of traditions of Stonehenge included information garnered locally. Just as he was regaled with legends of Tintagel by the neighbouring landowner Ulfin of Rosecraddock, so he could likewise have sought out legends of Stonehenge in its vicinity. After all, the famous monument lay within riding distance of Oxford.

With customary scepticism, Tatlock scouted any notion of Geoffrey's discovering anything at or near the site:

> The historical silence as to the stucture up to the twelfth century is the more natural considering its isolated position in the midst of Salisbury Plain, which till the nineteenth century was a remote and barren region, off the beaten track, frequented only by shepherds. That elaborate Celtic tradition survived here for six centuries is as improbable as that traditions as to Stonehenge survived so long in Wales. It is an unlikely spot for originating or perpetuating any early tradition connected with a great event in national history.[79]

Tatlock must be right to the extent that it is hard to imagine Geoffrey's seeking out legendary lore of Stonehenge from nut-brown maidens roaming the desolate plain, just as it would be implausible to envisage his interrogating uncomprehending fishermen on the beach below the bleak promontory of Tintagel. On the other hand, just as he obtained information concerning the latter from a nearby well-informed Cornish gentleman, there existed a correspondingly obvious source for preservation of ancient lore in the vicinity of Stonehenge. At several points in his *Historia*, Geoffrey alludes to *coenobium Ambrii abbatis*, 'the monastery of Abbot Ambrius', which he associates closely with Stonehenge.[80] The reference is to Amesbury Abbey, which had been founded by the tenth century, although the site must already have been important a century earlier when King Alfred bequeathed it to one of his sons.[81] In the 950s King Eadred bequeathed *Ambresbyrig* to his mother, and in or about 1002 King Æþelred confirmed the title of the site of the abbey to the nunnery of *Ambresbyrig*.[82] The importance of the convent in the late Saxon period is illustrated by the fact that in 995 Ælfric, Bishop of Wiltshire, was chosen Archbishop of Canterbury by King Æþelberht with his councillors *on Easter dæi on Ambresbyri*.[83]

If Geoffrey visited Stonehenge in the course of his researches, where more likely was he to have stayed than Amesbury Abbey? And it would have been there, if anywhere, that he could have been regaled with tales of the uniquely majestic monument lying a few miles to the west. It was about this very time, in distant Yorkshire, that Ailred of Rievaulx lamented in his *Speculum Caritatis* that novices in the great abbey wept more over 'fictitious tales of someone (I don't know who) called Arthur (*fabulis quae vulgo de nescio quo finguntur Arcturo*) than over pious books'. He himself dismissed them as 'fables and lies', but it is evident that he found himself in

79   Tatlock, *The Legendary History of Britain*, p. 41.

80   Reeve and Wright (ed.), *Geoffrey of Monmouth: The History of the Kings of Britain*, pp. 135, 171, 181, 193.

81   H. P. R. Finberg, *The Early Charters of Wessex* (Leicester, 1964), p. 76. There are indications that the abbey was in fact considerably older than the reputed date of its foundation in the latter half of the tenth century (Pauline Stafford, *Queen Emma and Queen Edith: Queenship and Women's Power in Eleventh-Century England* (Oxford, 1997), p. 139).

82   P. H. Sawyer, *Anglo-Saxon Charters: An Annotated List and Bibliography* (London, 1968), pp. 424–25; Finberg, *The Early Charters of Wessex*, pp. 103–4.

83   Charles Plummer and John Earle (ed.), *Two Anglo-Saxon Chronicles Parallel: With Supplementary Extracts from the Others; A Revised Text Edited, with Introduction, Notes, Appendices, and Glossary* (Oxford, 1892–99), i, p. 128.

a decided minority. Since Ailred was a friend of the monastery's founder Walter Espec, who is known to have been an early enthusiast for Geoffrey of Monmouth's *Historia*, it has been suggested that it was to this that Ailred referred.[84] However, it is implausible to suppose that Ailred would have been so tactless as publicly to denounce his patron's preferred reading. His language suggests rather tales related by ribald *conteurs*, such as those to whom Geoffrey himself alludes in his introduction.[85]

Writing at the beginning of the ninth century, Nennius appears to have been unaware of any identification of the site of the slaughter of the Britons with Stonehenge – which is natural enough, given his residence in remote North Wales. His identification of the protagonists of the episode with opposed Britons and Saxons of the fifth century AD represents a 'learned' interpretation, which replaced what was undoubtedly a much older mythological tradition. Overall, it seems likely that legends of the massacre, and association of the stones located at Stonehenge with the Omphalos of Uisneach in Ireland, existed long before Geoffrey came to write his dramatic account.

The youth without a name

A striking aspect of Nennius's version of the story of the prophetic youth is the emphasis laid on his lack of a name. Similarly, in *Math uab Mathonwy* Lleu initially bears no name, and only acquires it subsequently through Gwydion's deception of his mother Arianrhod.[86] In *Cyfranc Lludd a Lleuelys* his counterpart is as we know Lleuelys, i.e. the euhemerized deity Lleu. There existed a significant cult of Lleu not far from Dinas Emrys. Towards the conclusion of *Math uab Mathonwy* the mortally wounded Lleu flies off in the form of an eagle. Gwydion searches high and low for him, eventually arriving at the house of a swineherd at Maenor Penardd in Arfon. One of the swineherd's sows leads Gwydion to 'a valley that is now called Nantlleu' (*a eloir ʓeithon Nantlleʓ*), where she halts to graze. There Gwydion espies Lleu hanging from a oak in eagle-form, from which he conjures him down with *englynion* of enchantment.[87] One verse alludes to the oak as growing 'between two lakes' (*rong deu lenn*), which the author clearly identified with Llyn Nantlle Uchaf and Llyn Nantlle Isaf in the Nantlle valley.[88] Nantlle means 'Valley of Lleu', a toponym which finds its exact counterpart in the Thracian toponym Λουκουνάντα, 'Valley of Lugus'.[89] Sir John Rhŷs recorded a local folktale of a strange gilded beast slain at Dinlle called the *Aurwrychyn*, 'Gold Bristle', whom he identified with Lleu in his eagle guise.[90] To these Snowdonian associations may be added what is probably the earliest attested link of Lleu to the locality. In *Cyfranc Lludd a Lleuelys*, it is he who arranges for the stone containing the Fighting Dragons to be buried at Dinas Emrys.

84   Antonia Gransden, *Historical Writing in England c. 550 to c. 1307* (London, 1974), pp. 212–13. Cf. Tatlock, *The Legendary History of Britain*, pp. 207–10.

85   Roger Sherman Loomis, *Wales and the Arthurian Legend* (Cardiff, 1956), pp. 186–88; idem, *Arthurian Tradition & Chrétien de Troyes* (New York, 1949), pp. 17, 22.

86   Ian Hughes (ed.), *Math Uab Mathonwy: Pedwaredd Gainc y Mabinogi* (Aberystwyth, 2000), pp. 8, 9–10.

87   Ibid., pp. 14–16.

88   Ibid., p. 67.

89   Vladimir E. Orel, 'Thracian and Celtic', *The Bulletin of the Board of Celtic Studies* (Cardiff, 1987), xxxiv, p. 5.

90   Rhys, *Lectures on the Origin and Growth of Religion as Illustrated by Celtic Heathendom*, pp. 404–5.

It was noted earlier that Lleu is implicitly identified in Welsh tradition with the Divine Son of insular Celtic mythology, who was known as *Mabon mab Modron*, 'Son, son of Mother'. A verse in the Stanzas of the Graves commemorates

> *Y bedd yngorthir Nanllau*
> *ni wyr neb ei gynneddfau,-*
> *Mabon vag Mydron glau.*
> The grave on Nantlle's height,
> no one knows its innate quality,-
> Mabon son of Mydron the swift.[91]

In *Math uab Mathonwy*, Lleu is son of the maiden (originally goddess) Arianrhod, who conceives him without apparently coming into physical contact with a man. A similar story appears to have been told of Mabon, who is described as being abducted from his mother when three nights old.[92] Sir John Rhŷs believed the legends of Lleu and Mabon to be 'related stories, handed down to us in a fragmentary form which leaves it impossible to ascertain in what way they were related to one another'.[93]

In fact location of the grave of Mabon at Nantlle, where Lleu likewise died and was resurrected, suggests that they were alternative names for the same deity. It is not hard to envisage Lleu son of Arianrhod as being known also as 'Son, son of Mother', just as Christians allude to Christ as the Son and his mother as the Virgin.[94] Such veiling of the divine name might arise from considerations such as an expression of extreme reverence, or from concern not to antagonize the deity. Names comprised an integral part of a person, human or divine, which might be withheld in certain circumstances. The Romans held their city to be under the protection of a deity whose name was a closely guarded secret, and Rome herself possessed an alternative name which was uttered only in secret rites, in case an enemy should learn it and so acquire power to harm the city.[95] In Siberia,

> To prevent harm being done by means of malicious manipulations with a person's name, and at the same time to neutralize similar actions coming from evil spirits, the Tungus kept their personal names secret from outsiders and used them only to address one another among close relatives.[96]

Returning to Nennius's tale of Dinas Emrys, we are reminded of the child Ambrosius, who in the original version was addressed elliptically as a 'man without a father' (*homo sine patre*), i.e. son of a virgin (note the slip, betraying the fact that in an earlier version the mantic visitor was not a child but an adult). No reason is given for the requirement that the sacrificial child have no father. The rôle of the originally unnamed *puer* in the *Historia Brittonum* corresponds to that

---

91   *The Proceedings of the British Academy*, liii, p. 136.

92   Bromwich and Simon Evans (ed.), *Culhwch and Olwen*, p. 26.

93   Rhys, *Lectures on the Origin and Growth of Religion as Illustrated by Celtic Heathendom*, p. 404.

94   Christ is identified with Mabon in the poem *Llath Moessen* in the Book of Taliesin (J. Gwenogvryn Evans (ed.), *Facsimile & Text of the Book of Taliesin* (Llanbedrog, 1910), p. 47).

95   Johann Knobloch, 'Zum Geheimnamen Roms', in Michaela Ofitsch and Christian Zinko (ed.), *Studia Onomastica et Indogermanica: Festschrift für Fritz Lochner von Hüttenbach zum 65. Geburtstag* (Graz, 1995), p. 123; M. L. West, *Indo-European Poetry and Myth* (Oxford, 2007), p. 129. Names were held to confer life, being imbued with magical power (H. E. Plutschow, *Chaos and Cosmos: Ritual in Early and Medieval Japanese Literature* (Leiden, 1990), pp. 85–87).

96   V. A. Tugolukov, 'Some Aspects of the Beliefs of the Tungus (Evenki and Evens)', in V. Diószegi and M. Hoppál (ed.), *Shamanism in Siberia* (Budapest, 1978), p. 419.

of Lleuelys in *Cyfranc Lludd a Lleuelys*, i.e. the god Lleu, whose cult is attested in the vicinity of Dinas Emrys. In *Math uab Mathonwy* Lleu is depicted as a child born of a virgin mother. In *Cyfranc Lludd a Lleuelys* he, like the '*puer*' of the *Historia Brittonum*, arrives from what was originally the Otherworld in order to assist a beleaguered king of Britain by interpreting the mystery of the Fighting Dragons. In each version the resting place of the 'dragons' is Dinas Emrys. Furthermore, given the likely identity of Lleu with Mabon mab Modron, it might even be that the expression *homo sine patre*, 'man without a father', represents an elliptical version of Welsh *mabon mab modron*, 'son, son of mother'.[97]

Conjunction of the originally distinct themes of the Foundation Sacrifice and the Paired 'Dragons', both being associated with the *omphalos*, was effected by identifying the Fatherless Boy of the first with the sagacious figure of the second. The prophetic function of the warring creatures was also secondary, being adopted by Nennius from the Bible. In both tales it has become linked to the calamitous settlement of the Saxons in Britain, and there can be little doubt that the author of *Cyfranc Lludd a Lleuelys* adopted this interpretation from the *Historia Brittonum* – whether directly or at a remove. The youth Ambrosius explains the creatures' struggle as portending the outcome of the conflict between the indigenous inhabitants and the alien invader. Although the Saxons have occupied the greater part of the island, the day is coming when they will be overcome in war, and expelled across the sea. This interpretation originated in a passage from Gildas, with whose work Nennius was familiar. Describing the landing of the Saxons, Gildas explains that the event was accompanied by an omen and portents, indicating that their occupation would endure for three hundred years, during the first half of which they would inflict terrible ravages on the island.[98] The influence of this passage on the native legend is also apparent in the parallel episode in *Cyfranc Lludd a Lleuelys*. Lleuelys explains to Lludd that the native dragon is fighting with another of foreign extraction (*dreic estrawn genedyl arall*). The dragons having been reinterred in Snowdonia,

> *Sef ffuruf y gelwit y lle hwnnw gwedy hynny Dinas Emreis [a chyn no hynny Dinas Ffaraon Dande. Trydyd cynweissat uu hwnnw a torres y gallon [o] anniuiged].*
>
> After that the place was called *Dinas Emreis* [and before that it had been *Dinas Ffaraon Dande*. He was one of the Three Chief Officers who Broke his Heart from Sorrow].[99]

That the passage in brackets represents an explanatory gloss is confirmed by its omission from versions of the story contained in the Bruts.[100] The curious allusion to the stronghold's former name as *Dinas Ffaraon Dande* ('The Fort of Fiery Pharaoh') further betrays absorption of the legend into the saga of Vortigern. Describing how Vortigern's foolish counsellors urged him to invite the Saxons into Britain, Gildas compares them to the misguided advisers of Pharaoh in the Bible.[101] Futhermore, the epithet *dandde* ('fiery') and the reference to Vortigern's death from

---

97 However, it is problematic to what extent the attributes of the visitor at Vortigern's court should be assigned, on the one hand to the sacrificial child, and on the other to the prophet 'Emrys'.

98 Mommsen (ed.), *Chronica Minora*, iii, p. 38.

99 Roberts (ed.), *Cyfranc Lludd a Llefelys*, p. 5.

100 Cf. Parry (ed.), *Brut y Brenhinedd: Cotton Cleopatra Version*, p. 69; Acton Griscom (ed.), *The Historia Regum Britanniæ of Geoffrey of Monmouth with Contributions to the Study of its Place in Early British History* (London, 1929), p. 304.

101 'Stulti principes', ut dictum est, 'Taneos dantes Pharaoni consilium insipiens' (Mommsen (ed.), *Chronica Minora*, iii, p. 38). The allusion is to Isaiah 19,11 (Robert Weber (ed.), *Biblia Sacra iuxta Vulgatam Versionem* (Stuttgart, 1969), ii, p. 1115).

heartbreak reflect alternative traditions of his end recorded in the *Historia Brittonum*, which ascribe his end to destruction, either by fire from heaven, or from heartbreak.[102]

Overall, it can be seen that the account of the revelation of the *vermes* in the *Historia Brittonum* is in fact considerably closer to the parallel story in *Cyfranc Lludd a Lleuelys* than has been appreciated. The protagonists of Nennius's source were doubtless euhemerized divinities, as they plainly are in *Cyfranc Lludd a Lleuelys*. Moreover, with the contrived introduction of the historical Vortigern and Ambrosius removed from the picture, identification of the Saxons as the national foe improbably poised to overwhelm the whole of Britain outside the ramparts of the Snowdonian stronghold must likewise be dismissed as originating in the pseudo-historical transformation of the previously purely mythical tale. All other factors in the original story being supernatural, the omnipresent foes must have been similarly so in the original legend. They echo the universal threat posed to the kingdom by the elusive Otherworld race of Coraniaid in *Cyfranc Lludd a Lleuelys*, as also the Fomoire whom Conn annually frustrates through ritual action from overrunning the ramparts of Tara.

Merlin-Ambrosius and the 'circle'

Nennius was clearly unaware of the Otherworld origin of the prophetic youth, whom he inferred from the toponym *Dinas Emrys* to have been the historical Romano-British leader Ambrosius Aurelianus. Whatever the origin of the name, it seems from the early accounts that it was already attached to Dinas Emrys when Nennius came to compile the *Historia Brittonum*. It would be tempting to associate the unidentified *campus Elleti* from which the boy originated with the plain (*maes*) of the Otherworld, but in the absence of any satisfactory explanation for *Elleti* this can only remain matter for speculation.

Attention may be further drawn to a curious allusion in Geoffrey's description of the discovery of Merlin by Vortigern's messengers at Carmarthen – an association Geoffrey inferred from the name of the town, *Caerfyrddin*. Arrived at its gates, they come upon a group of boys playing. Wearied by their journey, they sit in a circle (*sederunt in circo*). There they remain for the greater part of the day (*cum multum diei praeterisset*), until a chance remark reveals the boy Merlin among the players.[103] The most recent translator of the *Historia Regum Britanniæ* renders the passage thus:

> At cum in urbem quae postea Kaermerdin uocata fuit uenisset, conspexerunt iuuenes ante portam ludentes et ad ludum accesserunt, fatigati autem itinere sederunt in circo, exploraturi quod quaerebant.
>
> When they arrived at the city afterwards called Kaermerdin, they discovered youths playing in front of the gate; they approached the players, but, tired by their journey, sat in a circle *around them*, looking for what they sought.

In fact, the words 'around them' do not reflect anything in the Latin text, and are presumably inserted in order to make sense of the passage.[104]

What can be the significance of this curious 'circle'? The translator's explanatory insertion only serves to emphasize the anomaly. It seems unlikely that the men spontaneously reclined

---

102 Mommsen (ed.), *Chronica Minora*, iii, pp. 191–92.

103 The revealing jeer that Merlin was a child without a father may be of Celtic provenance, since it occurs also in the Irish birth-tale of Cormac mac Airt (Vernam Hull, 'Geneamuin Chormaic', *Ériu* (1952), xvi, pp. 83–84).

104 Reeve and Wright (ed.), *Geoffrey of Monmouth: The History of the Kings of Britain*, pp. 136–37.

on the ground in a ring around the troop of youths. To have done so would have required them to be a score or so in number, which appears superfluous. In any case, why should the exhausted royal messengers resign themselves to squatting for hours *outside* the town, in so odd and uncomfortable a manner? If they thought the youth they sought was among those playing before them, why did they not question them at the outset? After all, they spent the greater part of a day 'looking for what they sought' among the romping boys – through the curious approach of refraining from questioning them!

Could the intrusive 'circle' represent another detail surviving from Geoffrey's source? A similar misunderstanding features in the *Vita Cadoci*, where the feasters at *Medgarth* ('the Middle Enclosure') are described as seated 'in the form of a circle' (*in modum circuli*). In Chapter Ten, I suggested that this curious detail originated in a description of the Otherworld feast enjoyed at the *omphalos*. In addition, it has been seen that the elaborate account in *Breudwydd Maxen* of Maxen's sleep in the midst of a circle of his kingly subordinates similarly reflected a *mandala* arranged for ritualistic purpose at the Centre of the world. Whether Geoffrey's wording *in circo* be read as 'in the circle', or 'inside a circle', I suggest that the discovery of the wonderful child originally occurred within a context of circularity, whose context escaped the author.

Circular imagery is fundamental to *omphalos* ideology, with which Dinas Emrys is linked in *Cyfranc Lludd a Lleuelys*. In early cosmologies the world was frequently envisaged in the form of a disc,[105] and its microcosmic counterpart the *omphalos* was likewise circular. According to Varro, the *pomerium* dug around Rome constituted a 'circle' (*orbis*).[106] In Anatolian and Tokharian the expressions for establishing a temple literally mean 'set up enclosure > encircle'.[107]

One might consider the central position held by the circle and the employment of its symbolism within the Indo-European tradition... Unquestionably, in Indo-European culture the family hearth was the sacred fire and it did symbolize the ancestors in the cult of the dead. Further, as the sacred fire, the domestic hearth was the representation of the sun on earth not only in essence, but even in physical shape. It was the earthly replica of the sun disc.[108]

---

105   *Tetraque mundanum obumbrat mersa girum* (Michael W. Herren (ed.), *Hisperica Famina: I. The A-Text; A new Critical Edition with English Translation and Philological Commentary* (Toronto, 1974), p. 86). Circularity was held to be manifest throughout creation (Whitley Stokes, 'The Evernew Tongue', *Ériu*, ii, pp. 106–8), and it was believed that the earth was encircled by a mighty river (J. Gwenogvryn Evans (ed.), *Facsimile & Text of the Book of Taliesin* (Llanbedrog, 1910), pp. 21, 36). The world in Norse mythology was conceived as circular around its edge (Anthony Faulkes (ed.), *Snorri Sturluson: Edda; Prologue and Gylfaginning* (Oxford, 1982), p. 12), and in early Israel it was believed that Yhwh drew a circle marking the bound between order and chaos (Carola Kloos, *Yhwh's Combat with the Sea: A Canaanite Tradition in the Religion of Ancient Israel* (Amsterdam, 1986), pp. 75–79, 81). In Vedic India the uniquely holy fire *gārhapatya* was round, complementing the world (Georges Dumézil, *Rituels indo-européens à Rome* (Paris, 1954), pp. 29–30), while pre-Mahāyāna Buddhist cosmology envisaged the universe as a single circular disc, surrounded by a wall of iron (*cakravāla*) at its perimeter (Dorothy C. Wong, 'The Mapping of Sacred Space: Images of Buddhist Cosmographies in Medieval China', in Philippe Forêt and Andreas Kaplony (ed.), *The Journey of Maps and Images on the Silk Road* (Leiden, 2008), p. 54). Greek pre-Socratic philosophers believed in a circular earth. Anaximander described its shape as curved, like the the drum of a column, with man living on its flat surface (G. S. Kirk and J. E. Raven, *The Presocratic Philosophers: A Critical History with a Selection of Texts* (Cambridge, 1957), p. 134).

106   C. Michiel Driessen, 'On the Etymology of Lat. *urbs*', *The Journal of Indo-European Studies* (Washington, 2001), xxix, pp. 41–46. Widespread etymological links exist between terms for 'temple' and 'circularity' (Mirek B. Polišenský, *The Language and Origin of the Etruscans* (Prague, 1991), p. 74).

107   *The Journal of Indo-European Studies*, xxix, pp. 64–66.

108   Angela Della Volpe, 'From the Hearth to the Creation of Boundaries', ibid. (1990), xviii, p. 167.

A substantial proportion of circular objects have been found in Kurgan graves in south Russia.

> Circles around burial sites indicate a preoccupation with *consecrated space* and imply the practice of religious rituals aimed at delineating an area as sacred.

The circle was at once symbol of the sun, deceased ancestors, the hearth, and consecrated space.

> But there is yet another connection with the family hearth which was also symbolized by the circle, that is, the earth … it was in fact the womb, the birthplace of all living things. Thus the family hearth symbolized also the earth, in fact, it was the navel from which all life sprang forth.[109]

Geoffrey located the discovery of Merlin at Carmarthen in consequence of a mistaken interpretation of the Welsh name of the town, Caerfyrddin, as *caer* + *Myrddin*, 'Merlin's town'.[110] The incongruous 'circle' introduced in his version of the Dinas Emrys legend may be explained as an allusion retained from a pre-existing source, which his narrative has incidentally preserved. A prophet discovered within a circle suggests a mandala-like pattern, like the protective circular rampart of Tara ascended by Conn when conducting his prophylactic ritual. The name of Tara, *Temair*, derives from an Indo-European root **tem-*, 'cut', signifying 'space demarcated or cut off for sacred purposes', hence 'sacred precinct, or temple'.[111]

In Chapter Four I suggested that Geoffrey's accounts of Merlin's preservation of Vortigern's tower at Snowdon, and his transfer of the stones of Uisneach in Ireland to ensure the integrity of Stonehenge, derived from variant versions of the same legend. The effective identity of Uisneach and Stonehenge arose, not from any actual transportation of monoliths, but in consequence of their fulfilling the function of the national Omphalos in Ireland and Britain respectively. In addition, the discovery of Merlin within an unexplained 'circle' suggests that the setting of his mantic intervention was envisaged in earlier tradition as a circle. This in turn recalls the circular structure of Stonehenge, in Geoffrey's version established by Merlin on Salisbury plain.

Circles were accorded magical protective power in Celtic society, as in other early cultures.[112] In the seventh century, St Samson is described as tracing a circle, which a flame-spewing serpent was unable to cross. The Irish St Adamnán similarly drew a protective circle on a flooding strand.[113] In Ireland a druid-smith placed five magic circles around the newborn hero Cormac,

---

109 Ibid., 167–69.

110 The name of Carmarthen derives from '*Moridūnon, 'Sea Fort', consisting exactly of Brit. **mori* "sea" and **dūnon* "fort"' (Kenneth Jackson, 'Romano-British Names in the Antonine Itinerary', *Britannia: A Journal of Romano-British and Kindred Studies* (London, 1970), i, p. 77).

111 Dónall Mac Giolla Easpaig, 'Significance and Etymology of the Placename *Temair*', in Bhreatnach (ed.), *The Kingship and Landscape of Tara*, pp. 440–48.

112 Christian holy men frequently appropriated powers of enchantment deployed by the heathen. In the latter part of the fifth century, St Remigius in Gaul created an enchanted circle which preserved Rheims from encroachment by the plague (Peter Brown, *Authority and the Sacred: Aspects of the Christianisation of the Roman World* (Cambridge, 1995), p. 72).

113 Pierre Flobert (ed.), *La vie ancienne de saint Samson de Dol* (Paris, 1997), pp. 194–96; Máire Herbert and Pádraig Ó Riain (ed.), *Betha Adamnáin: The Irish Life of Adamnán* (Cork, 1988), p. 54. Cf. Elissa R. Henken, *The Welsh Saints: A Study in Patterned Lives* (Cambridge, 1991), p. 182. Imaginary circles at Hallow-e'en provided protection from witches and fairies (M. Macleod Banks, *British Calendar Customs: Orkney &*

which protected him from drowning, fire, enchantment, and wolves. Of a celebrated wizard, we are told that 'Mug Ruith, i.e. the magician of the circles, i.e. he used to make his prediction making circles'. Roundness represented perfection and truth, in particular the delivery of sound judgments in law.[114]

Scores of prehistoric stone circles in Britain attest to the numinous quality of circularity.[115] Round enclosures, with accompanying rites, demarcated sacred from profane space in ancient religions: a concept perpetuated in the early Christian era by erection of circular vallums around monasteries. Etymological links feature in many cultures connecting words for 'temple' and 'circularity'.[116]

In early Wales and Ireland, kings displayed their royal authority by travelling on circuit (Welsh *cylch*, Irish *cúairt*) around their realms. In the early mediæval period this afforded occasion to receive rent in kind. However, it is likely that originally it represented a primarily symbolic rite, wherein the king established his protective function over the kingdom. In the literatures of both countries we find these circuits ascribed to euhemerized former divinities, without any suggestion of economic function.[117] A poem exalting the seventh-century King Cadwallon of Gwynedd enumerates sites around Wales where the king established his camps. The itinerary indicated is inapt to any historical context, and the fact that that the sites run clockwise around Wales suggests 'a symbolic conquest or overlordship of Wales'.[118] A similar consideration applies to a poetic account of the early tenth-century Irish King Muirchertach of the Leather Cloaks, in which he is described as performing an equally unhistorical circuit of the whole of Ireland.[119]

In early times a Welsh king's circuit of his realm is likely to have reflected the course of the sun, characteristic symbol of royalty. In early India, the king's chariot course undertaken at his inauguration 'corresponds to that of the sun, encompassing in its march the whole world'.

Shetland (London, 1946), p. 72). 'Our village is protected by a magic circle. Neither gipsies nor bears are allowed to enter it because were they to do so the protective magic would be dispelled' (Richard and Eva Blum, *The Dangerous Hour: The Lore of Crisis and Mystery in Rural Greece* (London, 1970), p. 37).

114 Máirín O Daly (ed.), *Cath Maige Mucrama: The Battle of Mag Mucrama* (Dublin, 1975), p. 68; Sharon Arbuthnott (ed.), *Cóir Anmann: A Late Middle Irish Treatise on Personal Names* (Dublin, 2005–7), i, p. 104; ii, p. 78; Kuno Meyer (ed.), 'Sanas Cormaic', in O. J. Bergin, R. I. Best, Kuno Meyer, and J. G. O'Keefe (ed.), *Anecdota from Irish Manuscripts* (Halle and Dublin, 1907–13), iv, pp. 101–2.

115 'From the end of the Neolithic period the image of the circle was all-pervading' (Richard Bradley, *Rock Art and the Prehistory of Atlantic Europe: Signing the Land* (London, 1997), p. 125).

116 Colin Burgess, *The Age of Stonehenge* (London, 1980), pp. 339–44; Mircea Eliade, *Patterns in Comparative Religion* (London, 1958), p. 371; *The Journal of Indo-European Studies*, xviii, p. 157; H. J. Lawlor, *Chapters on the Book of Mulling* (Edinburgh, 1897), pp. 167–81, 179–85. In the Book of Joshua the Lord instructs the Israelites to take stones from the Jordan and re-erect them as a sanctuary at Gilgal. It has been suggested that, since Gilgal 'means "circle," perhaps a megalithic stone circle stood there and gave rise to the story', John Pairman Brown, *Israel and Hellas* (Berlin, 1995–2001), ii, pp. 205–6.

117 R. L. Thomson (ed.), *Pwyll Pendeuic Dyuet: The First of the Four Branches of the Mabinogi edited from the White Book of Rhydderch with variants from the Red Book of Hergest* (Dublin, 1957), p. 21; Ian Hughes (ed.), *Manawydan Uab Llyr: Trydedd Gainc y Mabinogi* (Cardiff, 2007), p. 2; idem (ed.), *Math Uab Mathonwy: Pedwaredd Gainc y Mabinogi* (Aberystwyth, 2000), pp. 1, 5; Lilian Duncan, 'Altram Tige Dá Medar', *Ériu* (1932), xi, p. 185; Osborn Bergin and R. I. Best, 'Tochmarc Étaíne', ibid. (1938), xii, pp. 34–40.

118 R. Geraint Gruffydd, 'Canu Cadwallon ap Cadfan', in Rachel Bromwich and R. Brinley Jones (ed.), *Astudiaethau ar yr Hengerdd* (Cardiff, 1978), pp. 34–35; Jenny Rowland, *Early Welsh Saga Poetry: A Study and Edition of the Englynion* (Cambridge, 1990), pp. 170, 172.

119 Edmund Hogan (ed.), *Móirthimchell Éirenn Uile dorigne Muirchertach mac Néill* (Dublin, 1901), pp. 15–41. Cf. Donnchadh Ó Corráin, 'Muirchertach Mac Lochlainn and the Circuit of Ireland', in Alfred P. Smyth (ed.), *Seanchas: Studies in Early and Medieval Irish Archaeology, History and Literature in Honour of Francis J. Byrne* (Dublin, 2000), pp. 238–50.

Egyptian Pharaohs undertook ritual encirclement of a symbolic 'Egypt' at the annual festival of renewal, when they danced around a field. This circuit was explicitly considered a re-enactment of the sun's cycle. Similarly, in China royal circumambulations of the walls of major cities performed at imperial coronations represented ritual circuits of the cosmos.[120] Thus the concept of the central focus of the realm as a circular repository of spiritual power reflected its imagery as a microcosm of the kingdom, world, or cosmos.[121] Among the Siberian Evenk, 'the circle of ground occupied by the tent symbolized the middle world, or in other cases was interpreted as the shaman's island in the middle of the shamanistic clan-river.' The central pole of the tent correspondingly' represented the world tree, linking earth to heaven at the Centre.[122]

As noted above, the circular construction of many megalithic monuments suggests a cosmological purpose. The name of the Rollright Stones in Oxfordshire is thought to derive from 'Brittonic *Rodland rich* 'groove at/near Rodland (from Brittonic 'Wheel-Precinct' …)'.[123] The description 'Wheel-Precinct' suggests a solar sanctuary, the term being possibly employed in a generic sense for round temples. The Welsh name *Rhodri*, meaning 'Wheel King', has been interpreted as indicating solar attributes, but could equally mean 'King of the (Circular or Solar) Sanctuary'. After all, the king, who was held to be of divine parentage, was customarily focus of rites conducted at the Sacred Centre.

It will be recalled that the name *Ambrosius* belongs to the original version of the story of the revelation of the 'dragons' at the Centre, it being likely that its attachment to the site of Dinas Emrys preceded composition of the *Historia Brittonum*. It accounts for Nennius's obtrusion of the Romano-British leader Ambrosius into the legend, and with him Vortigern and the Saxons. But who then was this Ambrosius, whose stronghold was associated with legendary exposition of mysteries (*en revelatum est mihi hoc mysterium et ego vobis propalabo*) at the sacred centre in Snowdonia bearing his name, and whom Geoffrey of Monmouth independently located (under the name of Merlin) within an unexplained 'circle'? Whoever he was, it seems that he bore a name sufficiently close to that of *Ambrosius* to induce Nennius to identify him with the distinguished fifth-century British commander of that name.

Could it be that Dinas Emrys was named after some forgotten local Romano-British potentate of the fourth or fifth century? Several Welsh principalities, such as Meirionydd, Rhufoniog, and Dunoding, contain Roman personal names. While the traditional ascription of their foundation to sons of Cunedda may be discounted as an artificial construct, Sir John Lloyd aptly observed

---

120 J. C. Heesterman, *The Ancient Indian Royal Consecration: The Rājasūya Described According to the Yajus Texts and Annotated* (The Hague, 1957), pp. 134–36, 137–38, 198; J. Gwyn Griffiths, *Atlantis and Egypt: With other Selected Essays* (Cardiff, 1991), p. 176; C. J. Bleeker, *Egyptian Festivals: Enactments of Religious Renewal* (Leiden, 1967), pp. 96, 101, 119; Paul Wheatley, *The Pivot of the Four Quarters: A Preliminary Enquiry into the Origins and Character of the Ancient Chinese City* (Edinburgh, 1971), pp. 433–34; David Hawkes, 'The Quest of the Goddess', *Asia Major: A British Journal of Far Eastern Studies* (London, 1967), xiii, pp. 84–85; Mac Cana, *The Cult of the Sacred Centre*, pp. 109–34. For 'the magic circle of the city wall' in early societies, cf. W. F. Jackson Knight, *Cumaean Gates: A Reference of the Sixth Aeneid to the Initiation Pattern* (Oxford, 1936), pp. 97–105; Stephen Scully, *Homer and the Sacred City* (New York, 1990), pp. 16–53, 141–47.

121 H. P. L'Orange, 'Expressions of Cosmic Kingship in the Ancient World', in *La Regalità Sacra: Contributi al Tema Dell' VIII Congresso Internazionale di Storia delle Religioni (Roma, Aprile 1955)* (Leiden, 1959), pp. 481–92.

122 A. F. Anisimov, 'The Shaman's Tent of the Evenks and the Origin of the Shamanistic Rite', in Henry N. Michael (ed.), *Studies in Siberian Shamanism* (Toronto, 1963), pp. 87–88.

123 Richard Coates and Andrew Breeze (ed.), *Celtic Voices English Places: Studies of the Celtic Impact on Place-Names in England* (Stamford, 2000), pp. 199–212.

that 'Names like Ceredigion (Caraticiana), Rhufoniog (Romaniaca), Meirionydd (Mariana), require a Ceredig, a Rhufon, a Meirion to make them intelligible.'[124]

At the same time, it does not appear that this consideration applies to hill-forts, of which no other example bearing a name of Roman derivation is known to me.[125] In the case of Dinas Emrys, one might rather expect a name of Celtic provenance: that of a divinity, or legendary hero, to whom tradition assigned possession of the stronghold. Equally, the fact that Nennius took its name for that of the historical Ambrosius, with whose career he was familiar, indicates that the name of the stronghold approximated sufficiently closely to Old Welsh *Embreis* to account for the erroneous identification.

Here may tentatively be considered the name of *Ambiorix*, a Belgic prince mentioned by Caesar, who ruled over the people of the Eburones living between the Rhine and the Meuse.[126] The tribal name signifies 'men of the yew', and Caesar notes that the house of Ambiorix lay within a wood. His co-ruler Catuvolcus committed suicide by eating yew, and these circumstances have led to the suggestion that Ambiorix was a priest-king, presiding over a sacred yew-grove.[127]

The name *Ambiorix* means either 'king of the enclosure', or possibly 'king of the surrounding region', the first element of which probably derives from proto-Celtic *ambi-*, 'on both sides, around'.[128] *Ambiorix* is an apt enough appellation for the princely guardian of a sacred site. Whether 'around' relates to the bounds of a small or large space need not be significant in the context, given that sacred enclosures represent microcosmic simulacra of the greater world without. However, if Ambiorix dwelt within a sacred grove, the first interpretation appears more likely.

There is a further parallel between the function exercised by Ambiorix, and that of Lleuelys in *Cyfranc Lludd a Lleuelys*. The monarchy of the Eburones, as described by Caesar, constituted a dual kingship, the rule of Ambiorix being shared by Prince Catuvalcus. While Ambiorix features as an energetic warrior, Catuvalcus is described as being too old to engage in serious physical activity. While this conceivably implies no more than disparity in age and vigour, it is strikingly close to the classic institution of dual kingship found in Indo-European and other early societies.

---

124 John Edward Lloyd, *A History of Wales from the Earliest Times to the Edwardian Conquest* (London, 1911), p. 119. Cf. John T. Koch, *Cunedda, Cynan, Cadwallon, Cynddylan: Four Welsh Poems and Britain 383–655* (Aberystwyth, 2013), pp. 69–70.

125 Cf. Elwyn Davies, *Rhestr o Enwau Lleoedd: A Gazetteer of Welsh Place-Names* (Cardiff, 1957), p. 38; Melville Richards, 'Some Welsh Place-Names Containing Elements which are Found in Continental Celtic', *Études Celtiques* (Paris, 1972), xiii, pp. 379–89.

126 I should stress that I am suggesting the possibility (no more) that a Brittonic equivalent of *Ambiorix* was interpreted by Nennius as representing Old Welsh *Embreis*, not that the one name corresponds etymologically to the other. Professor Ellis Evans suggested to me that 'If the name were **Amborix* it might be reflected in Welsh *Emyr*, but the -io- stem/juncture makes this a little dubious, but I would not rule out the equation altogether' (letter of 9 March 1984).

127 Guyonvarc'h and Le Roux, *Les Druides*, pp. 230–31.

128 Cf. Julius Pokorny, *Indogermanisches Etymologisches Wörterbuch* (Berne, 1959–69), i, p. 34; D. Ellis Evans, *Gaulish Personal Names: A Study of some Continental Celtic Formations* (Oxford, 1967), pp. 48–49, 134–35; Helmut Birkhan, *Germanen und Kelten bis zum Ausgang der Römerzeit: Der Aussagewert von Wörtern und Sachen für die Frühesten Keltisch-Germanischen Kulturbeziehungen* (Vienna, 1970), 206–10; Patrick Sims-Williams, 'The Celtic Languages', in Anna Giacalone Ramat and Paolo Ramat (ed.), *The Indo-European Languages* (London and New York, 1998), p. 353; Wolfgang Meid, *Keltische Personennamen in Pannonien* (Budapest, 2005), pp. 77–78; Ranko Matasović, *Etymological Dictionary of Proto-Celtic* (Leiden, 2009), p. 32. Alternatively, it has been suggested that the first element derives from a postulated Indo-European root *$*H_2mbhi\text{-}péH_3\text{-}$* ('protector') > Celtic **ambio-* (Fredrik Otto Lindeman, 'Gaulish *ambiorix*', *Zeitschrift für celtische Philologie* (Tübingen, 2006), lv, pp. 50–55).

Indo-European languages preserve distinct terminologies of 'king, lord, god', the first signifying '(symbolic) generator (of his subjects)', and the second 'rule, ruler, regulate'.[129] This ideological concept of paired divinities (and hence kings) with disparate parallel functions is found also in Celtic mythology, where the Irish god Núadu (Welsh Nudd/Lludd) exemplifies the largely passive ideological concept of kingship, while the youthful Lug (Welsh Lleu) personifies intelligence and martial vigour.[130]

These paired rôles are clearly demarcated in *Cyfranc Lludd a Lleuelys*. Lludd, king of Britain, retains the dignified and wealth-preserving qualities of kingship. But when the kingdom is menaced by triple Otherworld scourges, it is his brother Lleu who saves the realm by dint of his intelligence and mastery of supernatural means of waging war. In the Irish saga of the Battle of Mag Tuiread (*Cath Maige Tuired*), which broadly corresponds to *Cyfranc Lludd a Lleuelys*, Lug engages in victorious combat with the Otherworld host of the Fomoire, while Núadu remains passive in the background.

While such possibilities may repay consideration, the original significance, if any, of the name *Ambrosius* in the saga of Dinas Emrys nevertheless appears hard to establish with certainty.

What remains striking, however, is the evident antiquity of a tradition associating the British *omphalos* with the name *Emrys/Ambrosius/Ambrius*. While Geoffrey of Monmouth's *Mons Ambrii* is effectively synonymous with *Dinas Emrys*, it seems all but certain that he did not borrow the one name from the other.[131] Unlike Nennius, he attempts no identification of the Gwynedd hill-fort with Emrys, whose name he replaced with that of Merlin. In any case, whether or not the hill on which Stonehenge stands was called the Hill of Ambrius before Geoffrey's day, the name is surely original, since it contains the same element as nearby Amesbury, *Ambresbyrig*.

It is clear that in an earlier version Dinas Emrys was menaced by an omnipresent supernatural Oppression (*gormes*) like the Coraniaid, which the historicizing Nennius awkwardly converted into a momentary Saxon conquest of the whole of Britain. The fact that Vortigern is represented as withdrawing to a single magically impregnable stronghold at the heart of his kingdom, of which the remainder has been overrun by a malign power, implies what is explicit in *Cyfranc Lludd a Lleuelys*: namely, that the fortress represented the Sacred Centre, or Omphalos, of Britain. By the same token, all associated events of the story were originally envisaged as occurring at that Centre.

The entire *mise-en-scène* is archaic, recalling significant elements of Indo-European cosmology. In ancient Persian mythology, Yima, the First Man and King, is instructed by the divinity Ahura Mazdāh to construct a fortified refuge called *Var*. He withdraws there, where he survives the terrible winter *Markūsān*. Throughout that time he preserves the germs of creation in the *Var*, so that on his emergence after 12,000 years he is able to restore creation to its original vigour and fertility. Yima's retreat is represented as punishment inflicted for the crime of incest with his sister.[132] (The primal couple of early cosmologies naturally comprises a brother and sister).

---

129 Calvert Watkins, *How to Kill a Dragon: Aspects of Indo-European Poetics* (New York and Oxford, 1995), pp. 8–9.

130 Heinrich Wagner, 'Studies in the Origins of Early Celtic Civilisation', *Zeitschrift für celtische Philologie* (Tübingen, 1971), xxxi, pp. 25–26; Christian-J. Guyonvarc'h (tr.), *Textes mythologiques irlandais I* (Rennes, 1980), i, p. 134.

131 Latin *mons* could represent Welsh *din* or *dinas*, 'fortress'. Of the site of Arthur's famous victory at *mons Badonicus*, Kenneth Jackson observed that 'Its name in Welsh was very likely *din Baðon* "the hill fort of Baðon"' ('The Site of Mount Badon', *The Journal of Celtic Studies* (Baltimore, Md., 1958), ii, p. 153).

·132 Arthur Christensen, *Les types du premier homme et du premier roi dans l'histoire légendaire de Iraniens* (Stockholm, 1917–34), ii, pp. 16–18, 55–62; Georges Dumézil, *Mythe et Épopée* (Paris, 1968–73), ii,

A similar eschatological concept is enshrined in the Norse *fimbulvetr*, that harsh winter before the end of the world, which will be evaded only by Líf and Lífðrasir (the primal male and female couple), who will survive by hiding in Hoddmímir's wood, where they rear men.[133]

That the story of Vortigern at Dinas Emrys reflects a comparable myth of destruction and renewal of the human race is further indicated by an early tradition that the son begotten by his incest with his daughter was named *Britu*.[134] This is an obvious eponym of the island of Britain, and Nennius himself identifies the original settler of Britain as *Britto*.[135] On this basis, the Dinas Emrys episode reflects a cosmic myth, which described the cataclysm at the world's ending, followed by the birth and survival at the Centre of a hero destined to establish a renewed cycle of existence.

Earlier I argued that the episode describing Vortigern's confrontation with Ambrosius, located by Nennius at Dinas Emrys, was originally attached to Stonehenge. It will be recalled that the version recounted in *Cyfranc Lludd a Lleuelys* explains that the 'dragons' were discovered at the original *omphalos* of the whole island, a site in central Southern Britain, whence they were transported to Gwynedd (Snowdonia) and interred in a stone coffer. Thus, the events described in §§40–42 of the *Historia Brittonum* may likewise have originated in a myth attached to the Omphalos of Britain, i.e. Stonehenge.

The survival of Eldol

To his account of the massacre at the site of Stonehenge, Geoffrey added a dramatic event absent from the earlier version contained in the *Historia Brittonum*. When the unarmed British nobles valiantly but ineffectually try to defend themselves from the the Saxon onslaught, one man alone proffers successful resistance. Eldol, Earl of Gloucester (*consul Claudiocestriae, uocabulo Eldol*), defends himself with a stake he happens to find (*palum quem forte inuenerat*), to such good effect that he succeeds in bursting through the murderous throng, and making his escape to his own city. Having slaughtered all his companions (save Vortigern, whom they make prisoner), the brutal Saxons occupy the major cities of Britain and lay waste the entire country (*quasque prouincias deuastantes*).[136]

It has been suggested that Geoffrey concocted the heroic figure of Eldol as a counterbalancing exception to the otherwise humiliating slaughter of the hapless Britons.[137] However, this appears a rather haphazard conjecture, and closer consideration indicates that here, as elsewhere in his dramatic account of the establishment of Stonehenge, Geoffrey adapted authentic legendary lore to his own dramatic ends.

In Chapter Fourteen it was shown that Welsh tradition in *Culhwch ac Olwen* preserved accounts of an heroic figure named *Eidoel mab Aer*, who like Geoffrey's Eldol was associated with Gloucester. In view of this, *Eldol* and *Eidoel* must surely be one and the same, given the facility with which the letters *i* (lacking the dot) and *l* were liable to be confused in mediæval

pp. 246–49; Jean Kellens, 'Yima et la mort', in Mohammad Ali Jazayery and Werner Winter (ed.), *Languages and Cultures: Studies in Honor of Edgar C. Polomé* (Berlin, 1988), pp. 329–34.

133 Tim William Machan (ed.), *Vafþrúðnismál* (Cambridge, 1988), pp. 67, 88.

134 V. E. Nash-Williams, *The Early Christian Monuments of Wales* (Cardiff, 1950), p. 123.

135 Mommsen (ed.), *Chronica Minora*, iii, pp. 149–53.

136 Reeve and Wright (ed.), *Geoffrey of Monmouth: The History of the Kings of Britain*, p. 137.

137 Faral, *La légende arthurienne*, ii, pp. 228–29.

manuscripts.[138] This is confirmed by the fact that puzzled Welsh translators of Geoffrey's *Historia* habitually replaced the unfamiliar *Eldol* with *Eidol* or *Eidiol*.[139]

It seems that Geoffrey of Monmouth and the author of *Culhwch* drew independently on early Welsh tradition. The names of *Eldol/Eidoel* and their common patrimonial city of Gloucester (*Claudiocestria/Gliui*) correspond too closely for coincidence. It may be further significant that, while Eldol alone escapes the slaughter of the long knives, Eidoel is known as 'son of Aer' – *aer* being Welsh for 'combat' or 'slaughter'.[140]

The massacre of the Britons cannot be regarded as an historical event, and has long been recognized as originating in an international popular tale. Its introduction into the history of the Saxon invasion of Britain is explained as 'a play on the etymology – felt and correct – of the word *Saxon*: OE. *Seaxe* "the Saxons" to OE. *seax* "knife"'. The story in the *Historia Brittonum* bears independent indications of drawing on Saxon tradition.[141]

The resistance and escape of Eldol feature only in Geoffrey's version of the event. However, Eldol cannot be dismissed as an invention by that ingenious author, given that Eidoel of Gloucester (*Cair Gliui*) features in early Welsh tradition independent of Geoffrey's work. Moreover, there are indications that the Welsh Eidoel was associated with an event comparable to that described by Geoffrey.

In *Culhwch ac Olwen* Eidoel is discovered languishing as a prisoner in *Caer Gliui* (Gloucester), while Geoffrey describes his Eldol as obtaining refuge in Gloucester after his escape from the Saxon assassins. A tradition of Eidoel as martial fugitive appears to have been known in Wales long before Geoffrey wrote his History. In the Black Book of Carmarthen 'Stanzas of the Graves', mention is made of Eidal (Eidoel), who is described both as leader of an army and a valiant exile.[142]

The Welsh Eidoel is clearly a figure of legend rather than history. The Gloucester in which he is incarcerated is the 'Shining City' of Celtic mythology, which had become identified with the fortress of *Glevum* built by the Romans. Eidoel himself is implicitly identified in *Culhwch*

---

138 Gwenogvryn Evans (ed.), *Facsimile & Text of the Book of Taliesin*, p. 133; Bromwich and Simon Evans (ed.), *Culhwch and Olwen*, pp. lxi-ii, 133.

139 Henry Lewis (ed.), *Brut Dingestow* (Cardiff, 1942), p. 99; John Rhŷs and J. Gwenogvryn Evans (ed.), *The Text of the Bruts from the Red Book of Hergest* (Oxford, 1890), p. 140; Acton Griscom (ed.), *The Historia Regum Britanniæ of Geoffrey of Monmouth with Contributions to the Study of its Place in Early British History* (London, 1929), p. 378; John Jay Parry (ed.), *Brut y Brenhinedd: Cotton Cleopatra Version* (Cambridge, Mass., 1937), p. 119.

140 Alexander Falileyev, *Etymological Glossary of Old Welsh* (Tübingen, 2000), p. 80.

141 Edwin Guest, *Origines Celticae (A Fragment) and other Contributions to the History of Britain* (London, 1883), ii, p. 183; Chadwick, *The Origin of the English Nation*, p. 42; H. Munro Chadwick and N. Kershaw Chadwick, *The Growth of Literature* (Cambridge, 1932–40), i, p. 286; Alan S. C. Ross, 'Hengist's Watchword', *English and Germanic Studies* (Kendal, 1948–49), ii, pp. 83–84. Cf. 'K811.1. Enemies invited to feast and killed' (Stith Thompson, *Motif-Index of Folk-Literature: A Classification of Narrative Elements in Folktales, Ballads, Myths, Fables, Mediaeval Romances, Exempla, Fabliaux, Jest-Books, and Local Legends* (Bloomington, Indiana, 1955–58), iv, p. 340; I. Glazunov (ed.), *Лѣтописъ Нестора: Со включенїемъ поученїя Владимира Мономаха* (St Petersburg, 1903), p. 28; Margaret Mackintosh of Mackintosh, *The Clan Mackintosh and the Clan Chattan* (Edinburgh, 1948), p. 9).

142 A. O. H. Jarman (ed.), *Llyfr Du Caerfyrddin gyda Rhagymadrodd Nodiadau Testunol a Geirfa* (Cardiff, 1982), p. 41. The names *Eidal* and *Eid(i)ol* are essentially identical (J. Lloyd-Jones, *Geirfa Barddoniaeth Gynnar Gymraeg* (Cardiff, 1931–63), p. 453).

with Mabon, the youthful saviour god of the Celts. His patronymic 'Son of Slaughter' suggests the survivor of an indiscriminate massacre. (It is intriguing to note the curious parallel with the story of the infant Jesus, the saviour-god whose flight into exile enabled him alone to survive the Massacre of the Innocents. The two traditions are of course of entirely distinct provenance.)

It is further possible that the escape of Eidoel, together with his imprisonment in the Shining City until his rescue by Arthur, reflects pagan seasonal myth. The great festival marking the beginning of the new Celtic year was known in Ireland as *Samain*, in Gaul as *Samo-*, and in Wales as *nos Galan Gaeaf*, 'Night of the Winter Calends'. It was celebrated on the night of 1 November (All Hallows Eve), when entrances to the Otherworld were temporarily opened, from which demonic hordes emerged to wreak malicious harm on humanity.[143]

The festival was precursor to winter, grim season of dearth and mortality. According to Welsh folk tradition, spirits in church could be heard calling out the names of folk destined to die during coming months of ice, snow, and bitter winds. It was a time of death and dissolution of the goods of this world, and the Welsh name for November, *Mis Tachwedd*, is 'Month of Slaughter'.[144] Death and winter marched together: the Irish word *samain* for the winter festival was understood to mean *sam-fuin*, 'the end (or death) of summer'.[145] In Indo-European cosmology, winter was regarded as a metaphor for death.[146]

These grim connotations are echoed in a passage of the account of Eidoel's imprisonment in *Culhwch ac Olwen*. When Arthur appears before the walls of Caer Gliui, an otherwise unidentified character named *Gliui* stands on top of the fort, and declaims these curious words:

> Arthur, what do you seek from me, since you will not leave me alone on this crag? No good comes to me here, and no pleasure; I have neither wheat nor oats, without you too seeking to do me harm.

Gliui is merely an eponym of *Caer Gliui*. Names of cities and fortresses in early Britain were commonly understood to derive from those of their founders, and the lament is implicitly descriptive of Caer Gliui. But what can be the relevance of this peculiar reproach? The incongruous allusion to absence of wheat and oats surely intimates that Caer Gliui is here envisaged as a place of winter, its crops depleted, and wretchedness afflicting humanity. However, spring eventually returns, and life begins afresh. After further adventures, Arthur and his men succeed in liberating Mabon mab Modron, Eidoel's alter ego, from his imprisonment.[147]

143 Marie-Louise Sjoestedt, *Gods and Heroes of the Celts* (London, 1949), pp. 53–56; Françoise Le Roux and Christian-J. Guyonvarc'h, *Les fêtes celtiques* (Rennes, 1995), pp. 35–87.

144 T. Gwynn Jones, *Welsh Folklore and Folk-Custom* (London, 1930), p. 152; Kenneth Jackson (ed.), *Early Welsh Gnomic Poems* (Cardiff, 1935), p. 42. November was the season for butchering stock (Trefor M. Owen, *Welsh Folk Customs* (Cardiff, 1974), p. 122), but the name of the month may well have borne wider resonance.

145 H. Wagner, 'Studies in Early Celtic Traditions', *Ériu* (1975), xxvi, p. 16; J. Vendryes, E. Bachellery, and P-Y. Lambert, *Lexique étymologique de l'irlandais ancien* (Dublin and Paris, 1959–96), S-22.

146 Uli Linke, 'Blood as Metaphor in Proto-Indo-European', *The Journal of Indo-European Studies* (1985), xiii, pp. 340–42.

147 Bromwich and Simon Evans (ed.), *Culhwch and Olwen*, p. 33.

There existed a popular belief in Wales that the bonfires (*coelcerthi*) traditionally lit at *nos Galan Gaeaf* commemorated the notorious massacre of the Britons by the Saxons. It is likely that the identification reflects historicization of an earlier mythological explanation. What closer parallel to winter dearth and spring recovery could there be than extinction of the British people, with but a solitary survivor left to bear the torch of humanity through the darkness until the affliction has passed away? This may also be reflected in a custom associated with the kindling of the fires:

> Those who assisted at the making of the bonfire watched until the flames were out, and then somebody would raise the usual cry, when each ran away for his life, lest he should be found last.[148]

Who was Eidoel mab Aer, and how did he come to be identified as lone survivor of the Celtic winter cataclysm? I suggest we need look no further than his name for the explanation. Welsh *eidol, idol* could have been borrowed in Romano-British times, either from Latin īdōlum, itself a borrowing from Greek εἴδωλον, 'ghost, departed soul',[149] or directly from the Greek. Demetrius, a distinguished Greek expert on oracles, visited Britain within a generation of the Roman conquest, seeking information concerning islands off the coast understood to be inhabited by the souls of the departed.[150] He presumably consulted appropriate British authorities (druids?) on the subject, and is in any case unlikely to have been the only Greek familiar with such matters to visit Britain during the centuries of Roman occupation. Alternatively, the loanword could have originated in a literary source: evidence attests to knowledge of Greek in Roman Britain.[151]

In Chapter Thirteen it was shown that insular Celts held that the span of human existence passed through regular cycles of death and rebirth, within which a single soul-bearer, human or emblematic, preserved the seed or embryo of life during its period of dissolution in the Otherworld. In Geoffrey's *Historia*, Eldol (*Eidoel*) is sole survivor of the slaughter of the British nobility (Vortigern, who is made prisoner by Hengest, represents an obvious intruder into the original tale). In Welsh tradition, Eidoel is called 'Son of Slaughter': effectively, 'lone survivor'. In *Culhwch* he is found confined in an Otherworld retreat, described as a place where no cereal crops are to be found. Eventually he is liberated from this imprisonment, being transformed

---

148   [John Humffreys Parry (ed.)], *The Cambro-Briton* (London, 1820–22), i, p. 172; John Rhŷs, *Celtic Folklore: Welsh and Manx* (Oxford, 1901), p. 225. The story of the Slaughter of the Long Knives was familiar to Welsh bards from at least the middle of the tenth century. The prophetic poem *Armes Prydein* recalls how the hated Saxons gained dominion in Britain *gwedy rin dilein*: 'after the secret slaughter' (Sir Ifor Williams and Rachel Bromwich (ed.), *Armes Prydein: The Prophecy of Britain From the Book of Taliesin* (Dublin, 1972), p. 4). Gunpowder Day, commemorating an attempted massacre of the assembled king and nobles of England, was also assimilated to *Kalan Gaeaf* (Gwynn Jones, *Welsh Folklore*, p. 147). Guy Fawkes commemorations in various parts of England were characterized by nocturnal outbreaks of chaotic crowd hooliganism (Hilda Ellis Davidson, *Patterns of Folklore* (Ipswich, 1978), pp. 56–57). This presumably arose from the coincidental proximity of the date of the plot's discovery to November Eve. (cf. ibid., pp. 74–75).

149   A. Ernout, A. Meillet, and Jacques André, *Dictionnaire étymologique de la langue latine: Histoire des mots* (Paris, 1994), p. 306.

150   W. Sieveking and Hans Gärtner (ed.), *Plvtarchvs Pythici Dialogi* (Stuttgart and Leipzig, 1997), p. 60. Two bronze plates found at York attest to Demetrius's reception in high places during his visit to Britain (R. G. Collingwood and R. P. Wright (ed.), *The Roman Inscriptions of Britain: I Inscriptions on Stone* (Oxford, 1965), p. 222).

151   R. G. Collingwood and R. P. Wright (ed.), *The Roman Inscriptions of Britain: II Instrumentum Domesticum: Combined Epigraphic Indexes and Concordance with Major Printed Sources Compiled by S.S. Frere* (Stroud, 1995), pp. 49–50.

into the divine founder of the human race, Mabon mab Modron, who corresponds to Yima (the First Man) in the Avestan myth discussed earlier.

Thus, it seems that the escape of Eldol in Geoffrey of Monmouth's *Historia* reflects an euhemerized myth of the survival of mankind, during those periodic cyclical cataclysms to which the world was believed to be subjected. During his 'winter' imprisonment, the sole survivor dwells as a shade in the Otherworld. With the world's vernal rebirth, the transient soul-spirit emerges as another Adam, founder of the revivified human race. The British prisoner resembles the Greek εἴδωλον, which

> is a wraith representing the living man's vitality and identity; but however it is defined, the crucial point for us is that Pindar identifies it both as the survivor of death and the spiritual core of the living – 'the part that comes from the gods'.[152]

The sanctuary of ancestral heroes

In early cosmologies, the First Man is born at the Navel of the Earth. I have sought to show from discrete sources that the Navel of Britain was originally located at Stonehenge. From the darkness of prehistory, archaic traditions associated with *omphalos* belief are preserved in mediæval legendary sources, principally the tenth-century Welsh tale *Cyfranc Lludd a Lleuelys*, and Geoffrey of Monmouth's *Historia Regum Britanniæ*. Other sources suggest that cognate legendary lore was associated with provincial *omphaloi*, such as Preseli Mountain in Dyfed and Dinas Emrys in Snowdonia. The author of the Life of St Illtud adapted traditions of the British *omphalos* – *Medgarth*, the 'Middle Enclosure' – to a local site fortuitously bearing the same name. In this way, he recorded for posterity an important body of oral lore originally associated with the British *omphalos*. §9 of the Life of St Cadog also appears to have incorporated a traditional account of the national *omphalos*.

Geoffrey's association of Stonehenge with heroic British dead recalls the uniquely impressive array of burial mounds distributed around Stonehenge. Since Welsh *cawr*, like the corresponding Irish *caur*, may mean equally 'giant' or 'hero', it could have been the latter meaning which Geoffrey or his source latinized as *gigas*, 'giant'.[153] The forebears of the Britons and Irish were traditionally envisaged as colossal figures.[154] Major man-made structures of the landscape surviving from early times, their origin forgotten, were ascribed to the labour of giants.[155]

Following erection of the mighty monoliths of Stonehenge, Geoffrey relates how king Aurelius summoned his leading subjects to the spot at Whitsun, when for three days he wore the royal crown. Subsequently, after Uther had defeated an invasion of Irish and Saxons in Wales, he hastened to report to Aurelius, who was lying sick at Winchester. There he discovered that

---

152 Michael Clarke, *Flesh and Spirit in the Songs of Homer: A Study of Words and Myths* (Oxford, 1999), p. 311. Cf. Jan Bremmer, *The Early Greek Concept of the Soul* (Princeton, 1983), pp. 78–80, 81, 83; Alfred Heubeck, Stephanie West, J. B. Hainsworth, and Arie Hoekstra, *A Commentary on Homer's Odyssey* (Oxford, 1988–92), ii, p. 82.

153 Ibid., p. 443; Quin *et al.* (ed.), *Dictionary of the Irish Language*, 'C', col. 93; Vendryes, Bachellery, and Lambert, *Lexique étymologique de l'irlandais ancien*, C-50–51; J. P. Mallory and D. Q. Adams, *The Oxford Introduction to Proto-Indo-European and the Proto-Indo-European World* (Oxford, 2006), p. 412.

154 Dáithí Ó hÓgáin, 'Magic Attributes of the Hero in Fenian Lore', in Bo Almqvist, Séamas Ó Catháin, and Pádraig Ó Héalaí (ed.), *The Heroic Process: Form, Function and Fantasy in Folk Epic* (Dun Laoghaire, 1987), pp. 209–14; Proinsias Mac Cana, *The Mabinogi* (Cardiff, 1992), pp. 84–85.

155 Chris Grooms, *The Giants of Wales: Cewri Cymru* (Lampeter, 1993), pp. 370–71.

the king was dead, and had already at his instruction been buried by his bishops at Stonehenge (*iam ab episcopis patriae sepultum fore prope coenobium Ambrii infra choream gigantum*). Later, Arthur was uniquely spirited away to the Isle of Avalon, but his successor Constantine was interred alongside his predecessors at Stonehenge.

Although Geoffrey of Monmouth was generally cavalier with historical facts, in view of the widespread association of king and *omphalos* it may nevertheless be significant that he associated Stonehenge so closely with the royal dynasty of Britain.

18

The Stones and the Seasons: Myths and Rituals of the *Omphalos*

In the arts nearly everywhere the most effective means of representing the numinous is 'the sublime'. This is especially true of architecture, in which it would appear to have first been realized. One can hardly escape the idea that this feeling for expression must have begun to awaken far back in the remote Megalithic Age. The motive underlying the erection of those gigantic blocks of stone, hewn or unworked, single monoliths or titanic rings of stone, as at Stonehenge, may well have been to localize and preserve and, as it were, to store up the numen in solid presence by magic; but the change to the motive of expression must have been from the outset far too vividly stimulated not to occur at a very early date.[1]

Calendrical rites at the Centre of Britain

A striking aspect of legends associated with the Centre in Celtic mythology is the extent to which they are found linked to significant dates and times in the Celtic calendar. In *Cyfranc Lludd a Lleuelys*, the deadly scream that echoes about every hearth in Britain, which can only be stifled by rituals performed at the *omphalos*, recurs '*every* May-day Eve' (*pob nos Kalan Mei*). In early times deadly scourges (*gormesoedd*) threatened the realm at twice-yearly festivals, when they were were averted through enactment of appropriate rites instituted by gods in the primal time. Although the date of the destructive visit of the giant wizard who absconded with the food and drink prepared in the royal courts is unspecified, we are told that it likewise occurred at night. This suggests that other fraught night of peril in the British calendar, *nos Galan Gaeaf* (All Hallows Een). Indeed, that 'nothing was ever had of it [the royal food and drink] *save what could be consumed on the very first night*', suggests a major royal feast followed by protracted dearth. This is precisely the significance of the feast celebrated at *nos Galan Gaeaf*, the eve of winter.

The Fomoire, Irish counterpart of the British Coraniaid, were wont to conduct their predatory assaults on humanity on the same ill-boding anniversary. It was at *Samain* (November Eve) that the people of Nemed were constrained to pay tribute of two-thirds of their corn, milk, and children to the Fomoire. And it was on the same day that the destructive tribe took tribute of goods, together with his daughter Derbforgaill, from Ruad, king of the Hebrides.[2] The

---

1   Rudolf Otto, *The Idea of the Holy: An Inquiry into the Non-rational Factor in the Idea of the Divine and its Relation to the Rational* (Oxford, 1926), p. 68.

2   R. I. Best, Osborn Bergin, M. A. O'Brien, and Anne O'Sullivan (ed.), *The Book of Leinster Formerly Lebar na Núachongbála* (Dublin, 195483), pp. 20, 23; A. G. van Hamel (ed.), *Compert Con Culainn and*

corresponding Irish tale of 'the Battle of Mag Tuired' (*Cath Maige Tuired*) is expressly structured on a calendrical basis. Emphasis is laid on the dates at which the two principal events take place. It was on the Calends of May that the divine race of the *Túatha Dé Danann* arrived in Ireland,[3] while their bloody overthrow of the Fomoire occurred at *Samain*.[4]

The calendrical basis of *Cyfranc Lludd a Lleuelys* appears as follows.

1. At *Kalan Mai* (1 May), a hideous scream echoed across every hearth in Britain. It heralded total destruction of the kingdom's wealth and fertility: men lost their strength, women miscarried, and kine and crops became barren.
2. At *nos Galan Gaeaf* (November Eve), the population feasted on the first night, but thereafter the disaster struck again, the wealth of the kingdom being this time abducted by a sinister unknown power.

    Initially, it appeared impossible for the country's king and people to frustrate these recurrent threats. It is clear that the authors of the first *gormes* were the malevolent supernatural race of the Coraniaid, against whom it was impossible to concert any defence, in view of their possession of an occult power enabling them to overhear every prophylactic measure planned.

Measures concerted by the gods for countering these successive inroads were as follows.

1. At *Kalan Mai* communication between King Lludd and his Otherworld counterpart Lleuelys is facilitated by pouring of wine through a horn.

    Lleuelys provides Lludd with *pryfed*, some of which are preserved 'for breeding', as a precaution against recurrence of the *gormes*.

    The population is assembled at a meeting (*dadleu*), where it is subjected to a lustration, which destroys the otherwise undetectable Coraniaid while preserving the native Britons.
2. At *nos Galan Gaeaf* the king adopts Lleu's prescribed precaution ensuring that he maintain vigil throughout the night. In this way he is enabled to confront the nocturnal intruder, and compel him to abandon his destructive project. The magical measures that this must originally have involved are obscured by the author's euhemerizing transformation of the encounter from what was earlier a contest between rival wizards, into a clash of arms.

Both events are commemorated at the Centre of Britain, which I have argued was originally located at Stonehenge, which, once the original site was abandoned and its especial function forgotten in Wales, became identified in Welsh eyes with Oxford.

Lug and the Stone of Destiny

Irish literary sources associate the god Lug (British *Lleu*) with megaliths to so significant an extent, that he might almost be known as the God of the Megalith. In 'The Battle of Mag Tuired'

Other Stories (Dublin, 1933), pp. 60–62; R. A. Stewart Macalister (ed.), *Lebor Gabála Érenn: The Book of the Taking of Ireland* (Dublin, 1938–56), iii, pp. 138, 172–74.

3   *Dia Luain hi kallann Mai* (ibid., iv, p. 140).

4   Elizabeth A. Gray (ed.), *Cath Maige Tuired: The Second Battle of Mag Tuired* (Naas, 1982), pp. 44, 46; Best, Bergin, O'Brien, and O'Sullivan (ed.), *The Book of Leinster*, p. 42.

(*Cath Maige Tuired*), Ogma, one of the company of the divine Túatha Dé Danann, flings a huge flagstone (*márlicc*) out through the wall of Tara. The newly arrived Lug promptly hurls it back, so that it lies in the centre of the royal hall, and restores the broken wall, which remains intact as before.[5] This singular detail recalls the widely recorded myth of the clashing rocks (*Planktai*), familiar as the *Sympligades* encountered by the Argonauts. The privileged hero Jason is enabled to pass between two mighty rocks, which open briefly, then crash together immediately after he has effected his passage between them.[6]

That this motif was associated with Tara is further suggested by a passage in the early Irish tract 'Concerning the Race of Conaire Mór'. There we find two stones, *Blocc* and *Bluigne*, which normally stood so close that a man could only pass his hand sideways between them. However, when approached by a lawful king of Tara, they open sufficiently wide to admit him and his chariot.[7]

These accounts were attached to particular stones at Tara, which provided a focus of both ritual practice and myths linked to the sanctuary. Moreover, emphasis on the great stone's coming to rest *in the centre* of the royal hall (*for lár an ríghthighi*) suggests that it was an *omphalos* pillar. The impression is conveyed of an outer ring of stones, through which only privileged persons may enter. At its centre stands a menhir, the *Lia Fáil*, which was believed to have been erected by Lug in the primal era.

Recently John Carey has pointed out that 'there is very little evidence which links Lug with Tara directly', from which he concludes:

> It seems safest to say that Lug was a god associated with the idea of kingship – an ideal which has always included the claim to Tara – rather than that he was specifically associated with the site of Tara itself.[8]

It seems likely that the legend was originally attached to the celebrated stone at Uisneach, primary Navel of Ireland, traditions of which became transferred to Tara when altered political circumstances led to the latter's identification with the national Kingship.[9]

---

5   Gray (ed.), *Cath Maige Tuired*, p. 40. Another version of Lug's exploit features in the story *Cath Chrionna* (Standish H. O'Grady (ed.), *Silva Gadelica: A Collection of Tales in Irish with Extracts Illustrating Persons and Places* (London, 1892), i, p. 325). The episode appears designed to account for the location of the stone *Fál*, symbolizing the sovereignty of Ireland, of which Lug was the presiding deity (Christian-J. Guyonvarc'h, *Magie, médecine et divination chez les Celtes* (Paris, 1997), p. 65).

6   Stith Thompson, *Motif-Index of Folk-Literature: A Classification of Narrative Elements in Folktales, Ballads, Myths, Fables, Mediaeval Romances, Exempla, Fabliaux, Jest-Books, and Local Legends* (Bloomington, Indiana, 1955–58), ii, p. 270 (D1553); Clive Tolley, *Shamanism in Norse Myth and Magic* (Helsinki, 2009), i, pp. 442–43. 'It is clear that the sea out of which the Planktai rise is no ocean of the ordinary world, for the moving rocks lie on the route traversed by the ambrosia-bearing doves on their way to Zeus: they are in the upper regions of the air. Thus Odysseus is being warned by Circe of the dangers of the ascent into heaven. Such a flight into the upper world is typical of shamanism, and the dangers encountered in the course of it make much of the material of shamans' narrations. The Planktai are characteristic of these risks', (E. A. S. Butterworth, *The Tree at the Navel of the Earth* (Berlin, 1970), p.181).

7   Lucius Gwynn, 'De Síl Chonairi Móir', *Ériu: The Journal of the School of Irish Learning* (1912), vi, p. 134. Cf. Robert H. Gartman, 'Mael, Bloc, and Bluiccniu', in D. K. Wilgus (ed.), *Folklore International: essays in traditional literature, belief, and custom in honor of Wayland Debs Hand* (Hatboro, Pa., 1967), pp. 67–70.

8   'Tara and the Supernatural', in Edel Bhreatnach (ed.), *The Kingship and Landscape of Tara* (Dublin, 2005), pp. 42, 44.

9   The principal rite in the inauguration of a Norse king involved his ascent of a sacral stone: 'the placing of the future ruler, with the consent of the people, upon the stone or in the highseat endowed him with

In the tale 'The Death of the Children of Tuireann' (*Oidhe Chlainne Tuireann*), King Núadu travels from Tara to the Hill of Uisneach to pay a weighty tribute extorted annually by the rapacious Fomoire. There he encounters Lug of the Long Hand (*Lugh Lámhfhada*). Shortly afterwards, a large ugly troop of envoys from the Fomoire appears. Lug angrily declares his intention of killing them, and fulfils his promise, leaving only nine alive to bear a defiant challenge to their king Balar.[10] The eschatological Battle of Mag Tuired (at which Lug slew Balor, king of the Fomoire) may originally have been located at Uisneach, appropriate setting for a national conflict of cosmic dimensions. Elsewhere, we read that Lug was mortally wounded at Uisneach and plunged to his death in nearby Lough Lugborta. Another version has him slain at Uisneach itself.[11]

All this indicates the Hill of Uisneach, the original Omphalos of Ireland, as the original setting for Lug's salvificatory exploits. His establishment of a great stone at the centre of the royal enclosure of Ireland recalls the action of his Welsh counterpart Lleuelys, who must originally have employed divinatory powers enabling King Lludd to establish the precise centre of his realm, where he discovered 'dragons' (originally paired soul-creatures, *vermes*, *pryfed*) which he required to be preserved within a *kistvaen* (menhir).

This association of Lug with a great stone is further indicated by curious accounts, which appear to identify him with a stone pillar. In the story of 'The Battle of Mag Mucrama' (*Cath Maige Mucrama*), the poet Ferches slays Lugaid (another name for Lug) by hurling a spear at him, which successively pierces his forehead and a pillar-stone (*coirthe*) behind him, which 'resounded' while Lugaid 'withered away lifeless'.[12] Evidently the fates of Lugaid and the stone were bound together.

Similar circumstances characterized the death of Lug's famous son, Cú Chulainn. Mortally wounded, the hero strapped himself by his belt to a stone pillar in order to remain upright. Afterwards Lugaid son of Cú Roí came up to him and cut off his head. Cú Chulainn's friend Conall Cernach, who was bound by a mutual oath to avenge Cú Chulainn, arrived and found his body attached to the pillar. Conall promptly arranged a tryst with Lugaid to accord with their destiny. Arrived at the agreed spot, Conall flung his spear at Lugaid, wounding him at a pillar stone which became known as the Pillar of Lugaid. Then Conall pursued the injured Lugaid, decapitated him, and deposited his head on another stone. Subsequently Conall returned to the spot, to find that 'the head had dissolved the stone, and it had passed through it'.[13]

Another version relates that the spear used by Lugaid to kill Cú Chulainn was one of a number forged on a particular day in each of seven successive years.[14] This was plainly a ritual undertaken in order to endow the missiles with lethal magical potency. The story contains striking parallels with the death of Lug's British counterpart Lleu, as described in *Math uab*

---

regal qualities and royal power. No other ritual was necessary for granting the qualities that belonged to the seated person' (Elisabeth Vestergaard, 'A Note on Viking Age Inaugurations', in János M. Bak (ed.), *Coronations: Medieval and Early Modern Monarchic Ritual* (Berkeley and Los Angeles, 1990), p. 121).

10   Seán Ua Ceallaig (ed.), *Trí Truaġa na Scéaluiḋeaċta* (Dublin, 1927), pp. 6–7.

11   Edward Gwynn (ed.), *The Metrical Dindshenchas* (Dublin, 1903–35), iv, p. 278; Macalister (ed.), *Lebor Gabála Érenn*, iv, pp. 124, 184.

12   O Daly (ed.), *Cath Maige Mucrama*, p. 60. Cf. Myles Dillon, 'The Death of Mac Con', *Publications of the Modern Language Association of America* (New York, 1945), lx, p. 341; David Comyn and Rev. Patrick S. Dinneen (ed.), *The History of Ireland by Geoffrey Keating, D.D.* (London, 1902–14), ii, p. 286.

13   Best, Bergin, O'Brien, and O'Sullivan (ed.), *The Book of Leinster*, 450–53.

14   Bettina Kimpton (ed.), *The Death of Cú Chulainn: A Critical Edition of the Earliest Version of Brislech Mór Maige Muirthemni* (Maynooth, 2009), p. 11.

Mathonwy. Lleu makes an appointment to meet his foe by a standing stone, and the spear prepared for the killing of Lleu is required to be forged during divine service on each Sunday of the year preceding the encounter.[15]

Most remarkable of all is the manner in which Lugaid's head is said to merge with the stone, which became celebrated throughout the region. The implication is that Lugaid was believed to be housed within a particular stone. There exists some overlap in treatments of Lug and his son Cú Chulainn. Elsewhere the latter is described as wrapping his cloak around himself and a pillarstone, which consequently received a sword stroke aimed at him. This again suggests an identity between hero and menhir.[16]

Association of Lug with a stone features in Irish folklore. In a version of Lug's slaying of his cyclopean grandfather Balor, Lui Lavada (i.e. *Lugh lámfada*, 'Lug the Long-handed') drives a red spear into his baneful single eye. The stricken Balor pursues his grandson until he becomes weary, when he summons him:

'Come here now. Take the head off me and place it above your own for a few moments. You will know everything in the world, and no one will be able to conquer you.'

Lui took the head off his grandfather, and, instead of putting it on his own head, he put it on a rock. The next moment a drop came out of the head, made a thousand pieces of the rock, and dug a hole in the earth three times deeper than Loch Foyle …[17]

In another version Balor decapitates his son-in-law Mac Aneely on a large white stone, which the blood permeated 'to its very heart'. The red veins remained visible in the stone. However Mac Aneely's son (i.e. Lug) subsequently avenged his father by driving a red-hot iron bar 'through the Basilisk eye of Balor'. The stone itself was re-erected by a local squire in 1774, its name being given to the surrounding district of Clogh-an-Neely.[18] In a further version of the story, the youthful hero's father Cian is transformed into a stone pillar, being afterwards liberated by his son by means of a magic wand.[19]

In British tradition this close affinity between deity and stone is equally apparent. The most archaic section of the old British poem *Y Gododdin*, which contains no allusion to Christianity,[20] and may have originated as early as the seventh century AD, opens with a passage describing preparations for a campaign against the Angles of Northumbria. A gathering was held at 'the rock of Lleu's tribe: the folk of Lleu's mountain stronghold'.[21]

This indicates the existence of a rock, apparently situated on a hilltop fortress, which from early times was regarded as palladium of Lleu's people. Its likely setting is the hill of Traprain Law near Edinburgh, which was surmounted by an important stronghold of the tribe of the

15   Ian Hughes (ed.), *Math Uab Mathonwy: Pedwaredd Gainc y Mabinogi* (Aberystwyth, 2000), pp. 13–14.

16   Best, Bergin, O'Brien, and O'Sullivan (ed.), *The Book of Leinster*, p. 309. A poet's elegy, uttered at the deposition of the hero's head and arm at Tara, hails him as 'beautiful pillar'(*caín tuir*) (ibid., p. 450).

17   Curtin, *Hero-Tales of Ireland*, pp. 293–94.

18   Michael Herity (ed.), *Ordnance Survey Letters Donegal: Letters Containing Information relative to the Antiquities of the County of Donegal Collected during the Progress of the Ordnance Survey in 1835* (Dublin, 2000), pp. 43–44.

19   Curtin, *Hero-Tales of Ireland*, pp. 28–32.

20   'Further confirmation of the stemma is obtained by looking at some general features of the three texts. A and B¹ have Christian references, some shared. B² has none' (Koch (ed.), *The Gododdin of Aneirin*, p. lxix).

21   Ibid., p. 3; cf. p. 131; T. M. Charles-Edwards, *Wales and the Britons 350–1064* (Oxford, 2013), p. 375.

Votadini (Old Welsh *Guotodin*) in the Roman period. It continued in use into the early Dark Ages.[22] The region was known in the Middle Ages as *Lleuddiniawn* (later Lothian), meaning 'the Country of Lugu-dūnon, i.e. of the Fort of [the God] Lugus'.[23]

The existence of a special stone associated with Lleu at the site is attested by the mediæval Life of Saint Kentigern, patron saint of Glasgow. The saint is described as grandson of a half-pagan King Leudonus, from whom his province of *Lleuddiniawn* received its name:

> *Rex ... Leudonus, vir semipaganus, a quo provincia quam regebat Leudonia nomen sortita in Brittannia septentrionali.*

Leudonus had a daughter Thaney, who became a Christian and determined to espouse a life vowed to virginity. A dashing young prince fell in love with her, whose suit was favoured by the king. On finding her intransigent, he angrily gave her the choice of wedding the prince or of being consigned to the household of a swineherd. Assured by the humble herd that he would respect her maidenhood, the girl infuriated her father by accepting the second choice. Subsequently the tyrannical monarch sought to slay the innocent swineherd. In the course of the pursuit, however, the latter managed to transfix his royal assailant with a spear. Members of his household erected a curious commemorative monument to their lord near a place named *mons Dumpelder*, which constituted 'a great royal stone' on top of which was set a smaller carved stone. This structure was still to be seen at the time of writing. Next, Thaney was violated by her princely suitor in bizarrely erotic fashion – an episode originating in the familiar theme of virgin birth.[24]

The curious detail of the stone balanced on a larger stone recalls Lug's placing the head of Balor on a pillar stone in the Irish folktale.

Mons Dumpelder was the British name for Traprain Law,[25] and it seems likely that the stone identified in popular lore as the memorial to King Leudonus was likewise that 'rock of Lleu's tribe', palladium of 'the folk of Lleu's mountain stronghold', which is mentioned at the outset of *Y Gododdin*. The name *Leudonus* is a latinized eponym of the province *Lleuddiniawn*, and evidently the Christian birthtale of St Kentigern was appropriated at some stage from a traditional pagan account of the birth of the eponymous presiding divinity of the region, Lleu.

The story of Lleu in the early eleventh-century Welsh story of *Math uab Mathonwy* conforms in material respects to the same mythological pattern. Lleu, like Kentigern, is son of a virgin (Arianrhod). Leudonus is killed by a javelin flung by a concealed adversary, who is a swineherd. Lleu is likewise slain by a spear hurled at him by a stealthy foe, and his body is discovered with the assistance of a swineherd.

The death-tale of Lleu is complicated in part by his resurrection, following which he slays his assailant, Gronwy Pebr. The circumstances are nonetheless revealing. Following his magical resuscitation, Lleu hunts down Gronwy. Rejecting the latter's proffer of compensation, he insists

---

22   A. H. A. Hogg, 'The Votadini', in W. F. Grimes (ed.), *Aspects of Archaeology in Britain and Beyond: Essays presented to O. G. S. Crawford* (London, 1951), p. 207; Lloyd R. Laing, *Settlement Types in Post-Roman Scotland* (Oxford, 1975), p. 10.

23   Koch, *The Gododdin of Aneirin*, p. 131.

24   Alexander Penrose Forbes (ed.), *Lives of S. Ninian and S. Kentigern. Compiled in the Twelfth Century* (Edinburgh, 1874), pp. 245–49.

25   Kenneth Hurlstone Jackson, 'The Sources for the Life of St Kentigern', in Nora K. Chadwick (ed.), *Studies in the Early British Church* (Cambridge, 1958), p. 289.

that they both repair to the place by the River Cynfael where Gronwy perpetrated his dastardly attack. However, their rôles are reversed, with Lleu casting his spear from the spot where Gronwy threw his, while Gronwy stands on the spot where he found his victim. Lleu accepts Gronwy's plea to be permitted to place a boulder from the river bank between him and Lleu. The latter then flings his spear, which passes through the stone and shatters Gronwy's spine. Thereafter the stone, which was still to be found at the time *Math uab Mathonwy* was composed, became known as *Llech Gronwy*, 'the Stone of Gronwy'.[26]

It is possible that the curious circumstances of the return bout between Lleu and Gronwy arose from misunderstanding of the fact that *originally they were one and the same divine figure*. The name *G(o)ronwy* is a suffixed form of the compound *gwron*, 'hero'.[27] Thus, it may be that, by the time the literary version of the myth in *Math uab Mathonwy* came to be composed, 'the Hero/ Lleu' had evolved into paired distinct individuals. This is evinced by their cohabiting with the identical wife/mistress (Blodeuedd), and their being killed in identical manner at an identical spot. A fifteenth-century genealogy makes Gronwy son of Gwydion, thereby effectively identifying him with Lleu, who was likewise Gwydion's son.[28] This must reflect a tradition independent of *Math uab Mathonwy*, knowledge of which should have precluded such an interpretation.

Finally, W. J. Gruffydd showed that

> The story of Blodeuwedd is an intrusion. It has no connection at all with the original history of Llew, which, as far as the three destinies are concerned, ended with the acquisition of a wife made from flowers ... In every case where Blodeuwedd in *Math* mentions her husband to Gronwy Pevr, she carefully avoids his name, and calls him simply *yr unben y llys*, 'the lord to whom the court belongs'.[29]

With the Owl Maiden's adulterous affair with Gronwy removed, we are left with the death of Lleu from a spear-cast, his hanging on a tree and metamorphosis into an eagle, and association of his death with the pierced Stone of the Hero by the river Cynfael.

Furthermore, Gronwy's epithet *pebr* (modern Welsh *pefr*), 'radiant', is singularly apt to Lleu. The latter's name could easily be taken for the common noun *lleu*, 'light, brightness'.[30] A traditional account of the betrayal and death of Lleu, recorded in the early seventeenth century and clearly independent of the version in *Math uab Mathonwy*, substitutes the name

---

26   Hughes (ed.), *Math Uab Mathonwy*, pp. 16–17.

27   John T. Koch, 'Further to Indo-European *g^{wh} in Celtic', in Joseph F. Eska, R. Geraint Gruffydd, and Nicolas Jacobs (ed.), *Hispano-Gallo-Brittonica: Essays in honour of Professor D. Ellis Evans on the occasion of his sixty-fifth birthday* (Cardiff, 1995), pp. 83–84. Cf. J. Loth, 'Remarques et additions à la grammaire galloise historique et comparée de John Morris Jones', *Revue Celtique* (Paris, 1915–16), xxxvi, p. 152; Patrick Sims-Williams, 'Indo-European *g^{wh} in Celtic, 1894–1994' (Eska, Gruffydd, and Jacobs (ed.), *Hispano-Gallo-Brittonica*, pp. 205–6).

28   *Gronwy m. Gwdion m. Don* (P. C. Bartrum (ed.), *Early Welsh Genealogical Texts* (Cardiff, 1966), p. 58); *Louhen . map . Guid gen* ... (Egerton Phillimore, 'The *Annales Cambriæ* and Old-Welsh Genealogies from *Harleian MS.* 3859', *Y Cymmrodor* (London, 1888), ix, p. 176).

29   Gruffydd, *Math vab Mathonwy*, pp. 258–59.

30   Sir John Morris-Jones, 'Taliesin', *Y Cymmrodor* (1918), xxviii, pp. 239–40; Ifor Williams (ed.), *Pedeir Keinc y Mabinogi* (Cardiff, 1930), pp. 275–76; Max Förster, *Der Flußname Themse und seine Sippe: Studien zur Anglisierung keltischer Eigennamen und zur Lautchronologie des Altbritischen* (Munich, 1941), pp. 62–63. '*Lugu-* "god Lug", perhaps originally "the shiny one"' (Ranko Matasović, *Etymological Dictionary of Proto-Celtic* (Leiden, 2009), p. 248).

Llech Gronwy.
(Courtesy Flickr Alicia Grosso)

Huan for that of Lleu.[31] *Huan* is Welsh for 'sun' or 'sunlight'. A folktale associated with Nantlle ('Valley of Lleu') in Snowdonia recounted the death-tale of the dazzling monster *Aurwrychyn*, 'Gold-bristle', who was hunted from his seat near Llyn y Gadair and killed at Nantlle. As Sir John Rhŷs observed:

> The coincidence which makes the beast die in Nant where also Gwydion discovered his son Lleu in the form of an eagle, makes it probable that the proper name of the beast in golden bristles was originally no other than that of Lleu.[32]

The monster's picturesque appearance suggests solar imagery. Moreover, his name recalls that bestowed at birth on the infant Pryderi, hero of the First Branch of the Mabinogi: *Gwri Wallt Euryn*, 'Gwri Goldenhair'. There are complementary reasons for identifying the parallel figures of Pryderi and Lleu as personifications of Maponos, the Divine Son.[33]

---

31   Gruffydd, *Math vab Mathonwy*, pp. 198–99.

32   John Rhys, *Lectures on the Origin and Growth of Religion as Illustrated by Celtic Heathendom* (London, 1888), pp. 404–5.

33   *Studia Celtica*, xxviii, p. 98.

The apparent identity of Lleu and his adversary 'Gronwy' suggests that it was originally Lleu who was slain in the peculiar circumstances ascribed to his alter ego Gronwy, and consequently he who interposed the stone between himself and his assailant. A slab with an appropriate hole in it, known as *Llech Gronwy* ('the Stone of Gronwy'), existed at the time the author of the *Mabinogi* wrote, and in 1934 was rediscovered lying in the River Cynfael not far from its original site.[34] From *Math uab Mathonwy* it is evident that traditions of Lleu abounded in the neighbourhood, where the ruined Roman fortress of Tomen y Mur was identified as his stronghold. It looks as though an appropriately shaped stone on the bank of the Cynfael, known as the Stone of the Hero, was popularly associated with the tragic death of Lleu.[35] Perhaps the stone was in an earlier age regarded as an *eidolon*, or lapidary personification, of Lleu himself, identified by the hole inflicted by his adversary's spear.

The insular Celts believed that potent beings resided within certain hallowed stones. Thus the hero Fergus mac Roig was chanted out of his gravestone to recite the epic tale *Táin Bó Cúalnge*. In the early ninth-century Martyrology of Oengus, St Mochutu is described as banishing Satan into a pillar-stone, the biblical Evil One having clearly replaced a heathen god. The concept is explicitly alluded to in the same source, where reference is made to a gilded stone, worshipped by the heathens, out of which its 'devil' spoke. Similarly, St Patrick expelled the demon inhabiting a stone pillar at Mag Slécht, according to one account employing his crozier as a magic wand, and in another energetically wielding a sledgehammer.[36]

As frequently occurred, the Christian Church appropriated the powers of the ousted heathen. St Finnchu was said to have resided inside a stone prison, *i gcarcair chloiche*, which the description suggests was probably originally a solid rock, from which he was reluctantly conjured forth by St Comgall of Bangor.[37] Rationalization of a dwelling within a stone into a coffer constructed of stone slabs is again all but explicit in the Irish Life of St Coemgen (*anglicé* Kevin). There we learn that at Glendalough the saint had 'for bed, only a pillar of stone under his head, and a flagstone under him, and a flagstone at each side of him … and he would often go to the cliff and to the bed called Coemgen's bed'.[38] St Kevin's Bed is in fact a natural cleft in the rock set just above the surface of the lake, within which he is traditionally held to have slept. In North Britain, St Kentigern was similarly said to have lain inside a stone (*jacebat in saxo*), which his twelfth-century biographer explained was hollowed out, adding a stone pillow for

34   Frank Ward, 'Llech Ronw', *The Bulletin of the Board of Celtic Studies* (Cardiff, 1935), vii, pp. 352–53.

35   Rachel Bromwich regarded the episode in *Math* as 'an onomastic tale purporting to account for *Llech G(o)ronwy* in Cwm Cynfal, near Ffestiniog' (Rachel Bromwich (ed.), *Trioedd Ynys Prydein: The Welsh Triads* (Cardiff, 1978), p. 62).

36   Best, Bergin, O'Brien, and O'Sullivan (ed.), *The Book of Leinster*, p. 1119; Whitley Stokes (ed.), *Félire Óengusso Céli Dé. The Martyrology of Oengus the Culdee* (London, 1905), pp. 94, 186; Kathleen Mulchrone (ed.), *Bethu Phátraic: The Tripartite Life of Patrick* (Dublin, 1939), pp. 55–56; Gwynn (ed.), *The Metrical Dindshenchas*, iv, pp. 18–22.

37   O'Grady (ed.), *Silva Gadelica*, ii, p. 465.

38   Charles Plummer (ed.), *Bethada Náem nÉrenn: Lives of Irish Saints* (Oxford, 1922), i, p. 156; Whitley Stokes and John Strachan (ed.), *Thesaurus Palaeohibernicus: A Collection of Old-Irish Glosses Scholia Prose and Verse* (Cambridge, 1901–1903), ii, p. 331.

good measure.[39] All this must have been designed to explain a local menhir identified in popular lore with the sanctified hero.[40]

In Ireland and Wales the theme of the expectant mother of a child destined for great things, who sits or lies on a stone when giving birth, suggests a belief that the stone was possessed of generative power.[41] Two great stones mysteriously appeared at St David's birth, and at the moment of delivery his mother grasped a stone on which the imprint of her fingers remained.[42] In Ireland numerous saints are described as being delivered on flagstones.[43] Heroes were likewise portrayed as being born in this manner,[44] suggesting that pre-Christian Ireland shared with early Greek and other Indo-European cultures a belief that humanity originated in birth from stones.

Around the world a belief is recorded of gods and ancestors inhabiting menhirs and cromlechs. The Armenian hero Mher is described as entering the Raven's Rock, where he remains until the Judgment Day, while both the Nart hero Sasruquo and the divine Mithras were born from from rocks. Among the early Semites, standing stones were revered as embodiments of divinity. The Turkic people of the Altai-Sayan region in Central Asia believe that the world of the dead may be visited within a rock. On the Pacific island of Vao, ghosts were understood to dwell within monoliths representing the islanders' ancestors. The Quiche of Mexico worshipped stones in which their gods had become immured at the beginning of time. In North America the Ingalik believed that stones possessed souls known as 'shadows'.[45] Just as a talking stone was worshipped

---

39   Forbes (ed.), *Lives of S. Ninian and S. Kentigern*, p. 184. Self-enclosure in a stone 'tomb', rock-hewn tunnel, or natural cave represented regular ascetic practice in the early Near East. The body being as it were imprisoned, the spirit is released to seek communion with God (Violet MacDermot, *The Cult of the Seer in the Ancient Middle East: A Contribution to Current Research on Hallucinations drawn from Coptic and other Texts* (London, 1971), i, pp. 34–35).

40   Among numerous Siberian peoples, 'Burial traditions gave rise to the practice that dead persons are pressed under stone ... They are buried inside a stone ... stuck to a stone, that they even became stones/rocks' (Maria M. Tátar, 'Mythology as an areal problem in the Altai-Sayan area: the sacred holes and caves', in Juha Pentikäinen (ed.), *Shamanism and Northern Ecology* (Berlin and New York, 1996), p. 268).

41   Dorothy Ann Bray, *A List of Motifs in the Lives of the Early Irish Saints* (Helsinki, 1992), p. 128.

42   J. W. James (ed.), *Rhigyfarch's Life of St. David: The Basic Mid Twelfth-Century Latin Text with Introduction, Critical Apparatus and Translation* (Cardiff, 1967), pp. 4, 5. The description appears designed to account for a stone bearing an ogam inscription.

43   Cf. Whitley Stokes (ed.), *Lives of Saints from the Book of Lismore* (Oxford, 1890), p. 2; O'Grady (ed.), *Silva Gadelica*, i, p. 19; ii, p. 460; Plummer (ed.), *Vitae Sanctorum Hiberniae*, i, p. 34; ii, pp. 34, 36, 132; Rev. P. Power (ed.), *Life of St. Declan of Ardmore and Life of St. Mochuda of Lismore* (London, 1914), p. 8; A. O'Kelleher and G. Schoepperle (ed.), *Betha Colaim Chille: Life of Columcille Compiled by Manus O'Donnell in 1532* (Urbana, Ill., 1918), pp. 36–38, 42; Plummer (ed.), *Bethada Náem nÉrenn*, i, p. 26; Mulchrone (ed.), *Bethu Phátraic*, p. 5.

44   Cf. Best, Bergin, O'Brien, and O'Sullivan (ed.), *The Book of Leinster*, p. 400; Tomás Ó Cathasaigh (ed.), *The Heroic Biography of Cormac mac Airt* (Dublin, 1977), p. 119; Máirín O Daly (ed.), *Cath Maige Mucrama: The Battle of Mag Mucrama* (Dublin, 1975), p. 50; Comyn and Dinneen (ed.), *The History of Ireland by Geoffrey Keating*, ii, p. 274.

45   Eliade, *Patterns in Comparative Religion*, pp. 219–20; J. A. Boyle, 'Mher in the Carved Rock', *Journal of Mithraic Studies* (London, 1976), i, pp. 107–18; John Colarusso (tr.), *Nart Sagas from the Caucasus: Myths and Legends from the Circassians, Abazas, and Ubykhs* (Princeton, NJ, 2002), pp. 327–35; Leroy A. Campbell, *Mithraic Iconography and Ideology* (Leiden, 1968), pp. 272–73, 380–81; Lucy Goodison and Christine Morris (ed.), *Ancient Goddesses: The Myths and the Evidence* (Madison, Wis., 1998), p. 87; Juha Pentikäinen (ed.), *Shamanism and Northern Ecology*, pp. 269–70; John Layard, *Stone Men of Malekula: Vao* (London, 1942), pp. 17–19, 699; Karen Bassie-Sweet, *At the Edge of the World: Caves and Late Classic Maya World View* (Norman and London, 1996), pp. 32, 33, 146; Åke Hultkrantz, *Conceptions of the Soul among North American Indians: A Study in Religious Ethnology* (Stockholm, 1953), p. 485.

at Druim Tairleime in Ireland, so a Paiute Indian walking on a mountainside overheard a voice uttering a prophecy emanating from a crack in a rock, from which obtruded a bubble of saliva.[46]

Reverting to the myth of Lleu, it appears that he was not only believed to have entered, or become, a rock at his death, but was likewise born within one. The account in *Math uab Mathonwy* is curious. When the virgin Arianrhod comes to the court of her brother Gwydion, she leaves behind what is enigmatically described as 'a small something' (*y ryw bethan*). Before anyone could see it, Gwydion wrapped a sheet of silk around it, and hid it in a small chest (*cist*) at the foot of his bed. Subsequently he heard a cry from the chest, and found within a baby boy who proved to be the infant Lleu.[47]

The 'small something' which Arianrhod left behind was clearly an embryo,[48] and the episode is redolent of pre-Christian mythology. When Arianrhod arrives, Gwydion challengingly enquires whether she be a maiden. Her reply is in the affirmative, although couched in oddly guarded wording. Gwydion tests her by requiring her to step over his magic wand, whereupon she lets drop a sturdy child who flees to the sea. Turning to depart, she leaves the 'small something' at the entrance.

The equivocal emphasis on Arianrhod's virginity evokes the familiar figure of the Maiden Sovereignty, that divine personification of the land who remains eternally a virgin, while simultaneously functioning as mother to successive kings and heroes. As personification of the sovereignty she is mother of royal posterity, but since each reign represents a fresh cycle her virginity is perpetually renewed.[49] Her liminal situation in the doorway, when delivered of the 'small something' destined to become the royal hero Lleu, reflects the barrier set between eternity, where she dwells in perpetuity, and terrestrial time and space, on the margin between which the conception occurs. The episode is closely paralleled by the birth-tale of Lug's son Cú Chulainn, whose mother Deichtine 'rejected a second time that which was in her bosom and became a virgin'.[50]

The doorway as liminal conjunction between time and eternity, the point where the worlds of divinity and mortality temporarily coalesce, features (like many other pagan motifs) in Welsh and Irish hagiography. When Nonnita (whose name means 'nun', i.e. 'virgin') becomes pregnant with the future St David, she is discovered by St Gildas concealed between 'the door and the wall' of his church.[51] In Ireland the birth of St Brigid, whose name and attributes are those of a

---

46 Stokes (ed.), *Félire Óengusso Céli Dé*, p. 186; Gwynn (ed.), *The Metrical Dindshenchas*, iv, pp. 296; Julian H. Steward, 'Panatübiji' an Owens Valley Paiute', *Bulletin of the Smithsonian Institution Bureau of American Ethnology* (Washington, 1938), cxix, p. 188.

47 Hughes (ed.), *Math Uab Mathonwy*, p. 8.

48 'On devine aussi que la petite chose y ryw bethan ohonei que perd Aranrhod … n'est pas le placenta comme on l'a cru jusqu'ici … mais un embryon séminale, une étincelle vitale qui ne s'était pas encore développé en elle' (Claude Stercckx, 'Les Têtes Coupées et le Graal', *Studia Celtica* (Cardiff, 1985–1986), xx/xxi, p. 26); idem, *Les mutilations des ennemis chez les celtes préchrétiens*, p. 139. Gruffydd's earlier contention that the 'small thing' was a placenta is unconvincing (Gruffydd, *Math vab Mathonwy*, pp. 228–32). A placenta does not grow into a child.

49 Françoise Le Roux, 'La courtoise d'Étain: Commentaire du texte', *Celticvm XV: Actes du Vᵉ Colloque International d'Études Gauloises, Celtiques et Protoceltiques* (Rennes, 1966), pp. 362–63.

50 A. G. van Hamel (ed.), *Compert Con Culainn and Other Stories* (Dublin, 1933), p. 6.

51 Theodor Mommsen (ed.), *Monvmenta Germaniae Historica* (xiii): *Chronica Minora saec. IV. V. VI. VII* (Berlin, 1894), iii, p. 108; James (ed.), *Rhigyfarch's Life of St. David*, p. 4. It has been suggested that *Nonnita* is masculine, being originally the name of a companion of David, subsequently converted into that of his mother (Andrew Breeze, 'St David and the Cult of St Non', *The Carmarthenshire Antiquary* (Carmarthen, 2013), xlix, pp. 5–15). While the thesis merits attention, I remain unconvinced. The conventional ascription of a saint's conception to the rape of a virgin by a king is a motif too widespread

Celtic goddess, occurred when her mother arrived at dawn (i.e. between night and day), bearing milk, and placing one foot on one side of the threshold and one on the other.[52]

There remains the curious detail of the deposition of the divinely engendered embryo in a box (*cist*), at the foot of Gwydion's bed (*gwely*). Neither detail serves any clear purpose in the narrative, yet each must originally have been included for a reason. The *cist* recalls a similar discovery in the story of *Culhwch ac Olwen*. The wife of the guardian of the wilderness, Custennin the Herdsman, 'opened a coffer (*cib*) at the end of the hearth (*pentan*), and out of it came a lad with yellow curly hair'. Echoing the birth-tale of Lleu, he bears no name until one is bestowed upon him in consequence of a play on words. Following a subsequent exploit, he is told 'you are the best (*goreu*)' – upon which he is accorded the name *Goreu*. In due course, again like Lleu, he slays an oppressor and becomes ruler of the land. *Goreu* may have been a modified form of Old Welsh *Gurou* or *Guorou*, from which derives also the name of Lleu's adversary and alter ego Gronwy.[53]

The Red Book of Hergest text of *Culhwch* describes the receptacle in which the child appears as a box made of stone (*kib uaen*).[54] But what precisely was this stone receptacle, which the context intimates was a permanent fixture? The answer, surely, is that it was the hearthstone, *pentanfaen*, of the courthouse, which in insular Celtic societies was imbued with especial ideological significance. Under Welsh law its possession provided one of three prescribed proofs of landholding.[55] The fact that it was commonly the sole indestructible component of a wooden hall is clearly relevant to this provision,[56] as also is the numinous symbolism of the hearth as generative centre of cosmos and kingdoms, familiar from Celtic and other cosmologies.[57]

It appears that the author of *Culhwch*, or an earlier author, perplexed by the notion of a child's emergence from a solid flagstone, converted it into a stone box – an unlikely object, however,

---

to be ignored, identification of the virgin as a nun representing an obvious rationalization of her continuing immaculate status. This is how the author of *Buched Dewi* understood it, who observes: *enw a lleian oed Nonn* (D. Simon Evans (ed.), *The Welsh Life of St David* (Cardiff, 1988), p. 2).

52 Whitley Stokes (ed.), *Lives of Saints from the Book of Lismore* (Oxford, 1890), p. 36. Brigid was famed as a sanctified midwife, and rituals in her honour were performed on doorsteps (Séamas Ó Catháin, *The Festival of Brigit: Celtic Goddess and Holy Woman* (Dublin, 1995), pp. 36–37).

53 Rachel Bromwich and D. Simon Evans (ed.), *Culhwch and Olwen: An Edition and Study of the Oldest Arthurian Tale* (Cardiff, 1992), pp. 17–18, 30, 42; cf. p. 140. On the other hand, a personal name GOREVS occurs in an inscription on a stone at Yealmpton in Devonshire, which has been compared with Irish *Gúaire* (Elisabeth Okasha, *Corpus of Early Christian Inscribed Stones of South-west Britain* (Leicester, 1993), pp. 338–40; Patrick Sims-Williams, *The Celtic Inscriptions of Britain: Phonology and Chronology, c. 400–1200* (Oxford, 2003), pp. 224–25, 236.

54 John Rhŷs and J. Gwenogvryn Evans (ed.), *The Text of the Mabinogion and other Welsh Tales from the Red Book of Hergest* (Oxford, 1887), p. 116.

55 Stephen J. Williams and J. Enoch Powell (ed.), *Cyfreithiau Hywel Dda yn ôl Llyfr Blegywryd (Dull Dyfed)* (Cardiff, 1942), pp. 117, 118; A. W. Wade-Evans (ed.), *Welsh Medieval Law: Being a Text of the Laws of Howel the Good, Namely the British Museum Harleian MS. 4353 of the 13th Century* (Oxford, 1909), p. 136; Hywel D. Emanuel (ed.), *The Latin Texts of the Welsh Laws* (Cardiff, 1967), p. 129.

56 The Welsh Laws imposed stringent punishment on anyone responsible for fire damage (L. A. S. Butler, 'Domestic Building in Wales and the Evidence of the Welsh Laws', *Medieval Archaeology* (London, 1987), xxxi, pp. 50, 52).

57 Angela Della Volpe, 'From the Hearth to the Creation of Boundaries', *The Journal of Indo-European Studies* (1990), xviii, pp. 157–84; eadem, 'On Indo-European Ceremonial and Socio-Political Elements Underlying the Origin of Formal Boundaries', ibid. (1992), xx, pp. 71–122. 'Agni's luminous energy (*varcas*) in the sky is the sun … and the fire on the fireplace is identical with that heavenly body' (J. Gonda, *Prajāpati and the Year* (Amsterdam, 1984), p. 43).

whether lodged by a royal fireside or in any other context. The notion of a large stone possessed of a hollow interior is implicit in the term *cistfaen* (literally 'stone chest'), employed to denote a dolmen or menhir. Possibly the concept originated as a rationalization of the belief that boulders of striking appearance might house a hero, giant, or divinity.[58]

The box in which Lleu was discovered was placed at the foot of Gwydion's bed (*gwely*). The word *gwely* evolved at an early date from the meaning 'bed', to that of 'marriage-bed', and so 'married couple *qua* ancestors or parents'.[59] The combined symbolism of (stone) box and marriage-bed suggests classic Indo-European myth, wherein the divinely engendered hero is born from a rock or stone.[60] The curious detail in *Math* of a box containing a newborn divinity 'under the foot of the *gwely*' (*is traed y wely*) further suggests mythical imagery of the tribe and its progenitor, recalling *inter alia* the Rock of Lleu, palladium of the Gododdin people of North Britain.

A parallel conception lay behind the marriage rite *Aśmāropana* in Vedic India. A significant stage of the ceremony involved the priest's leading the bridal couple clockwise around a fire. He then instructed them to stand on a stone, while he uttered the verse: 'Come, step you both on (this) stone; be firm like a stone; may all the gods make your lifetime a hundred autumns.'

The next verse calls upon the bridegroom to imitate the action of the god Indra and his wife Indrānī, who in the primal era stepped down from Gandhamādana (a sacred mountain in the Himalayas): 'Likewise you must descend from this stone together with your wife, and mount (and place) your feet on plain ground ... on attaining old-age, O woman, be rich in sons.'[61]

The human couple ensure the fecundity of their union, encircling the central fire of the universe, and descending from a stone, which provides a microcosmic representation of the sacred mountain from which the god descended *in illo tempore*. As sky-god and source of fertility on earth (implanted through rain and lightning-bolts), Indra was the ideal figure to invoke in such a context.

The name *Indra* derives from Old Indian *Indriyám*, 'skill, ability, power',[62] attributes which recall Lug's epithet *samildánach*, 'very gifted, skilled, accomplished, having many skills or accomplishments'. Indra's character broadly parallels that ascribed to Lug (as well as that of Apollo):

> He embodies the qualities of all the gods ... Ever young, Indra embodies all the virtues of youth: heroism, generosity, exuberance. He stands for action and service but also for the need of force which leads to power, to victory, and booty. He leads the warriors and protects them with his thunderbolt and his bow, the rainbow ... His color is gold or tawny

---

58   For these reasons it does not appear that the 'box' in which Goreu was found was primarily conceived as a receptacle for supplementary gestation or ritual revelation, as has been suggested (Stefan Zimmer, 'Indo-Celtic Connections: Ethic, Magic, and Linguistic', *The Journal of Indo-European Studies* (Washington, 2001), xxix, pp. 393–94; Leslie Ellen Jones, 'Boys in Boxes: The Recipe for a Welsh Hero', in Joseph Falaky Nagy and Leslie Ellen Jones (ed.), *Heroic Poets and Poetic Heroes in Celtic Tradition: A Festschrift for Patrick K. Ford* (Dublin, 2005), pp. 207–25).

59   Charles-Edwards, *Early Irish and Welsh Kinship*, p. 255.

60   Gregory Nagy, *Greek Mythology and Poetics* (Ithaca, NY, 1990), pp. 181–201; Calvert Watkins, *How to Kill a Dragon: Aspects of Indo-European Poetics* (New York and Oxford, 1995), pp. 161–64.

61   M. J. Dresden (ed.), *Mānavagrhyasūtra: A Vedic Manual of Domestic Rites* (Groningen, 1941), pp. 51–52.

62   Julius Pokorny, *Indogermanisches Etymologisches Wörterbuch* (Berne, 1959–69), i, p. 774.

like that of the horses drawing his car. In the Purānas he is shown as a fair young man riding a white horse or an elephant and bearing the thunderbolts in his right hand.[63]

Furthermore, just as Lug in Ireland and his Welsh counterpart Lleu were associated with magical cows, Indra was concerned with the rescue and preservation of cattle.[64]

The gestation and birth of Lleu in what was originally a stone chest at the foot of a *gwely*, a word meaning equally 'bed' and 'lineage', bears obvious metaphorical application. In Irish and Welsh mythology Lug or Lleu is envisaged both as dwelling within a stone and as divine progenitor of royal dynasties. In many mythologies the concept of the royal throne evolved from the sacred stone representing the Centre of the kingdom, creative matrix of life, and fount of the royal dynasty personifying humanity as a whole.[65] This ideology is reflected in the Welsh word *gorsedd*, which may mean equally 'mound/hill' (often the focus of a kingdom, affording access to the Otherworld), or 'throne'. The close correspondence between these respective meanings is illustrated by the frequency with which persons seeking an encounter with the supernatural are described as *seating* themselves on top of a *gorsedd*.[66]

In early Germanic societies a royal burial-mound was used alike as assembly point, central sanctuary of the kingdom, and formal seat of a king.[67] The king derived his authority or numen from his royal ancestors, who rested within the howe or barrow beneath him. In Ireland and Wales the god Lug, primal ancestor of royal dynasties, was widely believed to reside within a sacred stone situated at the heart of the kingdom. Whilst each provincial Irish kingdom possessed its own royal stone or throne, the most celebrated of all was the *Lia Fáil*, or Stone of Destiny, at Tara. Its most striking characteristic was confirmation of the legitimacy of a king of Tara or Ireland by utterance of a piercing scream or screams, when mounted by the lawful heir.[68] That it was regarded as embodying the land of Ireland is self-evident, *Fál* being both the name of the stone and an alternative name for Ériu, Ireland.[69] The royal capital

---

63   Alain Daniélou, *Hindu Polytheism* (London, 1964), pp. 107, 109.

64   Barend A. van Nooten and Gary B. Holland (ed.), *Rig Veda: A Metrically Restored Text with an Introduction and Notes* (Cambridge, Mass., 1994), pp. 152–54; J. C. Heesterman, *The Ancient Indian Royal Consecration: The Rājasūya Described According to the Yajus Texts and Annotated* (The Hague, 1957), pp. 136–37, 168, 170–71.

65   Ibid., pp. 101, 140, 141–42, 147-50; Jeannine Auboyer, 'Le caractère royal et divin du trône dans l'Inde ancienne', *La Regalità Sacra: Contributi al Tema Dell' VIII Congresso Internazionale di Storia delle Religioni (Roma, Aprile 1955)* (Leiden, 1959), pp. 181–88; A. J. Wensinck, *The Ideas of the Western Semites Concerning the Navel of the Earth* (Amsterdam, 1916), pp. 54–58. The throne on which the mediæval dukes of Carinthia were installed was constructed of large stone slabs (Joseph Felicijan, *The Genesis of the Contractual Theory and the Installation of the Dukes of Carinthia* (Cleveland, Ohio, 1967), pp. 63–64, 89).

66   Thomson (ed.), *Pwyll Pendeuic Dyuet*, pp. 8–9; Thomson (ed.), *Branwen uerch Lyr*, p. 6; Hughes (ed.), *Manawydan Uab Llyr*, pp. 2, 5; Bromwich and Simon Evans (ed.), *Culhwch and Olwen*, p. 15.

67   Hilda Roderick Ellis, *The Road to Hel: A Study of The Conception of the Dead in Old Norse Literature* (Cambridge, 1943), pp. 105–11; William A. Chaney, *The Cult of Kingship in Anglo-Saxon England: The Transition from Paganism to Christianity* (Manchester, 1970), pp. 96–105.

68   Gray (ed.), *Cath Maige Tuired*, p. 24; Best, Bergin, O'Brien, and O'Sullivan (ed.), *The Book of Leinster*, i, p. 34; James Henthorn Todd (ed.), *leabhar breathnach annso sis: The Irish Version of the Historia Brittonum of Nennius* (Dublin, 1848), p. 200; O'Grady (ed.), *Silva Gadelica*, i, p. 233; Comyn and Dinneen (ed.), *The History of Ireland by Geoffrey Keating*, i, p. 100.

69   E. G. Quin *et al.* (ed.), *Dictionary of the Irish Language: Based mainly on Old and Middle Irish Materials* (Dublin, 1913–76), 'F', col. 36.

of Munster at Cashel also housed a sacred stone, which played a central function in the elevation of kings of that country.[70]

There are intimations in the sources that the stone was understood in early times to house, or provide access to, a microcosmic world presided over by Lug. In the account mentioned earlier, we learn that the king was required to drive his chariot between two flagstones standing a hand's breadth apart, after which his chariot-axle screeched against the side of the prophetic stone *Fál*.[71] This looks like an attempt to rationalize an earlier version, in which the king was understood to enter and re-emerge from the stone.[72] The names of the stones through which he was obliged to pass, *Blocc* and *Bluigne*, appear devised to serve the tale (in another account they feature as names of the king's two druids).[73] The screeching of the axle against the stone *Fál* may have originated in an attempt to account for screams originally emanating from within the stone itself.

This belief is likewise suggested by the story of 'The Phantom's Frenzy' (*Baile in Scáil*). The tale begins with the primal King Conn of Tara setting out to stand guard at dawn against the malign hosts of the Otherworld. Arrived at the rampart, he treads on the stone *Fál*, which utters a scream which is heard across the plain of Meath. Conn asks his poet the meaning of this wonder, who replies that he will provide an explanation after meditating for fifty-three days. Once that time had passed, the poet described the significance of the stone as a national palladium, adding that the number of screams it uttered portended the number of Conn's descendants destined to reign over Ireland.

The poet further explained that he was not the one to expound their names. Thereupon a thick mist descended upon them, and they crossed a great plain until they arrived at a splendid house. Within they found a beautifully dressed maiden seated on a crystal chair, together with a man of more than human size and splendour. He explained to the visitors that he was Lug, son of Ethne, who would now foretell Conn's successors, together with the lengths of their reigns.[74]

It looks as though Conn originally obtained access to the realm of Lug by standing on the stone *Fál*, the Otherworld kingdom being implicitly situated within the stone. The significance of the number of screams it utters replicates the scene subsequently witnessed by Conn in the House of Lug. As the adventure makes plain, the stone was not envisaged as a minuscule kingdom inhabited by pygmies, but as an alternative world commensurate with the kingdom of Tara. Time and space operate on distinct dimensions in the Otherworld.

A similar belief obtained in Finland, where

the proper noun *Hiidenportti* (Gate of *Hiisi*) is based on the common noun *hiisi* ['cultic site'], with which the social community have adapted a large cleft in between two rocks into the conceptual sphere of the sacred. It is deemed sacred because it is perceived as

---

70   Edel Bhreathnach, '*Tara* and *Cashel*: Manifestations of the Centre of the Cosmos in the North and the South', in Jacqueline Borsje, Ann Dooley, Séamus Mac Mathúna, and Gregory Toner (ed.), *Celtic Cosmology: Perspectives from Ireland and Scotland* (Toronto, 2014), pp. 179–81.

71   *Ériu*, vi, p. 134.

72   This is not incompatible with my suggestion that the paired rocks correspond functionally to the Symplegades of classical tradition. In both cases the myth is likely to have reflected an earlier version, in which the divine hero enters an Otherworld housed within a rock.

73   Kevin Murray (ed.), *Baile in Scáil: 'The Phantom's Frenzy'* (Dublin, 2004), p. 33.

74   Ibid., pp. 33–35.

a gate on a borderline which marks the end of the differentiated and classified territory (profane) and the beginning of the undifferentiated, unclassified and unseen (sacred) sphere.[75]

That a parallel belief existed in Celtic Britain is indicated by a curious episode in the Welsh Arthurian romance of *Owein*. One day its eponymous hero *Owein uab Uryen* hears three loud screams uttered from within a forest. Approaching, he discovers amidst the trees a grey rock set in a huge cliff. To his surprise, he finds that the cries are uttered by a pure white lion inside a cleft of the rock, which is being attacked by a serpent. Owain slays the serpent, whereupon the lion becomes his inseparable companion and protector.[76]

Sir John Rhŷs pointed out that the description in the White Book of Rhydderch of the lion as 'pure white' (*lle6 pur6yn*)[77] 'is mythologically doubtless more correct' than the more natural 'pure black' (*lle6 purdu*) found in the later Red Book of Hergest text.[78] Although his interpretation is a little involved, he appears to have been first to note the significance of this curious encounter. Both its peculiar lair and unusual colour indicate that the lion was an Otherworld creature. The Welsh word for 'lion' is *lle6*, which was also the spelling widely though incorrectly employed in mediæval Welsh manuscripts for *Lleu*, counterpart of Irish *Lug*. As a common noun, *Lleu* might naturally be understood as 'light', which however makes no sense in the context. Consequently, it was interpreted as the similar-sounding *Lle6*, 'lion' – an apt enough name for a martial hero.[79]

Given the screams emanating from the rock that attracted Owain's attention, who then discovered *Llew* dwelling within it, it is not unlikely that the incident represents a late and confused interpretation of a myth comparable to that of Conn's adventure at Tara, wherein screams emanating from a stone led the king to an encounter with Lleu's Irish counterpart Lug. In addition, the lion's protective rôle echoes that of Lug as guardian of his son Cú Chulainn. Just as the brave *lle6* intervenes to save Owain at critical moments, so Lug arrives to heal the wounded Ulster hero and fight at his side.[80]

In the 'Herbertian' Life of Kentigern, the saint is conceived in consequence of seduction of the virgin daughter of *Leudonus, vir semipaganus* (i.e. Lleu), by a youthful prince *Ewen*

75   Veikko Anttonen, 'Rethinking the Sacred: The Notions of 'Human Body' and 'Territory' in Conceptualizing Religion', in Thomas A. Idinopulos and Edward A. Yonan (ed.), *The Sacred and its Scholars: Comparative Methodologies for the Study of Primary Religious Data* (Leiden, 1996), pp. 47–52. Cf. Veikko Anttonen, 'The Concept of Pyhä (Sacred) in Pre-Christian Finnish Religion', in Mihály Hoppál and Juha Pentikäinen (ed.), *Northern Religions and Shamanism* (Budapest, 1992), pp. 31–38.

76   R. L. Thomson (ed.), *Owein or Chwedyl Iarlles y Ffynnawn* (Dublin, 1968), pp. 24–25.

77   J. Gwenogvryn Evans (ed.), *The White Book Mabinogion: Welsh Tales & Romances Reproduced from the Peniarth Manuscripts* (Pwllheli, 1907), col. 254.

78   John Rhŷs and J. Gwenogvryn Evans (ed.), *The Text of the Mabinogion and other Welsh Tales from the Red Book of Hergest* (Oxford, 1887), p. 186.

79   Rhys, *Lectures on the Origin and Growth of Religion as Illustrated by Celtic Heathendom*, pp. 401–403; idem, *Studies in the Arthurian Legend* (Oxford, 1891), p. 97. For 'lion' as martial sobriquet, cf. Ifor Williams (ed.), *Canu Aneirin* (Cardiff, 1938), p. 126; Doris Edel, 'Geoffrey's So-called Animal Symbolism and Insular Celtic Tradition', *Studia Celtica* (1983/1984), xviii/xix, p. 103.

80   R. I. Best and Osborn Bergin (ed.), *Lebor na Huidre: Book of the Dun Cow* (Dublin, 1929), pp. 194–96; John Strachan and J. G. O'Keefe (ed.), *The Táin Bó Cúailnge from the Yellow Book of Lecan with Variant Readings from the Lebor na Huidre* (Dublin, 1912), pp. 66–67; Best, Bergin, O'Brien, and O'Sullivan (ed.), *The Book of Leinster*, p. 324.

filius regis Ulien (i.e. the North British prince Owain ap Urien).[81] Here we have evidence prior to the romance of *Owein* of a traditional association between the hero Owain and the god Lleu.

The pryfed in the rock

The second *gormes* described in *Cyfranc Lludd a Lleuelys* is the destructive scream, which proves to have been uttered by one of the two fighting dragons discovered at the Centre of Britain. There can be little doubt that the treatment of this episode in *Cyfranc Lludd a Lleuelys* rests on a misunderstanding, the scream having originally been no more than premonitory accompaniment to one or both *gormesoedd*. Fortunately, this factor can be compared with the earlier account of the dragons contained in the *Historia Brittonum*, whose influence on the Welsh tale is evident.

I have shown that in Nennius's version the paired creatures, which he terms in Latin *vermes*, were in Welsh *pryfed*, or tiny soul-creatures, featuring in Irish birth-tales under the cognate term *cruim*, or corresponding *dorb*. Puzzled by their mysterious nature, Nennius took the word in its non-specific sense of 'creatures', which he adapted to the political context of this section of his *History*, evoking biblical dragons from the Book of Esther as personifications of the warring races of Britons and Saxons. There is no scream in the *Historia Brittonum* account, nor does it occur in *Cyfranc Lludd a Lleuelys* at the moment foretold by Lleuelys. In the latter tale it is awkwardly distinguished from the revelation of the 'dragons' in order to make the *gormesoedd* accord with the traditional framework of a triad. In reality, the cosmic scream was not of itself a *gormes*, but a dreadful accompaniment either to the advent of a hostile Otherworld manifestion or to moments of catastrophic change in society, ranging from the downfall of a kingdom to the extinction of a family landholding. As the Welsh legal terminology *diasbad uwch Annwfn* indicates, the gates of the stygian Underworld gaped briefly open, from which resounded the eldritch wail.

Nevertheless, it is clear that the *pryfed* represented a distinctive factor in *omphalos* lore. They are central to both early accounts: being so entrenched, that their forgotten character required ingenious but revealingly divergent explanations. It is apparent from both versions that the nature of the *pryfed* was no longer understood.

In *Cyfranc Lludd a Lleuelys*, the author sought to reconcile this interpretation with awareness of authentic tradition, in which the *pryfed* were minuscule creatures, which (like their Irish counterparts *cruim* and *dorb*) were customarily found in water or mead. Lustration representing a potent means of destroying demons, whether in pagan or Christian tradition, the author guessed that it was their presence in holy water that conferred its purgative potency.[82] In view

---

81 Forbes (ed.), *Lives of S. Ninian and S. Kentigern*, p. 245.

82 Could the misunderstanding have been influenced by the identification of cloud-bearing plague as a *pryf*? In the corpus of pseudo-Taliesin poetry, the prophetic bard is made to declare that 'a most strange *pryf* will come from the Sea Marsh of Rhianedd' (*Fe ddaw pryf rhyfedd / O Forfa Rhianedd*) to destroy Maelgwn Gwynedd (Ifor Williams, 'Hen Chwedlau', (London, 1948): *Sessions 1946–47*, p. 57). The allusion is to the devastating sixth-century plague, known as the Yellow Death, in which King Maelgwn was believed to have died (Juliette Wood, 'Maelgwn Gwynedd: A Forgotten Welsh Hero', *Trivium* (Lampeter, 1984), p. 106). From the Lives of Saints Teilo and Oudoceus we learn that it acquired this sobriquet from the fact that its victims appeared yellow and bloodless. Significantly, it manifested itself in the form of a towering watery cloud (*incolumpna aquose nubis apparebat hominibus*), inflicting wholesale destruction across the landscape as it passed over (J. Gwenogvryn

of this, I suggest that the passage here rendered in bold represents a gloss on an earlier version of *Cyfranc Lludd a Lleuelys*.

> And after their speech was unobstructed, Lleuelys told his brother that **he would give him some *pryfed* and that he should keep some of them alive for breeding, lest by chance that sort of *gormes* come a second time, but he should take some others of the *pryfed* and crush them in water, and that he declared would be good for destroying the race of the Coraniaid. Namely,** after he returned home to his realm, he should summon all the people together, his people and the race of the Coraniaid [to one meeting on pretence of making peace between them], and when they were all together, he should take the charged water (*y dwuyr rinweddawl*) and sprinkle it over one and all, and he averred that the water would poison the race of the Coraniaid and would not kill and would not harm anyone of his own race.

This suggestion has the merit of distinguishing the *pryfed* from the *dwuyr rinweddawl*, the two representing disparate concepts with distinctive functions in British mythological lore. Destruction of evil spirits by means of lustration recurs in both pagan and Christian contexts, but nowhere else does the rite require distillation of creatures in the water. At the same time, the intrusive *pryfed* require an explanation. The likeliest is that they represented the life force of humanity, which was preserved at the heart of the kingdom. Omitting Nennius's introduction of the discrete motif of the sacrificial child, together with his conjectural explanation of the nature of the *vermes*, the following elements remain.

1. *Historia Brittonum.* The site of the royal fortress is identified as the safest (*tutissima*) spot in the kingdom. However, the emergent structure is nightly destroyed by an unseen power. A prophetic figure arrives before the king, to whom he reveals two vases or vats (*uases*) buried beneath the paving. The phraseology here is a little confusing, but essentially it seems that a tent is found between them, inside which are discovered two *vermes*. (I suggested earlier that the peculiar phrase 'in the midst' (*in medio*) derives from an earlier allusion to the Centre of the Kingdom (*y pwynt perued*). It is further likely that the *vermes* were originally contained in the 'vases',[83] which in turn were covered by the tent. Some confusion is likely enough, given Nennius's demonstrable ignorance of the nature of the *vermes*. Although the story then breaks off into the interpolated 'fighting dragons' explanation, and concludes with odd inconsequentiality, the implication seems to be that the *vermes* in their vase or vases constitute a palladium, retention of which ensured the security in perpetuity of the structure erected at the kingdom's Centre, and hence the kingdom itself.

2. *Cyfranc Lludd a Lleuelys.* Again excluding their erroneous transformation into dragons, two creatures of varying terminology are immersed in a vat of the best mead, covered by a sheet of brocaded silk. This in turn is contained within a stone chest, which is buried 'in the strongest place you can find in your kingdom', 'and

---

Evans and John Rhŷs (ed.), *The Text of the Book of Llan Dâv Reproduced from the Gwysaney Manuscript* (Oxford, 1893), pp. 107, 131).

83   It may be that an original single vase was duplicated in order to accommodate the paired *vermes*. This is suggested by the more logical account contained in the *Cyfranc*.

as long as they are in that secure place, no *gormes* shall come to *Ynys Prydein* from anywhere else'.

In its originally mythological context, the druids' injunction to Vortigern that he 'make a citadel in this place, which will be the most safe from barbaric races forever' (*arcem in isto loco fac, quia tutissima a barbaris gentibus in aeternum erit*) – i.e. one place, and one place only – must surely allude to the nation's indestructible *omphalos*.[84] The transfer of the *pryfed* from the Centre of Britain ('Oxford') to Dinas Emrys implies that the myth was attached alike to the Omphalos of Britain revealed by Lleuelys, and to its provincial counterpart at Dinas Emrys. Stripped of Nennius's speculative accretions, the security of the kingdom is envisaged as depending on preservation of a palladium held at the Sacred Centre.

With this, too, may be associated Lleuelys's explanation of the *pryfed* he bestows on Lludd, when he 'told his brother that he would give him some *pryfed* and that he should keep some of them alive for breeding, lest by chance that sort of *gormes* came a second time'. Here, it seems, lies a prime source of the confusion. In the *Historia Brittonum* it was a pair (male and female?)[85] of *pryfed*, that in *Cyfranc Lludd a Lleuelys* was directed to be preserved at the Centre 'for breeding', i.e. a paradigmatic pair, whose preservation at the *omphalos* ensured the continuing protection of the British race (*cenedl*) from destruction by a *gormes*. That some *pryfed* were to be preserved at the Centre 'for breeding' might appear to signify that they would when occasion required generate further *pryfed*. Given evidence that *pryf* originally designated the generative embryo, or 'soul-creature', I suggest rather that originally Lleuelys's injunction to 'keep some of them alive for breeding' (*a gadu rei onadunt yn vyw y hiliaw*) meant that they were to be preserved at the Centre for use in propagating (*hiliaf*) fresh generations of humanity.

Again, that they were envisaged as reposing within a receptacle containing mead recalls the medium in which they were ingested by a queen at her impregnation in the Irish tradition. Finally, their being housed within a stone at the *omphalos* suggests that a particular megalith was imbued with procreative potency ensuring the ultimate survival of the Britons, no matter what cataclysm might afflict the country as a whole.[86] The Irish *omphalos*-stone *Lia Fáil* at Tara was widely accorded phallic (i.e. generative) properties.[87] In Heinrich Wagner's words,

---

84 'The navel is the seat of natural and civil order, a symbol of the divine throne, the place where the order of the universe is regulated' (A. J. Wensinck, *The Ideas of the Western Semites Concerning the Navel of the Earth* (Amsterdam, 1916), p. 65).

85 'The union of the two serpents round the wand [*caduceus*] might for the Greeks represent the life-power complete by the union of male ψυχή and female ψυχή' (Richard Broxton Onians, *The Origins of European Thought about the Body, the Mind the Soul, the World Time, and Fate: New Interpretations of Greek, Roman and kindred evidence also of some basic Jewish and Christian beliefs* (Cambridge, 1954), p. 122). 'As messenger of the gods, Hermes carries the herald's staff, the *kerykeion*, which is really the image of copulating snakes taken over from ancient Near Eastern tradition' (Walter Burkert, *Greek Religion* (Cambridge, Mass., 1985), p. 158). Cf. the important discussion of the mythological rôle of the entwined serpents by Luc Brisson, *Le mythe de Tirésias: Essai d'analyse structurale* (Leiden, 1976), pp. 46–77.

86 Belief in the fertilizing power of sacred stones is widely attested in early Britain and Ireland, as in other primitive societies around the globe. Cf. Carolus Plummer (ed.), *Vitae Sanctorum Hiberniae: Partim Hactenvs Ineditae ad Fidem Codicvm Manvscriptorvm Recognovit Prolegominis Notis Indicibvs Instrvxit* (Oxford, 1910), i, p. clvi; Mircea Eliade, *Patterns in Comparative Religion* (London, 1958), pp. 220–26, 237; Elissa R. Henken, *The Welsh Saints: A Study in Patterned Lives* (Cambridge, 1991), pp. 244–25; Dorothy Ann Bray, *A List of Motifs in the Lives of the Early Irish Saints* (Helsinki, 1992), p. 128.

87 Jan de Vries, *Keltische Religion* (Stuttgart, 1961), pp. 239–40; Alwyn Rees and Brinley Rees, *Celtic Heritage: Ancient Tradition in Ireland and Wales* (London, 1961), pp. 146–47; Tomás Ó Broin, 'Lia Fáil:

> The *lía fáil*, the magic stone … originally meaning "penis-stone" [*ferp cluche*] … apparently represents the voice of the progenitor/ancestor-deity of Tara, which ultimately was *Lug/Mercurius*.[88]

The procreative power of the stone also recalls that implicitly ascribed the spot on Preseli Mountain, whither Pwyll and his nobles repaired to resolve the problem of his queen Rhiannon's infertility.

Was the original stone housing the *pryfed* at the Centre in *Cyfranc Lludd a Lleuelys* the so-called Altar Stone at Stonehenge, which 'could have formed a focal point, more or less facing the "entrance"'?[89] It is the most massive of the bluestones brought from Preseli, and was evidently revered as possessed of particular significance.[90] The fact that it appears to have been partially buried[91] recalls the instruction given by Lludd to Lleuelys, that he 'inter them [the 'dragons'] in a stone chest and hide it in the ground'.

It was seen earlier that a strikingly similar concept of the preservation of 'souls' occurs in Iranian mythology. Anticipating the potential destruction of mankind during the cosmic winter *Markūsān*, the god Yima constructs a subterranean refuge called *Var*, in which are preserved the germs of all creation: human, animal, and vegetable. When the dreadful winter passes away, Yima brings forth a new creation from the seeds of the old.[92]

In his account of the re-erection of the Irish stones from Uisneach at the site of Stonehenge on Salisbury Plain, Geoffrey of Monmouth reports of their former owners, the giants, that 'their purpose was to set up baths among them whenever they were ill. They used to wash the stones and pour the water into the baths to cure illnesses.'

I have suggested that this could reflect a confused version of the lustration described in *Cyfranc Lludd a Lleuelys*. Was water poured over a particularly numinous stone understood to house the paradigmatic *pryfed*, archetypal seeds of procreation, in order to be employed in a lustration ensuring fertility among worshippers congregated at the *omphalos* shrine? The birth-tale of the Irish hero Conall Cernach describes how Finnchaím, daughter of the druid Cathbad, encountered difficulty in conceiving. She was taken by a druid to a well in which, after chanting incantations and spells over it, he instructed her to wash, whereupon she could

Fact and Fiction in the Tradition', *Celtica* (Dublin, 1990), xxi, pp. 399–400; Helmut Birkhan, *Kelten: Versuch einer Gesamtdarstellung ihrer Kultur* (Vienna, 1997), pp. 574, 779, 885; Proinsias Mac Cana, *The Cult of the Sacred Centre: Essays on Celtic Ideology* (Dublin, 2011), p. 268. Ó Broin argues rather that the *lía fáil* was the epiphany of the Earth Goddess (*Celtica*, xxi, p. 401), but this seems doubtful.

88   'Studies in the Origins of Early Celtic Civilisation', *Zeitschrift für celtische Philologie* (Tübingen, 1971), xxxi, p. 58; cf. p. 19.

89   'This structure of a sacred stone affiliated with a sovereign figure is not unique to Rome, but is one which recurs on both the eastern and western fringes of the Indo-European world' (Roger D. Woodard, *Indo-European Sacred Space: Vedic and Roman Cult* (Urbana and Chicago, 2006), p. 60).

90   K. E. Walker, 'The monument today', in Rosamund M. J. Cleal, K. E. Walker, and R. Montague (ed.), *Stonehenge in its landscape: Twentieth-century excavations* (London, 1995), pp. 29–30; Rosamund M. J. Cleal, 'The stone monument, phase 3', in ibid., p. 188. 'Within the bluestone setting of Stonehenge 3i, the Altar Stone, placed on the south-west side, appears to have been the centre of attention' (Clive Ruggles, 'Astronomy and Stonehenge', in Barry Cunliffe and Colin Renfrew (ed.), *Science and Stonehenge* (Oxford, 1997), p. 218).

91   John North, *Stonehenge: Neolithic Man and the Cosmos* (London, 1996), pp. 424–27. 'Its shaped end shows that, at some point, in Stonehenge's past, it was probably a standing stone' (Mike Parker Pearson, *Stonehenge: Exploring the Greatest Stone Age Mystery* (London, 2012), p. 31).

92   Arthur Christensen, *Les types du premier homme et du premier roi dans l'histoire légendaire de Iraniens* (Stockholm, 1917–34), ii, pp. 17–18, 21–25, 28, 30, 41–43, 55–58.

be assured of conceiving a son. While drinking from the water, Finncháim swallowed a worm (*dorb*), and in due course gave birth to a boy.[93]

A rite such as that I have suggested might be expected to have taken place on the Calends of May, following perennial dearth and mortality undergone during the winter season, with survivors gathered at the kingdom's holiest spot to participate in solemn rituals ensuring the regeneration of humanity. That it took place at a designated megalithic site is suggested in the British legend by the divine admonition that the 'dragons' be preserved within a 'stone chest' (*kistvaen*), i.e. a menhir. Such an association is indicated in the cognate Irish version of the myth contained in *Cath Maige Tuired*, throughout whose narratives stones provide a remarkable running theme:

> The texts recounting the First and Second Battles of Mag Tuired use stones and pillars in sophisticated and strikingly similar ways. The geography of the battlefield is also a figurative, literary geography, inscribing history and narrative into the landscape; the symbolism of the stones encompasses history, memory, and sovereignty, and resonates with both Irish and biblical literary traditions. The poets who stand atop pillar-stones, and the poets who transform themselves into pillar-stones, textualize the landscape, and the texts in turn use the Irish landscape as a historical witness for the tales they depict.[94]

It will further be recalled that, in *Cyfranc Lludd a Lleuelys*, it is the god Lleu who instructs Lludd to secure the two 'dragons' within a monolith at the most secure point of his kingdom, while in *Cath Maige Tuired* it is his Irish alter ego Lug who deposits the Stone of Destiny (*Lia Fáil*) at the heart of the Sacred Centre at Tara.

In the earlier Welsh version of the story, the clerical scholar Nennius, baffled by the mysterious *vermes*, drew on the Bible for his explanation of them as rival British and Saxon dragons battling for hegemony over Britain. It was seen, too, that his *vermes* is the Latin translation of *pryfed*, those mysterious soul-creatures from which humanity is germinated. Originally a paradigmatic pair was believed to repose within a monolith (*kist vaen*) at the Centre of the island. In *Cyfranc Lludd a Lleuelys* this improbable receptacle appears rationalized into 'a vat of the best mead that can be made, and a sheet of brocaded silk over the top of the vat'. However, it seems it was not the author of the tale who improvised this explanation, since it is in a cloth-covered vessel of mead that the corresponding Irish *cruim* are discovered. The concept must surely have originated in prior Common Celtic traditions of the *omphalos*.

So long as the *pryfed* remained inviolate within their stone resting place, the safety of the British people was assured. Thus it looks as though *Cyfranc Lludd a Lleuelys* preserves a tradition of rites practised at the *omphalos* (Stonehenge) every May-day. Water was poured over the stone housing the *pryfed*, which was then used to perform a lustration over the crowd of worshippers. Privileged persons (the queen?) imbibed *pryfed* distilled in mead from a goblet. The rite evoked the deity's restoration of fertility to the land and its inhabitants, through the beneficent effect of spring showers. Dafydd ap Gwilym likens mist advancing across moorland

---

93   Sharon Arbuthnott (ed.), *Cóir Anmann: A Late Middle Irish Treatise on Personal Names* (Dublin, 2005–7), ii, p. 69.

94   Rebecca Blustein, 'Poets and Pillars in Cath Maige Tuired', in Joseph Falaky Nagy (ed.), *Myth in Celtic Literatures* (Dublin, 2007), p. 38; cf. pp. 22–38.

to 'a tin sieve that was rusting' (*rhidyll ystaen yn rhydu*), imagery that evokes sprinkling by an aspergillum (*siobo*).[95]

Pouring water through a sieve was widely employed as ritually imitative of showers: in Greece rain was envisaged as water passed by Zeus through a sieve.[96] Rain was likewise widely believed to represent the seminal fluid of the sky-god, a concept reflected in Indo-European etymology.[97] Given that in *Cyfranc Lludd a Lleuelys* it is Nudd who performs the lustration over the assembled people of Britain, it is noteworthy that his name has been derived by philologists from the Indo-European root *sneud(h)-, snoudho-*, 'cloud, mist'.[98]

Nudd was of course originally a divinity, prior to his euhemerized appearance as king of Britain in *Cyfranc Lludd a Lleuelys*, and the foregoing considerations suggest that in Celtic times he was the presiding deity at Stonehenge. At the Navel of the realm the renewal of the British people was assured by ritual lustrations, a 'baptism' which was simultaneously efficacious in destroying the demonic foes of mankind.

Does this, too, explain Geoffrey of Monmouth's account of the giants who originally erected Stonehenge? After all, the sole use to which they put the megaliths was 'to wash the stones and pour the water into the baths to cure illnesses'. In the Welsh translations of Geoffrey's work, Latin *gigantes* is rendered *cewri*, which derives from Celtic **kawaro-*, 'hero, champion'.[99] It may be that the 'giants' were conceived as the original ancestors of the Britons, who in a primæval era had brought the great stones from afar and erected the mighty *omphalos* temple. I suggested earlier that Geoffrey's incongruous 'baths' (*balnea*) originated in a mistranslation of Welsh *enneint*, the word used in Welsh translations of his *History*. This may mean equally 'bath' or 'unguent', the latter interpretation being more apt to the context. That the word might be employed on occasion to describe a lustration is suggested by Dafydd am Gwilym's description of fog as 'the ointment of the witches of Annwfn' (*ennaint gwrachïod Annwn*).[100] The term employed in the *Brutiau* for the giants' curative 'charged water' (*y dvuyr rynwedavl*)[101] is also that employed in *Cyfranc Lludd a Lleuelys* for the water in which the *pryfed* were dissolved.

Now that it has been established that the 'dragons' in the story were originally *pryfed*, it follows that the second *gormes* afflicting Britain in the primæval era has been conflated with its cure. The author's explanation that the deadly scream emanated from one of the fighting dragons is as artificially contrived as the dragons themselves, and was clearly not original to

---

95 Rachel Bromwich (ed.), *Dafydd ap Gwilym: A Selection of Poems* (Llandysul, 1982), p. 133.

96 Sir James George Frazer, *The Magic Art and the Evolution of Kings* (London, 1911), i, p. 285; Arthur Bernard Cook, *Zeus: A Study in Ancient Religion* (Cambridge, 1914–40), ii, p. 2; iii, pp. 333–54, 427–51.

97 Ibid., pp. 322, 451–54; Onians, *The Origins of European Thought about the Body, the Mind the Soul, the World Time, and Fate*, pp. 240, 288–89; Karin Stüber, *The Historical Morphology of N-Stems in Celtic* (Maynooth, 1998), p. 171. 'This idea of the rain actually fertilizing the earth may be of great antiquity' (G. S. Kirk and J. E. Raven, *The Presocratic Philosophers: A Critical History with a Selection of Texts* (Cambridge, 1957), p. 29; cf. p. 393).

98 E. Anwyl, 'The Value of the Mabinogion for the Study of Celtic Religion', in *Transactions of the Third International Congress for the History of Religions* (Oxford, 1908), ii, p. 241; Thomas F. O'Rahilly, *Early Irish History and Mythology* (Dublin, 1946), p. 495; Julius Pokorny, *Indogermanisches Etymologisches Wörterbuch* (Berne, 1959–69), i, p. 978. 'The iconography accords with O'Rahilly's view – against Tolkien's – that the name, cognate with *nubes*, 'cloud', should mean something like "cloud-maker"' (George C. Boon, 'The Pagans Hill Dog', *Britannia: A Journal of Romano-British and Kindred Studies* (London, 1989), xx, p. 212).

99 Ranko Matasović, *Etymological Dictionary of Proto-Celtic* (Leiden, 2009), p. 196.

100 Bromwich (ed.), *Dafydd ap Gwilym: A Selection of Poems*, p. 135.

101 Henry Lewis (ed.), *Brut Dingestow* (Cardiff, 1942), p. 127.

the story – at least, not in the context it is given. It has been shown from references in early Welsh literature and law that the scream was not of itself a *gormes*, but a sinister accompanying manifestation, in this case heralding the universal destruction threatened by the Coraniaid. In fact, the function of the *pryfed* was originally purely benign. They were distilled in water, to be used in a salvificatory lustration. Lleuelys's instruction that some should be held back in case the plague returned betrays the fact that the irruption of the Coraniaid was anticipated *every* Calends of May. Next (in the 'second' *gormes*), the *pryfed* are described as being *first* lodged in a vat of mead, covered by a cloth of brocaded silk, and *second* held within a great stone at the securest place in the kingdom, i.e. the *omphalos*. The latter concept is clearly the more archaic. Could the 'vat' or 'vases', with their silken covering, represent a subsequent ritual development, when a queen was presented by her king with a sacramental goblet of mead, containing *pryfed* ensuring her fertility, and consequent protection of the realm through preservation of the dynasty?

In early Irish literature *crumai* (singular *cruim*), corresponding to Welsh *pryfed*, bring about the impregnation of a queen through being ingested in mead from a goblet. The covering cloth provides an accompanying motif. Again, it will be recalled that the cloth symbolized the permeable barrier separating this world from the Otherworld. Since there is no indication that either tradition borrowed from the other, it is likely that both originate in Common Celtic mythological tradition. The underlying implication seems to be that the *pryfed* lay securely lodged within a particular sacred stone at the *omphalos*. Water poured over the stone (doubtless accompanied by appropriate rites) acquired the essence of the *pryfed* immured within the stone, which was transferred to an appropriate receptacle, and could then be employed equally to ensure the impregnation of a queen, or as a corresponding fertilizing lustration of all participants in the *Kalan Mai* ceremonial at the *omphalos*.[102]

The indications are that *all* the foregoing events were envisaged as occurring at the national *omphalos* at the festivals of May Eve (*Kalan Mai*) and November Eve (*nos galan gaeaf*). The artificially triadic form in which the myth is presented in the story has distinguished elements which originally comprised a single narrative. It was understood that *pryfed* (that is to say, soul-creatures, or embryos of humanity) reposed within a particular monolith at Stonehenge. At the appropriate calendrical occasions the stones were washed (as Geoffrey of Monmouth learned) with water, which became imbued with the power of the *pryfed* immured within the stone. This generative potion was sprinkled over the assembled worshippers, saining them from the destructive threat of demonic forces (Coraniaid), whose primary threats were those of causing pregnant women to miscarry, offspring of domestic animals to be aborted, and crops to fail. It is surely significant that the original purpose of lustration with *pryfed* distilled in water provided the effective counter-measure, *ensuring* as it did fertility of women, kine, and crops.

One aspect as yet unexplained is what happened to the vessel containing the mead in which the *pryfed* were contained. From it they ascended into the air (like the soul or spirit of Étaín, when she was transformed into a butterfly), and returned to the vat. This symbolized the aery asylum of the soul-creatures during intermittent periods of cosmic annihilation. Lludd then wrapped them in the brocaded cloth and lodged them within the stone, though it remains unclear whether they continued housed in the vat. Evidence from Irish stories cited earlier suggests that the queen of the land imbibed the soul-creature from a goblet in order to become impregnated with an heir

---

102 Libations were poured over stones in early Greece and other archaic societies (Walter Burkert, *Structure and History in Greek Mythology and Ritual* (Berkeley and Los Angeles, 1979), p. 42; idem, *Greek Religion* (Cambridge, Mass., 1985), p. 72).

to the kingdom. Since ceremonies at the *omphalos* must surely have been focussed on the king and his consort, who personified respectively divinity and the land, it seems not unlikely that the ceremony included a royal communion rite. In the Arthurian romances a dastardly intruder at the royal banquet dashes Guenevere's goblet from her hand. Was it the intent of this malevolent Otherworld character to prevent her begetting an heir to the kingdom?

A solemn ceremony, in which a queen's imbibing from a goblet plays an essential part, evokes comparison with the Grail procession witnessed by Perceval in the Grail Castle. That too centres on a beautiful maiden bearing a splendid vessel.[103] However, discussion of that alluring issue is reserved for a further book I have in preparation.

Turning from the description in *Cyfranc Lludd a Leuelys* to Geoffrey's account of the origins of Stonehenge, it is significant that the latter provides disparate explanations for the 'charged water'. In the first place, it is explained that what imbued it with its saining power was the fact that it was washed over the stones at Killare. Next, however, we learn instead that it was herbs mixed in the water that wrought the cure. That Geoffrey was uncertain how to account for its medicinal property suggests that he was in this instance refashioning pre-existing sources, rather than drawing on his imagination. Overall, it seems he was aware that *something* was distilled in the water to make it effectual.

There are obvious parallels between the versions in *Cyfranc Lludd a Lleuelys* and Geoffrey's *Historia Regum Britanniæ* of what appears to be an underlying common myth. In both, ceremonies are conducted, in which a monolith or monoliths play a significant part. Both involve distillation of mysterious entities in water, the resultant mixture being applied to the stones. In each case, the distillation is possessed of an arcane curative property which has proved effectual since first the stone(s) was placed *in situ* in the primæval era. The only distinction of note lies in the esoteric ingredient distilled in the water: *pryfed* in the Welsh account, and 'herbs' in the Latin.

That he sought to explain the tradition in disparate ways suggests that Geoffrey was puzzled by his sources of information. It has been seen that he or his source probably misinterpreted Welsh *enneint* by its alternative meaning – the incongruous Latin *balnea*. In view of these factors, it seems not unlikely that it was the baffling *pryfed* or *vermes* that he (or, as ever, a predecessor) attempted to explain in terms comprehensible to his Anglo-Norman readers as curative 'herbs'.

Again, I have suggested that the strange account of the colloquy between Lludd and Lleuelys through a long horn reflects a rite of libation through a funnel into the earth, whereby communication was established with a chthonic deity.[104] Given converging indications that the 'exact centre' of Britain discovered by the two gods was Stonehenge, it seems likely that the Otherworld access point was likewise to be found there.

Within a mile of the great stone circle lies a remarkable pit known as Wilsford Shaft, which when excavated was found to have been dug to a depth of a hundred feet. Although conceivably intended as a well (evidence of fluctuating water supply was found at the bottom of the shaft),[105] overall it is

---

103   Cf. Michael J. Enright, *Lady with a Mead Cup: Ritual, Prophecy and Lordship in the European Warband from La Tène to the Viking Age* (Dublin, 1996), pp. 69–96.

104   An essential property of the *omphalos* was its provision of access to the underworld (M. L. West, *The Orphic Poems* (Oxford, 1983), pp. 12, 147).

105   Paul Ashbee, Martin Bell, and Edwina Proudfoot, *Wilsford Shaft: excavations 1960–2* (London, 1989), pp. 35–36. Cf. Mark Bowden, Sharon Soutar, David Field, and Martyn Barber, *The Stonehenge Landscape* (Swindon, 2015), p. 68.

considered more probable that it served a ritual purpose.[106] Equally, absence of appropriate artefacts suggests that it was not employed as a repository for offerings to a chthonic deity.[107]

Could it have been designed as an access point to the underworld?[108] Such a provision would have been appropriate to the function of Stonehenge as *omphalos*, the focal point linking the upper, middle, and nether worlds. Although the Irish tale of the Gilla Decair (*Tóraidheacht an Gilla decair*) is a romantic adventure preserved in a late copy, like many of its category it preserves elements of earlier legendary material.[109] At one point in the tale, the Ossianic hero Diarmaid arrives at a mysterious land in the midst of the ocean. After penetrating a belt of wild woodland, he traverses a great plain 'from east and west, from south and north'. There he discovers a huge tree (*bile flescach*), beside which stood an equally colossal stone (*carraic commór*), at whose base burbled a well of pure drinking-water.

A harsh noise arose, which seemed to warn Diarmaid from drinking. Nevertheless, he drank – to find himself accosted by the guardian of the well, a terrifying wizard (*gruagach*), who accused him of stealing his water. After a succession of ferocious hand-to-hand combats, Diarmaid overcomes the wizard, and together they descend to the bottom of the well. There Diarmaid finds himself in a beautiful flowery land, in the midst of which stands a splendid royal city.[110]

Stripped of its romantic colouring, the setting of this episode exhibits fundamental attributes of the *omphalos*. That Diarmaid crossed 'from east and west, from north and south' (*do bhí mac úi Dhuibne ac siubal in mhaige anoir is aniar andes ocus adtuaid*) suggests that tree and menhir were situated where they might naturally be expected, viz. at the exact centre of the plain.[111] Both tree and stone represent archetypal *foci* of the Centre,[112] whose adjacent well afforded access to the supernatural realm in the Underworld. (A sacred well was believed to be located at Uisneach, the Omphalos of Ireland). The overthrow of the *gruagach* in the Ossianic adventure tale may have replaced an earlier version, in which the hero compelled the ruler of the Otherworld to accede to his wishes – just as Nudd in a similar swordfight overcame the giant

---

106 'Its proximity to Stonehenge and its great depth suggest that it was of a ritual nature and may perhaps have been connected with the cults practised at Stonehenge' (Anne Ross, *Pagan Celtic Britain: Studies in Iconography and Tradition* (London, 1967), p. 27).

107 Cf. ibid., pp. 132–33, 135–37, 255–58; eadem, 'Shafts, pits, wells – sanctuaries of the Belgic Britons?', in J. M. Coles and D. D. A. Simpson (ed.), *Studies in Ancient Europe: Essays presented to Stuart Piggott* (Leicester, 1968), pp. 275–78; Jane Webster, 'Sanctuaries and Sacred Places', in Miranda J. Green (ed.), *The Celtic World* (London, 1995), pp. 451–52.

108 Wells were traditionally regarded as providing access to the Underworld (Séamus Mac Mathúna, 'The Relationship of the Chthonic World in Early Ireland to Chaos and Cosmos', in Jacqueline Borsje, Ann Dooley, Séamus Mac Mathúna, and Gregory Toner (ed.), *Celtic Cosmology: Perspectives from Ireland and Scotland* (Toronto, 2014), pp. 55–57).

109 An earlier copy was known to Keating, writing in the reign of Charles I (David Comyn and Rev. Patrick S. Dinneen (ed.), *The History of Ireland by Geoffrey Keating, D.D.* (London, 1902–14), ii, p. 326).

110 Standish H. O'Grady (ed.), *Silva Gadelica: A Collection of Tales in Irish with Extracts Illustrating Persons and Places* (London, 1892), i, pp. 266–67. For a folktale version of this episode, cf. Jeremiah Curtin, *Hero-Tales of Ireland* (London, 1894), pp. 520–22.

111 Geographical attributes of the Sacred Centre are described thus in an early Irish tale: 'they came to Uisneach of Meath in the centre of Ireland (*Uisneach Midi a medon Erenn*), for 'there was Eochaid's house, Ireland stretching equally far from it on every side, to south and north, to east and west' (Osborn Bergin and R. I. Best, 'Tochmarc Étaíne', *Ériu: The Journal of the School of Irish Learning* (Dublin, 1938), xii, p. 144).

112 M. L. West, *Indo-European Poetry and Myth* (Oxford, 2007), pp. 345–47; Clive Tolley, *Shamanism in Norse Myth and Magic* (Helsinki, 2009), i, pp. 304–68; Proinsias Mac Cana, *The Cult of the Sacred Centre: Essays on Celtic Ideology* (Dublin, 2011), pp. 76–77.

magician in *Cyfranc Lludd a Lleuelys*. Finally, the flowery plain could stand for the restoration of the kingdom to fertility and prosperity.

Lastly, at the risk of appearing overly speculative, the tentative possibility may be considered that a liturgical fragment survives from the early Iron Age (if not earlier), which was recited at a high point during seasonal assemblages at Stonehenge and provincial *omphaloi* across Celtic Britain. Attention was drawn earlier to the three magical stanzas chanted by Gwydion in *Math uab Mathonwy*, whereby he draws the emaciated Lleu down from his treetop refuge, to be restored to his former health and beauty.

It was noted that such verses, in the metre known as *englynion*, are older than the prose in which they are embedded. Indeed, they may be much older. As Eve Sweeter points out, 'the native Welsh *englyn* can easily be seen as a possible descendant of the Indo-European short-line verse form, via combination with a catalectic variant ...'[113]

The language of the *englynion* in *Math* presents difficulties and ambiguities, and the translation which follows is intended as a guide rather than literal version. Thus, Kathryn A. Klar translates the first line as 'Oak that grows between two veils', taking the last word as *llen* ('veil'), rather than *llyn* ('lake').[114] Given the unmistakably Otherworld connotation of the verses, it is tempting to prefer Dr Klar's rendering. It has been widely assumed that the setting of the scene at Nantlle points to the twin lakes of that lovely valley. However, the geographical setting was presumably suggested to the author of *Math* by its name, 'Valley of Lleu'. The setting of the *englynion*, in contrast, is unmistakably the Otherworld, attained by ascent of the World Tree.[115] Dr Klar's 'veils' would in that case appear appropriate, the Otherworld being widely envisaged as separated by a veil from the world of mortal men.

> *Dar a dyf y rwng deu lenn,*
> *Gorduwrych ayr a glenn.*
> *Ony dywedaf i eu,*
> *O ulodeu Lleu ban yw hynn.*
>
> *Dar a dyf yn ard uaes,*
> *Nis gwlych glaw, nis mwy tawd* [tes].
> *Naw ugein angerd a borthes.*
> *Yn y blaen, Lleu Llaw Gyffes.*
>
> *Dar a dyf dan anwaeret,*
> *Mirein modur ymywet.*

113 Eve E. Sweeter, 'Line-Structure and *Rhan*-Structure: the Metrical Units of the *Gododdin* Corpus', in Brynley F. Roberts (ed.), *Early Welsh Poetry: Studies in the Book of Aneirin* (Aberystwyth, 1988), p. 150.

114 'Poetry and Pillowtalk', in Joseph Falaky Nagy and Leslie Ellen Jones (ed.), *Heroic Poets and Poetic Heroes in Celtic Tradition: A Festschrift for Patrick K. Ford* (Dublin, 2005), p. 240. Other useful translations are those by W. J. Gruffydd, *Math vab Mathonwy: An Inquiry into the Origins and Development of the Fourth Branch of the Mabinogi with the Text and a Translation* (Cardiff, 1928), p. 37; Patrick K. Ford (tr.), *The Mabinogi and other Medieval Welsh Tales* (Berkeley, 1977), p. 107; Sioned Davies (tr.), *The Mabinogion* (Oxford, 2007), p. 62.

115 The poem bears obvious resemblance to the early ninth-century Irish three-stanza poem ascribed to Suibne Geilt (counterpart of the British Merlin), which describes the poet's delightful (clearly Otherworld) treetop refuge as 'a house in which rain does not fall ... it is as bright as though one were in a garden' (Gerard Murphy (ed.), *Early Irish Lyrics: Eighth to Twelfth Century* (Oxford, 1956), p. 112).

Ony dywedaf i [eu]
Ef dydau Lleu y'm arfet.

An oak grows between two veils,
Very sombre is the sky and the valley.
If I speak not a falsehood,
This is on account of Lleu's members.

An oak grows on a high plain,
Rain wets it not, neither does heat melt it
It upheld one possessing nine-score skills.
In its top is Lleu of the Skilful Hand.

An oak grows on a slope
The sanctuary of a handsome prince.
Unless I am mistaken
Lleu will come to my lap.

Could poetry resembling such verses have been uttered at one time by a druid enacting the rôle of *Gwydion*, the Divine Druid of *Math uab Mathonwy*, as he conjures up the presence of the 'visiting' god Lleu among celebrants at annual calendrical high festivals?[116] It will be recalled that the leading participant at the Cornish Lughnasa festival interrupted by St Samson bore the name *Guedianus*, while the rites culminated with the resuscitation of a 'dead' youth – recalling *Lleu* (*lux*), with whom the festival was associated.

Overall, I have sought to show that the ancient stones of Stonehenge, although erected in an age long anterior to the arrival of the Celts in Britain, and much longer before the invention of writing in Europe, may yet reveal a residue of its secrets, primarily through the medium of Celtic mythology. As Rebecca Blustein writes,

Reviving the significance of old rocks and yet at the same time investing them with new meaning, Merlin – fronting for Geoffrey of Monmouth, the author of the *Historia* – uses these objects to construct both a living memorial to the dead and a bold claim of ownership – the same uses to which stones are put in the *Cath Maige Tuired*, as we have seen.[117]

* * *

---

116 'Verse and *roscad* depend for their effect on their form as much as on their content and are for that reason markedly resistant to change; this is sufficient to explain why our earliest verse remains often seem linguistically more archaic than the prose recorded in or about the same time'. (Proinsias Mac Cana, 'Notes on the Combination of Prose and Verse in Early Irish Narrative', in Stephen N. Tranter and Hildegard L. C. Tristram (ed.), *Early Irish Literature – Media and Communication* (Tübingen, 1989), p. 129.)

117 Nagy (ed.), *Myth in Celtic Literatures*, p. 30.

I ask you which is the extremity of the earth,

I ask where is the Navel (*nábhih*) of the Earth;
I ask you what is the sperm of the stallion,
I ask what is the apogee of the Word.

This altar is the extremity of the earth,
This sacrifice is the Navel of the Earth;
This *soma* is the sperm of the stallion,
This *brahmán* is the apogee of the Word.

(*Ṛg Veda*, §I.164,34–35)[118]

118 van Nooten and Holland (ed.), *Rig Veda*, p. 99. Cf. Françoise Bader, *La langue des dieux, ou l'hermétisme des poètes indo-européens* (Pisa, 1989), p. 136. 'As early as the *Ṛg Veda*, the word *brahman* (neuter) refers to a major aspect of the Word: the ritualistic word, the "formula" par excellence, the Supreme Word' (André Padoux, *Vāc: The Concept of the Word in Selected Hindu Tantras* (New York, 1990), p. 6). Cf. Leopold Sabourin, *Priesthood: A Comparative Study* (Leiden, 1973), p. 232.

Bibliography

Primary sources

Bjarni Aðalbjarnarson (ed.), *Heimskringla* (Reykjavik, 1941–51)

E. H. Alton, D. E. W. Wormell, and E. Courtney (ed.), *P. Ovidi Nasonis Fastorvm Libri Sex* (Leipzig, 1985)

Alan Orr Anderson and Marjorie Ogilvie Anderson (ed.), *Adomnan's Life of Columba* (Edinburgh, 1961)

W. B. Anderson (ed.), *Sidonius: Poems and Letters* (London, 1936–65)

C. Bruyn Andrews (ed.), *The Torrington Diaries: Containing the Tours through England and Wales of the Hon. John Byng (later Fifth Viscount Torrington) between the Years 1781 and 1794* (London, 1934–38)

Sharon Arbuthnott (ed.), *Cóir Anmann: A Late Middle Irish Treatise on Personal Names* (Dublin, 2005–7)

Ivor Arnold (ed.), *Le Roman de Brut de Wace* (Paris, 1938–40)

I. D. O. Arnold and M. M. Pelan (ed.), *La partie arthurienne du Roman de Brut: (Extrait du manuscrit B.N. fr. 794)* (Paris, 1962)

Robert Atkinson (ed.), *The Passions and the Homilies from Leabhar Breac: Text, Translation, and Commentary* (Dublin, 1887)

Germaine Aujac, François Lasserre, and Raoul Baladié (ed.), *Strabon: Géographie* (Paris, 1966–89)

D. R. Shackleton Bailey (ed.), *M. Annaei Lucani De Bello Civili Libri X* (Leipzig, 1988)

S. E. Banks and J. W. Binns (ed.), *Gervase of Tilbury: Otia Imperialia; Recreation for an Emperor* (Oxford, 2002)

P. C. Bartrum (ed.), *Early Welsh Genealogical Texts* (Cardiff, 1966)

E. S. de Beer (ed.), *The Diary of John Evelyn* (Oxford, 1955)

Alexander Bell (ed.), *L'Estoire des Engleis by Geffrei Gaimar* (Oxford, 1960)

H. Idris Bell (ed.), *Vita Sancti Tathei and Buched Seint y Katrin: Re-edited, after Rees, from the MSS. in the British Museum* (Bangor, 1909)

G. E. Bentley, Jr. (ed.), *William Blake's Writings* (Oxford, 1978)

John Beresford (ed.), *The Diary of a Country Parson: The Reverend James Woodforde* (London, 1924–31)

O. J. Bergin, R. I. Best, Kuno Meyer, and J. G. O'Keefe (ed.), *Anecdota from Irish Manuscripts* (Halle and Dublin, 1907–13)

Osborn Bergin and R. I. Best, 'Tochmarc Étaíne', *Ériu: The Journal of the School of Irish Learning* (1938), xii, pp. 137–96.

J. H. Bernard and R. Atkinson (ed.), *The Irish Liber Hymnorum* (London, 1898)

R. I. Best, 'The Adventures of Art son of Conn, and the Courtship of Delbchæm', *Ériu: The Journal of the School of Irish Learning* (Dublin, 1910), iii, pp. 149–73

R. I. Best, 'The Settling of the Manor of Tara', *Ériu: The Journal of the School of Irish Learning* (Dublin, 1910), iv, pp. 121–72

R. I. Best and Osborn Bergin (ed.), *Lebor na Huidre: Book of the Dun Cow* (Dublin, 1929)

Richard Irvine Best and Hugh Jackson Lawlor (ed.), *The Martyrology of Tallaght: from the Book of Leinster and MS. 5100-4 in the Royal Library, Brussels* (London, 1931)

R. I. Best, Osborn Bergin, M. A. O'Brien, and Anne O'Sullivan (ed.), *The Book of Leinster Formerly Lebar na Núachongbála* (Dublin, 1954–83)

Hans Dieter Betz, *The Greek Magical Papyri in Translation: Including the Demotic Spells* (Chicago, 1986)

Ludwig Bieler (ed.), *Libri Epistolarum Sancti Patricii Episcopi* (Dublin, 1952)

Ludwig Bieler (ed.), *The Irish Penitentials* (Dublin, 1963)

Ludwig Bieler (ed.), *The Patrician Texts in the Book of Armagh* (Dublin, 1979)

D. A. Binchy (ed.), *Críth Gablach* (Dublin, 1941)

Matthew Black (tr.), *The Book of Enoch or I Enoch: A New English Edition* (Leiden, 1985)

R. C. Blockley (ed.), *The Fragmentary Classicising Historians of the Later Roman Empire: Eunapius, Olympiodorus, Priscus and Malchus* (Liverpool, 1983)

R. C. Blockley (ed.), *The History of Menander the Guardsman* (Liverpool, 1985)

Franz Boas (ed.), *Kathlamet Texts* (Washington, 1901)

Franz Boas (ed.), *Tsimshian Texts* (Washington, 1902)

The History and Chronicles of Scotland: Written in Latin by Hector Boece, Canon of Aberdeen; and Translated by John Bellenden, Archdeacon of Moray, and Canon of Ross (Edinburgh, 1821)

W. N. Bolderston (ed.), *La vie de Saint Remi: Poème du XIIIe siècle par Richier* (London, 1912)

William Borlase, *Antiquities, Historical and Monumental, of the County of Cornwall* (London, 1769)

William Bottrell, *Stories and Folk-Lore of West Cornwall* (Penzance, 1870–80)

Helen E. Boulton (ed.), *The Sherwood Forest Book* (Nottingham, 1965)

Alan K. Bowman and J. David Thomas (ed.), *The Vindolanda Writing-Tablets: (Tabulae Vindolandenses II)* (London, 1994)

Caomhín Breatnach (ed.), *Patronage, Politics and Prose: Ceasacht Inghine Guile; Sgéala Muice Meic Dhá Thó; Oidheadh Chuinn Chéadchathaigh* (Maynooth, 1996)

J. S. Brewer, James F. Dimock, and George F. Warner (ed.), *Giraldi Cambrensis Opera* (London, 1861–91)

James Britten (ed.), *Remaines of Gentilisme and Judaisme. by John Aubrey, R.S.S. 1686–87* (London, 1881)

Rachel Bromwich, 'The Historical Triads: With Special Reference to Peniarth MS. 16', *The Bulletin of the Board of Celtic Studies* (Cardiff, 1946), xii, pp. 1–15

Rachel Bromwich, 'Trioedd Ynys Prydain: The *Myvyrian* "Third Series"', *The Transactions of the Honourable Society of Cymmrodorion: Session 1969* (London, 1969), pp. 127–56

Rachel Bromwich (ed.), *Trioedd Ynys Prydein: The Welsh Triads* (Cardiff, 1978)

Rachel Bromwich (ed.), *Dafydd ap Gwilym: A Selection of Poems* (Llandysul, 1982)

Rachel Bromwich and D. Simon Evans (ed.), *Culhwch and Olwen: An Edition and Study of the Oldest Arthurian Tale* (Cardiff, 1992)

G. L. Brook and R. F. Leslie (ed.), *Laȝamon: Brut* (Oxford, 1963–78)

C. F. Burgess (ed.), *The Letters of John Gay* (Oxford, 1966)

Aubrey Burl and Neil Mortimer (ed.), *Stukeley's 'Stonehenge': An Unpublished Manuscript 1721–1724* (Cambridge, 2005)

Keith Busby (ed.), *Chrétien de Troyes: Le Roman de Perceval ou Le Conte du Graal* (Tübingen, 1993)

The Rev. Canon Callaway, *The Religious System of the Amazulu. Izinyanga Zokubula; or, Divination, as Existing among the Amazulu, in their own Words, with a Translation into English, and Notes* (London, 1870)

William Camden, *Britannia* (London, 1600)

Rev. Alexander Cameron, *Reliquiæ Celticæ: Texts, Papers, and Studies in Gaelic Literature and Philology* (Inverness, 1894)

A. Campbell (ed.), *The Chronicle of Æthelweard* (London, 1962)

J. F. Campbell (ed.), *Leabhar na Feinne: Heroic Gaelic Ballads Collected in Scotland Chiefly from 1512 to 1871* (London, 1872)

J. F. Campbell, *Popular Tales of the West Highlands Orally Collected* (Paisley, 1890–93)

John Gregorson Campbell, *The Fians; or, Stories, Poems, & Traditions of Fionn and his Warrior Band* (London, 1891)

John Gregorson Campbell, *Superstitions of the Highlands & Islands of Scotland Collected entirely from Oral Sources* (Glasgow, 1900)

John Lorne Campbell (ed.), *Highland Songs of the Forty-Five* (Edinburgh, 1933)

John Carey, 'Scél Túain meic Chairill', *Ériu* (1984), xxxv, pp. 93–111

John Carey, 'An Edition of the Pseudo-Historical Prologue to the '*Senchas Már*', *Ériu* (1994), xlv, p. 1–32

Alexander Carmichael (ed.), *Carmina Gadelica: Hymns and Incantations with Illustrative Notes on Words, Rites, and Customs, Dying and Obsolete: Orally Collected in the Highlands and Islands of Scotland* (Edinburgh, 1900–71)

James Carney (ed.), *The Poems of Blathmac Son of Cú Brettan; Together with the Irish Gospel of Thomas and a Poem on the Virgin Mary* (Dublin, 1964)

Filippo Càssola (ed.), *Inni Omerici* (Milan, 1975)

T. M. Charles-Edwards (tr.), *The Chronicle of Ireland* (Liverpool, 2006)

Andrew Clark (ed.), '*Brief Lives,*' *chiefly of Contemporaries, set down by John Aubrey, between the Years 1669 & 1696* (Oxford, 1898)

Basil Clarke (ed.), *Life of Merlin; Geoffrey of Monmouth: Vita Merlini* (Cardiff, 1973)

Karl Clemen (ed.), *Fontes Historiae Religionum Primitivarum, Praeindogermanicarum, Indogermanicarum Minus Notarum* (Bonn, 1936)

John Colarusso (tr.), *Nart Sagas from the Caucasus: Myths and Legends from the Circassians, Abazas, and Ubykhs* (Princeton, NJ, 2002)

Bertram Colgrave (ed.), *The Life of Bishop Wilfrid by Eddius Stephanus* (Cambridge, 1927)

R. G. Collingwood and R. P. Wright (ed.), *The Roman Inscriptions of Britain: I Inscriptions on Stone* (Oxford, 1965)

David Comyn and Rev. Patrick S. Dinneen (ed.), *The History of Ireland by Geoffrey Keating, D.D.* (London, 1902–14)

Johan Corthals (ed.), '*Táin Bó Regamna*' *und* '*Táin Bó Flidais*' (Hamburg, 1979)

T. Crofton Croker, *Fairy Legends and Traditions of the South of Ireland: The New Series* (London, 1828)

Ch. Cuissard, 'Vie de Saint Pol de Léon', *Revue Celtique* (Paris, 1883), v, pp. 413–58

Jeremiah Curtin, *Hero-Tales of Ireland* (London, 1894)

Bror Danielsson (ed.), *William Twiti: The Art of Hunting 1327* (Stockholm, 1977)

Sioned Davies (tr.), *The Mabinogion* (Oxford, 2007)

Charles de Clercq (ed.), *Concilia Galliae A. 511 – A. 695* (Turnhout, 1963)

Phillip de Lacy (ed.), *Galeni De Semine* (Berlin, 1992)

Igor de Rachewiltz, *The Secret History of the Mongols: A Mongolian Epic Chronicle of the Thirteenth Century* (Leiden, 2006–13)

Vicomte Hersart de la Villemarqué (ed.), *Barzaz Breiz: Chants Populaires de la Bretagne* (Paris, 1867)

H. B. Dewing (ed.), *Procopius* (London, 1914–40)

D. R. Dicks (ed.), *The Geographical Fragments of Hipparchus* (London, 1960)

O. A. W. Dilke, *Greek and Roman Maps* (London, 1985)

Myles Dillon, 'The Death of Mac Con', *Publications of the Modern Language Association of America* (New York, 1945), lx, pp. 340–45

Myles Dillon (ed.), *Serglige Con Culainn* (Dublin, 1953)

Myles Dillon (ed.), *Stories from the Acallam* (Dublin, 1970)

Elliott van Kirk Dobbie (ed.), *The Anglo-Saxon Minor Poems* (New York, 1942)

Maigréad Ni C. Dobbs, 'Agallamh Leborchaim', *Études Celtiques* (Paris, 1949), v, pp. 148–61

M. J. Dresden (ed.), *Mānavagrhyasūtra: A Vedic Manual of Domestic Rites* (Groningen, 1941)

Ursula Dronke (ed.), *The Poetic Edda: Volume II Mythological Poems* (Oxford, 1997)

David N. Dumville, 'The Anglian collection of royal genealogies', *Anglo-Saxon England 5* (Cambridge, 1976), pp. 23–50

David N. Dumville (ed.), *Annales Cambriae, A.D. 682–954: Texts A-C in Parallel* (Cambridge, 2002)

David Dumville and Michael Lapidge (ed.), *The Annals of St Neots with Vita Prima Sancti Neoti* (Cambridge, 1985)

Lilian Duncan, 'Altram Tige Dá Medar', *Ériu: The Journal of the School of Irish Learning, Dublin* (1932), xi, pp. 184–225

Paul-Marie Duval and Georges Pinault (ed.), *Recueil des inscriptions gauloises (R.I.G.); Volume III: Les Calendriers (Coligny, Villards d'Héria)* (Paris, 1986)

L. Edelstein and I. G. Kidd (ed.), *Posidonius* (Cambridge, 1988–89)

J. K. Elliott (tr.), *The Apocryphal New Testament: A Collection of Apocryphal Christian Literature in an English Translation* (Oxford, 1993)

Sir Henry Ellis (ed.), *Polydore Vergil's English History, from an Early Translation Preserved among the MSS. of the Old Royal Library in the British Museum* (London, 1846)

David A. H. Evans and Anthony Faulkes (ed.), *Hávamál* (Kendal, 1986–87)

D. Simon Evans (ed.), *The Welsh Life of St David* (Cardiff, 1988)

J. G. Evans, 'Pedigrees from Jesus College MS. 20', *Y Cymmrodor* (London, 1887), viii, pp. 83–92

J. Gwenogvryn Evans, 'Extracts from Hengwrt MS. 34', *Y Cymmrodor* (1888), ix, pp. 325–33

J. Gwenogvryn Evans (ed.), *Facsimile of the Chirk Codex of The Welsh Laws* (Llanbedrog, 1909)

J. Gwenogvryn Evans (ed.), *Facsimile & Text of the Book of Taliesin* (Llanbedrog, 1910)

J. Gwenogvryn Evans (ed.), *The Poetry in the Red Book of Hergest* (Llanbedrog, 1911)

J. Gwenogvryn Evans (ed.), *Poetry by Medieval Welsh Bards* (Llanbedrog, 1926)

J. Gwenogvryn Evans and John Rhŷs (ed.), *The Text of the Book of Llan Dâv Reproduced from the Gwysaney Manuscript* (Oxford, 1893)

J. Gwenogvryn Evans (ed.), *The White Book Mabinogion: Welsh Tales & Romances Reproduced from the Peniarth Manuscripts* (Pwllheli, 1907)

Alfred Ewert (ed.), *Marie de France: Lais* (Oxford, 1947)

Maurice Exwood and H. L. Lehmann (ed.), *The Journal of William Schellinks' Travels in England 1661–1663* (London, 1993)

Anthony Faulkes (ed.), *Snorri Sturluson: Edda; Prologue and Gylfaginning* (Oxford, 1982)

Robert Fawtier (ed.), *La vie de Saint Samson: Essai de critique hagiographique* (Paris, 1912)

Allan Fea, *After Worcester Fight* (London, 1904)

Pierre Flobert (ed.), *La vie ancienne de saint Samson de Dol* (Paris, 1997)

Peter Foote and Humphrey Higgins (tr.), *Olaus Magnus: Historia de Gentibus Septentrionalibus* (London, 1996–98)

Jacques Fontaine (ed.), *Sulpice Sévère: Vie de Saint Martin* (Paris, 1967–69)

Alexander Penrose Forbes (ed.), *Lives of S. Ninian and S. Kentigern. Compiled in the Twelfth Century* (Edinburgh, 1874)

Patrick K. Ford (ed.), *The Poetry of Llywarch Hen* (Los Angeles, 1974)

Patrick K. Ford (tr.), *The Mabinogi and other Medieval Welsh Tales* (Berkeley, 1977)

Patrick K. Ford (ed.), *Ystoria Taliesin* (Cardiff, 1992)

Giovanni Forni (ed.), *Taciti De Vita Iulii Agricolae* (Rome, 1962)

John Knight Fotheringham (ed.), *Evsebii Pamphili Chronici Canones: Latine Vertit, Adavxit, ad sva Tempora Prodvxit S. Evsebivs Hieronimvs* (London, 1923)

Robert L. Fowler (ed.), *Early Greek Mythography* (Oxford, 2000–2013)

Hermann Fränkel (ed.), *Apollonii Rhodii Argonavtica* (Oxford, 1961)

J. Fraser, 'The First Battle of Moytura', *Ériu: The Journal of the School of Irish Learning, Dublin* (Dublin, 1915), viii, pp. 1–63

J. Fraser, P. Grosjean, and J. G. O'Keeffe (ed.), *Irish Texts* (London, 1931–34)

J. G. Frazer, *Pausanias's Description of Greece* (London, 1898)

Sir James George Frazer (ed.), *Apollodorus: The Library* (London, 1921)

Sir James George Frazer (ed.), *Publii Ovidii Nasonis Fastorum Libri Sex: The Fasti of Ovid* (London, 1929)

S. S. Frere and R. S. O. Tomlin (ed.), *The Roman Inscriptions of Britain: Volume II Instrumentum Domesticum; Fascicule 4* (Stroud, 1992)

R. G. Collingwood and R. P. Wright (ed.), *The Roman Inscriptions of Britain: II Instrumentum Domesticum: Combined Epigraphic Indexes and Concordance with Major Printed Sources Compiled by S.S. Frere* (Stroud, 1995)

Wilson Frescoln (ed.), *Guillaume Le Clerc: The Romance of Fergus* (Philadelphia, 1983)

Édouard Galletier (ed.), *Panégyriques latins* (Paris, 1949–52)

Édouard Galletier, Jacques Fontaine, Guy Sabbah, Marie-Anne Marié, and Laurent Angliviel de la Beaumelle (ed.), *Ammien Marcellin: Histoire* (Paris, 1978–99)

A. R. George (ed.), *The Babylonian Gilgamesh Epic* (Oxford, 2003)

P. Geyer, O. Cuntz, A. Francheschini, R. Weber, L. Bieler, J. Fraipont, and F. Glorie (ed.), *Itineraria et Alia Geographica* (Turnholt, 1965)

Joseph Gildea (ed.), *Durmart le Galois: Roman Arthurien du Treizième Siècle* (Villanova, Pa., 1965–66)

Stephen Gill (ed.), *The Salisbury Plain Poems of William Wordsworth* (Ithaca, New York, 1975)

Remo Giomini (ed.), *M. Tvlli Ciceronis Scripta qvae Manservnt Omnia: De Divinatione; De Fato; Timaevs* (Leipzig, 1975)

I. Glazunov (ed.), *Лѣтописъ Нестора: Со включенѴемъ поученѴя Владимира Мономаха* (St Petersburg, 1903)

Glenys Witchard Goetinck (ed.), *Historia Peredur vab Efrawc* (Cardiff, 1976)

J. H. C. Grattan and Charles Singer, *Anglo-Saxon Magic and Medicine: Illustrated Specially from the Semi-Pagan Text 'Lacnunga'* (Oxford, 1952)

Elizabeth A. Gray (ed.), *Cath Maige Tuired: The Second Battle of Mag Tuired* (Naas, 1982)

David Greene, Fergus Kelly, and Brian O. Murdoch (ed.), *The Irish Adam and Eve Story from Saltair na Rann* (Dublin, 1976)

R. P. H. Green (ed.), *The Works of Ausonius* (Oxford, 1991)

Diana Greenway (ed.), *Henry, Archdeacon of Huntingdon, Historia Anglorum: The History of the English People* (Oxford, 1996)

J. Gwyn Griffiths (ed.), *Plutarch's De Iside et Osiride* (Cambridge, 1970)

Acton Griscom (ed.), *The Historia Regum Britanniæ of Geoffrey of Monmouth with Contributions to the Study of its Place in Early British History* (London, 1929)

Lady Charlotte Guest (tr.), *The Mabinogion from the Welsh of the Llyfr Coch o Hergest (the Red Book of Hergest) in the Library of Jesus College, Oxford* (London, 1877)

Hubert Guillotel, André Chédeville, Bernard Tanguy, Jean-Pierre Brunterc'h, Alain Duval, Hélène Guicharnaud, and Sandrine Pagès-Camagna (ed.), *Cartulaire de l'abbaye Saint-Sauveur de Redon* (Rennes, 2004)

Christian-J. Guyonvarc'h (tr.), *Textes mythologiques irlandais I* (Rennes, 1980)

Christian-J. Guyonvarc'h, *Le Dialogue des deux sages* (Paris, 1999)

Edward Gwynn (ed.), *The Metrical Dindshenchas* (Dublin, 1903–35)

John Gwynn (ed.), *Liber Ardmachanus: The Book of Armagh, Edited with Introduction and Appendices* (Dublin, 1913)

Lucius Gwynn, 'De Síl Chonairi Móir', *Ériu: The Journal of the School of Irish Learning* (Dublin, 1912), vi, pp. 130–43

John W. Hales and Frederick J. Furnivall (ed.), *Bishop Percy's Folio Manuscript. Ballads and Romances* (London, 1867–68)

John Barrie Hall (ed.), *Clavdii Clavdiani Carmina* (Leipzig, 1985)

C. Halm (ed.), *Sulpicii Severi: Libri qui Supersunt* (Vienna, 1866)

Silas M. Harris, 'The Kalendar of the *Vitae Sanctorum Wallensium* (B.M. Cotton MS., Vespasian A.xiv)', *Journal of the Historical Society of the Church in Wales* (Cardiff, 1953), iii, pp. 3–52

Marged Haycock (ed.), *Legendary Poems from the Book of Taliesin* (Aberystwyth, 2007)

Marged Haycock (ed.), *Prophecies from the Book of Taliesin* (Aberystwyth, 2013)

W. W. Heist (ed.), *Vitae Sanctorum Hiberniae ex Codice olim Salmanticensi nunc Bruxellensi* (Brussels, 1965)

Joyce Hemlow (ed.), *The Journals and Letters of Fanny Burney (Madame d'Arblay)* (Oxford, 1972–84)

William Henderson, *Notes on the Folk Lore of the Northern Counties of England and the Borders* (London, 1866)

William M. Hennessy (ed.), *Chronicum Scotorum: A Chronicle of Irish Affairs, from the Earliest Times to A.D. 1135* (London, 1866)

Máire Herbert and Pádraig Ó Riain (ed.), *Betha Adamnáin: The Irish Life of Adamnán* (Cork, 1988)

Michael Herity (ed.), *Ordnance Survey Letters Donegal: Letters Containing Information relative to the Antiquities of the County of Donegal Collected during the Progress of the Ordnance Survey in 1835* (Dublin, 2000)

Michael W. Herren (ed.), *Hisperica Famina: I. The A-Text; A new Critical Edition with English Translation and Philological Commentary* (Toronto, 1974)

Douglas P. Hill (ed.), *The Bhagavadgītā: Translated from the Sanskrit with an Introduction an Argument and a Commentary* (Oxford, 1928)

Sir Richard Colt Hoare (tr.), *The Itinerary of Archbishop Baldwin through Wales, A.D. MCLXXXVIII. By Giraldus de Barri* (London, 1806)

Harry Angier Hoffner, Jr. (ed.), *The Laws of the Hittites: A Critical Edition* (Leiden, 1997)

Edmund Hogan (ed.), *Móirthimchell Éirenn Uile dorigne Muirchertach mac Néill* (Dublin, 1901)

T. Rice Holmes (ed.), *C. Iuli Caesaris Commentarii: Rerum in Gallia Gestarum VII; A. Hirti Commentarius VIII.* (Oxford, 1914)

Richard Howlett (ed.), *Chronicles of the Reigns of Stephen, Henry II, and Richard I* (London, 1884)

Benjamin T. Hudson, *Prophecy of Berchán: Irish and Scottish High-Kings of the Early Middle Ages* (Westport, Conn., 1996)

Ian Hughes (ed.), *Math Uab Mathonwy: Pedwaredd Gainc y Mabinogi* (Aberystwyth, 2000)

Ian Hughes (ed.), *Manawydan Uab Llyr: Trydedd Gainc y Mabinogi* (Cardiff, 2007)

Thomas Hughes, *The Scouring of the White Horse; or, the Long Vacation Ramble of a London Clerk* (Cambridge, 1859)

Vernam Hull (ed.), *Longes mac n-Uislenn: The Exile of the Sons of Uisliu* (New York, 1949)

Vernam Hull, 'Geanamuin Chormaic', *Ériu* (1952), xvi, p. 79–85

Robert Hunt, *Popular Romances of the West of England; or, The Drolls, Traditions, and Superstitions of Old Cornwall* (London, 1865)

Tony Hunt (ed.), *Les Gius Partiz des Eschez: Two Anglo-Norman Chess Treatises* (London, 1985)

Graham R. Isaac, 'Trawsganu Kynan Garwyn mab Brochuael: a Tenth-Century Political Poem', *Zeitschrift für celtische Philologie* (Tübingen, 1999), li, pp. 173–85

Kenneth Jackson (ed.), *Early Welsh Gnomic Poems* (Cardiff, 1935)

Kenneth Jackson (ed.), *Cath Maighe Léna* (Dublin, 1938)

J. W. James (ed.), *Rhigyfarch's Life of St. David: The Basic Mid Twelfth-Century Latin Text with Introduction, Critical Apparatus and Translation* (Cardiff, 1967)

A. O. H. Jarman (ed.), *Ymddiddan Myrddin a Thaliesin (O Lyfr Du Caerfyrddin)* (Cardiff, 1951)

A. O. H. Jarman (ed.), *Llyfr Du Caerfyrddin gyda Rhagymadrodd Nodiadau Testunol a Geirfa* (Cardiff, 1982)

Dafydd Jenkins (ed.), *Llyfr Colan: Y Gyfraith Gymreig un ôl Hanner Cyntaf Llawysgrif Peniarth 30* (Cardiff, 1963)

Dafydd Jenkins (tr.), *The Law of Hywel Dda: Law Texts from Medieval Wales Translated and Edited* (Llandysul, 1986)

Thomas Jones (ed.), *Brut y Tywysogion: Peniarth MS. 20* (Cardiff, 1941)

Thomas Jones, 'The Black Book of Carmarthen "Stanzas of the Graves"', *The Proceedings of the British Academy* (London, 1967), liii, pp. 97–137

Freerk C. Kamma (ed.), *Religious Texts of the Oral Tradition from Western New Guinea* (Leiden, 1975–78)

Thomas A. Kelly (ed.), *Sancti Ambrosii Liber de Consolatione Valentiniani: A Text with a Translation, Introduction and Commentary* (Washington, 1940)

Elspeth Kennedy (ed.), *Lancelot do Lac: The Non-Cyclic Old French Prose Romance* (Oxford, 1980)

Bettina Kimpton (ed.), *The Death of Cú Chulainn: A Critical Edition of the Earliest Version of Brislech Mór Maige Muirthemni* (Maynooth, 2009)

Mary H. Kingsley, *Travels in West Africa: Congo Français, Corisco and Cameroons* (London, 1897)

George Lyman Kittredge, 'Arthur and Gorlagon', *Studies and Notes in Philology and Literature* (Boston, 1903), viii, pp. 149–75

Fr. Klaeber (ed.), *Beowulf and the Fight at Finnsburg* (Boston, 1950)

Eleanor Knott (ed.), *Togail Bruidne Da Derga* (Dublin, 1936)

John T. Koch (ed.), *The Gododdin of Aneirin: Text and Context from Dark-Age North Britain* (Cardiff, 1997)

John T. Koch, *Cunedda, Cynan, Cadwallon, Cynddylan: Four Welsh Poems and Britain 383–655* (Aberystwyth, 2013)

Erich Koestermann (ed.), *P. Cornelii Taciti Libri qvi Svpersvnt: Ab Excessv Divi Avgvsti* (Leipzig, 1960)

Florian Kragl (ed.), *Ulrich von Zatzikhoven: Lanzelet* (Berlin, 2006)

George Philip Krapp (ed.), *The Junius Manuscript* (London and New York, 1931)

Hans Kuhn and Gustav Neckel (ed.), *Edda: Die Lieder des Codex Regius nebst Verwandten Denkmälern* (Heidelberg, 1962–68)

Matti Kuusi, Keith Bosley, and Michael Branch (ed.), *Finnish Folk Poetry Epic: An Anthology in Finnish and English* (Helsinki, 1977)

Karl Lachmann and Bernd Schirok (ed.), *Wolfram von Eschenbach: Parzival* (Berlin, 1999)

Pierre-Yves Lambert (ed.), *Recueil des inscriptions gauloises (R.I.G.); Volume II, fascicule 2: Textes gallo-romains sur instrumentum* (Paris, 2002)

William Larminie, *West Irish Folk-Tales and Romances* (London, 1893)

Robert Latham and William Matthews (ed.), *The Diary of Samuel Pepys* (London, 1970–83)

André Le Bœuffle (ed.), *Hygin: L'Astronomie* (Paris, 1983)

L. G. Wickham Legg (ed.), *A Relation of a Short Survey of the Western Counties: Made by a Lieutenant in the Military Company in Norwich in 1635* (*Camden Miscellany* (London, 1936), xvi)

Ruth Lehmann (ed.), *Fled Dúin na nGéd* (Dublin, 1964)

Henry Lewis (ed.), *Brut Dingestow* (Cardiff, 1942)

Henry Lewis, Thomas Roberts, and Ifor Williams (ed.), *Cywyddau Iolo Goch ac Eraill* (Cardiff, 1937)

Timothy Lewis (ed.), *The Laws of Hywel Dda: A Facsimile Reprint of Llanstephan MS. 116 in the National Library of Wales, Aberystwyth* (London, 1912)

Felix Liebermann (ed.), *Die Gesetze der Angelsachsen* (Halle, 1903–16)

Leslie Linder (ed.), *The Journal of Beatrix Potter 1881–1897* (London, 1989)

W. M. Lindsay (ed.), *Isidori Hispalensis Episcopi Etymologiarvm sive Originvm: Libri XX* (Oxford, 1911)

J. G. Lockhart, *Memoirs of the Life of Sir Walter Scott, Bart.* (Edinburgh, 1839–48)

Ferdinand Lot, *Nennius et l'Historia Brittonum: Étude critique suivie d'une édition des diverses versions de ce texte* (Paris, 1934)

Seán Mac Airt (ed.), *The Annals of Inisfallen (MS. Rawlinson B. 503)* (Dublin, 1951)

Seán Mac Airt and Gearóid Mac Niocaill (ed.), *The Annals of Ulster (to A.D. 1131)* (Dublin, 1983)

R. A. S. Macalister, 'The "Druuides" Inscription at Killeen Cormac, Co. Kildare', *Proceedings of the Royal Irish Academy* (Dublin, 1914), xxxii, pp. 227–38

R. A. Stewart Macalister (tr.), *The Latin & Irish Lives of Ciaran* (London, 1921)

R. A. Stewart Macalister (ed.), *Lebor Gabála Érenn: The Book of the Taking of Ireland* (Dublin, 1938–56)

R. A. S. Macalister, *Corpus Inscriptionum Insularum Celticarum* (Dublin, 1945–49)

Proinsias Mac Cana, *The Learned Tales of Medieval Ireland* (Dublin, 1980)

Rev. James MacDougall, *Folk Tales & Fairy Lore in Gaelic and English Collected from Oral Tradition* (Edinburgh, 1910)

Tim William Machan (ed.), *Vafþrúðnismál* (Cambridge, 1988)

L. MacKenna, 'A Poem by Gofraidh Fionn Ó Dálaigh', *Ériu: The Journal of the School of Irish Learning, Dublin* (Dublin, 1952), xvi, pp. 132–39

Séamus Mac Mathúna (ed.), *Immram Brain: Bran's Journey to the Land of the Women* (Tübingen, 1975)

Eoin MacNeill and Gerard Murphy (ed.), *Duanaire Finn: The Book of the Lays of Finn* (London and Dublin, 1908–53)

Leslie A. Marchand (ed.), *Byron's Letters and Journals* (London, 1973–82)

Didier Marcotte (ed.), *Géographes grecs: Ps. – Scymnos : Circuit de la Terre* (Paris, 2000)

Peter K. Marshall (ed.), *Hygini Fabvlae* (Stuttgart and Leipzig, 1993)

M. Martin, *A Description of the Western Islands of Scotland* (London, 1703)

T. P. McCaughey, 'Tract on the Chief Places of Meath', *Celtica* (Dublin, 1960), v, pp. 172–76

Kim McCone (ed.), *Echtrae Chonnlai and the Beginnings of Vernacular Narrative Writing in Ireland* (Maynooth, 2000)

Rev. L. McKenna (ed.), *iomarḃáǵ na ḃfileaḋ: The Contention of the Bards* (London, 1918)

Wolfgang Meid (ed.), *Táin Bó Fraích* (Dublin, 1967)

Wolfgang Meid (ed.), *Die Romanze von Froech und Findabair: Táin Bó Froích* (Innsbruck, 1970)

R. Merkelbach and M. L. West (ed.), *Fragmenta Hesiodea* (Oxford, 1967)

Hans Joachim Mette (ed.), *Pytheas von Massalia* (Berlin, 1952)

Kuno Meyer, 'Macgnimartha Finn inn so sis', *Revue Celtique* (Paris, 1882), v, pp. 197–204

Kuno Meyer (ed.), 'Irish miscellanies: Anecdota from the Stowe MS. n° 992', *Revue Celtique* (Paris, 1883), vi, p. 173–186

Kuno Meyer (ed.), *Hibernica Minora: Being a Fragment of an Old-Irish Treatise on the Psalter* (Oxford, 1894)

Kuno Meyer, 'Mitteilungen aus irischen Handschriften', *Zeitschrift für celtische Philologie* (Halle, 1901), iii, pp. 2–39

Kuno Meyer, 'The Expulsion of the Dessi', *Y Cymmrodor* (1901), xiv, pp. 101–35

Kuno Meyer, 'The Expulsion of the Déssi', *Ériu: The Journal of the School of Irish Learning, Dublin* (1907), iii, pp. 135–42

Kuno Meyer (ed.), *Fianaigecht: Being a Collection of Hitherto Inedited Irish Poems and Tales Relating to Finn and his Fiana, with an English Translation* (Dublin, 1910)

Kuno Meyer (ed.), *Betha Colmán maic Lúacháin: Life of Colmán son of Lúachan* (Dublin, 1911)

Alexandre Micha (ed.), *Lancelot: Roman en prose du XIIIᵉ siècle* (1978–83)

Alexandre Micha (ed.), *Robert de Boron: Merlin, Roman du XIIIᵉ siècle* (Geneva, 1979)

Theodor Mommsen (ed.), *Monvmenta Germaniae Historica* (xiii): *Chronica Minora saec. IV. V. VI. VII* (Berlin, 1894), iii.

Rupert H. Morris (ed.), *Parochialia: Being a Summary of Answers to "Parochial Queries in Order to a Geographical Dictionary, etc., of Wales" Issued by Edward Lhwyd* (London, 1909–11)

J. Morris Jones and John Rhŷs (ed.), *The Elucidarium and Other Tracts in Welsh from Llyvyr Agkyr Llandewivrevi, A.D. 1346 (Jesus College MS. 119)* (Oxford, 1894)

John Morris-Jones and T. H. Parry-Williams (ed.), *Llawysgrif Hendregadredd* (Cardiff, 1933)

Denis Murphy (ed.), *The Annals of Clonmacnoise: Being Annals of Ireland from the Earliest Period to A.D. 1408* (Dublin, 1896)

Kevin Murray (ed.), *Baile in Scáil: 'The Phantom's Frenzy'* (Dublin, 2004)

James A. H. Murray (ed.), *The Romance and Prophecies of Thomas of Erceldoune* (London, 1875)

Kathleen Mulchrone (ed.), *Bethu Phátraic: The Tripartite Life of Patrick* (Dublin, 1939)

Gerard Murphy (ed.), *Early Irish Lyrics: Eighth to Twelfth Century* (Oxford, 1956)

R. A. B. Mynors, R. M. Thomson, and M. Winterbottom (ed.), *William of Malmesbury, Gesta Regvm Anglorvm; The History of the English Kings: Volume I* (Oxford, 1998)

A. S. Napier and W. H. Stevenson (ed.), *The Crawford Collection of Early Charters and Documents* (Oxford, 1895)

V. E. Nash-Williams, *The Early Christian Monuments of Wales* (Cardiff, 1950)

William A. Nitze and T. Atkinson Jenkins (ed.), *Le Haut Livre du Graal: Perlesvaus* (Chicago, 1932–37)

Nessa Ní Shéaghdha (ed.), *Agallamh na Seanórach* (Dublin 1942–45)

Nessa Ní Shéaghdha (ed.), *Tóruigheacht Dhiarmada agus Ghráinne: The Pursuit of Diarmaid and Gráinne* (Dublin, 1967)

M. A. O'Brien, 'The Oldest Account of the Raid of the Collas (circa A.D. 330)', *Ulster Journal of Archaeology* (Belfast, 1939), ii, pp. 170–77

M. A. O'Brien (ed.), *Corpus Genealogiarum Hiberniae* (Dublin, 1962)

Tomás Ó Cathasaigh (ed.), *The Heroic Biography of Cormac mac Airt* (Dublin, 1977)

Brian Ó Cuív (ed.), *Cath Muighe Tuireadh: The Second Battle of Magh Tuireadh* (Dublin, 1945)

Máirín O Daly, 'A Poem on the Airgialla', *Ériu* (Dublin, 1952), xvi, pp. 179–88

Máirín O Daly (ed.), *Cath Maige Mucrama: The Battle of Mag Mucrama* (Dublin, 1975)

John O'Donovan (ed.), *leabhar na g-ceart, or The Book of Rights* (Dublin, 1847)

Richard O'Gorman (ed.), *Robert de Boron, Joseph d'Arimathie: A Critical Edition of the Verse and Prose Versions* (Toronto, 1995)

Standish H. O'Grady (ed.), *Silva Gadelica: A Collection of Tales in Irish with Extracts Illustrating Persons and Places* (London, 1892)

Seán Ó hEochaidh, Máire Mac Neill, and Séamas Ó Catháin (ed.), *Síscéalta ó Thír Chonaill: Fairy Legends from Donegal* (Dublin, 1977)

Elisabeth Okasha, *Corpus of Early Christian Inscribed Stones of South-west Britain* (Leicester, 1993)

J. G. O'Keeffe (ed.), *Buile Suibhne* (Dublin, 1931)

A. O'Kelleher and G. Schoepperle (ed.), *Betha Colaim Chille: Life of Columcille Compiled by Manus O'Donnell in 1532* (Urbana, Ill., 1918)

C. H. Oldfather (ed.), *Diodorus of Sicily* (London, 1953)

J. Olrik, H. Ræder, and Franz Blatt (ed.), *Saxonis Gesta Danorum* (Copenhagen, 1931–57)

John J. O'Meara, 'Giraldus Cambrensis in Topographia Hibernie: Text of the First Recension', *Proceedings of the Royal Irish Academy* (Dublin, 1949), lii, pp. 113–78

Toirdhealbhach Ó Raithbheartaigh (ed.), *Genealogical Tracts I.* (Dublin, 1932)

Hans Pieter Atze Oskamp (ed.), *The Voyage of Máel Dúin: A Study in Early Irish Voyage Literature* (Groningen, 1970)

Hans P. A. Oskamp, 'Echtra Condla', *Études Celtiques* (Paris, 1974), xiv, 207–28

Henry Owen (ed.), *The Description of Pembrokeshire, by George Owen of Henllys, Lord of Kemes* (London, 1892–1936)

Gaston Paris and Jacob Ulrich (ed.), *Merlin: Roman en prose du XIIIᵉ siècle* (Paris, 1886)

John Jay Parry (ed.), *Brut y Brenhinedd: Cotton Cleopatra Version* (Cambridge, Mass., 1937)

François Paschoud (ed.), *Zosime: Histoire Nouvelle* (Paris, 1971–89)

Lucy Allen Paton, *Les Prophecies de Merlin: Edited from MS. 593 in the Bibliothèque Municipale of Rennes* (New York, 1926)

W. R. Paton *et al.* (ed.), *Plvtarchi Moralia* (Leipzig, 1953–78)

Albert Pauphilet (ed.), *La Queste del Saint Graal: Roman du XIIIe siècle* (Paris, 1923)

Thomas Pennant, *A Tour in Scotland and Voyage to the Hebrides. MDCCLXXII. Part I.* (London, 1776)

Thomas Pennant, *A Tour in Scotland; MDCCLXIX* (London, 1776)

J. D. Pheifer (ed.), *Old English Glosses in the Épinal-Erfurt Glossary* (Oxford, 1974)

Egerton G. B. Phillimore, 'A Fragment from Hengwrt MS. No. 202', *Y Cymmrodor* (London, 1887), vii, pp. 89–154

Egerton Phillimore, 'The *Annales Cambriæ* and Old-Welsh Genealogies from *Harleian MS. 3859*', *Y Cymmrodor* (London, 1888), ix, pp. 141–83

William Plomer (ed.), *Kilvert's Diary: Selections from the Diary of the Rev. Francis Kilvert* (London, 1977)

Charles Plummer (ed.), *Venerabilis Baedae Historiam Ecclesiasticam Gentis Anglorum; Historiam Abbatum, Epistolam ad Ecgberctum una cum Historia Abbatum Auctore Anonymo* (Oxford, 1896)

Charles Plummer and John Earle (ed.), *Two Anglo-Saxon Chronicles Parallel: With Supplementary Extracts from the Others; A Revised Text Edited, with Introduction, Notes, Appendices, and Glossary* (Oxford, 1892–99)

Carolus Plummer (ed.), *Vitae Sanctorum Hiberniae: Partim Hactenvs Ineditae ad Fidem Codicvm Manvscriptorvm Recognovit Prolegominis Notis Indicibvs Instrvxit* (Oxford, 1910)

Charles Plummer (ed.), *Bethada Náem nÉrenn: Lives of Irish Saints* (Oxford, 1922)

K. R. Potter (ed.), *Gesta Stephani: The Deeds of Stephen* (London, 1955)

Rev. P. Power (ed.), *Life of St. Declan of Ardmore and Life of St. Mochuda of Lismore* (London, 1914)

Karl Preisendanz (ed.), *Papyri Graecae Magicae: Die Griechischen Zauberpapyri* (Stuttgart, 1973–74)

James B. Pritchard (ed.), *Ancient Near Eastern Texts Relating to the Old Testament* (Princeton, 1969)

H. Rackham, W. H. S. Jones, and D. E. Eichholz, (ed.), *Pliny: Natural History* (London, 1938–62)

Joan Newlon Radner (ed.), *Fragmentary Annals of Ireland* (Dublin, 1978)

Bruce Redford (ed.), *The Letters of Samuel Johnson* (Oxford, 1992–94)

Henry Reeve (ed.), *The Greville Memoirs (Second Part): A Journal of the Reign of Queen Victoria from 1837 to 1852* (London, 1885)

M. D. Reeve (ed.), *Vegetius: Epitoma Rei Militaris* (Oxford, 2004)

Michael D. Reeve and Neil Wright (ed.), *Geoffrey of Monmouth: The History of the Kings of Britain* (Woodbridge, 2007)

John Rhŷs and J. Gwenogvryn Evans (ed.), *The Text of the Mabinogion and other Welsh Tales from the Red Book of Hergest* (Oxford, 1887)

John Rhŷs and J. Gwenogvryn Evans (ed.), *The Text of the Bruts from the Red Book of Hergest* (Oxford, 1890)

Melville Richards (ed.), *Breudwyt Ronabwy: Allan o'r Llyfr Coch o Hergest* (Cardiff, 1948)

Melville Richards (ed.), *Cyfreithiau Hywel Dda o Lawysgrif Coleg yr Iesu Rhydychen LVII* (Cardiff, 1957)

N. J. Richardson (ed.), *The Homeric Hymn to Demeter* (Oxford, 1974)

William Roach (ed.), *The Didot Perceval: According to the Manuscripts of Modena and Paris* (Philadelphia, 1941)

William Roach, Robert H. Ivy, and Lucien Foulet (ed.), *The Continuations of the Old French Perceval of Chretien de Troyes* (Philadelphia, 1949–83)

Brynley F. Roberts (ed.), *Brut y Brenhinedd: Llanstephan MS. 1 Version* (Dublin, 1971)

Brynley F. Roberts (ed.), *Cyfranc Lludd a Llefelys* (Dublin, 1975)

Brynley F. Roberts (ed.), *Breudwyt Maxen Wledic* (Dublin, 2005)

Maria-Helena Rocha-Pereira (ed.), *Pavsaniae Graeciae Descriptio* (Leipzig, 1973–81)

Robert H. Rodgers (ed.), *Palladii Rvtilii Tavri Aemiliani Viri Inlvstris: Opvs Agricvltvrae de Veteniraria Medicina de Insitione* (Leipzig, 1975)

Ulrike Roider (ed.), *De Chophur in Da Muccida* (Innsbruck, 1979)

Duane W. Roller (tr.), *Eratosthenes' Geography* (Princeton and Oxford, 2010)

Mario Roques (ed.), *Erec et Enide* (Paris, 1955)

Christina Horst Roseman (ed.), *Pytheas of Massalia: On the Ocean* (Chicago, 1994)

Haiim B. Rosén (ed.), *Herodoti Historiae* (Leipzig, 1987–97)

Harry Rothwell (ed.), *The Chronicle of Walter of Guisborough* (London, 1957)

Jenny Rowland, *Early Welsh Saga Poetry: A Study and Edition of the Englynion* (Cambridge, 1990)

Eurys I. Rowlands, 'Y Tri Thlwys ar Ddeg', *Llên Cymru* (Cardiff, 1958) v, pp. 33–69

Eurys I. Rowlands (ed.), *Gwaith Lewys Môn* (Cardiff, 1975)

Paul Russell (ed.), *Vita Griffini Filii Conani: The Medieval Latin Life of Gruffudd ap Cynan* (Cardiff, 2005)

Ian Rutherford, *Pindar's Paeans: A Reading of the Fragments with a Survey of the Genre* (Oxford, 2001)

H. E. Salter (ed.), *Cartulary of Oseney Abbey* (Oxford, 1929–36)

Francesco Sbordone (ed.), *Strabonis Geographica* (Rome, 1963–2000)

A. B. Scott and F. X. Martin (ed.), *Expugnatio Hibernica: The Conquest of Ireland by Giraldus Cambrensis* (Dublin, 1978)

Forrest S. Scott (ed.), *Eyrbyggja Saga: The Vellum Tradition* (Copenhagen, 2003)

Otto Seel (ed.), *C. Ivlii Caesaris Commentarii Rervm Gestarvm: Bellvm Gallicvm* (Leipzig, 1961)

Carl Selmer (ed.), *Navigatio Sancti Brendani Abbatis from Early Manuscripts* (Notre Dame, Indiana, 1959)

Francis Shaw (ed.), *The Dream of Óengus: Aislinge Óenguso* (Dublin, 1934)

W. Sieveking and Hans Gärtner (ed.), *Plvtarchvs Pythici Dialogi* (Stuttgart and Leipzig, 1997)

A. Silberman (ed.), *Pomponius Mela: Chorographie* (Paris, 1988)

[Louis Simond], *Journal of a Tour and Residence in Great Britain, during the Years 1810 and 1811, by a French Traveller* (Edinburgh, 1815)

Walter W. Skeat (ed.), *The Complete Works of Geoffrey Chaucer* (Oxford, 1894)

William F. Skene (ed.), *Chronicles of the Picts, Chronicles of the Scots, and Other Early Memorials of Scottish History* (Edinburgh, 1867)

William F. Skene (ed.), *The Four Ancient Books of Wales: Containing The Cymric Poems attributed to the Bards of The Sixth Century* (Edinburgh, 1868)

William F. Skene (ed.), *Johannis de Fordun Chronica Gentis Scotorum* (Edinburgh, 1871–72)

D. Slay (ed.), *Hrólfs Saga Kraka* (Copenhagen, 1960)

S. R. Slings (ed.), *Platonis Rempvblicam* (Oxford, 2003)

Mark S. Smith and Wayne T. Pitard (ed.), *The Ugaritic Baal Cycle* (Leiden, 1994–2009)

Bruno Snell (ed.), *Pindari Carmina cvm Fragmentis* (Leipzig, 1964)

H. Oskar Sommer (ed.), *Le Roman de Merlin or the Early History of King Arthur: Faithfully Edited from the French MS. Add. 10292 in the British Museum (About A.D. 1316)* (London, 1894)

William Henry Stevenson (ed.), *Asser's Life of King Alfred: Together with the Annals of Saint Neots Erroneously Ascribed to Asser* (Oxford, 1904)

Dietrich Stichtenoth (ed.), *Rufus Festus Avienus: Ora Maritima* (Darmstadt, 1968)

Whitley Stokes (ed.), *The Tripartite Life of Patrick, with other Documents Relating to that Saint* (London, 1887)

Whitley Stokes (ed.), *Lives of Saints from the Book of Lismore* (Oxford, 1890)

Whitley Stokes and John Strachan (ed.), *Thesaurus Palaeohibernicus: A Collection of Old-Irish Glosses Scholia Prose and Verse* (Cambridge, 1901–3)

Whitley Stokes (ed.), *Félire Óengusso Céli Dé. The Martyrology of Oengus the Culdee* (London, 1905)

Whitley Stokes, 'The Evernew Tongue', *Ériu: The Journal of the Irish School of Learning, Dublin* (1905), ii, pp. 96–162

John Stow, *The Annales of England* (London, 1601)

John Strachan and J. G. O'Keefe (ed.), *The Táin Bó Cúailnge from the Yellow Book of Lecan with Variant Readings from the Lebor na Huidre* (Dublin, 1912)

Rev. Thomas Taylor (tr.), *The Life of St. Samson of Dol* (London, 1925)

Dennis Tedlock (tr.), *Popol Vuh: The Definitive Edition of the Mayan Book of the Dawn of Life and the Glories of Gods and Kings* (New York, 1985)

The Welsh History Review (Cardiff, 1963)

Derick S. Thomson (ed.), *Branwen uerch Lyr: The Second of the Four Branches of the Mabinogi edited from the White Book of Rhydderch with variants from the Red Book of Hergest and from Peniarth 6* (Dublin, 1961)

R. L. Thomson (ed.), *Pwyll Pendeuic Dyuet: The First of the Four Branches of the Mabinogi edited from the White Book of Rhydderch with variants from the Red Book of Hergest* (Dublin, 1957)

R. L. Thomson (ed.), *Owein or Chwedyl Iarlles y Ffynnawn* (Dublin, 1968)

Robert L. Thomson (ed.), *Ystorya Gereint uab Erbin* (Dublin, 1997)

Rudolf Thurneysen (ed.), *Scéla Mucce Meic Dathó* (Dublin, 1935)

James Henthorn Todd (ed.), *leabhar breathnach annso sis: The Irish Version of the Historia Brittonum of Nennius* (Dublin, 1848)

R. S. O. Tomlin (ed.), *Tabellae Svlis: Roman Inscribed Tablets of Tin and Lead from the Sacred Spring at Bath* (Oxford, 1988)

Örnólfur Thorsson (ed.), *Völsunga saga og Ragnars saga loðbrókar* (Reykjavík, 1985)

Werner Trillmich and Rudolf Buchner (ed.), *Quellen des 9. und 11. Jahrhunderts zur Geschichte der Hamburgischen Kirche und des Reiches* (Darmstadt, 1961)

G. J. Turner (ed.), *Select Pleas of the Forest* (London, 1901)

Seán Ua Ceallaiġ (ed.), *Trí Truaġa na Scéaluiḋeaċta* (Dublin, 1927)

R. D. Van Arsdell, *Celtic Coinage of Britain* (London, 1989)

A. G. van Hamel (ed.), *Compert Con Culainn and Other Stories* (Dublin, 1933)

A. G. van Hamel (ed.), *Lebor Bretnach: The Irish Version of the Historia Britonum Ascribed to Nennius* (Dublin, 1932)

Elisabeth M. C. van Houts (ed.), *The Gesta Normannorum Ducum of William of Jumièges, Orderic Vitalis, and Robert of Torigni* (Oxford, 1992–95)

Barend A. van Nooten and Gary B. Holland (ed.), *Rig Veda: A Metrically Restored Text with an Introduction and Notes* (Cambridge, Mass., 1994)

Helmut van Thiel (ed.), *Homeri Odyssea* (Hildesheim, 1991)

Joseph Vendryes (ed.), *Airne Fíngein* (Dublin, 1953)

Eugène Vinaver (ed.), *The Works of Sir Thomas Malory* (Oxford, 1948)

José Vives (ed.), *Inscripciones Latinas de la España Romana* (Barcelona, 1971)

A. W. Wade-Evans, 'Peniarth MS. 37, Fol. 61A–Fol. 76B', *Y Cymmrodor* (1904), xvii, pp. 129–63

A. W. Wade-Evans, 'The Brychan Documents', *Y Cymmrodor* (1906), xix, pp. 18–50

A. W. Wade-Evans (ed.), *Welsh Medieval Law: Being a Text of the Laws of Howel the Good, Namely the British Museum Harleian MS. 4353 of the 13th Century* (Oxford, 1909)

A. W. Wade-Evans (tr.), *Nennius's "History of the Britons"* (London, 1938)

A. W. Wade-Evans (ed.), *Vitae Sanctorum Britanniae et Genealogiae* (Cardiff, 1944)

Marshall Waingrow (ed.), *The Correspondence and Other Papers of James Boswell Relating to the Making of The Life of Johnson* (Edinburgh, 2001)

Georg Waitz (ed.), *Richeri Historiarum Libri IIII.* (Hanover, 1877)

G. Waitz (ed.), *Pauli Historia Langobardorum* (Hanover, 1878)

Arthur Waley, *The Nine Songs: A Study of Shamanism in Ancient China* (London, 1955)

G. S. M. Walker (ed.), *Sancti Columbani Opera* (Dublin, 1957)

Robert R. Wark (ed.), *Rowlandson's Drawings for a Tour in a Post Chaise* (San Marino, CA, 1964)

Jeanne Wathelet-Willem (ed.), *Recherches sur la chanson de Guillaume: Etudes accompagnées d'une édition* (Paris, 1975)

J. Carmichael Watson (ed.), *Mesca Ulad* (Dublin, 1941)

Robert Weber (ed.), *Biblia Sacra iuxta Vulgatam Versionem* (Stuttgart, 1969)

M. L. West (ed.), *Hesiod: Works & Days* (Oxford, 1978)

Nora White (ed.), *Compert Mongáin and Three Other Early Mongán Tales* (Maynooth, 2006)

Aled Rhys Wiliam (ed.), *Llyfr Iorwerth: A Critical Text of the Venedotian Code of Medieval Welsh Law Mainly from BM. Cotton MS. Titus Dii* (Cardiff, 1960)

Frederick Williams (ed.), *Callimachus: Hymn to Apollo* (Oxford, 1978)

Ifor Williams (ed.), *Breuddwyd Maxen* (Bangor, 1908)

Ifor Williams, 'Ymddiddan Arthur a'r Eryr', *The Bulletin of the Board of Celtic Studies* (Oxford, 1925), ii, pp. 269–86

Ifor Williams (ed.), *Pedeir Keinc y Mabinogi* (Cardiff, 1930)

Ifor Williams (ed.), *Canu Aneirin* (Cardiff, 1938)

Sir Ifor Williams and J.E. Caerwyn Williams (ed.), *The Poems of Taliesin* (Dublin, 1968)

Sir Ifor Williams and Rachel Bromwich (ed.), *Armes Prydein: The Prophecy of Britain From the Book of Taliesin* (Dublin, 1972)

J. E. Caerwyn Williams, 'Gildas, Maelgwn and the Bards', in R. R. Davies, R. A. Griffiths, I. G. Jones, and K. O. Morgan (ed.), *Welsh Society and Nationhood: Historical Essays Presented to Glanmor Williams* (Cardiff, 1984), pp. 19–34

J. E. Caerwyn Williams and Patrick K. Ford, *The Irish Literary Tradition* (Cardiff, 1992)

N. J. A. Williams (ed.), *The Poems of Giolla Brighde Mac Con Midhe* (Dublin, 1980)

Rev. Robert Williams (ed.), *Selections from the Hengwrt MSS. Preserved in the Peniarth Library* (London, 1876–92)

Stephen J. Williams and J. Enoch Powell (ed.), *Cyfreithiau Hywel Dda yn ôl Llyfr Blegywryd (Dull Dyfed)* (Cardiff, 1942)

James Willis (ed.), *Ambrosii Theodosii Macrobii: Satvrnalia* (Leipzig, 1963)

David M. Wilson (ed.), *The Bayeux Tapestry* (London, 1985)

Bartina H. Wind (ed.), *Les Fragments du Tristan de Thomas* (Leiden, 1950)

Neil Wright (ed.), *The Historia Regum Britannie of Geoffrey of Monmouth I: Bern, Burgerbibliothek, MS. 568* (Cambridge, 1984)

Neil Wright (ed.), *The Historia Regum Britannie of Geoffrey of Monmouth II: The First Variant Version: a critical edition* (Cambridge, 1988)

Wilmer Cave Wright (ed.), *The Works of the Emperor Julian* (London, 1913–23)

Joannes Zwicker (ed.), *Fontes Historiae Religionis Celticae* (Bonn, 1934–36)

Secondary works

Lesley Abrams and James P. Carley (ed.), *The Archaeology and History of Glastonbury Abbey: Essays in Honour of the Ninetieth Birthday of C.A. Ralegh Radford* (Cambridge, 1991)

Paul Acker and Carolyne Larrington (ed.), *The Poetic Edda: Essays on Old Norse Mythology* (New York and London, 2002)

J. N. Adams, *The Latin Sexual Vocabulary* (London, 1982)

J. N. Adams, *Bilingualism and the Latin Language* (Cambridge, 2003)

Tore Ahlbäck (ed.), *Old Norse and Finnish Religions and Cultic Place-Names* (Åbo, 1990)

N. B. Aitchison, *Armagh and the Royal Centres in Early Medieval Ireland: Monuments, Cosmology, and the Past* (Woodbridge, 1994)

Nick Aitchison, *Scotland's Stone of Destiny: Myth, History and Nationhood* (London, 2000)

Leslie Alcock, 'Excavations at South Cadbury Castle, 1969', *The Antiquaries Journal* (London, 1970), l, pp.14–25

Leslie Alcock, '*By South Cadbury is that Camelot ...': The Excavation of Cadbury Castle 1966–1970* (Aylesbury, 1972)

G. J. Alder, *British India's Northern Frontier 1865-95: A Study in Imperial Policy* (London, 1963)

Stephen Aldhouse-Green, *Paviland Cave and the 'Red Lady': A Definitive Report* (Bristol, 2000)

Caroline Alexander, 'If the Stones Could Speak: Searching for the Meaning of Stonehenge', *National Geographic* (Washington, June 2008), ccxiii, pp. 34–59

Rosamund Allen, Lucy Perry, and Jane Roberts (ed.), *Laȝamon: Contexts, Language, and Interpretation* (Exeter, 2002)

Bo Almqvist, Séamas Ó Catháin, and Pádraig Ó Héalaí (ed.), *The Heroic Process: Form, Function and Fantasy in Folk Epic* (Dun Laoghaire, 1987)

Marjorie O. Anderson, *Kings and Kingship in Early Scotland* (Edinburgh, 1973)

Edward Anwyl, *Celtic Religion in Pre-Christian Times* (London, 1906)

E. Anwyl, 'The Value of the Mabinogion for the Study of Celtic Religion', in *Transactions of the Third International Congress for the History of Religions* (Oxford, 1908), ii, pp. 234–44

Paul Ashbee, Martin Bell, and Edwina Proudfoot, *Wilsford Shaft: excavations 1960–2* (London, 1989)

Donald Atkinson, *The Roman-British Site on Lowbury Hill in Berkshire* (Reading, 1916)

Maria Eugenia Aubet, *The Phoenicians and the West: Politics, colonies and trade* (Cambridge, 1993)

Michel Aubineau, 'Une homélie grecque inédite sur la Transfiguration', *Analecta Bollandiana* (Brussels, 1967), lxxxv, pp. 401–27

G. Ausenda (ed.), *After Empire: Towards an Ethnology of Europe's Barbarians* (Woodbridge, 1995)

Emile Bachelier, 'Les Druides en Gaule romaine', *Ogam: Tradition celtique* (Rennes, 1959), xi, pp. 295–306

Françoise Bader, *La langue des dieux, ou l'hermétisme des poètes indo-européens* (Pisa, 1989)

Françoise Bader, 'Pan', *Revue de Philologie* (Paris, 1989), lxiii, pp. 7–46

N. Bailey, *An Universal Etymological Dictionary* (London, 1723)

János M. Bak (ed.), *Coronations: Medieval and Early Modern Monarchic Ritual* (Berkeley and Los Angeles, 1990)

Katharine C. Balderston (ed.), *Thraliana: The Diary of Mrs. Hester Lynch Thrale (Later Mrs. Piozzi) 1776–1809* (Oxford, 1951)

Philip Baldi, *The Foundations of Latin* (Berlin, 1999)

Martin J. Ball, James Fife, Erich Poppe, and Jenny Rowland (ed.), *Celtic Linguistics/Ieithyddiaeth Geltaidd; Readings in the Brythonic Languages: Festschrift for T. Arwyn Watkins* (Amsterdam and Philadelphia, 1990)

Alfred Bammesberger and Alfred Wollmann (ed.), *Britain 400–600: Language and History* (Heidelberg, 1990)

M. Macleod Banks, *British Calendar Customs: Orkney & Shetland* (London, 1946)

S. Baring-Gould, *Strange Survivals: Some Chapters in the History of Man* (London, 1892)

S. Baring-Gould and John Fisher, *The Lives of the British Saints: The Saints of Wales and Cornwall and such Irish Saints as have Dedications in Britain* (London, 1907–13)

Margaret Barker, *The Gate of Heaven: The History and Symbolism of the Temple in Jerusalem* (London, 1991)

John C. Barrett, P. W. M. Freeman, and Ann Woodward, *Cadbury Castle Somerset: The later prehistoric and early historic archaeology* (London, 2000)

G. W. S. Barrow, *Robert Bruce and the Community of the Realm of Scotland* (London, 1965)

Peter C. Bartrum, 'Was there a British 'Book of Conquests?', *The Bulletin of the Board of Celtic Studies* (Cardiff, 1968), xxiii, pp. 1–6

Karen Bassie-Sweet, *At the Edge of the World: Caves and Late Classic Maya World View* (Norman and London, 1996)

Janet Bately and Anton Englert (ed.), *Ohthere's Voyages: A late 9th-century account of voyages along the coasts of Norway and Denmark and its cultural context* (Roskilde, 2007)

J. D. Bateson, 'Roman Material from Ireland: A Re-Consideration', *Proceedings of the Royal Irish Academy* (Dublin, 1973), lxxiii, pp. 21–97

Rolf Baumgarten, 'A Crux in Echtrae Conlai', *Éigse: A Journal of Irish Studies* (1975), xvi, pp. 18–23

Curt W. Beck and Jan Bouzek (ed.), *Amber in Archæology: Proceedings of the Second International Conference on Amber in Archaeology, Lilice 1990* (Prague, 1993)

Roger Beck, 'Interpreting the Ponza Zodiac: II', *Journal of Mithraic Studies* (London, 1978), ii, pp. 87–147

Roger Beck, *Planetary Gods and Planetary Orders in the Mysteries of Mithras* (Leiden, 1988)

Joachim Becker, *Messianic Expectation in the Old Testament* (Philadelphia, 1980)

Gary Beckman, Richard Beal and Gregory McMahon (ed.), *Hittite Studies in Honor of Harry A. Hoffner Jr. on the Occasion of His 65th Birthday* (Winona Lake, Ind., 2003)

Jonathan Ben-Dov, Wayne Horowitz, and John M. Steele (ed.), *Living the Lunar Calendar* (Oxford, 2012)

Rev. J. A. Bennett, 'Camelot', *The Proceedings of the Somersetshire Archæological and Natural History Society* (Taunton, 1890), xxxvi, pp. 1–19

Fernand Benoit, *Le symbolisme dans les sanctuaires de la Gaule* (Brussels, 1970)

Émile Benveniste, *Le vocabulaire des institutions indo-européennes* (Paris, 1969)

Osborn Bergin and Carl Marstrander (ed.), *Miscellany Presented to Kuno Meyer by Some of his Friends and Pupils on the Occasion of his Appointment to the Chair of Celtic Philology in the University of Berlin* (Halle, 1912)

J. Bergman, K. Drynjeff, and H. Ringgren (ed.), *Ex orbe religionum: studia Geo Widengren* (Leiden, 1972)

Ronald M. Berndt, *Australian Aboriginal Religion* (Leiden, 1974)

William B. N. Berry, *Growth of a Prehistoric Time Scale: Based on Organic Evolution* (San Francisco, 1968)

Richard Bevins, Rob Ixer, and Nick Pearce, 'Carn Goedog is the likely source of Stonehenge doleritic bluestones: evidence based on compatible element geochemistry and Principal Component Analysis', *Journal of Archaeological Science* (London, 2014), xlii, pp. 179–93

Sukumari Bhattacharji, *The Indian Theogony: A Comparative Study of Indian Mythology from the Vedas to the Puranas* (Cambridge, 1970)

Martin Biddle, *King Arthur's Round Table: An archaeological investigation* (Woodbridge, 2000)

D. A. Binchy (ed.), *Studies in Early Irish Law* (Dublin, 1936)

D. A. Binchy, 'The Linguistic and Historical Value of the Irish Law Tracts' *The Proceedings of the British Academy* (London, 1943), xxix, pp. 195–227

D. A. Binchy, 'The Fair of Tailtiu and the Feast of Tara', *Ériu* (Dublin, 1958), xviii, pp. 113–38

D. A. Binchy, *Celtic and Anglo-Saxon Kingship* (Oxford, 1970)

Kaj Birket-Smith, 'Studies in Circumpacific Culture Relations: IV. The Double-Headed Serpent', *Historisk-filosofiske Meddelelser* (Copenhagen, 1973), xlvii, pp. 1–14

Helmut Birkhan, *Germanen und Kelten bis zum Ausgang der Römerzeit: Der Aussagewert von Wörtern und Sachen für die Frühesten Keltisch-Germanischen Kulturbeziehungen* (Vienna, 1970)

Helmut Birkhan, *Kelten: Versuch einer Gesamtdarstellung ihrer Kultur* (Vienna, 1997)

Helmut Birkhan, *Kelten/Celts: Bilder ihrer Kultur/Images of their Culture* (Vienna, 1999)

Anthony R. Birley, *The Fasti of Roman Britain* (Oxford, 1981)

Henrik Birnbaum and Jaan Puhvel (ed.), *Ancient Indo-European Dialects: Proceedings of the Conference on Indo-European Linguistics Held at the University of California, Los Angeles April 25–27, 1963* (Berkeley, 1966)

Ronald Black, William Gillies, Roibeard Ó Maolalaigh, and D. W. Harding (ed.), *Celtic Connections: Proceedings of the 10th International Congress of Celtic Studies* (Phantassie, East Linton, 1999–2005)

Carmen Blacker, *The Catalpa Bow: A Study of Shamanistic Practices in Japan* (London, 1975)

C. J. Bleeker, *The Sacred Bridge: Researches into the Nature and Structure of Religion* (Leiden, 1963)

C. J. Bleeker (ed.), *Initiation: Contributions to the Theme of the Study-Conference of the International Association for the History of Religions Held at Strasburg, September 17th to 22nd 1964* (Leiden, 1965)

C. J. Bleeker, *Egyptian Festivals: Enactments of Religious Renewal* (Leiden, 1967)

C. J. Bleeker, *The Rainbow: A Collection of Studies in the Science of Religion* (Leiden, 1975)

Roger Blench and Matthew Spriggs (ed.), *Archaeology and Language I: Theoretical and methodological orientations* (London, 1997)

Richard and Eva Blum, *The Dangerous Hour: The Lore of Crisis and Mystery in Rural Greece* (London, 1970)

Fanni Bogdanow, *The Romance of the Grail: A Study of the Structure and Genesis of a Thirteenth-Century Arthurian Romance* (Manchester, 1966)

Émile Boisacq, *Dictionnaire étymologique de la langue grecque: étudiée dans ses rapports avec les autres langues indo-européennes* (Heidelberg and Paris, 1916)

J. K. Bollard, 'The Role of Myth and Tradition in *The Four Branches of the Mabinogi*', *Cambridge Medieval Celtic Studies* (Cambridge, 1983), vi, pp. 67–86

Kees W. Bolle (ed.), *Secrecy in Religions* (Leiden, 1987)

J. D. P. Bolton, *Aristeas of Proconnessus* (Oxford, 1962)

Larissa Bonfante (ed.), *Etruscan Life and Afterlife: A Handbook of Etruscan Studies* (Detroit, 1986)

Giuliano Bonfante and Larissa Bonfante, *The Etruscan Language: An Introduction* (Manchester, 1983)

Yves Bonnefoy and Wendy Doniger (ed.), *Mythologies: A Restructured Translation of Dictionnaire des mythologies et des religions des sociétés traditionelles et du monde antique* (Chicago, 1991)

George C. Boon, 'The Pagans Hill Dog', *Britannia: A Journal of Romano-British and Kindred Studies* (London, 1989), xx, pp. 201–17

William Copeland Borlase, *The Age of the Saints: A Monograph of Early Christianity in Cornwall with the Legends of the Cornish Saints* (Truro, 1893)

Jacqueline Borsje, *From Chaos to Enemy: Encounters with Monsters in Early Irish Texts. An Investigation Related to the Process of Christianization and the concept of Evil* (Turnhout, 1996)

Jacqueline Borsje, Ann Dooley, Séamus Mac Mathúna, and Gregory Toner (ed.), *Celtic Cosmology: Perspectives from Ireland and Scotland* (Toronto, 2014)

A. P. Bos, *Cosmic and Meta-Cosmic Theology in Aristotle's Lost Dialogues* (Leiden, 1989)

Mark Bowden, Sharon Soutar, David Field, and Martyn Barber, *The Stonehenge Landscape* (Swindon, 2015)

E. G. Bowen, *The Settlements of the Celtic Saints in Wales* (Cardiff, 1956)

E. G. Bowen, *Saints, Seaways and Settlements in the Celtic Lands* (Cardiff, 1969)

G. W. Bowersock, *Augustus and the Greek World* (Oxford, 1965)

Alan K. Bowman, Edward Champlin, and Andrew Lintott (ed.), *The Cambridge Ancient History (Second Edition): The Augustan Empire, 43 B.C.–A.D. 69* (Cambridge, 1996), x.

Edel Bhreatnach (ed.), *The Kingship and Landscape of Tara* (Dublin, 2005)

Richard Bradley, *Rock Art and the Prehistory of Atlantic Europe: Signing the Land* (London, 1997)

Dorothy Ann Bray, *A List of Motifs in the Lives of the Early Irish Saints* (Helsinki, 1992)

Dorothy Ann Bray, 'Ireland's Other Apostle: Cogitosus' St Brigit', *Cambrian Medieval Celtic Studies* (Aberystwyth, 2010), lviii, pp. 55–70

Andrew Breeze, 'The Provenance of the Rushworth Mercian Gloss', *Notes and Queries* (London, 1996), ccxli, pp. 394–95

Andrew Breeze, 'The Name of Ganarew', *Journal of the English Place-Name Society* (Nottingham, 1999), xxxi, pp. 113–14

Andrew Breeze, *The Origins of the Four Branches of the Mabinogi* (Leominster, 2009)

Andrew Breeze, 'Welsh loanwords in the AB Language', in Yoko Wada (ed.), *Europe Without Boundaries* (Osaka, 2010), pp. 9–14

Andrew Breeze, 'St David and the Cult of St Non', *The Carmarthenshire Antiquary* (Carmarthen, 2013), xlix, pp. 5–15)

Andrew Breeze, 'Two Ancient Names: *Britanni* and *Londinium*', *Eos: Commentarii Societatis Philologae Polonorum* (Warsaw, 2014), ci, pp. 313–14

Jan Bremmer, *The Early Greek Concept of the Soul* (Princeton, 1983)

J. N. Bremmer and N. M. Horsfall, *Roman Myth and Mythography* (London, 1987)

Caroline Brett, 'Breton Latin Literature as Evidence for Literature in the Vernacular, A.D. 800–1300', *Cambridge Medieval Celtic Studies* (Cambridge, 1989), xviii, pp. 1–25

Jacques Briard, *The Bronze Age in Barbarian Europe: From the Megaliths to the Celts* (London, 1979)

Luc Brisson, *Le mythe de Tirésias: Essai d'analyse structurale* (Leiden, 1976)

Johanna Broda, Davíd Carrasco, and Eduardo Matos Moctezuma, *The Great Temple of Tenochtitlan: Center and Periphery in the Aztec World* (Berkeley, 1987)

Frank Brommer, *Heracles: The Twelve Labors of the Hero in Ancient Art and Literature* (New Rochelle, 1986)

Rachel Bromwich, 'Celtic Dynastic Themes and the Breton Lays', *Études Celtiques* (Paris, 1960–61), ix, pp. 441–74

Rachel Bromwich and R. Brinley Jones (ed.), *Astudiaethau ar yr Hengerdd* (Cardiff, 1978)

Rachel Bromwich (ed.), *The Beginnings of Welsh Poetry: Studies by Sir Ifor Williams, D.Litt., LL.D., F.B.A.* (Cardiff, 1980)

Rachel Bromwich, A. O. H. Jarman, and Brynley F. Roberts (ed.), *The Arthur of the Welsh: The Arthurian Legend in Medieval Welsh Literature* (Cardiff, 1991)

Arthur C. L. Brown, *The Origin of the Grail Legend* (Cambridge, Mass., 1943)

John Pairman Brown, *Israel and Hellas* (Berlin, 1995–2001)

Theo Brown, *The Fate of the Dead: A Study in Folk-Eschatology in the West Country After the Reformation* (Cambridge, 1979)

James Douglas Bruce, *The Evolution of Arthurian Romance: From the Beginnings Down to the Year 1300* (Göttingen, 1928)

R. L. S. Bruce-Mitford (ed.), *Recent Archaeological Excavations in Britain* (London, 1956)

Marie-Thérèse Brouland, *Le Substrat celtique du lai breton anglais Sir Orfeo* (Paris, 1990)

Peter Brown, *Authority and the Sacred: Aspects of the Christianisation of the Roman World* (Cambridge, 1995)

Jean-Louis Brunaux, *Les Druides: Des philosophes chez les Barbares* (Paris, 2006)

E. A. Wallis Budge, *Osiris and the Egyptian Resurrection* (London, 1911)

Colin Burgess, *The Age of Stonehenge* (London, 1980)

Constance Bullock-Davies, *Professional Interpreters and the Matter of Britain* (Cardiff, 1966)

Walter Burkert, *Structure and History in Greek Mythology and Ritual* (Los Angeles, 1979)

Walter Burkert, *Greek Religion* (Cambridge, Mass., 1985)

Titus Burckhardt, *Mirror of the Intellect: Essays on Traditional Science & Sacred Art* (Cambridge, 1987)

Aubrey Burl, *Prehistoric Avebury* (London, 1979)

Aubrey Burl, *Stonehenge: a new history of the world's greatest stone circle* (London, 2006)

L. A. S. Butler, 'Domestic Building in Wales and the Evidence of the Welsh Laws', *Medieval Archaeology* (London, 1987), xxxi, pp. 47–58

E. A. S. Butterworth, *The Tree at the Navel of the Earth* (Berlin, 1970)

Francis John Byrne, *Irish Kings and High-Kings* (London, 1973)

J. F. Campbell, *The Celtic Dragon Myth* (Edinburgh, 1911)

Leroy A. Campbell, *Mithraic Iconography and Ideology* (Leiden, 1968)

Joseph Campbell, *The Hero with a Thousand Faces* (Princeton, 1972)

John Carey, 'Nodons in Britain and Ireland', *Zeitschrift für celtische Philologie* (Tübingen, 1984), xl, pp. 1–22

John Carey, 'Sequence and Causation in *Echtra Nerai*', *Ériu: The Journal of the School of Irish Learning* (Dublin, 1988), xxxix, pp. 67–74

John Carey, 'Time, Memory, and the Boyne Necropolis', in William Mahon (ed.), *Proceedings of the Harvard Celtic Colloquium* (Cambridge, Mass., 1993), x, pp. 24–36

John Carey, 'On the Interrelationships of Some *Cín Dromma Snechtai* Texts', *Ériu* (1995), xlvi, pp. 71–92

John Carey, John T. Koch, and Pierre-Yves Lambert (ed.), *Ildánach Ildírech: A Festschrift for Proinsias MacCana* (Andover and Aberystwyth, 1999)

John Carey, Máire Herbert, and Pádraig Ó Riain (ed.), *Studies in Irish Hagiography: Saints and Scholars* (Dublin, 2001)

M. Cary and E. H. Warmington, *The Ancient Explorers* (London, 1929)

David L. Carmichael, Jane Hubert, Brian Reeves, and Audhild Schanche (ed.), *Sacred Sites, Sacred Places* (London, 1994)

James Carney, *Studies in Early Irish Literature and History* (Dublin, 1955)

James Carney, *The Irish Bardic Poet: A study in the relationship of Poet and Patron as exemplified in the persons of the poet, Eochaidh Ó hEoghusa (O'Hussey) and his various patrons, mainly members of the Maguire family of Fermanagh* (Dublin, 1967)

James Carney and David Greene (ed.), *Celtic Studies: Essays in memory of Angus Matheson 1912–1962* (London, 1968)

Jane Cartwright (ed.), *Celtic Hagiography and Saints' Cults* (Cardiff, 2003)

M. O. H. Carver (ed.), *The Age of Sutton Hoo: The Seventh Century in North-Western Europe* (Woodbridge, 1992)

P. J. Casey (ed.), *The End of Roman Britain: Papers arising from a Conference, Durham 1978* (Oxford, 1979)

P. J. Casey and J. L. Davies, with J. Evans, *Excavations at Segontium (Caernarfon) Roman Fort, 1975–1979* (London, 1993)

Elena Cassin, *La splendeur divine: Introduction à l'étude de la mentalité mésopotamienne* (Paris, 1968)

L. Luca Cavalli-Sforza, Paolo Menozzi, and Alberto Piazza, *The History and Geography of Human Genes* (Princeton, 1994)

H. Munro Chadwick, *The Origin of the English Nation* (Cambridge, 1907)

H. M. Chadwick, *Early Scotland: The Picts, the Scots & the Welsh of Southern Scotland* (Cambridge, 1949)

H. Munro Chadwick and N. Kershaw Chadwick, *The Growth of Literature* (Cambridge, 1932–40)

John Chadwick, *Lexicographica Graeca: Contributions to the lexicography of Ancient Greek* (Oxford, 1996)

N. Kershaw Chadwick, *Poetry & Prophecy* (Cambridge, 1942)

Nora K. Chadwick, 'The Lost Literature of Celtic Scotland', *Scottish Gaelic Studies* (Oxford, 1953), vii, p. 115–83

Nora K. Chadwick (ed.), *Studies in Early British History* (Cambridge, 1954)

Nora K. Chadwick, 'Pictish and Celtic Marriage in Early Literary Tradition', *Scottish Gaelic Studies* (Oxford, 1955), viii, pp. 56–115

Nora K. Chadwick (ed.), *Studies in the Early British Church* (Cambridge, 1958)

Nora K. Chadwick, *The Age of the Saints in the Early Celtic Church* (London, 1961)

Nora K. Chadwick (ed.), *Celt and Saxon: Studies in the Early British Border* (Cambridge, 1963)

Nora K. Chadwick, *Celtic Britain* (London, 1963)

Nora K. Chadwick, *The Druids* (Cardiff, 1966)

Nora K. Chadwick, *Early Brittany* (Cardiff, 1969)

Nora K. Chadwick and Victor Zhirmunsky, *Oral Epics of Central Asia* (Cambridge, 1969)

E. K. Chambers, *The Mediaeval Stage* (Oxford, 1903)

E. K. Chambers, *Arthur of Britain* (London, 1927)

William A. Chaney, *The Cult of Kingship in Anglo-Saxon England: The Transition from Paganism to Christianity* (Manchester, 1970)

Pierre Chantraine, *Dictionnaire* étymologique de la langue grecque: Histoire des mots; avec *un Supplément sous la direction de: Alain Blanc, Charles de Lamberterie, Jean-Louis Perpillou* (Paris, 1999)

B. G. Charles, *The Place-Names of Pembrokeshire* (Aberystwyth, 1992)

T. M. Charles-Edwards, 'Welsh *diffoddi, difa* and Irish *do-bádi* and *do-ba*', *The Bulletin of the Board of Celtic Studies* (Cardiff, 1969), xxiii, pp. 210–13

T. M. Charles-Edwards, 'The Date of the Four Branches of the Mabinogi', *The Transactions of the Honourable Society of Cymmrodorion: Session 1970* (London, 1971), pp. 263–98

T. M. Charles-Edwards, 'Kinship, Status, and the Origins of the Hide', *Past & Present* (Oxford, 1972), lvi, pp. 3–33

T. M. Charles-Edwards, *Early Irish and Welsh Kinship* (Oxford, 1993)

T. M. Charles-Edwards, *Early Christian Ireland* (Cambridge, 2000)

Thomas Charles-Edwards, *Wales and the Britons 350–1064* (Oxford, 2013)

T. M. Charles-Edwards, Morfydd E. Owen and D. B. Walters (ed.), *Lawyers and Laymen: Studies in the History of Law presented to Professor Dafydd Jenkins on his seventy-fifth birthday* (Cardiff, 1986)

T. M. Charles-Edwards, Morfydd E. Owen, and Paul Russell (ed.), *The Welsh King and his Court* (Cardiff, 2000)

M. P. Charlesworth, *The Lost Province or the Worth of Britain* (Cardiff, 1949)

M. P. Charlesworth and M. D. Knowles (ed.), *The Heritage of Early Britain* (London, 1952)

Jean Chélini and Henry Branthomme (ed.), *Histoire des pèlerinages non chrétiens: Entre magique et sacré: le chemin des dieux* (Paris, 1987)

V. Gordon Childe, *Prehistoric Communities of the British Isles* (London, 1940)

Julia Ching, *Mysticism and Kingship in China: The heart of Chinese wisdom* (Cambridge, 1997)

Christopher Chippindale, *Stonehenge Complete* (London, 1983)

Jamsheed Kairshasp Choksy, 'Purity and Pollution in Zoroastrianism', *The Mankind Quarterly* (Washington, 1986), xxvii, pp. 16791

Arthur Christensen, *Les types du premier homme et du premier roi dans l'histoire légendaire de Iraniens* (Stockholm, 1917–34)

Reidar Th. Christiansen, *The Dead and the Living* (Oslo, 1946)

Reidar Th. Christiansen, *Studies in Irish and Scandinavian Folktales* (Copenhagen, 1959)

Thomas Owen Clancy, 'The Needs of Strangers in the Four Branches of the Mabinogi', *Quaestio Insularis: Selected Proceedings of the Cambridge Colloquium in Anglo-Saxon Norse and Celtic* (Cambridge, 2006), vi, p. 1–24

M. T. Clanchy, *From Memory to Written Record: England 1066–1307* (London, 1979)

Katherine Clarke, 'In Search of the Author of Strabo's *Geography*', *The Journal of Roman Studies* (London, 1997), lxxxvii, pp. 92–110

Michael Clarke, *Flesh and Spirit in the Songs of Homer: A Study of Words and Myths* (Oxford, 1999)

Rosamund M. J. Cleal, K. E. Walker, and R. Montague (ed.), *Stonehenge in its landscape: Twentieth-century excavations* (London, 1995)

R. E. Clements, *God and Temple* (Oxford, 1965)

Richard J. Clifford, *The Cosmic Mountain in Canaan and the Old Testament* (Cambridge, Mass., 1972)

Richard Coates and Andrew Breeze (ed.), *Celtic Voices English Places: Studies of the Celtic Impact on Place-Names in England* (Stamford, 2000)

G. E. C[ockayne]. *et al.* (ed.), *The Complete Peerage: or a History of the House of Lords and all its Members from the Earliest Times* (London, 1910–59)

J. M. Coles and D. D. A. Simpson (ed.), *Studies in Ancient Europe: Essays presented to Stuart Piggott* (Leicester, 1968)

R. G. Collingwood and Ian Richmond, *The Archaeology of Roman Britain* (London, 1969)

C. F. Konrad, *Plutarch's Sertorius: A Historical Commentary* (Chapel Hill and London, 1994)

Danièle Conso, Nicole Fick, and Bruno Poulle (ed.), *Mélanges François Kerlouégan* (Paris, 1994)

Mary-Anne Constantine, 'Prophecy and Pastiche in the Breton Ballads: Groac'h Ahès and Gwenc'hlan', *Cambrian Medieval Celtic Studies* (Aberystwyth, 1995), xxx, pp. 87–121.

Arthur Bernard Cook, *Zeus: A Study in Ancient Religion* (Cambridge, 1914–40)

Gordon J. Copley, *An Archaeology of South-East England: A Study in Continuity* (London, 1958)

Altay Coşkun, *Die gens Ausoniana an der Macht: Untersuchungen zu Decimius Magnus Ausonius und seiner Familie* (Oxford, 2002)

James Cowan, *The Maori: Yesterday and To-day* (Auckland, 1930)

O. G. S. Crawford, *Man and his Past* (Oxford, 1921)

O. G. S. Crawford, *Archaeology in the Field* (Plymouth, 1953)

Julia C. Crick, *The Historia Regum Britannie of Geoffrey of Monmouth IV: Dissemination and Reception in the Later Middle Ages* (Cambridge, 1991)

J. Crofts, *Packhorse, Waggon and Post: Land Carriage and Communications under the Tudors and Stuarts* (London, 1967)

Frank Moore Cross, *Canaanite Myth and Hebrew Epic: Essays in the History of the Religion of Israel* (Cambridge, Mass., 1973)

Tom Peete Cross, *Motif-Index of Early Irish Literature* (Bloomington, Ind., 1952)

David Crouch, *The Reign of King Stephen, 1135–1154* (Harlow, 2000)

Barry Cunliffe (ed.), *Hengistbury Head Dorset; Volume 1: The Prehistoric and Roman Settlement, 3500 BC–AD 500* (Oxford, 1987)

Barry Cunliffe, *Iron Age Communities in Britain: An account of England, Scotland and Wales from the Seventh Century BC until the Roman Conquest* (London, 1991)

Barry Cunliffe, *Facing the Ocean: The Atlantic and its Peoples 8000 BC–AD 1500* (Oxford, 2001)

Barry Cunliffe and Colin Renfrew (ed.), *Science and Stonehenge* (Oxford, 1997)

Barry Cunliffe and John T. Koch (ed.), *Celtic from the West: Alternative Perspectives from Archaeology, Genetics, Language and Literature* (Oxford, 2010)

M. E. Cunnington, *An Introduction to the Archæology of Wiltshire from the Earliest Times to the Pagan Saxons* (Devizes, 1934)

Ernst Robert Curtius, *European Literature and the Latin Middle Ages* (London, 1953)

M. A. Czaplicka, *Aboriginal Siberia: A Study in Social Anthropology* (Oxford, 1914)

Catherine Daniel, *Les prophéties de Merlin et la culture politique (XIIᵉ-XVIᵉ siècle)* (Turnhout, 2006)

Glyn E. Daniel (ed.), *Myth or Legend?* (London, 1955)

Iestyn Daniel, 'The date, origin, and authorship of 'The Mabinogion' in the light of *Ymborth yr enaid*', *The Journal of Celtic Studies* (Turnhout, 2004), iv, pp. 117–52

Alain Daniélou, *Hindu Polytheism* (London, 1964)

K. R. Dark, *Civitas to Kingdom: British Political Continuity 300-800* (Leicester, 1994)

Ken Dark, *Britain and the End of the Roman Empire* (Stroud, 2000)

Timothy Darvill and Geoffrey Wainwright, 'Stonehenge Excavations 2008', *The Antiquaries Journal* (Cambridge, 2009), lxxxix, p. 1–18

Timothy Darvill and Geoff Wainwright, 'Beyond Stonehenge: Carn Menyn Quarry and the origin and date of bluestone extraction in the Preseli Hills of south-west Wales', *Antiquity: A Quarterly Review of World Archaeology* (Cambridge, 2014), lxxxviii, pp. 1099–1114

Sara Graça da Silva and Jamshid J. Tehrani, 'Comparative phylogenetic analyses uncover the ancient roots of Indo-European folktales', *Royal Society Open Science* (London, 2016)

Hilda Ellis Davidson, *Patterns of Folklore* (Ipswich, 1978)

Edward Davies, *Celtic Researches, on the Origin, Traditions & Language, of the Ancient Britons* (London, 1804)

Elwyn Davies, *Rhestr o Enwau Lleoedd: A Gazetteer of Welsh Place-Names* (Cardiff, 1957), pp. 56–67

Jonathan Ceredig Davies, *Folk-Lore of West and Mid-Wales* (Aberystwyth, 1911)

R. R. Davies, *Conquest, Coexistence, and Change: Wales 1063-1415* (Oxford, 1987)

R. R. Davies, *The First English Empire: Power and Identities in the British Isles 1093–1343* (Oxford, 2000)

Wendy Davies, *Wales in the Early Middle Ages* (Leicester, 1982)

Norman Davis and C. L. Wrenn (ed.), *English and Medieval Studies Presented to J. R. R. Tolkien on the Occasion of his Seventieth Birthday* (London, 1962)

R. R. Davies, *Conquest, Coexistence, and Change: Wales 1063-1415* (Oxford, 1987)

R. H. C. Davis and J. M. Wallace-Hadrill (ed.), *The Writing of History in the Middle Ages: Essays Presented to Richard William Southern* (Oxford, 1981)

Elwyn Davies (ed.), *Celtic Studies in Wales: A Survey* (Cardiff, 1963)

Oliver Davies, *Celtic Christianity in Early Medieval Wales: The Origins of the Welsh Spiritual Tradition* (Cardiff, 1996)

Sioned Davies and Nerys Ann Jones (ed.), *The Horse in Celtic Culture: Medieval Welsh Perspectives* (Cardiff, 1997)

Wendy Davies, *Wales in the Early Middle Ages* (Leicester, 1982)

W. Boyd Dawkins, 'The Retreat of the Welsh from Wiltshire', *Archæologia Cambrensis* (London, 1914), xiv, pp. 3–28

John Day, *God's Conflict with the dragon and the sea: Echoes of a Canaanite myth in the Old Testament* (Cambridge, 1985)

Pádraig de Brún, Seán Ó Coileán, and Pádraig Ó Riain (ed.), *Folia Gadelica: Essays presented by former students to R.A. Breatnach, M.A., M.R.I.A.* (Cork, 1983)

Javier de Hoz, 'The Mediterranean Frontier of the Celts and the Advent of Celtic Writing', *Cambrian Medieval Celtic Studies* (Aberystwyth, 2007), liii/liv, pp. 1–22

Javier de Hoz, Eugenio R. Luján, and Patrick Sims-Williams (ed.), *New Approaches to Celtic Place-Names in Ptolemy's Geography* (Madrid, 2005)

Xavier Delamarre, *Dictionnaire de la langue gauloise: Une approche linguistique du vieux-celtique continental* (Paris, 2001)

R. L. M. Derolez, *Les dieux et la religion des Germains* (Paris, 1962)

Jan de Vries, *Altgermanische Religionsgeschichte* (Berlin, 1956–57)

Jan de Vries, *Keltische Religion* (Stuttgart, 1961)

Jan de Vries, *Altnordisches Etymologisches Wörterbuch* (Leiden, 1961)

Ferdinand Jozef Maria de Waele, *The Magic Staff or Rod in Graeco-Italian Antiquity* (Ghent, 1927)

Miriam Robbins Dexter and Edgar C. Polomé (ed.), *Varia on the Indo-European Past: Papers in Memory of Marija Gimbutas* (Washington, 1997)

W. Howship Dickinson, *King Arthur in Cornwall* (London, 1900)

Myles Dillon, 'The Archaism of Irish Tradition', *The Proceedings of the British Academy* (London, 1947), xxxiii, pp. 245–64

Myles Dillon, *Early Irish Literature* (Chicago, 1948)

Myles Dillon, 'The Taboos of the Kings of Ireland', *Proceedings of the Royal Irish Academy* (Dublin, 1951), liv, pp. 1–36

Myles Dillon (ed.), *Irish Sagas* (Dublin, 1959)

Myles Dillon, *Celt and Hindu* (Dublin, 1973)

Myles Dillon and Nora Chadwick, *The Celtic Realms* (London, 1967)

V. Diószegi (ed.), *Popular Beliefs and Folklore Tradition in Siberia* (Bloomington and The Hague, 1968)

V. Diószegi and M. Hoppál (ed.), *Shamanism in Siberia* (Budapest, 1978)

Dorothy Disterheft, Martin Huld, John Greppin, and Edgar C. Polomé (ed.), *Studies in Honor of Jaan Puhvel* (Washington, 1997)

Gilbert H. Doble, *Saint Iltut* (Cardiff, 1944)

Gilbert H. Doble, *The Saints of Cornwall* (Chatham and Oxford, 1960–70)

Anne Dodd (ed.), *Oxford Before the University: The Late Saxon and Norman Archaeology of the Thames Crossing, the Defences and the Town* (Oxford, 2003)

E. R. Dodds, *The Greeks and the Irrational* (Berkeley, 1951)

Terence L. Donaldson, *Jesus on the Mountain: A Study in Matthean Theology* (Sheffield, 1985)

C. Michael Driessen, 'On the Etymology of Lat. *urbs*', *The Journal of Indo-European Studies* (Washington, 2001), xxix, pp. 41–68

Jan Willem Drijvers, *Helena Augusta: The Mother of Constantine the Great and the Legend of Her Finding of the True Cross* (Leiden, 1992)

J. F. Drinkwater, 'Lugdunum: 'Natural Capital' of Gaul?', *Britannia: A Journal of Romano-British and Kindred Studies* (London, 1974), vi, pp. 133–40

John Drinkwater and Hugh Elton (ed.), *Fifth-Century Gaul: a crisis of identity?* (Cambridge, 1992)

Stephen T. Driscoll, Jane Geddes and Mark A. Hall (ed.), *Pictish Progress: New Studies on Northern Britain in the Early Middle Ages* (Leiden, 2011)

S. R. Driver, *Modern Research as illustrating the Bible* (London, 1909)

Hans Peter Duerr, *Dreamtime: Concerning the Boundary between Wilderness and Civilization* (Oxford, 1985)

A. R. Dufty (ed.), *Ebvracvm: Roman York* (Leicester, 1962)

F. Duine, *Questions d'hagiographie et vie de S. Samson* (Paris, 1914)

Georges Dumézil, *Rituels indo-européens à Rome* (Paris, 1954)

Georges Dumézil, 'Remarques comparatives sur le dieu scandinave Heimdallr', *Études Celtiques* (Paris, 1959), viii, pp. 269–72

Georges Dumézil, *Mythe et Épopée* (Paris, 1968–73)

Georges Dumézil, *Archaic Roman Religion* (Chicago, 1970)

Georges Dumézil, 'The Vedic Mitra: a résumé of theses and references', *The Journal of Mithraic Studies* (London, 1976), i, pp. 26–35

Georges Dumézil, *Les dieux souverains des Indo-Européens* (Paris, 1986)

David N. Dumville, ''Nennius' and the *Historia Brittonum*', *Studia Celtica* (Cardiff, 1975–6), x–xi, pp. 78–95

David N. Dumville, 'Sub-Roman Britain: History and Legend', *History: The Journal of the Historical Society* (London, 1977), lxii, pp. 173–92

David Dumville, 'The 'Six' Sons of Rhodri Mawr: A Problem in Asser's *Life of King Alfred*', *Cambridge Medieval Celtic Studies* (Cambridge, 1982), iv, pp. 5–18

David N. Dumville, 'Brittany and «Armes Prydein Vawr»', *Études Celtiques* (Paris, 1983), xx, pp. 145–59

David Dumville, 'The Historical Value of the *Historia Brittonum*', *Arthurian Literature* (Cambridge, 1986), vi, pp. 1–26

David N. Dumville, *Saint Patrick, A.D. 493–1993* (Woodbridge, 1993)

David N. Dumville, *Saint David of Wales* (Cambridge, 2001)

G. R. Dunstan (ed.), *The Human Embryo: Aristotle and the Arabic and European Traditions* (Exeter, 1990)

Terence DuQuesne (ed.), *Hermes Aegyptiacus: Egyptological Studies for BH Stricker* (Oxford, 1995)

Paul-Marie Duval, *Les dieux de la Gaule* (Paris, 1957)

Doris Edel, 'Geoffrey's So-called Animal Symbolism and Insular Celtic Tradition', *Studia Celtica* (1983/1984), xviii/xix, pp. 96–109

Doris Edel (ed.), *Thracian Tales on the Gundestrup Cauldron* (Amsterdam, 1991)

J. Goronwy Edwards, 'Edward I's Castle-Building in Wales' *The Proceedings of the British Academy* (London, 1944), xxxii, pp. 15–81

Nancy Edwards and Alan Lane (ed.), *The Early Church in Wales and the West* (Oxford, 1992)

Eilert Ekwall, *The Concise Oxford Dictionary of English Place-Names* (Oxford, 1936)

Mircea Eliade, *Le mythe de l'éternel retour: Archétypes et répétition* (Paris, 1949)

Mircea Eliade, *Le chamanisme et les techniques archaïques de l'extase* (Paris, 1951)

Mircea Eliade, *Forgerons et alchimistes* (Paris, 1956)

Mircea Eliade, *Patterns in Comparative Religion* (London, 1958)

Mircea Eliade, *Yoga: Immortality and Freedom* (New York, 1958)

Mircea Eliade, *Birth and Rebirth: The Religious Meanings of Initiation in Human Culture* (London, 1961)

Mircea Eliade, *The Quest: History and Meaning in Religion* (Chicago, 1969)

Mircea Eliade, *Occultism, Witchcraft, and Cultural Fashions: Essays in Comparative Religions* (Chicago, 1976)

Mircea Eliade, *Myth and Reality* (Northampton, 1964)

Mircea Eliade, *A History of Religious Ideas* (London, 1979), i.

Hilda Roderick Ellis, *The Road to Hel: A Study of The Conception of the Dead in Old Norse Literature* (Cambridge, 1943)

Encyclopaedia Britannica; or, a Dictionary of Arts, Sciences, and Miscellaneous Literature (Edinburgh, 1810)

Ivan Engnell, *Studies in Divine Kingship in the Ancient Near East* (Uppsala, 1943)

Michael J. Enright, *Lady with a Mead Cup: Ritual, Prophecy and Lordship in the European Warband from La Tène to the Viking Age* (Dublin, 1996)

George Eogan, *Knowth and the passage-tombs of Ireland* (London, 1986)

George Eogan, 'Prehistoric and Early Historic Culture Change at Brugh na Bóinne', *Proceedings of the Royal Irish Academy* (Dublin, 1991), xci, pp. 106–32

Angelique Gulermovich Epstein, 'Miscarriages and Miraculous Births in Indo-European Tradition', *The Journal of Indo-European Studies* (Washington, 1994), xxii, pp. 151–63

A. Ernout, A. Meillet, and Jacques André, *Dictionnaire étymologique de la langue latine: Histoire des mots* (Paris, 1994)

Joseph F. Eska, R. Geraint Gruffydd, and Nicolas Jacobs (ed.), *Hispano-Gallo-Brittonica: Essays in honour of Professor D. Ellis Evans on the occasion of his sixty-fifth birthday* (Cardiff, 1995)

Lawrence E. Eson, 'Merlin's Last Cry: Ritual Burial and Rebirth of the Poet in Celtic and Norse Tradition', *Zeitschrift für celtische Philologie* (Tübingen, 2006), lv, pp. 180–200

D. Ellis Evans, *Gaulish Personal Names: A Study of some Continental Celtic Formations* (Oxford, 1967)

D. Ellis Evans, John G. Griffith, and E. M. Jope (ed.), *Proceedings of the Seventh International Congress of Celtic Studies* (Oxford, 1986)

J. Gwenogvryn Evans, *Report on Manuscripts in the Welsh Language* (London, 1898–1902)

E. E. Evans-Pritchard, *Nuer Religion* (Oxford, 1956)

Sally Exon, Vince Gaffney, Ann Woodward, and Ron Yorston, *Stonehenge Landscapes: Journeys through real-and-imagined worlds* (Oxford, 2000)

Anton Fägersten, *The Place-Names of Dorset* (Uppsala, 1933)

François Falc'hun, *Les noms de lieux celtiques* (Rennes, 1966)

Alexander Falileyev, *Etymological Glossary of Old Welsh* (Tübingen, 2000)

Alexander Falileyev, Ashwin E. Gohil and Naomi Ward, *Dictionary of Continental Place-Names: A Celtic Companion to the Barrington Atlas of the Greek and Roman World* (Aberystwyth, 2010)

Edmond Faral, *La légende arthurienne - Études et documents* (Paris, 1929)

Christopher A. Faraone and Dirk Obbink (ed.), *Magika Hiera: Ancient Greek Magic and Religion* (Oxford, 1991)

Isabelle Fauduet, *Les temples de tradition celtique en Gaule romaine* (Paris, 1993)

Leonard Charles Feldstein, *Homo Quaerens: The Seeker and the Sought; Method Become Ontology* (New York, 1978)

Leonard Charles Feldstein, *The Dance of Being: Man's Labyrinthine Rhythms; The Natural Ground of the Human* (New York, 1979)

Joseph Felicijan, *The Genesis of the Contractual Theory and the Installation of the Dukes of Carinthia* (Cleveland, Ohio, 1967)

John Ferguson, *The Religions of the Roman Empire* (London, 1970)

Paul Feuerherd, *Geoffrey of Monmouth und das Alte Testament mit Berücksichtigung der Historia Britonum des Nennius* (Halle, 1915)

P. J. C. Field, 'Nennius and his History', *Studia Celtica* (Cardiff, 1996), xxx, pp. 159–65

H. P. R. Finberg, *Roman and Saxon Withington: A Study in Continuity* (Leicester, 1955)

H. P. R. Finberg, *The Early Charters of Wessex* (Leicester, 1964)

Alec Fisher, *The logic of real arguments* (Cambridge, 2004)

I. L. Finkel (ed.), *Ancient Board Games in perspective: Papers from the 1990 British Museum colloquium* (London, 2007)

Raymond Firth, *Tikopia Ritual and Belief* (London, 1967)

A. P. Fitzpatrick, *The Amesbury Archer and the Boscombe Bowmen* (Salisbury, 2011)

Elizabeth FitzPatrick, *Royal Inauguration in Gaelic Ireland c. 1100-1600* (Woodbridge, 2004)

Robert Huntington Fletcher, *The Arthurian Material in the Chronicles especially those of Great Britain and France* (Boston, 1906)

H. J. Fleure, 'Archaeology and Folk Tradition', *The Proceedings of the British Academy* (London, 1932), xvii, pp. 369–90

Léon Fleuriot, *Les origines de la Bretagne: L'émigration* (Paris, 1980)

Pierre Flobert, 'La vie ancienne de saint Samson et l'histoire', *Études Celtiques* (Paris, 1992), xxix, pp. 183–89

Maxim Fomin, *Instructions for Kings: Secular and Clerical Images of Kingship in Early Ireland and Ancient India* (Heidelberg, 2013)

Joseph Fontenrose, *Python: A Study of Delphic Myth and its Origins* (Berkeley and Los Angeles, 1959)

Patrick K. Ford, 'Branwen: A Study of the Celtic Affinities', *Studia Celtica* (Cardiff, 1987/8), xxii/xxiii, pp. 29–41

J. Forde-Johnston, *Hillforts of the Iron Age in England and Wales: A Survey of the Surface Evidence* (Liverpool, 1976)

Max Förster, *Der Flußname Themse und seine Sippe: Studien zur Anglisierung keltischer Eigennamen und zur Lautchronologie des Altbritischen* (Munich, 1941)

Katherine Forsyth, *Language in Pictland* (Utrecht, 1997)

I. LL. Foster and Glyn Daniel (ed.), *Prehistoric and Early Wales* (London, 1965)

Cyril Fox, *The Archaeology of the Cambridge Region: A Topographical Study of the Bronze, Early Iron, Roman and Anglo-Saxon Ages, with an Introductory Note on the Neolithic Age* (Cambridge, 1923)

Sir Cyril Fox and Bruce Dickins (ed.), *The Early Cultures of North-West Europe (H. M. Chadwick Memorial Studies)* (Cambridge, 1950)

Sir Cyril Fox, *Life and Death in the Bronze Age: An Archaeologist's Field-Work* (London, 1959)

Sir Cyril Fox, *The Personality of Britain: Its Influence on Inhabitant and Invader in Prehistoric and Early Historic Times* (Cardiff, 1959)

Henri Frankfort, *Kingship and the Gods: A Study of Ancient Near Eastern Religion as the Integration of Society & Nature* (Chicago, 1948)

Sir James George Frazer, *Lectures on the Early History of the Kingship* (London, 1905)

Sir James George Frazer, *The Magic Art and the Evolution of Kings* (London, 1911)

Sir James George Frazer, *Taboo and the Perils of the Soul* (London, 1911)

Sir James George Frazer, *The Scapegoat* (London, 1913)

J. G. Frazer, *Balder the Beautiful: The Fire-Festivals of Europe and the Doctrine of the External Soul* (London, 1913)

Sir James George Frazer, *Adonis, Attis, Osiris: Studies in the History of Oriental Religion* (London, 1914)

Sir James George Frazer, *Folk-Lore in the Old Testament: Studies in Comparative Religion Legend and Law* (London, 1918)

Sir James George Frazer, *Myths of the Origin of Fire* (London, 1930)

David Noel Freeman, *Pottery, Poetry, and Prophecy: Studies in Early Hebrew Poetry* (Winona Lake, Ind., 1980)

Philip P. Freeman, 'The Earliest Greek Sources on the Celts', *Études Celtiques* (Paris, 1996), xxxii, pp. 11–48

Charles French, Rob Scaife, and Michael J. Allen, 'Durrington Walls to West Amesbury by Way of Stonehenge: A Major Transformation of the Holocene Landscape', *The Antiquaries Journal* (Cambridge, 2012), xcii, pp. 1–36

Roger French and Frank Greenaway (ed.), *Science in the Early Roman Empire: Pliny the Elder, his Sources and Influence* (Totowa, NJ, 1986)

W. H. C. Frend, 'Religion in Roman Britain in the Fourth Century A.D.', *The Journal of the British Archaeological Association* (London, 1955), xviii, pp. 1–18

W. H. C. Frend, 'Pagans, Christians, and 'the Barbarian Conspiracy' of A.D. 367 in Roman Britain', *Britannia* (1992), xxiii, pp. 121–31

Sheppard Frere, *Britannia: a history of Roman Britain* (London, 1967)

Paul Friedrich, *Proto-Indo-European Trees: The Arboreal System of a Prehistoric People* (Chicago, 1970)

Paul Friedrich, *The Meaning of Aphrodite* (Chicago, 1978)

Hjalmar Frisk, *Griechisches Etymologisches Wörterbuch* (Heidelberg, 1954–72)

Claude Gaignebet and Jean-Dominique Lajoux, *Art profane et religion populaire au Moyen Age* (Paris, 1985)

Alan Gailey and Dáithí Ó hÓgáin (ed.), *Gold Under the Furze: Studies in Folk Tradition Presented to Caoimhín Ó Danachair* (Dublin, 1982)

Pierre Gallais, 'Bleheri, la cour de Poitiers et la diffusion des récits arthuriens sur le continent', *Journal of the International Arthurian Society* (Berlin, 2014), ii, pp. 84–113

Thomas V. Gamkrelidze and Vjačeslav V. Ivanov, *Indo-European and the Indo-Europeans: A Reconstruction and Historical Analysis of a Proto-Language and a Proto-Culture* (Berlin and New York, 1995)

Geiriadur Prifysgol Cymru: A Dictionary of the Welsh Language (Cardiff, 1950–2002)

Margaret Gelling and Doris Mary Stenton, *The Place-Names of Oxfordshire* (Cambridge, 1953–54)

Margaret Gelling, *The West Midlands in the Early Middle Ages* (Leicester, 1992)

Peter Gelling and Hilda Ellis Davidson, *The Chariot of the Sun and other Rites and Symbols of the Northern Bronze Age* (London, 1969)

Karen George, *Gildas's De Excidio Britonum and the Early British Church* (Woodbridge, 2009)

Ilya Gershevitch (ed.), *The Avestan Hymn to Mithra* (Cambridge, 1959)

Alex Gibson, *Stonehenge & Timber Circles* (Stroud, 1998)

Marija Gimbutas, *The Language of the Goddess* (London, 1989)

Marija Gimbutas, *The Kurgan Culture and the Indo-Europeanization of Europe: Selected Articles from 1952 to 1993* (Washington, 1997)

P. G. W. Glare (ed.), *Oxford Latin Dictionary* (Oxford, 1968–82)

John S. Stuart Glennie, *Arthurian Localities; their Historical Origin, Chief Country, and Fingalian Relations* (Edinburgh, 1869)

Stephen O. Glosecki, *Shamanism and Old English Poetry* (New York, 1989)

Glenys Goetinck, 'Peredur ... Upon Reflection', *Études Celtiques* (Paris, 1988), xxv, pp. 221–32

Walter Goffart, *Rome's Fall and After* (London, 1989)

[Oliver Goldsmith], *The Geography and History of England: Done in the Manner of Gordon's and Salmon's Geographical and Historical Grammars* (London, 1765)

J. Gonda, *Ancient Indian Kingship from the Religious Point of View* (Leiden, 1966)

J. Gonda, *The Vedic God Mitra* (Leiden, 1972)

J. Gonda, *Prajāpati and the Year* (Amsterdam, 1984)

Lucy Goodison and Christine Morris (ed.), *Ancient Goddesses: The Myths and the Evidence* (Madison, Wis., 1998)

Joaquín Gorrochategui and Patrizia de Bernardo Stempel (ed.), *Die Kelten und ihre Religion im Spiegel der Epigraphischen Quellen (Akten des 3. F.E.R.C.AN.-Workshops (Vitoria-Gasteiz, September 2000)* (Bilbao, 2004)

J. E. B. Gover, Allen Mawer, and F. M. Stenton, *The Place-Names of Devon* (Cambridge, 1931–32)

J. E. B. Gover, Allen Mawer, and F. M. Stenton, *The Place-Names of Wiltshire* (Cambridge, 1939)

Linda M. Gowans, *Cei and the Arthurian Legend* (Cambridge, 1988)

Antonia Gransden, *Historical Writing in England c. 550 to c. 1307* (London, 1974)

Antonia Gransden, *Legends, Traditions and History in Medieval England* (London, 1992)

Elizabeth A. Gray, 'Cath Maige Tuired : Myth and Structure', *Éigse: A Journal of Irish Studies* (Naas, 1982), xix, pp. 1–35

Miranda Jane Green, *The Wheel as a Cult-Symbol in the Romano-Celtic World With Special Reference to Gaul and Britain* (Brussels, 1984)

Miranda Green, *Symbol and Image in Celtic Religious Art* (London, 1989)

Miranda J. Green (ed.), *The Celtic World* (London, 1995)

David Greene, *Makers and Forgers* (Cardiff, 1975)

J. Gwyn Griffiths, *Atlantis and Egypt: With other Selected Essays* (Cardiff, 1991)

Margaret Enid Griffiths, *Early Vaticination in Welsh with English Parallels* (Cardiff, 1937)

W.F. Grimes (ed.), *Aspects of Archaeology in Britain and Beyond: Essays presented to O. G. S. Crawford* (London, 1951)

Jakob Grimm, *Germanic Mythology* (Washington, 1997)

L. V. Grinsell, *The Folklore of Stanton Drew* (St Peter Port, Guernsey, 1973)

Chris Grooms, *The Giants of Wales: Cewri Cymru* (Lampeter, 1993)

Paul Grosjean, 'Trois pièces sur S. Senán', *Analecta Bollandiana* (Brussels, 1948), lxvi, p. 219–30

W. J. Gruffydd, 'The Mabinogion', *The Transactions of the Honourable Society of Cymmrodorion: Session 1912-1913* (London, 1913), pp. 14–80

W. J. Gruffydd, *Math vab Mathonwy: An Inquiry into the Origins and Development of the Fourth Branch of the Mabinogi with the Text and a Translation* (Cardiff, 1928)

W. J. Gruffydd, *Rhiannon: An Inquiry into the Origins of the First and Third Branches of the Mabinogi* (Cardiff, 1953)

W. J. Gruffydd, *Folklore and Myth in the Mabinogion* (Cardiff, 1958)

Jean Guilaine (ed.), *Mégalithismes de l'Atlantique à l'Ethiopie* (Paris, 1999)

G. B. Grundy, 'The Ancient Highways of Dorset, Somerset, and South-West England', *The Archaeological Journal* (London, 1938), xciv, pp. 257–90

Anita Guerreau-Jalabert, *Index des motifs narratifs dans les romans arthuriens français en vers (XIIᵉ-XIIIᵉ Siècles)* (Geneva, 1992)

Edwin Guest, *Origines Celticae (A Fragment) and other Contributions to the History of Britain* (London, 1883)

A. J. Gurevich, *Categories of Medieval Culture* (London, 1985)

Christian-J. Guyonvarc'h, 'Mediolanvm Bitvrigvm: Deux éléments de vocabulaire religieux et de géographie sacrée', *Celticvm I: Actes du Premier Colloque International d'Etudes Gauloises, Celtiques et Protoceltiques* (Rennes, 1961), pp. 137–58

Christian-J. Guyonvarc'h, 'La conception de Cúchulainn', *Ogam: Tradition celtique* (Rennes, 1965), xvii, pp. 363–91

Christian-J. Guyonvarc'h, 'La Courtise d'Étain', *Celticvm XV: Actes du Ve Colloque International d'Études Gauloises, Celtiques et Protoceltiques* (Rennes, 1966), p. 283–327

Christian J. Guyonvarc'h, 'Celtique commun *Letavia, gaulois LETAVIS, irlandais Letha; la porte de l'Autre Monde', *Ogam: Tradition Celtique* (Rennes, 1967), xix, pp. 490–94

Christian-J. Guyonvarc'h, 'Notes d'étymologie et de lexicographie gauloises et celtiques XXXII', *Ogam* (1969), xxi, pp. 315–30

Christian-J. Guyonvarc'h, *Magie, médecine et divination chez les Celtes* (Paris, 1997)

Christian-J. Guyonvarc'h and Françoise Le Roux, *Les Druides* (Rennes, 1986)

Martti Haavio, *Väinämöinen: Eternal Sage* (Helsinki, 1952)

Alfred Haldar, *The Notion of the Desert in Sumero-Accadian and West-Semitic Religions* (Uppsala, 1950)

C. R. Hallpike, *The Foundations of Primitive Thought* (Oxford, 1979)

Roberte Hamayon, *La chasse à l'âme: Esquisse d'une théorie du chamanisme sibérien* (Nanterre, 1990)

Jacob Hammer, 'Geoffrey of Monmouth's Use of the Bible in the "Historia Regum Britanniae"', *Bulletin of the John Rylands Library* (Manchester, 1947), xxx, pp. 293–311

Eric P. Hamp, 'The Element –tamo-', *Études Celtiques* (Paris, 1974), xiv, pp. 187–94

Eric P. Hamp, 'Mabinogi', *The Transactions of the Honourable Society of Cymmrodorion: Sessions 1974 and 1975* (London, 1975), pp. 243–49

Eric P. Hamp, '*Clas*: Lucus a non lucendo', in Kathryn A. Klar, Eve E. Sweetser, and Claire Thomas (ed.), *A Celtic Florilegium: Studies in Memory of Brendan O Hehir* (Andover, Mass., 1996), pp. 40–42

Robert W. Hanning, *The Vision of History in Early Britain: From Gildas to Geoffrey of Monmouth* (New York, 1966)

Bernhard Hänsel and Stefan Zimmer (ed.), *Die Indogermanen und das Pferd: Akten des Internationalen interdisziplinären Kolloquiums Freie Universität Berlin, 1.-3. Juli 1992* (Budapest, 1994)

Florence Emily Hardy, *The Later Years of Thomas Hardy 1892-1928* (London, 1930)

J. B. Harley and David Woodward (ed.), *The History of Cartography* (Chicago, 1987–2015)

Rendel Harris, *The Ascent of Olympus* (Manchester, 1917)

Jane Ellen Harrison, *Themis: A Study of the Social Origins of Greek Religion* (Cambridge, 1912)

Edwin Sidney Hartland, *The Science of Fairy Tales. An Inquiry into Fairy Mythology* (London, 1891)

Edwin Sidney Hartland, *The Legend of Perseus: A Study of Tradition in Story Custom and Belief* (London, 1894–96)

Gudmund Hatt, *Asiatic Influences in American Folklore* (Copenhagen, 1949)

F. Haverfield and George Macdonald, *The Roman Occupation of Britain* (Oxford, 1924)

C. F. C. Hawkes, 'Britons, Romans, and Saxons round Salisbury and in Cranborne Chase', *The Archaeological Journal* (London, 1947), civ, pp. 27–81

C. F. C. Hawkes, *Pytheas: Europe and the Greek Explorers* (Oxford, 1975)

Christopher Hawkes, 'Britain and Julius Caesar', *The Proceedings of the British Academy* (London, 1977), lxiii, pp. 125–92

David Hawkes, 'The Quest of the Goddess', *Asia Major: A British Journal of Far Eastern Studies* (London, 1967), xiii, pp. 84–85

David Boyd Haycock, *William Stukeley: Science, Religion and Archaeology in Eighteenth-Century England* (Woodbridge, 2002)

Marged Haycock, "Preiddeu Annwn' and the Figure of Taliesin', *Studia Celtica* (Cardiff, 1983-84), xviii–xix, pp. 52–78

Brian Hayden, *Shamans Sorcerers and Saints* (Washington, 2003)

J. C. Heesterman, *The Ancient Indian Royal Consecration: The Rājasūya Described According to the Yajus Texts and Annotated* (The Hague, 1957)

H. O'Neill Hencken, 'A Gaming Board of the Viking Age', *Acta Archaeologica* (Copenhagen, 1933), iv, pp. 85–104

Martin Henig, *Religion in Roman Britain* (London, 1984)

Martin Henig and Anthony King (ed.), *Pagan Gods and Shrines of the Roman Empire* (Oxford, 1986)

Elissa R. Henken, *Traditions of the Welsh Saints* (Cambridge, 1987)

Elissa R. Henken, *The Welsh Saints: A Study in Patterned Lives* (Cambridge, 1991)

David Henry (ed.), *The worm the germ and the thorn: Pictish and related studies presented to Isabel Henderson* (Balgavies, 1997)

P. L. Henry, *The Early English and Celtic Lyric* (London, 1966)

Michael W. Herren (ed.), *Insular Latin Studies: Papers on Latin Texts and Manuscripts of the British Isles* (Toronto, 1981)

Hans-Volkmar Herrmann, *Omphalos* (Münster, 1959)

Alfred Heubeck, Stephanie West, J. B. Hainsworth, and Arie Hoekstra, *A Commentary on Homer's Odyssey* (Oxford, 1988–92)

Thomas D. Hill, 'Woden as "Ninth Father": Numerical Patterning in Some Old English Royal Genealogies', in Daniel G. Calder and T. Craig Christy (ed.), *Germania: Comparative Studies in the Old Germanic Languages and Literature* (Woodbridge, 1988), pp. 161–74

A. M. Hocart, *Kingship* (Oxford, 1927)

N. J. Higham, *The English conquest: Gildas and Britain in the fifth century* (Manchester, 1994)

Ørnulf Hodne, *The Types of the Norwegian Folktale* (Oslo, 1984)

F. R. Hodson (ed.), *The Place of Astronomy in the Ancient World* (London, 1974)

Edmund Hogan, S.J., *Onomasticon Goedelicum: Locorum et Tribuum Hiberniae et Scotiae; An Index, with Identifications, to the Gaelic Names of Places and Tribes* (Dublin, 1910)

Christina Hole, *English Custom & Usage* (London, 1941)

Nils G. Holm (ed.), *Religious Ecstasy* (Uppsala, 1982)

T. Rice Holmes, *Ancient Britain and the Invasions of Julius Caesar* (Oxford, 1907)

F. Holthausen, *Altenglisches Etymologisches Wörterbuch* (Heidelberg, 1934)

S. H. Hooke (ed.), *The Labyrinth: Further Studies in the Relation between Myth and Ritual in the Ancient World* (London, 1935)

Mihály Hoppál and Juha Pentikäinen (ed.), *Uralic Mythology and Folklore* (Budapest, 1989)

Mihály Hoppál and Juha Pentikäinen (ed.), *Northern Religions and Shamanism* (Budapest, 1992)

Ray Howell, 'Roman Past and Medieval Present: Caerleon as a Focus for Continuity and Conflict in the Middle Ages', *Studia Celtica* (Cardiff, 2012), xlvi, pp. 11–21

David Howlett, 'Seven Studies in Seventh-Century Texts', *Peritia: Journal of the Medieval Academy of Ireland* (Turnhout, 1996), x, pp. 1–70

D. R. Howlett, *British Books in Biblical Style* (Dublin, 1997)

Mícheál Hoyne, 'The Political Context of Cath Muighe Tuireadh, the Early Modern Irish Version of the Second Battle of Magh Tuireadh', *Ériu* (Dublin, 2013), lxiii, pp. 99–116

J. H. Humphrey (ed.), *Literacy in the Roman world* (Ann Arbor, 1991)

Benjamin T. Hudson and Vickie Ziegler (ed.), *Crossed Paths: Methodological Approaches to the Celtic Aspect of the European Middle Ages* (Lanham, Md. and London, 1991)

Carl A. Huffman, *Philolaus of Croton: Pythagorean and Presocratic* (Cambridge, 1993)

Martin Huld, 'Albanian *gögel* and Indo-European 'acorns'', *The Journal of Indo-European Studies* (Washington, 2007), xxxv, pp. 121–28

Åke Hultkrantz, *Conceptions of the Soul among North American Indians: A Study in Religious Ethnology* (Stockholm, 1953)

Åke Hultkrantz (ed.), *The Supernatural Owners of Nature: Nordic symposium on the religious conceptions of ruling spirits (genii loci, genii speciei) and allied concepts* (Uppsala, 1961)

Ronald Hutton, *Blood and Mistletoe: The History of the Druids in Britain* (New Haven and London, 2009)

Ronald Hutton, 'Medieval Welsh Literature and Pre-Christian Deities', *Cambrian Medieval Celtic Studies* (Aberystwyth, 2011), lxi, pp. 57–85

Thomas A. Idinopulos and Edward A. Yonan (ed.), *The Sacred and its Scholars: Comparative Methodologies for the Study of Primary Religious Data* (Leiden, 1996)

Graham R. Isaac, 'Myrddin, Proffwyd Diwedd y Byd: Ystyriaethau Newydd ar Ddatblygiad ei Chwedl', *Llên Cymru* (Cardiff, 2001), xxiv, pp. 13–23

G. R. Isaac, 'The Nature and Origins of the Celtic Languages: Atlantic Seaways, Italo-Celtic and Other Paralinguistic Misapprehensions', *Studia Celtica* (Cardiff, 2004), pp. 49–58

Kenneth Jackson, *Studies in Early Celtic Nature Poetry* (Cambridge, 1935)

Kenneth Jackson, 'Nennius and the Twenty-Eight Cities of Britain', *Antiquity: A Quarterly Review of Archæology* (Gloucester, 1938), xii, p. 44–55

Kenneth Hurlstone Jackson, *A Celtic Miscellany: Translations from the Celtic Literatures* (London, 1951)

Kenneth Jackson, *Language and History in Early Britain: A Chronological Survey of the Brittonic Languages First to Twelfth Century A.D.* (Edinburgh, 1953)

Kenneth Jackson, 'The Site of Mount Badon', *The Journal of Celtic Studies* (Baltimore, Md., 1958), ii, pp. 152–55

Kenneth Jackson, 'Four Local Anecdotes from Harris', *Scottish Studies* (Edinburgh, 1959), iii, pp. 72–87

Kenneth Jackson, *The International Popular Tale and Early Welsh Tradition* (Cardiff, 1961)

Kenneth Jackson, 'Romano-British Names in the Antonine Itinerary', *Britannia: A Journal of Romano-British and Kindred Studies* (London, 1970), i, pp. 68–82

Kenneth Jackson, 'Varia: II. Gildas and the Names of the British Princes', *Cambridge Medieval Celtic Studies* (Cambridge, 1982), iii, pp. 30–40

Thorkild Jacobsen, *Toward the Image of Tammuz and Other Essays on Mesopotamian History and Culture* (Cambridge, Mass., 1970)

E. O. James, *Sacrifice and Sacrament* (London, 1962)

E. O. James, *The Worship of the Sky-God: A Comparative Study in Semitic and Indo-European Religion* (London, 1963)

E. O. James, *The Tree of Life: An Archaeological Study* (Leiden, 1966)

E. O. James, *The Tree of Life: An Archaeological Study* (Leiden, 1966)

Simon James, *The Atlantic Celts: Ancient People or Modern Invention?* (London, 1999)

William James, *The Varieties of Religious Experience: A Study in Human Nature* (Cambridge, Mass., 1902)

Karen Jankulak and Jonathan M. Wooding (ed.), *Ireland and Wales in the Middle Ages* (Dublin, 2007)

A. O. H. Jarman, *Sieffre o Fynwy: Geoffrey of Monmouth* (Cardiff, 1966)

Mohammad Ali Jazayery and Werner Winter (ed.), *Languages and Cultures: Studies in Honor of Edgar C. Polomé* (Berlin, 1988)

Dafydd Jenkins and Morfydd E. Owen (ed.), *The Welsh Law of Women: Studies presented to Professor Daniel A. Binchy on his eightieth birthday 3 June 1980* (Cardiff, 1980)

Erik Jensen, *The Iban and their Religion* (Oxford, 1974)

Gillian Fellows Jensen, 'Place-Names and Settlement in the North Riding of Yorkshire', *Northern History* (Leeds, 1978), xiv, pp. 19–46

Gillian Jondorf and D. N. Dumville (ed.), *France and the British Isles in the Middle Ages and Renaissance: Essays by Members of Girton College, Cambridge, in Memory of Ruth Morgan* (Woodbridge, 1991)

F. C. Johnson, 'An Edinburgh Prose Tristan: the 'Bret'', *The Modern Language Review* (Cambridge, 1933), xxviii, pp. 456–64

Gwilym T. Jones and Tomos Roberts, *Enwau Lleoedd Môn* (Bangor, 1996)

Karlene Jones-Bley, Martin E. Huld, and Angela della Volpe (ed.), *Proceedings of the Eleventh Annual UCLA Indo-European Conference: Los Angeles June 4-5, 1999* (Washington, 2000)

Karlene Jones-Bley, Martin E. Huld, Angela della Volpe, and Miriam Robbins Dexter (ed.), *Proceedings of the Seventeenth Annual UCLA Indo-European Conference: Los Angeles October 27-28, 2005* (Washington, 2006)

A. H. M. Jones, *The Later Roman Empire 284-602: A Social Economic and Administrative Survey* (Oxford, 1964)

A. H. M. Jones, J. R. Martindale, and J. Morris, *The Prosopography of the Later Roman Empire* (Cambridge, 1971–92)

Barri Jones and David Mattingly, *An Atlas of Roman Britain* (Oxford, 1990)

Francis Jones, 'An Approach to Welsh Genealogy', *The Transactions of the Honourable Society of Cymmrodorion: Session 1948* (London, 1948), pp. 303–466

Michael E. Jones, *The End of Roman Britain* (Ithaca and London, 1996)

T. Gwynn Jones, *Welsh Folklore and Folk-Custom* (London, 1930)

Thomas Jones, *Brut y Tywysogion* (Cardiff, 1953)

W. Lewis Jones, 'Geoffrey of Monmouth', *Transactions of the Honourable Society of Cymmrodorion: Session 1898-1900* (London, 1900), pp. 52–95

W. Lewis Jones, *King Arthur in History and Legend* (Cambridge, 1914)

François Jouan (ed.), *Visages du destin dans les mythologies: Mélanges Jacqueline Duchemin* (Paris, 1983)

C. G. Jung, *Alchemical Studies* (London, 1968)

Zena Kamash, Chris Gosden, and Gary Lock, 'Continuity and Religious Practices in Roman Britain: The Case of the Rural Religious Complex at Marcham/Frilford, Oxfordshire', *Britannia: A Journal of Romano-British and Kindred Studies* (London, 2010), xli, pp. 95–125

Rafael Karsten, *The Religion of the Samek: Ancient Beliefs and Cults of the Scandinavian and Finnish Lapps* (Leiden, 1955)

Arvid S. Kapelrud, *Baal in the Ras Shamra Texts* (Copenhagen, 1952)

Flemming Kaul, *Gundestrupkedlen: Baggrund og billedverden* (Copenhagen, 1991)

Sarah Larratt Keefer, 'The lost tale of Dylan in the Fourth Branch of *The Mabinogi*', *Studia Celtica* (Cardiff, 1989/90), xxiv/xxv, pp. 26–37

Laura Keeler, *Geoffrey of Monmouth and the Late Latin Chroniclers 1300–1500* (Berkeley, 1946)

Georgia Dunham Kelchner, *Dreams in Old Norse Literature and their Affinities in Folklore* (Cambridge, 1935)

Fergus Kelly, *A Guide to Early Irish Law* (Dublin, 1988)

Fergus Kelly, *Early Irish Farming: a study based mainly on the law-texts of the 7th and 8th centuries AD* (Dublin, 1997)

T. D. Kendrick, *British Antiquity* (London, 1950)

T. D. Kendrick, *The Druids: A Study in Keltic Prehistory* (London, 1927)

François Kerlouégan, *Le De Excidio Britanniae de Gildas: Les destinées de la culture latine dans l'île de Bretagne au VIᵉ siècle* (Paris, 1987)

Edmund King (ed.), *The Anarchy of King Stephen's Reign* (Oxford, 1994)

Peter Kingsley, *Ancient Philosophy, Mystery, and Magic: Empedocles and Pythagorean Tradition* (Oxford, 1995)

G. S. Kirk and J. E. Raven, *The Presocratic Philosophers: A Critical History with a Selection of Texts* (Cambridge, 1957)

Carola Kloos, *Yhwh's Combat with the Sea: A Canaanite Tradition in the Religion of Ancient Israel* (Amsterdam, 1986)

Jeremy K. Knight, 'An Inscription from Bavai and the Fifth-Century Christian Epigraphy of Britain', *Britannia* (London, 2010), xli, pp. 283–92

W. F. Jackson Knight, *Cumaean Gates: A Reference of the Sixth Aeneid to the Initiation Pattern* (Oxford, 1936)

R. Buick Know, *James Ussher Archbishop of Armagh* (Cardiff, 1967)

John T. Koch, 'A Welsh Window on the Iron Age: Manawydan, Mandubracios', *Cambridge Medieval Celtic Studies* (Cambridge, 1987), xiv, pp. 17–52

John T. Koch, 'Gleanings from the *Gododdin* and other Early Welsh Texts', *The Bulletin of the Board of Celtic Studies* (Cardiff, 1991), xxxviii, pp. 111–18

John Koch, 'The Loss of Final Syllables and Loss of Declensions in Brittonic', in James E. Doan and Cornelius G. Buttimer (ed.), *Proceedings of the Harvard Celtic Colloquium* (Cambridge, Mass., 1981), i, pp. 21–51

John T. Koch, 'Gallo-Brittonic *Tasc(i)ouanos* 'Badger-slayer' and the Reflex of Indo-European g^wh', *Journal of Celtic Linguistics* (Cardiff, 1992), i, pp. 101–18

John T. Koch, *Tartessian: Celtic in the South-west at the Dawn of History* (Aberystwyth, 2009)

John T. Koch and Barry Cunliffe (ed.), *Celtic from the West 2: Rethinking the Bronze Age and the Arrival of Indo-European in Atlantic Europe* (Oxford, 2013)

Helge Kökeritz, *The Place-Names of the Isle of Wight* (Uppsala, 1940)

Samuel Noah Kramer, *The Sacred Marriage Rite: Aspects of Faith, Myth, and Ritual in Ancient Sumer* (Bloomington, Indiana, 1969)

Stella Kramrisch, *The Presence of Śiva* (Princeton, 1981)

Alexander Heggarty Krappe, *Balor With the Evil Eye: Studies in Celtic and French Literature* (Columbia, 1927)

Alexander H. Krappe, 'Arturus Cosmocrator', *Speculum: A Journal of Mediaeval Studies* (Cambridge, Mass., 1945), xx, pp. 405–14

Josef Kroll, 'Elysium', in Leo Brandt (ed.), *Arbeitsgemeinschaft für Forschung des Landes Nordrhein-Westfalen* (Cologne, 1953), ii, pp. 7–35

Venceslas Kruta (ed.), *Les Celtes et l'écriture* (Paris, 1997)

V. Kruta, O. H. Frey, B. Raftery, and M. Szabó (ed.), *The Celts* (London, 1991)

F. B. J. Kuiper, *Aryans in the Rigveda* (Amsterdam, 1991)

Leslie Kurke, 'Pouring Prayers: A Formula of IE Sacral Poetry', *The Journal of Indo-European Studies* (Washington, 1989), xvii, pp. 113–25

Venceslas Kruta (ed.), *Les Celtes et l'écriture* (Paris, 1997)

Lloyd R. Laing, *Settlement Types in Post-Roman Scotland* (Oxford, 1975)

P.-Y. Lambert, '"Tribunal" et "praetorium" en vieux-breton', *The Bulletin of the Board of Celtic Studies* (Cardiff, 1987), xxxiv, pp. 120–22

Pierre-Yves Lambert, 'Magie et Pouvoir dans la Quatrième Branche du *Mabinogi*', *Studia Celtica* (1994), xxviii, pp. 97–107

Pierre-Yves Lambert and Georges-Jean Pinault (ed.), *Gaulois et celtique continental* (Geneva, 2007)

Vassilis Lambrinoudakis and Jean Ch. Balty (ed.), *Thesaurus Cultus et Rituum Antiquorum* (Los Angeles, 2004–6)

René Largillière, *Six saints de la région de Plestin: Saint Haran, saint Karé, saint Tuder, saint Nérin, saint Kémo, saint Kirio* (Rennes, 1922)

Joachim Latacz, *Troy and Homer: Towards a Solution of an Old Mystery* (Oxford, 2004)

R. E. Latham and D. R. Howlett (ed.), *Dictionary of Medieval Latin from British Sources* (London, 1975–2013)

John Layard, *Stone Men of Malekula: Vao* (London, 1942)

Anne E. Lea, 'Lleu Wyllt: an Early British Prototype of the Legend of the Wild Man?', *The Journal of Indo-European Studies* (Washington, 1997), xxv, pp. 35–47

R. William Leckie, Jr, *The Passage of Dominion: Geoffrey of Monmouth and the Periodization of Insular History in the Twelfth Century* (Toronto, 1981)

Jean-Michel Le Contel and Paul Verdier, *Un calendrier celtique: Le calendrier gaulois de Coligny* (Paris, 1997)

E. T. Leeds, 'The West Saxon Invasion and the Icknield Way', *History: The Quarterly Journal of the Historical Association* (London, 1925), x, pp. 97–109

M. Dominica Legge, 'Master Geoffrey Arthur', in Kenneth Varty (ed.), *An Arthurian Tapestry: essays in memory of Lewis Thorpe* (Cambridge, 1983), pp. 22–27

Les écrivains du deuxième siècle et l'Etrusca disciplina: Actes de la Table-Ronde de Dijon, 9 juin 1995 (Dijon, 1996)

Pierre-Yves Lambert, *La langue gauloise: Description linguistique, commentaire d'inscriptions choisies* (Paris, 1995)

G. W. H. Lampe, *God as Spirit: The Bampton Lectures, 1976* (Oxford, 1977)

Michael Lapidge and David Dumville (ed.), *Gildas: New Approaches* (Woodbridge, 1984)

Michael Lapidge (ed.), *H. M. Chadwick and the Study of Anglo-Saxon, Norse and Celtic at Cambridge* (Aberystwyth, 2015)

La Regalità Sacra: Contributi al Tema Dell' VIII Congresso Internazionale di Storia delle Religioni (Roma, Aprile 1955) (Leiden, 1959)

Donatien Laurent, *Aux sources du Barzaz-Breiz: La mémoire d'un peuple* (Douarnenez, 1989)

H. J. Lawlor, *Chapters on the Book of Mulling* (Edinburgh, 1897)

Anatole le Braz, *La légende de la mort chez les Bretons armoricains* (Paris, 1928)

Winfred P. Lehmann, *Die Gegenwärtige Richtung der Indogermanistischen Forschung* (Budapest, 1992)

Gwennolé Le Menn and Jean-Yves Le Moing (ed.), *Bretagne et pays celtiques: langues, histoire, civilisation; mélanges offerts à la mémoire de Léon Fleuriot* (Rennes, 1992)

Françoise Le Roux, 'Le *Celticvm* d'Ambigatvs et l'*omphalos* gaulois: La royauté suprême des *Bituriges*', *Celticvm I: Actes du Premier Colloque International d'Etudes Gauloises, Celtiques et Protoceltiques* (Rennes, 1961), pp. 159–84

Françoise Le Roux, 'Recherches sur les éléments rituels de l'élection royale Irlandaise et Celtique', *Ogam: tradition celtique* (Rennes, 1963), xv, pp. 245–54

Françoise Le Roux, 'Le dieu-roi NODONS/NUADA', *Celticvm VI: Actes du Troisième Colloque International d'Études Gauloises, Celtiques et Protoceltiques* (Rennes 1963), pp. 425–54

Françoise Le Roux, 'La Conception de Cúchulainn', *Ogam: Tradition Celtique* (Rennes, 1965), xvii, pp. 393–410

Françoise Le Roux, 'La Courtise d'Étain', *Celticvm XV: Actes du Premier Colloque International d'Etudes Gauloises, Celtiques et Protoceltiques* (Rennes, 1966), pp. 328–74

Françoise Le Roux, 'La mort de Cúchulainn', *Ogam: Tradition Celtique* (Rennes, 1966), xviii, p. 365–99

Françoise Le Roux and Christian-J. Guyonvarc'h, *Les fêtes celtiques* (Rennes, 1995)

T. C. Lethbridge, *Herdsmen & Hermits: Celtic Seafarers in the Northern Seas* (Cambridge, 1950)

Saul Levin, *Semitic and Indo-European: The Principal Etymologies with Observations on Afro-Asiatic* (Amsterdam and Philadelphia, 1995)

Lucien Lévy-Bruhl, *Primitives and the Supernatural* (London, 1936)

F. R. Lewis, 'Gwerin Ffristial a Thawlbwrdd', *Transactions of the Honourable Society of Cymmrodorion* (London, 1941), pp. 185–205

Henry Lewis, *Yr Elfen Ladin yn yr Iaith Gymraeg* (Cardiff, 1943)

Henry Lewis (ed.), *Angles and Britons* (Cardiff, 1963)

Hywel D. Lewis, *The Self and Immortality* (London, 1973)

Mark Edward Lewis, *The Early Chinese Empires: Qin and Han* (Cambridge, Mass., 2007)

M. J. T. Lewis, *Temples in Roman Britain* (Cambridge, 1966)

Timothy Lewis, *Mabinogi Cymru* (Aberystwyth, 1931)

Edward Lhuyd, *Archæologia Britannica, Giving some Account Additional to what has been hitherto Publish'd, of the Languages, Histories and Customs Of the Original Inhabitants of Great Britain* (Oxford, 1707)

Henry George Liddell and Robert Scott, *A Greek-English Lexicon* (Oxford, 1940)

Godfrey Lienhardt, *Divinity and Experience: The Religion of the Dinka* (Oxford, 1961)

Fredrik Otto Lindeman, 'Gaulish *ambiorix*', *Zeitschrift für celtische Philologie* (Tübingen, 2006), lv, pp. 50–55

W. M. Lindsay, *Early Welsh Script* (Oxford, 1912)

Uli Linke, 'Blood as Metaphor in Proto-Indo-European', *The Journal of Indo-European Studies* (Washington, 1985), xiii, pp. 333–43

Ivar Lissner, *Man, God and Magic* (London, 1961)

A. G. Little and F. M. Powicke (ed.), *Essays in Medieval History Presented to Thomas Frederick Tout* (Manchester, 1925)

B. A. Livitsky, Zhang Guang-da, and R. Shabani Samghabadi (ed.), *History of civilizations of Central Asia; Volume III The crossroads of civilizations: A.D. 250 to 750* (Paris, 1996)

John Edward Lloyd, *A History of Wales from the Earliest Times to the Edwardian Conquest* (London, 1911)

J. Lloyd-Jones, 'or, eryr, dygyfor, Eryri', *The Bulletin of the Board of Celtic Studies* (Cardiff, 1928), iv, pp. 140–41

J. Lloyd-Jones, *Geirfa Barddoniaeth Gynnar Gymraeg* (Cardiff, 1931–63)

Ceridwen Lloyd-Morgan, 'Narratives and Non-Narratives: Aspects of Welsh Arthurian Tradition', in eadem (ed.), *Arthurian Literature XXI: Celtic Arthurian Material* (Cambridge, 2004), pp. 115–36

Roger Sherman Loomis, *Arthurian Tradition & Chrétien de Troyes* (New York, 1949)

Roger Sherman Loomis, *Wales and the Arthurian Legend* (Cardiff, 1956)

Roger Sherman Loomis (ed.), *Arthurian Literature in the Middle Ages: A Collaborative History* (Oxford, 1959)

C. Scott Littleton, *The New Comparative Mythology: An Anthropological Assessment of the Theories of Georges Dumézil* (Los Angeles, 1966)

Charlotte R. Long, *The Twelve Gods of Greece and Rome* (Leiden, 1987)

H. P. L'Orange, *Studies on the Iconography of Cosmic Kingship in the Ancient World* (Oslo, 1953)

J. Loth, *Contributions à l'Étude des Romans de la Table Ronde* (Paris, 1912)

J. Loth, 'La vie la plus ancienne de Saint Samson de Dol d'après des travaux récents: remarques et additions', *Revue Celtique* (Paris, 1914), xxxv, pp. 269–300

J. Loth, *Remarques et additions à la grammaire galloise historique et comparée de John Morris Jones* (Paris, 1915-16), xxxvi, pp. 108–85, 391–410

J. Loth, 'Remarques à *l'Historia Brittonum* dite de Nennius', *Revue Celtique* (Paris, 1932), xlix, pp. 150–65

Meir Lubetski, Claire Gottlieb, and Sharon Keller (ed.), *Boundaries of the Ancient Near Eastern World: A Tribute to Cyrus H. Gordon* (Sheffield, 1998)

A. T. Lucas, *Cattle in Ancient Ireland* (Kilkenny, 1989)

Sophie Lunais, *Recherches sur la lune, I: Les auteurs latins de la fin des guerres puniques à la fin du règne des Antonins* (Leiden, 1979)

C. J. Lynn, 'Hostels, Heroes and Tale: Further Thoughts on the Navan Mound', *Emania: Bulletin of the Navan Research Group* (Belfast, 1994), xii, pp. 5–20

Rev. Daniel Lysons and Samuel Lysons, *Magna Britannia; Being A Concise Topographical Account of the Several Counties of Great Britain... Vol. I. – Part II. Containing Berkshire* (London, 1813)

Alexander Macbain, *Celtic Mythology and Religion* (Stirling, 1917)

Proinsias Mac Cana, *Branwen Daughter of Llŷr: A Study of the Irish Affinities and of the Composition of the Second Branch of the Mabinogi* (Cardiff, 1958)

Proinsias Mac Cana, 'Aspects of the Theme of King and Goddess in Irish Literature', *Études Celtiques* (Paris, 1958), viii, pp. 59–65

Proinsias Mac Cana, 'An Archaism in Irish Poetic Tradition', *Celtica* (Dublin, 1968), viii, pp. 174–81

Proinsias Mac Cana, *Celtic Mythology* (London, 1970)

Proinsias Mac Cana, 'Conservation and Innovation in Early Celtic Literature', *Études Celtiques* (Paris, 1972), xiii, pp. 61–119

Proinsias Mac Cana, 'The Sinless Otherworld of *Immram Brain*', *Ériu: The Journal of the School of Irish Learning* (Dublin, 1976), xxvii, pp. 95–115

Proinsias Mac Cana, *The Mabinogi* (Cardiff, 1992)

Proinsias Mac Cana, *The Cult of the Sacred Centre: Essays on Celtic Ideology* (Dublin, 2011)

Proinsias Mac Cana and Michel Meslin (ed.), *Rencontres de religions: Actes du colloque du Collège des Irlandais tenu sous les auspices de l'Académie Royale Irlandaise* (Juin 1981) (Paris, 1986)

Daniel McCarthy, 'The Chronology of St Brigid of Kildare', *Peritia: Journal of the Medieval Academy of Ireland* (Turnhout, 2000), xiv, pp. 255–81

J. A. MacCulloch, *The Religion of the Ancient Celts* (Edinburgh, 1911)

Violet MacDermot, *The Cult of the Seer in the Ancient Middle East: A Contribution to Current Research on Hallucinations drawn from Coptic and other Texts* (London, 1971)

Gearóid Mac Eoin (ed.), *Proceedings of the Sixth International Congress of Celtic Studies* (Dublin, 1983)

Margaret Mackintosh of Mackintosh, *The Clan Mackintosh and the Clan Chattan* (Edinburgh, 1948)

Gordon W. MacLennan (ed.), *Proceedings of the First North American Congress of Celtic Studies held at Ottawa from 26th-30th March 1986* (Ottawa, 1988)

Ramsay MacMullen, *Enemies of the Roman Order: Treason, Unrest, and Alienation in the Empire* (Cambridge, Mass., 1966)

Ramsay MacMullen, *Christianity and Paganism in the Fourth to Eighth Centuries* (New Haven and London, 1997)

Eoin MacNeill, *Phases of Irish History* (Dublin, 1919)

Eoin MacNeill, *Early Irish Laws and Institutions* (Dublin, 1935)

Eoin MacNeill, 'The Language of the Picts', *Yorkshire Celtic Studies* (Leeds, 1938–39), ii, pp. 3–45

Máire MacNeill, *The Festival of Lughnasa: A Study of the Survival of the Celtic Festival of the Beginning of Harvest* (Oxford, 1962)

John Mac Queen, 'Goreu son of Custennin', *Études Celtiques* (Paris, 1958), viii, pp. 154–63

John MacQueen, *Numerology: Theory and outline history of a literary mode* (Edinburgh, 1985)

Sarah Macready and F. H. Thompson (ed.), *Cross-Channel Trade between Gaul and Britain in the Pre-Roman Iron Age* (London, 1984)

Eóin MacWhite, 'Early Irish Board Games', *Éigse: A Journal of Irish Studies* (Dublin, 1945), v, pp. 25–35

Eóin MacWhite, 'Problems of Irish Archaeology and Celtic Philology', *Zeitschrift für celtische Philologie* (Tübingen, 1955), xxv, pp. 1–29

Lorraine Madway, 'Charles II and Royal Reshaping of Ancient British History', *Royal Stuart Journal* (Glanton, 2011), iii, pp. 1–27

William J. Mahon, 'The *Aisling* Elegy and the Poet's Appropriation of the Feminine', *Studia Celtica* (Cardiff, 2000), xxxiv, pp. 249–70

Adolf Mahr, 'New Aspects and Problems in Irish Prehistory: Presidential Address for 1937', *Proceedings of the Prehistoric Society* (Cambridge, 1937), iii, pp. 262–436

Bernhard Maier, 'Is Lug to be Identified with Mercury (*Bell. Gall.* VI 17, 1)? New Suggestions on an Old Problem', *Ériu* (Dublin, 1996), xlvii, pp. 127–35

Bernhardt Maier, 'Gaulish *Genā* 'Girl; Unmarried Woman'? A note on Pomponius Mela, *De Chorographia* III 48', *Studia Celtica* (1997), xxxi, p. 280

Bernhard Maier, *Die Religion der Kelten: Götter – Mythen – Weltbild* (Munich, 2001)

Bernhard Maier, Stefan Zimmer, and Christiane Batke (ed.), *150 Jahre »Mabinogion« - Deutsch-Walische Kulturbeziehungen* (Tübingen, 2001)

Victor H. Mair (ed.), *The Bronze Age and Early Iron Age Peoples of Eastern Central Asia* (Philadelphia, 1998)

Bronislaw Malinowski, *The Foundation of Faith and Morals: An Anthropological Analysis of Primitive Beliefs and Conduct with Special Reference to the Fundamental Problems of Religion and Ethics* (Oxford, 1936)

J. P. Mallory, *Navan Fort: The Ancient Capital of Ulster* (Belfast, 1985)

J. P. Mallory, *In Search of the Indo-Europeans* (London, 1989)

J. P. Mallory and Gerard Stockman (ed.), *Ulidia: Proceedings of the First International Conference on the Ulster Cycle of Tales* (Belfast, 1994)

J. P. Mallory and D. Q. Adams (ed.), *Encyclopedia of Indo-European Culture* (Chicago and London, 1997)

J. P. Mallory and D. Q. Adams, *The Oxford Introduction to Proto-Indo-European and the Proto-Indo-European World* (Oxford, 2006)

Ivan D. Margary, 'The North Downs' Main Trackways', *Surrey Archaeological Collections* (Guildford, 1952), lii, pp. 29–31

Ivan D. Margary, *Roman Roads in Britain* (London, 1955–57)

Alexander Marshack, *The Roots of Civilization: The Cognitive Beginnings of Man's First Art, Symbol and Notation* (London, 1972)

David J. P. Mason, *Roman Britain and the Roman Navy* (Stroud, 2003)

Ranko Matasović, *Etymological Dictionary of Proto-Celtic* (Leiden, 2009)

Colin Matheson, 'The Rabbit and the Hare in Wales', *Antiquity: A Quarterly Review of Archæology* (Gloucester, 1941), xv, pp. 371–81

A. T. E. Matonis and Daniel F. Melia (ed.), *Celtic Language, Celtic Culture: A Festschrift for Eric P. Hamp* (Van Nuys, California, 1990)

John Matthews, *The Roman Empire of Ammianus* (London, 1989)

David Mattingly, *An Imperial Possession: Britain in the Roman Empire, 54 BC–AD 409* (London, 2006)

Allen Mawer, *The Place-Names of Northumberland and Durham* (Cambridge, 1920)

Allen Mawer, *Place-Names and History* (Liverpool and London, 1922)

A. Mawer and F. M. Stenton, *The Place-Names of Bedfordshire & Huntingdonshire* (Cambridge, 1926)

Daniel McCarthy, 'Topographical Characteristics of the *Vita Prima* and *Vita Cogitosi Sanctae Brigitae*', *Studia Celtica* (Cardiff, 2001), xxxv, pp. 259–61

Edmund McClure, *British Place-Names in their Historical Setting* (London, 1910)

Kim McCone, 'Dubthach Maccu Lugair and a Matter of Life and Death in the Pseudo-Historical Prologue to the *Senchas Már*', *Peritia: Journal of the Medieval Academy of Ireland* (Galway, 1986), v, pp. 1–35

Kim McCone, *Pagan Past and Christian Present in Early Irish Literature* (Naas, 1990)

Kim McCone, *The Celtic Question: Modern Constructs and Ancient Realities* (Dublin, 2008)

Patrick McConvell and Nicholas Evans (ed.), *Archaeology and Linguistics: Aboriginal Australia in Global Perspective* (Melbourne, 1997)

Damian McManus, *A Guide to Ogam* (Maynooth, 1991)

Ian McKee, 'Gildas: Lessons from History', *Cambrian Medieval Celtic Studies* (Aberystwyth, 2006), li, pp. 1–36

Bernard Mees, 'The Celtic Inscriptions of Bath', *Studia Celtica* (Cardiff, 2005), xxxix, pp. 176–81

J. V. S. Megaw (ed.), *To illustrate the monuments: Essays on archaeology presented to Stuart Piggott* (London, 1976)

Wolfgang Meid, 'The Indo-Europeanization of Old European Concepts', *The Journal of Indo-European Studies* (Washington, 1989), xvii, pp. 297–307

Wolfgang Meid, *Gaulish Inscriptions* (Budapest, 1992)

Wolfgang Meid, *Die erste Botorrita-Inschrift: Interpretation eines keltiberischen Sprachdenkmals* (Innsbruck, 1993)

Wolfgang Meid, *Keltische Personennamen in Pannonien* (Budapest, 2005)

Wolfgang Meid and Peter Anreiter (ed.), *Die grösseren altkeltichen Sprachdenkmäler: Akten des Kolloquiums Innsbruck, 29. April-3. Mai 1993* (Innsbruck, 1993)

Gerhard Meiser, *Historische Laut- und Formenlehre der lateinischen Sprache* (Darmstadt, 1998)

Bernard Merdrignac, *Recherches sur l'hagiographie armoricaine du VIIème au XVème Siècle* (Saint-Malo, 1985-86)

B. Merdrignac, 'La première Vie de saint Samson: Étude chronologique', *Stvdia Monastica* (Barcelona, 1988), xxx, pp. 243–89

Alexandre Micha, *Étude sur le «Merlin» de Robert de Boron: Roman du XIIIe siècle* (Geneva, 1980)

Henry N. Michael (ed.), *Studies in Siberian Shamanism* (Toronto, 1963)

David Miles, Simon Palmer, Gary Lock, Chris Gosden, and Anne Marie Cromarty, *Uffington White Horse and its Landscape: Investigations at White Horse Hill, Uffington, 1989–95, and Tower Hill, Ashbury, 1993–4* (Oxford, 2003)

Alan Millard, *Reading and Writing in the Time of Jesus* (Sheffield, 2001)

A. D. Mills, *The Place-Names of Dorset* (Cambridge, 1977-)

Arnaldo Momigliano, *On Pagans, Jews, and Christians* (Middletown, Conn., 1987)

Paul Kléber Monod, *Jacobitism and the English people 1688–1788* (Cambridge, 1989)

Donald Moore (ed.), *The Irish Sea Province in Archaeology and History* (Cardiff, 1970)

Vincent Mora, *La symbolique de la création dans l'évangile de Matthieu* (Paris, 1991)

T. J. Morgan and D. Ellis Evans, 'Place-Names', in W. G. King and R. E. Takel (ed.), *The Scientific Survey of Swansea and its Region* (Swansea, 1971), pp. 195–200

Francis M. Morris, 'Cunobelinus' Bronze Coinage', *Britannia* (2013), xliv, pp. 27–83

Ian Morris and Barry Powell (ed.), *A New Companion to Homer* (Leiden, 1997)

John Morris, *The Age of Arthur: A History of the British Isles from 350 to 650* (London, 1973)

J. Morris Jones, *A Welsh Grammar: Historical and Comparative* (Oxford, 1913)

Sir John Morris-Jones, 'Taliesin', *Y Cymmrodor* (London, 1918), xxviii.

Richard Muir, *History from the Air* (London, 1983)

Alex Mullen, 'Evidence for Written Celtic from Roman Britain: A Linguistic Analysis of *Tabellae Sulis* 14 and 18', *Studia Celtica* (Cardiff, 2007), xli, pp. 31–45

Alex Mullen, 'Linguistic Evidence for 'Romanization': Continuity and Change in Romano-British Onomastics: A Study of the Epigraphic Record with Particular Reference to Bath', *Britannia* (London, 2007), xxxviii, pp. 35–61

Alex Mullen, *Southern Gaul and the Mediterranean: Multilingualism and Multiple Identities in the Iron Age and Roman Periods* (Cambridge, 2013)

Alex Mullen and Patrick James (ed.), *Multilingualism in the Graeco-Roman Worlds* (Cambridge, 2012)

Kiyohiko Munakata, *Sacred Mountains in Chinese Art* (Urbana and Chicago, 1991)

H. J. R. Murray, *A History of Board-Games other than Chess* (Oxford, 1952)

Kevin Murray, 'The Finding of the '*Táin*', *Cambrian Medieval Celtic Studies* (Aberystwyth, 2001), xli, pp. 17–23

Carla Corradi Musi, *Shamanism from East to West* (Budapest, 1997)

George E. Mylonas, *Eleusis and the Eleusinian Mysteries* (Princeton, 1962)

Harold Mytum, *The Origins of Early Christian Ireland* (London, 1992)

Gregory Nagy, *Greek Mythology and Poetics* (Ithaca, NY, 1990)

Joseph Falaky Nagy, *The Wisdom of the Outlaw: The Boyhood Deeds of Finn in Gaelic Narrative Tradition* (Los Angeles, 1985)

Joseph Falaky Nagy (ed.), *Myth in Celtic Literatures* (Dublin, 2007)

Joseph Falaky Nagy and Leslie Ellen Jones (ed.), *Heroic Poets and Poetic Heroes in Celtic Tradition: A Festschrift for Patrick K. Ford* (Dublin, 2005)

Vladimir Napolskikh, Anna-Leena Siikala, and Mihály Hoppál (ed.), *Komi Mythology* (Budapest, 2003)

Vladimir Napolskikh, Anna-Leena Siikala, and Mihály Hoppál (ed.), *Khanty Mythology* (Budapest, 2006)

Jeremy Narby, *The Cosmic Serpent, DNA and the origins of Knowledge* (London, 1998)

Joseph Needham (ed.), *Science and Civilisation in China* (Cambridge, 1954-)

Rodney Needham (ed.), *Imagination and Proof: Selected Essays of A. M. Hocart* (Tucson, 1987)

O. Neugebauer, *The Exact Sciences in Antiquity* (Providence, RI, 1957)

O. Neugebauer and D. Pingree (ed.), *The Pañcasiddhāntikā of Varāhamihira* (Copenhagen, 1970–71)

Jacob Neusner (ed.), *Religions in Antiquity: Essays in Memory of Erwin Ramsdell Goodenough* (Leiden, 1970)

Venetia Newall (ed.), *The Witch Figure: Folklore Essays by a group of scholars in England honouring the 75th birthday of Katharine M. Briggs* (London, 1973)

C. A. Newham, *The Astronomical Significance of Stonehenge* (Leeds, 1972)

Próinséas Ní Chatháin and Michael Richter (ed.), *Irland und Europa: Die Kirche im Frühmittelalter* (Stuttgart, 1984)

E. Williams B. Nicholson, 'The Dynasty of Cunedag and the 'Harleian Genealogies', *Y Cymmrodor* (London, 1908), xxi, pp. 63–104

E. Williams B. Nicolson, 'The Vandals in Wessex and the Battle of Deorham', *Y Cymmrodor* (London, 1906), xix, pp. 5–17

W. F. H. Nicolaisen, *Scottish Place-Names: Their Study and Significance* (London, 1976)

Máirín Ní Dhonnchadha, '*Caillech* and Other Terms for Veiled Women in Medieval Irish Texts', *Éigse: A Journal of Irish Studies* (Dublin, 1994-5), xxviii, pp. 71–96

E. R. Norman and J. K. St Joseph, *The Early Development of Irish Society: The Evidence of Aerial Photography* (Cambridge, 1969)

F. J. North, *Sunken Cities: Some legends of the coast and lakes of Wales* (Cardiff, 1957)

John North, *Stonehenge: Neolithic Man and the Cosmos* (London, 1996)

Richard North, *Heathen Gods in Old English Literature* (Cambridge, 1997)

Alfred Nutt and Kuno Meyer, *The Celtic Doctrine of Re-birth* (London, 1897)

Tore Nyberg, Iørn Piø, Preben Meulengracht Sørensen, and Aage Trommer (ed.), *History and Heroic Tale: A Symposium* (Odense, 1985)

Bruce R. O'Brien, *God's Peace and King's Peace: The Laws of Edward the Confessor* (Philadelphia, 1999)

M. A. O'Brien, 'Etymologies and Notes', *Celtica* (Dublin, 1956), iii, p. 168–84

Tómás Ó Broin, '"Craebruad": The Spurious Tradition', *Éigse: A Journal of Irish Studies* (Dublin, 1973), xv, pp. 103–13

Tomás Ó Broin, 'Lia Fáil: Fact and Fiction in the Tradition', *Celtica* (Dublin, 1990), xxi, pp. 393–401

Séamas Ó Catháin, *The Festival of Brigit: Celtic Goddess and Holy Woman* (Dublin, 1995)

Tomás Ó Cathasaigh, 'The Déisi and Dyfed', *Éigse: A Journal of Irish Studies* (Naas, 1984), xx, pp. 1–33

Tomás Ó Cathasaigh, 'The Eponym of Cnogba', *Éigse: A Journal of Irish Studies* (Dublin, 1989), xxiii, pp. 27–38

M. G. O'Connell and Joanna Bird, 'The Roman Temple at Wanborough, excavation 1985-1986', *Surrey Archaeological Collections Relating to the History and Antiquities of the County* (Guildford, 1994), lxxxii, pp. 1–168

Ailbhe Ó Corráin (ed.), *Proceedings of the Third Symposium of Societas Celtologica Nordica held in Oslo 1–2 November 1991* (Uppsala, 1994)

Donnchadh Ó Corráin, 'The Vikings in Scotland and Ireland in the Ninth Century', *Peritia: Journal of the Medieval Academy of Ireland* (Turnhout, 1998), xii, pp. 296–339

Donnchadh Ó Corráin, Liam Breatnach, and Kim McCone (ed.), *Sages, Saints and Storytellers: Celtic Studies in Honour of Professor James Carney* (Maynooth, 1989)

Brian Ó Cuív (ed.), *The Impact of the Scandinavian Invasions on the Celtic-speaking Peoples c. 800–1100 A.D.* (Dublin, 1975)

Eugene O'Curry, *Lectures on the Manuscript Materials of Ancient Irish History* (Dublin, 1861)

Robert O'Driscoll (ed.), *The Celtic Consciousness* (Toronto, 1981)

Michaela Ofitsch and Christian Zinko (ed.), *Studia Onomastica et Indogermanica: Festschrift für Fritz Lochner von Hüttenbach zum 65. Geburtstag* (Graz, 1995)

Dáithi Ó hÓgáin, *Fionn mac Cumhaill: Images of the Gaelic Hero* (Dublin, 1988)

Dáithi Ó hÓgáin, *The Sacred Isle: Belief and Religion in Pre-Christian Ireland* (Woodbridge, 1999)

J. G. O'Keeffe, 'Poem on the Observance of Sunday', *Ériu: The Journal of the Irish School of Learning, Dublin* (Dublin, 1907), iii, p. 143–47

Garrett S. Olmsted, *The Gundestrup Cauldron: Its Archaeological Context, the Style and Iconography of its Portrayed Motifs, and their Narration of a Gaulish Version of Táin Bó Cúailnge* (Brussels, 1979)

Garrett Olmsted, 'The Meter of the Gaulish Inscription from Larzac', *The Journal of Indo-European Studies* (Washington, 1989), xvii, 155–63

Garrett Olmsted, 'Gaulish, Celtiberian, and Indo-European Verse, *ibid.* (1991), xix, pp. 259–307

Garrett Olmsted, *The Gaulish Calendar: A Reconstruction from the Bronze Fragments from Coligny with an Analysis of its Function as a Highly Accurate Lunar/Solar Predictor as well as an Explanation of its Terminology and Development* (Bonn, 1992)

Garrett S. Olmsted, *A Definitive Reconstructed Text of the Coligny Calendar* (Washington, 2001)

Lynette Olson, *Early Monasteries in Cornwall* (Woodbridge, 1989)

B. Lynette Olson and O. J. Padel, 'A Tenth-Century List of Cornish Parochial Saints', *Cambridge Medieval Celtic Studies* (Cambridge, 1986), xii, pp. 33–71

John J. O'Meara and Bernd Naumann (ed.), *Latin Script and Letters A.D. 400–900: Festschrift presented to Ludwig Bieler on the occasion of his 70th birthday* (Leiden, 1976)

Richard Broxton Onians, *The Origins of European Thought about the Body, the Mind the Soul, the World Time, and Fate: New Interpretations of Greek, Roman and kindred evidence also of some basic Jewish and Christian beliefs* (Cambridge, 1954)

Jarich G. Oosten, *The War of the Gods: The social code in Indo-European mythology* (London, 1985)

Cecile O'Rahilly, *Ireland and Wales: Their Historical and Literary Relations* (London, 1924)

T. F. O'Rahilly, 'The Goidels and their Predecessors', *The Proceedings of the British Academy* (London, 1936), pp. 323–72

Thomas F. O'Rahilly, *Early Irish History and Mythology* (Dublin, 1946)

T. F. O'Rahilly, 'On the Origin of the Names Érainn and Ériu', *Ériu: The Journal of the School of Irish Learning, Dublin* (Dublin, 1943), xiv, pp. 7–28

T. F. O'Rahilly, 'Buchet the Herdsman', *Ériu* (Dublin, 1952), xvi, pp. 7–20

Vladimir E. Orel, 'Thracian and Celtic', *The Bulletin of the Board of Celtic Studies* (Cardiff, 1987), xxxiv, pp. 1–9

Pádraig Ó Riain, *The Making of a Saint: Finbarr of Cork 600-1200* (Dublin, 1997)

Nicholas Orme, *The Saints of Cornwall* (Oxford, 2000)

Archdeacon T. O'Rorke, *The History of Sligo: Town and County* (Dublin, 1889)

Seán Ó Súilleabháin, *A Handbook of Irish Folklore* (Wexford, 1942)

Thomas D. O'Sullivan, *The De Excidio of Gildas: Its Authenticity and Date* (Leiden, 1978)

Rudolf Otto, *The Idea of the Holy: An Inquiry into the Non-rational Factor in the Idea of the Divine and its Relation to the Rational* (Oxford, 1926)

A. J. Otway-Ruthven, *A History of Medieval Ireland* (London, 1968)

D. D. R. Owen, *The Evolution of the Grail Legend* (Edinburgh, 1968)

Edward Owen, 'An Episode in the History of Clynnog Church', *Y Cymmrodor* (1906), xix, pp. 66–88

Hugh Owen, 'Peniarth MS. 118, Fos. 829–837', *Y Cymmrodor* (London, 1917), xxvii, pp. 115–52

Trefor M. Owen, *Welsh Folk Customs* (Cardiff, 1974)

O. J. Padel, 'Geoffrey of Monmouth and Cornwall', *Cambridge Medieval Celtic Studies* (Cambridge, 1984), viii, pp. 1–28

O. J. Padel, *Cornish Place-Name Elements* (Cambridge, 1985)

O. J. Padel, *A Popular Dictionary of Cornish Place-Names* (Penzance, 1988)

Oliver Padel, 'The Nature of Arthur', *Cambrian Medieval Celtic Studies* (Aberystwyth, 1994), xxvii, pp. 1–31

O. J. Padel, *Arthur in Medieval Welsh Tradition* (Cardiff, 2000)

André Padoux, *Vāc: The Concept of the Word in Selected Hindu Tantras* (New York, 1990)

Denys Page, *Sappho and Alcaeus: An Introduction to the Study of Ancient Lesbian Poetry* (Oxford, 1955)

Denys Page, *Folktales in Homer's Odyssey* (Cambridge, Mass., 1973)

Robert E. A. Palmer, *The King and the Comitium: A Study of Rome's Oldest Public Document* (Wiesbaden, 1969)

H. W. Parke, *Greek Oracles* (London, 1967)

H. W. Parke and D. E. W. Wormell, *The Delphic Oracle* (Oxford, 1956)

[John Humffreys Parry (ed.)], *The Cambro-Briton* (London, 1820–22)

David Parsons, 'British *Caratīcos*, Old English Cerdic', *Cambrian Medieval Celtic Studies* (Aberystwyth, 1997), xxxiii, pp. 1–8

Adrian Pârvulescu, 'The Name of the Great Bear', *The Journal of Indo-European Studies* (Washington, 1988), xvi, pp. 95–120

Etienne Patte, *Les Hommes Préhistoriques et La Religion* (Paris, 1960)

Ivar Paulson, Åke Hultkrantz, and Karl Jettmar, *Die Religionen Nordeurasiens und der amerikanischen Arktis* (Stuttgart, 1962)

Susan M. Pearce, *The Kingdom of Dumnonia: Studies in History and Tradition in South-Western Britain A.D. 350–1150* (Padstow, 1978)

Susan Pearce, *South-western Britain in the Early Middle Ages* (London, 2004)

Mike Parker Pearson, *Stonehenge: Exploring the Greatest Stone Age Mystery* (London, 2012)

Mike Parker Pearson et al., 'The age of Stonehenge', *Antiquity: A Quarterly Review of World Archaeology* (Cambridge, 2007), lxxxi, pp. 617–39

J. J. Parry, 'The Welsh Texts of Geoffrey of Monmouth's *Historia*', *Speculum: A Journal of Mediaeval Studies* (Cambridge, Mass., 1930), v, pp. 424–31

Séamus Pender (ed.), *Féilscríbhinn Torna* (Cork, 1947)

Juha Y. Pentikäinen, *Kalevala Mythology* (Bloomington and Indianapolis, 1989)

Juha Pentikäinen (ed.), *Shamanism and Northern Ecology* (Berlin and New York, 1996)

W. M. Flinders Petrie, 'Neglected British History', *The Proceedings of the British Academy* (London, 1917–18), viii, pp. 251–78

Michael John Petry, *Herne the Hunter: A Berkshire Legend* (Reading, 1972)

Olof Petterson, *Jabmek and Jabmeaimo: A Comparative Study of the Dead and the Realm of the Dead in Lappish Religion* (Lund, 1957)

Gwynedd O. Pierce, *The Place-Names of Dinas Powys Hundred* (Cardiff, 1968)

Stuart Piggott, 'Nemeton, Temenos, Bothros: Sanctuaries of the Ancient Celts', in C. F. C. Hawkes, E. M. Jope, and Stuart Piggott (eds) *I Celti e la Loro Cultura nell'Epoca Pre-Romana e Romana nella Britannia* (Rome, 1978)

Stuart Piggott, 'The Sources of Geoffrey of Monmouth: I. The 'Pre-Roman' King-List', *Antiquity: A Quarterly Review of Archæology* (Gloucester, 1941), xv, pp. 269–86

Stuart Piggott, 'The Sources of Geoffrey of Monmouth. II. The Stonehenge Story', *Antiquity: A Quarterly Review of Archæology* (Gloucester, 1941), xv, pp. 305–19

Stuart Piggott, *Ancient Europe from the beginnings of Agriculture to Classical Antiquity* (Edinburgh, 1965)

Stuart Piggott, *The Druids* (London, 1968)

Murray G. H. Pittock, *Poetry and Jacobite Politics in Eighteenth-Century Britain and Ireland* (Cambridge, 1994)

H. E. Plutschow, *Chaos and Cosmos: Ritual in Early and Medieval Japanese Literature* (Leiden, 1990)

Julius Pokorny, 'The Origin of Druidism', *The Smithsonian Report for 1910* (Washington, 1911), pp. 583–97

J. Pokorny, 'Miscellanea Celtica', *Celtica* (Dublin, 1956), iii, p. 306–10

Julius Pokorny, *Indogermanisches Etymologisches Wörterbuch* (Berne, 1959–69)

Mirek B. Polišenský, *The Language and Origin of the Etruscans* (Prague, 1991)

John Polkinghorne, *The Faith of a Physicist: Reflections of a Bottom-Up Thinker* (Princeton, 1994)

Edgar Polomé (ed.), *Homage to Georges Dumézil* (Washington, 1982)

Edgar C. Polomé and Carol F. Justus (ed.), *Language Change and Typological Variation: In Honor of Winfred P. Lehmann on the Occasion of His 83rd Birthday* (Washington, 1999)

M. K. Pope, *From Latin to Modern French with Especial Consideration of Anglo-Norman: Phonology and Morphology* (Manchester, 1934)

Barry B. Powell, *Homer and the origin of the Greek alphabet* (Cambridge, 1991)

T. G. E. Powell, 'The Gold Ornament from Mold, Flintshire, North Wales', *Proceedings of the Prehistoric Society* (London, 1953), xix, pp. 161–179

K. D. Pringle, 'The Kings of Demetia', *The Transactions of the Honourable Society of Cymmrodorion: Session 1970* (London, 1971), pp. 140–44

Huw Pryce (ed.), *Literacy in Medieval Celtic Societies* (Cambridge, 1998)

Proceedings of the Second International Congress of Celtic Studies (Cardiff, 1966)

Jaan Puhvel, 'Greek ΑΝΑΞ', *Zeitschrift für vergleichende Sprachforschung auf dem Gebiete der Indogermanischen Sprachen* (Göttingen, 1956), lxxiii, pp. 202–22

Jaan Puhvel (ed.), *Myth and Law among the Indo-Europeans: Studies in Indo-European Comparative Mythology* (Berkeley and Los Angeles, 1970)

Jaan Puhvel, *Comparative Mythology* (Baltimore, 1987)

Benjamin C. Ray, *Myth, Ritual, and Kingship in Buganda* (Oxford, 1991)

E. G. Quin et al. (ed.), *Dictionary of the Irish Language: Based mainly on Old and Middle Irish Materials* (Dublin, 1913–76)

Christian Raffensperger, *Reimagining Europe: Kievan Rus' in the Medieval World* (Cambridge, Mass., 2012)

Philip Rahtz, 'The Roman Temple at Pagans Hill, Chew Stoke, N. Somerset', *Somersetshire Archaeological & Natural History Society: Proceedings during the Year 1951* (Dorchester, 1952), xcvi, pp. 112–42

Anna Giacalone Ramat and Paolo Ramat (ed.), *The Indo-European Languages* (London and New York, 1998)

Elizabeth Rawson, *Intellectual Life in the Late Roman Republic* (Baltimore, 1985)

D. H. Moutray Read, 'Hampshire Folklore', *Folk-Lore* (London, 1911), xxii, pp. 292–329.

Alwyn Rees and Brinley Rees, *Celtic Heritage: Ancient Tradition in Ireland and Wales* (London, 1961)

Martin Rees, *Before the Beginning: Our Universe and Others* (London, 1997)

Rice Rees, *An Essay on the Welsh Saints or the Primitive Christians Usually Considered to Have Been the Founders of Churches in Wales* (London, 1836)

Colin Renfrew, *Archaeology and Language: The Puzzle of Indo-European Origins* (London, 1987)

Colin Renfrew and Katie Boyle (ed.), *Archaeogenetics: DNA and the population prehistory of Europe* (Cambridge, 2000)

John Rhys, 'Welsh Fairy Tales', *Y Cymmrodor* (London, 1883), vi, pp. 155–221

J. Rhys, *Celtic Britain* (London, 1884)

John Rhys, *Lectures on the Origin and Growth of Religion as Illustrated by Celtic Heathendom* (London, 1888)

John Rhŷs, *Studies in the Arthurian Legend* (Oxford, 1891)

John Rhŷs, 'Notes on the Hunting of Twrch Trwyth', *The Transactions of the Honourable Society of Cymmrodorion: Session 1894–1895* (London, 1895), pp. 1–34

John Rhŷs, *Celtic Folklore: Welsh and Manx* (Oxford, 1901)

John Rhŷs, 'Studies in Early Irish History', *The Proceedings of the British Academy* (London, 1903), i, pp. 21–80

Sir John Rhys, 'President's Address', *Transactions of the Third International Congress for the History of Religions* (Oxford, 1908), ii, p. 201–25

John Rhŷs, 'All around the Wrekin', *Y Cymmrodor* (London, 1908), xxi, pp. 1–62

Sir John Rhŷs, 'Notes on The Coligny Calendar together with an Edition of the Reconstructed Calendar', *The Proceedings of the British Academy* (London, 1910), iv, pp. pp. 207–89

Sir John Rhŷs, 'Gleanings in the Italian Field of Celtic Epigraphy', *The Proceedings of the British Academy* (London, 1914), vi, pp. 315–69

Melville Richards, 'Nennius's 'Regio Guunnessi'', *Caernarvonshire Historical Society: Transactions* (Caernarvon, 1963), xxiv, pp. 21–27

Melville Richards, 'Some Welsh Place-Names Containing Elements which are Found in Continental Celtic', *Études Celtiques* (Paris, 1972), xiii, pp. 364–410

I. A. Richmond (ed.), *Roman and Native in North Britain* (Edinburgh, 1958)

Sir Ian Richmond, *Hod Hill* (London, 1968)

Michael Richter and Jean-Michel Picard (ed.), *Ogma: Essays in Celtic Studies in honour of Próinséas Ní Chatháin* (Dublin, 2002)

Helmer Ringgren, *Word and Wisdom: Studies in the Hypostatization of Divine Qualities and Functions in the Ancient Near East* (Lund, 1947)

Gisela Ripoll and Josep M. Gurt (ed.), *Sedes regiae (ann. 400-800)* (Barcelona, 2000)

A. L. F. Rivet (ed.), *The Roman Villa in Britain* (London, 1969)

A. L. F. Rivet and Colin Smith, *The Place-Names of Roman Britain* (London, 1979)

Brynley F. Roberts, 'Geoffrey of Monmouth and Welsh Historical Tradition', *Nottingham Mediaeval Studies* (Cambridge, 1976), xx, pp. 29–40

Brynley F. Roberts (ed.), *Early Welsh Poetry: Studies in the Book of Aneirin* (Aberystwyth, 1988)

Simon Rodway, 'Mermaids, Leprechauns, and Fomorians: A Middle Irish Account of the Descendants of Cain', *Cambrian Medieval Celtic Studies* (Aberystwyth, 2010), lix, p. 1–15

Erwin Rohde, *Psyche: The Cult of Souls and Belief in Immortality among the Greeks* (London, 1925)

James S. Romm, *The Edges of the Earth in Ancient Thought: Geography, Exploration, and Fiction* (Princeton, 1992)

Alan S. C. Ross, 'Hengist's Watchword', *English and Germanic Studies* (Kendal, 1948-49), ii, pp. 81–101

Anne Ross, *Pagan Celtic Britain: Studies in Iconography and Tradition* (London, 1967)

Anne Ross, *Everyday Life of the Pagan Celts* (London, 1970)

Anne Ross, 'Chartres: the *Locus* of the Carnutes', *Studia Celtica* (Cardiff, 1979/1980), xiv/xv, pp. 260–69

W. Rothwell, W. R. J. Barron, David Blamires, and Lewis Thorpe (ed.), *Studies in medieval literature and languages in memory of Frederick Whitehead* (Manchester, 1973)

Michel Rouche (ed.), *Clovis: histoire & mémoire* (Paris, 1997)

Marjorie Rowling, *The Folklore of the Lake District* (London, 1976)

E. H. Ruck, *An Index of Themes and Motifs in Twelfth-Century French Arthurian Poetry* (Cambridge, 1991)

Clive Ruggles (ed.), *Astronomy, Cosmology and Landscape: Proceedings of the SEAC 98 Meeting, Dublin, Ireland, September 1998* (Bognor Regis, 2001)

Clive Ruggles, *Astronomy in Prehistoric Britain and Ireland* (Yale, 1999)

Clive L. N. Ruggles and Nicholas J. Saunders (ed.), *Astronomies and Cultures* (Niwot, Colo., 1993)

John Ryan, *Irish Monasticism: Origins and Early Development* (London, 1931)

Rev. John Ryan (ed.), *Féilsgríbinn Eóin Mhic Néill* (Dublin, 1940)

Leopold Sabourin, *Priesthood: A Comparative Study* (Leiden, 1973)

H. E. Salter, 'Geoffrey of Monmouth and Oxford', *The English Historical Review* (London, 1919), xxxiv, pp. 382–85

Peter Salway, *Roman Britain* (Oxford, 1981)

Alan E. Samuel, *Greek and Roman Chronology: Calendars and Years in Classical Antiquity* (Munich, 1972)

L.-F. Sauvé, 'Formulettes et traditions diverses de la Basse-Bretagne', *Revue Celtique*, v, pp. 157–97

H. N. Savory, 'Excavations at Dinas Emrys, Beddgelert (Caern.), 1954–56', *Archaeologia Cambrensis* (Cardiff, 1960), cix, pp. 13–77

P. H. Sawyer, *Anglo-Saxon Charters: An Annotated List and Bibliography* (London, 1968)

William Sayers, "*Mani Maidi an Nem* ...": Ringing Changes on a Cosmic Motif', *Ériu* (Dublin, 1986), xxxvii, p. 99–117

Edward H. Schafer, *The Vermilion Bird: T'ang Images of the South* (Berkeley, 1967)

Edward H. Schafer, *Pacing the Void: T'ang Approaches to the Stars* (Berkeley, 1977)

Karl Horst Schmidt, *Celtic: A Western Indo-European Language?* (Innsbruck, 1996)

Karl Horst Schmidt and Rolf Ködderitzsch (ed.), *Geschichte und Kultur der Kelten: Vorbereitungskonferenz 25.-28. Oktober 1982 in Bonn* (Heidelberg, 1986)

Roseanne Schot, Conor Newman, and Edel Bhreatnach (ed.), *Landscapes of Cult and Kingship* (Dublin, 2011)

R. Mark Scowcroft, '*Leabhar Gabhála*: Part II: The Growth of the Tradition', *Ériu* (1988), xxxix, pp. 1–66

R. Mark Scowcroft, 'Abstract Narrative in Ireland', *Ériu* (1995), xlvi, pp. 130–37

Stephen Scully, *Homer and the Sacred City* (New York, 1990)

Frederic Seebohm, *The Tribal System in Wales: Being Part of an Inquiry into the Structure and Methods of Tribal Society* (London, 1904)

Myra Shackley, *Rocks and Man* (London, 1977)

Mosalam Shaltout and Juan Antonio Belmonte (ed.), *In Search of Cosmic Order: Selected Essays on Egyptian Archaeoastronomy* (Cairo, 2009)

Alfred K. Siewers, 'Writing an Icon of the Land: the *Mabinogi* as a Mystagogy of Landscape', *Peritia: Journal of the Medieval Academy of Ireland* (Turnhout, 2005), xix, p. 193–228

Anna-Leena Siikala, *The Rite Technique of the Siberian Shaman* (Helsinki, 1978)

Anna-Leena Siikala and Mihály Hoppál, *Studies on Shamanism* (Budapest, 1992)

Wirt Sikes, *British Goblins: Welsh Folk-Lore, Fairy Mythology, Legends and Traditions*. (London, 1880)

I. G. Simmons, *The Environmental Impact of Later Mesolithic Cultures: The Creation of Moorland Landscape in England and Wales* (Edinburgh, 1996)

Nicholas Sims-Williams (ed.), *Indo-Iranian Languages and Peoples* (Oxford, 2002)

Patrick Sims-Williams, *The Celtic Inscriptions of Britain: Phonology and Chronology, c. 400–1200* (Oxford, 2003)

Patrick Sims-Williams, 'anfab² 'illegitimate child': a ghost-word', *The Bulletin of the Board of Celtic Studies* (Cardiff, 1978), xxviii, pp. 90–93

Patrick Sims-Williams, *Rhai Addasiadau Cymraeg Canol o Sieffre o Fynwy* (Aberystwyth, 2011)

Patrick Sims-Williams, 'Celtic Civilization: Continuity or Coincidence?', *Cambrian Medieval Celtic Studies* (Aberystwyth, 2012), lxiv, pp. 1–45

Patrick Sims-Williams, 'Powys and Early Welsh Poetry', *Cambrian Medieval Celtic Studies* (Aberystwyth, 2014), lxvii, pp. 33–44

Patrick Sims-Williams, 'Bronze- and Iron-Age Celtic Speakers: What Don't We Know, What Can't We Know, and What Could We Know? Language, Genetics and Archaeology in the Twenty-First Century', *The Antiquaries Journal* (Cambridge, 2012), xcii, p. 427–49

Giulia Sissa, *Greek Virginity* (Cambridge, Mass., 1990)

Hagith Sivan, *Ausonius of Bordeaux: Genesis of a Gallic Aristocracy* (London, 1993)

Marie-Louise Sjoestedt, *Gods and Heroes of the Celts* (London, 1949)

William F. Skene, *The Coronation Stone* (Edinburgh, 1869)

William F. Skene, *Celtic Scotland: A History of Ancient Alban* (Edinburgh, 1876–80)

Paul Slack and Ryk Ward (ed.), *The Peopling of Britain: The Shaping of a Human Landscape* (Oxford, 2002)

A. H. Smith, *English Place-Name Elements* (Cambridge, 1956)

A. H. Smith, *The Place-Names of Gloucestershire* (Cambridge, 1964–65)

Bardwell Smith and Holly Baker Reynolds (ed.), *The City as a Sacred Center: Essays on Six Asian Contexts* (Leiden, 1987)

Mark S. Smith, *The Origins of Biblical Monotheism: Israel's Polytheistic Background and the Ugaritic Texts* (Oxford, 2001)

R. B. Smith and W. Watson (ed.), *Early South East Asia: Essays in Archaeology, History and Historical Geography* (Oxford, 1979)

Malcolm Smuts, *Court Culture and the Origins of a Royalist Tradition in Early Stuart England* (Philadelphia, 1987)

Alfred P. Smyth (ed.), *Seanchas: Studies in Early and Medieval Irish Archaeology, History and Literature in Honour of Francis J. Byrne* (Dublin, 2000)

Marina Smyth, *Understanding the Universe in Seventh-Century Ireland* (Woodbridge, 1996)

Maynard Solomon, *Beethoven Essays* (Cambridge, Mass., 1988)

Mark R. V. Southern (ed.), *Indo-European Perspectives* (Washington, 2002)

R. H. Spencer (ed.), *Gallica: Essays presented to J. Heywood Thomas by colleagues, pupils and friends* (Cardiff, 1969)

Luis I. J. Stadelmann, *The Hebrew Conception of the World* (Rome, 1970)

Pauline Stafford, *Queen Emma and Queen Edith: Queenship and Women's Power in Eleventh-Century England* (Oxford, 1997)

John Steane, 'How old is the Berkshire Ridgeway?', *Antiquity* (Cambridge, 1983), lvii, p. 103–8

Claude Sterckx, 'Les Têtes Coupées et le Graal', *Studia Celtica* (1985/1986), xx/xxi, pp. 1–42

Claude Sterckx, *Les dieux protéens des celtes et des indo-européans* (Brussels, 1994)

Claude Sterckx, 'De Cassivellaunos à Caswallon', *Studia Celtica* (Cardiff, 1998), xxxii, pp. 95–114

Claude Sterckx, *Les mutilations des ennemis chez les celtes préchrétiens* (Paris, 2005)

Claude Sterckx, *Mythologie du monde celte* (Paris, 2009)

Jaroslav Stetkevych, *Muḥammad and the Golden Bough: Reconstructing Arabian Myth* (Bloomington and Indianapolis, 1996)

Julian H. Steward, 'Panatübiji' an Owens Valley Paiute', *Bulletin of the Smithsonian Institution Bureau of American Ethnology* (Washington, 1938), cxix, p. 185–95

D. Stichtenoth, *Pytheas von Marseille: Über das Weltmeer* (Cologne, 1959)

John Strachan, *An Introduction to Early Welsh* (Manchester, 1909)

Clara Strijbosch, *The Seafaring Saint: Sources and Analogues of the Twelfth-Century Voyage of Saint Brendan* (Dublin, 2000)

Karin Stüber, *The Historical Morphology of N-Stems in Celtic* (Maynooth, 1998)

Margaret Stutley, *Ancient Indian Magic and Folklore: An Introduction* (London, 1980)

Rosemary Sweet, *Antiquaries: The Discovery of the Past in Eighteenth-Century Britain* (London, 2004)

Stanley J. Tambiah, *Culture, thought, and social action* (Cambridge, MA, 1985)

Michel Tardieu, *Les paysages reliques: Routes et haltes syriennes d'Isidore à Simplicius* (Louvain and Paris, 1990)

J. S. P. Tatlock, 'The Dates of the Arthurian Saints' Legends', *Speculum: A Journal of Mediaeval Studies* (Cambridge, Mass., 1939), xiv, pp. 345–49

J. S. P. Tatlock, *The Legendary History of Britain: Geoffrey of Monmouth's Historia Regum Britanniae and its Early Vernacular Versions* (Berkeley and Los Angeles, 1950)

Christopher Taylor, *Roads and Tracks of Britain* (London, 1979)

D. Ya. Telegin and J. P. Mallory, *The Anthropomorphic Stelae of the Ukraine: The Early Iconography of the Indo-Europeans* (Washington, 1994)

Emile Thevenot, *Sur les traces des Mars celtiques (entre Loire et Mont-Blanc)* (Bruges, 1955)

Paul Thieme, 'Mitra and Aryaman', *Transactions of the Connecticut Academy of Arts and Sciences* (New Haven, 1957), xli, pp. 6–96

Charles Thomas, 'The Early Christian Inscriptions of Southern Scotland', *Glasgow Archaeological Journal* (Glasgow, 1991–92), xvii, pp. 1–10

Charles Thomas, *Tintagel: Arthur and Archaeology* (London, 1993)

Charles Thomas, *And Shall These Mute Stones Speak?: Post-Roman Inscriptions in Western Britain* (Cardiff, 1994)

Charles Thomas, *Christian Celts: Messages & Images* (Stroud, 1998)

Rosalind Thomas, 'Written in Stone? Liberty, Equality, Orality and the Codification of Law', *Bulletin of the Institute of Classical Studies* (London, 1995), xl, pp. 59–74

E. A. Thompson, *Saint Germanus of Auxerre and the End of Roman Britain* (Woodbridge, 1984)

J. Eric S. Thompson, *Maya History and Religion* (Norman, Okla., 1970)

Stith Thompson, *The Folktale* (New York, 1946)

Stith Thompson, *Motif-Index of Folk-Literature: A Classification of Narrative Elements in Folktales, Ballads, Myths, Fables, Mediaeval Romances, Exempla, Fabliaux, Jest-Books, and Local Legends* (Bloomington, Indiana, 1955–58)

Derick Thomson, 'The Seventeenth-Century Crucible of Scottish Gaelic Poetry', *Studia Celtica* (Cardiff, 1991/92), xxvi/xxvii, pp. 155–62

David Thornton, *Kings, Chronologies, and Genealogies: Studies in the Political History of Early Medieval Ireland and Wales* (Oxford, 2003)

Rudolf Thurneysen, *Die irische Helden- und Königsage bis zum siebzehnten Jahrhundert* (Halle, 1921)

R. Thurneysen, 'Zu Nemnius (Nennius)', *Zeitschrift für Celtische Philologie* (Halle, 1936), xx, pp. 97-137

J. J. Tierney, 'The Celtic Ethnography of Posidonius', *Proceedings of the Royal Irish Academy* (1960), lx, pp. 189–275

Y. H. Toivonen, 'Le gros chêne des chants populaires finnois', *Journal de la Société Finno-Ougrienne* (Helsinki, 1947), liii, pp. 37–77

Clive Tolley, *Shamanism in Norse Myth and Magic* (Helsinki, 2009)

Nikolai Tolstoy, 'Early British History and Chronology', *The Transactions of the Honourable Society of Cymmrodorion: Session 1964* (London, 1964), pp. 237–312

Nikolai Tolstoy, *The Quest for Merlin* (London, 1985)

Nikolai Tolstoy, 'Geoffrey of Monmouth and the Merlin Legend', in Elizabeth Archibald and David F. Johnson (ed.), *Arthurian Literature XXV* (Cambridge, 2008), pp. 1–42

Nikolai Tolstoy, '*When and where was* Armes Prydein *Composed?*', *Studia Celtica* (Cardiff, 2008), xlii, pp. 145–49

Nikolai Tolstoy, *The Oldest British Prose Literature: The Compilation of the Four Branches of the Mabinogi* (Lampeter, 2009)

R. S. O. Tomlin, 'Was ancient British Celtic ever a written language? Two texts from Roman Bath', *The Bulletin of the Board of Celtic Studies* (Cardiff, 1987), xxxiv, pp. 18–25

Robert M. Torrance, *The Spiritual Quest: Transcendence in Myth, Religion, and Science* (Berkeley and Los Angeles, 1994)

Antonio Tovar, 'The God Lugus in Spain', *The Bulletin of the Board of Celtic Studies* (Cardiff, 1982), xxix, pp. 591–99

Stephen N. Tranter and Hildegard L. C. Tristram (ed.), *Early Irish Literature - Media and Communication* (Tübingen, 1989)

Marie Trevelyan, *Folk-Lore and Folk-Stories of Wales* (London, 1909)

F. R. Trombley, *Hellenic Religion and Christianization C. 370–529* (Leiden, 1993–94)

Robert Turcan, *The Gods of Ancient Rome: Religion in Everyday Life from Archaic to Imperial Times* (Edinburgh, 2000)

E. O. G. Turville-Petre, *Myth and Religion of the North: The Religion of Ancient Scandinavia* (London, 1964)

David Tylden-Wright, *John Aubrey: A Life* (London, 1991)

Gabriele Uelsberg, Michael Schmauder, and Stefan Zimmer (ed.), *Kelten am Rhein: Akten des dreizehnten Internationalen Keltologiekongresses* (Mainz am Rhein, 2009)

Jürgen Uhlich, *Die Morphologie der komponierten Personennamen des Altirischen* (Bonn, 1993)

A. G. van Hamel, 'Aspects of Celtic Mythology', *The Proceedings of the British Academy* (London, 1935), xx, pp. 207–48

Joan M. Vastokas and Romas K. Vastokas, *Sacred Art of the Algonkians: A Study of the Peterborough Petroglyphs* (Peterburgh, Ontario, 1973)

Joseph Vendryes, 'La religion des Celtes', *Mana: Introduction à l'histoire des religions* (Paris, 1948), iii, pp. 239–445

J. Vendryes, 'Les éléments celtiques de la légende du Graal', *Études celtiques* (Paris, 1949), v, pp. 1–50

J. Vendryes, E. Bachellery, and P-Y. Lambert, *Lexique étymologique de l'irlandais ancien* (Dublin and Paris, 1959-)

Christophe Vielle, *Le mytho-cycle héroïque dans l'aire indo-européenne: Correspondances et transformations helléno-aryennes* (Louvain, 1996)

Rainer Vollkommer, *Herakles in the Art of Classical Greece* (Oxford, 1988)

Angela Della Volpe, 'From the Hearth to the Creation of Boundaries', *The Journal of Indo-European Studies* (Washington, 1990), xviii, pp. 157–84

Angela Della Volpe, 'On Indo-European Ceremonial and Socio-Political Elements Underlying the Origin of Formal Boundaries', *The Journal of Indo-European Studies* (1992), xx, pp. 84–98

John Waddell, *Archaeology and Celtic Myth* (Dublin, 2014)

John Waddell and Elizabeth Twohig (ed.), *Ireland in the Bronze Age* (Dublin, 1995)

A. W. Wade-Evans, 'Parochiale Wallicum', *Y Cymmrodor* (London, 1910), xxii, pp. 22–124

Arthur W. Wade-Evans, *Welsh Christian Origins* (Oxford, 1934)

Heinrich Wagner, 'The Origin of the Celts in the Light of Linguistic Geography', *Transactions of the Philological Society 1969* (Oxford, 1970), lxviii, pp. 203–50

Heinrich Wagner, 'Studies in the Origins of Early Celtic Civilisation', *Zeitschrift für celtische Philologie* (Tübingen, 1971), xxxi, pp. 1–58

H. Wagner, 'Studies in the Origins of Early Celtic Traditions', *Ériu: The Journal of the School of Irish Learning* (Dublin, 1975), xxvi, pp. 1–26

Bernard Wailes, 'The Irish 'Royal Sites' in History and Archaeology', *Cambridge Medieval Celtic Studies* (Cambridge, 1982), iii, pp. 1–29

F. T. Wainwright (ed.), *The Problem of the Picts* (Edinburgh, 1956)

F. T. Wainwright, *Archaeology and Place-Names and History: An Essay on Problems of Co-ordination* (London, 1962)

G. J. Wainwright and I. H. Longworth, *Durrington Walls: Excavations 1966–1968* (London, 1971)

Martyn F. Wakelin, *Language and history in Cornwall* (Leicester, 1975)

Mary K. Wakeman, *God's Battle with the Monster: A Study in Biblical Imagery* (Leiden, 1973)

F. W. Walbank, *Speeches in Greek Historians* (Oxford, 1970)

Alexandra Walsham, *The Reformation of the Landscape: Religion, Identity, and Memory in Early Modern Britain and Ireland* (Oxford, 2011)

Frank Ward, 'Llech Ronw', *The Bulletin of the Board of Celtic Studies* (Cardiff, 1935), vii, pp. 352–53

H. L. D. Ward and J. A. Herbert, *Catalogue of Romances in the Department of Manuscripts in the British Museum* (London, 1883–1910)

Peter Warry, 'A Possible Mid-Fourth-Century Altar Platform at Marcham/Frilford, Oxfordshire', *Britannia: A Journal of Romano-British and Kindred Studies* (London, 2015), xlvi, pp. 273–79

R. Gordon Wasson, Stella Kramrisch, Jonathan Ott, and Carl A. P. Ruck, *Persephone's Quest: Entheogens and the Origins of Religion* (Yale, 1986)

D. M. Waterman, *Excavations at Navan Fort 1961-71* (Belfast, 1997)

Morgan Watkin, *La civilisation française dans les Mabinogion* (Paris, 1962)

Morgan Watkin, 'The Chronology of the White Book of Rhydderch on the Basis of its Old French Graphical Phenomena', *The National Library of Wales Journal* (Aberystwyth, (1964), xiii, pp. 349–52

Calvert Watkins, *How to Kill a Dragon: Aspects of Indo-European Poetics* (New York and Oxford, 1995)

Calvert Watkins, *The American Heritage Dictionary of Indo-European Roots* (Boston, 1985)

W. J. Watson, *The History of the Celtic Place-Names of Scotland* (Edinburgh, 1926)

Dorothy Watts, *Christians and Pagans in Roman Britain* (London, 1991)

Dorothy Watts, *Religion in Late Roman Britain: Forces of Change* (London, 1998)

Lorna Watts and Peter Leach, *Henley Wood, Temples and Cemetery Excavations 1962–69 by the late Ernest Greenfield & others* (York, 1996)

Graham Webster, *Rome Against Caratacus: The Roman Campaigns in Britain AD 48–58* (London, 1981)

Graham Webster, *The Cornovii* (Stroud, 1991)

W. J. Wedlake, *The Excavation of the Shrine of Apollo at Nettleton, Wiltshire, 1956–1971* (Dorking, 1982)

Kathryn Welch and Anton Powell (ed.), *Julius Caesar as Artful Reporter: The War Commentaries as Political Instruments* (London, 1998)

Derek A. Welsby, *The Romano-British Defence of the British Provinces in its Later Phases* (Oxford, 1982)

A. J. Wensinck, *The Ideas of the Western Semites Concerning the Navel of the Earth* (Amsterdam, 1916)

A. J. Wensinck, *The Ocean in the Literature of the Western Semites* (Amsterdam, 1918)

M. L. West, *The Orphic Poems* (Oxford, 1983)

M. L. West, *The East Face of Helicon: West Asiatic Elements in Greek Poetry and Myth* (Oxford, 1997)

M. L. West, *Indo-European Poetry and Myth* (Oxford, 2007)

Claus Westermann, *Genesis 1-11: A Commentary* (London, 1984)

Paul Wheatley, *The Pivot of the Four Quarters: A Preliminary Enquiry into the Origins and Character of the Ancient Chinese City* (Edinburgh, 1971)

Ann Woodward and Peter Leach, *The Uley Shrines: Excavation of a ritual complex on West Hill, Uley, Gloucestershire: 1977-9* (London, 1993)

R. E. Mortimer Wheeler, 'Segontium and the Roman Occupation of Wales', *Y Cymmrodor* (London, 1923), xxxiii.

R. E. M. Wheeler and T. V. Wheeler, *Report on the Excavation of the Prehistoric, Roman, and Post-Roman Site in Lydney Park, Gloucestershire* (Oxford, 1932)

Lady Wilde, *Ancient Legends, Mystic Charms, and Superstitions of Ireland. With Sketches of the Irish Past* (London, 1888)

D. K. Wilgus (ed.), *Folklore International: Essays in traditional literature, belief, and custom in honor of Wayland Debs Hand* (Hatboro, Pa., 1967)

G. J. Williams, *Iolo Morganwg* (Cardiff, 1956)

Hugh Williams, *Christianity in Early Britain* (Oxford, 1912)

Sir Ifor Williams, *Lectures on Early Welsh Poetry* (Dublin, 1944)

Sir Ifor Williams, 'Hen Chwedlau', *Transactions of the Honourable Society of Cymmrodorion: Sessions 1946-1947* (London, 1948), pp. 28-58

Olwen Williams-Thorpe, M. C. Jones, P. J. Potts, and P. C. Webb, 'Preseli Dolerite Bluestones: Axe-heads, Stonehenge Monoliths, and Outcrop Sources', *Oxford Journal of Archaeology* (Oxford, 2006), xxv, pp. 29-46

Lowry Charles Wimberly, *Folklore in the English & Scottish Ballads* (Chicago, 1928)

Ernst Windisch, *Das Keltische Brittannien bis zu Kaiser Arthur* (Leipzig, 1912)

Iwan Wmffre, 'Penrhyn *Blathaon* ac Amgyffred yr Hen Gymry o Eithafion Gogledd Prydain', *Studia Celtica* (Cardiff, 2004), xxxviii, pp. 59-68

John Edwin Wood, *Sun, Moon and Standing Stones* (Oxford, 1978)

Juliette Wood, 'Maelgwn Gwynedd: A Forgotten Welsh Hero', *Trivium* (Lampeter, 1984), xix, pp. 103-17

Roger D. Woodard, *Indo-European Sacred Space: Vedic and Roman Cult* (Urbana and Chicago, 2006)

Ann Woodward and Peter Leach, *The Uley Shrines: Excavation of a ritual complex on West Hill, Uley, Gloucestershire: 1977-9* (London, 1993)

Dorothy C. Wong, 'The Mapping of Sacred Space: Images of Buddhist Cosmographies in Medieval China', in Philippe Forêt and Andreas Kaplony (ed.), *The Journey of Maps and Images on the Silk Road* (Leiden, 2008)

W. G. Wood-Martin, *Traces of the Elder Faiths of Ireland: A Folklore Sketch; A Handbook of Irish Pre-Christian Traditions* (London, 1902)

C. L. Wrenn, 'Saxons and Celts in South-West Britain', *The Transactions of the Honourable Society of Cymmrodorion: Session 1959* (London, 1959), pp. 38-75

A. R. Wright and T. E. Lones, *British Calendar Customs* (London, 1936-40)

C. E. Wright, *The Cultivation of Saga in Anglo-Saxon England* (Edinburgh, 1939)

G. R. H. Wright, *As on the First Day: Essays in Religious Constants* (Leiden, 1987)

Thomas Wright, *The Celt, the Roman, and the Saxon: A History of the Early Inhabitants of Britain, Down to the Conversion of the Anglo-Saxons to Christianity* (London, 1852)

C. C. Wrigley, 'Stonehenge from without', *Antiquity* (Cambridge, 1989), lxiii, pp. 746-52

Stefan Zimmer, 'Indo-Celtic Connections: Ethic, Magic, and Linguistic', *The Journal of Indo-European Studies* (Washington, 2001), xxix, pp. 379-405

Paul Zumthor, *Merlin le Prophète: Un thème de la littérature polémique de l'historiographie et des romans* (Lausanne, 1943)

Index